WORLD CIVILIZATIONS

The Global Experience

SECOND EDITION

Volume I   Beginnings to 1750

Peter N. Stearns
Carnegie Mellon University

Michael Adas
Rutgers University

Stuart B. Schwartz
University of Minnesota

 HarperCollins*CollegePublishers*

Executive Editor: *Bruce Borland*
Developmental Editor: *Barbara Muller*
Project Coordination and Text Design: *Ruttle, Shaw & Wetherill, Inc.*
Cover Designer: *Kay Petronio*
Cover Illustrations: *Planet Art*
Art Studio: *Mapping Specialists Ltd.*
Photo Researchers: *Cheryl Kucharzak and Sandy Schneider*
Electronic Production Manager: *Christine Pearson*
Manufacturing Manager: *Helene G. Landers*
Electronic Page Makeup: *Americomp*
Printer and Binder: *R.R. Donnelley & Sons Company*
Cover Printer: *Phoenix Color Corp.*

WORLD CIVILIZATIONS: THE GLOBAL EXPERIENCE
Volume I   Beginnings to 1750, Second Edition

Library of Congress Cataloging-in-Publication Data
Stearns, Peter N.
     World civilizations : the global experience / Peter N. Stearns, Michael Adas, Stuart B. Schwartz.—2nd ed.
          p.   cm.
     Includes bibliographical references (p.   ) and index.
     Contents: v.   1. Beginnings to 1750—v.   2. 1450 to present.
     (v.1) ISBN 0-673-99427-9 (pbk.).—(v.2)ISBN 0-673-99428-7 (pbk.)
     1. Civilization—History.   2. Civilization—History—Sources.
I. Adas, Michael, [date–   ]   II. Schwartz, Stuart B.   III. Title.
CB69.S84   1996
909—dc20   95-22004
                                                                                                        CIP

97 98   9 8 7 6 5 4

WORLD CIVILIZATIONS

Brief Contents

Detailed Contents

PART I
THE ORIGINS OF CIVILIZATIONS

1

The Agrarian Revolution and the Birth of Civilization 4

2

The Rise of Civilization in the Middle East and Africa 22

3

Asia's First Civilizations: India and China 46

PART II
THE CLASSICAL PERIOD IN WORLD HISTORY

4
Nomadic Challenges and Civilized Responses   72

5
Unification and the Consolidation of Civilization in China   90

6
Classical Greece and the Hellenistic World   112

7
Religious Rivalries and India's Golden Age   136

PART III
THE POSTCLASSICAL ERA

17

The Americas on the Eve of Invasion   370

18

Reunification and Renaissance in Chinese Civilization: The Era of the Tang and Song Dynasties   392

19

The Spread of Chinese Civilization: Korea, Japan, and Vietnam   414

20

The Last Great Nomadic Challenges: From Chinggis Khan to Timur   438

PART IV
THE WORLD SHRINKS, 1450–1750

22

The Transformation of the West, 1450–1750   484

23

The West and the World   508

List of Maps

Preface

World history provides an exciting introduction to both the world and the historian's craft, and this text builds on these two themes. The survey course in world history has been gaining ground steadily as a staple of the history and social science curriculum. The reasons are immediately evident. First, the composition of the American population perpetually changes, adding to our need for international understanding. The European heritage, though still vital, now logically shares attention with our sources in Africa, various parts of Asia, and Latin America.

Second, American involvement in world affairs continues to grow. Long a Pacific, Caribbean, and Atlantic power, the United States nevertheless has tended to define its primary interests in terms of Europe. In the second half of the 20th century, after participation in three wars in Asia as well as massive economic and cultural interaction around the globe, the United States and its citizens have embraced a global perspective. This perspective involves emphasis on international currents and on a full range of civilizations.

The global coverage in the first edition of this text was extremely well received—an indication of growing confidence in the teaching of world history. Readers also appreciated the analytical emphasis, which this new edition retains. World history is not a parade of facts—one society after another. It involves vital interpretive issues, including comparative analysis, the balance between independent development in the major civilizations, and the results of international contacts and parallelisms.

GOALS

To meet the needs of a global perspective—to explain the emergence of the present world and its major civilizations—teachers of world history have created an increasingly sophisticated and comprehensive structure. Several decades of scholarship in world history and in area studies by historians and other social scientists and humanists have yielded a wealth of information and interpretive generalizations. This text reflects a synthesis of teaching and historical scholarship, a synthesis that grasps world history not as a list of facts recorded for routine memorization but as a set of processes open to analysis that builds an understanding of how study of the world has been shaped.

We have taught and written widely on topics central to world history. This text reflects our experience and our conviction of the role of world history in improving students' ability to handle issues of interpretation. By showing students how to assess change and continuity, the text helps them learn how to relate past to present.

As in many world history texts, we include excerpts from original documents in order to enhance students' contact with diverse voices of the past. With several other writers, we share a firm commitment to include social history that involves women, the nonelite, and experiences and events outside the spheres of politics and high culture.

This text is no clone, however. It offers several distinctive qualities that are pioneers in the presentation of world history.

APPROACH

The two most important and distinguishing features of this text involve the genuine global orientation and the attendant analytical style. This is a real *world* history text. It deals seriously with the Western tradition but does not allocate extra space to it that might blur the distinction between a Western civilization text and a world history text. Correspondingly, civilizations or societies sometimes slighted in world texts—such as the nomadic societies of Asia, Latin American societies, and nations and states of the Pacific Rim—receive additional attention here. This global orientation has made *World Civilizations: The Global Experience* a pioneer in the field. Its coverage is based on international criteria and gives the West its respectful due but not pride of place.

This text also seeks to upgrade the analytical level of the presentation of world history. Many world history texts function as factual compendia, leaving analytical challenge to the classroom. Our goal throughout has been to relate fact to interpretation while still allowing ample room for classroom exploration. Analytical emphasis is evident in the attention to periodization, which presents strands of interpretation amid the parade of facts. Comparative issues are strongly emphasized as a means both of raising the level of reading above that of memorization and of bridging the gap between discrete civilization segments.

By happy accident, this text was revised after one of those rare moments in world history (1989–1991) when all sorts of established patterns seem to change. Thus, the text incorporates the upheavals in Russia, Eastern Europe, and the Middle East—not as completed events, to be sure, but in integral relationship with other coverage. Recent developments in all these areas have been incorporated into this revised edition. The text is thus up to date not only in presenting facts but also in relating recent events to larger analytical patterns.

THEMES AND STRUCTURE

This text pays a great deal of attention to periodization. Some texts range through one civilization and then the next without much attention to coherent time periods. This book, in contrast, identifies themes for each major period of world history that help locate some common experiences or at least common forces in individual societies. Part introductions set clear definitions for each period, identifying new kinds of global contacts and parallel developments. Basic characteristics of each period are referred to in chapters dealing with specific civilizations and also in several crosscutting chapters that return to larger world trends.

The book is divided into six major parts, each defined by fundamental new characteristics in world history. After sketching the hunting-and-gathering phase of the human experience, Part I focuses on several major developmental stages. The rise of agriculture and then the development of civilization—with initial examples in different parts of Asia, Africa, Central America, and southeastern Europe—constitute the sequence that set world history in motion, from the origin of the human species until about 3000 years ago.

Part II deals with the elaboration of major civilizations in several parts of the world. Civilizations in this classical phase developed a new capacity to integrate large regions and diverse groups of people through overarching cultural and political systems. They also established many durable values that continue to mark the character of major societies to the present day. Part III of the book, covering the period from 500 C.E. to 1400

C.E., gains coherence by the spread of major religions to many different societies, by further expansion of the civilization form, and above all by the establishment of new commercial and cultural linkages that brought most civilizations into great contact with each other.

The final three parts of the book deal with world history in the past 550 years. During these years, previous international systems were fundamentally redefined, and well-established traditional civilizations encountered new forces of change. Part IV of the book deals with the three centuries after 1450, when new technology and modes of military and political organization allowed the establishment of a variety of important empires and when western Europe gained primary control of international trade, redefining its own society in the process. Western global power increased in the 170 years after 1750 (Part V), mainly through the ramifications of the Industrial Revolution. Other civilizations had to take a position toward Western power and toward industrialization—a common set of pressures that evoked diverse responses.

A new period of world history opened up in the middle decades of the 20th century with the retreat of Western imperialism, the rise of new political systems such as communism, the surge of the United States and the Soviet Union, and a variety of economic innovations including the achievements of Japan and the Pacific Rim. Part VI deals with this most recent period of world history and some of its portents for the future.

PEDAGOGICAL AIDS

Teachers (and students) of world history come from a wide range of backgrounds, personal and academic. To support the thematic and analytical features of the text and to make all facets of world history as accessible as possible, the authors have integrated several pedagogical features into the book. We have retained the following successful elements of the first edition.

In addition to narrative part openers that set forth key themes in each unit, parts begin with an extensive but manageable timeline that establishes the period under consideration. The timeline includes events in all the societies involved.

Chapters open with an outline for a quick overview of major topics and with a detailed timeline specific to the groups to be discussed. Chapter introductions highlight key themes and analytical issues to consider in reading.

Within each chapter, one or more documents appear

in a discrete section. The documents are preceded by a brief, scene-setting narration and followed by probing questions. Each chapter also contains an analytical essay on a topic of broad application; the essay is followed by questions intended both to probe student appreciation of the topic and to suggest questions or interpretive issues for further thought.

The text is accompanied by photographs, line drawings, and a series of maps specially developed to enhance the global orientation. Maps in the part introductions and in the chapters highlight major developments during each period and familiarize students with many non-Western areas.

Each chapter ends with a conclusion that goes beyond a mere summary of events. Conclusions reiterate the key themes and issues raised in the chapter and again suggest areas for reflection and anticipation. Obvious examples can be found in the unit on the 20th century, in which conclusions highlight developments leading to events of which students have had first-hand experience. Each chapter also includes several paragraphs of annotated suggested readings, so that readers can pursue additional topics on their own.

At the back of the book (in addition to the index) is a comprehensive glossary, another feature that sets this book apart. It includes conceptual terms, frequently used foreign terms, and names of important geographical regions and key characters on the world stage. Much of world history will be new to most students, and this glossary will greatly assist them in developing a global vocabulary.

In addition, several new pedagogical features have been added. In order to personalize the narrative, each chapter includes a closeup, usually with an illustration, focusing on an individual, an event, or an artifact. Further, each major chapter section begins with a Focal Point to help the student organize reading and interpretation. Finally, the text has been somewhat shortened to facilitate an expanded visual presentation.

ACKNOWLEDGMENTS

Grateful acknowledgment is made to the following colleagues and reviewers, who made many useful suggestions during the development of this revision.

Norman R. Bennett
Boston University

Wilfred J. Bisson
Keene State College

Laura Blunk
Cuyahoga Community College East

Francesco Cesareo
John Carroll University

Allen Cronenberg
Auburn University

Edward J. Davies
University of Utah

Janusz Duznkiewicz
William Penn College

Claybourne Foster
LeMoyne–Owen College

Christopher V. Hill
University of Colorado–Colorado Springs

Ramsay Kleff
Virginia Union University

Lysle E. Meyer
Moorhead State University

Melvin E. Page
East Tennessee State University

Oliver B. Pollak
University of Nebraska at Omaha

Dennis Reinhartz
University of Texas at Arlington

Cheryl Riggs
California State University–San Bernardino

James A. Saddington
Taylor University

Gershon Shafir
University of California–San Diego

Howard Spendelow
Georgetown University

Gordon C. Thomasson
Broome Community College

J. Malcolm Thompson
North Dakota State University

Peter N. Stearns
Michael Adas
Stuart B. Schwartz

Supplements

The following supplements are available for use in conjunction with this book.

FOR THE STUDENT

HarperCollins World History Atlas. This four-color atlas contains over 60 historical maps. It is available shrink-wrapped with *World Civilizations* at low cost.

Student Study Guide in two volumes. Volume I (Chapters 1 through 23) and Volume II (Chapters 22 through 42) prepared by John Paul Bischoff of Oklahoma State University. Each volume includes chapter outlines, time-lines, map exercises, multiple-choice practice tests, and critical thinking and essay questions.

World History Map Workbook in two volumes. Volume I (to 1600) and Volume II (from 1600) prepared by Glee Wilson of Kent State University. Each volume includes over 40 maps accompanied by over 120 pages of exercises. Each volume is designed to teach the location of various countries and their relationship to one another. Also included are numerous exercises aimed at enhancing students' critical thinking abilities.

Documents in World History in two volumes. Volume I, *The Great Tradition—From Ancient Times to 1500;* Volume II, *The Modern Centuries—From 1500 to the Present.* Edited by Peter N. Stearns of Carnegie Mellon University. A collection of primary source documents that illustrates the human characteristics of key civilizations during major stages of world history.

SuperShell II Computer Tutorial. An interactive program for computer-assisted learning, prepared by John Paul Bischoff of Oklahoma State University. Features multiple-choice, true-false, and completion quizzes; comprehensive chapter outlines; "flash cards" for key terms and concepts; and diagnostic feedback.

Timelink: World History Computerized Atlas by William Hamblin of Brigham Young University. A highly graphic,

Hypercard-based computerized atlas and historical geography tutorial for the Macintosh.

Mapping World Civilizations: Student Activities. A free student workbook by Gerald Danzer, University of Illinois, Chicago. Features numerous map skill exercises written to enhance students' basic geographical literacy. The exercises provide ample opportunities for interpreting maps and analyzing cartographic materials as - historical documents. The instructor is entitled to one free copy of *Mapping World Civilizations: Student Activities* for each copy of the text purchased from Harper-Collins.

FOR THE INSTRUCTOR

Instructor's Resource Manual by Norman Bennett of Boston University. Includes chapter summaries, discussion suggestions, critical thinking exercises, map exercises, primary source analysis suggestions, term paper and essay topics. Special "Instructor's Tool Kit" by George Jewsbury of Oklahoma State University includes numerous audiovisual suggestions.

Guide to Advanced Media and Internet Resources for World History by Richard Rothaus of St. Cloud State University. This guide provides a comprehensive review of CD-ROM, software, and Internet resources for world civilization including a list of the primary resources, syllabi and articles, and discussion groups available on-line.

Discovering World History Through Maps and Views, Second Edition, by Gerald Danzer, University of Illinois, Chicago, winner of the AHA's James Harvey Robinson Award for his work in the development of map transparencies. The second edition of this set of 100 four-color transparencies is completely updated and revised to include the newest reference maps and the most useful source materials. These transparencies are bound with introductory materials in a three-ring binder with an introduction about teaching history with maps and detailed commentary on each transparency. The collection includes source and reference maps, views and photos, urban plans, building diagrams, and works of art.

Test Bank by John Paul Bischoff of Oklahoma State University. A total of 2,300 questions, including 50 multiple-choice questions and five essay questions per chapter. Each test is referenced by topic, type, and text page number.

TestMaster Computerized Testing System. A test-generation software package available for DOS and Macintosh computers. Allows user to add, delete, and print test items.

Map Transparencies. A set of 48 two-color text map transparencies from the second edition of *World Civilizations: The Global Experience.*

Grades. A grade-keeping and classroom management software program that maintains data for up to 200 students.

The HarperCollins World Civilization Media Program. A wide variety of media enhancements for use in teaching world civilization courses. Offered to qualified adopters of HarperCollins's world civilization texts.

Prologue

The study of history is the study of the past. Knowledge of the past gives us perspective on our societies today. It shows different ways in which people have identified problems and tried to resolve them, as well as important common impulses in the human experience. History can inform through its variety, remind us of some human constants, and provide a common vocabulary and examples that aid in mutual communication.

The study of history is also the study of change. Historians attempt to describe major changes in the human experience over time and to examine the ways in which those changes connect the past to the present. They try to distinguish between superficial and fundamental change, as well as between sudden and gradual change. They also deal with causation, explaining why change occurs and what impact it has. Finally, they pinpoint continuities from the past along with innovations. History, in other words, is a study of human society in motion.

World history is not simply a collection of the histories of various societies but a subject in its own right. World history is the study of historical events in a global context. It does not attempt to sum up everything that has happened in the past. It focuses on two principal subjects: the evolution of leading civilizations and the framework for international contacts among different societies. In the first category, world history identifies major stages in the development of important societies. In the second category, world history emphasizes major stages in the interaction among different peoples and societies around the globe.

THE EMERGENCE OF WORLD HISTORY

Serious attempts to deal with world history are relatively recent. Many historians have attempted to locate the evolution of their own societies in the context of developments in a larger "known world": Herodotus, though particularly interested in the origins of Greek culture, wrote also of developments around the Mediterranean; Ibn Khaldun wrote of what he knew about developments in Africa and Europe as well as in the Muslim world;

and unsystematically, European historians in the 18th-century Enlightenment liked to compare the evolution of various societies with the evolution of their own. But not until the 20th century, with an increase in international contacts and a vastly expanded knowledge of the historical patterns of major societies, did a full world history become possible. In the West, world history depended on a growing realization that the world could not be understood simply as a mirror reflecting the West's greater glory or as a stage for Western-dominated power politics. This hard-won realization continues to meet some resistance. Nevertheless, at various times since 1900, historians in several societies have attempted to develop an international approach to the subject that includes but goes beyond merely establishing a context for the emergence of their own civilizations.

The surge of interest in world history has been fueled by three interrelated factors. The first factor has been an explosion of knowledge about the histories of societies outside the Western tradition, in some cases also older than that tradition. The known past is much larger than ever before. Analysis of a host of issues—the effects of a classical tradition on later cultural development, the relationship between religion and commerce, or the impact of the Industrial Revolution on women—simply cannot be confined to Western examples.

The second factor involves the realization of the increasingly international context in which we live. Much of what happens in the United States can still be explained by national or even local contexts, but our economy and culture, as well as our military and diplomatic framework, are vitally shaped by developments around the world. For example, wars and revolutions in the Middle East and economic and population trends in Latin America have a direct impact on the way we live. Living in an international context creates the need to understand this context and to apply to it the knowledge and perspectives of history. We need to know how other traditions besides our own have evolved, what beliefs and attitudes they produce, and what kinds of economic and political behaviors they generate.

One world historian has put the case this way: History in the United States first concentrated on the national experience alone, as part of an attempt at self-understanding and as a means of building agreed-upon national values. In the 20th century Americans realized that they were caught up in a network of which Europe was a vital part. One response was the creation of programs in the study of the history of Western civilization that made us better able to deal with European issues in the post–World War II era. Now we need, and are developing, the same types of programs on a wider international level—and world history plays a key role here.

The third factor follows from the growing analytical challenge posed by world history. Historians increasingly understand that key aspects of past and present alike have been shaped by global forces: exchanges of technologies, ideas, religions, foods, and diseases. Defining and assessing the emergence of global forces and tracing their interaction with individual societies stand at the forefront of the world history agenda as a research area. Our understanding of these forces, though still incomplete, is steadily improving.

WHAT CIVILIZATION MEANS

In dealing with *civilizations*—societies that generate and use an economic surplus beyond basic survival needs—world history focuses on only a tiny portion of the more than 2.5 million years since the genus *Homo* first appeared in the savanna of eastern Africa. The era of civilized life makes up about 9000 of the 40,000 years that our own human species, *Homo sapiens sapiens*, has inhabited the earth. Civilized life has made possible human population densities unimaginable in precivilized time periods: It has given human groups the capacity to reshape their environments in fundamental ways and to dominate most other living creatures. The history of civilizations embraces most of the people who have ever lived; their literature, formal scientific discoveries, art, music, architecture, and inventions; their most sophisticated social, political, and economic systems; their brutality and destruction caused by conflicts; their exploitation of other species; and their degradation of the environment—a result of advances in technology and economic organization.

To be truly global in scope, our inquiry into the history of civilizations must not be constricted by the narrow, Western-centric standards for determining what is civilized. Many "civilized" peoples have regarded outsiders with different physical features and cultures as uncouth "barbarians" or even subhumans. For example, in awarding a society civilized status, most European and American writers have insisted that monumental buildings, cities, writing, and a high level of technology be present. These criteria banished from the realm of the civilized many societies that were highly advanced in other areas but deficient in those the Western writers deemed critical. Clearly, another approach to the meaning of civilization has to be taken if one is to write a truly global history of the human experience.

Different civilizations have stressed and therefore excelled in different facets of human creativity. The Chinese have consistently demonstrated the capacity to build large and effective political systems. But Chinese thinkers have formulated only one major religion, Daoism, and this has had only a limited appeal within and beyond East Asia. By contrast, the peoples of India have produced some of humankind's most sophisticated and sublime religions, but they have rarely known periods of political unity and strong government. The civilizations of the Maya made remarkable discoveries in astronomy and mathematics, but their technology remained roughly equivalent to that of Stone-Age peoples as late as the arrival of the Spaniards in the 16th century. These examples suggest that rather than stressing particular attainments such as the capacity to build pyramids or wheeled vehicles, a genuinely global definition of what it means to be civilized should focus on underlying patterns of social development that are common to complex societies throughout history. The attributes that determine whether a particular society is civilized or not should be freed from *ethnocentrism*—the tendency to judge other peoples' cultural forms solely on the basis of how they compare with one'own.

For our purposes, civilization is a form of human social organization that arises from the capacity of certain peoples to produce food supplies beyond their basic needs and to develop a variety of specialized occupations, a heightened social differentiation on a class and gender basis, and regional and long-distance trading networks. Surplus agricultural production spurs the growth of large towns and then cities inhabited by merchants, artisans, ritual specialists, and political leaders. Both specialization and town life contribute to the increase in creativity and innovation that have been characteristic of all civilizations.

THE COMPARATIVE APPROACH TO THE HISTORY OF CIVILIZATIONS

Even in emphasizing major civilizations, world history must offer other ways to select and highlight significant developments. One vital step involves a comparative approach to the major societies. Much of world history can be organized through careful comparisons of the leading characteristics of the principal civilizations, such as formal governments, family structures, and art. Remembering what civilizations have in common helps us to manage the complexity of world history and to highlight key distinctions between major societies. Comparison gives us a means of connecting historical developments within different civilizations and allows us to identify key patterns that ought to be remembered and explained.

Comparison can also help capture the process of historical change. Aspects of a single civilization can be compared across time, before and after change. Furthermore, a situation new to one society can be compared with similar situations elsewhere. Consider the introduction of a new slave system, as happened in the Americas in the 16th and 17th centuries. By comparing the American slave system with slave systems developed elsewhere, one can get a better fix on what American slavery involved and what changes it brought to the emerging society.

INTERNATIONAL CONTACTS AND TIME PERIODS

World history is not, however, simply a progression of separate civilizations that can be compared in various ways. An understanding of the kinds of contacts different civilizations developed—and their responses to the forces that crossed their boundaries—is as important as the story of the great societies themselves. For example, when the rate of international trade picked up, it presented questions for each major society to answer: How would the society participate in the trading system? What domestic impact did international trade have? How did one society's reactions to the new levels of trade compare with those of other major societies?

Historians treat time not in terms of one event after another but by defining *periods* in which basic patterns emerge. Each period differs from the one before and the one after in terms of these basic patterns. In the case of world history, periodization depends primarily on changes in the nature and level of international exchange, though the earliest periods focus on regional rather than international links. Because of parallel developments as well as crosscutting global contacts, many civilizations display some common chronological features that suggest a shared framework. Some time periods see a particular trend toward the formation of empires; others involve the spread of major religions; others stress the impact of new technologies or production systems. Not all societies, in a given time period, neatly responded to the larger world forces—isolation from the wider world remained possible until just a few centuries ago—but enough did to enable us to define a coherent chronology for world history.

This book emphasizes six major time periods in world history. The first, covered in Part I, involved the emergence of civilization. Early civilizations arose after people had formed a wide variety of local societies over most of the inhabitable globe. The early civilizations were regional, but they pulled more localized groups together into some shared institutions and beliefs, and some of them developed limited contacts with other civilizations.

The second period of world history saw the formation of much larger civilization units: the great classical societies of China, India, and the Mediterranean. Emphasis in the classical period rests on the integration of these larger civilization areas, and the level of contact between them. This was the period when elites in many parts of the world created systems of thought and artistic styles that continue to have force today: Confucian ideas about polite behavior and the social good, Greek ideas about nature, and Buddhist ideas about spirituality.

The third, postclassical period in world history emerged as the classical civilizations underwent new challenge and decline. After about 500 C.E., civilization spread to new areas and new kinds of contact developed, involving the spread of novel religious systems, the increase of commercial exchange, and even the acceleration of international disease transmission.

The fourth period of world history, beginning around 1450 C.E., saw the Americas and other previously isolated areas brought into the international framework as trade and exchange reached yet another level of intensity. Humble American crops such as corn and potatoes encouraged massive population growth in many societies—a trend that continues into our own time.

Between about 1750 and 1920, the fifth period of world history was shaped particularly through the advent of industrial society in western Europe. Industrial technology brought new rates of international interaction and a new, and complex, balance of forces among the major civilization areas. Habits of work changed in response to new ideas of discipline and productivity; leisure changed as well. This was the time when key sports like soccer football won an international audience.

Finally, world history periodization took a sixth turn during the 20th century, again because of complicated changes in the nature of international contacts and the impact of those contacts on particular societies. The new global patterns of this century gain added meaning against the perspective of previous world trends.

The basic framework for managing and understanding world history resembles a weaving loom, in which two sets of threads interweave. One set consists of the major civilizations, identified through their principal characteristics and traced over time. The second set involves parallel processes and contacts that delineate the principal time periods of world history. The interaction between civilizations and international forces forms the warp and weave of world history, from civilization's origin to the present day.

ANALYSIS IN WORLD HISTORY

In addition to comparison and periodization, which link the historical experience of individual civilizations, some world historians have been fascinated by a third, even more sweeping formula: regularities in historical development that can be identified and applied on a global basis. Do all civilizations rise, mature, and then fall in a process like that of human growth? Is there a historical law to prove that societies that begin to neglect the welfare of their lowest classes are doomed to decay? A variety of historical laws have been proposed, and even if some of them prove simplistic, the more insightful ones can raise valid questions about the larger processes of world history.

World history involves comparison, assessment of global interaction, and consideration of more general formulas about how human societies operate. There are facts to be learned, but the greater analytical challenge is to use the facts to compare civilizations, to identify key periods of world history and the patterns of change from one period to the next, and to test general propositions about historical causation and development. When this approach is used, world history becomes something to think about, not simply something to regurgitate. With this approach the task of learning world history gains focus and purpose.

WORLD CIVILIZATIONS

PALEOLITHIC AGE		**1 million** Further development of species into *Homo erectus*, an upright, tool-using human	**30,000** Passage of people to America	**8500–3500** Neolithic Age; development of farming in Middle East
		600,000 Wide spread of species across Asia, Europe, Africa; development of fire use		**12,000** Domestication of dogs
	2.5 million Emergence of more humanlike species, initially in eastern Africa		**40,000** Completion to date of basic human evolution; *Homo sapiens sapiens* displaces other human species	**8500–6500** Domestication of sheep, pigs, goats, cattle
2.5 MILLION B.C.E.	**1.25** MILLION B.C.E.	**50,000** B.C.E.	**30,000** B.C.E.	**10,000** B.C.E. **8000** B.C.E.

INTRODUCTION

This first section focuses on how human societies started and particularly on how initial civilization emerged. The key markers are the advent of humankind's first production system—agriculture—and the achievements and diversities of the first complex societies that resulted. The section ends about 1000 B.C.E., when several civilizations were poised to develop more elaborate cultural and political forms and to embrace wider areas beyond their river-valley cores.

Though human beings first appeared over 2 million years ago, major stages in the physical development of the species ended only about 40,000 years ago. Long before this, it was clear that humans were capable of using tools and improving them.

It was this capacity that produced a particularly crucial break in the context of human history by allowing groups of people to move away from the hunting-and-gathering economy that had shaped human society from its inception. Hunting for meat and gathering nuts and seeds allowed people to form organized units, but only small ones. The system permitted people to locate in many areas, but it could not sustain large numbers of people.

The capacity to effect a major transformation in basic economic organization, by substituting agriculture for hunting and gathering as the primary source of food, constituted a decisive change in the human record. This transformation, based on the improved tools of the New Stone (Neolithic) Age, began after 9000 B.C.E. With this change, the possibility of more elaborate forms of social and political organization—civilization itself—gradually emerged. The Neolithic revolution ushered in agriculture and thus stands as a landmark of the human experience, as the prehistoric development moved toward the world history of more organized societies.

THE NEOLITHIC REVOLUTION

Focal Point: Agriculture produced more food and encouraged wider contacts than hunting-and-gathering economies allowed. New tensions between local identities and integrating forces quickly emerged. The advent of civilizations in several river valleys increased the scope of human organization still further.

Humankind had spread to all major continents and many island groups at least 15,000 years before agriculture was invented. The species proved able to adapt to a wide variety of climates and environments even before elaborate technologies further aided survival. Hunting and gathering encouraged dispersal of the population. When agriculture made larger cultural and political systems possible, the differences and divisions among segments of the far-flung population posed major barriers that could not completely be overcome.

In fact, many people resisted agriculture itself. The new economic system allowed more people to exist, but it also brought many disadvantages. These included changes in relationships between men and women and a need to work harder. Agriculture thus constituted progress only in some ways; it could be seen as deterioration in others. Also, by requiring settling down and more coordination between larger groups of people, it could arouse resentments based on attachments to a wandering life and small, scattered units of human organization.

Two other complexities that attended the emergence of agriculture and civilization are covered primarily in Chapters 1 and 2. First, while change sped up, it hardly rocketed. New political forms emerged very slowly. There is an agonizing gap of many centuries between the first signs of civilization in the Middle East and its full initial development. Technology did not develop at an even pace. Agriculture gave rise to the use of

6000 B.C.E.	5000 B.C.E.	4000 B.C.E.	3000 B.C.E.	
7000 Full-fledged town in Jericho	5000 Domestication of maize (corn)		3100–1087 Initial kingdoms, then flowering of Egyptian civilization	
5600 Beans domesticated in Western Hemisphere		4000–3000 Age of innovation in Middle East: writing, bronze metalworking, wheel, plow		2500–1500 Indus civilization in South Asia
	5000–2000 Yangshao culture in North China		3500–1800 Sumerian civilization, with some disruptions through conquest	

CONTINUED

new materials, particularly metals, and new manufacturing techniques, but the transformation of the production process took many centuries. For example, several thousand years passed between the discovery of grain growing and the invention of bread.

The second complexity involves place. The development of agriculture and then civilization did not proceed evenly across the globe. The dispersion of the species inhibited the rapid spread of new ideas, as did deliberate resistance to novelty. In some areas agriculture and then civilization emerged separately, well after their initial advent in western Asia (what we today call the Middle East). Several distinct "inventions" of agriculture occurred; other areas learned of agriculture from contact with one of the pioneering centers. Vast differences in timing help explain later historical patterns in the Asian and North African regions where innovation first occurred, and in Europe and the Americas.

CIVILIZATION'S FIRST PHASE: THE RIVER VALLEYS

Four major centers of early civilization developed by 2500 B.C.E.: Mesopotamia, Egypt, northwestern India, and northern China. All four were regional concentrations, though each exhibited some capacity to fan out slightly into adjacent territories. They had little contact with one another. These civilizations created basic devices to facilitate more effective government and trade, a system of writing, some bureaucratic forms and legal procedures, increasingly elaborate commercial practices, and characteristic styles in art and architecture. They can be seen as pioneers in generating basic elements common to later, more organized, more expansive civilizations. These key ingredients of civilized life would never have to be fully reinvented by later civilizations.

In some cases—most clearly Mesopotamia and China—the early civilizations also projected ideas about humanity and nature that would continue to shape civilization in these and other areas, long after these rather constricted river-valley societies had given way to great empires.

The pioneering phase of civilization in Asia and parts of Europe and Africa lasted for many centuries, up to 2500 years. Many early civilizations were deliberately conservative, which helps account for their durability and their lack of striking internal change. Yet, in part because of some widespread invasions, the early civilizations either ended or paused to regroup about 1000 B.C.E. This date signaled a definable break between the initial phase of civilization's history and a more mature phase.

ISSUES FOR INTERPRETATION: PROBLEMS IN ANALYZING EARLY WORLD HISTORY

Focal Point: The early phases of world history not only introduce key initial concepts, such as civilization, and vital early forms of what became separate civilized traditions, but also introduce analytical issues that can be tested in the first millennia of agriculture and metalworking.

The balance between technology and culture is one key issue. The focus in dealing with early societies deliberately oscillates between technology and culture—between tools and ideas—as people in those societies built a growing mastery over nature while also producing a wide variety of values and styles of art and science. Both facets of development involve important encounters between evolving forms of human society and their physical environments. Both technology and culture must be

1850 Shang kingdom in China	**1600 Beginning** of Indo-European invasions	**1000–500** Olmec civilization in Mesoamerica	**400** Potatoes domesticated (Andes)
1800 Babylonian Empire in Middle East	**1600** Spread of civilization to Crete (Minoan)	**800** Beginning of writing of Bible (Israel)	**700** Composition of first of the sacred Vedas (India)
	1122 Western Zhou kings, China; writing develops		
1700–1300 Rise of village culture in Mesoamerica		**1000** Kush independent kingdom in Africa (Upper Nile)	
	1250 Moses and Jewish exodus from Egypt	**770** Later Zhou kings	
		1000 Spread of Phoenician settlements, Western Mediterranean; Indo-European invasions of Greece	**550** Persian Empire (Middle East)

2000 B.C.E.   1000 B.C.E.

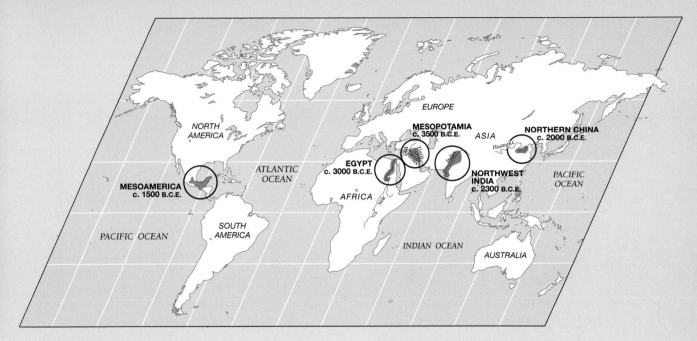

Early Civilizations

used to analyze how and why change occurred and to establish the characteristics of any civilization.

Comparison is another essential feature of analysis. The early civilizations all had to devise institutions and techniques. Although they had some characteristics in common, they also differed in political structure and cultural styles. Comparison centers on the exploration of those similarities and differences.

Heritage constitutes another important interpretive issue for these first periods in world history. For example, how much did later civilizations borrow from earlier examples, beyond basic techniques, and how much did they invent separately? Was a basic difference in outlook between the Middle East and eastern Asia set as early as 1000 B.C.E.?

Obviously, early civilizations introduced some techniques that have lasted to our own day—though by 1000 B.C.E. they had not yet spread to most areas of the world. These techniques included writing and the use of money. Whether the early civilizations also set the tone for later, larger societies is open to greater debate. A recent argument that Egypt, as an African society, really provided basic institutions and ideas for Greek and later European culture is an instance of this important effort to explore how much of the later shape of major civilizations was prepared during the long river-valley phase.

Defining the close of the first period of world history is considerably tougher than identifying its origins and main features. The four main river-valley civilizations met different fates. The first civilization in India

almost completely disappeared, while the Chinese civilization that still exists today is in some ways directly linked to its early river-valley phase.

One final analytical approach can be fruitfully applied to the first period of world history. Many people, including some who are dubious about outright historical laws, find in the past informative analogies that help them interpret later human experience. Two major potential analogies leap out from the formative period of civilization. First, the ways in which the initial civilizations arose set patterns that can be applied to the study of the genesis of civilization in other areas. This analogy applies particularly vividly to the Americas, where early civilizations, arising independently and somewhat later, are often compared with those of Egypt or Mesopotamia (see Chapter 9). It can also apply to early civilizations in Italy, Africa, or the Polynesian islands.

The second analogy is even more grandiose. With the development of agriculture the first period of civilized development produced one of the two basic shifts in human production methods ever developed. (Industrialization was the second.) The nature, causes, and limitations of the agrarian revolution of the late Neolithic period set patterns and raised questions that have helped us understand the much more recent Industrial Revolution. Because recent human history involves almost unprecedented alterations in basic living habits, we can only benefit from understanding prior experiences that are at all comparable.

1

The Agrarian Revolution and the Birth of Civilization

	LATE PALEOLITHIC	TRANSITION PHASE	NEOLITHIC AGE
EASTERN HEMISPHERE	18,000–10,000 Central Russian mammoth bone settlements	10,500–8000 Natufian settlements	8500–5000 Development of farming in the Middle East
			7000 Full-fledged town at Jericho
			6250–5400 Çatal Huyuk at its peak
	12,000 Domestication of dogs	8500 Domestication of sheep	
			7500–6500 Domestication of pigs, goats, cattle
WESTERN HEMISPHERE			5600 Beans domesticated
	18,000 B.C.E. 12,000 B.C.E.	10,000 B.C.E.	8000 B.C.E. 6000 B.C.E.

INTRODUCTION

This history of human civilizations focuses on only a tiny portion—roughly 9000 years—of the more than 2.5 million years since the genus *Homo* first appeared in the savannas of eastern Africa (and perhaps contemporaneously further east in parts of Asia). Within this 9000-year time span, we will concentrate on societies that we consider civilized by virtue of their reliance on sedentary agriculture for sustenance and their ability to produce crop surpluses that support specialized elites as well as nonfarming, trading, and manufacturing groups. In most civilizations, agricultural surpluses and specialization have also given rise to concentrations of human populations in towns and cities and to complex social divisions and social stratification based on a mix of birth, sex, and occupation. The era of civilized life so defined makes up less than a quarter of the 40,000 years that our own human species, *Homo sapiens,* has inhabited the earth. But within the civilized societies that developed in this limited time span, most of human history has been lived.

Our emphasis in defining *civilizations* on the basis of the economic circumstances that give rise to them and the social patterns that characterize them makes it necessary to explore the origins of early civilizations. We need to understand why humans opted for this form of organization and path of development, and how they were able to make the transition from small-scale, nonspecialized, subsistence societies to city-states with their increasingly complex division of labor. Before studying the varying patterns of civilized life that are the focus of world history, we will examine some of the alternative modes of human organization that had evolved by the end of the transition period between the *Paleolithic* (Old Stone) *Age* and the *Neolithic* (New Stone) *Age*. In this period, from roughly 12,000 to 8000 B.C.E., changes occurred in human organization and food production that made possible the surpluses and specialization that were essential to the first stirrings of civilized life in the eighth millennium B.C.E. The economic and social patterns that developed after 8000 B.C.E. were in turn critical to the surge of invention between 4000 and 3000 B.C.E. that laid the basis for the first civilizations.

The rise of farming in the Neolithic era (between roughly 8000 and 5000 B.C.E.) is generally regarded as the source of the first truly revolutionary transformations in human history. But the thousands of years over which this process occurred suggest that it was not revolutionary in the usual sense of a rapid or abrupt change. Rather, the development of agriculture profoundly altered the relationships between human societies and their environments and between humans and other, often competing, animal species. The shift to agriculture also altered the way humans lived their daily lives.

Sedentary farming was made possible by technological breakthroughs that made the survival of the human species more secure and gave humans a much greater capacity to remake their environments to suit their needs. The most visible signs of this capacity were the spread of regularly cultivated fields and especially the development of towns, such as Jericho between 8500 and 7500 B.C.E. and Çatal Huyuk around 5500 B.C.E. Human control over other animal species was evidenced by the growing herds of domesticated goats, sheep, and cattle that be-

METAL AGE		
5000–2000 Yangshao culture in North China	**c. 1766** Emergence of Shang kingdom in China	
c. 3100 Rise of Egyptian civilization		
3500–2350 Civilization of Sumer		
2500–1500 Indus civilization in South Asia		
4000–3000 Age of innovation in the Middle East: Introduction of writing, metalworking, the wheel, and the plow		
5000 Domestication of maize (corn)	**2000** Kotosh culture in Peru	**1000–500** Olmec civilization in Mesoamerica
		400 Potatoes domesticated
3500 Llama domesticated	**1700–1300** Rise of village culture in Mesoamerica	
4000 B.C.E.	**2000** B.C.E.	**1** C.E.

came important sources of food and materials for clothing and shelter. Trade between these centers of settlement and production greatly increased contacts between different human groups, enhancing the innovation and increase of resources that were key features of the Neolithic era. Transformations of this sort occurred in all the areas of the world where civilizations emerged in the last two or three millennia B.C.E. Indeed, these transformations proved to be an essential prelude to the emergence of a variety of civilizations.

ANALYSIS

The Idea of Civilization in World Historical Perspective

The perception that there are fundamental differences between civilized and "barbaric" or "savage" peoples is very ancient and widespread. For thousands of years the Chinese, the civilized inhabitants of the "Middle Kingdom," set themselves off from neighboring peoples, including the pastoral or nomadic cattle- and sheep-herding peoples of the vast plains or steppes to the north and west of China proper, whom they regarded as barbarians. To the Chinese, being civilized was cultural, not biological or racial. If barbarians learned the Chinese language and adopted Chinese ways—from the clothes they wore to the food they ate—these outsiders were admitted into the exalted circle of the civilized.

A similar pattern of demarcation and cultural absorption was found among the American Indian peoples of present-day Mexico. Those who settled in the valleys of the mountainous interior, where they built great civilizations, lived in fear of invasions by peoples they regarded as barbarous and referred to as *chichimecs,* meaning "sons of the dog." The latter were nomadic hunters and gatherers who periodically moved down from the desert regions of North Mexico into the fertile central valleys in search of game and settlements to pillage. The Aztecs were simply the last, and perhaps the most fierce, of a long line of *chichimec* peoples who entered the valleys and either destroyed or conquered the urban-based empires that had developed there. But after the conquerors settled down in the mountain valleys, they adopted many of the religious beliefs and institutional patterns and much of the material culture of the vanquished peoples.

The word *civilization* is derived from the Latin word *civilis* meaning "of the citizens." The term was coined by the Romans to distinguish between themselves as citizens of a cosmopolitan, urban-focused civilization and the "inferior" peoples who lived in the forests and deserts on the fringes of their Mediterranean empire. Centuries earlier, the Greeks, who had contributed much to the rise of Roman civilization, made a similar distinction between themselves and outsiders. Because the languages that non-Greek peoples to the north of the Greek heartlands spoke sounded like senseless blabber to the Greeks, they lumped all the outsiders together as *barbarians,* which meant literally "those who cannot speak Greek." As in the case of the Chinese and Aztecs, the boundaries between civilized and barbarian for the Greeks and Romans were cultural, not biological. Regardless of the color of one's skin or the shape of one's nose, it was possible for free individuals to become members of a Greek *polis*—city-state—or to become Roman citizens by adopting Greek or Roman customs and swearing allegiance to the polis or the emperor.

Until the 17th and 18th centuries C.E., the primacy of cultural attributes (language, dress, manners, etc.) as the means by which civilized peoples set themselves off from barbaric ones had been rarely challenged. But in those centuries, two major changes occurred among thinkers in western Europe. First, efforts were made not only to define systematically the differences between civilized and barbarian, but to identify a series of stages in human development that ranged from the lowest savagery to the highest civilization. Depending on the writer in question, candidates for civilization ranged from Greece and Rome to (not surprisingly) Europe of the 17th and 18th centuries. Most of the other peoples of the globe, whose "discovery" since the 15th century had prompted the efforts to classify them in the first place, were ranked in increasingly complex hierarchies. Peoples like the Chinese and the Arabs, who had created great cities, monumental architecture, writing, advanced technology, and large empires, usually won a place along with the Europeans near the top of these ladders of human achievement. Nomadic, cattle- and sheep-herding peoples, such as the Mongols, were usually classified as barbarians. Civilized and barbarian peoples were in turn pitted against various sorts of *savages.* These ranged from the hunters and gatherers who inhabited much of North America and Australia before the arrival of the Europeans to the slash-and-burn or migratory cultivators in the hill and forest zones on most of the continents.

The second major shift that European writers brought about in our ideas regarding civilization began at the end of the 18th century but did not really take hold until a century later. In keeping with a growing emphasis in European thinking and social interaction on racial or biological differences, modes of human social organization and cultural expression were increasingly linked to what were alleged to be the innate capacities of each human race. Though no one could agree on what a race was or how many races there were, most European writers argued that some races were more inventive, more moral, more courageous, more artistic—thus more capable of building civilizations—than others. White, or Caucasian, Europeans were, of course, considered by white European authors to be the most capable of all. The hierarchy from savage to civilized took on a color dimension from white at the top, where the civilized peoples clustered, to yellow, red, brown, and black in descending order.

Some authors sought to reserve all the attainments of civilization for whites, or as some preferred to call them, *Aryans.* Confronted with clear evidence of civilization in places such as China and the Middle East, these writers categorized Arabs as Caucasian and argued that Aryan migrants had carried the essence of civilization to places like India and China. As the evolutionary theories of thinkers such as Charles Darwin came into vogue, race and level of cultural development were seen in the perspective of thousands of years of human change and adaptation rather than as being fixed in time. Nevertheless, this new perspective had little effect on the rankings of different human groups. Civilized whites were simply seen as having evolved much further than backward and barbaric peoples.

The perceived correspondence between race and level of development and the hardening of the boundaries between civilized and "inferior" peoples affected much more than intellectual discourse about the nature and history of human society. These beliefs were used to justify European imperialist expansion, which was seen as a "civilizing mission" aimed at uplifting barbaric and savage peoples across the globe. In the last half of the 19th century virtually all non-Western peoples came to be dominated by the Europeans, who were confident that they, as representatives of the highest civilization ever created, were best equipped to govern lesser breeds of humans.

In the 20th century much of the intellectual baggage that once gave credibility to the racially embedded hierarchies of civilized and savage peoples has been jettisoned. Racist thinking has been discredited by 20th-century developments, including the revolt of the colonized peoples and the persistent failure of racial

supremacists to provide convincing proof for innate differences in mental and physical aptitudes between various human groups. These trends, as well as research that has resulted in a much more sophisticated understanding of the evolutionary process, have led to the abandonment of rigid and self-serving 19th-century ideas about civilization. Yet, even though non-European peoples such as the Indians and Chinese are increasingly given credit for their civilized attainments, much ethnocentrism remains in the ways social theorists determine who is civilized and who is not.

Perhaps the best way to avoid the tendency to define the term with reference to one's own society is to view civilization as one of several human approaches to social organization, rather than attempting to identify specific kinds of cultural achievement (writing, cities, monumental architecture, etc.). All peoples, from small bands of hunters and gatherers to farmers and factory workers, live in societies. All societies produce cultures: combinations of the ideas, objects, and patterns of behavior that result from human social interaction. But not all societies and cultures generate the surplus production that permits the levels of specialization, scale, and complexity that distinguish civilizations from other modes of social organization. All peoples are intrinsically capable of building civilizations, but many have lacked the resource base, historical circumstances, or, quite simply, the motivation for doing so.

Questions: Identify a society you consider to be civilized. What criteria did you use to determine that it was civilized? Can you apply those criteria to other societies? Can you think of societies that might not fit your criteria and yet be civilizations?

HUMAN LIFE IN THE ERA OF HUNTERS AND GATHERERS

Focal Point: During the Paleolithic (Old Stone) Age, *Homo sapiens,* one of several humanlike species, had gained clear advantages over its rivals. Superior intelligence, manual dexterity, and the tool making and language development they made possible were critical to this outcome. By 10,000 B.C.E., *Homo sapiens* had spread over much of the earth. Most human groups in this era supported themselves by *hunting and gathering,* but by the end of the Paleolithic Age, many peoples were experimenting with agriculture and permanent settlements.

By the end of the Paleolithic era in 12,000 B.C.E., humans had evolved in physical appearance and mental capacity to roughly the same level as today. Our species, *Homo sapiens,* had been competing with increasing success for game and campsites with other humanlike creatures for nearly 30,000 years. *Homo sapiens'* enlarged brain, critical to the survival of all of the branches of the genus *Homo,* was virtually the same size as that of modern humans. The erect posture of Stone Age humans freed their hands. The combination of these free hands with opposable thumbs and a large brain made it possible for different human species to craft and manipulate tools and weapons of increasing sophistication. These implements helped to offset the humans' marked inferiority in body strength and speed to rival predators, such as wolves and wild cats, as well as to many of the creatures that humans themselves hunted. A more highly developed brain also allowed humans to transform cries and grunts into the patterned sounds that make up language. Language greatly enhanced the possibilities for cooperation and a sense of cohesion within the small

bands that were the predominant form of human social organization in this era. By the last phase of the Paleolithic epoch, these advantages had made *Homo sapiens* a species capable of mastering the earth.

Paleolithic Culture

No matter how much *Homo sapiens* might have developed in physical appearance and brain capacity by around 12,000 B.C.E., its culture, with some exceptions, was not radically different from the cultures of rival human species such as the Neanderthals, who had died out thousands of years earlier. Fire, perhaps the most central element in the material culture of Paleolithic peoples, had been mastered nearly a half million years earlier. Originally snatched from conflagrations caused by lightning or lava flows, fire was domesticated as humans developed techniques to preserve glowing embers and to start fires by rubbing sticks and other materials together. The control of fire led to numerous improvements in the lives of Stone Age peoples. It rendered edible a much

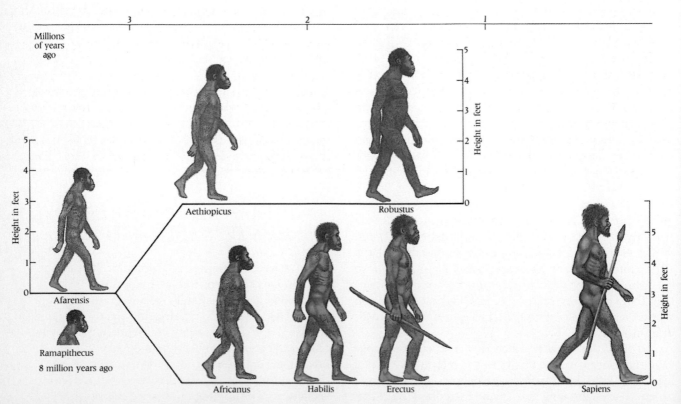

The hominoids' upright posture, which freed their hands, meant that over long periods of time Homo sapiens *could develop weapons and tools.*

Early human groups developed a variety of stone tools. The tools shown here include weapon points (second row from the top), scrapers for peeling off animal hides or working wood (third row from the top), and a hammerstone (lower left).

number of tools to assist them in these critical endeavors. Tools of wood and bone have perished; thus, surviving stone tools are our main evidence of the technology of this epoch. These tools had advanced considerably by the late Old Stone Age. Early human tools, discovered by archeologists at sites well over 2 million years old, were made by breaking off the edges of stone cores to create crude points or rough cutting surfaces. By the late Paleolithic period, humans had grown much more adept at working stone. They preferred to chip and sharpen flakes broken off the core stone. These chips could be fashioned into knife blades, arrow points, or choppers, which had a wide range of uses from hunting and warfare to skinning animal carcasses and harvesting wild plants.

Earlier human groups had produced evidence of artistic expression: small figurines and decorated implements. The late Paleolithic was a period of particularly intense creativity. Fine miniature sculpture, beads and other forms of jewelry, and carved bones were produced by Paleolithic peoples, but their most impressive artistic contributions were the cave paintings that have been discovered at sites like those in southern France and Spain. Other paintings—and in many cases small sculptures, including those found at a number of Middle Eastern sites—appear to have religious significance. They may have been intended, for example, to depict prominent deities or to promote fertility. There is also speculation that paintings at some sites may represent early counting systems or primitive calendars. Whatever their purpose, the art of the Old Stone Age era suggests quite a sophisticated level of thinking. It also indicates that humans were becoming increasingly interested in expressing themselves artistically and in leaving lasting images of their activities and concerns.

The Spread of Human Culture

The possession of fire and tools with which to make clothing and shelters made it possible for different human species to extend the range of their habitation far beyond the areas where they had originated. During the last Ice Age, which began about 2.5 million years ago and ended around 8000 B.C.E., humans first moved northward from Africa into Europe and eastward from the present-day Middle East into central Asia, India, and East Asia. Neanderthals and related peoples were found across this zone as late as 35,000 B.C.E., and some archeologists claim that by then they may also have begun to migrate across a land bridge into the continents we now call North and South America. Glaciation, which had

wider range of foods, particularly animal flesh, which was virtually the only source of protein in a culture without cows, goats, or chickens and thus lacking in milk, cheese, and eggs. Cooked meat, which was easier to digest, may also have been more effectively preserved and stored, thus giving Stone Age peoples an additional buffer against the constant threat of starvation. In addition, fire was used to treat animal hides for clothing and to harden wooden weapons and tools. Its light and warmth became the focal point of human campsites.

By late Paleolithic (Old Stone) Age times, human groups survived by combining hunting and fishing with the gathering of fruits, berries, grains, and root crops that grew in the wild. They had created a considerable

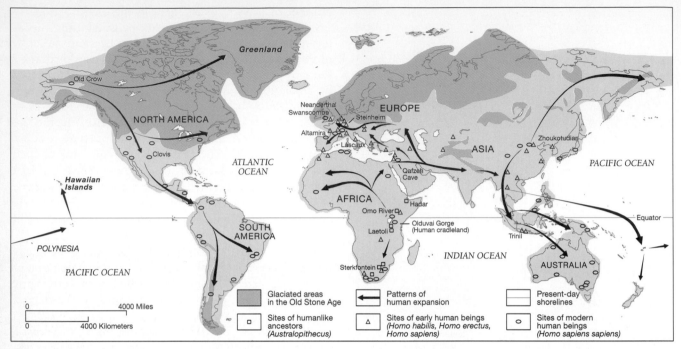

The Spread of Human Populations, About 10,000 B.C.E.

caused a significant drop in sea levels, resulted in land bridges to the New World and Australia. By around 12,000 B.C.E., human colonies were found in North and South America and in the south and west of Australia. Thus, by the late Paleolithic period, groups of the *Homo sapiens sapiens* species had colonized all of the continents except Antarctica.

Human Society and Daily Life at the End of the Old Stone Age

Most human societies in the Old Stone Age consisted of small groups that migrated regularly in pursuit of game animals and wild plants. But recent archeological research has shown that in some places, natural conditions and human ingenuity permitted some groups to establish settlements where they lived for much of the year, and in some cases for generation after generation. These settled communities harvested wild grains that grew in abundance in many areas. After surviving for centuries in this way, some of these communities made the transition to true farming by domesticating plants and animals near their permanent village sites. Many Paleolithic peoples who established enduring settlements did not advance to domesticated agricultural production; in fact, they often reverted to a migratory hunting-and-gathering existence.

The rejection of full-fledged agriculture and the reversion to migratory lifestyles caution us against seeing farming as an inevitable stage in human development. There was no simple progression from hunting-and-gathering peoples to settled foraging societies and then to genuine farming communities. Rather, human groups experimented with different strategies for survival. Climatic changes, the availability of water for crop irrigation, dietary preferences, and patterns of procreation affected the strategy adopted by a particular group. Only those groups involved in crop and animal domestication, however, have proved capable of producing civilizations.

However successful a particular group proved to be at hunting and gathering, few could support a band larger than 20 to 30 men, women, and children. Dependence on migrating herds of game dictated that these bands were nomadic, though many moved back and forth between the same forest and grazing areas year after year. The migration patterns meant that small numbers of humans needed an extensive land area to support themselves, and consequently human population densities were very low.

Though we imagine Stone Age peoples living in caves, recent research suggests that most preferred to live on open ground. The migratory peoples who lived on hilltops or in forest clearings built temporary shelters of skins and leaves or grass thatching. Their flimsy campsites were readily abandoned when herd movements or threats from competing bands prompted migration. Though it is likely that bands developed a sense of territoriality, boundaries were vague, and much interhuman strife focused on rival claims to sources of game and wild foods.

Within each band, labor was divided according to gender. Men hunted and fished in riverine or coastal areas. Because they became skilled in the use of weapons in the hunt, it is also likely that men protected the band from animal predators and raids by other human groups. Though women's roles were less adventuresome and aggressive, they were arguably more critical to the survival of the band. Women gathered the foods that provided the basic subsistence of the band and permitted its survival in times when hunting parties were unsuccessful. Women also became adept in the application of medicinal plants, which were the only means that Paleolithic peoples had to ward off disease. Because life expectancy was short—20 years or less on the average—and mortality rates for women in labor and infants were very high, women had to give birth many times in order for the band to increase its numbers even slightly.

Settling Down: Dead Ends and Transitions

Though most humans lived in small hunting-and-gathering bands until well into the era of the agrarian revolution between 8000 and 5000 B.C.E., some prefarming peoples worked out a very different strategy of survival. They managed to devise more intensive hunting-and-gathering patterns that permitted them to establish semipermanent and even permanent settlements and to

CLOSEUP

Tales of the Hunt: The Meanings of Paleolithic Cave Paintings

The first historical events recorded by humans were the animal hunts that are depicted in remarkably realistic and colorful cave paintings of a variety of animals from woolly mammoths to horses. These Paleolithic cave paintings have been discovered in diverse geographical regions from southern Europe and North Africa to the Middle East. Because writing would not be devised by any human group for many millennia to come, we cannot be certain of the meanings that those who created the paintings were trying to convey. Some of them may have been done purely for the sake of artistic expression. But others, which clearly depict animals in flight, pursued by human hunters, were probably painted to celebrate and commemorate actual incidents in particularly successful hunting expeditions. Their locations deep in cave complexes, and the rather consistent choice of game animals as subject matter, suggest that they also served a ritual purpose. Perhaps capturing the images of animals in art was seen as a way of assisting future hunting parties in the wild. In addition, it is possible that those who painted the animal figures hoped to acquire some of the strength and speed of the animals depicted in order to improve their chances in the hunt and to ward off animals that preyed on the human hunters themselves. Whatever their intentions, those who executed these remarkable works of art also created the first conscious historical accounts of the human experience.

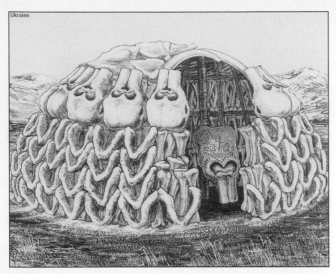

This sketch of a mammoth-bone hut suggests the ingenuity in the design and construction of these single-room structures.

support larger and more complex forms of social organization. Among the most spectacular of the Paleolithic settlements are those of central Russia. Apparently there was an abundance of large but slow woolly mammoths in that region some 20,000 years ago. The hunting techniques of the local peoples produced a supply of meat that, when supplemented by wild plant foods gathered in the area, made it possible for them to live in the same place throughout much of the year. Their dependence on the mammoths is suggested by the bones found in refuse pits at the settlement sites and by the bones of the larger mammoths that were used extensively for the walls and roofing of dwellings.

The storage pits for food and the other materials found at the sites of the central Russian settlements suggest that the mammoth-bone dwellers participated in trading networks that involved groups in the Black Sea region nearly 500 miles away. Burial patterns and differing degrees of bodily decoration also indicate that there were clear status differences among the groups that inhabited the settlements. Mammoth-bone communities lasted from about 18,000 to 10,000 B.C.E., when they suddenly disappeared for reasons that are still unknown.

Even more sophisticated than the central Russian settlements were those of the *Natufian complex,* which extended over much of present-day Israel, Jordan, and Lebanon. Climate changes, which occurred between 12,000 and 11,000 B.C.E., enabled wild barley and wheat plants to spread over much of this area. When supplemented with nuts and the meat of gazelles and other game, these wild grains proved sufficient to sup-

port numerous and quite densely populated settlements on a permanent basis. Between about 10,500 and 8000 B.C.E., the Natufian culture flourished. The population at Natufian settlement sites reached as high as six to seven times that of other early Neolithic communities. The Natufians developed quite sophisticated techniques of storing grain, and they devised pestles and grinding slabs to prepare it to eat. They built circular and oval dwellings of stone that were occupied year round for centuries.

The evidence we have from housing layout, burial sites, jewelry, and other materials indicates that, like the mammoth-bone dwellers of central Russia, Natufian society was stratified. Clothing appears to have been used to distinguish a person's rank, and grand burial ceremonies marked the passing of community chieftains. There is also evidence that Natufian society was *matrilocal*—young men went to live with their wives' families—and *matrilineal*—family descent and inheritance were traced through the female line. The fact that women gathered food crops in the wild may explain the power and influence they enjoyed in Natufian settlements.

The Natufian strategy for survival did not involve the development of new tools or techniques for production. It rested primarily on the intensification of gathering wild grains and the improvement of storage techniques. The Natufians' concentration on a couple of grain staples, gazelle meat, and nuts rendered the culture vulnerable through overspecialization. After 9000 B.C.E., the climate of the region where the Natufian settlements were located grew more and more arid. The grains and game on which they had grown dependent were reduced or vanished from many locations. One thousand years later, all the Natufian sites had been abandoned. Some villagers reverted to migratory hunting and gathering in an effort to broaden the range of animals they could hunt and the foods they could harvest from the wild. Other villagers—usually those located near large and reliable sources of water—domesticated the grains they had once gathered in the woodlands.

A Precarious Existence

Until the late Old Stone Age era, about 12,000 B.C.E., advances in human technology and social organization were remarkably slow compared with the advances that have occurred since about 8000 B.C.E. Millions of years of evolution of the genus *Homo* had produced small numbers of humans mostly scattered in tiny bands across six continents. On the average, the lives of members of these bands were—to paraphrase a cynical, 17th-century

English philosopher, Thomas Hobbes—violent and short. They crouched around their campfires in constant fear of animal predators and human enemies. They were at the mercy of the elements and helpless in the face of injury or disease. They had a few crude tools and weapons; their nomadic existence reflected their dependence on the feeding cycles of migrating animals.

The smaller numbers of human groups that lived in permanent settlements had better shelters, a more secure supply of food, and larger communities on which to draw in their relentless struggle for survival. But their lifestyles were precarious: their specialized hunting-and-gathering practices meant that shifts in grazing patterns or the climate could undermine their carefully developed cultures. Late Paleolithic humans had considerably improved on earlier, and by then extinct, versions of the species. But there was little to suggest that within a few thousand years they would radically transform the environments in which they lived and would dominate all other forms of life.

AGRICULTURE AND THE ORIGINS OF CIVILIZATION: THE NEOLITHIC REVOLUTION

Focal Point: In the Neolithic (New Stone) Age, between roughly 8000 and 3500 B.C.E., some human societies, in different areas over much of the globe, crossed one of the great watersheds in all of human history. They mastered sedentary agriculture and domesticated animals that would prove critical to human development, such as cattle, sheep and horses. These innovations produced the surpluses and rising populations that made possible the rise of genuine towns and the increasing specialization of occupations within human societies.

There was nothing natural or inevitable about the development of agriculture. Because cultivation of plants requires more labor than hunting and gathering, we can assume that Stone Age humans gave up their former ways of life reluctantly and slowly. In fact, peoples such as the Bushmen of Southwest Africa still follow them today. But between about 8000 and 3500 B.C.E., increasing numbers of humans shifted to dependence on cultivated crops and domesticated animals for their subsistence. By about 7000 B.C.E., their tools and skills had advanced sufficiently to enable cultivating peoples to support towns with over one thousand people, such as Jericho in the valley of the Jordan River and Çatal Huyuk in present-day Turkey.

By 3500 B.C.E., agricultural peoples in the Middle East could support sufficient numbers of noncultivating specialists to give rise to the first civilizations. As this pattern spread to or developed independently in other centers across the globe, the character of most human lives and the history of the species as a whole were fundamentally transformed.

Because there are no written records of the transition period between 8000 and 5000 B.C.E., when many animals were first domesticated and plants were cultivated on a regular basis, we cannot be certain why and how some peoples adopted these new ways of producing food and other necessities of life. Climatic changes associated with the retreat of the glaciers at the end of the last Ice Age (about 12,000 B.C.E.), may have played an important role. These climatic shifts prompted the migration of many big game animals to new pasturelands in northern areas. They also left a dwindling supply of game for human hunters in areas such as the Middle East, where agriculture first arose and many animals were first domesticated. Climatic shifts also led to changes in the distribution and growing patterns of wild grains and other crops on which hunters and gatherers depended.

In addition, it is likely that the shift to sedentary farming was prompted in part by an increase in human populations in certain areas. This population growth may have been caused by changes in the climate and plant and animal life, forcing hunting bands to move into the territories where these shifts had been minimal. It is also possible that population growth occurred within these unaffected regions because the hunting-and-gathering pattern reached higher levels of productivity. Peoples like the Natufians found that their human communities could grow significantly by intensively harvesting grains that grew in the wild. As the population grew, more and more attention was given to the grain harvest, which eventually led to the conscious and systematic cultivation of plants and thus the agrarian revolution.

The Domestication of Plants and Animals

The peoples who first cultivated cereal grains had long observed them growing in the wild and gleaned their seeds, as they gathered other plants for their leaves and roots. In late Paleolithic times, both wild barley and wheat grew over large areas in present-day Turkey, Iraq, Syria, Jordan, Lebanon, and Israel. Hunting-and-gathering bands in these areas may have consciously experimented with planting and nurturing seeds taken from the wild, or they may have accidentally discovered the principles of domestication by observing the growth of seeds dropped near their campsites.

However it began, the practice of agriculture caught on only gradually. Archeological evidence suggests that the first agriculturists retained their hunting-and-gathering activities as a hedge against the ever-present threat of starvation. But as Stone Age peoples became more adept at cultivating a growing range of crops, including various fruits, olives, and protein-rich legumes such as peas and beans, the effort they expended on activities outside agriculture diminished.

It is probable that the earliest farmers broadcast wild seeds, a practice that cut down on labor but sharply reduced the potential yield. Over the centuries, more and more care was taken to select the best grain for seed and to mix different strains in ways that improved both crop yields and resistance to plant diseases. As the time required to tend growing plants and the dependence on agricultural production for subsistence increased, some roving bands chose to settle down, while others practiced a mix of hunting and shifting cultivation that allowed them to continue to move about.

Though several animals may have been domesticated before the discovery of agriculture, the two processes combined to make up the critical transformation in human culture called the Neolithic revolution. Different animal species were tamed in different ways that reflected both their own natures and the ways in which they interacted with humans. Dogs, for example, were originally wolves that hunted humans or scavenged at their campsites. As early as 12,000 B.C.E., Stone Age peoples found that wolf pups could be tamed and trained to track and corner game. The strains of dogs that gradually developed proved adept at controlling herd animals like sheep. Relatively docile and defenseless herds of sheep could be domesticated once their leaders had been captured and tamed. Sheep, goats, and pigs (which also were scavengers at human campsites) were first domesticated in the Middle East between 8500 and 7000 B.C.E. Horned cattle, which could run faster and were better able to defend themselves than wild sheep, were not tamed until about 6500 B.C.E.

Domesticated animals such as cattle and sheep provided New Stone Age humans with additional sources of protein-rich meat, and in some cases, milk. Animal hides and wool greatly expanded the materials from which clothes, containers, shelters, and crude boats could be crafted. Animal horns and bones could be carved or used for needles and other utensils. Because plows and wheels did not come into use until the Bronze Age (c. 4000–3500 B.C.E.), most Neolithic peo-

ples made little use of animal power for farming, transportation, or travel. There is evidence, however, that peoples in northern areas used tamed reindeer to pull sledges, and those farther south used camels for transporting goods. More importantly, Neolithic peoples used domesticated herd animals as a steady source of manure to enrich the soil and thus improve the yield of the crops that were gradually becoming the basis of their livelihood.

The Spread of the Neolithic Revolution

The greater labor involved in cultivation, and the fact that it did not at first greatly enhance the peoples' security or living standards, caused many bands to stay with long-tested subsistence strategies. Through most of the Neolithic period, sedentary agricultural communities co-existed with more numerous bands of hunters and gatherers, migratory cultivators, and hunters and fishers. Even after sedentary agriculture became the basis for the livelihood of the majority of humans, hunters and gatherers and shifting cultivators held out in many areas of the globe.

The domestication of animals also gave rise to *pastoralism,* which has proved to be the strongest competitor to sedentary agriculture as a way of life throughout most of the world. Pastoralism has thrived in semiarid areas such as central Asia, the Sudanic belt south of the Sahara desert in Africa, and the savanna zone of East and South Africa. These areas were incapable of supporting dense or large populations. The nomadic, herding way of life has tended to produce independent and hardy peoples, well versed in the military skills needed not only for their survival but also to challenge more heavily populated agrarian societies. Horse-riding nomads who herd sheep or cattle have destroyed powerful kingdoms and laid the foundations for vast empires. The camel nomads of Arabia played critical roles in the rise of Islamic civilization. The cattle-herding peoples of Central, East, and South Africa produced some of the most formidable preindustrial military organizations. Only in the rather recent period of the Industrial Revolution has the power of nomadic peoples been irreparably broken and the continuation of their cultures threatened by the steady encroachment of sedentary peoples.

In the era of the Neolithic revolution (roughly 8000–5000 B.C.E.), agriculture was far from the dominant mode of support for human societies. But those who adopted it survived and increased in numbers. They also passed on their techniques of production to other peoples. The cultivation of wheat and barley spread throughout the Middle East and eastward to India.

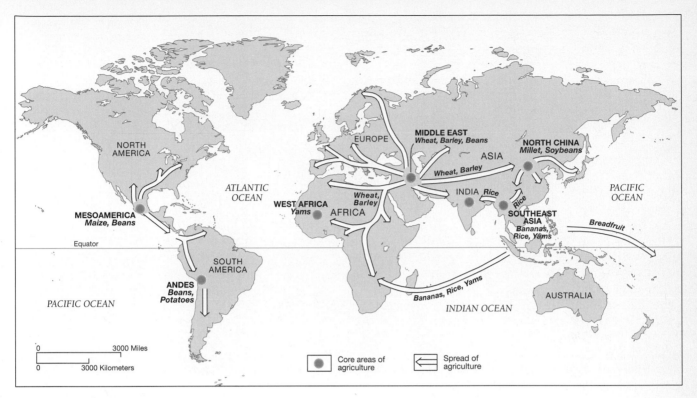

The Spread of Agriculture

These crops also spread northward to Europe, where oats and rye were added later. From Egypt, the cultivation of grain crops and fibers, such as flax and cotton used for clothing, spread to peoples along the Nile in the interior of Africa, along the North African coast, and across the vast savanna zone south of the Sahara desert.

Agriculture in the African rain forest zone farther south evolved independently in the 2nd millennium B.C.E. and was based on root crops such as cassava and tree crops such as bananas and palm nuts. In northern China during the Neolithic period, a millet-based agricultural system developed along the Huanghe or Yellow River basin. From this core region, it spread in the last millennium B.C.E. east toward the North China Sea and southward toward the Yangtze basin. A later but independent agricultural revolution based on rice began in mainland Southeast Asia sometime before 5000 B.C.E. and slowly spread into South China and India and to the islands of Southeast Asia. In the Americas maize-(corn-), manioc-, and sweet potato–based agrarian systems arose in Mesoamerica (Mexico and Central America today) and present-day Peru. Long before the arrival of Columbus in the Americas in 1492 C.E., these and other crops had spread through large portions of the continents of the Western Hemisphere, from the temperate woodlands of the North Atlantic coast to the rain forests of the Amazon region. Thus, varying patterns of agricultural production were disseminated on all the inhabited continents except Australia, to virtually all the regions of the globe with sufficient rainfall and suitable temperatures.

The Transformation of Material Life

With the development of agriculture, humans began to radically transform the environments in which they lived. A growing portion of humans became sedentary cultivators who cleared the lands around their settlements and controlled the plants that grew and the animals that grazed on them. The greater presence of humans was also apparent in the steadily growing size and numbers of settlements. These were found both in areas that they had long inhabited and in new regions that farming allowed them to settle. This great increase in the number of sedentary farmers is primarily responsible for the leap in human population during the Neolithic transition. For tens of thousands of years before agriculture was developed, the total number of humans had fluctuated between an estimated five and eight million persons. By 4000 B.C.E., after four or five millennia of farming, their

Interior of Skara Brae, a prehistoric dwelling.

number had risen to 60 or 70 million. Hunting-and-gathering bands managed to subsist in the zones between cultivated areas and continued to war and trade with sedentary peoples. But villages and cultivated fields became the dominant features of human habitation over much of the globe.

The growth of sedentary farming communities in the Neolithic era greatly accelerated the pace of technological and social change. The relatively sudden surge in invention and social complexity in the Neolithic era marks one of the great turning points in human history. Increased reliance on sedentary cultivation led to the development of a wide variety of agricultural implements, from digging sticks used to break up the soil and axes to clear forested areas to the introduction of the plow. Techniques of seed selection, planting, fertilization, and weeding improved steadily. By the end of the Neolithic period, human societies in several areas had devised ways of storing rainwater and rechanneling river water to irrigate plants. The reservoirs, canals, dikes, and sluices that permitted water storage and control represented another major advance in the ability of humans to remake their environment.

More and better tools and permanent settlements gave rise to larger, more elaborate, commodious housing and the construction of community ritual centers.

Building materials varied greatly by region, but sundried bricks, wattle (interwoven branches, usually plastered with mud), and stone structures were associated with early agricultural communities. Seasonal harvests made improved techniques of food storage essential. At first, baskets and leather containers were employed. By the early Neolithic period pottery—which protected stored foods better from moisture and dust—was known to several cultures in the Middle East.

Houses in early agricultural settlements usually included special storage areas, and most were centered on clay or stone hearths that were ventilated by a hole in the roof. The presence of stored food in early villages made the houses tempting targets for nomadic bands or rival settlements. For that reason they were increasingly fortified. More dependable and varied food supplies, walls, and sturdy houses greatly enhanced the security and comfort of human groups. These conditions spurred higher rates of procreation and lowered mortality rates, at least in times when crop yields were high.

Social Differentiation

The surplus production that agriculture made possible was the key to the social transformations that made up another dimension of the Neolithic revolution. Surpluses meant that cultivators could exchange part of their harvest for the specialized services and products of noncultivators, such as toolmakers and weavers. Human communities became differentiated on an occupational basis. Political and religious leaders arose and eventually formed elite classes, whose members intermarried and became involved in ruling and ceremonies on a full-time basis. But in the Neolithic period, the specialized production of stone tools, weapons, and perhaps pottery was a more important consequence of the development of agriculture than the formation of elites. Originally, each household crafted the tools and weapons it required, just as it wove its own baskets and produced its own clothing. Over time, however, families or individuals who proved particularly skilled in these tasks began to manufacture implements beyond their own needs and to exchange them for grain, milk, or meat.

Villages in certain regions specialized in the production of materials that were in demand in other areas. For example, flint, which is extremely hard, was the preferred material for the blades of axes. Axes were needed for forest clearing, which was essential to the extension of cultivation throughout much of Europe. The demand was so great that villagers who lived near flint deposits could support themselves either by mining the flint or by crafting the flint heads that were then traded, often with peoples who lived far from the sources of production. Such exchanges set precedents for regional specialization and interregional trade, but the emergence of full-time merchants appears to have been associated with the rise of cities in a later period.

It is difficult to know precisely what impact the shift to agriculture had on the social structure of the communities that made the transition. Social distinctions were most likely heightened by occupational differences but well-defined social stratification, such as that which produces class identity, was nonexistent. Leadership remained largely communal, though village alliances may have existed in some areas. It is likely that property in Neolithic times was held in common by the community, or at least that all households in the community were given access to village lands and water.

By virtue of their key roles as plant gatherers in pre-farming cultures, it can be surmised that women played a critical part in the domestication of plants. Nonetheless, there is evidence that their position declined in many agricultural communities. They worked the fields and have continued to work them in most cultures. But men took over tasks involving heavy labor, for example, land clearing, hoeing, and plowing. Men monopolized the new tools and weapons devised in the Neolithic era and

later times, and they controlled the vital irrigation systems that developed in most of the early centers of agriculture. As far as we can tell, men also took the lead in taming, breeding, and raising the large animals associated with both farming and pastoral communities. Thus, though Neolithic art suggests that earth and fertility cults, which focused on feminine deities, retained their appeal [see the Document that follows], the social and economic position of women may have begun to decline with the shift to sedentary agriculture.

THE FIRST TOWNS: SEEDBEDS OF CIVILIZATION

Focal Point: By about 7000 B.C.E., techniques of agricultural production in the Middle East had reached a level at which it was possible to support thousands of people, many of whom were not engaged in agriculture, in densely populated settlements. In these and other Middle Eastern Neolithic settlements, occupational specialization and the formation of religious and political-military elite groups advanced significantly. Trade became essential for the community's survival and was carried on with peoples at considerable distances, perhaps by specialized merchants. Crafts such as pottery, metalworking, and jewelry making were highly developed.

Two of the earliest of these settlements were at Jericho in what is today part of the autonomous Palestinian entity, and at Çatal Huyuk in present-day southern Turkey. With populations of about 2000 and from 4000 to 6000 people, respectively, Jericho and Çatal Huyuk would be seen today as little more than large villages or small towns. But in the perspective of human cultural development they represented the first stirrings of urban life.

Nonetheless, these earliest centers were quite isolated. They were merely tiny islands of sedentary cultivators and small numbers of townspeople, surrounded by vast plains and woodlands. The earliest town centers appear to have traded rather extensively but to have maintained only intermittent and limited contacts with neighboring hunting-and-gathering peoples. Though small in size and not highly specialized in comparison with the cities of Sumer and other early civilizations, the first towns played critical roles in continuing the Neolithic transformation. Their ruling elites and craft specialists contributed in major ways to the introduction in the 4th millennium B.C.E. of critical inventions—such as the wheel, the plow, writing, and the use of bronze—that secured

DOCUMENT

Women in Early Art

The earliest writing system that we know of was not introduced until around 3500 B.C.E. in the civilization of *Sumer* in Mesopotamia (see Chapter 2). Consequently, evidence for piecing together the history of human life in the Paleolithic and Neolithic eras comes mainly from surviving artifacts from campsites and early towns. Stone tools, bits of pottery or cloth, and the remains of Stone Age dwellings can now be rather precisely dated. When combined with other material objects from the same site and time period, they provide us with a fairly good sense of the daily activities and life cycle of the peoples who created them.

As we have seen in the earlier discussion of cave paintings, of all of the material remains of the Stone Age era, none provide better insights into the social organization and thinking of early humans than works of art. Much of what we know, for example, about gender relations, or the positions of males and females and the interaction between them, has been interpreted from the study of the different forms of artistic expression of Stone Age peoples. The early appearance (c. 25,000 B.C.E.) of rock carvings, such as the wonderfully robust and very pregnant "Venus of Laussel" shown here, indicates the importance of childbearing to the survival of the small bands of hunters and gatherers that once made up the whole population of the human species.

The "Venus" was found in the remains of an early campsite at St.-Germain-en-Laye in France. Figurines or

the future of civilized life as the central pattern of human history.

Jericho

Proximity to the Jordan River and the deep and clear waters of an oasis spring account for repeated human settlement at the place where the town of *Jericho* was built. By 7000 B.C.E., over ten acres at the site were occupied by round houses of mud and brick resting on stone foundations. Most early houses had only a single room with mud plaster floors and a domed ceiling, but some houses had as many as three rooms. Entry to these windowless dwellings was provided by a single wood-framed doorway and steps down to the floor of the main room underground. Although there is no evidence that the town was fortified in the early stages of its growth, its expanding wealth made the building of walls for protection from external enemies increasingly imperative. The town was enclosed by a ditch cut into the rocky soil and a wall reaching almost 12 feet in height. The extensive excavation required for this construction is quite impressive because the peoples who undertook it possessed neither picks nor shovels. The stones for the wall were dragged from a riverbed nearly a mile away. These feats of transport and construction suggest not only a sizable labor force but one that was well organized and disciplined.

carvings of fertility symbols of this sort are among the most common artifacts of early human cultures.

Such carvings and later figurines also suggest the existence of cults devoted to earth and mother goddesses. The centrality of female symbolism in early art and religion may also indicate the considerable influence that women wielded both within hunting and gathering bands and in the first cities and towns of the Neolithic era. As we have seen, the chief deity of Çatal Huyuk was a goddess, who is depicted in surviving sculptures as a young woman giving birth or nursing a small child and as an old woman accompanied by a vulture. The large number and diverse natures of the feminine figurines found at Hacilar, another early town uncovered in present-day Turkey, graphically illustrate the many roles that women played in this early town culture. Shown here in sketches made from the original baked-clay figurines, they include a mother goddess and several fertility figures.

Questions: Why do you think that women are more frequently depicted in early art forms than men? On the basis of the sample provided in these illustrations, which of women's roles in early human society were deemed the most important? Why might women have been seen as deities in these early societies, and what sort of requests might those who worshiped goddesses have made through their prayers and offerings?

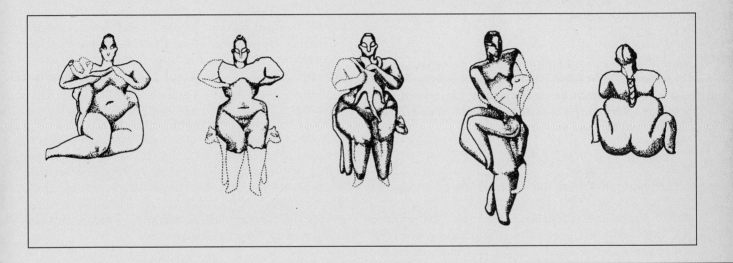

When Jericho was rebuilt in later centuries, the wall reached a height of nearly 15 feet, and the fortifications included a stone tower at least 25 feet high. The area covered by the town increased. Round houses gave way to rectangular ones, entered through larger and more elaborately decorated wooden doorways. Houses were built of improved bricks, were provided with plaster hearths and stone mills for grinding grain, and were furnished with storage baskets and straw mats. In addition, small buildings have been found that were used as religious shrines during the later stages of the town's history.

Though the economy of Jericho was based primarily upon the farming of wheat and barley, there is considerable evidence of reliance on both hunting and trade. Domesticated goats provided meat and milk, while gazelles and various marsh birds were hunted for their flesh, hides, and feathers. The town was close to large supplies of salt, sulfur, and pitch. These materials, which were in great demand during this era, were traded for obsidian, a dark, glasslike volcanic rock; semiprecious stones from Anatolia, turquoise from the Sinai; and cowrie shells from the Red Sea.

The ruins excavated at Jericho indicate that the town was governed by a distinct and quite powerful ruling group, which was probably allied to the keepers of the shrine centers. There were specialized artisans and a small merchant class. In addition to fertility figurines and animal carvings like those found at many other sites, the

This artist's reconstruction depicts the layout of living units in the town of Çatal Huyuk. A family dwelling included an open hearth and an oven in the wall, clearly demarcated and slightly raised sleeping areas, and benches along the walls.

inhabitants of Jericho sculpted life-sized, highly naturalistic human figures and heads. These sculptures, which may have been used in ancestor cults, give us vivid impressions of the physical features of the people who enjoyed the wealth and security of Jericho.

Çatal Huyuk

The first community at this site in southern Turkey was founded around 7000 B.C.E., somewhat later than the earliest settlements at Jericho. But the town that grew up at *Çatal Huyuk* was a good deal more extensive than that at Jericho and contained a larger and more diversified population. Çatal Huyuk was in fact the most advanced human center of the Neolithic period. At the peak of its power and prosperity the city occupied 32 acres and contained as many as 6000 people. Its rectangular buildings, which were centers of family life and community interaction, were remarkably uniform and were built of mud-dried bricks. They had windows high in their walls and were entered from holes in their flat roofs. These entryways also served as chimneys for the fireplaces within the houses. The houses were joined together to provide fortification for the town. Movement within the settlement was mainly across the roofs and terraces of the houses. Since each dwelling had a substantial storeroom, when the ladder to the roof entrance was pulled up, each became a separate fortress within the larger complex.

The standardization of housing and construction at Çatal Huyuk suggests an even more imposing ruling group than that found at Jericho. The many religious shrines at the site also indicate the existence of a powerful priesthood. The shrines were built in the same way as ordinary houses, but they contained sanctuaries surrounded by four or five rooms related to the ceremonies of the shrine's cult. The walls of these religious centers were filled with paintings of bulls and carrion eaters, especially vultures, suggesting fertility cults and rites associated with death. The surviving statuary indicates that the chief deity of the Çatal Huyuk peoples was a goddess.

The obvious importance of the cult shrines and the elaborate burial practices of the peoples of Çatal Huyuk reveal the growing role of religion in the lives of Neolithic peoples. The carefully carved sculptures associated with the sanctuaries, and the fine jewelry, mirrors, and weapons found buried with the dead, attest to the high level of material culture and artistic proficiency achieved by these town dwellers.

Excavations of the settlement also reveal an economic base that was much broader and richer than that of Jericho. Hunting remained a factor, but the breeding of goats, sheep, and cattle vastly surpassed that associated with Jericho. Çatal Huyuk's inhabitants consumed a wide range of foods, including several grains, peas, berries, berry wine, and vegetable oils made from nuts. Trade was extensive with the peoples in the surrounding hills and also in places as distant as present-day Syria and the Mediterranean region. Çatal Huyuk was also a major center of production by artisans. Its flint and obsidian weapons, jewelry, and obsidian mirrors were some of the finest produced in the Neolithic era. The remains of the town's culture leave little doubt that its inhabitants had achieved a civilized level of existence.

CONCLUSION

The Watershed of the 4th Millennium B.C.E.

Though Jericho, Çatal Huyuk, and similar settlements can best be seen as towns rather than cities, they displayed many of the characteristics that have come to be associated with urban life. Perhaps they were too small and too dependent on crops grown by their own inhabitants to be labeled cities. But they clearly set the patterns for layout, fortification, and standardization that would be found in the first cities in neighboring regions such as Sumer in Mesopotamia and Egypt, and in distant urban complexes such as Harappa in northwest India and Kush and Axum in Africa. The level of specialization and political organization these early townspeople had attained proved critical to the invention and dissemination of new tools and production techniques during the 4th millennium B.C.E. The years from 4000 to 3000 B.C.E. saw a second wave of major transformations in human culture in the Middle East and nearby regions. These shifts marked the transition from the last of the Stone Ages to the Bronze Age and succeeding epochs of metalworking.

During this transition era, the use of the plow significantly increased crop yields, and wheeled vehicles made it possible to carry a greater volume of food and other raw materials over greater distances. Both developments meant that larger noncultivating populations could be supported and concentrated in particular locales. Though copper had been used for spear and axe heads for millennia, accident and experiment revealed that when copper was mixed with other metals such as tin, it formed bronze, a harder and more durable material. The bronze tools that resulted further enhanced agricultural production. Trade-oriented, specialized, and wealthy urban peoples were also more likely than relatively isolated nomadic hunters and gatherers to acquire and manufacture bronze weapons, which were much lighter and more lethal than those made of stone. Finally, the development of writing, first in Mesopotamia and later in India, China, and other centers of agrarian production, greatly improved communications in ways that made it possible to expand trading networks and enlarge bureaucracies. Both were essential to the maintenance of large urban complexes.

The long isolation of American Indian peoples from the centers of civilization in Africa, Asia, and Europe prevented the diffusion of much of the new technology that was developed in a variety of centers at different times. This diffusion and ongoing exchange of objects and ideas between the civilized peoples of the Eastern Hemisphere had played a key role in the founding of new civilizations and the continued growth and development of those already established. Lacking these contacts, the peoples of the Americas built civilizations that were wonderfully sophisticated in many areas but were far behind those of the Old World in critical areas such as technological innovation and the harnessing of animal and machine power. Because their civilizations also developed in very different plant, animal, and disease environments from those in the Eastern Hemisphere, the peoples (and plant and animal life) of areas like the Americas, Australia, and the South Pacific proved highly vulnerable to the diseases introduced from Africa and Eurasia after 1492 C.E. These differences would eventually have catastrophic consequences for these peoples, who had long been isolated from the critical exchanges between the peoples of the Eastern Hemisphere.

FURTHER READINGS

A very considerable literature has developed in recent years on early humans and the critical Neolithic transformations. Sonia Cole's *The Neolithic Revolution* (1970) remains a concise and authoritative survey of this process in the Middle East and parts of Europe. For a broader overview that takes into account more recent research and includes early farming cultures in the Americas, see Robert J. Wenke's *Patterns in Prehistory* (1984). For a sense of the debates that have raged on various aspects of this process, see the sometimes quite technical essays in Stuart Streuver, ed., *Prehistoric Agriculture* (1971), which also covers the Americas extensively.

Even more lively, though often quite technical, are Donald O. Henry's *From Foraging to Agriculture* (1989) and Douglas Price and James A. Brown, eds., *Prehistoric Hunter-Gatherers: The Emergence of Cultural Complexity* (1986). M. C. and H. B. Quennell's *Everyday Life in the New Stone, Bronze and Early Iron Ages* (1955) is difficult to top for an imaginative reconstruction of life in the Neolithic epoch, though some of it is now dated. The most reliable treatment of technology in this era can still be found in volume one of C. Singer, et al., *A History of Technology* (1954). The best introduction to the earliest towns is in James Mellaart's *Earliest Civilizations of the Near East* (1965) and *The Neolithic of the Near East* (1975).

2

The Rise of Civilization in the Middle East and Africa

	7000–4000 Spread of agriculture through most of Middle East	**3000** Introduction of bronze tools	
	4000 Sumerians settle in Tigris-Euphrates valley		
	5000 Farming along Nile River	**3500** Early Sumerian alphabet	
MIDDLE EAST			**2400–2200** Akkadian empire conquers Sumer
EGYPT AND UPPER NILE		**3100–2700** Initial kingdoms **2600** First great pyramid	
		2700–2200 Old Kingdom period	
OTHER MEDITERRANEAN			
	7000 B.C.E.	**4000** B.C.E. **3000** B.C.E.	

INTRODUCTION

The central subject of this chapter is the nature of early civilization and its manifestations in two key places. The first full civilization emerged by 3500 B.C.E. in the Tigris-Euphrates valley in the Middle East. Relatively soon thereafter, civilization developed along the Nile in Egypt. The early civilizations that arose in the Middle East and northeastern Africa had several distinctive features, in political structure and cultural tone, for example. The early civilizations in the Middle East and North Africa generated a number of separate and durable traditions, which can still be found in civilizations around the Mediterranean, in parts of Europe, and even across the Atlantic.

Describing the first river-valley civilizations allows fuller understanding of what this form of human organization involves. But *Mesopotamian* civilization, around the Tigris-Euphrates valley, was quite different from Egyptian, which means some comparison is essential. Both civilizations encountered new problems about 1000 B.C.E. as the river-valley period came to an end. By 1000 B.C.E., both of the early civilizations had produced offshoots in eastern Africa and southern Europe, and additional centers in the Middle East. These smaller centers of civilization made important contributions of their own, for example, the monotheistic religion created among the Jewish people in Palestine.

THE MIDDLE EAST BY 4000 B.C.E.

Focal Point: Many features of civilization, as a form of social organization, emerged gradually on the basis of the consolidation of an agricultural economy. The first civilization also depended on the technical advance of the 4th millennium B.C.E. New tools brought about higher economic production, which facilitated new specializations and social inequalities. A more complex economy also created new needs for more formal governments and better methods of communication and record-keeping.

Agriculture and the Rise of Civilization

Much time elapsed between the development of agriculture and the rise of civilization in the Middle East and many other places. The successful agricultural communities that formed were based primarily on very localized production, which normally sustained a population despite recurrent disasters caused by bad weather or harvest problems. Localized agriculture did not consistently yield the kind of surplus that would allow specializations among the population, and therefore it could not generate civilization and the spread of agriculture to more and more regions in the Middle East. Even the formation of small regional centers, such as Jericho or Çatal Huyuk, did not assure a rapid pace of change. Agriculture did encourage new forms of social organization. Settled

---

1100 Spread of use of iron

2000 Gilgamesh epic written	1400–1200 Hittite empire; use of iron	665–617 Assyrian empire
1800 Babylonian empire; Hammurabi, 1796–1750		
	1600 Possible settlement of Jews in southeast Mediterranean	539 Persian empire

2052–1786 Middle Kingdom period; civilization to Upper Nile	1575–1087 New Kingdom period	100 C.E. Decline of Kush and its capital Meroe
	1000 Kush independent kingdom	
1700 Hyksos invasion	730 Kushite rule of Egypt	300 C.E. Rise of Axum (Ethiopia)

2000 Phoenician state		1000–970 Kingdom of Israel under King David
		800 Beginning of writing of Bible
1600 Minoan civilization (Crete)	1250 Moses and Jewish exodus from Egypt (traditional belief)	1000 Indo-European invasion of Greece
		1000 Spread of Phoenician settlements in western Mediterranean
		721 Assyrian invasion conquers northern Israel

2000 B.C.E.	1000 B.C.E.	1 C.E.

agriculture, as opposed to slash-and-burn varieties, usually implied some forms of property so that land could be identified as belonging to a family, a village, or a landlord. Only with property was there incentive to introduce improvements, such as wells or irrigation measures, that could be monopolized by those who created them or left to their heirs. But property required new kinds of laws and enforcement mechanisms, which in turn implied more extensive government. Here agriculture could create some possibilities for trade and could spur innovation: new kinds of regulations and some government figures who could enforce them.

In many early agricultural areas, including the Middle East, a key incentive to stability was the need for irrigation systems. Irrigated agriculture depended on arrangements that would allow farmers to cooperate in building and maintaining irrigation ditches and sluices. The needs of irrigation, as well as protection from marauders, help explain why most early agricultural peoples settled in village communities rather than on isolated farms. Villages that grouped several hundred people constituted the characteristic pattern of residence in almost all agricultural societies from Neolithic days to our own times. Some big rivers facilitated elaborate irrigation projects that could channel water to vast stretches of land. To create larger irrigation projects along major rivers such as the Tigris and Euphrates or the Nile, large gangs of laborers had to be assembled. Further, regulations had to assure that users along the river and in the villages near the river's source would have equal access to the water supply. This implied an increase in the scale of political and economic organization. A key link between the advantages of irrigation and the gradual emergence of civilization was that irrigated land produced surpluses with greater certainty and required new kinds of organization.

It is no accident that the earliest civilizations arose along large rivers and amid irrigation projects. Civilization in Mesopotamia, and then Egypt, involved not only the central fact of economic surplus but also the ability to integrate tens—even hundreds—of square miles along rivers. Regional coordination, based first on irrigation needs, could easily lead to other contacts: shared cultures, including artistic styles and religious beliefs; economic contacts, including trade; and common political institutions.

Innovation, Specialization, and Productivity

The first civilization also required the technological developments whose impact coalesced about 4000 B.C.E. Most of these inventions occurred in regions where agri-culture was best developed, notably the Middle East. At the same time, the new inventions enhanced the productivity of Middle Eastern agriculture, creating the consistent surpluses that would ultimately shape civilization itself. The result was a recurrent series of technological changes. The first potter's wheel was invented by about 6000 B.C.E. It encouraged faster and higher-quality ceramic pottery production, which facilitated food storage and improved the reliability of food supplies. Pottery production promoted the emergence of a group of specialized manufacturing workers who made pots to exchange for food produced by others.

Better tools allowed improvements in other products made out of wood or stone. Obsidian, a hard stone, began to be used for tools in the late Neolithic centuries. The wheel was another Middle Eastern innovation. Wheeled vehicles long remained slow, but they were vital to many monumental construction projects where large blocks of stone were moved to the construction sites of temples. Shipbuilding also gradually improved. Developments of this sort, enhancing production and possibilities for trade, set the framework for the outright emergence of civilization with the rise of Sumerian society along the Tigris-Euphrates valley.

The introduction of bronze allowed manufacture of a greater variety of tools than could be made of stone or bone, and the tools were lighter and more quickly made. The Middle East was the first region to move from the Neolithic (stone tool) Age to the Bronze Age, during which metal hoes, plows, and other implements were developed. Again, new technology promoted further specialization as groups of artisans concentrated on metal production, exchanging their wares for food. Widespread use of bronze also encouraged greater trade, because tin, in particular, was hard to find. By 2000 B.C.E. trade had become a motivation for extensive development of sea routes.

CIVILIZATION IN MESOPOTAMIA

Focal Point: The first civilization emerged about 3500 B.C.E. It generated several features characteristic of most civilizations including writing, expanded cities, and a complex social structure. The civilization also had distinctive features, including religious beliefs and artistic styles. Periodic invasions and the rise and fall of empires punctuated the history of this first civilization, foreshadowing the transition to more elaborate civilization forms after 1000 B.C.E.

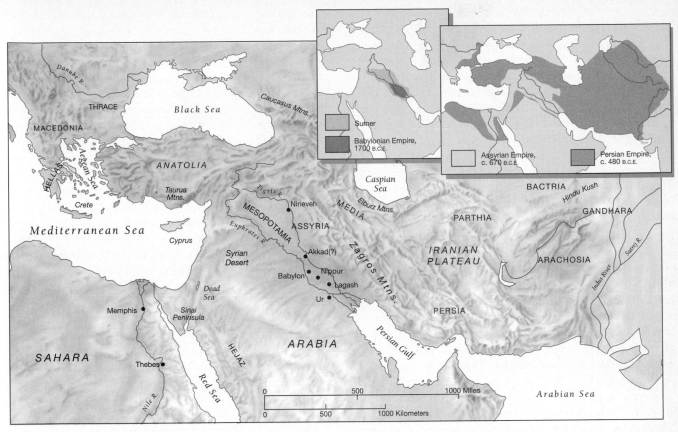

Mesopotamia and the Middle East

The Sumerians

The scene for the first civilization was the northeastern section of what we today call the Middle East, along the great rivers that led to the Persian Gulf. The agents were a newly arrived people called the Sumerians.

Between the northern hills and the deserts of the Arabian peninsula, running from the eastern Mediterranean coast to the fall plain of the Tigris and Euphrates rivers, lies a large swath of arable land called the Fertile Crescent. The rivers rise in the spring, depositing immensely fertile soil. Rainfall is scant in the region, so as population pressure increased, farming communities began to find ways to tame and use the rivers through irrigation ditches. Construction of the ditches required improved tools that were not available much before 4000 B.C.E., and from that point onward, developments in the region were swift. Irrigation plus the fertility of the Tigris-Euphrates region generated substantial food surpluses, promoting population growth and village expansion as well as increasing trade and specialization. The

region was vulnerable in one respect: it was so flat that it was open to frequent invasion.

By 3500 B.C.E., farmers in Mesopotamia, as the Tigris-Euphrates region is also called, were benefiting not only from rich agriculture but also from flourishing pottery and obsidian tool production. The wheel had been introduced, and community coordination was steadily improving to support the irrigation network.

The final boost toward establishing civilization was provided by the *Sumerians,* a people who had migrated into the area from the north about 4000 B.C.E. They settled in an area of about 700 square miles, where they mixed with other local races in a pattern of cultural mingling that has remained characteristic of the region. Sumerian culture early developed important religious values with centers of pilgrimage and worship. Well before 3000 B.C.E., many of these centers were provided with elaborately decorated temples built of mud brick. Sumerians were impressed with the power of grim gods who, they believed, ultimately controlled human destiny.

Sumerian Political and Social Organization

Sumerian civilization lasted intact until about 2000 B.C.E. Its political organization was based on tightly organized city-states, where the agricultural hinterland was ruled by an urban-based king who claimed great authority. In some cases, local councils advised the king. One of the functions of Sumerian states was to define boundaries, unlike the less formal territories of precivilized villages in the region. The government helped regulate religion and enforce its duties. It also provided a system of courts for justice. Kings were originally war leaders whose leadership of a trained army in defense and war remained vital in Sumerian politics where fighting loomed large. Kings, the noble class, and the priesthood controlled considerable amounts of land. Slaves, who had been conquered in wars with nearby tribes, were used to work this land.

Sumerian political and social organization set up traditions that would long endure in this region. City-state government established a tradition of regional rule, which would often be overlaid by larger empires but would frequently return as the principal organizational form. Reliance on slaves was maintained in the economy of many successor civilizations. The use of slaves along with the lack of natural barriers to invasion help explain recurrent warfare, for war was often needed to supply labor. At the same time, slavery in the Middle Eastern tradition was a variable condition, and many slaves were able to earn their own keep and even buy their freedom.

The Sumerians, aided by regional political stability and the use of writing, added to their region's economic prosperity. Agriculture gained as farmers learned how to cultivate date trees, onions, and garlic. Oxen were used to pull plows, donkeys carried goods. Wheeled carts helped transport goods as well. The Sumerians introduced the use of fertilizer and adopted silver as a means of exchange for buying and selling. Major cities expanded—one city reached a population of over 70,000—with substantial housing units in rows of flat-roofed, mud-brick shops and apartments. More commonly, cities contained as many as 10,000 people. The Sumerians improved the potter's wheel, and the production of pottery expanded. Because of the skill level and commercial importance involved, men began to take this trade away from women. The Sumerians also invented glass. Trade expanded to the lower Persian Gulf and to the western portion of the Middle East along the Mediterranean. By 2000 B.C.E., the Sumerians had trading contacts with India.

Sumerian Culture and Religion

Into this rich economy and culture, writing—the most important invention between the advent of agriculture and the age of the steam engine—was introduced about 3500 B.C.E. The Sumerian invention of writing was probably rather sudden, based on new needs for commercial, property, and political records, including a celebration of the deeds of proud local kings. Writing was preceded by the invention of clay cylinder seals, on which little pictures of objects could be recorded. The earliest Sumerian writing simply evolved from those pictures, baked on clay tablets, which were turned into symbols and gradually transformed into phonetic elements. The early Sumerian alphabet—a set of symbols representing sounds—may have had as many as 2000 symbols derived from the early pictures. Before long, writers began to use more abstract symbols to represent sounds, and this allowed the Sumerians and their successors to reduce the alphabet to about 300 symbols. Sumerian writers used a wedge-shaped stick to impress the symbols on clay tablets. The resulting writing is called *cuneiform*, meaning "wedge shaped," and it was used for several thousand years in the Middle East for many different languages. Cuneiform writing was difficult to learn, so specialized scribes monopolized most of it. The Sumerians believed that every object in nature should have a separate name to assure its place in the universe; knowing the name gave a person some power over the object. Writing, in other words, quickly took on essentially religious purposes, allowing people to impose an abstract order over nature and the social world.

The Sumerians also steadily elaborated their culture, again using writing to advance earlier forms. By about 2000 B.C.E., they managed to write down the world's oldest story, the *Epic of Gilgamesh*, which went back at least to the 7th millennium B.C.E. in oral form. Gilgamesh, a real person who had ruled a city-state, became the first hero in world literature. The epic describes a great flood that obliterated humankind except for a favored family, which survived by building an ark and producing descendants who formed a new race of people. The overall tone of the epic and of Sumerian culture (perhaps reflecting the frequently disastrous floods of the region) was somber. Gilgamesh does great deeds but constantly bumps up against the iron laws of the gods, ensuring human failure as the gods triumph in the end.

> The heroes, the wise men, like the new moon have their waxing and waning. Men will say, "Who has ever ruled with might and with power like Gilgamesh?" As in the dark month, the month of shadows; so without him there is no light. O Gilgamesh, this was the meaning of your dream. You were given the kingship, such was your destiny; everlasting life was not your destiny. . . . Gilgamesh, why do you search? The life you seek you will never find. When the gods created the world, they made death a part of human fate.

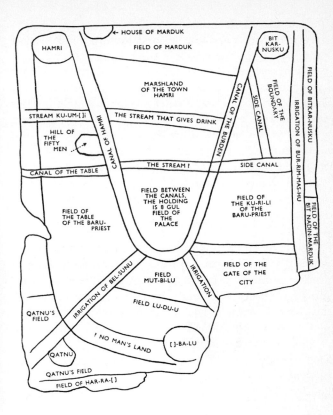

One of the early uses of writing involved marking property boundaries. This picture shows cuneiform writing on a Mesopotamian map from about 1300 B.C.E. The map focuses on defining the king's estate.

Along with early literature, Sumerian art developed steadily. Statues and painted frescoes adorned the temples of the gods, and statues of the gods decorated individual homes. Sumerian science aided a complex agricultural society, as people sought to learn more about the movement of the sun and stars—thus founding the science of astronomy—and to improve their mathematical knowledge. The Sumerians employed a system of numbers based on units of 12, 60, and 360, which we still use in calculations involving circles and hours. They also introduced specific systems, such as charts of major constellations, that have been used for 5000 years in the Middle East and, through later imitation, in India and Europe. In other words, Sumerians and their successors in Mesopotamia created patterns of observation and abstract thought about nature on which many later societies, including our own, still rely.

Religion played a vital role in Sumerian culture and politics. Gods were associated with various forces of nature. At the same time, gods were seen as having a human form and many of humanity's more disagreeable characteristics. Thus, the gods often quarreled and used their power in selfish and childish ways—which made for interesting stories but also created a fear that the gods might make life difficult and hard to control. The gloomy cast of Sumerian religious ideas also included an afterlife of suffering—an original version of the concept of hell. Because gods were believed to regulate natural forces such as flooding in a region where nature was often harsh and unpredictable, they were more feared than loved. Priests played a central role because of their responsibility for placating the gods through proper prayers, sacrifices, and magic. Priests became full-time specialists, running the temples and also performing the astronomical calculations necessary to run the irrigation systems. Each city had a patron god and erected impressive shrines to please and honor this god and other deities. Massive towers, called *ziggurats*, formed the monumental architecture for this civilization. Prayers and offerings to prevent floods as well as to protect good health were a vital part of Sumerian life. Sumerian ideas about the divine force behind and within natural objects—in rivers, trees, and mountains—were common among agricultural peoples. A religion of this sort is known as *animism*. More specifically, Sumerian religious concepts, notably their ideas about the creation of the earth by the gods from a chaos of water and about divine punishment of humans through floods, continue to have force in Jewish, Christian, and Muslim cultures, all of which were born much later in the Middle East.

Sumerian activities in trade and war spread beyond the regional limits of the civilization in the Middle East. The adoption of portions of the Gilgamesh tale in later literature such as the Jewish Bible developed well to the west of Sumer. Even after Sumer itself collapsed, the Sumerian language was still used in religious schools and temples, showing the power of this early culture and its decidedly religious emphasis.

What Civilization Meant in Sumeria

The emergence of the world's first civilization in Sumer brought to fruition the key features of this form of organization. Sumerian society certainly met the basic criterion of civilization: it built on fairly regular economic surpluses. Sumerian farmers produced enough to enable them to be taxed in order to support a small but crucial number of priests and government officials. They produced enough to allow some trade and specialization, thus encouraging groups of artisans and merchants who did not farm. The Sumerian economy also stretched out along the great irrigation systems of the Tigris-Euphrates valley. One of the tasks of regional government was to elaborate and maintain these systems; regional coordination was thus a vital feature.

The advent of civilization in Sumer also involved additional innovations. First, Sumerian civilization generated a clearly defined state, or government, replacing the much more loosely organized communities of previous agricultural societies. Second, civilization involved the creation of cities beyond scattered individual centers like Jericho. The economy remained fundamentally agricultural, and at least 80 percent of all people still lived in the countryside (as would be true in all civilizations until about 200 years ago). But the cities were crucial in promoting trade, more specialized manufacture, and the exchange of ideas. At the same time, cities depended on a well-organized regional economy that could provide food for urban areas and on a government capable of running essential services such as a court system to handle disputes.

The third key innovation pioneered by civilization in the Middle East was the invention of writing. Some historians and anthropologists urge against focusing too much on the development of writing, because concentrating only on this aspect can leave out some civilizations, such as the civilization of the Incas in the Andes region of South America, that produced significant political forms without this intellectual tool. We now appreciate the sophistication societies can attain without writing, and we rate the division of early human activities between hunting and gathering and agriculture as more fundamental than that between oral and literate societies.

The Importance of Writing   Nevertheless, writing was a genuinely important development. Societies with writing can organize more elaborate records, including the lists essential for effective taxation. Writing is a precondition for most formal bureaucracies, which depend on standardized communication and the ability to maintain some documentation. Societies with writing can also produce a more elaborate intellectual life because of their ability to record data and build on past written wisdom. For example, it is no accident that with writing many early civilizations began to generate more formal scientific knowledge. Societies before the development of writing typically depended on poetic sagas to convey their value systems; the poetry was designed to aid in memorization. With writing, the importance of sagas such as the Gilgamesh epic continued, but the diversity of cultural expressions soon increased and other kinds of literature supplemented the long, rhymed epics. Some experts argue that the very fact of becoming literate changes the way people think and encourages a greater sense that the world can be understood by organized human inquiry as opposed to a belief in whimsical magical spirits. Writing, in other words, can produce more abstract religious thinking as well as secular thinking that seeks to describe nature and human affairs in nonreligious terms.

Writing also promotes trade and manufacturing. Sumerian merchants used writing to communicate with their trading partners. Written records helped preserve manufacturing knowledge. One of the first recorded uses of Sumerian writing was to transmit a recipe for the brewing of beer.

Writing also created new divisions within the population of early civilizations. Only a small minority of people—namely priests, scribes, and a few merchants—had time to master writing skills.

The Importance of Cities   In Middle Eastern agricultural civilization most people did not live in cities. The cities that existed were vital, however, because they amassed wealth and power; allowed relatively easy exchange of ideas, encouraging intellectual and artistic changes; and promoted further specialization in manufacture and trade. Early Middle Eastern cities radiated considerable influence and power into the surrounding countryside. Cities also relied on broader attributes of civilization, the most notable being relatively extensive trade and political organization. Cities could not be founded until the Middle East produced a significant agricultural surplus above what farmer families needed to live on and until there were groups—merchants—to organize the trade that brought food to the city and carried urban-made goods to the countryside and to other cities. Cities could not be founded until there was a sufficiently solid political organization—a government, with some recognized legitimacy, and some full time officials—that could run essential urban services and help regulate the relationship between cities and the countryside.

Saying that early Middle Eastern civilizations were based on cities, then, even when most people remained in the countryside as agricultural producers, is partly saying that civilizations had generated more elaborate trade and political structures than initial agricultural societies had managed. This helps explain, also, why civilizations generally covered a fairly wide area, breaking out of the localism that described the economics and political activities of the initial agricultural communities.

Civilization: Gains and Losses Because civilizations are by definition well organized compared with the societies that preceded them, it is not surprising that almost all history is about what has happened to civilized societies. We know the most about such societies, and we are likely to be particularly impressed by their great art or powerful rulers. It is also true that civilizations tend to be far more populous than noncivilized societies. Because civilizations depend on some trade, they allow greater specialization, which increases the productivity and sustenance of larger populations. Their political structure allows whole regions or even several regions to be unified. But the history of civilization does not embrace everybody. In the days of the river-valley civilizations, even long after Sumer, most inhabited parts of the world were not in the civilized areas.

There is inevitable confusion between defining a society as a civilization and assuming that civilization produces a monopoly on higher values and controlled behavior. Civilization does not necessarily mean "progress." In the first place, civilization brings losses as well as gains. As the Middle East moved toward civilization, distinctions based on social class and wealth increased. This was clearly the case in Sumer, where social structure ranged from slaves, who were treated as property, to powerful kings and priests. Civilizations typically have firmer class or caste divisions and greater separations between ruler and ruled than "simpler" societies. Civilizations also often create greater inequality between men and women than noncivilized societies do. Many early civilizations, including those of the Middle East, went to considerable

pains to organize the supposed inferiority of women on a more structured basis than ever before, treating women as the property of fathers or husbands.

Furthermore, people in noncivilized societies may be exceptionally well regulated and possessed of interesting, important culture. They are not "merely" barbarians or uncouth wild men. Some societies that were most eager to repress anger and aggression in human dealings, such as several Eskimo groups, were not part of a civilization until recently. In contrast, many civilized societies produce a great deal of aggressive behavior and build warlike qualities into their list of virtues. Some noncivilized societies treat old people cruelly; others display respect and veneration. A civilized society does not invariably enhance the human capacity for restrained, polite behavior or an interest in the higher values of life. Civilizations do not even clearly promote greater human happiness.

The development of civilization continued the process of enhancing human capacity for technological and political organization, and the production of increasingly elaborate and diverse artistic and intellectual forms. In this quite restricted sense, the term *civilization* has meaning and legitimately commands the attention of most historians. Because of the power and splendor civilizations could provide, they tended to spread as other societies came under their influence or deliberately tried to imitate their achievements. Early civilizations, however, spread slowly because many peoples had no contact with them and because their disadvantages, such as greater social inequality, might have been repellent. During the river-valley civilization period, civilizations developed in particular geographical regions amid considerable isolation.

Later Mesopotamian Civilization: A Series of Conquests

The general characteristics of civilization, from economic surplus to writing, cities, and social inequality, are vital, but we must also consider their specific qualities. As an example, in Mesopotamia, writing was of a certain style; social organization was distinctive, for example, in the power of priests; and overall culture had some special qualities.

A key ingredient of Mesopotamian civilization was frequent instability as one ruling people gave way to another invading force. The Sumerians, themselves invaders of the fertile river valleys, did not set up a sufficiently strong and united political force to withstand pressures from outside, particularly when other peoples of the Middle East began to copy their key achievements, such as the formation of cities.

The Akkadian Empire   Shortly after 2400 B.C.E., a king from a non-Sumerian city, Akkad, conquered the Sumerian city-states and inaugurated an Akkadian Empire. This empire soon sent troops as far as Egypt and Ethiopia. The initial Akkadian ruler, *Sargon I*, the first clearly identified individual in world history, set up a unified empire integrating the city-states into a whole. He also added to Sumerian art a new style marked by the theme of royal victory. Professional military organization expanded, since Sargon maintained a force of 5400 troops. Extensive tax revenues were needed to support his operations. The Akkadians were the first people to use writing for more than commercial and temple records, producing a number of literary works. The Akkadian Empire lasted only about 200 years, however, and then it was overthrown by another invading force. Sumerian regional states reappeared in what turned out to be the final phase of this particular civilization. It was then that the Epic of Gilgamesh was written. By this time, around 2000 B.C.E., kingdoms were springing up in various parts of the Middle East, while new invading groups, including Indo-European tribes that came from the Balkans in southeastern Europe, added to the region's confusion. A civilization derived from Sumerian culture spread more widely in the Middle East, though political unity was rarely achieved in the expanded setting.

The Babylonian Empire   Another new empire arose around 1800 B.C.E., for the first time unifying the whole of Mesopotamia. This Babylonian empire was headed by *Hammurabi*, one of the great rulers of early civilized history. Hammurabi set up an extensive network of officials and judges while maintaining a separate priesthood. He also codified the laws of the region to deal with a number of criminal, property, and family issues. Large cities testified to the wealth and power of this new empire. At the same time, Sumerian cultural traditions were maintained and elaborated. The famous *Hammurabic Code* thus was built on earlier codifications by Sumerian kings.

A Babylonian poem testified to the continued sobriety of the dominant culture: "I look about me and see only evil. My troubles grow and I cannot find justice. I have prayed to the gods and sacrificed, but who can understand the gods in heaven? Who knows what they plan for us? Who has ever been able to understand a god's conduct?"

Finally, Babylonian scientists extended the Sumerian work in astronomy and mathematics. Scholars were able to predict lunar eclipses and trace the paths of some of the planets. Babylonians also worked out mathematical tables and an algebraic geometry of great practical utility. The modern 60-minute hour and 360-degree circle are heritages of the Babylonian system of measurement

This bronze head of Sargon, founder of the Akkadian dynasty, dates from about 2350 B.C.E. The elaborate metalwork displays the artistic talents acquired by leading craftsmen.

applied to earlier Sumerian numbering systems. The study of astronomy is another Babylonian legacy.

Indeed, of all the successors of the Sumerians, the Babylonians constructed the most elaborate culture, though their rule was not long-lived. The Babylonians expanded commerce and a common cultural zone, both based on growing use of cuneiform writing and a shared language. During the empire itself, new government strength showed in both the extensive legal system and

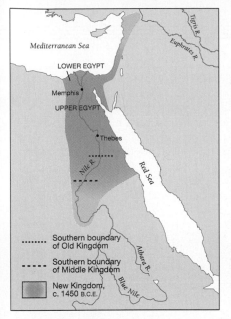
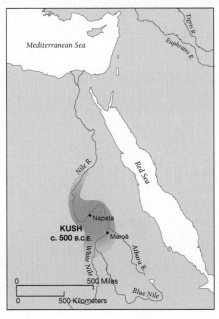
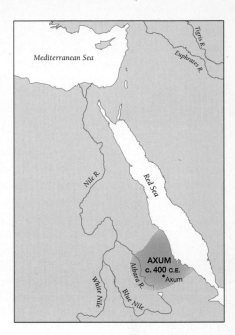

Egypt, Kush, and Axum, Successive Dynasties

the opulent public buildings and royal palaces. The hanging gardens of one king dazzled visitors from the entire region.

The Babylonian empire fell by about 1600 B.C.E. An invading Hittite people, one of the first of the Indo-European groups to press in from central Asia, adapted the Sumerian cuneiform script to their own Indo-European language and set up an empire of their own. The Hittites soon yielded, and a series of smaller kingdoms disputed the region for several centuries between about 1200 and 900 B.C.E. This period allowed several regional cultures, such as the Hebrew and the Phoenician, to develop greater autonomy, thus adding to the diversity and the achievements of the Middle East. Then, after about 900 B.C.E., another series of empires began in the Middle East, including the Assyrian Empire and later the Persian Empire, based on invasions of new groups from central Asia. These new invaders had mastered the production of iron weapons and also used horses and chariots in fighting, sketching a new framework for the development of empires and a new chapter in the history of the Middle East and of civilization more generally.

ANCIENT EGYPT

Focal Point: A second civilization grew up, in northeastern Africa along the Nile River. Egyptian civilization, formed by 3000 B.C.E., benefited from trade and technological influence from Mesopotamia, but it produced a

quite different society and culture. Thus, while Egypt generated standard features of civilization such as writing and a well-defined government, it also had its own distinctive flavor, expressed, for example, in its rich art and massive monuments. More stable than Mesopotamia, Egyptian civilization flourished for more than 2000 years before beginning to decline about 100 B.C.E. A small minority of people—mainly priests, scribes, and a few merchants—had time to master writing skills.

Basic Patterns of Egyptian Society

Unlike Mesopotamia and the Middle East, where an original river-valley basis to civilization ultimately gave way to the spread of civilization throughout an entire region, Egyptian civilization from its origins to its decline was focused on the Nile River and the deserts around it. The Nile focus also gave a more optimistic cast to Egyptian culture, for it could be seen as a source of never-failing bounty to be thankfully received, rather than as a menacing cause of floods. Egyptian civilization may have received some inspiration from Sumer at the outset, but a distinctive pattern soon developed in both religion and politics.

Farming had been developed along the Nile by about 5000 B.C.E., but some time before 3200 B.C.E. economic development accelerated, in part because of growing trade with other regions, including Mesopotamia. This economic acceleration provided the basis for the formation of regional kingdoms. Unlike Sumer,

DOCUMENT

Hammurabi's Law Code

Hammurabi, as king of Babylon, united Mesopotamia under his rule from about 1800 to 1750 B.C.E. His law code, the earliest such compilation still in existence, was discovered on a stone slab in Iran in 1901 C.E. Not a systematic presentation, it was a collection of exemplary cases designed to set general standards of justice. The code provides vital insights into the nature of social relations and family structure in this ancient civilization. Examples of the Hammurabic code follow:

> When Marduk commanded me to give justice to the people of the land and to let [them] have [good] governance, I set forth truth and justice throughout the land [and] prospered the people.

At that time:

> If a man has accused a man and has charged him with manslaughter and then has not proved [it against] him, his accuser shall be put to death.
>
> If a man has charged a man with sorcery and then has not proved [it against] him, he who is charged with the sorcery shall go to the holy river; he shall leap into the holy river and, if the holy river overwhelms him, his accuser shall take and keep his house; if the holy river proves that man clear [of the offense] and he comes back safe, he who has charged him with sorcery shall be put to death; he who leapt into the holy river shall take and keep the house of his accuser.
>
> If a man has come forward in a case to bear witness to a felony and then has not proved the statement that he has made, if that case [is] a capital one, that man shall be put to death.
>
> If he has come forward to bear witness to [a claim for] corn or money, he shall remain liable for the penalty for that suit.
>
> If a judge has tried a suit, given a decision, caused a sealed tablet to be executed, [and] thereafter varies his judgment, they shall convict that judge of varying [his] judgment and he shall pay twelvefold the claim

The Stele of Hammurabi shows the king in front of the sun god, Shamash. Hammurabi's code of law is carved below.

Egypt moved fairly directly from precivilization to large government units without passing through a city-state phase, though the first *pharaoh*, Narmer, had to conquer a number of petty local kings around 3100 B.C.E. Indeed, Egypt always had fewer problems with political unity than Mesopotamia did, in part because of the unifying influence of the course of the Nile River. By the same token, however, Egyptian politics tended to be more authoritarian as well as centralized, for city-states in the Mesopotamian style, though often ruled by kings, also provided the opportunity for councils and other participatory institutions.

By 3100 B.C.E., Narmer, king of southern Egypt, conquered the northern regional kingdom and created a unified state 600 miles long. This state was to last 3000 years. Despite some important disruptions, this was an amazing record of stability, even though the greatest vitality of the civilization was exhausted by about 1000 B.C.E. During the 2000-year span in which Egypt displayed its greatest vigor, the society went through three

in that suit; then they shall remove him from his place on the bench of judges in the assembly, and he shall not [again] sit in judgment with the judges.

If a free person helps a slave to escape, the free person will be put to death.

If a man has committed robbery and is caught, that man shall be put to death.

If the robber is not caught, the man who has been robbed shall formally declare whatever he has lost before a god, and the city and the mayor in whose territory or district the robbery has been committed shall replace whatever he has lost for him.

If [it is] the life [of the owner that is lost], the city or the mayor shall pay one maneh of silver to his kinsfolk.

If a person owes money and Adad [the river god] has flooded the person's field, the person will not give any grain [tax] or pay any interest in that year.

If a person is too lazy to make the dike of his field strong and there is a break in the dike and water destroys his own farmland, that person will make good the grain [tax] that is destroyed.

If a merchant increases interest beyond that set by the king and collects it, that merchant will lose what was lent.

If a trader borrows money from a merchant and then denies the fact, that merchant in the presence of god and witnesses will prove the trader borrowed the money and the trader will pay the merchant three times the amount borrowed.

If the husband of a married lady has accused her but she is not caught lying with another man, she shall take an oath by the life of a god and return to her house.

If a man takes himself off and there is not the [necessary] maintenance in his house, his wife [so long as] her [husband is delayed], shall keep [herself chaste; she shall not] enter [another man's house].

If that woman has not kept herself chaste but enters another man's house, they shall convict that woman and cast her into the water.

If a son strikes his father, they shall cut off his forehand.

If a man has put out the eye of a free man, they shall put out his eye.

If he breaks the bone of a [free] man, they shall break his bone.

If he puts out the eye of a villain or breaks the bone of a villain, he shall pay one maneh of silver.

If he puts out the eye of a [free] man's slave or breaks the bone of a [free] man's slave, he shall pay half his price.

If a man knocks out the tooth of a [free] man equal [in rank] to him[self], they shall knock out his tooth.

If he knocks out the tooth of a villain, he shall pay one-third maneh of silver.

If a man strikes the cheek of a [free] man who is superior [in rank] to him[self], he shall be beaten with 60 stripes with a whip of ox-hide in the assembly.

If the man strikes the cheek of a free man equal to him[self in rank], he shall pay one maneh of silver.

If a villain strikes the cheek of a villain, he shall pay ten *shekels* of silver.

If the slave of a [free] man strikes the cheek of a free man, they shall cut off his ear.

Questions: What can you tell from the Hammurabic code about the social and family structure of Mesopotamia? What is the relationship between law and trade? Why did agricultural civilizations such as Babylon insist on harsh punishments for crimes?

major periods of monarchy (the Old, the Intermediate, and the New Kingdoms), each divided from its successor by a century or two of confusion.

In all its phases, Egyptian civilization was characterized by the strength of the pharaoh. The pharaoh was held to be descended from gods and to him was attributed the power to assure prosperity and control the rituals that assured the flow of the Nile and the fertility derived from irrigation. Soon the pharaoh was regarded as a god. Much Egyptian art was devoted to demonstrating the power and sanctity of the king. From the king's authority also flowed an extensive bureaucracy, recruited from the landed nobles and specially trained in writing and law. Governors were appointed for key regions and were responsible for supervising irrigation and arranging for the great public works that became a hallmark of Egyptian culture. Most Egyptians were peasant farmers, closely regulated and heavily taxed. Labor requisition by the states allowed construction of the great pyramids and other huge public buildings. These monuments were triumphs of human coordination, for the Egyptians were not particularly advanced technologically. They even lacked pulleys or other devices to hoist the huge slabs of stone that formed the pyramids. Recent aerial discoveries reveal that early Egyptians built at least one roadway to the stone quarries, but roads were not used during the age of the pyramids. Masses of workers rolled stones over logs and onto Nile barges before assembling the massive monuments on the river's banks.

Given the importance of royal rule and the belief that pharaohs were gods, it is not surprising that each of the main periods of Egyptian history was marked by some striking kings. Early in each dynastic period, leading pharaohs conquered new territories, sometimes pressing up the Nile River into present-day Sudan and once even moving up the Mediterranean coast of the Middle East. One pharaoh, Akhenaton, late in Egyptian history, tried to use his power to install a new, one-god religion, replacing the Egyptian pantheon. It was to commemorate their greatness that many pharaohs built the pyramids to house themselves and their retinues after death, commanding work crews of up to 100,000 men to haul and lift the stones. The first great pyramid was built about 2600 B.C.E.; the largest pyramid followed about a century later, taking 20 years to complete and containing 2 million blocks of stone, each weighing $5\frac{1}{2}$ tons.

Some scholars have seen fundamental links between Egypt's stable, centralized politics and its fascination with an orderly death, which gave rise to massive funeral monuments and preservation through mummification. Death rituals suggested a concern with extending organization to the afterlife, based on a belief that through politics, death as well as life could be carefully controlled. A similar connection between strong political structures and careful funeral arrangements developed in Chinese civilization, though with quite different specific religious beliefs.

Egyptian Ideas and Art

Despite some initial inspiration, Egyptian culture separated itself from Mesopotamia in several ways other than politics and monument building. The Egyptians did not take to the Sumerian cuneiform alphabet and developed a hieroglyphic alphabet instead. *Hieroglyphs*, though more pictorial than Sumerian cuneiform, were based on simplified pictures of objects abstracted to represent concepts or sounds. As in Mesopotamia, the writing system was complex, and its use, for the most part, was, monopolized by the powerful priestly caste. Egyptians ultimately developed a new material to write on, papyrus, which was cheaper to manufacture and use than

clay tablets or animal skins and allowed the proliferation of elaborate record-keeping. Despite the elaboration of writing, Egypt did not generate an epic literary tradition.

Egyptian science focused on mathematics and astronomy, but its achievements were far less advanced than those of Mesopotamia. The Egyptians were, however, the first people to establish the length of the solar year, which they divided into 12 months, each with three ten-day weeks. The week was the only division of time not based on any natural cycles. The achievement of this calendar suggests Egyptians' concern about predicting the Nile floods and their abilities in astronomical observation. The Egyptians also made important advances in medicine, including knowledge of the workings of a variety of medicinal drugs and some contraceptive devices. Elements of Egyptian medical knowledge were gained by the Greeks and so passed into later Middle Eastern and European civilizations.

The pillar of Egyptian culture was not science, however, but religion, which was firmly established as the basis of a whole worldview. The Egyptian religion promoted the worship of many gods. It mixed magical ceremonies and beliefs with worship in a fashion common to early religions almost everywhere. A more distinctive focus involved the concern with death and preparation for life in another world, where—in contrast to the Mesopotamians—the Egyptians held that a happy, changeless well-being could be achieved. The care shown in preparing tombs and mummifying bodies, along with elaborate funeral rituals, particularly for the rulers and bureaucrats, was designed to assure a satisfactory afterlife, though Egyptians also believed that favorable judgment by a key god, Osiris, was essential as well. Other Egyptian deities included a creation goddess, similar to other Middle Eastern religious figures later adapted into Christian worship of the Virgin Mary, and a host of gods represented by partially animal figures. Egyptian art focused heavily on the gods, though earthly, human scenes were portrayed as well in a characteristic, stylized form that lasted without great change for many centuries.

Stability was a hallmark of Egyptian culture. Given the duration of Egyptian civilization, there were surprisingly few basic changes in styles and beliefs. The Egyptians' emphasis on stability was reflected in their view of a changeless afterlife, suggesting a conscious attempt to argue that persistence was a virtue. Change did occur, however, in some key areas. Egypt was long fairly isolated, and this isolation helped preserve continuity. The invasions of Egypt from Palestine toward the end of the Old Kingdom period (about 2200 B.C.E.) were distinct exceptions to Egypt's usual self-containment. They were

CLOSEUP

Amenhotep IV (1379–1362 B.C.E.)

One of the most intriguing pharaohs, Amenhotep IV (1379–1362 B.C.E.), attempted to use his power to overturn Egyptian religious beliefs, replacing the many deities with a single god, the sun god Aton (from whom he took a new name for himself, Akhenaton). His *Hymn to Aton* put his case clearly: "O sole god, like whom there is not other! Thou didst create the world according to thy desire." This early invention of monotheism foreshadowed the later development of religions that focused on one all-powerful divinity. But Akhenaton was not able to defeat the powerful priesthood, and after his death he was condemned and his name was removed from the monuments. Historians debate whether his vision was simply a fascinating historical accident or has some larger, if diffuse, significance. More pragmatically, Akhenaton's regime also weakened Egypt's control over conquered territories in the Middle East, leading to a series of later wars. The pharaoh's religious focus distracted him from effective foreign policy.

followed by attacks from the Middle East by tribes of Asian origin, which brought a period of division, chaos, and rival royal dynasties. But the unified monarchy was reestablished during the Middle Kingdom period, during which Egyptian settlements spread southward into what is now the Sudan, toward what later became the African kingdom of Kush.

Then followed another period of social unrest and invasion, ending in the final great kingdom period, the New Kingdom, about 1570 B.C.E. During this period, trade, and other contacts with the Middle East and the eastern Mediterranean, including the island of Crete, gained ground. These contacts spread certain Egyptian influences, notably in monumental architecture, to

other areas. It was during the New Kingdom that Egyptians first instituted formal slavery. Also during this period, the pharaoh Akhenaton tried to impose his new monotheistic religion—an attempt that reflects some foreign influence—but his effort was renounced by his successor, Tutankhamen, who restored the old capital city and built a lavish tomb to celebrate the return to the traditional gods. After about 1150 B.C.E., new waves of invasion, internal conspiracies, and disorganization, including strikes and social protest, brought fairly steady decline. It was around this period, according to Jewish legend, that one people, the Hebrews, followed their leader Moses out of Egypt and into the deserts of Palestine.

This tomb painting from about 1300 B.C.E. highlights black-skinned people from the rising kingdom of Kush, who interacted increasingly with Egyptian society and would at one point control Egypt directly.

EGYPT AND MESOPOTAMIA COMPARED

Focal Point: Because each civilization has its own characteristics, comparison is essential to highlight what the differences were among civilizations and also how they combined with important similarities.

Because of differences in geography, different degrees of exposure to outside invasion and influence, and different prior beliefs, Egypt and Mesopotamia contrasted with each other in many ways. Egypt emphasized strong central authority, while Mesopotamian politics shifted more frequently over a substructure of regional city-states. Mesopotamian art focused on less monumental structures and embraced a pronounced literary element that Egyptian art lacked.

These cultural differences can be explained partly by geography: Mesopotamians lacked access to the great stones that Egyptians could import for their monuments. The differences also owed something to different politics, for Egyptian ability to organize masses of laborers resulted from its centralized government structures and strong bureaucracy. The differences owed something, finally, to different beliefs, for the Mesopotamians lacked the Egyptian concern for preparations for the af-

terlife, which motivated the great tombs and pyramids that have made Egypt and some of the pharaohs live on in human memory.

Both societies traded extensively, but there was a difference in economic tone. Mesopotamia was more productive of technological improvements, because the environment was more difficult to manage than the Nile valley. Trade contacts were more extensive, and the Mesopotamians gave considerable attention to a merchant class and commercial law.

Social differences were less obvious, because it is difficult to obtain information on daily life for early civilizations. It is probable, though, that the status of women was greater in Egypt than in Mesopotamia (where women's position seems to have deteriorated after Sumer). Egyptians paid great respect to women, at least in the upper classes, in part because marriage alliances were vital to the preservation and stability of the monarchy. Also, Egyptian religion included more pronounced deference to goddesses as sources of creativity.

Comparisons in politics, culture, economics, and society suggest that the two civilizations varied substantially because of largely separate origins and environments. The distinction in overall tone was striking, with Egypt being more stable and cheerful than Mesopotamia not only in beliefs about gods and the afterlife but in the colorful and lively pictures the Egyptians emphasized in

A relief from the temple of Aten at Tel el Amarna shows the pharaoh Akhenaton, Queen Nefertiti, and one of their daughters adoring the god Aten in the form of the sun's disk. The Aten sends down tiny hands to accept the libations of the royal pair.

their decorative art. Also striking was the distinction in internal history: Egyptian civilization was far less marked by disruption than its Mesopotamian counterpart.

Differences were not the whole story, for as river-valley civilizations Egypt and Mesopotamia inevitably shared important features. Both emphasized social stratification, with a noble, landowning class on top and masses of peasants and slaves at the bottom. A powerful priestly group also figured in the elite. Although specific achievements in science differed, there was a common emphasis on astronomy and related mathematics, which produced durable findings about units of time and measurement. Both Mesopotamia and Egypt changed slowly by the standards of more modern societies. Details of change have not been preserved, but it is true that having developed successful political and economic systems, both societies tended strongly toward conservation.

Change, when it came, was usually brought by outside forces: natural disasters or invasions. Both civilizations demonstrated extraordinary durability in the basics. Egyptian civilization and a fundamental Mesopotamian culture lasted far longer than the civilizations that came later, because of relative isolation within each respective region and because of the deliberate effort to maintain what had been achieved rather than experiment widely.

Both civilizations, finally, left important heritages in their regions and adjacent territories. Several smaller civilization centers were launched under the impetus of Mesopotamia and Egypt, and some would produce important innovations of their own by about 1000 B.C.E.

ANALYSIS

Women in Patriarchal Societies

Most agricultural civilizations downgraded the status and potential of women, at least according to modern Western standards and to the implicit standards of hunting-and-gathering societies. Agricultural civilizations were characteristically *patriarchal*; that is, they were run by men and based on the assumption that men directed political, economic, and cultural life. Furthermore, as agricultural civilizations developed over time and became more prosperous and more elaborately organized, the status of women deteriorated from its initial level. Individual families were normally set up on a patriarchal basis. The husband and father determined fundamental conditions and made the key decisions, and the woman gave humble obedience to this male authority. Patriarchal family structure rested on men's control of most or all property, starting with land itself. Marriage was based on property relationships, and it was assumed that marriage, and therefore subordination to men, was the normal condition for the vast majority of women. A revealing symptom of patriarchy in families was the fact that after marrying, a woman usually moved to the orbit (and often the residence) of her husband's family.

Characteristic patriarchal conditions developed in Mesopotamian civilization. Marriages were arranged for women by their parents, and a formal contract was drawn up. The husband served as authority over his wife and children just as he did over his slaves. Early Sumerians may have given women greater latitude than they enjoyed later on. Their religion attributed considerable power to female sexuality, and their law gave women im-

This detail from tomb art shows a husband and wife doing harvesting work. Appropriately for patriarchial values, the husband takes the lead in work, the wife following to assist.

portant rights, so that they could not be treated as outright property. Still, even in Sumerian law the adultery of a wife was punishable by death, while a husband's adultery was treated far more lightly—a double standard characteristic of patriarchalism. Mesopotamian societies after Sumerian times began to emphasize the importance of a woman's virginity at marriage and to impose the veil on respectable women when they were in public to emphasize their modesty. These changes showed a progressive cramping of women's social position and daily freedoms. At all points, a good portion of Mesopotamian law (such as the Hammurabic code) was given over to prescriptions for women, assuring certain basic protections but clearly emphasizing limits and inferiority.

Patriarchal conditions also could vary from one agricultural civilization to another. Egyptian civilization gave women, at least in the upper classes, more credit and witnessed several powerful queens. The beautiful Nefertiti, wife of Akhenaton, seems to have been influential in the religious disputes in this reign. Some agricultural societies gave women a certain importance by tracing descendants from mothers rather than from fathers. This was true, for example, of Jewish law. But even these matrilineal societies held women to be inferior to men; for example,

Jewish law insisted that men and women worship separately. So while variety is truly important, it usually operated within a framework of basic patriarchalism. It was around 2000 B.C.E. that an Egyptian writer, Ptah Hotep, put patriarchal beliefs as clearly as anyone in the early civilizations: "If you are a man of note, found for yourself a household, and love your wife at home, as it beseems. Fill her belly, clothe her back. . . . But hold her back from getting the mastery."

Why was patriarchalism so pervasive? As agriculture improved with the use of better techniques, women's labor, though still absolutely vital, became less important than it had been in hunting-and-gathering or early agricultural societies. This was particularly true in the upper classes and in cities where men frequently took over the most productive work—craft production or political leadership, for example. The inferior position of women in the upper classes was usually more marked than in peasant villages, where women's labor remained essential. More generally, agricultural societies were based on concepts of property, beginning with the ways land was organized. Early law codes denied property relationships. It seemed essential in those circumstances for a man to be sure who his heirs were—that is, to try to make sure that he monopolized the sexual activities of his wife or wives. This situation helps account for the strong legal emphasis placed on women's sexual fidelity and the tendency to treat women themselves as part of a man's property. Within this framework, in turn, it became possible to think of women as inferior and partly ornamental, so that when groups achieved a certain prosperity they often tried to demonstrate it by further reducing the status of women. This pattern was very clear pattern in Chinese civilization and operated also in India and later in western Europe. Patriarchalism, in sum, responded to economic and property conditions in agricultural civilizations and might deepen over time.

Patriarchalism raises important questions about women themselves. Many women internalized the culture of patriarchalism, holding that it was their job to obey and to serve men and accepting arguments that their aptitudes were inferior to those of men. But patriarchalism did not preclude some important options for women. In many societies, a minority of women could gain some relief through religious functions, which could provide them a chance to operate independently of family structures. Patriarchal laws defined some rights for women even within marriage, protecting them in theory from the worst abuses. Sumerian law, for example, gave women as well as men the right to divorce under certain conditions when the spouse had not lived up to obligations. Women could also wield informal power in patriarchal societies by the emotional hold they gained over husbands or sons. Such power was indirect, behind the scenes, but a forceful woman might use these means to figure prominently in a society's history. Women also could form networks, if only within a large household. Older women, who commanded the obedience of many daughters-in-law as well as unmarried daughters, could powerfully shape the activities of the family.

The fact remains that patriarchalism was a commanding theme in most agricultural civilizations from the early centuries onward. Enforcement of patriarchalism, through law and culture, provided one means by which these societies regulated their members and tried to achieve order. While women were not reduced to literal servitude by most patriarchal systems, they might have come close. Their options were severely constrained. Girls were reared to accept patriarchal conditions, and boys were reared with full consciousness of their distinctiveness. In many agricultural civilizations, patriarchalism dictated that boys, because of their importance in carrying on the family name and the chief economic activities, were more likely to survive. When pop-

ulation excess threatened a family or a community, patriarchal assumptions determined that female infants be killed as a means of population control.

Questions: How do you think most women reared in a patriarchal society would react to their conditions? What might cause differences in women's conditions in patriarchal societies? Why were upper-class women often more inferior to men in power than peasant women were?

CIVILIZATION CENTERS IN AFRICA AND THE EASTERN MEDITERRANEAN

Focal Point: Toward the end of the early civilization period, about 1000 B.C.E., several partially separate centers of civilization sprang up on the fringes of the civilized world in Africa and the Middle East, extending also into parts of southern Europe. These centers utilized the achievements of the great early centers. They resulted in part from the expansion efforts of these centers, as in the Egyptian push southward during the New Kingdom period or the spread of Mesopotamian commerce. In the Middle East, separate societies emerged during the chaotic centuries following the collapse of the Hittite empire. The new centers also had characteristics of their own, often of lasting significance.

Kush and Axum: Civilization Spreads in Africa

The kingdom of *Kush* sprang up along the upper (southern) reaches of the Nile. Kush was the first African state other than Egypt of which there is record. It was a state on the frontiers of Egyptian activity, where Egyptian garrisons had been stationed from time to time. By 1000 B.C.E. it emerged as an independent political unit, though strongly influenced by Egyptian forms. By 730 B.C.E., as Egypt declined, Kush was strong enough to conquer its northern neighbor and rule it for several centuries. This conquest was ended by Assyrian invasion from the Middle East. After this point the Kushites began to push their frontiers farther south, gaining a more diverse African population and weakening the Egyptian influence. At this point the new capital was established at Meroe. Kushites became skilled in the use of iron and had access to substantial quantities of African ore and fuel. The use of iron tools extended the area that could be brought into agriculture. Kush formed a key center of metal technology in the ancient world, as a basis of both military and economic strength.

Kushites developed a form of writing derived from Egyptian hieroglyphics (and which has not yet been fully deciphered). They established several significant cities. Their political organization, also similar to that of Egypt, emphasized a strong monarchy with elaborate ceremonies based on the belief that the king was a god. Kushite economic influence extended widely in sub-Saharan Africa. Extensive trade was conducted with people to the west, and this trade may have brought knowledge of ironmaking to much of the rest of Africa. The greatest period of the kingdom at Meroe, where activities centered from the early 6th century onward, lasted from about 250 B.C.E. to 50 C.E. By this time the kingdom served as a channel for African goods—animal skins, ebony and ivory, gold and slaves—into the commerce of the Middle East and the Mediterranean. Many monuments were built during those centuries, including huge royal pyramids and an elaborate palace in Meroe. Much fine pottery and articles of jewelry were produced. Meroe began to decline from about 100 C.E. onward and was defeated by a kingdom to the south, *Axum,* about 300 C.E. Prosperity and extensive political and economic activity did not end in this region but extended into the formation of a kingdom in present-day Ethiopia.

The outreach of Kush is not entirely clear aside from its trading network set up with neighboring regions. Whether African peoples outside the Upper Nile region learned much from Kush about political forms is unknown. Certainly, there was little imitation of its writing, and the region of Kush and Ethiopia would long remain somewhat isolated from the wider stream of African history. Nevertheless, the formation of a separate society stretching below the eastern Sahara was an important step in setting the bases for technological and economic change throughout much of upper Africa. Though its achievements flow less fully into later African development, Kush did for sub-Saharan Africa what Sumer achieved for the Middle East: it set a wider process of civilization in motion.

Cultures in the Mediterranean Region

Smaller centers in the Middle East began to spring up after about 1500 B.C.E. Though dependent on the larger Mesopotamian culture for many features, these centers added important new ingredients and in some cases also extended the hold of civilization westward to the Asian coast of the Mediterranean. The smaller cultures also added to the diversity of the Middle East, creating a varied array of identities that would continue to mark the region even under the impetus of later empires, such as the Roman Empire, or the sweeping religion of Islam. Several of these smaller cultures proved immensely durable and influenced other parts of the world as well.

The Hebrews and Monotheism The most important of the smaller Middle Eastern groups were the Hebrews, who gave the world one of its most influential religions. The Hebrews were a Semitic people (a population group that also includes the Arabs). They were influenced by Babylonian civilization. They may have settled in the southeast corner of the Mediterranean about 1600 B.C.E., probably migrating from Mesopotamia. Some may have moved into Egypt, where they were treated as a subject people, although the first clear record of the Hebrews dates only to 1100 B.C.E. According to Jewish tradition, in the 13th century B.C.E., Moses led the Hebrews to Palestine in search of a homeland promised by the Hebrew God, Yahweh. This was later held to be the central development in Jewish history. The Jews began by 1100 B.C.E. to emerge as a people with a self-conscious culture and some political identity. At most points, however, the Jewish state was small and relatively weak, retaining independence only when other parts of the Middle East were disorganized. A few Jewish kings were able to unify their people, but at many points the Jews were divided into separate regional states. Most of Palestine came under foreign (initially Assyrian) domination from 722 B.C.E. onward, but the Jews were able to maintain their cultural identity and key religious traditions. A series of dynamic prophets elaborated Jewish beliefs and added to the rich religious literature.

The distinctive achievement of the Jews was the development of a strong *monotheistic* religion. Early Jewish leaders probably emphasized a particularly strong, creator god as the most powerful of many divinities—a hierarchy not uncommon in animism—but this encouraged a focus on the father God for prayer and loyalty. According to Mosaic tradition, Jews were increasingly urged to abandon the worship of all other gods and to receive from Yahweh the Torah (a holy Law), the keeping of which would assure divine protection and guidance. From this point onward Jews regarded themselves as a chosen people under God's special guidance. As Jewish politics deteriorated because of increasing foreign pressure, prophets sprang up to call Jews back to faithful observance of God's laws. By the 9th century B.C.E., some religious ideas and stories about the history of the Hebrews began to be written down in what would become the Jewish Bible (the Old Testament of the Christian Bible).

Besides the emphasis on a single God, Jewish religion had two important features. First was the idea of an overall divine plan. God guided Jewish history, and when disasters came they constituted punishment for failures to live up to divine laws. Second was the concept of a divinely organized morality. The Jewish God demanded not empty sacrifices or selfish prayers but righteous behavior. God, though severe, was ultimately merciful and would help the Jews to regain morality. This system was not only monotheistic but also intensely ethical; God was actively concerned with the doings of people and so enjoined good behavior. By the 2nd century B.C.E., these concepts were clearly spelled out in the Torah and the other writings that were formed into the Old Testament of the Bible. By their emphasis on a written religion the Jews were able to retain their identity under foreign rule and even under outright dispersion from their Mediterranean homeland.

The impact of Jewish religion beyond the Jewish people was complex. The Jews saw God's guidance in all of human history, not simply their own. Ultimately all peoples would be led to God. But God's special pact was with the Jews, and little premium was placed on missionary activity or converting others to the faith. This limitation helps explain the intensity and durability of the Jewish faith. It also kept the Jewish people a minority within the Middle East, though at various points the religion was spread somewhat more widely by substantial conversions to Judaism. Jewish monotheism, though a landmark in world religious history, is noteworthy for sustaining a distinctive Jewish culture to our own day, not for immediately altering a wider religious map.

Yet, the elaboration of monotheism had a wide significance. In Jewish hands the concept of God became less humanlike and more abstract—a basic change not only in religion but in overall outlook. Yahweh had a power and a planning quality far different from the attributes of the traditional gods of the Middle East or Egypt. The gods, particularly in Mesopotamia, were whimsical and capricious; Yahweh was orderly and just, and individuals could know what to expect if they adhered to God's rules. The link to ethical conduct and moral behavior was also central. Religion for the Jews was a system of life, not merely a set of rituals and ceremonies. The full impact of this religious transformation

This Jewish wall painting, from a synagogue at Dura Europas (about 239 C.E.) reflects the artistic style of the Roman Empire. The scene, though, is central to Jewish tradition, showing Abraham and the covenant of God, rejecting the apparatus of pagan idolatry symbolized by the material items of worship to the right.

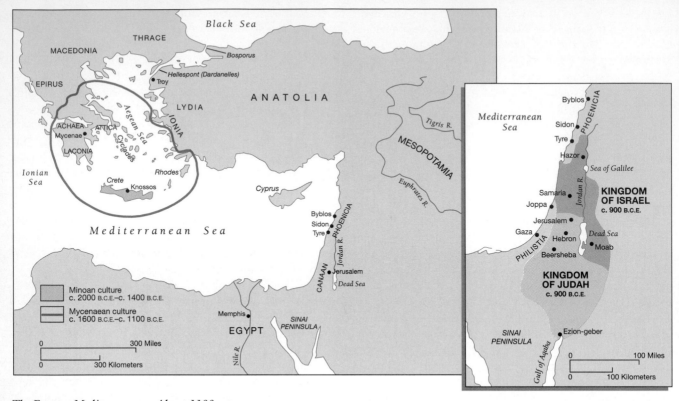

The Eastern Mediterranean, About 1100 B.C.E.

on Middle Eastern and Mediterranean civilization would come only later, when Jewish ideas were taken up by the proselytizing faiths of Christianity and Islam. But the basic concept formed one of the legacies of the twilight period between the first great civilizations and the new cultures that would soon arise in their place.

The Minoans   The Jews were not alone among the distinct societies popping up in the eastern Mediterranean. About 1600 B.C.E., a civilized society developed on the island of Crete. This *Minoan* society traded widely with both Mesopotamia and Egypt and probably acquired many of its civilized characteristics from this exchange. Minoan society, for example, copied Egyptian architectural forms and mathematics, though it developed important new artistic styles in the colossal palace built in the capital city, Knossos. The alphabet, too, was adapted from Egypt. Political structures similar to those of Egypt or the Mesopotamian empires emphasized elaborate bureaucratic controls, complete with massive record keeping, under a powerful monarch. Minoan navies at various points conquered parts of the mainland of Greece; these conquests eventually led to the establishment of the first civilization there. Centered particu-

larly in the kingdom of Mycenae, this early Greek civilization developed considerable capacity for monumental building and also conducted important wars with city-states in the Middle East, including the famous conflict with Troy.

Civilizations in Crete and in Greece were overturned by a wave of Indo-European invasions, culminating about 1000 B.C.E., that temporarily reduced the capacities of those societies to maintain elaborate artistic production or writing, or extensive political or economic organizations. While the civilization that would arise later to form classical Greece had somewhat separate origins, it would build extensively on the memories of this first civilized society and on its roots in Egyptian and Mesopotamian achievements.

The Phoenicians   Another distinct society grew up in the Middle East itself, in what is now the nation of Lebanon. Around 2000 B.C.E. a people called the *Phoenicians* settled on the Mediterranean coast. Like the Minoans, they quickly turned to seafaring because their agricultural hinterland was not extensive. The Phoenicians used their elaborate trading contacts to gain knowledge from the major civilization centers, and then in several key cases improved upon what they learned. About 1300 B.C.E. they devised a much simplified alphabet based on the Mesopotamian cuneiform. The Phoenician alphabet had only 22 letters and so was learned relatively easily. It served as ancestor to the Greek and Latin lettering systems. The Phoenicians also upgraded the Egyptian numbering system.

The Phoenicians were, however, a merchant people, not vested in extensive cultural achievements. They advanced manufacturing techniques in several areas, particularly the production of dyes for cloth. Above all, for commercial purposes, they dispersed and set up colonies at several points along the Mediterranean. They benefited from the growing weakness of Egypt and the earlier collapse of Minoan society and its Greek successor, for there were few competitors for influence in the Mediterranean by 1000 B.C.E. Phoenician sailors moved steadily westward, setting up a major trading city on the coast of North Africa at Carthage and lesser centers in Italy, Spain, and southern France. The Phoenicians even traded along the Atlantic coast of Europe and reached Britain, where they sought a supply of tin. Ultimately, Phoenicia collapsed in the wake of the Assyrian invasions of the Middle East, though several of the colonial cities long survived.

THE END OF THE EARLY CIVILIZATION PERIOD

Focal Point: About 1000 B.C.E. the river-valley civilization period came to an end in both the Middle East and Egypt. The decline of previous governments, particularly in Egypt, led to change. There was no complete upheaval like the invasions that ended the first civilization period in India. The continued development of the Kushite kingdom, the elaboration of the Jewish religion, and the sheer durability of many features of Mesopotamian society blurred the transition. Nevertheless, disruption, invasion, and innovation began to set the basis for the second major period in the history of civilization in the Middle East and the Mediterranean.

Innovations within some of the smaller civilization centers prepared for further change. The simplified alphabet, the major cultural shift described by the first great monotheistic system, and several quite practical improvements—such as the introduction by another Mediterranean coastal people, the Lydians, of coined money—considerably advanced the level of civilization itself. The spread of civilization into Kush and into some

European portions of the Mediterranean, fed by deliberate expansion and growing trade, pushed the major centers well beyond the original core. By 1000 B.C.E. the civilization zone initially established by separate developments in Mesopotamia and Egypt had fanned out widely, sketching the basis for later societies in the Middle East, Africa, and parts of Europe.

At the same time, about 1000 B.C.E., Mesopotamia underwent an unusual several-century span during which regional city-states and considerable internal warfare brought political chaos. Egyptian politics were also deteriorating. Early civilizations in Greece were overwhelmed (almost as completely as their counterpart in India) by waves of invasions by Indo-Europeans. These invasions for a time reduced politics to essentially tribal levels and virtually destroyed cultural activities that depended on writing or elaborate workmanship.

The series of Indo-European invasion form the clearest breaking point. These invaders were hunters and herders initially from central Asia, who pressed into western Asia and Europe in successive waves. The Hittites were an Indo-European people capable of assimilating Mesopotamian values to the extent of setting up a major empire. They also pushed back the Egyptian sphere of influence, launching the decline of the New Kingdom and also freeing up the southeastern Mediterranean corner for the rise of smaller states such as the Jewish kingdom. But by 1200 B.C.E. the Hittites were swept away by another invading force of Indo-Europeans (the same group that interrupted civilization in Greece).

The Indo-Europeans, beginning with the Hittites, introduced the use of iron, which gave rise to more powerful weaponry and the possibility of geographically more extensive empires based on military power. The first group to exploit this new weaponry were the Assyrians, who began a pattern of conquest from their base along the Tigris River. By 665 B.C.E. they had conquered the whole of the civilized Middle East down to the Persian Gulf as well as Egypt. They were a cruel people, eager to terrorize their enemies. The Assyrians used iron, a strong and widely available metal, to arm more men more cheaply than societies relying on bronze were able to do. Their empire was unprecedentedly large and also unusually systematic: they collected tribute, assimilated diverse cultural achievements, and even moved whole peoples (as they did the Jews) in order to maintain control. The Assyrian state was not long-lived. By 612 B.C.E. it fell to a combination of pressures from invading frontier tribes and internal revolt. Several smaller successor kingdoms followed until another great eastern empire, the Persian, arose in 539 B.C.E.

The key points are these: The characteristic boundaries of the early civilizations that had lasted so long amid a relatively slow pace of change were beginning to yield. Invading peoples brought new ideas. The Indo-Europeans, for example, ignored the Mesopotamian or Egyptian beliefs about the divine attributes of kings. Rather, kings were selected by councils formed by nobles and the army. Also, where Indo-European culture took deep root, as in Greece, political patterns began to diverge from those set in the earlier civilizations of the region. Geographical boundaries were shifting, too. Egypt faded as a major independent actor, while the Middle East was open to new empires with greater unifying potential than ever before; and new centers of vitality were beginning to be sketched in Africa and along the European coast of the Mediterranean.

The stage was beginning to be shaped for the emergence of a new set of civilizations, such as those in Persia and Greece, that would build on earlier precedents in many ways but also advance new cultural and political forms. Based on the new military technology brought by iron and on steady improvements in shipping, these new civilizations would reach out to wider regions than the early civilizations had usually managed. More extensive zones of civilization, and new cultural and political principles, both prepared by developments in the early civilization period, would define the era of classical civilizations in the Middle East and Mediterranean that began to emerge by about 800 B.C.E. with the recovery of civilization in Greece and, soon, the rise of the great Persian Empire.

CONCLUSION

The Issue of Heritage

The centuries in which early civilizations took hold and spread in Mesopotamia and Egypt, and then in surrounding regions, provide a fascinating insight into the ways civilization took shape, the reasons it developed, and the mixtures of advantages and disadvantages it involved. The period of early civilization, stretching over more than 2000 years, also allows a clear understanding of the mixtures of diversity and contact that would long shape history in the Middle East, northern Africa, and southern Europe. Separate centers arose, particularly along the Tigris-Euphrates valley and the Nile, that had relatively little interaction and differed in numerous ways.

Civilization, though it grouped unprecedented numbers of people in common cultures and common political structures, also created lasting divisions because of its diverse points of origin. Because of the way in which two distinct civilizations began in the Middle East and North Africa, supplemented by successive invasions and the formation of smaller regional cultures, the area would be permanently marked as a complex, vibrant, but often disputed and disputatious part of the world.

As a new set of civilizations began to emerge to replace the societies born of the river-valley achievements, it is important to ask more specifically what traces of the river-valley civilizations would survive. Diversity in the region is one important trace, as is the persistence of specific developments such as the Jewish religion. So too, at another level, were the monumental achievements of the early civilizations, notably, of course, the great Egyptian structures.

Beyond specifics, however, there were two levels of heritage from the river-valley civilizations: one vital and precisely measurable, the other vital but harder to assess.

The Durable Tools

The basic apparatus of civilization never had to be reinvented in the Middle Eastern or Mediterranean regions or in those areas that received civilization from these regions. This apparatus includes the idea of writing, calendars, basic mathematical and scientific discoveries, and improved technologies, such as irrigation, iron use, more productive grain seeds, the potter's wheel, and the wheel. Money and the idea of written, collected law did not have to be rediscovered in this part of the world, nor did the use of certain medicinal drugs. Many of the attributes or consequences of civilization were so obviously advantageous that they would be taken over by any successor society and carefully preserved amid vast political or cultural change. Other parts of the world had to invent some of these features separately, but in this considerable region the river-valley civilizations produced a framework that never had to be redone.

The Question of Cultural Impact

Whether the early civilizations also produced a set of basic political and cultural impulses that would survive into later societies is harder to determine. Certainly, there are some important traces. The flood story of Mesopotamia passed into the Jewish Bible and so into the cultural arsenal of both Christian and Muslim civilizations in the world today—some of them far distant, geographically, from the story's place of origin. We use words that come directly from the ancient Middle East or Egypt—such as the Sumerian-derived word *alcohol*—and suggest important transmissions. It is increasingly believed that modern music owes much to specific instruments (harps, drums, flutes) that have been discovered in early Mesopotamiam civilization as well as in the development of the seven- and eight-ton scales now used in the West and passed from Mesopotamia through Greece. Towers and columns now common in Muslim and in European and American architecture were based on the ziggurats and perhaps on Egyptian columns. These continuities in style or vocabulary were not, of course, unchanged as they were transmitted, but they show the ongoing influence of the early civilizations on societies that succeeded those of Mesopotamia and Egypt.

The heritage of the early civilizations in politics, though incomplete, is fairly obvious. Ideas of divine kingship, worked out in Mesopotamia and Egypt, were remembered and revived in the later Roman empire and may also have influenced later African monarchies. The importance of regional city-states recurrently marked Middle Eastern history and has had some bearing on the political fragmentation of the region even in recent times.

Some historians have gone further still in suggesting an ongoing link between certain modern civilizations and their river-valley progenitors. It has been argued, for example, that cultures that accepted Mesopotamian influence, including classical Greece and later Christian cultures, emphasized a division between humanity and nature quite different from the civilization traditions launched by early societies in India, China, and probably sub-Saharan Africa. Instead of seeing humanity as part of a larger natural harmony, the Mesopotamian tradition held humans to be separate from nature, capable of observing and exploiting it from a different vantage point, and seeing nature as antagonistic rather than seeking a peace within it. From this basic division in early cultures would come different scientific approaches, religions, and religious goals. The Middle East and Europe have long been centers of religions that encourage action and anxiety, as distinct from the religious traditions of greater tranquility that arose in India. Some of these characteristics may go back to the Sumerian worldview. Distinctive attitudes toward women might even result, as the Mesopotamian tradition tended to see women as closer to nature than men and so more inherently inferior. Whether this basic cultural divide holds up in general may be debated; it may presume too much on what is known about later scientific or religious outlooks, not on what is known about the early civilizations themselves.

Much depends, of course, on how any Mesopotamian core tradition was transmitted into subsequent cultures such as the Greek, the Christian, and the Muslim.

Nevertheless, the idea that some basic guidelines have passed down from the early civilizations is a fascinating one. Not fully provable and certainly not definite fact, the idea legitimately suggests the power and complexity of the values, not just the specific technical and social inventions, that early civilizations developed. One point may give support to the idea of distinctive, durable frameworks of values: The civilizations that inherited from Egypt and Mesopotamia were not all the civilizations in the world. Other, quite separate early civilization centers, notably those in India, China, and later the Americas, would send out different signals, duplicating through separate invention some of the practical features of Egypt and Mesopotamia but inevitably producing quite different versions of culture and politics. More people in the world today look back to those other early civilizations for points of origin than lay claim directly to the heritage of the Middle East and North Africa.

FURTHER READINGS

Two excellent studies can guide additional work on early civilization in Mesopotamia: C. L. Redman's *The Rise of Civilization: From Early Farmers to Urban Society in the Ancient Near East* (1988) and N. J. Nissen's *The Early History of the Ancient Near East, 9000–2000 B.C.* (1988). See also S. N. Kramer's *History Begins at Sumer* (1981). Two fine studies of Egypt are A. Gardiner's *Egypt of the Pharaohs* (1966), a very readable treatment, and A. Nibbi's *Ancient Egypt and Some Eastern Neighbors* (1981). Patterns of life with some useful comparison are the subject of J. Hawkes's *Life in Mesopotamia, the Indus Valley, and Egypt* (1973). Two recent books deal with important special topics: M. Silver's *Economic Structures of the Ancient Near East* (1987) and T. Jacobsen's *The Treasures of Darkness: A History of Mesopotamian Religion* (1976).

Two studies of Israel are J. Bright's *A History of Israel* (1981) and the first two volumes of W. D. Davies and L. Finkelstein, eds., *The Cambridge History of Judaism* (1984, 1987). For a study of Phoenicia, see N. K. Sandars's *The Sea Peoples* (1985). Early civilization in the Upper Nile is the subject of Roland Oliver, ed., *The Dawn of African History* (1968). On the influence of Africa and the Middle East, the much-debated *Black Athena* (1992) by M. Bernal is fascinating.

3

Asia's First Civilizations: India and China

	400,000 B.C.E.	8000 B.C.E.	4000 B.C.E.	3000 B.C.E.
INDIA			**4000–2500** Spread of farming and villages in western India	
CHINA	**400,000–350,000** Peking man	**8000–4000** Transition to sedentary agriculture; silk weaving **4000** Yangshao		

INTRODUCTION

Like Sumer and Egypt in the Middle East, civilizations first developed in East and South Asia in the vicinity of great river systems. When irrigated by the massive spring floods of the Yellow River, the rich soil of the North China plain proved a superb basis for what has been the largest and most enduring civilization in human history. Civilization first developed in the Indus River valley in present-day Pakistan in the middle of the 3rd millennium B.C.E., more than a thousand years earlier than in China. In fact, the civilization of the Indus valley, usually called Harappa after its chief city, rivals those of Sumer and Egypt as humanity's oldest. But like Sumer and its successor civilizations in the Middle East, Harappa was unable to survive natural catastrophes and nomadic invasions. Between about 1500 and 1200 B.C.E., Harappa vanished from history. Until the mid-19th century it was "lost" or forgotten, even by the peoples who lived in the vicinity of its sand-covered ruins. Important elements of Harappan society were transmitted to later civilizations on the Indian subcontinent. But unlike the contemporaneous Shang kingdom on the Yellow River, Harappa did not survive to be the core and geographical center from which a unified and continuous civilization developed, like that of China. The difference in the fates of these two great civilizations provides one of the key questions in dealing with the history of civilized societies: What factors permitted some civilizations to endure for millennia whereas others rose and fell within a few centuries?

The early sections of this chapter are devoted to the rise and decline of Harappan civilization in India and to the history of the nomadic peoples who supplanted the Harappans. Between about 1500 and 1000 B.C.E., as the great cities of the Indus region crumbled into ruins, nomadic Aryan invaders from central Asia moved into the fertile Indus plains and pushed into the Ganges River valleys to the east. It took these unruly, warlike peoples many centuries to build a civilization that rivaled that of the Harappans. As peoples who depended primarily on great herds of cattle to provide their subsistence, they had little use for the great irrigation works and advanced agricultural technology of the Indus valley peoples. Though they conserved some Harappan beliefs and symbols, the Aryan invaders did little to maintain or replace the great cities and engineering systems of the peoples they had supplanted.

Eventually, however, many of the Aryan groups began to settle down, and increasingly they relied on farming to support their communities. By about 700 B.C.E., their priests had begun to orally preserve the sacred hymns and ritual incantations that had long been central to Aryan culture. In the following centuries, strong warrior leaders built tribal units into larger kingdoms. The emergence of priestly and warrior elites signaled the beginning of a new pattern of civilization in South Asia. By the 6th century B.C.E., the renewal of civilized life in India was marked by the emergence of great world religions, such as Hinduism and Buddhism, and a renewal of trade, urban life, and splendid artistic and architectural achievements.

The early development of civilization in China combined the successive phases of advancement of Mesopotamian history with the continuity of Egyptian civilization. Civilization in China coalesced about 1500 B.C.E. Chinese civilization emerged gradually out of Neolithic farming and potterymaking cultures that had long been present in the Yellow River region of East Asia. The establishment of the Shang kingdom at this time gave political expression to a combination of civilizing trends. The appearance of a distinctive and increasingly specialized elite supported by the peasant majority of the Chinese people, the growth of towns and the first cities, the spread of trade, and the formulation of a written language all indicated that a major civilization was emerging in China.

Though the political dominance of the Shang came to an end in 1122 B.C.E., under the new royal house of the Zhou, civilized development in China was enriched and extended as the Chinese people migrated east and

c. 2500 Emergence of Harappan civilization	**1600–1500** Beginning of Aryan nomadic invasion	**600–500** Age of the Buddha, and Hindu-Buddhist rivalry
	1600–1200 Collapse of the Harappan civilization	**700** The composition of the first of the sacred Vedas
2200 Longshan	**1122** Former or western Zhou kings	**550–480** Age of Confucius
1766 Shang kingdom; writing develops	**770** Later or eastern Zhou kings	
2000 B.C.E.	**1000** B.C.E.	

Wheeled model clay carts, such as the one shown here that was found during the excavation at Mohenjo-daro, tell us a good deal about the main mode of land transport employed in South Asia's first civilization. Similar models have been found in almost all Indus valley settlements, and in some respects they resemble the ox-drawn, nearly solid-wheeled carts in use in India today.

south from their original Yellow River heartland. By the end of the Zhou era, which would last officially until 256 B.C.E., many of the central elements in Chinese civilization were firmly established. Some of those elements have persisted to the present day.

THE INDUS VALLEY AND THE GENESIS OF SOUTH ASIAN CIVILIZATION

Focal Point: In the 3rd millennium B.C.E., South Asia's first civilization, one of humankind's earliest, developed along the *Indus River* system in northeast India. Anchored on two great cities, *Harappa* and *Mohenjo-daro,* the Indus civilization excelled in urban planning and hydraulic engineering. Though its larger urban centers were fortified, Harappa's relatively low level of military development left it vulnerable to the depredations of nomadic peoples. Horse-riding, cattle-herding Indo-Europeans entered the Indian subcontinent in successives waves beginning about 1500 B.C.E., contributing to the decline of Harappa and its eventual disappearance from history until the mid-19th century C.E.

Great torrents of water from the world's highest mountain range, the *Himalayas,* carved out the vast Indus River system, which was to nurture the first civilization in the Indian subcontinent. As the rapidly running

mountain streams reached the plains of the Indus valley they branched out into seven great rivers, of which five remain today. These rivers in turn converge midway down the valley to form the Indus River, which runs for hundreds of miles to the southwest and empties into the Arabian Sea. The streams that flow from high in the Himalayas are fed by monsoon rains. Rain clouds are carried from the seas surrounding the Indian subcontinent by monsoons—seasonal winds—across the lowlands to the mountains, where, cooled and trapped, they release their life-giving waters. These "summer," or wet, monsoons, which blow toward central Asia from the sea, are also a critical source of moisture for the plains and valleys they cross before they reach the mountain barriers. The streams from the mountains also carry prodigious amounts of rich soil to the plains, constantly enlarging them and giving them the potential for extensive cultivation and dense human habitation. The Indus is only one of many river systems on the Indian subcontinent formed by melting snow and monsoon rains, but it was the first to nurture a civilization.

The lower Indus plains were a very different place in the 3rd millennium B.C.E. than they are today. Most of the region is now arid and desolate, crisscrossed by dried-up riverbeds and virtually devoid of forests. In Harappan times it was green and heavily forested. Game animals and pasturage for domesticated animals were plentiful. Long before the first settlements associated with the Harappan complex appeared, the plains were dotted with the settlements of sedentary agriculturists.

By at least 3000 B.C.E., these pre-Harappan peoples cultivated wheat and barley and had developed sophisticated agricultural implements and cropping techniques.

The pre-Harappan peoples knew how to make bronze weapons, tools, and mirrors, and they had mastered the art of pottery making. Recurring motifs, such as bulls and long-horned cattle on elaborately decorated bowls and storage urns, suggest links to early agricultural communities in the Middle East, while fish designs indicate a preoccupation with what was probably a major source of food. The long-horned bull was a central image in the Harappan culture and remains important in Indian *iconography* (the art of pictorial representation). Pre-Harappan peoples in the Indus valley also carved large numbers of small figurines of women. These statuettes differ from those found in many other early cultures in the detailed attention given to hairstyles and jewelry. Early village sites also contained tiny carts with clay wheels, which may be the earliest children's toys yet discovered.

The Discovery and Mystery of Harappa

In the late 1850s C.E., the British were directing the building of railway lines through the Indus valley. In need of materials for the railway bed, British engineers allowed their construction workers to plunder bricks found in the dirt mounds of long-abandoned cities in the valley. A British general named Cunningham, who would later be the head of the Indian Archeological Survey, visited one of these sites in 1856. While there, he was given several artifacts, some of which were soapstone seals imprinted with various carvings, including the figure of a bull and what were apparently letters in an unknown script. Cunningham was convinced that the artifacts were of ancient origin and was intrigued by the strange script, which bore little resemblance to that of any of the languages then used in various parts of India. As head of the archeological survey, Cunningham took steps to ensure the full-scale excavation of what came to be recognized as one of the earliest and most mysterious of all human civilizations.

Decades of extensive excavation at the original site and hundreds of other sites throughout the Indus valley uncovered a huge complex of cities and villages that made up the first civilization in South Asia. The evidence found so far indicates that Harappan civilization developed quite rapidly in the middle centuries of the 3rd millennium B.C.E. It diverged sharply from the village cultures that preceded it in levels of material culture, scale, and organization. Equally notable is the lack of

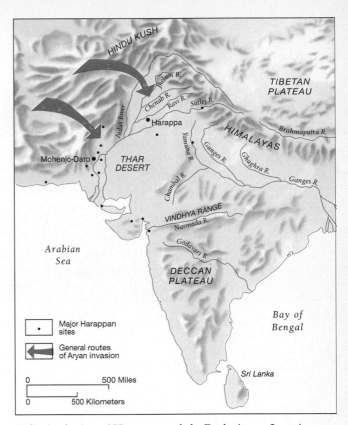

India in the Age of Harappa and the Early Aryan Invasions

strong resemblances to other early civilizations to the west in Mesopotamia, which indicates that Harappa was not a colony. Skeletal remains, however, show that the dominant human type of the peoples who built the civilization was a tall, long-faced, dark-haired strain much like those from the Mediterranean region.

The civilization was anchored on two cities: Harappa, in the north, on one of the five great rivers that forms the Indus, and Mohenjo-daro, 400 miles to the south, on the banks of the Indus proper. These cities formed the twin capitals of a civilization made up of smaller urban centers and villages that covered an area four times the size of Sumer and twice the size of Egypt during the Old Kingdom.

The Great Cities of the Indus Valley

Though hundreds of miles apart, Harappa and Mohenjo-daro were remarkably similar in layout and construction. Both were built on a square grid pattern that was divided by main thoroughfares into 12 smaller and precisely measured grids. Each city was surrounded by walls, which extended one mile from east to west and

CLOSEUP

The Mystery Writing on the Harappan Seals

Potentially some of the best evidence that has been found at Harappan archeological sites is provided by over two thousand seals, usually made of soft stone. As these illustrations of a sacred bull, an elephant, and what appears to be a rhinoceros suggest, these seals were carefully and finely crafted.

The seals apparently played a number of vital roles in Harappan life. They were used by merchants to ensure that bound crates or urns were not opened and pilfered while being transported. Many also appear to have had religious significance and perhaps were used as personal talismans, or magical charms.

Because no one has yet been able to decipher the writing that was usually inscribed across their top edge, we cannot know the meanings of the seals with any certainty, nor can we begin to tap their value as historical sources. Several European scholars have devoted whole careers, futilely, to decoding the mystery writing on the seals. We know that the script had hundreds of characters, but even these estimates vary. Like some modern languages, such as Arabic, the Harappan script was written and read from right to left. Like Chinese and ancient Egyptian, Harappan writing appears to have been pictographic, but no one has found a consistent pattern to tell us what various symbols meant. Perhaps more seals and characters will

be found that will allow us to decipher the script, using sophisticated computer programs. But until that breakthrough occurs, Harappan writing, like much of the civilization that produced it, will remain a mystery—a remnant of a vanished civilization that appears to have left only a limited legacy to those that followed it in South Asia.

one-half mile from north to south. The buildings of the cities and the surrounding walls were made of standardized kiln-dried bricks. Controlled building on such a massive scale would have required an autocratic government with the capacity to organize and supervise the daily tasks of large numbers of laborers. This control appears to have extended to the Harappans' domestic lives as well.

The existence of a strong ruling class is also indicated by the presence of large, well-fortified citadels in each of the capital cities. These citadels served as sanctuaries for the cities' populations in times of attack and as community centers in times of peace. The citadel at Mohenjo-daro included a very large building that may have been a palace. Both citadels contained what are believed to have been audience and assembly halls or places of

worship, and bathing tanks for public use. The elaborately decorated bath at Mohenjo-daro was surrounded by a cloister, which opened onto many small rooms that may have housed priests of the city's cults. Large granaries located near each of the citadels suggest that the state stored grain for ceremonial purposes, times of shortage, and possibly the regulation of grain production and sale.

Though the main avenues of the cities were straight and about 30 feet wide, the lanes and paths in the cities' quarters were narrow and twisting. Brick houses of one to three stories were jumbled together in these areas, which must have been densely populated at the height of Harappan civilization. The layout of the houses was strikingly uniform; each consisted of a courtyard surrounded by rooms for sleeping, cooking, and, in the larger homes, receiving visitors. Entrance to the houses was gained through a long passageway from the street, which in combination with few windows reflects a concern for security. The lack of ornamentation on the houses and the dun-colored brick walls must have given the cities a very drab appearance. Each of the homes had a bathing area and drains that emptied into a covered, citywide sewage system, which was the best in the ancient world. The Harappans apparently bathed standing up by pouring pitchers of water over their bodies.

Harappan Culture and Society

The great cities and many towns of the Harappan complex were supported by a rather advanced agricultural system based on the cultivation of wheat, rye, peas, and possibly rice. Cotton was widely cultivated, and numerous domesticated animals were reared. It is likely that irrigation systems were built to catch and control waters from the monsoon and the rivers, and that fish caught in the rivers provided an additional dietary staple.

The cities of Harappa were major trading centers. Indus seals have been found in urban ruins as far away as Sumer in Mesopotamia. Jade from present-day China and precious jewels from what is now Burma have been unearthed at various Indus sites. Despite these overseas contacts, Harappan peoples appear to have been intensely conservative and highly resistant to innovations introduced from the outside. They cast tools and weapons in bronze, but most of their tools were inferior to those of Mesopotamian peoples, with whom they had contacts. Their weapons were even more primitive. They lacked swords, tipped their spears with bronze points so thin that they would crumble on contact, and used stone for their arrowheads. These shortcomings may have proved fatal to the survival of the Harappan civilization.

Harappan society was dominated by a powerful priestly class, which ruled from the citadel of each of the capitals. The priests derived their impressive control from their role as the intermediaries between the Harappan populace and a number of gods and goddesses, whose provision of fertility was of paramount concern. Several of the gods are depicted on the undeciphered seals [see the illustrations in the Closeup on page 50] that are dominated by a naked male figure with a horned head and a fierce facial expression. On some of the seals he is pictured in a crossed-legged posture of meditation similar to that now known as the lotus position. Numerous figurines of women, also naked except for a great deal of jewelry, have been found. These "mother goddesses" appear to have been objects of worship for the common people, whereas the horned god was apparently favored by the priests and upper classes.

The obsession with fertility was also reflected in the veneration of sacred animals, especially bulls, and in the large quantity of phallic-shaped objects that have been found at Harappan sites. Along with a handful of superbly carved figurines of male notables, dancing girls, and animals, these cult objects represent the pinnacle of artistic expression for the rather unimaginative and practical-minded peoples of Harappa.

The control exhibited by the uniformity and rigid ordering of Harappan culture would not have been possible without an extensive administrative class serving the priests. It is probable that members of this class and possibly wealthy mercantile families lived in the large two- and three-story houses. Characteristically, size—not decoration—set their dwellings off from those of artisans, laborers, and slaves that made up the rest of the urban population. Outside of the two great cities, the subjects of the priest-rulers were agriculturists, whose surplus production was essential to urban life and the maintenance of very vulnerable defenses against natural calamities and human aggressors.

The Slow Demise of Harappan Civilization

It was once widely accepted that Harappan civilization was the victim of assaults by nomadic invaders eager to claim the rich Indus valley as pasturelands for their herds of cattle. A dramatic vision of a wave of "barbarian" invaders smashing town dwellers' skulls made for good story telling but bad history. Archeological investigations carried out in recent decades demonstrate rather conclusively that Harappa declined gradually in the middle centuries of the 2nd millennium B.C.E. The precise causes of that decline remain a matter of dispute.

It is likely that a combination of factors led to Harappa's demise. There is evidence of severe flooding at Mohenjo-daro and other sites. Short-term natural disasters may have compounded the adverse effects of long-term climatic changes. Shifts in the monsoon pattern and changes in temperature may have begun the process of desertification that eventually transformed the region into the arid steppe that it has remained for most of recorded history. Rapid changes in types of pottery suggest a series of sudden waves of migrants into the region. It is possible that the Harappans were too weak militarily to prevent these incoming peoples from settling in or taking over their towns and cities.

A photo of the excavation at Mohenjo-daro conveys a sense of the impressive size and well-planned layout of the city. Note the fortified walls and gates, and the fortress-like construction of the blocks of buildings within the city.

A marked decline in the quality of building and town planning indicates that the priestly elite was losing control. Some of the migrants probably were bands of Aryan herders who entered the Indus region over an extended period of time rather than in militant waves. But the Aryan pastoralists may have consciously destroyed or neglected the dikes and canals on which the agrarian life of the Harappan peoples depended. Extensive cattle raising would then have replaced intensive crop cultivation, further undermining the economic basis of the civilization. That there was a good deal of violent conflict in this transition cannot be ruled out. Groups of skeletons with smashed skulls or in postures of flight have been found on the stairways at some sites. Thus, environmental changes and related administrative decline combined with the effects of nomadic migrations to gradually undermine South Asia's first civilization.

THE ARYAN INVASIONS AND EARLY ARYAN SOCIETY IN INDIA

Focal Point: All through the centuries when Harappan civilization was crumbling from the blows dealt by natural calamities and human aggression, new peoples were moving into the Indus valley. Of these migrants, those of Aryan descent gradually gained the upper hand. Beginning as a rowdy and fragmented warrior culture,

the ascendant Aryans eventually built a sophisticated civilization on the Indian subcontinent. By the last centuries B.C.E., this new civilization had developed a written language, built sizable cities, and produced sophisticated art and literature, and it was nurturing two of the great world religions, Hinduism and Buddhism.

Despite the claims of 19th-century racist writers, such as Arthur Gobineau, and 20th-century demagogues, such as Adolf Hitler, the Aryans were not a race or distinct biological group. The term *Aryan* is properly a linguistic one. The Aryans were originally herders who spoke one variant of a group of related Indo-European languages and lived in the area between the Caspian and Black Seas. For reasons probably related to climatic shifts and conflicts over grazing lands, these nomadic, Indo-Aryan peoples began to migrate in large numbers from their homelands in the 3rd and 2nd millennia B.C.E. The first migrations were westward into Asia Minor and eventually Europe. The second waves were eastward toward Iran and the Indus valley.

The Indo-Europeans' mobility and military prowess made it possible for them to prevail over peoples who occupied the areas into which they moved. The remarkable extent of the zone affected by their expansion is illustrated by the great variety and prominence of modern languages that belong to the Indo-European family. From the Celtic, Germanic, and Romance languages of western Europe and the Slavonic tongues to the east, to the speech of the ancient Persians and modern Iranians and the Sanskrit-derived languages of North India, the ancient Indo-European invaders have left a lasting legacy. Despite millennia of separation and differing paths of cultural development on the part of Indo-European groups, the similarities between their widely dispersed languages remain striking. The word for *father,* for example, is *pater* in Latin, *vater* in German, *pitar* in Sanskrit, and *athir* in Celtic.

Aryan Warrior Culture

To the Aryan branch of the Indo-European nomads, the Indus and the valleys beyond were a veritable paradise of lush, well-watered, and underpopulated grasslands and forests. After spreading across the Indus plains (and probably driving the Harappan peoples farther south), the Aryans moved in waves of small bands to the southeast, into the rich plains and valleys formed by the Ganges River system, which surpassed the great Indus complex in size. Like the Indus plains in earlier times, the Ganges region provided the combination of monsoon rains and great river systems that made civilized life possible. The Aryans took many centuries to approach the level of civilization achieved by the Harappan peoples. But the potential for agriculture was so obvious that herding bands began to settle down and cultivate lands cleared from the forests in the first generations after their arrival.

The Aryans in India did not develop writing until long after they entered the subcontinent. But we can learn a good deal about their way of life from the hymns they composed for religious-based animal sacrifices, entertainment, and historical chronicles. Transmitted orally for centuries by priests and bards, the hymns were written down in sacred books called the *Vedas* in the 6th century B.C.E.

The Vedic hymns describe the Aryan invaders as a restless and warlike people organized at first in tribes and later in small kingdoms. The tribes and kingdoms fought constantly among themselves, often over cattle and pasturelands, and warred with the indigenous peoples. The chief deity of the Aryans was Indra, the god of battle and lightning. He was described as a colossal, hard-drinking warrior with a huge pot belly. Indra was revered as the smasher of dams and the destroyer of cities. The Aryans were superb horsemen, who also employed chariots in their wars. Their bows and arrows and metal-tipped spears were a good deal more effective than the weapons of the indigenous peoples. All together the Vedas de-

The Aryan god of war, Indra, seen riding an elephant and brandishing daggers, was considered king of heaven, in early times. Later Hindus gave Indra a lower status, but they continued to worship him as ruler of the skies and the god of rain and thunder.

scribe the Aryans as a rowdy crew, fond of beer, who engaged in and bragged about their gambling, fighting, horse racing, and womanizing.

Except for military hardware, early Aryan material culture represented a marked decline from the level reached during the Harappan period. Wood and thatch villages replaced stone and brick cities and towns. There is little evidence of interest in sculpture or painting, and thus it is unlikely that great works of art were produced. The Aryans were, however, extremely fond of music. They played flutes, harps, lutes, and a variety of cymbals and drums, and they delighted in singing and dancing. If the Vedic hymns are to be believed, they were also much addicted to gambling, particularly dice. One of the few secular poems in the early Vedic corpus, "The Gambler's Lament," vividly captures the pleasures and pitfalls of the gamblers' den. One passage reminds the tempted youth that

The dice are armed with hooks and piercing;
they are deceptive, hot and burning.

Like children they give and take again,
  they strike back at their conquerors.
They are sweetened with honey through the magic they
  work on the gambler.

Gambling has remained a recurring theme in Indian religious and philosophical discourses throughout South Asian history.

Aryan Society

When they entered the Indian subcontinent, the Aryan bands were divided into three main social groups: warriors, priests, and commoners. Conflict with the indigenous peoples added a fourth group: slaves, or serfs. Though social differentiation between the first three groups was pronounced, the dividing line between the Aryans, who were freeborn, and the enslaved population was particularly rigid. Apparently, there was also a physical dimension to the sharp division between the free and enslaved. The Aryans pictured themselves as light-skinned conquerors in a sea of dark-skinned *Dasas,* their name for the indigenous peoples. Attempts to prohibit miscegenation—sexual relations and procreation—between Aryans and Dasas gave rise to the caste system that came to form the basis for Indian social organization throughout subsequent history. Marriages between the two groups were forbidden. Penalties were prescribed according to the respective ranks of men and women who had sexual liaisons.

As the Aryans settled down, social divisions became more complex, with groups such as cultivators, merchants, and artisans joining the ruling groups of warriors, priests, and herders. Social distinctions were further complicated by the miscegenation that did in fact occur on a large scale. Over the centuries, four broad varnas—social classes—developed: brahmans (priests), warriors, merchants, and peasants. Beneath them were the outcaste and untouchable descendants of the Dasas and other non-Aryan migrants.

The culture of the Aryan invaders placed great emphasis on physical strength, martial skills, and heroic exploits. Descent and inheritance were patrilineal, through the male line. Elder males monopolized authority within the household, though it was possible for their mothers and wives to influence decisions behind the scenes. At marriage, brides left their own households and families and went to live with those of their husbands. Monogamous marriages were the norm, but *polygamy* (one husband with several wives) and *polyandry* (one wife with several husbands) are recounted in the Aryan epics.

Sizable dowries, or marriage payments, in the form of cattle, food, or precious objects were commonly given to the husband's family. In some cases, a prospective husband paid a "bride-price" to his wife-to-be's family, which suggests that female children had not yet become the economic burden that they have been considered through much of South Asian history. Nonetheless, sons were preferred to daughters because of the men's important family ritual roles and their key roles as warriors and priests. These positions were never held by women, nor were women allowed to be the chieftains of tribal bands or rulers of the kingdoms that developed in the early centuries of Aryan invasions.

Aryan Religion

The early Aryans were polytheists and worshiped a wide range of deities that physically resembled humans and displayed human emotions and needs. Like those of the ancient Greeks, each of the gods and goddesses of the Aryans had the power to assist their supplicants in a particular aspect of their lives. Thus, there were gods—or goddesses—to whom devotees offered sacrifices for success in business (the goddess Lakshmi), the means to overcome obstacles in their lives (Ganesha, the elephant-headed god), and the good fortune to conceive children (Shiva, as well as a number of feminine deities). Like the human society that propitiated these deities, the Aryan pantheon was dominated by males, particularly those gods relating to war, fire, and rain. Religious worship was centered on animal sacrifices and ritual offerings of food that were designed to win specific favors from individual deities. The major function of the Vedic priests was to perform these critical sacrifices, a role that later allowed them to amass great power.

In contrast to their Hindu and Buddhist descendants, there was apparently little inclination toward introspection among the early Aryans. The oldest of the Vedas consist mainly of songs, some quite beautiful, praising the various deities and giving incredibly detailed formulas for sacrifices. There is little speculation on issues that would later preoccupy Indian priests and philosophers such as the purpose of creation, the fate of the dead, and the nature of the soul. There was no concept of reincarnation or the transmigration of the soul. Much like the ancient Greeks, evildoers went to the "House of Clay" after death, while the virtuous were rewarded in the "World of the Fathers." In an early hymn to Vishvakarman, the creator god, however, there is a vision of a primal essence and oneness that prefigures later Indian thinking:

What was the germ primeval which the waters received
  where all the gods were seen together?

DOCUMENT

Aryan Poetry in Praise of a War-Horse

The following early Vedic hymn exults in the power of a great Aryan war-horse.

Rushing to glory, to the capture of herds,
Swooping down as a hungry falcon,
Eager to be first, he darts amid the ranks of
    the chariots
Happy as a bridegroom making a garland,
Spurning the dust and champing at the bit.

And the victorious steed and faithful,
His body obedient to his driver in battle,
Speeding on through the melee,
Stirs up the dust to fall on his brows.

And at his deep neigh, like the thunder of heaven,
The foemen tremble in fear,
For he fights against thousands, and none can
    resist him,
So terrible is his charge.

Questions: How did the Aryans regard war and fight their battles? What does the passage tell us about Aryan ideals of manliness and heroism, and their attitude toward death, loyalty, and the herd animals that were central to their culture?

The waters, they received that germ primeval
    wherein the gods were gathered all together.
It rested set upon the unborn's navel,
    that One wherein abide all things existing.

Harappa's Fall and Aryan Dominance

During the early centuries of the Aryan invasions, which began around 1500 B.C.E., civilization disappeared from India. Itinerant pastoralism dominated Indian economic life as sedentary agriculture retreated with the fleeing Harappan peoples. A well-defined elite gave way to rowdy chieftains chosen for their popularity among their warrior followers. A rather complex division of labor and responsibility gave way to tribal egalitarianism and occupational interchangeability. State control and standardization were replaced by fractious warrior bands and something resembling political chaos.

With the spread of cultivation among the invading tribes and the growth of trade some centuries after the fall of Harappa, the basis for civilization again emerged. The small kingdoms that arose in the foothills of the Himalayas and the upper Gangetic plains combined the ingredients that would give rise to India's great classical civilizations. These civilizations produced a succession of wealthy and far-flung empires; gave rise to two major religions, Hinduism and Buddhism, as well as a variety of lesser-known faiths; and produced splendid art, architecture, philosophy, and literature. But the new patterns of civilized life that developed in the last centuries B.C.E. diverged widely from those established by the Harappans. Though some of the Harappans' symbols and beliefs were adopted by the Aryans and other invaders, Harappan civilization became little more than a memory.

A BEND IN THE RIVER AND THE BEGINNINGS OF CHINA

Focal Point: At about the time the Aryan invasions began in South Asia in the middle of the 2nd millennium B.C.E., the first Chinese civilization was taking shape along the Huanghe or Yellow River. Established by nomadic warrior peoples similar in many ways to the Aryans, *Shang* civilization lasted over six centuries. Shang peoples greatly expanded and improved the vital irrigation systems that earlier inhabitants of the Yellow River basin had begun. They also developed a system of writing that has proved a critical source of identity, unity, and civilized development among the Chinese from Shang times to the present day.

Humanlike creatures as well as human beings have lived on the north China plain for hundreds of thousands of years. Peking man, one of the most famous of the hominids—two-legged primates—had campsites along the Fen River nearly 400,000 years ago, and several Paleolithic sites have been uncovered along the Yellow River where it arcs through the Ordos Desert. From Neolithic times (c. 8000–1800 B.C.E.) cultivating peoples gravitated to the lands that make up the base of the Ordos bulge, where conditions were surprisingly suitable for sedentary agriculture and human settlement.

The region abounded in rich *loess,* a fine-grained, yellowish-brown soil that has been deposited by powerful winds from central Asia in prehistoric times. In places, this extremely fertile soil had built up over thousands of millennia to depths of over 300 feet. The Yellow River derived its name from the peculiar color of the soil that permeates the river as it is carried eastward toward the sea. Rich soil and the abundant supplies of water in areas near the Yellow River and its tributaries made the southern portions of the Ordos bulge, and the areas eastward along the North China plain, suitable for intensive cultivation of grain crops and dense settlement. In addition, the region was shielded by mountains to the west and south but open to trade with the north and migratory movements from the grasslands there.

By 4000 B.C.E., human communities supported by sedentary agriculture were spread across the loess zone. These communities coalesced into two widely spread cultural complexes that laid the basis for the Shang dynasty and Chinese civilization. Both the Yangshao culture (c. 2500–2000 B.C.E.) and the Longshan culture (c. 2000–1500 B.C.E.) that followed it were based on very different mixes of agriculture and hunting. In the Yangshao period, hunting and fishing predominated, while foods supplied by shifting cultivation were supplementary. By the Longshan period, the cultivation of grain—millet in particular—was the central preoccupation, while sedentary cropping techniques made it possible for the inhabitants of the Yellow River region to support large, permanent villages surrounded by walls of stamped earth.

Increasingly elaborate irrigation systems were vital to the expansion of the agrarian base of society. Some of China's most ancient and venerated cultural heroes were linked to the building and restoration of the system of dikes and canals that grew up along the Yellow River. The shallow bed of the river after it empties onto the plains of north China, and the large quantities of silt it carries, render the river particularly treacherous in the springtime, when the melting snows of the Tibetan plateau and Kunlun mountains turn the river into a raging torrent. From ancient times, controlling the river by building and maintaining great earthen dikes has been a major preoccupation of peasants and rulers.

These concerns may have given rise to China's first rulers and prompted a high level of community and intervillage cooperation. It is significant that one of the most abused of China's early and semimythical leaders was a man named Kun, who proved incapable of controlling a succession of great floods. His son, Yu, who devised an effective system of flood control, has been revered for millennia as one of the great monarchs of China's mythical golden age. When later thinkers like Confucius searched China's past for leaders whose skill and virtue might be emulated in their own times, men such as Yu came readily to mind.

The Warrior Kings of the Shang Era

Semilegendary Chinese accounts tell us that Yu, the father of north China's great network of dikes and canals, also founded China's first kingdom, *Xia.* Because no archeological sites connected to Xia have been found, it is possible that the kingdom was purely the fabrication of later writers. But in the centuries before 1500 B.C.E., numerous small kingdoms had begun to emerge south of the Ordos bulge and east along the north China plain. Most of them were ruled by the nomadic tribal groups that continued to filter into the area from the north and west.

In this region of different ethnic and linguistic groups a distinctive Chinese culture formed. Key features of this culture included its cooking vessels and cuisine, its reliance on cracked animal bones for divination, its domestication of the silkworm and use of silk fabrics for clothing, and its practice of ancestor worship. The form of ancestor worship followed also suggests that Chinese culture was already patrilineal. By 1500 B.C.E., one of the tribes in the Ordos region, the Shang, conquered most of the other tribes and founded a kingdom that would lay the foundations of Chinese civilization.

Until recent decades we knew little more about the Shang than their Xia predecessors. But extensive excavation of Shang sites at Anyang, Zhengzhou, and elsewhere have given us insights into many aspects of Shang culture and society. In some respects they were very like those of the Aryans, who were in the process of conquering northern India during this same period. Like the Aryans, the Shang were warlike nomads. They fought on horseback and from chariots with highly lethal bronze weapons. Non-Shang subject peoples provided the foot soldiers that made up the bulk of their armies. Like those of Aryan India and Homeric Greece, Shang battles were wild melees that hinged on hand-to-hand combat between a few champions on each side. But unlike the Indo-Aryans and ancient Greeks, the Shang warriors were ruled by strong kings, who drew on their vassals' energies and military prowess to build a remarkably extensive empire.

The Shang monarch was seen as the intermediary between the Supreme Being, Shangdi, and ordinary mortals. His kingdom was viewed as the center of the world, and he claimed universal dominion over all humankind. Shang rulers directed the affairs of state and bore ritual responsibilities for the fertility of their kingdom and the well-being of their subjects. In the springtime, they participated in special ceremonies that included a symbolic mating with female fertility spirits. In times of drought and famine, Shang rulers, or perhaps designated surrogates, were obliged to perform ritual dances in the nude. The dancer—presumably the surrogate—was later burned alive to placate the spirits whose anger had caused the natural calamities.

Shang Society

Though Shang monarchs were served by a sizable bureaucracy in the capital city and the surrounding areas, most of the peasant and artisan population of the kingdom was governed by vassal retainers. These were recruited from the former ruling families and the aristocratic classes of the many small states. The vassals depended on the produce and labor from the commoners in these areas to support their families and military retainers. In return for these grants of control over the bonded peasants, warrior aristocrats collected tribute, which went to support the monarch and his court. They supplied soldiers for the king's armies in times of war, and they kept the peace and administered justice among the peasants and townspeople.

Shang rulers and their families, servants, and noble retainers lived within walled towns in large compounds that housed extended families. The extended families consisted of several generations of the family patriarch. As in Aryan India, family life, at least among the upper classes, was dominated by the elder males in the household. At marriage, a woman went to live with her husband's family, who were virtual strangers. Unswerving obedience was expected of both women and younger males. Within their own households and family spheres, patriarchs and husbands exercised absolute authority. Their wishes and commands were carried down the family hierarchy from elder to younger brother and from mother-in-law to young bride.

Judging from later social arrangements in China, the extended-family pattern was widespread only among elite groups who had the resources to support the large households and many servants it required. Ordinary peasants, who made up the great majority of the population, lived in modified nuclear families: households consisting of husband and wife, their children, and perhaps a grandmother or orphaned cousin. It is likely that peasant families were as male-dominated and patrilocal—the wife living with her husband's family—as those of the elite.

Peasants were in effect the servants of the nobles. By Shang times they were growing a wide range of crops, but their staple foods were millet, wheat, beans, and rice. They worked the land in the village in cooperative work teams using a variety of wooden hoes, spades, and crude plows. They lived in sunken houses of stamped earth and made offerings to local gods of the soil and kitchen hearth.

Though the peasants had only very limited opportunities for social and economic advancement, they were better off than most of the slaves who made up the lowest strata of society in the Shang era. The large numbers of slaves in the Shang era indicate that the Shang warrior elite relied on various systems to control and extract resources from the population of artisans, cultivators, and herders that came under their rule. Though it is likely that many of the artisans were slaves, some were free and quite prosperous. It is probable that this latter group was engaged in the manufacture of products that required a high degree of skill, such as weaving silk textiles and casting bronze. Though their dwellings were located outside the walls of Shang towns, some were surprisingly large and commodious.

Shang Culture

The Shang elites were preoccupied with rituals, oracles, and sacrifices. In addition to the fertility functions of the ruler, the entire elite was also involved in propitiating spirits to provide good crops and numerous offspring. Shang artistic expression reached its peak in the ornately carved and expertly cast bronze vessels that were used to make these offerings. Some offerings, such as fine grain, incense, wine, and animals, were a good deal more innocuous than others. Shang records tell of water festivals at which ritual contests were waged between rival boats, each attempting to sink the other. Those aboard the losing craft drowned when it capsized and were offered up to the deities responsible for fertility and good harvests.

War captives and servants were buried with deceased Shang rulers and major officials. Like the pharaohs of ancient Egypt, the kings of Shang went to the otherworld accompanied by their wives, servants, and loyal retainers as well as their favorite horses and hunting dogs, war chariots, and weapons. The ancestral veneration grew into a cult of the royal clan that involved sacrifices of war captives, mass burials, and the construction of tombs for each of the emperors.

This elaborately decorated, bronze incense vessel from the Shang era, with its whimsical horse and catlike figure, testifies to the high level of artistic expression that had been achieved very early in Chinese history.

Concern for abundant harvests and victory in war led the Shang elite to put great stock in the predictions provided by the shamans, priests who performed oracular rituals. Warriors about to go into battle, officials embarking on long journeys, or families negotiating marriage alliances routinely consulted the shamans to ensure that their enterprises would turn out well. This reliance on the shamans strongly influenced beliefs and behavior in the Shang era. The actual procedures followed by the shamans also gave rise to perhaps the single most important element in Chinese culture: writing.

Writing became the key to Chinese identity and the growth of civilization in China. The many and diverse peoples of the loess region and the north China plain spoke a bewildering variety of languages, which were often mutually unintelligible from one group to the next. They were surrounded by nomadic herders to the north and shifting cultivators to the south, whose contacts with and movements into the loess zone further complicated the linguistic muddle. But the written language that developed made communications possible between the educated elites of many of these peoples.

The use of increasingly standardized and more sophisticated characters provided the bond that gave growing numbers of the peoples of the loess zone a common identity. This sense of identity was felt most keenly by the elite groups, who monopolized the use of the characters, but eventually the sense of identity filtered down to the cultivating and artisan classes. After centuries of use, the characters gave the Chinese a powerful sense of continuity in time and space. With the persistence and growth of this identity, the Chinese people entered history for the first time. Increasingly distinct from the many nomadic herders and shifting cultivators with whom they continued to war, trade, and intermarry, the Chinese used their written language to build the educational and bureaucratic systems that would become the hallmarks of humankind's most extensive and enduring civilization.

THE DECLINE OF THE SHANG AND THE ERA OF ZHOU DOMINANCE

Focal Point: By the 11th century B.C.E., the decentralized Shang political system had long been in decline. In the west of the polyglot kingdom, a newly arrived nomadic people, the *Zhou*, had set up a vassal state that originally recognized Shang overlordship. The Zhou are believed to have been Turkic-speaking peoples from central Asia. By the end of the 12th century B.C.E., the Zhou had openly seized power and established a dynasty that was to last for nearly a millennium until late in the 3rd century B.C.E. In the early Zhou period, a distinct class of scholar-administrators, the *shi*, began to coalesce, and Chinese civilization expanded as far south as the Yangtze River. Attempts to build a centralized bureaucracy also prefigured developments under the short-lived Qin and pivotal Han dynastic rulers, who succeeded the Zhou as the overlords of Chinese civilization.

In the early centuries of their overlordship, the Zhou rulers exercised more power than their Shang predecessors. Under *Wu*, the military commander who had defeated the Shang, and his brother, the Duke of Zhou, the empire was greatly expanded, especially to the east and south. Because the original Zhou capital at Xian was too far to the west to effectively control these areas, a second capital was built at Loyang, hundreds of miles to the east. Wu and other early Zhou rulers governed their vast domains through a hierarchy of vassals, who were controlled to a much greater extent than had been the case under the Shang.

CLOSEUP

Oracle Bones and the Origins of Writing in China

Since pre-Shang times, Chinese oracles had made their prognostications on the basis of "readings" taken from animal bones or tortoise shells. Each of the bones or shells was drilled with a hole and seared with a red-hot iron poker. The bones or shells then cracked, and the patterns of the cracks were interpreted by a shaman or priest. Gradually the practice evolved of inscribing the bones and shells with painted designs that became part of the patterns the shamans "read." Over time, these designs became standardized and came to form the basis for a written Chinese language.

Like the hieroglyphics of the ancient Egyptians, early Chinese characters were pictographic. Thus, they readily conveyed the ideas they were intended to express. The original character for the sun, for example, was a circle with a dot in the center, while the character for a tree was a single tree, and a forest was a set of three tree characters. Combinations of characters made it possible for the Chinese literati to convey increasingly complex ideas. The character for emperor, for example, combined elements of the ideographs for *king, heaven, earth,* and *harmony.*

Over time the number of characters has increased substantially. By the end of the Shang period, there were an estimated 3000 characters. A well-educated scholar in the modern era would need to master some 8000 characters. The way they are written has also changed significantly. Many characters have been simplified, and most have been stylized so that they are less pictographic. The bones or bronze vessels on which the characters were originally carved, rather than written, gradually gave way to bamboo slips, silk scrolls, and wooden plates, and they in turn were sup-

planted in the 1st century C.E. by paper (another critical Chinese invention). Assorted fine brushes and inks were developed to "paint" the characters, which themselves became a major mode of artistic expression in later periods.

Many of the most powerful vassals were relatives, fellow clansmen, or long-standing allies of the Zhou household. Thus, ties of kinship cemented their loyalty and obedience to the Zhou overlords. In turn, the vassals held in check vassals further down the hierarchy, who were often their own subordinates or relations. In addi-

tion, the lords of Zhou formally annexed the vassal states. The Zhou overlords claimed ownership of all of the land in their domains and then parceled it out to their vassals for their support. Peoples whose loyalty to the Zhou dynasty was suspect were uprooted and forced to migrate to areas within the empire controlled by Zhou strongmen.

China in the Shang and Zhou Eras

Zhou Feudalism

In the Early Zhou period, formal oaths of allegiance and regularized fief-granting procedures transformed the Shang vassal system into a more genuine feudal order. Here, as in later political systems of this type, feudalism stressed mutual obligation and benefits within the ruling clan. The Zhou rulers granted to their loyal warrior retainers fiefs, or permission to extract revenue and services from varying numbers of peasant villages. In return, the favored vassals pledged their loyalty to the dynasty in a special ceremony in the ruler's palace. During the ceremony the new fiefholder was given a clump of earth, symbolizing the land and villages granted to him by the monarch. At the same time, a charter of his duties to his ruler and his rights as a fiefholder was presented to the assembled court.

Zhou monarchs had virtually no control over the fiefdoms beyond those in the central core regions. If a vassal stopped sending tribute to the capital or refused requests to muster troops for war or laborers for Zhou building projects, he was in effect declaring war and risking annihilation. As long as the Zhou overlords were strong, it was safer, and profitable enough, to pass on revenue to the court and to rally to the Zhou overlord's call to battle. But when the dynasty weakened, the flow of revenue from the vassals' domains dried up and their

troops were increasingly used for wars between the feudal lords or in alliances against the Zhou rulers.

Changes in the Social Order

Two developments worked against the continuance of the feudal system. The first was the elaboration of an ideology that the Zhou rulers used to legitimize their rule. When King Wu overthrew the Shang dynasty, he claimed that the Shang had lost the Mandate of Heaven and thus no longer deserved the allegiance of their vassals. The concept of the Mandate of Heaven provided a powerful rationale for the Zhou monarchs to strive to centralize authority. Wu charged that his successful bid for the throne was proof that the Zhou had the moral fiber and leadership potential to inherit the heavenly mandate the Shang had betrayed.

This appeal to a supernatural source of legitimation was a common feature of preindustrial monarchies throughout the world, and it became a pillar of the political system in China. It also meant that the Zhou had established the principle that supreme political authority was granted by Heaven, not by a ruler's vassals or the common people. This claim would greatly enhance the capacity of the Zhou and subsequent royal houses to rule as absolutist and authoritarian monarchs. But it also contained a potentially critical check on their powers, which was to be explored by Chinese social thinkers in the Late Zhou era. If a ruler governed by virtue of the Mandate of Heaven, it was possible—as the Shang precedent clearly demonstrated—for a monarch and royal house to fail in their duties and lose the mandate. In that case, it was legitimate for their subjects to overthrow them and replace them with a new imperial house.

The second development working against the persistence of feudalism in China involved the emergence of an alternative to the military retainers who governed most of the empire. During the Early Zhou era, the small corps of professional bureaucrats who had once served the Shang rulers began to grow in size and expertise. These administrators, who were the best educated men in the empire, came to be known in the Late Zhou period (c. 770–400 B.C.E.) as *shi,* or men of service. Their literacy and willingness to serve as scribes, clerks, advisors, and overseers won them a livelihood as administrators, both at the court and in the palaces of the fiefholders and their subordinate vassals. Some of these aspiring administrators were supported by grants of villages, but others, particularly those at the royal court, were paid regular salaries out of the imperial treasury. Many performed a wide range of services that at times could be embarrassingly menial; some even had to cultivate small plots of land to supplement their meager salaries. Increasingly, however, they came to specialize in keeping records; running particular departments, such as public works or war, or organizing palace rituals and ceremonies.

There is some evidence that even before the end of the Early Zhou era in the middle of the 8th century B.C.E., the most favored of these administrators had begun to amass considerable influence as advisors to the ruler and powerful nobles. As representatives of the great lords they sometimes exercised direct authority over lesser vassals. Though the rise of a large and skilled corps of professional bureaucrats did not occur until the Late Zhou era, these early administrators were the forerunners of a scholarly governing class that would become the chief guardian of civilization in China.

New Patterns of Life

In the Early Zhou era, the conquerors lived separately from the subjugated "black-haired people." This division appears to confirm the supposition that the Zhou were originally Turkic tribespeople with lighter hair and eye coloring than the peoples they found in the loess soil region and along the north China plain. In the twin capitals of Xian and Loyang, the Zhou and their servants lived in one side of the walled city, while peoples of other ethnic groups inhabited the rest.

Early in the Zhou period, some of the non-Zhou populace in Xian revolted against their foreign overlords. The revolt was brutally repressed, and large numbers of the deeply implicated artisans were forced to migrate to Loyang, where they lived for generations in poverty. With the passage of time, Loyang became the main seat of the royal house. The palace of Loyang was considered the center of the earth, and each spring critical sacrifices to Heaven and the fertility spirits were performed by the Zhou monarchs.

Zhou vassals lived away from the capitals and resided in walled garrison towns. Each town was laid out on a rectangular grid with two main roads that crossed at a central square. Servants, artisans, and slaves resided in or near the garrisons. Beyond them stretched the villages and tilled fields of the enserfed farmers who made up the great majority of the empire's population. Their staple crops remained millet and wheat, but rice was widely cultivated in the eastern and southern portions of the Zhou domains.

The introduction of iron farm implements and the extension of the irrigation system contributed to higher levels of productivity. But much of the increase went to fill the coffers of the lords and the Shang court rather than to the peasants themselves. The peasants were burdened by their lords' regular demands for labor on road, building, and irrigation projects. They were also obliged to feed and find shelter for the lords' retainers when they journeyed from the garrison towns. In times of war, the peasants marched on foot alongside the chariots and cavalry of the lords' army. As time passed, the lords' demands grew more and more oppressive. A rare insight into the peasants' plight is provided by a poem from the Book of Odes that was written in the Late Zhou era:

Big rat, big rat,
Do not eat my millet!
Three years I have served you,
But you will not care for me.
I am going to leave you
And go to that happy land;
Happy land, happy land;
Where I will find my place.

Big rat, big rat,
Do not eat my sprouts!
Three years I have served you
But you give me no comfort.
I am going to leave you
And go to those happy fields;
Happy fields, happy fields;
Who there shall long moan?

Peasants at some distance from their lords' garrison towns appear to have been the best off. In fact, communications were so poor in many parts of the empire that local lords were content to leave peasant communities alone if they regularly supplied tribute and gifts on special occasions. The peasants in the outlying villages were, in effect, free cultivators. Perhaps it was these peasant communities that later Chinese writers remembered in idyllic terms—peaceful, well-fed, living in harmony among themselves and with their kindly and protective overlords. It is likely, however, that the peasant lament just quoted captures the reality of peasant life in the Zhou period more accurately.

Migrations and the Expansion of the Chinese Core

Throughout the centuries of Zhou rule, both the area controlled by its vassals and the lands occupied by peoples who identified themselves as Chinese grew steadily. New agricultural tools and techniques of production

This carving from the Shang era depicts a two-pronged digging stick that probably was used to turn over the soil for cultivation. This wooden hoe is possibly the single most important tool of the Shang-Zhou era.

stimulated population growth, which in turn led to the extension of cultivation into new areas along the north China plain and then southward along the coast. Periodic nomadic raids and, at times, lasting conquests pushed Chinese peasant migrants to the south and east. Other peasants fled the oppression of feudal lords or sought large tracts of fertile frontier land.

Whatever their reasons for migrating, in the Zhou era hundreds of thousands of Chinese moved down the Yellow River, into the Shandong peninsula, and then south across the flatlands to first the Huai and later the great Yangtze River basins. As they advanced, non-Chinese peoples, who were hunters and gatherers and shifting cultivators, fell back into the hills to the west of the great plains and then to the mountainous region south of the Yangtze. By the end of the Zhou era, the two great river systems—the Yellow and the Yangtze—that have been the heart of Chinese civilization for thousands of years had been straddled. The basin of the Yellow River was securely Chinese, despite the continuing nomadic threat. The Yangtze had barely been reached, but the enormous agricultural potential of the rice-growing, monsoon-watered south had begun to be tapped.

Cultural Change in the Early Zhou Period

The Zhou influx into the loess heartland of early China strengthened the dominance of males within the family and in society. Perhaps the key roles played by males in ancestor veneration contributed to their increased authority. The cults of royal and familial ancestors became the central foci of religious observance. Human sacrifice ended, and philosophical speculation remained minimal as increasingly elaborate rites and ceremonies developed around the worship of deceased members of the family, clan, and dynasty. Family patriarchs and monarchs monopolized the role of celebrant in these ceremonies designed to win the blessings of the ancestors or Heaven, which was conceptualized rather abstractly and called *Tian*.

As in Aryan India, more and more stress was placed on the importance of performing these and other ceremonies flawlessly. An obsession with correctly performed rites led to the elite's more generalized concern with refined manners and proper decorum. The rough nomads had rapidly settled down to enjoy the amenities of the rich and powerful among the civilized.

The End of the Early or Western Zhou

By the 8th century B.C.E., Zhou power was in decline. Its control over its vassals had diminished dramatically and the size and strength of several of the vassals' domains had grown to the point where they were openly challenging the overlordship of the dynasty. In 771 B.C.E., an allied group of northern nobles attacked Xian. The Zhou ruler was killed in a battle, and in the months that followed, most of the western portions of the kingdom were lost to leaders of the vassal alliance or to nomadic invaders eager to take advantage of internal divisions among the Chinese. Retainers loyal to the Zhou managed to rescue a young prince and escort him safely to Loyang. The shift to the eastern capital marks the end of the Early or Western Zhou era.

A less powerful Zhou kingdom would survive for over five centuries more. The territories it effectively controlled shrank to little more than the capital and its immediate environs. Zhou vassals warred continuously, using the defense of the royal house to legitimize their attacks and conquests. Over time, successful lords annexed the holdings of defeated neighbors, and several rival kingdoms emerged in place of the fiefdoms that had existed in the Early Zhou era. The growing chaos and widespread suffering eventually produced a reaction on the part of the *shi* bureaucrats—a reaction that would produce some of China's greatest thinkers and radically alter the course of Chinese civilization.

ANALYSIS

The Legacy of Asia's First Civilizations

In their size, complexity, and longevity, the first civilizations to develop in South Asia and China match, and in some respects surpass, the earliest civilizations that arose in Mesopotamia and Egypt. But the long-term impact of the Harappan civilization in the Indus basin was strikingly different from that of the Shang-Zhou civilization in north China. The loess zone and north China plain where the Shang and Zhou empires took hold became the center of a continuous civilization that was to last into the 20th century C.E., and, many historians would argue, to the present day. Though regions farther south, such as the Yangtze basin, would in some time periods enjoy political, economic, and cultural predominance

within China, the capital and center of Chinese civilization repeatedly returned to the Yellow River area and the north China plain. By contrast, the Indus valley proved capable of nurturing a civilization that endured for over a thousand years. But when Harappa collapsed, the plains of the Indus were bypassed in favor of the far more lush and extensive lands in the basin of the Ganges River network to the east. Though the Indus would later serve, for much shorter time spans, as the seat of empires, the core areas of successive Indian civilizations were far to the east and south.

The contrast between the fates of the original geographical centers of Indian and Chinese civilizations is paralleled by the legacies of the civilizations themselves. Harappa was destroyed, and it disappeared from history for thousands of years. Though the peoples who built the Indus complex left their mark on subsequent Indian culture, they did not pass on the fundamental patterns of civilized life that had evolved. Their mother goddess and the dancing god of fertility endured, and some of their symbols, such as the swastika and the *lingam* (a phallic image, usually made of stone), were prominent in later artistic and religious traditions. The Harappans' tanks, or public bathing ponds, remain a central feature of Indian cities, particularly in the south. Their techniques of growing rice and cotton were preserved by cultivating peoples fleeing nomadic invaders and were later taken up by the newly arrived Indo-Aryan tribes.

Virtually everything else was lost. In contrast to the civilizations of Mesopotamia, which fell but were replaced by new civilizations that preserved and built on the achievements of their predecessors, much of what the Harappan peoples had accomplished had to be redone by later civilized peoples. The cities of the Indus civilization were destroyed, and comparable urban centers did not reappear in South Asia for hundreds or, by some scholars' reckoning, thousands of years. The Harappans' remarkably advanced standards for the measurement of distance and weight ceased to be used. Their system of writing was forgotten, and when rediscovered, it was celebrated as an intriguing but very dead language from the past. Harappan skills in community planning, sewage control, and engineering were meaningless to the nomadic peoples who took control of their homelands. The Harappan penchant for standardization, discipline, and state control was profoundly challenged by the brawling, independent-minded warriors who supplanted them as masters of the Indian subcontinent.

In contrast to the civilization of the Indus valley, the original civilization of China has survived nomadic incursions and natural catastrophes and has profoundly influenced the course of all Chinese history. Shang irrigation and dike systems, and millet and wheat cultivation, provided the basis for the innovations and expansion of subsequent dynasties. Shang and Zhou walled towns and villages surrounded with stamped earth have persisted as the predominant patterns of settlement throughout Chinese history. The founders of the Shang and Zhou dynasties have been revered by scholar and peasant alike as philosopher-kings who ought to be emulated by leaders at all levels. The Shang and Zhou worship of Heaven and their veneration of ancestors have remained central to Chinese religious belief and practice for thousands of years. The concept of the Mandate of Heaven has been pivotal in Chinese political thinking and organization.

Above all, the system of writing that was originally formulated for Shang oracles developed into the key means of communication between the elites of the many peoples who lived in the core regions of Chinese civilization. The scholar-bureaucrats, who developed this written language and also profited the most from it, soon emerged as the dominant force in Chinese culture and society. Chinese characters provided the basis for the educational system and bureaucracy that were to hold Chinese civilization together through thousands of years of invasions and political crises. In contrast to India, many of the key ingredients of China's early civilizations have remained central throughout Chinese history. This persistence has made for a continuity of identity that is unique to the Chinese people.

It has also meant that China, like the early civilizations of Mesopotamia, was one of the great sources of civilizing influences in human history as a whole. Though the area affected by ideas and institutions developed in China was less extensive than that to which the peoples of Mesopotamia bequeathed writing, law, and their other great achievements, Chinese contacts with other peoples led to the spread of civilization to Japan, Korea, and Vietnam. Writing and political organization were two areas in which the earliest formulations of Chinese civilization vitally affected other peoples. In later periods, Chinese thought and other modes of cultural expression such as art, architecture, and etiquette also strongly influenced the growth of civilized life throughout East Asia.

China's technological innovation was to have an impact on civilized development on a global scale comparable to that of early Mesopotamia. Beginning with increasingly sophisticated irrigation systems, the Chinese have devised a remarkable share of humankind's basic machines and engineering principles. In the Shang-Zhou era they also pioneered key manufacturing processes such as sericulture: the production of raw silk, later to be used in the manufacture of silk cloth, through the domestication of silkworms.

The reasons for the differing legacies of India and China are numerous and complex. But critical to the disappearance of the first and the resilience of the second were different patterns of interaction between the sedentary peoples who built early civilizations and the nomadic herders who challenged them. In India, the nomadic threat was remote—perhaps nonexistent—for centuries. The Harappan peoples were deficient in military technology and organization. When combined with natural calamities, the waves of warlike nomads migrating into the Indus region proved too much for the Harappan peoples to resist or absorb. The gap between the nomads' herding culture and the urban, agriculture-based Harappan civilization was too great to be bridged. Conflict between them may well have proved fatal to a civilization long in decline.

By contrast, the loess regions of northern China were open to invasions or migrations on the part of the nomadic herding peoples who lived to the north and west. Peoples from these areas were moving almost continuously into the core zones of Chinese civilization. The constant threat posed by the nomads forced the peoples of the north China plain to develop the defenses and military technology essential to defending against nomadic raids or bids for lasting conquest. Contrasting cultures and ways of life enhanced the sense of identity of the cultivating peoples. The obvious nomadic presence prodded these same peoples to unite under strong rulers against the outsiders who did not share Chinese culture. Constant interaction with the nomads led the Shang peoples to develop a culture that was malleable and receptive to outside influences, social structures, and political systems. Nomadic energies reinvigorated and enriched the kingdoms of the Shang and the Zhou, in contrast to India, where they proved catastrophic for the relatively isolated and unprepared peoples of Harappa.

Questions: Compare the early civilizations of India and China to that of Sumer in Mesopotamia and that which developed in Egypt. Which are more similar in terms of longevity? Are the factors that explain the persistence of Chinese civilization comparable to those responsible for the longevity of Egypt? Are there major differences between the two in terms of their interaction with nomadic peoples? Which of these four civilizations do you think has left the greatest legacy to civilized peoples throughout the world? What is the main legacy of each?

CONCLUSION

Beginnings and Transitions

The spread of the Aryan pastoralists into the hills and plains of northern and eastern India between 1500 and 500 B.C.E., and the establishment and decline of the Zhou kingdom in the latter half of the same time span, marked key transition phases in the development of civilization in India and China. But in each case a very different sort of transition occurred. Like Mesopotamia, the well-watered Indus valley had given rise to one of humankind's earliest civilizations. In contrast to the succession of more limited civilized centers that arose in Mesopotamia, Harappa extended over the largest territory of any of the first civilizations, and it existed without interruption for over a millennium. Its longevity invites comparison with Egypt. But Egypt proved more able than either Harappa or individual Mesopotamian civilizations to absorb massive invasions of nomadic peoples.

Faced with major climatic shifts, the Harappans proved unable to also withstand the steady and prolonged pressure of the Aryan incursions. Thus, the dominance of these invaders in the Harappan core regions and much of the rest of northern India by 1000 B.C.E. meant the end of India's first civilization.

The Zhou conquest and later the slow disintegration of the Zhou dynasty represented a continuation rather than a break in the development of civilization in China. Though civilization arose later in China than in the other three original centers in the Eastern Hemisphere, like the others it emerged independently and resulted in a distinctive pattern of development. In its capacity to endure, China resembled Egypt more than Mesopotamia or Harappa.

Of all the early civilizations, the Chinese proved the most adept at absorbing and assimilating outside invaders while preserving their own sense of identity and their basic beliefs and institutions. The conquering Zhou did not destroy Chinese society and culture; they were assimilated by them so thoroughly that they became Chinese. Thus, though the Zhou period brought major changes in the nature and direction of civilized development in China, fundamental themes and patterns persisted from the Shang era, and the Zhou rulers strove to conserve and build upon the achievements of their predecessors.

FURTHER READINGS

The best introduction to the Indus valley civilization remains that found in A. L. Basham's *The Wonder That Was India* (1954). Perhaps the best book-length studies that place Harappa in the context of Indian prehistory more generally are Stuart Piggot's *Prehistoric India* (1950) and Bridget and Stuart Allchin's *The Birth of Indian Civilization* (1968). For a sense of more recent findings on the Indus complex, see the sometimes quite technical essays in G. L. Possehl, ed., *Harappan Civilization: A Contemporary Perspective* (1982). Romilla Thapar's *History of India* (1966) has a superb chapter on Aryan culture and society. Also interesting are C. Chakraborty's account, *Common Life in the Rigeveda and Atharvaveda* (1977), and the lively and contentious analysis, *Ancient India* (1969), by D. D. Kosambi.

For ancient China, Wolfram Eberhard's *History of China* (1977 ed.) and the early portions of Michael Loewe's *Imperial China* (1965) are good places to start. More detailed (and technical) accounts of the formation of China through the Early Zhou include Kwang-chih Chang's *The Archeology of Ancient China* (1977) and *Shang Civilization* (1980); H. G. Creel's *The Origins of Statecraft in Ancient China* (1970); and Ping-ti Ho's *The Cradle of the East* (1975). K. C. Wu's *The Chinese Heritage* (1982) provides the fullest political history of the Shang and Early Zhou. While somewhat dated by recent archeological research, H. G. Creel's *The Birth of China* (1967 ed.) remains the liveliest and broadest account of these epochs.

	5000 B.C.E.	2000 B.C.E.	1000 B.C.E.	750 B.C.E.
CHINA		1122–770 Initial Zhou kingdom		770–403 Later Zhou kingdom; beginning of China's classical period
MEDITERRANEAN AND MIDDLE EAST			800 Rise of Greek city–states	600 Zoroastrian religion in Iran
INDIA		1200–700 Vedas composed		
THE AMERICAS			900 Maya begins / 850–250 Chavin culture (Andes)	
OTHER SOCIETIES	5000 Early Japanese settlement	2000 Germans settle in Denmark / 1500–500 Polynesian migration / 1000 Germans expand southward	800 B.C.E.–1000 C.E. Bantu migration, sub-Saharan Africa / 750–600 Meroe (Kush) rules Egypt / 600 Legendary ruler in Japan	

INTRODUCTION

Between 1000 and 500 B.C.E., a classical period took shape in several centers of Asia, North Africa, and southern Europe. These centers lasted until roughly the 5th century C.E. The classical civilizations built on the achievements of earlier river-valley civilizations. Originating in China, India, and the Mediterranean, each major classical civilization overlapped one or more of the earlier centers geographically. Because of the ability to build on earlier achievement, the pace of change accelerated in Asia, northern and northeastern Africa, and southern Europe.

The innovations of the classical civilizations were dramatic: empires developed as a political form, and great thinkers and religious leaders drew traditional cultural elements together in striking new statements that served as the basis for whole new cultures.

However, many regions and human societies were not connected to the classical centers or gained connections only as the period drew to a close. In these regions, too, important developments occurred during the classical period, yielding new civilizations, as in the Americas, or more advanced agricultural economies. To put it crudely, the world after 1000 B.C.E. divided into two main parts: one where the roots of civilization were well established and the other where complex societies were first forming. Coverage of the classical period must embrace both major sectors.

THE BOUNDARIES OF CLASSICAL CIVILIZATIONS

Focal Point: Classical civilizations differed from their river-valley ancestors in complexity. Their political institutions, their commerce, and their cultures became more elaborate. The classical civilizations also differed in geographic range: they extended over a much larger territory than the river-valley societies

---

551–c. 233 Period of the great Chinese philosophers: Confucius, Laozi, Menicus, the Legalists, etc.

202 B.C.E.–**9** C.E. Initial Han dynasty; key technical developments of horse collar and water mill

88 Beginning of Han decline

221 Shih Huangdi proclaimed first emperor of China

23–220 Later Han dynasty; invention of paper and the compass

500–449 Wars with Persia; Persia defeated

300–100 Hellenistic period

27 Augustus founds Roman Empire

500–450 Beginnings of Roman republic   **330** Alexander the Great

133 ff. Decline of Roman republic   **106** Height of Roman territory

30 Crucifixion of Christ

264–140 Roman expansion in North Africa (Punic wars) and eastern Mediterranean

550 Formation of Persian Empire

470–430 Height of Athenian culture; Socrates and Greek philosophical style

431 ff. Peloponnesian wars; decline of Greece

180 Beginning of the decline of Rome

327–325 Alexander's invasion   **200** B.C.E.–**200** C.E. Greater Buddhist influence

c. 542–483 Buddha

322–185 Mauryan Empire

300 B.C.E.–**900** C.E. Height of Maya

100 Germans begin contact with Rome; Slavs migrate into eastern Europe

| **500** B.C.E. | **250** B.C.E. | **1** C.E. | CONTINUED |

had done, which meant a major expansion not only of civilization but of the need to integrate diverse regions and peoples.

The nature of the classical period can be amplified in two ways: first, by sketching the currents that set the new period in motion and those that drew it to a close, and second, by defining the greater sophistication of the classical civilizations more precisely. Any period in history must be demarcated by reasonably clear starting and stopping points and must have some internal coherence in terms of definable main features.

No single event ushered in the classical period of history, which is one reason that pinning down a starting date is difficult. Too few connections existed among the civilization centers to make a clean single beginning very likely. Nor was there a dramatic set of technological breakthroughs of the sort that had prepared the rise of the first river-valley civilizations, though the growing use of iron weaponry played a role. The classical period be-

gan soon after 1000 B.C.E., because all the main centers of established civilization were then ripe for new developments. Indo-European invasions toppled empires in Mesopotamia and Egypt around 1200 B.C.E. as they had done earlier along the Indus River. One sign of the resultant change was the partial relocation of civilization centers: The heart of Indian civilization shifted from the Indus to the Ganges River valley as the Aryans cleared the dense forests of the northern Indian plains and spread cultivation. The expansion of China to the south had already begun under the early Zhou era, but it continued with the spread of Chinese culture and political forms into the Yangtze River valley and the mountain regions to the south and west. In the Middle East, a Persian state arose in Mesopotamia, recalling the earlier series of empires from Babylon onward.

Geographical change was more dramatic in the eastern Mediterranean. From 800 B.C.E. onward, an important new center began to develop in Greece, as the Indo-European peoples of the peninsula settled down. Greece

220 Last Han emperor deposed

300 Spread of Buddhism

589–618 Sui dynasty

618 Tang dynasty

312–337 Constantine; formation of Eastern Empire; adoption of Christianity

401 ff. Germanic invasions

527–565 Justinian Eastern emperor

476 Last Roman emperor in West

319–540 Gupta Empire

415 First Hun invasion

606–647 Harsha's Empire

200–1300 Anasazi in North American Southwest

200–700 Mochica culture (Andes)

200–500 Nasca culture (Andes)

800–1300 Mississippian culture

300–900 Intermediate Horizon period (Andes)

900–1200 Toltecs

300–1000 Second wave of Polynesian migrations to Hawaii

300–700 Rise of Axum; conversion to Christianity

401 ff. Large-scale Germanic invasion of Roman Empire

300–400 Yamato claim imperial control of Japan

580 ff. Spread of Buddhism in Japan

300 Decline of Meroe

400 Chinese script imported

700 ff. Spread of Islam; trans-Sahara trade in Africa

900 Polynesians to New Zealand

1000 Height of kingdom of Ghana, Africa

250 C.E.

500 C.E.

750 C.E.

used but greatly altered the scope of earlier civilization achievements from Crete, Mesopotamia, and Egypt, thus proving to be a major source of innovation throughout the Mediterranean region.

The expansion of the civilization centers also brought new peoples into contact with civilization on the fringes of the great empires. During the classical period, nomadic groups in Europe and agricultural peoples outside China in eastern Asia began to learn what civilization involved. Civilization had already moved into parts of sub-Saharan Africa through contacts with Egypt; some of the results now fanned out into other parts of Africa south of the desert.

The end of the classical period, between the 3rd and 6th centuries C.E., was clearer than its beginning, though hardly a unified event. Internal decay in the classical empires combined with a new surge of invasions from central Asia to topple great states from China in the east to Rome in the west. Civilization was not destroyed, but from Asia to Africa it was strongly threatened, forcing reassessments and redefinitions. This reworking of civilization patterns was the trigger for yet another new period in world history after about 500 C.E. The classical period was thus bounded at its beginnings by new sources of vigor and innovation, produced by

adaptations in the original river-valley centers after 1000 B.C.E., and at its end by huge dislocations caused by decay and invasion following a creative period stretching over a thousand years.

REGIONAL INTEGRATION IN THE CLASSICAL PERIOD

Focal Point: More important than sketching the boundaries of the classical era, however, is understanding its defining characteristics. Though each of the classical civilizations was very distinctive, all focused on the need to integrate large territories by building new political structures, extending a common culture, and expanding required commerce.

In the economic sphere, for example, classical civilizations created larger trading zones. The Mediterranean became a single economic region, first under Greek control and then under the imperial Romans. In this common market, local areas could maintain profitable specializations by trading with other Mediterranean areas. China helped link two major growing regions, one of wheat and millet and the other of rice, through rising in-

Romans' View of the World, c. 150 C.E.

ternal trade. Indian trade, both from the Ganges region and through the efforts of seagoing merchants, fanned out through the subcontinent and across the Indian Ocean into Sri Lanka and much of Southeast Asia. The economic interdependence of large regions was basic to the integration of large civilization zones.

The expansion of trading units also had wider implications. Trade with sub-Saharan Africa extended from the Mediterranean zone, while India traded with Southeast Asia. Some commerce also developed among major civilizations in Asia, North Africa, and Europe.

Cultural integration was also important in defining new civilization areas. Important cultural innovations emerged in the 6th and 5th centuries B.C.E. in all three classical centers and Persia. This cultural integration indicated a common need for a new definition of basic cultural values. Socratic philosophy and the great philosophical tradition in Greece, Confucianism and Daoism in China, and the spread of Zoroastrianism in Persia and Buddhism in India all emerged at roughly the same time, serving as major cultural orientations for the various regions involved. Basic classical styles in art and architecture also were shaped in this period and again would continue to define standard patterns. Hindu-derived art in India and classical Greco-Roman buildings in the West still shape artistic expression in the later 20th century.

Cultural innovation was matched by dissemination through each civilization. Indian religious values spread through the subcontinent and moved steadily southward from centers along the northern rivers. Chinese philosophies and religions also spread among elites throughout the Middle Kingdom, building on the unified elite language, Mandarin. Greek language, art, and philosophy spread through the Mediterranean basin and the Middle East. By no means was everyone in each major civilization brought into the same belief systems, for elite-commoner divisions remained crucial. Some civilizations were more fiercely assimilationist than others, for tolerance of internal diversity varied. Nevertheless, the emergence of wide cultural zones defined by distinctive styles and systems of thought was a crucial development.

Finally, there was substantial political integration. Each of the three centers of classical civilization managed to form huge regional empires for periods of several centuries. The ability to construct such large political units both reflected and promoted the other kinds of integration within each civilization.

Economic, cultural, and political integration meant that the great classical civilizations developed new abilities in internal communications, with enough shared language and shared technical systems to send messages, for example, across a wide expanse. Road systems fanned out in classical China and in the great Indian and Roman empires. Bureaucracies and laws provided new unity as well, and military forces moved easily within each of the civilization units. The precise nature of integration varied with the civilization.

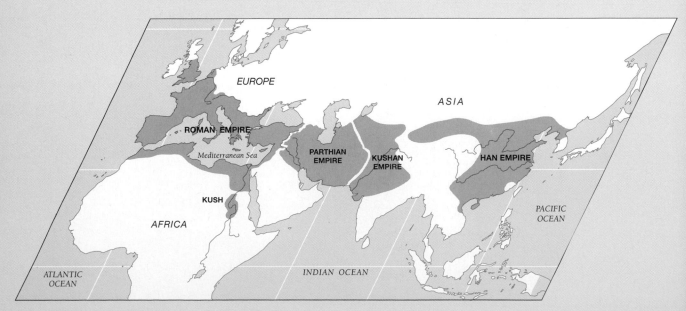

Centers of Classical Civilization, 1st Century C.E.

The growth of civilization's geographical scope allowed some important contacts among the major civilizations. In addition to trade from China to the Mediterranean, there were even more important cases of cultural borrowing or diffusion at several points in the classical period. India was particularly affected by cultural exchange from the Mediterranean region. More important was India's key role in facilitating international trade and cultural influence, westward and eastward alike, as the economies of the classical civilizations reached their high points in the first centuries C.E. Cross-civilizational contacts were limited still, and they did not shape the period as a whole. For example, while elite Romans bought silk cloth made in China, they did not know China directly—China was too distant, and regional traders controlled segments of the relevant trading route. Nevertheless, a rudimentary intercivilizational framework was established that has steadily increased in scale and intensity in each successive world history period to the present day.

The establishment of massive empires and cultural networks gave the classical era an awe-inspiring majesty to peoples who came later in time. This accounts for use of the word *classical* to describe this period. Though civilization was already well established, it was in this period that great monuments of thought, politics, and art were developed that would provide the foundations for most of humankind's later civilizations. The civilizations of the classical era set in motion fundamental patterns of development whose effects can still be felt today in art, philosophy, political institutions, and economic habits.

Each of the main classical civilizations differed greatly from the others in culture, politics, and economic and social forms. The chapters that follow will encourage a comparison between the great civilizations. The similarities between the classical civilizations are very general, but they are all the more important in determining a common framework of analysis. It is also vital to trace developments outside the classical orbit, including the rise of new civilizations in the Americas.

4

Nomadic Challenges and Civilized Responses

	7500 B.C.E.	5000 B.C.E.	2000 B.C.E.	1500 B.C.E.	1000 B.C.E.
EURASIA AND AFRICA	**7500–7000** Domestication of sheep and goats; first pastoralists	**7000–6500** Domestication of cattle	**2000–1500** Domestication of horse and camel **1800–1575** Hyksos invade Egypt **c. 3000** First use of donkeys as pack animals	**1900–1000** Hittite (Indo-European) expansion throughout the Middle East **c. 1600–600** Indo-European nomadic expansion	**1122** Zhou nomads establish dominance in China
THE AMERICAS		**c. 5000** Llama is domesticated by Andes mountain dwellers			

INTRODUCTION

By the end of the 2nd millennium B.C.E., civilizations based on the Neolithic innovations of livestock domestication and sedentary agriculture had evolved in several core regions across all the continents of the globe except Australia and Antarctica. The Middle East had proved to be the earliest and most fertile source of civilizations, having produced Sumer and the Akkadian and Babylonian empires. In South Asia, the great Harappan complex spread throughout the Indus valley and beyond during the middle centuries of the 3rd millennium B.C.E. In the Nile delta 500 years earlier, and in the bend in the Yellow River about a millennium later, two of the most durable civilizations, the Egyptian and the Chinese, had begun to flourish. Between about 2000 and 1500 B.C.E., Mesopotamian- and Egyptian-influenced civilizations also spread to the island of Crete in the Mediterranean and into what was to become Greece in southeastern Europe. At the very end of the 2nd millennium, a separate Kush civilization developed in Africa up the Nile from Egypt and for several generations dominated its older, northern neighbor. In the Americas, seed civilizations emerged on the eastern Mexican coast, at Monte Alban, also in Mexico far to the south at Chavin in the Andean highlands, and along the coast of present-day Peru.

The achievements of the peoples who established the centers of civilized development were truly impressive. But the total area occupied by civilized sedentary agriculturists and town dwellers remained only a small portion of the regions of the earth. Seen in this larger context, the different centers of civilization were rather constricted pools, usually separated by thousands of miles and surrounded by peoples whom the civilized regarded as distinct and hostile. Perhaps as high as 90 percent of the human population of the earth, which is estimated to have reached between 2 and 3 hundred million in this era, were sedentary agriculturists concentrated in the civilized cores.

However, most of the inhabited earth was occupied by migratory peoples who practiced shifting rather than sedentary cultivation, or were nomadic herders, or followed a hunting-and-gathering existence much like that of the Stone Age peoples before the Neolithic revolution. *Shifting cultivators* predominated in the rain-forest zones of Central and South America, West Africa, east and central India, and much of south China and the Southeast Asian mainland and islands. *Nomads,* who herded domesticated animals, ranged over the great swaths of grassy plains that stretched across central Eurasia and fringed desert areas, such as the central Arabian peninsula and the Sudanic zone in Africa. In the Americas, hunters and gatherers occupied similar areas as well as the arid wastes between the plains of North America and the fertile valleys of central Mexico.

Though none of the peoples following these migratory modes of existence produced its own civilization, many of them significantly influenced the course of development of the civilizations that arose in different areas. In some instances the impact of nonsedentary peoples was largely destructive, such as the nomadic Indo-Aryans' contribution to the decline of the Harappan complex in the Indus valley and the role of the hunting-and-gathering *chichimecs* in the collapse of early civilizations in Mesoamerica.

400–300 Hun invasions of China

400–500 Hun invasions in India

650–750 Bedouin Arabs spearhead Islamic expansion across North Africa and the Middle East and into central Asia

200–580 Era of nomadic dominance in China

170 B.C.E.–100 C.E. Waves of nomadic invasions into India

1050–1250 Age of nomadic dominance in Northwest Africa and the western Sudan

c. 370–480 First wave of nomadic incursions into western Europe

1050–1420 Prolonged phase of expansion by Turkic and Mongol nomads

c. 750–850 Nomad invasions from North Mexico central valley

1375–1440 Rise of the Aztecs

970–985 Toltec expansion throughout the central valley

c. 850 Teotihucan destroyed by invading nomads

1 C.E.   500 C.E.   1000 C.E.

Other incursions of migratory peoples into the zones occupied by sedentary agriculturists and towns-people were disruptive only initially. Eventually they led either to the establishment of new civilizations or to even stronger dynastic control over existing civilizations that had come under assault. Such was the case in Mesopotamia after the Hittite (Indo-European) invasions at the end of the 2nd millennium B.C.E., in China with the rise of the Zhou kingdom in roughly the same period, and in the Americas with the establishment of great Toltecan and Aztecan cities and empires. Finally, in key phases of global historical development, nomadic peoples served as links rather than barriers to civilization. Thus, they furthered the development of trading networks, carried new religious ideas far from the lands where they were first conceived, and transmitted key inventions between the different pools of human civilization.

In regions such as South India and China and Southeast Asia, where there were no great civilized centers until the last centuries B.C.E. and where sedentary agriculture was confined to small pockets in the lowland valleys, contacts with the practitioners of shifting cultivation in the hills were more limited and less dramatic. But peoples practicing the two patterns did exchange goods and periodically raided each others' domains in search of slaves and booty. They also clashed over the control of the river valleys, where irrigated wet-rice cultivation could be practiced on a large enough scale to support the cities and kingdoms that became the foci of early civilization in these areas. The outcome of these struggles often determined which people would go on to play major roles in the history of the regions in which they lived, and which would sink into obscurity and extended struggles to defend their territories from lowland dominance.

Migratory peoples have had such a great impact on human history that it is essential to have a clear sense of their lifestyles and the nature of their interaction with farming and urban populations. Migratory peoples can be divided into several main types according to the means by which they supported themselves and responded to different environments. After these basic types of migratory peoples have been discussed and their lifestyles and patterns of social organization have been contrasted with those of the sedentary agriculturists, the remainder of this chapter will be devoted to one variant of the migratory pattern: pastoral nomadism. Pastoral nomadism has had a great and continuing impact on the development of individual civilizations and on the contacts between the civilized cores. After the ways in which pastoralism shaped all aspects of nomadic life and culture have been explored and different forms of nomadic social and political organization have been considered, key patterns of interaction

Desert nomads trek with their heavily burdened camels through the arid terrain of sand and scrub near Tripoli in present-day Libya. The loss of one's camel or failure to keep one's bearings could prove fatal in such an unforgiving environment.

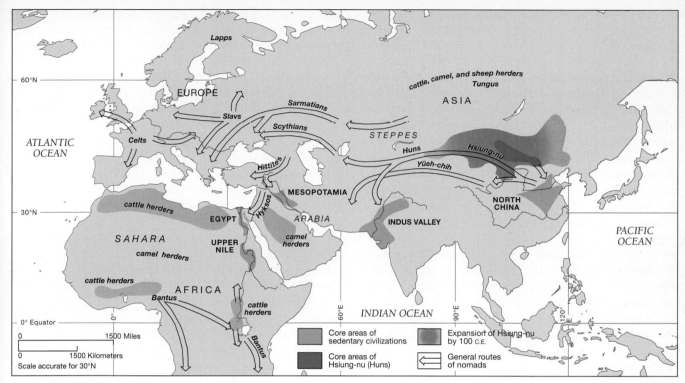

Earliest Civilizations and the Migration of Nomadic Peoples

between nomads and sedentary peoples will be identified. Insights into the nature of nomadic lifestyles and persistent modes of response to civilized peoples will prove essential to a full understanding of the history of virtually all civilizations, from the early ones we have already studied through those that flourished in the centuries just before the Industrial Revolution.

None of the variants of the migratory pattern posed as formidable a challenge to agrarian, town-based peoples as the pastoral nomads. These nomads raided and conquered the kingdoms and empires of the civilized peoples and on occasion forged huge empires of their own, which spanned several of the great civilizations. Though they remained powerful rivals of the civilized peoples until the advent of the Industrial Revolution just 200 years ago, the nomads were tied to patterns of economic sustenance and social and political organization that fundamentally constricted their ability to dominate agrarian and urban zones for long. Contacts between the two invariably led to the nomads' assimilation to sedentary cultures or their retreat to the grasslands or desert margins whence they had come.

ANALYSIS

Varieties of Human Adaptation and the Potential for Civilization

Perhaps the best way both to understand individual modes of human adaptation to environmental conditions and to compare these different responses is to relate them to the two extreme types of adaptation that ecologists call the *niche* and the *holding*. In the first instance, the human group works its way into the environment in which it lives rather than transforming that environment. Like the plants and other kinds of animals with whom they share a particular ecosystem, these peoples simply occupy one of many *niches* available in the overall ecosystem. Their activities have only a minimal impact on the other niches or the life-forms that occupy them. In the most extreme manifestations of the niche pattern, exhibited by rain-forest peoples of Central and South America, Southeast Asia, and Africa, small human groups, *forest farmers,* hunt game and gather fruits and vegetables in the jungle without altering the forest environment.

These peoples move continuously through large areas of the forest, ingeniously tapping the many sources of plant and animal food available. They seldom contact other bands, and when they do it is often to contest, frequently violently, the use of portions of the forest they consider part of the large territory from which they draw their livelihood. This pattern of subsistence is virtually identical to the pattern practiced by hunting and gathering peoples in the prefarming Stone Age. In addition to the forest farmers, the niche pattern has been adopted in the past by American Indian and African peoples in prairie and semidesert regions.

Before the Industrial Revolution, *sedentary agriculture,* which was dependent on elaborate irrigation systems, represented the most developed form of the holding approach to ecological adaptation. Peoples who practice variants of this approach transform the natural environments in which they live. Sedentary cultivators, for example, clear forests, haul away stones, and plow grasses and weeds to prepare large tracts of land for the cultivation of plants. In addition to land for cultivation, fields and forests are cleared to support the domesticated animals. Thus, both the original vegetation and animal life in regions brought under cultivation are supplanted by domesticated plants and livestock. The domesticated plants are arranged in patterns designated by human decision rather than natural processes. They are protected from wild animals, and rival plant life is removed by weeding.

Because a very large investment in labor hours is needed to prepare fields for farming and to grow and harvest the various crops, sedentary cultivators settle in permanent dwellings near the fields they work. In time, some of these settlements have grown into towns and cities, which have proved to be key elements in most civilizations. Thus, both farming and settlement in the holding mode have made for major transformations of the natural landscape in the regions in which they have been practiced.

Between the niche pattern and the holding pattern, several intermediary forms of human adaptation have developed. Two of the most important are closer to the niche than to the holding pattern. The first of these alternatives is represented by the *shifting cultivators* or *slash-and-burn* farmers, who are concentrated in the rain-forest zones of both the Eastern and Western Hemispheres. Shifting cultivators burn off the jungle undergrowth but leave the large trees and the cover they provide to protect the fragile tropical soils. Using the ashes created by their fires as a natural fertilizer, shifting farmers then cultivate the area cleared on the forest floor on a limited basis. The foods grown in this manner form the staples of their diet, which are supplemented by meat, wild berries, and other forest plants.

After working a particular clearing for a year or two, shifting cultivators move on to another patch in the forest, where they again begin the burning-cultivating sequence. Like the hunters and gatherers, shifting cultivators require large amounts of land because it takes anywhere from 20 to 30 years for burnt-off forest to be restored to the point where it can be reused. Generally, they move from patch to patch in a huge circle in the forest zone, eventually returning after 20 or so years to the patch originally worked. Though more substantial than those of the hunters and gatherers, their shelters tend to be flimsy because they are regularly abandoned.

The *pastoral nomads* provide the second major alternative between hunting-and-gathering and sedentary agriculture. Though nomadic groups differ according to the kinds of animals they herd and whether they ride horses or camels or work their herds on foot, their pattern of adaptation to their natural environment is similar. Like the shifting cultivators, nomads do not seek to transform their natural environments in major ways. In the steppe and savanna grasslands where they live in the winter and spring months, they introduce large herds of domesticated livestock. Their herds, in effect, harvest the plant cover in these areas. The nomads also set up temporary camps of tents or wagons near their herds. When the hot, dry summer season arrives, the nomads break camp and move with their herds to riverine or hilly areas where there is sufficient water and plant life to sustain their livestock.

The energy expended by the nomads in transforming their environment is minimal. Like the shifting cultivators and the hunters and gatherers, nomadic peoples need large tracts of land to maintain their subsistence lifestyle. But some nomadic groups, particularly those of the Eurasian steppes, have proved able to support far larger bands than either the shifting-farming or the hunting-and-gathering responses have allowed. Horse- and camel-riding nomads have also achieved a degree of mobility and a potential for large-scale organization that has proved impossible for shifting cultivators or hunters and gatherers. These advantages have given the nomads the capacity to challenge the peoples of the sedentary farming zones to a degree undreamed of by groups practicing any other migratory approach to ecological adaptation. In fundamental ways, human history until the Industrial Revolution can be seen as an extended contest between the nomadic peoples, who were the most expansive and warlike of all who followed migratory or nichelike adaptations, and the sedentary agriculturists, whose civilizations rested on their capacity to establish advanced holdings in fertile and well-watered areas.

Questions: Given the patterns of adaptation discussed, why would it be easier to build a civilization on the basis of the sedentary-farming holding pattern than on any of the migratory-niche responses described? What would a people gain in opting for the holding pattern and developing a civilization? What might they lose in giving up a nomadic or shifting-cultivating way of life?

THE RISE AND SPREAD OF PASTORAL NOMADISM

Focal Point: We do not know when genuinely nomadic societies first came into existence because the peoples who developed them had no written records. But it is likely that nomadic alternatives to sedentary agriculture emerged some time after the first civilizations and that nomadic herders were quite widely distributed by 1500 B.C.E. It is also probable that pastoral nomadism originated among peoples who had been driven with their herds from the fertile river valleys of the civilized cores or among hunting-and-gathering bands that captured domesticated livestock in raids on agricultural villages. In the following millennia, pastoral nomadism developed variants according to the animals that particular peoples domesticated.

The nomadic peoples led their herds into the grassy but sparsely inhabited plains of central Eurasia. In this vast area and in similar zones in Sudanic and East Africa, Arabia, and highland South America, refugees and raiders found ample pasturage for their herds and discovered that they could subsist on the products the animals supplied. The regions into which nomadism spread received enough rainfall (considerably more than today) to support the grasses and other plant life on which herd animals feed, but not nearly enough for sedentary farming. Thus, nomadic peoples occupied lands that could not be claimed by rapidly growing farming populations. As they spread through the steppes and savannas, the pastoralists displaced the original hunting-and-gathering peoples or prompted them to adopt the herding lifestyle, which was better suited to the plains environment. The pastoralists, in turn, continued to hunt the abundant game animals of the plains for both meat and fur.

The Horse Nomads

The first nomadic peoples about whom we know a good deal are the Indo-European tribes of the middle centuries of the 2nd millennium B.C.E. For over a millennium thereafter, they threatened the early civilizations of the Middle East and the Indus plains. Some Indo-European peoples, such as the Hittites and Hyksos, also established their own empires and centers of civilization, while others, such as the early Greeks, settled in the lands to which they migrated. As late as the last centuries B.C.E., these settled groups still struggled to fight off the incursions of later Indo-European migrants such as the Scythians, who invaded Europe and Asia Minor, and the Kushanas, who established an empire spanning northwest India and central Asia. Some Indo-European peoples migrated eastward, where they contested with other nomadic peoples for grazing lands, and invaded northwest India, where they proved an increasing menace to Harappan civilization.

Interestingly, the earliest Indo-European invaders did not ride the horses that they raised in great numbers and prized as symbols of wealth and status. Instead they fought from war chariots drawn by one or two horses. With the development of increasingly effective bridles and stirrups, however, Indo-European warriors began to ride horses during migrations or into battles.

Another nomadic group that played a major role in the age of classical civilizations was the Hsiung-nu (later known in Europe as the Huns). The devastation wrought by Hsiung-nu incursions into China, beginning in the 4th century B.C.E., presaged the calamities that would befall India and Europe centuries later when the Huns toppled the Gupta Empire and smashed into the crumbling Roman Empire. The eastern branches of the Hsiung-nu tribes also competed for pasturelands with peoples such as the Tungus, while the Huns to the west fought constantly with sheep- and goat-herding nomadic peoples speaking a variety of Turkic languages. From the era of the Indo-European migrations, droughts and intertribal warfare periodically drove large bands of central Asian nomads into the sedentary agricultural zones that fringed their far-flung steppe homelands. Their migrations played a major role in the rise and fall of empires in the civilized cores from the time of these first incursions to the era of the Turkic and Mongol explosions of the 11th through the 14th centuries C.E.

The Reindeer Herders of the North

It is possible that *reindeer-herding nomads* like the Lapps were migrating with their flocks across the tundra of northern Europe even before the nomadic pattern spread to the steppe regions of central Asia. In the bogs of Scandinavia, archeologists have found the remains of sledges dating as early as the late Paleolithic era. The earliest of these sledges were probably pulled by teams of dogs or men on rudimentary skis. But by the early Neolithic period, tamed reindeer were used, suggesting that pastoral nomadism had been established in the region. Despite their early appearance, the reindeer-herding nomads lived far from the centers of civilization. This isolation rendered their influence on the course of human history marginal at best.

The Camel Nomads

The spread of pastoral nomadism in the central Asian steppes had hinged largely upon the domestication of the horse. Farther west in the Arabian peninsula and the Sudanic zone that stretches across north-central Africa, another animal played the pivotal role in the diffusion of the nomadic pattern. As early as 1700 B.C.E., the camel was mentioned in Egyptian sources as a pack animal, but it had not yet been ridden by humans. It is likely that pastoralism based on the camel had been established in western Asia even before they were first ridden during the last centuries B.C.E.

Awkward-looking and peevish creatures, camels are remarkably well adapted to the barren and parched regions that fringe the Sahara and Arabian deserts. They can carry loads of up to 400 pounds and travel 60 miles a day. Once they have filled the reservoirs in their humps with water, camels are able to sustain this pace for over 20 days without water in temperatures averaging 120 degrees Fahrenheit. If they are occasionally fed a little green fodder on the journey, the camels will plod on indefinitely. Without the fodder, they will continue on for another five days before lying down to die. Though horses were introduced into both Arabia and the Sudan, and cattle-herding nomads came to predominate on the savannas south of the Sahara, the camel has remained central to most of the nomadic cultures that have developed in these regions. These "ships of the desert" have been essential to the great trading systems that developed in these areas and to the formidable capacity of their nomadic masters for making war.

The Cattle Herders

Beginning in the upper reaches of the Nile River in the central and southern portions of the present-day nation of Sudan, and expanding over the centuries from north to south across the rift valleys and plains of East and southern Africa, yet another major variant of pastoral nomadism developed. In this vast and varied expanse, warrior-dominated societies based on cattle herding coalesced and expanded. Because the climate and especially the disease environment posed major barriers to horse breeding, the cattle nomads migrated, hunted, and fought their wars on foot. But cattle provided their sustenance and the basis of their material culture. Cattle were the prime gauge of wealth and status, the focus of religious rituals, and the key item given to the bride's family in arranging a marriage alliance.

Like those of the reindeer herders of the northern tundras, the regions occupied by the cattle nomads were initially distant from major civilized centers. As a consequence, we know little of the early history of these peoples. However, in contrast to the Lapps and other subarctic pastoralists, the cattle herders of Africa were eventually to play major roles in the history of different areas of the continent.

Nomadic Peoples of the Americas

Because most of the large mammals of the Americas had died out by the end of the last Ice Age, pastoral nomadism played almost no part in the history of these continents until horses, cattle, and other domesticated animals were introduced by the Europeans after 1492 C.E. Only in the highlands of the Andes, where llamas and alpacas survived in large numbers, was it possible for truly nomadic cultures to develop. But even in this limited area, pastoralists played a minor and subordinate role. The prairie and semidesert regions of the Americas that might have supported pastoralists were occupied instead by hunting-and-gathering peoples.

The absence of large mammals prevented the nomadic peoples of the prairies and arid plains from fully tapping the potential of their environments and deprived them of the superior mobility necessary for raiding and conquering in the civilized heartlands. If the Aztecs can be taken as typical, however ferocious the *chichimecs* were in battle, they were impoverished wanderers until they established themselves in the sedentary zones. The

Aztecs' arrival in the central valley of Mexico was little noticed by the civilized peoples who lived in great cities along its lakes. During the decades when they struggled to establish themselves in the region, the hapless and weak Aztecs were beaten in battle, enslaved in large numbers, and finally driven to a marshy island refuge in Lake Texcoco. The contrast between the reception accorded in civilized Mesoamerica to incoming migratory peoples and the shock waves sent repeatedly through the civilized centers of Eurasia by invading horse- and camel-herding nomads is indeed striking evidence of the power that could be generated by pastoral adaptation.

NOMADIC SOCIETY AND CULTURE

Focal Point: More than any other feature, migratory patterns define and structure the lives of pastoral nomads. These movements reflect both the nomads' dependence on domesticated animals and the extent to which humans and animals have adapted to their environments. Nomads and herds migrate to survive. Their social systems, attitudes, and material culture are all shaped by the migratory patterns that dominate their existence.

The steppe and prairie areas, where nomads live, experience extreme fluctuations in temperature and weather conditions. Temperatures in the steppe regions of central Asia, for example, can range from 45 degrees Fahrenheit below zero in the winter to over 120 degrees in midsummer. In the steppe and in the desert fringes of the Sahara and Arabia, there are also extreme variations in temperature on a daily basis. Temperatures can soar well above 100 degrees in the heat of the midafternoon sun and then plummet after nightfall to below freezing. In both regions, powerful winds, easily able to throw a rider from the saddle, stir up dust and sand storms, which batter the sparse plant life that is able to survive in the thin and desiccated soils.

   In this harsh environment, nomadic peoples must regularly migrate to feed and water the herds on which their own survival depends. Year after year they usually follow the same routes between the different areas in which they pasture their herds. In late winter or early spring, they drive their herds onto the plains, where the seasonal rains provide a cover of rich vegetation to nourish their calving or lambing animals. When the dry winds and incessant heat of summer begin to wither the grasses and shrubs of the steppe or the desert fringe, the nomads drive their herds into hilly regions, to the lower slopes of distant mountains, or to riverine areas where

pasturage can still be found. After wintering in these regions, they return to the plains to celebrate rituals of renewal and fertility amid their feeding and growing herds.

   The distances nomadic groups migrate on a regular basis vary greatly, from tens to hundreds of miles depending on the size and needs of their herds and the environment in which they live. In addition to temperature and rainfall, their movements may be determined by other factors. In East Africa and the western Sudan, for example, cattle-raising peoples must drive their herds from areas where the tsetse fly thrives in certain seasons or risk the decimation of their livestock by disease. The camel-herding nomads of the Arabian peninsula must ensure that their animals feed regularly on the salt-laden grasses at the desert fringe, for without the salt the camels will sicken and die.

   Prolonged drought in regions where nomadic peoples normally pasture their animals can lead to temporary, and at times permanent, alterations in their routes and destinations. But shifts in migratory routines are adopted reluctantly because of the risks involved in moving into unknown regions as well as the potential for conflict with other nomadic groups. Though the nomad's sense of property is focused on livestock, pastoral groups stake out particular areas and watering places as their own. The use of another tribe's migration route, wells, or pasture lands has often provoked violent conflict and the expulsion or elimination of one of the competing groups. Thus, the nomads' struggle to survive in the harsh environment of the steppe and desert fringe is complemented by an ongoing contest to preserve their own pasturelands from rivals or to wrest control of additional or alternative areas in times of population increase or natural calamity.

Livestock and Survival

Though most nomadic peoples have traded with or raided the settlements of sedentary agriculturists, their survival has depended primarily on the well-being of their livestock. Whether cattle, camels, or sheep, the herds supply the meat, milk, and dairy products that are the nomads' staple foods. They use the hides or fleece of their livestock to make their clothing, tent and wagon covers, weapons, eating utensils, jewelry, and works of art. Animal sacrifices are at the center of the nomads' religious rituals, and the size and quality of a nomad's herd is the prime indicator of one's wealth and status.

   Peoples who raise camels and horses also depend on their animals to transport their worldly goods from one pastureland to another and to carry to market those items they wish to trade with sedentary peoples. The goods the nomads trade are in turn primarily products they derive from their herds: meat, milk products, skins, wool, and bone sculptures. The mobility they gain from the animals they raise plays a key role in their survival. It allows them to flee from powerful enemies or to reap the advantages of speed and surprise in attacks on rival encampments or town and village dwellers. To the horse- or camel-herding nomads, the loss of the animals they ride is in effect a sentence of death. For this reason, in the steppes and the desert fringe, horse and camel stealers are severely punished, very often by death.

"Courage Cultures" and Nomadic Patriarchy

The harsh environment in which nomadic peoples struggle to survive not only takes a very real physical toll, but it shapes virtually all aspects of their social organization and cultural expression. The lives of nomadic peoples have tended to be punctuated by intermittent violence. It is likely that the life expectancy of nomads, both male and female, has been considerably shorter than that of sedentary peoples at comparable points in time. The hard-skinned, sun- and wind-cracked faces of nomadic peoples testify to the constancy of their struggles for mere survival. Their history of intertribal feuds, warfare, and forced migrations reflects the ways in which these struggles set human group against human group. Their harsh environment and the chronic violence in their lives prompted nomadic peoples to develop what anthropologists have aptly labeled *courage cultures*. Cultures of this type are dominated by physically strong, warlike males

bound to each other by strong ties of personal loyalty. Members of such a society place a premium on personal honor and value physical courage and heroic deeds above all other human attributes and accomplishments.

Although there have been regional variations, most nomadic peoples have lived in kin-related bands that range in numbers from 10 or 20 to over 100. In times of crisis and exceptionally strong leadership, these bands have been brought together in great encampments numbering in the tens of thousands. But most nomads have lived most of their lives among their clanspeople, who were often linked to those in neighboring bands by tribal membership. This meant that each traced their origins back to a common, often mythical, ancestor. The fact or fiction of common origins did not prevent clans from clashing over pasturelands, campsites, or livestock. In fact, interclan quarrels accounted for much of the social violence experienced in a nomad's lifetime. Oral traditions suggest that these quarrels could erupt from the flimsiest of pretexts—a snub in the marketplace or a dispute over the ownership of a fine horse or camel.

Whether arising out of insults or competition for herds or pastureland, the violent confrontations that erupted from interclan rivalries set in motion cycles of raids, killings, and reprisals that could span generations and even centuries. The deep-felt hostility entrenched by these *vendettas* was a major barrier to interclan and tribal cooperation and alliances that would have allowed nomadic groups to project their power beyond the steppes and desert margins. They also had devastating effects on nomadic society, as the following Arab verse vividly illustrates:

In the daytime, the flaps of this nomad's tent, here pitched near an abandoned town in the central Arabian desert, are opened to catch desert breezes. At night, the flaps are closed to hold in warmth as the desert temperature falls sharply.

Clan Amir's broken and gone. Nothing is left of her good.
In the meadows of A'raf now—only ruined dwelling
    places.
Ragged shadows of tents and penfold-walls and shelters
Bough torn from bough, all spoiled by wind and weather.
All gone, the ancients gone, all her wise counsel gone.
None of us left but folk whose war-mares are only fillies
    [thus, timid people whose horses are not fit for war].

Cultures Made for War

Because stock raising did not require the labor that was involved in sedentary cultivation, men in nomadic society could devote long hours to honing the martial skills needed to fight these vendettas or conduct warfare with the armies of agrarian states. In horse and camel societies, young boys could ride almost as soon as they could walk. Man and animal came to function as one. Horse nomads, such as the Mongols, learned to depend on their legs alone to grip and direct their war steeds, thus freeing their arms and hands to make deadly use of their powerful bows and arrows. In the assault, a horseman could swing beneath the belly of the horse and let loose arrow after arrow while denying the enemy a clear target. Horse and camel nomads could literally live on their mounts for days, giving them a mobility denied to all other peoples until the advent of the railway.

This mobility has also proved critical in the nomadic peoples' ability to ward off the assaults of revenge-minded armies of sedentary peoples. In one of the earliest recorded instances of this capacity to defend themselves through retreat, the Scythians drew the Persian emperor Darius and a large army into a prolonged and futile chase through the steppes of western Asia in the 6th century B.C.E. As recently as the late 19th century, this pattern was followed by the cattle- and camel-herding nomads of the Sudan. They drew a British-led, Egyptian army of over 5000 soldiers into the desert wastes of the Upper Nile region. When the invaders were exhausted and dying of thirst and disease, the nomadic warriors ambushed and exterminated them.

Both mounted nomads and those who fought on foot displayed very considerable skills in battle, and thus they earned a reputation for ferocity among sedentary peoples. Many of the tales of their "barbarities" were hearsay or pure fiction, but some of them were quite accurate. The Scythians and Hsiung-nu, for example, had drinking cups fashioned from the skulls of defeated rivals. The leaders of the Huns lined these skull-goblets with gold. Some nomadic peoples regularly drank blood drained from their animals, which was quite rich in protein. Both the Scythians and Hsiung-nu practiced head-hunting, and on the death of a rival chief, a warrior would slit the throats of the deceased leader's wives and servants and bury them with him. The exploits of Turkic warriors (whom the Chinese called the T'u-chueh) were commemorated by stones piled on their tombs—one stone for every enemy they had killed in battle during their lifetime.

Family Ties and Social Stratification

Male monopolization of animal husbandry, band security, and warfare ensured that men would dominate gender relationships. Men controlled the herds that were the most valued property for pastoralists, traded with outside peoples for goods, and strictly controlled their households. Inheritance was through the male line. Though marriage patterns varied somewhat, young girls usually went to live in the households of older husbands. Polygamy was common, and a woman's position in her new household depended on her ability to produce healthy children, preferably sons.

Though the bards of many nomadic peoples told of young men's infatuation with legendary beauties and ill-fated romances, marriages were primarily alliances between families and clans. In some societies, the bride was virtually reduced to a piece of property as the men from her own family and her prospective in-laws haggled over the number of camels or mares to be included in her dowry or paid as a bride-price to her kinsmen. Once married, young women had little choice but to make the best of a life in transit dominated by domestic tasks such as breaking and reestablishing camp, cooking, sewing, and rearing children. Women of all ages had to endure the natural hardships and insecurities of nomadic life with little of the honor or excitement that could be enjoyed by their warrior fathers, husbands, and sons.

In some nomadic societies, women were given positions of prestige and power. The Samaritans, for example, expected their women to serve as priests, fight in wars, and even rule. Among the Mongols, it was the custom for the young widows of deceased tribal leaders to rule as regents until their infant or adolescent sons came of age. Instances of strong-willed and domineering women, such as the Mongol dowager Nomolun, who was slain attempting to avenge the death of six of her seven sons at the hands of a raiding band, do appear in nomadic tales and legends. But such instances of female dominance are remarkable for their rarity rather than suggestive of a recurring pattern or a social norm.

Despite the persistence of the belief that nomadic societies have been much more egalitarian and nurtur-

This drawing depicts a Mongol hunter in pursuit of wild game. Notice how the hunter's ability to ride and guide his horse with his legs alone leaves his arms free to shoot his bow and arrow.

ing of self-reliant individualism than sedentary, agrarian societies have been, pastoral groups have generally displayed both social stratification and dependence. Some households and kin groups control much larger herds and pasturelands than others; some families possess neither. The kin groups that control substantial resources become the patrons and protectors of weaker and less fortunate families within the band or tribal group. In exchange for access to the resources of their patrons, the less well-to-do become the loyal clients of clan and tribal notables and warrior-leaders. These clients assist in raising the patrons' livestock; rally to their side in times of feuding, raiding, or war; and defer to their decisions in matters of tribal politics or family difficulties.

Beyond gender and patron-client distinctions, there has been little social differentiation in nomadic societies, owing largely to the lack or low level of occupational specialization. Though smiths who could forge tools and weapons were revered specialists in some nomadic societies, in most only the shamans were distinguished by occupation from the rest of the population. In addition to their ceremonial roles, shamans also served as healers, soothsayers, and, in some cultures, keepers of the tribal traditions.

Animal Totems and Trousers

Like all else in their lives, the material culture of nomadic peoples has been dominated by the animals they herd and hunt. These animals also dictate artistic themes and styles. Much of the artwork of nomadic peoples, such as bone sculptures, wood carvings, and woven rugs, depicts stylized animals. Sometimes the animals are domesticated, such as bulls, hawks, and horses; more often they are wild creatures, such as lions, serpents, and deer. Often the animal depicted is a clan or tribal *totem*, which is seen as a mythic ancestor of the group and is venerated as progenitor and protector. Frequently the animal is shown fighting with one of its own kind, preying on another species, or struggling to free itself from a predator.

Nomadic artwork is largely utilitarian. Carvings are incorporated in the poles and entranceways of tents or in the sides of wagons. Animal motifs appear on belt buckles, jewelry, weapons, or the rugs used to pad and insulate the interiors of wagons or tents. It is rare to find art for art's sake because the highly mobile existence of pastoral peoples renders paintings or sculptures excessively burdensome.

CLOSEUP

Nomad Hospitality—Legends and Realities

The violence and suffering that periodically visited nomadic societies as a consequence of the vendetta cycle was offset to some extent by an emphasis on hospitality—to strangers as well as one's own friends and clanspeople—that has been characteristic of many nomadic cultures. In part, providing travelers or refugees from clans fallen on hard times with food, drink, and shelter made sense because it fit into a larger strategy of survival in the harsh environments where nomadic people lived. Those who refused hospitality to the weary or needy risked enduring infamy and retribution from other nomadic groups should they themselves become lost in a storm or wounded in an ambush. Once accepted as a guest within a nomadic encampment, an individual, even from a rival or enemy clan, was safe from bodily harm—a tradition that a nomad band broke at its own peril.

But often the nomads' hospitality went beyond the realities of their never-ending struggles for survival. Tribal legends celebrated leaders for their generosity as well as their aptitude for war. Arab nomads, for example, still delight in the tale of a young man who slaughtered the fattest of his father's rather meager supply of camels to feed some weary strangers who were passing by his encampment. Praised by the strangers for his lavish hospitality, and asking nothing in return, the young man proclaimed, "I have made you immortal." As this legend demonstrates, along with physical courage, endurance, and loyalty to one's clan, hospitality was one of the most valued of human qualities. In most nomadic societies, generosity was measured according to the power and wealth of the giver; the more one had, the greater the obligation to sponser feasts for guests or clan celebrations of important victories or rites of passage. As we shall see in the chapters that follow, on several occasions, the refuge provided by one nomadic leader for another—perhaps most famously the protection given to the future world conqueror, Chinggis Khan, by a friend of his murdered father—has proved pivotal to subsequent global history.

Like their art, the other aspects of nomadic culture are linked to their pastoral life cycle. Their housing, whether tent or wagon, is easily dismantled and reassembled. Their clothing is adapted to both their animals and the environment. Pants, or trousers, were an invention of the horse nomads of the central Asian steppes. The horse nomads also used skins or wool to fashion leather or felt shirts and pointed caps with ear flaps to protect them from the icy blasts of the winter steppe. Not surprisingly, nomadic peoples from central Asia also invented the stirrup, bits and reins, and the saddle.

DOCUMENT

Nomadic Verse and Nomadic Values

Much of what we know about nomadic attitudes and social interaction in the centuries before some of them adopted writing systems (based on languages such as Arabic and Chinese) has been gleaned from ancient myths, legends, and poetry. These works, which are among the finest artistic creations of nomadic peoples, were originally sung or declaimed at clan and tribal gatherings and passed down orally from one generation to the next. The three excerpts that follow are verses composed by camel-herding peoples of the Arabian peninsula. They provide some of our surest insights into pre-Islamic culture among the nomads of that region and reflect values characteristic of pastoral cultures in most areas of the globe.

1.   *Yet envy not even him of whom they say:*
     Ripeness and wisdom came with length of days.
     Love life—live long—live safely—
     All the same
     Long living leaves its furrow on thy face.

2.   *Time has taught me something; all other things*
     *   have lied;*
     The wasting of the days lets things unguessed
     *   stand clear.*
     And I know this at last: how powerful men use power.

All powerful men get praise, whatever shame they
*   earn.*
This too I know: poverty wears great hearts down,
And the wearing's like the lick of a rawhide whip.
A poor man looks at glories he can never climb
And sits among the rest silent, silent, silent.

3.   *Endure. For a man free-born only endurance is*
     *   honor.*
     Time is fell; there's neither help nor heal of his hurt.
     Even if it availed a man to obey his fear,
     Or a man could parry trouble by any low consent,
     Still to endure the full brunt, cut and thrust
     Of Fate with a manly front, to endure's the only
     *   honor.*

Questions: What sorts of attitudes toward life does the first verse reflect? Do these verses picture humans in charge of their own fate or at the mercy of some predetermined destiny? What does the second verse tell us about nomadic social structure among the early Arabs? Does it suggest that birth or merit decides one's place in the social order? How much social mobility do you think there is in this society? What sorts of values does the third verse express? How would you compare them to the values dominant in your own culture?

NOMADS AND CIVILIZATION

Focal Point: Though nomads have generally been regarded as cruel and destructive barbarians by the chroniclers of sedentary peoples, the actual history of their interaction with civilized centers has been many-sided and complex. Nomads have raided, pillaged, and conquered civilized centers, but they have also served as the protectors of failing dynasties and long-term rulers in their own right. Throughout human history, nomadic peoples have traded with sedentary peoples; exchanged ideas, weapons, and tools with them; and served as key links between the regional pools of civilized life.

The image of nomadic peoples in the millennia of recorded history has been created mainly by hostile town-dwelling writers. Not surprisingly, that image has rarely

been a flattering one. In Biblical times, prophets such as Jeremiah depicted the nomads as "cruel" and without mercy and declared that they were agents by which Yahweh, the God of the Hebrews, chastised his people for their wickedness. The peoples of the crumbling Roman Empire believed that the Huns were the offspring of evil spirits and witches and that their most infamous leader, Attila, was "the scourge of God." The Chinese regarded the many nomadic peoples who pressed in on their walled northern borders as uncouth and backward barbarians, whose brutality and delight in destruction posed a constant threat to the very life of their civilization. The coming of the *chichimecs* in Mesoamerica and the Mongols in the regions that fringed the steppes of central Asia was equated with great natural catastrophes, such as earthquakes in Mesoamerica and the spread of the plague in central Asia.

In fact, contacts between nomadic and farming or town-dwelling peoples were often more regular, peaceful, and mutually beneficial than these stereotypes would suggest. Many accounts of pastoral peoples depict them living in self-sufficient isolation. In this view, pastoralists have had little need of contacts with sedentary peoples in normal times. Thus, nomadic incursions into settled agrarian regions are routinely accounted for by either natural calamities, which push hard-pressed pastoralists into civilized domains, or political weaknesses in the latter, which tempt nomadic warriors to loot and pillage.

Recent research suggests that this view distorts the nature of the interaction between nomadic and sedentary people and greatly oversimplifies the motives that have periodically led nomads to move into areas dominated by agrarian-based states. In fact, all but the most isolated of nomadic peoples maintained regular contacts with farming villages and urban centers. Though nomads have attempted at times to take food and other products of the sedentary areas by force, more often they have gained them through peaceful exchanges or services provided.

Most nomadic peoples traded regularly with peasants and town dwellers for grains and vegetables that could not be grown on the steppes or desert fringe. They also bartered their animals and animal products for cotton or silk clothing, iron tools and weapons, and at times food for their animals. Sedentary peoples were normally less in need than the nomads of what the two exchanged in trade, but the meat and dairy products bartered by the pastoralists could provide important supplements to the largely vegetarian diet of many cultivating peoples. For sedentary peoples in areas such as China, India, and western Asia, the nomadic steppes were also a prime source of the horses their cavalry rode into war.

Nomads, Trade, and Contacts Between Civilizations

In addition to their involvement in regular local trade, nomads have played and continue to play critical roles in the development of long-distance trade. Nomadic peoples pioneered all the great overland routes that linked

For millennia, camel caravans like this one have made their way through the desert terrain of Arabia. Caravans have provided key links for trade and cultural exchange between the civilizations of Africa and Eurasia.

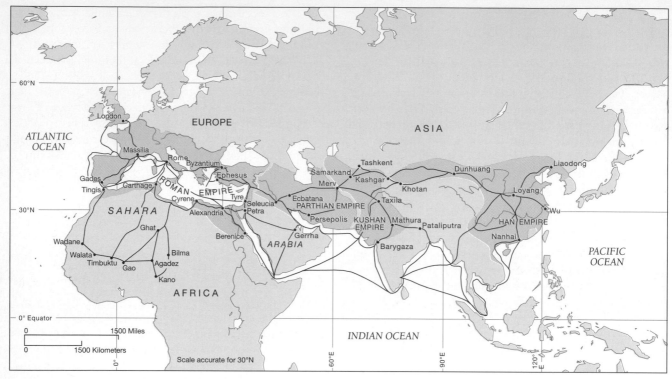

Main African-Eurasian Trade Routes in the Classical Age

the civilized cores of Eurasia in ancient times and the Middle Ages. The most famous were the fabled *silk routes* that ran from western China across the mountains and steppes of central Asia to the civilized centers of Mesopotamia in the last millennium B.C.E., and in the first millennium C.E. to Rome, the Islamic heartlands, and western Europe.

Chinese rulers at one end of these trading networks, and Roman emperors and later Islamic sultans at the other end, frequently had to send their armies to do battle with hostile nomads, whose raids threatened to cut off the flow of trade. But perhaps more often, pastoral peoples played critical roles in establishing and expanding trading links. For periodic payments by merchants and imperial bureaucrats, they provided protection from bandits and raiding parties for caravans passing through their grazing lands. For further payments, nomadic peoples would supply animals to transport both the merchants' goods and the food and drink needed by those in the caravan parties. At times, pastoralists themselves took charge of both transport and trading, but it was more common for the trading operations to be controlled by specialized merchants. These merchants were based either in the urban centers of the civilized cores or in the

trading towns that grew up along the Silk Road in central Asia, the oases of Arabia, and the savanna zones that bordered the vast Sahara desert in Africa on the north and south.

Until they were supplanted by the railroads and steamships of the Industrial Revolution, the overland trading routes of Eurasia and the Americas were, along with comparable networks established for sailing vessels, the most important channels for contacts between civilizations. Religions such as Buddhism and Islam spread peacefully along the trading routes throughout central Asia, Persia, and Africa. Artistic motifs and styles, like those developed in the cosmopolitan Hellenistic world created by Alexander the Great's conquests, were diffused by trading contacts in North Africa, northern India, and western China.

Inventions that were vital to the continued growth and expansion of the civilized cores were carried in war and peace by traders or nomadic peoples from one center to another. For example, central Asian steppe nomads who had been converted to Islam clashed with the armies of the Chinese Empire in the 8th century C.E. The victorious Muslims found craftsmen among their prisoners who knew the secrets of making paper, which

This 18th-century painting shows Kazak nomads bringing tribute horses to the emperor of China. Painted by an Italian artist Guiseppe Castiglione, this work exhibits a striking cross-civilizational mixture of European and Chinese artistic styles.

had been invented many centuries earlier by the Chinese. The combination of nomadic mobility and established trading links resulted in the rapid diffusion of papermaking techniques to Mesopotamia and Egypt in the 8th and 9th centuries and across North Africa to Europe in the centuries that followed.

Nomads as Mercenaries and Empire Builders

Despite ongoing contacts and nomadic contributions to civilized development, the predominant responses of settled peoples to pastoralists have been fear and hostility. Both the military prowess and the periodic ecological crises that have forced large numbers of nomads to raid sedentary areas go a long way to explain these reactions.

Very often, sedentary peoples have tried to ward off nomadic assaults by ensuring through tribute payments, which the Chinese aptly called "goodwill gifts," that their pastoral neighbors were well supplied with the goods they might covet in "civilized" towns and villages. Rulers of sedentary states have also paid generous sums for the services of nomadic peoples as mercenary soldiers. Those recruited in this manner rode into battle with the ruler's own armies and also served as frontier defenders against other pastoralists or the forces of rival empires. In the period before the rise of the first Islamic empires, for example, the rulers of Byzantium and Persia guarded their common borderlands with colonies of both sedentary and nomadic Arabs.

This practice could prove costly to the patron state. With the conversion of these frontier peoples to Islam in the 7th century C.E., Byzantium and Persia were both particularly vulnerable to attack by the very peoples who had once defended them. In China, border guardians, such as the Zhou, repeatedly built rival states of their own that overthrew the dynasties they had originally been used to protect. Even when nomadic mercenaries remained loyal to the sedentary rulers who recruited them, they proved difficult to tax or prevent from looting the peasants who lived near their encampments. These dangers may explain why strong dynasties were reluctant to recruit nomadic allies, preferring instead to build long walls, such as that in China, or chains of fortified garrisons, such as those of the Romans, to keep pastoral peoples beyond the boundaries of their empires.

Whether they had begun as mercenaries within sedentary zones or as raiders from without, again and again nomadic groups have overthrown dynasties established in the agrarian cores. At times, nomadic victories have meant interruptions in civilized development, as did the Hyksos' invasion of Egypt in the 2nd millennium B.C.E. In other instances, nomadic invasions have hastened the end of once-flourishing civilizations, as was the case with the Aryan incursions into India in the 1st millennium B.C.E. and the assaults of peoples such as the Hittites and Kassites into the empires of Mesopotamia throughout the ancient period.

Just as often, however, nomadic invaders have captured rather than destroyed the targeted empire and civilization. After seizing the throne of the defeated dynasty, nomads have governed largely through the institutions and personnel of the conquered peoples. When this pattern has been followed, the nomadic warriors who settled down in the sedentary zone have often gradually adopted elements of the culture of the farmers and town dwellers of the new empires they establish. Chinese history provides some of the best examples of this pattern, but as the experience of invaders like the Mongol conquerors of China in the 13th century C.E. demonstrates, often the nomads struggled with considerable success to remain culturally distinct from the subject peoples.

Despite the new rulers' attraction to the luxuries and sophistication of the civilized towns, nomadic peoples have been suspicious of, or downright antagonistic toward the "soft" living of city dwellers. The great Muslim historian, *Ibn Khaldun* (C.E. 1332–1406), incorporated this ambivalence in his theory of a three-generation cycle for dynasties founded by nomadic warriors. In the first generation, the ruler is vigorous and the kingdom strong. But each succeeding ruler, reared amid the temptations and luxury of palace and harem, is weaker and less occupied with the affairs of state that are the central concern of strong kings and emperors. By the third (or fourth) generation, the successor of the hearty nomadic warrior-conquerors is a dissolute wastrel, incapable of defending his throne from internal enemies and foreign invasions. The dynasty collapses, and another vigorous warrior dynasty is established by new invaders from the steppes or desert fringe.

Though the histories of dynasties founded by nomadic chieftains have varied greatly in duration and vigor, the general patterns that Ibn Khaldun discerned have proved remarkably accurate. At times, warrior-conquerors fled the soft living of the palace centers for the rugged life of their steppe or desert encampments. Some may have remained in the new capital but longed for the simpler life of their homelands—a sentiment that is wonderfully captured in the following verse by the wife of an early Islamic ruler:

A tent flapping in the desert air is dearer than this
    towering house;
Wind rustling over the sandy waste hath a sweeter sound
    than all the king's trumpets;
A crust in the nook of a wandering tent more relish than
    all these delicate cates [sweetmeats];
And a noble clansman's more to my lust than the paunchy
    longbeards about me here.

It is said that the great Mongol conqueror, *Chinggis Khan,* saw only potential pasturelands in the intensely cultivated millet fields of northern China. Most pastoral conquerors, such as the Aryans in India, tended to destroy or neglect the irrigation systems of the areas that came under their rule. Frequently, the dynasties established by nomadic conquerors were overthrown within a century or two by internal rebellions or the successful challenges of new invaders from the steppes or desert. Those who had not assimilated the culture of the conquered peoples or become mercenary troops in the armies of the new dynasty returned to the steppes from which their forebears had come.

CONCLUSION

Nomads and the Pattern of Global History

Their military prowess and greater dependence on the products of sedentary peoples have given nomadic pastoralists a far greater role in world history than other more isolated peoples who have followed variants of the niche pattern of ecological adaptation. But the harsh environments in which nomads lived and the limitations in scale and occupational restrictiveness imposed by their mode of adaptation have made it impossible for nomads to build civilizations of their own or to dominate, for long, those developed by sedentary peoples. Though steppe peoples, such as the Hittites, Mongols, and Turks, could forge great empires by winning political control over one or more of the civilized cores, their dynasties were usually short-lived and their rule dependent on the personnel, skills, and institutions of the conquered sedentary peoples. The more stable and productive economic base of sedentary peoples has allowed them to carry much larger populations on much more limited land areas than nomads. It has also led to an occupational diversity; a capacity to build enduring, large-scale state systems; and a level of accomplishment in invention, science, and the arts that was far beyond anything nomadic peoples could dream of matching.

As a result, nomadic peoples have periodically affected the course of civilized history and for brief periods have dominated it. For example, Indo-European nomadic invaders, such as the Aryans and Hittites, played major roles in the rise and fall of civilizations in western India, Egypt, and the Fertile Crescent. In China, nomadic peoples vitally affected the rise of the Shang and Zhou kingdoms, which laid the basis for civilization in eastern Asia. In later chapters we shall see that new waves of nomadic assaults in Eurasia, Africa, and the Americas had much to do with the rise of great classical dynasties, such as the Guptas in India and the Han in China, and even whole civilizations, such as the Roman Empire in the Mediterranean. This impact continued throughout the five continents where civilizations developed, building to the great Mongol and Turkic explo-

sions from the steppes of central Asia from the 11th to 14th centuries C.E. But most of human history has been lived and made by sedentary agrarian peoples and the city dwellers they supported. With the coming of the Industrial Revolution, and the greatly enhanced firepower and mobility that transformation gave to the already far more numerous peoples of the civilized zones from the late 18th century onward, the nomads' already subordinate position has been further reduced and their way of life increasingly threatened.

FURTHER READINGS

For a highly readable application of the holding and niche variants of ecological adaptation, see Lucien M. Hanks's *Rice and Man: Agricultural Ecology in Southeast Asia* (1972). The best general work on nomadic societies, which covers a wide range of different types over much of Eurasia and Africa, is A. M. Khazanov's *Nomads and the Outside World* (1984). A volume edited by Wolfgang Weissleder on *The Nomadic Alternative* (1978), contains several excellent case studies on different types of Afroasian nomads. For insights into the ecological underpinnings of both nomadic and sedentary societies and the interaction between the two, see Owen Lattimore's *Studies in Frontier History* (1962). René Grousset's *Empire of the Steppes: A History of Central Asia* (1970) covers some of the most important nomadic societies in terms of their impact on sedentary peoples from prehistoric times through the centuries of Mongol dominance. On the development of nomadism among the Middle Eastern Arabs, see Richard Bulliet's *The Camel and the Wheel* (1975). Jacques Maquet's *Civilizations of Black Africa* (1972) includes introductory sections on the cattle-herding nomads of Africa.

5

Unification and the Consolidation of Civilization in China

1122–770 Former or western Zhou kingdom	551–c. 233 Period of the "hundred philosophers" (including Confucius, Laozi, Menicus, Xunzi, the Legalists)
	221 Shi Huangdi proclaimed first emperor of China
770–403 Later or eastern Zhou kingdom	c. 400–320 Era of Sunzi	221 Great Wall completed
	403–221 Warring states period	221–207 Qin dynasty
1200 B.C.E.	600 B.C.E.	400 B.C.E.

INTRODUCTION

China formed one of the first areas where the interaction between nomadic pressure and the power of a river-valley civilization produced the characteristics of a larger, more complex classical society. The breakdown of the Zhou dynasty's ability to control its vassals in the 8th century B.C.E. led to an extended period of political conflict and social turmoil throughout China. In both the Yellow and the Yangtze river basins, numerous states rose and fell, each seeking to replace the Zhou as the paramount power in East Asia. Internal conflicts left China vulnerable to outside invaders, and between the 8th and 3rd centuries B.C.E., nomadic peoples frequently raided the farming areas of the north China plain. Many of the nomads settled down and eventually assimilated the distinct culture that had been developing in the region since the age of the Shang warrior kings. Some of these invaders captured existing states; others established new dynasties that further intensified the already complex political maneuvers and wars for supremacy.

Though the human suffering caused by the prolonged struggles between the warring states was enormous, these conflicts also provided the impetus for intellectual and political changes that, in the long run, greatly strengthened Chinese civilization. In the 6th and 5th centuries B.C.E., thinkers such as Confucius and his disciples tried to find ways to end the conflict and turmoil. They advocated changes that would both stabilize China's fluid social structure and promote the establishment of a strong and unified political system. Other philosophers, such as Laozi, the founder of Daoism, proposed contemplative ways of life that would put an end to the vicious rivalries and chaos.

The yearning for unity and an end to civil strife appeared to be answered in the 3rd century B.C.E. by the emergence of the warrior strongman Shi Huangdi. By 221 B.C.E., Shi Huangdi's state of Qin had vanquished all its rivals, and he founded a new imperial dynasty that promised to bring an end to the centuries of division and strife. But Shi Huangdi proved to be a tyrant. Driven by his own ambition and the advice of ruthless ministers, he embarked on a series of grandiose building projects. These exhausted the common people and angered the regional elites whose cooperation was vital to Qin rule. Shi Huangdi's death in 210 B.C.E. was the signal for resistance throughout the empire to the rule of his less despotic and less capable son and his inner circle of advisors. A rapidly spreading revolt, led by two peasants, toppled the Qin dynasty in 207 B.C.E. and gave rise to its much longer-lived successor, the Han.

The Han era, which was to last with a brief interruption for over 400 years, saw the consolidation of Chinese civilization. Unity was established in the old core regions, and Chinese political control was greatly extended in all directions. Perhaps more critically, the Han rulers founded what was to be the largest, most effective, and most enduring bureaucracy in the preindustrial world. They oversaw the development of the first civil service examinations and the professionalization of Chinese administration. The *shi,* or scholar-bureaucrats, were the greatest beneficiaries of these initiatives, and from the Han era onward they set the tone for Chinese social and cultural development. The shi were responsible for great achievements in literature and the arts. They provided the support and at times the creative ingenuity that were critical to great advances in technology. Above all, a sense of Chinese distinctiveness and identity was set, which was reflected in later centuries by Chinese references to themselves as the "sons of Han." This identity was to prove critical to the survival of Chinese civilization in the centuries of war, foreign invasion, and internal division that returned when the Han dynasty collapsed in the early 3rd century C.E.

---

200 B.C.E.–9 C.E. Former Han dynasty; development of the horse collar, stern-post rudder, and water mill

202–195 Reign of Liu Bang (Gaozu emperor)   **9–23** Interregnum of Wang Mang   **2nd century** C.E. Development of porcelain

141–87 Reign of Han Wudi   **23–220** Later Han dynasty; invention of paper and the compass

200 B.C.E.   **1** C.E.   **200** C.E.

PHILOSOPHICAL REMEDIES FOR THE PROLONGED CRISIS OF THE LATER ZHOU

Focal Point: The political rivalries, incessant warfare, and rebellions engendered by the long decline of the Zhou dynasty prompted much debate over remedies for China's political and social ills. In the last centuries of the Later or Eastern Zhou era, some of China's greatest thinkers, including Confucius and Laozi, attempted—in very different ways—to restore order and social harmony. Blended together by later scholars and administrators, the teachings of these great philosphers were worked into the composite ideology that for millennia would be central to civilized life in China.

The protracted warfare that raged throughout China after the Zhou rulers were reduced to powerless figureheads was a major setback for both the emerging shi elite and the ordinary people. Military skills and physical prowess were valued over the literary and ceremonial aptitudes of the shi. Local lords, whose kingdoms were constantly threatened by their neighbors, tended to concentrate all power in their own hands. They put little stock in the council of men who stayed behind in the palace while they risked their lives on the field of battle. The military leaders who wore trousers—which were widely adopted following the example of the horse-riding northern nomads—were contemptuous of the scholars who wore robes and gowns. In most kingdoms, the power of the old aristocratic families was strengthened, often at the expense of the shi, who were reduced to little more than clerks and fawning courtiers of the local strongmen. Rituals were neglected, and court etiquette, which had been so prized in the Early Zhou era, was replaced by the rough manners of nomadic invaders. Many shi found themselves without political positions and were forced to eke out a living as village schoolteachers and local scribes.

With rulers concentrating on the very survival of their kingdoms, most resources were consumed by expenditures on warfare. Public works, including dikes, canals, and regional granaries, were neglected, and some fell into ruin. Marauding armies confiscated or destroyed the crops on which the peasantry depended for its livelihood. Hard-pressed rulers taxed the farmers heavily and conscripted them to transport military supplies and, increasingly, to fight in the incessant wars of the Late Zhou period. Armies spread disease and destruction throughout China. The severity of the suffering caused by natural calamities was increased many times by the breakdown of public works and social support systems.

Perhaps because most of the kingdoms depended on outside areas for their supply of at least some vital materials—such as iron, horses, and salt—trade continued to increase despite political fragmentation and social disruption. The introduction of copper money and the growing acceptance of private property did much to advance the fortunes of the Chinese merchant class. By the end of the Zhou era, traders were growing wealthy as the suppliers of courts, armies, and town populations and as major investors in land ownership, which became widespread as the control of feudal vassals over villages and croplands broke down. The rulers of some kingdoms turned over the lucrative task of taxing the peasantry to prominent merchant families. Wealth and political connections brought these big traders considerable power. A legendary merchant named Zu Kung, for example, was said in the course of a single business trip to have saved one kingdom from destruction, strengthened two others, and caused the decline and fall of two more. As trade and production by artisans increased, towns, particularly walled administrative centers, grew in size. By the last centuries of the Zhou period, China could boast of several urban centers with hundreds of thousands of people. For many centuries to come, no other civilization could support cities of this size.

Confucius and the Restoration of the Shi

Threatened by the greatly enhanced power of the warrior overlords of rival kingdoms and the rising wealth and influence of the mercantile class, the aspiring shi scholar-bureaucrats found a champion in Kung Fuzi, or Confucius, as he has been known in the West. Confucius was born in the middle of the 6th century B.C.E into a poor shi family. Like many others, Confucius's father had lost his place at the local court, and the family had fallen on hard times. As a consequence, young Confucius had to take jobs, such as accounting, that were considered demeaning for a young man of his education and abilities. He was apparently an outspoken and opinionated individual who had a talent for putting people off by the brutally frank expression of his views. He had hoped for a high post in the state of Lu, near the present-day Shandung Peninsula, but having been passed over, he took to the road in search of the ideal ruler.

A portrait of Confucius painted by a Chinese prince in the mid-18th century. Here Confucius is idealized as a wise, fatherly member of the scholar-gentry class, replete with official headgear and robes of office.

He never found his ideal and thus spent most of his life traveling from one kingdom to another. But during his travels he met many leaders and local shi, supported himself by teaching, and earned a growing reputation for his learning and wisdom. Soon Confucius had attracted a considerable following. Some traveled with him as loyal disciples; others promoted his ideas at the courts of local rulers and compiled his sayings in what would come to be known as the Analects, meaning "the collected sayings"—thus, "Confucius says."

Though frustrated in his search for an ideal king to serve and unable to test his ideas as an actual administrator and advisor, Confucius developed ethical principles and a view of the proper ordering of society that would shape Chinese civilization for the next 2000 years. He was not a religious teacher like the Jewish prophets or the Buddha but rather a social philosopher. Ancestral veneration played a role, but his thinking was focused on the earthly realm and the proper ways to arrange social relationships and achieve good government. He was obsessed with the need for order and harmony. He believed that they could come about only if Chinese rulers relied on the advice of wise and educated men, who in Confucius's view could be recruited only from among the shi.

Confucius was convinced that a small minority of superior men were destined by their talents and sense of duty to govern and set an example for the common people. In a rather revolutionary bit of thinking, he argued that these men (women were quite explicitly excluded) were superior not by virtue of aristocratic birth but because of their education and training. In this view, superior men were made, not born, which meant that even a lowly peasant could aspire to this exalted status. However, most of the superior men were drawn from the elite classes, especially the old aristocracy and established shi households.

There was a strong ethical dimension to all of Confucian thought. Confucius believed that superior men should be given the power to rule, not to enrich or glorify themselves but to serve society as a whole; that the interests and welfare of the common people must be paramount in the decisions of good emperors and their advisors; and that in return for their concern and protection, the common people should respect, support, and acknowledge the superior status of their overlords. Social harmony depended on each person's accepting his or her allotted place and performing the tasks that his or her social station required. Obedience and deference were owed to one's superiors and elders, to males from females, and to teachers from students. A good man for Confucius was one who

Treats his betters as betters,
Wears an air of respect,
Who in serving father and mother
Knows how to put in his whole strength,
Who in the service of his prince will
*   lay down his life*
Who in intercourse with friends is
*   true to his word.*

Society, according to Confucius, was held together by personal ties of loyalty and obedience. Five links were stressed: three family links (father and son, elder brother and younger brother, husband and wife), one political link (ruler and subject), and one social link (friend and friend). If these links were faithfully honored, Confucius believed, only a minimum of intervention by the state in the lives of its subjects would be necessary.

The Confucian Gentleman

According to Confucius, the superior or educated man was a person of courage who made decisions on his own and then defended them no matter how strong the opposition. Shi in positions of power were to pay proper deference to rulers but not be afraid to criticize them for errors in judgment or for neglecting the welfare of their subjects. A superior man—a term that became synonymous with membership in the shi class—was moderate in demeanor and controlled his emotions. He presented a calm and composed "face" to rivals, subordinates, and friends. He was well mannered and observed the proper rituals and forms of address and behavior that varied depending on the social status of the person with whom he was interacting.

Above all, the shi gentleman was a generalist rather than a specialist. He strove to be equally accomplished at running a government department, directing the repair of irrigation works, composing poetry, or painting the plum blossoms in his garden. Power and status were accorded him as a moral exemplar, not for specific tasks he performed. Confucius reckoned that with such men in charge of China, war and social strife would be forever brought under control.

The Heirs of Confucius

During his lifetime and after his death in the early 5th century B.C.E., Confucius had many disciples, who spread his teachings and debated over their interpretation. The most important division arose between the followers of Mencius (Meng Ko) and those of Xunzi, who lived in the 3rd and 2nd centuries B.C.E. Mencius began with the assumption that humans were inclined to be good and thus ought to be ruled in such a way that their goodness could develop to the fullest extent. His thinking, which had a strong egalitarian strain, stressed the consent of the common people as the basis for political power. It provided the philosophical underpinnings for the long-standing Chinese belief that the people had the right to rise up and overthrow incompetent or oppressive rulers.

Xunzi rejected the basic assumption on which Mencius's system rested. Xunzi argued that humans were inclined to be lazy and evil. He concluded that a strong, authoritarian government was necessary to curb their selfish desires and their capacity to harm each other. Xunzi believed that humans could be improved through strong laws and education, but he had little sympathy with the view that the people were the ultimate source of political power. The ideas of both thinkers and those of Confucius continued to influence intellectual discourse in China for millennia. But in the short term, the views of Xunzi, bolstered by the arguments of later political philosophers known as the Legalists, would prove the most influential.

Daoist Alternatives

A very different sort of cure for China's ills in the Late Zhou era was offered by the recluse and philosopher Laozi (often called Lao Tsu in popular Daoist texts). Laozi's life history has been obscured by fantastic legends including those relating that his mother was pregnant with him for decades and that when he was finally born he was an old man with a white beard. Whatever his actual background, Laozi developed into a thinker who had little use for government or absolute ethical prescriptions in any form. As a solution for the sufferings brought on by human greed and ambition, Laozi recommended a retreat from society and civilization into nature. Through the contemplation of nature, he believed, the individual could become attuned with the Dao: the cosmic force and source of all creation. Laozi stressed nonaction over political power, and self-examination over the mastery of others. He taught:

It is wisdom to know others.
It is enlightenment to know one's self.

The conqueror of men is powerful.
The master of himself is stronger.

It is wealth to be content.
It is willful to force one's way on others.

Though much of Laozi's message concerned withdrawal from the world, he could not resist giving a good deal of advice to those who remained in society, particularly the rulers of China's many kingdoms. He chastised them for enjoying war and the excessive pursuit of pleasure in their palaces while the mass of the population went hungry. He wrote:

When the court is arrayed in splendor,
The fields are full of weeds,
And the granaries are bare.

DOCUMENT

Teachings of the Rival Chinese Schools

The brief passages quoted below are taken from the writings of Confucius, Mencius, Xunzi, and Laozi. Identify the author of each passage and explain why you believe it was written by the person you chose.

1. I take no action and the people are reformed.
    I enjoy peace and people become honest.
    I do nothing and people become rich.
    I have no desires and people return to the good and simple life.

2. The gentleman cherishes virtue; the inferior man cherishes possessions.
    The gentleman thinks of sanctions; the inferior man thinks personal favors.

3. The nature of man is evil; his goodness is acquired.
    His nature being what it is, man is born, first, with a desire for gain.
    If this desire is followed, strife will result and courtesy will disappear.

4. Keep your mouth closed.
    Guard your senses.
    Temper your sharpness.
    Simplify your problems.
    Mask your brightness.
    Be at one with the dust of the earth.
    This is primal union.

5. Personal cultivation begins with poetry, is made firm with rules of decorum, and is perfected by music.

6. When it is left to follow its natural feelings, human nature will do good. That's why I say it is good. If it becomes evil, it is not the fault of man's original capability.

Questions: Which of these ideas are most compatible? Which of them could best be termed religious? Which are most secular? Which philosophers propose ideas that are best suited to people who wish to build a strong and unified political order?

Laozi exhorted rulers and men of affairs to cultivate the virtues of patience, selflessness, and concern for the welfare of all creatures. He argued that these virtues were consistent with the nature of the Dao. Like Confucius, he believed that wise rulers and honest administrators made for happy and peaceful kingdoms. But Laozi differed from Confucius in his views on how a good ruler was made and what qualities he possessed. And where Confucius viewed a strong state and sound society as the primary goals, Laozi saw them as temporary concerns that were of little relevance to the wise man in search of the hidden meanings of creation and human life.

Like Confucius, Laozi had many disciples in his own lifetime and in later centuries as well. His poetic sayings were interpreted by these followers in widely varying ways. Some held to his original emphsis on withdrawal from the world, communion with nature, and meditation. Others mixed his ideas with magic, eroticism, and a search for a concoction that would bring bodily immortality to those who drank it. The meditative followers had the greatest appeal to the shi elite and courtiers of later ages, who drew on Daoist ideas to enhance their sensitivity to art and the natural world and to satisfy their interest in questions regarding the supernatural. In contrast, the masses were attracted by the magical solutions to everyday problems emphasized by conjurers and charlatans with rather dubious claims to being Laozi's disciples.

THE TRIUMPH OF THE QIN AND THE ESTABLISHMENT OF IMPERIAL UNITY

Focal Point: By the end of the 5th century B.C.E., the long wars had considerably reduced the number of states striving to supplant the house of Zhou. The failure of larger states, such as Ju and Wu based in the Yangtze river valley, to conquer the kingdoms of the

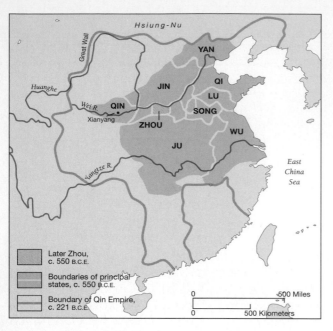

The Later Zhou and Qin Empires

The Transformation of a "Barbarian" Land

It is true that the Qin state lagged behind most of its rivals in the fine arts and refined etiquette. But from as early as the 5th century B.C.E., the rulers of Qin had initiated several critical social and political changes that greatly increased their capacity to wage war against their snobbish rivals to the east and south. The Qin state had long supported experimentation with bronze and iron-working that had transformed tool and weapons making in the Zhou era. In order to encourage the peasantry to adopt new tools and more productive cultivation techniques, the Qin freed them from bondage to local lords and allowed them to claim and hold their own land. Over time, these measures substantially increased the resource base on which Qin political ambitions depended. Because freeing the peasants undermined the support of the vassal warriors, who had originally carried out local administration, the Qin attempted to build a regular bureaucracy supported by the dynasty and totally loyal to it. These efforts attracted considerable numbers of migrant shi administrators, who were presumably willing to put up with bad manners if well-paying positions were to be had.

Qin power and military prowess were also increased by the many wars the state fought, first to survive and later to conquer the rest of China. The Qin conscripted for military service the peasants it had freed and given land, thus rendering its armies a good deal larger than those of rival states. The superior bureaucracy of the Qin meant that its forces were better supplied and organized. The nomadic background of the Qin elite ensured an ample supply of able military leaders. It also made the Qin more receptive to military innovations than many of their adversaries. They were, for example, one of the first states to use massed cavalry, which gave their armies a high degree of mobility, and to adopt the crossbow, which came into widespread use in the Late Zhou era. Good leadership and free peasants, who may have felt they had more to fight for than the vassals and serfs of other kingdoms, made the Qin armies famous for their ferocity and speed.

The Legalist Sanction

From at least the 4th century B.C.E., Qin efforts to break the power of their vassals were justified by the writings of some statesmen who came to be known collectively as the Legalists. The semilegendary Shang Yang, who served a Qin ruler of the mid-4th century B.C.E., was the

north China plain in the preceding centuries left only seven main rivals and the rump kingdom that was still ruled by the descendants of the Zhou dynasty. In the 4th and 3rd centuries B.C.E., one of these kingdoms, the westernmost state of the *Qin dynasty,* grew steadily more powerful at the expense of its rivals. At the end of the 3rd century, the Qin warlord, Shi Huangdi, defeated his rivals and unified China under Qin rule. Once in power, Shi Huangdi strove to build a highly centralized state and invested heavily in grandiose public works projects. His excesses in both efforts led to revolts against his weaker successor and the replacement of his short-lived but pivotal dynasty by the Han.

Like the original Zhou dynasty, the Qin rulers were of nomadic origins. The warriors of Qin had in earlier centuries served as the defenders of the western boundaries of the Zhou empire. As a backward land ruled by "barbarians," Qin was the object of ridicule by the rulers and administrators of states to the east, who considered themselves more civilized. Ambassadors and travelers from eastern states, such as Wei and Lu, complained of the crude living quarters in the Qin capital, the gross manners found even at the court, and the utter disregard for ceremony in the affairs of state. They failed to note the innovations in the kingdom of Qin that would, in time, give it greater political and military power than all of its rivals combined.

founder of the Legalist school of political philosophy. In *The Book of Lord Shang,* he contended that the power of China's rulers should be absolute. Their major objective as sovereigns should be to enhance the strength and wealth of the state. Shang Yang argued that the people existed to serve the state, and he had little to say about the ruler's duty to promote their welfare. He believed that the main responsibility of the state with regard to the people was to enforce strict laws with harsh punishments for offenders. Though the ruler was absolute, even he should not be above the law. To drive this point home, Shang Yang once had the crown prince punished for breaking the law—the cheek of the prince's tutor was tattooed in retribution for the offense.

As Shang Yang discovered at the end of his life, he too was subject to the strict laws. When he fled the court after the death of the ruler who was his patron and protector, the aged statesman sought refuge at a roadside inn. But a law had been enacted that in effect stated that a traveler could not stay at an inn without a permit, which Shang Yang did not have. The innkeeper, who faced death if he did not obey the law, turned out the old man. Shang Yang later led an unsuccessful rebellion, which resulted in his being tied to chariots and ripped apart in punishment.

Two of Shang Yang's intellectual heirs, Li Si and Han Feizi, were high officials at the court of a later Qin monarch, Shi Huangdi, who would conquer all of China at the end of the 3rd century B.C.E. They enlisted the Confucian philosopher Xunzi's supposition that humans were naturally evil to bolster the authoritarian claims of their master. They differed from Shang Yang in their contention that the ruler was above the law, but they followed his prescriptions for harsh punishments and strong state control over its subjects.

Shi Huangdi, Emperor of China

Shi Huangdi, the "tiger" of Qin, was extremely receptive to the Legalist approach to government. A man of unbounded ambition, energy, and physical courage, he was also a megalomaniac, who did not tolerate the slightest challenge to his absolute rule. Because of complaints from his officials, he once had hundreds of shi buried alive. His solution to "leaks" of news from the palace was similarly draconian. When his disapproval of the overuse of carriages by his courtiers became known throughout the capital and no one would admit to repeating comments he had made in confidence, Shi Huangdi executed all who were present when the criticism was made. After he became emperor, his megalomania knew no bounds. When it was reported that a chain of hills was blocking the critical wet monsoons, he had the trees on them cut down and their surface dyed red—the color associated with criminals in China.

By 221 B.C.E., Shi Huangdi had completed the work of his predecessors. He had defeated the last of rival

When kept in good repair and supplied with sufficient numbers of soldiers, the high walls and broad battlements of the Great Wall, which are clearly shown in this photo, presented a formidable obstacle for nomads who sought to invade China.

CLOSEUP

The First Attempt at Thought Control: Book Burning in Qin China

Within the empire, Shi Huangdi and his Legalist advisors tried to control all aspects of daily life. Laws were proclaimed for every possible occasion and activity, including statutes that regulated how many males could live in each dwelling and how parents and their children were to interact. In a series of measures that strikingly prefigured those of the great totalitarian regimes of the 20th century C.E., Qin efforts at control even extended to ideas. At Li Si's instigation, Shi Huangdi ordered the burning of all books. The campaign that followed was much more thorough than its Nazi counterpart in the 1930s and resembled that described by the science fiction writer Ray Bradbury in his novel *Fahrenheit 451*. All works, except an official political history of China, Legalist texts, and works on technology, medicine, and astrology, were to be confiscated by state officials and destroyed. At this time, books were written by hand on bamboo strips that were then bound together. Their high cost and the relatively small numbers of literate elite meant that books were scarce and easily located.

Provision was made for one copy of each of the works destroyed to be preserved in the imperial library, where the state could determine which works would be available and to whom. But the library was burned when the dynasty was overthrown in 207 B.C.E. Many precious works were lost, though some had been hidden in secret caches and were later recovered. During the early years of the Han dynasty, which followed the Qin, a systematic effort was launched to locate Confucian texts that had been hidden away during the book-burning campaign. Lost texts were reconstructed from memory, and official versions of the Confucian classics were inscribed in stone by a team of scholars and artisans. Thus, the thought control campaign of the Qin was eventually frustrated, but only because the regime itself fell and was replaced by one more open to the free exchange of ideas.

states of the Qin and had unified China under the upstart dynasty. To strengthen his hold over the vast domains that he now ruled, Shi Huangdi ordered all regional fortresses destroyed and the weapons of local warrior groups collected and melted down. Former states disappeared, and 36 provinces were created in their place. Vassal overlords and regional commanders were replaced by Qin bureaucrats. Surviving princes and aristocrats, as well as very wealthy merchants, were ordered to live in the capital at Xianyang, where Shi Huangdi's huge palace loomed over hundreds of others. The emperor's scribes developed a standard script and coinage, and weights and measures were unified throughout the empire.

Shi Huangdi's greatest passion was for building. His architects joined and expanded the walls that had been built by the northern kingdoms to keep out nomadic invaders, thus creating China's *Great Wall*. The Great Wall and other public works projects, such as canals and roadways, were constructed by millions of forcibly recruited peasant laborers, of whom 700,000 were said to have been used to build the emperor's palace alone. Even Shi Huangdi's death did not put an end to his building projects. As a final gesture of grandeur in preparing for his own burial, the emperor ordered the construction of a massive tomb at Mount Li, which was not uncovered until 1971.

The Collapse of a Tyrannical But Pivotal Regime

Shi Huangdi's building frenzy and the harsh rule of his Legalist administrators aroused resistance throughout the Qin's newly won empire. The shi were particularly angered by his book burning and the repression of any ideas that challenged those of the Legalists. The peasants were alienated by the Qin's endless demands for taxes and labor. In fact, Shi Huangdi's seemingly limitless appetite for building projects proved the immediate cause of the revolt that led to the abrupt collapse of the dynasty in 207 B.C.E., just three years after the emperor's death. The two peasants who began the revolt were conscripted for labor service on the Great Wall. On the journey from their village to the construction site, they realized that they could not arrive on time. Because the typical penalty for arriving late for a labor assignment was death, the two men concluded that they had little to lose by rousing others to revolt. Their calls for resistance found a ready audience among the weary peasantry and angry shi elite. The revolt spread rapidly, and within months the Qin dynasty was toppled. Shi Huangdi's son was murdered by a band of conspirators, and the emperor's huge palace was burned to the ground.

Although Qin rule over all of China lasted only a matter of decades, its short reign marked a watershed in Chinese history. Shi Huangdi not only unified China but governed it with a centralized bureaucracy staffed by salaried officials. This meant that he was not dependent on unsteady and potentially hostile vassals—a dependency that had been the undoing of earlier dynasties. It also involved strengthening the shi, who increasingly provided the social and political bonds that would hold China together through times of dynastic crisis and foreign invasion.

The public works projects of the Qin, though oppressive for the peasantry, provided the grid of roads and canals that made it possible for succeeding dynasties to hold far-flung territories together. The construction of the Great Wall reinforced the longstanding division between the nomads of central and north Asia and the farmers to the south. Improved communications and a unified currency advanced the efforts of China's merchants to establish interregional markets and the interdependence of the often very different geographical areas of the Chinese empire. Though the threat of a return to the warring states' anarchy loomed briefly after the sudden collapse of the Qin, the foundations that Shi Huangdi had laid for a centralized empire permitted another remarkable leader to establish a far milder and more lasting dynasty in China: the house of Han.

ANALYSIS

Sunzi and the Shift from Ritual Combat to "Real" War

For better or worse, the development of classical civilizations in the Middle East, Greece, China, and India

greatly advanced the business of making war. Agricultural surpluses made it possible to support specialized fighters and military commanders. Population growth made for larger armies, which required armor and weapons and a certain amount of training. Horses, and in some areas camels and elephants, were raised to carry men into battle or pull war chariots. Advances in metalworking meant steadily improving weaponry, and the art of fortification became a major concern for early engineers and architects. Warfare came to involve more soldiers, who fought for longer periods and suffered greater numbers of casualties. Frontier defenses and military campaigns became one of the prime concerns and main expenses for those who ruled civilized states.

Despite advances in weaponry and training, at least for warrior elites, warfare in most early civilizations was a combination of ritual and chaotic brawl. Wars were not fought during harvest times, winter months, or months when the monsoon rains arrived. A ruler was expected to announce his intention to attack a neighboring kingdom well in advance. Before battle, the high priests of each ruler offered sacrifices to the gods. Their readings of various sorts of omens, not strategic considerations, determined the time and place of combat. Battles consisted primarily of formal duels between trained and well-armed warriors in the midst of rather confused collisions of masses of poorly trained and armed foot soldiers, who were usually slaves or forcibly recruited peasants. Though often fierce, the warriors' duels were in theory regulated by codes of honor and fair play. It was unseemly, for example, for one champion to strike another from behind or when his opponent had fallen. Defeated champions, if they lived, were treated with great respect. Individual initiative and deeds of heroism were at a premium.

Duels between warrior champions were the set piece of a battle. As the great epics of early civilizations, such as the Indian *Mahabharata* and the Greek *Iliad*, demonstrate graphically, great warriors cut bloody swaths through the ranks of poorly prepared infantry and lesser fighters to get to each other and set up the hand-to-hand combats that normally determined the outcome of battle. The death of a commander, who was often the ruler of the kingdom at war or a renowned champion, meant the collapse of his forces and their chaotic flight from the field. Normally, the victorious army did not destroy or capture what remained of the opposing soldiers. The game had been played and won. The winners either retired with their booty to prepare for the next round or began negotiations to determine the terms on which the defeated party would submit to their overlordship.

The Shang and Early Zhou periods of Chinese history were filled with wars, most of which were fought according to this ritualized pattern. But by the Late Zhou period, some commanders and thinkers had become highly critical of the indecisiveness and waste of the endless conflicts between the warring states. In the 4th century B.C.E., Sunzi, an advisor to one of the warring monarchs, responded to these concerns with a treatise, *The Art of War*, which stands as one of the great classics of military theory. In opposition to the ritualized approach to war, Sunzi proposed a very different vision of military conflict. He argued that war was merely an extension of statecraft. Wars ought not to be games or macho contests for bragging rights; they ought to be fought only for ends that increased the territory, wealth, and power of the state. With these aims in mind, Sunzi insisted that speed was of the essence in warfare and that long wars burdened the subjects of the warring rulers and bred rebellions. He also urged that target kingdoms be captured swiftly and with as little damage as possible. Sunzi argued that war was a science; as such, it should be the object of extensive study. Rather than brawny warriors, commanders ought to be men well versed in organization, strategy, and tactics. He proposed, and Chinese rulers subsequently set up, special schools to train officers in the art of war.

Sunzi's ideas transformed warfare in China. Rulers made every effort short of war to bring down their rivals. Bluffs, spies, threats, and saboteurs were employed before armies were actually sent to war. Both before and after war was actually declared, substantial state resources and large bureaucracies were devoted to building and training armies and supplying them in the field. Sneak attacks were considered fair, and feints and ruses were regularly employed by field commanders. Weather conditions and advantageous terrain, rather than the auguries of soothsayers determined the time and place of battle.

Psychological devices were strongly recommended. For example, techniques were used to make the enemy commanders angry and cause them to make foolish moves that might demoralize their armies. Discipline was required, rather than individual heroics. This point was driven home by a ruler who had one of his commanders beheaded because the general's troops attacked ahead of schedule, despite the fact that this action was the key to victory. In combat, regular formations replaced mass brawls; soldiers fought as units under the direction of a chain of commanders. Good fighters were still valued, but now as unit leaders rather than as accomplished duelists. Quarter for a wounded enemy was less likely to be given. The main object of battle became the destruction of the enemy's forces as quickly as possible. The aim of warfare became the conquest of a rival kingdom or the defense of one's own.

Shi Huangdi's military and political successes demonstrated how effective the reorganization of warfare along the lines suggested by Sunzi might be. Halfway across the globe, the Greeks were independently developing comparable patterns of warfare. In roughly the same era as Sunzi and Shi Huangdi, the discipline and training of the smaller Greek armies culminated in Alexander the Great's unprecedented conquests. But these successes by no means put an end to ritual warfare between civilized peoples. Though Chinese armies tended to be organized and led according to the prescriptions of Sunzi and other theorists, the chivalric codes and battles centered on the duels of champions showed a remarkable staying power. This was particularly true of societies that were dominated by warrior elites, such as those that later developed in India, Japan, and Europe. But conditions in the warring states and the genius of Sunzi had led to a radically new vision of what wars were about and how they would be fought. The effects of this vision are still felt by civilized societies.

Questions: Do the ideas of Sunzi strike you as a force for the advance or retreat of civilized life? Why? What features of Chinese political systems and society may have contributed to the rise of this alternative way of warfare? If two societies—one employing Sunzi's brand of warfare, the other following ritual patterns—clashed, what advantages and disadvantages would each have?

THE HAN DYNASTY AND THE FOUNDATIONS OF CHINA'S CLASSICAL AGE

Focal Point: The sudden collapse of the Qin Empire threatened again to plunge China into incessant warfare and social strife. But one of the revolts against the Qin produced a leader, a man of peasant origins,

Hundreds of these clay warriors were found in the tomb of the first Chinese emperor, Shi Huangdi. Remarkably, each of the warriors has individualized facial features. Together with the clay horses also found in the tomb, these massed forces provide striking evidence of the power wielded by the founder of China's first and short-lived imperial dynasty.

who managed to reunify China and found a dynasty, the *Han dynasty,* that would consolidate most of the key elements of Chinese civilization. The Han era was also a time of great creativity and innovation. The long peace saw the growth of great cities, the expansion of trade and the mercantile classes, and a new surge of inventiveness that greatly advanced artisan and peasant productivity. The decline of the Han dynasty in the second and third centuries C.E. opened the way for the internal revolts, external invasions, and civil warfare that would dominate Chinese history for hundreds of years.

The pent-up anger produced by a decade and a half of harsh state demands and repression flared into regional riots and rebellions throughout the former Qin territories. Vassal chiefs fought former Qin bureaucrats for local control, and some dreamed of founding a renewed empire. The unlikely winner of these many-sided contests for power was a man of peasant birth named *Liu Bang.* Liu Bang's early life scarcely suggests that he would become the founder of one of China's longest-lived and most illustrious dynasties. In his youth Liu Bang was lazy, uneducated, and without work. He was best known for his fondness of wine and women—

tastes that remained pronounced throughout his life. In the years before the end of the Qin dynasty, Liu Bang, either because he had changed his shiftless ways or through clever maneuvers, had managed to establish himself as a village headman. In the confusion that followed the fall of the Qin, he built up a considerable following of soldiers, ex-bureaucrats, and disgruntled peasants.

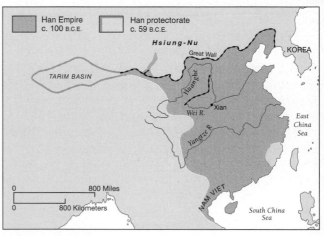

China in the Han Era

Liu Bang was apparently not much of a military commander; in fact, legend has it that he lost all the battles he fought for control of China except the last one. But he did have a gift for picking able subordinates and then giving them a real chance to exercise their talents. His skill at mediating between quarrelsome followers allowed him to hold his motley alliance of followers together while the forces of his enemies dissolved in violent factional fights. In 202 B.C.E., after years of campaigning and negotiation, Liu Bang proclaimed himself the new emperor of China, thus founding the Han dynasty that would rule China, with a brief interruption, for the next 400 years.

The Restoration of Imperial Control

For a time it looked as though the new emperor, whose official name was Gaozu, would restore the system of vassalage that had formed the basis for royal administration in the Zhou era. He raised many of his followers to the ranks of the nobility, and he rewarded them and existing lords, who had supported his efforts to win the throne, with grants of large estates. It soon became clear, however, that even his once-loyal followers were not above using the domains they had been granted to build up independent bases of power that could eventually threaten the dynasty itself. In addition to this threat, Liu Bang's determination to establish a more centralized imperial administration was promoted by the shi officials who attached themselves to his cause during his struggle for power and after he became emperor. Perhaps because Liu Bang was illiterate, he came to rely heavily on his shi advisors, even though he personally despised them. His efforts at bureaucratic centralization focused on enhancing their training and responsibilities.

Liu Bang's initiatives toward bureaucratic centralization were taken up by several strong and able rulers who succeeded him on the Han throne, most notably Han Wudi (140–87 B.C.E.). First, the larger fiefs granted to the highest nobles were broken up by a royal decree that required the domains of the vassals to be divided between all their sons at the time of their death rather than pass intact to their eldest son. At the same time, regular government appointees, especially regional governors and district magistrates, expanded their authority at the expense of local lords. In the time of Han Wudi, vassals were forbidden to bequeath their domains to heirs they had adopted. When a noble died without legitimate offspring, his estates were confiscated by the central government. Under a variety of pretexts, Han Wudi's administrators also seized the fiefs of many other vassals, who were then relegated to the status of commoners.

Han Expansion

The Han rulers used the impressive military might at their disposal to enlarge the empire and neutralize external threats. The most formidable of the external enemies were the Hsiung-nu nomads who lived north of the Great Wall. From the time of the first Han emperor, these skilled horsemen of Mongol descent had raided and looted territories south of the wall. Liu Bang attempted to buy them off by giving them presents and by marrying one of his daughters to the paramount Hsiung-nu chieftain. By the time of Han Wudi, it was clear that major expeditions would be necessary to put an end to the Hsiung-nu incursions. Han Wudi's forces defeated the nomads and annexed their pasturelands to the north and west of the Great Wall to the Han domains. But these great victories in the 120s B.C.E. provided only temporary relief. Under weaker Han rulers, and when divisions arose within the empire, the Hsiung-nu and other nomadic raiders repeatedly managed to breach the defenses of the Great Wall and raid deep into Han territory.

Han armies also expanded the empire to the east and south. In the east, the northern parts of Korea were conquered in 108 B.C.E., and were ruled by the Chinese for over 400 years. Conquests in the south extended Chinese civilization into the mountainous interior and down the coast of the South China Sea to Vietnam. The many different ethnic groups who lived in these areas either submitted to Han rule and assimilated to Chinese civilization or, like the various branches of the T'ai-speaking peoples, migrated farther south into present-day Burma, Thailand, and Laos. The southernmost of the peoples who resisted Han rule were subjects of the kingdom the Chinese called Nam Viet. After many attempts, Han armies finally managed to conquer this state and establish control over the Vietnamese people in 111 B.C.E.

The Revenge of the Shi

The majority of the shi, who were followers of Confucius and his disciples, had deeply resented the favoritism shown by Shi Huangdi for the Legalists. The fall of the Qin provided them an opportunity to strike back. At the urging of the advocates of the Confucian school, Liu Bang and his successors banned the works of the Legalists, and members of the school were hounded from the court and in some cases killed in local risings. The harsh law codes of the Qin were replaced by the milder edicts of the Han. Legalist ideas were eventually blended into the mix of philosophies and religious beliefs that came to make up China's official ideology.

Confucianism in its varying forms soon became the dominant thought system in Chinese civilization. Its full ascendancy was delayed in the early Han era by the suspicions of rulers, such as Liu Bang, who strongly favored Daoism, and the rivalry of non-Confucian thinkers. But by the end of the 2nd century B.C.E., the shi scholar-officials and the Confucian ideas they championed had won the preeminent place among the ruling classes of China that they would enjoy for much of the next 2000 years.

While downgrading the Legalists, Han rulers after Liu Bang increasingly promoted the Confucian cause. A thorough knowledge of Confucian teachings became essential to employment and promotion in the Han administrative hierarchy. This prerequisite for success in Han politics was institutionalized by the founding of an imperial university at the capital at Xian in 124 B.C.E. By the end of the Han era there were over 30,000 students at this state-supported center, which was designed primarily to turn out trained bureaucrats.

Education, Examinations, and Shi Dominance

Though students studying at the imperial university were expected to master law and a choice of specialized fields—including history, astronomy, and music—all concentrated on the memorization and interpretation of the Confucian classics. These were given even greater emphasis when formal examinations for government positions were established at the beginning of the last century B.C.E. The Chinese examination system marked the establishment of the first professional civil service in human history. Though exams were at first confined to the upper levels of government, local and regional exams were later established to identify and test local talent. Theoretically, any Chinese could take them. But no one could hope to pass them without a proper education, and education required considerable sums of money. This meant that members of established shi families, the old aristocracy, and local landlord households had a decisive advantage.

Each elite family supported the brightest of its sons. They were tutored at home as children and then en-

rolled in local schools, where they mastered the Chinese characters and the Confucian texts. On occasion a particularly bright child from a peasant household was adopted by a shi or landlord family and given the support he needed to do well on the exams and advance in the bureaucracy.

Though in general individuals from the lower classes lacked a proper education and the means to get it, several exceptional examples are recounted by Chinese historians of enterprising farmers or merchants who rose to high administrative posts. In one instance at the end of the 2nd century B.C.E., a dismissed police official, who had resorted to pig breeding to support himself, had in his later years so impressed the emperor with his responses to the examiners' questions that he was eventually elevated to the post of imperial chancellor.

In addition to the fact that education and success on the exams were monopolized by elite families, opportunities for government jobs were limited by the fact that only a small percentage of jobs were allotted by competitive examination. Though the Han rulers tried to put an end to hereditary rank, in fact many political positions automatically passed from father to son. Many offices were appointive, and an individual's chance of winning an office depended on personal links to the emperor or high official who distributed the political spoils. Thus, in the Han era, offices that were won by passing exams remained relatively limited. Despite this fact, the Han system nurtured a revolutionary idea: that administrative office and the exercise of political power ought to depend on personal merit and effort rather than birth alone.

The Emergence of the Scholar-Gentry

The growing influence of the shi in government circles was also felt in Chinese social life as a whole. In effect, three main social strata came to be recognized by those who wrote the official documents and histories: the literate shi, the ordinary but free subjects, and the underclass, referred to as the "mean people." Within each of these large groupings there were important occupational and status divisions. The shi ranged, for example, from the powerful families that served the imperial household to local tutors and petty clerks stationed in frontier provinces. The common people included groups that we would identify as separate classes. The majority were peasants, but even they varied greatly in wealth and social status. Some controlled large amounts of land, lived in extended family compounds, and aspired to provide their sons with the education that would elevate the family to shi status.

Increasingly, local landlord families were linked by marriage or the success of their sons to the shi. This combination gave rise to what was a new class configuration, the *scholar-gentry,* who superseded the shi. As their dual label suggests, the scholar-gentry upheld their position through both their landholdings in the rural areas and the political posts they won in the bureaucracy, which was housed mainly in the towns. Families tended to maintain branches in both areas. Wealth from landholding provided the means to educate the brightest males, who increased the family's fortunes by winning lucrative administrative positions. Well-placed family members in the town looked after the interests of their rural elders and cousins in such matters as tax quotas, military protection, or civil litigation. If bandits or nomads raided the area where the rural branch of the family resided, those family members could take refuge with their relatives in town. When towns became the object of warring armies, the city dwellers fled to the countryside. This double base and mutual support made for remarkable durability. Some families played major roles in Chinese politics and society for centuries. Some lasted for thousands of years—far longer than any imperial dynasty.

In both town and country, scholar-gentry families lived in large walled compounds, which often had separate buildings for each unit of the extended family. Surviving clay figurines of gentry homes show that they were multistoried structures with stucco or wooden walls and tiled roofs. Most compounds included an inner garden, where children could play and their elders could chat and enjoy nature. In times of peace, scholar-gentry families lived the good life. Family granaries ensured a ready supply of good food, and numerous household servants took care of tedious chores such as cleaning, cooking, and washing clothes. Male and female members of the family dressed in silks, which commoners, including merchants, were not permitted to wear (at least in public). A family's standing in the official and social hierarchy was further advertised by the color of the emblems and ribbons that males were permitted to wear.

When a member of a scholar-gentry household who held an administrative position left the compound for work or a night on the town, he rode in a horse-drawn carriage that, like his clothing, was of a size and design that indicated his government rank. Both male and female members of the family enjoyed the deference of the

Walls, strong gates, and numerous stories were prominent features of extended-family dwellings in the Han era, as this painted pottery model from the 1st century C.E. so clearly illustrates.

common people. Merchants plied them with their finest goods, servants scurried to do their bidding, and peasants bowed politely as they passed in their carriages. A commoner who forgot his place could expect to be chided by his peers or roughed up by the toughs that most gentry families employed to look after their physical safety.

Class and Gender Roles in Han Society

There is considerable evidence that women, particularly those from powerful scholar-gentry households, enjoyed more freedom and status in the Han era than they were to have in later periods of Chinese history.

Because marriages, especially among the elite, were arranged with family alliances rather than romantic concerns in mind, young men had as little say in the choice of their future spouses as women. Though the woman's father paid a dowry to the family of his son-in-law, and his daughter went to her husband's house to live, the young bride could usually rely on her powerful relatives to ensure that she was well treated in her new home. She was often allowed to take along her servants and even a sister as live-in companions. Widowed women were permitted to remarry, and all women participated in family ceremonies. Perhaps most important, women of upper-class families were often tutored in writing, the arts, and music. There were several important female poets in the Han era, and at least one prominent court historian was a woman.

Despite these promising trends, women at all social levels remained subordinated to men. Family households were run by the older males, and though women could inherit, male children normally received the greater share of family property. The following verse from the *Book of Poetry,* which indicates the appropriate responses to the birth into an aristocratic family of a son and a daughter, respectively, clearly illustrates the preference for and consequent privileges of males:

Sons shall be born to him—
They will be put to sleep on couches;
They will be clothed in robes;
They will have scepters to play with;
Their cry will be loud.
(Hereafter) they will be resplendent with red knee-covers,
The (future) king, the princes of the land.

Daughters shall be born to him—
They will be put to sleep on the ground;
They will be clothed in wrappers;
They will have tiles to play with.
It will be theirs neither to do wrong nor to do good. Only
    about the liquor and the food will they have to think,
And to cause no sorrow to their parents.

Political positions were reserved for males, though women could sometimes exert powerful influence from behind the throne. But this backstage plotting and scheming at the court merely served to confirm the view of the Confucian scholars that women were unfit for politics. Again, their shortcomings are bluntly set forth in the *Book of Poetry:*

A woman with a long tongue
Is a stepping-stone to disorder.
Disorder does not come down from Heaven—
It is produced by women.
Those from whom come no lessons, no instruction,
Are women and eunuchs.

At the level of the scholar-gentry, young married women were subjected to the demands and criticisms of notoriously domineering mothers-in-law. This was a lesser problem among the lower classes, where residence in extended households was not common. Nonetheless, women from peasant families were expected to cook, clean house, and labor long hours in the fields. Some found social outlets and even a degree of financial independence as market women in nearby towns. But all were legally subordinated to their fathers and husbands. At all class levels, women were expected to marry, and whatever their individual talents, their most vital social function remained the bearing of children, preferably male children.

Peasant Life

Ordinary cultivators held varying amounts of land, but few produced more than they needed to subsist and pay taxes. Moderately prosperous farmers sold their surplus to traders or their agents, or in a local market town. Most peasants who had a decent-sized plot of land lived well. But many peasants had little or no land of their own and were forced to labor for well-to-do landlords in order to earn a meager living. Peasants with plots that were too small to support their families complained to Han officials that they "did not have enough husks and beans to eat and [that] their coarse clothing was not in good condition." Those who worked the land of others as tenants or landless laborers were even more miserable. According to an official description, they "wore the coverings of oxen and horses and ate the food of dogs and pigs."

Key Chinese inventions, such as the shoulder collar (which permitted horses to pull greater loads) and the wheelbarrow, eased the physical burdens placed on farmers at all levels. These devices expanded irrigation networks, improved iron tools, and new cropping patterns made for larger agricultural yields that were mostly consumed by upper-class groups and the town populations. The governing classes required all peasants to devote a designated number of days each year to labor on public works. In addition, peasants were liable to conscription for the imperial armies.

The racing horses and decorated carriage shown on this rubbing from a stone carving from the Later Han era suggest the confidence and opulence of the elite classes, who alone could afford such a vehicle.

The existence of available, arable land in many areas, particularly the south, relieved population pressure and provided frontier outlets where hard-pressed laborers could clear land and start life anew. Some peasants took to banditry in the rugged hill country or the forested zones that still existed in large parts of the Yellow and Yangtze river basins. Others scraped by as beggars in provincial towns or lived with vagabonds who traveled the roads of the empire in search of temporary employment or vulnerable merchants and country houses to rob. Many more peasants joined secret societies, which provided financial support in times of shortage and physical protection in case of disputes with other cultivators or local notables. The most famous of the secret societies was called the Red Eyebrows because painted eyebrows served as its badge of membership. Usually the activities of the secret societies were localized, but in times of great social stress, groups such as the Red Eyebrows could play major roles in widespread popular insurrections.

The Han Capital at Xian

The urban growth that had been one of the most notable social developments in the Late Zhou era continued unabated in the Han period. The new capital city at *Xian* took on the basic features of Chinese imperial cities from that time forward. Laid out on a somewhat distorted grid, Xian had great roadways that gave access to and defined, the main quarters of the city. Much of the city was protected by long earth and brick walls broken at regular intervals by towers and gates. Estimates of Xian's population range from about 100,000, which probably refer to those people living within the walls, to 250,000, which probably include those people living outside the walls and in neighboring villages.

The emperor resided in an inner or forbidden city, which only his family, servants, and closest advisors were permitted to enter. The inner city was an impressive complex of palaces, towers, and decorated gateways. Each palace included audience halls, banquet rooms, large gardens and fishponds, and luxurious living quarters for the emperor, his wife and many concubines, and their numerous children. To the west of Xian, beyond the city walls, a large pleasure garden was laid out for the imperial family. It included, among other things, one of the earliest known zoos.

The forbidden city was surrounded by administrative buildings and the palaces of the most powerful aristocratic and scholar-gentry households. Under later dynasties, this zone would become a distinct imperial city within the capital. Some of the imperial palaces and government buildings were made of stone or brick, but many were made of clay covered with brightly colored plaster. Most were roofed with the glazed tiles with upturned edges that would become characteristic of Chinese architecture in the following millennia.

Towns and Traders

The Han capital at Xian was only one of many imposing cities found in China in this era. It is likely that China was the most urbanized civilization in the world at this time—a fact that tells us much about the productivity of its agricultural sector. There were large numbers of towns with over ten thousand people and several towns, such as Xian, with populations in the tens of thousands. Most towns were walled, and many were administrative centers dominated by the multistory residences and offices of imperial officials and scholar-gentry notables. But other towns grew up around mining and manufacturing centers, and many were centers of trade, which continued to grow in the Han era.

This growth was greatly advanced by Han military expansion to the west and south. It resulted in the establishment of new overland trade routes into central Asia and south China. Overseas links were also established with northern Vietnam, the rest of Southeast Asia, and westward to the rich trading towns of coastal India.

Large mercantile firms controlled these long-distance trading networks. They grew wealthy from the transport and sale of bulk items, such as grain and horses, as well as from supplying the elite classes with exotic luxury items, such as incense, fragrant woods, and rhinoceros horn, which when ground into an edible powder was believed to enhance male potency. Merchant families also made great fortunes by lending money and investing in mining, ship construction, sheep raising, and less legitimate enterprises such as gambling halls, brothels, and grave robbing.

A Han relief on a funeral tile found in the Chengdu region in Sichuan (Eastern Han dynasty, 25 B.C.E.–221 C.E.). The hunting scene in a luxuriant landscape in the upper panel is here linked with a scene (lower panel) of peasants working in the fields.

Though the merchant classes became wealthier and more numerous, they found it increasingly difficult to translate their profits into political power or social status. Fearing their rivalry, the scholar-gentry induced successive Han rulers to issue laws that restricted merchant activities and privileges. Under most Han rulers, for example, merchants were not permitted to hold administrative posts, though they often exerted considerable local influence. They were not allowed to own carriages, carry weapons, or wear silk clothing. Scholar-gentry writers consistently classed merchants below the peasants in terms of their social usefulness, arguing that peasants produced food and essential services, whereas traders produced nothing but rather lived off the labor of others.

A Genius for Invention and Artisan Production

Long before the Han, the Chinese had displayed a special aptitude for invention and technological innovation. They had built massive irrigation systems, canal networks, and fortifications. They devised cropping techniques that remained for millennia some of the most productive known to humanity. In the centuries of Han rule, however, their talent for invention reached new heights, and with it rose the excellence of their artisan production. There is little doubt that China was the most technologically innovative and advanced of all the classical civilizations.

At the level of the elite, the introduction of the brush pen and paper at the end of the 2nd century B.C.E. greatly facilitated the administrative work of the scholar-gentry and advanced their literary and artistic production. The Han Chinese also developed watermills to grind grain and power artisan workshops, and rudders and compasses to steer and guide ships (though in the Han era compasses were employed primarily for divination and not used by sailors until the 9th century C.E.). They devised ingenious mining techniques to allow them to fully exploit the iron and copper resources that had become critical to warfare and domestic artisan production. In the centuries of Han rule, silk making was carried to new levels of refinement, and techniques for making lacquerware and porcelain were pioneered, which allowed China to remain a leader in ceramics until well into the modern era.

All these advances, of course, promoted the growth of the artisan, manufacturing classes. Artisans tended to be clustered in special sectors of Chinese towns, but in some regions these were villages devoted almost exclusively to crafts such as silk-weaving or pottery manufacture. Skilled artisans were in high demand and probably had a higher living standard than most peasants, though the scholar-gentry accorded them a lower official social status. Again, the ideal and reality did not necessarily correspond, for some members of the artisan classes amassed wealth and were allowed to carry weapons, ride horses, and wear silk clothing.

The Arts and Sciences in the Han Era

Chinese art during the classical period was largely decorative. Careful detail and expert craftsmanship were most valued. Artistic styles often reflected the precision and geometric qualities of the many symbols of Chinese writing, and indeed, calligraphy itself became a highly prized art form. Chinese painting was much less developed than it was to become under later Chinese dynasties. But the bronzes and ceramic figurines, bowls, and vases produced in this era set a very high standard for later Chinese artists. Important work was also done in jade and ivory carving and woven silk screens.

In the sciences, the Chinese were more drawn to experimentation with practical applications than grand theorizing. By 444 B.C.E., court astronomers had developed an accurate calendar based on a year of 365.5 days. Later astronomers calculated the movements of the planets Saturn and Jupiter, and observed sunspots—more than 1500 years before comparable observations were made in Europe. The main purpose of Chinese astronomy was to make celestial phenomena predictable, as part of a wider interest in ensuring harmony between heaven and earth. In astronomy and other areas, Chinese scientists

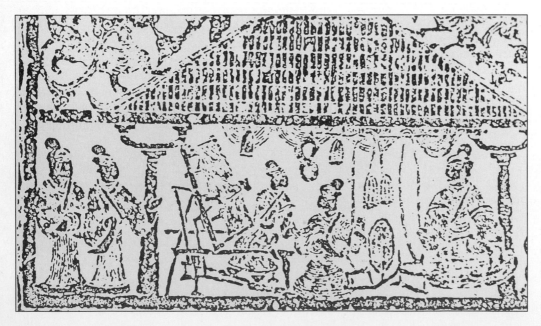

Rubbing from a stone carving of women weaving and spinning silk in the Later Han period.

steadily improved their instruments, even inventing a kind of seismograph to register the strength of earthquakes. The Chinese were also active in medical research. They made great strides in the diagnosis of diseases and in the prescription of herbal remedies and drugs to cure them. Recent evidence suggests that physicians in the Han era had begun to explore the principles of acupuncture, which remains the most distinctive and one of the most beneficial Chinese contributions to the advance of medicine.

Chinese mathematics also stressed the practical. Daoism encouraged some interest in studying the orderly processes of nature, but most research focused on how things work. For example, Chinese scholars studied the mathematics of music in ways that promoted advances in acoustics. They also sought to work out standards for the measurement of distance, volume, and weight. This kind of scientific and mathematical learning won substantial backing from the government and was generally approved by the shi scholar-officials.

Imperial Crisis and Han Restoration

For over two centuries the Han maintained its hold over a unified Chinese empire. But by the end of the 1st century B.C.E., problems centering on the court itself threatened to bring an end to Han rule. After Han Wudi, the quality of the emperors declined markedly. Many of his successors neglected the duties of government and, like the monarchs of the late Shang and Zhou, indulged heavily in the pleasures of food, drink, and concubines. As the hold of the emperors over state affairs weakened, the powerful families of their wives sought to take charge of imperial administration. In 6 C.E., the fact that the only male heir of the Han dynasty was a small child gave one of these families, the Wang, the opportunity to seize the throne in its own right.

With the initial support of the scholar-gentry and the general populace, an ambitious nephew of the Empress Dowager Wang, named Wang Mang, proclaimed himself emperor in 9 C.E. But Wang Mang's numerous and well-intended reforms rapidly alienated the very groups that had originally greeted his accession with great joy. Attempts to exert imperial control over land ownership angered the scholar-gentry. Government monopolies, which sent the price of food and other essentials soaring, led to widespread peasant unrest. In 23 C.E., the hapless Wang Mang was overthrown, and the Han dynasty was restored.

The Later Han and Imperial Collapse

The Later Han dynasty ruled a unified China for nearly 200 years. For a time the peace and prosperity of the Former Han era returned. Internal rebels were suppressed, and the nomads were again beaten into submission. The last centuries of the dynasty witnessed little of the innovation and creativity of the early centuries of Han rule. Inventions were improved, scholars commented on the works of earlier thinkers, the population of the empire continued to grow, and trading networks expanded. But major breakthroughs in government, the arts, and invention would have to wait for centuries and the next great dynasty, the Tang.

Politically, the Later Han was a period of steady decline. Han rulers were plagued by incessant struggles between factions at the court, which had been transferred from Xian eastward to the city of Loyang. Challenges from the families of the emperors' wives continued, but they were complicated by the growing power of the *eunuchs*—males who had been castrated in order to make them reliable guardians of the emperor's concubines. Some eunuchs were orphans, but many were sons of families who viewed their recruitment into the eunuch corps at the palace as a sure way to financial security and political advancement.

Over the years, the number of eunuchs increased, and after the Han dynasty was restored, they gained substantially in power as palace administrators and inner advisors of the later emperors. In the last decades of Han rule, these beleaguered monarchs attempted to use them to check the power of their wives' families. The three-way struggles that developed between the scholar-gentry, the families of the rulers' wives, and the eunuchs eventually ripped the court apart.

Divisions at the center of the empire weakened the emperor's ability to check nomadic incursions and remedy the worsening conditions of the mass of the people. An enfeebled imperial administration meant growing power for landlords and increasing autonomy for regional officials. Local notables pressed the peasantry that worked their lands for more taxes and higher rents. *Secret societies* spread like wildfire, and peasant risings broke out throughout the empire. Military commanders and regional lords seized power in their own right and fought against each other for the right to claim the Han throne.

The dynasty was not officially overthrown until 220 C.E., but decades earlier its power had been usurped. The end of the Han meant the return of the warring states and began nearly 400 years of division, strife, and turmoil that would end only with the rise of the Sui dynasty at the end of the 6th century C.E. (see Chapter 11).

CONCLUSION

An Era of Accomplishment and Affluence

The four centuries of Han rule from roughly 200 B.C.E. to 200 C.E., represented the first wave in a cyclic succession of dynasties that would rule China until the 20th century. Prolonged periods of political division and civil strife followed the fall of some dynasties, most notably the Han. Yet there was considerable social and institutional continuity from one dynasty to the next. Though Chinese civilization expanded and changed significantly in areas as fundamental as the social composition of the ruling elite, marriage arrangements, and religion, key elements came together in the Han period that persisted into the 20th century. Among them were the assumption that political unity was natural and desirable, the principle of rule by an emperor served by a professional bureaucracy, and the dominance in political, social, and cultural life of the educated scholar-gentry elite. Most Chinese also had a deep veneration for tradition and their ancestors, and they laid great stress on the importance of maintaining social harmony, self-restraint, and decorum in dealings within the family and in the wider society.

Classical China did not produce an entirely unified culture or complete social harmony. Major philosophical and religious schools disagreed widely about the nature of "man" and the goals of life. Many ordinary people knew little of the ideas of the great Chinese philosophers such as Confucius and Laozi. They continued to believe in a variety of gods and spirits, which were often associated with the home and kitchen, and developed rituals and offerings to placate these supernatural beings. The gap between elite and masses in Chinese culture was considerable, in part because Chinese writing was so difficult to master that only a small elite had time and money enough to learn to read and write.

Despite these divisions and differences, the short-lived Qin dynasty and four centuries of Han rule had established the basic components of a civilization that would last for thousands of years. As the achievements of the classical age demonstrate, it was to be one of the most creative and influential civilizations of all human history. The strength of its agrarian base has allowed China to carry about one-fourth of the total human population from the last centuries B.C.E. to the present day. The productivity of its peasants has allowed the Chinese to support some of the world's largest cities and one of history's largest and most creative elites. Over the centuries, Chinese textiles, porcelain, and inventions have been traded over much of the globe and have spurred technological revolutions in societies as diverse as those found in Japan and Europe. The civilization of China that came together in the classical age of the Qin and Han was destined to dominate the history of much of Asia and contribute significantly to the advance of civilized life throughout the globe.

FURTHER READINGS

Good introductions to life in China in the classical age can be found in Wolfram Eberhard's *A History of China* (1977), Dun J. Li's *The Ageless Chinese* (1965), and E. Reischauer's and J. K. Fairbank's *East Asia: The Great Tradition* (1960). *China's Civilization* (1976) by Arthur Cotterell and David Morgan contains useful illustrations and incorporates more recent interpretations of developments in early China. Two works deal extensively with the life and reign of Shi Huangdi: Arthur Cotterell's *The First Emperor of China* (1981) and Li Yu-Ning's *The First Emperor of China* (1975).

A relatively brief and clear introduction to Chinese thought is provided by Frederic Mote's *Intellectual Foundations of China* (1971). A much more detailed study that places Chinese thought in a comparative context can be found in Benjamin Schwartz's *The World of Thought in Ancient China* (1983). Michael Loewe's *Everyday Life in Early Imperial China* (1968) is excellent on Han society, as is the more detailed and scholarly work *Han Social Structure* (1972) by T'ung-Tsu Ch'u, which includes extensive quotations from Chinese texts and valuable insights into the position of women, merchants, artisans, and eunuchs. A detailed survey of the archeological work done on Han sites and what they tell us about Han society is provided by Wang Shongshu's *Han Civilization* (1982). Michele Pirazzoli-t'Serstevens's lavishly illustrated study, *The Han Civilization of China* (1982), contains the most comprehensive, up-to-date, and readable overview of Han civilization available. Edmund Capon's and William MacQuitty's *Princes of Jade* (1973) is less informative and reliable, but it also contains superb plates and illustrations. The most authoritative and detailed account of science and technology in the Han and later dynastic periods can be found in Joseph Needham's multivolume study, *Science and Civilization in China* (1954–). Burton Watson's *Courtier and* *Commoner in Ancient China* (1974), which is a translation of portions of Ban Ku's *History of the Former Han,* can be perused for examples and anecdotes that allow the student to gain a vivid sense of the day-to-day workings of Han society.

6

Classical Greece and the Hellenistic World

1600 Indo-European invasion

1000–800 Greek "Dark Ages" after Dorian invasion

800–700 Rise of Greek city–states and economy; Homeric epics, *Iliad* and *Odyssey*

600–500 Spread of commercial agriculture; rise of social protest

546–527 Pisistratus tyrant in Athens

1400 Kingdom of Mycenae; Trojan War

550 Cyrus the Great forms Persian Empire

1600 B.C.E.   **1200** B.C.E.   **800** B.C.E.   **600** B.C.E.

INTRODUCTION

Beginning about 800 B.C.E. on the peninsula and islands of Greece and in the surrounding territory in the eastern Mediterranean, a second center of classical civilization began to emerge.

Greek politics and culture flourished until about 400 B.C.E., then began to decline. A military empire emerged, initially forged by Alexander the Great, which set up what is called the Hellenistic period. *Hellenism* means "derived from the Greek." Under Alexander and then several regional kings, many Greek values and styles spread through the Middle East and much of North Africa, combining with local traditions for about 200 years.

As in China, classical Greek civilization built on earlier regional civilizations, which had constructed elaborate monuments, developed a form of writing, and produced strong monarchies. Influenced by cultures in the Middle East and Egypt, civilization on the island of Crete and around Mycenae on the Greek mainland had expanded for several centuries after 2000 B.C.E. These regional civilizations were able to assimilate initial Indo-European invaders who spoke the language that came to be known as Greek.

Internal warfare, however, plus a second wave of Indo-European invasions by a Greek-speaking people called the Dorians, virtually ended the first phase of civilization in this part of the Mediterranean by about 1100 B.C.E. Rich capital cities, including Mycenae, were abandoned. For a time agriculture itself deteriorated as some Greeks turned to nomadic life and purely local governments predominated. Greek-speaking people spread around the Aegean Sea, setting the basis for a culture that would include important parts of modern Turkey, Greece, and the Balkans, but a new civilization emerged only after 800 B.C.E.

GREECE AS A CLASSICAL CIVILIZATION

At this point, a full-fledged classical society began to take shape, exhibiting many basic features in common with the classical phase of civilization in China and India. Like the other classical societies, Greek civilization would extend over a wide region, embracing ultimately a far larger area than any of the earlier cultures of the eastern Mediterranean. Greek influence would spread well beyond the peninsula itself to much of the Middle East, part of North Africa, Sicily, and southern Italy. Greece began to sketch a Mediterranean civilization zone that combined earlier centers, notably in the Middle East, with more western shores new to civilization in any form. Classical Greece easily passed the test of geographical expansion, as classical China had done. The Greeks produced less tidy political unities than had the Chinese emperors, but their cultural and commercial outreach and periodic military forays affected a large portion of western Asia and southern Europe.

Classical Greece developed the second major feature of all the classical civilizations by demonstrating new political and cultural capacities compared with the earlier regional cultures of Egypt, Mesopotamia, and Greece. A greater diversity of philosophies and political forms developed; science and mathematics advanced, building on previous achievements; the ability to organize large empires arose, though somewhat haltingly. Many political traditions and cultural forms survived classical Greece itself, in the Mediterranean and elsewhere, making the long classical period in this part of the world a truly formative one like that in eastern and in southern Asia.

While Greek civilization had enduring impact, it was less clearly focused, geographically or institutionally, than that of China. Nothing like the Chinese cycles of dynasties described classical Greek history, for Greek political experience was more varied and underwent more

---

470–430 Athens at its height–Pericles, Phidias, Sophocles, Socrates, etc.		**338–323** Macedonian Empire; Alexander the Great
525–456 Aeschylus launches tradition of dramatic tragedy	**431–404** Peloponnesian Wars	**359–336** Philip II of Macedon
		300–100 Hellenistic period
500–449 Greek defeat of Persia; spread of Athenian Empire	**384–322** Aristotle	**250–126** Flourishing of Hellenistic astronomy and mathematics
	399 Socrates condemned	
500 B.C.E.	**400** B.C.E.	**300** B.C.E.

unexpected innovations. There were also important rivals to Greek civilization, and a distinct break within Greek history itself, that add further complexity.

THE PERSIAN EMPIRE: PARALLEL POWER IN THE MIDDLE EAST

Focal Point: As Greek civilization began to form, an important Persian empire developed, centered in the eastern portion of the Middle East. This empire, and several successor states, maintained separate political and cultural values. Ultimately less influential than Greek culture, the Persian tradition would surface at many points in world history and still affects the nation of Iran today.

After the fall of the great Babylonian and Hittite empires in the Middle East by 1200 B.C.E. and the ensuing regional states, including some Greek colonies in the Middle East, a series of new invasions took shape. First came the Assyrians and then an influx of Iranians. From a network of small kingdoms in this region, a great conqueror emerged by 550 B.C.E. Cyrus the Great established a massive Persian Empire, which ran across the northern Middle East and into northwestern India. The new empire formed the clearest successor to the great Mesopotamian states of the past, and Cyrus carefully tolerated traditional cultures. The Iranians advanced iron technology in the Middle East.

Persia was also the center of a major new religion. A religious leader, Zoroaster, revised the polytheistic religious tradition of the Sumerians by seeing life as a battle between two divine forces: good and evil. Zoroastrianism emphasized the importance of personal moral choice in picking one side or the other, with a Last Judgment ultimately deciding the eternal fate of each person. The righteous would live on in a heaven, the "House of Song," while the evil would be condemned to eternal pain. Zoroastrianism converted Persia's later emperors and added to the cultural richness of this civilization.

Later emperors expanded Persian holdings. They were unable to defeat Greece and enter Europe, but they long dominated the Middle East, providing an extensive period of peace and prosperity. Ultimately, the Persian Empire was toppled by Alexander the Great, a Greek-educated conqueror. Persian language and culture survived in the northeastern portion of the Middle East, periodically affecting developments in the region as a whole.

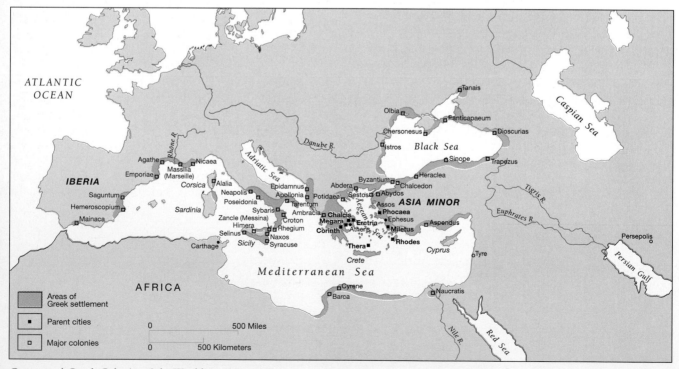

Greece and Greek Colonies of the World, c. 431 B.C.E.

Using ceremonial styles similar to those of earlier Mesopotamia, the great Persian Empire celebrated its powerful emperors. This wall relief is on the great ceremonial stairway leading to the royal Audience Hall of Darius and Xerxes.

The rise of classical civilization in Greece was thus in competition with a parallel and powerful classical civilization in Persia. Greek achievements would ultimately prove more influential—Zoroastrianism, for example, faded in importance—but they were not unrivaled.

THE POLITICAL CHARACTER OF CLASSICAL GREECE

Focal Point: Greek leaders valued an intense political life, and political forms—indeed, many of our terms, like *politics* itself—constituted a vital part of the Greek heritage. Greek politics was usually localized. It emphasized no one kind of government organization. Rule by aristocrats was most characteristic, but periods of tyranny were also important. The Greeks also sketched a dynamic version of democracy.

Greek civilization took a form very different from that of Persia. Its rapid development had two obvious roots by 800 B.C.E. First was the continued existence of small cities, as well as the memories of the earlier achievements of Crete and Mycenae, even during the Indo-European invasions. This heritage was combined with an Indo-European culture that included a vivid polytheistic religion. Oral poems chanted to local aristocracies preserved knowledge of a pantheon of gods and goddesses and of values from which more elaborate philosophies and ethical systems could be devised.

The second spur to Greek civilization was a general revival of trade in the eastern Mediterranean, abetted by the introduction of coined money. Trade allowed many Greek city-states (including Greek-dominated cities in Greece and Mediterranean Asia, particularly in what is now Turkey) to increase their wealth and their range of contacts. By 800 B.C.E., several Greek centers had trad-

ing connections around the Black Sea and also in Egypt and southern Italy. Economic revival, in turn, prompted population growth and social change in the Greek centers, which encouraged new political structures that challenged dominance by the owners of landed estates.

The Emergence of Greek Forms

Greek political evolution occurred at an often dizzying pace from the civilization's early days until a period of decline set in after a major internal war at the end of the 5th century B.C.E. Cultural development, in contrast, continued into the following Hellenistic centuries, while the civilization's geographical range widened on the heels of Alexander the Great's conquests. In the Greek and Hellenistic periods, political and cultural patterns depended on a complex social and economic structure that both explained and drove the Greek thirst for expansion.

During the 8th century B.C.E., the Greeks adapted the Phoenician alphabet for writing their own language, thereby creating the literal basis for a new civilization. This alphabet was easier to learn than any writing system previously devised. The advancement of literacy further stimulated trade by aiding in the exchange of commercial information and also enhancing cultural life. At this point two great poems, the *Iliad* and the *Odyssey*, which focused on the legendary Mycenean War with Troy, were written down, possibly by the poet Homer to whom they were attributed or by a larger group of writers gradually formalizing oral tradition. The Homeric achievement drew together many separate stories and set forth definitions of the gods and human nature that profoundly shaped later Greek thinking. Soon after the Homeric epics were written, other writers in several cities, including the famous woman poet Sappho, began writing poems that ranged from military songs to lyric statements. A distinctive Greek art also began to emerge.

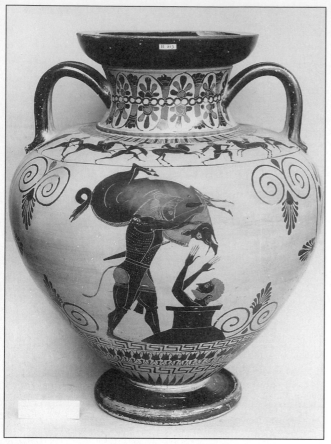

Vase art, with realistic figures from Greek legends surrounded by geometric designs, played a prominent role in Greece. In this myth, Hercules is bringing the Erymanthian boar back to Eurystheus, who is so frightened that he has hidden himself in a wine jar.

Architects defined the shape of the Greek temple as an oblong building framed by pillars. Early Greek sculptors used Egyptian models, but later sculptors moved toward more realistic portrayals including full-profile figures. Geometric designs on pottery similarly yielded to more realistic scenes of human activities, reflecting yet again the growing appreciation of human beauty and the centrality of human life.

The Polis (City-State) as a Political Unit

Greek politics also took shape in the three centuries after 800 B.C.E. Greek government in this early period and thereafter revolved around the city-state unit—that is, a regional government centered in a major city but embracing the agricultural hinterland as well. These units could be quite tiny, or like Sparta (one of the key city-states), they could embrace a substantial area. Athens, the most famous city-state, was about the size of the state of Rhode Island; by the 5th century B.C.E., Athens had a population of roughly 250,000, of whom 100,000 lived in the city proper. The city-state government came naturally to Greece, partly because of the traditions set in earlier Middle Eastern civilizations, where regional states often predominated, and partly because a mountainous terrain made larger connections difficult. Many city-states were formed in a valley or bay with a single city organizing the surrounding agricultural enclave. Greek settlements in other areas, however, such as the northern Middle East or southern Italy, also adopted the city-state form even when natural conditions did not require it. By 600 B.C.E., nearly 300 independent poleis had developed in Greece. While the city-state format promoted frequent wars, as no single unit predominated, it did encourage a political life of unusual intensity. So much was this the case that the Greek word for city-state government—*polis*—serves as the origin of our word *politics*.

Early Greek poleis were mainly ruled by landowning aristocrats, mostly descendants of the Indo-European warrior class who were still responsible for most military activities. Free farmers were also citizens, supporting the government and often participating in periodic assemblies, though not ruling directly. Councils of various sorts played a vital role in the early Greek city-states, even when there was a single king or other ruler. Warrior-aristocrats frequently met with the ruler to advise on matters of state, and they expected their advice to be taken seriously. Independent farmers also had a chance to meet occasionally to discuss political issues; one historian has described this form of government as a real peasant democracy.

This mixed system was increasingly challenged from about 700 B.C.E. onward. With the commercial expansion that began in the 8th century, aristocratic rule was often disputed. Some city-states escaped major contests, for they remained largely agricultural; Sparta, for example, maintained a strong militaristic rule under aristocratic leadership. But in active trading centers, merchants and a growing urban manufacturing group chafed under aristocratic rule. Furthermore, in many areas agriculture itself changed. Landlords began to specialize in growing olives and grapes and in manufacturing cooking oil and wines. These were commercial products, requiring substantial capital to develop; the landlords began importing cheap grain from colonies in Asia, Egypt, and Sicily in order to provide basic foodstuffs. These imports progressively squeezed out local independent farmers, creating a growing gulf between the rich and poor. The ideals of widespread citizenship were contradicted by these developments.

The result, by the 6th century B.C.E., was a growing crescendo of social protest, pitting urban groups and dispossessed farmers against the aristocratic elite. One common outcome was a series of *tyrants* who won popular support against the aristocratic interest. These tyrants often developed public works and other activities that benefited the lower classes and the cities, while maintaining pressures against aristocratic opposition. But the idea of one-man rule contradicted traditions of political legitimacy, which held that the community should govern itself, and of course it antagonized the aristocracy without destroying this class completely. Hence, in many cases, reformers arose to try to restore earlier ideals of citizenship while dealing with the new social tensions. Many reformers emphasized developing new laws to regulate economic relationships without resorting to tyrants. *Solon,* a reformer in Athens early in the 6th century, set up laws that would ease the burden of debts on the farmers by prohibiting slavery for such debts. The idea developed that laws could be written and revised, rather than being passed down unaltered from tradition; here was one source of new political interest and participation.

Other forces pressed for political change. Military activity increasingly involved larger numbers of citizens who formed tightly organized and well-coordinated lines of infantry. Naval forces in the port cities, such as Athens, also depended on extensive recruitment. This development increased the need for strong bonds among citizens within the polis. By 500 B.C.E., most poleis emphasized the importance of loyalty to the community, which itself would be regulated by law rather than by custom or purely personal relationships. Participation in public life became a widespread ideal, and it corresponded to the busy functions that grouped city dwellers together in the marketplace.

The dominant religion also supported this ideal of political unity and involvement. Each city-state had its own patron god or goddess, and regular rituals called forth prayer and ceremony on behalf of the city's well-being. These ceremonies included plays, choruses, sporting events, and religious exercises, all calling attention to the power and cohesion of the polis. In 399 B.C.E., the philosopher Socrates was condemned by a jury in Athens for corrupting his students by encouraging skepticism and doubt; he was given a choice between exile and death. He chose death because, as he said, the city had been the source of his character and he owed it obedience; better to die than to be apart.

The Rise of Democracy in Athens

After the period of greatest social tension, city-state governments continued to vary. Aristocratic councils returned in many places; Sparta had two kings to check each other, ruling on behalf of the military aristocracy. Generally, however, a democratic tendency gained ground by the 5th century, and here Athens proudly took the lead.

Athens had undergone a fairly standard, if highly dramatic, political evolution prior to its democratic flowering in the 5th century B.C.E. It started when smaller villages were unified into a single city-state as an aristocratic domain. Powerful nobles held the best land and dominated political and religious life through their council. There was no written law. During the 7th century, tensions between aristocrats and commoners mounted as family farmers increasingly went into debt when harvests failed, often losing their land and in some cases being enslaved when they could not repay. Solon's reforms, which limited indebtedness while also encouraging greater commerce, resolved this crisis and also expanded the citizenship rights of most adult males. Citizens could elect a council that monitored the aristocratic government. But these reforms did not prevent the rise of an outright tyranny as an aristocratic leader, *Pisastratus,* gained popular support against the traditional noble councils, ruling from 546 to 527 B.C.E. Pisastratus sponsored major new buildings and public works, which created new jobs, while dominating the major councils. Soon after his death, invaders from Sparta attempted to restore the aristocracy, but while the tyranny was toppled, the Athenian people refused to revert to traditional forms. A new reform leader, *Clisthenes,* reestablished a council, elected by all citizens, that prepared agendas for an assembly composed of the citizens themselves. Athens was ready to become not only the most powerful but also the most fully developed of the Greek democracies of the 5th century.

Full-blown Athenian democracy, after a few additional reforms about 462 B.C.E., continued to depend on the popular assembly as sovereign authority. All decisions of state emanated from this body or had to be approved by it, and there were no restrictions on who could debate or propose in assembly meetings. This was *direct democracy*—the word itself comes from the Greek word for people, *demos*—rather than rule through elected representatives. Since the assembly met frequently, only a minority of citizens actually had time to attend regularly, and a few leading speakers usually predominated.

The citizens' voice, however, had other outlets. The army was composed of citizens, whose active service and coordinated maneuvers expressed the spirit of the democratic polis. Citizens also served as jurors in court trials, and every judicial decision could be appealed to a citizen board. Most officials were selected by lot on the grounds that any citizen could and should serve as an administrator. A few key officials—the generals and imperial treasurers—were elected, usually from the nobility, but like all officials they were carefully assessed by the assembly and might be removed or punished for faulty service. Terms of office were brief, further to encourage popular control. Only a few positions in the area of military leadership were reserved for appointment.

This was a democracy of a different sort from the version common in the contemporary world. It depended on the small size of the city-state and the intensive participation of its citizens. Furthermore, many adults were excluded from political rights. Women, though they might be citizens in terms of treatment by the law, had no rights of political participation. Half of all adult males were not citizens in any sense, being slaves or foreigners. Even at its most democratic, the Athenian government was shaped by considerable behind-the-scenes control by the aristocracy. The Athenian leader *Pericles,* who guided Athens during its decades of greatest glory after the mid-5th century, was an aristocrat who managed to direct affairs year after year through wise manipulation of political groups and his own prestige, whether or not he held formal office. Many Athenians, and even more Greeks in city-states where democracy did not go as far, continued to believe that real political virtue lay in aristocratic rule (*aristocracy* being derived from the Greek word *aristos,* or "rule of the best"). Sparta continued to represent the aristocratic alternative.

Even though democracy was qualified, and far from general throughout Greece, its principles were articulated clearly. Athenian democracy rested far more directly on the public devotion and talent of those who were citizens than modern democracies do. Pericles offered a classic definition of the democratic ideal:

> The administration is in the hands of the many and not of the few. But while the law secures equal justice to all alike in their private disputes, the claim of excellence is also recognized; and when a citizen is in any way distinguished he is preferred to the public service, not as a matter of privilege but as the reward of merit. Neither is poverty a bar, but a man may benefit his country whatever be the obscurity of his condition.

In truth, politics could provide both excitement and responsibility for many Athenians. Huge juries handled crucial trials, including political cases such as that of Socrates. Officials judged to have served badly could be ostracized for ten years, a measure introduced to prevent tyranny. Names of politicians judged to be potential tyrants were inscribed on *ostraka*, or pottery fragments, and if one name was listed often enough the person was forced to leave.

By the end of the 5th century, when Athens plunged into a devastating war with Sparta, the polis demonstrated some of the weaknesses as well as the strengths of democracy. Ordinary citizens worked hard in the war, but the lower-class citizens, eager for government jobs and spoils, often pressed for reckless expeditions that weakened the state in its military efforts and contributed substantially to ultimate defeat.

A Comparison of Greek and Chinese Political Styles

The Greek political approach, overall, involved intense emphasis on political virtue and responsibility. Participation in politics was part of the ideal life, particularly in the aristocracy. In this approach, with its concern for a sound political system and well-defined relationships between various social elements, there was more than a hint of the values Confucianism emphasized in China. But in the decentralized atmosphere of Greek politics, a far larger array of political structures was tossed up than was true in China with its greater emphasis on a single centralized system. Also, in comparison with Chinese political principles, the Greeks placed more value on various councils and on participation rather than on hierarchy and obedience (including the very idea of citizenship); there was more emphasis on formal preparation of law (a theme the Romans would later extend); and far less emphasis on a bureaucracy and bureaucratic codes. Democracy was not a fully typical form, as even in Athens it proved short-lived. The idea of intense citizen involvement and responsibility—with the corollary that citizenship was restricted—was more characteristic of

Greek political life and was compatible with mixed aristocratic council systems as well as with democracy.

Greek Diplomacy and the Tensions of United Effort

During the four centuries when Greek political forms evolved, many city-states sent out additional colonics, which expanded exposure to Greek political values. Colonies helped relieve population pressure at home. They also provided vital grain supplies to the mainland while serving as markets for processed products, including wine, cooking oil, and manufactured goods. By the 5th century, Greek colonies dotted the Mediterranean coast of present-day Turkey, the entire coastline of the Black Sea, and key points in North Africa, Italy, and even southern France and Spain. By providing new wealth, colonies supported the political and cultural vigor of Greece itself.

At their best, from 750 to 420 B.C.E., Greek politics included some important common efforts in addition to the focus on separate government units. The Greek city-states were capable of sufficient coordination to deal with a variety of general problems. They joined in regular celebrations such as the athletic competitions of the *Olympic games,* which grouped wrestlers and runners in often bitter (and occasionally rigged) competitions. They supported some common religious organizations, such as the oracle priests at Delphi, whose predictions and advice were widely sought.

More important was the collaboration that allowed Greece to defeat its most pressing outside enemy, the great empire of Persia. Soon after Cyrus the Great created the Persian Empire, he turned against wealthy Greek colonies along the Asian side of the Mediterranean and conquered them by about 540 B.C.E. Persian power became an obvious threat to the Greek mainland, impelling cooperation between Athens and Sparta, the most powerful city-states. In 499 B.C.E., the conquered Greek cities rebelled against the Persians, and were aided by the Athenian navy. The rebellion failed, and the Persian kings (Darius I, then Xerxes) moved against Greece in punishment. In 480 B.C.E., a Persian army of 100,000 troops moved down the Greek peninsula, initially winning great success, and captured Athens, destroying much of the city. But the Athenians built a new fleet, which defeated the Persian navy and cut off supplies, and then a Spartan-led force bested the Persian army. While Persia continued to dominate the Middle East, Greek independence was preserved. The greatest age of Greek

This statue of a discus thrower by the sculptor Myron shows the Greek love for athletics and the realistic but heroic style adopted for human figures by the classical Greek artists.

politics and culture followed, including the perfection of Athenian political institutions and the Age of Pericles.

The *Persian Wars* provided some of the most dramatic moments in classical Greek history. In the battle at Thermopylae, 300 Spartans and a few thousand Greek soldiers blocked a huge Persian army until they were betrayed by local Greeks and caught from behind. After the Greek military triumph at Marathon, a runner labored nearly 23 miles to bring news to Athens, collapsing after the word was passed. Ultimate Greek victory, celebrated later by the historian Herodotus, who praised Greek justice over the excessive ambition of the Persians, helped the Greeks define their separate identity as a society different from the Asian empire.

In the years following the Persian defeat Athens began to form an empire of its own. The Athenians quickly rebuilt their city, enhancing Greek art and architecture. Athenian naval power helped organize an alliance of lesser Greek cities, which Athens quickly dominated. Officially designed to guard against the Persian threat, this *Delian league* was headed by an Athenian admiral and its treasury was controlled by Athens. Increasingly, many cities became completely dependent on Athenian rule without having a voice in policy. The empire provided great resources for Athens, but it also complicated Athenian politics because the city grew to include increasing numbers of noncitizens while the spoils of political office, given imperial wealth, became increasingly attractive and highly contested. Many Athenians wondered if authoritarian control of colonies based on military force and heavy tribute payment was compatible with free political life at home. Domestic political infighting to compete for the favor of the crowd became increasingly nasty as dependence on the empire increased.

For the Greek political structure was fragile. With so many different government units, division could easily override common purpose. Diversity also produced animosity, with democrats and aristocrats glaring at each other both within and among the poleis. A new and bitter conflict between the leading states set the stage for declining political vigor within Greece itself.

Athens vs. Sparta

The growing imperial power of Athens attracted competition from Sparta, which had its own alliance system of land-based city-states. Competition for power in the Greek peninsula in the later 5th century B.C.E.—each side fearing that the other might gain a dominant position—was heightened by ideological conflicts that some historians have compared in their intensity though not their precise nature to the "cold war" struggles between the capitalist United States and the communist Soviet Union in the decades after World War II. Sparta stood for the old Greece before its alteration by extensive commerce and massive political change. Aristocratic rule had been transformed into a highly military regime in which boys were trained for battle and girls for the bearing of brave sons. Spartan militarism was designed to keep a large force of near-slaves, who did the agricultural work, under control. Use of money was discouraged by minting coins of unwieldy size. Discipline and control were the themes of Spartan society.

Unlike Sparta, Athens encouraged extensive trade and a vibrant, creative culture, while its democracy contrasted with the narrow aristocratic dominance of Sparta. Both sides were quite aware of their differences and disliked the principles of the rival society intensely. Both also drew allies from like-minded poleis. Sparta had unexpected advantages because its traditional principles were widely admired, even by some conservative Athenians. The heavy-handedness of Athens's empire also drew hostility from many smaller cities.

For a few decades, around 450 B.C.E., an uneasy peace prevailed between the Greek rivals. Pericles, though aggressively proud of Athenian values, judged that Athenian welfare rested on a cautious foreign policy and in peace with the Spartans. But in 435 B.C.E., a revolt in a colonial city-state, Corcyra, disrupted the precarious balance. Corcyra had been neutral between Athens and Sparta, but it had a large navy that now risked coming under the control of a Spartan ally. Athens insisted that Corcyra was under its protection, for it feared a rival navy; but this persuaded Sparta that Athens was insatiably power-hungry. War broke out in 431 B.C.E. when Spartan forces marched into Athenian territory.

In the resultant *Peloponnesian War,* the Athenian strategy was to let Sparta invade its outlying lands while relying on its fleet to maintain supplies and to raid the Spartan coast. But during the second year of the war, a massive plague broke out in Athens, ultimately killing one-third of the population, including Pericles. Grievances rose in Athens, and there was no longer a leader to provide consistent guidance. A victory over Spartan troops brought a chance for peace, but a warlike faction in Athens insisted on continuing the war, seeking to conquer new territory while wasting precious Athenian resources. The attempt to invade Sicily failed, costing Athens over 200 ships, 4500 men, and the support of many allies. Finally, in 404 B.C.E., a Spartan general cut off the Athenian food supply, and the city had to surrender. Athens was deprived of its remaining fleet, and the city walls were torn down. A political age came to an end, not only in Athens but in all of Greece.

THE HELLENISTIC PERIOD

Focal Point: After a period of instability, a conquering empire took over Greece and then turned to further expansion in the Middle East and Egypt. While

CLOSEUP

Alcibiades

Alcibiades (c. 450–404) was an Athenian general and politician who exploited Athens' uncertainties during the Peloponnesian War. Wealthy, handsome, and dissipated, he was an aristocrat, a student of Socrates, and a relative of Pericles. Alcibiades helped keep the war going against Sparta, in 421, as a popular general. He then urged the expedition against Sicily, to fuel his ambition. His opponents in Athens finally brought him down, whereupon he fled to Sparta and joined the war against Athens. Later, having lost the confidence of the Spartans, he turned yet again and won a command in the Athenian navy, ultimately returning amid popular acclaim. When Athens lost he fled, but the Spartans arranged to have him murdered. His unscrupulous example contributed to Athenian charges against Socrates (in 399) as a corrupter of Athenian youth.

the unitary empire did not survive its creator, Alexander the Great, a series of regional kingdoms persisted in the region for two centuries under considerable Greek influence. This *Hellenistic period* produced few political institutions of lasting importance, but it solidified Greek cultural achievements while introducing new elements and expanding their geographical impact.

Spartan domination of Greece, after the collapse of Athens, did not work well. Periodic wars against the Persians and between key Greek states dominated the first half of the 4th century. An alliance between Athens and the city-state of Thebes successfully attacked the Spartans, briefly setting up a Theban Empire in northern Greece. Athens formed a new league of its own, but soon began to abuse its allies through interference and demands for tribute. Having defeated Thebes, Athens' federation collapsed amid revolt. By 355 B.C.E., Greece had returned to a setting of independent, disorganized city-states, many of them exhausted by decades of war and civil strife.

The Peloponnesian War destroyed the basis for informal Greek unity and weakened both the major combatants. It took only a few decades for Greeks to realize that Greek politics had lost its luster. The larger Greek empire began to break up as colonies were pulled away, while a dangerous vacuum of power opened in the mainland itself.

Macedonian Conquest

Into this vacuum came a new force from the kingdom of *Macedon* on the borders of Greece. Macedonian conquests in turn opened a period of three centuries in which Greek culture spread widely in Egypt and far into western Asia. Greek city-states persisted in this new Hellenistic world, but they were no longer the dominant forms. Greek culture also mixed with new elements from the Middle East and India, though on the whole Hellenistic culture built more clearly on Greek themes than Hellenistic politics did. In geography, politics, and to an extent culture, a new era opened in the 4th century B.C.E., just as Greek institutions lost their vitality. The roots of the new order lay in the rise of a Macedonian dynasty, which conquered first Greece and then the Persian Empire within two generations.

Macedon, a kingdom to the north of Greece, was semibarbaric by Greek standards and was loosely organized under a king. Its residents spoke Greek, and Macedonian kings had long been interested in Greek culture. When King *Philip II* (r. 359–336 B.C.E.) seized power, he strengthened the monarchy within Macedon and then turned his attention to the chaos of Greece. Skilled both as a general and as a diplomat, Philip soon developed a strong army that had more flexible tactics than the standard citizen force of the poleis. By seizing some northern Greek territory, he gained the resources to pay mercenary troops and peasant soldiers. Then he turned to the divided city-states of central Greece.

Despite warnings by insightful leaders, states such as Athens were no longer willing to make major sacrifices for self-defense. Philip also found allies in Greek statesmen who wanted a new unity even if it was imposed from the outside. Finally, in 338 B.C.E., Philip won a decisive battle, aided by a cavalry charge led by his 18-year-old son Alexander. Macedon now ruled the bulk of Greece, and while the city-states retained their governments with rights of internal administration, Macedonian garrisons assured tax tributes and loyalty to the new kingdom.

This bust of Alexander the Great is in the heroic style of Greek sculpture. The youthful emperor was one of the greatest conquerors of the world.

Alexander the Great

Philip's death left the next stage of Macedonian expansion to Alexander, who gained power at the age of 20. Alexander, eager to continue his father's thrust for conquest, logically turned to the target of the Persian Empire, still vast but now weakly ruled. In 334 B.C.E., Alexander moved into Asia with about 35,000 troops. Daring triumphs brought him control of the Persian side of the Mediterranean coast. Then, in 333 B.C.E., Alexander defeated the main Persian army led by its emperor in Syria.

Persian efforts to sue for peace were ignored: Alexander wanted the whole empire and more, if possible. He moved into Egypt, now a weakened regional state, where he was greeted as pharaoh and son of a god. By 331 B.C.E., he entered Babylon and then seized the vast Persian treasury, as the Greeks and Macedonians gained revenge for the many Persian threats to their homeland. Alexander pressed into India, but he finally had to stop because his men refused to go farther.

Alexander planned a dazzling future for his new empire, hoping to merge Greek and Asian institutions and values and add further conquests. He founded many cities bearing his name, the most famous one that of *Alexandria* in Egypt. He spread Macedonian and Greek officials through his vast new Middle Eastern holdings. Alexander also encouraged intermarriage with Persian and other local women, a practice in which he himself set an example. Eager to promote a Hellenistic culture, as evidenced by his founding centers of scholarship in Greek learning, *Alexander the Great* also recognized the need to accommodate various traditions in a multinational empire. Whether he could have succeeded in consolidating his unprecedented holdings, given his vision and organizational skills, cannot be known, for he died of a fever in Babylon at the age of 33.

Later Hellenistic States

Alexander's unexpected death quickly brought disunity to the new empire, though not an end to the Hellenistic enterprise. Quarrels among his successors allowed key generals to seize the major provinces as kings. Three major regional dynasties resulted: one in Egypt (the *Ptolemies*), which ended with the suicide of the famous queen, Cleopatra, in 31 B.C.E.; one in Mesopotamia (the *Seleucids*); and one in Macedonia, Greece, and the northern Middle East (the *Antigonids*).

The three major successor states enjoyed about 75 years of vigor and prosperity. Trade in Greek goods continued to flourish, and all the new kings encouraged commerce. Many Greeks moved toward the government jobs and merchant positions available in the Middle East. Wealth centered, however, on the city dwellers and the Hellenized upper classes (whether of Greek origin or not), while native peasants suffered from high taxes and the lack of adequate land. Internal divisions caused a decline in production and combined with warfare between the kingdoms to weaken the successor states and open them to outside attack. By the 2nd century B.C.E.—just as Rome was beginning to expand—all the Hellenistic kingdoms except the one in Egypt had vanished. Rome then moved actively into this vacuum in expanding its own empire.

The two centuries of *Hellenism* marked the end of the characteristically Greek political style. City-states continued officially to exist, and they would maintain some functions even later under Roman control. But they no longer served as intense focal points because of the control exercised by foreign monarchs. Hellenistic politics centered on military empires.

Hellenism did not bring cultural unity or political cohesion to the Middle East and eastern Mediterranean. There were new interchanges, however, and some common interests in Greek science and philosophy that would outlast the Hellenistic period, continuing into the Roman era and beyond. Contacts with India and with the African kingdom of Kush had important effects. Hellenistic leaders also generated innovations, particularly in science. The spread of a Greek-derived culture, then, set a new framework for intellectual life in a large and diverse portion of the civilized world. This heritage would have pleased the Hellenistic conquerors, who saw cultural expansion as part of their mission.

CREATIVITY IN GREEK AND HELLENISTIC CULTURE

Focal Point: The genius of Greek civilization lay more obviously in various facets of culture than in politics. It was Greek culture that determined the most lasting contributions of this civilization to the Mediterranean world, particularly in art and philosophy, and that served as the key linkage in the larger Hellenistic orbit sketched by Alexander.

Religion, Philosophy, and Science

The Greeks did not create a major religion, and in this they differed from India and to a lesser extent, from China. Greek ideas would ultimately influence great religions, particularly Christianity and to some degree Islam, but this came later. The characteristic Greek religion was a rather primitive affair, derived from animist belief in the spirits of nature elevated into a complex set of gods and goddesses who were seen as interfering in human life. The Greeks thus had a creator or father god, Zeus, who presided over an unruly assemblage of divinities whose functions ranged from regulating the daily passage of the sun (Apollo) or the oceans (Poseidon) to inspiring war or human love and beauty. Specific gods patronized other human activities such as metalworking, the hunt, literature, and history. Regular ceremonies to the gods had real political importance, and many individuals sought the gods' aid in foretelling the future or in assuring a good harvest or good health. Stories of the gods' activities provided rich entertainment and could drive home lessons about appropriate moral behavior, including courage and humility.

This was a religion, then, passed down from earlier Indo-European experience, that served many human needs and cemented community loyalties. It was not, however, intensely spiritual. Interestingly, the basic Indo-European pantheon was the same as that brought to India, which in both cases assumed human form. The Greek use of religion, however, differed considerably from the more other-worldly Indian outcome. Greek religion tended toward a human-centered, worldly approach. Stories of the gods allowed illustration of human qualities, rather like soap operas on a vaster scale; the gods could be jealous, sneaky, lustful, and powerful. Greek religion, like the Indian religion, helped engender an important literary tradition. In the Greek religion, the gods primarily provided good stories or served as vehicles for deeper inquiry into human passions and vulnerabilities. Greek gods were used mainly in terms of what they could do for humankind and what they could reveal about human nature, rather than as sources pushing people toward consideration of higher planes of spirituality or an ultimately divine experience.

Greek religion also had social limitations. Its lack of spiritual passion failed to satisfy many ordinary workers and peasants, particularly when times were hard because of political chaos or economic distress. Popular "mystery" religions, which had more exciting rituals and promised greater spiritual insight in contrast to worldly cares, often swept through Greece with their secret ceremonies, a strong sense of fellowship, and a greater implication of contact with unfathomable divine powers. The importance of mystery religions, to some extent, paralleled the role of Daoism in providing a contrast to more politically directed religion or philosophy, though none of the mystery religions won the currency or durability of Daoism in China.

The limitations of Greek religion also left many literate and educated people dissatisfied. The religion provided stories about how the world came to be as it is, but scant basis for systematic inquiry into nature or human society. And while the dominant religion promoted political loyalty, it did not provide an elaborate basis for ethical thought. Hence, from at least the 6th century onward, many Greek thinkers attempted to generate philosophical systems that were separate from a primarily religious base. The attempt to understand humankind, society, and nature by rational observation and deduction became one of the hallmarks of Greek and Hellenistic culture. The approach was not entirely dissimilar from that of Confucianism in China, but it had different specifics and a different and wider-ranging scope.

Many thinkers sought to generate ethical systems on the basis of rational definitions of right and wrong and some sense of the purpose of life on earth. Socrates (born in 465 B.C.E. and the tutor of Plato, who in turn would teach Aristotle) urged people to consider the bases of right action in terms of rational reflection on goals and consequences. In contrast to earlier Middle Eastern traditions, he thus formulated secular criteria rather than devising rewards and punishments from an otherworldly system. *Aristotle*, perhaps the most important of the Greek philosophers, maintained this ethical system through stressing the importance of moderation in human behavior against the instability of political life in Athens and the excesses of the gods.

During the Hellenistic period other ethical systems were devised. Thus a group called the *Stoics* emphasized an inner moral independence to be cultivated by strict discipline of the body and personal bravery. These ethical systems were major contributions in their own right, attracting many disciples and generating much literary debate; they also would later be blended with Christian religious thought.

Greek philosophy further devoted much attention to defining appropriate political structures. Various constitutional systems were discussed, often in the light of ongoing political disputes between Athens and Sparta. The Athenian philosopher Plato, in the 5th century, devised an ideal government structure in which philosophers would rule. Most Greek political theory stressed the importance of balance with due outlet for aristocratic principles and some popular contribution. Again, religious justifications for political behavior were played down in favor of arguments in terms of utility and practicality or more general definitions of justice. It was in this vein, also, that philosophers, such as Aristotle, discussed social topics like slavery or the conditions of women, providing vigorous defenses for the inevitability and usefulness of slavery and for family structures that would assume women's inferiority.

The idea of a philosophy separate from official religion, though not necessarily hostile to it, also generated considerable emphasis on the powers of human thought. In Athens, Socrates encouraged his pupils to question received wisdom on the ground that the chief human duty was "the improvement of the soul." Socrates himself ran afoul of the Athenian government in the aftermath of the tensions of the Peloponnesian War, for he seemed to be undermining political loyalty itself with his constant questions. But the Socratic principle of thinking things through by means of skeptical questioning, rather than assuming on the basis of authority or faith, became a recurrent strand in classical Greek thinking and education and was part of its bequest to later societies. Socrates' great pupil, *Plato*, accentuated the positive somewhat more strongly in suggesting that human reason could approach an understanding of the perfect forms—the absolutely True, Good, and Beautiful—that he believed underlay nature. Thus a philosophical tradition arose in Greece that tended to play down the importance of human spirituality in favor of a celebration of the human power to think. The result bore some similarities to Chinese Confucianism, though it placed greater emphasis on skeptical questioning and abstract speculations about the basic nature of humanity and the universe.

Greek interest in rationality carried over into inquiry into the underlying order of physical nature. The Greeks were not great empirical scientists, compared for example with the classical Chinese. Relatively few new scientific findings emanated from Athens, though philosophers such as Aristotle did collect large amounts of biological data. The Greek interest lay in speculations about nature's order, and many non-Westerners believe that this tradition continues to inform what they see as an excessive Western passion for seeking sweeping rationality in the universe. Greek belief in rational theorizing produced widespread philosophical commitment to a scientific method that would combine some observations with general concepts. In practice, the Greek concern translated into a host of theories about the motions of the planets and the organization of the elemental principles of earth, fire, air, and water, and into a considerable interest in mathematics as a means of rendering nature's patterns comprehensible. Greek and later Hellenistic work in geometry was particularly impressive, featuring among other achievements the basic theorems of Pythagoras and Euclid's compendium of geometry.

Scientists in the Hellenistic period added some important empirical contributions, especially in studies of anatomy; medical treatises by Galen were not improved upon in the Western world for many centuries. Less fortunately, the Hellenistic astronomer Ptolemy formalized an elaborate theory of the sun's motion around a stationary earth; this new Hellenistic theory contradicted much earlier Middle Eastern astronomy, which had recognized the earth's rotation. The idea of an earth-centered universe seemed to explain many observed phenomena, including eclipses, and this fact along with the sheer reputation of Greek science assured that Ptolemy's theory was long taken as fixed wisdom in Western thought.

Other Hellenistic scientists added more constructively to the observations about planetary motion. Archimedes (c. 287–212 B.C.E.) wrote about mathematics and the measurement of water power. He devised pulley systems to pump out flooded ships and fields and invented novel kinds of fortifications. Other Hellenistic scientists, using dissection on the corpses of criminals, made important discoveries about digestion and the vascular system.

Literature and the Visual Arts

Despite the importance of the rationalist tradition, science and mathematics loomed far less large than art and literature in conveying key cultural values in Greek and Hellenistic culture. The official religion inspired themes for artistic expressions and justifications for temples, statues, and plays devoted to the glories of the gods. But the human-centered qualities of the Greeks also showed through, as artists emphasized the beauty of realistic portrayals of the human form and poets and playwrights used the gods as vehicles for inquiries into the human condition.

All the arts received some attention in classical Mediterranean civilization. Performances of music and dance were vital parts of religious festivals, but their precise styles have not been preserved. Far more durable was the Greek interest in drama, for plays took a central role in this culture. Greek dramatists worked both on comedy and on tragedy, indeed making a formal division between the two approaches that is still part of the Western tradition. On the whole, in contrast to Indian writers, the Greeks placed greater emphasis on tragedy. Their belief in human reason and balance also involved a sense that these virtues were precarious, so that a person could easily overstep and be ensnared in situations of powerful emotion and uncontrollable consequences. The Athenian dramatist *Sophocles,* for example, so insightfully portrayed the psychological flaws of his hero Oedipus that modern psychology long used the term *Oedipus complex* to refer to potentially tragic attachments between a man and his mother. Another Athenian playwright, *Aristophanes,* used similar beliefs in the limitations of human experience to produce a sense of comedy, poking fun at the foibles of human nature.

In addition to defining the concept of drama, enriching the language, providing powerful themes, and maintaining a society that appreciated compelling plays, the Greeks established rules for future societies about how a drama should be written. These rules included an insistence on a coherent plot as opposed to a jumble of unrelated events. These specific precedents, along with the belief that the Greeks had perfected drama, helped shape dramatic writing in societies that looked back to the Greek example for inspiration.

Greek literature contained a strong epic tradition as well, starting with the beautifully crafted tales of the *Iliad* and the *Odyssey.* By the 5th century B.C.E., interest in human affairs led to a new kind of formal historical writing: Herodotus tried to sort out fact from myth in dealing with various Mediterranean cultures, and Thucydides composed a vivid account of the Peloponnesian War.

In the visual arts, the emphasis of classical Mediterranean civilization lay in sculpture and architecture, though Greek artists also advanced in ceramic work. In

Varied column designs marked the progression of Greek architecture from the square Doric sim-plicity (as shown in these pictures of the Parthenon), though Ionic, to the more ornate Corinthian.

Athens's brilliant 5th century B.C.E.—the age of Pericles, Socrates, Sophocles, Aristophanes, and many other intensely creative figures—sculptors such as Phidias developed unprecedented skill in simultaneously realistic and beautiful portrayals of the human form, from lovely goddesses to muscled warriors and athletes.

Greek architecture, from the 8th century B.C.E. onward, emphasized monumental construction, square or rectangular in shape, with columned porticoes. The Greeks devised three distinct styles for their massive buildings, each more ornate than the last: the *Doric,* the *Ionic,* and the *Corinthian.* The Greeks, in short, invented what Westerners and others in the world today still regard as "classical" architecture, though the Greeks themselves were influenced by Egyptian and Cretan models in their preferences. Greece provided abundant stone for ambitious temples, markets, and other public buildings. Many of these same structures were filled with products of the sculptors' workshops. They were also brightly painted, though over the centuries the paint faded so that later imitators came to think of the classical as involving unadorned stone.

Classical Mediterranean art and architecture were intimately linked with the society that produced them. It is tempting, because of the formal role of classical styles in later societies, to attribute a stiffness to Greek art that was not present in the original. Greek structures were built to be used. Temples and marketplaces were part of daily urban life. Classical art was also flexible, according to need. Classical dramas were not merely examples of high art performed in front of a cultural elite. Indeed,

Athens lives in the memory of many intellectuals because of the creativity of the writers and philosophers and of the large audiences that trooped to performances of plays by authors such as Sophocles. Literally thousands of people periodically gathered in the big hillside theaters of Athens and other cities for the new plays and the music and poetry competitions that simultaneously honored the gods.

The Principles of Greek Culture

Overall, the Greek and Hellenistic cultural achievement rested on four major principles. First, the interest in formal political theory, with a strong emphasis on debating the merits of different constitutional structures and assuming that government forms could be planned, obviously reflected the distinctive political atmosphere of Greece. If Greek politics faced frequent crises, its incorporation in political thought and history gave it a long life and wide subsequent influence.

Second, art and sculpture served on the whole to glorify human achievement, starting with a celebration of the beauties of the ideal human form, which was used also to represent the gods.

Third, drama and philosophy stressed the importance of human striving, though comedy might poke fun, and tragedy might emphasize the inevitable limits. This characteristic joined with the emphasis of the visual arts on secular over otherworldly themes. And while ethical philosophers might enjoin moderation, there was a fascination with human energy and striving rather differ-

Greek dramas were staged in this theater of Dionysus. This magnificent outdoor facility was nestled in a hillside, with the stage at the base of seating risers sculpted in stone. The location of the theater reflected its wide public functions.

ent from the more consistent restraint urged in secular Chinese thought.

Fourth, the philosophical and scientific tradition emphasized the validity of logical constructs in understanding the natural world.

The characteristics of Greek philosophy were not totally distinctive, of course, and they built on some earlier features of Middle Eastern culture. Nor was the resultant cultural package uniformly successful. Greek and Hellenistic science was open to more error than the more practical scientific traditions established in classical China and India. The Greek approach also tended to emphasize a significant cultural gap between the educated elite and the common masses. The debates of the philosophers formed part of an aristocratic tradition closed to the ordinary folk. The absence of a strong religious link helped to separate popular beliefs and folklore from the reasoning of the creative intellectuals.

Some degree of gap between literate and nonliterate culture was built into all the classical civilizations. But formal Greek culture was particularly uninterested in adopting popular values, which meant that the various levels of Greek and Hellenistic society shared fewer assumptions, in terms of styles of thought, than was true in China or India. Popular and widely accessible dramatic performances and the public art of the Greek cities narrowed this gap somewhat. With the decline of the city-states, however, and the rise of more general Hellenistic forms in which community art played a lesser role, the cultural gaps stood out in sharper relief.

Hellenistic Culture During and After Alexander

Greek intellectual and artistic life was not a constant. Literature changed considerably between the epic style of Homer and the more controlled dramatic forms of the great Athenian playwrights of the 5th century B.C.E. History writing, similarly, moved away from epic storytelling toward more analytical inquiries into the characteristics of different cultures or (with Thucydides) the causes of major developments such as the Peloponnesian War. In architecture, change was more limited, but there was a tendency to move toward more elaborate decorative motifs over time.

Inevitably, the decline of the Greek city-states and the emergence of the larger Hellenistic zone, from the 4th to the 3d centuries B.C.E., produced still more innovation in the Greek cultural tradition. Literature, for example, declined. Alexandria in Egypt became a dominant center of literary studies, based on a vast Greek library. Older stories and plays were preserved and ana-

DOCUMENT

The Power of Greek Drama

This section consists of two passages, one by the great tragedian, Aeschylus (525–456 B.C.E.), and one by Athens's leading writer of comedies, Aristophanes (c. 450–385 B.C.E.). Aeschylus's passage, from the play *Libation Bearers*, sees Orestes confront his mother Clytemnestra after having killed her lover and suspecting that she had earlier killed his father. Clytemnestra has learned what Orestes did and knows what is to come; she asks a slave:

Clytemnestra: Swift! Bring me an axe that can slay. I will know now if I am to win or lose. I stand here on the height of misery.

[Orestes *enters with his companion* Pylades.]

Orestes: It is you I seek. The other has had his fill. You love him—you shall lie in the same grave.

Clytemnestra: Stop—oh, my son. Look—my breast. Your heavy head dropped on it and you slept, oh, many a time, and your baby mouth where never a tooth was, sucked the milk and so you grew—

Orestes: Oh, Pylades, what shall I do? My mother—Awe holds me. May I spare?

Pylades: Where then Apollo's words and the dread compact? Make all men enemies but not the gods.

Orestes: Good counsel. I obey. You—follow me. I lead you where he lies to kill you there.

Clytemnestra: It seems, my son, that you will kill your mother.

Orestes: Not I. You kill yourself.

Clytemnestra: I am alive—I stand beside my grave. I hear the song of death. [*They go out and the* Chorus *sings that her fate is just.*] Lift up your head, oh, house. I see the light.

[*The palace doors roll back.* Orestes *stands over the two dead bodies.*]

Orestes: I am blameless of the one. He died the death adulterers must die. But she who planned this thing of horror against her husband by whom she had borne beneath her girdle the burden of children—what think you of her? Snake or viper was she? Her very touch would rot a man.

Chorus: Woe—woe—Oh, fearful, deeds!

Orestes: Did she do it or did she not? The proofs you know—the deed and the death. I am victor but vile, polluted.

Chorus: One trouble is here—another comes.

Orestes: Hear me and learn, for I know how it will end. I am borne along a runaway horse. My thoughts are out of bounds. Fear at my heart is leaping up. Before my reason goes—oh, you my friends, I say I killed my mother—yet not without reason—she was vile and she killed my father and God hated her—Look—look—women—there—there—black—all black, and long hair twisting like snakes. Oh, let me go.

Chorus: What fancies trouble you, O son, faithful to your father? Do not fear.

---

lyzed, often with great intelligence. Historical information was elaborated, and historical biography came into its own. There were also many disputes, some learned and some very petty, about the principles of literary excellence. But little new drama was produced.

Greek art and sculpture continued to dominate Hellenistic output, and the commercial wealth of the early Hellenistic kingdoms encouraged a vast amount of new building and decoration. While no new styles emerged, there was some movement toward more sentimental, emotional statuary.

Hellenistic intellectuals, in addition to their concerns with ethical systems, concentrated heavily on de-

veloping new knowledge in science and mathematics. Alexander and the Hellenistic dynasty in Egypt encouraged this work, and the expansion of cultural exchange in the Mediterranean in the Middle East also favored new research. Hellenistic thinkers thus preserved Greek scientific achievements and added significant new elements. Their work provided most of the scientific learning available to the Western world for almost 2000 years, and it also set a durable basis for scientific research in the Middle East and North Africa. Astronomical charts and maps improved greatly, despite the confusion about the earth as the center of the universe. Geography also improved, and one scientist was able to

Orestes: No fancies. My mother has sent them. They throng upon me and from their eyes blood drips, blood of hate. You see them not? I—I see them. They drive me. I cannot stay.

[*He rushes out.*]

Chorus: Oh, where will this frenzy of evil end.

Aristophanes' play *Plutus* mocks what he sees as the reigning values of Athens. The passage begins with a slave asking his respectable-looking master why they are following a blind man:

Chremylus: I'll tell you why, straight out. Of all my slaves I know that you are the best, most constant—thief. Well—I have been a good, religious man, but always poor—no luck.

Slave: And so you have.

Chremylus: So then I want to ask—not for myself, I've pretty well shot all my arrows now—but for my son, my only son. I prayed that he might change his ways and turn into a scoundrel, wicked, rotten through and through, and so live happily ever after. The god replied, the first man I fell in with to follow.

Slave: Yes—Quite good. Of course, a blind man can see it's better nowadays to be a rotten scoundrel.

[*The man in front proves to be Wealth himself, not aware of his power because he is blind. The two others proceed to enlighten him.*]

Chremylus: Why everything there is, is just Wealth's slave. The girls, now, if a poor man comes along, will they look at him? But just let a rich one, and he can get a deal more than he wants.

Slave: Oh, not the sweet, good, modest girls. They never would ask a man for money.

Chremylus: No? What then?

Slave: Presents—the kind that cost a lot—that's all.

Chremylus: Well, all the voting's done for Wealth of course. You man our battleships. You own our army. When you're an ally, that side's sure to win. Nobody ever has enough of you. While all things else a man can have too much of—of love.

Slave: Of loaves.

Chremylus: Of literature.

Slave: Of candy.

Chremylus: Of fame.

Slave: Of figs.

Chremylus: Of manliness.

Slave: Of mutton.

Questions: What were the purposes of comedy and tragedy in classical Athens? How does Aeschylus's passage move toward a starkly tragic view? How is a truly tragic situation for a person defined? What values might an Athenian audience have had in order to enjoy a satire such as that by Aristophanes? Are the Greek ideas of comedy and tragedy suggested in the passage different from American definitions today?

calculate the circumference of the earth within 200 miles. Little advancement occurred in biology and medicine, however, beyond summaries of Greek research in textbook fashion. In fact, interest in astrology and magic increased.

Though Hellenistic science won few new achievements after the end of the 3rd century, Hellenistic thinkers had done more than simply preserve knowledge and spread it. Their vigor, and the comprehensive art and philosophy they took over from the classical Greeks, greatly impressed the Romans as they moved into wider contacts with the Mediterranean world, just as the Hellenistic era was fading away.

ANALYSIS

Defining Social History

Over the past 30 years, historians have argued about the proper focus of their work. Should history focus on great achievements by major individuals? Or should social history, with its wider definition of significance, guide our view of the past?

Until fairly recently, many historians wrote as if the principal elements of the past that were worth recapturing involved formal politics—the changes in the structure of the state, the rise and fall of major political leaders, and their military battles—and the generation of major new ideas. Other elements of a society's structure might be recognized. How the masses of people lived was relevant insofar as it affected taxation levels (and thus what political leaders could do), political protest, and military service. New inventions or big changes in the economic or social system, such as an increase of slavery, could figure in. But the detailed work of the historian focused on charting and explaining what the leading statesmen and intellectuals were doing.

This type of historical focus has much to recommend it. Often, the key legacies of a major time period or civilization seem to lie in its dominant political forms, artistic styles, and religious concepts. In classical Greece, as we have seen, political and intellectual achievements not only commanded great attention at the time, at least in the upper classes, but also contributed greatly to later societies after the Greek and Hellenistic ages had ended. We may well look to Pericles, Socrates, or Phidias for example and inspiration.

Yet, modern historical research does not begin or end with the doings of the greatest statesmen and thinkers. The relatively new field of social history, which has gained momentum in the United States and elsewhere over the past quarter-century, increasingly defines a wider agenda. Social historians do not deny the significance of political structures, wars, or philosophical systems, but they argue that history also consists of the doings of ordinary people and other facets of life such as family activities, death, disease, work, and leisure. For social historians, the past is much larger than was once considered the case. It includes many groups of actors besides the elite: women, peasants and craftsmen, children and youth. Social historians integrate great ideas with the beliefs of large numbers of people about how the universe worked or what the good life was, and they combine attention to political forms with an understanding of the social structures and problems that helped generate these forms.

Social historians do not always have an easy time fleshing out their topics. Ordinary people, for example, did not conveniently describe their beliefs for posterity the way thinkers like Aristotle or Confucius did. Particularly for early and classical civilizations, when records have been lost and most people were illiterate, it is not easy to characterize work and family values beneath the elite.

Partly for this reason, many world histories until recently defined their domains in terms of formal governments and intellectual history alone. One world historian leaves ordinary people out simply because, in his view, only the groups that produce major milestones are worth attending to; the supporting cast is irrelevant. Another world historian once argued that the lives of ordinary people changed little, at least during the long reign of agriculturally based civilizations, so there is little to know about them in comparison with the obvious ups and downs of governments and artistic styles. Yet social history, for all its complexity, continues to gain ground, determining much of the subject matter of world history, for three major reasons.

First, the history of "unconventional" groups and topics helps us understand these same topics in societies today. It is just as important to have a historical perspective on women's roles, and to see how they changed and varied in the past, as it is to understand the evolution of judicial systems. We comprehend current work patterns better in our own society and elsewhere if we see what they emerged from. At certain times, work, women's roles, or family forms may change only gradually, even amid lively political developments. But the reverse may also be true, and there is no question that social-historical change can be charted and assessed.

Second, patterns and changes in the social history realm intimately affect the ways governments and intellectuals function, and the reverse is true as well. In classical civilizations, such as China and Greece, a substantial gulf often separated wealthy, literate aristocrats or bureaucrats and ordinary peasants or slaves. Yet, governments had to be organized in such a way as to keep ordinary people contented or repressed (or they had to contend with protest). Confucianism tried to deal with this issue; Greek city-state governments experimented almost constantly with systems that would preserve a class structure yet provide sufficient harmony for political life. Intellectuals might spin out new ideas from their own creative genius, but their ideas interacted in the long run with popular beliefs. One key way to grasp a civilization or the causes of change is to talk about how formal institutions and intellectual styles related to the masses of people and the basic structures of life.

Finally, ordinary people and the structures they were involved with could leave legacies, just as intellectual and political leaders did. Later periods or societies would thus build on earlier patterns of work, ways to treat children, or definitions of slavery.

Social history provides a means of testing the relationship between the people and their daily institutions, and the more heralded ideas and institutions of officialdom. We will see that the view of the world of a Greek slave or wife would differ substantially from that of Pericles or Aristotle. This is not just an isolated finding; it reflects a certain lack of coherence among different groups in overall Greek culture that limited the staying power of the civilization.

Among the social sciences during the past 30 years, social history has proved to be one of the most fruitful sources of new knowledge and analysis. The result is a redefinition of the past and of the kinds of questions to raise about how societies function.

Questions: What are some of the key problems of social history? What would a social historian emphasize in discussing the major features of classical Chinese civilization? Besides knowing about Greek and Hellenistic political development and intellectual styles, what else would the social historian try to pinpoint in summing up this classical civilization?

PATTERNS OF GREEK AND HELLENISTIC SOCIETY

Focal Point: Greek and Hellenistic society mirrored many standard social features of an agricultural economy, including a large peasantry but also a landowning aristocracy, and dependence on commerce combined with suspicion of it. Patriarchal family structures predominated. Distinctive features included the importance of slavery and a slightly greater ambivalence about women than was true in classical China.

Economic and Social Structure

The economic and social structure of classical Greece, including the colonies it sent out around the Mediterranean, had many features in common with other agricultural civilizations. It particularly resembled other civilizations in which an invading, warlike group settled down to agriculture. Thus, while 8th-century Greece clearly depended on farming, it had an aristocracy based on ownership of large estates and special claims to military service. At the same time, many farmers were independent, owning their plots of land and claiming some political and social status just as tribal soldiers had once done. But—again in a common pattern—the Greek economy evolved, particularly as trade rose and cities grew. Accordingly, social structure became more complex, and inequalities widened in many ways.

There were also, however, distinctive features in the Greek pattern. Because mainland Greece was so rocky and mountainous—a terrain unsuited to grain growing—many city-states came to depend unusually heavily on seagoing trade and colonies. Colonization and frequent wars produced abundant opportunities to seize slaves, and classical Mediterranean society maintained greater dependence on slavery than was true of Indian or Chinese civilizations in the same period. Correspondingly, while Greece developed many craft products, somewhat less attention was paid to the improvement of manufacturing technology than either China or India displayed. This reflected Greek concern for science as a philosophical system rather than as a collection of useful empirical data, as well as the availability of cheap slave labor.

The pronounced aristocratic tone, based on the importance of the landed elite, persisted in society as well as politics. Despite important differences among political forms, aristocratic assemblies and officials formed the most coherent single city-state theme in Greek politics. Aristocrats had the time to devote to political life as the Greeks defined it, and they argued that they brought special virtues, education and disinterest, to the political process. Aristocratic cultural patronage also helped give shape to Mediterranean art, literature, and the education of aristocratic youth—boys above all.

The aristocratic tenor of Greek society showed in the ambiguous position of merchants. Greece progressively became involved with the growth of trade. Yet, aristocratic suspicion of merchant values persisted, particularly among conservatives who blasted change in the name of traditional austerity. Sparta, which had unusually fertile land, tried to downplay trade altogether. Its deliberately cumbersome coinage discouraged commerce, while aristocratic estate owners concentrated on directing a semi-slave population of farm workers. Even in bustling Athens, most merchants were foreigners, mainly from the Middle East. Overall, merchants held higher status in the classical Mediterranean than in Confucian China, but their standing was less firm than in India (see Chapter 7).

Rural Life and Agriculture

The bulk of the population of the Greek and Hellenistic world was rural, even though the most important political and cultural activities occurred in cities. Rural peoples preserved distinctive rituals and beliefs. Many Greek farmers, for example, annually gathered for a spring passion play to celebrate the recovery of the goddess of fertility from the lower world. This event was seen as a vital preparation for planting and also carried hints of the possibility of life after death—a prospect important to many people who endured a life of hard labor and poverty. A substantial population of free farmers played a vital role in the early politics of the Greek city-states.

At the same time there was a constant tendency for large landlords to force these farmers to become tenants or laborers or to join the swelling crowds of the urban lower class. Tensions between tyrants and aristocrats, as well as between democratic reformers and aristocratic conservatives, often revolved around farmers' attempts to preserve their independence and shake off the heavy debts they had incurred. Waves of popular protest were not uncommon. Class tension was encouraged by special features of Greek agriculture. Farming was complicated by the fact that soil conditions were not ideal for grain growing, yet grain was the staple of life. As Greek society advanced, there was a natural tendency to specialize in cash crops, which would allow importation of grain from areas more appropriate to its production—parts of the northern Middle East, Sicily, and North Africa. In mainland Greece, the production of olives for cooking oil and grapes for wine making spread widely. The products were well suited to Greek soil conditions, but they required capital to install—a five-year wait was necessary before either vines or olive trees would begin to yield significant fruit. To convert to olives and grapes, farmers went into debt and often failed; aristocratic estate owners with more abundant resources converted more successfully, buying up the land of failed farmers in the process.

Mediterranean agriculture thus became unusually market oriented. In comparision with other agricultural civilizations, relatively few farmers produced simply for their own needs except in the early period before civilization fully developed. Imports of basic foods were more extensive here than in India or China. This was one obvious spur to empire: to try to assure access to adequate grain supplies. Greek expansion pushed out mainly toward sources of grain in Sicily and around the Black Sea.

Large estate agriculture gained further momentum in the Hellenistic kingdoms. Vast estates spread out in Egypt and the Middle East, requiring specialized banks and financial agents. Elements of this capitalistic agriculture affected Mediterranean history later under both the Roman Empire and Arab rule. The system also helped generate the surpluses needed for spreading Hellenistic culture and its urban monuments.

For peasants themselves, the importance of commercial farming created an unusual tendency of farming families to cluster in small towns of 3000 or more inhabitants rather than the villages with 4 to 600 people typi-

Greek commerce expanded along with the colonies. In the painting on the interior of the Arkesilas Cup, dating from 560 B.C.E., the king of Cyrene, a Greek colony in North Africa, is shown supervising the preparation of hemp or flax for export.

cal of other parts of Europe, Asia, and Africa. Mediterranean rural towns provided trading facilities for grain and other goods, while the peasants who lived there could still travel to the surrounding fields for work. These rural agglomerations would remain typical around the Mediterranean even after the classical period had ended and the region underwent new political and cultural divisions.

Slavery and Production

Slavery was a key ingredient of the classical Mediterranean economy. Philosophers like Aristotle produced elaborate justifications for the necessity of slavery to a proper society: without slaves, how would aristocrats learn what must be learned to maintain culture or have the time to cultivate political virtue? Slaves were acquired as a result of wars, unusually frequent in the Mediterranean world compared with China and India. Athenians used slaves for household service and also as workers in their vast silver mines, which hastened the progress of Athens's empire and commercial operations, although working conditions were appallingly bad. Sparta used *helots*, or unfree labor, extensively for agricultural work. The Spartan system relied less on prisoners taken from war, for it was imposed by Indo-European conquerors over previous residents in the area. Of the approximately 270,000 people in 5th-century Athens, 80,000 to 100,000 were slaves, while helots in Sparta outnumbered their masters by a ratio of nearly ten to one. In cities such as Athens some slaves enjoyed considerable independence and could earn money on their own. Manumission, or freeing, of valued slaves was also common. Yet, slave systems also required extensive military controls.

Slavery also helps explain why Greece was not especially interested in technological innovations applicable to agriculture or manufacturing. The Greeks made important advances in shipbuilding and navigation, which were vital to their trading economy. But technology designed to improve production of food or manufactured goods did not figure largely in this civilization. Abundant slave labor probably discouraged any concern for more efficient production methods. So did a sense that the true goals of humankind were artistic and political. One Hellenistic scholar, for example, refused to write a handbook on engineering because "the work of an engineer and everything that ministers to the needs of life is ignoble and vulgar." As a result of this outlook, Mediterranean society lagged behind both India and China in production technology. Population growth, also, was less substantial. A host of features of Greek life, including aspects of politics, thus hinged on the slave system and its requirements.

Men, Women, and Social Divisions

Greek society emphasized the importance of a tight family structure, with husband and father firmly in control. Women had vital economic functions, particularly in farming and artisan families. A woman with a powerful personality could command a major place within a household, and a free woman's responsibility for family possessions was protected by law. But in law and culture, women were held inferior. Even the activities of free women were directed toward their husbands' interests. The raping of a free woman, though a crime, was a lesser offense than seducing her, since seduction meant winning her affections away from her husband. Families burdened with too many children sometimes put female infants to death. Pericles stated common beliefs about women when he noted: "For a woman not to show more weakness than is natural to her sex is a great glory, and not to be talked about for good or for evil among

men." On the other hand, the oppression of women was probably less severe in this civilization than in China, for many Greek women were active in business and controlled a substantial minority of all urban property holdings.

Though Greek culture represented women abundantly as goddesses, often with revered powers, and celebrated the female form as well as the male form in art, the real cultural status of women was low. Aristotle even argued that women provided only an abode for a child developing before birth, as male seed alone contained the full germ of the child. Marriages were arranged by a woman's father; husbands could divorce wives at will, whereas women had to go to court. Adultery was tolerated for men but was grounds for divorce in the case of women. Even within the upper-class household, where women had vital functions including the supervision of domestic slaves, men entertained their guests in separate rooms.

Relations between men and women in Greek society, at least in the aristocracy, help explain the Greek attitude toward homosexuality. Upper-class boys and girls were often brought up separately, which increased the likelihood of homosexual relationships. While some Athenians ridiculed homosexual love, most saw love affairs between two young people of the same sex as a normal stage of life. Homosexuality was not defined as an exclusive preference, and many people in later life emphasized heterosexuality. Older men sometimes took younger men as partners, a practice that the philosopher Plato and others praised as a means of training the young in practical wisdom. Spartans stressed same-sex love as a means of inspiring heroic deeds in battle. Some contemporary psychologists have speculated that the Greeks' frank acceptance of homosexual impulses limited neurosis among adults, as it did not conflict with substantial devotion to marriage.

As with many aspects of Greek culture, homosexuality was almost certainly more pronounced in the aristocracy than in other social groups. Male and female peasants and urban workers worked together and generally mingled more freely, which may have promoted greater emphasis on heterosexuality, and these groups simply lacked the time for some of the more elaborate sexual arrangements.

Other cultural divisions complicated Greek society. Peasants shared beliefs in the gods and goddesses about which the playwrights wrote, but their religious celebrations were largely separate from those of the upper classes. At times, Greek peasants showed their interest in some of the more emotional religious practices imported from the Middle East, which provided more color than the official ceremonies of the Greek pantheon and spiced the demanding routines of work.

Different beliefs reflected and furthered the real social tensions of Greek and Hellenistic societies, particularly as these societies became more commercial and large estates challenged the peasants' desire for independent property ownership. Popular rebellions did not succeed in dislodging the landowning aristocracy, but they contributed to several political shifts in classical Greece and to the ultimate decline in the political stability of the city-states and later the Hellenistic kingdoms.

Interestingly, conditions for women improved somewhat in the Hellenistic period, in an atypical trend. Artists and playwrights began to display more interest in women and their conditions. Women in Hellenistic cities appeared more freely in public, and some aristocratic women gained new functions—for example, in forming cultural clubs. Several queens exercised great power, often ruling harshly. Cratesiclea, the mother of a Hellenistic king in Sparta, willingly served as a hostage to help form an alliance with a more powerful state; she reputedly said, "send me away, wherever you think this body of mine will be most useful to Sparta." More widely, Hellenistic women began to take an active role in commerce, though they still needed male guardianship over property.

CONCLUSION

A Complex Legacy

Classical Greece and its Hellenistic successors lasted for about 600 years. While major political and social changes took place during this span, some durable characteristics also developed. Durability resulted from the power of key cultural forms, the settled routines of the peasants, and the absence of major technological shifts.

Greece's political legacy obviously lay more in the realm of ideas and diverse examples than in enduring political institutions like China's emperor and bureaucracy, though the next leading Mediterranean city-state, Rome, replicated some Greek structures in part. Joined with shining ideals of citizenship was the equally important heritage of slavery. On the whole, Greek art and philosophy formed the most lasting contributions of this classical civilization. Here, interesting contrasts developed with the final center of classical civilization in India. India's cohesion also rested heavily on culture rather than on strong empires, but the culture was much more

religious than that of Greece and the Hellenistic kingdoms. Perhaps for this reason, India negotiated the problem of linking masses of ordinary people to its value system differently, as despite a rigid social hierarchy it offered a flexible culture in which a variety of groups could participate and gain identity. The impact of Greek thought on subsequent generations of intellectuals in various parts of the world was profound, but its relationship to ordinary people has often been complex.

A final complexity in dealing with classical Greece (and then Rome) involves its relationship to us—to contemporary residents of North America. For most Americans, Greece constitutes the first phase of "our own" classical past. The framers of the Constitution of the United States were intensely conscious of Greek precedents. Designers of public buildings in the United States have dutifully copied Greek and Roman models. Plato and Aristotle continue to be thought of as founders of our philosophical tradition, skillful teachers still imitate the Socratic method in seeking dialogues with students, and reliance on scientific methods of inquiry owes much to Greek formulations. The Western educational tradition has long invited elaborate explorations of the Greco-Roman past as part of the standard intellectual equipment for the educated person.

The world history approach requires the classical Mediterranean to be seen in a larger framework—one in which its development is compared with other great classical traditions. Although less familiar to the West, the classical patterns of China and India are no less important and no less valid. From a comparative standpoint, the civilization of the classical Mediterranean was inferior to that of China and India in key respects. The challenge is to comprehend the leading features of Greek and Roman civilization and recognize our debt to them while recognizing the vital importance of equally fascinating formative periods in other parts of the world. The sense of reverence to Greece and the Hellenistic world, which remains an identifiable feature of Western culture today, must not preclude comparisons with the other creative classical civilizations—civilizations to which even more people in southern and eastern Asia feel reverence as they define their own identities in the late 20th century.

FURTHER READINGS

Two good surveys on classical Greece are K. Dover's *The Greeks* (1981) and F. J. Frost's *Greek Society* (1980); both have bibliographies. An older study on Greek culture is extremely solid: H. D. F. Kitto's *The Greeks* (1957). On

Hellenism, M. M. Austin's *The Hellenistic World from Alexander to the Roman Conquest* (1981) is an excellent introduction.

Works on key special topics are M. Crawford and D. Whitehead's *Archaic and Classical Greece* (1983), A. R. Burn's *Persia and the Greeks* (1962), and M. M. Austin and P. Vidal-Naquet's *Economic and Social History of Ancient Greece* (1978). On Greek intellectual life, see W. Burkert's *Greek Religions* (1985) and G. E. R. Lloyd's *The Revolutions of Wisdom: Studies in the Claims and Practices of Ancient Greek Science* (1987). Particular features of Greek society are treated in Moses Finley's *Slavery in the Ancient World* (1972), an exciting study, and Sarah Pomeroy's *Goddesses, Whores, Wives, and Slaves: Women in Classical Antiquity* (1975).

An excellent way to approach Greek history is through documents from the period itself. See Herodotus's *The Histories* (trans. de Selincourt) (1972) and M. Crawford, ed., *Sources for Ancient History* (1983).

Though dealing with a later period, key social features of the region are explored in F. Braude's *The Mediterranean and the Mediterranean World* (2 v., 1972), a vivid illustration of what social history is.

7

Religious Rivalries and India's Golden Age

1600–1000 Period of Aryan invasions

1200–700 Sacred Vedas composed

c. 1500 Fall of Harappan civilization

700–c. 550 Era of unrivaled Brahman dominance

c. 542–483 Life of the Buddha

322–185 Time of the Mauryan Empire

322–298 Chandragupta Maurya rules

327–325 Alexander the Great's invasion

1600 B.C.E.   1200 B.C.E.   700 B.C.E.   500 B.C.E.

INTRODUCTION

The development of a new civilization in India after the long period of disruption following Harappa's fall around 1500 B.C.E. completed—along with those in China and the Mediterranean—the basic roster of classical civilizations that arose after 1000 B.C.E. The new foundations for this civilization were laid between 1500 and 500 B.C.E. by the nomadic Aryan invaders who were moving into India during the centuries when Harappa collapsed. By the end of this period, fairly large states, ruled by kings who claimed divine descent, controlled much of the fertile farmland that made up the Ganges River plains. Cities had developed, originally around the palaces of these monarchs and later at the sites of important religious shrines and regional market centers. A rich and increasingly influential merchant class joined the Aryan priests and warriors at the top of the Indian social hierarchy.

Ritual divisions and restrictions on intermarriage between these three groups grew more rigid as the increasingly complex caste hierarchy became a pervasive force in Indian life. Above all, the Vedic priests, or brahmans, emerged as the dominant force in Indian society and culture. Their literacy and the magical aura that surrounded the vital ceremonies they performed rendered them the makers and chief advisors of kings, the dispensers of the blessings (or curses) of the gods, and the most revered and privileged of India's elite social groups.

Even as the brahmans' power peaked, however, forces were building in Indian society that threatened to alter fundamentally the course of civilized development in South Asia. Weary of the empty rituals associated with sacrifices to the gods and the power-seeking and materialism of the priestly class, numerous holy men and religious seers had arisen by the 6th century B.C.E. From these holy men a number of major religious thinkers emerged who tried to discover and propagate more meaningful forms of religious belief and worship.

The most successful of these thinkers, the Buddha, founded one of the great world religions—a religion that for centuries provided a powerful challenge to the brahmans and many of the ancient Vedic beliefs and practices. The rivalry that developed between the brahmans and the followers of the Buddha helped define and reshape India's cultural core. The brahmans defended and reinvigorated the ancient Vedic rites and beliefs, and, drawing heavily on these beliefs, they promoted the growth of the religion we know as *Hinduism*. By the first centuries C.E., it was clear that a revived Hinduism had survived the Buddhist challenge. Though Buddhism would remain an important force in many parts of India for another millennium, it would eventually all but die out in the land of its birth.

The Buddha's teachings also contributed to the establishment of India's first genuine empire. Beginning in the late 4th century B.C.E., the rulers of a local dynasty in eastern India, the Maurya, began to build what would become the largest empire in premodern India. The most successful of the Mauryan monarchs, Ashoka (268–232 B.C.E.), converted to Buddhism and then tried to govern according to Buddhist precepts and to spread the religion to neighboring parts of Asia. The Mauryan Empire proved to be short-lived, however. When it collapsed, it was followed by another round of nomadic invasions through the Himalayan passes in the northwest, and the subcontinent was again fragmented politically. Many of the dynasties that followed the Mauryas dedicated themselves to the promotion of either Buddhism or the brahman counteroffensive. But in the early 4th century C.E., there arose in north India a powerful new dynasty, the Gupta, that was firmly committed to the reassertion of the brahmans' dominance.

The Gupta rulers' patronage of Hinduism reaffirmed the position of the brahmans as high priests and political advisors and led to an age of splendid Hindu achievement in architecture, painting, and sculpture as well as philosophy, literature, and the sciences. The Gupta Empire was considerably smaller than that estab-

268–237 Ashoka is emperor of India	170–165 Yueh-chi invasions	1–105 Kushana empire in the northwest	319–540 Gupta Empire
	200 B.C.E.–200 C.E. Period of greatest Buddhist influence		405 Fa-hsien's (Fa-xian's) pilgrimage
	c. 150 Indo–Greek invasions		541 First Hun invasion
c. 300 Kautilya's *Arthashastra* is written			606–647 Harsha's Empire
300 B.C.E.	100 B.C.E.	100 C.E.	300 C.E.

Perhaps the most frequently depicted Indian religious image is the god Shiva, here portrayed in a South Indian bronze. The position of the god's hands or the objects held in them each represent a different aspect of his power, which is simultaneously creative and destructive.

lished by the Mauryas, and the dynasty did not rule a good deal longer. But the ideas and institutions that were solidified during the Gupta era gave Indian civilization the strength and resilience to withstand the shock of yet another round of foreign invasions, beginning with the ravages of the Huns in the first half of the 6th century C.E.

This overview of the critical millennium of Indian history between c. 500 B.C.E. and 500 C.E. suggests several underlying patterns. One of the most critical of these patterns is the predominance in Indian history of political disunity and the short-lived character of even the most powerful Indian empires and dynasties. In con-

trast to China, where unity was the norm and disunity was viewed as unnatural and harmful, India has been divided into rival kingdoms throughout most of its history. This has meant that regional cultural diversity and local identities have been more pronounced in India than in China. In fact, the very name *India* and the idea of the continent as a single political unit did not exist until foreign rulers, the British, conceived them in the 19th century C.E.

Also in contrast to China, where scholar-bureaucrats and strong states were the mainstays of civilization, the brahmans, and social institutions such as the caste system, have been the key to the remarkable persistence of civilization in India. Rather than vanquish the brahmans and destroy the caste system, foreign invaders have frequently been converted by them and have established themselves as warrior-kings near the top of the caste hierarchy. Thus, despite periodic foreign invasions and persistent political divisions, common religious ideas and distinctive forms of social organization have provided the basis for an underlying unity for most of the diverse ethnic groups of South Asia, from Vedic times to the present. Religion and social organization held Indian civilization together durably but more loosely than political culture united China.

THE AGE OF BRAHMAN DOMINANCE

Focal Point: Over most of the areas in India where the Aryans settled, religious leaders or brahmans became the dominant force in Indian civilization in the millennium after about 1500 B.C.E. In this era, the *caste system* also came to form the backbone of the Indian social order, with brahman and warrior groups sharing political power and the highest social status. By about 500 B.C.E., several major challenges to this social order had emerged. The most enduring and serious of these proved to be the new religion that coalesced around the teachings of the Buddha.

The forces that made for the renewal of civilization in South Asia after the fall of Harappa were initially centered not on the great plains of the Ganges and Indus river systems but in the foothills of the *Himalaya Mountains.* Tribes of Aryan warrior-herders settled in the lush valleys of the cool hills. The hills provided abundant pasturage for their herds of horses and cattle, and the wooded valleys were easier to clear for farming than the jungle-covered plains along the Ganges and its tributaries. In the hill regions, single Aryan tribes or confederations of tribal groups developed small states—in many ways similar to those in Homeric Greece—that were based on a combination of sedentary agriculture and livestock breeding. The territories of most of these states extended no farther than the hills surrounding a single large valley or several adjoining valley systems. Most of the states were republics ruled collectively by a council made up of the free warrior elite. Individual leaders were usually called kings, even though their offices and powers more closely resembled those of tribal chieftains. They were elected or removed from office by a vote of the warriors' councils.

The hill republics provided an environment well suited to the preservation of traditional Aryan values and lifestyles. Wars between the numerous hill states were frequent, as were feuds and cattle raids. Thus, the warrior elites were kept busy at pastimes that brought them both wealth and honor. The republics nurtured the spirit of independence that had been strong among the invading Aryan tribes and hostility toward those who attempted to concentrate political authority in the hands of a single ruler.

The warrior elites were also careful to keep the power of the brahmans in check, and the hill cultures fostered a healthy skepticism with regard to the priests and the gods they worshiped. One early hymn reported, for example, that "One and another say, There is no Indra [the god of thunder and war]. Who hath beheld him? Whom then shall we honor?" In another hymn the brahmans, chanting their prayers, are compared to croaking frogs gathered about a pond in the rainy season. Given these trends, it is not surprising that the hill regions were major centers of religious ferment from the 6th century B.C.E. onward. One of the greatest religious reformers of all time, the Buddha, was from one of these republics, as were the founders of several other, less well-known Indian religions, such as Jainism.

The Kingdoms of the Ganges Plains

As Aryan settlement spread in the last millennium B.C.E. from the Indus region and Himalayan foothills to vast plains of the Ganges River system, republics and religious skeptics gave way to kings and powerful brahman priests. Though these regions eventually became the heartlands of great empires, in the middle centuries of the last millennium B.C.E. they were divided into a patchwork of rival kingdoms. The lowland rulers were usually drawn from the warrior elite, but they held power in their own right rather than deriving it from selection by warrior councils. Excepting their influential brahman advisors, there were no formal checks on the power and authority of the kings. Many kings claimed descent from divine ancestors, and their thrones were normally inherited by their sons. All considered themselves to be the supreme war leaders, chief judges, and protectors of the peoples in their domains.

As these roles suggest, the powers and privileges these kings enjoyed were justified by the duties they performed. The great Indian epic the *Ramayana* and other sources from this period stress the duties and obligations of righteous monarchs. They were expected to protect the realm from outside invaders and internal social conflicts. They were instructed to revere the brahmans and follow their advice, to patronize public works, and to rule in ways that promoted the welfare of their people. Ideally, Vedic kings were supposed to be hardworking, honest, and accessible to their most lowly subjects. There are even passages in the ancient texts that justify the violent overthrow of evil rulers.

It is highly unlikely that monarchs who lived up to all these high ideals would have long survived the court intrigues and the assaults of rival rulers that were commonplace in the Vedic era. In fact, the sources from this period suggest a darker side to kingship that may have been closer to the realities of the age. Kings lived in constant fear for their thrones and lives. They were threatened by internal rivals, including their own sons, and also by neighboring monarchs who periodically tested their strength in battle. A ruler's survival depended on the extensive use of spies and informers, a strong and loyal palace guard, and his courage and skills as a military commander.

Sources of Brahman Power

Though most of the rulers of the kingdoms on the Ganges plains were members of the warrior elite, brahmans residing at the court centers often exercised more real power. Their positions as the educators of the princes who would someday rule and as the chief advisors to the rulers themselves naturally made them influential figures in the ruling circles. Like the scholar-gentry in China, their literacy in a society where few could read or write made the brahmans obvious candidates for administrative positions, from heads of bureaucratic departments to judges and tax collectors. In addition, only the brahmans knew how to perform the sacred rituals that were essential to the coronation of a new king. They alone knew the rites that conferred divine status on a monarch—and without divine status a ruler's legitimacy was in doubt. Once the ruler was installed, brahman astrologers foretold his future and regulated his daily schedule, instructing him when to make war or mate with his wives.

As the brahmans' pivotal role in court ceremonies and prophecy indicates, their positions of power and prestige were linked above all to their capacity to mediate between the gods and humans. The key function of the priests of the early Aryan invaders was to offer sacrifices to the gods and spirits who intervened continuously in human affairs. By the 7th and 6th centuries B.C.E., the sacrifices themselves had in a very real sense become more powerful than the gods to whom they were offered. By this time it was widely believed that if the sacrifice was done correctly, the god to whom it was directed had no choice but to grant the wish of the petitioner for whom the brahmans had performed the ceremony. Thus, a king could ensure victory, a peasant village sufficient rainfall, or a barren woman fertility if the proper ceremony was conducted flawlessly. Only the brahmans were capable of performing the ceremony and allowed to read the sacred Vedic texts where the prayers and instructions for various types of sacrifices were set forth. Only they had memorized the steps of the sacrificial rituals and mastered the techniques of preparing the sacrificial offerings correctly. Their monopoly over the sacred rites ensured that brahmans would be honored and feared, even by the strongest of warrior-kings.

Only a small percentage of the brahmans in a given kingdom served as advisors at the court or as state administrators. Many were the personal priests or physicians of wealthy high-caste families; most were village priests, schoolteachers, and wandering ascetics. Some were alchemists and sorcerers, and even downright charlatans, living off the gullibility of the masses, who believed in their ability to tell fortunes and turn magic spells to good and evil purposes. But all brahmans, from the palaces of kings to the most remote villages, were privileged beings, exempt from taxes and protected from bodily injury by the harsh punishments meted out to those who dared to assault them. As the following passage from one of the ancient Vedas makes clear, not even kings were considered exempt from the horrible fate that befell those who did injury to a brahman.

Whenever a king, fancying himself mighty,
    seeks to devour a Brahman, [his] kingdom is broken up.
[Ruin] overflows that kingdom as water swamps
    a leaky boat;
Calamity smites that country in which a priest is wronged.
Even trees . . . repel, and refuse their shade to, the man
    who claims a right to the property of a Brahman.

In addition to the power exercised by the brahmans, and the services they provided, religion shaped the daily lives of the peoples of South Asia through the ethical prescriptions found in the sacred Vedic texts. These texts were orally compiled and systematically transmitted by the brahman priests between 1200 and 900 B.C.E. In the last centuries B.C.E., the *Vedas* were written in the Sanskrit language, which thereafter became the standard and scholarly language of India, akin to Greek and Latin in the West. From the chants and ritual formulas of the early Vedas, the texts were increasingly devoted to religious and philosophical speculation and moral prescriptions for the faithful. This highly religious culture provided the context for further changes as Indian civilization moved to even greater complexity.

An Era of Widespread Social Change

The rise of kings and increasing brahman dominance were only two of the many social changes that occurred as full civilization took shape for the second time in Indian history. Around the court centers of the lowland kings, towns grew up as servant, artisan, and merchant groups catered to the needs of the rulers, their courtiers, and often large numbers of brahman advisors and administrators. Along the Ganges and other rivers, towns developed that were mainly trading centers or were devoted to the specialized manufacture of key products such as pottery, tools, and cotton textiles. With the increase in commerce and specialized production, merchants and artisans became established as distinctive social groups. The great wealth amassed by the larger trading houses allowed the merchants to win a prominent place in the Indian social hierarchy, which became both more complex and more rigid in this era.

Another social stratum that assumed major importance in this period was the peasantry. As farming supplanted herding as the basis for the economies of the lowland kingdoms, peasants came to make up a large percentage of India's population. Mud-walled farming villages spread across the plains of northern India, though throughout the classical era they continued to be dwarfed in most places by massive primeval rain forests. Irrigation networks and new agricultural tools steadily increased productivity and hence the capacity of the peasants to support ever larger numbers of nonfarming specialists. Most peasants grew staples such as rice, millet, and wheat, but some villages specialized in cotton, plants for dyes such as indigo, and luxury crops such as sugar cane. Though presumably eager to market their surplus or specialized crops, the peasants only grudgingly paid the tribute demanded by the tax collectors of the lowland monarchs. If a ruler was weak and his court in disarray, it is likely that the peasants paid nothing at all.

The Caste System

The tripartite class division in India between warriors, priests, and commoners that made up the tribal social order of the early Aryan invaders had altered radically over the centuries. New social groups, such as merchants and peasants, were added to these broad social categories *(varnas),* and each was subdivided into occupational subgroups, or castes. Broad categories and occupational subgroups were arranged in a hierarchical pyramid based on the degree to which the tasks they performed were considered polluting. Those who dealt with human waste or slaughtered animals, for example, were regarded as extremely defiling, while scholars and wandering holy men who eschewed physical labor and refused to eat animal flesh were revered for their purity.

At the top of the pyramid were the brahman, warrior, and merchant castes, whose members made up only a small minority of the total population. The bulk of the population belonged to peasant and artisan castes, which made up most of the central and lower layers of the caste pyramid. Beneath the peasants and artisans were the untouchables, who performed the most despised tasks in Indian society, including removing human waste from towns and villages, sweeping the streets, and tanning leather hides. The Indians' reverence for cows, which may have been present in Harappan society, and their aversion to dead animals rendered the latter occupation particularly polluting. Even the untouchables were divided into caste subgroups, with sweepers looking down upon manure handlers, and they in turn despising leatherworkers.

Over the centuries, the boundaries between caste groups hardened. In addition to occupation, a caste's position in the Indian social hierarchy was distinguished by its diet and by the caste groups with which its members could dine or exchange different kinds of food. A caste's status also determined the social groups with which it was allowed to intermarry and whether or not it was permitted to read the Vedas. Only members of castes belonging to the three highest varnas (brahmans, warriors, and merchants) were allowed to read the texts. *Rama,* perhaps the greatest of Indian cultural heroes, was celebrated in the *Ramayana* for cutting off the head of a peasant holy man who presumed to recite hymns from the Vedas while hanging upside down from a tree.

A person was born into a caste group and could not change his or her caste status. Over considerable periods of time, a caste group could collectively rise or fall in status, but individuals were tied to the fortunes of their caste as a whole. An individual's refusal to accept the duties and status associated with the caste into which he or she was born could lead to beatings and other forms of physical abuse. If the rebellious individual continued to violate caste laws, he or she would be ostracized or quite literally outcast. This penalty normally meant certain

Like many of the larger Indian towns, the one portrayed in this artist's recreation (based on classical Indian stone sculptures from the last centuries B.C.E.) depicts an Indian city that has walls, a moat, and building constructed mainly of intricately carved wood.

death because no one, including a member of their own family, was allowed to pay them for labor or offer them food, drink, or other services.

In addition to physical punishment and local sanctions, the caste system was upheld by Indian rulers and the belief that it was supernaturally ordained. One of the chief duties of a righteous monarch was to preserve the caste hierarchy and see to it that persons at each level carried out the tasks and behaved in the manner appropriate to those at that rank. Ideally, the caste system was to provide for a harmonious exchange of products and services at all levels of Indian society. Peasants, for example, provided food for the brahmans, who saw to their religious and ritual needs, and for the warriors, who defended them from bandits and foreign invaders. In reality, high-caste groups, particularly brahmans and warriors, enjoyed a disproportionate share of wealth and power. But except in times of severe natural calamity or social crisis, even the lowliest of untouchables was guaranteed a livelihood, however meager.

The caste position and career determined by a person's birth was called one's *dharma*. The concept of transmigration of the soul helped to explain why some were given the enviable dharma of a brahman whereas others were consigned to the lowly status of an untouchable tanner. In the Vedic era, it was widely accepted that a person's soul existed through many human lives and was transferred from one body to another after death. In each of its lives, the soul accumulated varying amounts of merit and demerit, depending on the actions of the person in whose body it dwelled. The sum of these merits and demerits at any given point in time made up one's *karma*. An individual's karma in turn determined the sort of person that soul would be attached to in its next reincarnation. Thus, a person who was born as a brahman possessed a soul that had built up a large surplus of merit; a person born as a sweeper was paying the penalty for the sins of his or her past lives.

One of the greatest sins was to violate one's dharma—to refuse the duties and status attached to the caste into which one was born. The only way to ensure a better situation in the next rebirth was to accept one's situation in the present and fully perform the tasks one was allotted. Thus, the concepts of the transmigration of the soul and reincarnation provided not only an explanation for the inequities of the caste system but also a religious rationale for an individual's acceptance of his or her place in the caste hierarchy.

ANALYSIS

Inequality as the Social Norm

The Indian caste system is perhaps the most extreme expression of a mode of social organization that violates the most revered principles on which modern Western societies are based. Like the Egyptian division between a noble and a commoner and the Greek division between a freeperson and a slave, the caste system rests on the assumption that humans are inherently unequal and that their lot in life is determined by the families and social strata into which they are born. The caste system, like the social systems of all other classical civilizations, presumed that social divisions were relatively fixed and stable and that individuals ought to be content with the station they had been allotted at birth.

Furthermore, all classical social systems (with the partial exception of the Greeks, at least in Athens) played down the importance of the individual and stressed the primacy of collective obligations and loyalties that were centered in the family, extended kin groups, or broader occupational or social groupings. Family or caste affiliation, not individual ambition, determined a person's career goals and activities.

All of these assumptions, of course, directly contradict some of our most cherished beliefs. They run counter to one of the most basic organizing principles of modern Western culture that is rooted in a commitment to equality of opportunity. This principle is enshrined in our constitutions and legal systems, taught in our schools and churches, and proclaimed in our media from literature to television. The belief in human equality, or at least equality of opportunity, has also been one of the most important ideas that modern Western civilization has exported to the peoples of Africa, Asia, and Latin America.

The concept of equality rests on two assumptions. The first is that a person's place in society should be determined not by the class or family into which he or she is born but by personal abilities and hard work. The second is that the opportunity to rise—or fall—in social status should be open to everyone and protected by law. Some of our most cherished myths reflect these assumptions: that anyone can aspire to be president of the United States, for example, or that an ordinary person

has the right to challenge the actions of the politically and economically powerful.

Of course, equality is a social ideal rather than something any human society has achieved. No one pretends that all humans are equal in intelligence or talent, and in fact there are important barriers to equality of opportunity. But the belief persists that all humans should have an equal chance to better themselves by making use of the brains and skills they have. In the real world, race, class, and gender differences have often favored some individuals over others, and laws and government agencies have often not corrected these inequities. But the citizens of modern Western societies, and increasingly the rest of the world, champion the principles of equality of opportunity and the potential for social mobility as the just and natural bases for social organization and interaction.

What is just and natural for modern societies, however, would have been incomprehensible to the peoples of the classical age. In fact, most human societies through most of human history have been organized on assumptions that are much closer to those underlying the Indian caste system than those we assume to be the norm. Ancient Egyptians or Greeks, or for that matter medieval Europeans or early modern Chinese, believed that career possibilities, political power, and social privileges should be set by law according to the position of one's family in the social hierarchy. The Indian caste structure was the most rigid and complex of the systems by which occupations, resources, and status were allotted. But all classical civilizations had similar social mechanisms that determined the obligations and prerogatives of members of each social stratum from the aristocracy to the slaves.

In some ways, classical Chinese and Greek societies provided exceptions to these general patterns. In China, individuals from lowly social origins could rise to positions of great status and power, and well-placed families could fall on hard times and lose their gentry status. But "rags to riches" success stories were the exception rather than the rule, and mobility between different social strata was limited even in the best of times. In fact, Chinese thinkers made much of the distinctions between the scholar-gentry elite and the common people.

Though some of the Greeks, particularly the Athenians, developed the idea of equality for all citizens in a particular city-state, the great majority of the populations of their societies were not citizens, and many were slaves. By virtue of their birth the latter were assigned lives of servitude and physical drudgery. Democratic participation and the chance to make full use of their talents were confined only to the free *males* of the city-states.

In virtually all societies, these fixed social hierarchies were upheld by creation myths and religious beliefs that proclaimed their divine origins and the danger of supernatural retribution if they were challenged or altered. Elite thinkers stressed the importance of the established social order to human peace and well-being; rulers were duty bound to defend it with all the force at their disposal. Few challenged the naturalness of the hierarchy itself; fewer still proposed alternatives to it. Each individual was expected to accept his or her place and to concentrate on the duties and obligations required by that place, rather than worry about rights or personal desires. Males and females alike were required to subordinate their individual yearnings and talents to the needs of their families, clans, communities, or social superiors. In return for a person's acceptance of his or her allotted place in the hierarchy, he or she received material sustenance and a social slot. These benefits, of course, were denied to those people who fought the system. They were outcast or exiled, physically punished, imprisoned or killed.

Questions: What sorts of arguments did the thinkers of the classical civilizations of Greece, China, and India use to explain and justify the great differences in social status and material wealth that existed? Why did the vast majority of persons who lived in these societies, including oppressed groups such as slaves and untouchables, accept these divisions? Comparing this mode of social organization with the ideal in your own society, what do you see as the advantages and drawbacks of each?

The Family and the Changing Status of Women

Some of our best insights into family life and gender relationships in this era are provided by the two great Indian epics, the *Mahabharata* and the *Ramayana.* Though these tales of war and princely honor, love and social duty were not written down until the last centuries B.C.E., they were related in oral form long before. They suggest that by the middle centuries of the last millennium B.C.E., the extended family was increasingly regarded as the ideal. Those who could support the large household that extended family arrangements required, which normally meant only the highest caste groups, gathered all the male members of a given family and their wives and children under the same roof. At times up to four generations, from great-grandfathers and-grandmothers to great-grandsons and-granddaughters, lived together in the same dwelling or family compound.

Though these arrangements restricted individual privacy and often led to family quarrels, they also provided a high degree of security and human companionship. Lower-caste groups from the peasants and artisans rarely possessed the wealth required to support extended households. As a consequence, the great majority of Indian families were *nuclear families,* or made up of parents and their children, with perhaps a widowed grandparent sharing their dwelling.

Somewhat contradictory visions of the positions and roles of women emerge from the epics, which suggest that attitudes toward women may have been in flux. On one hand, women are seen as weak, passionate, frivolous, and fond of gossip and slander. Female demons in the *Ramayana* take on the roles of jealous temptresses and vengeful jilted lovers. Within the family, women remain clearly subordinated to men. Though youths are charged to obey and honor their mothers, parental veneration is focused on the father to whom complete obedience and loyalty are expected. Wives are instructed to be attentive to their husbands' needs and be ready to obey their every command. Rama's wife Sita is chosen for her physical beauty and absolute devotion to her husband. When he is forced into exile in the forest, she follows without question or complaint. When she is carried off to Sri Lanka by the demon Ravanna, Rama races to defend her honor and his own. Having rescued her after a mighty battle with Ravanna and his evil minions, Rama then refuses to take her back because he suspects that she may have been raped while in captivity. Only when she proves her virtue by walking unscathed through a fire will he accept her again as his wife. Throughout both epics, the fate of women is controlled by men, be they gods, demons, or mortal humans.

On the other hand, some passages in the epics (and other sources from this period) indicate that in certain ways women had greater freedom and opportunities for self-expression than was the case by the last centuries B.C.E. Women in the epics are often depicted as strong-willed and cunning. Sita and Draupadi, two of the wives of the five Pandava brothers who are the heroes of the *Mahabharata,* display remarkable courage and strength of character at various points in their respective ordeals. Contemporary sources mention women who were renowned scholars of the sacred Vedic texts, which later they would not even be permitted to read. Women in this era also made their mark as teachers, poets, musicians, and artists, though the last two activities were not highly esteemed. Like their brothers, girls from high-caste families were allowed to undergo the special cere-

An Indian village with its sacred tree. The thatched roofs of the cottages can be seen in the background as women bring their offerings of rice to the Buddha, who is not pictured in accord with early artistic practice.

monies that celebrated their twice-born or exalted status—an honor boys continued to enjoy but that gradually died out for young women. Women were even famed for their skills in the martial arts, as the amazon (female warrior) palace guards of several monarchs demonstrated.

The End of an Era

Roughly 1000 years after the first Aryan tribes entered India, a new civilization had come into being that was very different from the Harappan complex it replaced. Sedentary agriculture was well established and was productive enough to support a variety of specialized elites, true cities, extensive trade, and nonagrarian artisan manufacturers. In the caste system, the Indians had developed perhaps the most complex scheme of social stratification and labor division known to human history. They had also made notable accomplishments in philosophy and religious speculation, invention, and artistic creativity, though most of the art works were done in wood and thus have perished over time.

These considerable achievements, however, pale in comparison with what was about to occur in the final centuries B.C.E. The absolute and increasingly self-serving dominance of the brahmans, the endless succession of petty wars between the kings they advised, and the religious bankruptcy displayed by the excesses of the sacrificial cults all prompted major challenges. These challenges and the brahman responses to them would both remake and enrich Indian civilization in the millennium between 500 B.C.E. and 500 C.E.

RELIGIOUS FERMENT AND THE RISE OF BUDDHISM

Focal Point: For nearly a millennium, the Buddhist challenge to the brahmanical order was a central theme in South Asian history. Once institutionalized in monastic orders and great *stupas*, or temple mounds housing relics of the Buddha, the new religion provided a clear alternative to the sacrifice-oriented faith of the brahmans and the caste system that had been the dominant feature of Indian society for centuries. The Buddhist challenge was strengthened further by the patronage of the later rulers of the powerful Mauryan empire. Taking advantage of the political chaos left by the Greek invasions of northwest India beginning in the 4th century B.C.E., the Mauryas became the first dynasty to rule large portions of the subcontinent. The decline of the Mauryas, however, and changes within Buddhism itself, opened the way for a brahman counteroffensive that came to full fruition in the Gupta era in the first centuries C.E.

The 6th and 5th centuries B.C.E. were a time of great social turmoil and philosophical speculation throughout Eurasia. In China, Confucius and Laozi proposed very different views of the proper organization of human society and purposes of life. In Persia, Zoroaster founded a new religion, while the prophets Ezekiel and Isaiah strove to improve the Hebrews' understanding of the intentions of their single, almighty God. In Greece, the writings of Thales and Pythagoras laid the basis for unprecedented advances in philosophy, the sciences, and mathematics. India too was caught up in this transcontinental trend of social experimentation and intellectual probing.

Indian reformers questioned the brahmans' dominance and the efficacy of the sacrifices on which it ultimately rested. They sought to find alternatives to the caste system as the basis for India's social order. They posed questions about the nature of the universe and the end of life that the Vedic thinkers had debated for centuries, and often came up with very different answers. Some experimented with new techniques of meditation and self-mortification; others promoted new religions that would free the masses from what were viewed as the oppressive teachings of the brahmans. One holy man and thinker, the *Buddha,* did all of these things and in the process made the most influential religious and philosophical breakthroughs of an age of remarkable intellectual ferment. Though Zoroaster transformed Persian thinking and Confucius proclaimed an ethical system that was adopted in China and neighboring lands, the Buddha founded a religion that became a key ingredient in the life of civilized peoples throughout most of Asia.

The Making of a Religious Teacher

Accounts of the Buddha's life are so cluttered with myths and miracles that it is difficult to know what kind of man he actually was and what sort of message he originally preached. We are fairly certain, however, that he

lived from the middle of the 6th century to the second decade of the 5th century B.C.E. He was born into one of the warrior clans of the hill states south of the Himalayas, where, as we have seen, the rule of kings and the hold of the brahmans was weak. Buddhist traditions relate that he was the son of the local ruler who was haunted by a prophecy made by a religous seer, or holy person with prophetic powers, at the time of the Buddha's birth. The seer predicted that the child would someday become a wandering ascetic like himself, thus refusing his father's throne.

To prevent this, the king confined his son to the palace grounds and provided him with every imaginable human pleasure and comfort. But as he approached manhood the prince grew curious about the world beyond the palace gardens and walls. With the aid of a trusted servant, the Buddha ventured forth into the nearby countryside, where he encountered for the first time illness, old age, death, and a wandering ascetic (a holy person who has renounced the pleasures of the material world). Unsettled by these encounters with human suffering, the prince became moody and withdrawn. Finally, as the holy man had predicted, he renounced all claims to succeed his father as king and set off with a group of wandering ascetics to meditate and ponder the many questions posed by his discoveries beyond the palace walls.

In the wilderness, the Buddha experimented with the many ways Indian *gurus*, or religious teachers, had devised to reach a higher understanding of the nature of humanity and the supernatural world. He did yogic exercises, fasted almost to death, chanted sacred prayers for days on end, and conversed with every seer he encountered. Discouraged by his failure to find the answer to the questions that had driven him to take up the life of a wandering ascetic, and exhausted by the self-punishment he had inflicted, the Buddha collapsed, legend has it, under a huge Bo tree. Saved from death by the care of a young girl who took pity on him, the Buddha turned to meditation in his search for understanding. Ultimately, by disciplining his mind and body, he achieved enlightenment, which rested on his discovery of what Buddhists came to call the Four Noble Truths.

The central issue for the Buddha was the problem of suffering, which he believed all living things experience because all living things and the objects to which they are attached are impermanent. The moment we are born we begin to die, he reasoned. Individuals whom one loves or befriends may turn indifferent or hostile or simply move away; love and friendship are inevitably ended by death. The goals to which humans devote their lives,

This beautifully detailed sandstone statue of the enlightened Buddha meditating in a standing position was carved in the 5th century C.E. Note the nimbus or halo—which was commonly employed in later Buddhist iconography—as well as the calm and composure radiated by the Buddha's facial expression.

such as fame and wealth, are empty and, once attained, can easily be lost. These attachments to the illusory and impermanent things of the world are the source of suffering. One can escape suffering only by ceasing to desire the things of the world and realizing that even one's sense of self is part of the illusion. This realization, or enlightenment, can be achieved by following the eight-step process of right action, thinking, and meditation. Once enlightenment has been attained, the individual is released from suffering because she or he is free from desire and attachment. He or she has attained *nirvana*—not heaven in the Christian sense, but simply an eternal state of tranquility.

Having attained enlightenment, the Buddha, because of his great compassion for all living creatures, set out to spread his message to all humanity (and, Buddhist legends relate, to the creatures of the forest as well). He became the most successful of the numerous seers and gurus who traveled through the hill and lowland kingdoms in this era, challenging the teachings of the brahmans and offering alternative modes of worship and paths to salvation. The Buddha soon gained a considerable following, which ranged from exalted monarchs to humble sweepers and included both men and women. As he feared, his followers turned his teachings into an organized religion. In the process, what had begun as a starkly pessimistic and antiworldly vision of existence, without gods or a god or the promise of heaven, became one of the great salvationist faiths of all human history.

The Emergence of Buddhism as a Religion

After his death (again as he feared), the Buddha was worshiped as a deity. His most faithful disciples became monks who devoted their lives to spreading his message and achieving nirvana. They held conferences where they attempted to compile authoritative collections of his teachings and the traditions concerning his life. Not surprisingly, disagreements over points of doctrine and meaning arose at these sessions. These disputes led to the formation of rival schools of monks, who vied with each other, the brahmans, and other sects to build a popular following.

Over time, the rival schools created elaborate philosophical systems. But in their efforts to attract a broader following, the monks stressed more accessible aspects of what had become a new religion. They offered miraculous tales of the Buddha's life, which included traditions that his mother had been a virgin and that he had been visited by revered scholars from afar soon after his birth. In the popular mind, nirvana became equated with heaven. Graphic visions of heavenly pleasures and the tortures of hell became central features of popular Buddhism. The Buddha was worshiped as a savior who returned periodically to help the faithful find the way to heaven. Though within the monastic communities Buddhist monks continued their emphasis on meditation and the achievement of nirvana, lay people were encouraged to perform good deeds that would earn enough merit for their souls to go to one of the Buddhist heavens after death.

The Buddhist Challenge

Though other philosopher-ascetics criticized the religious beliefs and caste system that the brahmans had done so much to establish, none was as successful as the Buddha and the many monastic orders committed to his teachings at winning converts among the Indian people. The monks and monastic organizations provided a very viable alternative to the brahman priesthood as centers of scholarship, education, and religious ritual, and often directly opposed the beliefs that the brahmans championed. Though the Buddha retained the ideas of karma and reincarnation, he rejected the Vedas as divinely inspired teachings that ought to be accepted as the ultimate authority on all issues. He ridiculed the powers the brahmans claimed for their sacrifices and the gods for whom they were intended. He favored introspection and self-mastery over ritual. In so doing, he struck at the very heart of the brahmans' social and religious dominance.

The Buddha rejected the lifestyles of both the brahmans who had become addicted to worldly power and the brahman ascetics who practiced extreme forms of bodily mortification. He tried to do away with the caste system, an aim that gave his teachings great potential appeal among the untouchables and other groups. The Buddha also accepted women as his followers and taught that they were capable of attaining nirvana. These opportunities were institutionalized in Buddhist monastic organizations, which normally included provisions for communities of nuns. The evidence we have suggests that the monastic life became a fulfilling career outlet for women in many parts of India. This outlet proved doubly meaningful in an era when educational and other occupational opportunities for women were declining, and upper-caste women in particular were increasingly confined to the home. Thus, in virtually all spheres of life from religious worship to social organization, Buddhism offered potentially revolutionary challenges to the long-established brahmanical order.

The Greek Interlude

The intellectual and social ferment that swept northern India in the 6th century B.C.E. was intensified by political upheavals touched off by the invasion of northwestern India by Alexander the Great in 327 B.C.E. Alexander had several reasons for invading India. To begin with, he believed that except for India, Arabia, North Africa, and some remote and barbaric parts of Europe, he had run out of places to conquer. He knew of the Indians because some of them had fought with the Persians against his armies; he knew little or nothing of the Chinese. A new campaign would keep his soldiers in fighting trim and his generals from quarreling among themselves. It is also likely that Alexander found the prospect of further adventures in India a good deal more exciting than the humdrum tasks involved in administering the huge empire his armies had won in less than a decade.

Whatever his motives, in 327 B.C.E. Alexander's armies crossed the Hindu Kush into India, thus beginning what would be his last major campaign of conquest. It was a rousing success. His greatly outnumbered armies won a series of battles against the peoples living in the upper Indus valley. As had been the case in his Persian campaigns, Alexander's well-trained troops proved more than a match for the war chariots, archers, and massed cavalry of his Indian adversaries. Once the surprise wore off, his veteran soldiers also proved able to cope with the numbers of war elephants that had spooked their horses.

Victory stirred Alexander's passion for further conquests. But his soldiers, weary of endless battles and fearful of the stiffening resistance of numerous Indian princes in an exotic and very distant land, refused to go farther to the east. After considerable debate, Alexander agreed to lead his forces out of India. Those in his armies who survived an epic march through the desert wastes to the north and west of the Indus River returned to Persia in 324 B.C.E. Alexander's death a year later left his Indian conquests to be fought over by the commanders who divided up his empire.

Though several Greek rulers controlled territory in India's northwest for decades after Alexander's invasion, the impact of his campaign was largely indirect. It stimulated some trade and considerable cultural exchange between India and the Mediterranean region. Of particular importance was the flow of Greek astronomical and mathematical ideas to India as well as the impact of Indian thinking on religious movements in the Mediterranean. Greek Stoicism and the mystery religions that swept the eastern Mediterranean in the centuries around the birth of Christ owe much to Indian philosophical influences. In the arts, the combination of Indian and Greek styles led to an Indo-Greek school of sculpture that was both distinctive and influential in shaping approaches to the depiction of the Buddha. Indian motifs were blended with Greek physical features and artistic techniques.

The Rise of the Mauryas

Appropriately, the most lasting effects of Alexander's invasion were military and political. The defeats suffered by the kingdoms in the northwest created a political vacuum that was soon filled by the ablest of the regional lords, *Chandragupta Maurya* (322–298 B.C.E.). After some initial setbacks, Chandragupta embarked on a sustained campaign to build a great empire. After conquering much of the northwest and driving the Greek successors of Alexander out of India, his armies began the conquest of the kingdoms of the Ganges plain that would later form the heartland of the Maurya Empire.

As Chandragupta's empire grew, the folksy atmosphere of earlier localized court centers gave way to a new imperial style. He reigned from an elaborately carved and decorated palace set in large and well-tended gardens. Adopting the Persian example, Chandragupta proclaimed himself an absolute emperor and on state occasions sat on a high throne above hundreds of his splendidly attired courtiers. He was guarded by a special corps of amazons, and elaborate precautions were taken to safeguard his life. The food Chandragupta ate was first tasted by servants to ensure that *he* did not die of poisoning. Parrots were bred for the trees of the palace gardens to make sure that poisonous snakes did not find their way into the ruler's chambers. There were hollow pillars in which to hide palace spies, secret passages to enable the king to move about the palace undetected, and an obligatory bath and frisking for all who entered. Chandragupta built a standing army that Greek writers estimated (overly generously) was 500,000 strong, and he tried with some success to replace regional lords with his own administrators.

Chandragupta's son and successor, Bindusara, extended the Maurya Empire to the east along the Ganges plains and far to the south of the subcontinent. Little is known about Bindusara, but he was apparently a highly cultured man. He once requested wine, figs, and a philosopher as presents from one of the Greek rulers in western Asia. He received the wine and figs, but not the philosopher because, as the ruler informed him, the Greeks did not trade in philosophers. Bindusara's son, *Ashoka*, completed the conquests begun by his father and grandfather, and in his long reign from 268–232 B.C.E., northern India enjoyed a time of unprecedented political unity, prosperity, and cultural splendor.

Ashoka's Conversion and the Flowering of Buddhism in the Mauryan Age

In the early years of his rule, Ashoka showed little of the wisdom and tolerance that were to set off his reign as one of the great periods in Indian history. He won his throne only after a bloody struggle in which he eliminated several brothers. He was apparently bad-tempered and impetuous, as evidenced by his order that a woman from his harem be put to death for telling him that he was ugly. He also delighted in conquest—at least until he witnessed the horrible sufferings that were caused by his conquest of Orissa in eastern India. That experience, and regret for his earlier dissolute life, led to his conversion to Buddhism.

From the time of his conversion onward, Ashoka became a ruler who strove to serve his people and promote their welfare. He ceased to enlarge his domains by conquest; used his revenues to build roads, hospitals, and rest houses; and sought to reduce the slaughter of animals in his kingdom by encouraging vegetarianism. His attempts to curb the slaughter of cows were particularly important, since those attempts, in conjunction with a long-standing reverence for cattle, contributed to the sacred status that this animal attained in Indian civilization. Because Ashoka's edicts were also aimed at restricting animal sacrifices, they aroused the anxiety of the brahmans, who saw them as a threat to the rituals that were vital to their dominance in Indian society.

The influence of Buddhism on Ashoka's personal life spilled over into his state policy. Drawing on the Buddhist concept of a righteous world ruler spreading peace and good government, Ashoka attempted to build an imperial bureaucracy that would enforce his laws and sanctions against war and animal slaughter. Though his efforts to establish meaningful control by a centralized administration met with some success, they also aroused considerable opposition. The brahmans, resentful of their displacement as political advisors and administrators by Ashoka's bureaucrats, tried to stir up local resistance to imperial edicts. Warrior families that had once ruled the small states also sought to retain their control over local politics. They waited for signs of dynastic weakness in the hope of reviving their lost kingdoms.

CLOSEUP

The Arthashastra: A Treatise on Political Science for the Classical Age

In addition to nurturing some of the world's most sublime religious thought, the classical world produced many highly sophisticated and influential works on politics and political economy. India's contribution in this realm was the *Arthashastra*, a treatise on the art of statecraft that bore a much greater resemblance to Sunzi's *Art of War* than to Plato's *Republic*. Attributed to *Kautilya*, an astute advisor to Chandragupta Maurya, the work is actually a compilation over many generations of the political theory and practical advice of several authors. Writing in the atmosphere of intrigue and insecurity that dominated relations between the petty states that had ruled India since the fall of Harappa, those who contributed to the *Arthashastra* argued that in the pursuit of political power any measure was justified. Powerful kingdoms, they believed, must constantly expand, whereas weak rulers should accept the most humiliating terms in order to attach themselves to strong monarchs.

In great detail, Kautilya and his fellow political strategists described the techniques a ruler must use to attain and hold power. Spies disguised as beggars, barbers, and even holy men should be stationed everywhere in a king's own domains and those of his enemies. Crime and internal dissent must be harshly punished. The authors of the *Arthashastra* sanctioned the removal of rival rulers by bribery and assassination (for which specially trained prizefighters were recommended), and by employing traitors to undermine the resistance in neighboring kingdoms. Like Sunzi in China, they scorned the notion of chivalrous warfare in which great champions fought each other in single combat. Enemies wounded and fallen should be killed, they advised, lest they rise up again. Kautilya and his coauthors approved of the use of poison-tipped arrows and chariots with sword blades attached to their wheel hubs. With such advice, it is little wonder that Chandragupta and his successors rapidly conquered adversaries who were apparently operating by a much less ruthless set of rules.

Several social groups, however, gained greatly from Ashoka's attempts to recast Indian society in a Buddhist mold. The period of Maurya rule coincided with a great expansion from the Roman Empire in the west to China in the east. Indian merchants and artisans participated eagerly in this process. India established itself as one of the great preindustrial manufacturing centers of the classical world, specializing in cotton cloth and clothing. In fact, Indian cloth makers were so skilled that for many centuries Roman writers would lament the flow of gold to the east to pay for Indian textiles, for which the Romans had little else to exchange. Seeing in Buddhism an advantageous alternative to the caste system, merchants and artisans supported Ashoka's efforts. They generously patronized the different orders of Buddhist monks that increased greatly in wealth and membership. Women also had good reasons to support the Buddhist alternative. Their position within the family was strengthened under Buddhist law. In addition, the monastic life gave them opportunities for achievement and self-expression as nuns, scholars, and artists.

One of the chief signs of the Buddhist surge under Ashoka and his successors was the spread of great monastery complexes throughout the subcontinent. Most of the monasteries were made of wood and thus were lost in fires or destroyed by later invaders. But the Buddhist architectural legacy was preserved in the great stone shrines, or *stupas,* that were built to house pieces of bone or hair and personal possessions, which were said to be relics of the Buddha. Most of the freestanding stupas were covered mounds of dirt surrounded by intricately carved stone gateways and fences.

Another major effect of Ashoka's dedication to Buddhism resulted from his efforts to spread the faith beyond the Indian subcontinent. He sent missions, including one led by one of his sons, to Sri Lanka to the south and to the Himalayan kingdoms and the steppes of central Asia to the north. The establishment of Buddhism in

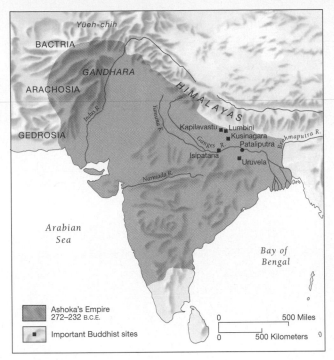

India at the Time of Ashoka

each region was critical, because converted rulers and monks in these areas were instrumental in spreading the religion to much of the rest of Asia. From Sri Lanka Buddhism was carried to Burma, Java, and many other parts of Southeast Asia. From Nepal and central Asia it was disseminated into Tibet, China, and the rest of East Asia.

Ashoka's Death and the Decline of the Mauryas

Ashoka's bold experiments in religious and social change and the empire that he and his forebears had established did not long survive his death. Weaker rulers followed him to the throne. The empire was first divided between rival claimants within the Maurya household and then pulled apart by internal strife and local lords who attempted to reestablish the many kingdoms that had been absorbed into the Maurya imperium. By 185 B.C.E., the Mauryan Empire had disappeared. Political fragmentation returned to the subcontinent, and new warrior invaders compounded the rapidly growing divisions. Though some of these conquerors built substantial empires and were devoted to the continued spread of Buddhism, none of them could match Ashoka in power and resolution. Within the fragmented political order that

emerged after the decline of the Mauryas, the brahmans initiated a religious revival that gradually, and usually without overt persecution, pushed Buddhism to the fringes of Indian social and intellectual life.

BRAHMANICAL RECOVERY AND THE SPLENDORS OF THE GUPTA AGE

Focal Point: Across the Indian subcontinent in the centuries between the fall of the Mauryas and the rise of the Guptas in the late 3rd century C.E., Buddhism and Hinduism, as the brahmanical beliefs and modes of worship would come to be known, vied largely without violence for the patronage of Indian rulers and the support of the Indian masses. By the time of the founding of the Gupta Empire in the 4th century C.E., it was clear that the brahmans would be able to meet the Buddhist challenge. Gupta patronage fortified the brahman revival, which in turn produced one of India's most glorious ages of philosophical and artistic creativity and social sophistication.

In the centuries after the end of the Mauryan Empire, new waves of invaders entered the Indian subcontinent. Indo-Greek rulers, whose kingdoms were based in central Asia, attempted to establish provinces in the northwest. Their kingdoms were attacked by Scythian nomads, who then raided and plundered and later settled in north India. The Scythians were overrun by a new wave of nomads, the *Yueh-chih,* from the eastern steppes. The Yueh-chih conquests gave rise to the Kushana dynasty, which was based in the northwest and was the most powerful in India between the end of the 1st and the early 3rd centuries C.E. Under the *Kushanas,* Buddhism experienced its last great era of imperial patronage. But the Kushanas' domains did not extend to the Ganges plains or central and south India, so in those areas kingdoms arose where the brahmans were able to reestablish their old political and religious dominance.

As the numbers of the converts to Buddhism multiplied in the last centuries B.C.E., the brahmans grew more and more sensitive to the challenge posed by the new faith. But they drew comfort from the fact that they still controlled the kings of the lowland states, where most of the population and Indian civilization was concentrated. The kings in turn were committed to upholding their positions and the caste hierarchy that was the key to the world they dominated. When, in the 4th and

The great Buddhist stupa at Sanchi in central India. Stupas were built to house relics of the Buddha, and they became major sites of pilgrimage for the Buddhist faithful.

3rd centuries B.C.E. these kings had been displaced by the powerful Mauryan Empire, and when the most talented ruler of that empire converted to Buddhism, the brahmans could no longer ignore their peril. The rise of the Mauryan Empire then was very much a precipitant of a largely peaceful, but nonetheless increasingly intense, struggle between the brahmans and the Buddhist monastic orders for dominance in Indian civilization.

Brahman Revival and Buddhist Decline

Even in the centuries immediately after the fall of the Mauryan dynasty, when the influence of Buddhism in Indian society was at its height, patterns had developed that rendered it quite vulnerable to a brahman counteroffensive. Over time, Buddhist monks became more and more concentrated in huge monasteries. Increasingly isolated from village and urban life, the monks grew obsessed with fine points of philosophy that often had little or no relevance to ordinary believers. Because Buddhism in India had not developed a sequence of family and life cycle rituals or folk festivals, the monks had little occasion to interact with the mass of the people. They focused their services more and more on wealthy patrons, whose donations supported the monasteries. This support made the daily rounds to collect alms unnecessary for the monks in many areas, and led to luxurious lifestyles and lax discipline at some of the more prominent Buddhist centers.

While the Buddhist monks became more remote from the Indian populace, the brahmans strove to effect changes in belief and worship that would make Hinduism more appealing to ordinary people. They played down the need for grand and expensive sacrifices and stressed the importance of personal worship and small, everyday offerings of food and prayers to the gods. Increasing emphasis was placed on intense devotion to gods such as Shiva and Vishnu and their female consorts Kali and Lakshmi. Special gods were allotted to particular occupational groups, such as Ganesh, the elephant-headed, pot-bellied deity who was especially revered by merchants.

Temples, both large and small, sprang up to house the multitude of statues that provided the focus for popular worship of the gods. Devotional cults were open to persons at all caste levels, including in some cases the untouchables. Women were also allowed to participate, at times, as cult poets and singers. In addition, the brahmans multiplied or enriched special festivals and rites-of-passage ceremonies, such as child-naming celebrations, weddings, and funerals, which enlarged the role they played in the everyday life of the Indian people. Over centuries, revived Hinduism simply absorbed the salvationist Buddhism that alone had a mass appeal. The brahmans treated the Buddha as another god of the Hindu pantheon and allowed their followers to worship him as one of the worldly forms of the preserver god Vishnu.

At the elite level, brahman philosophers and gurus placed increasing emphasis on the sophisticated and sublime philosophical ideas associated with the later books of the Vedas, the *Upanishads*. Not heavens or hells but the release of the soul from the endless cycle of rebirths was stressed in these teachings. Moderate asceticism and meditation were the means by which this release was achieved. In contrast to the Buddha, who preached that the soul itself was an illusion, the orthodox Hindu schools taught that the soul was real and its ultimate purpose was to fuse with the godhead from which it had come. The world was *maya*, or illusion, only because it was wrongly perceived by most humans. Those who had achieved realization and release understood that the world was in fact an extension of a single reality that encompassed everything.

In addition to monastic weaknesses and brahman reforms, Buddhism in India was weakened by underlying economic changes that altered the social circumstances that had favored the new religion. Most critical was the decline of the Rome-China trading axis with the fall of the Han empire in the 3rd century C.E. Not only did this undermine the position of the merchant groups that had been major patrons of Buddhism, it made large-scale traders more and more dependent on local kings and warrior households, which remained the chief allies of the brahmans.

The damage done to Buddhism by the losses of the mercantile classes was compounded by the collapse of the Mauryan and later the Kushana empires, which had been the monastic orders' supreme source of patronage. Their eventual replacement by the Guptas, who were enthusiastic supporters of the brahmans and Hinduism, all but sealed the fate of Buddhism in India. Its demise would be gradual and only occasionally hastened by violent persecution. But centuries of rule by the Guptas in north India and Hindu kingdoms in the south left only pockets of Buddhist strength, which would decay over time.

The Gupta Empire

In the last decades of the 3rd century C.E., a family of wealthy landholders in the eastern Ganges plains first infiltrated the court of the local ruler and then seized his throne. Through a succession of clever alliances and timely military victories, the Gupta family built an empire that by the end of the 4th century C.E. extended across most of northern India. The *Guptas'* domains were not nearly as extensive as those of the Mauryas, and they had far less control over the regional lords and villages that fell under their sway than had briefly been the case with the Mauryas, particularly under Ashoka. The Gupta rulers never attempted to build a genuine bureaucracy or to regulate affairs at the local level effectively. Their empire was in fact a massive tributary edifice, in which former kings were left to rule in the name of the Guptas, and regional warrior elites were virtually autonomous governors of all but the empire's heartlands in the Ganges basin.

The Guptas were content to be acknowledged as supreme overlords and to draw as much tribute as possible from the many vassals who were forced to accede to their rule. Weak control from the center meant that local lords periodically revolted or squabbled among themselves. Though internal warfare continued, it was at a low level compared to the centuries after the fall of the Mauryas. Until the 5th century, foreign invaders were kept beyond the Himalayas and internal conflicts were short and localized. Gupta dominance brought over two and a half centuries of relative peace and unprecedented prosperity to much of north India.

A Hindu Renaissance

From the outset, the Guptas had been staunch defenders of Hinduism and patrons of the brahmans. With the family's rise to power, the brahmans' roles as sanctifiers of and advisors to kings were fully restored. Buddhist monks were increasingly confined to their monasteries,

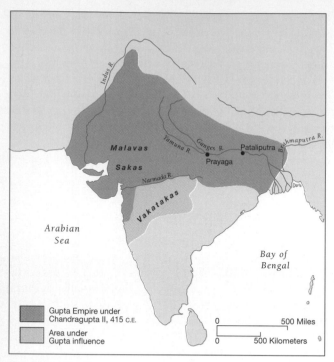

The Gupta Empire

Map legend:
- Gupta Empire under Chandragupta II, 415 C.E.
- Area under Gupta influence

500 Miles
500 Kilometers

which, lacking the patronage of the imperial court, had to depend on wealthy local merchants or landowners for support. The brahmans' roles as gurus, or teachers, for the princes of the imperial court and the sons of local notables also became entrenched. Brahmans regained the aura of mystery and supernatural power that they had enjoyed in the Vedic age. In *The Signet Ring of Rakshasa,* one of the great dramas that was produced in the Gupta epoch, King Chandragupta prostrates himself at the feet of his teacher and advisor, Chanyaka. The ruler lavishes presents on brahmans linked to the court and relies on their stratagems to thwart the schemes of his adversaries. With their power base and sources of patronage restored, brahman priests, poets, scholars, and patrons of the arts became the driving force behind an era of splendid achievement in literature, music, art, architecture, and the natural sciences.

The most dramatic expressions of the Hindu resurgence were the great temples that rose above the rapidly growing urban centers, both within the Gupta domains and in the independent kingdoms in the far south. In many cases the temples themselves provided the impetus for urban growth. Merchants, artisans, servants, and laborers migrated to the towns where the temples were located to serve the growing numbers of pilgrims who journeyed to the sacred sites to worship and win favors

from the Hindu deities. The intricately carved stone gateways and sanctuary towers of these edifices proclaimed the majesty of the Hindu gods and goddesses to the townspeople and peasants of the nearby villages. In eastern India and elsewhere, the temple towers literally teemed with sculptures of deities and friezes of their legendary exploits; with animals, which were often the vehicles or manifestations of major gods or goddesses; and with humans in all manner of activities, including explicit depictions of sexual intercourse.

The jumble of sculpture and the structure of the temples as a whole were very much reflections of the Hindu worldview. Compared with medieval European cathedrals and Muslim mosques, which soar to the heavens, Hindu temples were heavy and earthbound. These qualities were in part explained by limitations in construction techniques, but they resulted equally from the Hindu view that the divine is everywhere, not simply in the heavens. The towers, cluttered with statuary, mirrored the Hindu view of space as a realm alive with life. The worldly and even profane preoccupations of gods and goddesses (as well as ordinary mortals) depicted in temple sculptures suggest the Hindu conviction that divinity encompasses all life. It also reflects the symbolic parallels drawn in Indian religions between the union of male and female and the individual's search for oneness with the divine.

As these examples suggest, Hindu art stressed symbolism rather than accurate representation, which was so highly valued by the ancient Greeks. The sculpture and the god or goddess it depicted stood for something else—including creation (Brahma), destruction (*Shiva*), fertility (Lakshmi), and death (Kali as Durga). In fact, the temple complexes as a whole were massive *mandalas,* or cosmic diagrams, measured precisely and laid out according to established conventions.

Achievements in Literature and the Sciences

Though written languages had developed in India during the centuries before the rise of the Gupta dynasty, the Gupta reign initiated one of the great ages of Indian literary achievement. In the Gupta period and the following centuries, many of the great classics of *Sanskrit,* the sacred and classical Indian language, and Tamil, one of the major languages of the South, were written. The poet Kalidasa, who is acknowledged as the greatest of Sanskrit authors, lived in a period when Gupta power was at its height. In the "Cloud Messenger" and numerous other poems, he provided vivid pictures of life in the

An approaching pilgrim's view of the temple towers in the city of Madurai in south India. Like medieval cathedrals and Islamic mosques, these great structures attest to the intense faith and outpouring of devotion that were associated with the Hindu resurgence of the early centuries C.E.

Gupta age. In the following passage, for example, the clouds bringing the monsoon rains pass over a town where the poet exclaims:

> *Your body will grow fat with the smoke of incense from open windows where women dress their hair.*
> *You will be greeted by palace peacocks, dancing to welcome you, their friend.*
> *If your heart is weary from travel you may pass the night above mansions fragrant with flowers*
> *Whose pavements are marked with red dye from the feet of lovely women.*

In addition to poetry and drama, Hindu scholars in the classical era wrote treatises on the nature of time, space, and causality, which contain arguments that have much in common with the findings of modern science on these issues. In fact, the era of the Hindu revival was a time of great Indian achievement in both mathematics and the sciences. In addition to advances in geometry and algebra that were made quite independently of the work in these fields by the Greeks, Indian thinkers calculated the circumference of the globe and the value of π with remarkable accuracy. They also used the concept of zero and devised decimals, and, most critically, formulated the "Arabic" number system that we use today. In the Gupta age and afterward, the Indians also made major breakthroughs in medicine. They developed hospitals, surgical techniques, and sophisticated treatments for a variety of illnesses.

Intensifying Caste and Gender Inequities

As the brahmans recovered their earlier social dominance, the caste hierarchy they had long promoted was established as the backbone of the Indian social system. Caste divisions grew even more complex and came to vary significantly between different areas in the subcontinent. Styles of dress increasingly distinguished members of each varna grouping, and the restrictions on untouchables and other low-caste groups grew harsher and more pervasive. In some areas, for example, untouchables traveling on roadways between towns had to clap sticks together or continually shout that they were on the road in order to warn high-caste groups that they were in danger of being polluted. If a brahman or merchant was seen approaching, the untouchable was required to leave the road and pass by through the fields at a considerable distance. The untouchables were not allowed to use any wells but their own or to worship in the temples frequented by other caste groups. Even their living quarters were segregated from the rest of the towns and rural villages.

Like the untouchables, women at all caste levels suffered a further reduction of their status and restriction of career outlets. They were no longer allowed to read the sacred Vedas, though a few remained prominent in the devotional cults. Hindu law declared that women were legally minors, subject to the supervision and protection of their fathers, husbands, and, if widowed, their sons. Except for their personal clothing and jewelry, women were not allowed to inherit property. The fact that family fortunes could pass only from father to son and that large dowries were required to arrange marriages with suitable spouses meant that girls were increasingly seen as an economic liability. As popular sayings and poems from this period attest, sons were prized and pampered, while daughters were overlooked and neglected. In some regions where dowry amounts were highly inflated, female infanticide was practiced to save families from financial ruin.

Women were tied to the home, their lives decided by males. Marriages were primarily a means of establishing alliances between families. They were arranged with the groom having little say and the bride none. Child marriages were not uncommon among the upper castes. Young girls left the familiar surroundings of their own homes to live with their husband's families. In their new households, they were at the mercy of their mothers-in-law, who could be caring and reassuring but, if the literature from this and later periods is any gauge, were very often bossy and critical. A young girl's place in the new household depended almost wholly on her ability to bear sons, who would be devoted to her and would care for her in old age. A woman whose husband died before she bore him a son was doomed to a lonely life in the remote corners of the family compound. Even widows who bore sons were not to be envied. They were not allowed to remarry or go out alone lest they defile the memory of their deceased husbands.

Other than marriage, few avenues were open to women. A single woman was regarded as an economic liability and a blot on her family's honor. As the Buddhist monasteries shrank in numbers and size, the possibility of becoming a nun diminished sharply. Only by becoming a courtesan, or a woman accomplished in all the arts including sexual intercourse, could a woman establish some degree of independence. Courtesans, who are sometimes celebrated in the literature of this period, could become well educated, acquire wealth, and find outlets for their talents. But though they were far above the despised common prostitutes in status, they could not hope to have social respectability or raise families of their own. Unlike married women, whose husbands were duty bound to provide them with the requirements

of life, courtesans were dependent on the tastes and whims of males, who dominated all aspects of interaction between the sexes in the Gupta age.

The Pleasures of Elite Life

Though women were restricted in career options and largely confined to their households, life for those of the upper castes was not without its rewards—at least, once a woman had established her place in her husband's family by having sons. Well-to-do families lived in large compounds set in gardens filled with flowering plants and colorful birds. They were waited on by servants and entertained at periodic festivals and in their own compounds by swings, games such as chess and parchesi (both of which the Indians invented), and wandering musicians. Males and females dressed in silks and fine cottons and at mealtimes enjoyed one of the world's great cuisines. When they ventured away from the family compound, the very wealthy were carried in litters borne by servants and given the place of honor to which their caste rank entitled them.

Males from the upper castes were particularly privileged. They were expected to experience the four stages of the ideal Hindu life that were firmly established in this era for men only. In their youth they were to work hard as students, but many diversions and pleasures were available to the fashionable sons of well-to-do families. Many of these pastimes are described in the famous (or infamous) *Kamasutra* by Vatsayana, who lived in the Gupta era. Though often dismissed as little more than a glorified sex manual, Vatsayana's work in fact contains detailed instructions on virtually all aspects of the life of the young man-about-town. There are recommendations for grooming and hygiene, discussions of good etiquette in various situations, advice on the best way to select a wife, and, of course, instructions in making love to either a witty and knowledgeable courtesan or one's future wife. There was, of course, a double standard: young men were expected to come to marriage knowledgeable in the ways of love; girls who were not virgins were disgraced and unmarriageable.

The student was expected in the second stage of life to become a householder and, ideally, a faithful husband. Preserving or adding to the family fortune was a major task in this phase of life, and bearing sons to perform one's funeral rites and continue the family line was essential. At some point in middle age, the householder was supposed to bid farewell to his family and go off to the forest to join the hermits in meditation. In his final years, the upper-caste man was expected to enter the

DOCUMENT

A Guardian's Farewell Speech to a Young Woman About to Be Married

One of the great plays written during the Hindu revival of the early centuries C.E. was *Shakuntala,* by Kalidasa. The play is a Cinderella-style tale about a beautiful young woman, Shakuntala, who is loved by a king, and the travails she must endure before they are happily united. In the following exchange, as Shakuntala sets out to join her husband at his palace, she is instructed by her guardians (the hermits Kashyapa and Gautami) on the proper behavior for a young wife, in a manner that recalls the famous speech by Polonius to his son Laertes in Shakespeare's *Hamlet.*

Kashyapa: Now you Shakuntala . . . Respect your superiors,

Be friendly toward the ladies of the palace.

Never be angry with your husband, no matter what happens.

Be polite with the maids;

In everything be humble.

These qualities make a woman; those without them are black sheep in their families.

What is your opinion, Gautami?

Gautami: A bride needs nothing more. Remember his advice, Shakuntala.

Shakuntala: How will I ever manage in the palace? I feel so lost. I belong here, Father.

Kashyapa: Don't worry, my child; you are privileged.

You will be his great wife;

He is noble and great.

You will give him a son, as the East gives us light.

The pain of separation will then pass.

Questions: What does this conversation tell you about gender relationships and marriage in classical India? What does it say about attitudes toward women? How do these relationships and attitudes compare with those found in China and Greece in this era? How do they compare with those in our own society?

---

fourth stage of life by becoming a wandering holy man, completely dependent on the charity of others. Few individuals actually advanced beyond the householder stage. But the fact that the sequence had become the social ideal indicates that Indian religion and society could readily accommodate scholarship and worldly pursuits, bodily denial, and meditation as valid paths to self-fulfillment.

Lifestyles of the Ordinary People

For most Indians who labored as peasants, artisans, or sweepers at the lower levels of the caste system, the delights of upper-caste youths or the ability to set off as a wandering holy man were unattainable. Most Indians experienced lives of hard work, if not sheer drudgery. Most knew no deference from others but rather spent their lives bowing to and serving their caste superiors. At the lower-caste levels, women were somewhat freer in

their ability to move about the town and countryside and buy and sell in the local marketplace. But they had no servants to perform their many household chores and were required to do backbreaking farming tasks, such as weeding fields or transplanting rice.

There were, of course, small pleasures. Even low-caste groups could attend temple festivals, watch dances and dramatics performed in the open air, and risk their meager wages in dice games or betting on roosters specially bred to fight with each other. In an age when India was one of the most fertile and productive regions on the earth, it is probable that all but the untouchables lived as well as ordinary people did anywhere in the world.

The Indian economy continued to grow in the Gupta age, despite the decline of long-distance trade with China and Rome. Leadership in international commerce increasingly shifted to the trading cities on the east and west coasts and the southern seaports of the subcontinent. Strong trading links were maintained with

Gupta Decline and a Return to Political Fragmentation

For nearly 250 years, the Guptas managed to hold together the collection of vassal kingdoms that they passed off as an empire. Signs of future danger appeared in the northwest with the first of the Hun probes across the Himalayas in the early decades of the 5th century C.E. Preoccupied by the growing threat on their northern frontier, the later Gupta rulers failed to crush resistance from their vassals and challenges from states to the south of the Gupta domains. By the middle of the century, Gupta efforts to hold back repeated assaults by greater and greater numbers of Hun invaders were faltering. With the death of *Skanda Gupta,* the last of the truly able Gupta monarchs, a flood of nomadic invaders broke into the empire. Their pillaging and widely dispersed assaults finished off what remained of Gupta military might, and the empire dissolved into a patchwork of local kingdoms and warring states. From the mid-7th century until the establishment of the Delhi Sultanate in the early 13th century, northern India was divided and vulnerable to outside invasions.

CONCLUSION

The Legacy of the Classical Age in India

The civilization the Aryan invaders began to build in the centuries after settling in India in the middle of the second millennium B.C.E. proved a good deal more adaptable and long-lasting than the Harappan complex it replaced. Though its growth was marked by a couple of notable attempts to build a centralized political system to shield and nurture it, unlike China its genius and strength did not rest in political organization or military innovation. By the last centuries B.C.E., the central bulwarks of civilization in India were the caste system and the Hindu religion that provided its ideological underpinnings. What has come to be viewed as a system of social oppression served then as an intricate and ingenious mode of dividing labor and allotting social roles. The Hindu social order that rested on the caste hierarchy not only proved able to withstand the very formidable challenge of Buddhism but managed to absorb wave after wave of foreign invaders.

Though the contributions of the Buddhists and other nonbrahmanical religions were not inconsiderable, the brahman-dominated, caste-ordered civilization of India produced some of humanity's most sublime art

Stylized sculptures depicting young women from the Hindu temple at Khajuraho in eastern India. These figures represent a standardized form of feminine beauty in South Asian culture: large breasts, small waist, and ornate jewelry.

kingdoms in Sri Lanka and throughout Southeast Asia, which were strongly influenced by Indian cultural exports. In fact, India became the pivot of the great Indian Ocean trading network that stretched from the Red Sea and Persian Gulf in the west to the South China Sea in the east—a position it would maintain until the age of European overseas expansion after the 16th century C.E. It is no small wonder that India was known by the time of the Guptas as a land of great wealth as well as the home of many religions. A Chinese Buddhist, Fa-hsien, on a pilgrimage to India, exclaimed:

> The people are many and happy. They do not have to register their households with the police. There is no death penalty. Religious sects have houses of charity where rooms, couches, beds, food, and drink are supplied to travelers.

and philosophy; important breakthroughs in mathematics, the sciences, and technology; prosperous urban centers; and a population that in numbers has been second only to that of China through much of human history. Neither the rigidity of the caste system nor the pronounced religious emphasis of Indian culture prevented the range of diversity common in the achievements of the other classical civilizations. In India's case, these achievements included an often sensual art and literature, a sizeable corpus of tough-minded political theory, and a sophisticated trading system—all of which defy persisting characterizations of India as otherworldly and antimaterial.

FURTHER READINGS

Perhaps the most readable introductions to life and society in India's classical age can be found in A. L. Basham's *The Wonder That Was India* (1954) and Jeannine Auboyer's *Daily Life in Ancient India* (1961). The works of Romilla Thapar, especially her *Ashoka and the Decline of the Mauryas* (1961), are the best on the political history of the era. But even her more general *A History of India* (1966) is very detailed and quite technical—certainly a challenge for the beginner. Fine narrative histories of all aspects of Indian civilization in this period can be found in the appropriate chapters of *The History and Culture of the Indian People* (1964), ed. R. C. Majumdar, A. K. Majumdar, and D. K. Ghose. One of the best works on the position of women and social life more generally is Pandharinath Prabhu's *Hindu Social Organization* (1940). A wide range of other aspects of ancient Indian culture is covered in the fine essays in A. L. Basham's *A Cultural History of India* (1975).

Superb introductions to various branches of Indian religious and philosophical thinking, with well-selected portions of the appropriate texts, can be found in S. Radhakrishnan and Charles Moore, eds., *A Source Book in Indian Philosophy* (1957). Of the many books on Buddhism, Trevor Ling's *The Buddha* (1973) has the dual advantage of incorporating recent scholarship and being very readable. S. Radhakrishnan's *Hindu View of Life* (1927) provides a useful insider's view of Hindu religious beliefs and social organization. Heinrich Zimmer's *Philosophies of India* (1956), though somewhat dated, remains a good place to begin an exploration of the riches and diversity of Indian mythology and religious thinking. Benjamin Rowland's *The Art and Architecture of India* (1953) is the most objective and comprehensive work available in English on Indian art. For a taste of Indian literature in the classical age, there are English translations of the Ramayana and the Mahabharata and P. Lal's fine translations of *Great Sanskrit Plays* (1957).

8

Rome and
Its Empire

400 Rome completes control of central Italy   **146–133** Decline of Roman republic   **70–19** Vergil

167 Rome begins conquest in eastern Mediterranean   **44** Assassination of Caesar

500–450 Beginnings of Roman republic;
Twelve Tables of Law

106–43 Cicero

264–146 Rome's Punic Wars   **133–121** Gracchus brothers' reform attempts   **46** Julius Caesar dictator

107 ff. Increasing power of generals

500 B.C.E.   **300** B.C.E.   **100** B.C.E.

INTRODUCTION

Classical civilizations had taken shape in India and China by the 5th century B.C.E., and they maintained considerable coherence for the next 800 to 1000 years. This does not mean they were changeless: China experienced new dynasties and sharp debates among proponents of different ideologies. Change was even more pronounced in classical India, which saw recurrent invasions and the shifting fortunes of Buddhism and Hinduism. Nevertheless, many of the key issues and structures maintained continuity through the entire classical period, and while political boundaries shifted, the geographical cores of each of these Asian civilizations remained fairly constant.

This stability was not present in the Mediterranean. Greece, the cradle of classical Mediterranean civilization, had declined by the 4th century B.C.E., and its Hellenistic successor began to fade about two centuries later. This chapter deals with the final center of the classical Mediterranean, based around Rome. Rome preserved and extended many features of Greek and Hellenistic politics, culture, and economic organization; here too, as in southern and eastern Asia, there are some coherent classical themes. Rome also had a distinct tone and history, however, requiring separate treatment of the final 700 years of classical experience in the Mediterranean.

The earliest phases of Roman history occurred at a time when Greece and then Alexander and his successors held center stage to the east. It was during the 5th century B.C.E. that a new city-state near the middle of the Italian peninsula began to define a separate existence. Soon, Rome took on the trappings of a regional civilization, complete with its own language and an alphabet derived from the Greek alphabet. Rome was not the first center of civilization in Italy. Greek settlements had long occupied much of southern Italy, and an Etruscan culture, still poorly understood in key respects, had developed to the north of Rome. Roman influence in Italy gradually expanded, however, making Italy a focus of activity in the western Mediterranean.

As the Hellenistic kingdoms declined Rome prepared to advance further, soon taking over the dominant role in Mediterranean civilization. By the 2nd century B.C.E., Rome ruled Greece and the eastern Mediterranean directly, though it never penetrated fully into the Middle East's heartland where Hellenism had flourished. Yet, Rome established a zone of civilization around the Mediterranean that overlapped with much of the earlier Greek and Hellenistic orbit while extending it to the west and farther across North Africa. The Romans' massive empire flourished for four centuries and then limped through another 250 years in decline—an achievement in political organization and durability that the Greeks had never attained. Consequently, the fall of the Roman Empire about 476 C.E. had a far more dramatic quality than the more gradual evolution of Greece and the Hellenistic world.

Rome as Heir to Classical Mediterranean Civilization

Roman and Greek achievements were closely intertwined. Partly because of imitation, and partly because of shared Indo-European heritage, Roman religion, art and politics had much in common with those of Greece. Rome's genius differed somewhat, being focused more on engineering and less on philosophy or science. Nevertheless, Rome's achievements merged with those of Greece in developing Mediterranean civilization in the classical period. Rome served a vital role in preserving many features of Greek society. The Romans used and copied Greek science, monumental architectural styles, and drama. They built on Greek political and ethical theory and used Greek ideas to shape and explain their own constitutional structure. They revived many Greek commercial patterns and copied the Greek justifications of slavery. Rome had its own additions and modifications to make in many of these areas, but its eagerness to preserve and use Greek achievements was impressive.

Rome spread classical Mediterranean civilization to new parts of Europe and North Africa. Greek influence had touched mainly the coastal portions of the western

c. 4 B.C.E. Birth of Jesus	35 Paul converts to Christianity		180 Death of Emperor Marcus Aurelius; beginning of decline of empire
27 B.C.E. Augustus Caesar; rise of Roman Empire			476 Fall of Rome
	c. 30 Crucifixion of Jesus	101–106 Under Trajan, Rome's greatest territory	
			313 Constantine legalizes Christianity
1 C.E.	100 C.E.	200 C.E.	

Mediterranean. Rome moved inland, bringing all of North Africa, Spain, France, Romania, and important parts of present-day Britain, the Low Countries, and Germany into contact with Greco-Roman values and institutions—including writing in the Latin language. Rome did not create a permanent unity for Mediterranean civilization, nor was it able to control the bulk of the Middle East. However, its achievement in bringing a larger part of Europe and North Africa into the orbit of civilization did have lasting impact.

Along with preserving and adapting classical Mediterranean civilization and spreading it geographically, Rome sponsored major innovations in politics. Rome used Greek political ideas and paralleled many features of the Greek polis. But it also established an imperial administration that had its own principles particularly in law, providing an important new ingredient for the political legacy of Mediterranean civilization. This is why the *Roman Empire* was so much more durable than the colonial leagues of Athens or the Hellenistic kingdoms, leaving a more vivid impression.

Finally, the Roman Empire served as a breeding ground for one of the great religious changes in world history: the advent and initial dissemination of Christianity. Christianity did not spring directly from the mainstream principles of Greco-Roman civilization, but it did use many of these principles selectively and, in its spread and church structure, depended heavily on what Rome had achieved.

Overall, by preserving vital aspects of Greek and Hellenistic politics and culture, but also in its own major innovations, Rome created a new version of Mediterranean civilization—a final major statement of classical institutions in this part of the world. Greco-Roman civilization, in turn, would provide the classical background to several successor civilizations—in western Europe, where later medieval and Renaissance leaders harked back to what they understood from Greece and Rome; in eastern Europe, where Greek influence merged with Roman imperial government and Christianity; and to a degree in the next phase of civilization in the Middle East, under the spur of Islam.

This statue of a Roman patrician—the class that filled the Senate—comes from the time of the empire. The family patriarch, clad in his toga, holds busts of his two sons.

between expansion and established political values formed the key theme of Roman history by the 2nd century B.C.E. as the republic was wracked by a series of crises.

THE DEVELOPMENT OF ROME'S REPUBLIC

Focal Point: Building on the foundations of classical Mediterranean civilization, Rome early established firm political institutions, balancing aristocratic control with some popular voice. Rome also quickly began a pattern of expansion, first in Italy and then beyond. Tensions

Etruscan Beginnings and the Early Republic

The people of Rome were Indo-European and migrated to Italy about 2000 B.C.E. They gradually assimilated agriculture and, by about 800 B.C.E., gained some contact with Greek settlements farther south on the peninsula.

Rome was ruled for a time by the *Etruscans,* who provided powerful kings and organized tightly knit armies skilled in the use of horses and war chariots. The Etruscans imposed a strong government, but about 510 B.C.E., the local Roman aristocracy rebelled and devised a constitution carefully crafted to avoid tyrannical control. The Romans developed a *republic* because they had found monarchy contrary to the public good (*res publica*). By this time the Romans had also adapted the Greek alphabet to form their own Latin alphabet, which remains in use throughout western Europe and the Americas today.

The constitution of the early Roman republic favored the dominant aristocracy. Aristocrats staffed the powerful *Senate,* which advised on policy, and also served as magistrates. But lower-class citizens gained some voice. As in Greece, citizenship gave some people definite legal and political rights. At about 450 B.C.E., a law code was written to protect the property holdings of ordinary people and facilitate commerce. Soon, the ordinary citizens, or *plebeians*, won the right to elect their own representatives, the *tribunes*, to voice their interests. It was the Senate, however, that continued to serve as the center of Roman political life throughout the existence of the republic. The two chief executives, or *consuls,* were elected by an annual assembly in which the wealthy predominated. The rule of two consuls was designed to guard against arbitrary rule, and normally the consuls served for only a year, which meant that independent executive authority was hard to establish. This basic political structure, which balanced various interests to a degree but resembled many Greek city-states in depending heavily on the aristocratic voice, lasted for several centuries as Rome moved from a small local state to the center of a growing empire. The republic's balance of elements and the strong political loyalty it commanded from various classes not only was successful at the time, but also would inspire respect from later political reformers in Europe and the Americas seeking models for their own states and alternatives to monarchy.

Like its city-state politics, the early Roman economy resembled that of Greece about three centuries before. Aristocrats controlled large estates, but there were many grain-growing farmers, who were also independent citizens capable of military service. By introducing early the idea of written law (which placed some check on arbitrary aristocratic actions) and by allowing popular assemblies and elected officials to give some voice alongside the aristocratic Senate, the Roman republic constructed more explicit balances than most of the early Greek city-states had done. Social strife was long minimized as a result, even as many similar political ingredients appeared. More than the Greeks, the Romans emphasized *client-age* relationships by which landlords would aid and protect lesser citizens in return for loyalty and work.

Rome's diplomatic and military directions departed even more markedly from the patterns of the early Greek poleis, because there were fewer social tensions to distract the government and because no checkerboard of successful city-state rivals emerged to restrain the dynamic newcomer.

The Expansion of Rome

Rome's career differed most notably from that of its Greek counterparts by more promptly and wholeheartedly embracing expansion. Rome developed a solid army based on the service of citizen-farmers; while not as rigidly organized as Sparta, Rome stressed discipline and self-sacrifice within the framework of a largely agricultural economy. Rome was not, however, as sheltered from outside attack by natural boundaries as many of the Greek poleis had been. It faced challenges from other areas in Italy, including a league of city-states to the north. Rome dealt with these challenges, from 496 B.C.E. onward, through a combination of alliances and military attacks. By about 400 B.C.E. it had gained control over the whole of central Italy. A second wave of expansion, toward the southern end of the peninsula, began about 360 B.C.E., gradually winning over rival tribes by means of superior military organization and tight control over allied states.

Roman infantry units—the famous *Legions*—were disciplined and flexible fighting forces, trained never to give up; they endowed Rome with a deserved reputation for being able to bounce back from specific defeats through a persistent will to win. The Roman military was supported by the rich agricultural economy of central Italy, which provided an abundant population base; and each wave of expansion simply strengthened the military and economic resources available. Once established, Roman rule proved flexible, though it provoked some resentments and rebellions. Some areas were granted Roman citizenship, while others retained local self-governments; in a few cases colonies of Roman soldiers were planted to assure order.

By the early part of the 3rd century B.C.E., the Romans' expansion brought them in conflict with the Greek cities of the south, which soon accepted Roman governance. This made Rome a rival of the former Phoenician colony, *Carthage,* for control of the western Mediterranean. Carthage, located in North Africa in the modern nation of Tunisia, had a substantial navy and was quick to see the threat from Roman control over Sicily. A series of *Punic Wars* (*Punic* from the Roman word for *Phoenician*) began in 264 B.C.E. Thus, Rome developed its own navy for the first time; both Carthage and Rome generated new allies and colonies in Spain as competition steadily escalated. During the Second Punic War, the great Carthaginian general *Hannibal* brought a large army to Italy, including 50 war elephants. But gradually the Romans wore Carthage down. In the Third Punic War (146 B.C.E.), the Romans finally decided to kill or enslave every inhabitant of Carthage. Rome now had a substantial overseas empire, including much of Spain and substantial parts of North Africa, held either outright or through allied states.

Rome's growing power also drew the new empire toward the eastern Mediterranean, partly from a search for new conquests and partly because rival states in the region appealed for help. The collapse of the Hellenistic kingdoms left a vacuum of power in this region that Rome was more and more called to fill. From 167 B.C.E. onward, the Romans began to conquer Macedonia and Greece, and they soon set up a protectorate over the Asian coast of the Mediterranean and also Egypt.

The republic was often brutal in its treatment of the areas conquered outside Italy. Opponents of Roman rule in Greece were punished severely; much booty and many prisoners were taken. The conquest of Spain during the 2nd century B.C.E. produced repeated atrocities. In North Africa, Carthage was destroyed, its land was plowed up, and salt was scattered in its fields as a symbol of its abandonment.

Imperial expansion inevitably changed Roman society and politics, to the great dismay of traditionalists. New trade and wealth enriched the upper classes, creating new gaps between rich and poor and making it increasingly difficult to manage Rome's balanced constitution. Aristocrats bought out many farmers who could not compete with cheap grains imported from Sicily and later North Africa. Older clientage relationships deteriorated, sharpening class conflicts. The devastation caused by Hannibal's invasions also produced widespread indebtedness, allowing estate owners to buy out ordinary farmer-citizens. Central Italy, like Greece before it, turned into a grape and olive region, highly commercial and organized mainly in large estates. Ruined farmers either worked as rural laborers or moved to the city, swelling an impoverished urban lower class easily open to appeals from ambitious politicians. Adding to social complexity was the rise of an important business class, which also helped the state to collect taxes. Slavery also increased as a result of military conquests. Many slaves worked in households or craft production, even tutoring Roman children, but bands of slaves were used in mining and on some of the great agricultural estates. By 14 C.E. (after the republic's collapse), three million slaves—40 percent of the total population—worked in Italy.

The Crisis of the Republic

What was happening around Rome closely resembled earlier patterns in Greece, where accelerating social and economic tensions produced increasing political unrest. But the Roman crisis was in many ways greater, because the expanding empire created so many new opportunities for the upper classes to gain new lands and augment their supply of slaves. While some former farmers sank into debt-slavery, others flooded into the city of Rome,

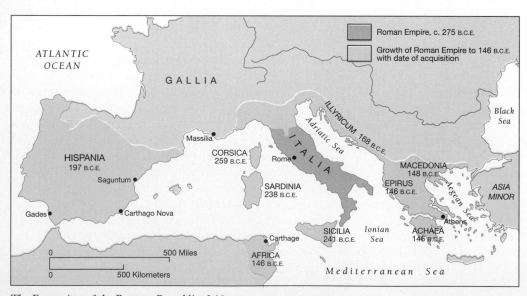

The Expansion of the Roman Republic, 146 B.C.E.

beginning a process that would push the city's population past one million, much of it consisting of poor, irregularly employed laborers.

Roman politics had long depended not only on some balance between farmers and landowners but also on the aristocrats' protection of the farmers as their clients. Thus, free farmers had direct participation in the Roman state through the popular assemblies. They could also count on aristocratic landlords to help them protect their interests in courts of law or even tide them over economically in bad times. Now this community of interest was split, as the landlords tried to buy out the farmers to add to their estates and as many farmers, though still citizens, massed in the city of Rome. The result, first economically and then politically, was a durable class conflict between popular leaders and aristocrats during the final decades of the republic. In this setting many ambitious leaders in both camps, including successful army generals, maneuvered for personal advantage.

In 133 B.C.E., a new tribune, *Tiberius Gracchus,* tried to limit the size of large estates, with the government redistributing some land to the poor. The Senate opposed the plan, and Tiberius was assassinated by conservatives. During the following decades, *Gaius Gracchus,* Tiberius's brother, tried to introduce land reforms and made a special attempt to appeal to the rising business class of wealthy men who were eager for greater power and continued expansion of the empire but who were below the aristocracy in status. Gracchus also proposed extending Roman citizenship to more of the Italian people, but the Roman masses opposed this dilution of their authority. The Senate decreed that Gracchus, undefended, was to be put to death; a servant helped him fall on his sword.

Soon after this, in 107 B.C.E., a successful army general, *Marius,* who had put down a rebellion in one of Rome's client kingdoms in North Africa, became consul. Marius began using paid volunteers from the lower classes for his army, creating a permanent military group with great political potential through their ability to coerce the Senate. Then another general, *Sulla,* siding with the Senate, which he packed with his supporters, drove out Marius and his followers. The republic, though most of its institutions were still intact, had become little more than a battleground for opposing ambitions. Clearly, a republican constitution designed for an agrarian city-state was proving unsuitable for governing a vast empire with a highly commercial economy.

In 77 B.C.E., another general, Pompey, came to the fore. Like his predecessors, he enhanced his power by winning new conquests—first in Spain, and then in the Middle East. His success, plus renewed civil war at home, prompted the Senate to give him special powers.

A middle-class political leader, *Cicero,* eloquently pleaded for a return to republican balance, arguing against the generals and popular demagogues, but he was not heeded. Pompey joined with other generals, including *Julius Caesar,* to form a new government that could override the Senate. Caesar, who won considerable support from the Roman lower classes, pursued his own goals through winning new territory across the Alps in Gaul (present-day France). He then defied Pompey and the Senate by bringing his troops back to Italy and taking over the government in 49 B.C.E. Effectively, Caesar's victory in the ensuing civil war ended the republic.

Caesar introduced few formal changes in government institutions. The Senate, which was packed with Caesar's men, still existed and debated, but its acts were a sham because of Caesar's control of the army. Caesar brought more Italians and other provincials into politics at the expense of old Roman families. Made dictator for ten years and then for life, Caesar named many new officials and judges and introduced important reforms, such as a more scientific calendar that formed the basis for the one we use today. Caesar was suspected of wanting to set up a monarchy, and was assassinated by traditionalist senators in 44 B.C.E.

Caesar's death led to 13 more years of civil war; his cause was defended by his grandnephew and adopted son *Octavian,* who fought the armies of the Senate. Octavian soon took the name "Caesar," which would come to mean emperor. In a series of wars, particularly in Egypt and the Middle East, Octavian finally won out. His last opponents, Mark Anthony and his wife Cleopatra, queen of Egypt, committed suicide, ending the civil strife and making Octavian absolute master of Rome and the entire Mediterranean world. Octavian then proceeded to create a new set of institutions that would be suited to Rome's altered position, including its vast empire, while not unduly offending the republican traditions still cherished by many citizens. His response was the creation of an outright empire, with himself as first emperor under the name of *Augustus Caesar.* This empire was a success, as Rome, unlike the earlier Greek poleis, made a successful transition to a new form of government that decisively broke with city-state bounds.

ROMAN CULTURE

Focal Point: As Rome struggled with its political crisis a major cultural transformation was taking place that merged earlier Roman values and the Latin language with the impressive heritage of Greek and Hellenistic learning. Roman leaders were increasingly schooled in

CLOSEUP

Caesar's Wives

Julius Caesar (100–44 B.C.E.) was married three times, and his marriages suggest to us several aspects of upper-class women's conditions at the end of the former republic. Caesar's first marriage was arranged for political reasons. He wedded with Cornelia, a daughter of the popular general Marius, to build support with Rome's more radical factions. He was genuinely devoted to her, though as a notorious philanderer he did not let this prevent him from having several affairs. Their daughter Julia was married to a leading general—another political alliance. Cornelia died in 69, and soon after Caesar married Pompeia, a granddaughter of the leading conservative general, Sulla. But in 62, Pompeia participated in a religious ceremony for women only at which her lover, the poet Clodius, appeared dressed as a woman and was discovered. The poet bribed his way out of a sacrilege trial, but Caesar divorced Pompeia, saying that "Caesar's wife must be above suspicion." His third wife, Calpurnia, seems to have been carefully domestic, and he stayed with her (again, along with renewed affairs, including one with Egypt's Cleopatra) until his assassination.

philosophy and a rich literary culture, blended with the earlier republican ideas of active citizenship.

Roman intellectual life was never as vibrant as that of the glory days of 5th-century Athens, in part because Roman writers and artists were so eager to adopt Greek forms. But Rome had its own strengths, while preserving and modifying many Greek cultural achievements.

The Range of Roman Art

Greek artistic styles and literary influence increasingly shaped Roman upper-class life, from the 2nd century into the days of the empire. Many aristocratic families were educated by Greek slaves, who as tutors had considerable independence and in a few cases produced important literary and historical works of their own. Imitation of Greece was aided by the similarity between Roman and Greek religions, in which essentially the same pantheon of gods and goddesses merely had different names. Roman religion was more political than Greek, bent toward divine protection of the state and colder in tone, but the similarities encouraged shared stories and literary symbolism. Rome's literary creativity was less impressive than that of the Greeks, partly because Greek authors were so widely read. The Roman poet *Vergil* picked up the Greek epic tradition and linked Roman history and mythology with the great stories of the *Iliad* and the *Odyssey*. Roman poets and biographers were also active, shaping the Latin language and providing stylistic models. Roman sculptors worked mainly in the Greek tradition, producing busts of great men and statues and scenes of heroic grandeur. Rome also developed active painters, who produced lively (and sometimes pornographic) decorations for the houses of the wealthy.

Roman architecture benefited as the city's wealth grew. Again, Greek styles provided primary inspiration, with the Romans preferring more ornate designs for columns and arches. But Rome added its own genius to Greek architecture, mainly through engineering advances that allowed structures of greater size to be built. Huge stadiums, public baths, temples, massive aqueducts to carry water to cities, great stretches of paved road, and huge port facilities began to appear in the later republic. Roman ability to construct elaborate arches, which allowed buildings to carry great structural weight, was unsurpassed anywhere in the world. Under Augustus, statues, fountains, and temples to the gods spread through Rome, making the city the showcase as well as the capital of the new empire, with its population of one million.

Greek influence and the practical issues of politics in an increasingly complex society prompted creativity in many other areas, though science advanced little beyond the compilation of Greek material into textbooks. Roman leaders valued skill in oratory, and they advanced discussions of the arts of rhetoric. Ethical philosophy received considerable attention. Hellenistic schools, including Stoicism, won many converts because Roman leaders were eager to develop arguments for moral behavior that had strong logical support. Writers such as Cicero discussed the joys and sorrows of human life, urging moderation and a dedication to the public good.

This photo shows the tombstone of a Roman centurion, Marcus Favonius Facilis (i.e., easy or skillful), son of Marcus, of the tribe of Pollia, Centurion of the 20th Legion.

Architecture expressed Roman power. Massive monuments, in the styles adapted from the Greeks, were built from England in the north to the desert fringes of North Africa, from Spain to present-day Hungary and Romania, and down the Middle Eastern coast of the Mediterranean. Temples, stadiums, villas for transplanted Romans or the local upper class, and the ubiquitous baths brought Roman styles and building knowledge through the expanded Mediterranean world. Awesome ruins of these structures, which still dot the

former empire, give testimony to Rome's power as a cultural disseminator.

Major Themes in Roman Literature

Prosperity and greater stability during the reign of Augustus and his successors brought growing attention to other cultural activities. While some of Rome's best poets flourished during the late republic as Greek themes were transmuted into Latin language and style, the early empire saw a flowering of history and biography. Many writers praised the new imperial house, but poets such as *Horace* combined this loyalty with considerable humor and creative skill in adapting Greek poetic meters to the Latin language. Horace, initially a republican, shifted his support to Augustus; his odes were lyrical poems, many of them praising the emperor and his family.

Another poet, *Ovid*, stressed the growing sensuality of the aristocracy in his writing on the arts of love. Exiled by the emperor, who wanted to defend family values, he also wrote about the Roman religion and translated Greek nature stories. Historians such as *Livy* wrote elaborate accounts of Rome, linking the empire to the republican past.

Vergil's great epic poem the *Aeneid* was itself dedicated to the glories of Augustus and his empire:

Now fix your sight, and stand intent, to see your Roman race, and Julian progeny.
There mighty Caesar waits his vital hour, Impatient for the world, and grasps his promised power.
But next behold the youth of form divine—Caesar himself, exalted in his line—Augustus, promised oft, and long foretold,
Sent to the realm that Saturn ruled of old; born to restore a better age of gold.
Africa and India shall his power obey;
He shall extend his propagated sway beyond the solar year, without the starry way . . .
But Rome! 'tis thine alone, with awful sway, To rule mankind, and make the world obey,
Disposing peace and war, thy own majestic way. . . .

After the cultural surge of the late republic and early empire, and having been spurred by the assimilation of Greek forms, Roman cultural activity declined somewhat. Intellectual life continued, but it stressed preservation, imitation, textbook summaries, and education of the upper classes. Dissemination and additional building continued, but well before the politics of the empire began to deteriorate, mainstream literary and artistic vitality began to decline. Only the new religious spur of

Rome and a Values Crisis

Rome's increasing contact with the eastern Mediterranean, particularly with Greece, brought important debates about culture. Many conservatives deplored Greek learning and argued that it would corrupt Roman virtue. Cicero, a leading politician in the Senate and a major Latin writer, here defends Greek literature, using Hellenistic justifications of beauty and utility. Cicero played a major role in the popularization of Greek culture during the 1st century B.C.E.

Do you think that I could find inspiration for my daily speeches on so manifold a variety of topics, did I not cultivate my mind with study, or that my mind could endure so great a strain, did not study to provide it with relaxation? I am a votary of literature, and make the confession unashamed; shame belongs rather to the bookish recluse, who knows not how to apply his reading to the good of his fellows, or to manifest its fruits to the eyes of all. But what shame should be mine, gentlemen, who have made it a rule of my life for all these years never to allow the sweets of a cloistered ease or the seductions of pleasure or the enticements of repose to prevent me from aiding any man in the hour of his need? How then can I justly be blamed or censured, if it shall be found that I have devoted to literature a portion of my leisure hours no longer than others without blame devote to the pursuit of material gain, to the celebration of festivals or games, to pleasure and the repose of mind and body, to protracted banqueting, or perhaps to the gaming-board or to ballplaying? I have the better right to indulgence herein, because my devotion to letters strengthens my oratorical powers, and these, such as they are, have never failed my friends in their hour of peril. Yet insignificant though these powers may seem to be, I fully realize from what source I draw all that is highest in them. Had I not persuaded myself from my youth up, thanks to the moral lessons derived from a wide reading, that nothing is to be greatly sought after in this life save glory and honour, and that in their quest all bodily pains and all dangers of death or exile should be lightly accounted, I should never have borne for the safety of you all the brunt of many a bitter encounter, or bared my breast to the daily onsets of abandoned persons. All literature, all philosophy, all history, abounds with incentives to noble action, incentives which would be buried in black darkness were the light of the written word not flashed upon them. How many pictures of high endeavor the great authors of Greece and Rome have drawn for our use, and bequeathed to us, not only for our contemplation, but for our emulation! These I have held ever before my vision throughout my public career, and have guided the workings of my brain and my soul by meditating upon patterns of excellence.

But let us for the moment waive these solid advantages; let us assume that entertainment is the sole end of reading; even so, I think you would hold that no mental employment is so broadening to the sympathies or so enlightening to the understanding. Other pursuits belong not to all times, all ages, all conditions; but this gives stimulus to our youth and diversion to our old age; this adds a charm to success, and offers a haven of consolation to failure. In the home it delights, in the world it hampers not. Through the night watches, on all our journeying, and in our hours of country ease, it is an unfailing companion.

If anyone thinks that the glory won by the writing of Greek verse is naturally less than that accorded to the poet who writes in Latin, he is entirely in the wrong. Greek literature is read in nearly every nation under heaven, while the vogue of Latin is confined to its own boundaries, and they are, we must grant, narrow. Seeing, therefore, that the activities of our race know no barrier save the limits of the round earth, we ought to be ambitious that whithersoever our arms have penetrated there also our fame and glory should extend; for the reason that literature exalts the nation whose high deeds it sings, and at the same time there can be no doubt that those who stake their lives to fight in honour's cause find therein a lofty incentive to peril and endeavor. We read that Alexander the Great carried in his train numbers of epic poets and historians. And yet, standing before the tomb of Achilles at Sigeum, he exclaimed, "Fortunate youth, to have found in Homer an herald of thy valor!" Well might he so exclaim, for had the *Iliad* never existed, the same mound which covered Achilles' bones would also have overwhelmed his memory.*

*Cicero, *Pro Archia Poeta*. Translated by N. H. Watts. Loeb Classical Library. Cicero, *Pro Archia* (Harvard University Press, 1965), 12–14, 16, 23–24.

Questions: What kind of objections to Greek learning is Cicero arguing against? Which of his arguments had the most lasting appeal to those who were reshaping Roman culture? Can you think of similar debates about foreign culture in other times and places in history?

These columns surround the Arch of Titus near the Colosseum in Rome. The use of decorative styles that originated in classical Greece was a central feature of Roman public design.

Christianity inspired new uses for Latin and Greek literary skill, elements of philosophy, and ultimately art.

THE INSTITUTIONS OF EMPIRE

Focal Point: Augustus and his successors had to create new policies to hold Rome's expanding empire together. Republican values were not forgotten, but the importance of military administration and effective laws gained ground. Rome did not, however, follow China's pattern in developing an elaborate bureaucracy or an integrating political culture.

Imperial Rule of Law

Rome's rule of its growing empire rested heavily on tolerance plus cohesion through law. Military force was used as needed, and in troubled periods, Rome briefly seized administration of a distant province.

In general, considerable autonomy was given to local governments, including the old Greek city-states, as the harsh colonial policies of the republic were revised. Some whole kingdoms, as in parts of North Africa, were preserved, though they were required to obey Roman foreign policy and obtain permission for any new succession to the throne. This policy of tolerance greatly facilitated Roman control, for an elaborate bureaucratic apparatus did not have to be developed. Only much later, in different circumstances, did lack of centralization prove to be a partial liability. At the same time, however, Rome maintained small military garrisons in most areas and large outposts in newly conquered or threatened regions. Army generals doubled as provincial governors in such cases, which gave them the possibility of building considerable regional power even to the point of challenging the consuls and Senate back in Rome. Again, in contrast to Chinese principles of imperial rule, Roman efforts were marked by the absence of coordinated bureaucratic hierarchies or formal training. In only a few cases, such as the forced dissolution of the independent Jewish state in 63 C.E. after a major local rebellion, did the Romans take over distant areas completely.

Rome's greatest addition to its principles of politics and empire was careful attention to the development of codes of law. While local laws continued to apply in many areas of the empire, Roman law provided an overarching system accessible to citizens in any part of the empire and capable of facilitating commercial exchange. Roman jurists carefully constructed statements of general legal principles—what they regarded as "natural law" and case precedents—that applied consistent standards to specific civil or criminal issues, building one of the most extensive legal systems anywhere. In the early republic they collected the statutes passed by the Roman assembly and the interpretations of judicial officials. As the republic expanded and encountered other legal systems, judicial officials had to formulate more general principles of equity. By the end of the republic, the idea of *natural law,* applicable to all societies and related to Stoic ethical theory, emerged as a result. Here was a substantial addition to the political traditions established by the Greek city-states and the early Roman republic.

Roman law was directed by praetors, some with the most able minds of the Roman world, who were elected annually. Along with concepts like natural law and the further idea that law should regulate human relations justly, the praetors worked to build precedent from actual, practical cases throughout the Roman Mediterranean. Roman law was too well established to be ignored by emperors. It defined rights as well as duties for citizens. Used later in Christianity and by many European states, its principles would enjoy a long life.

Roman law focused heavily on protection of private property and on family stability. It also carried forward some central concepts. Law, in the Roman view, should evolve to meet changing conditions without, however, fluctuating wildly. Rules and objective judgments, rather than personal whim, should govern social relationships; thus, Roman law steadily took over the judgment functions earlier reserved for fathers of families or landlords. Roman law also promoted the importance of common-sense fairness. In one case cited in the law texts, a slave was being shaved by a barber in a public square. Two men were playing ball nearby and one accidentally hit the barber with the ball, causing him to cut the slave's throat. Who was responsible: barber, catcher, or pitcher? According to Roman law, the slave himself, for anyone so foolish as to be shaved in a public place was asking for trouble and bore the responsibility himself.

The extension of Roman law was supplemented by a willingness to extend citizenship to important groups outside Rome and its environs. This was a marked contrast to earlier Greek policy, bent more on defending the primacy of the polis. Italians had gained this right during the republic, and a minority of people in France, Spain, North Africa, and the eastern Mediterranean acquired citizenship in the early decades of the empire. Paul, a key figure in early Christianity and born a Jew, was a Roman citizen and proud of it. Several North Africans served as emperors and were leaders in intellectual and religious life (including that of the early Christian church). More generally, citizenship gave selected individuals full access to Roman law and its courts and obviously encouraged loyalty.

The combination of systematic law, military organization, and tolerance for local autonomy (including a welter of diverse religions) allowed Rome to maintain its empire amid considerable internal peace for a long time—an achievement far greater than the conquest of the empire in the first place.

Augustus and His Successors

In building an imperial government after his final victory in 31 B.C.E., Octavian utilized tolerant principles of treatment for conquered provinces and the developing system of law. He also appealed carefully to remaining republican loyalties. He talked sincerely about the validity of republican virtues and the importance of discipline and family virtues. He also retained many of the agencies of the republic, including the Senate, while eviscerating most of them by installing his own supporters, who were in full control. Symbolizing the transition, in 27 B.C.E. the Senate voted Octavian the title *Augustus*—a word often applied to gods and appropriate to an office that now dominated the state. The emperor now controlled the apparatus of government, making major appointments and military decisions and establishing new laws and policies.

Augustus set about consolidating his new regime by instituting moral reforms, banning mystery religions, and insisting on adherence to traditional Roman ceremonies. He revised the law to strengthen family stability while encouraging people to have children by ruling, for example, that women with at least three children might gain new rights. Augustus launched an ambitious new building program in Rome, which brought new jobs to the Roman masses and new entertainments as well. Augustus also tried to regularize control over the provinces. He relied heavily on his army of 250,000 men, giving them abundant rewards for long service and loyalty. He maintained the earlier policy of allowing considerable local autonomy to accompany military strength while encouraging the development of Romanized colonies in many provinces, particularly in North Africa and western Europe.

The empire Augustus created maintained its basic organizational structure and its heady success for approximately two centuries. Incompetent emperors were no rarity in this period, in part because no clear lines of succession were established. Effectively, the army controlled basic power, which worked well when a strong emperor held the army's loyalty but badly when an emperor lost command of the troops. Succession battles among rival generals were common. By 96 C.E., emperors began to reduce succession problems by adopting their own successors. This practice yielded a series of five good emperors who brought Rome to its greatest power.

Beyond the idea of law, the Roman imperial state did not innovate, particularly in the functions ascribed to government. Regulation of commerce was essential to the Roman state's efforts to assure vital stocks of grain from Sicily and North Africa. The administration of food supplies and prices for huge cities, like Rome, required a substantial official staff. Public works in the form of roads and harbors facilitated military transport as well as commerce, while government-sponsored amenities, such as public baths and stadiums, attracted public loyalty. The building of aqueducts to carry water to cities was another major state activity. All these public works and regulations required substantial tax revenues.

Government-supported religious ceremonies continued,

This public lavatory was part of a new building in the prosperous Italian port city of Ostia Antica. Other buildings, some of which were made of brick, were used for commercial and storage purposes as well as for apartments.

but there was little attempt to impose this religion on all subjects, and various other religions were usually tolerated. Only Jews, and later, Christians found the state's claim to primary loyalty unacceptable, and only they drew Roman reprisals; the Roman government tolerated Jewish monotheism but reacted fiercely to Jewish revolt. Even the later Roman emperors, who as a means of shoring up authority enhanced the idea that the emperor himself was a god, were normally tolerant of other religions, inconsistently attacking Christianity because of the Christians' refusal to place the state first in their devotion.

Expansion continued during the early empire. The emperor *Trajan* adopted a particularly aggressive foreign policy in 101–106 C.E. The boundaries of the empire were pressed to the greatest extent ever; fortifications were built in northern England and along the Rhine and Danube rivers, signaling the inclusion of much of western Europe in the new geography of Mediterranean civilization. The empire also reached deeper into the Middle East, with new provinces in Armenia, Assyria, and Mesopotamia. But the expense of maintaining the vast boundaries placed growing burdens on the imperial economy. A turn from expansion to defense, though probably inevitable, mitigated some of the easy conquests characteristic of earlier years.

By 180 C.E., the empire was poised on a pinnacle of power that would quickly turn to descent. Foreign policy turned defensive—a matter of building walls and trying to finance border garrisons to keep invaders out. The later Roman Empire, though still capable of impressive achievements, was enmeshed in a pattern of gradual decline, which in turn was part of the general collapse of the classical world.

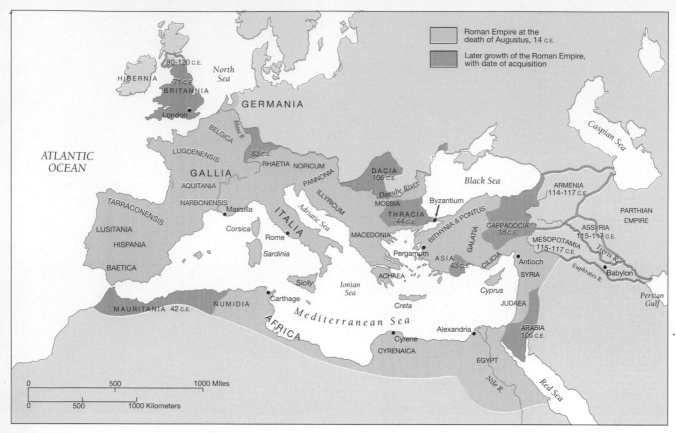

The Roman Empire from Augustus to 150 C.E.

ANALYSIS

The Classical Mediterranean in Comparative Perspective

The three great classical civilizations lend themselves to a variety of comparisons. The general tone of each differed from the others, ranging from India's otherworldly strain to China's emphasis on government centralization—though it is important to note the varieties of activities and interests and the changes that occurred within each of the three societies.

Basic comparisons embrace the substantial similarities that resulted from each classical society's effort to move toward empire or from the primary reliance on an agricultural economy. Greco-Roman interest in secular culture bears some resemblance to Confucian emphasis in China, though in each case religious currents, including popular animism, remained as well. But

Greco-Roman political values and institutions differed from the Confucian emphasis on deference and bureaucratic training. India differed greatly from Greece and Rome in its use of the Indo-European pantheon of gods. Greek definitions of science contrasted with those of India and China. Several focal points can be used for comparison.

Each of the classical civilizations emphasized a fairly rigid social hierarchy, with substantial distance between elites and the majority of people who did the manual and menial work. This vital similarity among the civilizations reflected common tensions between complex leadership demands and lifestyles and the limited economic resources of the agricultural economy. Groups at the top of the social hierarchy judged that they had to subordinate lower groups rather carefully to assure their own economic margins. Each classical society generated ideologies that explained and justified the great social divisions. Philosophers and religious leaders devoted considerable attention to this subject, either explicitly or by implication.

Within this common framework, however, there

were obvious differences. Groups at the top of the social pyramid reflected varied value systems. Hence, in India the priests, in China the bureaucrats, and in Greece the cultivated aristocrats ruled the roost, though in all cases this elite evolved from an earlier pattern that emphasized a warrior leadership. The status of merchants varied despite the vital role played by commerce in all three civilizations.

Opportunities for mobility varied also. India's caste system allowed movement within castes, if wealth was acquired, but little overall mobility. This was the most rigid classical social structure, because it tied people to their basic social and occupational position by birth. China's bureaucratic system allowed a very small number of talented people from below to rise substantially on the basis of education, though it must be emphasized that most bureaucrats continued to come from the landed aristocracy. Mediterranean society, with its aristocratic emphasis, limited opportunities to rise to the top, but the importance of acquired wealth (particularly in Rome) did give some nonaristocrats important economic and political opportunities. Cicero, for example, came from a family of merchant background. Various classes also shared some political power in city-state assemblies; the idea of basic political rights held by citizens (see "Analysis" in Chapter 7) was unusual in classical civilizations. Although most people were excluded even in the Greek democracies, this degree of mixing would have been impossible in a caste system.

Each classical civilization distinctively defined the position of the lowest orders. India's untouchables performed duties culturally evaluated as demeaning though often vital. So did China's "mean people"—who included actors. Classical Mediterranean society relied heavily on the legal and physical compulsions of slavery to provide both menial service and the most demanding kinds of labor, particularly as Greece and then Rome entered their expansion phases. Greece and Rome gave unusual voice to farmers when they maintained their own property, but tended to scorn manual labor per se—a view that helped justify slavery and was perpetuated by slavery in turn. The position of the peasantry tended to get worse over time in the Mediterranean when the economy became more complex. In this respect, India's caste system, which involved less direct control over labor, was more stable.

Finally, each of the classical civilizations developed a different kind of cultural "glue" to help hold its social hierarchy together. Greece and Rome left much of the task of managing the social hierarchy to local authorities; community bonds, as in the city-states, were meant to pull different groups into a sense of common purpose. They also relied on military force and clear legal statements that defined rights according to station. Force and legal inequalities played important roles in China and India as well, but there were additional inducements. India's Hinduism obviously helped justify and sustain the hierarchy by promising rewards through reincarnation for submission to one's place in any given existence. Within this framework, a network of caste laws and customs encouraged people to internalize their understanding of the jobs and social contacts permitted to them. China, in addition to government enforcement, urged general cultural values of obedience and self-restraint, creating some agreement—despite varied religions and philosophies—on the legitimacy of social ranks through the definition of how gentlemen and commoners should behave.

In no case did the social cement work perfectly; social unrest surfaced in all the classical civilizations, as in major slave rebellions in Rome or recurrent peasant uprisings in China. At the same time, the rigidity of all classical social structures gave many common people some leeway. Elites viewed the masses as being so different from themselves that they did not try to revamp all their beliefs or community institutions.

Differences in approach to social inequality nevertheless had important results. China and particularly India generated value systems that might convince people in the lower classes and the upper ranks that there was some legitimacy in the social hierarchy. Greece and Rome attempted a more difficult task in emphasizing the importance of aristocracy while offering some other elements a share in the political system. This combination could work well, though some groups, including slaves, were always excluded. It tended to deteriorate, however, when poorer citizens lost property. Yet, no sweeping new social theory emerged to offer a different kind of solace to the masses—at least until Christianity began to spread. It is no accident, then, that Indian and Chinese social structures survived better than Mediterranean structures did, lasting well beyond the classical period into the 20th century.

Questions: Why did the classical civilizations seem to need radical social inequalities? What was the relationship between wealth and social position in each of the classical civilizations? If India used religion to compensate for social inequalities, what did China and the Mediterranean use?

THE EVOLUTION OF ROME'S ECONOMIC AND SOCIAL STRUCTURE

Focal Point: Several basic features of Roman economic and social development closely paralleled earlier patterns in Greece. A local agricultural economy that yielded two social groups—aristocracy and free farmers—became increasingly complex as a result of urban and commercial growth.

As earlier in the Greek city-states, a class of merchants expanded during the final centuries of the republic. Many merchants were foreigners, for Romans did not take well to seafaring and built clumsy boats that hugged the shores. Traders from Greece and the Middle East played a vital role. But a native business group expanded as well, and its prestige was somewhat higher than its counterpart in classical Greece had been, even though aristocratic suspicion of merchants persisted in Rome. Merchants gained political voice in the Roman Senate in the later days of the republic, though they never matched aristocratic prestige.

Rome and other imperial cities also developed large artisanal and shopkeeping groups, and of course a substantial, sometimes troubling, propertyless lower class.

Rome's family structure resembled that of classical Greece and all the major classical civilizations that showed tendencies toward strong central government. The family structure was firmly patriarchal. Roman law stipulated that "the husband is the judge of his wife. If she commits a fault, he punishes her; if she has drunk wine, he condemns her; if she has been guilty of adultery, he kills her." Later, however, the power of husbands was modified by the need for approval by a family court composed of members of both families. If divorced because of adultery, a Roman woman lost one-third of her property and had to wear a special garment that set her apart like a prostitute. The oppression of women was less severe in Rome than in either Greece or China, however. As wives and mothers, many aristocratic Roman women wielded considerable political power, if only through their husbands. Women freely appeared in public and attended major entertainments; some were educated, though rarely as well as men in the same class.

As Roman agriculture became increasingly commercialized from the 2nd century B.C.E. onward, additional changes rocked Mediterranean society. The free-farming class declined, while slavery spread steadily. As in Greece, many Roman slaves performed household tasks.

Some were quite independent, particularly if they came from a civilized province such as Greece. Slaves were also used, however, for arduous manual labor, and large supplies of these slaves were brought in from Britain and Germany, the Slavic lands of the northern Balkans, and Africa. Slave labor manned the mines, amid brutal conditions. It also increasingly staffed the large estates, along with some paid laborers and tenant farmers. Far more than in Greece earlier on, the Roman economy became dependent on slave labor; grain supplies and other marketed agricultural products relied on this labor extensively. This pattern foreshadowed the use of slaves on commercial estates in the Americas from the 16th century onward, where slave labor provided the production on which the economy depended, but it was unusual in the classical world.

The spread of Roman slavery contributed further to the decline of free farmers and also to the unusual militarism of Rome in the late republic and early empire. Slave revolts, though not common, required a military presence. Displaced Italian farmers increasingly sought a longer-term career in the military, where they could earn pay and have some prospect of acquiring property as veterans. Most obviously, military expansion was a vital source of additional slaves, for the Roman slave population did not reproduce itself. Here was an obvious contrast to China and India, where an expansionist foreign policy was not a central issue in labor supply.

Finally, Roman slavery, like Greek slavery, helps explain the relatively stagnant production technology in manufacturing and agriculture. The Romans displayed real engineering genius in their buildings, roads, and city design, but they paid little attention to techniques of food supply or manufacturing. Estate agriculture and government organization of ports and markets, not production methods, seized center stage with abundant slave labor as a vital component.

In Harappa, the first river-valley civilization in India, ingenious city design had combined with stagnant technology in other fields. Although Roman methods were far superior to those of Harappa simply because of subsequent advances, particularly in ironworking, its combination was somewhat similar: innovative urban plans and systems but little attention to other technologies. A few engine designs were sketched but merely as exercises; there was no interest in building or using them. Some manufacturing operations used waterwheels for power, and there is evidence that these spread in the 2nd century C.E. Still, the number of new inventions was few. One result was an ongoing lag behind the economies of India and China in sophisticated manufacturing. The

This Roman painting features a young woman in an unusual role, as a student of the early Greek poetess Sappho.

Roman upper classes eagerly purchased silks and other processed goods that came from Asia arriving at the Mediterranean by overland routes through the Middle East. In return, the Romans offered exotic African animals, skins, and gold—not products they made.

The empire was not joined in a single economic and social structure. The social arrangements characteristic of Italy were not uniform through the Roman empire. Rome established vigorous cities in Spain, France, and England and populated them with the families of soldiers, who married local women, and with colonists. Only gradually and incompletely, however, did estate agriculture spread to Europe north of the Mediterranean. Many local farmers continued to practice subsistence agriculture—even hunting. The gap between new, Romanized cities and the rural population, who were usually ignorant of Latin as well as illiterate, was often

considerable. In the North African provinces, Romans pressed a policy of economic exploitation more ruthlessly. Peasants in Egypt and in other parts of North Africa were forced to produce grain for sale in the Italian markets, and large estates quickly predominated. There was little effort to set up Romanized cities or to encourage mutually beneficial trade. Even in the more prestigious North African provinces, agricultural exploitation was so intense that the resulting soil exhaustion and desert conditions have not been reversed in our own day. A third distinctive region was the portion of the empire in Greece and western Asia, where more active commerce and larger merchant groups maintained pre-Roman traditions and wielded greater wealth than existed in much of the Western Empire.

Because of the divisions of classical Mediterranean society, by region as well as class and gender, no easy generalizations about overall social achievement can be made. An 18th-century English historian called the high point of the Roman Empire before 180 C.E., the period in human history "during which the condition of the human race was most happy or prosperous." This is doubtful, given the technological accomplishments of China and India. And certainly many slaves, women, and ordinary male farmers might have disagreed, even in the Mediterranean world itself. Quite apart from the huge social divisions and stark gaps between the slaves and the free people, Mediterranean society, like most classical civilizations, was massively split between upper-class and urban populations on one hand and the rural majority on the other. Few farmers actively participated in the political structures or cultural opportunities that were the most obvious mark of this civilization. Many farmers continued to work largely as their ancestors had done, with quite similar tools and very similar poverty, untouched by the doings of the great or the bustle of the cities, except when wars swept over their lands.

We are tempted to remember particularly the urban achievements, for they carried the greatest influence on later ages that recalled the glories of Greece and Rome. The distinctive features of classical Mediterranean social and family structure had less enduring impact, though ideas about slavery or women were revived in subsequent periods. But the structures of ordinary life had their impact in helping to shape Roman politics and in contributing to new cultural changes and a declining vigor after about 180 C.E. in many facets of imperial life.

THE ORIGINS OF CHRISTIANITY

Focal Point: The early history of Christianity, ultimately one of the great world religions, is also part of the history of the Roman Empire. Early Christianity benefited from the sheer size of the empire and copied aspects of its organization. At the same time Christianity represented a new, un-Roman value system that could be accommodated only after many struggles and adjustments on both sides.

In the initial decades of the Roman Empire, at the eastern end of the Mediterranean, a new religion, Christianity, emerged. Much of the impetus for this new religion rested in issues in the Jewish religion, including a longstanding belief in the coming of a Messiah and rigidities that had developed in the Jewish priesthood. Whether or not Christianity was created by God, as Christians believe, the early stages of the religion focused on cleansing the Jewish religion of stiff rituals and haughty leaders. It

had little at first to do with Roman culture. Christianity arose in a remote province and appealed particularly to the poorer classes.

Life and Death of Jesus

Christianity originated with *Jesus of Nazareth,* a Jewish prophet and teacher who probably came to believe he was the Son of God and certainly was regarded as such by his disciples. Jesus preached in Israel during the time of Augustus, urging a purification of the Jewish religion that would free Israel and establish the kingdom of God on earth. He urged a moral code based on love, charity, and humility, and he asked the faithful to follow his lessons, abandoning worldly concern. Many disciples believed that a Final Judgment day was near at hand, on which God would reward the righteous with immortality and condemn sinners to everlasting hell.

Jesus won many followers among the poor. He also roused suspicion among the upper classes and the leaders of the Jewish religion. These people helped persuade the Roman governor, already concerned about unrest among the Jews, that Jesus was a dangerous agitator. As a result, Jesus was put to death, crucified along with common criminals, about 30 C.E. His followers believed that he was resurrected on the third day after his death—a proof that he was the Son of God. This belief helped the further spread of the religion among Jewish communities in the Middle East, both within the Roman Empire and beyond. As they realized that the Messiah was not immediately returning to earth to set up the Kingdom of God, the disciples of Jesus began to fan out, particularly around the eastern Mediterranean, to spread the new religious message.

Initially, converts were Jewish by birth and followed the basic Jewish law. Their belief that Christ was divine as well as human, however, roused hostility among other Jews. When one early convert, Stephen, was stoned to death, many disciples left Israel and traveled throughout western Asia.

Christianity Gains Converts and Religious Structure

Gradually over the next 250 years, Christianity won a growing number of converts. By the 4th century C.E., about 10 percent of the residents of the Roman Empire were Christian, and the new religion had also made converts elsewhere in the Middle East and Ethiopia. As it spread, Christianity connected increasingly with larger themes in Roman history.

With its particularly great appeal to some of the poor, Christianity was well positioned to reflect social grievances in an empire increasingly marked by inequality. Slaves, dispossessed farmers, and impoverished city dwellers found hope in a religion that promised rewards after death. Christianity also answered cultural and spiritual needs—especially but not exclusively among the poor—left untended by mainstream Roman religion and culture. Roman values had stressed political goals and ethics suitable for life in this world. They did not join peoples of the empire in more spiritual loyalties, and they did not offer many emotionally satisfying rituals. As the empire consolidated, reducing direct political participation, a number of mystery religions spread from the Middle East and Egypt—religions that offered emotionally charged rituals. Worship of gods such as Mithra or Isis, derived from earlier Mesopotamian or Egyptian beliefs, attracted some Roman soldiers and others with rites of sacrifice and a strong sense of religious community. Christianity, though far more than a mystery religion, had some of these qualities and won converts on this basis as well. Christianity, in sum, gained ground in part because of features of Roman political and cultural life.

The spread of Christianity also benefited from some of the positive qualities of Rome's great empire. Political stability and communications over a wide area aided missionary efforts, while the Roman example helped inspire the governmental forms of the growing Christian church. Early Christian communities regulated themselves, but with expansion, more formal government was introduced, with *bishops* playing a role not unlike that of Rome's provincial governors. Bishops headed churches in regional centers and supervised the activities of other churches in the area. Bishops in politically powerful cities, including Rome, gained particular authority. Roman principles also helped move what initially had been a religion among Jews to a genuinely cosmopolitan stance. Under the leadership of Paul, converted to Christianity about 35 C.E., Christian missionaries began to move away from insisting that adherents of the new religion must follow Jewish law. Rather, in the spirit of Rome and of Hellenism, the new faith was seen as universal, open to all whether or not they followed Jewish practices in diet, male circumcision, and so on.

Paul's conversion to Christianity proved vital. *Paul* was Jewish, but he had been born in a Greek city and was familiar with Greco-Roman culture. He helped explain basic Christian beliefs in terms other adherents of this culture could grasp, and he preached in Greece and Italy as well as the Middle East. Paul essentially created Christian theology as a set of intellectual principles that followed from, but generalized, the message of Jesus.

Paul also modified certain initial Christian impulses. Jesus himself had drawn a large number of women followers, but Paul emphasized women's subordination to men and the dangers of sexuality. It was Paul's stress on Christianity as a universal religion, requiring abandonment of other religious beliefs, and his related use of Greek—the dominant language of the day throughout the eastern Mediterranean—that particularly transformed the new faith.

Relations with the Roman Empire

Gradually, Christian theological leaders made further contact with Greco-Roman intellectual life. They began to develop a body of Christian writings beyond the Bible messages written by the disciples of Jesus. By the 4th century C.E., Christian writings became the most creative cultural expressions in the Roman Empire as theologians attempted not only to explain issues in the new religion but also to relate it to Greek philosophy and Roman ethics. Ironically, as the Roman Empire was in most respects declining, Christianity produced an outpouring of complex thought and often elegant use of language. In this effort, Christianity not only redirected Roman culture (never known for abundant religious subtlety) but also preserved many earlier literary and philosophical achievements.

Adherents of the new religion clashed with Roman authorities, to be sure. Christians, who put their duties to God first, would not honor the emperor as a divinity and seemed to reject the authority of the state in other spheres. Several early emperors, including the mad Nero, persecuted Christians, killing some and driving their worship underground. Persecution was not constant, however, which helps explain why the religion continued to spread. It resumed only in the 4th century, when several emperors tried to use religious conformity and new claims to divinity as a way of cementing loyalties to a declining state. Roman beliefs, including periodic tolerance, helped shape a Christian view that the state had a legitimately separate if subordinate sphere; Western Christians would often cite Christ as saying "Render unto Caesar that which is Caesar's, and unto God that which is God's."

The full story of early Christianity goes beyond the history of Rome, and we will turn to it again in Chapter 11. Christianity had more to do with opening a new era in the history of the Mediterranean region than with shaping the later Roman Empire. Yet important connections did exist that explain features of Christianity and of later Roman history. Though not a Roman product and though benefiting in part from the empire's decline,

This sarcophagus, or tomb, from the 4th century shows Christ and the apostles in typical Roman dress.

Christianity in some of its qualities can be counted as part of the Greco-Roman legacy.

CONCLUSION

The Mediterranean Heritage

Well before Christianity became a major factor in Mediterranean life, the Roman Empire began to show important signs of decay. Its political-social framework became increasingly vulnerable. Defending the borders of the empire and maintaining government establishments was a costly business, yet many regions and groups found it difficult to meet their tax requirements. Further expansion of the empire became impossible after 180 C.E., because the government could not afford the troops needed to keep order in more distant provinces and because pressures from border groups, particularly the Germanic tribes in central Europe, began to increase. Yet, without expansion, the necessary labor supplies and rewards for army units became more difficult to come by.

Other economic disruptions followed from regional changes. The Italian economy, for example, began to suffer by the 3rd century C.E. as African grain and French-grown wine cut into local production, reducing

prosperity and tax revenues at the empire's core. Disruptions of this sort contributed to political weakness, which forced new, more subsistence-oriented economic arrangements. More estates turned into local economic and political units rather than commercial operations as connections that had cemented the empire at its height began to come undone.

Economic problems were not alone. Assuring high-quality emperors, never easy, became more difficult after the final series of able leaders at the end of the 2nd century C.E. The declining authority of the imperial government began to reduce the willingness of upper-class individuals to sacrifice individual interest for service to the public good. Exactly what mixture produced Rome's gradual unraveling is not easy to determine. Rome was not eternal. Yet even as its fortune waned, it had established a legacy that would survive the empire itself. Roman institutions and values, Greek ideas and artistic forms that Rome had used and preserved, indeed the Greco-Roman ingredients in the ascending Christian religion—all would help shape successor societies around the Mediterranean.

Each of the classical civilizations created institutions and values that survived the classical period itself, helping to shape distinctive societies identifiable today. Each inspired great awe and veneration, causing later generations to look back on the classical period with genuine reverence.

Classical Mediterranean civilization fit that pattern neatly. Greece and Rome together generated traditions in science and philosophy and in political theory and definitions of citizenship. These traditions, continuing or later revived after the fall of Rome, are valued as part of Western civilization today. Other values, such as those concerning the roles of women, also had lingering influence, though in ways we now regard as less beneficent. Important features of classical Mediterranean society did not survive, however. On the whole, cultural emphases and artistic styles traveled best, though even here important features, such as the dominant Greco-Roman religion, were largely jettisoned. Political traditions were significant also, but they were more selectively used and certainly were combined with other, subsequent innovations.

In contrast to India and to an extent China, where caste or social ranking systems long endured, the characteristic social structure of the classical Mediterranean did not have much ongoing impact—though it had more impact in the eastern Mediterranean region than the west. It was already blurring, in fact, as Rome declined.

One of the key means of approaching the later history of China, India, or the Mediterranean region involves asking what happened to the basic features of the classical period: what persisted, what lasted if in modified form, and what was uprooted through change.

A recognition of the force of change is particularly important in the case of Greece and Rome. Classical Mediterranean society, along with its important positive qualities, had one final impact on world history: its rather messy collapse. Unlike China, classical civilization in the Mediterranean region was not simply disrupted only to revive. Unlike India, there was no central religion derived from the civilization itself to serve as the link between the classical period and what followed. Furthermore, the fall of Rome was not a uniform decline; in essence, Rome "fell" more in some parts of the Mediterranean than in others. The result, among other things, was that no single civilization ultimately arose to claim the mantle of Greece and Rome. At the same time, there was no across-the-board maintenance of the classical Mediterranean institutions and values in any of the civilizations that later claimed a relationship to the Greek and Roman past. Greece and Rome would live on, in more than idle memory, but their heritage was unquestionably more complex and more selective than proved to be the case for India or China.

We will turn to the process of Mediterranean decline under Rome in Chapter 11, and there we will determine more fully the initial process through which some Greco-Roman achievements survived while others perished. Two other phenomena need attention first, as part of an awareness that much of the world remained outside the orbit of the most extensive classical civilizations. In the Americas, something like a classical civilization period took shape though slightly later than the Chinese, Indian, and Mediterranean versions. In several other key regions, an initial and sometimes halting penetration of early civilization held center stage.

FURTHER READINGS

Two solid recent surveys with bibliographies are K. Christ's *The Romans: An Introduction to Their History and Civilization* (1984) and M. Grant's *The World of Rome* (1990). See also M. Crawford's *The Roman Republic* (1982) and B. W. Cunliffe's *Rome and Her Empire* (1978). On Rome's early history, see H. H. Scullard's *A History of the Roman World 753–146 B.C.* (1961).

An excellent analysis of the basic features of Roman cultural and social life is P. Garnsey's and R. Saller's *The Roman Empire: Economy, Society and Culture* (1987). See also R. MacMullen's *Roman Social Relations 50 B.C. to A.D. 284* (1981). A bold quantitative study is R. Duncan-Jones's *The Economy of the Roman Empire* (1982). On slavery, the best recent works are K. Hopkins's *Conquerors and Slaves, Slaves and Masters in the Roman Empire* (1987) and K. R. Bradley's and W. Philips, Jr.'s *Slavery from Roman Times to the Early Transatlantic Trade* (1985). On women, see J. F. Gardner's *Women in Roman Law and Society* (1986).

For war and diplomacy, see Y. Garlan's *War in the Ancient World* (1975) and E. N. Luttwak's *The Grand Strategy of the Roman Empire* (1976).

Collections of source materials include M. Crawford, ed., *Sources for Ancient History* (1983) and C. Fornara's *Translated Documents of Greece and Rome* (1977).

The rise and spread of Christianity are treated in two outstanding studies: R. MacMullen's *Christianizing the Roman Empire* (1984) and Peter Brown's *The World of Late Antiquity, A.D. 150–750* (1971). (Brown has also written several more specialized studies on early Christianity in the West.)

9

The Peoples and Civilizations of the Americas

	20,000 B.C.E.	9000 B.C.E.	5000 B.C.E.	1000 B.C.E.
GENERAL AMERICAS and NORTH AMERICA	20,000–8000 Earliest migration from Asia	9500 Earliest evidence of human occupation	7000 Evidence of agriculture; Guitarrero cave in Peru	2000 B.C.E.–500 C.E. Early southwestern cultures
			5000 Plant domestication becoming widespread	2000 Pottery in use in Mesoamerica
		9000–7000 "Clovis" and "Folsom" style weapons and tools in North America	4000 Maize domesticated in Mexico	3000 Early pottery of Puerto Hormiga, Colombia
MESOAMERICA			4000–2000 Archaic cultures	1500–800 Olmec civilization flourishes · 300 B.C.E.–900 C.E. Height of Maya civilization
				900 Maya civilization beginnings; classic period in Mesoamerica
ANDEAN REGION				c. 3000–1500 B.C.E. Initial period; evidence of cotton cultivation, metallurgy, ceramics · 200 B.C.E.–500 C.E. Nasca culture
				1800–1200 Ceremonial centers in the highlands · 850–250 Early Horizon; Chavin flourishes

INTRODUCTION

This chapter, covering the diverse cultures and early civilizations in the Americas, pulls well away from the classical world of Asia, North Africa, and southern Europe. Although the advent of civilization in the Americas displayed some parallels with developments in Asia and North Africa in terms of the earlier river-valley stages and the contemporary elaboration of classical forms, what took place in the Americas seems to have had no connection whatsoever to that classical world. This was, however, a vital period in the history of the Americas, setting certain institutional, cultural, and social patterns that outlasted the formative period itself.

American separateness was vital also, making the achievements of civilization all the more impressive but constraining them as well. Separateness meant that American chronology had only accidental connections with the classical civilizations, based on the regional interchanges and the similar problems of internal deterioration and outside attack. Civilization in the New World moved to its own rhythm. While crucial developments in American civilization occurred during the classical period of world history, our exploration of American developments in this chapter will also range before and after the 1000 B.C.E.–500 C.E. span.

When Europeans set foot in the Americas in 1492, the criteria they used to describe and evaluate the peoples they encountered were drawn directly from their own heritage and understanding of their past. Use of the known and familiar to explain the unknown and strange was perhaps inevitable, but it has continued into recent times in evaluations of the Americas and their peoples. The separate chronology of civilization in the Americas and the physical resources available there were essential differences. America, for example, had no horses or cattle, but American Indians had domesticated many plants whose caloric output was greater than that of any of the grains raised in Europe or Asia. The different resources available had a definite impact on the development of American societies.

The history of the Western Hemisphere is part of the greater story of human development, and the cultures and civilizations of the Americas bear marked similarities to those of the Old World. But there were also important differences in the pace of development and the level of technology that ultimately placed the inhabi-

---

800–1300 Mississippian culture in Cahokia flourishes

100–600 Mound Builders of Adena

c. 100–700 Hopewell culture

200–1300 Anasazi culture in Southwest

900–1500 Post-classic era

1–650 Teotihuacan flourishes in central Mexico

900–1500 Maya cities under Mexican influence flourish in Yucatan

400–800 Monte Alban flourishes in Oaxaca

900–1200 Toltec empire in central Mexico   1350 Rise of the Aztecs

600–1000 Huari state

200–700 Mochica culture

1200–1400 Chimu state

300–900 Intermediate Horizon

300–900 Tihuanaco

1 C.E.   500 C.E.   1000 C.E.

tants of the Americas at a disadvantage. By the time Europeans arrived in the early 16th century, they encountered great empires, such as that of the Aztecs, with a technology not much different from those of earlier American civilizations that had preceded them by 1000 years, and in some ways similar to the civilizations of the ancient Near East.

ORIGINS OF AMERICAN SOCIETIES

Focal Point: During the last Ice Age, peoples from Asia entered the Americas. These ancient hunters eventually created diverse societies and with the development of agriculture in the cultural hearths of *Mesoamerica* and Peru, they formed civilizations organized as chiefdoms, states, and sometimes empires.

The Americas were originally populated by peoples from Asia who moved during the period of the last Ice Age when the level of the oceans fell. Possibly because of increasing population pressure, *Homo sapiens* in Europe and Asia had been able to move onto the northern steppes and tundra by about 20,000 B.C.E. and by that time were hunting large game, wearing clothes, and living in small groups. These people moved across the land bridge that formed in the present Bering Strait between Siberia and Alaska. During the last period of the Pleistocene, or Ice Age (Wisconsin glaciation), the capture of great quantities of water in the ice lowered the level of the oceans and made it possible to cross from Siberia to Alaska on dry land.

Perhaps one-third of the earth's surface was under ice during the greatest extent of the expanding glacial sheets. The land bridge itself was not covered with ice but was probably a grassy tundra. The mammoths, mastodons, ancestors of the bison, and other large game probably crossed this route, and the hunters followed after them. A subsequent rise in the world's temperature about 10,000 years ago caused the ice to melt and eventually raised the level of the oceans so that the land bridge disappeared and the land migrations from Asia stopped. The last migrations by the ancestors of the Inuit (Eskimos) and Aleuts were probably made in boats or across the polar ice.

The Ancient Hunters

These migrations took place over a long period between about 20,000 B.C.E. and 8000 B.C.E. The earliest definite archeological evidence of people in the Americas dates from about 9500 B.C.E., but many scholars believe that occupation is much older than that. How long it took for the area of the American continents to be occupied is open to question; it may have taken thousands of years, but one scholar has estimated that from a group of only 25 original migrants that doubled every generation, a population of 10 million would result in 500 years. A population of 10 million, or about 1 person per square mile, seems reasonable for these peoples given what we know about more modern hunting societies, but other scholars have estimated the whole world's population before agriculture at only 10 million.

The earliest migrants may have had a technology that did not include projectiles (spears), since the only evidence of their tools is provided by small stones used for scraping or cutting. Crude spearheads, associated with the remains of animals that became extinct about 12,000 years ago, document the presence of hunting bands in the Americas. By about 11,000 years ago, stone tools and simple spear points associated with these early hunters were widely dispersed over North America. Other tool traditions followed, some of them relatively localized.

As the climate became dryer and warmer the ice began to melt. The great mammal herds diminished and some of the species disappeared. The ancient Americans seem to have been particularly successful hunters, and it has been argued that the disappearance of such animals as the mammoth, the ancient horse, the camel, and the giant anteater was, at least in part, due to the hunters' skills. After all, the climate changed in Eurasia as well, but nowhere else in the world did the number of mammals that became extinct equal that in the Americas, especially North America.

Little is known about the society of these early Ice Age hunters. Most likely, they lived in small groups or bands of 20 to 25 people, following the game in a seasonal pattern. Sites where the bones of the hunters' kills are found indicate that these people probably hunted the mammals in large groups. Kinship provided the basis of social organization, and there was little specialization or hierarchy in society. Age and gender were the main determinants of a person's roles and his or her contributions to the group.

American Diversity

Over the long period of the migrations, different peoples of different physical types and languages came out of Asia. Some of the first migrants came into the Western Hemisphere prior to the predominance of the Mongoloid peoples in Asia. Consequently, there were Cauca-

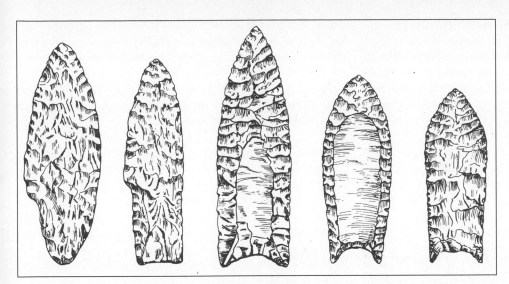

Early spearheads indicating the presence of human populations in the Americas by 10,000 B.C.E. were discovered at Folsom (second from right) and Clovis (center), New Mexico. Folsom points found in 1927 in conjunction with extinct bison species changed scientific thinking about the timing of human occupation in the New World.

soid and Australoid genetic features in the ancestors of the first Americans, or what are sometimes called the Paleo-Indians. The fact that all Indians of South America are of blood type O while in Asia type B predominates indicates the diversity of physical types involved in the migration and perhaps the early date of the migration prior to the creation of the present genetic situation of Asian populations. The Eskimos (Inuit), who genetically are most like contemporary Asians, were probably the last group to migrate.

While there was considerable physical variation between the American Indian populations, the genetic and physical similarities between them is very strong. This indicates a large degree of common ancestry and a relative isolation from other human populations. The variations between Indians can be attributed to adaptations and localized natural selection. Growing diversity is also indicated by American Indian languages; these languages seem to have developed from a few parent stocks into a myriad of languages, which can sometimes be used to trace migrations. The Navajo and Apaches of the American Southwest, for example, speak Athapascan languages that are related to the speech of the inhabitants of northwestern Canada and Alaska, and are quite unlike that of their Pueblo neighbors. It is assumed that they were later migrants who split off from their linguistic relatives to the north.

Outside Contacts?

The problem of later contacts with the Americas across the Pacific or the Atlantic continues to fascinate archeologists and cause heated debate. Definite mysteries and gaps in the history of pre-Columbian cultures remain unresolved. Artistic motifs and styles in the Americas similar to those of Shang China and Southeast Asia seem to indicate contact. Plants such as cotton and bottle gourds seem to be of definite Old World origin, and their presence in the Americas suggests diffusion by human agents. While many scholars admit the possibility of sporadic transoceanic contacts with Chinese, Phoenicians, Africans, Polynesians, and others, the evidence is still mostly circumstantial. No identifiable Old World object has ever been positively identified in a pre-Columbian archeological site, and if Phoenicians or Chinese introduced pottery or writing to the Americas, why they failed to introduce the wheel or bronze at the same time remains an unanswered question.

The biological and archeological records indicate that the peopling of the Americas had taken place long before the beginnings of agriculture in the Old World and that with the disappearance of the Bering land bridge, this population had lived in comparative isolation from the rest of humankind. While some archeologists have argued that the invention of agriculture and pottery may have taken place only once and then been diffused all over the world, most scholars believe that the peoples of the Americas developed agriculture, domestication of animals (except perhaps the dog, which came with them), weaving, ceramics, complex societies, urbanism, numerical systems, and religious ideas—in short, their cultures—independently of the Old World. Still, occasional contacts were possible, and the introduction of ideas and material things from elsewhere into American Indian cultures certainly may have taken place.

The processes of cultural development and the growth of Indian civilizations were long and complex, and they gave American Indian societies and cultures great resilience and an ability to survive even the shock of conquest. This independent development and relative isolation also had some negative results when American Indian populations came into contact with the peoples of Europe, Africa, and Asia. The development of a technology that did not include the wheel, the plow, or iron tools and weapons put American Indians at a disadvantage. Dogs, turkeys, and guinea pigs were domesticated, but with the exception of llamas in the Andes, the lack of large mammals, cattle, and horses was also a disadvantage in terms of diet, transportation, and power. With the exception of a limited area in the high Andes, pastoralism, so important in the Old World, was not a way of life in the Americas. Most importantly, the relative isolation of American populations from the disease environment of the larger Old World populations left the inhabitants of the Americas with no immunities to several diseases that became endemic in Asia, Europe, and Africa. This would prove disastrous after permanent contact was established.

The Archaic Cultures

By about 9000 B.C.E., small bands of hunters were widely dispersed over the American continents. Changes in climate with the ending of the last Ice Age may lie behind changes in diet and ways of life. The disappearance of large game animals was probably compensated for by the less specialized hunting of smaller game, fishing, and increased dependence on gathering wild fruits and other plant foods. The culture of these early, or *Archaic*, populations represented an adaptation to the changing environment. People made baskets and used stone grinding tools to prepare the roots and plants they collected for food. They used a wide range of animals and plants. As the seacoasts stabilized between 5000 and 4000 B.C.E., populations became concentrated around lagoons and river mouths to exploit fish and shellfish. Enormous shell middens, or debris mounds, found in Chile and Tierra del Fuego indicate long human dependence on these maritime resources. In Brazil, the middens indicate intensive use of these resources and permanent sites of occupation.

Agriculture in the Americas   The move toward agriculture was a natural extension of a process in which a wide range of animal and plant resources was used with less dependence on big game hunting. Agriculture may thus have been brought about first by women, since in many simple hunting societies women are responsible for gathering plant foods. There is early evidence from highland Peru of cultivation as early as 7000 B.C.E., and by 5000 B.C.E., plant domestication had taken place in many regions in the Americas.

The introduction of agriculture, the American version of the Neolithic revolution, was not as complete and drastic a change as we once thought, and many peoples continued to practice hunting and gathering along with some cultivation. In many places, agriculturalists and hunter-gatherers eventually lived in close contact with each other as a result of social choices and of different adaptations to environments and opportunities.

Eventually, agriculture was practiced all over the Americas from the woodlands of eastern North America to the tropical forests of the Amazon basin. American Indians eventually cultivated over 100 different crops from peppers, squash, and tomatoes to amaranth and quinoa. Some crops, particularly maize, potatoes, and manioc, became essential sources of food to dense populations. As in Asia earlier, agriculture imposed restrictions on human behavior and the patterns of human action; as American societies depended increasingly on agriculture, a series of processes was sometimes set in motion that resulted in complex social, economic, and political systems.

Maize, Manioc, and Potatoes   By about 4000 B.C.E., the domestication of maize had taken place in central Mexico. Along with it came the cultivation of peppers, squash, and beans. These expanded and more dependable food resources resulted in population growth (although some scholars argue that the growth of populations may have stimulated the search for new food sources and the domestication of plants). The cultivation of maize spread far and wide. By 2000 B.C.E., it was grown in Peru, along with the potato and other crops native to that region. Maize spread northward to the present southern United States, and by about 1000 C.E. it was grown by groups such as the Iroquois in Canada.

In the tropical forests of the Orinoco and Amazon basins, people had developed an agriculture based on varieties of manioc or cassava, a root that could be made into a flour. The introduction of maize in areas that had depended only on manioc probably resulted in population growth and with it the rise of more complex societies. While varieties of potatoes were the staple in highland South America, and manioc was the principal crop of peoples of the lowlands of South America and the islands of the Caribbean, maize cultivation spread in all directions and was often practiced in those areas in conjunction with the cultivation of other staples. In Mesoamerica, the area from north central Mexico to Nicaragua, maize dominated the diet of agricultural peoples.

It seems clear that in most cases, agriculture allowed societies to achieve the surplus production and complexity needed to develop those elements usually associated with civilization. With the adoption of agriculture and a sedentary way of life, the process of civilization was set in motion in the Americas.

Cultural Hearths and Social Systems

Traditionally, archeologists have seen two major areas of cultural development, or "hearths," in the Americas: Mesoamerica and the Peruvian orbit, including the coastal areas of Ecuador and Peru and the Andean highlands. In these two areas, processes of development, based on intensive agriculture and including most of the features usually associated with Old World civilizations, could be seen. In both areas, several cycles of cultural advance and sometimes of empire building took place long before the rise of the Incas and Aztecs, who were in power when the Europeans arrived. Artistic styles flourished and declined, and states rose and fell over thousands of years.

Some scholars have suggested that the area between these cultural hearths, including present-day Panama and Colombia, also contained advanced societies with considerable cultural achievements (especially in metallurgy and goldworking) that differed only in that they did not build large stone buildings. Thus, the whole region from central Mexico southward to Chile formed a continuous nucleus of American civilizations. On the peripheries of this nucleus, by influence and imitation, other Indian peoples adopted features characteristic of the civilizations.

Types of American Indian Societies

The idea of a relatively contiguous area of cultural development makes more sense than the previous concept of independent centers. That earlier concept produced an image of the Americas in which isolated civilizations and cultural traditions developed along parallel lines with little contact or interchange. Emphasis on artistic variation and regional diversity contributed to this view, but

Cultural Hearths—Regions in the Americas

scholars are increasingly beginning to examine the broad similarities between ancient American cultures. While many differences and variations existed, there were also uniformities of organization, subsistence, technology, and belief that made them more alike to one another than any one of them was to the civilizations of the Old World.

To some extent we can make distinctions between ancient American societies on the basis of their economic and political organization. Sedentary agriculture, and with it population density, was a key. Hunters and gatherers continued to occupy large portions of the continents, dividing in small bands and moving seasonally to take advantage of the resources. These peoples sometimes were organized in larger tribes and might recognize a chief, but generally their societies were organized around family groups or clans, and there was little hierarchy or specialization of skills. With some exceptions, the material culture of these people tended to be relatively simple.

Peoples who had made a partial transition to agriculture lived in larger and more complex societies. Here the village of 100 or 200 rather than the band of 25 was more common. Men often continued to hunt or make war, but women tilled the fields. Agricultural techniques tended to be simple and often necessitated periodic migration when soils played out. The villages of these tribes of semisedentary farmers and hunters have been found on the Brazilian coast and in the woodlands of eastern North America.

It was among peoples who had made a full transition to sedentary agriculture that the complex societies emerged most clearly, for it was here that surplus production was most firmly established. These populations could reach the millions. Men shifted into agriculture, forming a peasant base for a hierarchical society that might have included classes of nobles, merchants, and priests. Strong states and even empires could result, and the extraction of tribute from subject peoples and redistribution by central authority formed the basis of rule.

Chiefdoms and States

Sedentary peoples and hunters often lived near one other and shared mutual hostility and disregard, but, in fact, the categories of sedentary, semisedentary, and hunter-gatherers were never clearcut, and many aspects of life were shared by them all. To some extent, the large imperial states with highly developed religious and political systems and monumental architecture (which we call civilizations) were variants of a widely diffused pattern, the *chiefdom*.

From the Amazon to the Mississippi valley, populations—sometimes in the tens of thousands—were governed by hereditary chieftains who ruled from central towns over a large territory, including smaller towns or villages, which paid tribute to the ruler. The predominant town often had a ceremonial function, with large temples and a priest class. Beautiful pottery and other goods indicate specialization of labor.

The existence of a social hierarchy with classes of nobles and commoners was also characteristic of many of the chiefdoms. It is sometimes argued that in the state-building societies, ceremonial centers became true cities, and clan or family relations were replaced by social classes. The scale of the society was greater, but the differences are not always so obvious. Both the Aztecs and the Incas, with their complex social hierarchies, maintained aspects of earlier clan organization. In fact, in terms of social organization, warfare, and ceremonialism, little seems to differentiate the Maya city-states from some of the chiefdoms in South America or southeastern North America. Cahokia, near St. Louis, an important town of the Mississippian culture (c. 1050–1200 C.E.), with its great earthen mounds covering an area of five square miles, probably supported a population of over 30,000—as large as the great cities of the Maya civilization.

A distinction between sedentary agriculturists and nomadic hunters may be more useful than the distinctions between "civilized" and "uncivilized." Building and carving in stone, and thus the ability of archaeologists to reconstruct a culture, seem to have become a major feature in determining the difference between a state or a chiefdom—and by extension between "civilizations"—and societies that do not seem to merit the title. At the same time, we should recognize that the settled peoples and the hunters recognized the difference between their ways of life, and when they were in contact, they often experienced mutual jealousy and hostility toward one other. The Incas looked down on the peoples of the Amazonian rain forest, but they could never conquer them. Instead, they traded with them and sometimes used them as mercenaries. To some extent, the Old World pattern of tension between the nomad and the "civilized" was reproduced in the Americas.

SPREAD OF CIVILIZATION IN MESOAMERICA

Focal Point: The *Olmec* civilization, which appeared abruptly, spread certain elements of culture over the Mesoamerican region. This led to a classic era of great cultural achievment in art, architecture, and astronomy at *Teotihuacan* and especially in the Maya city-states, where a complex system of writing and mathematics also developed. These classic civilizations collapsed for partially unexplained reasons.

Geographically, the region of Mesoamerica is a complex patchwork of zones that is also divided vertically into cooler highlands, tropical lowlands and coasts, and an intermediate temperate zone. These variations created different environments with different possibilities for human exploitation. They also created a basis for trade, as peoples attempted to acquire goods not available locally. Much trade flowed from the tropical lowlands to the cooler central plateau.

The long slow process of change by which the hunters and gatherers of Mexico began to settle into small villages and domesticate certain plants is poorly known. Beginning about 5000 B.C.E., gathering and an increasing use of plant foods eventually led to the domestication of certain plants. Beans, peppers, avocados, squash, and eventually maize served as the basis of agriculture in the region. Later innovations such as the introduction or development of pottery took place about 2000 B.C.E., but there was little to differentiate one small village from the next.

When the Shang dynasty ruled in China, permanent sedentary villages based to some extent on agriculture were first beginning to appear in Mesoamerica. These were small and modest settlements without much hierarchy or social differentiation and an apparent lack of craft specialization. But the number of these Archaic period villages proliferated, and population densities rose.

The Olmec Mystery

Quite suddenly a new phenomenon appeared. On the southeastern coast of Mesoamerica (Veracruz and Tabasco), without much evidence of gradual development in the archeological record, a cultural tradition emerged that included irrigated agriculture, monumental sculpture, urbanism, an elaborate religion, and the beginnings of calendrical and writing systems. The origin of the Olmecs remains unknown, but their impressive settlements attest to a high degree of social organization and artistic skill. The major Olmec sites at San Lorenzo (1200–900 B.C.E.) and La Venta (900–500 B.C.E.) are in the wet tropical forests of the Gulf coast of eastern Mexico, but Olmec objects and art style spread to the drier highlands of central Mexico and toward the Pacific coast to the south.

The Olmecs have been called the "mother civilization" of Mesoamerica. Maize cultivation, especially along the rivers, provided the basis for a state ruled by a hereditary elite and in which the ceremonialism of a complex religion dominated much of life. About the time that Tutankhamen ruled in Egypt, the Olmec civilization flourished in Mesoamerica.

The Olmecs remain a mystery. Some of their monumental sculptures seem to bear Negroid features; others appear to be representations of humans with feline attributes. They were great carvers of jade, and they traded or conquered to obtain it. They developed a vigesimal numerical system—based on 20—and a calendar that combined a 365-day year with a 260-day ritual cycle. This became the basis of all Mesoamerican calendar systems. What language they spoke and what became of their civilization remain unknown, but some scholars believe that they were the ancestors of the great Maya civilization that followed.

During this preclassic period (c. 2000–300 B.C.E.), other civilizations were developing elsewhere in Mesoamerica. Olmec objects and, probably, Olmec influence

The origins of the Olmecs remain shrouded in mystery, but some of the enormous stone sculptures seem to have definite African features that indicate trans-Atlantic contact.

and religious ideas spread into many areas of the highlands and lowlands such as the Zapotec ceremonial center at *Monte Alban* in Oaxaca, creating the first generalized culture in the region. Farther to the south, some early Maya centers began to appear. In the central valley of Mexico, Olmec artistic influence could be seen in expanding communities.

Much of what we know about these cultures must be interpreted from their architecture and art and the symbols they contain. Art, especially public art, was both decorative and functional. It defined the place of the individual in society and in the universe. It had political and religious functions; in the Americas, as in many civilizations, these aspects were usually united. The interpretation of artistic styles and symbols presents a variety of problems in the absence of written sources. The diffusion of Olmec symbols is a good example of the problem. Did the use of these symbols by other peoples in

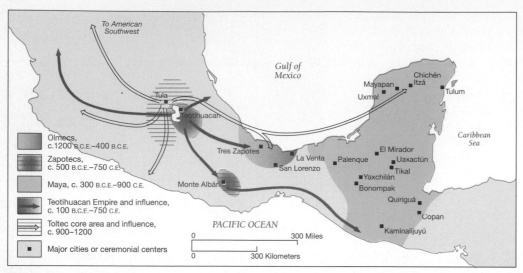

Mesoamerican Settlements

distant places indicate trade networks, missionary activity, colonies, conquest, or aesthetic appreciation? We do not know, but clearly Olmec influence was widely felt throughout the region.

The Classic Era of Mesoamerican Civilization

After the Olmec initiative, the period from about 150 to 900 C.E. was a great age of cultural achievement in Mesoamerica. Archaeologists refer to it as the *classic* period, and during it great civilizations flourished in a number of places. The two main centers of civilization were the high central valley of Mexico and the more humid tropical lands of southern Mexico, Yucatan, and Guatemala.

The Valley of Mexico: Teotihuacan   In central Mexico, the city of Teotihuacan, near modern Mexico City, emerged as an enormous urban center with important religious functions. It was supported by intensive agriculture in the surrounding region and probably by crops planted around the great lake in the central valley of Mexico. Teotihuacan's enormous temple pyramids rival those of ancient Egypt and suggest a considerable state apparatus with the power to mobilize large numbers of workers. Population estimates for this city, which covered nine square miles, are as high as 200,000. This would make it greater than the cities of ancient Egypt or Mesopotamia and probably second only to ancient Rome of the cities of classical antiquity.

Certain trades and ethnic groups had there own residential districts, and there is considerable evidence of wide social distinctions between the priests, the nobles, and the common folk. The many gods of Mesoamerica, still worshiped when the Europeans arrived in the 16th century, were already honored at Teotihuacan. The god of rain, the feathered serpent, the goddess of corn, and the goddess of waters are all apparent in the murals and decorations that adorned the palaces and temples. In fact, almost all Teotihuacan art seems to have been religious in nature.

The influence of Teotihuacan extended as far south as Guatemala, and tribute was probably exacted from many regions. Teotihuacan objects, such as pottery and finely worked obsidian, and Teotihuacan artistic styles are found in many other areas. Teotihuacan influence was strong at Monte Alban in Oaxaca. Warriors dressed in the style of Teotihuacan can be found far to the south in the Maya region.

Teotihuacan represented either a political empire or a dominant cultural and ideological style that spread over much of central Mexico. The lack of battle scenes on the walls of Teotihuacan has led some scholars to believe that the dominance of Teotihuacan led to a long period of peace maintained by the authority and power of the great city. Internally, the fact that the later buildings tend to be secular palaces rather than temple pyramids may indicate a shift in power and orientation from religious to civil authority.

The Classic Maya   Between about 300 and 900 C.E., at roughly the same time when Teotihuacan dominated the central plateau, the *Maya* peoples were developing Mesoamerican civilization to its highest point in southern Mexico and Central America. While the Tang dynasty ruled China, Charlemagne created his domain in Europe, and Islam spread its influence from Spain to India, after the classical period had ended in the Old World, a great civilization flourished in the American tropics. The American classic period, launched as the Old World classical civilizations were coming to an end, lasted well into the next period of world history. We can use the Maya as an example of the classic period in Mesoamerican development, for while their civilization was distinctive, it was based on some principles common to the area.

The Maya culture extended over a broad region that now includes parts of five different countries: Mexico, Guatemala, Belize, Honduras, and El Salvador. It included several related languages, and it had considerable regional variation, as can be seen in its art styles. The whole region shared a common culture that included monumental architecture, a written language, a calendrical and mathematical system, a highly developed religion, and concepts of statecraft and social organization. With an essentially Neolithic technology in an area of dense forests plagued by insects and often poor soils, as many as 50 city-states flourished.

How did the large classic Maya urban-religious centers, such as Tikal, Copán, Quirigua, and Palenque, with populations between 30,000 and 80,000, support themselves? Slash-and-burn agriculture as practiced today in the region was not enough. The classic Maya used several agricultural systems. Evidence of irrigation, swamp drainage, and a system of artificially constructed "ridged fields" at river mouths (where intensive agriculture was practiced) has now appeared and seems to explain the Maya ability to support large urban centers and a total population of perhaps five million. While some authorities still believe that the Maya centers were essentially ceremonial and were occupied primarily by rulers, artisans, and an elite, it seems clear that populations were concentrated in and around these centers to create a densely occupied landscape. The Maya cities vary in size and layout, but almost all include large pyramids surmounted by temples, complexes of masonry buildings that served administrative or religious purposes, elite residences, a ritual ball court, and often a series of altars and memorial pillars. These memorial monuments, or *stelae,* were erected to commemorate triumphs and events in the lives of the Maya rulers or to mark ceremonial occasions. The stelae were usually dated and were inscribed with hieroglyphic script. A complex calendar and a sophisticated writing system were two of the greatest Maya achievements.

Religion, Writing, and Society The calendar system and sophisticated astronomical observations were made possible by a vigesimal system of mathematics. The Maya knew the concept of zero and used it in conjunction with the concept of place value or position. With elegant simplicity and with signs for only one, five, and zero, they could make complex calculations. As among all the Mesoamerican peoples, the Maya calendar was based on a concept of recurring cycles of different length. The Maya had a sacred cycle of 260 days divided into months of 20 days each, within which there was a cycle of 13 numbers. This ritual calendar meshed with a solar calendar of 365 days, or 18 months of 20 days each with a remainder of 5 "dead" or inauspicious days at the end of the year. The two calendars operated simultaneously, so any day would have two names, but the particular combination of those two days would recur only once every 52 years. Thus, among the Maya and most Mesoamericans, cycles of 52 years were sacred.

The classic Maya, however, differed from their neighbors in that they also kept a *long count* or a system of dating from a fixed date in the past. This date, 3114 B.C.E. by our calendar, probably marked the beginning of a great cycle of 5200 years since the creation of the world. Like other Mesoamericans and the ancient Peruvians, the Maya believed in great cycles of creation and destruction of the universe. The long count enabled the Maya to date events with precision. The earliest recorded Maya date that survives is 292 C.E., and the last is 928 C.E.

A second great Maya accomplishment was the creation of a writing system. The Maya "wrote" on stone monuments, murals, and ceramics and in books of folded bark paper and deerskin, only four of which survive. Scribes were honored and held an important place in society. Although we still cannot read many of these inscriptions, recent advances now permit the reading of many texts. The Maya written language, like Chinese and Sumerian, was a logographic system, which combined phonetic and semantic elements. With this system and about 287 symbols, the Maya were able to record and transmit complex concepts and ideas. The few remaining books are religious and astronomical texts, and many inscriptions on ceramics deal with the cult of the dead and with the complex Maya cosmology.

The Maya viewed the universe as a flat earth, whose cardinal points and center were each dominated by a god who supported the sky. Above the sky extended 13 levels of heavens, and below were 9 underworlds, each

The great pyramids of classic Maya cities like this one at Tikal demonstrate the architectural ability of the builders and the ability of the Maya states to mobilize labor.

dominated by a god. Through these levels the sun and the moon, also conceived as deities, passed each day. A basic concept of Mesoamerican dualism—male and female, good and bad, day and night—emphasized the unity of all things, similar to that found in some Asian religions. Each god often had a parallel female consort or feminine form and often an underworld equivalent as well. In addition, there were patron deities of various occupations and classes. Thus, the number of deities in the inscriptions seems overwhelming, but they should be understood as manifestations of a more limited set of supernatural forces, much like the avatars, or incarnations, of the Hindu gods.

While the few surviving books are religious in character, the majority of inscriptions on monuments are historical records of the ruling families of the Maya cities. The major Maya centers were the cores of city-states, which controlled outlying territories. There was constant warfare, and rulers, such as Pacal of Palenque (who died in 683 C.E.), expanded their territories by conquest. Pacal's victories were recorded on his funerary monuments and in his lavish tomb discovered inside a pyramid at Palenque.

The rulers exercised considerable civil and probably religious power, and their rule was aided by an elite that exercised administrative functions. A class of scribes, or perhaps priests, tended to the cult of the state and specialized in the complex calendrical observations and calculations. The ruler and the scribes organized and participated in rituals of self-mutilation and human sacrifice that among the Maya, as in much of Mesoamerica, formed an important aspect of religion. Also, as a form of both worship and sport, the Maya, like other Mesoamerican peoples, wagered on and played a ritual *ball game* on specially constructed courts in which players moved a ball with their hips or elbows. Losers might forfeit their possessions or their lives.

Builders, potters, scribes, sculptors, and painters worked in the cities for the glory of the gods and the rulers. Most people, however, were peasant farmers whose labor supported the elaborate ritual and political lives of the elite. Captives were enslaved. Patrilineal families probably formed the basis of social life as they did among the Maya of later days. The elite, however, traced their families through both their fathers and their mothers. Elite women are often represented in dynastic monuments in

Ball courts like this one at Copan existed throughout Mesoamerica. The ball game was both a sport and a religious ceremony.

positions of importance. State marriages were important, and elite women retained considerable rights. Among the common folk, women were responsible for the preparation of food and domestic duties, including the production of fine cloth on backstrap looms. The division of tasks by gender was probably supported by religious belief and custom, if present-day Maya practices are a guide.

Classic Collapse

Between about 700 and 900 C.E., the Mesoamerican world was shaken by the cataclysmic decline of the great cultural centers. The reasons for this collapse are not fully understood, but the phenomenon was general. In the central plateau, Teotihuacan was destroyed about 650 C.E. by outside invaders, probably nomadic hunters from the north, perhaps with the collaboration of some of the groups under the dominance of Teotihuacan. The city may have already been in decline due to increasing problems with agriculture. Whereas the fall of Teotihuacan seems to have been sudden, Monte Alban, the Zapotec center, went into a phase of slow decline and eventual abandonment.

The most mysterious aspect of the collapse was the abandonment of the Maya cities. During the 8th century C.E., Maya rulers stopped erecting commemorative stelae and large buildings, and population sizes dwindled.

By 900 C.E., most of the major Maya centers were deserted. Scholars do not agree whether this process was the result of ecological problems and climatic change, agricultural exhaustion, internal revolt, or foreign pressure. The collapse took place at different times in different places and seems to have been the result of several processes, of which increasing warfare was either a cause or a symptom. The warfare may be related to the decline of Teotihuacan and the attempt of Maya city-states to position themselves to control old trade routes.

Chief among the explanations for the Maya collapse has been agricultural exhaustion. The ability of the Maya to create a civilization in the dense rain forest of the Peten in Guatemala and in the Chiapas lowlands had been based on a highly productive agricultural system. By the 8th century, the limits of that system, given the size and density of population, may have been reached. Tikal had an estimated density of over 300 people per square mile. Maintaining the great population centers was an increasing burden. Epidemic disease has also been suggested as a cause of the collapse, perhaps indicating some unrecorded contact with the Old World. Others believe that the peasantry simply refused to bear the burdens of serving and feeding the political and religious elite and that internal rebellion led to the end of the ruling dynasties and their cities.

DOCUMENT

Deciphering the Maya Glyphs

Of all the peoples of ancient America, the Maya developed the most complex system of writing to record their history, religion, philosophy, and politics. Maya hieroglyphs have baffled and fascinated researchers since the 1820s, when the first steps toward deciphering the rich glyphs and symbols of Maya monuments, ceramics, and the few surviving Maya books were made. This process continues, and although we are not yet able to read all the surviving texts, those that have been deciphered have altered our view of Maya society and its underlying beliefs.

One of the problems of decipherment was a false start. In the 16th century, a Spanish bishop of Yucatan, Diego de Landa, burned many books in an attempt to stamp out Maya religion. Landa's attempt to describe the Maya writing based on his questioning of Indian informants was badly flawed. Landa thought the glyphs were letters, not syllables, and so his description confused scholars for many years. Despite his deficiencies, however, Landa provided the only guide available for many years. Unlike the decipherment of Egyptian hieroglyphs, no text with Maya and some other known language side by side exists, and so the problem of reading the Maya glyphs remains difficult.

The first modern advances were made in reading Maya numbers and identifying glyphs for the months in the calendar cycle. By the 1940s, scholars could read the dates rather well, and because so many inscriptions and the four remaining books seemed to be numerical and related to the calendar, most specialists believed that the Maya writing was primarily about the calendar system and that the Maya were obsessed with time. Many things complicated the reading of the other glyphs, such as the fact that scholars were not sure which of the various Maya languages that survive was the language of the inscriptions. In 1952, a young Russian researcher argued that the Maya glyphs combined signs that stood for whole words with others that represented sounds. In this, the Maya script was like ancient Egyptian and cuneiform writings. Althouh the theory was not fully accepted at first, it has proved to be accurate.

A major breakthrough took place in 1960, when art historian Tatiana Proskouriakoff noted that on certain sets of monuments the earliest and last dates were never more than 62 years apart, and that the first date was always accompanied by one certain glyph and the next always by another. She recognized that the images on the monuments were not gods or mythical figures, but kings, and that the first glyph indicated birth and the second accession. Sixty-two years was consistent with a human life span. With this approach, scholars have figured out the names of the rulers and their families and something about the dynastic history of a number of Maya cities.

Scholars now understand that despite regional variations, the texts were written in a language widely understood throughout the Maya region. The glyphs combine syllables, symbols, emblems, and ideas in what is basically a complex phonetic system. Now that we are able to read numbers, dates, place or city emblems, and a few nouns and verbs, a new window has been opened on the ancient Maya.

Art historians Linda Schele and Mary Ellen Miller, in their excellent volume, *The Blood of Kings: Ritual and Dynasty in Maya Art* (1986), provide a reading and interpretation of a famous Maya sculpture (see the figure on page 193). Here Lord Shield-Jaguar, a ruler of Yaxchilan who was between 40 and 60 years old at the time, holds a torch to illumine a ceremony of bloodletting self-sacrifice. His wife, Lady Xoc, draws a rope with thorns through her tongue, after which he too will sacrifice his blood to sustain the gods. This ceremony took place on October 28, 709. The short accompanying text in glyphs dates the ceremony, identifies the people portrayed, and describes their actions.

Questions: What do the elaborate ritual life and sumptuous clothing suggest about the nature of Maya society? Do the complex calendar and writing system indicate widespread literacy or the power of an elite class that controlled this esoteric knowledge? Does the role of writing in Mesoamerican civilization seem similar to that in ancient Egypt, Sumer, and China?

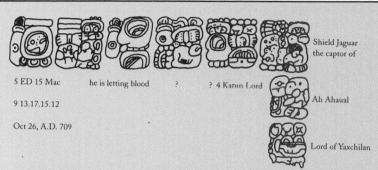

Shield Jaguar
the captor of

5 ED 15 Mac   he is letting blood   ?   ? 4 Katun Lord

9 13.17.15.12   Ah Ahaual

Oct 26, A.D. 709

Lord of Yaxchilan

This relief from the Mayan palace complex at Yaxchilan shows a kneeling woman pulling a rope barbed with thorns through her tongue to draw blood. Her husband, a king named Shield-Jaguar, holds a torch above her head. The king's hair is adorned with the shrunken head of a sacrificial victim.

she is
letting blood

name or titles

Lady Xoc

Lady Batab

The cultural achievements of the classic period were not attained again. Long-count dating ended, the stelae cult ceased, and the quality of ceramics and architectural accomplishments declined. But as the great Maya centers of the southern lowlands and highlands were abandoned or declined, Maya cities in the Yucatan and in the Guatemala highlands expanded and carried on some of the traditions, also receiving considerable cultural influences from central Mexico. Mexicanized ruling families established themselves at *Chichen Itzá* and other towns in Yucatan. The northern Maya area was able to accommodate these influences and create a new synthesis of Maya and central Mexican culture. In the great southern Maya cities, such as Tikal and Palenque, the rain forest soon overran the temples and palaces.

After 1000 C.E., the *Nahuatl*-speaking *Toltecs,* one of the new groups that occupied the central plateau after the fall of Teotihuacan, established political control over a large territory and eventually extended their influence into Maya territory. Their genius seems to have been military, and much of their culture was derived from classic traditions. From their capital at Tula in central Mexico, Toltec influence and trade may have spread as far as the American Southwest, where the cliff-dwelling Anasazi people, the ancestors of the Pueblo Indians, produced beautiful ceramics and cultivated maize in the desert valleys. In Yucatan, the ruling families claimed descent from Toltec invaders. Even when the Toltec empire fell, about 1200 C.E., the cultural traditions of Mesoamerica did not die, for imperial states and civilization do not necessarily go together. Eventually, however, a new power, the *Aztecs,* rose in the central plateau of Mexico. The Aztecs initiated yet another cycle of expansion based on the deep-rooted ways of life and thought of Mesoamerica.

THE PEOPLES TO THE NORTH

Focal Point: To the north of Mesoamerica, complex cultures developed, often based on agriculture. The extent of their contact with Mesoamerica is not clear, but in the Mississippi basin and in the American Southwest, the ancestors of the later Indian peoples formed complex societies with large populations.

Archaeologists have been able to distinguish various stages of Archaic culture, from Alaska to northern Mexico, among the ancestors of the North American Indians. We cannot deal in detail with the many cultural traditions that evolved from those cultures of the Archaic period, but two broad regions in North America

merit special attention because of the complex, sedentary agricultural societies that developed there: the eastern woodlands of what is now the southern United States and the arid Southwest.

The Mound Builders

In the valleys of the Mississippi and Ohio rivers, people began to practice agriculture by 2000 B.C.E. By 700 B.C.E., a society that combined hunting and agriculture had begun to emerge. The *Adena culture,* which developed in southern Ohio and neighboring areas, was characterized by large earthen constructions and mounds. Some of the mounds were defensive, whereas others served as places for burials. These burials contain pottery, pipes (indicating the use of tobacco), jewelry, and copper objects that indicate long-distance trade from as far away as Michigan. The Adena tradition may have been spread by migrants or by trade contacts to other places, such as New York State and Maryland, where it lasted as late as 700 C.E. In Ohio and southern Illinois, however, Adena was then already being replaced by a more complex culture.

The *Hopewell culture* (c. 200–500 C.E.) introduced new levels of scale and complexity. Elaborate mounds, some of great size and often organized into groups, were characteristic of this mound-builder culture. Some of the mounds, such as Serpent Mound in Ohio, were built as effigies of animals. Burials contained jewelry, personal items, weapons, and religious symbols of copper, quartz, galena, and mica. Conch shells and shark teeth indicate long-distance trade to the Gulf coast, and other materials were brought from as far away as the Rocky Mountains. Hopewell artisans worked in stone and clay and produced beautiful luxury items of pottery, pipes, and effigies, many seemingly designed specifically for the cult of the dead. By about 400 C.E., large-scale construction of mounds had ceased in the main centers of Hopewell culture, and the trade network had begun to break down.

After a hiatus of about 400 years, the Hopewell culture was succeeded by a new complex that spread widely throughout the Mississippi valley. Between 800 and 1300 C.E., very large towns and ceremonial centers, such as Moundville (Alabama) and Cahokia (Illinois), flourished throughout the southeastern region. Mound building here was not only for burials or effigies but also for fortification and large pyramid platforms. Cahokia had one temple mound over 30 meters high, containing over 600,000 cubic meters of earth. These Mississippian centers were surrounded by large populations and other smaller towns. For example, at least 50 communities seem to have been under Cahokia's influence. Except for the absence of stone architecture, Cahokia seemed to parallel the urban development of Mesoamerica.

The rich variety of artifacts of excellent workmanship indicates social divisions within this society, but in fact we know little about its social organization. The best clues come from the 18th-century observations of the Natchez Indians, who carried on the Mississippian tradition. They were organized as a powerful chiefdom under a ruler known as the Great Sun, who ruled a society composed of four distinct social classes, the lowest of which were called the stinkards. The Natchez were the last remnants of a culture that had mostly disappeared by 1400 C.E.

One explanation for the rise of *Mississippian culture* was the introduction of new strains of maize from Mesoamerica and the adoption of the maize-beans-squash agricultural complex developed there. Mississippians depended more fully on agriculture than their Hopewell and Adena predecessors. Mississippian populations were larger than those of previous cultures, and the search for new agricultural lands seems to have been a motive for political expansion. The large towns and urban centers, temple complexes, pyramid mounds, religious symbols, and crops appear to reflect a strong Mesoamerican influence, but no identifiable Mesoamerican artifacts have been found in Mississippian sites.

The Desert Peoples

Across the American Southwest a different cultural tradition developed with considerable local variation. By about 300 B.C.E., settled communities developed in this region, living first in pit houses partially beneath the ground and later in stone structures. Irrigation was used to grow maize, beans, and other crops, and ball courts and temple mounds that appeared by 600 C.E. suggest the influence of Mesoamerican cultures. Distinctive pottery developed in each cultural region, and there seems to have been trade between these areas and with Mexico. In southern New Mexico by about 1000 C.E., multi-room stone dwellings were being used.

Perhaps the most famous of the southwestern regional traditions is that of the *Anasazi* (Navajo for "the ancient ones"), who lived in the Four Corners region of New Mexico, Arizona, Colorado, and Utah. Settled in the region from about 200 B.C.E., they began to live in large, multistory adobe and stone dwellings by 700 C.E. Apparently, pressure from hostile neighbors caused them to construct these groups of buildings in protected canyons or in cliffs where access is difficult. The existing cliff-dwelling ruins at Mesa Verde and Canyon de Chelly are excellent examples of Anasazi settlements. A characteristic feature of these villages and towns is the circular pit, or *kiva,* used for religious meetings by the men of the community. This structure is still used today by the Pueblo Indians of the region.

Kivas are also found in another type of Anasazi settlement. The ruins of about 125 towns in New Mexico's Chaco Canyon and the surrounding areas are remarkable for their planning and the care of their construction in stone or adobe. Many of these towns were connected by an extensive system of what seem to be roads or ritual lines, which linked the city to celestial or natural phenomena. The Anasazi produced excellent pottery without the potter's wheel, and they had trading contacts with Mesoamerica, where the turquoise of their region was traded for items such as parrots, valued for their feathers.

A long period of drought in the late 13th century seems to explain the decline of the Anasazi and other southwestern peoples. This decline, followed by pressure from nomads like the Navajo and Apache, eventually led to the abandonment of the towns, but many scholars believe that the traditions of the Anasazi have continued in the culture of the modern Hopi and other Pueblo Indians of the American Southwest.

Among the ancient peoples of the southwestern United States, the contacts with Mesoamerican civilization are clearer than in the eastern woodlands. Both regions, however, demonstrate the diffusion of many aspects of civilization and the development of settled, agricultural societies throughout the Americas.

ANALYSIS

Different Times for Different Peoples

In this presentation of the indigenous civilizations of the Americas that were often so concerned with time, it is appropriate to examine the importance of time and its measurement in world history. The calendar and the keeping of time are so much a part of everyday life that we often think of these measures only as aspects of nature and of the natural order. We divide the day into 24 hours of 60 minutes each, and the year into 12 months or 365 or so days, without much reflection on the meaning or origins of these divisions. Our lives are guided by the clock and marked by its division into working hours, doctor's appointments, class periods, and TV time slots—all of which reflect a widely accepted system not only of measurement but also of an ideology of time and its value.

The marking and division of time is a complex matter with cultural, political, and even biological aspects (as anyone who has flown across the international date line or suffered from jet lag can testify). The concept and meaning of time have varied greatly from culture to culture and have changed historically within cultures. The leaders of both the French Revolution of 1789 and the Russian Revolution of 1917 created new calendar systems to represent what they hoped were to be the beginnings of new historical ages. Calendar systems and time measurement reflect ideas about politics and history as well as perceptions of the natural world.

Observation of the cyclical motion of the heavens was the key for constructing a yearly calendar by which agriculture could be regulated and religious cycles could be set. Early peoples observed the recurring patterns of the stars and planets. Clearly observed stages of the moon provided the guide for the ancient Babylonians, but because the annual cycle of the moon differed from the *solar cycle,* the lunar calendar did not provide an accurate guide to the seasons. The *lunar-cycle* calendar was in constant need of adjustment, or intercalation, which added extra days or months so that the seasons would occur in the same place in the cycle in each calendar year. Despite its difficulties, the lunar calendar was adopted by the Hebrews. It is still in use by Jews and is also the basis of the Muslim calendar.

The ancient Egyptians were the first to use a solar year, and as early as 4000 B.C.E. they had devised a calendar of 12 months of 30 days each, to which they added 5 days of celebration at the start of each year. (The Maya and other peoples of Mesoamerica had a similar solution but added their 5 "inauspicious" days at the end of the year.) The Egyptian solar calendar, while not exact and also in need of periodic adjustments, served as the basis for the Julian calendar of the Roman Empire established by Julius Caesar in 45 B.C.E. This calendar was modified and improved in the Gregorian calendar, instituted by Pope Gregory XIII in the late 16th century and adopted slowly thereafter throughout Europe.

Other peoples and civilizations also worked out calendar systems based on observation of the heavens, and these in turn were related to concepts about time and history. Among the ancient peoples of Mesoamerica, India, and Sumer, time was cyclical. Thus the events of history fit into recurring patterns that might reveal a divine purpose or plan but did not lead in any particular direc-

tion. Both the ancient Hindus and the Maya calculated great cycles of thousands of years as part of a divine plan.

The ancient Chinese were concerned with the measurement of time, and water clocks were in use during the Shang period, about 1500 B.C.E. By the 11th century, an elaborate clock regulated by the flow of water had been designed for the emperor by Su Sung, a court official. But Chinese interest in mechanical clocks did not continue, and time did not figure prominently in Chinese philosophical thought or in the lives of most people. A new emperor often introduced a new calendar, for control of the calendar was viewed as an attribute of power. The Chinese concept of history was marked by belief in a divine mandate that was given to each dynasty and then withdrawn when it failed in its duties and obligations. Thus, time and history recurred as each dynasty attempted to fulfill this Mandate of Heaven.

For the ancient Hebrews and Christians, history was not cyclical but linear: it moved toward an end, the revelation of God's will. The present was influenced by the past and the future. It has been suggested that a concept of the future and of progress depends on a linear view of time and history.

Prior to the 19th century, the vast majority of the world's people, including the peasants of the most technologically advanced societies, measured time by the cycle of work and daily tasks: when the cows had to be milked, how much time until dinner, how many hours of daylight remained. These "natural" rhythms kept work and life close together, and there was little concern for time as a separate "thing" that could be precisely measured and accounted, or "lost" or "gained." The day might be divided by the hours of daily prayer or by the duration of a task, but exact time was of little importance.

Although the Chinese had experimented with clocks, and other cultures had used sundials, candles, and water clocks to measure the passage of time, the synchronization and precision of these instruments was difficult. Clocks were curiosities and vehicles for artistic expression, more likely to be found in royal collections than in private homes. In 807 C.E., for example, Europeans marveled at a mechanical water clock sent as a gift by the Muslim leader Haroun al-Rashid to Charlemagne, but despite such wonders, the inaccurate instruments of antiquity were of limited use.

It was in Europe that the transformation of time measurement took place. Perhaps the deficiencies of sundials and water clocks in the cloudy and frosty climates of northern Europe bought about the perfection of the mechanical clock. The cause simply could have been Europe's growing interest in machines.

Between the 14th and 17th centuries, the measurement of time experienced a profound if gradual transformation. Church and town clocks appeared in the major urban centers, and clocks began to appear in private homes, especially after the introduction of pendulum clocks about 1660. By the end of the 17th century, pocket watches based on balance springs made accurate timekeeping a "private" matter, and the aristocrats, master craftsmen, and merchants of Europe began to live their lives by the clock. When Catholic missionaries arrived in China in the 17th century, the Chinese were amazed by the complexity and accuracy of the clocks they brought. Some authors see Europe's fascination with time and perfection of the clock as a symbol of changes in attitudes about labor and nature. Moreover, accurate clocks were precise machines and symbolized the development of technology that accompanied the scientific revolution of the 17th century and then the Industrial Revolution of the 18th century.

The "revolution in time," as historian David Landes has called it, was related to changes in work discipline needed in the new industries, where the synchronization of tasks in a factory called for precision and a sense of time different from that of rural labor. Such coordination had already begun to appear in activities such as shipbuilding and on sugar plantations. Time became something that workers sold and employers bought, and the concept of productivity measured by the amount of work done in a specific amount of time became a basic part of the industrial work ethic. The shift was difficult, however. Older working patterns were slow to change, and industrialists complained that workers still honored "Saint Monday" by not showing up for work on that day, or that they preferred to work not by the hour but by the task. Early industrial workers were not eager to become captives of the machine and the clock.

Those earlier preindustrial attitudes toward work—the rhythm of intense labor at some times of year and less work at others, labor measured by the job and not by the amount of time it took to do it—persisted in most of the world outside Europe in the 19th century. European travelers to Asia, Africa, the Pacific, and the Americas commented on the natives' lack of punctuality, the natural or religious rhythms of their life, their inability to measure time, and often their seeming disregard for it. The "myth of the lazy native" was being born. The clock became a measure of what Europeans and North Americans valued and what set them apart. When

an English missionary in southern Africa wrote in his diary, "Today we have unpacked our clock and we seem a little more civilized," he summarized a great deal of modern world history.

Questions: To what extent did the measurement of time become important in the early civilizations of Egypt, the Near East, and China? Do concepts of time influence a people's view of history? What are the implications of the technological changes in keeping time?

THE ANDEAN WORLD

Focal Point: The rise of civilization in South America paralleled many of the processes in Mesoamerica. Periods of broadly shared culture were followed by periods of regional diversity. The civilization of Chavín spread along the Peruvian coast and created a horizon of widely shared culture. It was followed by vibrant regional cultures like Nazca and Moche and then by another horizon centered on the highland states of Huari and Tihuanaco. The decline of these states led to new regional developments.

The Andean world presented to men and women a peculiar geography of complex microregions with extreme changes in altitude and temperature. The narrow and arid strip on the western coast, cut by a few rivers that flow to the Pacific, gives way quickly to the high Andes, where some peaks rise to over 15,000 feet. Between the two major chains of the Andes lie high valleys and steppes, or *puna,* that form the highlands, or altiplano. On these cool uplands (usually above 10,000 feet), the land is relatively level and there is adequate water. Here potatoes and maize could be grown, and the puna provided good grazing for *llamas* and *alpacas,* the "sheep of the Andes." Andean populations were concentrated here or down on the arid coast in the river valleys that made irrigation possible. On the eastern slopes of the Andes, large rivers run down into the tropical rain forest concentrated at the basins of the Amazon and La Plata rivers. This is the humid *montaña,* where tropical fruits and coca leaf can be obtained.

This rugged topography imposed limitations and created opportunities for civilization to develop. The arid coastal valleys demanded irrigation, and this spurred population growth and social complexity. In the highlands, irrigation and terracing increased the food supply

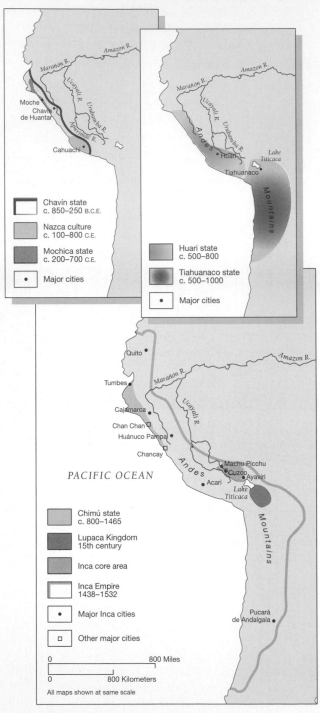

Andean Societies

Trade and communication were difficult. It took large, well-organized projects to build roads, bridges, and agricultural terraces. The reasons for state building were good. The warfare, military images, and trophy heads seen in much ancient Peruvian art represent a world of limited resources and competition.

Recall that in the Andean world, sharp vertical changes created microclimates within relatively short distances. Peoples and even individual communities or families strove to control the different ecological zones where different kinds of crops could be raised. A community might reside in the altiplano growing potatoes and quinoa (an Andean grain), but could also have fields in the lower valleys to grow maize, pastures miles away at a higher elevation for the llamas, and even an outer colony in the montaña to provide cotton, coca, and other tropical products. In fact, access to a variety of these ecological zones by colonization, occupation, conquest, or trade seems to have been a constant feature in Andean life—a feature that determined pre-Columbian patterns of settlement and influenced the historical development of the Andean world.

Early Developments and the Rise of Chavín

Much of early Andean history fits a pattern of alternation between periods of decentralization, in which various local or regional centers developed distinctive cultures, and periods when one of these centers seems to have spread its control over very large areas, establishing a cultural horizon under centralized authority. Between 3000 and 2000 B.C.E., permanent agricultural villages were established in the Andean highlands and on the arid Pacific coast. Maize was introduced from Mesoamerica and was grown along with indigenous crops such as the potato. By about 2700 B.C.E., pottery was produced, first on the north coast in present-day Ecuador and then in the highlands of central Peru. This early pottery, called Valdivia ware, indicates advanced techniques of production. It is remarkably similar to Japanese Jomon-period ceramics, and this has led some scholars to hypothesize a trans-Pacific contact by Japanese fishermen. Whatever the origins of pottery in the region, the presence of sedentary agriculture, ceramics, weaving, and permanent villages marked a level of productivity that was soon followed by evidence of political organization. Early sites, such as El Paraíso on the Peruvian coast, contain monumental buildings of great size, but we know little of the societies that built them.

in regions where the amount of arable land was limited. Populations were concentrated in the fertile valleys but were separated from one other by steep mountains.

CLOSEUP

Water Management in Ancient American Agriculture

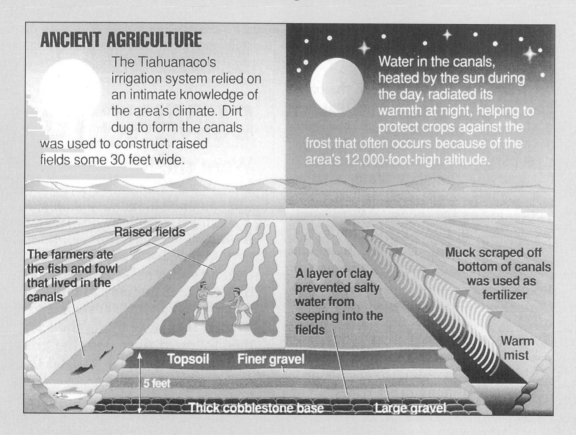

ANCIENT AGRICULTURE

The Tiahuanaco's irrigation system relied on an intimate knowledge of the area's climate. Dirt dug to form the canals was used to construct raised fields some 30 feet wide.

Water in the canals, heated by the sun during the day, radiated its warmth at night, helping to protect crops against the frost that often occurs because of the area's 12,000-foot-high altitude.

Raised fields

The farmers ate the fish and fowl that lived in the canals

A layer of clay prevented salty water from seeping into the fields

Muck scraped off bottom of canals was used as fertilizer

Warm mist

Topsoil   Finer gravel

5 feet

Thick cobblestone base   Large gravel

The ancient peoples of the Americas devised complex systems of irrigation, combining their knowledge of agriculture and hydrology to produce high yields in areas of drought, frost, or difficult soil that even today present great challenges to modern agriculture. Some of the projects were enormous, involving miles of canals and ditches. In the Maya areas of Central America, in the lowlands of Bolivia, and in arid coastal Peru there is evidence of "ridged" fields in which irrigation apparently supported dense populations. At Tihuanaco, near the shores of Lake Titicaca in the Andes, canals were dug, and the mud from them was used to fertilize the fields alongside. Fish and aquatic birds occupied the canals, providing protein. The water heated by the sun during the day helped protect the fields at night. Estimates are that productivity in such fields was as much as seven times greater than in nonirrigated fields. Similar systems were developed elsewhere in the Americas.

The role of water management has often been suggested as crucial in the development of early states in Mesopotamia, Egypt and Peru, but recent research suggests that in some cases the state came before irrigation. Thus, the "hydraulic theory" as an explanation of the rise of civilization is being questioned, but the ingenuity and importance of irrigation for many American Indian civilizations seems clear.

Between 1800 and 1200 B.C.E., ceremonial centers with large stone buildings were constructed in the highlands and on the coast. Pottery was now widely distributed, the domestication of the llama had taken place, and agriculture had become more complex, with evidence of simple irrigation at some places. The most important of these centers was Chavín de Huantar (850–250 B.C.E.) in the Peruvian highlands. Chavín contained several large temple platforms and adobe and stone constructions. Its craftsmen worked in ceramics, textiles, and gold. *Chavín culture* was characterized by artistic motifs that were widely diffused through much of the Andean region and seem to represent a cult or a system of religious beliefs. Jaguars, snakes, birds of prey, and humans with feline characteristics were used as decorations, often along with scenes of war and violence.

The Chavín artistic style was so widely diffused that archeologists refer to this epoch as a horizon, a period when there seems to have been a broad central authority that integrated a widely dispersed region. In truth, we do not know whether the religion of Chavín was spread by conquest, trade, or missionary activity, nor do we know its origins. It does have some remarkable stylistic similarities with Olmec art in Mesoamerica; some archeologists have pointed out certain tropical features in both and have suggested the Amazonian lowlands as a possible point of origin for both traditions.

The evidence of warfare in early Peruvian agricultural societies may indicate a general process. With the development of intensive agriculture and a limited amount of arable land, it became vitally necessary to organize irrigation and create political authority and eventually states that could mobilize to protect or expand the available land.

Regional Cultures and a New Horizon

By 300 B.C.E., Chavín was in decline, and whatever unity the widely spread Chavín style indicated was lost. The Andean world was now characterized by regional centers, each with its own cultural and artistic traditions. This was a period without political unity, but it produced some of the Andean world's finest art. Irrigated agriculture that produced a wide variety of crops, the domestication of llamas and related animals, dense populations, and hierarchical societies could be found in many places. Some societies, such as those in Nazca on the south coast and Moche to the north, produced remarkable pottery and weaving.

Nazca weaving reached a high point for the Americas. Discovery in the 1920s of a group of richly dressed mummies at Paracas near Nazca revealed the artistic accomplishments of these ancient weavers. Over 100 colors were used, and many techniques of weaving and cloth types were produced; the designs were often abstract. The plain near Nazca is also the scene of great figures of various animals, which cover many hundreds of feet and can be seen only from the air. There are also great straight lines or paths that cut across the plain and seem to be oriented toward distant mountains or celestial points. Why these lines and designs were drawn is unknown.

The *Mochica state* (200–700 C.E.), in the Moche valley and on the coast to the north of Chavín, mobilized workers to construct great clay-brick temples, residences, and platforms. Artisans produced gold and silver jewelry and copper tools. The potter's art reached a high point; scenes on Mochica ceramics depict rulers receiving tribute and executing prisoners. Nobles, priests, farmers, soldiers, and slaves are also portrayed in remarkably lifelike ways; many vessels are quite clearly portraits of individual members of the elite. The Mochica also produced a great number of pottery vessels showing a variety of extremely explicit sexual activities. These scenes are almost always in a domestic setting and indicate descriptions of everyday life rather than ritual unions.

Moche expanded its control by conquest. Mochica art contains many representations of war, prisoners, and the taking of heads as trophies. There is also archeological evidence of hilltop forts and military posts. Politically, Moche and the other regional states seem to have been military states or chiefdoms, supported by extensive irrigated agriculture and often at war.

Some idea of life in Moche society has been spectacularly revealed with the discovery in 1988 of the tomb of a warrior-priest. Buried with retainers, servants, and his dog, this nobleman was covered with gold, silver, and copper ornaments; fine cloth; and jewelry. The scenes on these objects and in the pottery buried with him include depictions of captive prisoners, ritual sacrifice, and warfare.

This pattern of regional development continued until about 300 C.E., when two large centers, *Tihuanaco* on the shores of Lake Titicaca, and *Huari,* farther to the north in southern Peru, began to emerge as large states. How much centralized political control they exerted is unclear, but as in the earlier case of Chavín, the religious symbols and artistic style associated with these centers

At the plain of Nazca on the southern Peruvian coast, mysterious geometric designs and the shapes of animals, like this spider, were traced on the ground. The purpose of these shapes, which can only be seen from the air, remains unknown.

became widely diffused in the Andean world, creating perhaps a second or Intermediate Horizon (c. 300–900 C.E.) roughly contemporary with the classic Maya and Teotihuacan in Mesoamerica.

Tihuanaco was an urban ceremonial center with a population of perhaps 40,000, supported by extensive irrigated agriculture. Recent archeological work has revealed an extensive system of raised fields, irrigated by canals, that could produce high yields. Tihuanaco's inhabitants probably spoke Aymara, the language of the southern Andes that is spoken today in Bolivia. The art style of Tihuanaco and the representations of its gods, especially the Staff God, spread all over the southern Andean zone.

In typical Andean fashion, Tihuanaco extended its political control through colonies as far away as Chile and the eastern Andean slopes in order to assure access to fish, coca, and tropical plants—the products of dif-

ferent ecological zones. Huari may have begun as a colony of Tihuanaco, but it eventually exercised wide influence over much of the North Andean zone. While the period of its control was relatively short, the urban area of Huari eventually covered over six square miles, and its influence was spread by the construction of a system of roads.

The Intermediate Horizon, represented by Tihuanaco and Huari, came to an end in the 9th century C.E., about the same time as the end of the classic period in Mesoamerica. Whether these two processes were connected remains unknown. With the decline of these expansive cultures in Peru, another period of regional development followed as different peoples, especially those along the coast, tried to establish control over their neighbors. The *Chimu state* on the north coast eventually controlled over 600 miles of the coastal zone.

The Chimu state, founded about 800 C.E., was still expanding when it fell to the Incas in 1465. During this period other small states had formed. From Lake Titicaca westward to the Pacific coast, the Lupacqa created a kingdom. On the eastern margins of the lake and into the rich valleys on the eastern slope of the Andes, other small chiefdoms formed. In the highlands, meanwhile, various ethnic groups were struggling for control of their neighbors. One of these, a group of Quechua-speaking clans, or *ayllus,* took control of the highlands around Cuzco and began to expand, especially after 1400 C.E. These were the Incas, who were in the midst of creating a new horizon of centralized control and considerable cultural influence over the various ethnic and linguistic groups of the Andean world from Ecuador to Chile when the Europeans arrived in 1532.

Andean Lifeways

Although it is difficult to reconstruct much of the social and political organization of early Andean societies on the basis of archeological evidence, by using later observations from Inca times along with archeological materials we can identify some characteristic features. We have already spoken of verticality, or the control of several economic niches at different altitudes, as a principle of Andean life. This control and related self-sufficiency was sometimes the objective of states, but it was also the goal of families and communities. Kin groups were another constant of the Andean world.

Andean peoples were divided into ethnic groups and spoke several languages, although Aymara came to predominate in the Bolivian highlands, and the Incas later spread Quechua from the central Andes to the coast and north to Ecuador. Despite ethnic and linguistic differences, communities were generally composed of households, which together recognized some form of kinship. Members of a kinship unit, or ayllu, traced their descent from a common, sometimes mythical ancestor, and they referred to other members of the ayllu as brother and sister. People usually married within their ayllu. The ayllu assigned land and access to herds and water to each household. But rights and access were not equal for every household or family within an ayllu. Ayllus were often divided into halves, which might have different functions or roles. The peoples of the highland civilizations shared this form of organization with many tribes of the Amazonian forests.

There were also community leaders and ayllu chiefs, or *curacas,* who had privileges of dress and access to resources. Groups of ayllus sharing a similar dialect, customs, and distinctive dress were bound together into ethnic groups, and sometimes several of these were forged into a state. The ties of kinship were used to mobilize the community for cooperative labor and war. The ayllu was a basic organization, and kinship provided an understanding of cooperation and conflict from the village to the empire. Some authors have suggested that even in the large states, conflicts were more often between ayllus or groups of ayllus than between secondary social classes.

The principle of reciprocity that lay beneath the cooperative organization of the ayllu infused much Andean social life. Reciprocal obligations existed at many levels—between men and women within the family, between households within the ayllu, and between the curacas, who were expected to represent the interests of the ayllus. Eventually, in theory at least, reciprocity also existed between communities and a large state such as Huari, which in return for labor and tribute was expected to provide access to goods or to mobilize large projects, such as irrigation or terracing, that would benefit the community. Reciprocity also infused religious belief. Andean peoples lived in a world where sacred spirits and powers, or *huacas,* were apparent in caves, mountains, rocks, rivers, and other natural phenomena. Worship of the huacas and of the mummies of ancestors (which were also considered holy and part of Andean religious life), at least from the Nazca period, was a matter of reciprocal exchange as well.

CONCLUSION

American Civilizations

There are striking parallels in the cultural development and the chronology of the two major areas of civilization in the Americas. This may be due to convergence—that is, people in different places often work out similar solutions to the same problems—but there also seems to have been considerable contact between these regions over a long period of time. Much of this contact was probably indirect, funneled through the intermediate areas of Colombia and Panama. Peoples such as the Tairona and Muisca of Colombia created large-scale chiefdoms based on intensive cultivation. Their societies were hierarchical, and their artisan crafts, especially metallurgy, were highly developed: South American gold artifacts turn up in offerings at Mayan shrines in Yucatan. Through such intermediate societies, contact between Mesoamerica and the Andean world may have been made. There are other examples of cultural diffusion and contact. The ritual ball game that was played for sport and worship on special courts throughout Mesoamerica and the Maya area has been found as far away as the American Southwest and even among the peoples of the Caribbean islands.

American Indian peoples and civilizations shared much, but there were differences as well. The Peruvian cultures developed metallurgy to a greater degree than other cultures in the Americas and eventually produced bronze tools. The puna supported herds of llamas and permitted a form of pastoralism unknown in Mesoamerica. Unlike the Maya, the ancient peoples of the Andes never invented a writing system. Still, in many ways the civilizations of the Americas had more in common with each other than with those of the Old World, and that fact probably indicates their shared origins and their contacts over thousands of years.

In this brief survey, it should be clear that we have not done justice to the variety and complexity of American Indian cultures and civilizations. It should also be clear that there is much we do not know about the history of the Western Hemisphere. The long history of civilization in the New World; the strength of Indian languages, traditions, and beliefs; and the crops of the Americas domesticated by the ancestors of the Indians all had an impact on the subsequent history of these continents. The long relative isolation of the Americas from the populations, and therefore from the diseases, of the Old World and the inability of the Americas to share in the technological advances of the Old World proved disastrous after the first contact with Europeans. Ultimately, however, the resilience of Indian cultures would shape the societies of the Americas in many ways.

FURTHER READINGS

An excellent, up-to-date survey of the early history of the Americas is Stuart Fiedel's *Prehistory of the Americas* (1987). Also extremely useful for its information and for its excellent maps is Michael Coe, et al., *Atlas of Ancient America* (1986).

On the early history of Peru, Edward P. Lanning's *Peru Before the Incas* (1967) remains, despite its age, a classic account, sensitive to the geography and ecology of the Andean region. Nigel Davies's *The Ancient Kingdoms of Mexico* (1983) offers a broad overview, which combines archeology, art history, and history.

One of the best books on the Maya is Norman Hammond's *Ancient Maya Civilization* (1982). Well illustrated and well written, this book covers the major aspects of classic Maya culture and is especially good on the calendar system. An excellent short survey is Michael D. Coe's *The Maya*, 4th ed. (1987).

Two good introductions to the ancient cultures of North America are Robert Silverberg's *Mound Builders of Ancient America* (1968) and George G. Gumerman, ed., *The Anasazi in a Changing Environment* (1988). George S. Stuart's *America's Ancient Cities* (1988) uses a good text and excellent photos to emphasize the continuity between the peoples of North America and Mesoamerica.

A fine example of a scholarly monograph, and one that demonstrates that exciting discoveries about the ancient Americas do not all center on great cities and "lost" civilizations, is Anna C. Roosevelt's *Parmana: Prehistoric Maize and Manioc Subsistence along the Amazon and Orinoco* (1980). This scientific study shows how archeologists are probing questions such as the origins and diffusion of agriculture.

10

The Spread of Peoples and Civilizations

AFRICA		**3200** Unification of Upper and Lower Egypt	**800** B.C.E.–**1000** C.E. Migration of Bantu-speakers throughout sub-Saharan Africa
	7000–3000 Desiccation of the Sahara		**600** B.C.E.–**1000** C.E. Iron diffused throughout Africa
		c.1500–300 Horses introduced to Africa by way of Egypt	
		3000–1000 Spread of agriculture south of the Sahara **750–666** Kings of Meroe rule Egypt	
NORTHERN EUROPE	*Germans*	**2000** B.C.E. **ff.** Germanic peoples settle in Scandinavia (present-day Denmark)	**100** Germans in southern Germany, on Roman borders
		1000 B.C.E. **ff.** Germans spread though Germany, displacing Celts	
	Slavs	**7th–3rd centuries** Scythian state in southern Russia	
JAPAN	**c. 5000** Early migrations and settlement of Japan		**600** Legendary Emperor Jimmu establishes state in Japan
	3000–2000 Jomon culture		
POLYNESIA		**1500–500** Beginnings of Polynesian migrations; Lapita pottery found in Fiji, Tonga, Samoa	
	7000 B.C.E.	**1000** B.C.E.	**500** B.C.E.

INTRODUCTION

We have concentrated thus far on the centers of civilization and their internal developments in the classical societies of the Old World and the emerging civilizations in the Americas. In this chapter we will explore the connections between the established centers and the rest of the world's peoples. The major civilizations have historically been expansive, and their innovations and cultures have influenced their immediate neighbors and sometimes peoples who lived at great distances from them. While scholars still debate the issue of diffusion versus independent development, many believe that important early breakthroughs, such as agriculture, the domestication of animals, pottery, and metallurgy, were not repeatedly reinvented across the globe but were rather diffused by contacts and migration. Agriculture, for example, may have been "invented" more than once, but most people learned about it by contact with those who already practiced it.

Throughout history, the process and means of cultural expansion have varied greatly. At times, as with Rome, conquest has been the means of imposing ideas, language, and institutions. Roman culture and law were carried to the far ends of the empire in the wake of the conquering Roman legions. In other places, long-distance traders have carried ideas as well as goods. The ship, the caravan, and the sword have thus been instruments of cultural diffusion.

The later history of Rome after the empire was invaded demonstrates another possibility. It is not always conquerors who spread their culture; sometimes it is the conquered. In late Rome, as in pre-Columbian Mesoamerica and China, the "barbarian" conquerors of a civilization absorbed its culture and adopted its ways. The result was a new fusion of cultural elements. In other places, trade or missionary activity has been the means by which civilization has spread. In this chapter, for example, our discussion of early Japanese society will demonstrate the peaceful diffusion of Chinese culture and its transformation in Japan, a process in which Buddhism played a major role.

In this chapter we cannot deal with all the peoples of the globe who were influenced by the spread of civilization or who contributed to that process. Instead we shall examine four areas of the world—sub-Saharan Africa, northern Europe, Japan, and the Pacific islands—which at the time their cultures took shape were not among the civilization centers. Nevertheless, the peoples of these areas were influenced by developments or innovations in

---

1076 Ghana conquered by Almoravids

1000 Ghana at height of its power

100–200 Camels introduced from Asia   **300** Meroe declines   **985** Conversion to Islam of king of Gao

700–800 Islam sweeps across North Africa

100 Rise of kingdom of Axum   **300–700** Conversion to Christianity of Nubian kingdoms in Axum

800–1100 Growth of the trans-Sahara trade for gold

c. 55–112 Tacitus writes about Germans   **401 ff.** Larger Germanic invasions of Roman Empire

100 ff. Improvements in German political organization, rise of local kings; movement of some Germans into Roman Empire

4th c. Germans pressed by Huns

100 ff. Increasing movement of Slavs into eastern Europe   **679** Bulgars (Turkic people) migrate to Balkans, become largely Slavicized, set up first Slavic kingdom in Balkans

300–400 Yamato clan establishes imperial control

580s Buddhism adopted

400 Chinese script introduced

300–1000 Polynesian migrations; settlement of Hawaii and Easter Island   **900** New Zealand settled   **1100–1300** Series of voyages from Hawaii to Tahiti

1 C.E.   **500** C.E.   **1000** C.E.

those centers, or, in the case of Polynesia, by earlier cultural developments on the Asian mainland. In each case, we will also see how ideas, techniques, and material objects were adapted to new environments and different social circumstances so that the spread of civilization and the contact of cultures was usually a creative process, not simply a matter of copying. Finally, important developments occurred during the classical period, though in Polynesia and the Americas there was no connection with the major Old World centers.

It may at first seem strange to discuss peoples as different as the Polynesians, the Germanic tribes, the Slavs, the Japanese, and the early sub-Saharan Africans together. But we should remember that the processes of migration, diffusion, and cultural development are the basis for our discussion. Moreover, unlike earlier chapters, in which the chronological limits have been relatively precise, our discussion will have to range more broadly over time because the pace and rhythm of the diffusion process varied greatly in these widely separated parts of the world. Here, too, the story of how these peoples began to develop their distinctive cultures, often in contact with centers of civilization, should be our focus, rather than a limited time frame. Finally, this chapter also serves the purpose of in-

troducing some peoples whose role in world history would later become particularly important.

THE SPREAD OF CIVILIZATION IN AFRICA

Focal Point: Africa, where earliest humans developed and the home of Egypt's remarkable civilization, experienced climatic changes such as the drying of the Sahara, and foreign influences like the introduction of the horse and of iron, which set in motion a series of cultural changes. The migration of *Bantu*-speaking peoples from West Africa across the continent was often accompanied by the diffusion of iron and agriculture. Kingdoms like Axum in Ethiopia and Ghana in the western Sudan represented the growth of African civilizations.

Africa is a continent of great size, almost 12 million square miles, or about three times the size of the United States. Most of it lies in the tropics, and although we often think of Africa in terms of its rain forests, less than 10 percent of the continent is covered by tropical forests—and those are mostly in West Africa. Much of the African surface is cov-

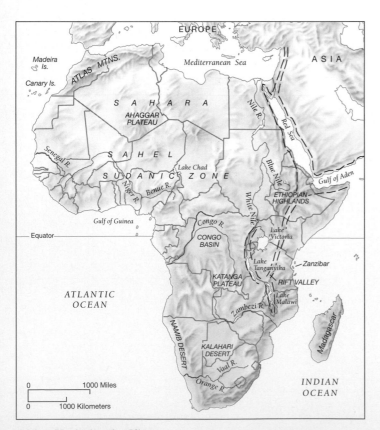

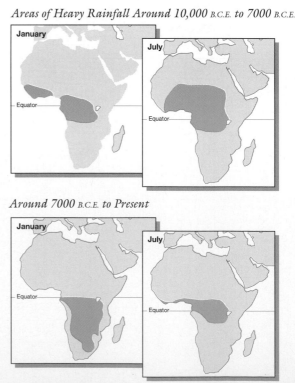

Areas of Heavy Rainfall Around 10,000 B.C.E. to 7000 B.C.E.

Around 7000 B.C.E. to Present

Africa: Variations in Climate

ered by savannas, or open grasslands, and by arid plains and deserts. In geological terms, the continent is really formed by a series of high plateaus broken in the east by the Great Rift Valley and the mountains that surround it. Large rivers—the Congo, the Nile, the Zambezi, and the Niger—begin in the interior of the continent and flow to the sea over great falls and cataracts that mark the passage from plateau to coast. These falls have historically made movement from the coast to the interior difficult, but the great river systems have also provided the interior of Africa with routes of communication.

We have already noted the origins of humankind in East Africa, where some of the earliest fossil remains of protohominids have been found. Even before the appearance about 300,000 years ago of *Homo sapiens,* the ancestors of modern human beings—other hominid species, such as *Homo erectus*—had moved outward from Africa to Asia and Europe. Africa, therefore, holds a special place in the development of the human species. It was the scene of human origins. Moreover, in cultural terms, Africa participated in the early development of civilization. In Chapter 2 we discussed the remarkable civilization of Egypt in the Nile valley and its extension to the Upper Nile kingdoms of Kush and Ethiopia. In this chapter, we will examine the spread of elements of civilization to other areas of Africa.

Despite the false image of Africa as the "dark" and isolated continent, it was, in fact, often in contact with other areas of the world. It received from them technology, crops, ideas, and material goods, which in turn stimulated social and cultural innovations. Moreover, the contacts were not always in the same direction, and there is now considerable evidence that not only early humans but also certain languages, crops, political, and cultural influences spread outward from Africa.

It is useful to begin this discussion by noting the climatic change that altered the appearance of the African continent and seems to have set a whole series of historical processes in motion. That change centers on the area of the Sahara, which during the Late Stone Age appears to have been far better watered than it is today, receiving between 10 and 50 times as much rain as at present. Archeological evidence indicates that several peoples inhabited the area of the Sahara during this period, including the ancestors of the modern-day Berbers and Tuaregs of North Africa, who speak languages related to ancient Egyptian, and the ancestors of the Negro peoples of sub-Saharan Africa, some of whom also spoke these Afro-Asiatic languages and others of whom did not. About 9000 years ago, this situation began to change as temperatures rose and rainfall became erratic. By about 3000 B.C.E., much of the area was desert. The droughts that have recently affected Africa indicate that the desiccation, or drying up, of the Sahara is continuing and the desert is growing.

As the *Sahara* became less habitable the populations moved north toward the Mediterranean coast and south into the area of the dry sahel, or fringe, and especially onto the grassy savannas suitable for agriculture and grazing. Savannas stretch across Africa from the mouth of the Senegal River on the west coast to Lake Chad and the Upper Nile valley. This broad region, the Sudan, became a center of cultural development. The movement of peoples into the Sudan and toward the Nile valley and the Mediterranean set the stage for major developments in the subsequent history of Africa.

Although an obstacle, the Sahara could be traversed, especially after the introduction of the camel, and an active trade developed between black Africa and the Mediterranean world.

Agriculture, Iron, and the Bantu Peoples

Agriculture may have developed independently in Africa, but many scholars believe that the spread of agriculture and iron throughout Africa linked that continent to the major centers of civilization in the Near East and the Mediterranean world. The drying up of the Sahara had pushed many peoples to the south into sub-Saharan Africa. These were the ancestors of the Negro peoples. They settled at first in scattered hunting-and-gathering bands, although in some places near lakes and rivers, people who fished, with a more secure food supply, lived in larger population concentrations. Agriculture seems to have reached these people from the Near East, since the first domesticated crops were millet and sorghum, whose origins are not African but West Asian. The route of agricultural distribution may have gone through Egypt or Ethiopia, which long had contacts across the Red Sea with the Arabian peninsula. There is evidence of agriculture prior to 3000 B.C.E.

Once the idea of planting became diffused, Africans began to develop their own crops, such as certain varieties of rice, and they demonstrated a continued receptiveness to new imports. The presumed areas of the domestication of African crops lie in a band that extends from Ethiopia across the southern Sudan to West Africa. Subsequently, other crops, such as bananas, were introduced from Southeast Asia, and in the 16th century C.E., American crops, such as maize and manioc, spread widely throughout Africa.

Livestock also came from outside Africa. Cattle were introduced from Asia, as probably were domestic sheep and goats. Horses were apparently introduced to Africa from West Asia by the Hyksos invaders of Egypt (1780–1560 B.C.E.) and then spread across the Sudan to West Africa. The camel was introduced from Asia about the 1st century C.E. This was an important innovation, because the camel's ability to thrive in harsh desert conditions and to carry large loads cheaply made it an effective and efficient means of transportation. The camel transformed the desert from a barrier into a still difficult, but more accessible, route of trade and communication.

Livestock provided a living to peoples in the arid portions of the savanna belt and the Sahara, and permitted a nomadic (seasonally moving, *transhumant*) way of life to flourish in certain inhospitable regions. In some areas, it appears that livestock and agriculture arrived about the same time. The spread of livestock was seriously limited in some places by the tsetse fly, dangerous to humans and especially livestock.

Iron also came from West Asia, although its routes of diffusion were somewhat different from those of agri-culture. Most of Africa presents a curious case in which societies moved directly from a technology of stone to iron without passing through the intermediate stage of copper or bronze metallurgy, although some early copperworking sites have been found in West Africa. Iron had been worked in the Near East and Anatolia for at least a thousand years before it began to penetrate into sub-Saharan Africa. The Phoenicians carried the knowledge of iron smelting to their colonies, such as Carthage in North Africa, and from there to their trading ports along the coast of Morocco. By sea down the coast or by land across the Sahara, this knowledge penetrated into the forests and savannas of West Africa during the last millennium B.C.E., or at roughly the same time that iron-making was reaching western Europe. Evidence of iron-making has been found in Nigeria, Ghana, and Mali, and iron implements seem to have slowly replaced stone ones at several sites.

This technological shift could cause profound changes in the complexity of African societies. Iron represented power. In West Africa, the blacksmith who made tools and weapons had an important place in society, often with special religious powers and functions. Iron hoes, which made the land more productive, and iron weapons, which made the warrior more powerful, had symbolic meaning in many West African societies. Those who knew the secrets of ironmaking gained ritual and sometimes political power.

Iron entered Africa by other routes as well. Ironmaking seems to have traveled from the Red Sea into Ethiopia and East Africa and down the Nile from Egypt into the Sudan, where, as we have seen, large African states such as Meroe were in close contact with dynastic Egypt. Meroe's contact with peoples to the south led to the further diffusion of iron technology. By the 1st century C.E., iron was known in sub-Saharan Africa, and within about a thousand years, it had reached the southern end of the continent. Iron tools and weapons increased the efficiency of both agriculture and war. In the later stages of this story, the adoption of agriculture and the use of iron tools and weapons were roughly simultaneous processes.

Unlike the peoples of the Americas, where metallurgy was a very late and limited development, Africans had iron from a relatively early date, developing ingenious furnaces to produce the high heat (1100°F) needed for production and to control the amount of air that reached the carbon and iron ore necessary for making iron. Except for those regions directly influenced by the great Bronze Age civilization of Pharaonic Egypt, much of Africa skipped right into the Iron Age, taking the basic technology and adapting it to local conditions and resources. The working of bronze was also known

CLOSEUP

African Horsemen

After its introduction into Egypt, the horse spread quickly in Africa. Rock paintings in the Sahara show the use of horses and chariots to traverse the desert, and by 300 to 200 B.C.E., there were trade routes across the desert. In the West African savanna, horses became a symbol of kingly authority and the basis of military power as some states organized large cavalry regiments. At ancient *Ghana,* the king gave audiences accompanied by ten horses caparisoned in gold. Horses had symbolic power and were used in sacrifices, processions, and other forms of conspicuous display. Archeological sites have yielded equestrian figures, especially in the period after about 1000 B.C.E. The horse was also a military asset. One observer wrote that the empire of *Mali* could field 10,000 riders. The association between cavalry forces and the growth of the Islamicized states of the savanna was strong, but the earliest West African states did not form because of the horse or outside influence. At *Ife,* traditionally the oldest state of the region, horses were not represented.

The obvious power and utility of the horse might have led to its further distribution throughout Africa, but the spread of new cultural elements and technology was always limited by the physical environment. The horse was widely adopted in the West African grassland regions, but wherever the *tsetse fly* thrived in humid tropical forests and brush, livestock raising became almost impossible. The tsetse fly carried "sleeping sickness," or trypanosomiasis, and horses and cat-

tle could not be used effectively in these regions. Cavalry campaigns could not be carried out in the rainy season when the range of the flies increased. The armies of African horsemen, which had often swept away their opponents, had met a tiny but tenacious foe.

to Africans, and by 1000 C.E., remarkably lifelike bronze sculptures of great technical virtuosity were cast at the city-state of Ife in Nigeria by the Yoruba people.

The Bantu Dispersal

The diffusion of agriculture and later of iron was accompanied by a great movement of people, who may have carried these innovations. These people probably originated in eastern Nigeria in West Africa. Their migration may have been set in motion by an increase in population caused by a movement into their homelands of peo-

ples fleeing the desiccation of the Sahara. They spoke a language, proto-Bantu (bantu means "the people"), which is the parent tongue of many related Bantu languages still spoken throughout sub-Saharan Africa. In fact, about 90 percent of the languages south of a line from the Bight of Benin on the west coast to Somalia on the east coast are part of the Bantu family.

Why and how these people spread out into central and southern Africa remains a mystery, but archeologists believe that at some stages their iron weapons allowed them to conquer their hunting-and-gathering opponents, who still used stone implements. Still, the process is uncertain,

Remarkable bronze figures were cast at Ife (Nigeria) by Yoruba craftsmen.

and peaceful migration—or simply rapid demographic growth—may have also caused the Bantu expansion.

The migrations moved first to the central Sudan and then into the forests of west and central Africa. The rivers, especially the Congo basin, provided the means of movement; the migration was a long, gradual, and intermittent process. Moving outward from central Africa, Bantu peoples arrived at the east coast, where they contacted cattle-raising peoples of a different linguistic tradition. By the 12th century, the Bantu speakers—the ancestors of the Shona and Nguni peoples—pushed south of the Zambezi River into modern Zimbabwe and eventually into South Africa.

From the study of the related Bantu languages, it is possible to learn something about the original culture of the proto-Bantu speakers. The early Bantu depended on agriculture and fishing. They raised goats and perhaps cattle. They were village dwellers who organized their societies around kinship ties. Leadership of the villages was probably in the hands of a council of elders. The spirits of the natural world played a large role in the lives of these people. They looked to their ancestors to help deal with those spirits, and they depended on village religious specialists to deal with calamity and to combat witchcraft, which they greatly feared.

In about a thousand years the Bantu-speaking peoples expanded over much of the continent, spreading their languages and cultures among the existing populations, absorbing those original peoples and being absorbed by them. By the 13th century C.E., cattle-raising, iron-using Bantu peoples had reached the southern end of the continent. By that time, black Africa's major features were in place. A few purely hunting peoples remained, such as the *Pygmies* of central Africa, but their way of life was not that of most Africans. Agricultural and herding societies with knowledge of iron metallurgy could be found throughout sub-Saharan Africa. While pockets of peoples still speaking non-Bantu languages existed, such as the Khoi-Khoi and Bushmen of southern Africa, and in East Africa the influence of Ethiopian culture was still strong, Bantu languages predominated all over southern and central Africa and marked the trail of one of the world's great migrations.

Africa, Civilization, and the Wider World

We have viewed the development of Egyptian civilization in conjunction with the parallel developments of the Fertile Crescent; yet, we should also recognize that many aspects of Egyptian life, such as ideas about religion and kingship, strongly resembled those of other African societies. There is much debate on whether the Egyptian idea of the king as a divine being with special powers over natural phenomena (an idea also found in some West African kingdoms) is due to the common origins of both or whether these concepts were diffused from Egypt to other areas of Africa. There are other striking parallels, such as brother-sister marriage among rulers, and the rituals of taking authority, that seem to tie the cultures of sub-Saharan Africa to Egypt. Whatever the African origins of Egyptian civilization (a matter of considerable controversy), there is no doubt of extensive contact between Egypt and peoples living southward along the Nile valley in the Sudan and northern Ethiopia.

Axum: A Christian Kingdom   We discussed the Egyptian contacts with Kush in Chapter 2 and the fact that the Kushites and their capitals became thoroughly influenced by Egyptian culture. For a short period, from 751 B.C.E. until the invasion of Egypt by the Assyrians in 666 B.C.E., the kings of Meroe also ruled as pharaohs of Egypt. Meroe possessed the ores and fuels needed to produce iron on a large scale. That technology, and its extensive trade with Egypt and the Mediterranean, allowed Meroe to flourish. But Meroe was not alone. Other town-based societies also existed in the region of the Sudan and Ethiopia.

The kingdom of *Axum* in the Ethiopian highlands, which eventually surpassed Meroe in importance around the 1st century C.E., introduces another cultural stream into the history of Africa. Axum seems to have received strong influences and perhaps settlers from the Arabian peninsula. Its population probably consisted of a mixture of these immigrants and peoples of Eritrea and the Ethiopian highlands. Axum became a great city with large palaces and monuments. It developed a writing system based on a South Arabian script. Geez, the language of the people of Axum, is a Semitic language, but Axum's rulers also spoke Greek and perhaps used it as a language of trade.

Axum was a powerful state. It controlled several ports, such as Adulis along the Red Sea coast, and it participated in the commerce of the Indian Ocean, where its ivory, salt, and slaves were in great demand. It also traded with Alexandrian Egypt and eventually with Rome, Byzantium, and India. Those contacts led to a fusion of cultural elements. By about 200 C.E., Axum was involved in military and political affairs across the Red Sea on the Arabian peninsula. By the middle of the 3rd century C.E., Axum had defeated Meroe and emerged as the dominant power in the horn of Africa. The history of the kingdom of Axum underlines the cross-fertilization of cultures across the Red Sea.

Axum, a large state in the Ethiopian highlands, received cultural influences from Arabia and traded widely in the Indian Ocean. Its capital contained large buildings and monuments like this 70-foot high solid granite obelisk.

About 350 C.E., Ezana, the king of Axum, converted to Christianity, and that religion spread among Axum's peoples over the following centuries. Monasteries and churches were established, the Bible was translated, and a religious literature was developed that linked the Queen of Sheba, wife of the biblical King Solomon, to Axum and demonstrated the area's supposed progression from Judaism to Christianity. All this established a certain religious legitimacy to the negus, or ruler of Axum. The form of Christianity that spread among the Axumites during the 5th and 6th centuries C.E. increased the kingdom's ties to the Greeks of the eastern Mediterranean, although eventually Ethiopian Christianity became somewhat isolated.

All this indicates considerable influence and contact between this African kingdom and the outside world well before the arrival of Islam. The civilization

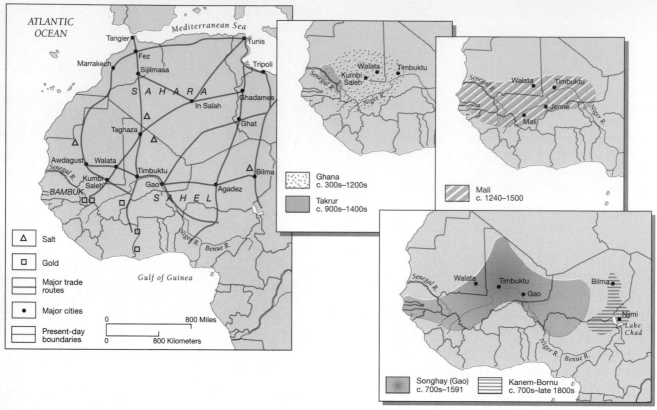

West African States

of Axum became the basis for much of the distinctive culture of Christian Ethiopia in the centuries that followed. Here, as along the Mediterranean coast of Africa where Phoenician, Greek, and Roman settlements were established, or up the Nile valley, the ideas, techniques, and material goods from the Mediterranean and western Asia mixed with African peoples and practices.

Finally, we can mention the area of the grassy savanna extending across the Sudan into West Africa. The defeated leaders of Meroe apparently moved westward into the Sudan and reestablished themselves at Darfur and Kordofan in the 4th century C.E. Their influence may have extended even farther to the west. Several accounts and myths associated with royal families and ancient kingdoms in West Africa point to Egypt, Arabia, and even Persia as the original home of the founders. But in West Africa, there is also evidence of long-term contact with the Mediterranean world directly across the Sahara. These long-distance external influences were paralleled by an extended period of internal development among the peoples of West Africa such as the Yoruba, Mande, and Fulbe.

Golden Ghana: A Trading State   The peoples of the savanna took advantage of their location to serve as intermediaries between the southern gold-producing forest zone in the region of the Niger and Senegal river valleys and the markets of North Africa. Trading salt for gold to the peoples of the forest, and then sending the gold northward along established caravan routes that crossed the Sahara, several states took form before the 8th century C.E. Strung in a line across the southern edge of the desert, the states of Takur, Ghana, Gao, and Kanem were located to serve as intermediaries in the trans-Sahara trade.

The trans-Sahara trade was the basis for the growth of the first great sub-Saharan state, the empire of Ghana, which lay squarely astride the route of exchange. This was a trading state created by the West African Soninke people, perhaps with some participation by the nomadic North African Tuaregs. Early Arab chroniclers wrote that in Ghana, 20 kings had ruled prior to the time of Muhammad, which was a way of saying that the kingdom was an ancient one. By the time Arab visitors began to write about Ghana and other Sudanic states in the 9th century C.E., these states were already well-established kingdoms—the product of their advantageous geographical position and apparently a joint heritage of internal development and external influences and trade. The external influences increased considerably with the arrival of Islam. In 985 C.E., the king of Gao converted to Islam and set in motion a series of conversions among the elite of the West African states. Conversion of the masses proceeded at a slower rate.

The ancient kingdom of Ghana (not to be confused with the modern nation of Ghana) lay mostly within the boundaries of the present-day Republic of Mali. It became a major trading state, receiving salt, cloth, and manufactured goods from North Africa and the Mediterranean in return for gold. The power of Ghana depended on its location and control over subject states and provinces, especially Bambuk and other gold-producing regions in the forest zones to the south. By the 9th century C.E., Ghana was known as a major source of gold within the Mediterranean world. In 1067 C.E., al-Bakri, a scholar from Muslim Spain, wrote a description of Ghana that provides us with a view of its life and power. At that time, the capital of Ghana, *Kumbi Saleh,* appears to have been divided into two adjoining cities about six miles apart. One was occupied by the king and his court, surrounded by the dwellings of the people. This city also contained buildings for worship and shrines to the local deities. The adjoining city was inhabited by long-distance Muslim traders, religious leaders, and scholars. Its mosques and houses were built in the style of the mud-walled architecture of North Africa. Together, the population of these cities may have reached 20,000.

The gold and salt trades were taxed by the king of Ghana, and these taxes provided the revenues of the kingdom. The wealth allowed for growth of the kingdom and thus its power. The historian al-Bakri reported that Ghana could field an army of 200,000 men. Even if we allow for exaggeration, it should be noted that the Normans invaded England at about this time with fewer than 5000 men, so al-Bakri's statement indicates the existence of a powerful and well-organized kingdom. The accounts of Ghana suggest the existence of a large kingdom dominated by the royal family and a group of elite retainers, whose strength rested on control of the trade and on the tribute collected from neighboring peoples.

The image of Ghana in contemporaneous Arab sources was one of fabled wealth. The account of al-Bakri stated that the king had a monopoly on all gold nuggets found, but the people could gather as much gold dust as they wanted for trade. His description of a royal audience noted guards with gold and silver ornaments and weapons, the royal princes in attendance splendidly attired with gold plaited in their hair, and the doors of the chamber guarded by "dogs of excellent breed, who never leave the king's seat; they wear collars of gold and silver, ornamented with the same metals." The king was known as Kaya-Maghan, or "the king of Gold."

While a certain amount of fantasy was mixed in these accounts, Ghana was obviously a powerful kingdom. Its influence eventually spread into the Sahara, and major trading towns like Awdagust were brought under its control. The Berber and Tuareg tribes of the Sahara had converted to Islam in the 7th century, and by the 11th century a new movement, whose followers were called the Almoravids had begun to sweep across the western desert, Morocco, and Spain. One branch of this movement under Abu Bakr ibn Umar (d. 1087) launched a series of campaigns in the western Sudan. The Almoravids controlled the gold trade across the Sahara and began to move toward its sources. Ghana was conquered in 1076, and a new fusion of Sudanic and Saharan peoples took place.

While Ghana continued to exist, its power was considerably weakened, and other states emerged to challenge its leadership. Islamization weakened the kingdom and perhaps caused a deepening division between its elite and the common folk. Former provinces broke away, and a period of political instability and fragmentation followed, during which new states emerged among the Soninke, Fulbe, and Malinke peoples. The power of Ghana ended, but its tradition of trade and military power and the fusion of African and Islamic traditions continued among the successor states. Eventually, a new kingdom, Mali, emerged from this struggle. In many ways Mali was the heir to the power in the region, and it ruled a territory that extended from the bend of the Niger River to the Atlantic coast, which included much of the ancient kingdom of Ghana.

ANALYSIS

Language as a Historical Source

Historians constantly search for new ways to understand the past and penetrate the haze that separates us from it. For much of the early history of the world we must depend on the archeological record. Cultures leave their traces not only in pottery, weapons, temples, and mummies but also in language, written or not. Language is a guide to the thought patterns of a people and to their society and their institutions. Language, moreover, is a guide to its speakers' historical relationships to others. The development of historical linguistics has greatly furthered our understanding of the past and has provided a set of theories and techniques that along with archeology have become indispensable aids to the study of both preliterate and literate societies.

The early study of languages was motivated by a recognition of the intimate relation between thought and language and the relationship between the structure of thought and language and the overall culture of a people. Early students of language, such as the French thinker Condillac, who wrote in the mid-18th century, believed that "each language expresses the character of the people that speak it." However, linguistic insights were sometimes influenced by cultural bias. Some later linguists shared the opinion of the learned Wilhelm von Humboldt, who wrote in his essay "On Language" (1836), that some languages were "more perfect" and better suited to the "mental cultivation of mankind." Not surprisingly, von Humboldt believed that the Sanskritic languages (what we would call Indo-European) best fit that definition. By the 20th century, however, the early work of people like von Humboldt had laid the foundation for the modern study of historical linguistics.

We have already discussed (in Chapter 4) the great migration of the Indo-European peoples from central Asia into India and western Europe. In this chapter we examine two other great migrations in human history: the movement of the Bantu peoples throughout southern Africa and the spread of the Polynesians across the Pacific. To a large extent, much of what can be said in all three cases—and in the study of the early settlement of the Americas—is based on a study of the vocabulary, structure, and diffusion of languages.

The study of language as a historical record is based on some fundamental ideas. Languages change over time, as any reading of Chaucer or Shakespeare immediately reveals. As they change they may diverge from related languages. Languages with strong similarities in structure and vocabulary that cannot be explained by borrowing or contacts are considered to be part of the same family, and it is assumed that sometime in the past an original language was the parent of all the languages in that family. As groups of people separated, their language changed and diverged. Further separation resulted in further divergence, so that over time a large number of related languages could result from the original language. The proto-Indo-European language was the parent of both Persian and Latin, but Latin later split into French, Italian, Rumanian, Portuguese, and other related languages. By looking at structural and vocabulary similarities, we can establish linguistic subgroups and their relationship to each other as well as to the parent language.

It can be assumed that the more diversity between languages, the longer the time that has elapsed since their separation from each other. For a while, some linguists thought that if they could establish the rate at which linguistic changes took place, they could calculate the time that had elapsed since one language and its speakers had separated from another. On the basis of 100 or 200 basic words, they attempted to calculate the percentage of change or loss from one language to another. This technique, called glottochronology, is no longer popular, since it is clear that languages do not change at a constant rate of speed but probably in spurts, and such change depends on many factors. Still, rates of change in written languages can be studied, and when used in conjunction with archeology, language can provide another and corroborating kind of historical evidence.

It is simple enough to see that the similarity of words in languages (barring random coincidence or words borrowed directly from a foreign language) can indicate a common origin. *Mother* in English, *mater* in Latin, and *mata* in Hindi all point to their common Indo-European origin. The word for *eye* in Tahiti was *mata*, in Hawaii, *maka,* and among the New Zealand Maori, *mata;* these similarities point to their common heritage as Polynesian languages. Despite the similar sounds involved in these two sets, the meanings indicate that we are dealing with two different language families.

In other cases, similarities and differences are less apparent and are based not only on a common vocabulary but on structure and pronunciation. While historical linguistics has developed various techniques and methods for establishing these relationships, explaining the divergence or the reason for the separation of the peoples that speak the languages is another story. Without the help of archeology, oral traditions, or written records, historical linguistics cannot describe the course of change.

The study of languages can tell us much about the values, social structure, and material life of peoples in the past. A language with 12 adjectives to describe the color of the sea between the speaker and the horizon, or another language that has 20 ways of describing the color of a llama's coat, indicates the importance of those things to the people involved. A language that has no word for private property or nobility probably lacked those concepts. The grammar and pronunciation of a language can be relatively independent of the physical world of its speakers, but the vocabulary cannot. It reflects what people knew and thought about. It can be assumed that if all the languages that split off from a parent tongue have the same word for iron, dog, cattle, or canoe, then the original speakers must have possessed these things. This kind of reasoning lies behind much of what we can say about the early Polynesians, the Bantu, and the Indo-Europeans. For example, by studying the distribution of words in various Polynesian languages, linguists have argued that even though we do not know the original home of the Polynesians, the original speakers of the parent language were inhabitants of some mountainous tropical island or islands in the western Pacific islands, and they grew taro, yams, bananas, and sugar cane before their expansion and dispersal.

Of course, such analysis is a complicated and risky enterprise. A word may have existed at one point for a thing that no longer exists and thus the word disappeared or was transformed to mean something else, leaving no trace of its past use. Putting the linguistic evidence together with the historical record is a challenging task. When that record is available, as in the case of Aztec and Roman expansion, we can see that language change and diffusion is sometimes the result of intentional policy rather than undirected change.

Historical linguistics also concerns itself with variations and subdivisions within languages, or dialects, and with their geographical distribution. What is the difference between a dialect and a language? Linguists argue on this point, but some unknown skeptic once said, "a language is a dialect with an army behind it." That comment should focus our attention on the social and historical reasons for the predominance of some languages. It also underlines the necessary relationship between linguistics and other methods of knowing the past, as tools that should be used together whenever possible.

Questions: In what ways are language and literacy expressions of social or political power? What are some ways in which changes in our own language indicate broad historical changes? Is there a problem in using language as historical evidence because spoken language often differs from formal written forms and usage?

THE SLAVS AND THE GERMANS ON THE NORTHERN RIM

Focal Point: Beyond the boundaries of the Hellenistic kingdoms in the Middle East and southern Europe, and to the north of the expanding Roman Empire, lived a mixture of peoples mostly of Indo-European origin. The major groups included *Celts, Germans,* and *Slavs,* all of whom developed some agriculture by the classical period. Political organization in northern Europe developed some significant features but—outside of Rome's boundaries—lagged behind the kingdoms of sub-Saharan Africa.

Celtic peoples, for example, formed Europe's first culture, which stretched from Spain northward. They were organized in small regional kingdoms with fierce warrior leaders, and they mixed agricultural and hunting economies. They had no cities and no writing, and their most impres-

The great religious monuments of Stonehenge was a centerpiece of pre-Celtic worship in England.

sive buildings were crude stone forts and arrays of stone set up to honor the gods of nature. The Romans considered the Celtic peoples barbarians, but as Rome expanded its empire into Gaul, Spain, and Britain, various Celtic peoples came under Roman influence. A population of Romanized Celts developed in villages and towns across western Europe.

The Germans in Northwestern Europe

Much of the northwestern portion of the European continent was populated by Germanic peoples, whose culture and institutions in many ways resembled that of the Celts (whom they had in some regions displaced). Certainly, to Roman observers, the Germanic tribes north of the empire's boundaries were undistinguished barbarians, pure and simple. As the Roman historian Tacitus wrote, "Who, indeed, would leave Asia, Africa, or Italy to seek Germany, with its desert scenery, its harsh climate, its sullen manners and aspect?" He might have added "and its warlike people," for by Tacitus's time the Romans had already developed a wary respect for the German warriors.

Tacitus had other comments on the Germans, although at times he emphasized their virtues as a way of criticizing what he considered to be Rome's moral degeneracy. The strength and bravery of the German warriors impressed him. He pointed out that warriors were pledged to support their chiefs and that the chiefs in turn led by example and tried to outdo their men in battle. The size of a chief's retinue was a measure of his power and distinction, and men strove to gain a place in such a following.

The role of women was particularly notable. Agriculture and all household duties were carried out by women, the elderly, and slaves. Women were thought to have an element of holiness and the gift of prophecy. Their advice was sought and respected. Men and women married rather late, and usually a bride-price was paid to the woman. This included oxen, a horse, and arms, which symbolized the union of the couple and their shared responsibilities. Women were supposed to pass these gifts on to their children. Strong matrilineal ties existed, and the relation between a man and his sisters' sons was particularly strong. The married state was respected, adultery was rare, and infanticide was not practiced. In a criticism of the Rome of his day, Tacitus said: "Good morality is more effective in Germany than good laws are elsewhere."

But Tacitus also commented on the rude material life of the Germans, their lack of cities, their simple dwellings, their lack of writing, and their constant fighting. Judgments of this sort accurately reflected the fact that the peoples of northwestern Europe had not formulated a civilization. They overlooked, however, several important achievements and also changes among some groups, such as the Germanic tribes, that accelerated during the final centuries of the classical era. Like the Celts, the Germanic peoples typically mixed agriculture and hunting, and they also herded cattle in a nomadic pattern. They had no cities. Among many Germans, however, agriculture steadily improved in the 1st centuries C.E. There were also marked improvements in iron use and the manufacture of cloth and other items. Some of these improvements resulted from knowledge of Roman skills, which spread gradually and incompletely northward beyond the empire's boundaries.

Political cohesion among some German groups improved by the 3rd and 4th centuries C.E. As with many traditionally nomadic peoples, the Germans had long been organized in decentralized tribes of a few thousand members each, and even the tribes were loosely organized, with individual family groups settling most disputes. A tribe might have a king or an assembly of warrior chiefs; in either case, vigorous discussion of any policy issue among all fighting men was essential. Group loyalty and a certain amount of political equality were important parts of this tradition and would affect European institutions in the centuries after the classical era. After about 200 C.E., some German tribes coalesced into larger units as they learned to copy Roman military structure somewhat and were forced by Roman pressure to improve their organizational ability. The power of individual kings increased as they ruled large confederations of tribes. Thus, even apart from the Germans who filtered into the Roman Empire or joined its armies, thus integrating portions of Roman civilization directly, there were important changes in the Germanic lands during the classical era, with improvements in agriculture, trade, manufacture, and politics.

Germanic culture, however, seems to have changed little outside Rome's boundaries. The German religion, like that of the Bantu, was animistic, with sacrifices and worship to the spirits of nature. Horses were the most common sacrifice, leading to a prejudice against eating horsemeat, which is still lively in German-influenced parts of the world today.

The Germans would make their first clear mark in world history as growing bands began to move southward into the Roman Empire, ultimately probing into Italy, Spain, and North Africa. Their movement, the *Völkerwanderungen,* resulted from population growth in their own lands, the nomadic tradition, Rome's attractiveness and growing weakness, and, finally, invasions by Asian groups on the eastern flanks of the Germanic region. German pressure within the Roman Empire played a major role in toppling the empire, as we will see in the following chapter.

Growing coherence among some Germanic groups, however, had an influence beyond the pressures on Rome. It helped prepare larger areas of Europe for the gradual development of civilization in the centuries after Rome's fall. This new civilization would reflect many Roman legacies and a strong Christian influence, but it would also build on some Germanic elements. Even as Rome fell, in fact, a new Germanic center was taking shape in Scandinavia that would have wide influence in the following centuries. Far from Roman influence, Scandinavian populations were growing, and political confederations were being formed by the 5th century. This would soon lead to invasions and trade throughout much of the Mediterranean world.

The Slavs in Eastern Europe

While developments among various Germanic peoples held the stage in northwestern Europe, a somewhat similar pattern of precivilizational advance emerged in various parts of eastern Europe, with some influence from the Hellenistic kingdoms and then the eastern portions of the Roman Empire. As early as 3000 B.C.E., agriculture had been established in the southern part of what is now Russia, spreading from the Middle East. Bronze tools were also introduced, and then a wave of Indo-European invasions, about 1000 B.C.E., brought iron. Several new invasions from central Asia followed, and a loosely organized Scythian state controlled the region from the 7th to the 3rd centuries B.C.E. The Scythians were nomadic warriors, but agriculture continued to flourish in the plain north of the Black Sea. Scythian rule was followed by an invasion by a people known as the Sarmatians, some of whose descendants live in the central Caucasus region of Russia today. Under both Scythians and Sarmatians, Greek and Persian trade and cultural influence, including artistic styles, spread into this region.

By the final centuries of the classical era, Slavic peoples were increasingly migrating into Russia and other parts of eastern Europe. Some Slavs had been in this region before, and the origin of these people is disputed. What is known is that the Slavic people were an Indo-European group, that they had become increasingly noticeable in Russia and the Balkans by the time of the early Roman Empire, and that they would ultimately dominate much of eastern Europe from the Balkans northward. While Slavic political organization was perhaps a bit less well developed than Germanic, by the 5th century C.E. some regional kingdoms had been formed, notably in Bulgaria. Agriculture and manufacturing, including skilled ironwork, gained ground steadily, and (in

advance of the Germanic northwest) some trading cities had been formed.

Again, as with the Germans to the west, it would be premature to refer to a civilization of eastern Europe beyond the Mediterranean zone at the time of Rome's fall—and the Slavic peoples were severely disrupted, along with Rome itself, by invasions from central Asia as the Huns and others cut across their lands. Nevertheless, an increasingly prosperous agricultural economy and rudiments of political organization beyond the tribal level described parts of the Slavic world toward the end of the classical era and presaged more important developments to come.

THE SPREAD OF CHINESE CIVILIZATION TO JAPAN

Focal Point: Although its full impact on global history has not been felt until the last century or so, the transmission of key elements in Chinese culture to the offshore islands that came to make up Japan clearly provides one of the most important examples of the spread of civilization from a central core area to neighboring or overseas peoples. In the first centuries C.E., the peoples of Japan imported a wide range of ideas, techniques of production, institutional models, and material objects from the Chinese mainland. After adapting these imports to make them compatible with the quite sophisticated culture they had previously developed, the Japanese used what they had borrowed from China to build a civilization of their own. New patterns of rice growing and handicraft production enhanced the economic base of the Yamato clan chieftains, who, beginning in the 3rd century C.E., extended their control over the most populous regions of the main Japanese island of Honshu.

The Japanese developed a unique civilization from a blend of their own culture and a selective importation and conscious refashioning of Chinese influences. The extension of Chinese influences to the Japanese islands was necessarily by sea rather than overland. Instead of conquering armies, merchants and traveling monks—and eventually Japanese students who studied in China—were the most important agents by which elements of Chinese culture were transmitted. Especially in the early centuries of borrowing, from the 1st to the 5th centuries C.E., interchange between China and Japan was largely indirect. It was mediated by the peoples and kingdoms of Korea, who had grafted key aspects of Chinese civilization to their own cultures somewhat earlier than the Japanese.

In contrast to the Vietnamese, who were ruled by the Chinese for nearly a millennium, and the peoples of South China, who were eventually absorbed by Chinese civilization, the Japanese initiated and controlled the process of cultural borrowing from China. Despite a willingness to acknowledge the cultural superiority of the Chinese Middle Kingdom, the Japanese retained political independence throughout the centuries of intense borrowing. Consequently, they could be more selective in their adoption of Chinese ideas and institutions than most of the other peoples who came under the influences emanating from China.

Natural Setting and the Peopling of the Islands

The four main islands that make up the homeland of the Japanese people rise abruptly and dramatically from the Pacific Ocean along the northeast coast of Asia. Formed by volcanic eruptions that still occur periodically, the islands are dominated by mountains and rugged hills. Only a small portion of their surface area is level and extensive enough for the cultivation of wet rice, which from prehistoric times has been the staple of the Japanese diet. Thus, from the time of the earliest settlements, the Japanese have mainly occupied the coastal plains, especially in the south central portions of the largest island of *Honshu*, which remain the most heavily populated areas of the islands today.

Though poor in natural resources, the islands are difficult to match in their combination of temperate climate and subtle natural beauty. Their forest-covered and mist-shrouded hills and glittering inland seas have instilled in the Japanese people a refined aesthetic sensibility and sensitivity to the natural world that have been reflected in their religion, art, and architecture from prehistoric ages to the present. At the same time, the islands' limited resource base nurtured a disciplined, hard working population that was regulated by strict legal codes and ruled through much of the islands' history by warrior elites. These characteristics of the Japanese people have been commented on repeatedly by foreign visitors, from the Chinese in the early centuries C.E. to Europeans and Americans in the modern era.

Archeological evidence suggests that as early as 5000 B.C.E., the ancestors of the Japanese people had begun to migrate to the islands. Drawn from numerous and diverse East Asian ethnic groups (and perhaps Southeast Asia and Polynesia), the migrants came in small bands and periodically in larger waves over many centuries. One of these waves of migrants produced the *Jomon culture* in the 3rd millennium B.C.E. The Jomon

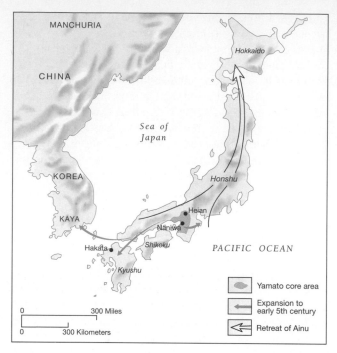

The Rise of Japanese Civilization

were a hunting-and-gathering people, who lived in pits dug in the ground. They produced a distinctive pottery, whose cordlike decoration gave the people their name.

Most of the new settlers crossed to the islands from the Korean peninsula and Manchuria. Because they were relatively isolated from political upheavals and social transformations occurring on the mainland, by the first centuries C.E. the diverse migrant streams had blended into a relatively homogenous population with a distinctive Japanese language, culture, and physical appearance. By then they had driven the Ainu, who had settled the islands before them, into northern Honshu and Hokkaido. Over the past two millennia, the Japanese have gradually displaced or absorbed nearly all the remaining Ainu, building in the process a strong sense of cultural and ethnic identity.

Indigenous Culture and Society

Long before distinctively Chinese cultural influences began to shape Japanese historical development, the indigenous peoples of the islands had taken significant steps toward the creation of a civilization of their own. In the last centuries B.C.E., migrants from the mainland introduced wet-rice agriculture and ironworking into Japan. In this period, which is known as the *Yayoi epoch*, the Japanese also produced wheel-turned pottery and very sophisticated bronzeware, including elaborately decorated bells that were sometimes 4 and 5 feet high.

Until the early 5th century C.E., most of the Japanese population was divided into hundreds of clans, whose members worshiped a clan deity and claimed common descent from a real or fictitious ancestor. Each of these clans was dominated by a small warrior aristocracy. The clan elites drew their support from the peasantry, which made up over 90 percent of the population of the islands. They were also served by slaves, who like their counterparts in China were only a small minority of the Japanese people. Early visitors from the mainland noted the rigid social distinctions, including different sorts of tattoos and other body markings, that separated the warrior elite from the mass of the people. They also remarked on the strong position women enjoyed in early Japanese culture, in marked contrast to their clear subordination in China. Early Japanese households appear to have been matriarchal—that is, dominated by childbearing women. Women also played key roles as shamans—who were central to Japanese religious ceremonies and worship; as leaders of some of the clans; and later as empresses.

The importance of women in early Japanese culture is also indicated by their legends regarding the creation of the world. In these tales the sun goddess, *Amaterasu*, played a central role, and her worship became the central element in the Shinto religion developed by the island peoples. *Shinto* devotees worshiped numerous gods and spirits associated with the natural world. Some of these deities were identified with objects, such as huge trees or mountains like the famous Mount Fuji. Others were linked to animals, such as foxes and snakes, that were believed to possess special powers. Gods and spirits were believed to be capable of doing good or evil to humans. To ensure that they brought blessings rather than misfortune, the Japanese made offerings of food and prayers to the gods and nature spirits at special shrines. These structures were built of unfinished wood and were notable for their simple lines and lack of ornamentation. They gave rise to a unique Shinto style of Japanese architecture, which persists to the present day and has had a considerable impact on architecture in the modern world.

The most venerated of the Shinto shrines is that dedicated to the sun goddess, Amaterasu, at Ise in central Honshu. The thatched roof, unpainted cypress wood, simplicity of design, and the beautiful forest setting in which the shrine is located are characteristics of Shinto architecture.

In the 4th and 5th centuries C.E., when one of the clans, the *Yamato,* gained increasing dominance over the others, an imperial cult developed around the sun goddess and Shinto worship. A central shrine was established on the island of Ise, and the priest-chief heads of the Yamato clan claimed descent from the sun goddess herself. Building upon this powerful source of legitimacy, the Yamato brought most of the lowland plains of the southern islands under their control through alliances and conquest. By the late 4th century C.E., their sway also extended to southern Korea. Though marginal in the amount of territory involved, this overseas extension of the Yamato domains brought intensified contacts with Chinese civilization, then about to enter into one of its most illustrious phases. The combination of these contacts and the Yamatos' successful campaigns to unify the Japanese people led to profound transformations in Japanese society and culture in the following centuries.

The Chinese Model and the Remaking of Japan

Though trade and the continued influx of migrants from the mainland had brought the Japanese peoples into contact with Chinese civilization from the last centuries B.C.E., the introduction of the Chinese script in the 4th century C.E. marks a major turning point in Japanese cultural development. Writing with the Chinese characters, which were adapted only with great difficulty to the Japanese language, made it possible for the Yamato to begin to build a real bureaucracy and thus more firmly establish their control over vassal clan heads and the peasantry. The use of the Chinese written language also meant that the Japanese could learn from Chinese texts on all manner of subjects, from science and philosophy to art and religion. These works, as well as Chinese scribes to make additional copies and interpret them, were imported from the 5th century onward. Later, Japanese students and scholars who were fluent in Chinese were sent to China to acquire new learning firsthand.

From the middle of the 6th century, the Buddhist religion became a pivotal factor in the transmission of Chinese influence to Japan. In the period of disunity and chaos that followed the fall of the Han dynasty in the early 3rd century C.E., Buddhism was widely adopted by the distressed populace of China and the rulers of the warring kingdoms that succeeded the Han. The pervasive influence of the religion in China in this era and the powerful position of Buddhist monks at the courts of Chinese rulers gave great impetus to its spread to Korea and Japan. In the middle of the 6th century, a Korean ruler

The critical role played by Buddhism in the transmission of key elements of Chinese civilization to Japan is strikingly illustrated by early Buddhist monasteries and temples such as this one at Nara. Comparison with the Shinto shrine at Ise underscores the contrast between the sparse indigenous art and architectural styles and the more ornate Buddhist structures that were modeled on Chinese prototypes.

sent Buddhist images and scriptures as presents to the Japanese emperor and urged him to adopt the religion and convert his subjects to it. After considerable debate and even open strife among the families serving the imperial household over the advantages and dangers of introducing Buddhism into Japan, it was officially adopted as the religion of the Yamato domains in the late 580s.

From that time onward, Japanese rulers attempted to propagate the new religion among their subjects. Warrior aristocrats and peasants converted to the new beliefs, but without giving up their long-standing reverence for Shinto spirits and deities. Thus, Shintoism and Buddhism developed side by side as twin pillars of state and society in Japan. The Japanese elite supported the efforts of Buddhist monks to spread their faith, and the monks in turn served as advisors to the emperor and regional lords. In their teachings of Buddhism, the monks stressed scriptural passages and Buddhist ethical prescriptions that supported rule by a strong monarch and a unified and centralized state.

Though converts from aristocratic Japanese families studied the complex beliefs of Buddhist philosophy and practiced its highly developed meditation techniques, to the illiterate mass of the Japanese people Buddhism was little more than a magical cult. Buddhist monks provided colorful rituals that enriched the peasants' monotonous lives, and charms to ward off sickness or evil spirits, but the common people knew little of Buddhist teachings beyond highly mythologized versions of the Buddha's life.

Political and Social Change

Beginning in the early 7th century, the Yamato rulers proclaimed themselves absolute monarchs in imitation of the emperors of China. They styled themselves the "emperors of the rising sun" in official letters to (one imagines) the somewhat dismayed Chinese "emperors of the setting sun." Inspired by Chinese examples, they established councils and government departments and tried to introduce genuine bureaucratic control at the local level. At *Nara* and later *Heian,* the Japanese emperors laid out courts and capital cities patterned after the ancient imperial centers of China. The Yamato rulers strove to build a peasant conscript army and impose legal codes and a landholding system similar to those in China.

In the centuries after the introduction of Buddhism, Chinese influences were felt in virtually all spheres of Japanese society. Alongside the traditional warrior elite, a class of monks and scholars developed that for several centuries exercised considerable power at the imperial court. Trade with China and Korea and improved communications within Japan enriched existing merchant groups and led to their emergence as a distinct class. New tools and techniques imported from the mainland increased the output of Japanese cultivators and made possible a great expansion of the islands' previously marginal mining industry.

The introduction into Japan of the ideal of the patriarchal and patrilineal family, which had long been dominant in China, presented a major challenge to traditional Japanese approaches to gender roles and relationships. For several centuries, the position of women within the family remained strong, and the ideal of wives and lovers who were accomplished in literature and the arts was preserved by the courtly elites at the imperial capitals of Nara and Heian. But the adoption of Chinese law codes eroded first the control that Japanese women were able to exercise over their own children, and eventually their overall status relative to males. These changes were reflected in the spread of polygamy among the Japanese aristocracy. From the early 9th century, the changes were even more emphatically underscored by the elite's refusal to allow women from the imperial family to rule in their own right, as they had periodically in the early centuries of Japanese history. Japanese women, like those in China and India, were increasingly subordinated to their fathers and husbands and were valued mainly for their domestic skills and ability to produce many healthy sons. As in China and India, entry into religious orders or successful careers as courtesans provided virtually the only alternatives to careers as subordinated wives and mothers.

Chinese Influence and Japanese Resistance

Contacts with China and innovations based on the Chinese model were pushed, from the 4th century C.E. onward, by those at the top of Japanese society. Japanese rulers and their chief advisors were motivated mainly by the desire to increase the power of the state to control the warrior nobles and to extract resources from the peasantry. Buddhist ethics and Confucian legal codes enhanced the rulers' legitimacy, Chinese rituals gave a new dignity and luster to court routines, and the growth of a Chinese-style bureaucracy provided the means for the creation of the first genuine state in Japanese history. Because the Japanese remained politically independent from China, their rulers could convincingly argue that the adoption of Chinese ways was voluntary and carefully controlled. Only imports that would strengthen the Japanese state or contribute to the well-being of the Japanese populace need be accepted. Chinese ideas and institutions could be reworked to suit conditions in Japan and fit the needs of the Japanese people. Selective borrowing from their ancient and advanced Chinese neighbors, the innovators argued, allowed the Japanese to become fully civilized without destroying their own culture and identity.

Because Japanese rulers lacked the resource base of the Chinese emperors and worked with a society that differed greatly in scale and organization, many of their efforts to imitate Chinese patterns ended in failure. The bloated bureaucracies that resulted from the imitation of China were top-heavy and a growing burden for the peasants who had to support them. Efforts to establish local control and reorganize landholding along Chinese lines floundered because of the opposition of regional lords and their retainers. The warrior elite also frustrated the attempt to make soldiers of the peasantry. Conscripts in Japan in this era were little more than forced laborers. Many of the imported Chinese legal injunctions bore lit-

DOCUMENT

Myths of Orgin

Legends and myths have long fascinated anthropologists, literary scholars, and folklorists because they offer an opportunity to see how various peoples have explained the universe and themselves within it. The noted French anthropologist Claude Levy-Strauss believed that all myths were constructed around certain basic structures of human thought and that those structures could be revealed by the comparative study of myths. He also argued that for some cultures, such as those of South American Indians, myths with their essentially recurring structures were the primary means of explaining life, while in other cultures, such as those of western Europe and China, a sense of change and of history, came to predominate in these explanations. Recent scholarship has begun to question the separation of myth and history and has begun to look at the possible historical context and content of myths.

In this chapter, we have examined several peoples whose origins are shrouded in mystery and about whom many questions remain unanswered. The following excerpts provide these peoples' explanations of their own origins or those of their world.

A Bantu Myth of Migration

A series of origin epics and tales among the Luba peoples, who lived in central Africa to the east of the Kongo kingdom, were collected in the 20th century. The concept of splitting off from an existing village and settling in new territory is part of many African origin myths.

In the country of the east, on the right bank of the Lualaba River, there once was a man and a woman. Their names mean respectively "he who builds many houses," and "she who makes much pottery." They lived in ignorance of each other. Guided by the sound of chopping, the man discovered the woman, who was preparing firewood. They lived for a long time under the same roof, sleeping in separate beds. The copulation of a pair of jackals gave them the idea of sleeping together. They brought forth twins of opposite sex, who became inseparable companions. One day the twins found a locality that was exceptionally rich in fish. They finally obtained permission from their parents to leave the village and devote themselves entirely to fishing. In their turn, they brought forth twins, who lived in the same incestuous manner, far from their parents. This new generation took up trapping. So pairs of twins, moving each generation a little farther westward, populated the country.*

A Germanic Myth: The Birth of the Gods

This tale from the rich Norse mythology deals with the birth of the gods. Drawn from the songs and sagas of the Germanic peoples, these stories were part of an oral literature until about the 12th century, when they were committed to writing.

In the beginning of the ages there lived a cow, whose breath was sweet and whose milk was bitter. The cow was called Audhumla and she lived by herself in a frosty, misty plain, where there was nothing to be seen but heaps of snow and ice. A giant named Ymir came out of the dark north and lay down on the ice near Audhumla. "You must let me drink of your milk," said the giant to the cow; and though her milk was bitter, he liked it well. The cow saw a few grains of salt sprinkled over the ice, so she licked the salt and breathed with her sweet breath. Then long golden locks rose out of the ice, and the southern day shone on them, making them bright and glittering. The giant frowned but the cow continued to lick the salt, and after three licks an entire man arose—a hero strong and beautiful.

When the giant looked full in the face of that beautiful man, he hated him with all his heart and he took a terrible oath that he would never cease fighting until either he or Bur, the hero, should lie dead on the ground. He kept this vow.

Afterwards when the sons of the hero began to grow up, the giant and his sons fought against them too, and were very near conquering them many times. There was one of the sons of these heroes, called Odin, who after many combats, did at last slay the great old giant Ymir, and pierced his body with a keen spear. The blood poured forth in a torrent and drowned all the hideous brood, except for one who fled.

After this, Odin gathered around him his sons, brothers, and cousins and spoke to them thus:

"Heroes, we have won a great victory; our enemies are dead, or have fled. We cannot stay any longer here where there is nothing evil for us to fight against." The heroes looked around them at the words of Odin. They spoke out with one voice, "It is well spoken, Odin; we will follow you."

"Southward," answered Odin, "heat lies, and northward night. From the dim east the sun begins his journey westward home."

"Westward home!" they shouted all.

Odin rode in the midst of them, and they all paid to him reverence and homage as to a king and father. On his right hand rode Thor, Odin's strong, warlike, eldest son. On his left hand rode Baldur, the most beautiful of his children. After him came Tyr, the Brave; the silent Vidar; and many more mighty lords and heroes; and then came a shell chariot, in which sat Frigga, the wife of Odin, with all her daughters, friends, and maids.†

The Birth of Japan

According to Japanese legend, the Lord of Heaven sent two young gods, Izanagi and his consort, Izanami, to subdue chaos and create beauty after the earth had been created. Descending on a carriage of clouds, Izanagi took the divine spear given to him by the Lord of Heaven and, stirring the fog, created a beautiful island in the midst of the sea. But the island was too small for goodness to grow. Izanagi and Izanami became man and wife and built a shrine.

When Izanagi and his wife came out of the shrine, they stood transfixed. Before them stretched the long, curving shore of a vast island, and on the far horizon were the shapes of others. In great joy the two set out to view their new domains. From island to island they went, marveling at each new land; and when they had traveled them all, they found that there were eight, and to them they gave these names in the order of their birth; first the island of Shikoku, followed by Kyushu, Oki and Sado which [each] were born as twins, Tsushima, and finally Iki. Together they were called the country of the eight great islands, and as time passed they became known as Japan.

More and more islands appeared, and every day Izanagi traveled the land and sea watching over them. Sometimes Izanami went with him, but serving in the shrine took much of her time and she found the long journeys exhausting. . . .

"My dear husband, there is nothing I wish to do more than to live here with you in peace and contentment. But now that so many islands have been born I pray that we too may bear children for our help and delight."

Her prayers were answered and in the years that followed many children were born to them. The first

was the Sea Spirit, the next a Mountain Spirit, and then in succession, the spirits of fields, trees, rivers, and all natural things. Under their care and guidance the islands grew more and more verdant and beautiful. Soon the seasons were born, and the breaths of the winds and rains brought their changing cycles to the mountains and fields. Everywhere the forests grew thick and dense, and in the groves flocks of birds gathered and sang. Crops and harvests multiplied and flowers and bushes bloomed in profusion.

Izanagi and his wife lived in utmost contentment among their family, and when a daughter was born to them, who was the goddess of the Sun, their joy was unbounded. She was the most beautiful and radiant being . . . everywhere she went she filled the darkest air with light and brilliance. Her they named Amaterasu.‡

A Polynesian Creation Story

In this tale from Tahiti, Tangaroa, the ancestor of all the gods and the creator of Havaiki, the birthplace of the land, the gods, and chiefs, and humanity, creates the world. This version of the story was collected in Tahiti in 1822.

For a long time Tangaroa lived within his shell. It was round like an egg and in the lasting darkness it revolved in the void. There was no sun, there was no moon, there was no land nor mountain, all was moving in the void. There was no man, no fowl, no dog, no living thing; there was no water, salt or fresh.

At the end of a great time Tangaroa flicked his shell, and it cracked and fell apart. Then, Tangaroa stepped forth and stood upon that shell and called:

"Who is above there? Who is below there?"

No voice replied. He called again:

"Who is in front there? Who is behind there?"

Still no voice answered. Only Tangaroa's voice was heard; there was no other.

Then Tangaroa said, "O rock, crawl here!"

But no rock was to crawl to him.

He therefore said, "O sand, crawl here!"

There was no sand to crawl to him. And Tangaroa became angry because he was not obeyed. He therefore overturned his shell and raised it up to form a dome for the sky, and he named it Rumia, that is, Overturned.

After a time great Tangaroa, wearied from confinement, stepped out from another shell that covered him; and he took this shell for rock and sand.

But his anger was not finished, and so he took his backbone for a mountain range and his ribs for the ridges that ascend. He took his innards for the broad floating clouds and his flesh for the fatness of the earth, and his arms and legs for the strength of the earth. . . . Of his feathers he made trees and shrubs and plants to clothe the land.

And the blood of Tangaroa became hot, and it floated away to make the redness of the sky, and also rainbows. All that is red is made from Tangaroa's blood.

Tangaroa called forth gods. It was only later that he called forth man [people], when Tu was with him.

As Tangaroa had shells, so everything has a shell. The sky is a shell, which is endless space, where the gods placed the sun, the moon, the constellations, and the other stars.

The land is a shell to the stones and the water, and to the plants that spring from it. The shell of a man is woman, since it is from her that he comes forth. And a woman's shell is woman, since it is from here that she comes forth.

No one can name the shells of all the things that are in the world.§

Questions: Do myths seem to encode history or are they an alternative way to explain the past? What are the roles of men and women in the myths recorded here and what do they indicate about these early societies? Do the origin myths of the civilizations, such as China, Greece, and Rome, differ greatly from those recorded here?

*Luc de Heusch, *The Drunken King or the Origin of the State* (Bloomington: Indiana University Press, 1982), 11–12.
†Adapted from A. and E. Keary, *The Heroes of Asgard: Tales from Scandinavian Mythology* (New York: Macmillan Co, 1909), 1–4.
‡Helen and William McAlpine, *Japanese Tales and Legends* (London: Oxford University Press, 1958), 13–14.
§Anthony Alpers, *Legends of the South Seas* (New York: Thomas Crowell, 1970), 51–54.

tle relation to social conditions in Japan and were simply not enforced. The impressive capital cities laid out by the emperors' architects remained half-built and underpopulated, even at the height of the early dynasties' power.

More than differences in scale and social compatibility limited the extent to which Japan could be remade in the image of China. From the outset, the introduction of writing, Buddhism, and other imports from China had given rise to concerns about preserving Japan's own culture and produced continuing opposition to foreign influences.

At times, as in the 580s and the mid-7th century, controversy over the extent of foreign influences became a central element in violent factional struggles between the aristocratic families closest to the throne. But until the 8th century each struggle resulted in the victory of the forces favoring continuing imports from abroad and the further transformation of Japan along Chinese lines.

THE SCATTERED SOCIETIES OF POLYNESIA

Focal Point: Peoples from Asia migrated across the vast expanse of the Pacific, occupying many of the islands. Masters of navigation, they adapted to a variety of environments. On the island groups of Polynesia, like Hawaii and New Zealand, these peoples created complex societies based on agriculture and maritime resources, mostly in isolation from the rest of humankind.

The cultural interaction between China and Japan was paralleled in other areas of Asia by the outward spread of ideas, products, skills, and peoples from China or India. Sometimes this diffusion was accomplished through trade and borrowings, and sometimes it was the result of military action, but the spread of Indian civilization into Southeast Asia or of Chinese civilization into Vietnam and Korea underlined the process.

The peoples of the far Pacific who had departed the Asian mainland prior to the rise of classical China and India were unaffected by the spread of Chinese and Indian civilization. They had brought with them the cultural features of Late Neolithic Asia, and in relative isolation they had developed these features on the islands of the vast Pacific.

Certainly one of the great epics of human achievement for which we have only fragmentary evidence is the peopling of the islands of the Pacific Ocean. The distance across the Pacific from Southeast Asia to Central America is some 20,000 miles, and the waters of that ocean are dotted with thousands of islands. These islands vary in size from tiny atolls formed by coral reefs, to large "high" islands with volcanic peaks and lush valleys, to the great continent of Australia. Most of these islands lie in the tropics, although some, like New Zealand, do not. They are inhabited by a variety of peoples whose physical appearance, language, and culture are quite different but whose origins for the most part seem to be in Asia.

We cannot deal with all the peoples of the Pacific, but the remarkable story of the Polynesians can serve as a case study of the spread of culture by long-distance maritime migration. Here we are not dealing with the spread from a great center of civilization but with the migration of peoples and their adaptation to new challenges in relative isolation.

Between roughly 1500 B.C.E. and 1000 C.E., almost all the major islands west of New Guinea were visited, and many were settled, by the ancestors of the peoples we call Polynesians. They left no written records, so we must depend on the evidence of archeology and linguistics, their own oral traditions, and the observations of Europeans who first contacted them in order to reconstruct the history of their societies.

Linguistic evidence is a starting point. The Polynesians speak about 30 related languages from a family of languages called *Austronesian*, which is also found in the Philippines, Indonesia, and Southeast Asia. The Austronesians were clearly peoples from Asia, but they were not the first migrants in the Pacific. By the time of their

expansion about 4000 years ago, New Guinea and Australia had already long been settled (probably since 38,000 B.C.E.) by dark-skinned peoples who spoke languages unrelated to Austronesian.

The Great Migration

Groups of these Austronesians, speaking a language ancestral to the Polynesian languages, began to expand eastward from Melanesia to Fiji, Tonga, and Samoa. By the time of this expansion, these people practiced agriculture of yams, taro (a tuber), and other crops; raised dogs, pigs, and chickens; and had already developed a variety of complex fishing techniques. Archeologists can identify their scattered settlements by a distinctive type of pottery called Lapita, with stamped decorations, and by polished stone adzes, fishhooks, and other implements.

From Tonga and Samoa these peoples began to spread eastward to *Polynesia* proper. Polynesia includes the islands contained in a rough imaginary triangle whose points lie at Hawaii to the north, New Zealand to the south, and Easter Island far to the east. Another group of these peoples seems to have moved westward, eventually settling on the island of Madagascar off the African coast.

On the widely dispersed islands of the Pacific, each culture and language began to adapt and evolve differently and thus to diverge from the ancestral Polynesian

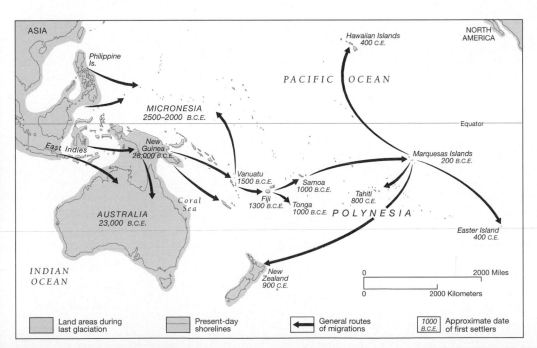

The Spread of Polynesian Peoples

forms. There remained some constants in the shared heritage of the ancestral Polynesian culture that also provided similarities. For example, the English explorer Captain James Cook, in the 18th century, was surprised to find that the words he had learned from the Tahitians were understandable to the Hawaiians, although almost 2500 miles separated those two island groups. Also, a Tahitian named Tupia served Captain Cook effectively as a translator when he contacted the *Maoris* of New Zealand.

Basic principles of economy and social organization could also be found throughout Polynesia, especially on the larger islands. From relatively small groups of original colonists, island populations grew in size and density. By the late 18th century, the island populations totaled perhaps 700,000. While the making of pottery was abandoned or forgotten, in many places agriculture became increasingly complex and intensive. Stratified societies with powerful chiefdoms based on lineage characterized many Polynesian islands, and in some places, such as Hawaii, they became extremely hierarchical. Chiefs were able to mobilize their followers to build ceremonial and public architecture, or for wars and inter-island raiding. Ritual and religion oriented many aspects of life and served as the basis of the chiefs' power.

The Voyagers of the Pacific

How did these ancient Polynesians discover and occupy the islands of the vast Pacific? The Polynesians knew how to make a variety of seaworthy vessels. Small outrigger canoes were used for fishing and moving along island coasts, but for long-distance voyaging, they used great double canoes, or *pahi*. These vessels usually carried a platform between the two hulls on which shelter could be given to the passengers—people, animals, and plants. With large triangular sails, these vessels, some of which were between 60 and 100 feet long, were capable of long voyages at sea and could travel over 200 kilometers a day in good weather. They were capable of sailing to the windward, against the winds and tides of the Pacific, which tend to move from east to west. They were impressive craft, as the first European visitors to Hawaii and Tahiti noted enthusiastically.

Naturally, navigation was a problem. Some scholars have held that the voyages were accidental—boats were blown off course, which led to the occupation of new islands—but Polynesian traditions and the continuing ability of some Pacific islanders to navigate long distances by observing the stars, wave patterns, and other techniques of observation support the idea that voyages of colonization were planned. Moreover, sometimes

Petroglyph lava rock.

they were two-way. For example, Hawaiian traditions commemorate the arrival of Tahitian chiefs who made voyages to and from Hawaii for about 200 years (1100–1300 C.E.). In 1976, to establish the possibility of such voyaging, the Hōkūlé, a reconstructed double canoe based on traditional proportions and using only traditional navigational techniques, was sailed from Hawaii to Tahiti in about 35 days. In the main, however, much of the voyaging seems to have been sporadic, as groups pushed by war, population pressure, famine, or a spirit of exploration followed a chief or a navigator into the unknown. In the 18th century, when the Europeans arrived, in much of Polynesia such long-range voyaging was rarely practiced. By that time, however, the Polynesians had explored and colonized almost every habitable island in the vast Pacific.

Ancient Hawaii

We can use the widely separated large islands, New Zealand and Hawaii, as examples of Polynesian societies that developed in relative isolation in response to particular environmental conditions. Hawaii includes eight major islands in a chain about 300 miles long. The volcanic nature of the islands and the tropical climate created an environment of great beauty and majesty that impressed the early inhabitants. The islands were probably settled in at least two migratory waves beginning about 300 C.E. There, early Polynesian culture was adapted and elaborated in relative isolation over a long period of time. The islands had good soil, and the population grew large, reaching, at contact in the 1700s, about 200,000 people. Towns and cities were absent, and houses, here as elsewhere in Polynesia, were scattered along the coast and in valleys leading to the higher interior. Islands were divided politically into wedge-shaped territories, broadest at the coast and narrowing toward the less desired interior. A number of chiefly families competed for control of the islands. It was not until after European contact that King *Kamehameha* I united all the islands under his control in 1810.

Of all the Polynesian societies, Hawaii became the most hierarchical. The high chiefs, or *ali'i*, claimed descent from the gods and rested their claims on their ability to recite in great detail their genealogical lineages. In some cases, marriage to their sisters ensured the purity of the chiefly family. Their power, authority, and sacredness, or *mana*, emanated from their lineages and enabled them to extract labor or tribute from their subjects or even take their land. Feathered capes and helmets as well as tattoos distinguished the chiefs. The ali'i were revered and feared. They were above and beyond the constraints of society. "The chief is a shark that swims on land" was a Hawaiian proverb. A class of lesser nobility and subchiefs of their relatives supported the rule of the ali'i.

Society rested on the commoners, who tilled the fields of taro and sweet potatoes, raised the pigs and chickens, and exploited the resources of the sea. Hawaiian society was intensely agricultural, and the community's control of land was a central aspect of social and political relations. Within the hierarchy, commoners were viewed almost as a separate people or at least as a people lacking in lineage. Their lives were constrained and limited by a complex set of *kapu* (tapu in Tahiti), or taboo, which forbade certain activities and regulated social discourse. It was kapu for women to eat certain foods, to enter the house of a chief, to eat together with men, to view certain ceremonies limited to the chiefs, or even to cast a shadow on a chief. And many other limits were imposed according to rank. Violations could lead to death. The number of kapu surrounding a chief was a measure of his status and his sanctity—as much a sign of his position in his society as material goods might be in our society.

Many aspects of life were ritualized. The numerous gods were honored at ceremonial centers, whose precincts were sacred. Ritual feasting and hula, or dancing, accompanied many ceremonies. Human and other sacrifices were offered to Ku, the god of war, and to the other deities. Lono, the god of fertility and agricultural rebirth, held special importance to the Hawaiians. The great Makahiki festival of thanksgiving, which lasted for four months and at which the chiefs received their tribute from the commoners, was celebrated in honor of the annual return of Lono. During this time war was kapu, hulas were danced, and sexual activity was engaged in frequently in the hope of stimulating fertility. In fact, lovemaking was an art and a preoccupation of the Hawaiians, with important religious, kinship, and political meanings.

Of the various Polynesian societies, Hawaii perhaps can be seen as the most successful in terms of its political and social complexity, its economic foundations, its art and material culture, and its religion. With a Neolithic technology, the Hawaiians created a complex culture on their islands. Though they lacked a written language, their legends and oral histories, which could trace the genealogies of chiefly families back to the original canoes of the first migrants, were remarkable achievements that formed and preserved their culture.

The New Zealand Landfall and the Development of Maori Culture

Perhaps as early as the 8th century C.E., the crews of canoes or rafts from the Society Islands and other parts of eastern Polynesia had sailed thousands of miles to the southwest and by chance discovered the two large islands that today make up New Zealand. Over the centuries additional bands of seafarers reached the islands, where they embarked on a struggle to survive in an environment that was colder and harsher than their home islands in Polynesia. Their success is evidenced by the large numbers of Maoris—the people descended from the Polynesian seafarers—who lived in the islands when the Europeans first came to stay in the late 18th century. If the high estimates of 200,000 people at this point in time are correct, the islands contained the highest concentration of Polynesian peoples anywhere in the world.

The "land of the long white clouds," as the Polynesians referred to the mist-covered islands that made up New Zealand, had few edible plants beyond berries and fern roots. There were no native land mammals except bats and various kinds of *moa*, or large wingless birds. However, overhunting led to the extinction of the moa, and both early settlers and later migrants had to find new sources of subsistence. Fishing and the introduction by later migrants of many of the staple crops of Polynesia, including the sweet potato, taro, and yam, filled the dietary gap left by the disappearance of the moa. Perhaps to compensate for the shortage of protein in their diet, settlers ate dogs and rats, which had also been brought to the islands by migrants from Polynesia, and human flesh, usually carved from enemies killed in war.

The relatively moderate climate and rich soils of the north island rendered it more suitable for settlement than the cold and desolate south island, which stretched beneath the 40th parallel toward the South Pole. Consequently, Maori tribes numbering in the thousands warred over control of the forests and croplands on the north island. Long before the arrival of the Europeans, tribal territories with clearly defined boundaries had been established throughout most of the north island.

Maori Culture and Society

Maori tribes were given the names of the semimythical canoes that were believed to have carried their ancestors to the islands. Each tribe was divided into subgroups called *hapu,* the primary unit of identity and community. Within hapu villages the Maori lived in extended families, which included up to five generations, in large, elaborately carved wooden houses. All the land the Maoris farmed for their subsistence was owned by the hapu village and allotted by a communal council to each of the extended families for their support.

Each hapu was led by a male chief, who was not a specialized political leader but rather a particularly skillful warrior. Chieftainships were hereditary, although weak leaders were soon displaced by more able warriors. Despite the magical aura associated with the hapu and tribal chieftains, their actual power was limited by village and tribal councils made up of the free males of a given group. Virtually all hapu communities also included slaves, who were usually prisoners of war or their descendants.

Though they had a strong voice within the family, women were clearly subordinated to men. Male dominance was evidenced by the monopoly they enjoyed with regard to positions of leadership and to highly prestigious activities such as making war and wood carving.

Maori society had not reached the level of development at which full-time specialists could be supported, but many kinds of religious and craft experts were recognized. Priests were of several kinds, varying according to social status and functions. The most esteemed were the chiefs who were also trained as priests. The chief-priest presided over communal ceremonies and knew the special prayers designed to protect the tribe or hapu from human or supernatural enemies. The Maori world was alive with spirits, gods, and goddesses, who intervened constantly in human affairs. At the other end of the social scale were shamans, who specialized in healing and served as the mediums by which gods and spirits made their desires known to humans.

A Society Oriented to War

In addition to priests, Maori society had a wide variety of experts, ranging from those who built canoes and made the ornate wood carvings that decorated Maori homes to those who tattooed the men's faces, thighs, and buttocks and women's lips and chins. The most important experts, however, were those with skills relating to making war. Maori society was obsessed with war. During the appropriate season, tribes and hapus fought regularly with their neighbors or distant confederations. Young males proved their worth as warriors, and leaders could not long maintain their positions without demonstrating their martial prowess. Much of the time and energy of Maori males was devoted to planning campaigns against neighboring tribes or building the intricate hilltop fortresses found throughout the north island. Though the loss of life in Maori wars was low by European standards, their combats were fierce. Hand-to-hand fighting with spears and exquisitely carved war clubs was the preferred mode of combat. Successful ambushes and surprise attacks were highly admired. The priest-leader of a hapu or tribe would cut out the heart of the first enemy killed in battle and offer it to the gods of his people. Enemy casualties were sometimes eaten; enemy prisoners, including women and children, were enslaved.

On the Threshold of Civilization

Polynesian seafarers had accomplished much in the harsh but beautiful environment of their New Zealand landfall. Mainly on the basis of imported crops, they had developed a fairly steady and productive agricultural system. Though they did not work metals, their material culture was quite impressive. In wood working and decoration, in particular, they surpassed the Polynesian societies from which their ancestors had come. They had also developed a wonderfully rich oral tradition, which placed a premium on oratorical skills and produced a complex and fascinating collection of myths and legends. Though divided and politically decentralized, the Maori had developed closely knit and well-organized communities within the hapu and the tribe.

Their isolation and limited resource base prevented the Maoris from achieving the full occupational specialization that, as we have seen, was critical to the advance to true civilization elsewhere. Isolation limited the Maori's technological advance and their resistance to disease. These limits rendered them vulnerable to peoples such as the Europeans, who possessed more sophisticated tools and weapons and transmitted diseases that decimated the tribes of New Zealand severely. Though their skills in war and their adaptability allowed the Maori to survive in the long run, they could do little to prevent the disintegration of their culture and the destruction of much of the world they had known before the coming of the Europeans.

CONCLUSION

The Emerging Cultures

Two important features were shared by the societies that formed on the fringes of the major core of world civilizations during the classical period and slightly beyond. First, as they adopted or imported agriculture, they were able to form more structured political units and develop a more complex social hierarchy. Second, that each of the emerging societies exhibited important characteristics from its own past. These characteristics would carry forward into the subsequent history of these regions, even as other influences were encountered.

The four emerging areas also displayed one vital difference in addition to particular distinctions in art, language, and the like. Three of the areas—northern Europe, Japan, and sub-Saharan Africa—were in contact with more established civilization centers, at least to some extent. Polynesia stood apart by its early separation from Asia. This resulted in an impressive set of independent achievements as Polynesian society advanced and spread, but also in important constraints, most obviously in technology. The availability of outside influence, in other words, can explain important differences between societies.

Further development of contacts with more established centers for the Japanese, the Slavs and the Germans, and the Sudanic kingdoms of Africa depended on changes in the classical civilizations themselves. The explosion of the great classical empires after the 2nd century C.E., then the new influences that helped reestablish vigorous societies in the same areas, had a vital spillover effect in northern Europe and Asia and in sub-Saharan Africa. This fact returns us to the classical centers, as they declined but also birthed dynamic new forces capable of transforming wide stretches of the Old World.

FURTHER READINGS

The general process of cultural migration and the problems of interpreting archeological and linguistic evidence are the subjects of Irving Rouse's *Migrations in Prehis-* *tory* (1986), which includes excellent chapters on the Japanese and the Polynesians.

Geography, society, and history of Africa are all treated in an informative way in Paul Bohannan's and Philip Curtin's *Africa and the Africans,* 3rd ed. (1988). A very useful introduction to and synthesis of Africa's ancient past is provided by David Phillipson's *African Archaeology* (1985). *The Horizon History of Africa* (1971) contains excellent articles by specialists and integrates these with original texts, well-chosen illustrations, and good maps. Philip Curtin et al., *African History* (1978), contains excellent chapters on various regions. Nehemia Levitzion's *Ancient Ghana and Mali* (1973) provides a succinct survey based on the original sources.

Justine Davis Randers-Pehrson's *Barbarians and Romans: The Birth Struggle of Europe,* A.D. *400–700* (1983) gives a broad overview of the Germans and Slavs during this period. Tacitus's classic on the Germans is easily available in the translation by H. Mattingly, *The Agricola and the Germania* (1970).

The fullest, though now somewhat dated, account of early Japanese cultural development available in English is included in G. B. Sansom's *A History of Japan to 1334* (1958). Useful introductions to the early period can also be found in Mikiso Hane's *Japan: A Historical Survey* (1972), E. O. Reischauer's *Japan: The Story of a Nation* (1974), and (especially for political developments) John W. Hall's *Japan from Prehistory to Modern Times* (1970). The best introductions to society and culture in the early period are provided by G. B. Sansom's *Japan: A Short Cultural History* (1943) and H. Paul Varley's *Japanese Culture: A Short History* (1973).

Peter Bellwood's *The Polynesians: Prehistory of an Island People* (rev. ed., 1978) is an excellent short introduction to the Polynesians. Jesse D. Jennings, ed., *The Prehistory of Polynesia* (1979) contains survey articles on various areas of Polynesia. Patrick Vinton Kirch's *Feathered Gods and Fishhooks* (1985) surveys the archeology of Hawaii. Classic accounts of Maori society and customs include Te Rangi Hiroa's (Peter Buck), *The Coming of the Maori* (1949) and the works of Elsdon Best, especially *Some Aspects of Maori Myth and Religion* (1923).

11

The End of the Classical Era: World History in Transition, 200–700 C.E.

	100 C.E.	200 C.E.	300 C.E.
CHINA	88 Beginning of Han decline	184 Daoist Yellow Turban rebellion 220 Last Han emperor deposed; "Time of Troubles" begins; nomadic invasions in north	300–700 Spread of Buddhism
INDIA			
ROME and CHRISTIANITY		180 ff. Beginning of Rome's decline; population decline 231 Initial Germanic invasion effort	284–305 Diocletian emperor 312–337 Constantine; division of empire administration; toleration of Christianity 330–379 Basil organizes Eastern monasticism
MIDDLE EAST			

INTRODUCTION

Between 200 and 600 C.E., all three of the great classical civilizations collapsed, at least in part. The western portion of the Roman Empire declined and fell, suffering major eclipse. The fates of Han China, Gupta India, and indeed the eastern part of the Roman Empire were less dire, but in those places too, there was substantial change. The coincidence of these developments in time raises one of the principal issues in world history: What causes civilizations to lose vigor? It also focuses attention on the close of one major period in time—characterized by the development and flowering of the classical societies—and the opening of a new, postclassical era in world history. For while decline and fall rivet our attention on the time from the 3rd through the 6th centuries, important new developments, including the spread of great religions, also set up many of the leading characteristics of the next stage in world history. This transitional aspect, as well as classical decline, requires analysis, as we examine developments that began to emerge around 200 C.E. and reached fruition between the 5th and the 8th centuries from Asia through North Africa and Europe.

This chapter returns to a primary focus on the centers of classical civilization in Eurasia and North Africa. The end of the classical era is predicated on changes in Asia and the Mediterranean, not the whole world. Nevertheless, the fading of the great classical empires did have consequences beyond their borders. The reshuffling of civilization boundaries that resulted would soon unleash new kinds of expansive forces that would touch sub-Saharan Africa, northern Europe, and various additional parts of Asia. Africans in the Sudan, Germans, Slavs, and Japanese were all affected. The changing map of civilization would still leave certain parts of the world entirely separate, but the number of isolated areas dropped.

It is worth remembering also that the classical period in American Indian civilizations, notably the Maya, ended not long after the collapse of the great empires in Asia and the Mediterranean, though the processes had no direct connection. We know much more about the nature and causes of decline in Rome or China because of available records, but some of the factors may have been similar.

All three classical civilizations in Asia, North Africa, and Europe suffered from outside invasions during the centuries of decline, the common results of growing incursions by nomadic herding groups from central Asia. This renewed wave of nomadic expansion was neither as sweeping nor as damaging as the Indo-European attacks on the civilization of the Indus valley many centuries before, but the new pressure severely tested the civilized regimes. Western Rome, including the capital city itself, fell to Germanic invaders from northern Europe, though there was one fierce incursion by Asiatic Huns. The Ger-

589–618 Sui dynasty   **618** Tang dynasty

606–647 Loose empire under Harsha

400–500 Decline of Buddhism; evolution of popular Hinduism

657 ff. Rajput (regional princes) predominate; periodic clashes with Islamic armies in northwest

c. 540 Collapse of Gupta dynasty

450 Hun invasions begin

401 ff. Increased Germanic invasions

527–565 Justinian, Eastern emperor

354–430 Augustine

480–547 Benedict and Western monasticism

410 Rome sacked by Germanic tribe

476 Last Roman emperor in West deposed

610 Beginning of Islam

400 C.E.   **500** C.E.   **600** C.E.

manic peoples pressed in partly because they were harassed by these same Huns and moved south for greater safety. Another Hun group from central Asia overthrew the Gupta dynasty in India, while similar nomadic tribes had earlier contributed to the disorder of China after the Han dynasty.

The central Asian nomads may have been spurred by population increase in their native lands, which prompted them to seek new territory. They were certainly encouraged by a growing realization of the weakness of the classical regimes. Han China, as well as the later Roman Empire, suffered from serious internal problems long before the invaders applied additional blows, and the Guptas had not permanently resolved India's tendency to political fragmentation. Thus, although outside invasion by warlike nomads forms the clearest common thread in the pattern of classical decline, the whole phenomenon invites consideration of some shared processes of internal decay that humbled once-proud empires before small but fierce bands of barbarian invaders.

In addition, then, to a study of what happened in the final centuries of the great classical empires of Rome, Han China and Gupta India, some assessment of causation—of the factors that explain roughly simultaneous decline—is essential. While invasions are part of the explanation, they would have been brushed aside with relative ease a few centuries before. Other changes had occurred, which accounted for the invaders' devastating success.

The process of decline, however, was far from identical across civilization boundaries. Everywhere the crisis was severe; even in China, which ultimately recovered most completely, the collapse of the Han dynasty led to an unusual period of disarray. But the image of destruction many Westerners learn on the basis of Rome's demise is really atypical. Most civilizations retained more of their earlier achievements than the Roman Europe managed to do. Differential patterns of revival and continuity raise additional prospects for a comparative analysis that sums up many of the emphases of the larger classical era that now drew to a close. What survived from classical China was different from the continuities in India, and both contrasted sharply with the much more complex Mediterranean patterns after the collapse of the Roman Empire. These differences must be explained, and they must also be used to anticipate subsequent developments.

The collapse or temporary eclipse of the classical civilizations forms a significant break in world history, and this too must be explored. The fall of the Han dynasty and the Guptas in India rather clearly ended formative periods in each civilization's history. This did not preclude further change. Indeed, the period of decline ushered in new forces, such as a novel Chinese interest in Buddhism. Each civilization had to alter somewhat, simply in reaction to invasion and extensive chaos. What the period of decline did in India and China, and to some extent in the eastern Mediterranean, was to define the essentials of the classical achievement that could endure or revive and to establish the crucial heritage, even as other features of the classical period were winnowed away. India, to use the clearest example, found it relatively easy to build on the religious tradition already sketched in the classical era and to amplify the distinctive social structure; here was a heritage that would survive, though with modifications and adjustments, into India's postclassical period and beyond. But other features of the classical achievement did not continue. Buddhism faded in the religious tradition, while India's recurrent ability to form internal empires lapsed. India began a long experience in which political fragmentation alternated with larger structures established by invasion from the outside. The next time Indians formed more than large regional kingdoms was in 1947 C.E.; here was a major change from the classical precedents set by the Mauryans and then the Guptas. In China as well as India, the centuries of decline brought important changes but also a process of selection in which crucial characteristics maintained the civilizations' definitions into a new age.

THE DECLINE OF CIVILIZATION AND THE RISE OF RELIGIONS

Focal Point: Fundamentally new periods in world history do not occur often, and they must be defined carefully. At the end of the classical period, the stage for periodization is set not only by the decline of empires but also by the rise of religions.

Defining the New Period

Generally, three overlapping shifts must occur for a new period to be identified in world history and not just in some individual societies. First, the world map must change significantly, which means that at least some civilization areas are divided in new ways, and new patterns of dynamism are established. Second, new kinds of contacts must be established among civilization areas. Third, perhaps in part because of new contacts, some new parallelisms must arise in the patterns displayed by the major civilization areas. Obviously, additional features may develop as part of world history periodization, including some important new technologies. Nevertheless, the three guidelines provide at least a minimum checklist.

The fall of the great empires and its consequences easily meet the three tests. Cultural and political boundaries shifted with the renewed openness of India to invasion and with the irrevocable division of the Mediterranean world. Boundary changes encouraged several civilizations to seek new outlets for expansion and influence, thus radiating contacts from the old classical core to new parts of Europe, Africa, and East and Southeast Asia. India's role as the most expansive civilization in terms of trade and cultural influence also declined in favor of the newcomer Muslim civilization based in the Middle East.

New contacts among civilizations developed after the 5th century C.E., through patterns of warfare that brought Middle Easterners briefly to the borders of China, where among other things they learned about the manufacture of paper and spread this knowledge westward. New contacts developed also from new trade patterns and from the unprecedented outreach of great world religions—Buddhism, Christianity, and Islam—which spread across civilization boundaries without, however, erasing them.

Finally, new parallelisms developed among civilizations from Europe and North Africa through Japan, in addition to numerous developments within individual societies. Most civilizations witnessed important changes in their belief systems in the aftermath of classical decline. More systematic religious movements spread increasingly, and they challenged, replaced, or merged with more traditional polytheism.

Surge in the Great Religions

All of this means that the end of the classical period was not simply a story of decay and collapse. As the great empires fell or receded after 200 C.E., the major world religions—the same religions practiced today—arose or spread. From Spain to China, growing political instability clearly prompted many people to seek solace in the joys of the spirit, and while this religious surge was not entirely new, the resulting changes in the religious map of Europe, Africa, and Asia, plus the nature and intensity of religious interests, were significant new forces. Christianity became an extensive religion through the Mediterranean region as the Roman Empire's political strength weakened, though it used the empire's political structure to form its own institutional framework and channels of communication. Buddhism's surge into East Asia accompanied the growing problems of Han China in decline. Thus two major world faiths, different in many ways but similar in their emphasis on the spiritual life and the importance of divine power, began to reshape major portions of Europe and Asia precisely as the political edifice of the classical period declined or disappeared. Even in India, Hinduism continued an evolution that produced new levels of spirituality among large sectors of the population. Finally, shortly after 600 C.E., an entirely new religion, *Islam,* started a career that would make it the most dynamic force in world history during the next several centuries; its early expansion owed much to the political disunity and uncertainty in the eastern Mediterranean after Rome's demise.

In sum, the religious map of the world, while by no means complete in the aftermath of classical decline, began to take on new contours, many of which are recognizable today in the areas of Christian, Islamic, or Buddhist influence. The chronological coincidence of this set of religious changes suggests the importance of classical decline in setting in motion new opportunities for missionaries and new needs for ordinary people to reassess what and why they believed. Never before had single religions spread so widely, crossing so many previous cultural and political boundaries. Not since before the classical era had masses and elites been so joined in common religious institutions and interests.

The decline and fall of the great empires thus marks more than parallel processes of political change. The differences among civilizations remained substantial, and in some ways the collapse of the great empires and the rise of new religious divisions made international contacts more complex than before. Yet, the centuries of decline did create something of a common moment in the history of most major civilizations, which not only brought certain patterns to an end but launched a new dynamic.

UPHEAVALS IN EASTERN AND SOUTHERN ASIA

Focal Point: The decline of the Han dynasty in China and, later, the Gupta Empire in India, and pressure from nomadic invaders, mark the key transition in the Asian civilization.

Decline and Fall in Han China

After a brief faltering following the reign of Wudi, the Han dynasty seemed to recover, and by about 100 C.E., the central government was about as effective and the economy about as prosperous as before. The Chinese launched a new expansion campaign, pushing westward with attacks in central Asia across the Gobi desert, that may have helped spark the westward and then southward movement of the groups known in Europe as the Huns. After about 88 C.E., however, the quality of the individual emperors began to decline. Most reigns were short and full of plotting; empresses and officials joined in the fray (see Chapter 5). On several occasions, numerous bureaucrats and popular protesters were massacred.

At a basic level, conditions among the peasantry began to deteriorate. Large landowners, always powerful under the Han, grew more so, avoiding taxes and forming private armies. Taxes on peasants increased, and many farmers, forced into serfdom, provided labor service and turned over much of their own produce as fees to the landlords. Social protest increased, often laced with Daoist beliefs.

Peasant unrest culminated in a great revolutionary effort led by the Daoists in 184 C.E. Leaders called the *Yellow Turbans* promised a golden age to be brought about by divine magic. Han generals suppressed this rebellion but set themselves up as regional rulers—a clear sign of the collapse of the central state. The last Han emperor was deposed in 220 C.E. China was divided into three kingdoms for several decades, but finally even these began to collapse. For several centuries, China was ruled by the landowning class, who ran huge numbers of serfs and directed private armies, operating beyond the control of formal government. Southern and northern China also pulled apart, with the south maintaining higher levels of economic growth and continuing to absorb tribal peoples into Chinese culture.

No firm dynasties could be established in this 350-year period, though there were short-lived regimes in the south. Northern China was pressed by invasions from central Asia. Nomadic peoples had been incorporated into Chinese armies, much as later Roman rulers tried to use Germanic troops, but as the government deteriorated the nomads broke loose and began to invade the Middle Kingdom. Several nomad-dominated states were formed, though all lasted only briefly. Internal warfare became endemic in what was an unusually long breakdown in Chinese stability.

Into this chaos came the new fascination with Buddhism, which responded to political uncertainty and eco-

The spread of Buddhism produced major new themes in Chinese art, many of which focused on stylized figures of Buddha himself. Buddha became an object of worship in this process, with statues great and small conveying his majesty.

nomic distress by offering spiritual solace and which also, like Christianity in Europe, provided a form of cultural cohesion at a time when political links had broken down. Imported from India—the only case until modern times when China borrowed a major idea from abroad—and disseminated by silk merchants and missionaries, Buddhism spread among both the Chinese and the nomadic warriors, helping gradually to mold a common culture in which Chinese ingredients predominated. Buddhist influence also brought to China a new impetus for art and sculpture, altering the established styles and themes.

Buddhism came under periodic attack by Daoist regional rulers, but the faith reached throughout China by the 5th century C.E. Buddhist monasteries for women as well as men gained ground. Many Chinese monks made pilgrimages to India, and Buddhist literature and philosophy spread widely. Chinese Buddhists blended practices from many Indian Buddhist sects, using meditation, recitation of prayers, and devotional exercises. The Chinese imposed some of their own values on Buddhism as well; for instance, they insisted on the importance of forming families so that the ancestral line could be preserved. Typically, as a result, only second sons became Buddhist monks, and first sons maintained the family responsibilities. Buddhists were also pressed into political loyalty, paying taxes to the government and submitting to government regulations on the formation of monasteries.

The growing Buddhist influence also had an impact on Daoism, forcing greater formalization of Daoist doctrine and more efforts to reach the common people. Many Chinese found great similarities between the two faiths, though Buddhism continued to have the advantage of offering a clearer doctrine of personal salvation—the chance of holy life after death—and a firmer set of personal ethics. Daoist leaders developed a variety of practices, including meditation and dietary restrictions, that might bring immortality. Popular Daoism, mixing Daoist beliefs with an animistic pantheon of many gods, tended to hold that good or evil done in this life would be compensated by heavens or hells hereafter. Of course, popular Daoism also could have political implications in protesting social injustice, and Daoism often provided priests and shamans who practiced faith healing in cases of disease. These ramifications of Daoism proved quite durable among the Chinese peasantry, lasting in some parts of eastern Asia even today.

Confucianism, obviously, lost ground during this confused period in Chinese history, eclipsed by the more otherworldly interests. But the legacy of Chinese institutions and secular beliefs did not disappear, and as nomadic invaders were partly converted to Chinese ways, the opportunity for political revival reemerged toward the end of the 6th century. A series of strong rulers in the north drove out nomadic bands and then merged, under a general of Chinese-Turkish background, into a new *Sui* dynasty. Under this brief dynasty, the whole of northern China was united and South China was reconquered. New canals were built and the Great Wall was repaired. Attempts to expand into Korea and central Asia brought financial collapse, however, along with new rebellions, and only in 618 C.E. was the more durable *Tang* dynasty established. The time of troubles had ended.

The decline and fall of the Han had thus brought important disruption to China and had opened the civilization to new religious influences. But old values survived as well. Even the competing landlords retained some training in Confucianism and with that training the idea of a united empire. New religious interests, though important, did not capture people's full attention. In this sense, China, with its greater cultural homogeneity established in the classical era, differed markedly from the Mediterranean, where Christianity and Islam came close to displacing older philosophical concerns while challenging earlier political loyalties. Many nomadic invaders found that they could do little better than to imitate Chinese styles, and this process ultimately encouraged the revival of older political habits. Chaos and innovation must not be forgotten, but eventually the main Chinese characteristic was the ability to recapture continuity.

The End of the Guptas: Decline in India

The decline of classical civilization in India was in one sense less drastic than the collapse of Han China in that India had not depended so heavily on political structures to hold its civilization together. The fall of the Guptas, in other words, did not initially entail an opening to dramatic new cultural or social influences. Yet, the Gupta collapse left more durable traces in later Indian history, for internally generated political unity became more difficult than ever before.

While the high point of Gupta rule came under Chandragupta II early in the 5th century, his immediate successors managed to sustain considerable prosperity. India about 450 C.E. was probably the most stable and peaceful area in the world. However, in 440 C.E., the nomadic Huns began a series of invasions that would gradually reduce the empire's strength. The Gupta pattern of somewhat decentralized rule, whereby vassal princes were treated as partial allies rather than subject to direct central administration, may have made response to invasion more difficult. The Huns controlled much of northwestern India—the classic invasion route of the subcontinent—by 500 C.E. By this juncture, the quality of Gupta kings was also diminishing, and this added to the problem (see Chapter 7). It was a regional prince, not the Guptas themselves, who broke the hold of the Huns in the northwest about 530 C.E., and the Guptas were too weak to restore their claims. The dynasty collapsed entirely about 550 C.E.

A few echoes of Gupta splendor were heard during the 7th century. Harsha, a descendant of the Guptas through his grandmother, constructed a loose empire across northern India between 616 and 657. But he died without heirs, and his empire broke up again. From this point onward, until a better-organized series of outside invasions began, northern India was politically divided. Regional dynasties were occasionally

DOCUMENT

The Popularization of Buddhism

Chinese Buddhism, unlike most Chinese beliefs, spread among all regions and social groups. While it divided into many sects that disagreed over details of theology and rituals by commenting on earlier Buddhist scriptures (the Sutras), many ordinary Chinese believers cared little for such niceties, and were concerned rather with direct spiritual benefits. Often they arranged to have Buddhist sermons copied, as a means of obtaining merit, while adding a note of their own. The following passages come from such notes, written mainly in the 6th century.

Recorded on the 15th day of the fourth month of 531.

The Buddhist lay disciple Yuan Jung—having lived in this degenerate era for many years, fearful for his life, and yearning for home—now makes a donation of a thousand silver coins to the Three Jewels [the Buddha, the Law, and the Monastic Order]. This donation is made in the name of the Celestial King Vaisravana. In addition, he makes a donation of a thousand to ransom himself and his wife and children [from their earthly existence], a thousand more to ransom his servants, and a thousand more to ransom his domestic animals. This money is to be used for copying sutras. It is accompanied by the prayer that the Celestial King may attain Buddhahood; that the disciple's family, servants, and animals may be blessed with long life, may attain enlightenment, and may all be permitted to return to the capital.

Dated the 29th day of the fourth month of 550.

Happiness is not fortuitous: pray for it and it will respond. Results are not born of thin air: pay heed to causes and results will follow. This explains how the Buddhist disciple and nun Tao-jung—because her conduct in her previous life was not correct—came to be born in her present form, a woman, vile and unclean.

Now if she does not honor the awesome decree of Buddha, how can future consequences be favorable for her? Therefore, having cut down her expenditures on food and clothing, she reverently has had the Nirvana Sutra copied once. She prays that those who read it carefully will be exalted in mind to the highest realms and that those who communicate its meaning will cause others to be so enlightened.

She also prays that in her present existence she will have no further sickness or suffering, that her parents in seven other incarnations (who have already died or will die in the future) and her present family and close relatives may experience joy in the four realms

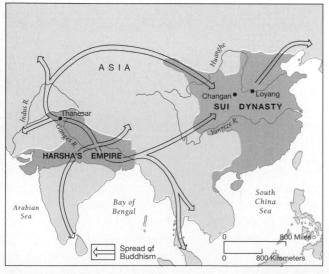

Asia, c. 600 C.E.

powerful, but none controlled a large region, and few managed to last very long. The regional princes, collectively called the *Rajput,* emphasized military prowess; but while there were many local wars, few political events had great significance.

In this localized framework, Indian culture continued to evolve. Buddhism declined steadily in India proper. The Guptas had preferred Hinduism, and the Hun invaders disliked the pronouncedly otherworldly tone of the Buddhists as well. Military-minded princes had little sympathy for the Buddhist principles of calm and contemplation. Hindu beliefs, in contrast, gained ground, converting the Hun leaders, among other groups. Within Hinduism, worship of a mother goddess, *Devi,* spread widely, which encouraged a new popular emotionalism in religious ritual. In essence, India partially redefined its core culture by emphasizing the Hindu strain more clearly while relying primarily on cul-

[earth, water, fire, and air], and that whatever they seek may indeed come to pass. Finally, she prays that all those endowed with knowledge may be included within this prayer.

Recorded on the 28th day of the fifth month of 583.

The Army Superintendent, Sung Shao, having suffered the heavy sorrow of losing both his father and mother, made a vow on their behalf to read one section each of [many] sutras. He prays that the spirits of his parents will someday reach the Pure Land [paradise] and will thus be forever freed from the three unhappy states of existence and the eight calamities and that they may eternally listen to the Buddha's teachings.

He also prays that the members of his family, both great and small, may find happiness at will, that blessings may daily rain down upon them while hardships disperse like clouds. He prays that the imperial highways may be open and free of bandits, that the state may be preserved from pestilence, that wind and rain may obey their proper seasons, and that all suffering creatures may quickly find release. May all these prayers be granted!

The preceding incantation has been translated and circulated.

If this incantation is recited 7, 14, or 21 times daily (after having cleansed the mouth in the morning with a willow twig, having scattered flowers and incense before the image of Buddha, having knelt and joined the palms of the hands), the four grave sins, the five wicked acts, and all other transgressions will be wiped away. The present body will not be afflicted by untimely calamities; one will at last be born into the realm of immeasurably long life; and reincarnation in the female form will be escaped forever.

Now, the Sanskrit text has been reexamined and the Indian Vinaya monk Buddhasangha and other monks have been consulted; thus we know that the awesome power of this incantation is beyond comprehension. If it is recited 100 times in the evening and again at noon, it will destroy the four grave sins and five wicked acts. It will pluck out the very roots of sin and will ensure rebirth in the Western Regions. If, with sincerity of spirit, one is able to complete 200,000 recitations, perfect intelligence will be born and there will be no relapses. If 300,000 recitations are completed, one will see Amita Buddha face to face and will certainly be reborn into the Pure Land of tranquility and bliss.

Copied by the disciple of pure faith Sun Szu-chung on the 8th day of the fourth month of 720.

Questions: Why did Buddhism spread widely in China by the 6th century? How did popular Buddhism compare with original Buddhist teachings (see Chapter 7)? How did Chinese Buddhists define holy life?

---

tural cohesion to maintain the civilization at a time when political life became more difficult. The reassertion of Hinduism also helped the caste system, now spreading to southern India. The number and complexity of castes increased as invaders were assimilated into the system, but the basic principles persisted from the classical period.

India's economic activity also continued at a relatively high level, though in periods of outright invasion there were new hardships. Here too, Indian civilization did not collapse to the extent of Han China or the western Mediterranean. Indeed, the decades after the fall of the Guptas saw new outreach in trade and even some conquest by southern Tamil kingdoms, which were trying to establish firmer strongholds along the Indian Ocean in Southeast Asia.

While Indian civilization substantially maintained its position, though with new political disunity, another threat was to come after 600 C.E. from the new Middle Eastern religion of Islam (see Chapters 12 and 13). At first, India's contacts with this new force were somewhat tangential. Arab armies, fighting under the banners of their god Allah, reached India's porous northwestern frontier during the 7th century, and while there was initially little outright conquest as opposed to raids for booty, Islam did win some converts in the north, particularly among lower-caste Indians drawn to the Islamic message of spiritual equality.

The challenge of Islam continued the evolutionary process within mainstream Hinduism. Hindu leaders strengthened their emphasis on religious and popular devotion, playing down some traditional intellectual interests. Popularization involved language change, as would occur in Christianity in western Europe several centuries later. Hindu texts began to be written in vernacular languages such as Hindi, while the old classical

Hindu statues gave vivid forms to holy figures, many of them female. This scene portrays a goddess subduing a mythological cosmic monster.

language, Sanskrit, declined in usage. These reactions helped prevent more than a minority of Indians from abandoning Hinduism, but they also tended to narrow Indian culture more strictly toward the religious focus. Earlier Indian achievements in science and mathematics were not matched by new work.

By the 8th century, Islamic competition also began to hit hard at India's international economic position. Arab traders soon wrested control of the Indian Ocean from Tamil merchants, and India, though still prosperous and productive, saw its commercial dynamism reduced. No political response to these new challenges emerged, and with persistent regionalism, the subcontinent was open by the 11th century to conquest by Muslim rulers from the outside. Clearly, the glory days of the Guptas were long past, and while classical traditions survived through Hinduism, the caste system, and active patterns of internal trade, the focus of the civilization, and its larger impact on Asia, were seriously reduced.

Here, then, is an important pattern of decline, though one rather different from that of China. India's political retreat from empire was longer lasting than China's political setbacks; only in the 20th century did India regain an ability to form large states on the basis of internal rule rather than regimes imposed from the outside. Obviously, earlier weaknesses in the classical past help explain this Indian-Chinese contrast. Classical India had generated neither a set of political values nor a durable institution like the Chinese bureaucracy that could allow a large political unit to bounce back from a period of invasion and chaos. Though India's regional states were often well run, combining the power of a prince with some sort of wider council, they were not strong enough to prevent the recurrent threat of invasion, mainly by Muslim forces coming in from the northwest. On the other hand, India's culture and caste system showed great resiliency, for they did not depend on any single pattern of political support. India in this sense experienced fewer sharp cultural shifts, and showed more ability to modify itself gradually, than did China under the Buddhist influence. Indian identity and key traditions could thus be preserved amid political disunity or even under foreign rule.

THE DECLINE AND FALL OF THE ROMAN EMPIRE

Focal Point: The decline of the Roman Empire fit chronologically between the collapse of the Han and that of the Gupta dynasty. It was more disruptive than either of these Asian developments. For many educated Westerners (like some Indians who view the Gupta dynasty as India's finest era and its collapse therefore as an unredeemed misfortune), the fall of Rome has a powerful impact on the imagination and commands a particular effort of explanation.

The Causation of Roman Decline

Signs of decay began to emerge in the Roman Empire from the late 2nd century onward, at various levels. The statistical symptoms were declining population size, as birth rates no longer kept pace with mortality rates, and growing difficulties in recruiting effective armies. The political symptoms showed in the greater brutality and arbitrariness of many later Roman emperors—victims, according to one commentator at the time, of "lustful and cruel habits." Tax collection became increasingly difficult as residents of the empire fell on hard times. The governor of Egypt complained that "the once numerous inhabitants of the aforesaid villages have now been reduced to a few, because some have fled in poverty and others have died . . . and for this reason we are in danger owing to impoverishment of having to abandon the tax-collectorship." Above all there were the human symptoms. Inscriptions on Roman tombstones increasingly ended with the motto "I was not, I was, I am not, I have no more desires," suggesting a pervasive despondency at the futility of this life and despair at the absence of any life after death. As the structures of the empire deteriorated, meaning in life became harder to find—and this mood made efforts at structural revival all the more difficult.

The signs of change in the quality of political and economic life in the empire began to emerge after about 180 C.E., at which point the empire's geographical expansion had already slightly receded from its high point. The end of expansion was itself a problem, though the results would only gradually become apparent. Unlike Han China or Gupta India, the Roman Empire had depended extensively on expansion, not simply to provide prestige but to recruit the necessary slave labor force. With the empire's boundaries now pushed to the limits it could support, and with resistance emerging to further expansion on the part of tribes in northern Europe and the Parthian Empire in the Middle East, Rome almost inevitably had to restructure its labor policies on the great commercial estates and in the mines. This restructuring gradually occurred, but it involved a reduction of economic vitality and market production.

More pressing, initially, were the internal issues of politics and population. Growing political confusion, including disputes over how emperors should be appointed and controlled, produced a series of weak rulers and many battles over succession to the throne. Intervention of the army in the selection of emperors, as the army became an increasingly separate but vital institution, complicated political life and contributed to the worsening of rule from the top. The deterioration of the state, in other words, was not simply an accident in terms of personalities.

Still more important in launching the process of decline was a series of plagues that swept over the empire toward the end of the 2nd century C.E. These plagues decimated the population and severely disrupted economic life. Some authorities have argued that Rome's urban population also suffered lead poisoning from the pipes leading from the aqueducts, which further weakened people and reduced their numbers. Lower population, obviously, added to the problems of finding labor. Recruiting of troops became more difficult as the empire was increasingly reduced to hiring Germanic soldiers to guard its frontiers. The need to pay troops added to the demands on the state's budget, just as declining production cut into tax revenues and the absence of new conquests cut into other rewards for soldiers.

Here, perhaps, is the key to the process of decline: a set of general problems, triggered by a cycle of plagues that could not be prevented, resulting in a rather mechanistic spiral that steadily worsened. But there is another side to Rome's downfall, though whether as cause or as result of the initial difficulties is hard to say. Rome's upper classes became steadily more pleasure-seeking and individualistic, turning away from the political devotion and economic vigor that had characterized the republic and early empire. Cultural life decayed. Aside from some truly creative Christian writers—the fathers of Western theology—there was very little sparkle to the art or literature of the later empire. Many Roman scholars contented themselves with writing textbooks that rather mechanically summarized earlier achievements in science, mathematics, and literary style. Writing textbooks is not, of course, proof of absolute intellectual incompetence—at least not in all cases—but the point is that new knowledge or artistic styles were not being generated, and

This plaque portrays Stilicho, a Vandal by birth, who rose to be Master of Soldiers and Consul of Rome.

even the levels of previous accomplishment began to slip. The later Romans wrote textbooks about rhetoric instead of displaying rhetorical talent in actual political life, they wrote simple compendiums about animals or geometry that barely captured the essentials of what earlier intellectuals had known, and they often added superstitious beliefs that previous generations would have scorned. This cultural decline, finally, was not clearly due to disease or economic collapse, for it began in some ways before these larger problems hit. Something was happening to the Roman elite, perhaps because of the deadening hand of authoritarian political rule, perhaps because of a new commitment to luxuries and sensual indulgence. It is revealing that the upper classes were no longer willing to reproduce themselves, for bearing and raising children seemed incompatible with a pleasure-seeking life. Military service became less attractive to these groups, which again forced the recruitment of paid soldiers from groups such as the Germanic tribes along the northern borders of the empire.

Rome's fall, in other words, can be blamed on large, impersonal forces that would have been hard for any society to control, or on moral and political decay that reflected growing corruption among the society's leaders. Probably elements of both were involved. Thus, the plagues would have weakened even a vigorous society but would not necessarily have produced an irremediable downward spiral had not the morale of the ruling classes been sapped by unproductive values. Cultural stagnation and even the fall of a particular ruling group might have been survivable had the larger problems of population decline and waning prosperity prevented the ability to rebound. It is certainly noteworthy that Rome's economic disruption ran much deeper than the problems of Han China or Gupta India, causing not just temporary hardships but a real regression in the levels of production and forms of economic organization, at least in the empire's western half.

The Process of Roman Decline

Regardless of precise causes, the course of Roman decay is quite clear. As the quality of imperial rule declined, and as life became more dangerous and economic survival more precarious, many farmers clustered around the protection of large landlords, surrendering full control over their plots of land in the hope of military and judicial protection. The decentralization of political and economic authority, which was greatest in the western, or European, portions of the empire, foreshadowed the manorial system of Europe in the Middle Ages. The estate system gave great political power to the landlords and could provide some local stability. But it weakened the hold of the emperor and also tended to drive the economy away from the elaborate trade patterns of Mediterranean civilization in its heyday. Many estates attempted to produce almost everything needed on the spot. Trade and production declined further, causing tax revenues to drop and cities to shrink in size. The empire was locked in a vicious circle, in which the responses to initial deterioration merely lessened the chances of recovery.

Some later emperors tried vigorously to reverse the flow. *Diocletian,* who ruled from 284 to 305 C.E., tightened up the administration of the empire and tried to improve tax collection. Regulation of the dwindling economy increased. Diocletian also attempted to concentrate political loyalties on his own person, enhancing the pressure to worship the emperor as god. This was what prompted him to persecute Christians with particular viciousness, for they would not give Caesar preference over their God. The emperor *Constantine,* who

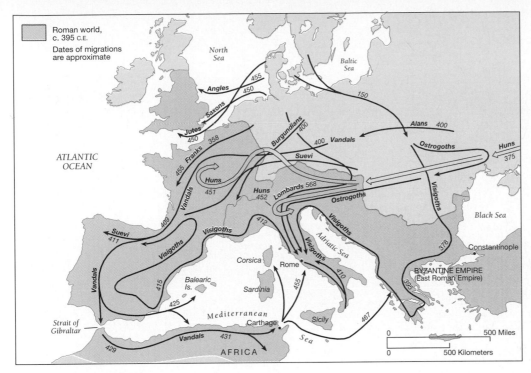

Patterns of Germanic Invasions

ruled from 312 to 337, tried other experiments. He set up a second capital city, Constantinople, to regulate the eastern half of the empire more efficiently. He tried to use the religious force of Christianity to unify the empire spiritually, extending toleration and adopting it as his own faith. These measures were not without result. The eastern empire, ruled from Constantinople (formerly the Greek colony of Byzantium, now the Turkish city of Istanbul), remained an effective political and economic unit. Christianity spread under official sponsorship, though some new problems were attached to success.

But none of these measures revived the empire as a whole. Division merely made the weakness of the western half worse. Attempts to regulate the economy reduced economic initiative and lowered production; ultimately, tax revenues declined once again. The army deteriorated further. And when the Germanic invasions began in earnest in the 400s, there was scant basis for resistance. Many peasants, burdened by the social and economic pressures of the decaying empire, actually welcomed the barbarians. A priest noted that "in all districts taken over by the Germans, there is one desire among all the Romans, that they should never again find it necessary to pass under Roman jurisdiction." German kingdoms were set up in many parts of the empire by 425, and the last Roman emperor in the West was displaced

in 476. The Germanic invaders numbered, at most, 5 percent of the population of the empire, but so great was the earlier decline that this small, uncoordinated force put an end to one of the world's great political structures.

The fall of Rome echoes some of the same questions that apply to China and India. Do civilizations inevitably fall, or at least undergo cycles of decline? When the collapse involves outside invading forces, does one look primarily at internal decay? Germanic or central Asian invaders were less civilized than the Roman, Indian, or Chinese areas they attacked. Their reliance on hunting and herding gave them some skills, including excellent horsemanship in the case of the Huns, that allowed them to easily overrun more populous peasant settlements where people were unaccustomed to battle. From their contacts on the Roman borders, the Germans had also learned new organizational methods that made them a more formidable force. But there is no question that in their glory days, the professional armies of Rome or Han China could have contained the invaders; it was internal weakness that allowed the invaders to have such disruptive effects. Rome, indeed, seemed headed for downfall even before the Germanic intruders applied the final blows. At the same time, ironically, the luxurious living of the upper classes and the

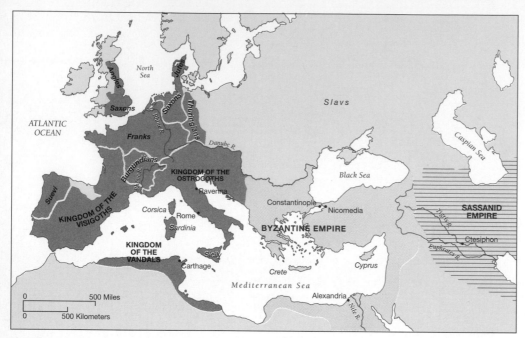

The Mediterranean, Middle East, Europe, and North Africa, c. 500 C.E.

impressive reputation of the classical empires helped lure the invaders in.

Results of the "Fall" of Rome

The collapse of Rome echoed mightily through the later history of Europe and the Middle East. Rome's fall split the unity of the Mediterranean lands that had been so arduously won through Hellenistic culture and then the Roman Empire itself. This was one sign that the end of the Roman Empire was a more serious affair than the displacement of the last classical dynasties in India and China. Greece and Rome, unlike China, had not produced the shared political culture and bureaucratic traditions that could allow revival after a period of chaos. Nor had Mediterranean civilization, for all its vitality, generated a common religion that reached deeply enough, or satisfied enough needs, to maintain unity amid political fragmentation, as in India. Such religions would reach the Mediterranean world as Rome fell, but they came too late to save the empire, and they produced a deep rift in this world, between Christian and Muslim, that has not been healed to this day. Rome's collapse, though profound, was uneven. In effect, the fall of Rome divided the Mediterranean world into three zones—the starting point of three distinct civilizations that would develop in later centuries.

In the northeastern part of the empire, centered now on Constantinople, the empire in a sense did not fall. Civilization was more deeply entrenched here than in some of the western European portions of the empire, and there were fewer pressures from invaders. Emperors continued to rule Greece and other parts of southeast Europe, plus the northern Middle East. This eastern empire—later to be known as the *Byzantine Empire*—was a product of the Hellenistic era and late imperial Rome, not a balanced result of the whole span of classical Mediterranean civilization. Thus, though its language became Greek, the eastern empire maintained the authoritarian tone of the late Roman rulers. Yet, the empire itself was vibrant, artistically creative, and active in trade. Briefly, especially under the emperor *Justinian* (who ruled from 527 to 565), the eastern emperors tried to regain the whole heritage of Rome. But Justinian was unable to maintain a hold in Italy, after some conquests at great cost, and a reconquered province of North Africa soon split away. He did issue one of the most famous compilations of Roman law in the code that bore his name. But his was the last European-based effort to restore Mediterranean unity.

Still, Rome's fall did not disrupt the northern Middle East or southeastern Europe as much as might have been expected. The *Sassanid* (Persian) *Empire*, which had replaced the Parthian Empire in 227 C.E., maintained considerable strength in the northeastern portion of the Middle East. As the Roman Empire weakened, the Sassanids joined the attack, at times pushing into parts of southeastern Europe. Ultimately, however, the Byzantine Empire managed to create a stable frontier, dividing the northern Middle East into Byzantine and Sassanid zones. This division, in turn, would last until the Persians were overwhelmed by Arab Islamic armies in the 7th century. In Byzantium, which proved able to withstand even the Arab onslaught, though with further loss of Middle Eastern territory, many of the important traditions of the later Roman Empire persisted, not only in the imperial political structure of the empire but through maintenance of many aspects of classical Greek culture, now conjoined with Christianity.

The second zone that devolved from Rome's fall was more seriously disrupted, though more in political terms than in terms of a marked economic or cultural decline. This zone consisted of North Africa and the southeastern shores of the Mediterranean. Here, several regional kingdoms briefly succeeded the empire. And while Christianity spread in the area—indeed, one of the greatest Christian theologians, Augustine, was a bishop in North Africa—it was not so uniformly triumphant as in the Byzantine Empire or western Europe. Furthermore, variant beliefs and doctrines soon split North African Christianity from the larger branches, producing most notably the Coptic church in Egypt, which still survives as a Christian minority in that country, and in Ethiopia. And soon much of North Africa would be filled with the still newer doctrines of Islam and a new Arab Empire.

Finally, there was the western part of the empire: Italy, Spain, and points north. Here is where Rome's fall not only shattered unities but reduced the level of civilization itself. Crude, regional Germanic kingdoms grew in parts of Italy, in France, and elsewhere. The only clearly vital force in this region emanated not from Roman traditions but from the spread of Christianity. Even Christianity could not sustain a sophisticated literature or art or even theology, however. In the mire of Rome's collapse, this part of the world forgot for several centuries what it had previously known.

In this western domain, what we call the fall of Rome was scarcely noted at the time, for decay had been progressing for so many decades that the failure to name a new emperor meant little. There was some comprehension of loss, some realization that the present could not rival the past. Thus, Christian scholars were soon apologizing for their inability to write well or to under-

stand some of the sophisticated doctrines of such earlier theologians as Augustine. This sense of inferiority to classical achievements would long mark the culture of this western zone—even as times got better.

ANALYSIS

The Problem of Decline and Fall

Explaining the decline of civilizations has fascinated observers since civilizations began to decline. As Rome's vitality ebbed, many writers tried to figure out what was going on. Christian theologians, like Augustine, wrote massive tomes to prove that Christianity was not to blame, for some non-Christian philosophers had argued that the religion's otherworldly emphasis and primary loyalty to the church had sapped Rome's strength. Both Christian and pagan writers worried that the cause of Rome's collapse was immorality, a loss of the virtues of self-denial and devotion to the common good that had made Rome great in the first place.

Many of these arguments have been taken up by world historians in more recent times. In the 18th century, Edward Gibbon, a British philosopher-historian who was hostile to religion, returned to the attack on Christianity, holding that it contradicted key Roman qualities of military valor and civic devotion and so brought the empire's fall. Several 20th-century historians have preferred to examine Rome's moral decline—the growing self-indulgence and pleasure-seeking of the aristocracy and the urban masses—that led them to accept forms of government in which they no longer participated, caused them to turn away from a willingness to serve in the army, and removed them from concern about the common good. This argument is interesting because it corresponds to some undeniable changes in the culture of the later Roman Empire. It also has won attention because of anxieties contemporary Westerners have about their own society—too materialistic, too much drawn to sexual indulgence, too much dominated by the tastes of the masses. Analogy—that is, real or imagined similarities between situations so that a historical phenomenon is seen to correspond to a current one, and vice versa—plays a big role in the concern about moral decline.

Both the religious and the moral decline arguments point to factors that in principle might have been addressed before the Roman Empire fell. A society deteriorating morally might pull itself together, accept a sterner set of virtues, and recover its earlier vigor. Those who point to analogies between Roman decay and Western self-indulgence, may, of course, hope that Westerners might regain their earlier self-control and reverse their presumed decline.

Another approach to the problem of decline, however, argues that it is almost inevitable. Civilizations, like individual humans, go through a period of vigor and reach the mature height of their powers, but then inevitably begin to lose their grip and deteriorate. At the civilization level, this means that governments become stultified, and their officials are bent on protecting their position rather than seeking new ways to do things; that aristocracies, once bent on military glory and willing to endure hardships in its quest, become soft and leave the fighting to others; that territories expand farther than a society can really control, leaving supply routes and armaments overextended and vulnerable to attack. An American diplomatic historian has recently argued that this last process of overextension, which reduces internal economic vitality through its sheer costliness, occurred not only in Rome but in 19th-century Britain and now the United States and Russia.

World history certainly lends itself to a search for patterns in the life cycles of civilizations. But it also generates some warnings. Civilizational decline does not occur in the same ways in all cases. It does seem true that many civilizations go through periods of confusion, when leadership worsens and new troubles ensue. The result, however, is not necessarily the death of a civilization but rather a period of regrouping, after which the civilization may reemerge with new combinations of tradition and innovation. Rome's fall, after all, was unusual at the end of the classical era and really occurred only in the western portion of the empire. Eastern Rome remained highly civilized and successful. China and India, though not unchanged by the decline of the great classical empires, did not suffer a full loss of achievement and certainly did not perish as civilizations. So the question of decline needs to be phrased carefully, with awareness of the diverse examples world history yields.

Some special features of the western Roman Empire may have made it an exceptional case. The advent of new epidemic diseases, producing population loss and economic decline, may have underlain the peculiar experience of the western Roman Empire. Certainly, relatively sparse populations left the Roman Empire far more vulnerable than China, India, or even the eastern Mediterranean to the disruptive effects of relatively small numbers of outside invaders. Dense populations, undiminished by new epidemics, help explain the resiliency of Chinese and Indian cultures, which could be disrupted but not destroyed by outside attack.

Many people seek laws in history. Perhaps there are some laws, or at least high probabilities, making it likely that civilizations will experience some normal growing phases, which will produce serious weaknesses in the course of time. But world history also complicates many of the attempts that have been made to find laws, because so much depends on the characteristics of each particular society. Predictable patterns, such as inevitable rises and falls, are hard to find. Western historians, long mesmerized by the undeniable collapse of Rome and perhaps uncomfortable with some of the changes they see in their own society, may sometimes have generalized too widely from a single case.

Questions: How great a role did moral decline play in the collapse of the classical empires? What historical "laws" accurately describe what happened not only in Rome but in Gupta India and Han China? Why can it be argued that the eastern part of the Roman Empire did not decline?

THE DEVELOPMENT AND SPREAD OF WORLD RELIGIONS

Focal Point: The decline of the classical empires contributed several ingredients to the spread of what turned out to be the great world religions. Buddhism and Christianity, soon to be joined by Islam, became the first and only world religions, spreading well beyond the boundaries of a single region. Even religions still essentially regional, such as Daoism in China and Hinduism in India, won new levels of active popular adherence. Just as the 5th century B.C.E. saw the clustering of the origins of major philosophical systems for the educated elites in China and the Mediterranean, so the period 200 to 700 C.E. saw the grouping of fundamental changes in religious alignments.

Christianity and Buddhism Compared

As during the period of chaos in China, Rome's decline brought vital new religious influences to societies around the Mediterranean. Christianity moved westward from its original center in the Middle East, just as in

CLOSEUP

Pope Leo I

Leo I (d. 461) was the most important pope of the early Christian church; he served from 440 to 461. His pontificate established the supremacy of the papacy in the West. Leo was born a Roman aristocrat, and his early work focused on France, where he had close ties to monastic leaders. As pope, Leo faced the rapid collapse of the Roman Empire. He had to negotiate personally with a Germanic leader to save Rome from complete destruction. Backed by the Roman emperor, Leo successfully asserted his authority over church leaders in Gaul (France) and elsewhere. He also fought for doctoral orthodoxy against a variety of heresies while engaging an ongoing rivalry with the patriarch of Alexandria for spiritual primacy in Christianity as a whole. Eager to centralize the Western church, Leo wrote widely on standardizing liturgy and prayer.

Asia, Buddhism was spreading east from India. Though initially less significant then Buddhism in terms of numbers of converts, Christianity would ultimately prove to be one of the two largest world faiths. It would play a direct role in the formation of two postclassical civilizations: those of eastern and western Europe.

Christianity resembled Buddhism in important ways. It could stress the unimportance of things of this world, urging the centrality of people's spiritual destiny and the focus on divinity. Not surprisingly, Christianity, like Buddhism, produced an important monastic movement, in which individuals seeking holiness came together in groups to live a spiritual life and serve their religion through their search for sanctity. Christianity resembled the version of Buddhism that spread to China (and later Korea and Japan) by stressing the possibility of an afterlife and the role that holy leaders could play in helping to attain it.

The Chinese version of Buddhism, called *Mahayana*, or the Greater Vehicle, placed considerable emphasis on Buddha as god or savior. Statues of the Buddha as god violated the earlier Buddhist hostility to religious images, but they served to emphasize the religion as a channel of salvation. Well-organized temples, with priests and rituals, also helped bring religious solace to ordinary people in East Asia. The idea developed also that Buddhist holy men, or *bodhisattvas,* built up such spiritual merit that their prayers, even after death, could aid people and allow them to achieve some reflected holiness. Christianity in many respects moved in similar directions. It too came to emphasize salvation, with well-organized rituals designed to promote its achievement. Religious images, though contrary to Jewish beliefs against idol-worship, helped focus popular belief in most versions of Christianity. Holy men and women, sometimes granted the title *saint* after their death, were revered not only as models but also because their spiritual attainments could lend merit to the strivings of more ordinary folk. The broad similarities between Christianity and the evolving Buddhism of East Asia remind us of the common processes apparently at work as new religions spread amid the ruins of great empires.

Yet, Christianity had a flavor of its own. More than any of the forms of Buddhism, it came to place great emphasis on church organization and structure, copying the example of the Roman Empire. It also placed greater value on missionary activity and widespread conversions, believing that error must be actively combated in God's name. More perhaps than any other major religion— certainly more than the contemplative and tolerant Buddhism—Christianity stressed its possession of exclusive truth and its intolerance of competing beliefs. Such fierce confidence was not the least of the reasons for the new religion's success. The common dynamic and chronology shared by Christianity and spreading Buddhism suggest a similar process at work, as ordinary people sought a well-organized spiritual outlet that was different from traditional animism and was more focused on otherworldly salvation. Christianity must also be understood, however, in the particular context of earlier Mediterranean religious traditions and the declining Roman Empire. Its emphasis on doctrines and exclusive loyalty differentiated it from the more tranquil religions of eastern and southern Asia—India as well as China— where a larger variety of beliefs and practices could be combined with Buddhism or Hinduism.

Christianity began, as was discussed in Chapter 8, as part of a Jewish reform movement. Initially, there seems to have been no intent to found a new religion. After Jesus' crucifixion, the disciples expected his imminent return and with it the end of the world. Only gradually, when the Second Coming did not transpire, did the disciples begin to fan out and, through preaching, pick up growing numbers of supporters in various parts of the Roman Empire.

The message of Jesus and his disciples seemed clear: There was a single God, who loved humankind despite earthly sin. A virtuous life should be dedicated to the worship of God and fellowship with other believers; worldly concerns were secondary, and a life of poverty might be most conducive to holiness. God sent Jesus, called "Christ," from the Greek word *Christos* for "God's anointed," to preach his holy word and through his sacrifice to prepare for the possibility of wider attainment of an afterlife of heavenly communion with God. Belief, good works, and discipline of fleshly concerns would lead toward heaven; rituals, such as commemorating Christ's Last Supper with wine and bread, would promote the same goal.

This message spread at an opportune time. The official religion of the Greeks and Romans had long seemed rather sterile, particularly to many of the poor. The Christian emphasis on the beauty of poverty and the spiritual equality of all people, plus the fervor of the early Christians and the satisfying rituals they provided, gained growing attention. The wide reach of the Roman Empire made it relatively easy for Christian missionaries to travel extensively in Europe and the Middle East and spread the new word. Then, when conditions began to deteriorate in the empire, the solace of this otherworldly religion won even wider response.

The adjustments effected by early Christian leaders maximized their conversions. Under the guidance of Paul, Christians began to see themselves as part of a new religion rather than a Jewish reform movement, and they welcomed non-Jewish converts. Paul also encouraged more formal organization in the new church, with local groups selecting elders to govern them; soon, a single leader, or bishop, was appointed for each major city. This structure paralleled the provincial government of the empire. Finally, Christian doctrine became increasingly well organized as the writings of several disciples and others were collected into what became the New Testament of the Christian Bible.

Christianity Gains Ground

During the first three centuries after Christ, the new religion competed with several Eastern mystery religions. It also faced, as we have seen, periodic persecution from the normally tolerant imperial government. Even so, by the time Constantine converted to the religion and accepted it as a legitimate faith, Christianity had won perhaps 10 percent of the empire's population. One convert was Constantine's mother, who visited the Holy Land and founded many churches there. Constantine's tolerant favor brought some new troubles to Christianity, particularly some interference by the state in matters of doctrine. But it became much easier to spread Christianity with official backing. Christian writers began to claim that both church and empire were works of God. At the same time, continued deterioration of the empire added to the motives to join this amazingly successful new church. In the eastern Mediterranean, where imperial rule remained strong, state control of the church became a way of life. But in the west, where conditions were far more chaotic, bishops had a freer hand. A centralized church organization under the leadership of the bishop of Rome, called *pope* from the Latin word *papa*, or father, gave the Western church unusual strength and independence.

By the time Rome collapsed, Christianity had thus demonstrated immense spiritual power and possessed a solid organization, though one that differed from East to West. The new church faced several controversies over doctrine but managed to promote certain standard beliefs as against several heresies. A key tenet involved a complex doctrine of the Trinity, which held that the one God had three persons, the Father, the Son (Christ), and the Holy Ghost. In 325 C.E., the church *Council of Nicaea,* under imperial sponsorship, met to debate a doctrine known as Arianism, which argued that Christ was divine but not of the same nature as God the Father. Ruling against Arianism, the resultant Nicene Creed insisted on the shared Godhead of all three parts of the Trinity. An important if complex decision in itself, the council also showed how important unified doctrine was to Christianity, in contrast to the greater toleration of diversity in Hinduism and Buddhism. Experience in fighting the heresies promoted the Christian interest in defending a single belief and strengthened its intolerance for any competing doctrine or faith.

Early Christianity also produced an important formal theology through formative writers such as *Augustine*. This theology incorporated many elements of classical philosophy with the Christian belief and helped the church gain respectability among intellectuals. Theologians like Augustine grappled with such problems as freedom of the will: If God is all-powerful, can mere human beings have free will? And if not, how can human beings be justly punished for sin? By working out these issues in elaborate doctrine, the early theologians, or church fathers, provided an important role for formal, rational thought in a religion that continued to emphasize the primary importance of faith.

Like all successful religions, Christianity combined several appeals. It offered blind devotion to an all-powerful God. One church father, denying the validity of human thought, simply stated, "I believe because it is absurd." But Christianity also developed its own complex and fascinating intellectual system for those so inclined. Mystical holy men and women flourished under Christian banners, particularly in the Middle East. In the West, soon after the empire's collapse, this impulse was partially disciplined through the institution of monasticism, which gained ground in Italy under *Benedict of Nursia* early in the 6th century. Benedict started a monastery to demonstrate the true holy life to Italian peasants in a region still (to Benedict's horror) practicing the worship of the sun-god Apollo. The Benedictine rule, which soon spread to many other monasteries and convents, urged a disciplined life with prayer and spiritual development alternating with hard work in agriculture and in study. Monastic movements also developed in the eastern empire, in Greece and Turkey, and also in Egypt. Eastern monasticism was organized by St. Basil in the 4th century.

Thus, Christianity attempted to encourage but also to discipline intense piety and to avoid a complete gulf between the lives of saintly men and women and the spiritual concerns of ordinary people. Christianity's success and organizational strength obviously appealed to political leaders. But the new religion never became the creature of the upper classes alone, as its popular message of ritual and salvation continued to draw the poor. Rather like Hinduism in India, Christianity provided some religious unity among different social groups. It even held special interest for women. Christianity did not create equality among men and women, but it did preach the equal importance of women's and men's souls, and it encouraged men and women to worship together, unlike many other faiths.

Christianity promoted a new culture among those who were won to its banners. The rituals, the otherworldly emphasis, the interest in spiritual equality—these were far different from the central themes of classical Mediterranean civilization. Christianity modified classical beliefs in the central importance of the state and political loyalties. Though Christians accepted the state, they did not put it first. Christianity also worked against other classical institutions, such as slavery, in the name of brotherhood (though later Christians would accept slavery in other contexts). Particularly through the values

The conversion of kings, such as Clovis, king of the Franks, helped inspire wider conversions and gave churchmen some symbolic power over the state.

promoted by Western monasticism, Christianity may have fostered a greater respectability for disciplined work than had been current in the aristocratic ethic of Mediterranean civilization.

Certainly, Christianity sought some changes in classical culture, including greater emphasis on sexual restraint, beyond its central religious message. But Christianity preserved important classical values in addition to the interest in solid organization and some of the themes of classical philosophy. Church buildings in western Europe retained Roman architectural styles, though often with greater simplicity if only because of the poverty of the later empire and subsequent Germanic states. Latin remained the language of the church in the West, Greek the language of most Christians in the eastern Mediterranean. Monasticism played an immensely valuable role in preserving classical as well as Christian learning through the patient librarianship of the monks.

The Emerging Religious Map

When the Roman Empire fell, Christian history was still in its infancy. The Western church would soon spread its missionary zeal to northern Europe, and the Eastern church would reach into the Slavic lands of the Balkans and Russia. But Christianity was already established as a significant world religion—one of the few ever generated. A world religion is defined by unusual durability and drawing power and by a complexity that can win adherence from many different kinds of people. Major world religions, such as Christianity and Buddhism, show some ability to cut across different cultures and to win converts in a wide geographical area amid considerable diversity.

One final world religion remained to enter the lists. Islam, launched in 610 C.E., would initially surpass Christianity in geographical extent and has remained Christianity's most tenacious rival. With Islam added, the roster of world religions was essentially complete. Changes would follow, but no totally new religion of major significance arose—unless one counts some of the secular faiths, such as communism, that have appeared in the past century. The centuries after the rise of Christianity, the spread of Buddhism, and the inception of Islam would see the conversion of most of the civilized world to one or another of the great faiths, producing a religious map that in Europe, Asia, and even parts of Africa would not alter greatly until our own time.

Table 11–1
Religions and Their Distribution in the World Today

Religion	Distribution*
Christianity	1.9 billion
Roman Catholic	(1 billion)
Protestant	(458 million)
Eastern Orthodox	(173 million)
Other	(195 million)
Islam	1 billion
Hinduism	751 million
Buddhism	334 million
Shintoism	3 million
Daoism	31 million
Judaism	18 million

*Figures for several religions have been reduced over the past 50 years by the impact of communism in Eastern Europe and parts of Asia.

The spread of major religions—Hinduism in India, Buddhism in East and Southeast Asia, a more popular Daoism in China, Christianity in Europe and parts of the Mediterranean world, and ultimately Islam—was a vital result of the changes in the classical civilizations brought on by attack and decay. Common difficulties, including invading forces that pressed out from central Asia and contagious epidemics that knew no boundaries, help explain parallel changes in separate civilizations. Contacts among the societies through trade and travel also provided common bonds. Chinese travelers learned of Buddhism through trading expeditions to India. Trade and diffusion of artistic styles linked the Mediterranean world to the Middle East and India.

There was a world framework, in other words, that affected the separate currents of the major civilizations. The new religions brought to each of the major civilizations and other parts of the world a greater interest in speculation about spiritual matters and a greater tendency to focus on a single basic divinity instead of a multitude of gods.

Obviously, some regions were still exempt: the great religions had yet to touch the Americas or parts of Africa and central Asia, and they spread only gradually northward in Europe. Obviously also, each religion had its own flavor; the idea of common process must not be exaggerated. And even where the new religions spread, they often merged with important polytheistic elements. Thus, Islam long would leave rural beliefs intact, concentrating on urban religious practice; Christianity often compromised with beliefs in magic and in the ritual properties of natural objects, such as mistletoe or the bones of saints.

Nevertheless, the spread of the great religions subjected many people in many different societies to a tendency to shift their beliefs away from age-old adherence to the idea of a host of divine spirits in nature to concentration on a powerful, single divine force and often the spirituality attendant on new hopes for an afterlife. Not only Hindu civilization, but also Christianity and Islam, provided shared beliefs that could transcend divided, bickering political units. The great religions could facilitate international trade, for they did not depend on local customs but on an ever-present God as organizer of all nature or at least a coherent divine order; successful trade could, in turn, help spread the new religions.

CONCLUSION

In the Wake of Decline and Fall

By 600 C.E., the major civilizations looked much different from the classical world at its height, and many of the differences would never be erased. The results of classical decline showed, obviously, in the new belief patterns, in the opportunities created for an amazing set of shifts in religious allegiance. They showed also in important revisions of the civilization map and in some related shifts in characteristic political styles.

The first geographical change resulted from the differential effects of classical decline: Some areas, as we have seen, altered far more than others. China proved unique in its ability to recapture so many classical ingredients. China and India shared, in contrast to the Mediterranean, an ability to maintain substantial cultural cohesion, based on widespread beliefs as well as—in China's case—restored politics. Traditional continuities would as a result play a more obvious role in eastern and southern Asia than in western Asia and Europe, though this fact resulted in part from the greater cultural homogenization achieved even earlier. Today, Indian and Chinese civilizations remain located in essentially the same places where they had taken root by late classical times, and at least until quite recently, they still abundantly reflected the classical heritage: India in the caste system and an otherworldly cultural tone, China in Confucian beliefs and a fascination with a strong, bureaucratic state.

The case was quite different in the Mediterranean zone. The Roman Empire split asunder without repair, in part because it had not been able to spread shared beliefs very widely. China and India developed an ability to change without deep disruption, whereas the diverse heirs of Rome would often oscillate between innovative dynamism and sheer confusion. Classical Mediterranean civilization left a very real heritage, but in part because geographical unity was lost, this heritage was used by successor civilizations, far more selectively, with considerably more new and diverse ingredients than was true in eastern or southern Asia.

The geographical changes resulting from classical decline also promoted outreach to new areas. Powerful civilization centers, once they recovered from internal confusion and invasion, tended to reach out for new areas of influence. Given the larger changes in the geography of civilizations, this often prompted them to look to areas not previously involved in the civilizational orbit. Thus, China, once it rebounded from the centuries of chaos, extended new levels of influence to Vietnam, Korea, and even Japan. Also, regional states in southern India, already molded in a seagoing tradition and unable to expand northward because of the confusion in the upper part of the subcontinent, briefly increased their activities in Southeast Asia.

The division of the Mediterranean world prompted still more general effects of diffusion. The Byzantine Empire, regarding itself as Rome's heir but blocked from recovering Rome's territory (particularly because of the powerful Arab presence in most of the eastern Mediterranean and north Africa), pushed its influence northward into the vast Slavic lands. The Arab Empire, less interested or less able than Rome to press into Europe beyond Spain and southern Italy, turned not only to some attacks on India and incursions into central Asia but also to a wider array of contacts with Africa below the Sahara than Rome had ever developed. Finally, the clearest organizational heir to Rome in the West, the Catholic church, unable because of Byzantine and Arab power to control most previous imperial territory religiously, itself turned northward, sending missions that brought civilization to the fierce peoples of northwestern Europe.

These extensions of civilization resulted directly from the tensions produced by the remaking of the classical map and from new forces such as the great missionary religions.

The centuries of transition at the end of the classical age must thus be seen not simply in terms of decline and confusion, though this element was definitely present, but in terms of a considerable reshuffling of peoples, boundaries, and beliefs that would soon give rise to a new period in world history. Elements of the classical era were irretrievably lost, particularly Mediterranean unity and, in western Europe and in India, the ability to form durable empires. In a few cases—again, most notably in western Europe—the levels of economic and cultural activity deteriorated for several centuries. Elsewhere, however, key features of civilization proved extremely resilient, even as new beliefs or boundaries were added to the mix. The ability to extend civilization's range to new regions was one sign of this ongoing vitality. Redefinition and realignment formed the key challenge for most of the civilized world in the new period beginning to take shape by the 6th century.

FURTHER READINGS

The fall of the Roman Empire has generated rich and interesting debate. For recent interpretations and discussion of earlier views, see A. H. M. Jones's *The Decline of the Ancient World* (1966), J. Vogt's *The Decline of Rome* (1965), and F. W. Walbank's *The Awful Revolution— The Decline of the Roman Empire in the West* (1960).

On India and China in decline, worthwhile sources include R. Thaper's *History of India*, vol. I (1966), R. C. Majumdar, ed., *The Classical Age* (1966); Raymond Dawson's *Imperial China* (1972), and J. A. Harrison's *The Chinese Empire* (1972). See also Twitchett and Fairbanks, eds., *The Cambridge History of China*, vol. 3, part I (1979).

On the role of disease in imperial decline, W. McNeill's *Plagues and Peoples* (1977) is provocative and useful.

For the rise and spread of new religions, a good introduction is Geoffrey Parinder, ed., *World Religions* (1971); see also Lewis M. Hopke's *Religions of the World* (1983) and Jamail Ragi al Farugi, ed., *Historical Atlas of the Religions of the World* (1974). On Hinduism, see N. C. Chandhuri's *Hinduism, A Religion to Live By* (1979); see also C. Eliot's *Hinduism and Buddhism* (1954). Two good studies of Buddhism are C. Humphreys's *Buddhism* (1962) and A. F. Wright's *Buddhism in Chinese History* (1959). Christianity's spread is the subject of S. Renko's *Pagan Rome and the Early Christians* (1986) and M. Hengel's *Acts and the History of Earliest Christianity* (1986). Important special topics are covered in J. Bowker's *Problems of Suffering in Religions of the World* (1975), a fascinating comparative effort; A. Sharma, ed., *Women in World Religions* (1987); and on Christianity, B. Witherington's *Women in the Earliest Churches* (1988).

PART

III

THE POSTCLASSICAL ERA

527–565 Justinian, Eastern Roman (Byzantine) emperor

610–613 Origins of Islam

570–632 Muhammad

634–750 Arab invasions in Middle East; spread of Islam in North Africa

589–618 Sui dynasty (China)

668 Korea becomes independent from China

618–907 Tang dynasty

711 First Islamic attack in India

661–750 Ummayad Caliphate

777 Independent Islamic kingdoms begin in North Africa

718 Byzantines defeat Arab attack on Constantinople

750 Abbasid caliphate

c. 855 Russian kingdom around Kiev

960–1127 Song dynasty (China)

864 Cyril and Methodius missionaries in eastern Europe

878 Last Japanese embassy to China

800–814 Charlemagne's Empire in western Europe

980–1015 Conversion of Vladimir I of Russia

968 Tula established by Toltecs (Mesoamerica)

1000 Ghana Empire at its height (Africa)

1055 Seljuk Turks control Abbasid caliphate

1054 Schism between Eastern and Western Christianity

500 C.E.   **700** C.E.   **900** C.E.

THE CHRONOLOGY OF THE POSTCLASSICAL PERIOD

The next ten chapters concentrate primarily on the time period that runs from the 5th to the 15th century C.E., or from about 450 to about 1450. Most of the individual chapters deal with specific civilizations, for there were many changes occurring in old civilization centers (in the aftermath of the decline of the great classical empires) and in newer ones. Before we turn to individual cases, however, it is vital to get a sense of some overall patterns in this thousand-year period, for many developments cut across single civilization boundaries. The postclassical period witnessed the emergence of an international framework, so that instead of the parallelisms and tentative contacts between individual civilizations that described the classical period, a genuine world-historical dynamic was taking shape.

The tension between the proliferation of new civilization areas and the network of world contacts is a vital characteristic of the postclassical period, and we will come back to it. Instead of a single, if diverse, Mediterranean civilization, for example, the Mediterranean world split into three segments: the Middle East and North Africa, eastern Europe and what is now Turkey, and western Europe. Yet, all three of these now distinct areas were linked through economic, cultural, and sometimes military contacts, and not only with each other but with other parts of Asia and Africa.

Focal Point: As with the classical period, there are two ways to define the postclassical age: first, in terms of what events opened and closed it, and second, in terms of coherent trends that lay between the overture and the finale.

The stage for the postclassical era was set by the same developments that ended its predecessor: the collapse of the Roman Empire and thus the end of Mediterranean unity, and the decline of classical empires in Asia. The 5th century saw most of these developments draw together, though India's full transition with the fall of the Guptas occurred slightly later, and China's period of chaos occurred a bit earlier. Capped by invasions of nomadic peoples, the classical decline produced huge changes in the map of the world's civilizations.

The end of the postclassical era was heralded by another set of invasions from central Asia, even more powerful than the surge of the Huns that had helped close the classical period. During the 13th and 14th centuries, Mongol invaders poured through much of Asia and eastern Europe, ending or altering a host of specific governments and also encouraging new kinds of exchanges across civilization borders, thanks to the vast if brief unity the Mongols produced in much of the civilized

1150–1350 Spread of Gothic style; scholasticism in western Europe

1066 Norman conquest of England; rise of feudal monarchy in western Europe

1231–1392 Mongols rule Korea

1258 Capture of Baghdad by Mongols; end of Abbasid caliphate

1150 Disintegration of Toltec Empire

1236 Capture of Russia by Mongols

1200 Rise of empire of Mali

c. 1100 Invention of explosive powder (China)

1260 Death of Sundiata

1206 Delhi sultanate in India

1096–1099 First Christian Crusade to Palestine

1185–1333 Kamakura Shogunate (Japan)

1265 First English parliament

1100 C.E.

1392–1910 Yi dynasty (Korea)

1320–1340 Bubonic plague breaks out in Gobi desert and spreads to other parts of Asia

1453 Turks capture Constantinople; end of Byzantine Empire

1405–1433 Chinese trading expeditions

1400 End of Polynesian expeditions

1279–1368 Mongol Empire in China

1439 Portugal acquires Azores

1325 Rise of Aztec Empire

1290s Islam begins to spread to Southeast Asia

1350 Rise of Incas (Andes)

1471–1493 Peak of Inca Empire

1338–1453 Hundred Years' War in Europe

1320s Europeans first use cannon in war

1300 C.E.

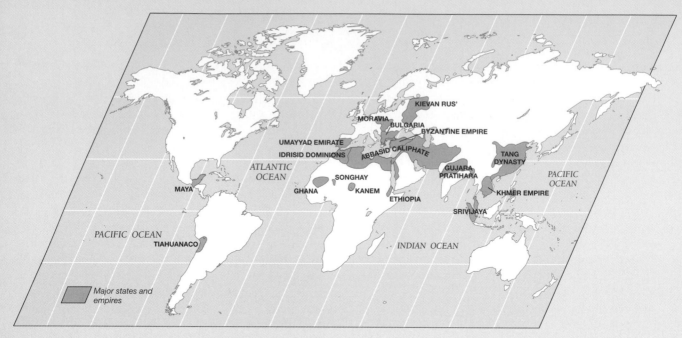

The Postclassical World Takes Shape, c. 900 C.E.

world. By 1400, much of Asia was beginning to recover from the Mongol onslaught, but a series of new empires and expansions was taking shape, including the beginning of the West's explorations into the wider world. These developments spanned about two centuries, from the early 13th to the mid-15th century; as before, the end of a world history period was not an overnight affair. The postclassical period closes, then, with Mongol invasions and subsequent realignments. The realignments included the collapse of two key political units in the Middle East—the Arab caliphate and the Byzantine Empire—as well as the advent of a new empire under the Ottoman Turks, new stirrings in Russia, and the first phases of the West's explosion into the mainstream of world history. By about 1450, the emergence of new empires and the beginnings of Europe's global expansion provide clear evidence of a shift to another phase of world development.

THE POSTCLASSICAL MILLENNIUM AND THE WORLD NETWORK

Four overarching developments define the postclassical centuries as they were shaping key trends amid the individual societies. The expanding influence of the Arabs and Islam, within their Middle Eastern base and well beyond, is one basic feature. The sheer spread of civiliza-

tion to additional regions of the world is another. A widespread trend toward a shift in basic belief systems, from polytheism to one of several great world religions, is a third. Finally, the development of a world network, consisting of increasingly regular and influential relations among many of the individual civilizations, constitutes the fourth general theme.

The Rise of Islam

Soon after the period began, a "leading civilization" emerged in terms of its expansionist capacity and ability to influence other civilizations. Islamic civilization, initially spread by the Arabs, spearheaded the creation of a new empire in the Middle East and North Africa as well as important political initiatives in India, southern Europe, and central Asia. Its missionary outreach brought conversions to Islam over other parts of Africa and Asia. Arab commerce spread through the Indian Ocean to the western Pacific, down the east coast of Africa, and across the Sahara desert. In the classical period, the three major civilization areas had been roughly balanced in dynamism, though India's outreach was particularly impressive. The postclassical era reshuffled the balance of power and created a definite world leader. Correspondingly, the decline of the Islamic imperial system was one of the key features leading to the end of this period and the emergence of a new era in world history.

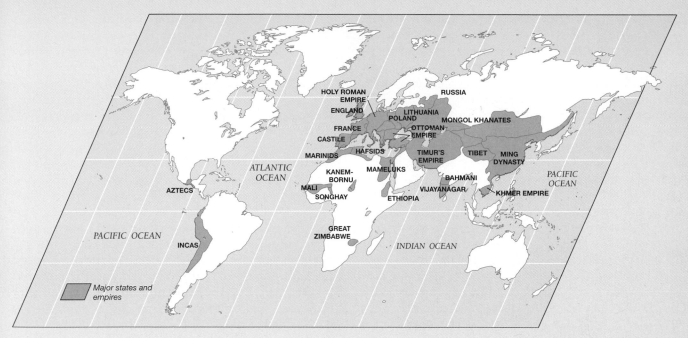

The Postclassical World in Transition, c. 1400 C.E.

The Expansion of Civilization

In the postclassical era, civilization began to spread geographically, covering many parts of the world not previously embraced by this system of social organization. These were the centuries, for example, when the structures of civilization, including great regional trading kingdoms, spread across sub-Saharan Africa, in contrast to the previous concentration in a few centers such as the Upper Nile River basin. Civilization also spread widely in northern Europe, both east and west, and became more fully established in Japan. The zones of civilization expanded in the Americas, while Polynesian culture in the Pacific fanned out to include important new areas. The "civilization map" of the world was much larger in 1450 than it had been a thousand years before. At least eight diverse areas command attention during the postclassical era: the Middle East and North Africa; India; China and East Asia; eastern Europe; western Europe; sub-Saharan Africa; Southeast Asia (where various influences from other civilizations intermingled); and the Americas.

The World Religions

The postclassical era was also defined by the spread of major religions across much of Asia, Europe, and Africa. While this process had already begun in the later phases of the classical era, it defined the new period far more clearly. While Hinduism took fuller shape as the majority religion in India and a few pockets in Southeast Asia, Buddhism spread to China and other parts of central and East Asia, including Japan, and also to much of Southeast Asia. Islam ran across the Middle East and North Africa and became an important minority religion in India, western China, and parts of sub-Saharan Africa. It also began to make inroads in Southeast Asia toward the end of the period. Finally, Christianity spread northward in Europe, both east and west. The major world religions differed widely in many respects, but they did bring a new focus on issues of spirituality and an afterlife, and a new concentration on an overarching divine force. Relatedly, they shared an ability to extend beyond local cultures and win the adherence of diverse peoples to a core of beliefs and rituals. The world religions competed, with increasing success although amid many compromises, with previous traditions of popular belief, particularly animism and, in many areas, polytheism.

The postclassical era, in other words, saw widespread and quite fundamental shifts in religious belief and practices that encompassed elites and ordinary people alike. In many cases, this huge change brought new institutions to the fore, such as the leading Christian churches, Buddhist monasteries, and the religious and legal experts of Islam. People began to move away from a belief in a multiplicity of nature spirits or gods, activating various forces of nature, and toward a greater concentration on an overriding divinity or single supernatural force. This involved more abstraction, in that the universe now came to be envisaged as part of a large divine plan. Various devices were used to modify this abstraction, thus making it more accessible to the ordinary populace. Some religions stressed intermediaries between humanity and divinity, including the powers of holy people and a few continued beliefs in magical forces.

Why did so many people in different areas change their basic beliefs? Pressed by political confusion after the fall of the classical empires, many people looked for new religious meaning. Other people were converted to one of the new religions by the persuasion of missionaries—the greatest world religions (Islam, Christianity, and Buddhism) were active missionary faiths—and by the powerful example of political and commercial splendor in the seats of the new religious authority. Thus, Russia moved toward Christianity in part because of its leaders' awe of the civilized power of the Byzantine Empire and in part because of missionary preachments, while Islam won converts through a combination of missionary zeal and the political and commercial strength of the Arab Empire. A growth in international trade also encouraged religious change, for local gods made less sense to people who exchanged goods with diverse and distant areas. The result was no agreement on belief—several of the new religions competed fiercely, with mutual detestation—but a vital underlying pattern nonetheless.

The World Network

The fourth major characteristic of the postclassical period, emerging with great force by about 1000 C.E., was ultimately the most important of all. An increasing level of interchange developed among the major civilizations of Asia, Europe, and parts of Africa. International trade grew, particularly thanks to the surge of Arab commerce but also as a result of continued activity by Indian merchants, Chinese exchanges with other parts of eastern and Southeast Asia, the development of new north–south trading connections in both eastern and western Europe, and the rise of African merchant routes along the eastern coast and overland through the Sahara. With growing trade and periodic military encounters as civilizations new and old redefined their boundaries, other kinds of exchanges occurred across civilizations. Technology spread. Thus, the knowledge of paper, developed earlier in China, was gained by Muslim troops fighting on China's western border in the 9th century. Paper production in the Middle East resulted, and as western Europeans gained new links with this region through trade and religious wars, they learned of the new product as well. The first European paper manufacture was set up in Italy in the 13th century. Technological dissemination of this sort was hardly speedy, but it did occur at a more rapid pace than previous innovations had.

Cultural exchange was another vital source of contact. Religious ideas spread from India to China and thence to Japan, Korea, and Indochina; they spread from the Middle East to Africa and many parts of Asia. This was part of the great missionary wave. Other kinds of ideas spread as well. Arabs gained knowledge of Indian mathematics, including the number system; later in the period, western Europeans began to learn Arab mathematics, including the same number system, and they elaborated their philosophy by using and reacting to Arab thought.

In contrast to the very limited international trade of the classical period, wealthy Westerners in 1300 bought silks and other goods from Asia in large quantities. They also could identify key agents of international trade, notably Arab merchants. Further, Western leaders were beginning to wish they could control the source of the trade, which they would soon be able to do thanks to improved mapmaking pioneered by the Arabs, navigational techniques devised by the Chinese and transmitted via the Arabs, and shipbuilding and artillery innovations developed in the West itself. The world network steadily intensified. World trade continued to involve luxury products, for the most part, but the volume was higher, the geographical range was more extensive, and the impact on the economies of many civilizations was greater.

Civilizations still defined key differences in institutions and values; new contacts did not destroy separate cultures and political institutions. Most people were still far removed from any direct involvement with international trade. Increasingly, however, many civilizations operated in a genuinely international framework in which the world network of commercial, technological, and cultural exchanges had real influence.

One qualification: The world network was a phenomenon of the Old World, extending an active framework of exchange among the various societies of Asia; northern, central, and eastern Africa; and Europe. It was not yet literally international, as the Americas, Polynesia, Australia, and several other regions were entirely excluded.

The postclassical era was not a time of fundamental technological innovation, though important advances occurred, particularly in China and at the end of the period in the West. Existing technical knowledge spread more widely. The postclassical era witnessed a great variety of political forms but no dominant political definition. Empire declined as a common political form, partly because religious ties became more important in holding civilizations together. Yet, the period was clearly defined by dramatic new religious cultures, a new civilization map, and an active if still rudimentary world network.

INTERACTION AND FRAGMENTATION IN THE POSTCLASSICAL WORLD

Focal Point: The postclassical world was divided among three major categories of civilizations, defined according to new contacts with the emerging world network. Lines of interaction extended between the eastern Mediterranean and northeastern Europe, including Russia; between China and Korea, Vietnam and Japan; between the Arab Middle East and North Africa, and important parts of sub-Saharan Africa; and among various parts of the Mediterranean world and the rising civilization of western Europe.

The best established civilizations sat essentially in the same centers that had witnessed the key developments in the classical period. Arab society took over much of the Middle East and North Africa; China dominated East Asia; India, though slightly in eclipse, continued to sponsor extensive trade and cultural development; and the Byzantine Empire took over the heritage of classical Greece and the eastern part of the Roman Empire. All the civilization centers differed to some extent from their classical predecessors; even China, with the greatest continuity, added new elements. The other centers were even more clearly marked by the impact of new religions and by new geographical boundaries. But they all built on previous strengths in art, commerce, and politics. They were, as a result, wealthier, more populous, and more sophisticated in style and manners than most other civilizations, particularly in the early centuries of the postclassical era. They embraced the greatest cities of the age: Constantinople, Baghdad, Zhangan, and Hangzhou.

Hovering around these centers were areas in which civilization was newer and many activities were less strongly organized. Japan, much of Southeast Asia, northern Europe, and parts of sub-Saharan Africa were defining their characteristics as civilizations while also imitating key features of one of the more established centers. These areas participated to some degree in the world network, though their level of participation changed over time (as with the West's growing involvement from the 12th century onward). Societies in this second zone usually participated in world exchange at some disadvantage, receiving more influence than they sent out.

There was a third zone of civilizations where important developments occurred with no link whatsoever to the world network; isolation prevailed. Neither technological exchange nor the kinds of shared cultural impulse involved in the replacement of polytheism by a new religion occurred. Civilizations in the Americas and Polynesian societies best illustrate this third zone where no contacts modified an independent existence despite frequent exchanges within each area. Some parts of sub-Saharan Africa also saw the creation of vigorous cultures that were largely isolated. For the important civilizations evolving outside the world network, the main features of the postclassical era have little salience. Important developments occurred but within separate frameworks and with only a few, accidental parallels to patterns elsewhere. As was true in even larger parts of the world earlier, the dynamics of change were only regional.

The chapters dealing with the postclassical millennium are arranged as follows in relation to the major themes. Three initial chapters explore the emergence of the Arabs as major historical actors, the rise of Islam, and the spread of Islam to key regions such as India, Southeast Asia, and Africa. The parts of the world particularly influenced by Islam illustrate all the overriding themes of the period: the rise of a world-class civilization, expansion of civilization, change in beliefs, and the impact of international exchange in the four civilization areas covered in these chapters. Civilization expansion, religious change, and complex links to the world network focus the treatment of eastern and western Europe in Chapters 15 and 16. The separate expansion of civilizations in the Americas is covered in Chapter 17. Chapter 18 turns to China, linked to larger patterns and the world network but in distinctive ways. The expansion of East Asian civilization—another part of the expansion-of-civilization theme—and the rise of the Mongol Empire (Chapters 19 and 20) lead to a final chapter on the changing world balance at the end of the postclassical period in the 15th century.

12

The First Global Civilization: The Rise and Spread of Islam

c. 570–632 Lifetime of the prophet Muhammad

597–626 Wars between the Byzantine and Sasanian (Persian) Empires

610 Muhammad's first revelations

613 Muhammad begins to preach the new faith

628 Muslim-Meccan truce

622 Muhammad's flight (*hijra*) from Mecca to Medina

624–627 Wars between the followers of Muhammad and the Quraysh of Mecca

630 Muhammad enters Mecca in triumph

632–634 Caliph Abu Bakr

632 Death of Muhammad

633–634 Ridda Wars in Arabia

634–644 Caliph Umar

634–643 Early Muslim conquests in the Byzantine Empire

637 Arab invasion and destruction of Sasanian Empire

600 C.E.

620 C.E.

INTRODUCTION

Although there were important contacts between the civilized centers of the classical world, no single civilization had bound together large portions of the ancient world in either the Western or the Eastern Hemisphere. But in the 7th century C.E., the followers of a new religion, *Islam* (which literally means "submission, the self-surrender of the believer to the will of the one, true God, *Allah*") charged out of the Arabian peninsula and began a sequence of conquest and conversion that would forge the first truly global civilization. Until then, Arabia had been a nomadic backwater on the periphery of the civilizations of the eastern Mediterranean. Within decades, the *Muslims* (as the followers of the new faith and its prophet, *Muhammad,* were called) had conquered an empire extending from Spain in the west to central Asia in the east—an empire that combined the classical civilizations of Greece, Egypt, and Persia. In succeeding centuries, Islamic civilization would be spread by merchants, wandering mystics, and warriors across the steppes of Asia (including most of what is today southern Russia) to western China, into the Indian subcontinent and across maritime Southeast Asia, and down the eastern coast of Africa as well as into the vast savanna zone to the west. Muslim conquerors would also capture Asia Minor and advance into the European heartland of Islam's great rival, Christendom.

During most of the millennium after the 7th century C.E., this great civilization, which cut a huge swath across the middle of the continents of Africa and Asia, provided key links and channels for exchange among the civilized centers of the classical era in the Eastern Hemisphere. Muslim merchants, often in cooperation with Jewish, Armenian, Indian, and other regional commercial groups, became key middlemen in the trade between civilizations from the western Mediterranean to the South China Sea. Muslim traders and conquerors became the prime agents for the transfer of food crops, technology, and ideas among the many centers of civilization in the Eastern Hemisphere. Muslim scholars studied, preserved, and improved on the learning of the ancient civilizations of the Old World, including most critically those of Greece, Persia, and Egypt. For several centuries, Muslim works in philosophy, literature, mathematics, and the sciences elevated Arabic (the language of the *Quran,* the holy book containing God's revelations to Muhammad) to the status of the international language of the educated and informed. Thus, building on the achievements of earlier civilizations, Muslim peoples forged a splendid new civilization that excelled in most areas of human endeavor, from poetry and architecture to the sciences and urban development. Islam not only joined existing centers of civilization but provided the foundations on which a truly global civilization would eventually be built.

Although unified by a common allegiance to the religious rituals and teachings proclaimed by Muhammad and to some extent by the Arabic language, the Islamic world was divided by political rivalries, vast cultural and linguistic diversity, and religious sectarianism. The agrarian cores of earlier civilizations provided the base of support for Muslim empires and kingdoms, which fought to expand their territorial control at one another's expense and warred for the right to claim that their rulers were the true leaders of the Islamic world. It was unrealistic to expect that such a large area as that encompassed by Islamic civilization could be united under a single ruler, particularly given the primitive state of sea and overland communications. In any case, from the 7th to the 14th centuries, political rivalries prompted technological and organizational innovations that strengthened the Islamic world as a whole. Diversity and the continuing influx of

	656–661 Caliph Ali; first civil war	**680–692** Second civil war
		744–750 Third civil war; Abbasid revolt
644–656 Caliph Uthman	**661–680** Mu 'awiya	**750** Abbasid caliphate
		680 Karbala; death of Ali's son Husayn
	661–750 Ummayad caliphate	
640 C.E.	**660** C.E.	**680** C.E.

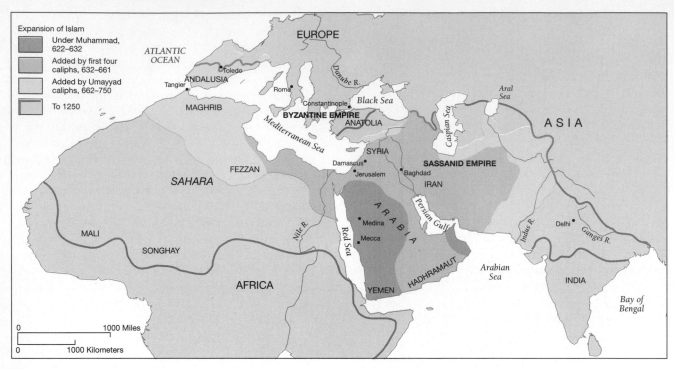

The Expansion of Islam from the 7th to the 13th Centuries

new ideas, objects, and peoples from areas newly brought into the Islamic fold enriched Muslim civilization and enhanced its accomplishments in the arts, invention, and the sciences.

Only with the rise of Europe, beginning in the 14th century, from a besieged and peripheral outlier on the western fringes of the Islamic empires to a mighty aggressor on a global scale, did the divisions within the Islamic world begin to undermine seriously the continued strength and prosperity of Muslim civilization. By playing rival Islamic rulers and sects against each other, the emerging Christian powers could further their designs for territorial expansion. In the 15th and 16th centuries, Muslim divisions and rivalries allowed the Europeans to gain footholds, however precarious, in Africa and the East Indies.

This chapter begins with an exploration of the Arabian origins of Muhammad and the Islamic faith. It traces the emergence of the Muslim religion and the community of Muhammad's faithful followers in the middle decades of the 7th century C.E. It then presents the early conquests of the Arabs, united by the new religion, and examines the achievements of early Islamic civilization. The chapter concludes with an account of a major shift in leadership that occurred within the Islamic community in the mid-8th century and the early history

of the Abbasid Empire, which was a product of that shift. Chapter 13 focuses on the later centuries of Abbasid rule and the spread of Islam into South and Southeast Asia from the 10th through the 14th centuries.

DESERT AND TOWN: THE ARABIAN WORLD AND THE BIRTH OF ISLAM

Focal Point: In the 7th century C.E., a new religion arose in the Arabian peninsula, a nomadic zone that had long been on the periphery of powerful neighboring civilizations in the eastern Mediterranean and the Middle East. Built on the revelations of the prophet Muhammad, originally a trader from the town of Mecca, the new faith won the adherence of many of the camel-herding tribes of the peninsula within decades. Though initially an Arab religion, in both beliefs and practices Islam contained a powerful potential appeal that would in the following centuries elevate it to the status of one of the great world religions.

The Arabian peninsula was a very unlikely birthplace for the first global civilization. Much of the area is covered by some of the most inhospitable desert regions in the world. An early traveler wrote of the region:

With their supply of portable water, shade, and date palms, oases like this one in central Arabia have long been key centers of settlement and trade in the desert.

> All about us is an iron wilderness; a bare and black shining beach of heated volcanic stones . . . a vast bed and banks of rusty and basaltic bluish rocks . . . stubborn as heavy matter, as iron and sounding like bell metal; lying out eternally under the sand-driving desert wind. . . .

In the scrub zones on the edges of the empty quarters, or uninhabitable desert zones, a wide variety of *bedouin*, or nomadic cultures, had developed over the centuries on the basis of camel and goat herding. In the oases that dotted the dry landscape, towns and agriculture flourished on a limited scale. Only in the far south, on the Yemen and Hadramaut coasts, had extensive sedentary agriculture, sizeable cities, and regional kingdoms developed in ancient times. Over much of the rest of the peninsula, the camel nomads, organized in tribes and clans, were dominant. Yet, in the rocky regions adjacent to the Red Sea, several trading towns had developed that would play pivotal roles in the emergence of Islam.

Though the urban roots of Islam have often been stressed by writers on Muslim civilization, the bedouin world in which the religion arose shaped the career of its prophet, his teachings, and the spread of the new beliefs in major ways. In fact, key towns, such as Mecca and Medina, were largely extensions of the tribal culture of the camel nomads. Their populations were linked by kinship to bedouin peoples. Mecca, for example, had been founded by bedouins and at the time of Muhammad was ruled by former bedouin clans. The safety of the trade routes on which the towns depended for their livelihood was in the hands of the nomadic tribes that lived along the vulnerable caravan routes to the north and south. In addition, the town dwellers' social organization, which focused on clan and family, as well as their culture, including language and religion, were much like those of the nomads.

Clan Identity, Clan Rivalries, and the Cycle of Vengeance

The harsh desert and scrub environment of Arabia gave rise to forms of social organization and a lifestyle that were similar to those of other nomadic peoples. Bedouin herders lived in kin-related clan groups that dwelt in highly mobile tent encampments. Clans, in turn, were clustered in larger tribal groupings, but these were rarely, if ever, congregated together and then only in times of war or severe crisis. The struggle for subsistence in the unforgiving Arabian environment resulted in a strong dependence on and loyalty to one's family and clan. Survival literally depended on cooperation with and support from kin. To be cut off from them or expelled from the clan encampment was in most cases fatal.

The use of watering places and grazing lands, which were essential to maintaining the herds on which bedouin life depended, was regulated by clan councils. But there could be wide disparities of wealth and status within clan groups and between clans of the same tribe. Though normally elected by councils of elder advisors, the *shaykhs*, or leaders of the tribes and clans, were almost always men with large herds, several wives, many children, and numerous retainers. The shaykhs' dictates were enforced by bands of free warriors, whose families made up a majority of a given clan group. Beneath the warriors were slave families, often the remnants of rival clans defeated and decimated by war, who served the shaykhs or the clan as a whole.

Clan cohesion and loyalty was reinforced by fierce interclan rivalries and struggles to control vital pasturelands and watering places. If the warriors from one clan found those from another clan drawing water from one

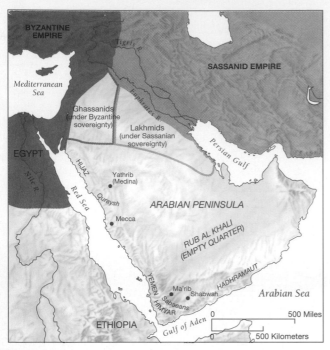

Arabia and Surrounding Areas Before and During the Time of Muhammad

of their wells, they were likely to kill them. Wars very often broke out as a result of one clan encroaching on the pasture areas of another clan. In a culture where one's honor depended on respect for one's clan, the flimsiest of pretexts could lead to interclan violence. For instance, an insult to a warrior in a market town, the theft of a prize stallion, or one clan's drubbing in a horse race by another clan could end in pitched battles between clan groups. All the males of a given clan joined in these melees, which were normally won by the side that could field several champions who were famed for their strength and skill with spears or bows and arrows.

These battles were fought according to a code of chivalry that was quite common in early cultures. Though battles were usually small in terms of the numbers involved, they were hard-fought and often bloody affairs. Almost invariably the battles either initiated or perpetuated clan feuds, which could continue for hundreds of years. The deaths of the warriors of one clan required that revenge be taken on the clan that had killed them. Their deaths led in turn to reprisals. This constant infighting drained resources and energies that might have been put to constructive ends. It also weakened the bedouins vis-à-vis the neighboring peoples and empires and allowed them to be manipulated and set against each other.

Towns and Long-Distance Trade

Though bedouin herders occupied most of the habitable portions of Arabia, agriculturists and town dwellers carved out small enclaves in the western and southern parts of the peninsula in the classical era. Foreign invasions and the inroads of bedouin peoples had all but destroyed these civilizations centuries before the birth of Muhammad. But a number of cities had developed farther north as entrepôts in the transcontinental trading system that stretched from the Mediterranean to East Asia. The most important of these cities was *Mecca,* which was located in the mountainous region along the Red Sea on the western coast of Arabia. The town had been founded by the *Umayyad* clan of the *Quraysh* bedouin tribe, and members of the clan dominated its politics and commercial economy.

The wealth and status of both Mecca and its merchant elite were also enhanced by the fact that the city was the site of the *Ka'ba,* one of the most revered religious shrines in pre-Islamic Arabia. Not only did the shrine attract pilgrims and customers for Mecca's bazaars, but at certain times of the year it was the focus of an obligatory truce in the interclan feuds. Freed from fears of assault by rival groups, traders and bedouin herdsmen flocked to the town to trade, exchange gossip, and partake in the delights (however limited in such a provincial environment) of city life.

Northeast of Mecca was a second town, *Yathrib* or *Medina,* which—like most of the other towns in the peninsula—was established in an oasis. Wells and springs made sedentary agriculture possible. In addition to wheat and other staples, Medina's inhabitants grew date palms, whose fruit and seeds (which were fed to camels) they traded to the bedouins. Medina was also engaged, though on a much smaller scale than Mecca, in the long-distance caravan trade that passed through Arabia. In contrast to Umayyad-dominated Mecca, control in Medina was contested by two bedouin and three Jewish clans. Their quarrels left the city a poor second to Mecca as a center of trade, and these divisions proved critical to the very survival of the prophet Muhammad and the Islamic faith.

Marriage and Family in Pre-Islamic Arabia

Though the evidence is thin, there are several indications that women in pre-Islamic Arabian bedouin culture enjoyed greater freedom and higher status than those who lived in neighboring civilized centers, such as the Byzantine and Sassanid empires that then dominated the Middle East. Women played key economic roles in clan life, from milking camels and weaving cloth to raising children. Because male members of the clan were often on the move, many tribes traced descent through the mother rather than the father. In some tribes, both males and females were allowed multiple marriage partners, and the male was required to pay a bride-price, rather than the father of the female paying a dowry, in order to seal a marriage contract. In contrast to women (especially elite women) in neighboring Syria and Persia, women in pre-Islamic Arabia were not secluded and went about without veils. Their advice was highly regarded in clan and tribal councils, and they often authored the poems that were the focus of bedouin cultural life in the pre-Islamic era.

However, women were not by any means the equals of men. They could not gain glory as warriors, the most prized occupation of the bedouins; and often they were little more than drudge laborers. Their treatment and status depended on the custom of individual clans and tribes rather than on legal codes and thus varied widely from one clan or family to the next. Customary practices regarding property control, inheritance, and divorce heavily favored males. In the urban environment of trading centers like Mecca, the rise of a mercantile elite and social stratification appear to have set back the position of women on the whole. The more stable family life of the towns led to the practice of tracing descent through the male line, and while males continued to practice polygamy, females were expected to be monogamous.

Poets and Neglected Gods

Because of the relative isolation of Arabia in the pre-Islamic age and the harshness and poverty of the natural environment (no one knew of, or had any use for, the vast reservoirs of oil hidden beneath its sands), Arab material culture was not highly developed. Except in the far south, there was little art or architecture of worth, and even Mecca made little impression on the cosmopolitan merchants who passed through the city in caravans from the fabled cities of the ancient civilizations farther north.

The main focus of bedouin cultural creativity in the pre-Islamic era was poetry, which was composed and transmitted orally, as there was as yet no written language. Clan and tribal bards narrated poems that told of their kinsmen's heroics in war and the clan's great deeds. Some poets were said to possess magical powers or to be possessed by demons. More than any other source, their poems provide a vision of life and society in pre-Islamic Arabia. They tell of lovers spurned and passion consummated, war and vendettas, loyalty, and generosity.

Bedouin religion was for most clans a blend of animism and polytheism, or the worship of many gods and goddesses. Some tribes, such as the Quraysh, recognized a supreme God named Allah. But they seldom prayed or sacrificed to Allah, concentrating instead on less abstract spirits who seemed more relevant to their daily lives. Both spirits and gods (for example, the moon god Hubal) tended to be associated with night, a cool period when dew covered the earth, which had been parched by the blaze of the desert sun. Likewise, the worship of nature spirits focused on sacred caves, pure springs, and groves of trees—places where the bedouins could take shelter from the heat and wind. Religion appears to have had little to do with ethics. Rather, standards of morality and proper behavior were rooted in tribal customs and unwritten codes of honor.

How seriously the bedouins took their gods is also a matter of some doubt. Their lukewarm adherence is illustrated by the famous tale of a bedouin warrior who had set out to avenge his father's death at the hands of a rival clan. He stopped at an oracle along the way to seek advice by means of drawing arrows that indicated various courses of action he might take. Three times he drew arrows that advised him to abandon his quest for revenge. Infuriated by this counsel, he hurled the arrows at the idol of the oracle and exclaimed, "Accursed one! Had it been thy father who was murdered, thou would not have forbidden my avenging him."

THE LIFE OF MUHAMMAD AND THE GENESIS OF ISLAM

Focal Point: By the 6th century C.E., the camel nomads were dominant throughout much of Arabia. The civilized centers to the south were in ruins, and trading centers, such as Mecca and Medina, depended on alliances with neighboring bedouin tribes to keep the caravan routes open. The constricted world of clan and kin, nomadic camp, blood feud, and local gods persisted despite the lure of the extensive empires and cosmopolitan urban centers that stretched in a great arc to the north and east of the Arabian peninsula. But pressures for change were mounting. Both the Byzantine and Sassanian empires struggled to assert greater control over the nomadic tribes of the peninsula, and Arab peoples migrated into Mesopotamia and other areas to the north, where they came increasingly under foreign influences. From these regions, the influence of monotheistic religions, especially Judaism and Christianity, entered Arabia, and Arab prophets urged the bedouin tribes to renounce idol worship and rely on a single, almighty

God. The prophet Muhammad and the new religion, which he propagated in the early decades of the 7th century, responded both to the influences flowing into Arabia and to related social dislocations that were disrupting Arab life.

The hardships of Muhammad's early life underscore the importance of clan ties in the Arabian world. He was born around 570 C.E. into a prominent clan of the Quraysh tribe, the Banu Hashim, in a bedouin encampment where he would spend the first six years of his life. Because his father died before he was born, Muhammad was raised by his father's kinsmen. The loss of his father was compounded by the death of Muhammad's mother shortly after he went to live with her some years later. Despite these early losses, Muhammad had the good fortune to be born into a respected clan and powerful tribe. His paternal uncle, Abu Talib, was particularly fond of the boy and served as his protector and supporter through much of his early life. Muhammad's grandfather, who like other leading members of the clan was engaged in commerce, educated the young man in the ways of the merchant. With Abu Talib, Muhammad made his first caravan journey to Syria, where on this and later trips he encountered adherents of the Christian and Jewish faiths whose beliefs and practices were to have such a great impact on his own teachings.

In his adolescence, Muhammad took up residence in Mecca, and by his early 20s he was working as a trader for Khadijah, the widow of a wealthy trader, whom he married some years later. His life as a trader in Mecca and on the caravan routes not only exposed Muhammad to the world beyond Arabia but made him acutely aware of the clan rivalries that had divided the peoples of the region for millennia. He was also increasingly concerned about new forces undermining solidarity within the clans. The growth of the towns and trade had enriched some clan families and left others behind, often in poverty. It had also introduced a new source of tension between clan and tribal groupings, because some clans, such as the Umayyads, grew rich on the profits from commerce, whereas others maintained their herding lifestyle.

As a trader and traveler, Muhammad would have been aware of the new religious currents that were sweeping the region in the early 7th century, particularly the spread of monotheistic ideas and the growing dissatisfaction with the old gods. In Muhammad's time, several prophets had arisen proclaiming a new faith for the Arabs. Some of these prophets would continue to compete with him for adherents after he received the divine revelations that would provide the basis for Islam.

Though socially prominent, economically well off, and widely admired for his trading skills and trustworthiness, the middle-aged Muhammad grew increasingly distracted and dissatisfied with a life focused on material gain. He took to spending increasing amounts of time in meditation in the hills and wilderness that surrounded Mecca. In 610 or earlier, he received the first of many revelations, which his followers believe God transmitted to him through the angel Gabriel. These revelations were later written in Arabic and collected in the Quran. The teachings and injunctions of the Quran were to form the basis for the new religion that Muhammad began to preach to his clanspeople and the population of Mecca.

Persecution, Flight, and Victory

At first Muhammad's following was small, consisting mainly of his wife, several clanspeople, and some servants and slaves. As his message was clarified with successive revelations, the circle of the faithful grew to the point where he began to be seen by the Umayyad notables who dominated Meccan life as a threat to their own wealth and power. Above all, the new faith threatened to supplant the gods of the Ka'ba, whose shrines had done so much to establish the city as a center of commerce and bedouin interchange. Though he was protected for a time by his own clan, Muhammad was increasingly threatened by the Umayyads, who plotted with other clans to murder him. It was clear that Muhammad must flee Mecca, but where was he to find refuge?

Muhammad's reputation as a skillful and fair negotiator prepared the way for his successful flight from Umayyad persecution. The quarrels between the clans in the nearby city of Medina had increasingly precipitated violent clashes, and the oasis community was on the verge of civil war. Leaders of the bedouin clans in Medina sent a delegation to invite Muhammad, who was related to them on his mother's side, to arbitrate their disputes and put an end to the strife that had so long plagued the town. Clever ruses and the courage of his clansman *Ali*—who at one point took Muhammad's place and thus risked becoming the target of assassins—secured in 622 the safe passage of Muhammad and a small band of followers from Mecca to Medina. In Medina he was given a hero's welcome, which he soon earned by deftly settling the quarrels between the bedouin clans. His wisdom and skill as a political leader won him new followers, who joined those who had accompanied him from Mecca as the core believers of the new faith.

CLOSEUP

Khadijah: Prophet's Wife and First Convert to Islam

Perhaps the most important person in Muhammad's young adult life and early years as a prophet was his wife Khadijah. What we know of Khadijah's own life tells us something of the situation of women—at least upper-class women—in Arabian society in the years before the prophet's teachings reordered gender relationships in fundamental ways. Khadijah's position as a wealthy widow in charge of a thriving trading enterprise reveals that women were able to remarry and to own and inherit property as well as pursue careers, such as business. After Muhammad had been working for Khadijah for some time, she tested him by giving him charge of a caravan to Syria. When he returned successfully, *she* asked him to marry her, which apparently neither surprised nor scandalized her family or Meccan society. It is also noteworthy that Khadijah was 10 to 15 years older than the prophet, who was 25 at the time of their betrothal.

All accounts agree that the marriage was a great success. The two made superb business partners, and Khadijah gave birth to six children. The marriage brought Muhammad financial security and thus the freedom to pursue his prophetic calling, which began with his first revelations some 15 years later. Through Khadijah's cousin, Waraqah, Muhammad also became somewhat familiar with the Bible and the Judeo-Christian prophetic traditions. When his revelations first began, about 610, Khadijah assured him that they were divinely sent and not signs of madness as he at first feared. Waraqah, who was probably a Christian, compared Muhammad's visions to those of Moses and other Biblical prophets. Khadijah steadfastly supported Muhammad, who struggled to accept his calling in the early years, and she was the first to convert to the new religion that he began to preach.

Muhammad's attachment to Khadijah is evidenced by the fact that she remained his only wife until her death in 619. More in accord with Arab practice at the time and his own teachings, after her death he took several wives. According to later traditions, Muhammad severely chided Aisha, the most beloved of these, for criticizing his continuing devotion to the deceased Khadijah. Khadijah, the prophet declared, had believed in his prophetic calling from the start and later sustained him when he was doubted and ridiculed by most of the Quraysh tribespeople.

Muslim pilgrims visiting the Ka'ba in Mecca, the most sacred of all Muslim shrines, are depicted in this 15th-century Persian miniature.

In the eyes of the Umayyad notables, Muhammad's successes made him a greater threat than ever. Not only was he preaching a faith that rivaled their own, but his leadership was strengthening Mecca's neighbor and competitor, Medina. Muslim raids on Meccan caravans provided yet another source of danger. Determined to put an end to these threats, the Quraysh launched a series of attacks in the mid-620s on Muhammad and his followers in Medina. These attacks led to several pitched battles. In these clashes, Muhammad proved an able leader and courageous fighter. He was also an innovative strategist: at one point he broke the "rules" of the local brand of chivalric-style warfare by having a ditch dug to protect the flanks of his badly outnumbered followers.

The ultimate victory of Muhammad and his followers was signaled by a treaty in 628, which included a provision granting them permission to visit the shrine at Ka'ba in Mecca during the season of truce. By then Muhammad's growing community had won numerous bedouin allies, and over 10,000 converts accompanied him on his triumphal return to his hometown in 629. After proving the power of Allah, the single God he proclaimed, by smashing the idols of the shrine, Muhammad converted the Umayyads and most of the other inhabitants of Mecca to the new faith.

Arabs and Islam

Although Islam was soon to become one of the great world religions, the beliefs and practices enjoined by the prophet Muhammad were initially adopted only by the Arab town dwellers and bedouins among whom he had grown up—just as very early Christianity had focused on Jewish converts. The new religion had much to offer the divided peoples of Arabia. It gave them a form of pristine monotheism that belonged to no single tribe and transcended clan and class divisions. It provided a religion that was distinctly Arab in origin and yet the equal of the monotheistic faiths held by the Christians and Jews, who lived in the midst of the bedouin tribes. If anything, the monotheism preached by Muhammad was even more uncompromising than that of the Christians because it allowed for no intermediaries between the individual and God. God was one; there were no saints, and angels were nothing more than messengers; nor were there priests in the Christian or Jewish sense.

Adherence to Islam offered the possibility of an end to the vendettas and feuds that had so long divided the peoples of Arabia and undermined their attempts to throw off the domination of neighboring empires. The

In this miniature painting, Muhammad is shown joining his disciples in laying the brick foundation for the large house where the Prophet lived with his family after his flight to Yathrib, or Medina, three years after Khadijah's death. The house also served as the main mosque until Mecca was captured.

umma, or community of the faithful, transcended old tribal boundaries and made possible a degree of political unity undreamed of before Muhammad's time. The new religion provided a single and supernaturally sanctioned source of authority and discipline. With unity, the skills and energies that the bedouins had once channeled toward warring with each other were turned outward in a burst of conquest that is perhaps unmatched in human history in its speed and extent. From vassals, march warriors, or contemptible "savages" of the desert waste, the Arab bedouins were transformed into the conquerors and rulers of much of the Middle Eastern world.

The new religion also provided an ethical system that did much to heal the deep social rifts within Arabian society that had appeared in the time of the prophet. Islam stressed the dignity of all believers and their equality in the eyes of Allah. It promulgated an ethical code that stressed the responsibility of the well-to-do and strong for the poor and weak, the aged and infirm. Payment of the *zakat,* a tax for charity, was obligatory in the new faith. In both his revelations and his personal behavior, Muhammad enjoined his followers to be kind and generous to their dependents, including slaves. He forbade the rich to exploit the poor through exorbitant rents or usurious rates of interest charged for loans. The prophet's teachings and the revelations of the Quran were soon incorporated into an extensive body of law that regulated all aspects of the lives of the Muslim faithful. Held accountable before Islamic law on earth, they lived in a manner that would prepare them for the Last Judgement, which in Islam, as in Christianity, would determine their fate in eternity. A stern but compassionate God and a strict but socially minded body of law set impressive standards for the social interaction between adherents of the new faith.

Universalistic Elements in Islam

Although it was almost exclusively a religion of the Arabs in its early years, from the outset Islam contained beliefs and practices that would give it a strong appeal to peoples at virtually all stages of social development and in widely varying cultural settings. Some of these beliefs—Islam's uncompromising monotheism, highly developed legal codes, egalitarianism, and strong sense of community—were the same as the attributes that had won it support among the peoples of Arabia. Its potential as a world religion was enhanced by the fact that most of the attributes of Islam were to some degree anticipated by the other Semitic religions with which Muhammad had contact. Muhammad accepted the validity of the earlier divine revelations that had given rise to the Jewish and Christian faiths. He taught that the revelations he had received were a refinement and reformulation of earlier ones, and that they were the last and culminating divine instructions for human behavior and worship.

In addition to the beliefs and practices that have given Islam a universal appeal, its "five pillars," which must be accepted and followed by all believers, provided the basis for an underlying religious unity. (1) The confession of faith was simple and powerful: "There is no God but Allah, and Muhammad is his Prophet." The injunctions (2) to pray, facing the holy city of Mecca, five times a day and (3) to fast during the month of Ramadan enhanced community solidarity and allowed the faithful to demonstrate their fervor. (4) The zakat, or tithe for charity, also strengthened community cohesion and won converts from those seeking an ethical code that stressed social responsibility and the "brotherhood" of all believers. (5) The *hajj*, or pilgrimage to the holy city of Mecca, to worship Allah at the Ka'ba (which was converted from an idolaters' shrine into the sacred center of the Islamic world) drew together the faithful from Morocco to China. No injunction did more to give Islam a truly cosmopolitan and universalistic character.

THE ARAB EMPIRE OF THE UMAYYADS

Focal Point: Muhammad's victory over the Umayyads and the resulting allegiance of many of the bedouin tribes of Arabia created a wholly new center of power in the Middle Eastern cradle of civilization. A backward, nonagrarian area outside the core zones of Egypt, Mesopotamia, and Persia suddenly emerged as the source of religious and political forces that would eventually affect the history of much of the known world. But when the prophet Muhammad died quite suddenly in 632, it appeared that his religion might altogether disappear. Despite internal disputes, the Muslim community held together and soon expanded beyond Arabia. Muhammad's old adversaries, the Ummaya clan, emerged after several years' struggle as the dominant force within the Islamic community. Under Umayyid rule, the Arabs rapidly built a vast empire, which had established the foundations for an enduring Islamic civilization by the time of its fall in the middle of the 8th century C.E.

Many of the bedouin tribes that had converted to Islam renounced the new faith in the months after Muhammad's death, and his remaining followers quarreled over who should succeed him. Though these quarrels were never fully resolved, the community managed to find new leaders who directed a series of campaigns to force those who had abandoned Islam to return to the fold. Having united most of Arabia under the Islamic banner by 633, Muslim military commanders began to mount serious expeditions beyond the peninsula, where only probing attacks had occurred during the lifetime of the prophet and in the period of tribal warfare after his death. The courage, military prowess, and religious zeal of the warriors of Islam, and the weaknesses of the empires that bordered on Arabia, resulted in stunning conquests in Mesopotamia, North Africa, and Persia, which dominated the next two decades of Islamic history. The empire built from these conquests was Arab rather than Islamic. Most of it was ruled by a small Arab warrior elite, led by the Umayyads and other prominent clans, who had little desire to convert the subject populations, either Arab or otherwise, to the new religion.

Consolidation and Division in the Islamic Community

The leadership crisis brought on by Muhammad's death in 632 was compounded by the fact that he had not appointed a successor or even established a procedure by which a new leader might be chosen. Opinion within the Muslim community was deeply divided as to who should succeed him. In this moment of extreme danger, a strong leader who could hold the Islamic community together was urgently needed. On the afternoon Muhammad died, one of the clans that remained committed to the new faith called a meeting to select a new leader who would be designated as the *caliph*, the political and religious successor to Muhammad. Several choices were possible, and a deadlock between the clans appeared likely—a deadlock that would almost certainly have been fatal to a community threatened by enemies on all sides. One of the main candidates, Ali, the cousin and son-in-law of Muhammad, was passed over because he was considered too young to assume a position of such great responsibility. This decision was later to prove a major source of division in the Islamic community. But in 632, it appeared that a difficult reconciliation had been won by the choice of one of Muhammad's earliest followers and closest friends, Abu Bakr (caliph from 632 to 634).

In addition to his personal courage, warmth, and wisdom, Abu Bakr was well versed in the genealogical histories of the bedouin tribes, which meant that he was well placed to determine which tribes could be turned against each other and which ones could be enticed into alliances. Initially at least, his mandate was very limited. He received no financial support from the Muslim community. Thus, he had to continue his previous occupation as a merchant on a part-time basis, and he only

loosely controlled the better military commanders of the faithful.

These commanders turned out to be very able indeed. After turning back attacks on Mecca, the Islamic faithful routed one after another of the bedouin tribes. The defeat of rival prophets and some of the larger clans in what were known as the *Ridda Wars* soon brought about the return of the Arabian tribes to the Islamic fold. Emboldened by the proven skills of his generals and the swelling ranks of the Muslim faithful, *Abu Bakr* oversaw raids to the north of Arabia into the sedentary zones in present-day Iraq and Syria and eastward into Egypt.

The unified bedouin forces had originally intended merely to raid for booty and then retreat back into the desert. But their initial probes revealed the deep-seated rot and vulnerability of the Byzantine and Persian empires, which dominated or ruled directly the territories into which the Muslim warriors rode. The invaders were also prodded onward by the growing support of the Arab bedouin peoples who had been migrating into the Fertile Crescent for centuries. These peoples had long served as the vassals and frontier guardians of the Byzantine and Persian empires. Now they joined their Arab brethren in a combined assault on the two empires.

Motives for Arab Conquests

The Arab warriors were driven by many forces. The unity provided by the Islamic faith gave them a new sense of common cause and strength. United, they could stand up to the non-Arab rulers who had so long played them against each other and despised them as unwashed and backward barbarians from the desert wastelands. It is also probable that the early leaders of the community saw the wars of conquest as a good way to release the pent-up energies of the martial bedouin tribes they now sought to lead. Above all, the bedouin warriors were drawn to the campaigns of expansion by the promise of a share in the booty to be won in the rich farmlands raided and the tribute that could be exacted from the towns and cities that came under Arab rule. As an early Arab writer observed, the bedouins forsook their life as desert nomads not out of a promise of religious rewards, but because of a "yearning after bread and dates."

The chance to glorify their new religion may have been a motive for the Arab conquests, but they were not driven by a desire to win converts to it. In fact, other than fellow bedouin tribes of Arab descent, the invaders had good reason to avoid mass conversions. Not only would Arab warriors have to share the booty of their military expeditions with ever larger numbers if converts were made, but Muslims were exempted from some of the more lucrative taxes levied on Christian and other non-Muslim groups. Thus, the vision of Islamic *jihads*, or holy wars, launched to forcibly spread the faith, which has long been associated with Islam in the Christian West, distorts the forces behind the early Arab expansion.

Weaknesses of the Adversary Empires

Of the two great empires that had once contested for dominance in the Fertile Crescent transit zone, the Sassanian Empire of Persia proved the more vulnerable. Power in the extensive Sassanian domains was formally concentrated in the hands of an autocratic emperor. By the time of the Arab explosion, the emperor was manipulated by a landed, aristocratic class that harshly exploited the cultivators who made up most of the population of the empire. *Zoroastrianism,* the official religion of the emperor, lacked popular roots. By contrast, the religion of a visionary reformer named Mazdak, which had won considerable support among the peasantry, had been brutally suppressed by the Sassanian rulers in the period before the rise of Islam.

At first, the Sassanian commanders had little more than contempt for the Arab invaders and set out against them with poorly prepared forces. By the time the seriousness of the Islamic threat was made all too clear by decisive Arab victories in the Fertile Crescent region and the defection of the Arab tribes on the frontier, Muslim warriors had broken into the Sassanian heartland. Further Muslim victories brought about the rapid collapse of the vast empire. The Sassanian rulers and their forces retreated eastward in the face of the Muslim advance. The capital was taken, armies were destroyed, and generals were slain. When, in 651, the last of the Sassanian rulers was assassinated, Muslim victory and the destruction of the empire were ensured.

Despite an equally impressive string of Muslim victories in the provinces of their empire, the Byzantines proved a more resilient adversary (see Chapter 15). Their ability to resist the Muslim onslaught, however, was impeded both by the defection of their own frontier Arabs and the support the Muslim invaders received from the Christians of Syria and Egypt. Members of the Christian sects dominant in these areas, such as the Copts and Nestorians, had long resented the rule of the Orthodox Byzantines, who taxed them heavily and openly persecuted them as heretics. When it became clear that the Muslims would not only tolerate the Christians but tax them less heavily than the Byzantines did, these Christian groups rallied to the Arabs.

Weakened from within and exhausted by the long wars fought with Persia in the decades before the Arab explosion, the Byzantines reeled from the Arab assaults. Syria, western Iraq, and Palestine were quickly taken by the Arab invaders, and by 640 a series of probes had been made into Egypt, one of the richest provinces of the empire. In the early 640s, the ancient center of learning and commerce, Alexandria, was taken, most of Egypt was occupied, and Arab armies extended their conquests into Libya to the west. Perhaps even more astounding from the point of view of the Byzantines, by the mid-640s the desert bedouins were putting together war fleets that increasingly challenged the long-standing Byzantine mastery of the Mediterranean. The rise of Muslim naval supremacy in the eastern end of the sea sealed the loss of Byzantium's rich provinces in Syria and Egypt and opened the way to further Muslim conquests in North Africa, the Mediterranean islands, and even southern Italy. For a time the Byzantines managed to rally their forces and stave off further inroads into their Balkan and Asia Minor heartlands. But the early triumphs of the Arab invaders had greatly reduced the strength and magnificence of the Byzantine Empire. Though it would survive for centuries, it would henceforth be a kingdom under siege.

The Problem of Succession and the Sunni–Shi'i Split

The stunning successes of Muslim armies and the sudden rise of an Arab empire covered over, for a time, continuing divisions within the community. The old division between the tribes of Mecca and Medina was compounded by differences between the tribes of north and south Arabia as well as between those who came to identify Syria as their homeland and those who settled in Iraq. Though these divisions were often generations old and the result of personal animosities, resentments had also begun to build over how the booty from the conquests ought to be divided among the tribal blocks that made up the Islamic community. In 656, just over two decades after the death of the prophet, the growing tensions broke into open violence.

The spark that began the conflict was the murder of the third caliph, *Uthman,* by mutinous warriors returning from Egypt. His death was the signal for the supporters of Ali to proclaim him as caliph. Uthman's unpopularity among many of the tribes, particularly those from Medina and the prophet's earliest followers, arose in part from the fact that he was the first caliph to be chosen from Muhammad's early enemies, the Umayyad clan. Already angered by the murder of their kinsman, the Umayyads rejected Ali's claims and swore revenge when he failed to punish Uthman's assassins. Warfare erupted between the two factions.

Ali was a famed warrior and experienced commander, and his deeply committed supporters soon gained the upper hand. After his victory at the Battle of the Camel in late 656, most of the Arab garrisons shifted to his side in opposition to the Umayyads, whose supporters were concentrated in the province of Syria and the holy city of Mecca. Just as Ali was on the verge of routing the Umayyad forces at the *Battle of Siffin* in 657, he was won over by a plea for mediation of the dispute. His decision to accept arbitration was fatal to his cause. Some of his most fervent adherents repudiated his leadership and had to be violently suppressed. While representatives of both parties tried unsuccessfully to work out a compromise, the Umayyads regrouped their forces and added Egypt to the provinces backing their claims. In 660, *Mu'awiya,* the new leader of the Umayyads, was proclaimed caliph in Jerusalem, thereby directly challenging Ali's position. A year later, Ali was assassinated, and his son, Hasan, was pressured by the Umayyads into renouncing his claims to the caliphate.

In the decades after the prophet's death, the question of succession generated deep divisions within the Muslim community. The split between the *Sunnis,* who backed the Umayyads, and the *Shi'is,* or dissenters who supported Ali, remains to this day the most fundamental in the Islamic world. Hostility between these two branches of the Islamic faithful was further heightened in the years after Ali's death by the continuing struggle between the Umayyads and Ali's second son, Husayn. After being abandoned by the clans in southern Iraq, who had promised to rise in a revolt supporting his claims against the Umayyads, Husayn and a small party were overwhelmed and killed at *Karbala* in 680. From that point on, the Shi'is mounted determined and sustained resistance to the Umayyad caliphate.

Over the centuries, factional disputes about who had the right to succeed Muhammad, with the Shi'ites recognizing none of the early caliphs except Ali, have been compounded by differences in belief, ritual, and law that have steadily widened the gap between Sunnis and Shi'is. These divisions have been further complicated by the formation of splinter sects within the Shi'i community in particular, beginning with those who defected from Ali when he agreed to arbitration of his and the Umayyads' claims.

The Umayyad Imperium

After a pause to settle internal disputes over succession, the remarkable sequence of Arab conquest was renewed in the last half of the 7th century. Muslim armies broke into central Asia, thus inaugurating a rivalry with Buddhism in the region that continues to the present day. By the early 8th century, the southern prong of this advance had reached into northwest India. Far to the west, Arab armies swept across North Africa and crossed the Straits of Gibraltar to conquer Spain and threaten France. Though the Muslim advance into western Europe was in effect checked by the hard-fought victory of Charles Martel and the Franks at Poitiers in 732, the Arabs did not fully retreat beyond the Pyrenees into Spain until decades later. Muslim warriors and sailors dominated much of the Mediterranean—a position that would be solidified by the conquest of key islands, such as Crete, Sicily, and Sardinia, in the early decades of the 9th century. By the early 700s, the Umayyads ruled an empire that extended from Spain in the west to the steppes of central Asia in the east. Not since the Romans had there been an empire to match it; never had an empire of its size been built so rapidly.

Though Mecca remained the holy city of Islam, under the Umayyads the political center of community shifted to *Damascus* in Syria, where the Umayyads chose to reside after the murder of Uthman. From Damascus a succession of Umayyad caliphs strove to build a bureaucracy that would bind together the vast domains they claimed to rule. The empire was very much an Arab conquest state. Except in the Arabian peninsula and in parts of the Fertile Crescent, a small Arab and Muslim aristocracy ruled over peoples who were neither Arab nor Muslim. Only Muslim Arabs were first-class citizens of this great empire. They made up the core of the army and imperial administration, and only they received a share of the booty derived from the ongoing conquests. They could be taxed only for charity. The Umayyads sought to keep the Muslim warrior elite concentrated in garrison towns and separated from the local population. It was hoped that isolation would keep them from assimilating to the subjugated cultures, because intermarriage meant conversion and the loss of taxable subjects.

Converts and "People of the Book"

Umayyad attempts to block extensive interaction between the Muslim warrior elite and the mass of their non-Muslim subjects had little chance of succeeding. The citified bedouin tribesmen were soon interacting intensively with the local populations of the conquered areas and intermarrying in considerable numbers with them. Equally critical, increasing numbers of these peoples were voluntarily converting to Islam, despite the fact that conversion did little to advance them socially or politically in the Umayyad period. *Mawali*, or Muslim converts, in this era still had to pay property taxes and in some cases the *jizya*, or head tax, levied on nonbelievers. They received no share of the booty and found it difficult, if not impossible, to acquire important positions in the army or bureaucracy. They were not even considered full members of the umma but were accepted only as clients of the powerful Arab clans. As a result, the number of conversions in the Umayyad era was low.

By far the greater portion of the population of the empire were *dhimmis,* or people of the book. As the title suggests, it was originally applied to Christians and Jews who shared the Bible with the Muslims. As Islamic conquests spread to other peoples, such as the Zoroastrians of Persia and the Hindus of India, the designation "dhimmi" was necessarily stretched to accommodate the majority groups within these areas of the empire. The Muslim overlords generally displayed tolerance toward the religions of dhimmi peoples. Though they had to pay the jizya and both commercial and property taxes, their communities and legal systems were left intact, and they were allowed to worship as they pleased. This approach made it a good deal easier for these peoples to accept Arab rule, particularly since many had been oppressed by their pre-Muslim overlords.

Family and Gender Roles in the Umayyad Age

Broader social changes within the Arab and widening Islamic community were accompanied by significant shifts in the position of women, both within the family and in society at large. In the first centuries of Arab expansion, the greatly strengthened position of women under Islam prevailed over the seclusion and domination by males

A congregation of Spanish Jews worshiping in their synagogue is depicted in this fourteenth-century manuscript page. One remarkable aspect of Spanish Islam was its treatment of the Jews. Like Christians, Jews were assessed a head tax and then allowed to pursue their lives unmolested. Many Jews rose to high office; others were distinguished scientists and philosophers.

that were characteristic features of women's lives through much of the rest of the Middle East. Muhammad's teachings and the dictates of the Quran stressed the moral and ethical dimensions of marriage. The kindness and concern the prophet displayed for his own wives and daughters did much to strengthen the bonds between husband and wife and the nuclear family in the Islamic community. Muhammad encouraged marriage as a replacement for the casual and often commercial sexual liaisons that had been widespread in pre-Islamic Arabia. He vehemently denounced adultery on the part of both husbands and wives, and he forbade female infanticide, which had apparently been widely practiced in Arabia in pre-Islamic times.

Though men were allowed to take up to four wives, the Quran forbade multiple marriages if the husband was not able to support more than one wife or treat all of his wives equally. Women could not take more than one husband, but Muhammad gave his own daughters a say

Whether in a nearby mosque or in their homes and shops, Muslims are required to pray five times a day, facing the holy city of Mecca.

Ali, while Zainab, Ali's daughter, went into battle with the ill-fated Husayn. Through much of the Umayyad period, little is heard of veiled Arab women, and they appear to have pursued a wide range of occupations, including scholarship, law, and commerce. Perhaps one of Zainab's nieces best epitomizes the independent-mindedness of Muslim women in the early Islamic era. When chided for going about without a veil, she replied that God in His wisdom had chosen to give her a beautiful face and that she intended to make sure that it was seen in public so that all might appreciate God's grace.

ANALYSIS

Civilization and Gender

Within a century of Muhammad's death, the relatively strong position women had enjoyed as a result of the teachings and example of the prophet had begun to erode. We do not fully understand all the forces that account for this decline. But almost certainly critical were the beliefs and practices of the urbanized, sedentary peoples in the areas the Arabs conquered and where many of them settled from the mid-7th century onward. The example of these ancient and long-civilized peoples increasingly influenced the Arab bearers of Islam. They developed a taste for city life and attempted to partake of the superior material and artistic culture of the peoples they ruled. In terms of gender roles, most of these influences weakened the position of women.

We have seen this apparent connection between increasing political centralization and urbanization and the declining position of women in many of the ancient and classical civilizations. In China, India, Greece, and the Middle East, women appear (on the basis of the limited sources available) to have enjoyed broader occupational options and a stronger voice within the family and also in society as a whole before the emergence of centralized kingdoms and highly stratified social systems. In each case, the rise of what we have termed civilizations strengthened paternal control within the family, inheritance through the male line, and male domination of positions of power and the most lucrative occupational roles. Women in these societies became more and more subjected to men—their fathers and brothers, husbands and sons—and more and more confined to the roles of homemakers and bearers of children. Women's legal

as to whom they might marry, and greatly strengthened the legal rights of women regarding inheritance and divorce. He insisted that the bride-price paid by the husband's family be given to his future wife, rather than to her father as before.

The prophet's teachings proclaimed the equality of men and women before God and in Islamic worship. Women were some of Muhammad's earliest and bravest followers. They accompanied his forces to battle (as did the wives of their adversaries) with the Meccans, and a woman was the first martyr for the new faith. Many of the *hadiths*, or traditions of the prophet, which have played such a critical role in Islamic law and ritual, were recorded by women, and Muhammad's wives and daughters played an important role in the compilation of the Quran. Though women were not allowed to be prayer leaders, they played an active role in the politics of the early community. Muhammad's widow, Aisha, actively promoted the claims of the Umayyad party against

rights were reduced, at times almost to the vanishing point, and various ways were devised to shut them off from the world.

As we have seen, women played active and highly valued roles in the bedouin tribes of pre-Islamic Arabia. They experienced considerable freedom (in terms of sexual and marriage partners), occupational choices (within the limited range available in a rather isolated pastoral society), and opportunities to influence clan decisions. The impact of the bedouin pattern of gender roles and relationships is clear in the teachings and personal behavior of Muhammad. Islam did much to legalize the rather strong, but by no means equal, status of women vis-à-vis men and gave greater uniformity to their position from one tribe, town, or region to the next. For a century or two after the prophet's death, women in the Islamic world enjoyed unprecedented opportunities for education, religious expression, and social fulfillment.

Then the influences of the cultures into which the Arabs had expanded began to take hold. The practices of veiling and female seclusion that were long followed by the non-Arab dwellers of Syria and Persia were increasingly adopted by Muslim women. Confined more and more to the home, women saw their occupational options decrease, and men served as their go-betweens in legal and commercial matters.

The erosion of the position of women was especially pronounced among those who lived in the cities that became the focus of Islamic civilization. Upper-class women, in particular, felt growing restrictions on their movement and activities. In the great residences that sprang up in the wealthy administrative centers and trading towns of the Middle East, the women's quarters were separate from the rest of the household and set off by high walls and gardens. In the palaces of Islamic rulers and provincial governors, this separation was marked by the development of the harem, or forbidden area. In the harem, the notables' wives and concubines lived in seclusion, guarded by the watchful eyes and sharp swords of corps of eunuchs, who were males castrated specifically to qualify them for the task. When women of the upper classes went forth into the city, they were veiled from head to toe and were often carried in covered sedan chairs by servants who guarded them from the glances of the townsmen and travelers. In their homes, upper-class women were spared the drudgery of domestic chores by large numbers of female slaves, who, if we are to judge from stories such as those related in the Arabian Nights, were fair game for their male masters.

Though veiling and seclusion and other practices that limited the physical and occupational mobility of women also spread to the lower urban classes and rural areas, they were never as stringently observed there as in urban, upper-class households. Women from poorer families had to work to survive. Thus, they had to go out—veiled but often unchaperoned—to the market or to work as domestic servants. Lower-class women also worked hard at home, not just at housekeeping but at weaving, rug making, and other crafts that provided key supplements to the family income. In rural areas and in towns distant from the main urban centers, veiling and confinement were also less strictly observed. Peasant women worked the family or local landlord's fields, planted their own kitchen gardens, and tended the livestock.

Because of Islamic religion and law, in all locales and at all class levels the position of women in the Middle East never deteriorated to the same extent as in India, China, and many other civilized centers. And because of the need to read the Quran, women continued to be educated, family resources permitting, even if they rarely were able to use their learning for scholarship or artistic expression. Islamic law preserved for women property, inheritance, divorce, and remarriage rights that were frequently denied in other civilized societies. Thus, the strong position women had enjoyed in bedouin cultures and that in many respects had been built into Islam was never entirely undone by the customs and practices of the civilized centers in the rest of the Middle East.

The fact that the position of women has also been relatively strong in other cultural areas where authority is decentralized and social organization not highly stratified, such as West Africa, suggests that at least in certain stages of its development, civilization works against the interests of women. The control women in decentralized societies have over their own property; the necessity, given limited labor power, for them to become involved in key economic activities; and their important roles in political councils (which are closely tied to each family in the clan or village) suggest areas that might be explored in the attempt to understand why there has been a greater balance in gender roles and power in precivilized societies. The very immediate connection between women and agriculture or stock-raising chores, which are central to survival in these societies, may also account for the greater respect accorded them as well as their often prominent roles in fertility rituals and religious cults. Whatever the explanation, until the present era, higher degrees of centralization and social stratification—both characteristic features of civilized societies—have almost always favored males in the allotment of power and career opportunities.

Questions: Compare the position of women in classical Indian, Chinese, Roman, and Greek societies with regard to their ability to hold property, opportunity to pursue careers outside the home, rights in marriage and divorce, and level of education. Why were women relatively better off in such societies as the Islamic and the Roman? Were differences in the position of women at various class levels similar among these societies? In what ways were women better off in decentralized pastoral or forest-farming societies? What advantages have they enjoyed in urbanized and centralized civilizations?

Umayyad Decline and Fall

The ever-increasing size of the royal harem was just one manifestation of the Umayyad caliphs' growing addiction to luxury and soft living. Their legitimacy had been disputed by various Muslim factions from the outset of their seizure of the caliphate. But the Umayyads further alienated the Muslim faithful as they became more aloof in the early decades of the 8th century and retreated from the dirty business of war into their pleasure gardens and marble palaces. Their abandonment of the frugal, simple lifestyle followed by Muhammad and the earliest caliphs—including Abu Bakr, who made a trip to the market the day after he was selected to succeed the prophet—enraged the dissenting sects and sparked revolts throughout the empire. The uprising that would prove fatal to the short-lived dynasty began among the frontier warriors who had fought and settled in distant Iran.

By the middle decades of the 8th century, more than 50,000 warriors had settled near the oasis town of Merv in the eastern Iranian borderlands of the empire. Many of them had married local women, and over time they had come to identify with the region and to resent the dictates of governors sent from distant Damascus. The warrior settlers were also angered by the fact that they were rarely given the share of the booty, which was now officially tallied in the account books of the royal treasury, that they had earned by fighting the wars of expansion and defending the frontiers. They were contemptuous of the Umayyads and the Damascus elite, whom they viewed as corrupt and decadent. In the early 740s, an attempt by Umayyad palace officials to introduce new troops into the Merv area touched off a revolt that soon spread over much of the eastern portions of the empire.

Marching under the black banners of the *Abbasid* party, which traced its descent from Muhammad's uncle, al-Abbas, the frontier warriors were openly challenging Umayyad armies by 747. Deftly forging alliances with Shi'ite rebels and other dissident groups that challenged the Umayyads throughout the empire, their leader, Abu al-Abbas, the great-great-grandson of the prophet's uncle, led his forces from victory to victory. Persia and then Iraq fell to the rebels. In 750, they met an army led by the Umayyad caliph himself in a massive *Battle on the River Zab* near the Tigris. The Abbasid victory resulted in the conquest of Syria and the capture of the Umayyad capital.

Desiring to eliminate the Umayyad family altogether to prevent recurring challenges to his rule, Abu al-Abbas invited numerous members of the clan to what was styled as a reconciliation banquet. As the Umayyads were enjoying the feast, guards covered them with carpets and they were slaughtered by Abbas's troops. An effort was then made to hunt down and kill all the remaining members of the family throughout the empire. Most were slain, but the grandson of a former caliph fled to distant Spain, and founded there the Caliphate of Cordoba, which was to live on for centuries after the rest of the empire had disappeared.

FROM ARAB TO ISLAMIC EMPIRE: THE EARLY ABBASID ERA

Focal Point: The sudden shift from Umayyad to Abbasid leadership within the Islamic Empire reflected a series of even more fundamental transformations within the evolving Islamic civilization. The revolts against the Umayyads were fundamentally a product of growing regional identities and divisions within the Islamic world. As Islamic civilization spread even farther under the Abbasids, these regional interests and religious divisions made it increasingly difficult to hold together the vast areas the Arabs had conquered. They also gave rise to new cleavages within the Islamic community that have sapped its strength from within, from Abbasid times to the present day. The victory of the Abbasids led to bureaucratic expansion, absolutism, and luxury on a scale beyond the wildest dreams of the Umayyads. The Abbasids also championed a policy of active conversion and the admission of converts as full members of the Islamic community. As a result, Islam was transformed from the religion of a small, Arab warrior elite into a cosmopolitan and genuinely universal faith with tens of millions of adherents from Spain to the Philippine islands.

The rough treatment the Umayyad clan had received at the hands of the victorious Abbasids ought to have forewarned their Shi'i and mawali allies of what was to come. But the Shi'i and other dissenting groups continued the support that allowed the Abbasids to level all other centers of political rivalry until it was too late. Gradually, the Abbasids rejected many of their old allies, becoming in the process more and more righteous in their defense of Sunni Islam and increasingly less tolerant of what they termed the heretical views of the various sects of Shi'ism. With the Umayyads all but eliminated and their allies brutally suppressed, the way was clear for the Abbasids to build a centralized, absolutist imperial order.

The fact that they chose to build their new capital, *Baghdad,* in Iraq near the ancient Persian capital of Ctesiphon was a clear sign of things to come. Soon the Abbasid caliphs were perched atop jewel-encrusted thrones, reminiscent of those of the ancient Persian emperors, gazing down on the great gatherings of courtiers and petitioners who bowed before them in their gilt and marbled audience halls. The caliphs' palaces and harems expanded to keep pace with their claims to absolute power over the Islamic faithful as well as the non-Muslim subjects of their vast empire.

The ever-expanding corps of bureaucrats, servants, and slaves who strove to translate Abbasid political claims into reality lived and worked within the circular walls of the new capital at Baghdad. The bureaucratization of the Islamic Empire was reflected above all in the growing power of the *wazir,* or chief administrator and head of the caliph's inner councils, and of the sinister figure of the royal executioner, who stood close to the throne in the public audiences of the Abbasid rulers. The wazirs oversaw the building of an administrative infrastructure that allowed the Abbasids to project their demands for tribute to the most distant provinces of the empire. Sheer size, poor communications, and collusion between Abbasid officials and local notables meant that the farther the town or village was from the capital, the less effectively royal commands were carried out. But for well over a century, the Abbasid regime was fairly effective at collecting revenue from its subject peoples and preserving law and order over much of the empire.

The presence of the executioner perhaps most strikingly symbolized the absolutist pretensions of the Abbasid rulers. With a wave of his hand, a caliph could condemn the highest of Muslim nobles to death. Thus, even in matters of life and death, the Abbasids claimed a status above the rest of the Muslim faithful and even above Islamic law that would have been rejected as heretical by

In this 15th-century Persian miniature, the Tigris River is shown flooding portions of the Abbasid capital at Baghdad.

the early community of believers. Though they stopped short of declaring themselves divine, the Abbasid rulers styled themselves the "shadow of God on earth," beings clearly superior to ordinary mortals—Muslim or otherwise. The openness and accessibility of the earlier caliphs, including the Umayyads, had become more and more unimaginable. The old days, when members of the Muslim community could request an audience with the caliph merely by ringing a bell announcing their presence in the palace, were clearly gone. Now, just to get into the vast and crowded throne room, one had to bribe and petition numerous officials, and more often than not the best result would be to win a few minutes with the wazir or one of his assistants. If an official or notable were lucky enough to buy and beg an audience with the caliph, he had to observe an elaborate sequence of bowing and prostration in approaching the throne.

The "Good Life" in the Abbasid Age

The luxurious lifestyle of the Abbasid rulers and their courtiers reflected the new wealth of the political and commercial elites of the Islamic Empire and also intensified sectarian and social divisions within the Islamic community. As the compilation of folk tales, *The Thousand and One Nights* from many parts of the empire testifies, life for much of the elite in Baghdad and other major urban centers was luxurious and was oriented to the delights of the flesh. Caliphs and wealthy merchants lived in palatial residences of stone and marble, complete with gurgling fountains and elaborate gardens, which served as retreats from the glare and heat of the southern Mediterranean climate. In the Abbasid palaces, luxurious living and ostentation soared to fantastic heights. In the Hall of the Tree, for example, there was a huge artificial tree, made entirely of gold and silver and filled with gold mechanical birds that chirped to keep the caliph in good cheer.

Sexual enjoyment, which within the confines of marriage had been condoned rather than restricted by the Quran, often degenerated into eroticism for its own sake. The harem, replete with fierce eunuchs, insatiable sultans, and veiled damsels, provided outside observers with a stereotypic image of the Abbasid world that had little to do with the life of the average citizen of the empire—and often even little to do with that of the caliph and high officials. Yet, as is illustrated by the following passage from *The Thousand and One Nights* describing the interior of the mansion of a Baghdad notable, the material delights of the Abbasid era were enjoyed beyond the confines of the palace:

> They reached a spacious ground-floor hall, built with admirable skill and beautified with all manner of colors and carvings, with upper balconies and groined arches and galleries and cupboards and recesses whose curtains hung before them. In the midst stood a great basin full of water surrounding a fine fountain, and at the upper end on the raised dais was a couch of juniper wood set with gems and pearls, with a canopy-like mosquito curtain of red satin-silk looped up with pearls as big as filberts and bigger.

Since the tales were just that—tall stories—there is some exaggeration of the wealth, as well as the romantic exploits and human excesses, of the world depicted. But for the free-living members of the elite classes, the luxuries, frivolities, and vices of the Abbasid age were very real indeed.

Islamic Conversion and Mawali Acceptance

The Abbasid era saw the full integration of new converts, both Arab and non-Arab, into the Islamic community. In the last decades of the Umayyad period, there was a growing acceptance of the mawali as equals and some effort to win new converts to the faith, particularly among Arab peoples outside the Arabian peninsula. In the Abbasid era, mass conversions to Islam were encouraged for all peoples of the empire, from the Berbers of North Africa in the west to the Persians and Turkic peoples of Central Asia in the east. Converts were admitted on an equal footing with the first generations of believers, and over time the distinction between mawali and the earlier converts all but disappeared.

Most converts were won over peacefully, owing to the great appeal of Islamic beliefs and to the considerable advantages they enjoyed over non-Muslim peoples in the empire. Not only were converts exempt from paying the head tax, but greater opportunities were open to them to get advanced schooling and launch careers as administrators, traders, or judges. No group demonstrated the new opportunities open to converts as dramatically as the Persians, who soon came to dominate the upper levels of imperial administration. In fact, as the Abbasid rulers became more dissolute and consequently less interested in affairs of state, several powerful Persian families close to the throne became the real locus of power within the imperial system.

Commercial Boom and Urban Growth

The rise of the mawali was paralleled in the Abbasid era by the growth in wealth and social status of the commercial and landlord classes of the empire. The Abbasid age was a time of great urban expansion that was linked to a revival of the Afro-Eurasian trading network, which had declined with the fall of the Han dynasty in China in the early 3rd century C.E. and the slow collapse of the Roman Empire in the 4th and 5th centuries. The Abbasid domains in the west and the great Tang and Song empires in the east became the pivots of the revived commercial system. From the western Mediterranean to the South China Sea, Arab *dhows*, or sailing vessels with triangular, or lateen, sails that later strongly influenced European ship design, carried the goods of one civilized core to be exchanged with those of another.

Muslim merchants, often in joint ventures with Christians and Jews (which, because each merchant had a different Sabbath, meant that the firm could carry on business all week), grew rich by supplying the cities of the empire with provisions and by taking charge of the long-distance trade that specialized in luxury products for the elite classes. The great profits made from the trade were reinvested in new commercial enterprises, the purchase of land, and the construction of the great mansions that dominated the central quarters of the political and commercial hubs of the empire. Some wealth also went to charity, as required by the Quran. A good deal of the wealth was spent on building and running mosques and religious schools, baths and rest houses for weary travelers, and hospitals, which in the numbers of patients served and the quality of their medical care surpassed those of any other civilization to that time.

Town and Country

In addition to the expanding bureaucracy and servant classes and the boom in commerce, the growth of Abbasid cities was fed by a great increase in artisan handicraft production. Both government-run and privately owned artisan workshops expanded or were established for the production of a wide range of products, from necessities such as furniture and carpets to luxury items such as glassware, jewelry, and tapestries. Though the artisans were frequently poorly paid and some worked in great workshops, they were not slaves or drudge laborers. They owned their own tools and were often highly valued for their craft skills. The most skilled of the artisans formed guildlike organizations, which negotiated wages and working conditions with the merchant oligarchy and provided support for their members in times of financial difficulty or personal crisis.

In towns and the countryside, much of the unskilled labor was left to slaves, who were frequently attached in considerable numbers to prominent families as domestic servants. Large numbers of slaves were also in the service of the caliphs and their highest advisors. It was possible for the more clever and ambitious of these to rise to positions of considerable power, and many were able eventually to be granted their freedom or to buy it. Less fortunate were the slaves forced into lives of hard labor under the overseer's whip on rural estates and government projects, such as those devoted to draining marshlands, or into a lifetime of labor in the nightmare conditions of the great salt mines in southern Iraq. Most of these drudge laborers, who were called the *Zanj* slaves, were non-Muslims captured on slaving raids in East Africa. With little hope of mobility, much less manumis-

sion, they had little reason to convert to Islam, and from the middle of the 9th century they became a major source of social unrest.

In the countryside, a wealthy and deeply entrenched landed elite, referred to as the *ayan*, emerged in the early decades of Abbasid rule. Many of the landlords had been long established. Others were newcomers: Arab soldiers who invested their share of the booty in land, or merchants and administrators who funneled their profits and kickbacks into the acquisition of sizable estates. In many regions, the vast majority of the peasantry did not own the land they worked. They occupied it as tenants, sharecroppers, or migrant laborers who were required to give the greater portion of the crops they harvested to the estate owners.

The First Flowering of Islamic Learning

When the Arabs first came out of the desert, they were for the most part illiterate and ignorant of the wider world. Their provincialism and cultural backwardness was no better revealed than at the moment when the victorious Muslim armies came within sight of the city of Alexandria in Egypt. Chroniclers of the great conquests record how the veteran Arab warriors halted and sat on their horses, mouths literally open in wonderment, before the great walls of the city that stretched across the horizon from the Pharos lighthouse in the north to perhaps the greatest library in the ancient world in the south.

As this confrontation suggests, the Arab conquerors burst quite suddenly into some of the most ancient and highly developed centers of civilization known to human history. Within the confines of the Islamic domains were located the centers of the Hellenistic, Persian, Indian, Egyptian, and Mesopotamian civilizations as well as the widely dispersed Christian and Jewish traditions of thought and learning. The rather sparse cultural tradition of the Arabs, which one author has fittingly captured with reference to their "mental virginity," made them highly receptive to influences percolating from the subject peoples and remarkably tolerant of the great diversity of their styles and approaches to thought and artistic creativity.

In the first phase of Abbasid rule, the Islamic contribution to human artistic expression focused on the great mosques and palaces. In addition to advances in religious, legal, and philosophical discourse, the Islamic contribution to learning was focused on the sciences and mathematics. In the early Abbasid period, the main tasks were recovering and preserving the learning of the ancient civilizations of the Mediterranean and Middle East. Beyond the works of Plato, for example, much of Greek

The Mosque as a Symbol of Islamic Civilization

From one end of the Islamic world to the other, Muslim towns and cities could (and can today) be readily identified by the domes and minarets of the mosques where the faithful were (and are) called to prayer five times daily. The following illustrations trace the development of the mosque and the refinement of mosque architecture—the crowning glory of Islamic material culture—during the early centuries of Muslim expansion. As you look at these photos and follow the development of the mosque, consider what the functions of the mosque and the evolving style of mosque architecture can tell us about Muslim beliefs and values and the impact of Islam on earlier religions, such as Judaism and Christianity.

Given the low level of material culture in pre-Islamic Arabia, it is not surprising that the earliest prayer houses were simple in design and construction. In fact, these first mosques were laid out along the lines suggested by Muhammad's own house. They were square enclosures with a shaded porch on one side, a columned shelter on the other, and an open courtyard in between. The outer perimeter of the earliest mosques were made of reed mats, but soon more permanent stone walls surrounded the courtyard and prayer areas. After Mecca was taken and the Ka'ba became the central shrine of the new faith, each mosque was oriented to the qibla, or Mecca wall, which always faced in the direction of the holy city.

In the last years of the prophet, his chair was located so that the faithful could see and hear him during prayer sessions. During the time of the first caliphs, the raised area became the place from which sermons were delivered. From the middle of the 8th century, this space evolved into a genuine pulpit. Somewhat earlier, the practice of building a special and often elaborately decorated niche in the qibla had developed.

Over time the construction of the mosque became more elaborate. Very often the remains of Greek or Roman temples or abandoned Christian churches formed the core of major mosques, or the ruins of these struc-

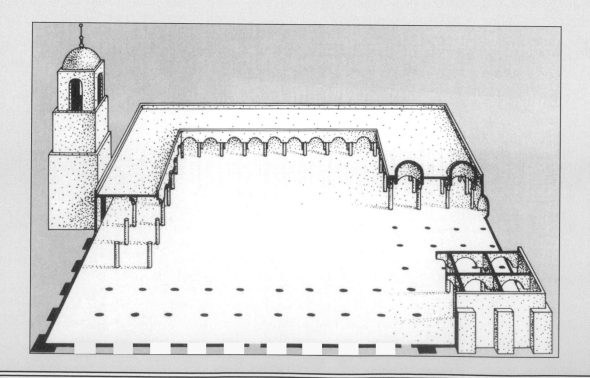

tures were mined for stone for mosque construction. In the larger cities, the courtyards of the great mosques were surrounded by columns and arches, and eventually they were enclosed by great domes such as that at the Dome of the Rock in Jerusalem.

The first minarets, or towers from which the faithful were called to prayer, were added in the early 8th century and soon became a key feature of the mosque complex. As mosques grew larger and more architecturally refined, elaborate decoration in brightly colored ceramic tiles, semiprecious stones, and gold and silver filigree adorned their sides and domes. Because human and animal images were forbidden, geometric designs, passages from the Quran in swirling Arabic, and flower and plant motifs were favored. Nowhere were these decorations more splendid than in the great mosques of Persia. Thus, in the early centuries of Islam, these great houses of worship became the focal points of Islamic cities, key places of community worship and socialization, and, with the schools that were often attached, vital intellectual and educational centers of the Islamic world.

Questions: What do the design and decoration of Muslim mosques tell us about the Islamic view of God and the relationship between God and humans? Discuss the Christian and Jewish influences you detect in mosque design and the pattern of the religious worship conducted there. What do you think is the significance of the lavish application of color and the frequent use of floral and plant motifs and Arabic verses from the Quran in the decoration of mosques through much of the Muslim world?

learning had been lost to the peoples of western Europe, Thanks to Muslim and Jewish scholars in the Abbasid domains, the priceless writings of the Greeks on key subjects such as medicine, algebra, geometry, astronomy, anatomy, and ethics were saved, recopied in Arabic, and dispersed throughout the empire. From Spain in the west, Greek writings found their way into Christendom. Among the authors rescued in this manner, one need only mention Aristotle, Galen, Hippocrates, Ptolemy, and Euclid to demonstrate the importance of the preservation effort.

In addition, scholars working in Arabic played a role as transmitters of ideas that paralleled the rise of Arab traders and merchants as the carriers of goods and inventions. Indian numbers, for example—which, along with Greek mathematics, would prove critical to the development of scientific thinking in western Europe—were learned by Muslim invaders of India, carried to the Middle Eastern centers of Islamic civilization, and eventually transmitted across the Mediterranean to Italy and from there to northern Europe.

CONCLUSION

The Measure of Islamic Achievement

By the 9th century, growing social stratification, sectarian divisions, and regional separatism had noticeably eroded the hold of the Abbasid caliphs on their vast empire. Non-Arab peoples such as the Turks, who had converted to Islam and migrated into the Muslim heartlands of Mesopotamia and North Africa, increasingly dominated political life. These newcomers carved out kingdoms within the Abbasid realm that soon outstripped the nominally sovereign caliphate in real military and political power. As we shall see in Chapter 13, Turkic peoples, and on occasion new Arab contenders for influence, became the chief defenders of Islamic civilization against growing challenges from western Europe and central Asia.

Though political power steadily passed to other groups within the Muslim community, the Arab accomplishment had been stunning. Not only had the largely nomadic peoples from the Arabian backwater managed to build one of the greatest empires of the preindustrial world, they had laid the basis for the first truly global civilization—if one excludes the Americas, which they cannot be expected to have influenced, since the Americas were as yet unknown to the Old World. Building on earlier religious traditions, especially Christianity and Judaism, Arab culture had nurtured Islam—one of the great universal religions of humankind. The mosques, the prayer rituals and pilgrimages of the faithful, and the influence of Islamic law proclaimed the pervasive effects of this new creed on societies from Spain to eastern Indonesia and from central Asia to the savannas of West Africa.

Religion and politics had been conjoined from the time of the prophet Muhammad in the early 7th century. But under the Umayyad caliphs (661–750) and the early Abbasids who followed them, religious legitimacy was used to build a powerful, absolutist political order to govern the vast domains won by Islamic armies. Again, the Muslims drew on the bureaucratic institutions, the royal precedents, and even the personnel of preexisting civilizations, particularly those of Persia and the Byzantine Empire.

In the arts and sciences, the Muslims also initially relied heavily on the achievements of the classical civilizations of Greece and Mesopotamia. But the work of preserving and combining the discoveries of earlier peoples soon led to reformulation and innovation. As in religion and politics, Muslim peoples were soon making important original contributions to learning, invention, and artistic creativity, which were carried by their armies and religious teachers to other civilizations in Europe, Africa, and Asia.

Never before had a civilization spanned so many different cultures and combined such a patchwork of linguistic groups, religions, and ethnic types. Never before had a single civilization mediated so successfully between the other centers of civilized life. Never had a civilized lifestyle so deeply affected so many of the nomadic cultures that still surrounded the pools of sedentary agriculture and urban life. Ironically, the contacts Islamic mediation made possible between the civilized cores of the Eastern Hemisphere would contribute much to the transformations in technology and organization that would increasingly tilt the balance of power against the Muslim

peoples. But those reversals were still far in the future. In the short run, Islamic conversion and contact appeared to have ushered in an age of unprecedented nomadic intervention in and dominance over global history.

FURTHER READINGS

There are many accounts of Muhammad's life and the rise of Islam. A sense of these pivotal historical events from different perspectives can be gained from W. Montgomery Watt's *Muhammad: Prophet and Statesman* (1961), Tor Andrae's *Mohammed: The Man and His Faith* (1960), Maxime Rodinson's *Mohammad* (1971), and the more recent revisionist (and somewhat less accessible for the general reader) writings of Elizabeth Crone and Michael Cook. Despite its unfortunate title, H. A. R. Gibb's *Mohammedism* (1962) remains a useful introduction to Islam as a religion. On early Islamic expansion and civilization through the first centuries of the Abbasid caliphate, see G. E. von Grunebaum's *Classical Islam* (1970), M. A. Shaban's *Islamic History: An Interpretation* (1971), and *The Abbasid Revolution* (1970). On virtually all of these topics, it is difficult to surpass Marshall G. S. Hodgson's brilliant analysis, *The Venture of Islam* (1974, vol. 1), but some grounding in the history and beliefs of the Muslims is highly recommended before one attempts this sweeping and provocative work. More accessible to the nonspecialist reader, but still authoritative and highly interpretive, are Ira M. Lapidus's *A History of Islamic Societies* (1988) and Albert Hourani's recent *A History of the Arab Peoples* (1991).

On early Islamic society generally, see M. M. Ahsan's *Social Life Under the Abbasids* (1979). On women in Islam specifically, there is a superb essay by Guity Nashat, "Women in the Middle East, 8000 B.C.—A.D. 1800," in the collection titled *Restoring Women to History*, published in 1988 by the Organization of American Historians. See also the relevant portions of the essays in Lois Beck and Nikki Keddi, eds., *Women in the Muslim World* (1978). For insights into Islamic culture and civilization from a literary perspective, a good place to begin is Eric Schroeder's delightful *Muhammad's People: A Tale by Anthology* (1955) and N. J. Dawood's translation, of the *Tales from the Thousand and One Nights* (1954). Of the many works on Muslim architecture, John D. Hoag's *Western Islamic Architecture* (1963) gives a good overview, but K. A. Creswell's *Early Muslim Architecture*, 2 vols. (1932–1940) provides greater detail and far better illustrations.

13

Abbasid Decline and the Spread of Islamic Civilization to South and Southeast Asia

604–646 Harsha's empire in India

711–713 First Muslim raids into India

661–750 Umayyad caliphate (Damascus)

775–785 Reign of al-Mahdi

750 Establishment of the Abbasid caliphate (Baghdad)

786–809 Reign of al-Rashid

777 Independent dynasty established in Algeria

788 Independent dynasty established in Morocco

800 Independent dynasty established in Tunisia

813–833 Reign of al-Ma'mun; first mercenary forces recruited

809 First war of succession between Abbasid princes

865–925 Life of al-Razi; physician and scientist

700 C.E.

800 C.E.

INTRODUCTION

By the middle decades of the 9th century C.E., the Abbasid dynasty had clearly begun to lose control over the vast Muslim Empire that had been won from the Umayyads a century earlier. From North Africa in the west to the Iranian heartlands in the east, rebellious governors and new dynasties arose to challenge the Abbasid caliphs' claims to be the rightful overlords of all Islamic peoples. As had been the case with the Umayyads before them, the Abbasids' ability to hold together the highly diversified empire they claimed in the 750s was greatly hampered by the difficulties of moving armies and compelling local administrators to obey orders across the great distances that separated the capital at Baghdad from the far-flung provinces they sought to rule. Travel by land and sea was slow and often dangerous. Most of the peoples of the empire maintained regional identities rather than an attachment to the caliphal regime at Baghdad. In addition, Abbasid control was constricted by the fact that the military technology of the rebel forces was often on a par with, and at times superior to, their own.

In addition to the splintering of the empire into often hostile states, the Abbasids had to contend with periodic revolts within the regions where they managed to maintain their rule. Here Shi'i dissenters, belonging to an ever-proliferating variety of sects, were particularly troublesome. Major slave revolts and more localized peasant risings also sapped the strength of the empire. The Abbasids' capacity to meet these challenges was steadily diminished by the decline in the quality of Abbasid leadership. In addition, there was a sharp decrease in resources available to even the more able of the later caliphs, owing to losses in territory and control over the revenues collected by regional officials. When Mongol invasions finally put an end to the caliphate in the middle of the 13th century, it was only a shadow of the great empire that had once ruled much of the Islamic world.

Paradoxically, even as the political power of the Abbasids declined and the Muslim world broke into a patchwork of rival kingdoms and empires, Islamic civilization reached new heights of creativity and entered a new age of expansion in both the east and west. In architecture and the fine arts, in literature and philosophy, and in mathematics and the sciences, the centuries during which the Abbasid Empire was slowly dismembered were an era of remarkable achievement. At the same time, political fragmentation did little to slow the process of the growth of the Islamic world through political conquest and more enduring peaceful conversion. From the 10th to the 14th century, Muslim warriors, traders, and wandering mystics carried the faith of Muhammad into the savanna and desert of West Africa, down the coast of East Africa, to the Turks and numerous other nomadic peoples of central Asia, and into South and Southeast Asia. For over five centuries, the spread of Islam played a central role in the rise, extension, or transformation of civilization in much of the Afro-Asian world.

In the early sections of this chapter, we will consider the forces that led to the prolonged disintegration of the Abbasid caliphate and the resulting political fragmentation of the Islamic world. The next sections focus on the great artistic and scientific accomplishments that Muslim peoples managed in the midst of political and social turmoil, and often in defiance of it. Central to these achievements were contacts between the many ancient centers of civilization that had been or were being brought into the Muslim orbit. New converts, such as the Turkic peoples of central Asia, brought a revival of military and political strength. This restored the authority of the caliphal regime for a time and enabled the Muslims to fend off the assaults of the crusading Europeans. Muslim trading contacts and conversions in other areas—Africa, India, Malaya, and the Indonesian archi-

973–1050 Life of al-Biruni, scientist

998 Beginning of Ghanzi raids into western India

c. 1020 Death of Firdawsi, author of the *Shah-Nama*

945 Persian Buyids capture Baghdad; caliphs made into puppet rulers

1055 Seljuk Turks overthrow Buyids, control caliphate

1096–1099 First Christian Crusade in Palestine

1206 Establishment of the Delhi sultanate in India

1111 Death of al-Ghazali, philosopher and scientist

1123 Death of Omar Khayyam, scientist and poet

1290s Beginning of the spread of Islam in Southeast Asia

1291 Fall of Acre; last Crusader stronghold in Middle East

1258 Fall of Baghdad to Mongols; end of Abbasid caliphate

900 C.E.   1000 C.E.   1200 C.E.

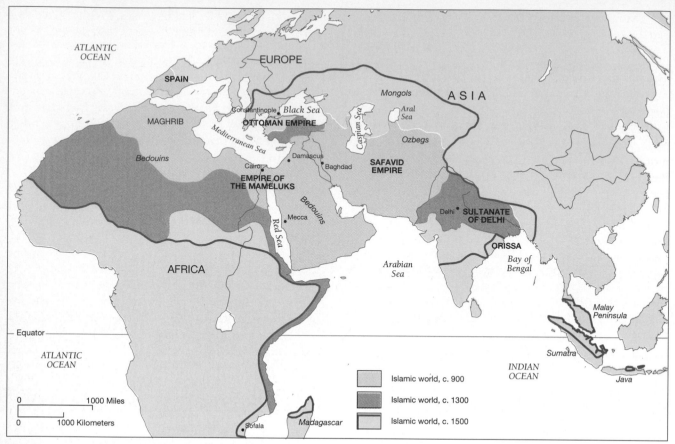

The Spread of Islam from the 10th to the 16th Centuries

pelago—drew new peoples, food crops, tools, and knowledge into the Islamic heartland areas. At the same time, the influx of conversion-minded Muslim peoples with their own very substantial cultural baggage brought fundamental transformations to virtually all these regions. In the latter sections of this chapter, we will explore the patterns and impact of Islamic expansion into South and Southeast Asia. In the next chapter, we will examine the ways in which the coming of Islam affected the development of civilization in various parts of Africa.

THE ISLAMIC HEARTLANDS IN THE MID- AND LATE-ABBASID ERA

Focal Point: The vast Abbasid empire gradually disintegrated between the 9th and 13th centuries. Revolts spread among the peasantry, slavery increased, and the position of women was further eroded. Divisions within the empire opened the way for Christian crusaders from western Europe to invade and, for a short period of time, carve out warrior kingdoms in the Muslim heartlands. Political decline and social turmoil were offset for many by the urban affluence, inventiveness, and artistic creativity of the Abbasid age.

As early as the reign of the third Abbasid caliph, *al-Mahdi* (775–785), the courtly excesses and political divisions that would eventually contribute significantly to the decline of the empire were quite apparent. Al-Mahdi's efforts to reconcile the moderates among the Shi'i opposition to Abbasid rule ended in failure, and Shi'i revolts and assassination attempts against Abbasid officials would plague the dynasty to the end of its days. Al-Mahdi abandoned the frugal ways of his predecessor and, in the brief span of his reign, established the taste for luxury and monumental building and the habit of surrounding himself with a multitude of dependent wives, concubines, and courtiers that would prove an ever greater financial drain in the reigns of succeeding caliphs.

Perhaps most critically, al-Mahdi failed to find a solution to the vexing problem of succession. Not only did he waver between which of his older sons ought to succeed him, he allowed his wives and concubines, the mothers of different candidates, to become involved in the palace intrigues that henceforth became a standard feature of the transfer of power from one caliph to the next. Though a full-scale civil war was avoided after al-Mahdi's death, within a year his eldest son and successor was poisoned. That perfidious act cleared the way for one of the most famous and enduring of the Abbasid caliphs, *al-Rashid* (786–809), to ascend the throne.

Imperial Extravagance and Succession Disputes

Emissaries sent in the early years of the 9th century to Baghdad from Charlemagne, then the most powerful monarch in Christian Europe, provide ample evidence that al-Rashid continued and enhanced his father's precedents for sumptuous and costly living among the courtly elite. Al-Rashid dazzled the Christians with the splendor of Baghdad's mosques, palaces, and treasure troves, and he also sent them back to Charlemagne with presents, including an intricate water clock and an elephant, that were quite literally worth a king's ransom. The luxury and intrigue of al-Rashid's court have also been immortalized by the tales of *The Thousand and One Nights*, which are set in the Baghdad of his day. The plots and maneuvers of the courtesans, eunuchs, and royal ministers related in the tales suggest yet another source of dynastic weakness. Partly because he was only 23 at the time of his accession to the throne, al-Rashid became heavily dependent, particularly in the early years of his reign, on a family of Persian advisors. Though he eventually put a halt to their usurpation of his powers and had these ambitious ministers executed or imprisoned, the growth of the power of royal advisors at the expense of the caliphs became a clear trend in succeeding reigns. In fact, from the mid-9th century onward, most of the caliphs were pawns in the power struggles between different factions at the court.

Al-Rashid's death was the signal for the first of several full-scale civil wars over succession. In itself, the precedent set by the struggle for the throne was deeply damaging to the dynasty, but it had an additional conse-

quence that would all but put an end to the real power of the caliphs. The first civil war convinced the sons of al-Ma'mun (813–833), the winner, that they needed to build personal armies in anticipation of the fight for the throne that would break out on the death of their father. One of the sons, significantly the victor in the next round of succession struggles, recruited a "bodyguard" of some 4000 slaves, mostly Turkic-speaking nomads from central Asia. On becoming caliph, he increased this mercenary force to over 70,000.

Not surprisingly, this impressive force soon became a power center in its own right, much like the Praetorian Guard in the later centuries of the Roman Empire. In 846, slave mercenaries murdered the reigning caliph and placed one of the caliph's sons on the throne. In the

The richness and vitality of urban life in the Islamic world in the Abbasid age and succeeding eras are wonderfully captured in this 16th-century Persian illustration from the Khamsah (Five Poems) *of Nizami.*

next decade, four more caliphs were assassinated or poisoned by the mercenary forces. From this time onward, the leaders of the slave mercenary armies were often the real power behind the Abbasid throne and were consistently major players in the factional contests for control of the capital and empire.

Between stints of military service, which the mercenaries became more and more adept at keeping to a minimum or avoiding altogether, they became a rowdy and volatile element in the capital and garrison towns into which they crowded. They bullied the local populace and quarreled, often violently, among themselves. When their salaries and provisions were meager or late in coming (a situation that became increasingly frequent as the central government's share of the revenues fell to a small fraction of the taxes actually collected), they sacked and pillaged or became a leading element in the food riots that broke out periodically in the urban centers.

Imperial Breakdown and Agrarian Disorder

In the last decades of the 9th century, the dynasty brought the slave armies under control for a time, but at a great cost. Incessant civil violence drained the treasury and alienated the subjects of the Abbasids. A further strain was placed on the empire's dwindling revenues by some caliphs' attempts to escape the perils and turmoil of Baghdad by establishing new capitals in the vicinity of the original capital. The construction of palaces, mosques, and public works for each of these new imperial centers added to the already exorbitant costs of maintaining the court and imperial administration. The burden of footing the bill, of course, fell heavily on the already hard-pressed peasantry of the central provinces of the empire, where some semblance of imperial control still remained.

The need to support growing numbers of mercenary troops also increased the revenue demands on the peasantry. Lacking the bureaucratic means to pay a regular salary to the commanders of the mercenary forces and stipends for their troops, the Abbasid regime farmed out the revenues from various parts of the empire to these military chiefs and their retainers. Some of the commanders were concerned for the welfare of the village populations under their control and tried to make improvements in irrigation and cropping patterns that would enhance the revenues they received over the long term. Unfortunately, the majority of the mercenary leaders tried to exact as much as possible from the hapless peasants.

Spiraling taxation and outright pillaging led to the destruction or abandonment of many villages in the richest provinces of the empire. The great irrigation works that had for centuries been essential to agricultural production in the fertile Tigris-Euphrates basin fell into disrepair and in some areas collapsed entirely. Some peas-

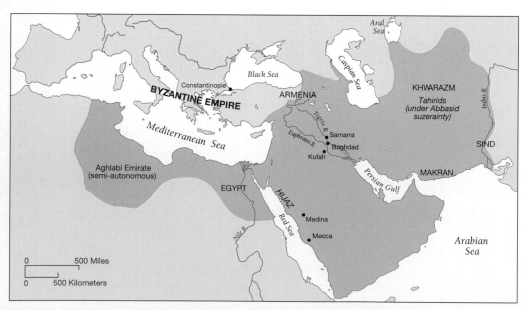

The Abbasid Empire at Its Peak, c. 900 C.E.

ants perished through flood, famine, or violent assault; others fled to wilderness areas beyond the reach of the Abbasid tax farmers or to neighboring kingdoms. Some formed bandit gangs that grew in size and audacity or joined the crowds of vagabonds that trudged the highways and camped in the towns of the imperial heartland. At times, bandits and vagabonds were involved in the food riots in the towns or the local peasant rebellions that broke out periodically during the later Abbasid period. In many cases, dissident religious groups, such as the various Shi'i sects, instigated these uprisings, thereby making them movements that not only challenged the legitimacy of the Abbasid regime but were dedicated to its utter destruction.

The Declining Position of Women in the Family and Society

The harem and the veil became the twin emblems of women's increasing subjugation to men and confinement to the home in the Abbasid era. Though the seclusion of women had been practiced by some Middle Eastern peoples since ancient times, the harem was a creation of the Abbasid court. Both the wives and the concubines of the Abbasid caliphs were restricted to the forbidden quarters of the imperial palace. Many of the concubines were slaves, who could win their freedom and amass considerable power by bearing healthy sons for the rulers. The growing wealth of the Abbasid elite generated a large demand for female and male slaves, who were found in the tens of thousands in Baghdad and other large cities. Most of these urban slaves continued to perform domestic services in the homes of the wealthy. One of the 10th-century caliphs is reputed to have had 11,000 eunuchs among his slave corps; another is said to have kept 4000 slave concubines.

Most of the slaves had been captured or purchased in the non-Muslim regions surrounding the empire, including the Balkans, central Asia, and Sudanic Africa. They were purchased, with the highest prices going for the most physically appealing, in the slave markets found in all of the larger towns of the empire. Female and male slaves were prized for both their beauty and their intelligence. Some of the best educated men and women in the Abbasid Empire were slaves, and caliphs and high officials frequently spent a good deal more time with their clever and talented slave concubines than with their less well-educated wives. Slave concubines and servants often also had a good deal more personal liberty than freeborn

wives. Slave women could go to the market and were not required to wear the veils and robes that free women wore in public.

Over the centuries, the practice of veiling spread from women of the urban elite to all classes in town and country. As the stories in *The Thousand and One Nights* make clear, seclusion and veiling were seen as essential ways of curbing the insatiable lust that supposedly possessed all women from puberty. Because men were considered incapable of resisting the lures and temptations of women, men needed to be segregated from all women except those in their own families.

Though women from poor households farmed, wove clothing and rugs, or raised silkworms to help support their families, rich women were allowed virtually no career outlets beyond the home. Often married at puberty (which was legally set at the age of 9) women were raised to devote their lives to running a household and serving their husbands. But at the highest levels of society, wives and concubines cajoled their husbands and plotted with eunuchs and royal advisors to advance the interests of their sons and win for them the ruler's backing for succession to the throne. Despite these brief incursions into power politics, by the end of the Abbasid era, the considerable freedom and influence—both within the family and in the wider world—that women had enjoyed in the first centuries of Islamic expansion had been severely curtailed.

Nomadic Incursions and the Eclipse of Caliphal Power

Preoccupied by struggles in the capital and central provinces, the caliphs and their advisors were powerless to prevent further losses of territory in the outer reaches of the empire in addition to areas as close to the capital as Egypt and Syria. More alarmingly, by the mid-10th century, kingdoms that had formed in areas once part of the empire had begun to aspire to supplant the Abbasids as paramount lords of the Islamic world. In 945, the armies of one of these regional splinter dynasties, the *Buyids* of Persia, invaded the heartlands of the Abbasid Empire and captured Baghdad. From this point onward, the caliphs were little more than puppets controlled by families such as the Buyids, whose heads took the title of sultan and became the real rulers of what was left of the Abbasid Empire.

The Buyids controlled the caliph and the court, but

they could not prevent the further disintegration of the empire. In just over a century, the Buyids' control over the caliphate was broken, and they were supplanted in 1055 by another group of nomadic invaders from central Asia via Persia, the *Seljuk Turks*. For the next two centuries, Turkic military leaders ruled the remaining portions of the Abbasid Empire in the name of caliphs, who were usually of Arab or Persian extraction. The Seljuks were staunch Sunnis, and they moved quickly to purge the Shi'i officials who had risen to power under the Buyids and to rid the caliph's domains of the Shi'ite influences the Buyids had tried to promote.

For a time, the Seljuk military machine was also able to restore political initiative to the much-reduced caliphate. Seljuk victories ended the threat of conquest by a rival Shi'i dynasty centered in Egypt, and it humbled the Byzantines, who had hoped to take advantage of Muslim divisions to regain some of their long-lost lands. The Byzantines' crushing defeat was particularly important because it opened the way to the settlement of Asia Minor, or Anatolia, by nomadic peoples of Turkic origins. The region later formed the nucleus for the powerful Ottoman Empire, and it comprises today the greater part of Turkey, the national home of the Turkic peoples.

The Impact of the Christian Crusades

Soon after seizing power, the Seljuks were confronted by another and very different challenge to Islamic civilization. It came from Christian Crusaders, knights from western Europe (see Chapter 16) who were determined to capture the portions of the Islamic world that made up the Holy Land of biblical times. Muslim divisions and the element of surprise made the first of the Crusaders' assaults between 1096 and 1099 by far the most successful. Much of the Holy Land was captured and divided into Christian kingdoms. In June 1099, the main objective of the Crusade, Jerusalem, was taken while its Muslim and Jewish inhabitants were massacred by the rampaging Christian knights.

For nearly two centuries, the Europeans, who eventually mounted eight *Crusades* that varied widely in strength and success, were able to maintain their precarious beachhead in the eastern Mediterranean. But they posed little threat to the more powerful Muslim princes, whose disregard for the Christians was demonstrated by the fact that they continued to quarrel among themselves despite the intruders' aggressions. When united under a strong leader, as they were under Saladin in the

last decades of the 12th century, the Muslims rapidly reconquered most of the crusader outposts. *Saladin's death in 1193* and the subsequent breakup of his kingdom gave the remaining Christian citadels some respite, but the last of the crusader kingdoms was lost with the fall of Acre in 1291.

Undoubtedly, the impact of the Crusades was much greater on the Christians who launched them than on the Muslim peoples who had to fend them off. Because there had long been so much contact between western Europe and the Islamic world through trade and the Muslim kingdoms in Spain and southern Italy, it is difficult to be sure which influences to attribute specifically to the Crusades. But the Crusaders' firsthand experiences in the eastern Mediterranean certainly intensified the European borrowing from the Muslim world that had been going on for centuries. Muslim weapons, such as the famous damascene swords (named after the city of Damascus), were highly prized and sometimes copied by the Europeans, who were always eager to improve on their methods of making war. Muslim techniques of building fortifications were adopted by many Christian rulers, as can be seen in the castles built in Normandy and coastal England by William the Conqueror and his successors in the 11th and 12th centuries. Richard the Lionhearted's legendary preference for Muslim over Christian physicians was but one manifestation of the Europeans' avid and centuries-old interest in the superior scientific learning of Muslim peoples.

From Muslims and Jews in Spain, Sicily, Egypt, and the Middle East, the Europeans recovered much of the Greek learning that had been lost to northern Europe during the waves of nomadic invasions after the fall of Rome. They also mastered Arabic numerals and the decimal system, and they benefited from the great advances Arab and Persian thinkers had made in mathematics and many of the sciences. The European demand for Middle Eastern rugs and textiles is amply demonstrated by the Oriental rugs and tapestries that adorned the homes of the upper classes in Renaissance and early modern paintings as well as by such names for cloth as *fustian, taffeta, muslin,* and *damask,* which are derived from Persian terms or the names of Muslim cities where the cloth was produced and sold.

Muslim influences, from Persian and Arabic words and games such as chess (passed on from India) to chivalric ideals, troubadour ballads, and foods like dates, coffee, and yogurt, permeated both the elite and popular cultures of much of western Europe in this period. Some of these imports—namely, the songs of the troubadours—can be traced quite directly to the contacts the

DOCUMENT

Ibn Khaldun on the Rise and Decline of Empires

Although he lived in the century after the Abbasid Caliphate was destroyed in 1258, *Ibn Khaldun* was very much a product of the far-flung Islamic civilization that the Abassids had consolidated and expanded. He was also one of the greatest historians and social commentators of all time. After extensive travels in the Islamic world, he served as a political advisor at several of the courts of Muslim rulers in North Africa. With the support of one of his royal patrons, Ibn Khaldun wrote a voluminous universal history, which began with a very long philosophical preface called *The Muqaddimah*. Among the subjects he treated at length in this tour de force of political philosophy and social theorizing were the causes for the rise and fall of dynasties. The shifting fortunes of the dynasties he knew well in his native North Africa, as well as the fate of the Abbasids and earlier Muslim regimes, informed his attempts to discern persistent patterns in the confusing political history of the Islamic world. The following passages have been selected from one of the most celebrated sections of *The Muqaddimah* on the "natural life span" of political regimes.

We have stated that the duration of the life of a dynasty does not as a rule extend beyond three generations. The first generation retains the desert qualities, desert toughness, and desert savagery. [Its members are used to] privation and to sharing their glory [with each other]; they are brave and rapacious. Therefore, the strength of group feeling continues to be preserved among them. They are sharp and greatly feared. People submit to them.

Under the influence of royal authority and a life of ease, the second generation changes from the desert attitude to sedentary culture, from privation to luxury and plenty, from a state in which everybody shared in the glory to one in which one man claims all the glory for himself while the others are too lazy to strive for [glory], and from proud superiority to humble subservience. Thus, the vigor of group feeling is broken to some extent. People become used to lowliness and obedience. But many of [the old virtues] remain in them, because they had direct personal contact with the first generation and its conditions . . .

The third generation, then, has [completely] forgotten the period of desert life and toughness, as if it had never existed. They have lost [the taste for] group feeling, because they are dominated by force. Luxury reaches its peak among them, because they are so much given to a life of prosperity and ease. They become dependent on the dynasty and are like women and children who need to be defended [by someone else]. Group feeling disappears completely. People forget to protect and defend themselves and to press their claims. With their emblems, apparel, horseback riding, and [fighting] skill, they deceive people and give them the wrong impression. For the most part, they are more cowardly than women upon their backs. When someone comes and demands something from them, they cannot repel him. The ruler, then, has need of other, brave people for his support. He takes many clients and followers. They help the dynasty to some degree, until God permits it to be destroyed, and it goes with everything it stands for.

Three generations last one hundred and twenty years . . . As a rule, dynasties do not last longer than that many years, a few more a few less, save when, by chance, no one appears to attack [the dynasty]. When senility becomes preponderant [in a dynasty], there may be no claimant [for its power, and then nothing will happen] but if there should be one, he will encounter no one capable of repelling him. If the time is up [the end of the dynasty] cannot be postponed for a single hour, no more than it can be accelerated.

Questions: What do these passages reveal about Ibn Khaldun's views of the contrasts between nomads and urban dwellers? Why does he see the former as a source of political strength? What are the key forces that undermine dynasties in later generations? How well do these patterns correspond to the history of the Ummayad and Abbasid dynasties we have been studying? How well do they work for other civilizations we have examined? Can elements of Ibn Khaldun's theory be applied to today's political systems? If so, which and how? If not, why?

A forest of graceful arches fills the interior of the mosque at Cordoba in Spain. Such an architectural feat testifies to the depth and expansive power of Islamic civilization.

AN AGE OF LEARNING AND ARTISTIC REFINEMENT

Focal Point: The avid interest in Muslim ideas and material culture displayed by European knights and merchants who journeyed to the centers of Islamic civilization in this era cautions us against placing too great an emphasis on the political divisions and struggles that were such a prominent feature of the later Abbasid era. It also invites comparison with neighboring civilizations, such as those of India and western Europe, that were a good deal more fragmented and racked by endless warfare in late Abbasid times. In the midst of the political turmoil and social tensions of the Abbasid age, Muslim thinkers and craftsmen living in kingdoms from Spain to Persia created, refined, and made discoveries in a remarkable range of fields. Their collective accomplishments mark one of the great ages of human ingenuity and creativity. Their thought and techniques influenced their counterparts in virtually all the civilized centers of the Old World, from the Sudanic peoples of Africa to the Iberians and Franks of western Europe, and from the Hindus of India to the distant and relatively isolated Chinese.

Though town life became somewhat more dangerous, the rapid growth and increasing prosperity that had been dominant trends in the first centuries of Muslim expansion continued until quite late in the Abbasid era. Expanding bureaucracies and caliphal building projects meant that employment opportunities for the well-educated and for skilled craftsmen remained surprisingly abundant. Despite the declining revenue base of the caliphate and deteriorating conditions in the countryside, there was a great expansion of the professional classes, particularly doctors, scholars, and legal and religious experts. Muslim, Jewish, and in some areas Christian entrepreneurs amassed great fortunes supplying the cities of the empire with staples such as grain and barley, essentials such as cotton and woolen textiles for clothing, and luxury items such as precious gems, citrus fruits, and sugar cane. Long-distance trade with coastal India and island Southeast Asia, as well as the overland caravan trade with China, flourished through much of the Abbasid era. Trade across the Mediterranean to western Europe, from both North Africa and the Middle East, also increased.

Among the chief beneficiaries of the sustained urban prosperity were the artists and artisans, who continued the great achievements in architecture and the crafts that

Crusaders made in the Holy Land. But most were part of a process of exchange that extended over centuries. In fact, the Italian merchant communities that remained after the political and military power of the Crusaders had been extinguished in the Middle East probably contributed a good deal more to this exchange than all the forays of Christian knighthood.

Of perhaps even greater significance, the "exchange" was largely a one-way process. Though they imported items such as fine glassware, weapons, and horses from Christian Italy and Byzantium, and beeswax, slaves, and timber from Russia and the Balkans, Muslim peoples in this era displayed little interest in the learning and products of the West. The Crusades reflected this imbalance. They had only a marginal effect on political and military developments in the Middle East, and, if anything, their cultural impact on Islamic civilization was even less.

The artisan who crafted this bronze incense burner from 12th-century Iran molded the burner into a caricature of a lion and intricately decorated the creature's body. The holes in the body allow smoke from the incense to escape.

had begun in the Umayyad era. Mosques and palaces grew larger and more ornate in most parts of the empire. Even in outlying areas, such as Cordoba in Spain, Muslim engineers and craftsmen created some of the great architectural treasures of all time. The tapestries and rugs of Muslim peoples, such as the Persians, were in great demand from Europe to China. To this day, Muslim rugs have rarely been matched for their exquisite designs, their vivid colors, and the skill with which they are woven. Muslim craftsmen also produced superb ceramics. Particularly stunning were the blue-glazed tiles, which were used to decorate the mosques and palaces of Persia, and the wonderfully designed pitchers and bowls, which were fashioned for everyday use in the Abbasid era but have become museum pieces in our day.

The Full Flowering of Persian Literature

As Persian wives, concubines, advisors, bureaucrats, and—after the mid-10th century—Persian caliphs came to play central roles in imperial politics, Persian gradually

replaced Arabic as the primary written language at the Abbasid court. Arabic remained the language of religion, law, and the natural sciences. But Persian was favored by Arabs, Turks, and those of Persian descent as the language of literary expression, administration, and scholarship. In Baghdad and major cities throughout the Abbasid Empire and in neighboring kingdoms, Persian was the chief language of "high culture," the language of polite exchanges between courtiers as well as of history, poetic musings, and mystical revelations.

Written in a modified Arabic script and drawing selectively on Arabic vocabulary, the Persian of the Abbasid age was a supple language as beautiful to look at when drafted by a skilled calligrapher as it was to read aloud. Though catch phrases ("A jug of wine, a loaf of bread—and Thou") from the *Rubiyat* of Omar Khayyam are certainly the pieces of Persian literature best known in the West, other writers from this period surpassed Khayyam in profundity of thought and elegance of style. Perhaps the greatest single work was the lengthy epic poem *Shah-Nama* (Book of Kings), written by Firdawsi in the late 10th and early 11th centuries. The work relates the history of Persia from Creation to the Islamic conquests, and it abounds in dramatic details of battles, intrigues, and illicit love affairs. Firdawsi's Persian has been extolled for its grand yet musical virtuosity, and portions of the *Shah-Nama* and other Persian works were actually read aloud to musical accompaniment. Brilliantly illustrated manuscripts of Firdawsi's epic history are among the most exquisite works of Islamic art.

In addition to historical epics, Persian writers in the Abbasid era wrote on all manner of subjects, from doomed love affairs and the elements of statecraft to incidents from everyday life and mystical striving for communion with the divine. One of the great poets of the age, Sa'di, fuses an everyday message with a religious one in the following relation of a single moment in his own life:

Often I am minded, from the days of my childhood,
How once I went out with my father on a festival;
In fun I grew preoccupied with all the folk about,
Losing touch with my father in the popular confusion;
In terror and bewilderment I raised up a cry,
Then suddenly my father boxed my ears:
"You bold-eyed child, how many times, now,
Have I told you not to lose hold of my skirt?"
A tiny child cannot walk out alone,
For it is difficult to take a way not seen;

You too, poor friend, are but a child upon
*   endeavour's way:*
Go, seize the skirts of those who know the way!

This blend of the mystical and commonplace was widely adopted in the literature of this period. It is epitomized in the *Rubiyat*, whose author is much more concerned with finding meaning in life and a path to union with the divine than with extolling the delights of picnics in the garden with beautiful women.

Achievements in the Sciences

From the preservers and compilers of the learning of the ancient civilizations they had conquered in the early centuries of expansion, Muslim peoples—and the Jewish scholars who lived peacefully in Muslim lands—increasingly became creators and inventors in their own right. For several centuries, which spanned much of the period of Abbasid rule, Islamic civilization outstripped all others in scientific discoveries, new techniques of investigation, and the innovation and dissemination of technology. The many Muslim accomplishments in these areas include major corrections to the algebraic and geometric theories of the ancient Greeks and great advances in the use of basic concepts of trigonometry: the sine, cosine, and tangent.

Among numerous discoveries in chemistry, two that were fundamental to all subsequent investigation were the creation of the objective experiment and al-Razi's scheme of classifying all material substances into three categories: animal, vegetable, and mineral. The sophistication of Muslim scientific techniques is indicated by the fact that in the 11th century, al-Biruni was able to calculate the exact specific weight of 18 major minerals. This sophistication was also manifested in the astronomical instruments and observations made through the cooperation of Muslim scholars and skilled craftsmen. Muslim technicians greatly improved devices, such as the astrolabe and armillary sphere, for measuring and mapping the position of celestial bodies. Muslim astronomers devised the names, which we still use today, of many of the constellations and individual stars. Their astronomical tables and maps of the stars were in great demand among scholars of other civilizations, including those of Europe and China.

As these breakthroughs suggest, much of the Muslims' work in scientific investigation had very practical applications. This practical bent was even more pro-

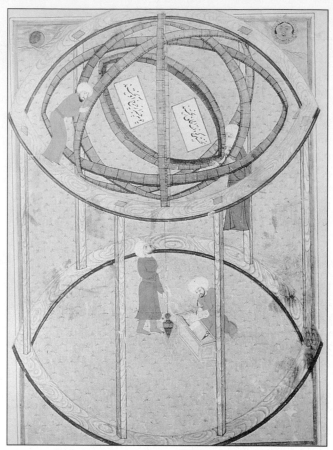

Muslim scientific instruments, such as this intricately designed armillary sphere for mapping the stars and planets, were among the most advanced in the world as late as the 13th and 14th centuries. Muslim prototypes inspired European artisans, cartographers, and scientists to develop instruments and maps, which were essential to European overseas expansion from the 14th century onward.

nounced in other fields. In medicine, for example, Muslim cities, such as Cairo, boasted some of the best hospitals in the world. Doctors and pharmacists had to follow a regular course of study and pass a formal exam before they were allowed to practice. Muslim scientists did important work on optics and bladder ailments. Muslim traders and craftsmen introduced into the Islamic world and Europe many basic machines and techniques—namely, paper-making, silk weaving, and ceramic firing—that had been devised earlier in China. In addition, Muslim scholars made some of the world's best maps, which were envied and copied by geographers from Portugal to Poland.

Religious Trends and the New Impetus for Expansion

The contradictory trends in Islamic civilization—social strife and political divisions versus expanding trading links and intellectual creativity—were strongly reflected in divergent patterns of religious development in the later centuries of the caliphate. On one hand, Sufist mysticism injected Islam with a new vibrancy and expansiveness; on the other hand, orthodox religious scholars, such as the *ulama,* grew increasingly suspicious of and hostile to non-Islamic ideas and scientific thinking. The Crusades had given great impetus to the latter trend, particularly with regard to Muslim borrowing from ancient Greek learning that the ulama associated with the aggressive civilizations of Christian Europe. Many orthodox scholars came to suspect that the propensity for empirical testing and seemingly endless questioning of the Greek tradition posed potential challenges to the absolute authority of the Quran, which they insisted was the final, perfect, and complete revelation of an all-knowing divinity. Brilliant thinkers like *al-Ghazali,* who was perhaps the greatest of Islamic theologians and whose ideas indirectly influenced major European philosophers such as Thomas Aquinas, struggled to fuse the Greek and Quranic traditions, achieving mixed success in terms of acceptance by orthodox scholars.

Much of the religious vitality in Islam in the later Abbasid period was centered in the Sufist movement. Like the Buddhist and Hindu ascetics earlier in India, *Sufis* (whose title was derived from the woolen robes they wore) were wandering mystics who sought a personal union with God. In its various guises—including both Sunni and Shi'i manifestations—Sufism was a reaction against the impersonal and abstract divinity that many ulama scholars argued was the true God of the Quran. Like the Indian mystics, the Sufis and their followers sought to see beyond what they believed to be the illusory existence of everyday life and to delight in the presence of God in the world. True to the uncompromising monotheism of Islam, most Sufis insisted on a clear distinction between God and humans—a distinction Hindu and Buddhist mystics tended to deny or blur. But in some Sufist teachings, God permeated the universe in ways that appeared to compromise his transcendent status.

Some Sufis gained reputations as great healers and workers of miracles; others led militant bands that attempted to spread Islam to infidel peoples. Some Sufis used asceticism or bodily denial to find God; others used meditation, songs, drugs, or (in the case of the famous dervishes) ecstatic dancing. Most Sufis built up a sizable popular following, and the movement as a whole was a central factor in the continuing expansion of the Muslim religion and Islamic civilization in the later centuries of the Abbasid caliphate.

New Waves of Nomadic Invasions and the End of the Caliphate

As we have seen, in the 10th and 11th centuries, the Abbasid domains were divided by ever-growing numbers of rival successor states. In the early decades of the 13th century, a new threat arose at the eastern extremities of the original Abbasid domains. Another central Asian nomadic people, the *Mongols,* united by their great war commander, *Chinggis Khan,* first raided in the 1220s and then smashed the Turko-Persian kingdoms that had developed in the regions to the east of Baghdad. Chinggis Khan died before the heartlands of the Muslim world were invaded, but his grandson, Hulegu, renewed the Mongol assault on the rich centers of Islamic civilization in the 1250s. In 1258, the Abbasid capital at Baghdad was taken by the Mongols, and much of it was sacked. The thirty-seventh and last Abbasid caliph was put to death by the Mongols, who continued westward until they were finally defeated by the *Mameluks,* or Turkic slaves, who then ruled Egypt. Baghdad never recovered from the Mongol depredations. In 1401 a second capture of the city and another round of pillaging by the even fiercer forces of Tamerlane. Baghdad shrank from the status of one of the great cities of the world—from the cultural, if not the political center of Islamic civilization—to a provincial backwater, supplanted by Cairo to the west and soon thereafter Istanbul to the north.

THE COMING OF ISLAM TO SOUTH ASIA

Focal Point: From the 7th century onward, successive waves of Muslim invaders, traders, and migrants carried the Islamic faith and elements of Islamic civilization to much of the vast Indian subcontinent. By the 12th and 13th centuries, Muslim dynasties ruled much of north and central India. Muslim conquests and growing numbers of conversions elicited a variety of Hindu responses, and efforts on the part of some of the adherents of both religions to reconcile their very significant differences. Though these efforts resulted only in an uneasy standoff between the two communities, Islamic influences had clearly become a major force in South Asian historical development. They added further layers of richness and complexity to Indian civilization as well as some of its most enduring channels to the peoples and cultures of neighboring lands.

All through the millennia when a succession of civilizations from Harappa to the Brahmanic Empire of the Guptas developed in the subcontinent, foreigners had entered India in waves of nomadic invaders or as small bands of displaced peoples seeking refuge. Invariably, those who chose to remain were assimilated into the civilizations they encountered in the lowland areas. They converted to the Hindu or Buddhist religion, found a place in the caste hierarchy, and adopted the dress, foods, and lifestyles of the farming and city-dwelling peoples of the subcontinent. This capacity to absorb peoples moving into the area owed much to the strength and flexibility of India's civilizations and also to the fact that India's peoples usually enjoyed a higher level of material culture than peoples entering the subcontinent. As a result, the persistent failure of Indian rulers to unite in the face of aggression on the part of outsiders meant periodic disruptions and localized destruction, but not fundamental challenges to the existing order. All of this changed with the arrival of the Muslims in the last years of the 7th century C.E.

With the coming of the Muslims, the peoples of India encountered for the first time a large-scale influx of bearers of a civilization as sophisticated, if not as ancient, as their own. They were also confronted by a religious system that was in many ways the very opposite of their own. Hinduism, the predominant Indian religion at that time, was open, tolerant, and inclusive of widely varying forms of religious devotion—from idol worship to meditation in search of union with the supernatural source of all creation. Islam was doctrinaire, proselytizing, and committed to the exclusive worship of a single, transcendent God.

In contrast to the egalitarianism of Islam, which proclaimed all believers equal in the sight of God, Hindu beliefs did much to validate the caste hierarchy, which rested on the acceptance of inborn differences between individuals and groups and the widely varying levels of material wealth, status, and religious purity these differences produced. Thus, where the faith of the invading Muslims was religiously more rigid than that of the absorptive and adaptive Hindus, the caste-based social system of the great majority of the indigenous peoples was much more compartmentalized and closed than those of the Muslim invaders, with their emphasis on mobility and the community of believers.

Because growing numbers of Muslim warriors, traders, Sufi mystics, and ordinary farmers and herders were able to enter the subcontinent and settle in it, extensive interaction between invaders and the indigenous peoples was inevitable. In the early centuries of the Muslim influx, conflict—often involving violent clashes between the two—predominated. But there was also a good deal of trade and even religious interchange between them. As time passed, peaceful (if wary) interaction became the norm. Muslim rulers employed large numbers' of Hindus to govern the largely non-Muslim populations they ruled; mosques and temples dominated different quarters within Indian cities; and Hindu and Muslim mystics strove to find areas of agreement between their two faiths. Tensions remained, and periodically they erupted into communal rioting or sustained warfare between Hindu and Muslim lords.

North India on the Eve of the Muslim Invasions

In the years after the collapse of the Gupta Empire at the end of the 5th century, the heads of numerous regional dynasties aspired to restore imperial unity in North India. But until *Harsha* in the early 7th century, all imperial ambitions were frustrated by timely alliances of rival lords that checked the rise of a single and unifying power center. Harsha was the second son of one of these rival kings, who through a series of wars had carved out a modest domain in the Panjab region to the southeast of the Indus River system. Upon his father's death in 604, Harsha's elder brother ascended the throne. He was soon killed—some accounts say he was treacherously murdered by the agents of a rival confederation of kings centered in Bengal. Although still a youth, Harsha agreed to accept the imperiled throne and was soon at war with the kingdoms of Bengal. The young king proved skillful at forging alliances with other rulers who were the enemies of those in the Bengali confederation; he also was a talented military commander. Soon after ascending the throne, he won a series of battles that both avenged the murder of his brother and led to a great increase in the territories under his control. Within a matter of years, he had pieced together the largest empire India had seen since the fall of the Gupta dynasty over a century earlier.

At the height of his power, Harsha ruled much of the central and eastern Gangetic plain, but his "empire" was a good deal smaller than that of the Guptas. He beat the Bengali lords in battle but was unable to control their lands on a sustained basis, and his attempts to expand into southern and northwest India were unsuccessful. Thus, though he was one of the most powerful rulers India was to know from the time of the Guptas until the establishment of the Delhi sultanate in the 13th century, Harsha's conquests fell far short of uniting even the northern regions of the Indian subcontinent.

The wars that dominated the early years of Harsha's reign gave way to a long period of peace and prosperity for his empire. Content with his early conquests, and too greatly feared by rival rulers to be attacked, Harsha turned his considerable energies to promoting the welfare of his subjects. Like Ashoka, he built roads and numerous rest houses for weary travelers, established hospitals, and endowed temples and Buddhist monasteries. A Chinese pilgrim named Xuan Zang, who visited the Buddhist shrines of India during Harsha's reign, wrote that as the king toured the provinces he would hold audiences for the common people in a special pavilion that was set up alongside the main roads. Judging from Xuan Zang's account, the prosperity of the Gupta age had been largely restored during Harsha's reign. This was particularly true in large towns such as the capital, *Kanauj*, which had formidable walls, palatial homes, and beautiful gardens with artificial tanks or pools. Some of the artistic creativity of the Gupta age was also revived during Harsha's long reign. The ruler was an author of some talent and wrote at least three Sanskrit plays, and he befriended and generously patronized philosophers, poets, artists, and historians.

Though he was probably a Hindu devotee of the god Shiva in his early years, Harsha was tolerant of all faiths and became increasingly attracted to Buddhism. His generous patronage of Buddhist monasteries and the Buddhist monastics attracted pilgrims like Xuan Zang. If Xuan Zang's account can be trusted, Harsha came close to converting to Buddhism in the last years of his life. He sponsored great religious assemblies, which were dominated by Buddhist monks and religious rituals, and he prohibited eating meat and putting an end to human life. His lavish patronage of the Buddhists led on one occasion to a Brahmin-inspired assassination attempt, which appears only to have strengthened his preference for Buddhist ceremonies and beliefs.

Political Divisions and the First Muslim Invasions

Harsha died without a successor in 646, and his kingdom was quickly pulled apart by ambitious ministers who were attempting to found new dynasties of their own. Though Hindu culture flourished in both north and south India in the centuries after Harsha's death—as evidenced by the great temples that were constructed and the works of sculpture, literature, and music that were produced—no paramount kingdom emerged. Political divisions in the north and west-central regions of the subcontinent proved the most significant, because they left openings for a succession of invasions by different Muslim peoples.

The first and least enduring Muslim intrusion, which came in 711, resulted indirectly from the peaceful trading contacts that had initially brought Muslims into contact with Indian civilization. Since ancient times, Arab seafarers and traders had been major carriers in the vast trading network that stretched from Italy in the Mediterranean to the South China Sea. After converting to Islam, these traders continued to frequent the ports of India, particularly those on the western coast. An attack by pirates sailing from Debul (in Sind in western India) on ships owned by some of these Arab traders prompted *Hajjaj,* the viceroy of the eastern provinces of the Umayyad Empire, to launch a punitive expedition against the king of Sind. An able Arab general, *Muhammad ibn Qasim,* who was only 17 years old when the campaign began, led over 10,000 horse- and camel-mounted warriors into Sind to avenge the assault on Arab shipping.

After victories in several fiercely fought battles and successful sieges of the great stone fortresses that stood guard over various parts of the arid and thinly peopled Sind interior, Muhammad ibn Qasim declared the region, as well as the Indus valley to the northeast, provinces of the Umayyad Empire. Soon after the territories had been annexed, a new caliph, who was a bitter enemy of Hajjaj, came to power in Damascus. He purged Hajjaj, and he recalled and executed his son-in-law, Muhammad ibn Qasim. Though the personnel of the ruling Arab elite shifted as a result, the basic policies established by Muhammad ibn Qasim were followed by his Umayyad and Abbasid successors for several centuries.

In these early centuries, the coming of Islam brought little change for most of the inhabitants of the Indian subcontinent. In fact, in many areas, local leaders and the mass of the populace had surrendered towns and districts willingly to the conquerors, who offered the promise of lighter taxation and greater religious toler-ance. The Arab overlords decided to treat both Hindus and Buddhists as protected "people of the book," de-spite the fact that their faiths had no connection to the Bible, the book in question. This meant that although they were obliged to pay special taxes, non-Muslims en-joyed the freedom to worship as they pleased and to maintain their temples and monasteries.

As in other areas conquered by the Arabs, most of the indigenous officials and functionaries retained their positions, which did much to reconcile them to Muslim rule. The status and privileges of the Brahmin castes were also respected. Virtually all the Arabs, who made up only a tiny minority of the population, lived in the cities or special garrison towns. Because little effort was expended in converting the peoples of the conquered ar-eas, they remained overwhelmingly Hindu or Buddhist and, initially at least, displayed scant interest in the be-liefs or culture of their new overlords.

Indian Influences on Islamic Civilization

Though the impact of Islam on the Indian subcontinent in this period was limited, the Arab foothold in Sind provided contacts by which Indian learning could be transmitted to the Muslim heartlands in the Middle East. As a result, Is-lamic civilization was enriched by the skills and discoveries of yet another great civilization. Of particular importance was Indian scientific learning, which rivaled that of the Greeks as the most advanced of the ancient world. Hindu mathematicians and astronomers traveled to Baghdad after the Abbasids came to power in the mid-8th century. Their works on algebra and geometry were translated into Ara-bic, and their instruments for celestial observation were copied and improved upon by Arab astronomers.

Most critically, Arab thinkers in all fields began to use the numerals that Hindu scholars had devised cen-turies earlier. Because these numbers were passed on to the Europeans through contacts with the Arabs in the early Middle Ages, we call them Arabic numerals today, but they originated in India. Due to the linkages be-tween civilized centers established by the spread of Is-lam, this system of numerical notation has proved central to two scientific revolutions: the first in the Middle East, which was discussed previously, and a second, in Europe and subsequently in much of the rest of the world from the 16th century onward, which was a more sustained and fundamental transformation.

In addition to science and mathematics, Indian trea-tises on subjects ranging from medicine to music were translated and studied by Arab scholars. Indian physicians were brought to Baghdad to run the well-endowed hos-pitals that the Christian Crusaders found a source of wonderment and a cause for envy. On several occasions, Indian doctors were able to cure Arab rulers and high of-ficials whom Greek physicians had pronounced beyond help. Indian works on statecraft, alchemy, and palmistry were also translated into Arabic, and it is believed that some of the tales in the Arabian Nights were based on an-cient Indian stories. Indian musical instruments and melodies made their way into the repertoires of Arab per-formers, and the Indian game of chess became a favorite of both princes and ordinary townspeople.

Arabs who emigrated to Sind and other Muslim-ruled areas often adopted Indian dress and hairstyles, ate Indian foods, and rode on elephants as the Hindu rajas (kings) did. In this era, additional Arab colonies were es-tablished in coastal areas, such as Malabar to the south and Bengal in the east. These trading enclaves would later provide the staging areas from which Islam was transmitted to island and mainland Southeast Asia.

From Booty to Empire: The Second Wave of Muslim Invasions

After the initial conquests by Muhammad ibn Qasim's armies, little territory was added to the Muslim foothold on the subcontinent. In fact, disputes between the Arabs occupying Sind and quarrels with first the Umayyad and later the Abbasid caliphs gradually weakened the Muslim hold on the area and led to the reconquest of parts of the lower Indus valley by Hindu rulers. The slow Mus-lim retreat was dramatically reversed by a new series of military invasions, this time launched by a Turkish slave dynasty that in 962 had seized power in Afghanistan to the north of the Indus valley. The third ruler of this dy-nasty, *Mahmud of Ghazni,* led a series of expeditions that initiated nearly two centuries of Muslim raiding and conquest in northern India. Drawn by the legendary wealth of the subcontinent and a zeal to spread the Mus-lim faith, Mahmud repeatedly raided northwest India in the first decades of the 11th century. He defeated one confederation of Hindu princes after another, and he drove deeper and deeper into the subcontinent in the quest of ever richer temples to sack and loot.

The raids mounted by Mahmud of Ghazni and his successors gave way in the last decades of the 12th century to sustained campaigns aimed at seizing political control in north India. The key figure in this transition was a tena-cious military commander of Persian extraction, *Muham-mad of Ghur.* The breakup of the *Ghazni Empire* as a re-sult of the ceaseless quarrels of Mahmud's successors made it possible for the small mountain kingdom of Ghur, near Herat in western Afghanistan, to emerge as a formi-

Built in 1626 at Agra, this exquisite tomb of white marble encrusted with semiprecious stones provides a superb example of the blending of Islamic and Hindu architectural forms and artistic motifs.

dable regional power center. After barely surviving several severe defeats at the hands of Hindu rulers, Muhammad put together a string of military victories that brought the Indus valley and much of north-central India under his control. In the following years, Muhammad's conquests were extended along the Gangetic plain as far as Bengal, and into west and central India, by several of his most gifted subordinate commanders. After Muhammad was assassinated in 1206, *Qutb-ud-din Aibak,* one of his slave lieutenants, formed a separate kingdom in the Indian portions of the Ghuri Empire.

Significantly, the capital of the new kingdom was at Delhi along the Jumna River on the Gangetic plain. Delhi's location in the very center of northern India graphically proclaimed that a Muslim dynasty rooted in the subcontinent itself, not an extension of a central Asian empire, had been founded. For the next 300 years, a succession of dynasties would rule much of north and central India. Alternately of Persian, Afghan, Turkic, and mixed descent, the rulers of these imperial houses, who proclaimed themselves the sultans of Delhi, fought each other, Mongol and Turkic invaders, and the indigenous Hindu princes for control of the Indus and Gangetic heartlands of Indian civilization.

All the dynasties that laid claim to the sultanate based their power on large military machines, which were anchored on massive contingents of cavalry and increasingly on corps of war elephants patterned after those that indigenous rulers had used for centuries. The support of their armies and sumptuous court establishments became the main objectives of the extensive bureaucracies that each of the rulers at Delhi attempted to maintain. Though some rulers patronized public works projects, the arts, and charitable relief, most concentrated on maximizing the revenues they could collect from the peasants and townspeople in their domains. Throughout the Delhi sultanate era, however, factional struggles among the ruling Muslims, and their dependence on Hindu lords and village notables in administration at the local level, greatly limited the actual control exercised by any of the dynasties that emerged.

Patterns of Conversion and Accommodation

Though the Muslims literally fought their way into India, their interaction with the indigenous peoples soon came to be dominated by accommodation and peaceful

This Indian miniature painting of milkmaidens serving the Hindu god, Krishna, reflects the highly personalized, devotional worship that was characteristic of the bhaktic movement.

exchanges. Over the centuries when much of the north was ruled by dynasties centered at Delhi, sizable Muslim communities developed in different areas of the subcontinent, particularly in Bengal to the east and in the northwestern provinces in the Indus valley that were the points of entry for most of the Muslim peoples who migrated into India. Few of these converts were won by forcible conversion. The main carriers of the new faith were traders, who played a growing role in both coastal and inland trade, and especially Sufi mystics, who shared much with Indian gurus and wandering ascetics, in both style and message. Belief in their magical and healing powers did much to enhance the Sufis' stature and increase their following. Their mosques and schools often became centers of regional political power. Sufis organized their devotees in militias to fend off bandits or the depredations of rival princes, oversaw the clearing of forests for farming and settlement, and welcomed low and outcaste Hindu groups into the Muslim brotherhood. After their deaths, the tombs of Sufi mystics became objects of veneration for Indian Muslims as well as Hindu and Buddhist pilgrims.

Most of the indigenous converts, who came to form a majority of the Muslims living in India, were drawn from specific regions and social groups. Surprisingly small numbers of converts were found in the Indo-Gangetic centers of Muslim political power—a fact that suggests the very limited importance of forced conversions. Most Indians who converted to Islam were from Buddhist or low-caste groups. In areas such as western India and Bengal, where Buddhism had survived as a popular religion until the era of the Muslim invasions, esoteric rituals and corrupt practices had debased Buddhist teachings and undermined the morale of the monastic orders. This decline was accelerated by Muslim raids on Buddhist temples and monasteries, which provided vulnerable and lucrative targets for the early invaders. Without monastic supervision, local congregations sank further into orgies and experiments with magic, and in some areas into practices, such as human sacrifice, that also disregarded the Buddha's social concerns and religious message. Disorganized and misdirected, Buddhism proved no match for the confident and vigorous new religion the Muslim invaders carried into the subcontinent, particularly when those who were spreading the new faith possessed the charisma and organizing skills of the Sufi mystics.

Though Buddhist converts probably made up the larger portion of the Indians who converted to Islam, untouchables and low-caste Hindus, as well as animistic tribal peoples, were also attracted to the more egalitarian social arrangements promoted by the new faith. As was the case with the Buddhists, group conversions were essential, since those who remained in the Hindu caste system would have little to do with those who converted. Some conversions were also prompted by the desire of Hindus or Buddhists to escape the hated head tax the Muslim rulers levied on unbelievers, and by intermarriage between the indigenous peoples and Muslim migrants. The migrants themselves also increased the size of the Muslim population in the subcontinent. This was particularly true in periods of crisis in central Asia, as in the 13th and 14th centuries when Turkic, Persian, and Afghan peoples retreated to the comparative safety of India in the face of the Mongol and Timurid conquests.

Although Islam won large numbers of converts in certain areas and communities, it initially made little impression on the Hindu community as a whole. Despite military reverses and the imposition of Muslim political rule over large areas of the subcontinent, high-caste Hindus in particular persisted in regarding the invaders as the bearers of an upstart religion and as polluting outcastes. Al-Biruni, one of the chief chroniclers of the Muslim conquests, complained openly about the prevailing Indian disdain for the newcomers:

> The Hindus believe that there is no country but theirs, no nation like theirs, no kings like theirs, no religion like theirs, no science like theirs. They are haughty, foolishly vain, self-conceited and stolid.

Many Hindus were quite willing to take positions as administrators in the bureaucracies of Muslim overlords or as soldiers in their armies and to trade with Muslim merchants. But they remained socially aloof from their conquerors. Separate living quarters in both cities and rural villages were established everywhere Muslim communities developed. Genuine friendships between members of high-caste groups and Muslims were rare, and sexual liaisons between them were severely restricted.

During the early centuries of the Muslim influx, the Hindus were convinced that like so many of the peoples who had entered the subcontinent in the preceding millennia, the Muslims would soon be absorbed by the superior religions and more sophisticated cultures of India. Many signs pointed to that outcome. Hindus staffed the bureaucracies and made up a good portion of the armies of Muslim rulers. In addition, Muslim princes adopted regal styles and practices that were Hindu-inspired and contrary to the Quran. Some Hindus proclaimed themselves to be of divine descent, while others minted coins decorated with Hindu images such as Nandi, the bull associated with a major Hindu god, Shiva.

More broadly, Muslim communities became socially divided along caste lines. Recently arrived Muslims were generally on top of the hierarchies that developed, and even they were divided depending on whether they were Arab, Turk, or Persian. High-caste Hindu converts came next, followed by "clean" artisan and merchant groups. Lower-caste and untouchable converts remained at the bottom of the social hierarchy, which may well explain why conversions in these groups were not as numerous as one would expect from the original egalitarian thrust of Islam. Muslims also adopted Indian foods and styles of dress and took to chewing pan, or betel leaves. The Muslim influx had unfortunate consequences for women in both Muslim and Hindu communities. The invaders increasingly adopted the lower age of women at the time of their marriage, and the prohibitions against the remarriage of widows found especially at the high-caste levels of Indian society. Some upper "caste" Muslim groups even performed the ritual of *sati*, the immolation of widows with the bodies of their deceased husbands.

Islamic Challenge and Hindu Revival

Despite a significant degree of acculturation to Hindu lifestyles and social organization, Muslim migrants to the subcontinent held to their own quite distinctive religious beliefs and rituals. The Hindus found Islam impossible to absorb and soon realized that they were confronted by an actively proselytizing religion with great appeal to substantial segments of the Indian population. Partly in response to this challenge, the Hindus placed ever greater emphasis on the devotional cults of gods and goddesses that earlier had proved so effective in neutralizing the challenge of Buddhism. Membership in these devotional, or *bhaktic*, *cult* groups was open to all, including women and untouchables. In fact, some of the most celebrated writers of religious poetry and songs of worship were women, such as Mira Bai. Saints from low-caste origins were revered by warriors and brahmans as well as by farmers, merchants, and outcastes. Because many songs and poems were composed in regional languages, such as Bengali, Marathi, and Tamil, they were more accessible to the common people and became prominent expressions of popular culture in many areas.

Bhaktic mystics and gurus stressed the importance of a strong emotional bond between the devotee and the god or goddess who was the object of veneration. Chants, dances, and in some settings drugs were used to reach the state of spiritual intoxication that was the key to individual salvation. Once one had achieved the state of ecstasy that came through intense emotional attachment to a god or goddess, all past sins were removed and caste distinctions were rendered meaningless. The most widely worshiped deities were the gods *Shiva* and *Vishnu* (particularly in the guise of Krishna the goatherder) and the goddess Kali in any of several manifestations. By increasing popular involvement in Hindu worship and by enriching and extending the modes of prayer and ritual, the bhaktic movement may have done much to stem the flow of converts to Islam, particularly at the level of low-caste groups. Once again, the Hindu tradition demonstrated its remarkable adaptability and tolerance for widely varying modes of divine worship.

Stand-Off: The Muslim Presence in India at the End of the Sultanate Period

The attempts of mystics like Kabir to minimize the differences between Hindu and Islamic beliefs and worship won only small numbers of the followers of either faith. They were also strongly repudiated by the guardians of orthodoxy in each religious community. Sensing the long-term threat to Hinduism posed by Muslim political dominance and conversion efforts, the Brahmins denounced the Muslims as infidel destroyers of Hindu temples and polluted meat-eaters. Later Hindu mystics, such as the 15th-century holy man Chaitanya, composed songs that focused on love for Hindu deities and set out to convince Indian Muslims to renounce Islam in favor of Hinduism.

CLOSEUP

Kabir: Mystic Mediator Between Religions

The similarities in style and religious message between the Sufis, who attempted to spread Islam to the Indian masses, and the gurus, who championed bhaktic devotion to the Hindu gods and goddesses, led to a number of attempts to find common ground between the two communities. One of the most remarkable of these efforts was expressed through the teachings of a 15th-century mystic named *Kabir*. A man of humble origins, Kabir was raised by Muslim weavers in Banaras, one of the most sacred Hindu cities. He played down the importance of ritual differences between Hinduism and Islam. In one of his religious poems, Kabir declared:

O servant, where do thou seek Me?
Lo! I am beside thee.
I am neither in temple nor in mosque:
Neither am I in rites and ceremonies, nor in Yoga and
renunciation.

Though he saw both Hinduism and Islam as valid paths to God, Kabir taught that the ultimate truths transcended them both. Sheer devotion, not prayers or sacrifices, he argued, would lead the devotee to divine bliss:

If you have not drunk of the nectar of that One Love, what does it matter that you purge yourself of all sins?

The Kazi [judge] is searching the words of the Koran [Quran], and instructing others but if his heart is not steeped in that love, what does it avail, though he be a teacher of men? The Yogi dyes his garments with red: but if he knows nothing of the color of love, what does it avail though his garments be tinted?

For Kabir and other mystics who bridged the two great religious traditions, all paths to salvation were valid, and mixing religious beliefs and approaches enhanced one's chances of communion with the divine.

For their part, Muslim ulama, or religious experts, grew increasingly aware of the dangers that Hinduism posed for Islam. Attempts to fuse the two faiths were rejected on the grounds that though Hindus might argue that specific rituals and beliefs were not essential, they were fundamental for Islam. If one played down the teachings of the Quran, prayer, and the pilgrimage, one was no longer a true Muslim. Thus, the ulama and even some Sufi mystics stressed the teachings of Islam that separated it from Hinduism. They worked to promote unity within the Indian Muslim community and to strengthen its contacts with Muslims in neighboring lands and the Middle Eastern centers of the faith.

After centuries of invasion and migration, a sizable Muslim community had been established in the Indian subcontinent. Converts had been won, political control had been established throughout much of the area, and strong links had been forged with Muslims in other lands such as Persia and Afghanistan. But non-Muslims, particularly Hindus, remained the overwhelming majority of the population of the vast and diverse lands south of the Himalayas. Unlike the Zoroastrians in Persia or the animistic peoples of the Maghrib and the Sudan, most of the Indians showed little inclination to convert to the religion of the Muslim conquerors.

On the contrary, despite their subjugation, they remained convinced that they possessed a superior religion and civilization and that the Muslims would eventually be absorbed into the expansive Hindu fold. The Muslim adoption of Hindu social forms and Indian customs certainly pointed in this direction. The teachings of Hindu and Muslim mystics threatened to blur the religious boundaries between the two faiths—a process that favored the ascendancy of the more amorphous faith of the Hindu majority. Thus, though Muslim conquests and migration had carried Islam into the heart of one of the most ancient and populous centers of civilization,

India remained, after centuries of political dominance and missionary activity, one of the least converted and integrated of all the areas to which the message of Muhammad had spread.

THE SPREAD OF ISLAM TO SOUTHEAST ASIA

Focal Point: The spread of Islam to various parts of coastal India set the stage for its further expansion to island Southeast Asia. Arab traders and sailors regularly visited the ports of Southeast Asia long before they converted to Islam. From the 13th century, these traders, and the Sufi mystics they sometimes carried aboard their ships, spread Islam to Java and much of the rest of island Southeast Asia. As was the case in India, conversion was generally peaceful, and the new believers combined Islamic teachings and rituals with elements of the animist, Hindu and Buddhist religions that had spread through the area in preceding centuries.

From a world history perspective, island Southeast Asia had long been mainly a middle ground, where the Chinese segment of the great Euroasian trading complex met the Indian Ocean trading zone to the west. At ports on the coast of the Malayan peninsula, east Sumatra, and somewhat later north Java, goods from China were transferred from East Asian vessels to Arab or Indian ships, and products from as far west as Rome were loaded into the emptied Chinese ships to be carried to East Asia. By the 7th and 8th centuries C.E., sailors and ships from areas within Southeast Asia—particularly Sumatra and Malaya—had become active in the seaborne trade of the region. Southeast Asian products, especially luxury items—such as aromatic woods from the rain forests of Borneo and Sumatra and spices such as cloves, nutmeg, and mace from the far end of the Indonesian archipelago—had also become important exports to both China in the east and India and the Mediterranean regions in the west. These trading links were to prove even more critical to the expansion of Islam in Southeast Asia than they had earlier been to the spread of Buddhism and Hinduism.

As the coastal trade of India came to be controlled (from the 8th century onward) increasingly by Muslims from such regions as Gujarat and various parts of south India, elements of Islamic culture began to filter into island Southeast Asia. But only in the 13th century after the collapse of the far-flung trading empire of *Shrivijaya*, which was centered on the Strait of Malacca between Malaya and the north tip of Sumatra (see map on p. 284), was the way open for widespread proselytization by Islam. Indian traders, Muslim or otherwise, were welcome to trade in the chain of ports controlled by Shrivijaya. But since the rulers and officials of Shrivijaya were devout Buddhists, there was little incentive for the traders and sailors of Southeast Asian ports to convert to Islam, the religion of growing numbers of the merchants and sailors from India. With the fall of Shrivijaya, the way was open for the establishment of Muslim trading centers and efforts to preach the faith to the coastal peoples.

Trading Contacts and Conversion

As was the case in most of the areas to which Islam spread, peaceful contacts and voluntary conversion were far more important than conquest and force in spreading the faith in Southeast Asia. Throughout the islands of the region, trading contacts paved the way for conversion. Muslim merchants and sailors introduced local peoples to the ideas and rituals of the new faith and impressed on them how much of the known world had already been converted. Muslim ships also carried Sufis to various parts of Southeast Asia, where they were destined to play as vital a role in conversion as they had in India. The first areas to be won to Islam in the last decades of the 13th century were several small port centers on the northern coast of Sumatra. From these parts, the religion spread in the following centuries across the Strait of Malacca to Malaya.

On the mainland the key to widespread conversion was the powerful trading city of *Malacca*, whose smaller trading empire had replaced the fallen Shrivijaya. From Malacca, Islam spread along the coasts of Malaya to east Sumatra and to the trading center of *Demak* on the north coast of Java. From Demak, the most powerful of the trading states on north Java, the Muslim faith was disseminated to other Javanese ports and, after a long struggle with a Hindu-Buddhist kingdom in the interior, to the rest of the island. From Demak, Islam was also carried to the Celebes and the spice islands in the eastern archipelago, and from the latter to Mindanao in the southern Philippines.

This progress of Islamic conversion shows that port cities in coastal areas were particularly receptive to the new faith. Here the trading links were critical. Once one of the key cities in a trading cluster converted, it was in the best interest of others to follow suit in order to enhance personal ties and provide a common basis in Muslim law to regulate business deals. Conversion to Islam also linked these centers, culturally as well as economically, to the merchants and ports of India, the Middle East, and the Mediterranean.

Islam made slow progress in areas such as central Java, where Hindu-Buddhist dynasties contested its spread. But the fact that the earlier conversion to these Indian religions had been confined mainly to the ruling elites in Java and other island areas left openings for mass conversions to Islam that the Sufis eventually exploited. The island of Bali, where Hinduism had taken deep root at the popular level, remained largely impervious to the spread of Islam. The same was true of most of mainland Southeast Asia, where centuries before the coming of Islam, Theravada Buddhism had spread from India and Ceylon and won the fervent adherence of both the ruling elites and the peasant masses.

Sufi Mystics and the Nature of Southeast Asian Islam

Because Islam came to Southeast Asia primarily from India and was spread in many areas by Sufis, it was often infused with mystical strains and displayed a high tolerance for coexistence with earlier animist, Hindu, and Buddhist beliefs and rituals. Just as they had in the Middle East and India, the Sufis who spread Islam in Southeast Asia varied widely in personality and approach. Most were believed by those who followed them to have magical powers, and virtually all Sufis established mosque and school centers from which they traveled in neighboring regions to preach the faith.

In winning converts, the Sufis were willing to allow the inhabitants of island Southeast Asia to retain pre-Islamic beliefs and practices that orthodox scholars would clearly have found contrary to Islamic doctrine. Pre-Islamic customary law remained important in regulating social interaction, whereas Islamic law was confined to specific sorts of agreements and exchanges. Women retained a much stronger position, both within the family and in society, than they had in the Middle East and India. Trading in local and regional markets, for example, continued to be dominated by small-scale female buyers and sellers. In such areas as western Sumatra, lineage and inheritance continued to be traced through the female line after the coming of Islam, despite its tendency to promote male dominance and descent through the male line.

Perhaps most tellingly, pre-Muslim religious beliefs and rituals were incorporated into Muslim ceremonies. Indigenous cultural staples, such as the brilliant Javanese puppet shadow plays that were based on the Indian epics of the Brahmanic age, were refined, and they became even more central to popular and elite belief and practice than they had been in the pre-Muslim era.

ANALYSIS

Conversion and Accommodation in the Spread of World Religions

Although not all great civilizations have produced world religions, the two have tended to be closely associated throughout human history. World religions are those that have the capacity to spread across many cultures and societies, to forge links between civilized centers, and to diffuse civilized lifestyles to nomadic pastoral or shifting-cultivating peoples. Religions with these characteristics had appeared before the rise of Islam. As we have seen, India alone produced two of these faiths in ancient times: Hinduism, which spread to parts of Southeast and central Asia, and Buddhism, which spread even more widely in the Asian world. At the other end of the Eastern Hemisphere, Christianity spread throughout the Mediterranean region before claiming northern and western Europe as its core area. Judaism spread not because it won converts in non-Jewish cultures but because the Jewish people were driven from their homeland by Roman persecution and scattered throughout the Middle East, North Africa, and Europe.

Because religious conversion affects all aspects of life, from the way one looks at the universe to more mundane decisions about whom one may marry or how one ought to treat others, a world religion must be broad and flexible enough to permit the retention of much of the existing culture of peoples who are potential converts. At the same time, it must possess core beliefs and practices that are well enough defined to allow its followers to maintain a clear sense of common identity despite their great differences in culture and society. These beliefs and practices must also be sufficiently profound and sophisticated to convince potential converts that their own cultures can be enriched and their lives improved by adopting the new religion.

Until the 16th century, when Christianity claimed the two continents of the Western Hemisphere, no world religion could match Islam in the extent to which it spread across the globe and in the diversity of peoples and cultures that identified themselves as Muslims. Given its uncompromising monotheism, very definite doctrines, and elaborately prescribed rituals and principles of social organization, Islam's success at winning converts from very different cultural backgrounds is at first glance quite surprising. This is particularly true if it is compared with the much more amorphous beliefs and more variable ceremonial patterns of earlier world religions such as Buddhism and Hinduism. Closer examination, however, reveals that the apparent rigidity of Islamic beliefs and social practices, as written in the Quran and interpreted in the abstract by the ulama, proved much more flexible and adaptable in the actual situations in which the religion was introduced into new, non-Islamic cultures. Like all world religions, Islam had the capacity to adjust to widely varying cultural norms and modes of expression even as it was converting the peoples who exhibited these differences to a common set of religious beliefs, ritual forms, and social practices.

The fact that Islam won converts overwhelmingly through peaceful contacts between long-distance traders and the preaching and organizational skills of Sufis exemplifies this capacity for accommodation in the conversion process. Those adopting the new religion did not do so because they were pressured or forced to convert but because they saw Islam as a way to enhance their understanding of the supernatural, enrich their ceremonial expression, improve the quality of their social interaction, and establish ongoing links to a transcultural community beyond their local world.

Because Islam was adopted rather than imposed, those who converted had a good deal to say about how much of their own cultures they would change and which aspects of Islam they would emphasize or accept. Certain beliefs and practices were obligatory for all true believers—the worship of a single God, adherence to the prophet Muhammad and the divine revelations he received as recorded in the Quran, observance of the five pillars of the faith, etc.—but even these were liable to reinterpretation and reworking. In virtually all cultures to which it spread, for example, Islamic monotheism supplanted but did not eradicate the animistic veneration of nature spirits or personal and place deities. Allah was acknowledged as the most powerful and all-purpose of supernatural forces, but people continued to make offerings to spirits that could heal, bring fertility, protect their home, or punish their enemies. In such areas as

Africa and western China, where the veneration of ancestral spirits was a key aspect of religious life, the spirits were retained not as powers in themselves but as emissaries to Allah. In cultures like those found in India and Southeast Asia, Islamic doctrines were recast in a heavily mystical, even magical, mode.

The capacity of Islam for accommodation was exhibited in the social as well as the religious sphere. In Islamic Southeast Asia and, as we shall see in the next chapter, sub-Saharan Africa, the position of women remained a good deal stronger in critical areas, such as occupational outlets and family law, than it had become in the Middle East and India. In both regions, the male-centric features of Islam that had grown more pronounced through centuries of accommodation in ancient Middle Eastern and Persian cultures were played down as Islam adapted to societies where women had traditionally enjoyed considerable influence, both within the extended family and in occupations such as farming, marketing, and craft production. Even an institution like the caste system of India, which in principle is so opposed to the strong egalitarian strain in Islam, developed among Muslim groups that migrated into the subcontinent and survived in indigenous South Asian communities that converted to Islam.

Beyond basic forms of social organization and interaction, Islam accommodated diverse aspects of the societies into which it spread. The African solar calendar, for example, which was essential for the coordination of the planting cycle, was retained alongside the Muslim lunar calendar. In India, Hindu-Buddhist symbols of kingship were appropriated by Muslim rulers and acknowledged by both their Hindu and Muslim subjects. In island Southeast Asia, exquisitely forged knives, called *krises*, which were believed to have magical powers, were among the most treasured possessions of local rulers both before and after they converted to Islam.

There was always the danger that accommodation could go too far—that in winning converts, Islamic precepts and rituals would be so watered down and remolded that they no longer resembled and, in fact, actually contradicted the teachings of the Quran. Sects that came to worship Muhammad or his nephew Ali as godlike, for example, had clearly moved beyond the Muslim pale. This danger was a key source of the periodic movements for purification and revival that have been a notable feature of virtually all Islamic societies, particularly those on the frontier fringes of the Islamic world. But even these movements, which were built around the insistence that the Muslim faith had been corrupted by alien ideas and practices and that there had to be a return to Islamic fundamentals, were invariably cast in the modes of cultural expression of the peoples who rallied to them. What was considered fundamental varied according to culture, and perhaps more important, the ways in which basic beliefs were interpreted and rituals enacted differed significantly from one Islamic culture to the next.

Questions: Can you think of ways in which world religions, such as Christianity, Hinduism, and Buddhism, changed to accommodate the cultures and societies to which they spread? Do these religions strike you as more or less flexible than Islam? Why? Do you think it is possible for a set of religious beliefs and practices to become a world religion without changing as it moves from one culture to the next? If not, why? If so, can you think of a religion that has?

CONCLUSION

The Legacy of the Abbasid Age

Though problems of political control and succession continued to plague the kingdoms and empires that divided the Muslim world, the central position of Islamic civilization in global history was solidified during the centuries of Abbasid rule. Its role as the go-between for the other, more ancient civilizations of the Eastern Hemisphere grew as Arab trading networks expanded and reached into new areas. More than ever, it became the civilizer of nomadic peoples, from the Turks and Mongols of central Asia to the Berbers of North Africa and the camel herders of the Sudan. Equally critically, Islam's original contributions to the growth and refinement of civilized life greatly increased. From its great cities and universities and the accomplishments they generated in the fine arts, sciences, and literature to its vibrant religious and philosophical life, Islam pioneered patterns of organization and thinking that would affect the development of human societies in major ways for centuries to come.

In the midst of all this achievement, however, there were tendencies that would put the Muslim peoples at a growing disadvantage, particularly in relation to their long-standing European rivals. Muslim divisions would leave openings for political expansion that the Europeans would eagerly exploit, beginning with the island Southeast Asian extremities of the Islamic world and

then working their way across Muslim North India. The Muslims' inclination to leave commerce and entrepreneurship increasingly in the hands of non-Muslim groups, such as Jews and Christians, would hamper effective responses to their growing economic dependence on the West and other civilizations, particularly China, and their increasing backwardness relative to them. Above all, the growing orthodoxy and intolerance of the ulama, as well as the Muslim conceit that the vast Islamic world contained all requirements for civilized life, caused Muslim peoples to grow less receptive to outside influences and innovations. These tendencies became increasingly pronounced at precisely the time when their Christian rivals were entering a period of unprecedented curiosity, experimentation, and exploration of the world beyond their own civilized regions. The combination of these trends would put the Islamic world at a growing disadvantage vis-à-vis the West and would eventually engender a profound crisis in Islamic civilization that continues in the present day.

FURTHER READINGS

M. A. Shaban's *Islamic History: An Interpretation*, 2 vols. (1971) contains the most readable and thematic survey of early Islam, concentrating on the Abbasid period. Though Philip Hitti's monumental *History of the Arabs* (1967) and J. J. Saunders's *A History of Medieval Islam* (1965) are now somewhat dated, they contain much valuable information and some fine insights into Arab history. Also useful are the works of G. E. von Gruenebaum, especially *Classical Islam* (1970), which covers the Abbasid era. On changes in Islamic religion and the makeup of the Muslim community, Marshall Hodgson's *Venture of Islam* (1974, vol. 2) is indispensable, but again it should not be tackled by the beginner. *The Cambridge History of Islam*, 2 vols. (1970), Ira Lapidus's *A History of Islamic Societies* (1988), and Albert Hourani's *A History of the Islamic Peoples* (1991) provide excellent reference works for the political events of the Abbasid era and Muslim achievements in various fields. D. M. Dunlop's *Arab Civilization to A.D. 1500* (1971) also contains detailed essays on the latter aspects of Islamic culture as well as an article on the accomplishments of Muslim women in this era.

On social history, B. F. Musallam's *Sex and Society in Islam* (1983) has material on the Abbasid period, and Ira Lapidus's study, *Muslim Cities in the Later Middle Ages* (1967), remains the standard work on urban life in the premodern era. Two essential works on the spread of Islam to India are S. M. Ikram's *Muslim Civilization in India* (1964) and Aziz Ahmad's *Studies in Islamic Culture in the Indian Environment* (1964). For the role of the Sufis in Islamic conversion, Richard Eaton's *Sufis of Bijapur* (1978) and *The Rise of Islam and the Bengal Frontier* (1993) are particularly revealing. The best introduction to the pattern of Islamic conversion in Southeast Asia is H. J. de Graaf's essay in *The Cambridge History of Islam* (1976, vol. 2). Clifford Geertz's *Islam Observed* (1968) provides a sweeping and provocative interpretation of the process of conversion in general and of the varying forms Islam takes in the Javanese and Moroccan milieux in particular.

14

African Civilizations and the Spread of Islam

100–200 Camels introduced for trade in the Sahara   **600–700** Islam spreads across North Africa

300 Origins of the kingdom of Ghana

1000 Ghana at height of its power

1100 Almoravid movement in the Sahara

100 C.E.   **600** C.E.   **1000** C.E.

INTRODUCTION

The spread of Islam, from its heartland in the Middle East and North Africa to India and Southeast Asia, revealed the power of the religion and its commercial and sometimes military attributes. Civilizations were altered without being fully drawn into a single Islamic statement. A similar pattern developed in sub-Saharan Africa as Islam provided new influences and contacts without amalgamating African culture as a whole to the Middle Eastern core. New religious, economic, and political patterns developed in relation to the Islamic surge, but great diversity remained.

Africa below the Sahara was never totally isolated from the centers of civilization in Egypt, west Asia, or the Mediterranean, but for long periods the contacts were difficult and intermittent. During the ascendancy of Rome, sub-Saharan Africa, like northern Europe, was on the periphery of the major centers of civilization. After the fall of Rome, the civilizations of Byzantium and the Islamic world provided a link between the civilizations of the Middle East and the Mediterranean as well as the areas, such as northern Europe and Africa, on their frontiers. In Africa, between roughly 800 and 1500 C.E., the frequency and intensity of contact with the outside world increased as part of the growing international network. Social, religious, and technological changes took place that influenced many of the different peoples throughout the vast and varied continent. Chief among these changes was the arrival of the followers of the Prophet Muhammad.

The spread of Islam across much of the northern third of Africa produced profound effects on both those who converted and those who resisted the new faith. Islamization also served to link Muslim Africa even more closely to the outside world through trade, religion, and politics. Trade and long-distance commerce, in fact, was carried out in many parts of the continent and linked regions beyond the orbit of Muslim penetration. Until about 1450, however, Islam provided the major external contact between sub-Saharan Africa and the world.

State building took place in many areas of the continent under a variety of conditions. West Africa, for example, experienced both the cultural influence of Islam and its own internal dynamic of state building and civilizational developments that produced, in some places, great artistic accomplishments. The formation of some powerful states, such as Mali and Songhay, depended more on military power and dynastic alliances than on ethnic or cultural unity. In this aspect and in the process of state formation itself, Africa paralleled the roughly contemporaneous developments of western Europe. The development of city-states, with strong merchant communities in West Africa and on the Indian Ocean coast of East Africa, bore certain similarities to the urban developments of Italy and Germany in this period. However, disparities between the technologies and ideologies of Europeans and Africans by the end of this period also created marked differences in the way in which their societies developed. The arrival of western Europeans—the Portuguese—in the 15th century set in motion a series of exchanges that would draw Africans increasingly into the world economy and create a new set of relationships that would characterize African development for centuries to come.

Several emphases thus highlight the history of Africa in the postclassical centuries. Northern Africa and the East African coast became increasingly incorporated into the Arab Muslim world, but even other parts of the continent reflected the power of Islamic thought and institutions. New centers of civilization and political power arose in several parts of sub-Saharan Africa, illustrating the geographical diffusion of civilization. African civilizations, however, built somewhat less clearly on prior precedent than was the case in other postclassical societies. Some earlier themes, such as the Bantu migration and the formation of large states in the western Sudan, persisted. Overall, sub-Saharan Africa remained a varied and distinctive setting; parts of it were drawn into new

---

1200 Rise of the empire of Mali

1260 Death of Sundiata; earliest stone buildings at Zimbabwe; Lalaibela rules in Ethiopia; Yoruba culture flourishes at Ile-Ife

1300 Mali at its height; Kanem Empire as a rival

1324 Pilgrimage of Mansa Musa

1400 Flourishing of cities of Timbuktu and Jenne; Ethiopian Christian kingdom; Swahili cities flourish on East Africa coast

1417, 1431 Last Chinese trade voyages to East Africa

1500 Songhai Empire flourishes; Benin at height of its power

1200 C.E.   **1400** C.E.

contacts with the growing world network, but much of it retained a certain isolation.

AFRICAN SOCIETIES: DIVERSITY AND SIMILARITIES

Focal Point: African societies developed diverse forms from large centralized states to stateless societies organized around kinship or age sets rather than central authority. Within this diversity were many commonly shared aspects of language and beliefs. Universalistic faiths did penetrate the continent and serve as the basis for important cultural developments in Nubia and Ethiopia.

The continent of Africa is so vast and its societies are so diverse that it is almost impossible to generalize about them. Differences in geography, language, religion, politics, and other aspects of life contributed to the diversity and to Africa's lack of political unity over long periods of time. Unlike many parts of Asia, Europe, and North Africa, neither universal states nor universal religions characterized the history of sub-Saharan Africa. Yet universal religions, first Christianity and later Islam, did find adherents in Africa and sometimes contributed to the formation of large states and empires.

Stateless Societies

While some African societies had rulers who exercised control through a hierarchy of officials in what can be called states, other African societies were "stateless": organized around kinship or other forms of obligation and lacking the concentration of political power and authority we normally associate with the state. The African past reveals that the movement from stateless to state societies was not necessarily an evolutionary development. Stateless peoples who lived in villages organized around either lineages or age sets—that is, groups of people of the same age who are considered to have similar responsibilities to society—did not need rulers or bureaucracies and existed side by side with states. Sometimes the *stateless societies* were larger and more extensive than the neighboring states. Stateless societies had forms of government, but the authority and power normally exercised by a ruler and his court in a kingdom could be held instead by a council of families or by the community, with no need to tax the population to support the ruler, the bureaucrats, the army, or the nobles as was usually the case in state-building societies. Stateless societies had

little concentration of authority, and that authority affected only a small part of the peoples' lives. In these societies, government was rarely a full-time occupation.

Other alternatives to formal government were also possible. Among peoples of the West African forest, secret societies of men and women exercised considerable control over customs and beliefs and were able to limit the authority of rulers. Especially among peoples who had sharp rivalries between lineages or family groupings, secret societies developed that cut across the lineage divisions. The secret societies incorporated their members after an initiation that might have been based on knowledge, skills, physical tests, an initiation fee, or all of these. Members took on an allegiance to the society that transcended their lineage ties. The secret societies settled village disputes; enforcement or punishment was carried out by masked junior members acting on behalf of the secret society so that no feuding between families resulted. The secret societies acted to maintain stability within the community, and they served as an alternative to the authority of state institutions.

Throughout Africa many stateless societies thrived, perhaps aided by the fact that internal social pressures or disputes could often be resolved by the splitting off of dissidents and the establishment of a new village in the relatively sparsely populated continent. Fragmentation and a "frontier" open to new settlement were constant features in much of African history. Still, stateless societies found it difficult to meet external pressures, mobilize for warfare, organize large building projects, or create stable conditions for continuous long-distance trade with other peoples. All these needs or goals contributed in various ways to the formation of states in sub-Saharan Africa.

Common Elements in African Societies

Even amid the diversity of African cultures, certain similarities in language, thought, and religion provided some underlying unities. As we saw in Chapter 10, the spread of the Bantu-speaking peoples provided a linguistic base across much of Africa, so that even though specific languages differed, structure and vocabulary allowed for some mutual understanding between neighboring Bantu speakers.

The same might be said of the animistic religion that characterized much of Africa. The belief in the power of natural forces personified as spirits or gods and the role of ritual and worship—often in the form of dancing, drumming, divination, and sacrifice—in influencing their actions was central to the religion of many African peoples, although local practice varied widely. African religions had well-developed concepts of good and evil. Africans, like Europeans, believed that some evil, disasters, and illnesses were produced by witchcraft. Specialists were needed to combat the power of evil and eliminate the witches. This led in many societies to the existence of a class of diviners or priests who guided religious practice and helped protect the community. Above all, African religion provided a cosmology—a view of how the universe worked—and a guide to ethics and behavior.

Many African peoples shared an underlying belief in a creator deity whose power and action were expressed through spirits or lesser gods and through the founding ancestors of the group. The ancestors were often viewed as the first settlers and thus the "owners" of the land or the local resources, and through them the fertility of the land, the game, the people, and the herds could be ensured. Among some groups, working the land took on religious significance, so the land itself had a meaning beyond its economic usefulness.

Religion, economics, and history were thus closely intertwined. Then too, the family, lineage, or clan around which many African societies were organized had an important role in dealing with the gods. Deceased ancestors were often a direct link between their living relatives and the spirit world. Veneration of the ancestors and gods was part of the same system of belief. Such a system was strongly linked to specific places and people. It showed remarkable resiliency even in the face of contact with the more generalized principles of religions such as Islam and Christianity.

The economies of Africa are harder to describe in common terms than some basic aspects of politics and culture. North Africa, fully involved in the Mediterranean and Arab economic world, stands clearly apart. Sub-Saharan Africa varied greatly from one region to the next. In many areas, settled agriculture and skilled ironwork had been established before the postclassical period or advanced rapidly during the period itself. Specialization encouraged active local and regional trade, the basis for many lively markets and the many large cities that grew both in the structured states and in the decentralized areas. The bustle and gaiety of market life were important ingredients of African society, and women as well as men participated actively. Trade was handled by professional merchants, in many cases in hereditary kinship groupings. Participation in international trade increased in many regions in this period, mainly toward the Islamic world and often through the intermediary of Arab traders.

While African states benefited from their ability to tax the trade, they stood at some disadvantage in trading unprocessed goods, such as gold, ivory, salt, or slaves, for more elaborate products made elsewhere. International trade stimulated political and cultural change and furthered the growth of African merchant groups, but it did not induce rapid technical or manufacturing shifts within Africa, except for some important innovations in the excavation of mines.

Finally, we should note that one of the least known aspects of African societies prior to the 20th century is the size and dynamic of their populations. This is true not only of Africa but of much of the world. Archeological evidence, travelers' reports, and educated guesses are used to estimate the population of early African societies, but in truth, our knowledge of how Africa fits into the general trends of the world population is very slight. By 1500, Africa may have had 30 to 60 million inhabitants.

The Arrival of Islam in North Africa

Africa north of the Sahara had long been part of the world of classical antiquity, where Phoenicians, Greeks, Romans, and Vandals traded, settled, built, battled, and destroyed. The Greek city of Cyrene (c. 600 B.C.E.) in modern Libya and the great Phoenician outpost at Carthage (founded c. 814 B.C.E.) in Tunisia attest to the part North Africa played in the classical world. After the age of the Pharaohs, Egypt (conquered by Alexander in 331 B.C.E.) had become an important part of the Greek world and then later a key province in the Roman Empire, valued especially for its grain. Toward the end of the Roman Empire, Christianity had taken a firm hold in Mediterranean Africa, but in the warring between the Vandals and the Byzantines in North Africa in the 5th and 6th centuries C.E., considerable disruption had taken place. During that period, the Berber peoples of the Sahara had raided the coastal cities. As we have seen with Egypt, North Africa was also linked across the Sahara to the rest of Africa in many ways. With the rise of Islam, those ties became even closer.

Between 640 and 700 C.E., the followers of Muhammad swept across North Africa from Suez to the Pillars of Hercules on Morocco's Atlantic shore. By 670 C.E., Muslims ruled Tunisia, or *Ifriqiya*—what the Romans had called Africa. (The Arabs originally used this word as the name for eastern North Africa and *Maghrib* for lands to the West.) By 711, Arab and Berber armies had crossed into Spain. Only their defeat in France by Charles Martel at Poitiers in 732 brought the Muslim advance in the West to a halt. The message of Islam found fertile ground among the populations of North Africa. Conversion took place rapidly within a certain political unity provided by the Abbasid dynasty. This unity eventually broke down, and North Africa divided into several separate states and competing groups.

In opposition to the states dominated by the Arabic rulers, the peoples of the desert, the Berbers, formed states of their own at places such as Fez in Morocco and at Sijilimasa, the old city of the trans-Saharan caravan trade. By the 11th century, under pressure from new Muslim invaders from the East, a great puritanical reformist movement, whose followers were called the *Almoravids,* grew among the desert Berbers of the western Sahara. Launched on the course of a jihad—a holy war waged to purify, spread, or protect the faith—the Almoravids moved southward against the African kingdoms of the savanna and westward into Spain. In 1130 another reformist group, the *Almohadis,* followed the same pattern. These North African and Spanish developments were an essential background to the penetration of Islam into sub-Saharan Africa.

Islam offered many attractions within Africa. Its fundamental teaching that all Muslims are equal within the community of believers made the acceptance of conquerors and new rulers easier. The Islamic tradition of uniting the powers of the state and religion in the person of the ruler or caliph appealed to some African kings as a way of reinforcing their authority. The concept that all members of the umma, or community of believers, were equal put the newly converted Berbers and later Africans on an equal footing with the Arabs, at least in law. Despite these egalitarian and somewhat utopian ideas within Islam, practices differed considerably at local levels. Social stratification remained important in Islamicized societies and ethnic distinctions also divided the believers. Despite certain teachings on the relative equality between men and women, the law recognized that the monetary penalty for killing a man was twice that for killing a woman. The disparity between law and practice—between equality before God and inequality within the world—sometimes led to reform movements of a utopian type. Groups like the Almohades are characteristic within Islamic history, often developing in peripheral areas and dedicated to a purification of society by returning to the original teachings of the Prophet.

The Christian Kingdoms: Nubia and Ethiopia

Islam, of course, was not the first universalistic religion to take root in Africa, and the wave of Arab conquests across northern Africa had left behind it islands of Christianity at various places. Christianity had made converts in Egypt and Ethiopia even before the conversion of the Roman Empire in the 4th century C.E. Aside from the Christian kingdom of Axum, Christian communities thrived in Egypt and Nubia. The Christians of Egypt, the *Copts,* developed a rich tradition in contact with Byzantium, translating the gospels and other religious literature from Greek to Coptic, their own tongue, which was based on the language of ancient Egypt. On doctrinal and political issues they eventually split from the Byzantine connection. When Egypt was conquered by Arab armies and then converted to Islam, the Copts were able to maintain their faith; they were recognized by Muslim rulers as followers of a revealed religion and thus entitled to a certain tolerance. The Coptic influence had already spread up the Nile into Nubia, the ancient land of Kush. Muslim attempts to penetrate Nubia were met with such stiff resistance in the 9th century that the Christian descendants of ancient Kush were left in relative peace as independent Christian kingdoms until the 13th century.

The *Ethiopian kingdom* that grew from Axum was perhaps the most important of the African Christian outposts. Cut off from Christian Byzantium by the Muslim conquest of Egypt and the Red Sea coast, surrounded by pagan neighbors, and probably influenced by pagan and Jewish immigrants from Yemen, the Christian kingdom turned inward. Its people occupied the Ethiopian highlands, living in fortified towns and supporting themselves with agriculture on terraced hillsides. Eventually, through a process of warfare, conversion, and compromise with non-Christian neighbors, a new dynasty appeared, which under King Lalaibela (d. 1221) sponsored a remarkable building project in which 11 great churches were sculpted from the rock in the town that bore his name.

In the 13th and 14th centuries, an Ethiopian Christian state emerged under a dynasty that traced its origins back to the marriage of Solomon and Sheba. Using the Geez language of Axum as a religious language and Amharic as the common speech, this state maintained its brand of Christianity in relative isolation while facing constant pressure from its increasingly Muslim neighbors.

The struggle between the Christian state in the Ethiopian highlands and the Muslim peoples in Somalia and on the Red Sea coast shaped much of the consequent history of the region and continues to do so today. When one of these Muslim states, with help from the Ottoman Turks, threatened the very existence of the Ethiopian kingdom, a Portuguese expedition arrived in 1542 at Massawa on the Red Sea and turned the tide in

The 13th-century churches of Lalaibela, some cut from a single rock, represent the power of early Christianity in Ethiopia.

favor of its Christian allies. Portuguese attempts thereafter to bring Ethiopian Christianity into the Roman Catholic church failed, and Ethiopia remained isolated, Christian, and fiercely independent.

KINGDOMS OF THE GRASSLANDS

Focal Point: In the sahel grasslands, several powerful states emerged that combined Islamic religion and culture with local practices. The kingdoms of *Mali* and *Songhay* and the *Hausa states* represented an African adaptation of Islam and its fusion with African traditions.

As the Islamic wave spread across North Africa, it sent ripples across the Sahara, not in the form of invading armies but at first in the merchants and travelers who trod the dusty and ancient caravan routes toward the savanna. Africa had three important "coasts" of contact: the Atlantic, the Indian Ocean, and the savanna on the southern edge of the Sahara.

On the edge of the desert, where several resource zones came together, African states such as Ghana had already formed by the 8th century by exchanging gold from the forests of West Africa for salt or dates from the Sahara or for goods from Mediterranean North Africa. Camels, which had been introduced from Asia to the Sahara between the 1st and 5th centuries C.E., had greatly improved the possibilities of trade, but these animals, which thrived in arid and semiarid environments, could not penetrate into the humid forest zones because of disease. Thus, the *Sahel,* the extensive grassland belt at the southern edge of the Sahara, became a point of exchange between the forests to the south and North Africa—an active "coast" where ideas, trade, and people from the Sahara and beyond arrived in increasing numbers. Along that coast, several African states developed between the trading cities, taking advantage of their position as intermediaries in the trade. But location on the relatively open plains of the dry Sahel also meant that these states were subject to attack and periodic droughts.

In Chapter 10 we discussed the rise of the kingdom of Ghana among the Soninke peoples of the western Sudan. Founded probably in the 3rd century C.E., Ghana

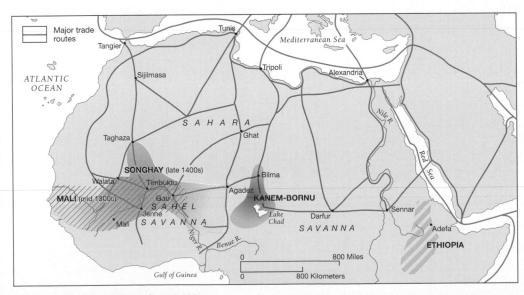

The Savanna Kingdoms, About 1400 C.E.

rose to power by taxing the salt and gold exchanged within its borders. By the 10th century, its rulers had converted to Islam, and Ghana was at the height of its power. At a time when William the Conqueror could muster perhaps 5000 troops for his invasion of England, Muslim accounts reported that the king of Ghana could field an army many times that size. Eventually, however, Almoravid armies invaded Ghana from North Africa in 1076, and although the kingdom survived, its power was in decline so that by the beginning of the 13th century, new states had risen in the savanna to take its place of leadership.

Sudanic States

There were several Sudanic kingdoms, and even during the height of Ghana's power, neighboring and competing states persisted, such as Takrur on the Senegal River to the west and Gao (Kawkaw) on the Niger River to the east. Before we deal with the most important kingdoms that followed Ghana, it will be useful to review some of the elements these states had in common.

The *Sudanic states* were often led by the patriarch or council of elders of a particular family or group of lineages that established control over its neighbors. Usually these states had a territorial core area in which the people were of the same linguistic or ethnic background, but their power extended over subordinate communities. These were conquest states, which drew on the taxes, tribute, and military support of the subordinate areas, lineages, and villages. The effective control of subordinate societies and the legal or informal control of their sovereignty are the usual definition of empires. Ghana, Mali, and Songhay and some of their neighbors were imperial states.

The rulers of these states were considered to be sacred individuals and were surrounded with rituals that separated them from their subjects. With the conversion of the rulers of Ghana and Takrur after the 10th century, Islam was used to reinforce indigenous ideas of kingship, so that Islam became something of a royal cult. Much of the population never converted, and the Islamicized ruling families also drew on their traditional powers to fortify their rule.

Several savanna states rose among the various peoples in the Sudan. We can trace the development and the culture of two of the most important, Mali and Songhay, as an example of the fusion of Islamic and indigenous African cultures, within the context of trade and military expansion, that these states represented.

The spread of Islam and the importance of trade in Africa is represented by the great mosque at Jenne on the Niger River in the modern Republic of Mali.

The Empire of Mali and Sundiata, the "Lion Prince"

The empire of Mali, centered between the Senegal and Niger rivers, was the creation of the Malinke peoples, who in the 13th century broke away from the control of Ghana, which was by then in steady decline. In Mali the old forms of kingship were reinforced by Islam. As in many of the Sudanic states, the rulers supported Islam by building mosques, attending public prayers, and supporting preachers. In return, sermons to the faithful emphasized obedience and support of the king. Mali became a model of these Islamicized Sudanic kingdoms. The economic basis of society in the Mali Empire was successful agriculture. This was combined with an active tradition of trade in many products, although like Ghana, Mali also depended on its access to gold-producing areas to the south. Malinke merchants, or *juula*, formed small partnerships and groups to carry out trade throughout the area. They spread beyond the borders of the empire and throughout much of West Africa.

The beginning of Malinke expansion is attributed to *Sundiata* (sometimes written Sunjata), a brilliant leader whose exploits serve as the foundation of a great oral tradition. The griots, professional oral historians who also served as keepers of traditions and advisors to kings, began their epic histories of Mali with Sundiata, the "Lion Prince."

Listen then sons of Mali, children of the black people, listen to my word, for I am going to tell you of
Sundiata, the father of the Bright Country, of the
savanna land, the ancestor of those who draw the
bow, the master of a hundred vanquished kings. . . .
He was great among kings, he was peerless among
men; he was beloved of God because he was the last
of the great conquerors.

After a difficult childhood, Sundiata emerged from a
period of interfamily and regional fighting to create a
unified state. Oral histories ascribed to him the creation
of the basic rules and relationships of Malinke society
and the outline of the government of the empire of Mali.
He became the mansa, or emperor. Sundiata, it was said,
"divided up the world," which meant that he was considered the originator of social arrangements. Sixteen
clans of freemen were entitled to bear arms and carry the
bow and quiver of arrows as the symbol of their status,
five clans were devoted to religious duties, and four clans
were specialists and tradesmen, such as blacksmiths and
griots. Division and grouping by clans had apparently
existed and represented traditional patterns among the
peoples of the savanna in ancient Ghana as well, but
Sundiata as the hero of origins was credited with the creation of this social arrangement. While he created the
political institutions of rule that allowed for considerable
regional and ethnic differences in the federated
provinces, he also stationed garrisons to maintain loyalty
and security. Travel was secure and crime was severely
punished, as *Ibn Batuta,* the Arab traveler, reported:
"Of all peoples," he said, "the Blacks are those who
most hate injustice, and their emperor pardons none
who is guilty of it." The security of travelers and their
goods was an essential element in a state where commerce played so important a role.

Sundiata died about 1260, but his successors expanded the borders of Mali until it controlled most of
the Niger valley almost to the Atlantic coast. A sumptuous court was established and hosted a large number of
traders. Mali grew wealthy from the trade. Perhaps the
most famous of Sundiata's successors was Mansa Kankan
Musa (c. 1312–1337), who made a pilgrimage to Mecca
in 1324 and brought the attention of the Muslim world
to Mali.

City Folk and Villagers

The cities of the western Sudan began to resemble
those of North Africa, but with a distinctive local architectural style. The towns were commercial and often

included craft specialists and a resident foreign merchant community. The military expansion of states
such as Ghana, Mali, and later Songhay contributed to
their commercial success because the power of the state
protected traders.

A cosmopolitan court life developed as merchants
and scholars were attracted by the power and protection of Mali. Mandinka juula traders ranged across the
Sudan and exploited their position as middlemen.
"Port" cities flourished, such as Jenne and *Timbuktu,*
which lay just off the flood plain on the great bend in
the Niger River. Timbuktu was reported to have a
population of 50,000, and by the 14th century, its
great Sankore mosque contained a library and an associated university where scholars, jurists, and Muslim
theologians studied. The book was the symbol of civilization in the Islamic world, and it was said that the
book trade in Timbuktu was the most lucrative business of all.

For the vast majority of people in the empire of
Mali and the other Sudanic states, life was not centered on the royal court, the great mosque, or long-
distance trade but rather on the agricultural cycle and
the village. Making a living from the land was the preoccupation of most people, and about 80 percent of
the villagers lived by farming. This was a difficult life.
The soils of the savanna were sandy and shallow.
Plows were rarely used. The villagers were people of
the hoe, who looked to the skies in the spring for the
first rains to start their planting. Rice in the river valleys, millet, sorghums, some wheat, fruits, and vegetables provided the basis of daily life in the village and
supplied the caravan trade. Even a large farm would
rarely exceed ten acres and most were much smaller.
Clearing land was often done communally, accompanied by feasts and competition, but the farms belonged to families and were worked by them. A man
with two wives and several unmarried sons could work
more land than a man with one wife and a smaller family. Polygamy, or the practice of having multiple wives,
was therefore, common in the region, and it remains
so today.

Given the difficulties of the soil, the periodic
droughts, insect pests, storage problems, and the limitations of technology, the farmers of the Sudanic states—
by the methods of careful cultivation, crop rotation, and,
in places like Timbuktu, the use of irrigation—were able
to provide for their people the basic foods that supported them and the imperial states on which they were
based. The hoe and the bow became symbols of the
common people of the savanna states.

CLOSEUP

The Hajj of Mansa Musa

Although Sundiata died around 1260, his successors expanded the borders of Mali almost to the Atlantic coast. A sumptuous court hosted many foreign traders, and Mali grew rich from the trade. Perhaps the most famous of Sundiata's successors was Mansa Kankan Musa (c. 1312–1337). As a Muslim he decided to make the hajj, or pilrimage to Mecca, in 1324, and his trip brought the glory and wealth of Mali to the attention of the Muslim world. The trip caused a sensation across the Sudan and in Egypt, where it was said that so much gold was distributed by his retinue that a devaluation of currency took place.

In 1375, Abraham Cresques, a Jewish mapmaker in Spain, illustrated a map with the image of the Emperor of Mali holding a golden scepter in his hand.

Mansa Musa brought back from Mecca the poet and architect Ishak al-Sahili, who came from Muslim Spain. The architect directed the building of several important mosques and expanded the use of sun-dried bricks. A distinctive form of Sudanic architecture developed, which made use of local materials, especially beaten clay. This can still be seen in the great mosque of Jenne. Mali's contact with the outer world had brought change and innovation.

The Songhay Kingdom

As the power of Mali began to wane, a successor state from within the old empire was already beginning to emerge. The people of Songhay dominated the middle reaches of the Niger valley. Traditionally, the society of

Songhay was made up of "masters of the soil," that is, farmers, herdsmen, and "masters of the waters," or fisher-folk. Songhay had begun to form in the 7th century as an independent kingdom, perhaps under a Berber dynasty. By 1010, a capital was established at Gao on the Niger River, and the rulers had become

Muslims, although the majority of the population remained pagan. Dominated by Mali for a while, by the 1370s Songhay had established its independence again and began to thrive as new sources of gold from the West African forests began to pass through its territory. Gao became a large city with a resident foreign merchant community and several mosques. Under a dynamic leader, Sunni Ali (1464–1492), the empire of Songhay was forged.

Sunni Ali was a great tactical commander and a ruthless leader. His cavalry expanded the borders and seized the traditional trading cities of Timbuktu and Jenne. The whole middle Niger valley fell under his control, and he developed a system of provincial administration to mobilize recruits for the army and rule the far-flung conquests. Although apparently a Muslim, he met any challenge to his authority even when it came from the Muslim scholars of Timbuktu, whom he persecuted. Sunni Ali was followed by a line of Muslim rulers who took the military title of askia. These rulers, especially Askia *Muhammad the Great,* extended the boundaries of the empire so that by the mid-16th century Songhay dominated the central Sudan.

Life in the Songhay Empire followed many of the patterns established in the previous savanna states. The fusion of Islamic and pagan populations and traditions continued. Muslim clerics and jurists were sometimes upset by the pagan beliefs and practices that continued among the population, and even more by the local interpretation of Islamic law. They wanted to impose a strict interpretation of the law of Islam and were shocked that men and women mixed freely in the markets and streets, that women went unveiled, and that at Jenne young girls went naked.

Songhay remained the dominant power in the region until the end of the 16th century. In 1591, a Muslim army from Morocco, equipped with muskets, crossed the Sahara and defeated the vastly larger forces of Songhay. This sign of weakness stimulated internal revolts against the ruling family, and eventually the parts of the old empire broke away.

The demise of the Songhay imperial structure did not mean the end of the political and cultural tradition of the western Sudan. Other states that combined Muslim and pagan traditions rose among the Hausa peoples of northern Nigeria, based on cities such as Kano. The earliest Muslim ruler of Kano took control in the late 14th century and turned the city into a center of Muslim learning. In Kano, Katsina, and other Hausa cities of the region, an urbanized royal court in a fortified capital ruled over the essentially animistic villages, where the majority of the population lived. With powerful cavalry forces these states were able to extend their rule and protect their active trade in salt, grains, and cloth. While these later Islamicized African states tended to be small in size and local in their goals, they reproduced many of the social, political, and religious forms of the great empires of the grasslands.

Beyond the Sudan, Muslim penetration came in various forms. Merchants became established in most of the major trading cities, and religious communities developed in each of these, often associated with particular families. Networks of trade and contact were established widely over the region as juula merchants and groups of pastoralists established their outposts in the area of Guinea. Muslim traders, herdsmen, warriors, and religious leaders became important minorities within these segmented African societies, composed of elite families, occupational groups, free men, and slaves. Intermarriage often took place, but Muslim influence varied widely from region to region. Nevertheless, families of juula traders and lineages that became known as specialists in Muslim law spread widely through the region, so that by the 18th century there were Muslim minorities scattered widely throughout West Africa, even in those areas where no Islamicized state had emerged.

Political and Social Life in the Sudanic States

We can generalize from these brief descriptions of Mali and Songhay about the nature of the Sudanic states. The village communities, clans, and various ethnic groups continued to organize many aspects of life in the savanna. The development of unified states provided an overarching structure that allowed the various groups and communities to coexist. The large states usually represented the political aims and power of a particular group and often of a dominant family. Many states pointed to the immigrant origins of the ruling families, and in reality the movement and fusion of populations was a constant feature in the Sudan. Islam provided a universalistic faith that served the interests of many groups. Common religion and law provided solidarity and trust to the merchants who resided in the cities and whose caravans brought goods to and from the savanna. The ruling families used Islamic titles, such as emir or caliph, to reinforce their authority, and they surrounded themselves with literate Muslim advisors and scribes, who aided in the administration of government. The Muslim concept of a ruler who

DOCUMENT

The Great Oral Tradition and the Epic of Sundiata

Oral traditions are of various kinds. Some are simply the shared stories of a family or people, but in many West African societies, the mastery of oral traditions is a skill practiced by *griots*. Although today's griots are professional musicians and bards, historically they held important places at the courts of West African kingdoms. The epic of Sundiata, the great ruler of Mali, has been passed down orally for centuries. In the following excerpts from a version collected among the Mandingo (Malinke) people of Guinea by the African scholar D. T. Niane, the role of the griot and the advantages of oral traditions are outlined.

> We are now coming to the great moments in the life of Sundiata. The exile will end and another sun will rise. It is the sun of Sundiata. Griots know the history of kings and kingdoms and that is why they are the best counsellors of kings. Every king wants to have a singer to perpetuate his memory, for it is the griot who rescues the memories of kings from oblivion, as men have short memories. Kings have prescribed destinies just like men, and seers who probe the future know it. They have knowledge of the future, whereas we griots are depositories of the knowledge of the past. But whoever knows the history of a country can read its future.

Other peoples use writing to record the past, but this invention has killed the faculty of memory among them. They do not feel the past any more, for writing lacks the warmth of the human voice. With them everybody thinks he knows, whereas learning should be a secret. The prophets did not write and their words have been all the more vivid as a result. What paltry learning is that which is concealed in dumb books!

The following excerpt describes the preparation for a major battle fought by Sundiata against the forces of Soumaoro, king of the Sossos, who had taken control of Mali and who is referred to in the epic as an evil sorcerer. Note the interweaving of proverbs, the presence of aspects of Muslim and animist religion, the celebration of Sundiata's prowess, the recurring references to iron, and the high value placed on the cavalry, the key to military power in the savanna. Note how the story of Alexander the Great inspires this "African Alexander."

> Every man to his own land! If it is foretold that your destiny should be fulfilled in such and such a land, men can do nothing against it. Mansa Tounkara

united civil and religious authority reinforced traditional ideas of kingship. It is also important to note that in Africa, as elsewhere in the world, the formation of states heightened social differences and made these societies more hierarchical.

In all the Sudanic states, Islam was fused with the existing traditions and beliefs. Rulership and authority were still based on the ability to intercede with local spirits, and while Sundiata or Sunni Ali might be nominally Muslim, they did not ignore the traditional basis of their rule. Because of this, Islam in these early stages in the Sudan tended to accommodate pagan practice and belief. Large proportions of the populations of

Mali and Songhay never converted to Islam, and those who did convert often maintained many of the old beliefs as well.

We can see this fusion of traditions clearly in the position of women. Several Sudanic societies were matrilineal, and some recognized the role of women within the lines of kinship, contrary to the normal patrilineal customs inscribed in the *Sharia*, or Islamic law. As we have just noted in the case of Songhay, North African visitors to the Sudan were shocked by the easy familiarity between men and women and the freedom enjoyed by women.

Finally, we must also take note that slavery and the

could not keep Sundiata back because the destiny of Songolon's son was bound up with that of Mali. Neither the jealousy of a cruel stepmother, nor her wickedness could alter for a moment the course of great destiny.

The snake, man's enemy, is not long-lived, yet the serpent that lives hidden will surely die old. Djata (Sundiata) was strong enough now to face his enemies. At the age of eighteen he had the stateliness of the lion and the strength of the buffalo. His voice carried authority, his eyes were live coals, his arm was iron, he was the husband of power.

Moussa Tounkara, king of Mema, gave Sundiata half of his army. The most valiant came forward of their own free will to follow Sundiata in the great adventure. The cavalry of Mema, which he had fashioned himself, formed his iron squadron. Sundiata, dressed in the Muslim fashion of Mema, left the town at the head of his small but redoubtable army. The whole population sent their best wishes with him. He was surrounded by five messengers from Mali, and Manding Bory [Sundiata's brother] rode proudly at his side. The horsemen of Mema formed behind Djata a bristling iron squadron. The troop took the direction of Wagadou, for Djata did not have enough troops to confront Soumaoro directly, and so the king of Mema advised him to go to Wagadou and take half the men of the king, Soumaba Cissé. A swift messenger had been sent there and so the king of Wagadou came out in person to meet Sundiata and his troops. He gave Sundiata half of his cavalry and blessed the weapons. Then Manding Bory said to his brother, "Djata, do you think yourself able to face Soumaoro now?"

"No matter how small a forest may be, you can always find there sufficient fibers to tie up a man. Numbers mean nothing; it is worth that counts. With my cavalry I shall clear myself a path to Mali."

Djata gave out his orders. They would head south, skirting Soumaoro's kingdom. The first objective to be reached was Tabon, the iron-gated town in the midst of the mountains, for Sundiata had promised Fran Kamara that he would pass Tabon before returning to Mali. He hoped to find that his childhood companion had become king. It was a forced march and during the halts the divines, Singbin Mara Cissé and Mandjan Bérété, related to Sundiata the history of Alexander the Great and several other heroes, but of all of them Sundiata preferred Alexander, the king of gold and silver, who crossed the world from west to east. He wanted to outdo his prototype both in the extent of his territory and in the wealth of his treasury.

Questions: Can "oral" traditions be used like other sources? Even if they are not entirely "true," do they have historical value? Judging from this epic, how did people of the Sudan define the qualities of a king? What aspects of the epic reveal contacts between this part of Africa and the wider world?

slave trade between black Africa and the rest of the Islamic world had a major impact on women and children in these societies. Various forms of slavery and dependent labor had existed in Africa prior to the arrival of Islam. While we know little about slavery in central Africa in this period, slavery had been a relatively marginal aspect of the Sudanic states. Africans had been enslaved by others before, and Nubian (African) slaves had been known in the classical world, but with the Muslim conquests of North Africa and commercial penetration to the south, slavery became a more widely diffused phenomenon, and a slave trade in Africans developed on a new scale.

In theory, slavery was viewed by Muslims as a stage in the process of conversion—a way of preparing pagans to become Muslims—but in reality, conversion did not guarantee freedom. Slaves in the Islamic world were used in a variety of occupations, such as domestic servants and laborers, but they were also used as soldiers and administrators who, having no local ties and affiliations, were considered to be dependent and thus trustworthy by their masters. Slaves were also used as eunuchs and concubines; thus the emphasis on women and children. The trade caravans from the Sahel across the Sahara often transported slaves as well as gold, and as we shall see, other slave-trade routes developed from the

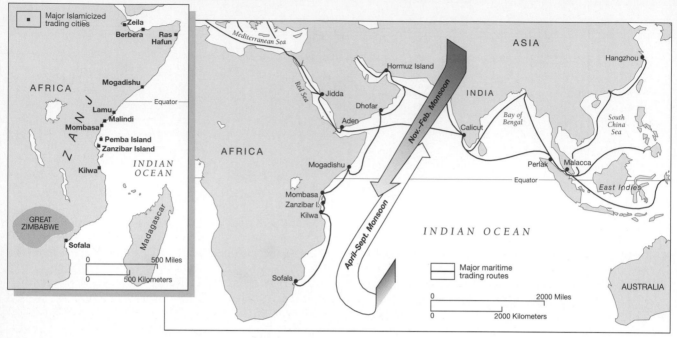

The Swahili Coast; African Monsoon Routes and Major Trade Routes

African interior to the east African coast. The tendency for the children of slave mothers to eventually be freed and integrated into Muslim society, while positive in one sense, also meant a constant demand for more slaves. Estimates of the volume of this trade vary widely. One scholar places the total in the trans-Saharan trade at 4.8 million, with another 2.4 million sent to the Muslim ports on the Indian Ocean coast. Actual figures may have been considerably lower, but the trade extended over 700 years and affected a large area. In a way, it was one more fashion in which the Islamic civilization touched and modified sub-Saharan Africa.

THE SWAHILI COAST OF EAST AFRICA

Focal Point: A string of Islamicized African ports tied to the trade of the Indian Ocean dotted the East African coast. Although these cities were Islamicized, African customs and the Bantu Swahili language remained so strong that they represented a cultural fusion, mostly limited to the coast.

While the kingdoms of West Africa came under the influence of Islam from across the Sahara, another center of Islamic civilization was developing on the seaboard

and offshore islands of Africa's Indian Ocean coast. Along that coast, extending southward from the horn of Africa to modern-day Mozambique, a string of Islamicized trading cities developed that reflected their cosmopolitan contacts with trading partners from Arabia, Persia, India, and China. Islam provided the residents of these towns a universal set of ethics and beliefs that made their maritime contacts easier, but in East Africa, as in the savanna kingdoms of West Africa, Islamization was slow to penetrate among the general population. When it did, the result was often a compromise between indigenous ways and the new faith.

The Coastal Trading Ports

A 1st-century Greek account of the Indian Ocean, *The Periplus of the Erythraean Sea,* mentioned some ports in East Africa but was somewhat vague about the nature of the local inhabitants—that is, whether they were Africans or immigrants from the Arabian peninsula. From that century to the 10th century, the wave of Bantu migration had clearly reached the East African interior. Bantu-speaking pastoralists in the north and agriculturalists in the south mixed with older populations in the region. Other peoples were also moving to the African coast. Contact across the Indian Ocean dated back to at least the 2nd century B.C.E. From Indonesia or Malaya, seaborne immigrants settled on the large island of Madagascar and from there introduced foods such as bananas and coconuts to the African coast. These were widely adopted and spread rapidly along the coast and into central Africa. Small coastal villages of fishermen and farmers, making rough pottery and working iron, dotted this coast. By the 8th and 9th centuries, visitors and refugees from Oman and the Persian Gulf had established themselves at some of these villages, attracted by the possibilities of trade with the land of *Zanj,* the Arabic term for the East African coast. The villages were transformed from relatively homogeneous and egalitarian societies with shared language, ancestors, and traditions into more cosmopolitan and diverse communities.

By the 13th century, a string of urbanized *East African trading ports* had develpoed along the coast. These towns shared the common Bantu-based and Arabic-influenced Swahili language and other cultural traits, although they were governed by separate Muslim ruling families. Towns such as Mogadishu, Mombasa, Malindi, Kilwa, Pate, and Zanzibar eventually contained mosques, tombs, and palaces of cut stone and coral. Ivory, gold, iron, slaves, and exotic animals were exported from these ports in exchange for silks from Persia and porcelain from China for the ruling Muslim families. The Arab traveler Ibn Batuta was impressed with the beauty and refinement of these towns. He described Kilwa as "one of the most beautiful and well-constructed towns in the world" and was also impressed by the pomp and luxury of its ruler. Kilwa, in fact, was particularly wealthy because it controlled the southern port of Sofala, which had access to the gold produced in the interior (near "Great Zimbabwe"), and because of its location as the farthest point south at which ships from India could hope to sail and return in a single monsoon season.

From the 13th to the 15th centuries, Kilwa flourished in the context of international trade, but it was not alone. At their height, perhaps as many as 30 of these port towns dotted the coast. These were tied to each other by an active coastal commerce and, in a few places, to the interior by a caravan trade, although it was usually Africans who brought the goods to the coast. Textiles from India and porcelain from China were brought by Arab traders. Some Chinese ports sent goods directly to Africa in the 13th century, and as late as 1417 and 1431, state-sponsored expeditions sailing directly from China stopped at the East African coast to load ivory, gold, and rare woods. Such contact was discontinued after 1431 by the Chinese, and goods from China came to the coast thereafter in the ships of Arab or Indian traders.

The Mixture of Cultures on the Swahili Coast

The Islamic overlay in these towns benefited this long-distance commerce. The 13th century was a period of considerable Islamic expansion, and as that faith spread eastward to India and Indonesia, it provided a religious bond of trust and law that facilitated trade throughout ports of the Indian Ocean. The ruling families in the East African trading ports built mosques and palaces; the mosque at Mogadishu was begun in 1238. Many of these ruling families claimed to be descendants of immigrants from Shiraz in Persia—a claim intended to legitimize their position and orthodoxy. In fact, some evidence indicates that the original Muslim families had emigrated to the Somali coast and from there to other towns farther south.

The institutions and forms of the Muslim world operated in these cities. While Islam tended to be the faith of the rulers and the merchants, the majority of the population on the East African coast, and perhaps even in the towns themselves, retained their previous beliefs and culture.

African culture remained strong throughout the area. The Swahili language was essentially a Bantu language containing a large number of Arabic words, though many of these words were not incorporated until the 16th century. The language was written in an Arabic script some time prior to the 13th century; the ruling families could also converse in Arabic. Islam itself penetrated very little into the interior among the hunters, pastoralists, and farmers. Even the areas of the coast near the trading towns remained relatively unaffected. In the towns, the stone and coral buildings of the Muslim elite were surrounded by mud and thatch houses of the non-Muslim common people, so that Islamization was to some extent class based. Still, a culture developed that fused Islamic and traditional elements. Family lineage, for example, was traced both through the maternal line, which controlled property (the traditional African practice), and through the paternal line, as was the Muslim custom. Swahili culture was a dynamic hybrid, and the Swahili people spread their language and culture along the coast of East Africa.

By the time the Portuguese arrived on this coast around 1500, the Swahili culture was widely diffused. Kilwa was no longer the predominant city, and the focus of trade had shifted to Malindi and Mombasa on the Kenya coast; but the commerce across the Indian Ocean continued. Eventually, the Portuguese raided Kilwa and Mombasa in an attempt to shift the focus of trade into their own hands. Their outpost on Mozambique island

and their control of Sofala put much of the gold trade in their hands. Although the Portuguese built a major outpost at Fort Jesus in Mombasa in 1592, they were never able to control the trade on the northern Swahili coast. The East African patterns, as established by 1500, persisted even more straightforwardly than those of the Sudanic kingdoms.

ANALYSIS

Two Transitions in the History of World Population

In this chapter and in those dealing with the ancient Americas, it is clear that establishing the size and structure of the historical populations is very difficult. Estimates based on fragmentary sources, the amount of available resources, and analysis of agricultural or hunting techniques have been used to make rough guesses about population size. The results are often inadequate or controversial, but historians believe that the question is important.

Demography, the study of population, has increasingly become a valued tool of historical inquiry. Clearly, unless we have knowledge of the size, density, age structure, health, and reproductive capacity of a population, it is difficult to understand many aspects of its society, politics, and economy. In the contemporary world, most nations conduct periodic censuses in order to know the present situation of their populations and to plan for the future. Before the mid-18th century, when census taking became a regular procedure, population estimates and counts were sporadic and usually highly inaccurate. Estimating populations in the past, especially in nonliterate societies, is therefore a highly speculative exercise in which archeological evidence and estimates of productive capacity of agricultural practices and technology are used. The earliest date for a population estimate with a margin of error less than 20 percent is probably 1750.

The history of human population can be divided into two basic periods: a long era—almost all of human history—of very slow growth, and a very short period—about 250 years from 1750 to the present—of very rapid growth. For most of this history, the human population was very small and grew very slowly. Before the development of agriculture, the hunting-and-gathering economies of the world's populations supported between 5 and 10 million people, if modern studies of such populations can be used as a guide. After about 8000 B.C.E.,

when domestication of plants and animals took place, population began to increase more rapidly but still at a modest level. Agriculture provided a more secure and larger food supply, but population concentration in villages and towns may have made people more susceptible to disease and thus reduced their numbers. Other historians believe that the settled agricultural life also led to intensified warfare (because of the struggle for land and water) and increasing social stratification within societies. Still, the Neolithic revolution and the development of agriculture stimulated population growth. It was the first major transition in the history of world population. One estimate, based on Roman and Chinese population counts and some informed guesses about the rest of the world, is an annual growth rate of about 0.36 per million. By 1 C.E., the world population may have been about 300 million people. It increased between 1 C.E. and 1750 C.E. to about 500 million people. We should bear in mind that during this period of general increase, there were always areas that suffered decline, sometimes of a violent nature because of warfare, epidemics, or natural catastrophes. The disastrous decline of American Indian populations after contact with Europeans, because of disease, conquest, and social disruption, is a case in point. The effect of the slave trade on Africa, while still debated, is another.

A second and extremely important transition took place between the mid-17th and the mid-18th centuries. Initially based on new food resources, this transition is often associated with the Industrial Revolution, when new sources of energy were harnessed to production. The growth rate greatly increased during this period in those countries most affected. Between 1750 and 1800, the population grew at a rate of over 4 percent a year to more than a billion people. By the mid-20th century, the world growth rate had tripled, and by 1990 world population had risen to over 5 billion.

This *Demographic Transition* took place first in Europe and is still more characteristic of the developed world. Most premodern agrarian economies were characterized by a relative balance between the annual number of births and deaths; both were high. Life expectancy was usually less than 35 years, and the high mortality was compensated by high fertility—that is, women had many children. Improvements in medicine, hygiene, diet, and the general standard of living contributed to a decrease in mortality in the 18th century. This allowed populations to begin to grow at a faster rate. By the 19th century in most of western Europe, the decline in mortality was followed by a decline in fertility brought about by contraception. In some countries such as France, these two transitions took place at about the same time, so the growth of population was limited. In much of Europe, however, the decline in fertility lagged behind the decrease in mortality, so there was a period of rapid population growth. Until the 1920s, population growth in western Europe and the United States was higher than in the rest of the world, especially the "less developed countries." In recent times, that situation has been reversed.

Some demographers believe that the Demographic Transition is part of the process of shifting from a basically agrarian society to an industrial, urbanized one and that the improvements in medicine, technology, and higher standards of living will necessarily result in a change to a modern demographic regime. They believe that a decreasing need for children as part of the family economic unit, laws against child labor, and state intervention in family planning will eventually lower the birth rate and decrease the pressure of population on economic growth. This assumption remains to be proved, and responses may vary greatly from one region of the world to another because of economic conditions and cultural attitudes about proper family size.

Finally, we should also note that responses to the Demographic Transition can vary greatly according to historical conditions. In the 18th and 19th centuries, Europe resolved the problem of population growth by an enormous wave of emigration to the Americas, Australia, and various colonies around the globe. Present-day political circumstances make this solution less possible.

Still, it is clear that the Demographic Transition has begun to take place in the developing world of Latin America, Africa, and Asia. Mortality has dropped very rapidly since 1950 because of modern medical technology, and life expectancy has doubled. To cite a single example, in Sri Lanka the mortality rate was almost cut in half between 1945 and 1952 simply by the elimination of malarial mosquitoes. Fertility has declined in many places in Asia and Latin America, but in Africa, where children have an important economic and social role in the extended family, it remains high. It is difficult to project how the Demographic Transition will take place in these areas of the world. However, all countries are faced with the problem of balancing their population's growth against the ability of the society to feed and provide an adequate standard of living to their people.

At present, the world's population is growing because of a moderate rate of growth in the industrialized nations and a high rate in the developing countries. In the 1970s, demographer Ansley Coale pointed out that the rate of growth, about 2 percent a year, is 100 times greater than it had been for most of human history. At this rate the world's population would be multiplied by 1000 every 350 years. The results of such growth would be disastrous. Coale concluded, therefore, that the present period of growth is a transitory one in the history of the world's population. Some concerned with the "population explosion" believe that the fundamental answer is to limit population growth in the developing nations by state intervention, through incentives to have smaller families and education about birth control. Others believe that a redistribution of resources from rich nations to poor nations would alleviate the human misery created by population pressure and eventually lead to political and social conditions that would contribute to a gradual lowering of the birth rates. Clearly, the demographic questions must always be set in political, economic, and social contexts.

Questions: Why do nations differ about the need to control population growth? Why has the rate of population growth varied in different areas of the world? Is "population" essentially a biological, social, or political problem?

PEOPLES OF THE FOREST AND PLAINS

Focal Point: Across Central Africa, kingdoms developed that were supported by complex agrarian societies capable of great artistic achievements. At Benin, in the Kongo, in the Yoruba city-states, and at Great Zimbabwe, royal authority—often considered divinely inspired—led to the creation of powerful states.

As important as the Islamic impact was on the societies of the savanna and the East African coast, other African peoples in the continent's interior and in the forests of West Africa were following their own trajectories of development. By 1000 C.E., most of these societies were based on a varied agriculture sometimes combined with herding, and most societies used iron tools and weapons. Many were still organized in small village communities. In various places, however, states had formed. Some of them began to resolve the problems of integrating large territories under a single government and ruling subject peoples. While Egypt, Kush, and Ethiopia had developed writing, and other areas borrowed the Arabic script, many sub-Saharan African societies were preliterate and transmitted their knowledge, skills, and traditions by oral methods and direct instruction. The presence or absence of writing has often been used as a measure of civilization by western observers, but as in pre-Columbian Peru, various

African societies produced considerable accomplishments in the arts, building, and statecraft—sometimes in the context of highly urbanized settings without a system of writing.

Artists and Kings: Yoruba and Benin

In the forests of central Nigeria, objects in terra-cotta of a realistic and highly stylized form have been discovered near the village of *Nok*. These objects, most of which date from about 500 B.C.E. to 200 C.E., display considerable artistic skill. The inhabitants of ancient Nok and its region practiced agriculture and used iron tools. They remain something of a mystery, but it appears that their artistic traditions spread widely through the forest areas and influenced other peoples. Nevertheless, there is a long hiatus in the historical and archeological record between the Nok sculptures and the renewed flourishing of artistic traditions in the region after about 1000 C.E.

Among the Yoruba-speaking peoples of Nigeria, at the city of Ile-Ife, remarkable terra-cotta and bronze portrait heads of past rulers were produced in the period after 1200 C.E. The lifelike representations of these portraits and the skill of their execution place them among the greatest achievements of African art. The craftsmen of Ile-Ife also worked in wood and ivory. Much of the art seems to be associated with kings and the authority of kingship. Ile-Ife, like other *Yoruba* states, seems to have been an agricultural society supported by a peasantry and dominated by a ruling family and an aristocracy. Ile-Ife was considered by many peoples in the region to be the original cultural center, and many of them traced their own beginnings to it.

Yoruba origins are, in fact, obscure. Ile-Ife was seen as the holiest city of the Yoruba, their place of birth. Another legend maintained by the royal historians was that Oduduwa, a son of the king of Mecca, migrated from the east and settled in Yoruba. Modern historians have suggested that the real origins were perhaps Meroe and Nubia, or at least in the savanna south of the Sahara. In any case, the Yoruba spoke a non-Bantu language of the West African Kwa family and recognized a certain affinity between themselves and neighboring peoples, such as the Hausa, who spoke Afro-Asian languages.

The Yoruba were organized in small city-states, each controlling a radius of perhaps 50 miles. The Yoruba were, in fact, highly urbanized, although many of the town inhabitants farmed in the surrounding countryside. These city-states developed under the strong authority of regional kings, who were considered divine. The person of the king was surrounded with a royal court of great size that included secondary wives, musicians, ma-

In the 13th and 14th centuries, Ife artists worked in terra-cotta, as well as bronze, and produced personalized portraits.

gicians, and bodyguards of soldier-slaves. His rule was not absolute, however, and it was limited by other forces in society. We can use the example of the Yoruba state of Oyo, which had emerged by the 14th century. Its king, the alafin, controlled subject peoples through "princes" in the provinces, drawn from local lineages, who were allowed to exercise traditional rule as long as they continued to pay tribute to Oyo. In the capital a council of state, made up of nobles from the seven city districts, advised the ruler and limited his power, and the Ogboni, or secret society of religious and political leaders, reviewed decisions of the king and the council. The union of civil and supernatural powers in the person of the ruler was the basis of power. The highly urbanized nature of Yoruba society and the flourishing of artisan traditions within these towns bear some similarity to the city-states of medieval Italy or Germany.

Patterns similar to the Yoruba city-states could be found among Edo peoples to the east of Yoruba. A large city-state called *Benin* was formed sometime in the 14th century under Ewuare the Great (1440–1473). Benin's control extended from the Niger River to the coast near modern Lagos. Benin City was described by early European visitors in the 16th century as a city of great population and broad avenues. The Oba, or ruler, lived in a large royal compound surrounded by a great entourage, and his authority was buttressed by ritual and ceremony.

That authority was also the theme of the magnificent artistic output in ivory and cast bronze that became characteristic of Benin. Tradition had it that Iguegha, an artisan in bronze casting, was sent from Ile-Ife to introduce the techniques of making bronze sculptures. Benin then developed its own distinctive style, less naturalistic than that of Ile-Ife but no less impressive. Celebration of the powers and majesty of the royal lineage as well as objects for the rituals surrounding kingship were the subjects of much of this art. When the first Europeans, the Portuguese, visited Benin in the 1480s, they were impressed by the power of the ruler and the extent of his territory. Similarly, the artists of Benin were impressed with the Portuguese, and Benin bronzes and ivories began to include representations of Portuguese soldiers and other themes that reflected the contact with outsiders.

Central African Kingdoms

South of the rain forest that stretched across Africa almost to Lake Victoria lay a broad expanse of savanna and plain, cut by several large rivers such as the Kwango and the Zambezi. From their original home in Nigeria, the Bantu peoples had spread into the southern reaches of the rain forest along the Congo River, then southward onto the southern savannas, and eventually to the east coast. By the 5th century C.E., Bantu farmers and fishermen had reached beyond the Zambezi, and by the 13th century they were approaching the southern end of the continent. Mostly beyond the influence of Islam, many of these central African peoples had begun their own process of state formation by about 1000 C.E., replacing the pattern of kinship-based societies with forms of political authority based on kingship.

Whether the idea of kingship developed in one place and was diffused elsewhere or had multiple origins is unknown, but the older system based on seniority within the kinship group was replaced with rule based on the control of territory and the parallel development of rituals that reinforced the power of the ruler. Several important kingdoms developed. In Katanga, the Luba peoples modified the older system of village headmen to a form of divine kinship in which the ruler and his relatives were thought to have a special power that ensured fertility of people and crops; thus, only the royal lineage was fit to rule. A sort of bureaucracy grew to administer the state, but it was hereditary, so that brothers or male children succeeded to the position. In a way, this system was a half step toward more modern concepts of bureaucracy, but it provided a way of integrating large numbers of people in a large political unit.

The Kingdoms of Kongo and Mwene Mutapa

Beginning about the 13th century, another kingdom was forming on the lower Congo River. By the late 15th century this kingdom of the *Kongo* was flourishing. On a firm agricultural base, its people also developed the skills of weaving, pottery, blacksmithing, and carving. Individual artisans, skilled in the working of wood, copper, and iron, were highly esteemed. There was a sharp division of labor between men and women. Men took responsibility for clearing the forest and scrub, producing palm oil and palm wine, building houses, hunting, and long-distance trade. Women took charge of cultivation in all its aspects, the care of domestic animals, and household duties. On the seacoast, women made salt from sea water, and they also collected the seashells that served as currency in the Kongo kingdom. The population was distributed in small family-based villages and in towns. The area around the capital, Mbanza Kongo, had a population of 60,000 to 100,000 by the early 16th century.

The kingship of the Kongo was hereditary but local chieftainships were not, and this gave the central authority considerable power to control subordinates. In a way, the Kongo kingdom was a confederation of smaller states brought under the control of the manikongo, or king, and by the 15th century it was divided into eight major provinces. The word *mani* means "blacksmith," and it demonstrated the importance of iron and the art of working it in its association with political and ritual power.

Farther to the east, another large Bantu confederation developed among the farming and cattle-herding Shona-speaking peoples in the region between the Zambezi and Limpopo rivers. Beginning in the 9th century C.E., migrants from the west began to build royal courts in stone, to which later immigrants added more polished

Great Zimbabwe was one of several stone settlement complexes in southeastern Africa. Added to at different times, it served as the royal court of the Monomotapa empire.

constructions. There were many of these zimbabwe, or stone house, sites (about 200 have been found) that housed local rulers and subchiefs, but the largest site, called *Great Zimbabwe,* was truly impressive. It was the center of the kingdom and had a religious importance as well, associated with the "bird of God," an eagle that served as a link between the world and the spirits. The symbol of the "bird of God" is found at the ruins of Great Zimbabwe and throughout the area of its control. Great Zimbabwe (not to be confused with the modern nation of Zimbabwe) included several structures, some with strong stone walls 15 feet thick and 30 feet high, a large conical tower, and extensive cut-stone architecture made without the use of mortar to join the bricks together. Observers in the 19th century suspected that Phoenicians or Arabs had built these structures, but archeologists have since established that a Bantu kingdom had begun construction in stone by the 11th century C.E. and had done its most sophisticated building in the 14th and 15th centuries.

By the 15th century, a centralized state centered on Great Zimbabwe had begun to form. It controlled a large portion of the interior of southeast Africa all the way to the Indian Ocean. Under a king who took the title of Mwene Mutapa (which the Portuguese later pronounced as Mono-motapa), this kingdom experienced a short period of considerable expansion in the late 15th and 16th centuries. Its dominance over the sources of gold in the interior eventually gave it great advantages in commerce, which it developed with the Arab port of Sofala on the coast. Evidence of this trade is found in the glass beads and porcelain unearthed by archeologists at Great Zimbabwe. By the 16th century, internal divisions and rebellion had split the kingdom apart, but control of the gold fields still provided a source of power and trade. Representatives of the Mwene Mutapa called at the East Coast ports to buy Indian textiles, and their regal bearing and fine iron weapons impressed the first Europeans who saw them. As late as the 19th century, a much reduced kingdom of Muenemutapa survived in the interior and provided some leadership against European encroachment.

CONCLUSION

Internal Development and External Contacts

This chapter has concentrated on the Sudanic states and the Swahili coast, where the impact of Islam was the most profound and where, because of the existence of written sources, it is somewhat easier to reconstruct the region's history. Sub-Saharan Africa had never been totally isolated from the Mediterranean world or other outside contacts, but the spread of Islam obviously brought large areas of Africa to the global community more intensely, even though Africa remained something of an Islamic frontier. Still, the fusion of Islamic and indigenous African cultures created a synthesis that restructured the life of many Africans.

While the arrival of Islam in Africa in the period from 800 to 1500 was clearly a major event, it would be wrong to see Africa's history in this period exclusively in terms of the Islamic impact. Great Zimbabwe and the Kongo kingdom, to cite only two examples, represented the development of Bantu concepts of kingship and state building relatively independently of trends taking place elsewhere on the continent. Similar processes and accomplishments could also be noted in Benin and among the Yoruba of West Africa. Meanwhile in Ethiopia, East Africa, and the eastern Sudan, the impact of the pre-Islamic Mediterranean world had been long felt.

By the late 15th century when the first Europeans, the Portuguese, began to arrive on the west and east coasts of Africa, they encountered in many places well-developed, powerful kingdoms that were able to deal with the Portuguese as equals from a position of strength. This was even more the case in those parts of Africa that had come under the influence of Islam and through it had established various links with other areas of Muslim civilization. In this period, Africa had increasingly become part of the general cultural trends of the wider world, even though many of these contacts had been brought by outsiders rather than Africans. Moreover, the intensification of the export trade in ivory, slaves, and especially gold from Africa drew Africans, even those far from the centers of trade, into a widening network of relations. With the arrival of Europeans in sub-Saharan Africa in the late 15th century, the pace and intensity of the cultural and commercial contacts became even greater, and many African societies were presented with new and profound challenges.

FURTHER READINGS

Several of the books recommended on Africa in Chapter 10 are also useful for further reading in relation to this chapter. The period covered in this chapter is summarized in Roland Oliver's and Anthony Atmore's The

African Middle Ages, 1400–1800 (1981). Basil Davidson has produced many excellent popular books that provide a sympathetic view of African development. A good example, prepared to accompany a television series, is *The Story of Africa* (1984). A readable book that gives an overview of African history and emphasizes broad common themes and everyday life is Robert W. July's *Precolonial Africa* (1975). Essential reading on Central Africa is Jan Vansina, *Paths in the Rainforests* (1990).

A very good survey of the early history of Africa with interesting comments on the Nok culture is Susan Keech McIntosh's and Roderick J. McIntosh's "From Stone to Metal: New Perspectives on the Later Prehistory of West Africa," *Journal of World History* vol. 2, no. 1 (1988), 89–133. Basil Davidson has also written, with F. K. Buah, *A History of West Africa* (1966), which presents a good introduction for that region. More detailed, however, is J. F. Ade Ajayi's and Michael Crowder's *History of West Africa,* 2 vols. (1971), which contains excellent review chapters by specialists. For the East African coast, an excellent survey and introduction is provided by Derek Nurse and Thomas Spear in *The Swahili: Reconstructing the History and Language of an African Society* (1985).

Two good books on the Kongo kingdom are Anne Hilton's *The Kingdom of the Kongo* (1985), which shows how African systems of thought accommodated the arrival of Europeans and their culture, and Georges Balandier's *Daily Life in the Kingdom of the Kongo* (1969), which makes good use of travelers' reports and other documents to give a rounded picture of Kongo society. David Birmingham's and Phyllis Martin's *History of Central Africa,* 2 vols. (1983) provides an excellent regional history.

Two multivolume general histories of Africa, which provide synthetic articles by leading scholars on many of the topics discussed in this chapter, are *The Cambridge History of Africa,* 8 vols. (1975–1986) and the UNESCO *General History of Africa,* 7 vols. to date (1981–).

Some important source materials on African history for this period are D. T. Niane's *Sundiata, an Epic of Old Mali* (1986); G. R. Crone, ed., *The Voyages of Cadamosto,* 2d series, vol. 80 (1937), which deals with Mali, Cape Verde, Senegal, and Benin; and H. A. R. Gibb's *The Travels of Ibn Batuta,* 2 vols. (1962), which in vol. 2 includes his visit to the Swahili coast.

15

Civilization in Eastern Europe: Byzantium and Orthodox Europe

1st century C.E.–**650** Slavic migrations into eastern Europe

527–565 Justinian

718 Defeat of Arab attack on Constantinople

330s Constantinople made capital of Eastern Roman Empire

855 According to legend, Rurik king of Kievan Russia

864 Beginning of missionary work of brothers Cyril and Methodius in Slavic lands

896 Magyars settle in Hungary

870 First kingdom in what is now Czech and Slovak Republics

c. 960 Emergence of Polish state

100 C.E.   **600** C.E.   **800** C.E.

INTRODUCTION

During the postclassical period, in addition to the great civilizations of Asia and North Africa, two major, though related, civilizations took shape in Europe. One was anchored in the Byzantine Empire, which straddled western Asia and southeastern Europe but expanded with the spread of Orthodox Christianity to eastern Europe. The other was defined above all by the beliefs and institutions of Catholicism in western and central Europe. Both European civilizations were colored by Islamic dynamism, but they operated according to different principles. Comparable to African civilization in some ways—for example, in building political institutions in areas where formal states had not existed before—these civilizations carved out many distinctive features as well.

The Byzantine Empire maintained particularly high levels of political, economic, and cultural life during much of the period from 500 to 1450 C.E. It controlled an important, though somewhat fluctuating, swath of territory in the Balkans, the northern Middle East, and the eastern Mediterranean. The leaders of the empire regarded themselves as Roman emperors, and indeed their government was in many ways a direct continuation of the eastern portion of the late Roman Empire. This was not really Rome moved eastward, however, though the governmental structure built on traditions of late Roman emperors such as Diocletian and Constantine. The term *Byzantine*, though not used at the time, accurately suggests the distinction from Rome itself: This was a political heir to Rome, but with geography and focus of its own.

The real significance of the Byzantine Empire goes well beyond its ability to keep Rome's memory alive. The empire lasted for almost a thousand years, between Rome's collapse in the West and the final overthrow of the regime by Turkish invaders. The empire's capital,

Constantinople, was one of the truly great cities of the world, certainly the most opulent and important city in Europe in this period. From Constantinople radiated one of the two major branches of Christianity: the Orthodox Christian churches that became dominant throughout most of eastern Europe.

Like the other great civilizations of the period, the Byzantine Empire spread its cultural and political influence to parts of the world that had not previously been controlled by any major civilization. Just as Muslim influence helped shape civilization in parts of Africa south of the Sahara, and Indian and Chinese dynamism helped define cultural zones in Southeast Asia, the Byzantines began to create a new civilization area in the Balkans and particularly in western Russia (present-day Ukraine and Belarus as well as western Russia proper). Here was a major case, indeed, of the remaking of the civilizational map that formed such an important characteristic of the early centuries of the postclassical millennium.

Ultimately, the empire's most important stepchild was Russia, whose rise as a civilized area relied heavily on influences from the Byzantines to the south. Russia took many initial cultural and political characteristics from the Byzantine Empire and would ultimately claim to inherit the mantle of the empire itself. However, the postclassical millennium formed a preliminary, somewhat tentative gestation period for civilization in Russia, and historians must be cautious in drawing too many parallels between the patterns displayed at this point and subsequent developments when Russia more fully hit its stride. A Byzantine or Byzantine-influenced heritage would remain, but it was highly selective.

The history of civilization in eastern Europe in this period involves one other interpretive issue in addition to the complexity of the relationship between Byzantine flourish and decline and the patterns to the north. This issue consists, quite simply, of how to frame the story of the spread of Christianity in Europe between the eastern

1019–1054 Yaroslav king of Russia

1203–1204 Capture of Constantinople during the Fourth Crusade

1054 Schism between Eastern and Western Christianity

1480 Expulsion of Tatars from Russia

980–1015 Conversion of Vladimir I of Russia to Christianity

1100–1453 Byzantine decline; growing Turkish attack

1018 Defeat of first Bulgarian Empire, taken over by Byzantines

1237–1241 Capture of Russia by Mongols (Tatars)

1453 Capture of Constantinople by Ottoman Turks; end of Byzantine Empire

1000 C.E.   **1200** C.E.   **1400** C.E.

and western portions of the continent. There were many commonalities between developments in eastern Europe and those of the Christian West. In both cases, civilization spread northward, because of the missionary appeal of the religion itself. In both cases, polytheism gave way to monotheism—though important compromises were made, particularly at the popular level. In both cases, more northerly political units, such as Russia, Poland, Germany, and France, struggled for political definition without as yet being able to rival the political sophistication of the more advanced civilization areas in Asia and North Africa—or in Byzantium itself. In both cases, new trading activities brought northern regions into contact with the major centers of world commerce, including Constantinople, with important long-range as well as short-term results. In both cases, newly civilized areas looked back to the Greco-Roman past, as well as to Christianity, for cultural inspiration, using as a result some of the same political myths and, with due modifications, artistic styles.

Yet, with all these shared ingredients, the civilizations that expanded in the East and developed in the West operated largely on separate tracks. They produced different versions of Christianity, which culturally as well as organizationally were rather separate—even hostile. The civilizations had little mutual contact, particularly in the formative centuries before western Europe became strong enough to trade significantly with Constantinople. Commercial patterns in both cases ran south–north, rather than east–west. Political evolution was also somewhat distinct. The fact was that during most of the postclassical millennium, major portions of eastern Europe were significantly more advanced than the West in political sophistication, cultural range, and economic vitality. Even the relationship with the classical Mediterranean past differed, as eastern Europe maintained important features of the late Roman Empire explicitly, whereas western leaders ultimately turned to a much more selective borrowing and imitation. Thus, eastern Europe worked directly from the classical architectural tradition, whereas western Europe, after a modest classicism, developed a much different dominant style.

By 1400, essentially two civilizations existed in Europe, with very few contacts and only a handful of basic similarities. This relationship would later change, with new contacts developing on the basis of contiguous geography, the common adherence to Christianity, and new commercial exchanges. In this formative period, however, the distinct paths must be emphasized along with the undeniably greater importance, in terms of larger world history before 1450, of the eastern European civilization. The boundary line between East and West was somewhat fuzzy, embracing important regions, such as Hungary, where overlapping and competing influences between western and eastern Europe helped define a special identity—where indeed a special identity exists to this day. In the major centers of the two European civilizations, however—in Byzantium and Russia, or France and the Low Countries—different paths were defined after the fall of Rome, marked by different cycles of dynamism and decline. When the two civilizations did meet, in this period as later, they met as distant cousins, related but not close kin.

THE BYZANTINE EMPIRE

Focal Point: The Byzantine Empire unfolded initially as part of the greater Roman Empire. Then, as this framework shattered with Roman decline, it took on a life of its own, particularly from the reign of the emperor Justinian onward. It centered on a territory both different from and smaller than the eastern Mediterranean as Rome had defined it. This was the result of new pressures, particularly the surge of Islam throughout North Africa and the bulk of the Middle East. Despite many attacks, the Empire largely flourished until the 11th century.

Origins of the Empire

The *Byzantine Empire* in some senses began in the 4th century C.E., when the Romans set up their eastern capital in Constantinople. This city quickly became the most vigorous center of the otherwise fading imperial structure. The emperor Constantine constructed a host of elegant buildings, including Christian churches, in his new city, which was built on the foundations of a previously modest town called Byzantium. Soon, separate Eastern emperors ruled from the new metropolis, even before the western portion of the empire fell to the Germanic invaders. They warded off invading Huns and other intruders while enjoying a solid tax base in the peasant agriculture of the eastern Mediterranean. Constantinople was responsible for the Balkan peninsula, the northern Middle East, the Mediterranean coast, and North Africa. Although for several centuries Latin served as the court language of the eastern empire, Greek was the common tongue, and after the emperor

Justinian in the 6th century, it became the official language as well. Indeed, in the eyes of the easterners, Latin became an inferior, barbaric means of communication. Knowledge of Greek enabled the scholars of the eastern empire to read freely in the ancient Athenian philosophical and literary classics and in the Hellenistic writings and scientific treatises.

The new empire benefited from the high levels of civilization long present in the eastern Mediterranean. Commerce continued at a considerable pace, though the merchant classes declined and state control of trade increased. New blood was drawn into administration and trade as Hellenized Egyptians and Syrians, long excluded from Roman administration, moved to Constantinople and entered the expanding bureaucracy of the Byzantine rulers. The empire faced many foreign enemies, though the pressure was less severe than that provided by the Germanic tribes in the West. It responded, however, by recruiting armies in the Middle East itself, not by relying on barbarian troops. And the empire increasingly turned from the emphasis on army power, so characteristic of Rome in its later phases, to add a growing, highly trained civilian bureaucracy. Tensions between strong generals and bureaucratic leaders remained, but the empire did not rely primarily on force for its internal rule. Complex administration around a remote emperor, who was surrounded by elaborate ceremonies, increasingly defined the empire's political style.

Eastern Orthodox Christianity

As an Eastern Empire took shape politically, Christianity also began to split between East and West. In the West, the pope, based in Rome, officially headed the framework of church organization. He claimed control over bishops, sent missionaries to the north, and tried to regulate doctrine. No comparable single leader developed in the Eastern church. For several centuries, the Eastern church acknowledged the pope's authority as first among equals, but in practice, papal directives had no hold over the Byzantine church. Rather, it was the emperors themselves who regulated church organization, creating a pattern of state control over church structure far different from the tradition that developed in the West, where the church insisted, though not always successfully, on its independence. Byzantine emperors used their claim to be God's representative on earth to cement their own power. Correspondingly, they kept a close eye on church affairs while trying to

force non-Christians to convert. From the time of Justinian, the number of non-Christians allowed in Constantinople was carefully limited.

Furthermore, the Eastern church experienced several different influences from those prevalent in Western Christianity. Monasticism developed earlier in the East than in the West. Many individuals and groups of monks tried to follow Christ in a more complete way through special lives of fasting, celibacy, and prayer, staying apart from worldly concerns. Several leaders undertook to regulate this holy life, and a rule for monasteries developed by *Basil*, the patriarch of Constantinople in the mid-4th century, became particularly important in the East. Basil's rule helped formalize the separation between monasteries and ordinary people, pledging monks to lives of poverty, charity, and prayer. Unlike Western monastic orders, Eastern monks devoted little attention to scholarship. Their social role was great, however, for Eastern people venerated holy men and gave them considerable authority in the larger affairs of the church. Monasteries, along with traveling missionaries, provided food and medical care while seeking to drive away demons; they were far closer to popular Christianity than the official religion of the imperial court.

Orthodox Christianity, in sum, shared a host of features with its Western cousin, including intolerance for other beliefs. Different political organizations, however, launched a largely separate pattern of religious development in terms of specific church structures, monasticism, religious art, and theology. These differences, in turn, caused ongoing mutual suspicion and hostility. A late 12th-century church patriarch in Constantinople even argued that Muslim rule would be preferable to that of the pope: "For if I am subject to the Muslim, at least he will not force me to share his faith. But if I have to be under the Frankish rule and united with the Roman Church, I may have to separate myself from God."

Justinian's Achievements

The early history of the Byzantine Empire was marked by a recurrent threat of invasion. Eastern emperors, relying on their local military base plus able generalship by upper-class Greeks, beat off attacks by the Sassanian Empire in Persia and by Germanic invaders.

Then, in 533 C.E., with the empire's borders reasonably well assured, a new emperor, Justinian, attempted to reconquer western territory in a last, futile effort to

Mosaics in Ravenna, Italy, from the early period of the Byzantine Empire, illustrate some of the highest achievements of Byzantine religious art and provide a dazzling, ornate environment for worship. This mosaic features a rather militant Christ the Redeemer.

restore an empire like that of Rome. Ironically, Justinian's reign would confirm Byzantium's basis in the Greco-Roman heritage, through massive architectural and legal achievements in the classical mode, while also furthering the empire's relocation toward the *Balkans* and the western part of present-day Turkey, away from the Mediterranean coast.

Justinian himself, who faced and brutally suppressed serious social unrest, has been variously judged by contemporaries and later historians alike. He was a somber personality, autocratic, and prone to grandiose ideas. A contemporary historian named Procopius, no friend of the emperor, described him as "at once villainous and amenable; as people say colloquially, a moron. He was never truthful with anyone, but always guileful in what he said and did, yet easily hoodwinked by any who wanted to deceive him." The emperor was also heavily influenced by his wife Theodora, a courtesan connected

with Constantinople's horse-racing world, who was eager for power. It was Theodora who stiffened Justinian's backbone in response to popular unrest and who prodded the plans for expansion.

Justinian's positive contributions to the Byzantine Empire lay in rebuilding Constantinople, ravaged by earlier riots against high taxes, and systematizing the Roman legal code. Extending later Roman architecture, with its addition of domes to earlier classical styles, Justinian's builders constructed many new structures—the most inspiring of which was the huge new church, the *Hagia Sophia*, long one of the wonders of the Christian world. This was an achievement in engineering as well as architecture, for no one had previously been able to construct the supports for a dome of comparable size. Justinian's codification of Roman law reached a goal earlier emperors had sought but not achieved. Unified law not only reduced confusion but also served to unite and organize the new empire itself, paralleling the state's bureaucracy. Justinian's code, called the *Body of Civil Law*, stands as one of the clearest and most comprehensive systems created by any culture. The code summed up and reconciled a host of Roman edicts and decisions, making Roman law a coherent basis for political and economic life throughout the empire. Recurrently updated by later emperors, the code would also ultimately help spread Roman legal principles in various parts of Europe.

Justinian's military exploits had more ambiguous results. The emperor wanted to recapture the old Roman Empire itself. With the aid of a brilliant general, *Belisarius*, new gains were made in North Africa and Italy. The Byzantines hoped to restore North Africa to its role as grain producer for the Mediterranean world, while Italy would be the symbol of past imperial glories. Unable to hold Rome against the Germans, Justinian's forces made their temporary capital, Ravenna, a key artistic center, embellished by some of the most beautiful Christian mosaics known anywhere in the world. But the major Italian holdings were short-lived, unable to withstand Germanic pressure, while North African territory was soon besieged as well.

Furthermore, Justinian's westward ambitions had weakened the empire in its own sphere. Persian forces attacked in the northern Middle East, while new Slavic groups, moving into the Balkans, pressed on another front. Justinian finally managed to create a new line of defense and even pushed Persian forces back again, but some Middle Eastern territory was irretrievably lost. Furthermore, all these wars, offensive and defensive alike, created new tax pressures on the government and forced Justinian to exertions that almost literally wore him to his death in 565 C.E.

Arab Pressure and the Empire's Defenses

Justinian's successors, after some renewed hesitations and setbacks, began to concentrate more fully on defending the Eastern Empire itself. Persian successes in the northern Middle East were reversed in the 7th century, and the population was forcibly reconverted to Christianity. The resultant empire, centered in the southern Balkans and the western and central portions of present-day Turkey, was a far cry from Rome's greatness—far even from the wealth of the Eastern Empire itself when it had a firmer hold on the fertile lands of the northern Middle East. It was sufficient, however, to amplify a rich Hellenistic culture and blend it more fully with Christianity while advancing Roman achievements in engineering and military tactics as well as law.

The Byzantine Empire was also sufficiently strong to withstand the great new threat of the 7th century, though not without massive loss: the surge of the Arab Muslims. The Arabs, by the mid-7th century, had built a fleet that challenged Byzantine naval supremacy in the eastern Mediterranean while repeatedly attacking Constantinople. They quickly swallowed the empire's remaining provinces along the eastern seaboard of the Mediterranean and soon cut into the northern Middle Eastern heartland as well. Considerable Arab cultural and commercial influence also affected patterns of life in Constantinople.

The Byzantine Empire, however reduced, held out nevertheless. A major siege of the capital in 717–718 C.E. was beaten back, partly owing to a new weapon called *Greek fire* (a petroleum, quicklime, and sulfur mixture) that devastated Arab ships. The Arab threat was never entirely removed. Furthermore, wars with the Muslims had added new economic burdens to the empire, as invasions and taxation, weakening the position of small farmers, resulted in greater aristocratic estates and new power for aristocratic generals. The free rural population that had served the empire during its early centuries—providing military recruits and paying the bulk of the taxes—was forced into greater dependence. Greater emphasis was given to careful organization of the army and navy. The history of the empire, after the greatest Arab onslaughts had been faced and their results assimilated, offered a dizzying series of weak and strong emperors. Periods of vigor alternated with seeming decay. Arab pressure continued. Conquest of the island of Crete in the 9th century allowed the Muslims to harass Byzantine shipping in the Mediterranean for several centuries. Slavic kingdoms, especially *Bulgaria*, periodically pressed Byzantine territory in the Balkans, though at times military success and marriage alliances brought Byzantine control over the feisty Bulgarian kingdom. Thus, while a Bulgarian king in the 10th century took the title of *tsar*, a Slavic version of the word *Caesar*, steady Byzantine pressure through war eroded the regional kingdom. In the 11th century, the Byzan-

Imperial cavalry, detail from "Chronicle" of John Scylitzes, 14th century.

tine emperor Basil II, known appropriately enough as *Bulgaroktonos,* or slayer of the Bulgarians, used the empire's wealth to bribe many Bulgarian nobles and generals. He defeated the Bulgarian army in 1014, blinding as many as 15,000 captive soldiers—the sight of whom brought on the Bulgarian king's death. Bulgaria became part of the empire, its aristocracy settling in Constantinople and merging with the leading Greek families. Thus, despite all its problems, the imperial core displayed real strength, governing a territory about half the size of the previous eastern portion of the Roman Empire and withstanding a series of enemies. More than a long-standing barrier to the Arabs, the empire would soon make its greatest contributions to subsequent world history by reaching northward in trade and culture, creating a new zone of civilization precisely because so much of the Mediterranean had fallen to Arab hands.

The Empire's High Point

The Byzantine Empire entered a particularly stable period during the 9th and 10th centuries, when a new ruling dynasty managed to avoid the quarrels over succession to the imperial throne that had bedeviled many heirs before and after Justinian. The result was growing prosperity and solid political rule. The luxury of the court and its buildings steadily increased. Elaborate ceremonies and rich imperial processions created a magnificence designed to dazzle the empire's subjects. Briefly, at the end of the 10th century, the Byzantine emperor may have been the most powerful single monarch on earth, with a capital city whose rich buildings and abundant popular entertainments awed visitors from western Europe and elsewhere, while giving Eastern rulers a growing confidence in the validity of their own institutions and values.

Byzantine Society and Politics

The Byzantine political system bore unusual resemblance to the earlier patterns in China. The emperor was held to be ordained by God—head of church as well as state. He appointed church bishops and passed religious and secular laws. The elaborate court rituals symbolized the ideals of a divinely inspired, all-powerful ruler, though they also often immobilized rulers and inhibited innovative policy. At key points, women held the imperial throne, while maintaining the ceremonial power of the office.

Supplementing the centralized imperial authority was one of history's most elaborate bureaucracies. Trained in Greek classics, philosophy, and science in a secular school system that paralleled but contrasted with church education for the priesthood, Byzantine bureaucrats could be recruited from all social classes. As in China, aristocrats predominated, but there was some openness to talent among this elite of highly educated scholars. Bureaucrats were specialized into various offices, and officials close to the emperor were mainly eunuchs. Provincial governors were appointed from the center and were charged with keeping tabs on military authorities. An elaborate system of spies helped preserve loyalty while also creating intense distrust even

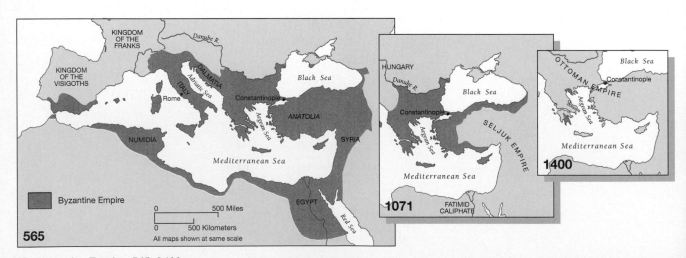

The Byzantine Empire, 565–1400 C.E.

CLOSEUP

Empress Theodora

Empress Theodora (981–1056), namesake of Justinian's powerful wife, was twice a Byzantine empress. She illustrates the complex nature of Byzantine politics and also the whims of fate that circumscribed women rulers. Daughter of an emperor, Theodora had a strong and austere character; she refused to marry the imperial heir, who then wed her sister Zoë. Zoë remained fearful of Theodora's influence and had her confined to a monastery. A popular rebellion against the new emperor installed Theodora and Zoë jointly (and one assumes uneasily) as empresses. But Theodora soon yielded power to Zoë's new husband. When he died, however, Theodora reasserted her rights, at the age of 70. After brief turmoil, she checked unruly nobles and limited bureaucratic corruption, though her severe retaliation against personal enemies brought criticism. Theodora also had trouble building a reliable staff and was attacked for her reliance on "menials."

among friends. It is small wonder that the word *Byzantine* came to refer to complex and convoluted institutional arrangements. At the same time, the system was sufficiently successful to constitute one of the cements that preserved the longest-lived single government structure the Mediterranean world has ever known.

Much of the empire's success depended on careful military organization. Byzantine rulers adapted the later Roman system by recruiting troops locally and rewarding them with grants of land in return for their military service. The land could not be sold, but sons inherited its administration in return for continued military responsibility. Many outsiders, particularly Slavs and Ar-

menian Christians, were recruited for the army in this fashion. Increasingly, hereditary military leaders assumed considerable regional power, displacing more traditional and better-educated aristocrats. One emperor, Michael II, was a product of this system and was notorious for his hatred of Greek education and his overall personal ignorance. On the other hand, the military system had obvious advantages in protecting a state recurrently under attack from Muslims of various sorts—Persians, Arabs, and later Turks—as well as nomadic intruders from central Asia. Until the 15th century, the Byzantine Empire effectively blocked the path to Europe for most of these groups.

Socially and economically, the empire depended on Constantinople's control over the countryside, with the bureaucracy regulating trade and controlling food prices. The large peasant class was vital in supplying goods and also in providing the bulk of tax revenues. Food prices were kept artificially low, in order to content the numerous urban lower classes, in a system supported largely by taxes on the hard-pressed peasantry. Other cities were modest in size—Athens, for example, dwindled—as the focus was on the capital city and its food needs. The empire developed a far-flung trading network with Asia to the east and Russia and Scandinavia to the north. Silk production expanded in the empire, with silkworms and techniques initially imported from China, and various luxury products, including cloth, carpets, and spices, were sent northward. This gave the empire a favorable trading position with less sophisticated lands. Only China produced luxury goods of comparable quality. The empire also traded actively with India, the Arabs, and East Asia while receiving simpler products from western Europe and Africa. At the same time, the large merchant class never gained significant political power, in part because of the elaborate network of governmental controls. In this, Byzantium again resembled China and differed notably from the looser social and political networks of the West, where merchants were rising and gaining greater voice.

Byzantine cultural life centered on the secular traditions of Hellenism, so important in the education of bureaucrats, and on the evolving traditions of Eastern, or Orthodox, Christianity. While a host of literary and artistic creations resulted from this climate, there was little fundamental innovation except in art and architecture. The Byzantine strength lay in preserving and commenting on past forms more than in developing new ones. A distinct Byzantine style had developed fairly early in art and architecture. The adaptation of Roman domed buildings, the elaboration of powerful and richly colored religious mosaics, and a tradition of *icon* painting—paintings of saints and other religious figures, often richly ornamented—expressed this artistic impulse and its marriage with Christianity. The blue and gold backgrounds set with richly dressed religious figures were meant to display on earth the unchanging brilliance of heaven. The important controversy over religious art arose in the 8th century, when a new emperor attacked the use of religious images in worship (probably responding to Muslim claims that Christians were idol-worshipers). This attack, called *iconoclasm*

In this mosaic of Christ, dating from about 1100 C.E., note the difference from the images of Christ common in Western Christianity, which place more emphasis on suffering and less on divine majesty.

because of the breaking of images, roused huge protest from Byzantine monks, which briefly threatened a split between church and state. After a long and complex battle, the use of icons was gradually restored, while the tradition of state control over church affairs was also reasserted. Cultural issues in Byzantium reflected strong feelings, in part the fruit of the great diversity of peoples and cultural habits under the empire's sway, even if major new intellectual principles did not result. A certain amount of diversity could be accepted because of common allegiance to Christianity and the military and administrative effectiveness of the empire at its best.

The Schism Between East and West

Byzantine culture and politics, as well as its economic orientation toward Asia and northeastern Europe, helped explain the growing break between its Eastern version of

Christianity and the Western version headed by the pope in Rome. There were many milestones in this rift. Different rituals developed as the West translated the Greek Bible into Latin in the 4th century. Later, Byzantine emperors deeply resented papal attempts to interfere in the iconoclastic dispute, for the popes, understandably enough, hoped to loosen state control over the Eastern church in order to make it conform more fully to their own idea of church-state relations. There was also scornful hostility to efforts by a Frankish ruler, Charlemagne, to proclaim himself a Roman emperor in the 9th century. Byzantine officials knew full well that they were the true heirs of Rome and that Western rulers were crude and unsophisticated. They did, however, extend some recognition to the "Emperor of the Franks."

Contact between the two branches of Christianity trailed off, though neither East nor West cared to make a definitive break. Then, in 1054, an ambitious church patriarch in Constantinople raised a host of old issues, including a quarrel over what kind of bread to use for the celebration of Christ's last supper in the church liturgy. He also attacked the Roman Catholic practice, developed some centuries earlier, of insisting on celibacy for its priests; Eastern Orthodox priests could marry. Delegations of the two churches discussed these disputes, but this led only to new bitterness. The Roman pope finally excommunicated the patriarch and his followers—that is, banished them from Christian fellowship and the sacraments. The patriarch, no slouch, responded by excommunicating all Roman Catholics. Thus the split between the Roman Catholic church and Eastern Orthodoxy—the Byzantine or Greek, as well as the Russian Orthodox, Serbian Orthodox, and others—became formal and has endured to this day.

The East–West split fell short of complete divorce. A common Christianity with many shared or revived classical traditions and frequent commercial and cultural contacts continued to enliven the relationship between the two European civilizations. The split also reflected significant distinctions in political systems, most obviously in the principles of church–state relations but also between an imperial administration and the more divided Western state system. And it reflected the different patterns of development followed by the two civilizations during the postclassical millennium. Byzantium, for all its ups and downs, was well aware of its advantages over the West during the early centuries following Rome's collapse. The East–West split occurred right at the end of Byzantium's period of greatest glory. By this point, however, the West was beginning to develop new strengths of its own, and over the next few centuries, its dynamism would eclipse that of most of eastern Europe.

The Empire's Decline

Shortly after the schism between East and West, the Byzantine Empire entered a long period of decline. Turkish invaders who had converted to Islam in central Asia began to press on its eastern borders, having already gained increasing influence in the Muslim caliphate. In the later 11th century, Turkish troops, the Seljuks, seized almost all the Asiatic provinces of the empire, thus cutting off the most prosperous sources of tax revenue as well as the territories that had supplied most of the empire's food. The Byzantine emperor lost the disastrous battle of Manzikert in 1071, his larger army was annihilated, and the empire never recovered. It staggered along for another four centuries, but its doom, at least as a significant power, was virtually sealed.

Eastern emperors appealed to Western leaders for help against the Turks, but their requests were largely ignored. The appeal helped motivate Western Crusades to the Holy Land, but this did not help the Byzantines. At the same time, Italian cities, blessed with powerful navies, gained in Constantinople increasing advantages, such as special trading privileges—a sign of the shift in power balance between East and West. One Western Crusade, in 1204, ostensibly set up to conquer the Holy Land from the Muslims, actually turned against Byzantium. Led by greedy Venetian merchants, the Crusade attacked and conquered Constantinople, briefly unseating the emperor altogether and weakening the whole imperial structure. But the West was not yet powerful enough to hold this ground, and a small Byzantine Empire was restored, able through careful diplomacy to survive for another two centuries. Not only Western and Turkish pressure but also the creation of new, independent Slavic kingdoms in the Balkans, such as Serbia, showed the empire's diminished power. Turkish settlements pressed ever closer to Constantinople in the northern Middle East—in the area that is now Turkey—and finally, in 1453, a Turkish sultan brought a powerful army, equipped by artillery purchased from the West, against the city, which fell after two months. By 1461, the Turks had conquered remaining pockets of Byzantine control, including most of the Balkans, bringing Islamic power farther into eastern Europe than ever before. The great Eastern Empire was no more.

The Byzantine Empire developed a distinctively stylized religious art, adapted from earlier Roman painting styles and conveying the solemnity of the holy figures of the faith. This 11th-century miniature features the holy women at the sepulchre of Christ.

The fall of Byzantium was one of the great events in world history, and we will deal with its impact in several later chapters. It was a great event because the Byzantine Empire had been so durable and important, anchoring a vital corner of the Mediterranean even amid the rapid surge of Islam. The empire's trading contacts and its ability to preserve and disseminate classical and Christian learning made it a vital unit during the whole postclassical period. After its demise, its influence would affect other societies, including the new Ottoman empire.

THE SPREAD OF CIVILIZATION IN EASTERN EUROPE

Focal Point: Missionary attempts to spread Christianity, new Byzantine conquests in the Balkans (particularly Bulgaria), and trade routes running north and south through western Russia and Ukraine created abundant contacts with key portions of eastern Europe. A number of regional states formed. Kievan Rus', in a territory including present-day Ukraine, Belarus, and western Russia, developed some of the formative features of Russian culture and politics. Mongol invasions ended this period of early Russian history, redividing parts of eastern Europe in the process.

Long before the Byzantine decline after the 11th century, the empire had been the source of a new northward surge of Christianity. Orthodox missionaries sent from Constantinople busily converted most people in the Balkans—in what is now Bulgaria, Yugoslavia, and parts of Romania and Hungary—to their version of Christianity, and some other trappings of Byzantine culture came in their wake. In 864, the Byzantine government sent the missionaries *Cyril* and *Methodius* to the territory that is now the Czech and Slovak republics. Here the effort failed, in that Roman Catholic missionaries were more successful. But Cyril and Methodius continued their efforts in the Balkans and in southern Russia, where their ability to speak the Slavic language greatly aided their efforts. One of the Catholic objections to Methodius was in fact his insistence on using Slavic rather than Latin in church services. The two missionaries devised a written script for this language, derived from Greek letters; to this day, the Slavic alphabet is known as Cyrillic. Thus, the possibility of literature and some literacy developed in eastern Europe along with Christianity, well beyond

East European Kingdoms in the 12th Century

the political borders of Byzantium. Byzantine missionaries were quite willing to have local languages used in church services—another contrast with Western Catholicism.

Orthodox Missionaries and Other Influences

Eastern missionaries did not monopolize the borderlands of eastern Europe. Roman Catholicism and the Latin alphabet prevailed not only in the Czech area but also in most of Hungary (which was taken over in the 9th century by a Turkic people, the Magyars) and in Poland. Much of this region would long be an area of competition between Eastern and Western political and intellectual models. During the centuries after the conversion to Christianity, this stretch of eastern Europe north of the Balkans was organized in a series of regional monarchies, loosely governed amid a powerful, landowning aristocracy. The kingdoms of Poland, Bo-

hemia (Czechoslovakia), and Lithuania easily surpassed most western kingdoms in territory. This was also a moderately active area for trade and industry. Ironworking, for example, was more developed than in the West until the 12th century. Eastern Europe during these centuries also received an important influx of Jews, who were migrating away from the Middle East but also fleeing intolerance in western Europe. Poland gained the largest single concentration of Jews. Eastern Europe's Jews, largely barred from agriculture and often resented by the Christian majority, gained strength in local commerce while maintaining their own religious and cultural traditions. A strong emphasis on extensive education and literacy, though primarily for males, distinguished Jewish culture not only in eastern Europe but also compared with most societies in the world at this time.

This was an early phase of the development of eastern Europe beyond the Byzantine heartland, for by Asian (or Byzantine) standards the region remained backward, lightly populated, and not yet able to produce a significant written or artistic culture beyond rudimentary church buildings and monkish chronicles of events. Many features of Byzantium, including its elaborate bureaucracy, were irrelevant to what was, like most of western Europe at the same time, a developing region.

The Emergence of Kievan Rus'

Russia shared many features with the rest of northeastern Europe before the 15th century, including rather hesitant advances in economy and politics. A full-fledged Russian civilization had yet to emerge. Yet, as with much of eastern Europe, the centuries of Byzantine influence were an important formative period that would influence later developments considerably.

Slavic peoples had moved into the sweeping plains of Russia and eastern Europe from an Asian homeland during the time of the Roman Empire. They mixed with and incorporated some earlier inhabitants and some additional invaders, such as the Bulgarians who adopted Slavic language and customs. The Slavs already knew the use of iron, and they extended agriculture in the rich soils of what is now Ukraine and western Russia, where no durable civilization had previously taken root. Slavic political organization long rested in family tribes and villages. The Slavs maintained an animist religion with gods for the sun, thunder, wind, and fire. The early Russians also had a rich tradition of folk music and oral legends, and they developed some very loose regional kingdoms.

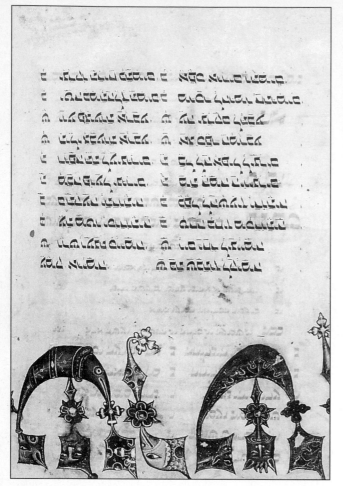

This 14th-century illustrated German-Jewish prayer book is a remnant from the spread of Jews and Jewish culture during the postclassical period.

During the 6th and 7th centuries, traders from Scandinavia began to work through the Slavic lands, moving along the great rivers of western Russia, which run south to north—particularly the Dnieper. Through this route the Norse traders were able to reach the Byzantine Empire, and a regular, flourishing trade developed between Scandinavia and Constantinople. Luxury products from Byzantium and the Arab world traveled north in return for furs and other relatively crude products. The Scandinavian traders, militarily superior to the Slavs, gradually set up some governments along their trade route, particularly in the city of *Kiev.* A monarchy emerged, and according to legend a man named *Rurik,* a native of Denmark, became the first prince of Kievan Rus' about 855 C.E. The Kievan principality, though still loosely organized through al-

liances with regional, landed aristocrats, flourished until the 12th century. It was from the Scandinavians also that the word *Russia* was coined, possibly from a Greek word for "red," which applied to the hair color of many of the Norse traders. In turn, the Scandinavian minority gradually mingled with the Slavic population, particularly among the aristocracy.

Contacts between Kievan Rus' and Byzantium extended steadily. Kiev, centrally located, became a prosperous trading center, and from there many Russians visited Constantinople. These exchanges led to growing knowledge of Christianity. Prince *Vladimir I,* a Rurik descendant who ruled from 980 to 1015, finally took the step of converting to Christianity—not only in his own name but on behalf of all his people. He was eager to avoid the papal influence that came with Roman Catholicism, which he knew about through the experiences of the Polish kingdom. Orthodox Christianity gave a valid alternative that still provided a sophisticated replacement for the prevailing animism. Islam was rejected, according to one account, because Vladimir could not accept a religion that forbade alcoholic drink. Russian awe at the splendor of religious services in Constantinople also played a role. Having made his decision, Vladimir proceeded to organize mass baptisms for his subjects, forcing conversions by military pressure. Early church leaders were imported from Byzantium, and they helped train a literate Russian priesthood. As in Byzantium, the king characteristically controlled major appointments, and a separate *Russian Orthodox church* soon developed.

As Kievan Rus' became Christian, it was the largest single state in Europe, though highly decentralized. Rurik's descendants managed for some time to avoid damaging battles over succession to the throne. Following Byzantine example, they issued a formal law code, which among other things reduced the severity of traditional punishments and replaced community vendettas with state-run courts, at least in principle. The last of the great Kievan princes, *Yaroslav,* issued the legal codification while also building numerous churches and arranging the translation of religious literature from Greek to Slavic.

Institutions and Culture in Kievan Rus'

Kievan Rus' borrowed much from Byzantium, but it was in no position to replicate major institutions such as the bureaucracy or an elaborate educational system. Major princes were attracted to Byzantine ceremonials and lux-

This painting shows the Russian king, Vladimir, accepting Christianity.

ury and to the concept (if not yet the reality) that a central ruler should have wide powers.

Many characteristics of Orthodox Christianity gradually penetrated Russian culture. Fervent devotion to the power of God and to many Eastern saints helped organize worship. Churches were relatively ornate, filled with icons and the sweet smell of incense. A monastic movement developed that stressed prayer and charity. Traditional practices, such as polygamy, gradually yielded to the Christian family ethic that insisted on only one wife. The emphasis on almsgiving as a manifestation of religious feeling long described the sense of obligation felt by wealthy Russians toward the poor, and it would actually delay the formation of more institutionalized welfare arrangements.

The Russian literature that developed, which used the Cyrillic alphabet, mainly summed up a mixture of religious and royal events and was filled with praises to the saints and invocations of the power of God. Disasters were seen as expressions of the just wrath of God against human wickedness, while success in war followed from the aid of God and the saints in the name jointly of Russia and the Orthodox faith. This tone also was common in Western Christian writing during these centuries, but in Kievan Rus' it monopolized formal culture more fully; a distinct, additional philosophical or scientific current did not emerge in the postclassical period.

Russian and Ukrainian art focused on the religious also, with icon painting and illuminated religious manuscripts becoming something of a Kievan specialty. Orthodox churches, built in the form of a cross surmounted by a dome, similarly aped Byzantine styles, though frequently the building materials were wood rather than stone. Religious art and music were rivaled by continued popular entertainments in the oral tradition, which combined music, street performances, and some theater. The Russian church tried to suppress these forms, regarding them as pagan, but with incomplete success.

Overall, this formative period in Russian society saw the development of a powerful religious sentiment, with particular cultural emphasis on art and music. This cultural development, although parallel to some features in emerging Western culture because of the common process of creating a new literary tradition from a polytheistic background and because of shared Christian beliefs, operated quite separately from specific patterns in the West. Russian–Western contacts, at this point and for several centuries to come, were virtually nonexistent, though Yaroslav, interestingly, married his daughter to a French king, indicating his awareness of possible beneficial interchange.

The same separate development marked Russian social and economic patterns. Russian peasants at this juncture were fairly free farmers, though an aristocratic landlord class existed. Russian aristocrats, called *boyars*, had less political power than their counterparts in western Europe, though the Kievan princes had to negotiate with them.

Kievan Decline

The Kievan principality began to fade in the 12th century. Rival princes set up regional governments, while the royal family frequently squabbled over succession to

DOCUMENT

Russia Turns to Christianity

This document from a monk's chronicle, describing King Vladimir's conversion policy, indicates what was officially believed about the power of Russian princes, Russian social structure, and the relationship between Christianity and earlier animism. These official claims are important, but they may not reflect the whole reality of this important transition in Russia history.

> For at this time the Russes were ignorant pagans. The devil rejoiced thereat, for he did not know that his ruin was approaching. He was so eager to destroy the Christian people, yet he was expelled by the true cross even from these very lands. . . . Vladimir was visited by Bulgars of the Mohammedan faith. . . . [He] listened to them for he was fond of women and indulgence, regarding which he heard with pleasure. But . . . abstinence from pork and wine were disagreeable to him. "Drinking," said he, "is the joy of the Russes. We cannot exist without that pleasure." [Russian envoys sent to Constantinople were astonished by the beauty of the churches and the chanting], and in their wonder praised the Greek ceremonial. . . .
>
> [Later, Vladimir was suffering from blindness; a Byzantine bishop baptized him] and as the bishop laid his hand upon him, he straightway recovered his sight. Upon experiencing this miraculous cure, Vladimir glorified God, saying, "I have now perceived the one true God." When his followers beheld this miracle, many of them were also baptized. . . . Thereafter Vladimir sent heralds throughout the whole city to proclaim that if any inhabitant, rich or poor, did not betake himself to the river [for mass baptism] he would risk the Prince's displeasure. When the people heard these words, they wept for joy and exclaimed in their enthusiasm, "If this were not good, the Prince and his nobles would not have accepted it." . . . There was joy in heaven and upon earth to behold so many souls saved. But the devil groaned, lamenting, "Woe is me. How am I driven out hence . . . my reign in these regions is at an end." . . .
>
> He [Vladimir] ordered that wooden churches should be built and established where [pagan] idols have previously stood. He founded the Church of Saint Basil on the hill where the idol of Perun and the other images had been set, and where the prince and the people had offered their sacrifices. He began to found churches, to assign priests throughout the cities and towns, and to bring people in for baptism from all towns and villages. He began to take the children of the best families and send them for instruction from books.

Questions: In what ways might the account be oversimple in describing royal powers and popular response? What explanations does this religious chronicler offer for the conversion of Russians to Christianity? Which of the explanations are most likely, and which are the results of some kind of bias? What kind of church–state relationship did this conversion procedure predict?

---

the throne. Invaders from Asia whittled at Russian territory. The rapid eclipse of Byzantium reduced Russian trade and wealth, for the kingdom had always depended heavily on the greater prosperity and sophisticated manufacturing of its southern neighbor. A new kingdom was briefly established around a city near what is now Moscow, but by 1200, Russia was weak and disunited. The final blow in this first chapter of Russian history came in 1237–1238 and 1240–1241, when two invasions by Mongols from central Asia moved through Russia and into other parts of eastern Europe. The initial Mongol intent was to add the whole of Europe to their growing empire. The Mongols, or *Tatars* as they are called in the Russian tradition, easily captured the major Russian cities, but they did not penetrate much farther west because of political difficulties in their Asian homeland. For over two centuries, however, much of Russia would remain under Tatar control.

This control, in turn, further separated the dynamic of Russian history from that of western Europe. Russian literature languished under Tatar supervision. Trade lapsed in western Russia, and indeed, the vigorous north–south commerce of the Kievan period never returned. At the same time, loose Tatar supervision did not destroy Russian Christianity or a native Russian aristocratic class. So long as tribute was paid, Tatar over-

St. Sophia in Kiev, though built after the postclassical period, utilized artistic themes developed earlier in Byzantium.

lords left day-to-day Russian affairs alone. Thus, when Tatar control was finally forced out in the second half of the 15th century, a Russian cultural and political tradition could reemerge, serving as a partial basis for the further, fuller development of Russian society.

Russian leaders, moreover, retained during the period of eclipse an active memory of the glories of Byzantium. When Constantinople fell to the Turks in 1453, just as Russia was beginning to assert its independence from the Tatars, it was logical to claim that the mantle of east European leadership had fallen on Russia. A monk, currying favor, wrote the Russian king in 1511 that while heresy had destroyed the first Roman Empire, and the Turks had cut down the second, Byzantium—a "third, new Rome,"—under the king's "mighty rule" "sends out the Orthodox Christian faith to the ends of the earth and shines more brightly than the sun." "Two Romes have fallen, but the third stands, and there will be no fourth." This sense of an Eastern Christian mission, inspiring a Russian resurgence, was not the least

of the products of this complicated formative period in the emergence of a separate European civilization in the Slavic lands.

ANALYSIS

Eastern and Western Europe: The Problem of Boundaries

Deciding where one civilization ends and another begins is not always easy, particularly when (as is usually the case) many political units and some internal cultural differences are involved within each civilization. Deciding about the territory of the two admittedly related civilizations that developed in Europe is particularly difficult. A number of states sat, and still sit, on the borders of the two civilizations, sharing some characteristics of each. Further, political disputes and nationalist attachments, fierce in this border territory of east-central Europe during the past two centuries, make definitions an issue of great emotionalism as well. So the question of defining Europe's civilizations is a particularly thorny case of a larger problem.

If civilization is simply mainstream culture, then east and west Europe in the postclassical period divide logically according to Orthodox and Catholic territories (and relatedly, use of the Cyrillic and Greek or of the Latin alphabets). By this reckoning, Poland, the Czech areas, and the Baltic states (these latter not converted to Catholicism until the 14th century) are western, and Hungary is largely so. South Slavs are mainly but not entirely Orthodox, a regional division that can provoke recurrent violence. Russia and Ukraine are decidedly Orthodox in tradition. Religion matters. Poland and other Catholic regions have long maintained much more active ties with western Europe than Russia has. At the end of the postclassical period, a Czech religious dissenter, named Hus, even foreshadowed the later Protestant Reformation in his attacks on the Catholic church.

Politically, however, the case is more complicated. Poland, Hungary, and Lithuania formed large regional kingdoms at various times during the postclassical period and beyond. But these kingdoms were very loosely organized, much more so than the feudal monarchies that were developing in western Europe. This was one reason German influence grew strongly in Poland and the Baltic during the postclassical period, just as Russian influence would grow by the 18th century. Exceptionally large aristocracies in Poland and Hungary (by western or by Russian standards) helped limit these states. By this measurement, a part of east-central Europe seems different both from the Byzantine strong-state tradition and from western Europe.

Trade patterns also did not elaborately unite Poland or Hungary with western Europe until much later, when the two regions were quite clearly very different in economic structure. Relatedly, Polish and Hungarian societies often shared more features with Russia than with western Europe.

Russian expansion later pulled parts of eastern Europe, including Poland, into its orbit, though it never eliminated a strong Polish national identity. During the postclassical period, it is important to realize that the main characteristics of east European civilization affected the borderlands, like Hungary or Poland, but did not predominate. Borders can change, furthermore. The Mongol invasions that swept through Russia also conquered Poland and Hungary, but there the armies did not stay. Part of the Ukraine was also free from direct Mongol control, which helped differentiate it from Russia proper. For two centuries, at the end of the classical period, the divisions within eastern Europe intensified. Since 1989, many east European countries have again achieved full independence from Russia, and they justifiably wish to claim their distinctive pasts. Not an easy border area to characterize in terms of a single civilization, east-central Europe has also been a victim of many conquests interspersed with periods of proud independence.

Questions: What were the main characteristics of east European civilization as it first emerged in the postclassical period? In what ways did Poland, Hungary, and the Czech lands differ from these characteristics? Are there other civilization border areas, in the postclassical period or later, that are similarly difficult to define because of their intermediate position between two other areas?

CONCLUSION

The End of an Era in Eastern Europe

With Byzantium and Russia both under siege, east European civilization unquestionably fell on hard times at the end of the postclassical era. Brighter days were ahead, though the struggle to define anew a full civilization af-

ter 1453 would not prove easy. In the meantime, the connection of key border territories, such as Poland, to the west European cultural zone would deepen—another complication for the subsequent history of the region—while the Balkans lay under Turkish rule.

These difficulties confirmed the largely separate trajectories of West and East in Europe, for western Europe remained free from outside control and, despite some new problems, maintained a clearer vigor in politics, economy, and culture. When eastern Europe did reemerge, it would be at some disadvantage to the West, in terms of power and economic-cultural sophistication—a quite different balance from that which had prevailed during the glory days of Byzantium and the cruder vigor of Kievan Russia.

At the same time, the disruption caused by Tartar invasion and Byzantine collapse warns against projecting too much continuity between these early east European centuries and what would come later. Byzantine patterns were never recaptured. Key features of Kievan social structure would not characterize the later development of imperial Russia. Yet continuity was not entirely lost. Not only Christianity but the particular east European assumptions about political rulers and church-state relations as well as the pride in a lively artistic culture would serve as organizing threads when Russia and other Slavic societies turned to rebuilding.

The Byzantine Empire was one of the great centers of civilization during the postclassical period, though smaller than the other three centers in the Middle East (plus North Africa), India, and China. Alone of the great centers, it did not simply decline but disappeared, and this suggests some of the limitations of its final centuries of existence. Yet the empire was not simply a random feature of the postclassical period that must be inserted to keep the historical record straight. Its role in shaping one of the major versions of Christianity and its active effort in spreading religion, commerce, and the trappings of civilization northward helped prepare for later developments in the east European region. These developments, headed by the rise of Russia, began to take shape when the shock of Byzantium's fall and the Mongol invasions finally wore off.

FURTHER READINGS

J. M. Hussey's *The Byzantine World* (1982) provides a useful overview. Byzantine Christianity is studied in G. Every's *The Byzantine Patriarchate, 451–1204* (1978) and S. Runciman's *The Byzantine Theocracy* (1977); see also D. M. Nicol's *Church and Society in the Last Centuries of Byzantium* (1979). On culture, see E. Kitzinger's *Byzantine Art in the Making* (1977). Byzantine relations with the West form the main topic in H. J. Magoulias's *Byzantine Christianity: Emperor, Church and the West* (1982).

On Byzantine influence in eastern Europe, D. Obolensky's *The Byzantine Commonwealth: Eastern Europe, 500–1453* (1971) is an excellent analysis. See also S. Runciman's *A History of the First Bulgarian Empire* (1930).

On Russian history, the best survey is Nicholas Riasanovsky's *A History of Russia* (5th ed., 1992), which has a good bibliography. Three books deal with early Russian culture: N. P. Kondakov's *The Russian Icon* (1927), J. H. Billington's *The Icon and the Axe: An Interpretive History of Russian Culture* (1966), and Arthur Voyce's *The Art and Architecture of Medieval Russia* (1967).

Two source collections are also very helpful on early Russian history: T. Riha, ed., *Readings in Russian Civilization*, vol. 1, *Russia before Peter the Great, 900–1700* (1969); and especially S. A. Zenkovsky, ed. and trans., *Medieval Russia's Epics, Chronicles and Tales* (1963).

16

A New Civilization Emerges in Western Europe

500–900 Recovery period after Rome's fall; missionary work in northern Europe

900–1000 Spread of new plows; use of horses in agriculture, transport

1066 Norman conquest of England, strong feudal monarchy

1096–1270 Crusades

732 Franks defeat Muslims in France

800–814 Charlemagne's empire

962 Germanic kings "revive" Roman Empire

1018 Beginning of Christian reconquest of Spain

1073–1085 Gregory VII, reform pope

1070–1141 Peter Abelard

500 C.E.

800 C.E.

1000 C.E.

INTRODUCTION

The postclassical period in western Europe began with the decline and fall of the Roman Empire and extended until the 15th century. Known as the Middle Ages in European history, the period featured gradual recovery from the shock of Rome's collapse and growing interaction with other societies, particularly around the Mediterranean.

Developments in Western civilization during the Middle Ages reflected many of the larger themes of postclassical world history. The spread of civilization underlay medieval history. Although western Europe had been touched by the Roman Empire at its height, contacts had been somewhat superficial outside the Mediterranean zone. And much of the north—most of Germany, northern Britain, and Scandinavia—had been entirely outside the Roman orbit. During the Middle Ages, civilization extended, gradually, to the whole of western Europe.

Western Europe also witnessed the spread of new religious beliefs. The missionary activity of Christianity was the chief bearer of civilization to northwestern Europe in the early centuries of the Middle Ages. Most western Europeans converted from polytheistic faiths to Christian monotheism as part of this process, though in fact many produced an amalgam in which beliefs in magic and supernatural spirits coexisted with often fervent Christianity.

Finally, medieval western Europe participated in the emerging international community, the network of expanding contacts between major societies in Asia, Europe, and parts of Africa. From such contacts medieval Europeans learned new technologies. New implements introduced from Asia by invading tribes helped spur medieval agriculture from the 10th century onward. Trade in the Mediterranean, bringing contacts with the Arabs, yielded other technological gains, such as the first European paper factory. Medieval culture was at least as powerfully shaped by connections with the wider world. From the Byzantines and the Arabs, Western scholars by the 11th and 12th centuries learned new and challenging lessons in mathematics, science, and philosophy that spurred them to change and elaborate their own world view. The medieval West unquestionably took more from the emerging world network than it contributed, but it was also challenged by its international position to seek new world roles.

THE FLAVOR OF THE MIDDLE AGES: INFERIORITY AND VITALITY

Focal Point: Western Europe changed rapidly during the postclassical period, but it remained commercially and culturally backward compared to Islam and the Byzantine Empire. But its development did usher in certain political and cultural forms that made this civilization distinctive, not only in this period, but subsequently.

Medieval western Europe was not simply an illustration of larger themes. It had its own characteristics, both positive and negative. The West, during this entire period, was a backward society by the standards of the great civilizations of the Middle East and Asia. Muslims, for example, scorned the west Europeans as barbarians, incapable of knowing science. "Their bodies are large, their manners harsh, their understanding dull and their tongues heavy . . . those of them who are farthest to the north are the most subject to stupidity, grossness and brutishness," said a 10th-century Arab geographer. It is small wonder that before 1100, Europeans were not infrequently seized as slaves, or that even as their medieval society gained in strength, its international reputation

---

1303 Seizure of papacy by French king

1150–1300 Gothic style spreads

1180 University of Paris

1200–1274 Thomas Aquinas and flowering of scholasticism

1338–1453 Hundred Years' War

1265 First English parliament

1469 Formation of single Spanish monarchy

1215 Magna Carta

1226–1270 Louis IX of France

1348 Black Death (bubonic plague)

1150 C.E.   **1300** C.E.   **1450** C.E.

rested mainly on the prowess of its warriors, not on more sophisticated achievements. Western Europe's inferior position explains why contacts with the wider world proved so important.

Medieval backwardness certainly accounts for a long-standing anxiety about, as well as hostility toward, the more powerful Muslim world. Fears of Arab invasion did not die with the end of the actual Arab threat, and Arab control of Spain and portions of southern Italy constituted a long-standing challenge to Europe's Christian leaders. Only toward the end of the Middle Ages could Europeans even begin to presume they were capable of grappling with Arab learning, and superior Arab wealth and commerce caused medieval traders no small concern. Yet, inferiority was galling in that Europeans believed Islam to be a false religion (despite many features shared with Christianity) and looked for ways to push back or circumvent Muslim power. The Crusades were one result of this belligerent outlook; explorations that sought trade routes free from Muslim power at the end of the Middle Ages were another.

Medieval Europe's backwardness means, finally, that it can most fruitfully be compared with other societies in which civilization was a fairly new achievement in these centuries, rather than with the more established centers. Western political structures had interesting points in common with those of Japan and sub-Saharan Africa.

The Middle Ages also served western Europe as something of a crucible for institutions and values that helped propel Western civilization forward. The postclassical West advanced mightily, by almost all relevant measurements, after centuries of serious instability following the fall of the Roman Empire. Population grew, the economy blossomed, political units became more effective and covered larger territories, and a complex artistic and intellectual life took shape. Technological innovations included the use of new water-driven mills and improvements in iron casting for the manufacture of great church bells. The postclassical centuries also formed a seedbed for certain new values and institutions that would outlast the medieval period itself. In politics and social structure, particularly, the Middle Ages contributed more to the ongoing heritage of Western civilization than the classical era had done. And even in intellectual life, where medieval thinkers grappled with the legacy of classical philosophy and science, the distinctive contributions of the Middle Ages would leave a durable mark. It was thus from the Middle Ages that the Western world gained the institution of the university (including the rituals and degrees still associated with university life), the architectural forms (towers and vaulting arches of the Gothic style) we still associate with intellectual and religious life, and some new concepts of limited government.

STAGES OF POSTCLASSICAL DEVELOPMENT

Focal Point: Medieval European development unfolded in two subperiods up to about 1300. Between the 6th and the 10th centuries, chaotic conditions prevailed, despite gains made by the church and Charlemagne's brief empire. Then, improvements in trade and agriculture brought new strength and diversity. Feudal monarchy developed as a stronger political form. During this period, western Europe also developed expansionist tendencies, particularly in the Crusades.

From about 550 C.E. until about 900, western Europe seemed to be groping for civilization. Rome's decline had left Italy fragmented—its cities and commerce shrinking and its intellectual life in tatters. Rome continued to serve as the center of the growing Catholic church, in turn the most powerful institution and the central Christian agency in the West. And Italy's trade and urban life continued to surpass the levels of the remainder of western Europe, as the area retained stronger links with the Roman past than did newer centers such as France. But Italy could hardly claim anything but a shadow of the Roman Empire's grandeur, and its political weakness would indeed last until the later 19th century. Spain, another key region of the Roman Empire in the West, lay in the hands of the Muslims through much of the Middle Ages. A vibrant intellectual and economic life was focused there, and it would have an important influence on Western developments by dint of its superiority, but it was for the time being out of the Western mainstream. The center of the postclassical West lay in France, the Low Countries, and southern and western Germany, with England increasingly drawn in—areas where civilization was relatively recent.

Frequent invasions reflected and prolonged the West's weakness, making it difficult to develop durable government or economic forms. Raids by the seagoing *Vikings* from Scandinavia periodically disrupted life from Ireland to Sicily. The Scandinavians attacked several coastal areas, while other invaders from the east also disrupted politics, trade, and production. With weak rulers and little more than subsistence agriculture, it was small wonder that intellectual activity almost ground to a halt.

The few who could read and write were concentrated in the hierarchy and the monasteries of the Catholic church, where they provided signal service simply by keeping learning alive. But they could do little more than copy older manuscripts, including those of the great Christian thinkers of the later Roman Empire. They could not, by their own admission, understand much of the philosophy involved, and they often apologized for their inability even to write good Latin.

The Manorial System: Obligations and Allegiances

Between Rome's fall and the 10th century, effective political organization was largely local, though Germanic kings ruled some territories such as a portion of what is France today. *Manorialism* was the system of economic and political relations between landlords and their peasant laborers. Most people were *serfs*, living on self-sufficient agricultural estates called manors. Serfs were agricultural workers who received some protection, including the administration of justice, from the landlords; in return, they were obligated to turn over part of their goods and to remain on the land. The manorial system had originated in the later Roman Empire; it was strengthened by the decline of trade and the lack of larger political structures. Serfs needed the military forces the landlords could muster, given the instability of society. Without much market economy to stimulate production and specialization, these same landlords used the serfs' produce and labor to support their own modest establishments.

Manorialism thus involved a hierarchy of reciprocal obligations between the masses and the ruling class. Life for most serfs was difficult. Agricultural equipment was limited, and production was therefore kept low. The available plows, copied from Mediterranean models, were too light to work the heavy soils of France and Germany effectively. Only from the 9th century onward was a better plow, the *moldboard*, introduced that allowed deeper turning of the soil. Most Western peasants early in the postclassical period also left half their land uncultivated each year to restore nutrients. This again limited productivity, though by the 9th century, a new *three-field system*, reserving only one-third of the land for *fallow*, improved the situation.

The obligations of the manorial system bore as heavily on most serfs as did the technological limitations. Serfs had to give their lord part of their crops in return for grazing their animals on his land or milling their grain. They also provided many days of labor repairing the lord's castle or working the lands under his control. Serfs were not slaves—they could not be bought or sold, and they retained essential ownership of their houses and lands so long as they kept up with their obligations; they could also pass their property rights on through inheritance. Peasants also grouped themselves in their own villages, which provided them a rich community life of festivals and a political structure through which they could resolve most internal disputes. Nevertheless, life remained hard, particularly during the early postclassical centuries. Some serfs escaped landlord control, creating a host of vagabond wanderers, who added to the disorder of the early Middle Ages.

The Church: Political and Spiritual Power

During the recovery centuries after 500 C.E., the Catholic church provided the only extensive example of solid organization. Roman popes built a partial hierarchy by trying to control some of their local bishops. The popes did not always appoint the bishops, for monarchs and local lords often claimed this right, but they did send directives and receive information. The popes also regulated doctrine, beating back several heresies that threatened a unified Christian faith. Moreover, they sponsored extensive missionary activity. Papal missionaries converted the English to Christianity. They brought the religion to northern and eastern Germany, beyond the borders of the previous Roman Empire, and ultimately, by the 10th century, to Scandinavia. They were active, of course, in the border regions of eastern Europe, sometimes competing directly with Orthodox missionaries. In theory, and to an extent in fact, the Church copied the government of the Roman Empire in order to administer Christendom. The pope in Rome was the top authority. Regional churches were headed by bishops, who were supposed to owe allegiance to the Church's central authority; bishops, in turn, appointed and to some degree supervised local priests.

The interest of early Germanic kings in Christianity was a testimony to the political as well as spiritual power of the Church. A warrior chieftain, *Clovis,* converted to Christianity about 496 C.E. in order to gain greater prestige over local rivals who were still pagan. This authority, in turn, gave him a vague dominion over the Franks, located in much of what is France today. Conversion of this sort also strengthened beliefs by Western religious leaders, particularly the popes, that they had a legitimate authority separate from and superior to the political sphere.

The Church also developed an important chain of monasteries during the Dark Ages. Western monasteries helped discipline the intense spirituality felt by some individual Christians, expressed by a desire to escape the limits of ordinary material life. By locating those particularly dedicated to piety in groups and subjecting them to common rules, the Church could use the monastic movement to promote Christian unity in the West. The most important set of rules for monasteries was developed by *Benedict of Nursia* (in Italy) in the 6th century. Monasteries also served ordinary people as examples of a holy life, adding to the spiritual focus that formed part of the fabric of medieval society. They served more prosaic functions as well. Many monasteries helped improve the cultivation of the land at a time when agricultural techniques were at a low ebb. Benedict urged the holy importance of productive work. Study and prayer formed part of the monastic discipline, and Western monks, in copying and pondering ancient manuscripts by Roman authors as well as Christian theologians, helped set the basis for later intellectual inquiry in this emerging civilization. Thus, monasteries also provided some education and promoted literacy.

Charlemagne and His Successors

One significant development occurred during the early postclassical centuries in the more strictly political sphere. The royal house of the Franks grew in strength during the 8th century. A new family, the *Carolingians,* took over this monarchy, which was based in northern France, Belgium, and western Germany. One founder of the Carolingian line—*Charles Martel,* or Charles the Hammer—was responsible for defeating the Muslims in the battle of Tours in 732, though his victory had more to do with Arab exhaustion and an overextended invasion force than Carolingian strength. This defeat helped confine the Muslims to Spain and, along with the Byzantine defeat of the Arabs in the same period, preserved Europe for Christianity.

A later Carolingian ruler in this same royal line, Charles the Great, or *Charlemagne,* established a substantial empire in France and Germany around the year 800. Briefly, it looked as if a new Roman Empire might revive in the West, and indeed, the imperial title continued to be used by Charlemagne's successors in Germany. Charlemagne helped to restore some church-based education in western Europe, and the level of intellectual activity began a slow recovery, in part because of these efforts. When Charlemagne died in 814, however, his empire did not long survive him. Rather, it was split into three portions: the outlines of modern France, Germany, and a middle strip consisting of the Low Countries, Switzerland, and northern Italy. Several of Charlemagne's successors, with nicknames like "the Bald" or "the Fat," were not models of political dynamism even in their regional kingdoms. Emperors in Germany claimed Charlemagne's mantle, later terming their realm the "holy Roman Empire," but in fact they only ruled a regional state, rather loosely coordinated.

From this point onward, the essential political history of western Europe consisted of the gradual emergence of regional monarchies; a durable empire proved impossible, given competing loyalties and the absence of a strong bureaucracy. Western Europe proved to be a civilization with strong cultural unity, initially centered in Catholic Christianity, but with pronounced political divisions. No single language united this civilization, any more than did a single government. Latin was used by intellectuals and by the church officials, but during the Middle Ages separate spoken languages evolved, usually merging Germanic and Latin elements. These separate languages, such as French and English, in turn helped form the basis of halting national identities when political and national boundaries roughly coincided—which is what began to happen in key cases after the 9th century.

The royal houses of several lands gained new visibility soon after Charlemagne's empire split. At first, the rulers who reigned over Germany and northern Italy were in the strongest position. It was they who claimed the title "emperor," beginning around the 10th century. Later they called themselves "*holy Roman emperors,*" merging Christian and classical claims. By this time, however, their rule had become increasingly hollow, precisely because they relied too much on their imperial claims and did not build a solid monarchy from regional foundations. Local feudal lords often went their own way in Germany, while city-states showed independence in northern Italy. The future lay elsewhere, with the rise of monarchies in individual states—states that ultimately would become nations.

New Economic and Urban Vigor

A series of developments began, by the 9th and 10th centuries, to introduce new sources of strength into Western society that ultimately had clear political and cultural repercussions. New agricultural techniques developed from contacts with eastern Europe and with Asian raiders into central Europe. The new moldboard plow and the three-field system were crucial gains; so was a new horse collar that allowed horses to be yoked without choking. The use of horse collars and stirrups also confirmed the military dominance of the feudal

The pope's coronation of the emperor Charlemagne was a vital precedent for the idea that Church approval was essential for a legitimate state in Western Europe, though in fact Charlemagne's power greatly exceeded the pope's.

lords, who monopolized fighting on horseback. But better plows aided the ordinary people by allowing deeper working of heavy soil and the opening of new land. Monasteries also promoted better agricultural methods (in contrast to the less worldly orientation of monks in eastern Europe).

Shortly after this time, in the 10th century, Viking raids began to taper off, partly because regional governments became stronger (sometimes when the Vikings themselves took over, as in the French province of Normandy) and partly because the Vikings, now Christianized, began to settle down. Greater regional political stability and improved agriculture went hand in hand to encourage population growth, an important fact of Western history from the 10th through the 13th centuries.

Population growth, in turn, encouraged further economic innovation. More people created new markets. There was a wedge here for growing trade, which in turn encouraged towns to expand. During the early postclas-

sical centuries, towns had barely held on in most of western Europe outside of Italy, serving mainly as church centers. Now, however, by 1000 C.E., they began to serve as regional centers of trade, developing a merchant class and some craft production. Growing towns required more food. Landlords and serfs alike began to look to lands that had not previously been converted to agriculture. Whole regions, such as northeastern Germany, became colonized by eager farmers, and new centers sprang up throughout settled regions such as France. To woo labor to the new farms, landlords typically had to loosen the bonds of serfdom and require less outright labor service, sometimes simply charging a money rent. Harsh serfdom still existed, but most serfs gained greater independence, and some free peasants emerged. The pace of economic life, in other words, created a less rigid social structure, and more commercial, market-oriented economic motives began to coexist with earlier feudal and Christian ideals.

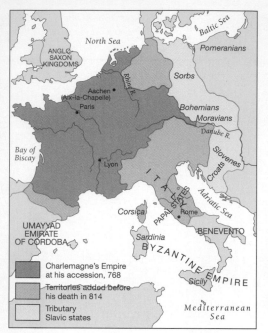

Charlemagne's Empire and Successor States

The growth of towns reflected the new vigor of West Europe's agriculture. In parts of Italy and the Low Countries, where trade and urban manufacturing were especially brisk, urban populations soared to almost 20 percent of the total by the 13th century. Overall, they constituted about 5 percent of the West's population—a significant figure, though below the levels of the advanced Asian civilizations. Few European cities approached a population level of 100,000 people (in contrast to China, which had 52 still larger cities), but the multiplicity of modest regional centers was an important development. Literacy spread in the urban atmosphere, spurring the popular languages; professional entertainers introduced new songs as well as dazzling tricks like fire-eating or bearbaiting; urban interests spurred new forms of religious life, including city-based monastic orders dedicated to teaching or hospital work. These new orders relished interaction with society to promote religious goals, in contrast to the more isolated traditional monasteries.

Europe's economic and urban surge helped feed formal cultural life, which had already gained somewhat under Charlemagne's encouragement. By the 9th and 10th centuries, schools began to form around important cathedrals, particularly training children who were destined for church careers. By the 11th century, there was enough demand for educated personnel to allow the first

universities to emerge. Italy offered universities to train students in medicine and law; the legal faculties profited from a growing revival in knowledge of Roman law, while medicine benefited from new learning imported from the Arabs and from revived Greek and Hellenistic science. By the 12th century, a more characteristic university was forming in Paris. It specialized in training churchmen, with theology as the culminating subject but with faculties in other subjects as well. The Parisian example in turn inspired universities in England (Oxford and Cambridge), Germany, and elsewhere. Solid educational institutions, though destined for only a small minority of Europe's population, undergirded increasingly diverse and sophisticated efforts in philosophy and theology. At the same time, medieval art and architecture reached a new high point spurred by the same prosperity, which also fed further political developments, particularly in the form of the expanding monarchies of France and Britain.

Feudal Monarchies and Political Advances

From the 6th century onward, the key political and military relationships in Western Europe evolved in a system called *feudalism*. Feudal relationships linked military elites, mostly landlords, who could afford the horses and

This scene, from a manuscript of the 15th century, shows peasant labor and tools in France, near a stylized great palace.

the Holy Roman emperor. Throughout much of Europe (including Poland and the Czech lands, feudal relationships crisscrossed, as inheritances and marriage alliances added complexity. On the whole, European feudalism inhibited the development of strong central states, but it also gradually reduced purely local warfare.

Furthermore, kings could use feudalism to build their own power. Feudal monarchies developed as western Europe began to stabilize and as kings combined their own revenues to become major landowners, with a growing array of feudal ties to powerful regional vassals (who of course had vassals of their own).

Kings of France began to win growing authority, from the 10th century onward. At first they mainly exploited their position as regional feudal lords in the area around Paris. They controlled many serf-stocked manors directly, and they held most other local landlords as vassals. More attentive administration of this regional base produced better revenues and armies. The kings also formed feudal links with great lords in other parts of France, often through marriage alliances, gradually bringing more territory under their effective control. They experimented with the beginnings of bureaucratic administration by separating their personal accounts from government accounts, thus developing a small degree of specialization among the officials who served them. The growth of a strong feudal monarchy in France took several centuries, but it provided a clear evolutionary thread throughout the later postclassical centuries.

Feudal monarchy in England was introduced more abruptly. The Duke of Normandy, of Viking descent, who had already built a strong feudal domain in his French province, invaded England in 1066. The Duke, now known as *William the Conqueror,* extended his tight feudal system to his new kingdom. He tied the great lords of England to his royal court by bonds of loyalty, giving them estates in return for their military service. But he also utilized throughout the kingdom some royal officials, called sheriffs, to help supervise the administration of justice. He and his successors created, in essence, a merger of feudal principles with a slightly more centralized approach, including more standardized national law codes issued by the royal court.

England's political gains spurred the French monarchy to further consolidation. English kings had long held territories in France, including Normandy, as feudal lords. French kings wanted to press them back. This effort required greater attention to tax revenues and organization of armies, though these were still drawn mainly from the ranks of the king's feudal vassals. Success in

iron weaponry necessary to fight. Greater lords provided protection and aid to lesser lords, called *vassals;* vassals in turn owed their lords military service, some goods or payments, and advice. Early feudalism after Rome's fall was very local; many landlords had armed bands of five or ten local vassals, easily converted into raiding parties. But feudal relationships could be extended to cover larger regions and even whole kingdoms.

Charlemagne's empire boosted this more stable version of feudalism. He could not afford to pay his own bureaucracy, so he rewarded most of his military leaders with estates, which they quickly converted into family property in return for pledges of loyalty and service. Many German duchies were created by powerful lords with their own armies of vassals, ostensibly deferring to

wars gave the French kings new territory that they administered directly, including wealthy urban areas in northern France. Mistreatment of a French vassal by King John of England (who was also lord over many French lands, including Normandy) allowed the Capetian king to deprive him of his French fiefs under feudal law, as a disobedient vassal. Local lords supported this effort, and Normandy was gained for France. At this point, the Capetian king began to send out his own officials to aid in regional administration, while allowing the provinces to keep their own laws and courts.

By the 13th century, France's feudal monarchy was essentially complete. Louis IX (1226–1270) inherited a stable kingdom. He improved the quality and particularly the ethical standards of royal bureaucrats sent to check on activities in distant provinces. The king gained a reputation as a provider of justice. Louis was also extremely pious and was ultimately sainted; many French people believed that such kings had virtually miraculous powers, including the ability to heal illness by the laying on of hands. Louis also sponsored vicious attacks on religious heretics in southern France and organized two futile Crusades against the Arab Muslims; he died of a fever during the second effort, but his memory continued to support the prestige of the French monarchy.

By the early 14th century, the process of cautious centralization had gone so far in France that a king could claim rights to make the Church pay taxes (an issue that caused great conflict). The king could print money and employ some professional soldiers apart from the feudal armies that still did most of the fighting.

Strong monarchies did not, to be sure, develop evenly throughout Europe. The West remained politically divided and diverse. Germany and Italy, though nominally controlled by the Holy Roman emperor, were actually split into dukedoms and city-states. The pope directly ruled the territory of central Italy. The Low Countries, a vigorous trade and manufacturing region, remained divided into regional units. Spain formed somewhat larger, though still regional, monarchies as Christian lords began to push back the Muslims from 1018 onward; but a national royal house was formed only in the 15th century with the marriage of Ferdinand and Isabella.

Europeans did develop more capacity for central administration during the later Middle Ages, though they built on, rather than displaced, the powers of feudal lords, and though the results were clearly uneven and by Asian standards still woefully limited. Local wars gave way to larger conflicts, like the conflicts between the proud rulers of France and England. In the 14th century, a long battle began—the *Hundred Years' War*, between the national monarchies of France and England—over territories the English king controlled in France and relatedly over feudal rights versus the emerging claims of national states.

The West's Expansionist Impulse

During the period of political development and economic advance, Western Europe began to show its muscle beyond its initial postclassical borders. Population growth spurred the expansionist impulse, as did the memory of Rome's lost greatness and the righteous zeal provided through Christianity.

The most concrete expansion took place in east central Europe from the 11th century onward. Germanic knights and agricultural settlers poured into sparsely settled areas in what is now eastern Germany and Poland, changing the population balance considerably. Another important surge occurred in Spain. Small Christian states remained in northern Spain by the 10th century, and they gradually began to attack the Muslim government that held most of the peninsula. The "reconquest" stepped up in pace by the 11th century, as Christian forces, swelled by feudal warriors from various areas, pushed into central Spain, conquering the great Muslim center of Toledo. Full expulsion of Muslim rulers occurred only at the end of the Middle Ages in 1492, but the trend of the Christian offensive was clear even earlier. At Europe's other extreme, Viking voyagers, along with their raids to the south, had pushed out into the northern Atlantic, establishing settlements in Iceland. By the 11th century, other voyages had pushed to Greenland and the Hudson Bay area in what is now Canada, where short-lived outposts were created. By the 13th century, Spanish and Italian seafarers entered the Atlantic from the Mediterranean, though without much initial result except several lost expeditions.

The most dramatic expansionist move involved the great *Crusades* against the Muslim control of the Holy Land. Pope *Urban II* called for the First Crusade in 1095, appealing to the undeniable piety of the West's rulers and common people. Crusaders were promised full forgiveness of sins if they died in battle, assuring them entry to heaven. The attraction of winning spoils from the rich Arab lands added to the inducement, as did the thirst for excitement among the West's feudal warriors. Three great armies, with tens of thousands of Crusaders from various parts of the West, assembled in Constantinople in 1097—much to the distress of the Byzantine government. The Western Crusaders moved

This imaginary duel between the noble Christian champion King Richard of England and the Muslim leader Saladin shows "good guys" and "bad guys" without hesitation.

toward Jerusalem, winning it from the Turkish armies that held the area by that time. For almost a century, Western knights ruled the "kingdom of Jerusalem," losing it to a great Muslim general, Saladin, during the 12th century. Several later Crusades attempted to win back the Holy Land, though many subsequent efforts turned toward other goals—or toward pure farce. The Third Crusade at the end of the 12th century led to the death of the German emperor and the imprisonment of the English king, though it did produce a brief truce with Saladin that allowed Christian pilgrims to visit Jerusalem. The Fourth Crusade was manipulated by merchants in Venice, who turned it into an attack on their commercial rivals in Constantinople.

The Crusades did not demonstrate a new Western superiority in the wider world, despite some limited successes. But as an expression of a combination of religious zeal and growing commercial and military vigor on the part of the knights and merchants who organized the largest efforts, the Crusades unquestionably showed the distinctive spirit of the Western Middle Ages at their height. They also helped open the West to new cultural and economic influences from the Middle East—a major spur to further change and to the West's interaction with the larger world.

Religious Reform and Evolution

As medieval society developed, the Catholic church went through several periods of decline and renewal. At times, church officials and the leading monastic groups became preoccupied with their land holdings and their political interests. The Church was a wealthy institution; it was tempting for many priests and monks to behave like ordinary feudal lords in pursuit of greater worldly power. A reform movement arose in the 11th century to combat this growing secularism. Purified monastic orders, centered in *Cluny* in France, inspired fresh vigor to this branch of the Church. Later, in the 13th century, another monastic reform movement created orders such as the Franciscans, devoted to poverty and service in Europe's bustling cities.

Reform-minded popes, such as *Gregory VII* (1073–1085), attempted to purify the Church generally and free it from interference by feudal lords. One technique was insistence on the particularly holy character of the priesthood. Reformers stipulated that all priests remain unmarried, to separate the priesthood from the ordinary world of the flesh. Gregory also endeavored to free the Church from any vestige of state control. He quarreled vigorously with the Holy Roman Emperor Henry IV over the practice of state appointment, or *investiture*, of bishops in Germany. Ultimately, by excommunicating the emperor from the Church, Gregory won his point. The emperor appealed on his knees in the snow of a northern Italian winter, and the investiture controversy ended, apparently in the Church's favor. Gregory and several later popes made clear their beliefs that the Church not only was to be free from state interference but was superior to the state in its function as a direct channel of God's word. These claims were not entirely accurate, as governments influenced religious affairs still, but they were not hollow. It was this sort of affirmation, indeed, that enabled the Church to inspire kings and warriors to fight in the Crusades and also to war against several heresies that broke out during the same centuries. Independently of the state, a network of church courts developed to rule on matters of religious, or canon, law and to bring heretics to trial and occasionally to execution. Here, in long-run terms, was the origin of recurrent Western beliefs in church–state separation.

The High Middle Ages

The postclassical version of Western civilization reached its high mark in the 12th and 13th centuries. Fed by the growing dynamism of western Europe's population, agriculture, and cities, the High Middle Ages were characterized above all by a series of creative tensions. Feudal political structures, which derived from local and personal allegiances, were balanced by nascent central monarchies. The unquestionable authority of the Church and the cultural dominance of Christianity jostled with the intellectual vitality and diversity that formed part of university life. A social order and economy, based primarily on agriculture and the partially free labor of serfs, now had to come to terms with important cities, merchants, and some new opportunities even for ordinary farmers.

ANALYSIS

The Sources of Vitality in the Postclassical West

Why did Western Europe begin to demonstrate new vigor about 1000 C.E.—forming new schools and a more elaborate culture; expanding trade and towns, while loosening the most restrictive aspects of manorial social organization; and launching new, sometimes aggressive contacts with other areas, as in the Crusades? The question is really the reverse of the more familiar analysis of societal decline. It is at least as important to know what causes civilizations to rise as to probe the reasons for their fall. At various points in history (including the 20th century), certain societies begin to be more dynamic than they had been before—sometimes more dynamic also than many other societies in the same period. Determining the causes in one case may help in evaluating other cases. Furthermore, an understanding of causes may help explain directions of new vigor—what kinds of new cultural forms are generated, for example, or why some dynamic societies are more expansionistic than

others. The causes that produced new energy in the medieval West are particularly interesting in that they galvanized a society that not only was backward but that in some respects—in levels of trade and learning, for instance—had retrogressed from previous achievements.

The legacy of Greece and Rome had something to do with the medieval surge. Key Europeans knew the empire had existed; a sense of lost greatness might have inspired them. More concretely, the revival of specific political achievements like Roman law helped stabilize medieval politics by the 11th century, starting with the organization of the Church itself. The continued use of Latin for intellectual life facilitated encounters with classical learning. One approach to an explanation, then, might suggest a certain inevitability: Classical achievements were so inspiring that after a few centuries of chaos, the West almost automatically resurrected key elements of the Greco-Roman experience. By the 12th century, medieval writers suggested this pattern, arguing that though they could not rival the sheer intellectual power of the classical philosophers, they actually could forge beyond them by "standing on their shoulders." This model suggests a Western experience similar to that of China after its centuries of chaos subsequent to the fall of the Han dynasty, for here new vigor was based directly on the ability to revive past strengths (see Chapter 18).

Another model for the West stresses the impact of cultural change, notably the results of conversions to Christianity. To be sure, Christianity incorporated elements of classical learning and the institutional patterns of the Roman Empire, but it was in many ways a new force. It took some time for Christianity to be assimilated, but ultimately it began to reshape habits in important ways. Thus, Christian pleas for peace, while they did not end war in Europe, did have a taming effect, allowing more stable political structures to develop by about 1000 C.E. The example of the Church as a bureaucratic institution similarly helped inspire secular rulers to improve their administrations, while the interest in reading and interpreting the Bible and the writings of the church fathers spurred medieval intellectual and educational life. Some scholars have even argued for a special, unanticipated technological result of assimilation of Christianity. By arguing that humankind is superior to the animal world—made in God's image—the new religion encouraged medieval people toward a less reverent, more utilitarian view of nature as something to be exploited. It prepared medieval Europeans' receptivity to new technologies that would subdue nature. More specifically, Christian interest in bells, for use in church celebrations, stimulated medieval interest in metalworking, with results that were applied to other fields by the 15th century. The development of clocks, a major technological advance, followed from an interest in timing the start of religious services. Certainly, Christianity encouraged some of the expansionist tone of a more dynamic western Europe as part of a desire to convert unbelievers and beat back the infidel.

A third line of explanation stresses more purely technological factors. The use of moldboard plows began to spread in northwestern Europe by the 9th century, though they had been introduced earlier by Celtic or Germanic farmers. The moldboards worked much better in the moist, clinging soil of northern Europe than the lighter models the Romans had used. The moldboard in turn encouraged better ironwork and also improved village organization, for the new plows were costly and required cooperation. At the same time food production improved, spurring population growth, the rise of cities, and the important push into sparsely populated lands in eastern Germany. The growing use of horses, thanks to the new collar, also encouraged land transport and roads.

Western Europe was not of course the only dynamic new society to emerge in the later centuries of the postclassical era. Russia, parts of Africa, Japan, and other areas showed vigor as well, and in some of the same ways, such as more stable politics and commercial expansion. Whatever the specific combination of factors operating in western Europe, it is important to remember the larger typology: Several societies were able to blend their own cultural traditions and the advantages of new contacts with more established centers of civilization to produce various kinds of growth and innovation. The motivation of trying to catch up with the richer centers, along with sufficient contacts to allow some hope of figuring out how to advance, played no small role in this general process.

Questions: Which of the causation models—heritage, religious change, or technology—seems more appealing, and why? Which of the causes began to have an impact first? Do the models contradict each other, or can they be combined? Which models might also be applied to explain the rise of medieval Russia or the kingdoms of sub-Saharan Africa?

WESTERN CULTURE IN THE POSTCLASSICAL ERA

Focal Point: Christian culture formed the clearest unifying element in Western Europe at this point. Theologians and artists both developed distinctive expres-

sions, though there were other philosophical and artistic currents as Europe's cultural creativity increased.

Theology: Assimilating Faith and Reason

During the centuries before about 1000, a small number of churchmen continued the efforts of preserving and interpreting past wisdom, particularly the writings of church fathers like Augustine, but also some non-Christian Latin authors. During Charlemagne's time, a favorite practice was to gather quotations from ancient writers around key subjects. Efforts of this sort showed little creativity, but they gradually produced a fuller understanding of past thought as well as improvements in Latin writing style and in organizing philosophical materials. Interest in classical principles of rhetoric, particularly logic, reflected the concern for coherent organization; Aristotle, known to the Middle Ages as *the* philosopher, was valued because of his clear exposition of rational thought.

From 1000 onward, a series of outstanding clerics advanced the logical exposition of philosophy and theology to new levels. They stressed the importance of absolute faith in God's word, but they believed that human reason could move toward an understanding of some aspects of religion and the natural order as well. Thus, according to several theologians, it was possible to prove the existence of God, to use logic to help explain the *Trinity,* and to develop certain moral principles. A concomitant interest in collecting Roman law and in codifying canon law also promoted the use of careful logical exposition. Fascination with logic led some intellectuals to a certain zeal in pointing out inconsistencies in past wisdom, even in the writings of the church fathers. In the 12th century, *Peter Abelard* in Paris wrote a treatise called "Yes or No," in which he showed several logical contradictions in established interpretations of doctrine. Though Abelard protested his faith, saying, "I would not be an Aristotle if this were to part me from Christ," he clearly took an impish delight in suggesting skepticism.

This logical-rationalist current in Western philosophy was hardly unopposed. Quite apart from the fact that most ordinary Christians knew nothing of these debates, seeing their religion as a matter of received belief and appointed sacraments that would remove sin and promote salvation, many church leaders emphasized the role of faith alone. A powerful monk, *St. Bernard of Clairvaux,* successfully challenged Abelard. Bernard, an intellectual of a different sort, stressed the importance of mystical union with God, attainable even on this earth in brief blissful glimpses, rather than rationalist endeavor.

Gothic architecture constituted one of the creative expressions of postclassical western Europe and was used particularly in churches great and small. This major cathedral in Amiens, France, was built over many centuries and dwarfs the surrounding buildings.

Bernard believed that reason was dangerous and prideful and that God's truth must be received through faith alone.

The debates over how, and whether, to combine the classical Mediterranean philosophical and scientific tradition with revealed religious faith had much in common with debates among Arab intellectuals during the 10th and 11th centuries. Both Christianity and Islam relied heavily on faith in a revealed word, through the Bible or Koran, respectively, yet some intellectuals in both cultures strained to include other approaches. Arab philosophers who had already advanced rationalist arguments helped shape the most characteristic Western approach. At the same time, because Christian thinkers interpreted the Bible in terms of allegories as well as literal truths, their theological speculations could range even more widely.

The thirst to assimilate rational philosophy and Christian faith was the dominant intellectual theme in the postclassical West. It represented the need to come to terms with both Christian and classical heritages. This assimilation of rational philosophy and Christian faith also posed formidable and fascinating problems of reconciliation. By the 12th century, the zeal for this kind of knowledge produced several distinctive results. It explained the intellectual vitality of most of the emerging universities, where students flocked to hear the latest debates by leading theologians. Higher education certainly benefited students through resultant job opportunities; trained lawyers, for example, could hope for advancement in the growing bureaucracies of church or state. In contrast to China, however, the new universities were not directly tied into a single bureaucratic system, and the excitement they engendered during the Middle Ages did not follow from opportunism alone. A large number of students, from the whole of western Europe, sought out the mixture of spiritual and rational understanding that leading thinkers were trying to work out. Many early universities had their students pay the teachers directly if they were interested in attending a given set of lectures, and the eagerness for learning could make this system work.

The postclassical intellectual drive also motivated a growing interest in knowledge newly imported from the classical past and from the Arab world, and this knowledge in turn fed the highest achievements of medieval learning. By the 12th century, Western scholars were consuming vast amounts of material translated from Greek in centers in the Byzantine Empire, Italy, and Muslim Spain. They gained familiarity with the bulk of ancient Greek and Hellenistic philosophy and science. They also read translations of Arab and Jewish learning, particularly those works in which Middle Eastern thinkers had wrestled with the problems of mixing human reasoning with truths gained by faith. Translators in Spain and Constantinople could barely keep up with the growing Western demand to discover everything there was to know.

With much fuller knowledge of Aristotelian and Hellenistic science, plus the work of Arab rationalists, such as Ibn-Rushd (known in the West as Averroës), Western philosopher-theologians in the 13th century proceeded to the final great synthesis of medieval learning. The leading figure was *Thomas Aquinas,* an Italian-born monk who taught at the University of Paris. Aquinas maintained the basic belief that faith came first, but he greatly expanded the scope given to reason. Through reason alone, humans could know much of the natural order, of moral law, and of the nature of God. Thomas had complete confidence that all essential knowledge could be coherently organized, and he produced a host of *Summas,* or highest works, that disposed through careful logic of all possible objections to truth as revealed by reason and faith. Here was a masterful demonstration of medieval confidence in the fundamental orderliness of learning and God's creation. Essentially, this work restated in Christian terms the Greek efforts to seek a rationality in nature that would correspond to the rational capacities of the human mind. To be sure, a few philosophers carried the interest in logic to absurd degrees; after the 13th century, *scholasticism*—as the dominant medieval philosophical approach was called because of its base in the schools—sometimes degenerated into silly debates such as the one over the conundrum of how many angels could dance on the head of a pin. But at its

height, and particularly with Aquinas, scholasticism demonstrated an unusual confidence in the logical orderliness of knowledge and in human ability to know clearly most of what needed to be known.

Medieval philosophy did not encourage a great deal of new scientific work. The emphasis on mastering past learning and organizing it logically could lead to overemphasis on previous discoveries, rather than empirical research. Thus, university-trained doctors stressed memorization of Galen, the Hellenistic authority, rather than systematic practical experience. Toward the end of the 13th century, a current of practical science developed. In Oxford, members of the clergy, such as Roger Bacon, did experimental work with optics, pursuing research done earlier by Muslim scholars. An important by-product of this interest was the invention of eyeglasses, an indispensable aid to many Western (and other) scholars ever since. During the 14th and 15th centuries, experimenters also advanced knowledge in chemistry and astronomy. This early work set the stage for the flourishing of Western science later on.

Popular Religion

Far less is known about popular beliefs than about formal intellectual life in the Middle Ages. Christian devotion undoubtedly ran deep and may well have increased with time among many ordinary people. The rise of cities saw the formation of laymen's groups to develop spirituality and express their love of God. The content of popular belief evolved as well. Enthusiasm for the veneration of Mary, the mother of Jesus, expanded by the 12th century, showing a desire to stress the merciful side of Christianity, as against the supposed sternness of God the Father, and new hopes for assistance in gaining salvation. The worship of various saints showed a similar desire for intermediaries between people and God. At the same time, ordinary people continued to believe in various magical rituals, and they celebrated essentially pagan festivals, which often involved much dancing and merriment. They blended their version of Christianity with considerable earthiness and spontaneity, some of which was conveyed by late medieval writers such as the English writer Geoffrey Chaucer.

Religious Themes in Art and Literature

Christian art in many ways reflected both the popular outlook and the more formal religion of theologians and church leaders. Religious art was another cultural area in which the medieval West came to excel, as was the case in other societies such as the Islamic Middle East or Hindu India, where religious enthusiasm ran strong. As

CLOSEUP

St. Clare of Assisi

St. Clare of Assisi (1194–1253) was deeply influenced by St. Francis, also from Assisi, who had converted to a life of piety and preaching in 1207. A new monastic order quickly formed around St. Francis, known for his gentle mysticism. Clare refused to marry, as her parents wished, and in 1212 she fled to a chapel, where Francis received her vows. This was the beginning of a women's Franciscan order, later known as the Order of St. Clare, or the Poor Clares. Clare, like many women in Europe, found in monasticism a vital means of personal expression. Her order, living by rules she composed, lived a severe life of total piety. Many women joined, including Clare's mother and sister. The order's aim was to use penitential prayer to help both church and society. Her prayers were credited with turning two invading armies away from Assisi, and she was held to perform many other miracles in her life and after death. She was canonized in 1255. In 1958, Pope Pius XII declared her the patron saint of television, for during her last illness she miraculously heard and saw a Christmas mass being performed on the other side of Assisi.

---

with philosophy, medieval art and architecture were intended to serve the glory of God. Western painters used religious subjects almost exclusively. Painting mainly on wooden panels, artists in most parts of western Europe depicted Christ's birth and suffering and the lives of the saints, using stiff, stylized figures. By the 14th and 15th centuries, artists improved their ability to render natural scenes realistically and portrayed a host of images of medieval life as backdrops to their religious subjects. Designs and scenes in stained glass for churches constituted another important artistic expression.

Medieval architecture initially followed Roman models, particularly in church building, using a rectangular, or Romanesque, style sometimes surmounted by domes. During the 11th century, however, a new style took hold that was far more original, though it benefited from knowledge of Muslim design plus advances in structural engineering in the West itself. *Gothic* architects, taking advantage of growing engineering expertise, built soaring church spires and massive, arched windows. While their work focused on the creation of churches and great cathedrals, some civic buildings and palaces also picked up the Gothic motif. The Gothic was one of the three main architectural styles (the others being the earlier classical and the later modern) developed in Western culture. It is not far-fetched to see the Gothic style as representative of Western postclassical culture more generally. Its spiritual orientation showed in the towers cast up to the heavens. It built also on growing technical skills and deep popular devotion, expressed by the monies collected to build the huge monuments as well as the patient labor required for construction that often lasted many decades. The originality of the Gothic reflected the growing Western ability to find suitable new means of expression, just as the Gothic heritage in the later Western world showed the ongoing power of medieval models.

Medieval literature and music reflected strong religious interests. Most Latin writing dealt with points of philosophy, law, or political theory. There was little concern for stylistic niceties for their own sake. However, alongside writing in Latin came the development of a growing literature in the spoken languages, or vernaculars, of western Europe. The pattern was not unlike that of India a few centuries earlier after the fall of the Gupta empire, when Sanskrit served as a scholarly language but increasing power was given to popular languages such as Hindi. Several oral sagas, dealing with the deeds of great knights and mythic figures in the past, were written down. From this tradition came the first known writing in early English, *Beowulf*, and in French, *The Song of Roland.* Late in the Middle Ages, a number of writers created adventure stories, comic tales, and poetry in the vernacular tongues, such as Chaucer's *Canterbury Tales.* Much of their work, and also plays written for performance in the growing cities, reflected the tension between Christian values and a desire to portray the richness and coarseness of life on this earth. Chaucer's narrative thus shows a fascination with bawdy behavior, a willingness to poke fun at the hypocrisy of many Christians, and an ability to capture some of the tragedies of human existence. In France, a long poem, called *The Romance of the Rose,* used vivid sexual imagery, and the poet Villon wrote, in largely secular terms, of the terror and poignancy of death. Finally, again in vernacular language, a series of courtly poets, or troubadours, based particularly in southern France in the 14th century, wrote hymns to the love that could flourish between men and women. While their verses stressed platonic devotion rather than sexual love and paid homage to courtly ceremonies and polite behavior, their concern with love was the first sign of a new valuation of this emotional experience in the Western tradition.

Medieval intellectual and artistic life, in sum, created a host of important themes. Religion served as the centerpiece, but it did not prevent a growing range of interests—from science to romantic poetry. Medieval culture was a rich intellectual achievement in its own right. It also set in motion a series of developments—in rationalist philosophy, science, artistic representations of nature, and vernacular literature—that would serve as building blocks for later Western thought and art.

CHANGING VALUES IN THE POSTCLASSICAL CENTURIES

Focal Point: With the revival of trade and agriculture, commercial ties spread through most of western Europe. Urban merchants gained unusual power, but early capitalism was disputed by the different economic values of the guilds.

While culture provided the most obvious cement for Western society during the medieval centuries, framed of course by the institutional sweep of the Catholic church, common features also described economic activity and social structure. Here too, the postclassical West demonstrated impressive powers of innovation, for the hold of classical patterns was slight. As trade revived by the 10th century, the West became something of a common commercial zone. Most regions produced primarily for local consumption, as was true in agricultural societies generally. But Italian merchants actively sought cloth manufactured in the Low Countries, and merchants in many areas traded for wool grown in England or timber supplies and furs brought from Scandinavia and the Baltic lands. Great ports and trading fairs, particularly in the Low Countries and northern France, served as centers for Western exchange as well as markets for a few exotic products such as spices brought in from other civilizations.

New Strains in Rural Life

The improvements in agriculture after 800 C.E. brought important new ingredients to rural life. Some peasants were able to shake off the most severe constraints of manorialism, becoming almost free farmers with only a few obligations to their landlords, though rigid manorialism remained in place in many areas. Noble landlords still served mainly military functions, for ownership of a horse and armor were prerequisites for fighting until the end of the medieval period. But while most nobles shunned the taint of commerce—like aristocrats in many societies, they found too much money-grubbing demeaning—they did use trade to improve their standard of living and adopt more polished habits. The courtly literature of the late Middle Ages reflected this new style of life.

As many lords sought improved conditions they were often tempted to press their serfs to pay higher rents and taxes—even as serfs themselves were gaining a new sense of freedom and control over their own land. This tension produced, from the late Middle Ages until the 19th century, a recurrent series of peasant–landlord battles in Western society. Peasants sought what they viewed as their natural and traditional right to the land, free and clear of any exactions. They talked of Christian equality, turning such phrases as "When Adam delved and Eve span, Who was then a gentleman?" A more complex economy clearly brought new social strains, not totally unlike the recurrent wave of popular unrest in China or the rural risings in the Middle East, where religion helped prompt egalitarian sentiments as well.

Yet, on the whole, the condition of Western peasants improved during the most dynamic part of the Middle Ages. Landlord controls were less tight than they had become in other societies, such as the Middle East. Western agriculture was not yet particularly advanced technologically, compared for example with East Asia, but it had improved notably over early medieval levels and also surpassed the productivity of the classical Mediterranean world.

Growth of Trade and Banking

Gains in agriculture, of course, promoted larger changes in medieval economic life. Urban growth allowed more specialized manufacturing and commercial activities, which in turn promoted still greater trade. Spearheaded by Italian businessmen, banking was introduced to the West to facilitate the long-distance exchange of money and goods. The use of money spread steadily, to the dismay of many Christian moralists and many ordinary people who preferred the more direct, personal ways of traditional society. The largest trading and banking operations, not only in Italy but in southern Germany, the Low Countries, France, and Britain, were clearly capitalistic. Big merchants invested funds in trading ships and the goods they carried, hoping to make large profits on this capital. Profit making was not judged kindly by Christian thinkers like Thomas Aquinas, who urged that all prices should be "just," reflecting only the labor put into the good; but it clearly, sometimes avidly, occurred.

Rising trade took several forms. There were exchanges between western Europe and other parts of the known world. Wealthy Europeans developed a taste for some of the spices and luxury goods of Asia; the Crusades played a role in bringing these products to wider attention. A Mediterranean trade redeveloped, mainly in the hands of Italian merchants, in which European cloth and some other products were exchanged for the more polished goods of the East. Commerce within Europe involved exchanges of timber and grain from the north for cloth and metal products manufactured in Italy and the Low Countries. England, at first an exporter of raw wool, developed some manufactured goods for exchange by the later Middle Ages. Commercial alliances developed. Cities in northern Germany and southern Scandinavia grouped together in the *Hanseatic League* to encourage trade. With growing banking facilities, it became possible to organize commercial transactions throughout much of western Europe. Bankers, including many Jewish businessmen, were valued for their service in lending money to monarchs and the papacy.

The growth of trade and banking in the Middle Ages served as the genesis of capitalism in Western civilization. The greater Italian and German bankers, the long-distance merchants of the Hanseatic cities, were clearly capitalistic in their willingness to invest considerable sums of money in trading ventures with the expectation of substantial profit. Given the continued dangers of trade by land and sea, the risks in these investments were substantial, but profits of up to 100 percent or more were also possible. In many cities, such as London, groups of powerful merchants banded together to invest in international trade, each buying shares in the venture and profiting or losing accordingly.

This was not, by world standards, a totally unprecedented merchant spirit. European traders were still less venturesome and less wealthy than some of their Muslim counterparts. Nor was Western society yet as tolerant of merchants as Muslim or Indian societies were. Yet, Western commercial endeavors were clearly gaining in dynamism. Because Western governments were weak, with few economic functions, merchants had a freer hand than in many other civilizations. Many of the growing cities, in particular, were ruled by commercial leagues. Monarchs liked to encourage the cities as a counterbalance to the power of the landed aristocracy, and in the later Middle Ages and beyond, traders and kings were typically allied. However, aside from taxing merchants and using them as sources of loans, royal governments did not interfere extensively with trading activities. Merchants even developed their own codes of commercial law, administered by city courts. Thus, the rising merchant class, though not unusual in strength or venturesomeness, was staking out an unusually powerful and independent role in European society.

Capitalism was not yet typical of the Western economy, even aside from the moral qualms fostered by the Christian tradition. Most peasants and landlords had not become enmeshed in a market system. In the cities, the dominant economic ethic stressed group protection, not untrammeled profit seeking. The characteristic institution was not the international trading firm but the merchant or artisan guild. *Guilds* grouped people in the same business or trade in a single city, sometimes with loose links to similar guilds in other cities. These organizations were new in western Europe, though they resembled guilds in various parts of Asia but with greater independence from the state. They stressed security and mutual control. Merchant guilds thus attempted to as-

CLOSEUP

Jacques Coeur

Jacques Coeur (c. 1395–1456) was one of the most extraordinary merchants in Europe. His father was a furrier. Jacques married well, to the daughter of a royal official. For a time he was a tax official, but he was caught minting adulterated coins. Then he founded a trading company that began to compete with Italians and Spaniards in dealing with the Middle East. He visited Damascus to buy spices; shipwrecked on the way home, he had to be ransomed. But he set up a regular trade in rugs, Chinese silk, and Indonesian spices and sugar. He also became a financial advisor and supplier to the French king and was ennobled. With the largest fleet ever owned by a French subject, Jacques Coeur surrounded himself with splendor, even arranging with the pope for his 16-year-old son to become an archbishop. But he also had enemies, many of them nobles in debt to him, and they turned the king against him. He was tortured, and admitted to various crimes (including sup-

plying arms to Muslims). His property was confiscated, and he died on a Greek island, serving in a papal fleet against the Turks.

sure all members a share in any endeavor. If a ship pulled in loaded with wool, the clothiers' guild of the city insisted that all members participate in the purchasing so that no one member would monopolize the profits.

Artisan guilds were composed of the people in the cities who actually made cloth, bread, jewelry, or furniture. These guilds tried to limit their membership so that all members would be assured of work. They regulated apprenticeships to guarantee good training but also to make sure that no member would employ too many apprentices and so gain undue wealth. They discouraged new methods because security and a rough equality, not maximum individual profit, were the goals; here was their alternative to the capitalistic approach. Guilds also tried to guarantee good workmanship so that consumers would not have to worry about shoddy quality on the part of some unscrupulous profit-seeker. Guilds played an important political and social role in the cities, assuring their members of recognized status and often a voice in city government. Their statutes were in turn upheld by municipal law and were often backed by the royal government as well.

Despite the traditionalism and security-mindedness of the guilds, manufacturing as well as commercial methods improved in medieval Europe. Western Europe was not yet as advanced as Asia in ironmaking and textile manufacture, but it was beginning to catch up. In a few areas, such as clockmaking—which involved both sophisticated technology and an interesting concern for precise time—European artisans in fact had forged a world lead. Furthermore, some manufacturing spilled beyond the bounds of guild control. Particularly in the Low Countries and parts of Italy, groups of manufacturing workers were employed by capitalists to produce for a wide market. Their techniques were simple, and they worked in their own homes, often alternating manufacturing labor with agriculture. Their work was regulated not by the motives of the guilds but by the inducements of merchant capitalists, who provided them with raw materials and then paid them for their production.

The simple fact was that by the later Middle Ages, western Europe's economy and society embraced many contradictory groups and principles. Commercial and capitalist elements jostled against the slower pace of eco-

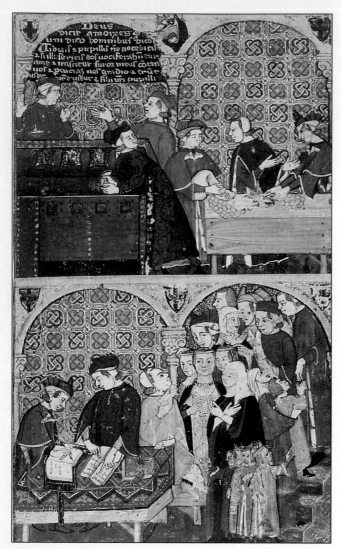

This 14th-century miniature shows views of a banking house.

Limited Sphere for Women

The increasing complexity of medieval social and economic life may have had one final effect, which is familiar from patterns in other agricultural societies: setting new limits on the conditions of women. Women's work, of course, remained vital in most families. The Christian emphasis on the equality of all souls, and the practical importance of monastic groups organized for women, giving some an alternative to marriage, continued to offer distinctive features for women's lives in Western society. The veneration of Mary and other female religious figures gave women real cultural prestige, counterbalancing the Biblical emphasis on Eve as the source of human sin. In some respects, women in the West had higher status than their sisters under Islam: They were less segregated in religious services (though they could not lead them) and were less confined to the household. Still, women's effective voice in the family may have declined in the Middle Ages. Urban women often played important roles in local commerce and even operated some craft guilds, but they found themselves increasingly hemmed in by male-dominated organizations. By the late Middle Ages, a literature arose that stressed women's roles as the assistants and comforters to men, listing supplemental household tasks and docile virtues as women's distinctive sphere. Patriarchal structures seemed to be taking deeper root.

POLITICAL VALUES OF THE MIDDLE AGES

Focal Point: While monarchical power grew, in some specific ways Western political institutions imposed a number of limits on the central state. A medieval version of parliament was a lasting contribution of this period in Western history.

The key values and tensions of medieval society and culture were expressed in characteristic styles and institutions: the Gothic cathedral, the scholastic *Summas,* the manors, and the guilds. Medieval politics produced a similar summary expression in the feudal monarchy as it flowered during the High Middle Ages.

The postclassical West developed implicit political principles that were carried over, though also modified, when more sophisticated government structures began to emerge with the rise of monarchies. Principle number one, clearly articulated in Church writings, held that laws of God were superior to those of humans. The

nomic life in the countryside and even against the dominant group protectionism of most urban guilds. Most people remained peasants, but a minority had escaped to the cities, where they found more excitement—though also increased danger and higher rates of disease. Medieval tradition held that a serf who managed to live in the city for a year and a day became a free person. A few prosperous capitalists flourished, but most people operated according to quite different economic values, directed toward group welfare rather than individual profit. This was neither a static society nor an early model of a modern commercial society. It had its own flavor and its own tensions—the fruit of several centuries of economic and social change.

DOCUMENT

Changing Roles for Women

A late 14th-century Parisian manual entitled *The Good Wife* revealed the kind of thinking about gender that became more pronounced as medieval society developed in the West. It invites comparison with patriarchal views you have studied in other agricultural civilizations. Is any room left for initiatives by women?

Wherefore I counsel you to make such cheer to your husband at all his comings and stayings, and to persevere therein; and also be peaceable with him, and remember the rustic proverb, which saith that there be three things which drive the goodman from home, to wit, a leaking roof, a smoky chimney, and a scolding woman. And therefore, fair sister, I beseech you that you keep yourself in the love and good favour of your husband, you be unto him gentle, and amiable, and debonair. Do unto him what the good simple women of our country say hath been done to their sons, when these have set their love elsewhere and their mothers cannot wean them therefrom.

Wherefore, dear sister, I beseech you thus to bewitch and bewitch again your husband that shall be, and beware of roofless house and of smoky fire, and scold him not, but be unto him gentle and amiable and peaceable. Have a care that in winter he have a good fire and smokeless and let him rest well and be well covered between your breasts, and thus bewitch him. . . .

And thus shall you preserve and keep your husband from all discomforts and give him all the comforts whereof you can bethink you, and serve him and have him served in your house, and you shall look to him for outside things, for if he be good he will take even more pains and labour therein than you wish, and by doing what I have said, you will cause him ever to miss you and have his heart with you and your loving service and he will shun all other houses, all other women, all other services and households.

Questions: Is this a distinctively "Christian" view of women? How does it compare with Muslim or Chinese views of women in the postclassical period? Why might postclassical values have become more rigorous in the late medieval centuries in the West?

Church, as an instrument of God, was separate from the state and in some ways above it, even though in the rough and tumble of actual medieval politics, secular rulers often seized the upper hand. Principle number two involved the ineradicable local and regional divisions. Effective imperial governments could not be formed, as the collapse of Charlemagne's empire demonstrated; the West would be politically divided. Even regional governments had to recognize the strength of the local interests and power clusters. Principle number three, closely related to the impediments to centralization, involved the values embodied in feudalism. Feudal bonds—the relationships between lords and vassals—stressed mutuality. Each party in the relationship should contribute, each should gain. Vassals received protection and, usually, land (the fief or *feudum*, from which feudalism took its name) from their lord; lords won some payments, military service, and loyalty from their vassals. While feudalism permitted hierarchy among lords, it did not permit, at least in theory, unilat-

eral assertions of power. It also encouraged mutual consultation. Vassals were supposed to advise their lords on judicial matters or issues of policy; lords were supposed to consult their vassals rather than acting arbitrarily.

Monarchy and Its Limits

The new ingredient in medieval politics, as medieval society developed greater vigor from the 10th century onward, was of course the growth of royal power (or in some regions, such as much of present-day Belgium, ducal power). Here the key steps are in many ways familiar, for they duplicated, unwittingly, the centralization principles developed earlier and more extensively in China and elsewhere. Medieval kings followed particular patterns of alliances and gradual aggrandizement because of their initially weak positions, and important specific events were involved, such as the Norman Conquest of England. Centralization is centralization, however, and though often reinvented, it has some standard features.

Thus, as they began to expand their resources and aspirations, medieval kings developed small armies of their own, paid for by lands under their direct control, and they ventured a small central bureaucracy. Often they chose urban business or professional people to serve in this bureaucracy, partly because such people had expertise in financial matters and partly because they unlike the aristocracy, would owe allegiance to the crown alone. French and English monarchs began to introduce bureaucratic specialties, so that some of their ministers would handle justice, others finance, and still others military matters. They found ways to send centrally appointed emissaries to the provinces to supervise tax collection and the administration of justice. It was in this vein that English kings, from the Norman Conquest onward, appointed local sheriffs to oversee the administration of justice. None of these activities gave the monarchs extensive contacts with ordinary subjects; for most people, effective governments were still local. Once the principle of central control was established, however, steady growth of state-sponsored rule followed. By the end of the Middle Ages, monarchs were gaining the right to tax their subjects directly, and they were beginning to recruit professional armies instead of relying solely on an aristocratic cavalry whose loyalties depended on feudal bonds or alliances. Several medieval kings, such as Louis IX in France, also gained solid reputations as lawgivers, which allowed a gradual centralization of legal codes and court systems. The rediscovery of Roman law in countries like France encouraged this effort toward centralization.

Feudal monarchy was always a delicately balanced institution, of which the central government formed only one of the key ingredients. The power of the Church served to check royal ambitions. As we have seen, the Church could often win in a clash with the state by excommunicating rulers and thus threatening to turn the loyalties of the population against them. Although the Church entered a period of decline at the end of the Middle Ages, the principle was rather clearly established that there were areas of belief and morality not open to manipulation by the state.

The second limitation on the royal families came from the traditions of feudalism and from the landed aristocracy as a powerful class. Aristocrats tended to resist too much monarchical control in the West, and they had the strength to make their objections heard. These aristocrats, even when vassals of the king, had their own economic base and their own military force—sometimes, in the case of great nobles, they had an army greater than that of the king. The growth of the monarchy cut into aristocratic power, but this led to new statements of the limits of kings. In 1215, the unpopular English King John faced opposition to his taxation measures from an alliance of nobles, townspeople, and church officials. Defeated in his war with France and then forced down by the leading English lords, John was compelled to sign the Great Charter, or *Magna Carta*, which confirmed basically feudal rights against monarchical claims. John promised to observe restraint in his dealings with the nobles and the Church, agreeing, for example, not to institute new taxes without the lords' permission or to appoint bishops without the Church's permission. A few modern-sounding references to the general rights of the English people against the state that were included in the Magna Carta largely served to show where the feudal idea of mutual limits and obligations between rulers and ruled could later expand.

This same feudal balance led, late in the 13th century, to the creation of *parliaments* as bodies representing not individual voters but privileged groups such as the nobles and the Church. (Even earlier, in 1000, the regional kingdom of Catalonia created a parliament.) The first full English parliament convened in 1265, with the House of Lords representing the nobles and the church hierarchy, and the Commons made up of elected representatives from wealthy citizens of the towns. The parliament institutionalized the feudal principle that monarchs should consult with their vassals. In particular, parliaments gained the right to rule on any proposed changes in taxation; through this power, they could also advise the crown on other policy issues. While the parliamentary tradition became strongest in England, similar institutions arose in France, Spain, Scandinavia, and several of the regional governments in Germany. Here too, parliaments represented the key *three estates*: Church, nobles, and urban leaders. They were not widely elected.

Feudal government was not modern government. People had rights according to the estate into which they were born; nobles transmitted membership in their estate to their children. There was no general concept of citizenship and no democracy. Thus, parliaments represented only a minority, and even this minority only in terms of the three or four estates voting as units (nobles, clergy, urban merchants, and sometimes wealthy peasants), not some generalized collection of voters. Still, by creating a concept of limited government and some hint of representative institutions, Western feudal monarchy produced the beginnings of a distinctive political tradition. This tradition differed from the political results of Japanese feudalism, which emphasized group loyalty more than checks on central power.

Western Europe Toward the End of the Middle Ages, c. 1360 C.E.

THE DECLINE OF THE MEDIEVAL SYNTHESIS

Focal Point: Amid new problems of overpopulation and disease, the postclassical version of Western civilization declined after 1300. This decline was evident in the feudal aristocracy, the church, and theology.

After about 1300, some of the characteristics of medieval life at its height began to give way. One problem, both a symptom and a cause of larger issues, was the major war that engulfed France and England during the 14th and 15th centuries. The Hundred Years' War, which sputtered into the mid-15th century, lasted even longer than its name and initially went very badly for France—a sign of new weakness in the French monar-

chy. Not very bloody, the war nevertheless consumed precious resources, brought confusion to key medieval centers in France, and ultimately demonstrated the futility of some of the military and organizational methods attached to feudalism. As the war dragged on, kings reduced their reliance on the prancing forces of the nobility in favor of paid armies of their own. New military methods challenged the key monopoly of the feudal lords, as ordinary paid archers learned how to unseat armored knights with powerful bows and arrows and with crossbows. The war ended with a French victory, sparked in part by the heroic leadership of the inspired peasant woman Joan of Arc, but both its devastation and the antifeudal innovations it encouraged suggested a time of change.

Concurrently, from about 1300 onward, key sources

Burying plague victims in coffins at Tournai before mass burial became the only way to keep up with the deaths.

of Western vitality threatened to disappear. Medieval agriculture could no longer keep pace with population growth; the readily available new lands had been used up, and there were no major new technological gains to compensate. The result included severe famines and an actual decline in population levels until the end of the century. A devastating series of plagues that persisted for several centuries, beginning with the *Black Death* in 1348, further challenged Europe's population and social structure. The West's economy did not go into a tail-spin; in some respects, as in manufacturing technology, progress may even have sped up. Again, the contours were novel. The 150 to 200 years after 1300 form in Western history something of a transition period in which the features of the Middle Ages began to blur while new problems and developments began to take center stage. Western civilization was not in a spiral of decline as a result, but the postclassical version of this civilization was.

Signs of Strain

The decline of medieval society after about 1300 had two facets. The first was that several sources of vigor that had sustained a varied culture and political life during the High Middle Ages stagnated or even changed course. The downward population trends showed the limits of Western resources at this point. Plagues cut into the labor force. Ironically, as the West developed new international contacts it became more vulnerable to epi-

demic disease. New social disputes arose, heightening some of the tensions noted earlier between peasants and landlords, artisans and their employees. Not until the 16th century would the West begin to work out a new social structure.

The second aspect of decline involved the increasing challenges to—or compromises of—several typical medieval institutions. Here decline was not absolute but rather a sign of change, as Western society began to shed part of its earlier skin only to emerge, with renewed dynamism, in somewhat different garb by the middle of the 15th century. The fading of medievalism showed in many key areas, three of which we will present here.

During the 14th century, the ruling class of medieval society, the landowning aristocracy, began to show signs of confusion of function. It had long staked its claim to power on its control of much of the land and also on its military prowess, but its skill in warfare was now open to question. The growth of professional armies and new weaponry—such as the crossbow and, by the 15th century, the cannon and gunpowder—made traditional fighting methods, including fortified castles, increasingly irrelevant. The aristocracy did not, as a result, simply disappear. Rather, the nobility chose to emphasize a rich ceremonial style of life, featuring tournaments in which military expertise could be turned into competitive games. The spread of courtly love poems signaled another new interest in a more refined culture. The idea of chivalry—carefully controlled, polite behavior, including behavior toward women—gained ground.

In the Hundred Years' War, English archers fought France's feudal cavalry—this was the beginning of the end of feudal warfare in Europe. This 14th-century battle of Crécy was a resounding defeat for France's noble army, though it outnumbered the English army.

This was a potentially fruitful development of increased cultivation among the upper class. We have seen similar transformations in dealing with earlier changes in the Chinese and Muslim aristocracy. Yet, at the time of transition in the West, some of the elaborate ceremonies of chivalry seemed rather hollow, even a bit silly—a sign that medieval values were losing hold, without being replaced by a new set of purposes.

Another key area involved decisive shifts in the balance between church and state that had characterized medieval life. For several decades in the aftermath of the taxation disputes in the early 14th century, French kings wielded great influence on the papacy, which they relocated from Rome to Avignon, a town surrounded by French territory. Then, rival claimants to the papacy confused the issue further. Ultimately a single pope was returned to Rome, but the Church was clearly weakened. Moreover, the Church began to lose some of its grip over Western religious life. Church leaders were so preoccupied with their political involvement that they tended to neglect the spiritual side. Religion was not declining; indeed, signs of intense popular piety continued to blossom, and new religious groups formed in the towns. But devotion became partially separated from the institution of the Church. One result, again beginning from the 14th century, was a series of popular heresies, with leaders in places like England and Bohemia preaching against the hierarchical apparatus of the Church in favor of direct popular experience of God. Another result was an important new series of mystics, many of them women, who claimed direct, highly emotional contacts with God.

A third area in which medievalism faded was the breaking down of the intellectual and even artistic synthesis. After the work of Aquinas, the sterile philosophical pursuits of the later scholastics seemed petty. Church officials became less tolerant of intellectual daring, and they even declared some of Aquinas's writings heretical. The earlier blend of rationalism and religion no longer seemed feasible. Ultimately, this would turn some thinkers away from religion, but this daring development took time to coalesce. In art, growing interest in realistic portrayals of nature, though fruitful, suggested the beginnings of a shift away from medieval artistic standards. Some medieval artistic styles became trite—a symptom of waning creativity. The various constraints on forms of postclassical culture prompted many Western intellectuals to look for different emphases. In Italy most clearly, new kinds of literature and art took shape that differed from the styles and subjects of the postclassical centuries.

CONCLUSION

The Postclassical West and Its Heritage: A Balance Sheet

The term *Middle Ages* long suggested a rather unpleasant, backward period in Western history between the glories of classical Greece and Rome and the return of vigorous civilization in the 15th century. In this view, the Middle Ages might be regarded as an unfortunate interlude in which Westerners were dominated by poverty and superstition, pulled away from mainstream Western values. Western leaders might be given credit for keeping a few classical ideals alive, copying documents and venerating the glories of the past, but for little else.

The harsh view of the Middle Ages is not entirely wrong, though it neglects the extent to which much activity centered in parts of Europe that had never before been integrated into a major civilization and therefore were building appropriate institutions and culture for the first time. Postclassical Europe was backward in some re-

spects, even at its height. It did not participate in world contacts as an equal to the great Asian societies. The Middle Ages was not simply an awkward interlude in Western history, however. It had a formative force of its own.

In culture, medieval thinkers did recapture and repackage key elements of the classical heritage, particularly in their view of humanity's rational powers and their definition of reason in terms of logic. By linking classical rationalism with a strong belief in a divine plan, they may indeed have advanced the idea of a fundamentally orderly universe and so set the stage for further advances in rationalistic scientific thought. Stylistically, medieval artists did not mainly work in classical modes, and their contributions added important ingredients to the larger cultural heritage. William Shakespeare, for example, writing in the later 16th century, borrowed freely from Greek literary themes, but he owed still more to the earthy popular drama that began in the Middle Ages.

In politics, the Middle Ages largely bypassed the classical heritage despite a few longings for empire and the important usage of principles of Roman law. The most characteristic institutions were built on the Church and feudalism, and their bequest to later Western political developments was almost certainly greater than that of Greece or Rome. Medieval politics did not, of course, take the final Western form, but in ideas of higher law and in the parliamentary restraints on central government, they did prefigure values and institutions that have had enduring impact in the West. Similarly, medieval economics, with the new interest in merchant life and technical innovation that developed by the 10th century, set a much more direct stage for subsequent Western developments than classical economic patterns had done. Here, too, medieval patterns were quite different from their Greek and Roman analogues, as was evident from the greater prestige of merchants and the absence of extensive slavery.

The Middle Ages, in sum, created its own culture, relying only in part on earlier classical models. Preservation of classical patterns was important, and Western leaders would later select a larger number of Greek and Roman ingredients to challenge certain medieval impulses. Medieval precedents would remain strong as well, even for periods in which Western pacesetters professed to scorn the Middle Ages. One world historian has suggested that a key historical source of Western vitality in more modern centuries has been the ability to select from a quite diverse set of pasts, rather than building, Chinese fashion, upon more unified traditions. Certainly, the Middle Ages contributed greatly to the range of options available for later Western development, even as specifically medieval syntheses began to come apart by the 14th century.

Postclassical Europe can also be compared with other societies in several developmental respects. Over time, growing complexity brought tensions between the merchant spirit and older agricultural values, which other civilizations had faced before; it also brought some familiar changes in the conditions of women. Conversion to Christianity had features that resembled conversion to Islam elsewhere, though Christian religious institutions differed considerably from Muslim institutions. Christian and Muslim thinkers shared problems in coming to terms with other intellectual traditions, though ultimately the balance struck turned out to differ. On another front, as feudal monarchies developed more specialized bureaucracies they unwittingly duplicated elements pioneered much earlier by Chinese rulers, and they copied contemporary bureaucracies they learned about in the Byzantine Empire and Muslim Spain.

The most important comparisons involve juxtaposing western Europe with other areas where civilization was partially novel in this period and where change was correspondingly rapid. Divided political rule in Europe resembled conditions in African regions and, even more obviously, in Japan, the only other feudal society in this period. Rapidly growing trade and an orientation toward richer, more established centers was another common feature, shared also with Russia's north–south links. The West's contact levels were higher than those of most of sub-Saharan Africa, however, and its expansionist interests—witness the Crusades—were much greater than Japan's. Again, the postclassical West constituted a type of civilization with many similarities to other emerging regions but with its own distinctive combinations, including aggressive interest in the wider world.

FURTHER READINGS

For the Middle Ages generally, Joseph Strayer's *Western Europe in the Middle Ages* (1982) is a fine survey with an extensive bibliography. Key topics are covered in R. S. Lopez's *The Commercial Revolution of the Middle Ages, 950–1350* (1976) and C. H. Lawrence's *Medieval Monasticism: Forms of Religious Life in Western Europe in the Middle Ages* (1984). National histories are important for the period, particularly on political life: see J. W. Baldwin's *The Government of Philip Augustus: Foundations of French Royal Power in the Middle Ages* (1986), G. Barraclough's *The Origins of Modern Germany* (1984), and M. Chibnall's *Anglo-Norman England, 1066–1166* (1986).

Social history has dominated much recent research on the period. See P. Ariès and G. Duby, eds., *A History of Private Life*, vol. 2 (1984) and Barbara Hanawalt's *The Ties That Bound: Peasant Families in Medieval England* (1986) for important orientation in this area. David Herlihy's *Medieval Households* (1985) is a vital contribution, as is J. Chapelot's and R. Fossier's *The Village and House in the Middle Ages* (1985). J. Kirshner and S. F. Wemple, eds., *Women of the Medieval World* (1985) is a good collection. On tensions in popular religion, see C. Bynum's *Jesus as Mother: Studies in the Spirituality of the High Middle Ages* (1982) and L. Little's *Religious Poverty and the Profit Economy in Medieval Europe* (1978). A highly readable account of medieval life is E. Leroy Ladurie's *Montaillou: The Promised Land of Error* (1979).

Several excellent studies take up the theme of technological change: J. Gimpel's *The Medieval Machine: The Industrial Revolution of the Middle Ages* (1977); Lynn White, Jr.'s *Medieval Technology and Social Change* (1962); and David Landes's *Revolution in Time: Clocks and the Making of the Modern World* (1985).

On intellectual and artistic life, E. Gilson's *History of Christian Philosophy in the Middle Ages* (1954) is a brilliant sketch, while his *Reason and Revelation* (1956) focuses on key intellectual issues of the age. S. C. Ferruolo's *The Origins of the University* (1985) and N. Pevsner's *An Outline of European Architecture* (1963) deal with other important features; see also H. Berman's *Law and Revolution: The Formation of the Western Legal Tradition* (1983). An intriguing classic, focused primarily on culture, is J. Huizinga's *The Waning of the Middle Ages* (1973).

17

The Americas on the Eve of Invasion

MESOAMERICA		1200–1500 Mississippian culture flourishes
	1000 Toltec conquest of Chichén Itzá and influence in Yucatan	
		1150 Fall of Tula, disintegration of Toltec Empire
	968 Tula established by Toltecs	
ANDEAN WORLD	900–1465 Chimor Empire based on Chan Chan on north coast	
	900 End of Intermediate Horizon and decline of Tihuanaco and Huari	
	900 C.E.	1150 C.E.

INTRODUCTION

During the postclassic period, societies in the Americas remained entirely separate from those of the Old World. Some displayed features similar to the great centers of Asia and the Mediterranean in that they were able to build on earlier precedents from the classic period. Thus, Mesoamerican civilizations formed large cities, based on elaborate political and economic organization, that would later dazzle European intruders much as Constantinople or the great cities of China did. But these similarities were accidental, and they were outweighed by the vast differences that resulted from American isolation.

As in the classical centuries, American societies continued to display extraordinary diversity. Other continuities marked the pre-Columbian experience up to the year of Columbus's arrival and indeed beyond. Great American civilizations were marked by elaborate cultural systems and a highly developed agriculture, yielding a distinctive array of foods. The postclassic period saw significant changes in the Americas also, particularly in the increasingly extensive organization of agriculture and in the people's ability to form larger political units.

By 1500, the Americas were densely populated in many places by Indian peoples long indigenous to the New World. The term *Indian* is, of course, a misnomer created by Columbus when he thought he had reached the Indies, but the label is also somewhat misleading because it implies a certain recognition of commonality among the peoples of the Americas that did not exist until after the arrival of Europeans. *Indian* as a term to describe all the peoples of the Americas could have a meaning only when there were non-Indians to apply it. Still, the term has been used for so long—and is still in use by many Native Americans today—that we will continue to use it.

As should already be clear, there were many Indian peoples with a vast array of cultural achievements. This variety of cultural patterns and ways of life of pre-Columbian civilizations prohibits a detailed discussion of each, but we can concentrate our attention on a few areas where major civilizations developed, based on earlier achievements. By concentrating on these regions we can demonstrate the continuity of civilization in the Americas. We shall examine in some detail Mesoamerica, especially central Mexico, and the Andean heartland. In both these areas great imperial states were in place when European expansion brought them into direct and continual contact with the Old World. We shall also discuss in less detail a few areas influenced by the centers of civilization—and some whose development seems to have been independent of them—in order to provide an overview of the Americas on the eve of invasion.

POSTCLASSIC MESOAMERICA, 1000–1500 C.E.

Focal Point: Chief among the civilizations that followed the collapse of Teotihuacan and the abandonment of the classical Maya cities in the 8th century C.E. were the Toltecs and later the Aztecs, who built on the achievements of their classic predecessors but rarely surpassed them except in the areas of political and military organization. The Toltecs created a large empire whose influence extended far beyond central Mexico. In the 15th century, the Aztecs rose from humble beginnings to create an extensive empire organized for war, motivated by fervent religious zeal, and based on a firm agrarian base.

As noted in Chapter 9, the collapse of Teotihuacan in central Mexico and the abandonment of the classical

---

1325 Aztecs established in central Mexico; Tenochtitlan founded

1434–1472 Rule of Nezhualcoyotl at Texcoco

1502–1520 Moctezuma II

1434 Creation of triple alliance **1440–1469** Moctezuma I

1471–1493 Inca Topac Yupanqui increases areas under control

1434–1471 Great expansion under Inca Pachacuti

1350 Incas established in Cuzco area

1493–1527 Huayna Capac expands into Ecuador; his death results in civil war

1438 Incas dominate Cuzco and southern highlands

1300 C.E.

1450 C.E.

Maya cities in the 8th century C.E. signaled a significant political and cultural change in Mesoamerica.

In central Mexico, nomadic peoples from beyond the northern frontier of the sedentary agricultural area took advantage of the political vacuum to move into the richer lands. Among these peoples were the *Toltecs,* who established a capital at Tula in about 968. They adopted many cultural features from the sedentary peoples and added to them a strongly militaristic ethic. This included the cult of sacrifice and war that is often portrayed in Toltec art. Later Mesoamerican peoples, such as the *Aztecs,* had some historical memory of the Toltecs and thought of them as culture heroes, the givers of civilization. Thus, being able to trace one's lineage back to the Toltecs later became a highly prized pedigree. The archeological record, however, indicates that Toltec accomplishments were often fused or confused with those of Teotihuacan in the memory of the Toltec's successors.

The Toltec Heritage

Among the legends that survived about the Toltecs were those of *Topiltzin,* a Toltec leader and apparently a priest dedicated to the god *Quetzalcoatl* (the Feathered Serpent), who later became confused with the god himself in the legends. Apparently, Topiltzin, a religious reformer, was involved in a struggle for priestly or political power with another faction. When he lost, Topiltzin and his followers went into exile, promising to return in the future to claim his throne on the same date according to the cyclical calendar system. Supposedly, Topiltzin and his followers sailed for Yucatan; there is considerable evidence of Toltec influence in that region. The legend of Topiltzin-Quetzalcoatl was well known to the Aztecs and may have influenced their response when the Europeans later arrived.

The Toltecs created an empire that extended over much of central Mexico, and their influence spread far beyond the region. About 1000 C.E., *Chichén Itzá* in Yucatan was conquered by Toltec warriors, and it and several other cities were then ruled for a long time by central Mexican dynasties or by Maya rulers under Toltec influence. Some Maya states in Guatemala, such as the Quiché kingdom, also had Toltecized ruling families.

Toltec influence spread northward as well. Obsidian mines were exploited in northern Mexico, and the Toltecs may have traded for turquoise in the American Southwest. It has been suggested that the great Anasazi adobe town at Chaco Canyon in New Mexico was abandoned when the Toltec Empire fell and the trade in local turquoise ended.

How far eastward that influence spread is a matter of dispute. Was there contact between Mesoamerica and

The Toltec political and cultural influence spread from its capital at Tula in northern Mexico (shown here) to places as far south as Chichén Itzá in Yucatan.

the elaborate culture and concentrated towns of the Hopewell peoples of the Ohio and Mississippi valleys, discussed in Chapter 9? Scholars disagree. Eventually, in the lower Mississippi valley from about 700 C.E., elements of Hopewell culture seem to have been enriched by external contact—perhaps with Mexico. This Mississippian culture, which flourished between 1200 and 1500 C.E., was based on maize and bean agriculture. Towns, usually located along rivers, had stepped temples made of earth, and sometimes large burial mounds. Some of the burials include well-produced pottery and other goods and seem to be accompanied by ritual executions or sacrifices of servants or wives. This indicates social stratification in the society. Cahokia, near East St. Louis, Illinois, covered 5 square miles and may have had over 30,000 people in and around its center. Its largest earthen pyramid, called Monk's Mound, covers 15 acres and is comparable in size to the largest pyramids of the classic period in Mexico. Many of these cultural features seem to suggest contact with Mesoamerica, although no definitely Mexican object has been found in a Mississippian site. Still, certain artistic traits and subjects, including the feathered serpent, strongly suggest contact.

The Aztec Rise to Power

The Toltec Empire lasted until about 1150, at which time it was apparently destroyed by nomadic invaders from the north, who also seem to have sacked Tula about that date. After the fall of Tula, the center of population and political power in central Mexico shifted to the valley of Mexico and especially to the shores of the large chain of lakes in that basin. The three largest lakes were connected by marshes; together they provided a rich aquatic environment. While the eastern lakes tended to be brackish from the minerals that emptied in them from the surrounding rivers, the southern and western portions contained fresh water. The shores of the lakes were dotted with settlements and towns. A dense population lived around the lakes to take advantage of their life-giving water for agriculture, the fish and aquatic plants and animals, and the advantages of transportation. Of the approximately 3000 square miles in the basin of the valley, about 400 square miles were under water.

The lakes became the cultural heartland and population center of Mexico in the postclassic period. In the unstable world of post-Toltec Mesoamerica, various peoples and cities jockeyed for supremacy of the lakes and the advantages they offered. The winners of this struggle, the Aztecs (or as they called themselves, the Mexica), eventually built a great empire, but when they emerged on the historical scene they were the most unlikely candidates for power.

From their obscure origins, the Aztec rise to power and their formation of an imperial state was as spectacular as it was rapid. According to some of their legends, the Mexica had once inhabited the central valley and had known agriculture and the "civilized" life but had lived in exile to the north in a place called Aztlan (from whence we get the name Aztec). This may be an exaggeration by people who wished to lay claim to a distinguished heritage. Other sources indicate that the Aztecs were simply one of the nomadic tribes that used the political anarchy, following the fall of the Toltecs, to penetrate into the area of sedentary agricultural peoples. Like the ancient Egyptians, the Aztecs rewrote history to suit their purposes.

What seems clear is that the Aztecs were a group of about 10,000 people who migrated to the shores of Lake Texcoco in the central valley of Mexico around the year 1325. After the fall of the Toltec Empire, the cen-

tral valley was inhabited by a mixture of peoples—Chichimec migrants from the northwest and various groups of sedentary agriculturalists. These peoples were divided into small political units that claimed greater or lesser authority on the basis of their military power and their connections to Toltec culture or Toltec descendants. Many of these peoples spoke *Nahuatl*, the language the Toltecs had spoken. The Aztecs too spoke this language, a fact that made their rise to power and their eventual claims to legitimacy more acceptable.

In this period, the area around the lake was dominated by several tribes organized into city-states. The city of Azcapotzalco was the real power but was challenged by an alliance centered in the city of Texcoco. Another city, Culhuacan, which had been part of the Toltec Empire, used its position as legitimate heir to the Toltecs as a means of creating alliances by marrying its princes and princesses to more powerful but less distinguished states. This was a world of political maneuver and state marriages, competing powers and shifting alliances.

An intrusive and militant group, such as the Aztecs, were distrusted and disliked by the dominant powers of the area, but their fighting skills could be put to use, and this made them attractive as mercenaries or allies. For about a century the Aztecs wandered around the shores of the lake, being allowed to settle for a while and then driven out by more powerful neighbors.

In a period of militarism and warfare, the Aztecs had a reputation as tough warriors and fanatical followers of their gods, to whom they offered continual human sacrifices. This reputation made them both valued and feared. Their own legends foretold that their wanderings would end when they saw an eagle perched on a cactus with a serpent in its beak. Supposedly, this sign was seen on a marshy island in Lake Texcoco, and there, on that island and one nearby, the Aztecs settled. The city of *Tenochtitlan* was founded about 1325, and on the neighboring island the city of *Tlatelolco* was established shortly thereafter. The two cities eventually grew together, although they maintained separate administrations.

From this secure base the Aztecs began to take a more active role in regional politics. Azcapotzalco and Texcoco, two powerful city-states, were locked in a struggle, and the Aztecs now began to serve Azcapotzalco as mercenaries. This alliance brought prosperity to the Aztecs, especially to their ruler and the warrior nobility, which was now acquiring lands and tribute from conquered towns. By 1428, however, the Aztecs had rebelled against Azcapotzalco and had joined with Texcoco in destroying it. From that victory the Aztecs emerged as an independent power. In 1434, Tenochtitlan, Texcoco, and a smaller city, Tlacopan, joined to-

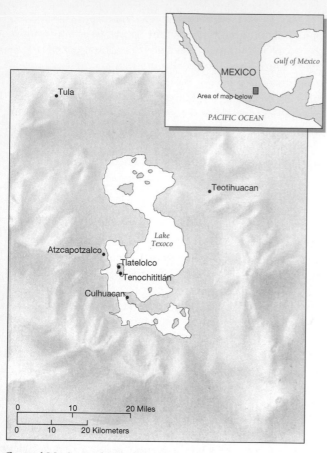

Central Mexico and Lake Texcoco

gether in a triple alliance that exercised control over much of the central plateau. In reality, Tenochtitlan and the Aztecs dominated their allies and controlled the major share of the tribute and lands taken.

The Aztec Social Contract

According to the Aztec accounts of this history, a social and political transformation had also taken place. The conquest of Azcapotzalco assured the position of the nobility. Moreover, the ruler of Tenochtitlan emerged from this process no longer as a spokesman for a general council but as a supreme ruler with wide powers. Succeeding rulers expanded that power and the boundaries of Aztec control, although a few independent states remained within central Mexico. Aztec domination extended from the Tarascan frontier southward to the Maya area. Subject peoples were forced to pay tribute, surrender lands, and sometimes do military service for the growing Aztec Empire.

Aztec society had been transformed in the process of expansion and conquest. From a loose association of clans, the Mexica had become a stratified society under the authority of a supreme ruler of great power. A central figure in these changes was *Tlacaelel*, a man who served as a sort of prime minister and advisor under three rulers from 1427 to his death around 1480. Under his direction, the histories were rewritten and the Mexica were given a self-image as a people chosen to serve the gods. Human sacrifice, long a part of Mesoamerican religion, was greatly expanded under his direction into a cult of enormous proportions in which the military class played a central role as suppliers of war captives to be used as sacrificial victims. It was also a policy of Tlacaelel to leave a few territories unconquered so that periodic "flower wars" could be staged in which both sides could obtain captives for sacrifice. Whatever the religious motivations of this cult, Tlacaelel and the Aztec rulers manipulated it as an effective means of political terror. By the time of Moctezuma II, the Aztec state was dominated by a king who represented civil power and served as a representative of the gods on earth. The cult of human sacrifice and conquest was united with the political power of the ruler and the nobility.

Religion and the Ideology of Conquest

Aztec religion incorporated many features that had long been part of the Mesoamerican system of beliefs. Religion was a vast, uniting, and sometimes oppressive force in which little distinction was made between the world of the gods and the natural world. The traditional deities of Mesoamerica—the gods of rain, fire, water, corn, the sky, and the sun, many of whom had been worshiped as far back as the time of Teotihuacan—were known and venerated among the Aztecs. There were at least 128 major deities, but the number of gods, in fact, seemed innumerable, for often each deity had a female consort or feminine form, because a basic duality was recognized in all things. Moreover, gods might have different forms or manifestations, somewhat like the avatars of the Hindu deities. Often each god had at least five aspects, each associated with one of the cardinal directions and the center. Certain gods were thought to be the patrons of specific cities, ethnic groups, or occupations. This extensive pantheon was supported by a round of yearly festivals and a highly complex ceremonialism that involved various forms of feasting and dancing along with penance and sacrifice.

This bewildering array of gods can be organized into three major themes or cults. The first were the gods of fertility and the agricultural cycle, such as *Tlaloc*, or the god of rain (called Chac by the Maya), and the gods and goddesses of water, maize, and fertility. A second theme centered on the creator deities, the great gods and goddesses who had brought the universe into being. The story of their actions played a central role in Aztec cosmography. Tonatiuh, the warrior god of the sun, and Tezcatlipoca, the god of the night sky, were among the most powerful and respected gods among the peoples of central Mexico. Much of Aztec abstract and philosophical thought was devoted to the theme of creation. Finally, the cult of warfare and sacrifice built on the preexisting Mesoamerican traditions that had been expanding since Toltec times but which, under the militaristic Aztec state, became the cult of the state. *Huitzilopochtli,* the Aztec tribal patron, became the central figure of this cult, but it included Tezcatlipoca, Tonatiuh, and other gods as well.

The Aztecs revered the great traditional deities—such as Tlaloc and Quetzalcoatl, the ancient god of civilization—so holy to the Toltecs, but their own tribal deity, Huitzilopochtli, became paramount. The Aztecs identified him with the old sun god, and they saw him as a warrior in the daytime sky fighting to give life and warmth to the world against the forces of the night. In order to carry out that struggle, the sun needed strength—and just as the gods had sacrificed themselves for humankind, the nourishment the gods needed most was that which was most precious: human life in the form of hearts and blood.

The great temple of Tenochtitlan was dedicated to both Huitzilopochtli and Tlaloc. The tribal deity of the Aztecs and the ancient agricultural god of the sedentary peoples of Mesoamerica were thus united.

In fact, while human sacrifice had long been a part of Mesoamerican religion, it had expanded considerably in the postclassic period of militarism. Warrior cults and the militaristic images of jaguars and eagles devouring human hearts were characteristic of Toltec art. The Aztecs simply took an existing tendency and carried it to an unprecedented scale. Both the types and frequency of sacrifice increased, and a whole symbolism and ritual, which included ritual cannibalism, developed as part of the cult. How much of Aztec sacrifice was the result of religious conviction and how much was imposed as a tactic of terror and political control by the rulers and the priest class is a question still open to debate (see "Analysis" in this chapter).

Beneath the surface of this polytheism, there was, however, also a sense of spiritual unity. *Nezhualcoyotl,* the king of Texcoco, composed hymns to the "lord of the close vicinity," an invisible creative force that supported all the gods. Yet, his conception of a kind of monotheism, much like that of Pharaoh Akhnaten in Egypt, was too abstract and never gained great popularity.

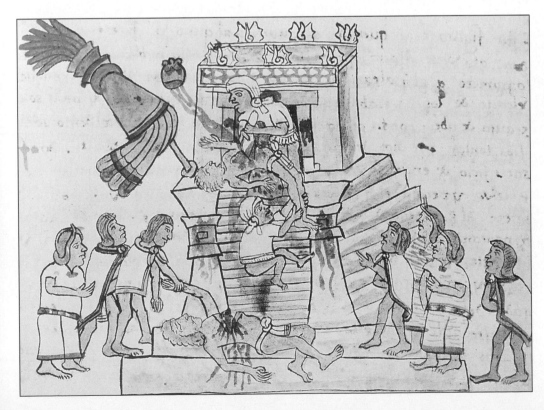

Human sacrifice existed among many Mesoamerican peoples, but the Aztecs apparently expanded its practice for political reasons and religious beliefs.

While the bloody aspects of Aztec religion have gained much attention, we must also realize that the Aztecs concerned themselves with many of the great religious and spiritual questions that have preoccupied other civilizations: Is there life after death? What is the meaning of life? What does it mean to live a good life? Do the gods really exist?

Nezhualcoyotl, whose poetry survived in oral form and was written down in the 16th century, wondered about life after death:

Do flowers go to the land of the dead?
In the Beyond, are we dead or do we still live?
Where is the source of light, since that which gives life hides
    itself?

He also wondered about the existence of the gods:

Are you real, are you fixed?
Only You dominate all things
The Giver of Life.
Is this true?
Perhaps, as they say, it is not true.

Aztec religious art and poetry is filled with images of flowers, birds, and song—all of which the Aztecs greatly admired—as well as human hearts and blood: the "precious water" needed to sustain the gods. It is this mixture of images that makes the symbolism of Aztec religion so difficult for modern observers to understand.

Aztec religion depended on a complex mythology that explained the birth and history of the gods and their relation to peoples and on a religious symbolism that infused all aspects of life. As we have seen, the Mesoamerican calendar system was a religious one, and many ceremonies coincided with particular points in the calendar cycle. Moreover, the Aztecs also believed in a cyclical view of history and believed that the world had been destroyed four times before and would be destroyed again. Thus, there was a certain fatalism in Aztec thought and a premonition that eventually the sacrifices would be insufficient and the gods would again bring catastrophe.

Feeding the People: The Economy of the Empire

Feeding the great population of Tenochtitlan and the Aztec confederation in general depended on traditional forms of agriculture and on innovations developed by the Aztecs. Lands of conquered peoples were often appropriated, and food was sometimes demanded as tribute. In fact, the quantities of maize, beans, and other foods brought into Tenochtitlan annually were staggering. In and around the lake, however, the Aztecs adopted an ingenious system of irrigated agriculture by constructing *chinampas* for agriculture. These were beds of aquatic weeds, mud, and earth that had been placed in frames made of cane and rooted to the lake floor. They formed artificial floating islands about 5 meters long and 30 to 100 meters wide. This narrow, striplike construction allowed the water to reach all the plants, and willow trees were also planted at intervals to give shade and help fix the roots. Much of the land of Tenochtitlan itself was chinampa in origin, and in the southern end of the lake, over 20,000 acres of chinampas were constructed.

The yield from chinampa agriculture was high: four corn crops a year were possible. Apparently, this system of irrigated agriculture had been used in preclassic days, but a rise in the level of the lakes had made it impossible to continue. After 1200, however, lowering of the lake levels once again stimulated chinampa construction, which the Aztecs carried out on a grand scale. They also constructed dikes to close off the fresh waters in the southern and western parts of the lake from the brackish waters elsewhere. Today, the floating gardens of Xochimilco represent the remnants of the lake agriculture.

Production by the Aztec peasantry, and tribute, provided the basic foods. In each Aztec community, the local clan apportioned the lands, some of which were also set aside for support of the temples and the state. In addition, individual nobles might also have private estates, which were worked by servants or slaves from conquered peoples. Each community had periodic markets—according to various cycles in the calendar system, such as every 5 and 13 days—in which a wide variety of goods were exchanged. Cacao beans and gold dust were sometimes used as currency, but much trade was done as barter. The great market at Tlatelolco operated daily and was controlled by the special merchant class, or *pochteca*, which specialized in long-distance trade in luxury items such as plumes of tropical birds and cacao. The markets were highly regulated and under the control of inspectors and special judges. Despite the existence and importance of markets, this was not a market economy as we usually understand it.

The state controlled the use and distribution of many commodities and served to redistribute the vast levies of tribute received from subordinate peoples. Tribute levels were assigned according to whether the subject peoples had accepted Aztec rule or had fought against it. Those who surrendered paid less. Tribute payments, such as food, slaves, and sacrificial victims, served political and economic ends and provided a wide variety of commodities. Over 120,000 mantles of cotton cloth alone were collected as tribute each year and sent to

Agriculture was the basis of Aztec society and a diet centered on maize sustained the dense populations of the Valley of Mexico.

Tenochtitlan. The Aztec state redistributed these goods. After the original conquests, it rewarded its nobility richly, but the commoners received far less. Still, the redistribution of many goods by the state interfered with the normal functioning of the market and created a peculiar state-controlled mixed economy.

AZTEC SOCIETY IN TRANSITION

Focal Point: Aztec society became increasingly hierarchical as the empire grew and social classes with different functions developed, although the older organization based on calpullis never disappeared. Tribute was drawn from subject peoples, but Aztec society confronted technological constraints that made it difficult to maintain the extensive population of central Mexico.

Widening Social Gulf

During their wanderings, the Aztecs had been divided into seven calpulli, or clans—a form of organization that they would later expand and adapt to their imperial position. By the 16th century there were about 20 major calpulli; 40 associated ones were in Tenochtitlan alone. The calpulli were no longer only kinship groups but also residential groupings, which might include neighbors, allies, and dependents. Much of Aztec local life remained based on the calpulli, which performed important functions such as distributing land to heads of households, organizing labor gangs and military units in times of war, and maintaining a temple and school. Calpulli were governed by councils of family heads, but not all families were equal, nor were all calpulli of equal status.

The calpulli had obviously been the ancient and basic building block of Aztec society. In the origins of Aztec society every person—noble and commoner—had belonged to a calpulli, but Aztec power increased and the rule of the empire expanded. The calpulli had been transformed, and other forms of social stratification had emerged. Legends of the Aztecs' origins emphasized that at one time they had all been peasants and had worked for others. As Aztec power expanded, a class of nobility, the *pipiltin,* emerged, based on certain privileged families in the most distinguished calpulli. Originating from the lineages that headed calpulli—especially those that had married into non-Mexica families or could claim Toltec background—and by marriages, military achievements, or service to the state, this group of nobility accumulated high office, private lands, and other advantages. The most prominent families in the calpulli, those who had dominated leadership roles and formed a kind of local

Tenochtitlan, the Foundation of Heaven

The city-state with its ruler-spokesman was a key central Mexican concept, and it applied to Tenochtitlan, the Aztec capital. Tenochtitlan became a great metropolis, with a central zone of palaces and whitewashed temples surrounded by adobe brick residential districts, smaller palaces, and markets. The craftsmanship and architecture were outstanding. Hernán Cortés, the Spanish conqueror who viewed the city, personally reported, "The stone masonry and the woodwork are equally good; they could not be bettered anywhere." There were gardens, and a zoo was kept for the ruler. The nobility had houses two stories high, sometimes with gardens on the roofs.

Tlatelolco, at first a separate island city, was eventually incorporated as part of Tenochtitlan. It too had impressive temples and palaces, and its large market remained the most important place of trade and exchange. By 1519, the city covered about five square miles. It had a population of 150,000, larger than contemporary European cities such as Seville or Paris.

Its island location gave Tenochtitlan a peculiar character. Set in the midst of a lake, the city was connected to the shores by four broad causeways and was crisscrossed by canals that allowed the constant canoe traffic on the lake access to the city. Each city ward, controlled by a *calpulli*, or kin group, maintained its neighborhood temples and civic buildings. The structural achievement was impressive. A Spanish foot soldier who saw it in 1519 wrote:

> Gazing on such wonderful sights, we did not know what to say, or whether what appeared before us was real, for on one side, on the land, there were great cities, and in the lake ever many more, and the lake was crowded with canoes, and in the causeway were many bridges at intervals, and in front of us stood the great city of Mexico. . . .

Tenochtitlan was the heart of an empire and drew tribute and support from its allies and dependents, but in theory it was still just a city-state ruled by a headman, just like the other 50 or more city-states that dotted the central plateau. Even so, the Aztecs called it the "foundation of heaven," the basis of their might. Present-day Mexico City rises on the site of the former Aztec capital.

The great Aztec capital of Tenochtitlan was dominated by the pyramid and twin temples of Huitzilopochtli shown here in a modern miniature reconstruction.

nobility, were eventually overshadowed by the military and administrative nobility of the Aztec state.

While some commoners might receive promotion to noble status, most nobles were born into the class—although birth merely qualified an individual for high position, which ultimately depended on performance and ability. Nobles controlled the priesthood and the military leadership. The military, in fact, was organized into various ranks based on experience and success in taking captives. Military virtues were linked to the cult of sacrifice and infused the whole society; they became the justification for the nobility's predominance and the ideology of the nobility's identity. The "flowery death," or death while taking prisoners for the sacrificial knife, was the fitting end to a noble life and assured eternity in the highest heaven—a reward also promised to women who died in childbirth. The military was highly ritualized. There were orders of warriors: the jaguar, eagle, and other groups each had a distinctive uniform and ritual and fought together as units. Distinctive banners, cloaks, and other insignia marked off the military ranks.

The social gulf that separated the nobility from the commoners was widening as the empire grew and the pipiltin accumulated the lands and tribute that the expansion implied. Egalitarian principles that may have once existed in Aztec life disappeared—a situation similar to what happened among the warring German tribes of early medieval Europe. Social distinctions were made apparent by the use of, and restrictions on, clothing, hairstyles, uniforms, and other outward symbols of rank. The imperial family became the most distinguished of the pipiltin families.

As the nobility broke free from their old calpulli and acquired private lands, a new class of workers was created to serve as laborers on these lands. These *mayeques,* or serfs, were sometimes from dependent clans or more often from conquered peoples. Unlike the commoners attached to the land-controlling calpulli, the mayeques did not control land and worked at the will of others. Their status was low, but it was still above that of the slaves, who might have been war captives, persons punished for crimes, or those who had sold themselves into bondage to escape hunger. The mayeques often did domestic work, and while they could buy their freedom, they could also be offered as sacrifices by their owner. Together, the mayeques and the slaves formed a growing sector of the population, whose situation was directly tied to the fortunes of the nobility and the strength of the Aztec Empire and who had little to gain from its success. Finally, there were other social groups. The scribes, artisans, and healers all constituted part of a kind of intermediate group, es-

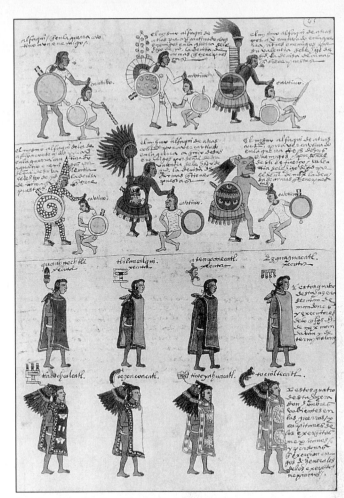

In the militarized society of the Aztec Empire, warriors were organized into regiments and groups distinguished by their distinctive uniforms. They gained rank and respect by capturing enemies for sacrifice.

pecially important in the larger cities. The long-distance merchants formed a sort of calpulli with their own patron gods, privileges, and internal divisions. They sometimes served as spies or agents for the Aztec military, but despite this role and their wealth, they were subject to restrictions that hindered their entry into or rivalry with the nobility.

It is possible to see an emerging conflict between the nobility and the commoners and to interpret this as a class struggle, but some specialists emphasize that to interpret Aztec society on that basis is to impose Western concepts on a different reality. Corporate bodies, such as the calpulli, temple maintenance associations, and occupational groups, cut across class and remained important in Aztec life. Competition between corporate groups was often more apparent and more violent than competition between social classes.

DOCUMENT

Aztec Women and Men

In the mid-16th century, Bernardino de Sahagún, a Spanish missionary, prepared an extraordinary encyclopedia of Aztec culture. His purpose was to gather this information to learn the customs and beliefs of the Indians and their language in order to better convert them. While Sahagún hated the Indian religion, he came to admire many aspects of their culture. His work, *The General History of the Things of New Spain*, is one of the first ethnographies and a remarkable compendium of Aztec culture. Sahagún used numerous Indian informants to tell him about the days before the European arrival, and so, even though this work dates from the postconquest era, it contains much useful information about earlier Aztec life.

In the following excerpts, the proper behavior for different roles of both women and men in Aztec society are described by the Aztecs themselves.

Father

One's father is the source of lineage. He is the sincere one. One's father is diligent, solicitous, compassionate, sympathetic, a careful administrator of his household. He rears, he teaches others, he advises, he admonishes one. He is exemplary; he leads a model life. He stores up for himself; he stores up for others. He cares for his assets; he saves for others. He is thrifty; he saves for the future, teaches thrift. He regulates, distributes with care, establishes order.

The bad father is incompassionate, negligent, unreliable. He is unfeeling . . . a shirker, a loafer, a sullen worker.

Mother

One's mother has children; she suckles them. Sincere, vigilant, agile, she is an energetic worker—diligent, watchful, solicitous, full of anxiety. She teaches people; she is attentive to them. She caresses, she serves others; she is apprehensive for their welfare; she is careful, thrifty—constantly at work.

The bad mother is evil, dull, stupid, sleepy, lazy. She is a squanderer, a petty thief, a deceiver, a fraud. Unreliable, she is one who loses things through neglect or anger, who heeds no one. She is disrespectful, inconsiderate, disregarding, careless. She shows the way to disobedience; she expounds nonconformity.

The Ruler

The ruler is a shelter—fierce, revered, famous, esteemed, well-reputed, renowned.

The good ruler is a protector: one who carries his subjects in his arms, who unites them, who brings them together. He rules, he takes responsibilities, assumes burdens. He carries his subjects in his cape; he bears them in his arms. He governs; he is obeyed. To him as a shelter, as refuge, there is recourse. . . .

The bad ruler is a wild beast, a demon of the air, an ocelot, a wolf—infamous, avoided, detested as a respecter of nothing. He terrifies with his gaze; he makes the earth rumble; he implants; he spreads fear. He is wished dead.

The Noble

The noble has a mother, a father. He resembles his parents. The good noble is obedient, cooperative, a follower of his parents' ways, a discreet worker; attentive, willing. He follows the ways of his parents; he resembles his father; he becomes his father's successor; he assumes his lot.

Overcoming Technological Constraints

Membership in society was defined by participation in various wider groups, such as the calpulli or a specific social class, and by gender roles and definitions. Aztec women assumed a variety of roles. Peasant women helped in the fields, but their primary domain was the household, where child-rearing and cooking took up much time. Above all, skill at weaving was highly regarded. The responsibility for training young girls fell on the mature and elderly women of the calpulli. Marriages were often arranged between lineages, and virginity at marriage was highly regarded for young women. Polygamy existed among the nobility, but the peasants were monogamous. Aztec women could inherit property and pass it to their heirs. The rights of Aztec women

One of noble lineage is a follower of the exemplary life, a taker of the good example of others, a seeker, a follower of the exemplary life. He speaks eloquently; he is soft-spoken, virtuous, deserving of gratitude. He is noble of heart, gentle of word, discreet, well-reared, well-taught. He is moderate, energetic, inquiring, inquisitive. He scratches the earth with a thorn. He is one who fasts, who starves his entrails, who parches his lips. He provides nourishment to others. He sustains one, he serves food, he provides comfort. He is a concealer [of himself], a belittler of himself. He magnifies and praises others. He is a mourner for the dead, a doer of penances, a gracious speaker, devout, godly, desirable, wanted, memorable.

The bad noble is ungrateful and forgetful, a debaser, a disparager of things, contemptuous of others, arrogant, bragging. He creates disorder, glories over his lineage, extols his own virtues.

The Mature Common Woman

The good mature woman is candid. She is resolute, firm of heart, constant—not to be dismayed; brave like a man; vigorous, resolute, persevering—not one to falter. She is long-suffering; she accepts reprimands calmly—endures things like a man. She becomes firm—takes courage. She is intent. She gives of herself. She goes in humility. She exerts herself.

The bad woman is thin, tottering, weak—an inconstant companion, unfriendly. She annoys others, chagrins them, shames, oppresses one. She becomes impatient; she loses hope, becomes embarrassed—chagrined. Evil is her life; she lives in shame.

The Weaver of Designs

She concerns herself with using thread, works with thread. The good weaver of designs is skilled—a maker of varicolored capes, an outliner of designs, a blender of colors, a joiner of pieces, a matcher of pieces, a person of good memory. She does things dexterously. She weaves designs. She selects. She weaves tightly. She forms borders. She forms the neck. . . .

The bad weaver of designs is untrained—silly, foolish, unobservant, unskilled of hand, ignorant, stupid. She tangles the thread, she harms her work—she spoils it.

The Physician

The physician is a knower of herbs, of roots, of trees, of stones; she is experienced in these. She is one who conducts examinations; she is a woman of experience, of trust, of professional skill: a counselor.

The good physician is a restorer, a provider of health, a relaxer—one who makes people feel well, who envelops one in ashes. She cures people; she provides them health; she lances them; she bleeds them . . . pierces them with an obsidian lancet.

Questions: In what ways do the expectations for men and women differ in Aztec society? To what extent do the roles for men and women in Aztec society differ from our own? Did the Aztecs value the same characteristics as our own and other historical societies?

seem to have been fully recognized, but in political and social life their role, while complementary to that of men, remained subordinate.

The technology of the Americas limited social development in a variety of ways. Here we can note a significant difference between the lives of women in Mesoamerica and in the Mediterranean world. In the maize-based economies of Mesoamerica, women spent six hours a day grinding corn by hand on stone boards, or metates, to prepare the household's food. Although similar hand techniques were used in ancient Egypt, they were eventually replaced by animal- or water-powered mills that turned wheat into flour. The miller or baker of Rome or medieval Europe could do the work of hundreds of women. Maize was among the simplest and most productive cereals to grow but among the most time-consuming to prepare. Without the wheel or suitable animals for power, the Indian civilizations were unable to free women from the 30 to 40 hours a week that went into the preparation of the basic food.

Finally, we must consider the size of the population of the Aztec state. Estimates have varied widely from as little as 1.5 million to over 25 million, but there is now considerable evidence that population density was high, resulting in a total population that was far greater than previously suspected. Historical demographers now estimate that the population of central Mexico under Aztec control reached over 20 million, excluding the Maya areas. This underlines the extraordinary ability of the Aztec state to intimidate and control such vast numbers of people.

A Tribute Empire

Each of the city-states was ruled by a speaker chosen from the nobility. The Great Speaker, the ruler of Tenochtitlan, became first among supposed equals. He was in effect the emperor, with great private wealth and public power, and was increasingly attributed with the symbols and status of a living god. His court was magnificent and surrounded with elaborate rituals. Those who approached him could not look him in the eye and were required to throw dirt upon their heads as a sign of humility. In theory he was elected, but his election was really a choice between siblings of the same royal family. The prime minister held a position of tremendous power and was usually a close relative of the ruler. There was a governing council; in theory, the rulers of the other cities of the triple alliance also had a say in government, but in reality most power was in the hands of the Aztec ruler and his chief advisor.

Over the course of a century of Aztec expansion, a social and political transformation had taken place. The position and nature of the old calpulli clans had changed radically, and a newly powerful nobility with a deified and virtually absolute ruler had emerged. Under the sponsorship of the prime minister, Tlacaelel, the ancient cult of military virtues had been elevated to a supreme position as the religion of the state, and the double purpose of securing increasing tribute for the state and obtaining more victims for Huitzilopochtli combined to drive further Aztec conquests.

The empire was never integrated, and local rulers often stayed in place to act as surrogates and tribute collectors for the Aztec overlords. In many ways the Aztec Empire was simply an expansion of long-existing Mesoamerican concepts and institutions of government, and it was not unlike the subject city-states over which it gained control. These city-states, in turn, were often left relatively unchanged, provided they recognized Aztec supremacy and met their obligations of labor and tribute. Tribute payments served both an economic and a political function, concentrating power and wealth in the Aztec capital. Archeologists at the recent excavations of the Great Temple beneath the center of Mexico City have been impressed by the large number of offerings and objects that came from the farthest ends of the empire and beyond. At the frontiers, neighboring states, such as Michoacan, preserved their freedom; while within the empire, independent kingdoms, such as Tlaxcala, maintained a fierce opposition to the Aztecs. There were many revolts against Aztec rule or a particular tribute burden, which the Aztecs often put down ruthlessly.

In general, the Aztec system was a success because it aimed at exerting political domination and not necessarily direct administrative or territorial control. In the long run, however, the increasing social stresses created by the rise of the pipiltin and the system of terror and tribute imposed over subject peoples were internal weaknesses that ultimately contributed to the Aztec Empire's collapse.

The Aztecs, then, represented a continuation of the long process of civilization in Mesoamerica. The civilizations of the classic era did not simply disappear in central Mexico or among the Maya in Yucatan and Central America, but they were reinterpreted and adapted to new political and social realities. When Europeans arrived in Mexico, they assumed that what they found was the culmination of Indian civilization, when in fact it was the militarized afterglow of earlier achievements.

ANALYSIS

The "Troubling" Civilizations of the Americas

From the first encounter with the peoples of the Americas, European concepts and judgments about civilization, barbarism, morality, power, politics, and justice were constantly called into question. The American Indian societies had many religious ideas and practices that shocked Christian observers, and there were aspects of their social and familial arrangements that also clashed with European sensibilities. Those sensibilities were often influenced by religious and political considerations. Many of those who most condemned human sacrifice, polygamy, or the despotism of Indian rulers were also those who tried to justify European conquest and control. Other European voices were also heard. Not long after the Spanish conquests in the 16th century, defenders of Indian rights came forward to argue that despite certain "unfortunate" habits, Indian civilization was no less to be admired than that of the ancient (and pagan) Romans and Greeks. Not only conquest and power were involved in the ways Europeans viewed and used Indian cultures. Occasionally, European thinkers, such as the French writer Michel de Montaigne in his essay "On Cannibals" (1580), might ironically contrast Indian cultures with European society in order to point out the deficiencies of Europe. By the 18th and 19th centuries, aristocratic whites in Mexico, Brazil, and Peru extolled the glories of the Indian past as a way of criticizing the colonial present. For them, Indian civilization became a justification and metaphor for American liberty.

For Western civilization, evaluating and judging non-Western or past societies has always been a complex business, which has mixed elements of morality, politics, religion, and self-perception along with the record of what is observed or considered to be "reality." That complexity is probably just as true for Chinese, Persian, or any culture trying to understand the "other." Still, Western society seems to have been particularly troubled by the American civilizations, with their peculiar combination of Neolithic technology and imperial organization. At times this has led to abhorrence and rejection— as of Aztec sacrifice—but at other times it has led to a kind of utopian romanticism in which the accomplishments of the Indian past are used as a critique of the present and a political program for the future.

The existence of *Inca socialism* is a case in point. While some early Spanish authors portrayed Inca rule as despotic, others saw it as a kind of utopia. Shortly after the conquest of Peru, Garcilaso de la Vega, the son of a Spaniard and an Indian noblewoman, wrote a glowing history of his mother's people in which he presented an image of the Inca Empire as a carefully organized system in which every community collectively contributed to the whole and the state regulated the distribution of resources on the basis of need and reciprocity. In the 20th century, Peruvian socialists, faced with the problems of underdevelopment and social inequality in their country, used this view of Inca society as a possible model for their own future. Their interpretation and that of historians who later wrote of Inca "socialism" tended to ignore the high degree of hierarchy in the Inca Empire and the fact that the state extracted labor and goods from the subject communities to support the nobles who held extensive power. The utopian view of the Incas was no less political

than the despotic view. Perhaps the lesson here is that what we see in the past often depends on what we think about the present or what we want for the future.

But if Inca socialism and despotism have fascinated students of the past, Aztec religion has caught the imagination of historians and of the general public. It causes us to ask how a civilization as advanced and accomplished as this could engage in a practice so cruel and, to us, so morally reprehensible. Perhaps nothing challenges our appreciation of the American civilizations more than the extensive evidence of ritual torture and human sacrifice, which among the Aztecs reached staggering proportions—on some occasions thousands of people were slain, usually by having their hearts ripped out.

First, we must put these practices in some perspective. Cruelty and violence can be found in many cultures, and to a world that has witnessed genocide, mass killings, and atomic warfare, the Aztec practices do not stand in such marked contrast to what our own age has seen. Certain customs in many past civilizations and in present cultures seem to us strange, cruel, and immoral. We find Aztec human sacrifice particularly abhorrent, but we should be aware that such practices were found among the ancient Canaanites and the Celtic peoples and that the story of Abraham and Isaac in the Old Testament, while its message is against such sacrifice, reflects what was a known practice. Human sacrifice was practiced in pre-Christian Scandinavia and in ancient India. Although by the time of Confucius, human sacrifice of wives and retainers at the burial of a ruler was no longer practiced in China, the custom had been known. The issue of sati, the Hindu ritual suicide of the widow on the funeral pyre of her husband, raged in India in the 20th century. The Aztecs were certainly not alone in the taking of human life as a religious rite. Whatever our moral judgments about such customs, it remains the historian's responsibility to understand them in the context of their own culture and time.

How have historians tried to explain or understand the extent of Aztec human sacrifice? Some defenders of Aztec culture have seen it as a limited phenomenon, greatly exaggerated by the Spanish for political purposes. Many scholars have seen it as essentially a religious act central to the Aztec's belief that humans must sacrifice that which was most precious to them, life, in order to receive in return the sun, rain, and other blessings of the gods that make life possible. Others have viewed Aztec practice as the intentional manipulation and expansion of a widespread phenomenon that had long existed among many American peoples. In other words, the Aztec rulers, priests, and nobility used the cult of war and large-scale human sacrifice for political purposes, to terrorize their neighbors, and to keep the lower classes subordinate. Another possible explanation is demographic. If central Mexico was as densely populated as we believe, then the sacrifices may have served as a kind of population control.

Other interpretations have been even more startling. Anthropologist Marvin Harris has suggested that Aztec sacrifice, accompanied by ritual cannibalism, was in fact a response to the lack of available protein. He argued that in the Old World, human sacrifice was replaced by animal sacrifice, but in Mesoamerica, which lacked cattle and sheep, that transformation never took place. The Aztec Empire was, as Harris called it, a *cannibal kingdom*. Other scholars have strongly objected to Harris's interpretation of the evidence. But it is clear that the shadow of human sacrifice shades all assessments of Aztec civilization.

These debates ultimately raise important questions about the role of moral judgments in historical analysis and the way in which our vision of the past is influenced by our own political, moral, ethical, and social programs. In thinking about the past and about societies other than our own, we cannot and perhaps should not abandon those programs, but we must always try to understand other times and other peoples in their own terms.

Questions: What special features of Aztec civilization have to be explained? Are they really distinctive? What explanations are most persuasive in terms of historical sensitivity and contemporary standards? Are there features of 20th-century society that are similar to those of Aztec civilization and that will require explanation for later generations?

TWANTINSUYU: WORLD OF THE INCAS

Focal Point: After about 1300 C.E. in the Andean cultural hearth, a new civilization emerged and eventually spread its control over the whole region. The *Inca* empire, or *Twantinsuyu,* was a highly centralized system, which integrated various ethnic groups into an imperial state. Extensive irrigated agriculture supported a state religion and a royal ancestor cult. With notable achievements in architecture and metallurgy, the Incas, like the Aztecs, incorporated many elements of the civilizations that preceded them.

Almost at the same time that the Aztecs extended their control over much of Mesoamerica, a great imperial state was rising in the Andean highlands, and it eventually held sway over an empire some 3000 miles in extent. The Inca Empire incorporated many aspects of previous Andean cultures but fused them together in new ways—and with a genius for state organization and bureaucratic control over peoples of different cultures and languages, it achieved a level of integration and domination previously unknown in the Americas.

Throughout the Andean cultural hearth, during the period following the breakup or disintegration of the large "horizon" states of Tihuanaco and Huari (c. 550–1000 C.E.), several smaller regional states continued to exercise some power. Rather than the breakdown of power that took place in postclassic Mesoamerica, in the Andean zone many relatively large states continued to be important. Some states in the Andean highlands on the broad open areas near Lake Titicaca, and those states along rivers on the north coast, such as in the Moche valley, remained centers of agricultural activity and population density. This time in the ultimate development of the Andean imperial state was a period of considerable warring between rival local chiefdoms and small states and in some ways was an Andean parallel to the post-Toltec militaristic era in Mesoamerica. Of these states, the coastal kingdom of Chimor, centered on its capital of Chan Chan, emerged as the most powerful. Between 900 and its conquest by the Incas in 1465, it gained control of most of the north coast of Peru.

The Inca Rise to Power

While Chimor spread its control over 600 miles of the coast, in the southern Andean highlands, where there were few large urban areas, ethnic groups and politics struggled over the legacy of Tihuanaco. Among these groups were several related Quechua-speaking clans, or ayllus, living near Cuzco, an area that had been under the influence of Huari but had not been particularly important. Their own legends stated that ten related clans emerged from caves in the region and were taken to Cuzco by a mythical leader. Wherever their origins, by about 1350 C.E. they resided in and around Cuzco, and by 1438 they had defeated their hostile neighbors in the area. At this point under their ruler, or Inca, *Pachacuti* (1438–1471), they launched a series of military alliances and campaigns that brought them control of the whole area from Cuzco to the shores of Lake Titicaca.

Over the next 60 years, Inca armies were constantly on the march, extending control over a vast territory. Pachacuti's son and successor, *Topac Yupanqui* (1471–1493) conquered the northern coastal kingdom of Chimor by seizing its irrigation system, and he extended Inca control into the southern area of what is now

The great mud-walled city of Chan Chan in northern Peru, capital of the Chimu state, covered an area of six square kilometers. The Chimu Empire dominated the region prior to the rise of the Incas.

Ecuador. At the other end of the empire, Inca armies reached the Maule River in Chile against stiff resistance from the Araucanian Indians. The next ruler, Huayna Capac (1493–1527) consolidated these conquests and suppressed rebellions on the frontiers. By the time of his death, the Inca Empire—or, as they called it, Twantinsuyu—stretched from what is now Colombia to Chile and eastward across Lake Titicaca and Bolivia to northern Argentina. Between 9 million and 13 million people of different ethnic backgrounds and languages came under Inca rule, a remarkable feat given the extent of the empire and the technology available for transportation and communication.

Conquest and Religion

What impelled the Inca conquest and expansion? The usual desire for economic gain and political power that we have seen in other empires provides one suitable explanation, but there may be others more in keeping with Inca culture and ideology. The cult of the ancestors was extremely important in Inca belief. Deceased rulers were mummified and then treated as intermediaries with the gods, paraded in public during festivals, offered food and gifts, and consulted on important matters by special oracles. From the Chimor kingdom the Incas adopted the practice of royal *split inheritance* whereby all the po-

litical power and titles of the ruler went to his successor, but all his palaces, wealth, land, and possessions remained in the hands of his male descendants, who used them to support the cult of the dead Inca's mummy for eternity. Each new Inca, then, in order to ensure his own cult and place for eternity, needed to secure land and wealth, and these normally came as part of new conquests. In effect, the greater the number of past Inca rulers, the greater the number of royal courts to support and the greater the demand for labor, lands, and tribute. This system created a self-perpetuating need for expansion, tied directly to ancestor worship and the cult of the royal mummies, as well as tensions between the various royal lineages. In a way, the cult of the dead weighed increasingly heavily on the living.

Inca political and social life was infused with religious meaning. Like the Aztecs, the Incas held the sun to be the highest deity and considered the Inca to be the sun's representative on earth. The magnificent *Temple of the Sun* in Cuzco was the center of the state religion, and in its confines the mummies of the past Incas resided. The cult of the sun was spread throughout the empire, but the Inca did not prohibit the worship of local gods.

Other deities were also worshiped as part of the state religion. Viracocha, a creator god, was a favorite of Inca Pachacuti and remained important. Popular belief was based on a profound animism that endowed many nat-

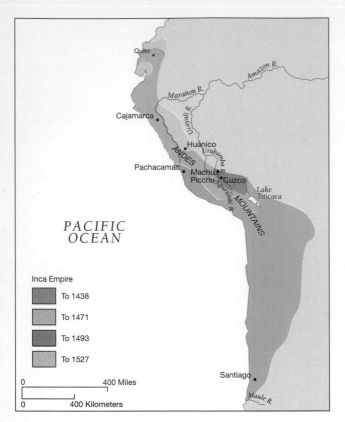

Inca Expansion

ural phenomena with spiritual power. Mountains, stones, rivers, caves, or tombs and temples were considered to be huacas, or holy shrines. At these places, prayers were offered and sacrifices of animals, goods, and humans were made. In the Cuzco area, imaginary lines running from the Temple of the Sun organized the huacas into groups for which certain ayllus took responsibility. The temples were served by many priests and women dedicated to the preparation of cloth and food for sacrifice. The temple priests were mainly responsible for the great festivals and celebrations and for the divinations upon which state actions often depended.

The Techniques of Inca Imperial Rule

The Inca were able to keep control over their vast empire by using techniques and practices that assured either cooperation or subordination. The empire was ruled by the Inca, who was considered virtually a god. He ruled from his court at Cuzco, which was also the site of the major temple; the high priest was usually a close relative. Twantinsuyu was divided into four great provinces, each under a governor, and then divided again. The Incas developed a state bureaucracy in which almost all the nobility played a

role. While some chroniclers spoke of a state organization based on decimal units of 10,000, 1,000, 100, and smaller numbers of households to mobilize taxes and labor, recent research reveals that many local practices and variations were allowed to continue under Inca rule. Local rulers, or curacas, were allowed to maintain their position and were given privileges by the Inca in return for their loyalty. The curacas were exempt from tribute obligations and usually received labor or produce from those under their control. For insurance, the sons of conquered chieftains were taken to Cuzco for their education.

The Incas intentionally spread the Quechua language as a means of integrating the empire. The Incas also made extensive use of *mitmaq,* or colonists. Sometimes Quechua-speakers from Cuzco might be settled in a newly won area to provide an example and a garrison. On other occasions, a restive conquered population was moved to a new home. Throughout the empire, a complex system of roads was constructed, with bridges and causeways when needed. Along these roads, way stations, or *tambos,* were placed about a day's walk apart to serve as inns, storehouses, and supply centers for Inca armies on the move. Tambos also served as relay points for the system of runners who carried messages throughout the empire. The Inca probably maintained over 10,000 tambos.

The Inca Empire functioned to extract land and labor from subject populations. Conquered peoples were enlisted in the Inca armies under Inca officers and were rewarded with goods from new conquests. Subject peoples received access to goods not previously available to them, and the Inca state undertook large projects of building and irrigation that formerly would have been impossible. In return, the Incas demanded loyalty and tribute. The state claimed all resources and redistributed them. The Incas divided conquered areas into lands for the people, lands for the state, and lands for the sun—that is, for religion and the support of priests. There were also private estates held by some nobles.

With few exceptions the Incas, unlike the Aztecs, did not demand tribute in kind, but rather exacted labor on the lands assigned to the state and the religion. Communities were expected to take turns working on state and church lands and sometimes on building projects or in mining. These labor turns, or *mita,* were an essential aspect of Inca control. In addition, the Inca required women to weave high-quality cloth for the court and for religious purposes. The Incas provided the wool, but each household was required to produce cloth. Woven cloth, a great Andean art form, had political and religious significance. Some women were taken as concubines for the Inca; others were selected as servants at the temples, the so-called Virgins of the Sun. In all this, the

The role of women in Inca agriculture is emphasized in this 16th-century drawing of the symbolic irrigation of the fields. Complex Inca irrigation systems permitted the farming of steep hillsides and marginal lands.

Inca had an overall imperial system but remained sensitive to local variations, so that its application accommodated regional and ethnic differences.

In theory, each community aimed at self-sufficiency and depended on the state for goods difficult to acquire. The ayllus of each community controlled the land, and the vast majority of the male population were peasants and herdsmen. Women aided in the fields, wove cloth, and cared for the household. Roles and obligations were gender specific and theoretically equal and interdependent. Andean peoples recognized parallel descent, so that property rights within the ayllu and among the nobility passed in both the male and female lines. Women passed rights and property to daughters, men to sons. Whether in pre-Inca times women may have served as leaders of ayllus is open to question, but under the Incas this seems to have been uncommon. The Inca emphasis on military virtues reinforced the inequality of men and women, even though an ideology of complementarity of the sexes was very strong.

The concept of close cooperation of men and women was also reflected in the Inca view of the cosmos. Gods and goddesses were worshiped by men and women, but women felt a particular affinity for the moon and the goddesses of the earth and corn—the fertility deities. The Inca queen, the Inca's senior wife (who was usually also a sister of the Inca), was viewed as a link to the moon. Queen and sister of the sun, she represented imperial authority to all women. But despite an ideology of gender equality, Inca practice created a hierarchy of gender relationships that meshed with the dominance of the Inca state over subject peoples. This fact is supported, and the power of the empire over local ethnic groups is demonstrated, by the Incas' ability to select the most beautiful young women to serve the temples or be given to the Inca.

The integration of imperial policy with regional and ethnic diversity was a political achievement. Ethnic headmen were left in place, but over them were Inca administrators drawn from the Inca nobility in Cuzco. Reciprocity and verticality continued to characterize Andean groups as they came under Inca rule; reciprocity between the state and the local community was simply an added level. The Inca state could provide roads, irrigation projects, and hard-to-get goods. Maize, for example, was usually grown on irrigated land and was particularly important as a ritual crop. State-sponsored irrigation added to its cultivation. The Inca state manipulated the idea of reciprocity to extract labor power, and it dealt harshly with resistance and revolt. In addition to the ayllu peasantry, there was also a class of people, the *yanas,* who were removed from their ayllus and served permanently as servants, artisans, or workers for the Inca or the Inca nobility.

Members of the Inca nobility were greatly privileged, and those related to the Inca himself held the highest positions. The nobility were all drawn from the ten royal ayllus. In addition, the residents of Cuzco were given noble status to enable them to serve in high bureaucratic posts. The nobles were distinguished by dress and custom. Only they were entitled to wear the large ear spools that enlarged the ears and caused the Spaniards to later call them *orejones,* or "big ears." Noticeably absent in most of the Inca Empire was a distinct merchant class. Unlike Mesoamerica, where long-distance trade was so important, the Incas' emphasis on self-sufficiency and state regulation of production and surplus limited trade. Only in the northern areas of the empire, in the chiefdoms of Ecuador, the last region brought under Inca control, did a specialized class of traders exist.

The Inca imperial system, which controlled an area

almost 3000 miles in extent, was a stunning achievement of statecraft, but like all empires it lasted only as long as it could control its subject populations and its own mechanisms of government. A system of royal multiple marriages as a way of forging alliances created rival claimants for power and the possibility of civil war. That is exactly what happened in the 1520s, just before the arrival of the Europeans. When the Spanish first arrived in Peru, they saw an empire weakened and wasted by civil strife.

Inca Cultural Achievements

The Incas drew on the artistic traditions of their Andean predecessors and the skills of subject peoples. Beautiful pottery and cloth were produced in specialized workshops. Inca metallurgy was among the most advanced in the Americas, and Inca artisans worked gold and silver with great technical skill. The Incas also used copper and some bronze for weapons and tools. Like the Mesoamerican peoples, the Incas made no practical use of the wheel, but unlike them, they had no system of writing. The Incas, however, did make use of a system of knotted strings, or *quipu,* with which numerical and perhaps other information could be recorded. It functioned something like an abacus, and with it the Incas took censuses and kept financial records. The Incas had a passion for numerical order, and the population was divided into decimal units from which population, military enlistment, and work details could be calculated. The existence of so many traits associated with civilization in the Old World and yet the absence of a system of writing among the Incas should make us realize the variations of human development and the dangers of becoming too attached to certain characteristics or cultural features in defining civilizations.

The Incas' genius was best displayed in their statecraft and in their architecture and public buildings. Inca stonecutting was remarkably accurate; the best buildings were constructed of large fitted stones without the use of masonry. Some of these buildings were immense. These constructions, the large agricultural terraces and irrigation projects, and the extensive system of roads were among the Incas' greatest achievements, displaying their technical ability and workmanship as well as their ability to mobilize large amounts of manpower.

Comparing Incas and Aztecs

Both the Inca and the Aztec empires were based on a long development of civilization that preceded them; and while in some areas of artistic and intellectual achievement, earlier peoples had surpassed their accomplishments, both represented the success of imperial and military organization. Both empires were based on intensive agriculture organized by a state that accumulated surplus production and then controlled the circulation of goods and their redistribution to groups or social classes. In both states, older semikinship-based institutions, the ayllu and the calpulli, were being transformed by the emergence of a social hierarchy in which the nobility was increasingly predominant. In both areas, this nobility was also the personnel of the state, so that the state organization was almost an image of society.

While the Incas attempted to create an overarching political state and made conscious attempts to integrate their empire as a unit (the Aztecs did less in this regard), both empires recognized local ethnic groups and political leaders and were willing to allow considerable variation from one group or region to another—that is, provided that Inca or Aztec sovereignty was recognized and tribute paid. Both the Aztecs and the Incas, like the Spaniards who followed them, found that their military power was less effective against nomadic peoples who lived on their frontiers. Essentially, the empires were created by the conquest of sedentary agricultural peoples and the extraction of tribute and labor from them.

We cannot overlook the considerable differences between Mesoamerica and the Andean region in terms of climate and geography nor ignore the differences between the Inca and Aztec civilizations. Trade and markets, for example, were far more developed in the Aztec Empire and earlier in Mesoamerica in general than in the Andean world. There were considerable differences in metallurgy, in writing systems, and in social definition and hierarchy. But within the context of world civilizations, it is probably best to view these two empires and the cultural areas they represent as variations of similar patterns and processes, of which sedentary agriculture is the most important. Basic similarities underlying the variations can also be seen in systems of belief and cosmology and in social structure. Whether similar origins, direct or indirect contact between the areas, or parallel development in Mesoamerica and the Andean area explains the similarity remains to be explored. But the American Indian civilizations shared much with each other, and that factor plus their relative isolation from external cultural and biological influences gave them their peculiar character and ultimately their vulnerability. At the same time, their ability to survive the shock of conquest and to contribute to the formation of societies after conquest demonstrates much of their strength and resiliency. Long after the Aztec and Inca empires had ceased to exist, the peoples of the Andes and Mexico continue to draw on these cultural traditions.

THE OTHER INDIANS

Focal Point: The civilizations of Mesoamerica and the Andes, and the imperial states in place at the moment of contact with the wider world, were high points of an Indian cultural achievement cut short by subsequent contact and conquest. The Americas, however, continued to be occupied by a wide variety of peoples who lived in different ways, ranging from highly complex sedentary agricultural empires to simple kin-based bands of hunters and gatherers.

Rather than a division between "primitive" and "civilized" Indians, it is more useful to consider series of gradations according to material culture and social complexity that also recognize similarities. Groups like the Incas had many things in common with the tribal peoples of the Amazon basin, such as the division into clans or into halves—that is, a division of villages or communities into two major groupings with mutually agreed-upon roles and obligations. Moreover, as we have seen, the diversity of ancient America forces a reconsideration of ideas of human development based on Old World examples. If social complexity is supposedly dependent on an agricultural base for society, that theory is not supported by the existence in the Americas of some groups of fishermen and hunters and gatherers, such as the Indians of the northwest coast of the United States and British Columbia, who developed hierarchical societies. For those who see control of water for agriculture as the starting point for political authority and the state, exceptions are provided by such societies as the Pimas of Colorado and some of the chiefdoms of South America, who practiced irrigated agriculture but did not develop states.

How Many Indians?

A major issue that has fascinated students of the Americas for centuries is the question of population size. For many years after the European conquests, many people discounted the early descriptions of large and dense Indian populations as the exaggeration of the conquerors and missionaries who wished to make their own exploits seem more impressive. In the early 20th century, the most repeated estimate of Indian population about 1492 was 8.4 million (4 million in Mexico, 2 million in Peru, and 2.4 million in the rest of the hemisphere). Since that time, new archeological discoveries, a better understanding of the impact of disease on indigenous populations, new historical and demographic studies, and improved estimates of agricultural techniques and productivity have led to major revisions. Estimates still vary widely,

Table 17.1
A Population Estimate for the Western Hemisphere, 1492

Area	Population in thousands
North America	4,400
Mexico	21,400
Central America	5,650
Carribbean	5,850
Andes	11,500
Lowland South America	8,500
Total	57,300

Sources: William M. Deneven, *The Native Population of the Americas in 1492* (1976), 289–292; John D. Durand, "Historical Estimates of World Population," *Population and Development Review,* 3 (1957), 253–296; Russell Thornton, *American Indian Holocaust and Survival* (1987).

and some have gone as high as 112 million at the time of contact. Despite disagreements, most scholars agree that Mesoamerica and the Andes supported the largest populations. Table 17.1 summarizes one of the most careful estimates, which places the total figure at over 57 million, although an American Indian demographer has adjusted this figure upward to 72 million.

These figures should be set in a global context. About 1500, the population of the rest of the world was probably about 500 million, of which China and India each had 75 to 100 million people and Europe had 60 to 70 million, a figure roughly equivalent to the Americas. The peoples of the Americas clearly made up a major segment of humanity.

Differing Cultural Patterns

While it is impossible to summarize the variety of cultural patterns and lifeways that existed in the Americas on the eve of contact, we can mention the major patterns outside the main civilizational areas. In Chapter 9 we noted that the area of northern South America and part of Central America was an intermediate area, which shared many features with the Andes and some with Mesoamerica and perhaps served at times as a point of cultural and material exchange between the two regions. In the mountain valleys of central Colombia large chiefdoms of the Muisca and Tairona peoples, based on sedentary agriculture, mobilized large numbers of peasant agriculturalists for building projects and extracted surpluses from them. Warfare seems to have been endemic in these soci-

Table 17.2
World Population c. 1500

Area	Population in thousands
China	100,000–150,000
Indian subcontinent	75,000–150,000
Southwest Asia	20,000–30,000
Japan	15,000–20,000
Rest of Asia (except Russia)	15,000–30,000
Europe (except Russia)	60,000–70,000
Russia (USSR)	10,000–18,000
Northern Africa	6,000–12,000
Remainder of Africa	30,000–60,000
Oceania	1,000–2,000
Americas	57,000–72,000
Total	389,000–614,000

Sources: William M. Deneven, *The Native Population of the Americas in 1492* (1976), 289–292; John D. Durand, "Historical Estimates of World Population," *Population and Development Review,* 3 (1957), 253–296; Russell Thornton, *American Indian Holocaust and Survival* (1987).

eties, and there was a strong religious cult associated with political authority. In fact, with the exception of monumental architecture, the intermediate-zone chieftainships resemble the sedentary agriculture states in many ways.

Similar kinds of chieftainships based on sedentary agriculture were found elsewhere in the Americas. There is strong evidence of large and populous chieftainships along the Amazon, where the rich aquatic environment supported complex and perhaps hierarchical societies. The island Arawaks that Columbus first encountered in the Caribbean on the island of Hispaniola were agriculturalists organized in a hierarchical society and divided into chiefdoms. These Indian chiefdom-level societies bear a strong resemblance to the societies of Polynesia. On the bigger Caribbean islands, such as Hispaniola and Puerto Rico, chieftainships ruled over dense populations, which lived primarily from the production of manioc.

Agriculture was widely diffused throughout the Americas by 1500. Some peoples, like those of the eastern North American woodlands and the coast of Brazil, combined agriculture with hunting and fishing. Techniques such as slash-and-burn farming led to the periodic movement of villages when production declined. Social organization in these societies often remained without strong class divisions, craft specializations, or the demographic density of people who practiced per-

manent, intensive agriculture. Unlike Europe, Asia, and Africa, nomadic herdsmen were lacking in the Americas. However, throughout the Americas from Tierra del Fuego to the Canadian forests, peoples remained who lived in small, mobile, kin-based groups of hunters and gatherers. Their material culture was simple and their societies were more egalitarian.

Nowhere is the problem of American Indian diversity more apparent than in North America. In that vast continent perhaps as many as 200 languages were spoken by 1500, and a variety of cultures reflected Indian adaptation to different ecological situations. By that time, the concentrated towns of the Mississippian Mound Builder cultures had mostly been abandoned, and only a few groups in southeastern North America still maintained the social hierarchy and religious ideas of those earlier cultures. In the Southwest, the descendants of the Anasazi and other cliff dwellers had taken up residence in the adobe pueblos along the Rio Grande, where they practiced various forms of terracing and irrigation to support their agriculture. Their rich religious life, their artistic ceramic and weaving traditions, and their agricultural base reflected their own historical traditions.

Elsewhere in North America, most groups were hunters and gatherers or combined those activities with some agriculture. Sometimes an environment was so rich that complex social organization and artistic specialization could develop without an agricultural base. This was the case among the Indians of the northwest coast, who depended on the rich resources of the sea. In other cases, technology was a limiting factor. The tough grasses of the prairies could not be easily farmed without the use of metal plows, nor could the buffalo be effectively hunted prior to the European introduction of the horse. Thus, the Great Plains were only sparsely occupied.

Finally, we should note that while there was great variation among the Indian cultures, some aspects stood in marked contrast to contemporary societies in Europe and Asia. With the exception of the state systems of Mesoamerica and the Andes, most Indian societies were strongly kin-based. Communal action and ownership of resources, such as land or hunting grounds, were emphasized, and material wealth was often disregarded or placed in a ritual or religious context. It was not that these societies were necessarily egalitarian but rather that ranking was usually not based on wealth. Women, although often subordinate, in some societies held important political and social roles and usually played a central role in crop production. Indians tended to view themselves as part of the ecological system and not in control of it. These attitudes stood in marked contrast to those of the contemporary Eurasian civilizations.

CONCLUSION

American Indian Diversity in World Context

By the end of the 15th century, two great imperial systems had risen to dominate the two major centers of civilization in Mesoamerica and the Andes. Both of these empires were built on the achievements of their predecessors, and both reflected a militaristic phase in their area's development. These empires proved to be fragile—weakened by their own internal strains and the conflicts that any imperial system creates, but also limited by their technological inferiority when challenged by Eurasian civilization.

The Aztec and Inca empires were one end of a continuum of cultures that went from the most simple to the most complex. The Americas contained a broad range of societies, from great civilizations with millions of people to small bands of hunters. In many of these societies, religion played a dominant role in defining the relationship between people and their environment and between the individual and society. How these societies would have developed and what course the American civilizations might have taken in continued isolation remains an interesting and unanswerable question. The first European observers were simultaneously shocked by the "primitive" tribesmen and astounded by the wealth and accomplishments of civilizations like that of the Aztecs. Europeans generally saw the Indians as curiously anachronistic. In comparison with Europe and Asia, the Americas did seem strange—more like ancient Babylon or Egypt than contemporary China or Europe—except that without the wheel, large domesticated animals, the plow, and to a large extent metal tools and written languages, even that comparison is misleading. The relative isolation of the Americas had remained important in physical and cultural terms, but that isolation came to an end in 1492—often with disastrous results.

FURTHER READINGS

Alvin M. Josephy, Jr.'s *The Indian Heritage of America* (1968) is a broad, comprehensive history that deals with North and South America and provides much detail without being tedious. It is a logical starting point for further study. Frederick Katz's *The Ancient Civilizations of the Americas* (1972) is now somewhat out of date, but it still provides the best overall survey that compares Mesoamerica and Peru. It traces the rise of civilization in both areas.

The literature on the Aztecs is growing rapidly. Sahagún's Florentine Codex: *The General History of the Things of New Spain,* Charles Dibble and Arthur J. O. Anderson, eds. and trans., II vols. (1950–1968) is a fundamental source. A good overview is Jacques Soustelle's *Daily Life of the Aztecs* (1961), but more recent is Frances Berdan's *The Aztecs of Central Mexico: An Imperial Society* (1982). Miguel Leon-Portilla's *Aztec Thought and Culture* (1963) deals with religion and philosophy in a sympathetic way. Burr Cartwright Brundage has traced the history of the Aztec rise in several books such as *A Rain of Darts* (1972); his *The Jade Steps* (1985) provides a good analysis of religion. Nigel Davies's *The Aztec Empire* (1987) is a political and social analysis. Susan D. Gillespie's *The Aztec Kings* (1989) views Aztec history in terms of myth.

On Peru, a good overview through solid scholarly articles is provided in Richard W. Keatinge, ed., *Peruvian Prehistory* (1988). The article on Inca archeology by Craig Morris is especially useful. Alfred Metraux's *The History of the Incas* (1970) is an older but still useful and very readable book. John Murra's *The Economic Organization of the Inca State* (1980) is a classic that has influenced much thinking about the Incas. J. Hyslop's *The Inka Road System* (1984) examines the building and function of the road network. The series of essays in John V. Murra, Nathan Wachtel, and Jacques Revel, eds., *Anthropological History of Andean Polities* (1986) shows how new approaches in ethnohistory are deepening our understanding of Inca society. Interesting social history is now being done. Irene Silverblatt's *Moon, Sun, and Witches: Gender Ideologies and Class in Inca and Colonial Peru* (1987) is a controversial book on the position of women before, during, and after the Inca rise to power.

From a comparative perspective is Geoffrey W. Conrad's and Arthur A. Demerest's *Religion and Empire: The Dynamics of Aztec and Inca Expansionism* (1984). These two archeologists compare the political systems of the two empires and the motivations for expansion. The authors find more similarities than differences. Excellent studies on specific themes on Mexico and Peru are found in George A. Collier, et al., eds., *The Inca and Aztec States,* 1400–1800 (1982).

18

Reunification and Renaissance in Chinese Civilization: The Era of the Tang and Song Dynasties

220–589 Era of the Six Dynasties; political division in China; time of greatest Buddhist influence

220 End of the Han dynasty

589–618 Sui dynasty; building of the Grand Canal

618–907 Tang dynasty

618–626 Gaozu emperor

627–649 Tang Taizong emperor

690–705 Empress Wu; Buddhist influence in China peaks

668 Korean conquest; vassal state of Silla

712–756 Xuanzong emperor

840s Period of Buddhist persecution

200 C.E.   **600** C.E.   **800** C.E.

INTRODUCTION

The postclassical period saw a vital consolidation of basic themes in Chinese civilization, whereby the ability to innovate on the basis of tradition was unparalleled. Less fundamental innovation occurred in China than in civilization areas such as the Americas or the two parts of Europe. Yet, Chinese civilization contributed important new developments, some of which, notably in technology, soon affected the wider world network. Attention to postclassical China obviously returns to the core civilization areas of Asia and to the network of relationships that developed among societies in Asia and around the Mediterranean. Chinese achievements—for example, the size of cities—are best compared with the Middle East or India. China also formed its own wider orbit in eastern Asia. Relatively isolated compared with the Islamic world and India, China nevertheless contributed vitally to other areas as it flourished under two vigorous dynasties.

In the era of political division and civil strife after the breakdown of the Han dynasty in the last decades of the 2nd century C.E., most of the advances of the Qin–Han era (221 B.C.E. to 220 C.E.) appeared to have been lost. Writers in the *period of the Six Dynasties* (220–589 C.E.) feared that the very basis for maintaining civilization in China had been swept away by a new wave of nomadic invasions and the seemingly endless wars fought by the patchwork of regional kingdoms that vied with each other to claim the imperial throne of the fallen Han. The bureaucratic apparatus of the empire collapsed, though many of the successor states aspired to the Qin–Han ideal of state centralization. In most kingdoms the position of the scholar-gentry declined sharply as landed families with aristocratic pretensions dominated regional rulers.

The reemergence of bickering and self-serving aristocratic elites could not help but remind the scholars who recorded China's history of the chaos and suffering of the Warring States period before the rise of the Qin.

In the centuries after the fall of the Han, non-Chinese nomads ruled much of China, and a foreign religion, Buddhism, eclipsed Confucian teachings as the prime force in Chinese political and cultural life. The Great Wall was divided between kingdoms and usually poorly defended as nomadic peoples raided and conquered across the north China plain. Trade and city life declined, technology stagnated, and with mainly Buddhist exceptions, thought degenerated into the quest for magical cures and the elixir of immortality.

Given the magnitude of these reverses and the fact that Chinese civilization was battered and dislocated for nearly four centuries, its revival at the very end of the 6th century C.E. appears at first glance abrupt and incomprehensible. But the reestablishment of a centralized empire under the short-lived Sui dynasty, and the restoration and growth of Chinese civilization during the 300-year Tang reign (618–907) that followed, demonstrated convincingly the great strength of the patterns of civilized life that had coalesced in the Qin–Han era. The rapid revival of empire and civilization under the Tang was also made possible by the preservation, in the kingdoms that carved up the Han Empire, of the Confucian institutions and ideas that had been so central to the development of civilization in China. Not only did the rulers of these kingdoms aspire to reunify China—an ideal that was a key ingredient of civilization as it had come to be understood in China—but the destruction and human suffering of the Six Dynasties era led to an intense longing at all social levels for a return to imperial order.

The victories of the two Sui emperors laid the basis for political unity that would be fully exploited by the early Tang rulers. Under the Tang, the Chinese imperial regime was again able to extend its control over the nomadic peoples who lived on the fringes of the empire as well as over the quarrelsome nobles who competed for political power. The first sections of this chapter will trace the rise of Sui–Tang rule and focus on the process of bureaucratic reconstruction that these dynasties undertook to solidify their power. The next sections will

960–1279 Song dynasty; Neo-Confucian revival

907 End of the Tang dynasty

1127–1279 Southern Song dynasty

1279–1368 Mongol (Yuan) dynasty rules all China

1067–1085 Shenzong emperor; reforms of Wang Anshi

c. 1050 Invention of block printing

c. 1100 Invention of gunpowder

1119 First reference to the use of the compass for sea navigation

1115 Jurchen (Qin) kingdom in North China

950 C.E.

1100 C.E.

1250 C.E.

cover the major changes in Chinese economic and social life that occurred in the Tang era, with emphasis on the monumental shifts in the center of population, production, and trade from the north China plain to the Yangtze valley and coastal areas to the south. With political unification and the rapid expansion of the agricultural and commercial sectors came a renaissance in the arts, scholarship, and invention. These developments, with an emphasis on the often creative tensions between Chinese Buddhism and a revived Confucianism, will be discussed in the final sections on the Tang.

In a very real sense, particularly in thought and the arts, the revival begun in the Tang was continued and in some ways brought to full fruition under the Song dynasty (960–1279), which came to power after Tang authority collapsed in the first decades of the 10th century. The Song Empire never attained the size of the Tang, and Song political control at home was not as effectively exercised. But the Song era saw the full restoration of the scholar-gentry and the Confucian order. It was also perhaps the most glorious age of Chinese artistic and literary production as well as a period of technological innovation that has few parallels in all human history. These latter accomplishments will be the focus of the section on the Song, which will end with a discussion of the underlying political failings of the dynasty. These shortcomings left China open to new nomadic incursions and, finally, to the conquest in 1279 of what was left of the Song Empire by the Mongols.

REBUILDING THE IMPERIAL EDIFICE IN THE SUI–TANG ERA

Focal Point: The emergence at the end of the 6th century C.E. of the Sui dynasty from the patchwork of warring states that had dominated Chinese history for nearly four centuries signaled a return to strong dynastic control. In the Tang era that followed the Sui interlude, the bureaucratic institutions begun under the Han were restored, improved, and greatly expanded. A Confucian revival significantly enhanced the position of the scholar-gentry administrators and provided the ideological underpinnings for a return to highly centralized rule under an imperial dynasty.

The initial steps of the rise of the Sui dynasty in the early 580s appeared at first to be just another factional struggle of the sort that had occurred repeatedly in the splinter states fighting for control of China in the centuries after the fall of the Han. *Wendi,* a member of a promi-

nent north Chinese noble family that had long been active in these contests, struck a marriage alliance between his daughter and the ruler of the northern Zhou empire, who had only recently defeated several rival rulers and united much of the north China plain. After considerable intrigue, Wendi seized the throne of his son-in-law and proclaimed himself emperor. Though Wendi himself was ethnic Chinese, he secured his power base by winning the support of neighboring nomadic military commanders. He did this by reconfirming their titles and showing little inclination to favor the Confucian scholar-gentry class at their expense. With their support, Wendi completed the extension of his empire across north China, and in 589 attacked and conquered the weak and divided Chen kingdom, which had long ruled much of the south. With his victory over the Chen, Wendi reunited the traditional core areas of Chinese civilization for the first time in three and a half centuries.

Wendi won widespread popular support by lowering taxes and establishing ever-ready granaries throughout his domains. These bins for storing grain were established in all the large cities and in each village of the empire to ensure that there would be a reserve food supply in case floods or drought destroyed the peasants' crops and threatened the people with famine. Large landholders and poor peasants alike were taxed a portion of their crop to ensure that the granaries were filled for times of crisis. Beyond warding off famine, the surplus grain was dumped on the market in times of food shortages to hold down the price of the people's staple food.

Sui Excesses and Collapse

The foundations Wendi laid for political unification and economic prosperity were at first strengthened even further by his son *Yangdi,* who murdered his father to reach the throne. Yangdi extended his father's conquests and drove back the nomadic intruders who threatened the northern frontiers of the empire. He promulgated a new and milder legal code and devoted considerable resources to upgrading Confucian education and restoring the examination system for regulating entry into the bureaucracy. These latter measures were part of a broader policy of promoting the scholar-gentry in the imperial administration, often to the detriment of the great aristocratic families and nomadic military commanders.

Yangdi was overly fond of luxury and delighted in construction projects that reached megalomaniacal proportions. He forcibly conscripted hundreds of thousands of peasants to build numerous palaces, a new capital city at Loyang, and above all a series of great canals to link

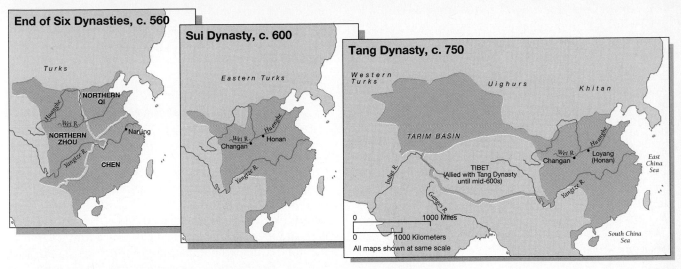

China During the Periods of the Six Dynasties, the Sui Dynasty, and the Tang Dynasty

the various parts of his empire. His demands on the people seemed limitless. In his new capital at Loyang, for example, Yangdi had a vast, heavily forested game park laid out. Because there were not enough trees on the site chosen, tens of thousands of laborers were forced to dig up huge trees in the nearby hills and cart them miles to be replanted in the artificial mounds that tens of thousands of other laborers had built.

Even before work on his many construction projects had been completed, Yangdi led his exhausted and angry subjects into a series of unsuccessful wars to bring Korea again under Chinese rule. His failures in the Korean campaigns between 611 and 614, and the near-fatal reverse he suffered in central Asia at the hands of Turkic nomads in 615, set in motion widespread revolts throughout the empire. Provincial governors declared themselves independent rulers, bandit gangs roved and raided at will, and nomadic peoples again established control over large sections of the north China plain. Faced with a crumbling empire, an increasingly deranged emperor retreated to his pleasure palaces in the city of Yangzhou on the Yangtze River to the south. When Yangdi was assassinated by his own ministers in 618, it looked very much as if China would return to the state of political division and social turmoil it had endured in the preceding centuries.

The Emergence of the Tang and the Restoration of the Empire

The dissolution of the imperial order was averted by the military skills and political savvy of one of Yangdi's most illustrious officials, *Li Yuan*, the Duke of Tang. Of no-

ble and mixed Chinese-nomadic origins, Li Yuan was for many years a loyal supporter of the Sui ruler. In fact, on one occasion, Li Yuan had rescued the impetuous Yangdi, whose forces had been trapped by a far larger force of Turkic cavalry in a small fort that was part of the Great Wall defenses. But as Yangdi grew more and more irrational and unrest spread from one end of the empire to another, Li Yuan was convinced by his sons and allies that only rebellion could save his family and the empire. From the many-sided struggle for the throne that followed Yangdi's death and continued until 623, Li Yuan emerged the victor.

Together with his second son, Tang Taizong, in whose favor he abdicated in 626, Li Yuan, who took the imperial name Gaozu, laid the basis for the golden age of the Tang. Tang armies conquered deep into central Asia as far as present-day Afghanistan, thereby forcing many of the nomadic peoples who had dominated China in the Six Dynasties era to submit to Tang overlordship. Of all the nomadic peoples on the empire's borders, the Turkic tribes posed the greatest threat. Therefore, the early Tang rulers sought to play one Turkic people off another, a stratagem that very often succeeded. They also completed the repairs begun by the Sui and earlier dynasties on the Great Wall and created frontier armies, partly recruited from the nomadic peoples, that gradually became the most potent military forces in the empire. Leaders of Turkic tribes were compelled to submit as vassals to the Tang rulers, who took the title "heavenly khan." The daughters of the Turkic khans were often married into the imperial family. The sons were sent to the capital both as hostages to guarantee the good behavior of the tribe in question and as students who were to be educated in Chinese ways in the hope of their eventual assimilation into Chinese culture.

The empire was also extended to parts of Tibet in the west, the Red River valley homeland of the Vietnamese in the south (see Chapter 19), and Manchuria in the north. In the Tang period, the Yangtze River basin and much of the south were fully integrated with north China for the first time since the Han. In 668, under the emperor Kaozong, Korea was overrun by Chinese armies, and a vassal kingdom called Silla was established that long remained loyal to the Tang. In a matter of decades, the Tang had built an empire that was far larger than even that of the early Han—an empire whose boundaries in many directions extended beyond the borders of present-day China.

Rebuilding the Bureaucracy

Crucial for the restoration of Chinese unity were the efforts undertaken by the early Tang monarchs to rebuild and expand the imperial bureaucracy. A revived scholar-gentry elite and reworked Confucian ideology played central roles in this process. From the time of the second Sui emperor, Yangdi, the fortunes of the scholar-gentry had begun to improve markedly. This trend continued under the early Tang emperors, who desperately needed loyal and well-educated officials to govern the vast empire they had put together in a matter of decades. The Tang rulers also used the scholar-gentry bureaucrats to offset the power of the aristocracy.

As the control of the aristocratic families over court life and administration declined, their role in Chinese history was much reduced. From the Tang era onward, political power in China was shared by a succession of imperial families and the bureaucrats of the civil service system. Members of the hereditary aristocracy continued to occupy administrative positions, but the scholar-gentry class came to staff most of the posts in the secretariats and executive department that oversaw a huge bureaucracy.

This bureaucracy reached from the imperial palace down to the subprefecture, or district level, which was roughly equivalent to an American county. One secretariat drafted imperial decrees; a second monitored the reports of regional and provincial officials and the petitions of local notables. The executive department, which was divided into six ministries—including war, justice, and public works—ran the empire on a day-to-day basis. In addition, there was a powerful Bureau of Censors, whose chief task was to keep track of officials at all levels

and report their misdeeds or failures to perform their duties. Finally, there was a very large staff to run the imperial household, both the palaces in the capital at *Changan* and the subsidiary residences of the princes of the imperial line and other dignitaries.

The Growing Importance of the Examination System

Like Yangdi, the Tang emperors patronized academies to train state officials and educate them in the Confucian classics. In the Tang era, and under the Song dynasty that followed, the numbers of the educated scholar-gentry rose far above those in the Han era, though this elite and its dependents remained only a tiny fraction of the total Chinese population. In the Tang and Song periods, the examination system was also greatly enlarged, and the pattern of advancement in the civil service was much more regularized. Several different kinds of examinations were administered by the *Ministry of Rites* to students from the government schools or to those recommended by distinguished scholars.

The highest offices could be gained only by those who were able to pass exams on the classics or the even more difficult exams on Chinese literature. Those who passed the latter earned the title of *jinshi*. Their names were announced throughout the empire, their families' positions were secured by the prospect of high office that was opened up by their success, and they became overnight dignitaries, whom even their former student friends addressed formally and treated with deference. A further round of written and oral examinations determined the jinshi holder's ranking in the pool of civil servants who were eligible for the highest positions in the imperial administration, and thus the office he actually received. Success in exams at all levels won the candidate special social status, which included the right to wear certain types of clothing, freedom from corporal punishment, and the power to demand services and outward signs of respect, such as bowing, from the common people.

Even though a much higher proportion of Tang bureaucrats won their positions through success in civil service examinations than had been the case in the Han era, birth and family connections continued to be important in securing high office. Established bureaucrats not only saw that their sons and cousins got into the imperial academies but could pull strings to see that even failed candidates from their families received government posts. Ethnic and regional ties also played a role in the staffing of bureaucratic departments. This meant that al-

As shown in this ink drawing of Chinese philosophers during the Song dynasty, board games and musical recitals were highly esteemed leisure activities for the scholar-gentry class.

though bright commoners could rise to upper-level positions in the bureaucracy, the central administration was dominated by a rather small number of established families. Sons followed fathers in positions of power and influence, and prominent households bought a disproportionate share of the places available in the imperial academies. Many positions were reserved for members of the old aristocracy and the low-ranking sons and grandsons of lesser wives and concubines belonging to the imperial family. Merit and ambition counted for something, but birth and family influence often counted for a good deal more.

State and Religion in the Tang–Song Era

The Confucian revival threatened not only the old aristocratic families, whose power diminished as that of the scholar-gentry bureaucrats grew, but also the Buddhists, who had become a major force in Chinese life in the Six Dynasties era. Many of the rulers in the pre–Tang era, particularly those from nomadic origins, had been devout Buddhists and strong patrons of the Buddhist establishment. In the centuries after the fall of the Han, Buddhist sects had proliferated in China. The most popular were those founded by Chinese monks, in part because they soon took on distinctively Chinese qualities. Among the masses, the salvationist *pure land* strain of Mahayana *Buddhism* won widespread conversions as a refuge from an age of war and turmoil. Members of the elite classes, on the other hand, were more attracted to the *Chan* variant of Buddhism, or Zen as it is known in Japan and the

West. With its stress on meditation and the appreciation of natural and artistic beauty, and its Daoist hostility to written texts and scholasticism, Zen had great appeal for the educated classes of China. The riddlelike quality of Zen sayings was apparently particularly intriguing to Chinese intellectuals. The following sequence of questions and answers provides a fairly typical example:

> The Master asked the monk: "What are you doing?"
> The monk answered: "Sweeping the floor."
> The Master said: "In front of the Buddha figure or behind it?"
> The monk answered: "Both at the same time."
> The Master said: "Give your sandals to Ts'ao-shan."

The combination of royal patronage and widespread conversion at both the elite and mass levels had made Buddhism a strong social, economic, and political force by the time of the Tang unification. The early Tang rulers continued to patronize Buddhism while attempted to promote education in the Confucian classics. Emperors like Taizong endowed monasteries, sent emissaries to India to collect texts and relics, and commissioned Buddhist paintings and statuary. No Tang ruler, however, matched the empress Wu (690–705) in supporting the Buddhist establishment. Not only did she contribute large sums to build or improve monasteries and reward Buddhist cooperation with impressive grants of land, at one point she sought to elevate Buddhism to

At sites such as Lungmen near the Yangtze River and Yunkang far to the north, massive statues of the Buddha were carved out of rocky cliffsides beginning in the 6th century A.D.

the status of a state religion. Empress Wu also commissioned numerous Buddhist paintings and sculptures.

The sculptures are particularly noteworthy for their colossal size. She had statues of the Buddha, which were as much as two and three stories high, carved from stone or cast in bronze. Some of these statues were housed in great caves near her capital at Loyang; for others she had equally huge pagodas built. With this sort of support, it is not surprising that Buddhism flourished in the early centuries of Tang rule. By the middle of the 9th century, there were nearly 50,000 monasteries and hundreds of thousands of Buddhist monks and nuns in China.

The Anti-Buddhist Backlash

Buddhist successes inevitably aroused the envy and enmity of both Confucian and Daoist rivals. Some of these attacked the religion as alien, even though the faith followed by most of the Chinese was very different from that originally preached by the Buddha or that practiced in India or Southeast Asia. Daoist monks sought to counter Buddhism's appeals to the masses by stressing their own magical and predictive powers—a tendency that led to a continuation of the long-standing Chinese fascination with alchemy and potions for fertility and longevity. Most damaging to the fortunes of Buddhism, however, was the growing campaign of Confucian scholar-administrators to convince the Tang rulers that

the large Buddhist monastic establishment posed a fundamental economic challenge to the imperial order. Because monastic lands and resources were not taxed, the Tang regime lost huge amounts of revenue because of imperial grants to Buddhist monasteries or the wills of ordinary Chinese, which turned family properties over to Buddhist monasteries as an act of religious devotion. The state was also denied labor power, because it could neither tax nor conscript peasants who worked monastic estates.

By the mid-8th century, it was clear that the rapidly growing Buddhist monastic orders were a major drain on China's resources and an obvious economic competitor of the Tang dynasty. Measures to limit the flow of land and resources to the monastic orders gave way in the 840s to open persecution of Buddhism under the emperor *Wuzong* (841–847). Thousands of monasteries and Buddhist shrines were destroyed, and hundreds of thousands of monks and nuns were forced to abandon their monastic existence and return to ordinary civilian lives. They and the slaves and peasants who worked their lands were again subject to taxation, and monastery lands were parceled out to taxpaying landlords and peasant smallholders.

Though Chinese Buddhism survived this and other bouts of repression, it did so in a much reduced state. Never again would the Buddhist monastic orders possess the political influence and control the wealth they had enjoyed in the first centuries of Tang rule. The great age

DOCUMENT

Ties That Bind: Paths to Power

The following letter was included in a short story by the Tang author Niu Su. It was sent by a local functionary named Wu Bao to a high official to whom Wu hoped to attach himself and thus win advancement in the imperial bureaucracy. What can this letter tell us about the ways in which the Chinese bureaucracy worked in the Tang and Song eras?

To my great good fortune, we share the same native place, and your renown for wise counsel is well known to me. Although, through gross neglect, I have omitted to prostrate myself before you, my heart has always been filled with admiration and respect. You are the nephew of the Prime Minister, and have made use of your outstanding talents in his service. In consequence of this, your high ability has been rewarded with a commission. General Li is highly-qualified both as a civil and a military official, and he has been put in full command of the expedition [to put down "barbarian" rebellions in the southern parts of the empire]. In his hands he unites mighty forces, and he cannot fail to bring these petty brigands to order. By the alliance of the General's heroic valor and your own talent and ability, your armies' task of subjugation will be the work of a day. I, in my youth, devoted myself to study.

Reaching manhood, I paid close attention to the [Confucian] classics. But in talent I do not compare with other men, and so far I have held office only as an officer of the guard. I languish in this out-of-the-way corner beyond the Chien [mountains], close to the haunts of the barbarians. My native place is thousands of miles away, and many passes and rivers lie between. What is more, my term of office here is completed, and I cannot tell when I shall receive my next appointment. So lacking in talent, I fear I am but poorly fitted to be selected for an official post; far less can I entertain the hope of some meager salary. I can only retire, when old age comes, to some rustic retreat, and "turn aside to die in a ditch." I have heard by devious ways of your readiness to help those in distress. If you will not overlook a man from your native place, be quick to bestow your special favour on me, so that I may render you service "as a humble groom." Grant me some small salary, and a share however slight in your deeds of merit. If by your boundless favour I could take part in this triumphal progress, even as a member of the rear-most company, the day would live engraved on my memory.

Questions: What techniques does Wu employ to win the high official's favor? How does Wu expect the official to help him? What does he promise in return? Does birth or merit appear to be more important in his appeals? What does this suggest about the place of the examinations in the political system? What dangers to the imperial system are contained in the sorts of ties that Wu argues bind him to the high official?

---

of Buddhist painting and cave sculptures gave way to art dominated by Daoist-Confucian subjects and styles in the late Tang and the Song dynastic era that followed. The Zen and "pure land" sects of Buddhism continued to attract adherents, those of the latter numbering in the millions. But Confucianism emerged as the central ideology of Chinese civilization for most of the period from the 9th to the early 20th century. Buddhism left its mark on the arts, the Chinese language, and Chinese thinking about things such as heaven, charity, and law, but it ceased to be a dominant influence. Buddhism's fate in China contrasts sharply with its ongoing and pivotal impact on the civilizations of mainland Southeast Asia, Tibet, and parts of central Asia.

TANG DECLINE AND THE RISE OF THE SONG

Focal Point: After several centuries of strong rule, the Tang dynasty fell on hard times. Beset by internal rebellions and nomadic incursions, the Tang gave way to the Song in the early 10th century. Though the Song domains were considerably smaller than the Tang, the Confucian revival flourished under the successor dynasty. Following new waves of nomadic invasions, in the mid-12th century the Song lost control of north China. A century and a half later, their rump empire in the south of China fell, after a prolonged struggle, to the Mongols under Kubilai Khan.

Because many of the great Buddhist temples and monasteries in China were destroyed in various waves of persecution, some of the best surviving examples of East Asian Buddhist architecture, such as this monastery at Kyoto, are found in Japan.

The motives behind the mid-9th century Tang assault on the Buddhist monastic order were symptomatic of a general weakening of imperial control that had begun almost a century earlier. Following the decades of controversial but strong rule between 690 and 705 by Empress Wu, who actually sought to establish a new dynasty, a second attempt to control the throne was made by a highborn woman who had married into the imperial family. Backed by her powerful relatives and an extensive clique of prominent courtiers, Empress Wei poisoned her husband, the son of Empress Wu, and placed her own small child on the throne. But Empress Wei's attempt to seize power was thwarted by another prince, who led a palace revolt that ended with the destruction of Wei and her supporters. The early decades of the long reign of this prince, who became the emperor Xuanzong (713–756), marked the peak of Tang power and the high point of Chinese civilization under the Tang dynasty.

Initially, Xuanzong took a strong interest in political and economic reforms, which were pushed by the very capable officials he was able to appoint to high positions. Increasingly, his interest in running the vast Tang Empire waned, and he devoted himself more and more to patronizing the arts and to the enjoyment of the considerable pleasures available within the confines of the imperial city. These diversions included music, which he played and also had performed by the numerous musi-

cians he summoned. Thousands of concubines vied in the imperial apartments for the attention of the monarch. After the death of his second wife, the aged and lonely emperor became infatuated with *Yang Guifei*, a beautiful young woman from the harem of one of the imperial princes.

Their relationship proved to be one of the most famous and ill-starred romances in all of Chinese history. While Xuanzong promenaded in the imperial gardens and gave flute lessons to Yang, who was raised to the status of royal concubine, she packed the upper levels of the government with her avaricious relatives and assumed an ever greater role in court politics. The arrogance and greed of Yang Guifei and her family angered members of the rival cliques at court who took every opportunity to turn Yang's excesses into a cause for popular unrest. Xuanzong's long neglect of state affairs resulted in economic distress, which fed this unrest. It also led to chronic military weaknesses, which rendered the government unable to deal with the disorders effectively. The deepening crisis came to a head in 755, when one of the emperor's main military leaders, a general of nomadic origins named An Lushan, led a widely supported revolt with the aim of founding a new dynasty to supplant the Tang.

Though the revolt was eventually crushed and the Tang dynasty preserved, victory was won at a very high cost. Early in the rebellion, Xuanzong's retreating and

This painting of Yang Guifei gives a vivid impression of the opulence and refinement of Chinese court life in the late-Tang era.

demoralized troops mutinied, first killing several members of the Yang family and then forcing the emperor to do away with Yang Guifei herself. Xuanzong lived on for a time, but his grief and disillusionment rendered him utterly incapable of continuing as emperor. None of the Tang monarchs who followed him could compare with the able leaders the dynasty had rather consistently produced in the first century and a half of its rule.

Equally critical, in order to defeat the rebels the Tang had both sought alliances with nomadic peoples living on the northern borders of the empire and delegated resources and political power to regional commanders. As had happened so often in the past, in the late 8th and 9th centuries the nomads used political divisions within China to gain entry into and eventually assert their control over large areas of the north China plain. At the same time, many provincial governors became in effect independent rulers. They collected their own taxes, passing little or none on to the imperial treasury; raised their own armies; and bequeathed their titles to their sons without asking for permission from the Tang court. Worsening economic conditions led to a succession of revolts in the 9th century, some of which were popular risings led by peasants.

The Founding of the Song Dynasty

By the end of the 9th century, little remained of the once-glorious Tang Empire. By 907, when the last emperor of the Tang dynasty was forced to resign, China appeared to be entering yet another era of nomadic dominance, political division, and social strife. In 960, however, a military commander emerged to reunite China under a single dynasty. *Zhao Kuangyin* had established a far-flung reputation as one of the most honest and able of the generals of the last of the "Five Dynasties" that had struggled to control north China after the fall of the Tang. Though a fearless warrior, Zhao was a man of scholarly leanings, who collected books rather than booty while out campaigning. In the midst of the continuing struggles for control in the north, Zhao's subordinates and regular troops insisted that he proclaim himself emperor. In the next few years, Zhao, renamed Emperor Taizu, routed all his rivals except one, thus founding the Song dynasty that was to rule most of China for the next three centuries.

The one rival Taizu could not overcome was the northern Liao dynasty, which had been founded in 907 by the nomadic Khitan peoples from Manchuria. This

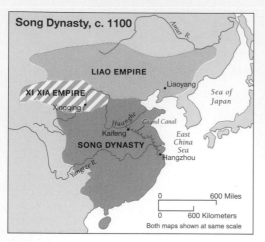

China in the Song and Southern Song Dynastic Periods

failure set a precedent for weakness in dealing with the nomadic peoples of the north that would plague the Song dynasty from its earliest years to its eventual destruction by the Mongols in the late 13th century. Beginning in 1004, the Song were forced by military defeats at the hands of the Khitans to sign a series of humiliating treaties with their smaller but more militarily adept northern neighbors. These treaties committed the Song to paying what was in effect a very heavy tribute to the Liao dynasty to deter it from raiding and possibly conquering the Song domains. The Khitans, who had been highly Sinified during a century of rule in north China, were apparently content with this arrangement. They clearly regarded the ethnic Chinese empire of the Song as culturally superior—an area from which they could learn much in statecraft, the arts, and economic organization.

Song Politics: Settling for Partial Restoration

A comparison of the boundaries of the early Song Empire with that of the Tang domains reveals that the Song never matched its predecessor in political or military strength. The relative weakness of the Song resulted in part from imperial policies that were designed to ward off the conditions that had destroyed the Tang Empire. From the outset, the military was clearly subordinated to the civilian administrators of the scholar-gentry class. Only civil officials were allowed to be governors, thereby removing the temptation of regional military commanders to seize power in their own right. In addition, all military commanders were rotated to prevent them from building up a power base in the areas where they were stationed.

At the same time, the early Song rulers strongly promoted the interests of the Confucian scholar-gentry, who touted themselves as the key bulwark against the revival of warlordism. Officials' salaries were significantly increased and numerous perks—including additional servants and payments of luxury goods such as silk and wine—made government posts more lucrative than ever before. The civil service exams were fully routinized. They were given every three years at three levels: district, provincial, and imperial. Song examiners passed a far higher percentage of those taking the exams than the Tang examiners had, and these successful candidates were much more likely to receive an official post than their counterparts in the Tang era. As a result, the bureaucracy soon became bloated with well-paid officials who often had little to do. In this way, the ascendancy of the scholar-gentry class over its aristocratic and Buddhist rivals was fully secured in the Song era.

The Revival of Confucian Thought

The great influence of the scholar-gentry in the Song era was mirrored in the revival of Confucian ideas and values that dominated intellectual life. Many scholars tried to recover long-neglected texts and decipher ancient inscriptions. New academies devoted to the study of the classical texts were founded, and impressive libraries were established. The adherents of new schools of philosophy propounded rival interpretations of the teachings of Confucius and other ancient thinkers and sought to prove the superiority of indigenous thought systems, such as Confucianism and Daoism, over imported ones, especially Buddhism. The most prominent thinkers of the era, such as *Zhu Xi*, stressed the importance of applying philosophical principles to everyday life and action.

These neo-Confucianists believed that the cultivation of personal morality was the highest goal to which humans could aspire. They argued that virtue could be attained through the acquisition of knowledge gained by book learning and personal observation as well as through contact with men of wisdom and high morality. In these ways, the basically good nature of humans could be cultivated, and superior *men*, fit to govern and teach others, could be developed.

Neo-Confucian thinking, which would have a great impact on Chinese intellectual life during the eras of all the dynasties that followed the Song, affected many aspects of Chinese life. Its hostility to foreign philosophical systems, such as Buddhism, rendered Chinese rulers and bureaucrats less receptive to outside ideas and influences at a time when it was increasingly critical for them to be aware of developments in other civilizations. The neo-Confucian emphasis on tradition and past precedents was one of a number of forces that eventually did much to stifle innovation and critical thinking among the Chinese elite. The neo-Confucian emphasis on rank, obligation, deference, and the performance of traditional rituals reinforced class, age, and gender distinctions, particularly as these were expressed in occupational roles. Great importance was given to upholding the authority of the patriarchal head of the Chinese household, who was compared to the male emperor of the Chinese people as a whole. If men and women kept to their place and performed the tasks allotted by their age and social rank, the neo-Confucians argued, there would be social harmony and prosperity. If problems arose, the best solutions could be found in examples drawn from the past; historical experience was thought to be the best guide for navigating the uncertain terrain of the future.

Roots of Decline: Attempts at Reform

The means by which the Song emperors had secured their control over China did much to undermine their empire in the long run. The weakness they had shown in the face of the Khitan challenge encouraged other nomadic peoples to carve out kingdoms on the northern borders of the Song domains. By the mid-11th century, Tangut tribesmen, who had originally come from Tibet, had established a kingdom named Xi Xia to the northwest of the Khitan kingdom of Liao. The tribute that the Song had to pay to each of these peoples for "protection" of their northern borders was a great drain on the resources of the empire and a growing burden for the Chinese peasantry. Equally burdensome was the cost of the army, numbering nearly 1 million soldiers by the

middle of the 11th century, that the Song had to maintain to guard against invasion from the north.

The emphasis on civil administration and the scholar-gentry and the growing disdain among the Song elite for the military also took their toll. Though Song armies were large, their commanders were rarely the most able men available, and funds needed to upgrade weapons or repair fortifications were often diverted to the scholarly pursuits and entertainments of the court and gentry. At the court and among the ruling classes throughout the empire, painting and poetry, which account for some of the most splendid achievements of the Song era, were cultivated, while the horsemanship and hunting that had so preoccupied earlier rulers and their courtiers went out of fashion.

In the 1070s and early 1080s, *Wang Anshi,* the chief minister of the Song Shenzong emperor, attempted to ward off the impending collapse of the dynasty through the introduction of sweeping reforms. Wang, who was a celebrated Confucian scholar, ran the government on the basis of the Legalist (see Chapter 5) assumption that an energetic and interventionist state could greatly increase the resources and strength of the dynasty. For 20 years, in the face of strong opposition from the conservative ministers who controlled most of the administrative apparatus, Wang sought to correct the grave defects in the imperial order. He introduced cheap loans and government-assisted irrigation projects to encourage agricultural expansion. He taxed the landlord and scholarly classes, who had regularly exempted themselves from military service. Wang used the revenue received to establish well-trained mercenary forces to replace armies that had formerly been conscripted from the unprepared and unwilling peasantry. Wang even attempted to reorganize university education and reorient the examination system so that analytical skills were given precedence over the rote memorization of the classics that had long been key to success.

Reaction and Disaster: The Flight to the South

Unfortunately, Wang's ability to propose and enact reforms was totally dependent on continuing support from the Shenzong emperor. In 1085 that emperor died, and his successor favored the conservative cliques that had long opposed Wang's changes. The neo-Confucians came to power, reform halted, and many of Wang's initiatives were reversed. As a result, economic conditions continued to deteriorate, and peasant unrest grew throughout the empire. Faced by banditry and rebellion from within, an unprepared military proved no match for the increasing threat from beyond the northern borders of the empire. In 1115, a new nomadic contender, the *Jurchens,* had overthrown the Liao dynasty of the Khitans and established the Qin kingdom north of the Song Empire. After successful invasions of Song territory, the Jurchens annexed most of the Yellow River basin to what had become the Qin Empire and forced the Song to flee to the south. With the Yangtze River basin as their anchor and their capital transferred to Hangzhou, the Song dynasty would survive for another century and a half. Politically the *southern Song* dynasty (1127–1279) was little more than a rump state carved out of the much larger domains ruled by the Tang and Northern Song. Culturally, its comparatively brief reign was to be one of the most glorious in Chinese history—perhaps in the history of all humankind.

TANG AND SONG PROSPERITY: THE BASIS OF A GOLDEN AGE

Focal Point: In addition to being the era in which China was reunified under strong imperial regimes, the Tang and Song period was a time of major transitions in Chinese history. Shifts in the balance of population within China, new patterns of trade and commerce, renewed urban expansion, novel forms of artistic and literary expression, and a series of further technological breakthroughs all contributed to new directions in the development of Chinese civilization. These shifts became particularly pronounced in the late-Tang period and the centuries of rule by the Song dynasty (960–1279). The China that emerged from this era was vastly more wealthy and market-oriented and much more bureaucratized, urbanized, and cosmopolitan than the civilization that had first come to fruition in the Han epoch.

The attention given to canal building by the Sui emperors and the Tang rulers who followed them was compelled by a major shift in the population balance within Chinese civilization. The Grand Canal, which Yangdi imperiled his throne to have constructed, was designed to link the original centers of Chinese civilization on the north China plain with the Yangtze River basin more than 500 miles to the south. Because the great river systems that were essential to China's agrarian base ran from west to east—from the mountains of central Asia to the sea—the movement of people and goods in that direction was much easier than from north to south. Though no major geographical barriers separated the

The farming methods that were developed in the Song era are illustrated by this 17th-century engraving. Note the overseer, protected by an umbrella from the hot sun.

millet-growing areas of northern China from the rice-producing Yangtze basin, travel overland was slow and difficult, and the transport of bulk goods like millet or rice was prohibitively expensive. The great increase of the ethnic Chinese population in the southern regions in the later Han and Six Dynasties periods made the improvement of communications between north and south imperative once the two regions were joined by the Sui conquests. Not only did more and more of the emperor's subjects live in the southern regions, but the Yangtze basin and other rice-growing areas in the south were fast becoming the major food-producing areas of the empire. By late Tang and early Song times, the south had surpassed the north in both crop production and total population.

Yangdi's Grand Canal was intended to facilitate control over the southern regions by courts, bureaucracies, and armies centered in ancient imperial centers such as Changan and Loyang in the north. The canal made it possible to transport revenue collected in the form of grain from the fertile southern regions and to transfer food from areas in the south to districts threatened by drought and famine in the north. No wonder that Yangdi was quite literally obsessed with canal construction. By the time the Grand Canal was finished, well over 1 million forced laborers had worked, and many had died, on its locks and embankments.

The completed canal system was an engineering achievement every bit as impressive as the Great Wall. It joined the Yellow River to the cities of the northeast and to the Yangtze basin and the sea on the south central coast. Most stretches of the canal, which totaled nearly 1200 miles in length, were 40 paces wide, and imperial highways lined with willow trees ran along the banks on both sides. Its construction not only created a bridge to join north and south China but opened up the south to migration and commercial development on a scale unimaginable in previous centuries.

A New Phase of Commercial Expansion

Tang conquests in central Asia and the building of the canal system did much to promote commercial expansion in the Tang and Song centuries. The extension of Tang control deep into central Asia meant that the overland silk routes between China and Persia to the west were reopened and protected—a vital step in the intensification of international contacts in the postclassical period. This facilitated mutually beneficial exchanges between China and Buddhist centers in the nomadic lands as well as with the Islamic world farther west. Horses, Persian rugs, and tapestries passed to China along these routes, while fine silk textiles, porcelain, and paper were exported to the centers of Islamic civilization.

As in the Han era, China exported mainly manufactured goods to overseas areas, such as Southeast Asia, while importing mainly luxury products such as aromatic woods and spices. Trading ships for oceanic, canal, and river transport improved dramatically, and their numbers multiplied many times in the Tang and Song eras. In late Tang and Song times, Chinese merchants and sailors increasingly carried Chinese trade overseas instead of being content to let foreign seafarers come to them. Along with the dhows of the Arabs, Chinese *junks* were the best ships in the world in this period. They were equipped with watertight bulkheads, sternpost rudders, oars, sails, compasses, bamboo fenders, and gunpowder-propelled rockets for self-defense. With such vessels, Chinese sailors and merchants became the dominant force in the Asian seas east of the Malayan peninsula.

The heightened role of commerce and the money economy in Chinese life was readily apparent in the numerous and enlarged market quarters found in all cities and major towns. These were filled with shops and stalls that sold products drawn from local farms, regional centers of artisan production, and entrepôts as distant as the Mediterranean. The Tang and Song governments supervised the hours and methods in these centers, while merchants specializing in products of the same kind banded together in guilds to promote their interests with local officials and to regulate competition within the trading community.

This expansion in scale was accompanied by a growing sophistication in commercial organization and forms of credit available in China. The proportion of exchanges involved in the money economy expanded greatly, and deposit shops, an early form of bank, were found in many parts of the empire. The first use of paper money also occurred in the Tang era. Merchants deposited their profits in their hometown before setting out on trading caravans to distant cities. They were given credit vouchers, or what the Chinese called *flying money,* which they could then present for reimbursement at the appropriate office in the city of destination. This arrangement greatly reduced the danger of robbery on the often perilous journeys merchants made from one market center to another. In the early 11th century, the government itself began to issue paper money when an economic crisis made it clear that the private merchant banks could no longer handle the demand for the new currency.

The World's Most Splendid Cities

The expansion of commerce and artisan production was complemented by a surge in urban growth in the Tang and Song eras. At nearly 2 million, the population of the Tang capital and its suburbs at Changan was far larger than that of any other city in the world at the time. The imperial city, which was an inner citadel within the walls of Changan, was divided into a highly restricted zone dominated by the palace and audience halls and a section crowded with the offices of the ministries and secretariats of the imperial government. Near the imperial city, but outside Changan's walls, elaborate gardens and a hunting park were laid out for the amusement of the emperors and favored courtiers.

The spread of commerce and the increasing population also fed urban growth in the rest of China. In the north and especially the south, old cities mushroomed in size as suburbs spread in all directions from the original city walls. Towns grew rapidly into cities, and the proportion of the empire's population living in urban centers grew steadily. China had numerous cities with over

CLOSEUP

Hangzhou: Savoring the Delights of a Great City

Of all China's remarkable urban centers in this era, perhaps none surpassed the Late Song capital of *Hangzhou* in size, beauty, and sophistication. Located between a large lake and a river in the Yangtze delta, Hangzhou was criss-crossed by canals and bridges. The city's location near the Yangtze and the coast of the East China Sea allowed its traders and artisans to prosper through the sale of goods or the manufacture of products from materials drawn from both north and south China as well as overseas. By Late Song times, Hangzhou had a population that exceeded a million and a half, and was famed for its wealth, cleanliness, and the number and variety of diversions it offered to visitors and residents alike.

A visitor to Hangzhou could wander through its ten great marketplaces—each stocked with products from much of the then-known world. The less consumption-minded visitor could enjoy the city's many parks and delightful gardens, or go boating on the great Western Lake, where the pleasure craft of the rich mingled with special barges for gaming, dining,

or listening to Hangzhou's famous "singing-girls." By late afternoon, it would be time to take advantage of the bath houses that were found throughout the city. At these establishments, one could also get a massage and sip a cup of tea or rice wine. In the evening, one might dine with family and friends at one of the city's many fine restaurants, which specialized in the varied and delicious cuisines of the different regions of China. After dinner, there was a variety of entertainments from which to chose. One could take in the pleasure parks, where acrobats, jugglers, and actors performed for the passing crowds. Other options included one of the city's ornate tea houses, an opera performance by the lake, or a viewing of landscape paintings by artists from the city's famed academy. Having spent such a day, it would be hard for a visitor to disagree with Marco Polo—who himself hailed from another beautiful city of canals, Venice—that Hangzhou was "the most noble city and the best that is in the world."

100,000 people, whereas most other preindustrial civilizations were fortunate to have more than a handful of large urban centers and some had none. The number of people living in large cities in China, which may have been as high as 10 percent, was also far greater than that found in any civilization until after the Industrial Revolution.

Expanding Agrarian Production and Life in the Country

The movement of the population southward to the fertile valleys of the Yangtze and other river systems was part of a larger process of agrarian expansion in the Tang and Song period. The expansion of Chinese settlement and agricultural production was promoted by the rulers of both dynasties, who actively encouraged peasant groups to migrate to uncultivated areas or those occupied by shifting cultivators or peoples of non-Chinese

descent. The state supported military garrisons in these areas to protect the new settlements and to complete the task of pacifying indigenous non-Chinese peoples. State-regulated irrigation and embankment systems also advanced agrarian expansion, and the great canals made it possible for peasants who grew specialized crops, such as tea, or those who cultivated silkworms to market their produce over much of the empire. The introduction of new seeds, such as the famed Champa rice from Vietnam; better use of human, animal, and silt manures; more thorough soil preparation and weeding; and multiple-cropping and improved techniques of water control increased the yields of peasant holdings. Inventions such as the wheelbarrow eased somewhat the laborious tasks linked to plowing, planting, weeding, and harvesting that occupied much of the time of the great majority of the Chinese people.

The rulers of both the Sui and Tang dynasties had adopted policies aimed at breaking up the great estates of the old aristocracy and distributing land more equitably among the free peasant households of the empire. These policies were, of course, designed in part to reduce if not eliminate the threat that the powerful aristocracy posed for the new dynasties. They were also intended to bolster the position of the ordinary peasants, whose labors and well-being had long been viewed by Confucian scholars as essential to a prosperous and stable social order. To a point, these agrarian measures succeeded. For a time the numbers of the free peasantry increased, and the average holding size in many areas rose. The fortunes of many of the old aristocratic families also declined, thus removing many of them as independent centers of power. They were gradually supplanted in the rural areas by the gentry side of the scholar-gentry combination that dominated the imperial bureaucracy.

The extended-family households of the gentry that were found in rural settlements in the Han era increased in size and elegance in the Tang and Song. The widespread use of the graceful curved roofs with upturned corners that one associates with Chinese civilization dates from the Tang period. By imperial decree, curved roofs were reserved for persons of high rank, including the gentry families. With intricately carved and painted roof timbers topped with glazed tiles of yellow or green, the great dwellings of the gentry left no doubt about the status and power of the families who resided in them. At the same time, their muted colors, wood and bamboo construction, and simple lines blended beautifully with nearby gardens and groves of trees.

Family and Society in the Tang–Song Era

Though Chinese family organization at various class levels in the Tang and Song centuries closely resembled that found in earlier periods, the position of women showed signs of improving under the Tang and Early Song, and then deteriorated steadily in the Late Song. As in the classical age, extended-family households were preferred, but they could normally be afforded only by the upper classes. The male-dominated hierarchy promoted by Confucius and other early thinkers held sway at all class levels. In the Tang period, the authority of elders and males within the family was buttressed by laws that, for example, prescribed beheading as a punishment for children who struck their parents or grandparents in anger, and two and one-half years of hard labor for younger brothers or sisters who hit their older siblings.

Over the centuries, a very elaborate process of forging marriage alliances developed. Professional go-betweens, who were almost invariably women, assisted

Manufacturing silk was a laborious process that required several distinct operations. Here a woman and a small girl put the finishing touches on a roll of embroidered cloth.

both families in negotiating such prickly issues as matching young men and women and the amount of the dowry to be paid to the husband's family. In contrast to India, brides and grooms were generally approximately the same age, probably because of the Confucian abhorrence of mixing generations. In the rural areas, some potential sons-in-law were adopted by their prospective parents-in-law at birth, though the marriage ceremony did not actually take place until both parties had at least reached puberty. Among the urban upper classes, marriages were consummated somewhat later. It was not uncommon for the son of a scholar-gentry family, who was busy with studies for the state examinations, to delay his marriage until he was 30 or older.

Both within the family and in society at large, women remained clearly subordinate to males. But some of the evidence suggests that at least for women of the upper classes in urban areas, the opportunities for personal expression increased in the Tang and early Song. As the example of the empresses Wu and Wei and the concubine Yang Guifei make clear, Tang women could wield considerable power at the highest levels of Chinese society. That they also enjoyed access to a rather broad range of activities, if not career possibilities, is indicated by a surviving pottery figure from the early Tang period of a young woman playing polo.

Some semblance of women's rights is evidenced by provisions in Tang and Song law for divorce by mutual consent of both husband and wife, as well as those prohibiting a man from setting aside his wife if her parents were dead or if he had been poor when they were married and later became rich. These suggest that Chinese wives had more defenses against capricious behavior by their spouses than was the case in India at this time. A remarkable degree of female independence is also indicated by the practice, reported in late Song times, of wealthy women in large cities like Hangzhou taking lovers (or what were politely called "complementary husbands") with the silent though presumably unwilling complicity of their spouses.

The Neo-Confucian Assertion of Male Dominance

Evidence of the independence and legal rights enjoyed by a small minority of privileged women in the Tang–Song era is all but overwhelmed by broader trends that point emphatically to the worsening condition of Chinese women in general. The assertion of male dominance within the family and beyond it was especially pronounced in the thinking of the neo-Confucian philosophers, who, as we have seen, became a major force in the later Song period. The neo-Confucians stressed the woman's role as housemaker and mother—particularly as the bearer of sons to continue the patrilineal family line. They advocated the physical confinement of women and emphasized the importance of virginity for young brides, fidelity for wives, and chastity for widows, who like their counterparts in India were discouraged from remarrying.

At the same time, men were permitted to have premarital sex without scandal, to take numerous concubines if they could afford them, and to remarry if one or more of their wives died. The neo-Confucians attacked the Buddhists for promoting career alternatives for women, such as the monastic life and female scholarship, to marriage and raising a family. They drafted laws that favored males in inheritance, divorce, and familial interaction, and they excluded females from the sort of education that would allow them to enter the civil service and rise to positions of political power.

No practice better exemplifies the degree to which

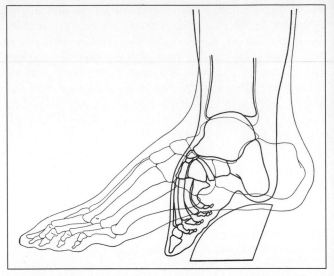

The contrast between the bone structure of a normal foot and that of a Chinese woman whose foot has been bound since she was a young girl is graphically illustrated in this diagram.

women in Chinese civilization had been constricted and subordinated by the end of the Song era as dramatically as *foot-binding*. This counterpart of the veil and seclusion in Islam may have had its origins in the delight that one of the emperors had taken in the tiny feet of his favorite dancing girl. Whatever its origins, by the later Song era upper-class males displayed a decided preference for small feet. This preference later spread to lower-class groups, including the peasantry. In response to male demands, on which the successful negotiation of a young woman's marriage contract might hinge, mothers began to bind the feet of their daughters as early as the age of 5 or 6. The young girl's toes were turned under and bound with silk, which was wound more tightly as the child grew. By the time she reached marriageable age, the woman's foot had been transformed into the "lotus petal" or "golden lily" shapes that were presumably preferred by prospective marriage partners.

Not only were bound feet a constant source of pain for the rest of a woman's life; they greatly restricted her mobility by making it very difficult to walk even short distances. Restricted physical mobility, of course, made it easier for husbands to confine their wives to the family compound and made it impossible for women to engage in most occupations. For the latter reason, the lower classes, whose households were often dependent on female labor to make ends meet, were slow to adopt the practice. But once it was in fashion among the scholar-gentry and other elite classes, foot-binding became vital to winning a suitable husband for a young girl. Since a good marriage for her daughters was the primary goal of any self-respecting mother, the practice was unquestioningly passed from one generation of women to the next. The constricted vision of upper-class women regarding the possibilities for self-fulfillment, and their willingness to endure a painful and unnecessary physical deformity to achieve it, say a great deal about the lowly position to which women had been relegated in China by the end of the Song era.

A Glorious Age: Invention and Artistic Creativity

Perhaps even more than for political and economic achievements, the Tang–Song eras are remembered as a time of remarkable accomplishment in science, technology, literature, and the fine arts. Major technological breakthroughs and scientific discoveries were made under each dynasty. Some of them, particularly those involving the invention of new tools, production techniques, and weapons, would gradually be disseminated to other civilizations and fundamentally alter the course of human development as a whole. Until recent centuries, the arts and literature of China were less well known beyond its borders. Their impact was confined mainly to areas such as central Asia, Japan, and Vietnam, where Chinese imports had long been a major impetus for cultural advance. But the poetry and short stories of the Tang and the landscape paintings of the Song represent some of the most splendid artistic creations of all human history.

As we have seen, new agricultural implements and innovations, such as banks and paper money, contributed a great deal to economic growth and social prosperity in the Tang–Song era. In this respect, the engineering feats of the period are particularly noteworthy. In addition to constructing the Grand Canal, Tang and Song engineers made great advances in building dikes and dams and regulating the flow of water in complex irrigation systems. They also devised ingenious new ways to build bridges, long a major focus of engineering efforts in a land dominated by mountains and waterways. From arched and segmented to suspension and trussed, most of the basic bridge types known to humans were pioneered in China.

One of the most important of the many technological advances made in the Tang era, the invention of explosive powder, had at first little impact on warfare. For centuries, the Chinese used these potent chemical mixtures mainly for fireworks, which delighted emperors and the masses alike. By the late Song, however, explosive powder was widely employed by the imperial armies in a variety of grenades and bombs that were hurled at the enemy by catapults. Song armies and warships were also equipped with naphtha flamethrowers, poisonous gases, and rocket launchers, which were perhaps the most effective weapons the dynasty employed in its losing struggle to check nomadic incursions. On the domestic scene, chairs—modeled on those encountered in India—were introduced into the household, the habit of tea drinking swept the empire, coal was used for fuel for the first time, and the first kite soared into the heavens.

Though the number of major inventions in the Song era was lower than in the Tang, several were pivotal for the future history of all civilizations. Compasses, which had been used since the last centuries B.C.E. by Chinese military commanders and magicians, were applied to sea navigation for the first time in the Song period. The abacus, the ancestor of the modern calculator, was introduced to help merchants count their profits and tax collectors keep track of the revenues due. And in the middle of the 11th century, a remarkable artisan named Bi Sheng devised the technique of printing with movable type. Though block printing had been perfected in China in the preceding centuries, the use of movable type represented a great advance in the production of written records and scholarly books. Combined with paper, which the Chinese had also invented much earlier in the Han period, printing made it possible for them to attain a level of elite literacy that excelled that of any preindustrial civilization.

Scholarly Refinement and Artistic Accomplishment

The reinvigorated scholar-gentry elite was responsible for much of the artistic and literary creativity of the Tang–Song era. Buddhist art and architecture had been heavily patronized by the court and wealthy monasteries in the Tang period. But scholar-administrators and Confucian teachers wrote much of the literature for which the Tang is best remembered, and they painted the landscapes that were the most sublime cultural productions of the Song. Confucian thinkers highly esteemed skillful writing and painting, and educated individuals were expected to be involved in these activities on an ongoing basis. The Chinese educational establishment was geared to turning out generalists rather than the specialists who are so revered in our own society. A well-educated man was a dilettante: a person who dabbled with varying degrees of success in many fields. Thus, after a hard day at the Ministry of Public Works, a truly accomplished official was expected to spend the evening composing songs on his lute, admiring a new painting or creating his own, or sipping rice wine while composing a poem to the harvest moon. Thus, talented and often well-trained amateurs wrote most of the poems, composed much of the music, and painted the landscapes for which the Tang–Song era is renowned.

As the Confucian scholar-gentry supplanted the Buddhists as the major producers of art and literature, devotional objects and religious homilies gave way to a growing fixation on everyday life and the delights of the natural world. Much of the short story literature was focused on the doings of the common folk, popular beliefs in witchcraft and demons, ill-fated romances, and even detective stories about brutal murders. Tang poetry moved from early verses that dwelt on the "pleasant breezes that envelope[d] the emperor's chair" to a seemingly endless variety of ways of celebrating the natural world. No one was better at the latter than the most famous poet of the Tang era, *Li Bo*. As the following illustrates, his poems, like those of the great Persian authors, blend images of the mundane world with philosophical musings:

The rain was over, green covered the land.
One last cloudlet melted away in the clear sky.
The east wind came home with the spring
Bearing blossoms to sprout on the branches.
Flowers are fading now and time will end.
All mortal men perceive it and their sighs are deep.

But I will turn to the sacred hills
And learn from Tao [Dao] and from magic how to fly.

This intense interest in nature came to full artistic fruition in the landscape paintings of the Song era. Most of them were produced by the cultivated gentlemen of the scholar-gentry class, and they pulled together diverse aspects of Chinese civilization. The brushes and techniques employed were similar to those used in writing the Chinese language, which itself was regarded as a high art form. The paintings were symbolic, intended to teach moral lessons or explore philosophical ideas. The objects depicted were not only beautiful in themselves but stood for larger concepts: A crane and a pine tree, for example, represented longevity; bamboo shoots were associated with the scholar-gentry class; and a dragon could call to mind any number of things including the emperor, the cosmos, or life-giving rain. There was an abstract quality to the paintings that gives them a special appeal in the present day. The artists were not concerned with depicting nature accurately but rather with creating a highly personal vision of natural beauty. A premium was placed on subtlety and suggestion. The winner of an

The simplicity of the composition, the use of empty space, and the emphasis on nature are all characteristic of Chinese landscape painting at its height.

imperial contest, for example, painted a lone monk drawing water from an icy stream to depict the subject announced by the emperor: a monastery hidden deep in the mountains during the winter. Song landscapes were often painted on scrolls that could be "read" as the viewer unfolded them bit by bit. Most were accompanied by a poem, sometimes composed by the painter, that complemented the subject matter and was aimed at further elucidating the artist's ideas.

ANALYSIS

Artistic Expression and Social Values

In its many forms, artistic creativity provides one of the most effective ways of probing the beliefs and values of a civilization. In some cases where the civilization in question did not develop writing, or at least writing that we can now decipher, art and architecture provide much of the evidence by which we can learn about the attitudes and lifestyles of vanished peoples. Some of the most notable examples include the ancient Indus civilization of South Asia and many of the high civilizations of the

Americas and sub-Saharan Africa. Even in civilizations where written records have survived, we can learn a good deal about social structure by discovering who produced the art and for whom it was created, about technology by studying artistic techniques and materials, and about worldview by exploring the messages the art was intended to convey. In comparing some of the major forms of artistic expression of the great civilizations, we can also identify underlying similarities and differences in the values by which the peoples who developed them organized their societies and responded to the natural and supernatural worlds.

The fact that members of the ruling political elite produced many of the landscape paintings of the Song era is a rather exceptional occurrence in the history of civilization. The sculptures that adorned the temples of India, and the statues, paintings, and stained glass that graced the cathedrals of medieval Europe, were created mainly by specialized and highly trained craftsmen, whose skills were passed down from father to son over many generations. By contrast, the Song artists were often amateurs, who painted in their leisure time. Even the most talented, who won sufficient patronage to devote themselves to painting full time, began as Confucian scholars and very often administrators. It is not just the amateur and "master of all fields" ideals that are remarkable here but the fact that so much art was produced by the men who also ran the country. In most of the other civilizations we have studied, political life has been dominated by warrior and priestly classes, not artistic scholar-bureaucrats like those who governed China.

Even in civilizations like those of medieval Europe and Islam, where priests and religious teachers produced fine art in the form of manuscript illuminations, the individuals involved were seldom persons with political responsibilities or power. Thus, the artistic creativity of China's political elite underscores the importance of the preference for civil over military leaders in Chinese society. It also tells us a good deal about the qualities the Chinese associated with a truly civilized and superior person—a person who was deemed worthy to rule the Middle Kingdom.

Song landscapes were aimed at expressing the reactions and ideals of individual persons, whom we can identify by the distinctive seals with which they stamped their paintings. The paintings were clearly elitist, intended for the pleasure and edification of members of the Chinese educated classes, not for museum viewing or mass consumption. Landscape painting served to reinforce the identity and values of this scholarly elite across the vast spaces of the Chinese empire as well as across time. In one of the most famous incidents illustrating the latter, the Confucian philosopher Ju Xi remarked on the nobility and loyalty that he saw so clearly displayed by the calligraphy of scholars from the Warring States era.

This individualism and elitism in the art of Chinese civilization can be contrasted with the anonymous creation of the works of sculpture and religious paintings in Hindu and Buddhist civilizations and medieval Europe, or the mosaic decorations of the mosques of Islam. In each of these other civilizations, artistic works that adorned temples, cathedrals, and mosques were intended for a mass audience. The moral instruction for the scholarly few that was contained in the Song landscapes had a very different purpose than the religious sculptures or mosaics of other civilizations. The sculptures and mosaics were created to convey a religious message, to remind the viewers of a key event in the life of Christ or the Buddha, or to impress upon them the horrors of hell or the delights of heaven.

Thus, the highest art forms, linked to a common religion, served to bridge the gulf between elites and the masses in Hindu, Buddhist, Christian, and Muslim civilizations. Though imported Buddhist art forms performed this function in some periods in Chinese history, the more enduring Confucian-Daoist artistic creativity, as best exemplified by landscape painting, accentuated the differences that separated the educated scholar-gentry and the common people. Whereas in most preindustrial civilizations religion was a central source of legitimacy for elites, in China it was present in fertility sacrifices and ancestral veneration but was much less vital to the legitimacy of the ruling elites. The knowledge and administrative skills of the educated Confucian bureaucrats and their concern for the common people provided the primary justification for their power and privileges.

Questions: What do you think the diminutive size of the people in Chinese landscape paintings can tell us about Chinese views on the relationship between humans and the natural world? What political functions might be served by monumental art like that of Hindu, Islamic, and Christian civilizations beyond reminding the masses of their religious ties to the elite? Which forms of artistic expression exact the highest toll from the mass of the people; which best serve their interests? Can you think of American or European politicians who have created great works of art? Do we expect this sort of creativity from our elected officials? If not, what does this tell us about the values of our own civilization?

CONCLUSION

The End of the Song: The Legacy of Two Great Dynasties

By retreating to the south, the Song rulers had managed to survive the assaults of the nomads from the north. They could not retreat far enough to escape the onslaught of the most brilliant nomadic commander of them all, Chinggis Khan, who directed perhaps the most powerful military machine the world had seen up to that time. The Song rulers bought time by paying tribute to the Mongol Khan and striking alliances with him against their common enemies, the Tanguts and the Jurchens. But as we shall see in Chapter 20, by the late 1260s, another Mongol leader, Kubilai Khan, who had long had a strong interest in Chinese civilization, had emerged as the paramount Mongol lord, and he was ready to launch a sustained effort to conquer the southern refuge of the Song dynasty. By 1279, decades after Kubilai had proclaimed himself emperor of China, the south had been completely conquered and the last claimant to the Song throne had drowned attempting to escape to Vietnam. Though nomads once again ruled China, the wisdom of Kubilai and the strength of the early Mongol, or Yuan, regime meant that China was spared the period of division and chaos that had marked earlier transitions from one dynasty to the next.

The long Tang–Song epoch proved to be truly pivotal in Chinese and world history. Centralized administration and the great Chinese bureaucratic apparatus were not only restored but strengthened. The scholar-gentry elite, which had for so long been the critical binding force for Chinese civilization, triumphed over its aristocratic, nomadic, and Buddhist monastic rivals. Under nomadic and indigenous dynasties, the scholar-gentry would continue to define and direct Chinese civilization for the next six and a half centuries. During the nearly seven centuries of Tang and Song rule, the area that comprised Chinese civilization had grown dramatically as the south was fully integrated with the north.

From the Tang era until the 18th century, the Chinese economy would be one of the world's most advanced in terms of market orientation, volume of overseas trade, productivity per acre, and the sophistication of its tools and techniques of craft production. No civilization, with the possible exceptions of those of the Romans and the Incas, could match its system of roads, and certainly none had such an extensive and sophisticated canal and irrigation network. Until the 18th century, the imperial dynasties of China possessed political power and drew on economic resources unmatched by any other civilization.

The great changes that occurred in the Tang–Song era caution us against the temptation to equate the remarkable continuity displayed by Chinese civilization with stagnation. China did retain or revive key ideas, institutions, and patterns of political and social organization from the classical age. But it also changed dramatically in the balance between regions within the empire, in its level of commercial and urban development, in technology, in the impact of outside influences such as Buddhism, and even in the degree to which the scholar-gentry exercised political power and social dominance. Part of the genius of Chinese civilization has clearly arisen from their ability to incorporate far-reaching changes into ancient traditions and time-tested patterns of social interaction and political organization.

As we will see in the next chapter, beyond its borders China continued to dominate culturally the peoples of the East Asian world—Korean, Tibetan, Vietnamese, Japanese, and nomadic—even though it did not control them politically for most of the centuries after the fall of the Tang dynasty. Chinese inventions such as paper, printing, and gunpowder would fundamentally alter the course of development in all other human civilizations, including those as yet unknown in the Americas. If the Qin and Han epochs had established and defined the meaning of civilization in China, the Tang and Song had restored and redefined it. The persisting importance of the Tang–Song era for the Chinese people is indicated by the fact that even to the present day, they identify themselves as both the "sons of Han" and the "men of Tang."

FURTHER READINGS

In addition to the general histories of China suggested in Chapter 5, several important works are devoted to the Tang and Song eras. The volume, edited by Denis Twitchett, devoted to the Tang and Song in the *Cambridge History of China* is an essential reference work. There are detailed works on the founding of the Tang dynasty by C. P. Fitzgerald (1970) and Woodbridge Bingham (1940), but these should be read in conjunction with the more recent *Mirror to the Son of Heaven* (1974), which provides valuable correctives to the interpretations of these earlier authors. Useful insights into political and cultural life in the Tang era can be gleaned from the specialized essays in the volume *Perspectives on the Tang* (1973), edited by Arthur Wright and Denis

Twitchett. Much less has been written specifically on society and politics in the Song than the Tang, but Jacques Gernet's *Daily Life in China on the Eve of the Mongol Invasion, 1250–1276* (1962) is both highly entertaining and informative. On the great social and economic transitions of the Song era, Mark Elvin's *The Pattern of the Chinese Past* (1973) is insightful, provocative, and controversial.

Of the numerous works on Chinese art and painting, perhaps the best place to start is with the standard work by Mai-mai Sze, *The Way of Chinese Painting* (1956), which quotes extensively from Chinese manuals.

Of more recent works, the general survey by Laurence Sickman and Alexander Soper, as well as James Cahill's study of landscape painting, stand out. Though there is as yet no full-scale study of gender roles in Tang or Song China, Elisabeth Croll's *Feminism and Socialism in China* (1980) has a superb introductory chapter on the position of women in traditional China, which can be supplemented by the appropriate sections in Gernet and other works on social life in the period. A wonderful sampler of Li Bo's poetry can be found in a volume entitled *Bright Moon, Perching Bird* (1987), edited by J. P. Seaton and James Cryer.

19

The Spread of Chinese Civilization: Korea, Japan, and Vietnam

206 B.C.E.–**220** C.E. Reign of the Han dynasty in China

222–589 Period of Six Dynasties in China

618–907 Tang dynasty in China

646 Taika reforms in Japan

668 Korea wins independence from Tang conquerors

960–1279 Song dynasty in C

918–1392 Koryo dynasty in Kore

111 B.C.E. Vietnam conquered by the Chinese

589–618 Sui dynasty in China

794 Japanese capital shifts to Heian (Kyoto)

939 Vietnam wins its independence from China

838 Last Japanese embassy to China

109 B.C.E. Choson (Korea) conquered by Chinese

39 C.E. Trung sisters revolt in Vietnam

668–918 Silla kingdom in Korea

710–784 Imperial Japanese capital at Nara

857–1160 Period of Fujiwara dominance in Japan

200 B.C.E.   **600** C.E.   **800** C.E.

INTRODUCTION

By the time of the Han dynasty (206 B.C.E–220 C.E.), the peoples who had come to identify themselves as Chinese had demonstrated a capacity for civilized development that was equaled by few other societies. Not only had the Chinese built one of the largest, most powerful, and most prosperous of all human societies, they had found ways of maintaining their patterns of civilized life over long periods of time. While the great civilizations of Egypt, Mesopotamia, Persia, India, and the Americas rose and fell, China persisted. Sometimes divided, often challenged by the warlike peoples beyond their frontiers, the Chinese managed to preserve a sense of identity, to absorb the nomadic peoples that periodically broke through their defenses, and to build continuously on the institutions, ways of thought, and modes of social organization devised in the last millennium B.C.E.

The Chinese did much more than endure; they managed to excel in virtually all areas of human endeavor. Their agrarian system was able to support a far larger population, both in absolute terms and per acre, than any other preindustrial civilization. They fashioned centralized administrative systems that effectively controlled a massive empire that dwarfed most of their civilized rivals. The Chinese led the classical and postclassical world in technological innovation, made great strides in scientific understanding, excelled in engineering and architectural design, supported one of the most advanced educational systems and scholarly elites in the civilized world, and consistently produced brilliant works in literature and the fine arts.

Such splendid achievements were not likely to go unnoticed by China's neighbors. It was perhaps inevitable that surrounding peoples would strive to emulate the Chinese model of civilized development. As we have seen, Japan, the most important of these neighbors in terms of its subsequent impact on global history, began to borrow heavily from China in the critical 5th and 6th centuries C.E., when its own pattern of civilization started to coalesce. China's influence upon the nomadic peoples to the north and west and upon areas such as Tibet has also been noted in earlier chapters. But the peoples most drawn to the Chinese model over long periods of time lived in the sedentary, wet-rice growing societies that flanked China on the east—Korea and Japan—and in the south, Vietnam.

This chapter will focus on the interaction and exchanges between China and these three regions. In each area, Chinese influences were blended with local conditions, preferences, and creativity to produce related but very distinctive patterns of civilized development. In the case of the Japanese, we will examine the strategies they adopted to build on the foundations laid in the first centuries C.E., which were discussed in Chapter 10. For Korea and Vietnam, we will begin with the first contacts between the expansive Chinese and the peoples of these areas, and then examine the quite different paths to civilization followed by each. In all of these areas, Chinese influences and regional reactions to them led to particularly significant patterns of civilized development in the postclassical era. Each case forms an important example of the larger theme of the expansion of civilization and the growing number and depth of the linkages that bound civilized societies across the globe.

Owing partly to geography and partly to historical circumstances, each of these three areas interacted with its giant neighbor and common source of civilization in a very different way. Despite intermittent efforts of the Chinese, particularly under the Mongol Yuan dynasty, to assert direct control over the islands, the Japanese man-

---

980–1009 Le dynasty in Vietnam

1160–1185 Taira clan dominant in Japan

1185–1333 Kamakura Shogunate in Japan

1180–1185 Gempei Wars in Japan

1279–1368 Mongol rule in China

1231–1392 Mongol rule in Korea

1336–1573 Ashikaga Shogunate in Japan

1392–1910 Yi dynasty in Korea

1467–1477 Onin War in Japan

1500 Nguyen dynasty in central/south Vietnam founded

1600 Founding of the Tokugawa Shogunate in Japan

1539–1787 Trinh dynasty in Vietnam/Red River area

1000 C.E.   1200 C.E.   1400 C.E.

aged to retain political independence. This meant that they had much greater control than the Koreans or Vietnamese over which aspects of Chinese civilization they wished to borrow and, equally important, over how these aspects were introduced into Japanese culture. As a result, though Chinese influences continued to shape Japanese life, particularly at the level of the court and aristocracy, distinctive Japanese approaches to social organization, thought, and artistic creativity became more and more pronounced.

In contrast to the Japanese, the Koreans and Vietnamese, both of whom could be reached overland by Chinese forces, were conquered and directly ruled by various Chinese dynasties. This meant that they had less control over the introduction and effects of Chinese cultural influences than the Japanese. But both peoples managed to preserve a strong sense of their own identity, which was forged to a large extent by prolonged resistance to Chinese political domination and their fear of absorption by their larger neighbor. In the first centuries C.E., the Koreans broke free from the Chinese yoke and managed to remain independent for most of the centuries thereafter. The Vietnamese struggled violently to escape Chinese rule for more than 1000 years. Ethnically and culturally, both the Koreans and the Vietnamese preserved key elements in their preconquest cultures and societies. These were blended with Chinese imports to produce unique variants of a broader East Asian pattern of civilization.

As we shall see, in each of the satellite areas of Chinese civilization, Buddhism in a variety of forms played key roles in the transmission of Chinese civilization and in the development of the indigenous cultures. Because Buddhism originated in India, the layers of cross-cultural interaction in the satellite areas are all the more complex and profound. In each case, ideas and rituals originating in India were filtered through Chinese society and culture before being passed on to Korea, Japan, and Vietnam. Historically, Buddhism also provided a critical link between two of the satellite civilizations: Korea and Japan.

Chinese influence in Japan, Korea, and Vietnam meant, finally, that each of these societies emphasized links to China more than links to the wider world network, which was encountered mainly through China itself. This fact, along with the struggle to define some autonomy in relationship to China, imposed considerable isolation on Japan and Korea in terms of wider international contacts. The East Asian zone thus differed from Europe, where contacts were more open-ended, despite basic similarities in the processes of borrowing and self-definition.

JAPAN: THE IMPERIAL AGE

Focal Point: Chinese influence on Japan peaked in the 7th and 8th centuries as Japanese rulers and their courtiers attempted to build a Chinese-style bureaucracy and army and to emulate Chinese etiquette and aesthetic sensibilities. But the isolated and ultracivilized court centers at Nara and later Heian lost political control to powerful aristocratic families and local warlords, who plunged Japan into a long series of civil wars from the 12th to the 17th centuries.

By the 7th and 8th centuries C.E., the Japanese court at Nara was awash in Chinese imports. Indigenous cultural influences, particularly those linked to Shinto views of the natural and supernatural world, remained central to Japanese cultural development. But in the Taika (645–710), Nara (710–784), and Heian (794–857) periods, Japanese borrowing from China—though selective—peaked. This borrowing touched virtually all aspects of Japanese life, particularly at the level of the elites and among the populace of the court towns.

In 646, the emperor and his advisors introduced the far-reaching *Taika reforms,* which were aimed at completely revamping the imperial administration along Chinese lines. Japanese court scholars struggled to master thousands of Chinese characters, which bore little relationship to the language they spoke. They wrote dynastic histories patterned after those commissioned by the emperors of China, and followed an elaborate court etiquette that somewhat uneasily combined Chinese protocol with ancient Japanese ideas about politeness and decorum. The Japanese aristocracy struggled to master Confucian ways, worshiped in Chinese-style temples, and admired Buddhist art that was Chinese in subject matter and technique.

Even the common people were affected by the steady flow of influence from the mainland. In the towns they stared in awe at the great Buddhist temples and bowed to passing aristocrats striving to present themselves as Confucian scholars. The peasants turned to Buddhist monks for cures when they were sick or to Buddhist magic when they needed a change of luck. They had begun to mesh the worship of Buddhist deities with that of the ancient kami, or nature spirits, of Japan.

Just as Chinese influence in Japan peaked, it began to be challenged: directly by the aristocracy, who increasingly argued for a return to Japanese ways, and silently by the peasantry, who steadily reworked Chinese Buddhism into a distinctly Japanese religion. In part, the erosion of support for Chinese ways reflected the failure

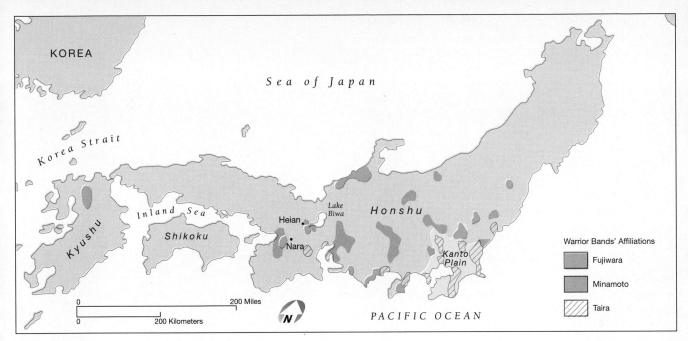

Japan in the Imperial and Warlord Periods

of the ambitious reforms introduced by the emperor in 646. That failure led to a gradual seepage of power from the emperor and his administrators to first the aristocratic families in attendance at court and later local lords in the provinces. As this shift of power occurred, those who argued for a revival and strengthening of Japanese traditions at the expense of Chinese influence slowly gained the upper hand.

Crisis at Nara and the Shift to Heian (Kyoto)

If they had succeeded, the Taika reforms of 646 would have represented the culmination of centuries of Japanese borrowing from China. The central objectives of the proposed changes were to remake the Japanese monarch into an absolutist Chinese-style emperor (even to the point of adding "Son of Heaven" to the Japanese ruler's many titles). The reforms were also intended to create a genuine professional bureaucracy and peasant conscript army in Japan to match those of Han–Tang China. But the changes necessary for these goals to be achieved were largely frustrated by the resistance of the aristocratic families and the Buddhist monastic orders, who dominated both the emperor and the capital as a whole. A century later, the Buddhist monks in particular had grown so bold and powerful that the court and aristocracy lived in fear of street demonstrations by "rowdy monks" and of

the escalating demands of the heads of the monastic orders. Their influence even threatened to engulf the throne in the 760s, when a clever Buddhist prelate worked his way into the inner circle of the empress Koken. Though his schemes to marry her and claim the throne were uncovered and foiled, it was now clear to the emperor's advisors that measures had to be taken to ensure that women could never rule Japan and to check the growing influence of the monastic orders at court.

The emperor, Koken's husband, literally fled some 28 miles and established a new capital city at *Heian,* or what was later called Kyoto. The Buddhists were forbidden to build monasteries in the new capital. But to get around this restriction, the monks established monasteries in the hills surrounding the new capital, and they soon reemerged as a potent force at court as royal advisors.

In addition to his efforts to control the Buddhist monks, the emperor abandoned all pretense of continuing the Taika reforms, which in any case had long been stalled by aristocratic and popular opposition. He fully restored the great aristocratic families, whose power the reforms had been intended to curb. The elaborate system of ranks into which the aristocrats were divided (patterned after that in China) was maintained. But like the Koreans, the Japanese broke with Chinese precedent in determining rank primarily by birth and by allowing little mobility between the various orders. The aristocrats had already taken over most of the positions in the central

From this artist's impression of the elaborate dress and studied poses of Heian courtiers, as well as the carefully cultivated trees and the tasteful decor, one gains a vivid sense of the formality and the attention to aesthetic pleasures that dominated the lives of the Japanese elite in this era.

government; now, their formal right to build up rural estates was restored as well. The emperor also gave up an ambitious scheme to build up a peasant conscript army. In its place, local leaders were ordered to organize militia forces, which would soon play a critical role in further eroding the actual control of the imperial household.

Ultracivilized: Court Life in the Heian Era

Though the basis of imperial political power had been severely compromised within decades of the shift to Heian, court culture soared to new levels of refinement. For several centuries more, the Japanese emperors and their courtiers continued to inhabit a closed world of luxury and aesthetic delights. Males and females of the aristocratic classes lived out their lives in accordance with strict codes of polite behavior, under the constant scrutiny of their peers and superiors. In this hothouse atmosphere, social status was everything, love affairs were a major preoccupation, and gossip was rampant. By our standards, life in this constricted and very artificial world was false and suffocating. Yet, rarely in human history has so much energy been so focused on the pursuit of beauty, or has social interaction—on the surface at least—been so gracious and well mannered.

At the Heian court, members of the imperial household and the leading aristocratic families lived in a complex of palaces and gardens. The buildings were of unpainted wood, which Japanese taste found the most appealing, with sliding panels, matted floors, and wooden walkways running between the separate residences where the many dignitaries lived. Fish ponds, artificial lakes with waterfalls, and fine gardens were interspersed among the courtiers' living quarters. Writing original verse was perhaps the most valued of arts at the court. The poems, which were often written on painted fans or scented paper and were sometimes sent in little boats down the streams that ran through the palace grounds, were brief and full of allusions to Chinese and Japanese verse and classical writings. In the following couplet, for example, a young courtier expresses his disappointment at being denied access to a pretty young girl:

Having come upon an evening blossom
The mist is loath to go with the morning sun.

Partly to accommodate the need for literary expression of this nature, the written script the Japanese had borrowed from the Chinese was simplified, making it more compatible with spoken Japanese. One result of these changes was an outpouring of poetic and literary works that were more and more distinctively Japanese. In addition to novels like Lady Murasaki's, discussed in the Closeup, some of the most elegant poetry in the Japanese language was written in this era. Again, it is characteristically sparing in words but rich in imagery and allusions to the natural world:

This perfectly still
Spring Day bathed in the soft light
From the spread-out sky,
Why do the cherry blossoms so restlessly scatter down?

Although I am sure
That he will not be coming
In the evening light
When the locusts shrilly call
I go to the door and wait.

As the female authorship of this poem clearly illustrates, women at the Heian court were expected to be as poised and cultured as men. They too wrote poems, played flutes or stringed instruments in informal concerts, and became embroiled in elaborate schemes to snub or disgrace rivals. Like their counterparts in China and the Islamic world, they also became involved in palace intrigues and power struggles.

The Decline of Imperial Power

While the emperor and his courtiers admired the plum blossoms and the newest fashions in court dress, some of the aristocratic families at court were busy running the rapidly shrinking imperial bureaucracy. By the middle of the 9th century, one of these families, the *Fujiwara*, exercised exceptional influence over imperial affairs. Not only did they pack the upper administration with family members and shape imperial policy, they increasingly married Fujiwaras into the imperial family. By the middle of the 10th century, one aged Fujiwara chief minister had seen four of his daughters married to emperors.

Families like the Fujiwara also took advantage of the wealth and influence their high office ensured to buy up large estates that provided a stable financial base for their growing power. Especially in the vicinity of the capital, they had to compete in these purchases with the Buddhist monasteries. But both could work together in the steady campaign to whittle down imperial control and increase their own. As the lands under their control expanded, both the monks and the court nobility greatly increased the number of peasants and artisans they effectively ruled. Cooperation between monastic orders and

court aristocrats was promoted by the introduction of the secret texts and ceremonies of esoteric Buddhism in this period. These teachings and techniques to achieve salvation through prayers and meditation, which were focused by mystical diagrams and special hand positions, were the rage among the Heian elite. As aristocrats and monks steadily built up their own power in the capital, however, they failed to reckon with the growing power of the local lords.

The Rise of the Provincial Warrior Elite

The pursuit of landed estates that increasingly preoccupied the court aristocracy was also taken up by elite families in the provinces. Some of these families were originally from aristocratic origins, but most had risen to power as landowners, estate managers, or local state officials. These families not only came to control land and labor and to deny these resources to the court, but gradually carved out little kingdoms, ruled by "house" governments, in various parts of the islands. They ruled their kingdoms within the larger Japanese state from small fortresses surrounded by wooden or earthen walls and moatlike ditches. The local lord and his retainers were housed within the fortress, constantly on the alert for an attack by a neighboring lord or the forces of one of the powerful families at court. Granaries for storing the rice provided by local peasants, blacksmith forges and stables, wells for water, and even armories made the fortresses self-contained worlds.

Within the little kingdoms ruled from the forts, the warrior leaders, or *bushi*, administered law, supervised public works projects, and collected revenue—for themselves, not the court. The failure of the court's plans to build conscript armies also left the way open for the bushi to build up their own armies, which soon became the most effective military forces in the land. Though these mounted troops, or *samurai*, were loyal to the local lord, not to the court or high aristocratic officials, they were increasingly called in to protect the emperor and his retainers and to keep the peace in the capital. As the imperial government's control over the country weakened in the 11th and 12th centuries, bandits freely roamed the countryside and the streets of the capital. Buddhist monasteries employed armed toughs to protect themselves and strike at rival sects. In this atmosphere of rampant crime and civil strife, both the court and high officials hired provincial lords and their samurai retainers to serve as bodyguards and to protect their palaces and mansions from robbery and arson.

These trends proved critical to the emergence of a warrior class. Counting on peasant dependents to supply

CLOSEUP

The First Novel: Lady Murasaki's The Tale of Genji

Life in the sheltered world of the Heian court is vividly depicted in the diaries and fiction written by a number of courtiers, but none captured its charm and its underlying tensions and sadness as wonderfully as Lady Murasaki's *The Tale of Genji*. In this, the first novel in any language, she relates the life history of a prominent and amorous son of the emperor and the fate of his descendants. As the story makes clear, Genji's life is almost wholly devoted to the pursuit of aesthetic enjoyment, whether found in affairs with beautiful women or in musical entertainments in a garden scented with blooming flowers. Uncouth commoners and distasteful things, such as dirt, cheap pottery, and rough popular entertainments, are to be avoided at all costs. When her rivals at the court wish to insult Genji's mother, for example, they leave spoiled fruit in the passages where she or her maidservants must pass. An encounter with a shriveled piece of fruit contributes to the illness that leads to her premature death.

Everyone who matters in Genji's world is obsessed with the social conventions that govern everything, from which gown is proper for a given ceremony to the composition of a suitable poem to woo a potential lover or win the emperor's favor. Though women rivaled men as poets, artists, and musicians and in their pervasive cultivation of aesthetic pleasure, it was unseemly for them to openly pursue princely lovers. Nonetheless, as Lady Murasaki's poignant novel makes clear, some women did court prospective lovers with great guile and passion. It was also not unheard of for a highborn woman to spurn a suitor and humiliate him in front of her maidservants. Thus, in the hothouse world of the Heian court, a tiny minority of Japanese women enjoyed outlets for the expression of emotion and creativity that have been denied to most women through much of civilized history.

them with food and other necessities, the bushi and samurai devoted their lives to hunting, riding, archery practice, and other activities that sharpened their martial skills. Until the 12th century, the main weapons of the mounted warriors were powerful longbows, though they also carried straight swords. From the 12th century on, they increasingly relied in combat on the superbly forged, curved steel swords that we commonly associate with the Japanese samurai. The bushi and the samurai warriors who served them rode into battles that increasingly hinged on the man-to-man duels of great champions. These combats represented heroic warfare in the extreme. The time and location of battles were elaborately negotiated beforehand, and each side strove to demonstrate the justice of its cause and the perfidy of its enemies. Before charging into battle, Japanese warriors would proudly proclaim their family lineage and its notable military exploits to their adversaries, who often missed the details because they were shouting back their own.

A warrior code developed that stressed family honor and death rather than retreat or defeat. Beaten or disgraced warriors turned to ritual suicide, which they called *seppuku* (disembowelment) but which is commonly known in the West by the more vulgar *hara-kiri* (belly splitting), to prove their courage and restore their family's honor. Battles were chaotic affairs—lots of shouting and clashing but relatively few fatalities—that were won or lost depending on the performance of the champions on each side. Though a full chivalric code did not develop until some centuries later, Japan was steadily moving toward a feudal order that was remarkably similar to that developing in western Europe in this era.

The rise of the samurai frustrated all hopes of creating a free peasantry. In fact, Japanese peasants were reduced in the next centuries to the status of serfs, bound to the land they worked and treated as the property of the local lord. They were also separated by rigid class barriers from the warrior elite, which was physically set off by its different ways of dressing and by prohibitions against the peasants' carrying swords or riding on horseback. In their growing poverty and degradation, the peasants turned to popular Buddhism in the form of the salvationist "pure lands" sect, which offered the promise of bliss in heaven for those who lived upright lives on earth. Colorful figures, such as the dancing monk Kuya, and Genshin, whose *Essentials of Salvation* outlined in great detail the pleasures of paradise and the horrible tortures of hell, strove to make Buddhist teachings comprehensible and appealing to both the peasantry and the artisans in the towns.

The latter were concentrated at the court center in Heian and the fortress towns of some of the more powerful bushi. Though their skills in potterymaking, painting, and textile manufacture were celebrated by subsequent generations, the artisans were paid almost as poorly as the peasants and accorded little status. In contrast to China, where these activities were often pursued by the scholar-gentry, in Japan they were usually undertaken by professional craftsmen who had inherited their skills from their fathers.

The imposing presence of a fully armed samurai warrior is captured in this pen-and-ink drawing.

THE ERA OF WARRIOR DOMINANCE

Focal Point: From the 12th century onward, Japanese history was increasingly dominated by civil wars between shifting factions of the court aristocracy and local warlords. Chinese influence declined steadily through the following centuries. But the warrior elite and the artisan classes that served them managed, in the midst of strife and social dislocation, to produce sublime creations in fields as diverse as ceramics, landscape architecture, and religious poetry. This creativity was obscured, however, by continuing civil strife, which

The horrible demons waiting to inflict torture on those who violate Buddhist teachings and fall into sin are graphically depicted in this painting of hell.

peaked in the late 15th and 16th centuries and ended only with the rise to paramountcy of the upstart Tokugawa warlord family in the early 1600s.

As the power of the provincial lords grew, that of the imperial household and court aristocracy declined. Powerful families at the court, such as the Fujiwara, increasingly depended on alliances with regional lords to bolster them in disputes with their rivals. By the 11th and 12th centuries, the provincial families had begun to pack the court bureaucracy and to contest power in their own right. By the mid-12th century, competition turned to open feuding between the most powerful of these families, the Taira and the Minamoto. For a time, the Taira gained the upper hand by controlling the emperor and dominating at court. But when rivalry turned to open warfare in the early 1180s, the Minamoto commanders and their powerful network of alliances with provincial lords in various parts of the country proved

vastly superior to the leaders or allies the Taira could muster. More fundamentally, the Tairas' concentration of their power-grabbing efforts in the capital led to the breakdown of critical links with rural notables, who often sided with the Minamoto in the factional struggles.

For five years, the *Gempei Wars* raged in the heartland of the main island of Honshu. This conflict brought great suffering to the peasantry, whose farmlands were ravaged and who fought, forcibly conscripted but poorly armed and untrained, against each other, while the samurai clashed in their ritual combats. By 1185, the Taira house faction had been destroyed. The Minamoto then established the *bakufu* (which literally means "tent"), or the military government at Kamakura, in their base area on the Kanto plain, far east of the capital at Heian (see map on p. 417). The emperor and his court were preserved—in fact all the military houses would derive their legitimacy from the descendants of the sun goddess—but real power now rested with the

Minamoto and their samurai retainers. The feudal age in Japan had begun.

ANALYSIS

Comparing Feudalisms

Two societies in the world developed fully feudal political systems in the postclassical period: western Europe and Japan. To heighten the coincidence, they both did so at approximately the same time. Both used feudal relationships in situations where they could not sustain more complex political forms. The West had the example of Rome's empire, but medieval leaders could simply not reconstruct the elements that had allowed the empire to exist and flourish. They could not organize or afford the necessary armies, they could not generate agreement on standardized laws, and they could not produce an independent bureaucracy that could cut across tribes and language groups except through the important but somewhat specialized mechanism of the Church. The Japanese had the example of the Chinese imperial system available to them, and they did briefly attempt a comparable kind of bureaucratic development, using Confucianism to promote the proper political attitudes. But again, the system did not take root in Japanese soil.

Both the West and Japan would develop more elaborate political forms, with the Japanese again making great use of Confucianism after the 16th century. But these innovations came late, after intermediate experience with feudal monarchy or the shogunate, and they had to incorporate centuries of feudal heritage, which meant, among other things, that they still did not replicate the imperial political structures of Rome or China.

In one sense, the existence of feudalism requires no elaborate assessment. Many societies generated only weak central government structures, simply because they lacked the resources, the shared political values, and the bureaucratic experience to develop alternatives. China under the Zhou dynasty is sometimes called feudal. The Russian kings from Rurik onward exercised only loose overlordship over powerful landlords. Kings in the divine monarchy systems of sub-Saharan Africa, which flourished from about the 9th to the 19th century in various parts of the continent, similarly relied on deals and compromises with local and regional leaders. Indeed, African historians have often noted with some justice, that kingdoms such as Ghana or Mali were ruled about

as effectively as were Western monarchies during the Middle Ages. A comparison of this sort reminds us that feudal systems were in many ways early, somewhat unsophisticated versions of political societies that were gradually moving from purely local toward more elaborate organization, and that almost all civilizations have experienced long periods of this sort of semicentralized rule. In all such cases, including the feudal cases, the claims of central authorities are not matched by effective power (which is why central authorities so often rely on the idea of divine backing). Regional leaders have armies of their own and do much of the effective administration of their localities. Kings have to make deals with such leaders, relying on personal negotiation and pledges of mutual respect, marriage alliances, lots of negotiation, and a willingness to give the local princes much free rein in practice.

The feudal systems that arose in the West and Japan had some features that were different from the many other decentralized cases they admittedly resemble. These differences make it desirable, analytically, not to call all such cases *feudal,* lest a term extremely useful for comparison be diluted beyond recognition. Russia, for example—while it was often decentralized and frequently saw its rulers, whatever their grandiose claims, make concessions to regional nobles because they depended on their loyalty and service to rule—never developed a real feudal tradition, which is one of the features that distinguished it from the West. The same holds true for China in comparison with Japan, or for sub-Saharan Africa.

Japan and the medieval West developed in feudalism a set of political values that embraced, however imperfectly, most of the participants in the system—primarily, of course, the aristocratic landlords. The idea of mutual ties and obligations, and the rituals and institutions that expressed them, went beyond more casual local deals and compromises. In both cases, feudalism was exceedingly militaristic. Both the medieval West and Japan went through long centuries of unusually frequent and bitter internal warfare, based in large part on feudal loyalties and rivalries. In both cases, fighting was largely confined to the landlord class, and feudalism summed up a host of military virtues—bravery, allegiance in battle—that long discouraged more stable, centralized government. The military aura of feudalism in both cases survived the feudal era, giving Japan the problems of dealing with its samurai class after the worst periods of internal conflict had passed (by the 17th century), and giving the West a strong belief that one purpose of the state was to make war and provide opportunities for military leaders to demonstrate their prowess.

The legacy of feudalism was not simply military, however. The idea of mutual ties as a foundation of political activity would continue to affect political life and institutions in both the West and Japan, even after the specifically feudal period ended. Here is where feudalism, with its elaborate rituals and the requirement that young leaders be initiated into its value system, differed most markedly from other decentralized systems.

Adding to complexity, however, the characteristics of feudalism in Japan and in the West were not identical. Western feudalism emphasized contractual ideas more strongly than did Japanese. While mutual ties were sincerely preached, the idea was that individuals contracted with each other and obtained fairly careful assurance of the advantages they would extract from the situation as individuals. Japanese feudalism stressed group loyalties more purely than did the Western form. Probably for this reason, the clearest ongoing legacy of feudalism in the West proved to be parliamentary institutions, where individual aristocrats (as well as townsmen and clergy) could join to defend their interests against the central monarch. In Japan, feudalism's legacy involved a less institutionalized group consciousness, propelling individuals to function as part of collective decision-making teams that ultimately could be linked to the state. In both cases, feudalism helped shape a distinctive political style that would be combined with later centralizing tendencies, but the styles themselves were not the same.

Can the common fact of a feudal heritage be used to explain another similarity between the West and Japan that emerged clearly only in the 20th century? Both societies have proved to be unusually successful in industrial development, leading the world in this regard by the final quarter of our own century. It would certainly be tempting, and convenient, to point to feudalism—the medieval feature the two societies uniquely shared—as a partial explanation for the otherwise unexpected 20th-century resemblance.

When the Japanese talent for group cohesion is identified so strikingly as an ingredient in 20th-century economic success, or when Western nations painfully win political stability through use of parliamentary forms, it surely seems legitimate to point to some persistent threads that, though greatly altered with new circumstances, run through the experience of the two societies. Whether one can push further to treat the common experience of feudalism as a basis for later economic dynamism is a matter for speculation. It need not, however, be excluded from a list of provocative uses of comparative analysis simply because the links are challenging.

Questions: Do you think the characteristics of feudalism help explain the later success of Western and Japanese societies? What other factors must be considered? Why might Arab or Chinese historians be skeptical about any claims for feudalism's special importance in world history?

The Declining Influence of China

As the power of the imperial house weakened and that of the aristocracy grew, the relevance of Chinese precedents and institutions for the Japanese diminished. Pretensions to a heavenly mandate and centralized power became ludicrous; the emergence of a scholar-gentry elite was stifled by the reassertion of aristocratic power and prerogatives. Grand designs for an imperial bureaucracy never materialized. The central Confucian precept that civilian administrators should rule and soldiers serve and keep out of the way was utterly violated by the growing influence of the provincially based bushi elite and their samurai retainers. Even Buddhism, which from the outset had been a central channel for the transmission of Chinese influence, was increasingly transformed by both aristocrats and peasants into a distinctively Japanese religion.

With the decline of the Tang and a return to decades of political uncertainty and social turmoil in China, the Chinese model seemed even less relevant to the Japanese. As early as 838, the Japanese court decided to discontinue its embassies to the much-reduced Tang court. Japanese monks and traders still made the dangerous sea crossing to China, but the emperor's advisors no longer deemed official visits and groveling before the Son of Heaven to be worth all the bother.

The Breakdown of Bakufu Dominance and the Age of the Warlords

Yoritomo, the leader of the victorious Minamoto, gravely weakened the Kamakura regime because of his obsessive fear of being overthrown by members of his own family. Close relatives, including his brother Yoshitsune, whose courage and military genius had much to do with the Minamoto triumph over the Taira, were murdered or driven into exile. Fear of spies and uncertainty about what one could do in order to be above suspicion lent an element of paranoia to elite life under the first of the Kamakura *shoguns,* or the military leaders of the bakufu. Though Yoritomo's rule went unchallenged, the measures he had adopted to protect his throne left him without an able heir. His death and the weakness of those who succeeded him led to a scramble on the part of the bushi lords to build up their own power and en-

Himeji Castle was one of the most formidable of the many fortresses that dominated the Japanese landscape in the age of warlord dominance. Though the inner buildings were often built of wood, these more vulnerable structures were defended by walls and long, fortified passageways made of stone at the entrances.

large their domains. The *Hojo,* one of the warrior families that had long been closely allied to the Minamoto, soon dominated the Kamakura regime, though they were content to leave the Minamoto as the formal rulers. Thus, a curious and confusing three-tiered system arose. Real power rested in the Hojo family, who manipulated the Minamoto shoguns, who in turn claimed to rule in the name of the emperor who resided at Kyoto.

In the early 14th century, the situation became murkier still when the head of one of the branches of the Minamoto family, *Ashikaga Takuaji,* led a revolt of the bushi that overthrew the Kamakura regime and established the Ashikaga Shogunate (1336–1573) in its place. Because the emperor at the time of Ashikaga's seizure of power refused to recognize the usurper and tried to revive imperial power, he was driven from Kyoto to the mountain town of Yoshino. There, with the support of several warlords, he and his heirs fought against the Ashikaga faction and the puppet emperors they placed on the throne at Kyoto for much of the rest of the 14th century.

Though the Ashikaga were finally successful in destroying the rival Yoshino center of imperial authority, the long period of civil strife seriously undermined whatever authority the emperor had left and that of the shogunate. The bushi vassals of the warring factions were free to crush local rivals and to seize the lands of the peasantry as well as the agents of the old aristocracy and the competing warlords. As the power of the warlords grew, the court aristocracy, which was impoverished by its inability to defend its estates, was virtually wiped out. The lands the warlords acquired were parceled out to their samurai retainers, who in turn pledged their loyalty and were expected to provide military support whenever their lord called on them.

The collapse of any semblance of centralized authority was sharply accelerated by the outbreak of the *Onin War,* which raged for over a decade between 1467 and 1477. Rival heirs to the Ashikaga Shogunate called on the warlord chiefs to support their claims. Samurai flocked to the rival headquarters in different sections of Kyoto, where feuding soon broke into all-out warfare. Within a matter of years, the old imperial capital had been reduced to rubble and weed-choked fields. While the shogunate self-destructed in the capital, the provincial lords continued to amass power and plot new coalitions to destroy their enemies. Japan was divided into nearly 300 little states, whose warlord rulers (the successors of the bushi) were called *daimyos.* Unlike the bushi domains of earlier centuries, the daimyos' holdings, which varied greatly in size, were consolidated into unified and bounded ministates. In the place of mud-walled forts, there arose the massive wood and stone castles that would dominate the Japanese landscape for centuries.

Toward Barbarism? Military Division and Social Change

Though the rituals became more elaborate, the armor heavier, and the swords more superbly forged, the chivalrous qualities of the bushi era deteriorated noticeably in the 15th and 16th centuries. Spying, sneak attacks, ruses, and timely betrayals became the order of the day. The pattern of warfare was fundamentally transformed as large numbers of peasants armed with pikes became a critical component of daimyo armies. Battles hinged less and less on the outcome of samurai combat. Victory depended on the size and organization of a warlord's forces and on how effectively his commanders employed them in the field. The badly trained and poorly fed peasant forces became a major source of the growing misery of the common people. As they marched about the countryside to fight the incessant wars of their overlords, they looted and pillaged with impunity. Often in response to the depredations of warlord armies, the peasantry in different areas sporadically rose up in hopeless but often ferocious revolts, which fed the trend toward brutality and destruction. It is no wonder that contemporary accounts of the era, as well as those written in later centuries, are dominated by a sense of pessimism and foreboding—a conviction that Japan was reverting from civilized life to barbarism.

Despite the chaos and suffering of the warlord period, there was much economic and cultural growth. Most of the daimyos clearly recognized the necessity of building up their petty states if they were to be strong enough to survive in the long run. The more able daimyos attempted to stabilize village life within their domains by introducing regular tax collection, supporting the construction of irrigation systems and other public works, and building strong rural communities. Incentives were offered to encourage the settlement of unoccupied areas, and new tools, the greater use of draft animals, and new crops—especially soybeans—contributed to the well-being of the peasantry in the better-run domains. Peasants were also encouraged to produce items such as silk, hemp, paper, dyes, and vegetable oils, which were highly marketable and thus were potential sources of household income. Daimyos vied with one other to attract merchants to their growing castle towns. Soon a new and quite wealthy commercial class emerged as the purveyors of goods for the military elite and the intermediaries in trade between Japan and overseas areas, especially China. As in medieval Europe, guild organizations for craftsmen (carpenters, thatchers, smiths, potters, etc.) and merchants were strong in this era. They helped provide social solidarity and group protection in a time of political breakdown and insecurity.

There is considerable evidence that the growth of commerce and the handicraft industries gave a minority of Japanese women opportunities to avoid the sharp drop in status that most experienced in the age of the warring daimyos. Women in merchant and artisan families apparently exercised a fair degree of independence, which was reflected in their participation in guild organizations and business management and by the fact that their positions were sometimes inherited by their daughters. But the position of women in the emerging commercial classes contrasted sharply with that of women of the warrior elites. In earlier centuries, the wives and daughters of the provincial bushi households learned to ride and to use a bow and arrow, and they often joined in the hunt. By the 14th and 15th centuries, however, the trend among the daimyo families toward primogeniture, or the restriction of inheritance to the eldest son, dealt a heavy blow to women of the elite classes. The wives and daughters of warrior households, who had hitherto shared in the division of the family estate, now received little or no land or income.

Patronage of landscape painting and the other fine arts made it possible for artistic expression to survive in the long centuries of political division and civil war.

Disinheritance was part of a larger pattern that saw women increasingly treated as defenseless appendages of their warrior fathers or husbands. They were given in marriage to cement alliances between warrior households, reared to anticipate their warrior husband's every desire, and taught to slay themselves rather than dishonor the family line by being defiled by illicit suitors or enemy soldiers. That the restrictions and loss of status felt by women at the level of the warrior elite were shared by Japanese women more generally is suggested by their loss of the role of the celebrant in village religious ceremonies and their replacement in Japanese theatrical performances by males specially trained to impersonate women.

Fears that the constant wars between the swaggering samurai might drag Japan back to barbarism were somewhat mollified by continuing cultivation of the arts in the warring-houses era. Zen Buddhism, which because of its stress on simplicity and discipline had a special appeal to the warrior elite, played a critical role in securing the place of the arts in an era of strife and destruction. Zen monasteries provided key points of renewed diplomatic and trade contacts with China, which in turn led to a revival of Chinese influence in Japan, at least at the cultural level. Though much of the painting of the era imitated contemporary Chinese work, the monochrome ink sketches of Japanese artists were both brilliant and original. Also notable were screen and scroll paintings, some of which capture the natural beauty of Japan, while others provide us with invaluable glimpses into Japanese life in this period. Zen sensibilities are also prominent in some of the splendid architectural works of this period, including the Golden and Silver Pavilions that Ashikaga

The Golden Pavilion, also called the Kinkaku-ji Pavilion, is a relic of the cultural golden age of the 15th century.

shoguns had built in Kyoto. Each pavilion was designed to blend into the natural setting in which it was placed, to create a pleasing shelter from which one might contemplate nature.

This contemplative mood is also evident in the design of some of the more famous gardens of this era, such as that at the Ryoanji Temple, which consists entirely of islands of volcanic rock set amid white sand, which is periodically raked into varying patterns. The influence of Zen and the related Japanese ability to find great beauty in the rough and simple were also present in the tea ceremony that developed in the era of warrior dominance. The graceful gestures, elaborate rituals, and subtly shaped and glazed pots and cups that came to be associated with the service of tea on special occasions all lent themselves to composure and meditation. When

one walks the paths near the Golden Temple or sits in the wooden gallery that looks out into the garden at Ryoanji, it is hard to imagine that places of such beauty were created in an era so dominated by violence and civil strife.

Seeds of Unity and Japanese Nationhood

The economic and cultural growth of the warlord era demonstrated that Japan would not slip back into chaos and barbarism. Interestingly, these developments, combined with measures taken by the daimyos to improve administration within their domains, laid the basis for the lasting unification of Japan. Though often tied to particular lords and castle towns, the emerging commercial and artisan classes would in later centuries readily transfer their capital reserves and talents to building a unified economy under political leaders determined to break down regional trade barriers and to create a unified currency and system of weights and measures. Though the fact was long disguised by the rivalries and warfare among the daimyo lords, the legal and administrative systems established within each of the feudal domains could, if linked together, provide the bureaucratic infrastructure for a unified Japanese state. Within the domains, there also began to emerge professional government functionaries, who were slowly acquiring the skills that would eventually enable them to man a centralized bureaucracy.

KOREA: BETWEEN CHINA AND JAPAN

Focal Point: Of all the areas to which the Chinese formula for civilized development spread, Korea was the most profoundly influenced for the longest period of time. Because the Korean peninsula is no more than a physical extension of the Chinese mainland, and because historically Korean kingdoms were dwarfed by their giant neighbor to the west, most observers have treated Korea as little more than an appendage of China. But lumping Korea together with China overlooks the fact that the peninsula was ruled by indigenous dynasties through most of its history, even though these dynasties often paid tribute to the reigning Chinese emperor. Equally important, the Korean people, like the Vietnamese and Japanese, developed a separate identity that was expressed in distinctive forms of dress, cuisine, and a class system that varied significantly from that in China.

The peoples who occupied the Korean peninsula represented quite a different ethnic blend from those who, centuries earlier, came to identify themselves as Chinese. The Koreans descended from the hunting and herding peoples of eastern Siberia and Manchuria rather than the Mongolian and Turkic-speaking tribes to the west. By the 4th century B.C.E., the peoples who moved into the Korean peninsula had begun to acquire sedentary farming and metalworking techniques from the Chinese. From this point onward, the Koreans played a role in the dynastic struggles that preoccupied the peoples of the north China plain. In 109 B.C.E., the earliest Korean kingdom, *Choson*, was conquered by the Han emperor Wudi, and parts of Korea were colonized by Chinese settlers who would remain for nearly four centuries. These colonies soon became a channel by which Chinese influences began to filter into Korean culture in the critical centuries of its early development. A small Japanese enclave in the southeast of the peninsula provided contact with the islands as well, though cultural influences in this era ran overwhelmingly east from China to Korea and then on to Japan.

Despite conquest and colonization under the Han, the tribal peoples of the peninsula, particularly the *Koguryo* in the north, soon rose in resistance to Chinese rule. As Chinese control weakened, the Koguryo established an independent state in the northern half of the peninsula that was soon at war with two southern rivals, *Silla* and Paekche. Contacts between the splinter kingdoms that ruled north China after the fall of the Han and Koguryo resulted in the first wave of *Sinification*—that is, the extensive adoption of Chinese culture—in Korea. As was the case in Japan, Buddhism supplied the key links between Korea and the successors of the Han dynasty in northeast China. Korean rulers patronized Buddhist artists and financed the building of monasteries and pagodas. Korean scholars traveled to China, and a select few went to the source of the Buddhist faith, India.

In addition to Sinified variants of Buddhism, Chinese writing was introduced, even though the spoken Korean language was as ill suited for adaptation to the Chinese characters as the Japanese language had been. The Koguryo monarch imposed a unified law code patterned after that of Han China. He established universities, where Korean youths struggled to master the Confucian classics and their teachers wrote histories of China rather than their own land. With the intent of expanding his power and improving revenue collection, the Koguryo ruler also attempted to put together a Chinese-style bureaucracy. But the noble families who supported

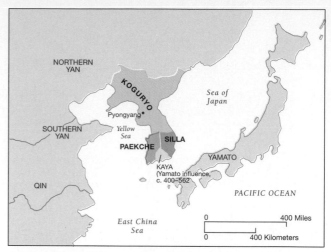

The Korean Peninsula During the Three Kingdoms Era

him had little use for a project that posed such an obvious threat to their own power. Without their support, the monarch did not have the resources for such an ambitious undertaking. Thus, full implementation of these policies had to wait for a more powerful dynasty to emerge some centuries later.

Tang Alliances and the Conquest of Korea

Centuries of warfare between the three Korean kingdoms weakened each without giving paramount power in the peninsula to any. Internal strife also left Korea vulnerable to further attacks from the outside. In addition to the unsuccessful campaigns of the Sui (see Chapter 18), the founders of the more lasting Tang dynasty included Korea in the territories they staked out for their empire. But it was several decades before one of them could finally mount a successful invasion. The stubborn warriors of the Koguryo kingdom bore the brunt of the Tang assaults, just as they had borne those launched by the Sui rulers. Finally, Tang strategists hit on the idea of taking advantage of Korean divisions to bring the troublesome region into line. Striking an alliance with the rulers of the Silla kingdom to the southeast, they destroyed the Paekche kingdom and then defeated the Koguryo and put an end to the long-lived dynasty that had played such a key role in Korea's early development.

The Chinese conquerors now began to quarrel with their Silla allies over how to divide the spoils. When the Silla proved able to fight the larger Chinese forces in the peninsula to a standstill, and revolts broke out in the former Paekche and Koguryo territories already conquered, the Tang decided it was time to strike a deal. In return for regular tribute payments and the Silla monarch's submission as a vassal of the Tang emperor, the Chinese withdrew their armies in 668, leaving the Silla in effect the independent rulers of a united Korea. Despite brief lapses, the Koreans were to maintain this independence and roughly the same boundaries established by the Silla until the occupation of their land by the Japanese in the early 20th century.

Sinification: the Tributary Link

Under the Silla monarchs, who ruled from 668 until the late 9th century, and the Koryo dynasty (918–1392) that followed, Chinese influences peaked and Korean culture achieved its first full flowering. The Silla rulers consciously strove to turn their kingdom into a miniature of the Tang Empire. They regularly sent embassies and tribute to the Tang court, where Korean scholars collected Chinese texts and noted the latest fashions in court dress and etiquette. The Koreans' regular attendance on the Chinese emperors was a key manifestation of their prominent and enduring participation in the Chinese tribute system. At various times, the participants in the system included nomads from central and North Asia, the Tibetans, many of the kingdoms of Southeast Asia, and the emperors of Japan. None of these participants were more committed to the tributary arrangements than the Koreans. Rather than attempt to conquer the Koreans and other surrounding peoples, most Chinese emperors were content to receive embassies from them. These emissaries offered tribute in the form of splendid gifts and acknowledged the superiority of the Son of Heaven by their willingness to kowtow to him (kowtowing involved a series of ritual bows in which the supplicant prostrated himself before the throne).

To most of the peoples involved, this seemed a small price to pay for the benefits they received from the Middle Kingdom. Not only did submission and tribute guarantee continuing peace with the Chinese, it brought far richer gifts in return for those offered to the Chinese ruler, as well as privileged access to Chinese learning, art, and manufactured goods. Tribute missions normally included merchants, whose ability to buy up Chinese manufactures and sell their own goods in the lucrative Chinese market hinged on their country's participation in the tribute system. Missions from heavily Sinified areas, such as Japan, Korea, and Vietnam, also included contingents of scholars, who studied at Chinese academies or Buddhist monasteries and busily purchased Chinese scrolls and works of art to fill the libraries and embellish

the palaces back home. Thus, the tribute system became the major channel of trade and intercultural exchange between China and its neighbors.

The Sinification of Korean Elite Culture

The Silla rulers rebuilt their capital at Kumsong on the Kyongju plain to look like its Tang counterpart. The streets were laid out on a regular grid; there were central markets, parks, lakes, and a separate district to house the imperial family. Fleeing the tedium of the backward rural areas and provincial capitals, the aristocratic families who surrounded the throne and dominated imperial government crowded their mansions in the areas around the imperial palace. With their large extended families and hundreds of slaves and hangers-on, they made up a sizeable portion of the capital's population. Some of the aristocracy studied in Chinese schools, and a minority even submitted to the rigors of the Confucian examination system introduced under the Silla rulers. Most of the aristocracy opted for the artistic pursuits and entertainments available in the capital. They could do so because most positions in the government continued to be occupied by members of the aristocratic families by virtue of their birth and family connections rather than their knowledge of the Confucian classics.

Partly out of self-interest, the Korean elite continued to favor Buddhism over Confucianism. They and the Korean royal family lavishly endowed monasteries and patronized works of art, which became major forms of Korean cultural creativity. The capital at Kumsong soon became crowded with Buddhist temples, which were usually built of wood. Buddhist monks were constantly in attendance on the ruler as well as on members of the royal family and the more powerful aristocratic households. But the schools of Buddhism that caught on among the elite were Chinese. Korean artwork and monastic design reproduced, sometimes splendidly, Chinese prototypes; and even the location of monasteries and pagodas in high places followed Chinese ideas about the need to mollify local spirits and balance supernatural forces.

Sometimes the Koreans borrowed from the Chinese and then outdid their teachers. Most notable in this regard was the pottery produced in both the Silla and Koryo eras. The Koreans first learned the techniques of porcelain manufacture from the Chinese. But in the pale green–glazed celadon bowls and vases of the late Silla and Koryo, they created masterworks that even Chinese connoisseurs admired and collected. They also pioneered in making oxide glazes that were used in the manufac-

These Korean ceramic cups, formed in the shape of lotus flowers with decorative stands, are from the time of the Koryo dynasty (918–1392).

ture of the black- and rust-colored stoneware of this era, which is still recognized as some of the finest pottery ever crafted.

Civilization for the Few

With the exception of Buddhist sects like the "pure land" that had strong appeal to the ordinary people, imports from China in this and later eras were all but monopolized by the tiny elite. The aristocratic families were divided into several ranks that neither intermarried nor socialized with each other, much less the rest of the population. They not only filled most of the posts in the Korean bureaucracy but also dominated the social and economic life of the entire kingdom. Much of Korea's trade with the Chinese and Japanese was oriented to providing the aristocrats with the fancy clothing, special teas, scrolls, and artwork that occupied such an important place in their idle lives. In return, Korea exported mainly raw materials, such as forest products and metals like copper, which was mined by virtual slaves who lived in horrendous conditions. Members of the royal family and the aristocratic households often financed artisan production for export or to supply the court; some backed mercantile expeditions and even engaged extensively in money-lending. All of this, of course, constricted the ac-

tivities of artisans and traders. The former were usually considered low in status and were poorly paid for their talents and labor. The latter were so weak that they did not really form a distinct class.

The aristocratic "ranks" were the only people who really counted for anything in Korean society. The classes beneath them were oriented to their service. These included government functionaries, who were recognized as a separate social category; commoners, who were mainly peasants; and virtual slaves, who were known as the "low born" and ranged from miners and artisans to servants and entertainers. Buddhist festivals periodically relieved the drudgery and monotony of the lives of the common people, and Buddhist salvationist teachings gave them hope for bliss in the afterlife. But much of what the peasants, artisans, and miners produced went to support the outsized court and aristocracy in the capital, where the wealth and cultural creativity of an otherwise impoverished and backward land was concentrated.

Koryo Collapse, Dynastic Renewal

Periodically, the common people and the "low born" found their lot too much to bear and rose up against a ruling class that was obviously much more devoted to pursuing its own pleasures than to their well-being. Most of these risings were local affairs and were ruthlessly repressed by armies of the ruling class. But collectively they weakened both the Silla and Koryo regimes, and in combination with quarrels between the aristocratic households and outside invasions, they contributed to the fall of both dynasties. In the absence of real alternatives, the aristocratic families managed to survive these crises and elevate one of their number above the others to the royal throne. After nearly a century and a half of conflict and turmoil triggered by the Mongol invasion in 1231, the Yi dynasty was established in 1392. Remarkably, it would rule Korea until 1910. Though there would be some modifications, the Yi quickly restored the aristocratic dominance and links to China that had predominated under their predecessors. Of all of the peoples who received higher civilization from China, none would be as content to live in the shadow of the Middle Kingdom as the Koreans.

BETWEEN CHINA AND SOUTHEAST ASIA: THE MAKING OF VIETNAM

Focal Point: From the Chinese point of view, the Red River valley, which became the heartland of the Vietnamese people in the first millennium C.E., was just another rice-growing area to be annexed to their ever-expanding civilization. So much territory and so many peoples had already been absorbed in the fertile southern regions that it was natural to anticipate the same fate for the Red River area and its inhabitants. But the Viets, who lived there, differed in critical ways from the other "southern barbarians" the Chinese had encountered. For one thing, their homeland was farther away from the main centers of Chinese political power on the northern plains than that of any people whom the Chinese had sought to absorb up to that point. For another, the Viets had already developed a fairly sophisticated and, as it turned out, very resilient culture of their own—a culture that shared much with the other peoples of Southeast Asia.

The preconquest culture of the Vietnamese gave them a strong sense of themselves as a distinct people with a common heritage that they did not want to see overwhelmed by an expanding China. Thus, though the Viets were well aware of the benefits they derived from the superior technology, modes of political organization, and ideas they received from China, their gratitude was tempered by their fear of losing their own identity and

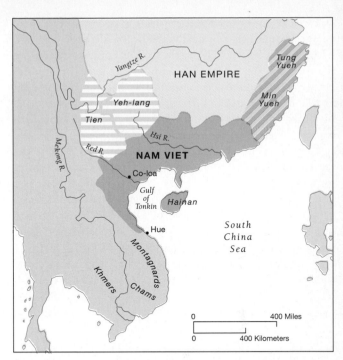

South China and Vietnam on the Eve of the Han Conquest

becoming just another part of China's massive civilization. Ironically, the Viets first appear in recorded history as a group of "southern barbarians" mentioned by Chinese scholars in accounts of Qin raids in South China in the 220s B.C.E. At that time, their kingdom, which the Chinese called Nam Viet, meaning "people in the south," extended along the southern coastal area of what is now China. The initial raids by Qin forces left little lasting Chinese presence, but they probably gave a boost to the lively trade that had been conducted between the Viets and the peoples of South China for centuries. In exchange for silk manufactured by the Chinese, the Viets traded ivory, tortoise shells, pearls, peacock feathers, aromatic woods, and other exotic products drawn from the sea and tropical forests. Some decades after the Qin raids, the Viet rulers defeated the feudal lords who controlled the Red River valley and brought their lands under the control of the Viet kingdom. In the following centuries, the Viets intermarried and blended with the Mon-Khmer and Tai-speaking peoples who occupied the Red River area. This proved to be a crucial step in the formation of the Vietnamese as a distinct ethnic group.

As the Viets' willingness to intermarry with ethnic groups like the *Khmers* (today's Cambodians) and the Tais suggests, before their conquest by the Han they possessed a culture that exhibited many features characteristic of Southeast Asia. Their spoken language was not related to Chinese. They enjoyed a strong tradition of village autonomy, physically symbolized by the bamboo hedges that surround northern Vietnamese villages to the present day. The Vietnamese favored the nuclear family to the extended household preferred by the Chinese, and they never developed the clan networks that have been such a prominent feature of south Chinese society. Vietnamese women have historically possessed greater freedom and more influence, both within the family and in society at large, than their Chinese counterparts.

Vietnamese customs and cultural forms also differed very significantly from Chinese. The Vietnamese dressed quite differently; women, for example, preferred long skirts to the black pants that nonelite women wore in China. The Vietnamese delighted in the archetypical Southeast Asian pastime, the cockfight; they chewed betel nut, which the Chinese found disgusting; and they blackened their teeth, which the Chinese also considered repulsive. In the centuries when they were dominated by the Chinese politically, the Vietnamese managed to preserve most of these original features of their society. They also became much more fervently attached at the grass-roots level to Buddhism, and they developed art and literature, especially poetry, that was refined and quite distinct from that of the Chinese.

Conquest and Sinification

As the Han rulers who succeeded the Qin attempted to incorporate South China into their empire, they inevitably came into conflict with the Viets. Though the Han emperor initially settled for the Viet ruler's admission of his vassal status and periodic payments of tribute, by 111 B.C.E., the Han thought it best to conquer the feisty Viets outright and to govern them directly by Chinese officials. The Red River area was garrisoned by Chinese troops, and Chinese administrators set to work co-opting the local lords and encouraging them to adopt Chinese culture. Because the Viet elite realized that they had a great deal to learn from their powerful neighbors to the north, they cooperated with the agents of the new regime. Sensing that they had found another barbarian people ripe for assimilation, the Chinese eagerly introduced essential elements of their own culture into the southern lands.

In the centuries after the Chinese conquest, the Vietnamese elite were drawn into the bureaucratic machine that the Han emperors and the shi had developed to hold together the empire won by the Qin. They attended Chinese-style schools, where they wrote in the Chinese script and read and memorized the classical Chinese texts of Confucius and Mencius. They took exams to qualify for administrative posts, whose responsibilities and privileges were defined by Chinese precedents. They introduced Chinese cropping techniques and irrigation technology, which soon made Vietnamese agriculture the most productive in Southeast Asia. This meant that Vietnamese society, like the Chinese, could support larger numbers of people. The result was the high population density characteristic of the Red River valley and the lowland coastal areas to the south.

The Vietnamese also found that Chinese political and military organization gave them a decisive edge over the Indianized peoples to the west and south, with whom they increasingly clashed over the control of lands to settle and cultivate. Over time, the Vietnamese elite adopted the extended family ideal and took to venerating their ancestors in the Confucian manner. Their Chinese overlords had every reason to assume that the barbarians were well on their way to becoming civilized—that is, like the Chinese.

Roots of Resistance

Sporadic revolts led by members of the Vietnamese aristocracy, and the failure of Chinese cultural imports to make much of an impression on the Vietnamese peasantry, ultimately frustrated Chinese hopes for the absorption of the Viets. Though they had learned much from the Chinese, the Vietnamese lords chafed under their overlordship, in part because the Chinese often found it difficult to conceal their disdain for local customs in what they considered a backward and unhealthy outpost of the empire. Vietnamese literature attests to the less than reverent attitudes felt by Vietnamese collaborators toward Chinese learning and culture. In the following poem, a teacher mocks himself and doubts his usefulness to the people he serves:

I bear the title "Disciple of Confucius."
Why bother with blockheads, wearing such a label?
I dress like a museum piece:
I speak only in learned quotations (poetry and prose);
*   Long since dried out, I still strut like a peacock;*
*   Failed in my exams, I've been dropped like a*
*   shrivelled root.*
Doctorate, M. A.: all out of reach,
So why not teach school, and beat the devil out of
*   my students.*

Elsewhere in Vietnamese writings, self-doubts and mockery turn to rage and a fierce determination to resist Chinese dominance, whatever the cost. The following

DOCUMENT

Literature as a Mirror of the Exchanges Between Civilized Centers

The following passages from Lady Murasaki's classic Japanese account of court life, *The Tale of Genji* (Vintage Press, ed., 1985), and from perhaps the most popular and beloved work of Vietnamese literature, Nguyen Du's *The Tale of Kieu* (Vintage Press, ed., 1973), provide superb examples of the important and far-reaching exchanges between the civilizations of South and East Asia. Not surprisingly, Chinese influences, including numerous allusions to Chinese writings and historical events, are paramount, but Buddhist (hence originally Indian) themes are pervasive in both works. As one of the following passages illustrates, there is also evidence of significant exchanges between the satellite civilizations of China.

[Kieu] dreamed a girl appeared hard by her side and murmured: "Kieu! Your Karma's still undone. How can you shirk your debt of grief to fate? You yet have to play out your woman's role."

The moderator was a man of considerable learning. There was much of interest in his exchanges with the Korean. There were also exchanges of Chinese poetry, and in one of his poems the Korean succeeded most skillfully in conveying his joy at having been able to observe such a countenance on this the eve of his return to his own land. . . . Summoning an astrologer of the Indian school, the emperor was pleased to learn that the Indian view coincided with the Japanese and the Korean; and so he concluded that the boy should become a commoner with the name of Minamoto or Genji.

Looking at the keepsakes Myobu had brought back, [Genji] thought what a comfort it would be if some wizard were to bring him, like that Chinese emperor, a comb from the world where his lost love was dwelling. . . . There are limits to the powers of the most gifted artist. The Chinese lady in the paintings did not have the luster of life. Yang Kuei-fei was said to have resembled the lotus of the Sublime Pond, the willows of the Timeless Hall. No doubt she was very beautiful in her Chinese finery.

"You are well-famed as a lute-player," he said. "Like Chung Tzu-ch'i I've longed to hear you play." . . . Now [Kieu] began to play. A battle scene—oh how they clashed and clanged, Han and Ch'u swords! The Ssu-ma tune, A Phoenix Seeks His Mate—it sounded like an outburst of pure grief. Then Hsi K'ang's masterpiece, Kuang-ling, was heard: it rushed on like a stream or flew like clouds. Next came what Chao-chin played—she mourned her Prince and all her kinsfolk she must leave behind as she crossed the Great Wall to wed a Hun.

The [abbot] talked of this ephemeral world and of the world to come. His own burden of sin was heavy, thought Genji, that he had been lured into an illicit and profitless affair. He would regret it all his life and suffer even more terribly in the life to come. What a joy to withdraw to such a place [a mountain monastery] as this!

When one must weigh and choose between one's love and filial duty, which will turn the scale? Kieu brushed aside her solemn vows to [the young student] Kim—she'd pay a daughter's debt before all else. Resolved on what to do, she spoke her mind: "Hands off my father, please! I'll sell myself and ransom him."

"A happy home where love will reign," said Kieu, "who does not dream of it? But I believe a bride must bring her man the purity of an unopened flower, the perfect shape of a full moon. Priceless is chastity."

Questions: From these passages can you identify Chinese precedents in terms of place names and historical personages, allusions to Chinese literary works, and more general attitudes toward gender or social organization that can be traced to Chinese models? Can you detect passages that convey Buddhist ideas about the nature of the world and human existence?

sentiments of a Vietnamese caught up in resistance to the reimposition of rule from China by the Mongols in the 13th century provide a dramatic case in point:

> I myself often forget to eat at mealtime, and in the middle of the night I wake up and caress my pillow. My intestines hurt me incessantly, as if they had been cut off, and tears flow abundantly from my eyes. My only grief is that I have not yet succeeded in hacking apart the enemy's body, peeling off his skin, swallowing his liver, drinking his blood.

The intensity and ferocity contained in this passage give some sense of why the Chinese failed in the end to hold or assimilate the Vietnamese. They also failed because the peasantry rallied again and again to the call of their own lords to rise up and drive off the alien rulers. The fact that the most famous of these risings was led in 39 C.E. by the *Trung sisters,* who were children of a deposed local leader, points to the importance of the more favored position of women in Vietnamese society, in contrast to the Chinese, as a source of resistance to Chinese domination.

Vietnamese women were understandably hostile to the Confucian codes and family system that would have confined them to the household and subjected them to male authority figures. We do not know whether this resentment figured in the Trung sisters' decision to revolt, but poetry written in later centuries by female authors leaves little doubt about the reactions of Vietnamese women to Confucian norms or male dominance. One of the most famous of these writers, Ho Xuan Huong, flaunts Confucian decorum in her ribald verse and mocks her male suitors:

> *Careful, careful where are you going:*
> *You group of know-nothings!*
> *Come here and let your older sister*
> *teach you to write poems.*
> *Young bees whose stingers itch*
> *rub them in wilted flowers.*
> *Young goats who have nothing to do with their horns butt*
> *them against sparse shrubbery.*

In the following poem, entitled "Sharing a Husband," Huong ridicules those who advocate the practice of polygamy, a practice favored by any self-respecting Confucian:

> *One wife is covered by a quilted blanket, while one wife is*
> *left in the cold.*

> *Cursed be this fate of sharing a common husband.*
> *Seldom do you have an occasion to possess your husband,*
> *Not even twice in one month.*
> *You toil and endure hardships in order to earn your*
> *steamed rice, and then the rice is cold and tasteless.*
> *It is like renting your services for hire,*
> *and then receiving no wages.*
> *How is it that I have turned out this way,*
> *I would rather suffer the fate of remaining unmarried*
> *and living alone by myself.*

Winning Independence

In addition to a strong sense of prior identity and motives for resistance that crossed class and gender barriers, the Vietnamese people's struggle for independence was assisted by the fragility of the links that bound them to China. Great distances and mountain barriers created nightmare conditions for Chinese administrators responsible for supplying military expeditions to the far south. Only small numbers of Chinese—mostly bureaucrats, soldiers, and merchants—resided in the Red River area, and few of them remained permanently. Most critically, Chinese control over the distant Vietnamese depended on the strength of the ruling dynasties in China itself.

The Vietnamese were quick to take advantage of political turmoil and nomadic incursions in northern China to assert their independence. After failing to completely free themselves on several occasions, they mounted a massive rebellion during the period of chaos in China following the fall of the Tang dynasty in 907. By 939, they had won political independence from their northern neighbors. Though both the Mongol and Ming rulers of China later attempted to reassert control over the Vietnamese, both efforts ended in humiliating retreats. From 939 until the conquests by the French in the 19th century, the Vietnamese were masters of their own land.

The Continuing Chinese Impact

Though the Chinese political hold was broken, Chinese cultural exports continued to play central roles in Vietnamese society. A succession of Vietnamese dynasties beginning with the Le (980–1009), which became the source of legitimacy for the rest, built Chinese-style palaces in the midst of forbidden cities patterned after those in Changan and Beijing. They ruled through a bureaucracy that was a much smaller copy of the Chinese administrative system, with secretariats, six main ministries, and a bureau of censors to keep graft and corrup-

As this view of the moat and part of the palace of the Vietnamese emperors at Hue illustrates, Chinese taste and architectural style strongly influenced the construction and decoration of Vietnamese court centers.

tion in check. Civil service exams were reintroduced, and an administrative elite schooled in the Confucian classics sought the emperor's favor and commanded deference from the common people.

But the Vietnamese equivalent of the Chinese scholar-gentry never enjoyed as much power or influence. For one thing, their control at the village level was much less secure than that of their Chinese counterparts. Much more than those in China, local Vietnamese officials tended to identify with the peasantry rather than with the court and higher administrators. To a much greater degree, they looked out for local interests and served as leaders in village risings against the ruling dynasty if its demands on the common people became too oppressive.

As in China during the period of division following the fall of the Han, the power of the scholar-bureaucrats in Vietnam was also limited in the reign of many dynasties by competition from well-educated Buddhist monks. The fact that the Buddhists sought and gained much stronger links with the Vietnamese peasantry than the monastic orders had in China strengthened them in their struggles with the Confucian scholars. The relatively high esteem in which women were held in Buddhist teachings and institutions also enhanced the popularity of the monks in Vietnam. Thus, countervailing centers of power and influence prevented most Vietnamese dynasties from enjoying the authority of their Chinese counterparts. They also frustrated efforts by Confucian bureaucrats to control the peasantry as firmly as the Chinese scholar-gentry whom they tried to emulate.

The Vietnamese Drive to the South

However watered down, the Chinese legacy gave the Vietnamese great advantages in the struggles within Indochina that became a major preoccupation of independent Vietnamese rulers. Because the Vietnamese refused to settle in the malarial highlands that fringed the Red River area and rose abruptly from the coastal plains farther south, their main adversaries were the *Chams* and Khmers, who occupied the lowland areas to the south that the Vietnamese coveted themselves. The Vietnamese launched periodic expeditions to retaliate for raids on their villages by the hill peoples. They also regularly traded with the hill dwellers for forest products, but the Vietnamese sought to minimize cultural exchange with these hunters and shifting agriculturists, whom they regarded as "nude savages."

As they moved out in the only direction left to them—south along the narrow plain between the mountains and the sea—the Vietnamese made good use of the larger population and superior bureaucratic and military organization that the Chinese connection had done much to foster. From the 11th to the 18th centuries, they fought a long series of generally successful wars against the Chams, an Indianized people living in the lowland areas along the coast. Eventually the Chams were driven into the highlands, where their descendants, in much diminished numbers, live to the present day.

Having beaten the Chams and settled on their former croplands, the Vietnamese next clashed with the Khmers, who had begun to move into the Mekong delta region during the centuries of the Vietnamese drive south. Again, Indianized armies, this time marching under Khmer rulers, whose power had declined markedly from that of the monarchs who had overseen the building of the great temples of Angkor Wat and the Bayon, proved no match for the Chinese-inspired military forces and weapons of the Vietnamese. By the time the French arrived in force in the Mekong area in the late 18th century, the Vietnamese had occupied much of the upper delta and were beginning to push into territory that today belongs to Cambodia.

Expansion and Division

As Vietnamese armies and peasant colonists moved farther and farther from the capital at Hanoi, the dynasties centered there found it increasingly difficult to control the commanders and peasants fighting and living in the frontier areas. As the southerners intermarried with and adopted some of the customs of the Chams and Khmers, differences in culture and attitude developed between them and the northerners. Though both continued to identify themselves as Vietnamese, the northerners (much like their counterparts in the United States) came to see the Vietnamese who settled in the frontier south as less energetic and slower in speech and movement. As the hold of the Hanoi-based dynasties over the southern regions weakened, regional military commanders grew less and less responsive to orders from the north and slower in remitting taxes due to the court. Bickering turned to violent clashes, and by the end of the 16th century a rival dynasty, the *Nguyen,* had emerged to challenge the legitimacy of the Trinh family that ruled the north.

The territories of the Nguyen at this time were centered on the narrow plains that connected the two great rice bowls of Vietnam along the Red and Mekong rivers. Their capital was at Hue, far north of the Mekong delta region that in this period had scarcely been settled by the Vietnamese. For the next two centuries, these rival dynastic houses fought for the right to rule Vietnam. None accepted the division of Vietnam as permanent; each sought to unite all of the Vietnamese people under a single monarch. This long struggle not only absorbed much of the Vietnamese energies but also prevented them from recognizing the growing external threat to their homeland. For the first time in history, the danger came not from the Chinese giant to the north but from a distant land and religion about which the Vietnamese knew and cared nothing—France and the conversion-minded Roman Catholic church.

CONCLUSION

Divergent Paths in East Asian Development

The first millennium C.E. was a pivotal epoch in the history of the peoples of East Asia. The spread of ideas, organizational models, and material culture from a common Chinese center spawned the rise of three distinct satellite civilizations in Japan, Korea, and Vietnam. In contrast to the lands of the nomadic peoples who had long been in contact with China from the north and west, each of these regions contained fertile and well-watered lowland areas that were suited to sedentary cultivation, which was essential to the spread of the Chinese pattern of civilized development. Each, in fact, provided an ideal environment for the cultivation of wet rice, which was increasingly replacing millet and other grains as the staple of China.

Common elements of Chinese culture, from modes of writing and bureaucratic organization to religious teachings and art, were transmitted to each satellite. In all three cases, Chinese imports, with the important exception of popular Buddhism, were all but monopolized by court and provincial elite groups, the former prominent in Japan and Korea, the latter in Vietnam. In all three cases, Chinese thought patterns and modes of social organization were actively and willingly cultivated by these local elites, who were well aware that they were the key to a higher level of development.

Thus, for a time at least, all three satellites shared prominent aspects of political organization, social development, and intellectual creativity. But the differing ways in which Chinese influences were transmitted to each area resulted in very divergent outcomes in terms of the mix of Chinese-derived and indigenous elements that were blended to produce distinctive variations of a common pattern of civilized life. In Korea, where the period of direct Chinese rule was relatively brief but China's physical presence and military power all too apparent, the need for symbolic political submission was obvious and the desire for long-term cultural dependence firmly implanted. In Vietnam, where Chinese conquest and control lasted over a thousand years, a hard-fought struggle for political independence gave way to a growing attachment to Chinese culture as a counterbalance to the Indian influences that had brought civilization to the Southeast Asian rivals of the Vietnamese.

In Japan, where all attempts by Chinese dynasties to assert direct control had failed miserably, Chinese culture was emulated by the courtly elite that first brought civilization to Japan. But the rise of a rival aristocratic class, which was based in the provinces and which championed military values that were fundamentally opposed to Chinese Confucianism, led to the gradual limitation of Chinese influence in Japanese culture and society and the reassertion of Japanese traditional ways. Japanese political patterns, in particular, formed a marked contrast with the predominance of rule by a centralized bureaucracy in China. Nonetheless, in Japan as in the rest of East Asia, China remained the epitome of civilized development; Chinese ways were the standard by which all peoples "ought" to be judged.

In Korea and Japan, as in China itself, interaction in the East Asian sphere led to many beneficial exchanges that were similar to those occurring in other centers of civilized life during the postclassical centuries. In East Asia, however, these exchanges occurred in semi-isolation, with a lower level of awareness of larger world currents than was the case among the peoples of the Islamic empires, Christian Europe, and the Buddhist kingdoms of mainland Southeast Asia. Thus, East Asia provides an important variant on the general theme of cross-cultural contact that was a dominant feature of the postclassical age.

FURTHER READINGS

In comparison with Korea, there is a wealth of good secondary works on early Japanese and Vietnamese history. The most accessible works on Korea are William Henthorn's *History of Korea* (1971), which gives some attention to the arts in addition to rather standard accounts of political and social changes, Hatada Takashi's *A History of Korea* (1969), and the sections by Albert Craig in Fairbank and Reischauer's *East Asia: The Modern Transformation* (1965). The best introductory works on Japanese history and culture are the writings of Reischauer; J. W. Hall's *Japan from Prehistory to Modern Times* (1970); and Mikisio Hane's superb overview, *Japan: A Historical Survey* (1972). H. Paul Varley's *Japanese Culture: A Short History* (1973) has fine sections on the arts, religion, and literature of the warlord era. Also good on this period are Peter Duus's *Japanese Feudalism* (1969); Varley's *Samurai* (1970), which was coauthored with Ivan and Nobuko Morris; and the first and second volumes of George Sansom's *A History of Japan* (1958, 1960).

For an understanding of the Chinese impact on Vietnam, there is no better place to begin than Alexander Woodsides' *Vietnam and the Chinese Model* (1971). The best works on the earliest period in Vietnamese history are translations of the writings of the French scholar Georges Coedes and the superspecialized *Birth of Vietnam* (1983) by Keith Taylor. Thomas Hodgkin's survey of Vietnamese history has the virtues of being highly readable as well as making extensive use of Vietnamese literature. Troung Buu Lam's edited volume, *Patterns of Vietnamese Response to Foreign Intervention* (1967), along with the Genji and Kieu tales cited in the "Document" of this chapter, provide wonderful ways for the student to get inside Japanese or Vietnamese culture.

20

The Last Great Nomadic Challenges: From Chinggis Khan to Timur

1130–c. 1250 Almohads rule North Africa and Spain

1215 First Mongol attacks on North China; Beijing captured

1236–1240 Mongol conquest of Russia

1234 Mongols take all of North China; end of Qin dynasty

1037–1194 Seljuk Turks dominant in the Middle East

1235–1279 Mongol conquest of South China; end of southern Song dynasty

1115–1234 Jurchens (Qin dynasty) rules North China

1227 Death of Chinggis Khan; Ogedei named successor

907–1118 Khitan conquest of North China

1219–1223 First Mongol invasions of Russia and the Islamic world

1126 Song dynasty flees to South China

1206 Temujin takes the name of Chinggis Khan; Mongol state is founded

900 C.E.　　　　**1100** C.E.　　　　**1200** C.E.

INTRODUCTION

From the first explosion of Mongol military might from the steppes of central Asia in the early decades of the 13th century to the death of Timur in 1405, the nomads of central Asia made a last, stunning return to center stage in world history. Mongol invasions ended or interrupted many of the great empires of the postclassical period and also extended the world network that had increasingly defined the period. Under Chinggis Khan—who united his own Mongol tribesmen and numerous nomadic neighbors into the mightiest war machine the world had seen to that time—central Asia, northern China, and eastern Persia were brought under Mongol rule. Under Chinggis Khan's sons and grandsons, the rest of China, Tibet, Persia, Iraq, much of Asia Minor, and all of southern Russia were added to the vast Mongol imperium. Though the empire was divided between Chinggis Khan's sons after his death in 1227, the four *khanates* or kingdoms—which emerged in the struggles for succession—dominated most of Asia for the next one and a half centuries. The Mongol conquests and the empires they produced represented the most formidable nomadic challenge to the growing global dominance of the sedentary peoples of the civilized cores since the great nomadic migrations in the first centuries C.E. Except for Timur's devastating but short-lived grab for power at the end of the 14th century, nomadic peoples would never again mount a challenge as massive and sweeping as that of the Mongols.

In most histories, the Mongol conquests have been depicted as a savage assault by backward and barbaric peoples on many of the most ancient and developed centers of human civilization. Much is made of the ferocity of Mongol warriors in battle; their destruction of great cities, such as Baghdad, in reprisal for resistance to Mongol armies; and their mass slaughters of defeated enemies. Depending on the civilization from whose city walls a historian recorded the coming of the Mongol "hordes," they were depicted as the scourge of Islam, devils bent on the destruction of Christianity, persecutors of the Buddhists, or defilers of the Confucian traditions of China. Though they were indeed fierce fighters and capable of terrible acts of retribution against those who dared to defy them, the Mongols' conquests brought much more than death and devastation.

At the peak of their power, the domains of the Mongol khans, or rulers, made up a vast realm in which once hostile peoples lived together in peace and virtually all religions were tolerated. From the Khanate of Persia in the west to the empire of the fabled Kubilai Khan in the east, the law code first promulgated by Chinggis Khan gave order to human interaction. The result was an important new stage in international contact. From eastern Europe to southern China, merchants and travelers could move across the well-policed Mongol domains without fear for their lives or property. The great swath of Mongol territory that covered or connected most of Europe, Asia, and the Middle East served as a bridge between the civilizations of the Eastern Hemisphere. The caravans and embassies that crossed the Mongol lands transmitted new

1240–1241 Mongol invasion of western Europe

1271–1368 Reign of the Yuan (Mongol) dynasty in China

1368 Yuan dynasty overthrown; Ming period in China begins

1258 Mongol destruction of Baghdad

1271–1295 Journey of Marco Polo to central Asia, China, and Southeast Asia

1336–1405 Life of Timur

1274, 1280 Failed Mongol invasions of Japan

c. 1370 Gunpowder weapons effectively deployed in China and Europe

1253 Mongol victory over Seljuk Turks; rise of Ottoman Turks in Middle East

1290s First true guns used in China

1260–1294 Reign of Kubilai Khan in China

mid-14th century Spread of the Black Death in Eurasia

1380 Russian victory at Kulikova; power of the (Mongol descended) Golden Horde is broken

1260 Mamluk (slave) rulers of Egypt defeat Mongols at Ain Jalut; end of drive west

1250 C.E. **1300** C.E. **1350** C.E.

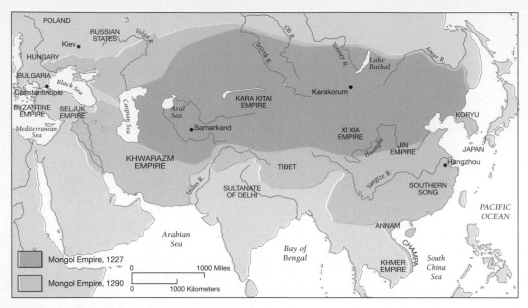

The First Mongol Empire of Chinggis Khan

foods, inventions, and ideas from one civilized pool to the others and from civilized pools to the nomadic peoples who served as intermediaries. Like the Islamic expansion that preceded it, the Mongol explosion did much to lay the foundations for more human interaction on a global scale, extending and intensifying the world network that had been building since the classical age.

This chapter will explore the sources of the Mongol drive for a world empire and the course of Mongol expansion. Particular attention will be given to the nomadic basis of the Mongol war machine and the long-standing patterns of nomadic–sedentary interaction that shaped the character, direction, and impact of Mongol expansion. After a discussion of the career and campaigns of Chinggis Khan, separate sections of this chapter will deal with the Mongol conquest and rule in Russia and eastern Europe, the Middle East, and China. The chapter will conclude with an assessment of the meaning of the Mongol interlude for the development of civilization and the growth of cross-cultural interaction on a global scale. In both their destructive and constructive roles, the Mongols generated major changes within the framework of global history.

THE MONGOL EMPIRE OF CHINGGIS KHAN

Focal Point: The Mongols had long been one of the nomadic peoples that intervened periodically in Chinese history. But tribal divisions and rivalries with neighbor-ing ethnic groups—particularly Turkic peoples—had long blunted the expansive potential of Mongol warrior culture. In the early 13th century, these and other obstacles to Mongol expansion were overcome, primarily because of the leadership of an astute political strategist and brilliant military commander who took the title *Chinggis Khan*. Within decades, the Mongols and allied nomadic groups built an empire that stretched from the Middle Eastern heartlands of the Islamic world to the China Sea.

In most ways, the Mongols epitomized nomadic society and culture. Their survival depended on the well-being of the herds of goats and sheep they drove from one pasture area to another according to the cycle of the seasons. Their staple foods were the meat and milk products provided by their herds, supplemented in most cases by grain and vegetables gained through trade with sedentary farming peoples. They also traded hides and dairy products for jewelry, weapons, and cloth manufactured in urban centers. They dressed in sheepskins, made boots from tanned sheep hides, and lived in round felt tents that were processed from wool sheared from their animals. The tough little ponies they rode to round up their herds, hunt wild animals, and make war were equally essential to their way of life. Both male and female Mongol children could ride as soon as they were able to walk. Mongol warriors could literally ride for days on end, sleeping and eating in the saddle.

Though it was a cumbersome process, even large Mongol tents could be moved when mounted on huge wagons, which were pulled by large teams of oxen.

Like the Arabs and other nomadic peoples we have encountered, the basic unit of Mongol society was the tribe, which was divided into kin-related clans whose members camped and herded together on a regular basis. When threatened by external enemies or in preparation for raids on other nomads or invasions of sedentary areas, clans and tribes could be combined in great confederations. Depending on the skills of their leaders, these confederations could be held together for months or even years. But when the threat had passed or the raiding was done, clans and tribes invariably drifted back to their own pasturelands and campsites. At all organizational levels, leaders were elected by the free males of the group. Though women exercised considerable influence within the family and had the right to be heard in tribal councils, males dominated positions of leadership.

Courage in battle, usually evidenced from youth by bravery in the hunt, and the capacity to forge alliances and attract dependents were vital leadership skills. A strong leader could quickly build up a large following of chiefs from other clans and tribal groups. Some of these subordinates might be defeated rivals who had been enslaved by the victorious chief, though often the lifestyles of master and slave differed little. Should the leader grow old and feeble or suffer severe reverses, his once loyal subordinates would quickly abandon him. He ex-

pected this to happen, and the subordinates felt no remorse. Their survival and that of their dependents hinged on attaching themselves to a strong tribal leader.

The Making of a Great Warrior: The Early Career of Chinggis Khan

Indo-European and then Turkic-speaking nomads had dominated the steppes and posed the principal threat to Asian and European sedentary civilizations in the early millennia of recorded history. But peoples speaking Mongolian languages had enjoyed moments of power and had actually carved out regional kingdoms in north China in the 4th and 10th centuries C.E. In fact, in the early 12th century, Chinggis Khan's great-grandfather, Kabul Khan, led a Mongol alliance that had won glory by defeating an army sent against them by the Qin kingdom of north China. Soon after this victory, Kabul Khan became ill and died, and his successors could neither defeat their nomadic enemies nor hold the Mongol alliance together. Divided and beaten, the Mongols fell on hard times.

Chinggis Khan, who as a youth was named Temujin, was born in the 1170s into one of the splinter clans that fought for survival in the decades after the death of Kabul Khan. Temujin's father was an able leader, who managed to build up a decent following and negotiate a promise of marriage between his eldest son and the daughter of a stronger Mongol chief. According to Mongol accounts, just when the family fortunes seemed to be on the upswing, Temujin's father was poisoned by the agents of a rival nomadic group. Suddenly, Temujin, who was still a teenager, was thrust into a position of leadership. But most of the chiefs who had attached themselves to his father refused to follow a mere boy, whose prospects of survival appeared to be slim.

In the months that followed, his much-reduced encampment was threatened and finally attacked by a rival tribe. Temujin was taken prisoner in 1182, locked into a wooden collar, and led in humiliation to the camp of his enemies. After a daring midnight escape, Temujin rejoined his mother and brothers and found refuge for his tiny band of followers deep in the mountains. Facing extermination, Temujin did what any sensible nomad leader would have done: he and his people joined the camp of a more powerful Mongol chieftain, who had once been aided by Temujin's father. With the support of this powerful leader, Temujin avenged the insults of the clan that had enslaved him and another that had taken advantage of his weakness to raid his camp for horses and women. These successes and Temujin's growing reputation as a warrior and military commander soon won him allies and clan chiefs eager to attach themselves to a leader with a promising future. Within a decade, the youthful Temujin had defeated his Mongol rivals and routed the forces sent to crush him by other nomadic peoples. In 1206, at a *kuriltai*, or meeting of all of the Mongol chieftains, Temujin—renamed Chinggis Khan—was elected the *khagan*, or supreme ruler, of the Mongol tribes. United under a strong leader, the

Mongols prepared to launch a massive assault on an unsuspecting world.

Building the Mongol War Machine

The men of the Mongol tribes that had elevated Chinggis Khan to leadership were in many ways natural warriors. Trained from youth not only to ride but also to hunt and fight, they were physically tough, mobile, and accustomed to killing and death. They wielded a variety of weapons, including lances, hatchets, and iron maces. None of their weapons was as devastating as their powerful short bows. A Mongol warrior could fire a quiver of arrows with stunning accuracy without breaking the stride of his horse. He could hit enemy soldiers as distant as 400 yards (compared with a range of 250 yards for the English longbow) while charging straight ahead, ducking under the belly of his pony, or leaning over the horse's rump while retreating from superior forces. The fact that the Mongol armies were entirely cavalry meant that they possessed speed and a mobility that were demoralizing to enemy forces. Leading two or three horses to use as remounts, Mongol warriors could spend more than one week in the saddle and, when pressed, cover 80 or 90 miles per day. They could strike before their enemies had prepared their defenses, hit unanticipated targets, retreat back to the steppes after suffering temporary reverses, and then suddenly reappear in force.

To a people whose very lifestyle bred mobility, physical courage, and a love of combat, Chinggis Khan and his many able subordinate commanders brought organization, discipline, and unity of command. The old quarrels and vendettas between clans and tribes were overrid-

This Chinese painting of a Mongol warrior clearly enjoying hunting small game suggests the well-deserved reputation the Mongols had earned for their skills as riders and archers.

A 14th-century miniature painting from Rashid al-Din's History of the World *depicts Mongol horsemen charging into battle against retreating Persian forces.*

den by loyalty to the khagan, and energies once devoted to infighting were now directed toward conquest and looting in the civilized centers that fringed the steppes on all sides. The Mongol forces were divided into armies made up of basic fighting units called *tumens*, each consisting of 10,000 cavalrymen. Each tumen was further divided into units of 1000, 100, and 10 warriors. Commanders at each level were responsible for the training, arming, and discipline of the cavalrymen under their charge. The tumens were also divided into heavy cavalry, which carried lances and wore some metal armor, and light cavalry, which relied primarily on the bow and arrow and leather helmets and body covering. Even more lightly armed and protected were the scouting parties that rode ahead of Mongol armies and, using flags and special signal fires, kept the main force apprised of the enemy's movements.

Chinggis Khan also created a separate messenger force, whose bodies were tightly bandaged to allow them to remain in the saddle for days, switching from horse to horse to carry urgent messages between the khagan and his commanders. Military discipline had long been secured by personal ties between commanders and ordinary soldiers. Mongol values, which made

courage in battle a prerequisite for male self-esteem, were also buttressed by a formal code that dictated the immediate execution of a warrior who deserted his unit. Chinggis Khan's swift executions left little doubt about the fate of traitors to his own cause or turncoats who abandoned enemy commanders in his favor. His generosity to brave foes was also legendary. The most famous of the latter, a man named Jebe, nicknamed "the arrow," won the khagan's affection and high posts in the Mongol armies by standing his ground after his troops had been routed and fearlessly shooting Chinggis Khan's horse out from under him.

A special unit supplied Mongol armies with excellent maps of the areas they were to invade, based largely on information supplied by Chinggis Khan's extensive network of spies and informers. New weapons, including a variety of flaming and exploding arrows, gunpowder projectiles, and later bronze cannons, were also devised for the Mongol forces. By the time Chinggis Khan's armies rode east and west in search of plunder and conquest in the second decade of the 13th century, they were among the best armed and trained and the most experienced, disciplined, and mobile soldiers in the world.

DOCUMENT

A European Assessment of the Virtues and Vices of the Mongols

As we have seen, much of what we know about the history of nomadic peoples is based on the records and reactions of observers from sedentary cultures that were their mortal enemies. Some of the most famous of these observers were those, including Marco Polo, who visited the vast Mongol domains at the height of the khans' power in the 12th and 13th centuries. Many tried to assess the strengths and weaknesses of this people who were suddenly having such a great impact on the history of much of the known world. One of the most insightful of these observers was a Franciscan friar named Giovanni de Piano Carpini. In 1245, Pope Innocent IV sent Piano Carpini as an envoy to the "Great Khan" to protest the assaults his Mongol forces had recently launched against Christian Europe. The Pope's protest had little effect on the Mongol decision to strike elsewhere in the following years. But Piano Carpini's extensive travels produced one of the most detailed and insightful accounts of Mongol society and culture to be written in the mid-13th century. As the following passages suggest, like other visitors from sedentary areas, he gave the Mongols a very mixed review:

> In the whole world there are to be found no more obedient subjects than the Tartars [Mongols] . . . they pay their lords more respect than any other people, and would hardly dare lie to them. Rarely do they revile each other, but if they should, the dispute hardly ever leads to blows. Wars, quarrels, the infliction of bodily harm, and manslaughter do not occur among them, and there are no large-scale thieves or robbers among them. . . .
>
> They treat one another with due respect; they regard each other almost as members of one family, and, although they do not have a lot of food, they like to

Conquest: The Mongol Empire Under Chinggis Khan

When he was proclaimed the khagan in 1206, Temujin was probably not yet 40 years old. At that point, he was the supreme ruler of nearly one-half million Mongol tribesmen and the overlord of 1 to 2 million more nomadic tribesmen who had been defeated by his armies or had voluntarily allied themselves with this promising young commander. But Chinggis Khan had much greater ambitions. He once remarked that his greatest pleasure in life was making war, defeating enemies, forcing "their beloved [to] weep, riding on their horses, embracing their wives and daughters." He came to see himself and his sons as men marked for a special destiny: warriors born to conquer the known world. In 1207, he set out to fulfill this ambition. His first campaigns humbled the *Tangut* kingdom of Xi-Xia in northwest China, whose ruler was forced to declare himself a vassal of the khagan and pay a hefty tribute. Next, the Mongol armies attacked the much more powerful Qin Empire, which the Manchu-related Jurchens had established a century earlier in north China.

In these campaigns, the Mongol armies were confronted for the first time with large, fortified cities that their inhabitants assumed could easily withstand the assaults of these uncouth tribesmen from the steppes. Indeed, the Mongol invaders were thwarted at first by the intricate defensive works that the Chinese had perfected over the centuries to deter nomadic incursions. But the adaptive Mongols, with the help of captured Chinese artisans and military commanders, soon devised a whole arsenal of siege weapons. They included battering rams, catapults that hurled rocks and explosive balls, and bamboo rockets that spread fire and fear in besieged towns.

Chinggis Khan and the early Mongol commanders had little regard for these towns, whose inhabitants they regarded as soft and effete. Therefore, when resistance was encountered, the Mongols adopted a policy of terrifying retribution. Though the Mongols often spared the lives of famed scholars—whom they employed as advisors—and artisans with particularly useful skills, towns that fought back were usually sacked once they had been taken. The townspeople were slaughtered or sold into slavery; their homes, palaces, mosques, and temples were reduced to rubble. Towns that surrendered without a fight were usually spared this fate, though they were required to pay tribute to their Mongol conquerors as the price of their deliverance.

share it with one another. . . . When riding they can endure extreme cold and at times also fierce heat; they are neither soft, nor sensitive [to the weather]. They do not seem to feel in any way envious of one another, and no public trials occur among them. No one holds his fellow in contempt, but each helps and supports the other to the limits of his abilities.

They are extremely arrogant toward other people and look down on all others with disdain. In fact, they regard them, both noble and humble people alike, as little better than nothing. . . . Toward other people the Tartars tend to anger and are easily roused. . . . They are the greatest liars in the world in dealing with other people [than the Tartars], and hardly a true word escapes from their mouths. Initially they flatter but in the end they sting like scorpions. They are crafty and sly, and wherever possible they try to get the better of everybody else by false pretenses. . . .

They are messy in their eating and drinking and in their whole way of life. Drunkenness is honorable among them. . . . At the same time they are mean and greedy, and if they want something, they will not stop begging and asking for it, until they have got it. They cling fiercely to what they have, and in making gifts they are extremely miserly. They have no conscience about killing other people. In short, if one tried to enumerate all their bad characteristics there would be too many to put on paper.

Questions: What might the qualities, pro and con, of the Mongols that Piano Carpini emphasizes tell us about his own society and its values or shortcomings? How are the Mongol virtues he extols linked to the achievements of Chinggis Khan and the stunning Mongol wars of conquest? To what extent would they be typical of nomadic societies more generally? In what ways might his enumeration of Mongol vices be simply dismissed as "sour grapes" resulting from European defeats? In what ways might these vices be linked to the hardships of Mongol life? How useful do you think this stereotyping is? Why have observers from virtually all cultures resorted to these sorts of generalizations when describing other peoples and societies?

First Assault on the Islamic World: Conquest in China

Once he had established a foothold in north China and solidified his empire in the steppes, Chinggis Khan sent his armies westward against the Kara-Khitai Empire established by a Mongolian-speaking people a century earlier. Having overwhelmed and annexed the Kara-Khitai, in 1219 Chinggis Khan sent envoys to demand the submission of *Muhammad Shah II*, the Turkic ruler of the Khwarazm Empire to the west. Outraged by the audacity of the still little-known Mongol commander, one of Muhammad's subordinates had some of Chinggis Khan's later envoys killed and sent the rest with shaved heads back to the khagan. These insults, of course, meant war—a war in which the Khwarazm were overwhelmed. Their great cities fell to the new siege weapons and tactics the Mongols had perfected in their north China campaigns. Their armies were repeatedly routed in battles with the Mongol cavalry. Again and again, the Mongols used their favorite battle tactic in these encounters. Cavalry were sent to attack the enemy's main force. Feigning defeat, the cavalry retreated, drawing the opposing forces out of formation in the hope of a chance to slaughter the fleeing Mongols. Once the enemy's pursuing horsemen had spread themselves over the countryside, the main force of Mongol heavy cavalry, until then concealed, attacked them in a devastating pincers formation.

Within two years, his once flourishing cities in ruin and his kingdom in Mongol hands, Muhammad Shah II, having retreated across his empire, died on a desolate island near the Caspian Sea. In addition to greatly enlarging his domains, Chinggis Khan's victories meant that he could incorporate tens of thousands of Turkic horsemen into his armies. With his forces greatly enlarged by these new recruits, he once again turned eastward, where in the last years of his life his armies destroyed the Xi-Xia kingdom and overran the Qin Empire of north China. By 1227, the year of his death, the Mongols ruled an empire that stretched from eastern Persia to the North China Sea.

Life Under the Mongol Yoke

Despite their fury as warriors and the horrible destruction they could unleash on those who resisted their demands for submission and tribute, the Mongols proved remarkably astute and tolerant rulers. Chinggis Khan himself set the standard in this enterprise. He was a complex man, capable, as we have seen, of gloating over the ruin of his enemies. But he was also open to new ideas and committed to building a world where the diverse peoples of his empire could live together in peace. Though illiterate, Chinggis Khan was neither the ignorant savage nor the cultureless vandal often depicted in the accounts of civilized writers—usually those who had never met him. Once the conquered peoples had been subdued, he took a keen interest in their arts and learning, though he refused to live in their cities. Instead he established a new capital at *Karakorum* on the steppes and summoned the wise and clever from all parts of the empire to the lavish palace of tents with gilded pillars where he lived with his wives and closest advisors.

At Karakorum, Chinggis Khan consulted with Confucian scholars about how to rule China, with Muslim engineers about how to build siege weapons and improve trade with the lands farther west, and with Daoist holy men, whom he hoped could provide him with an elixir that would make him immortal. Though he himself followed the shamanistic (focused on the propitiation of nature spirits) beliefs of his ancestors, all religions were tolerated in his empire. An administrative framework that drew on the advice and talents of both Muslim and Chinese bureaucrats was created. A script was devised for the Mongolian language in order to facilitate record keeping and the standardization of laws. Chinggis Khan promulgated a legal code that was enforced by a special police force. Much of the code was aimed at putting an end to the divisions and quarrels that had so long occupied the Mongols. Grazing lands were systematically allotted to different tribes, and harsh penalties were established for rustling livestock or stealing horses.

The Mongol conquests brought a peace to much of Asia that in some areas persisted for generations. In the towns of the empire, handicraft production and scholarship flourished and artistic creativity was allowed free expression. Chinggis Khan and his successors actively promoted the growth of trade and travelers by protecting the caravans that made their way across the ancient Asian silk routes and by establishing rest stations for weary merchants and fortified outposts for those harassed by bandits. One Muslim historian wrote of the peoples within the domains of the khagan that they "enjoyed such a peace that a man might have journeyed from the land of sunrise to the land of sunset with a golden platter upon his head without suffering the least violence from anyone."

Secure trade routes made for prosperous merchants and wealthy, cosmopolitan cities. They also facilitated the spread of foods such as sorghum, sugar, citrus fruits, and grapes; inventions such as firearms, printing, and windmills; and techniques ranging from papermaking to the improvement of irrigation, from one civilization to another. Paradoxically, Mongol expansion, which sedentary chroniclers condemned as a "barbarian" orgy of violence and destruction, became a major force for economic and social development and the enhancement of civilized life.

The Death of Chinggis Khan and the Division of the Empire

When the Mongols had moved west to attack Kara Khitai in 1219, support was demanded from the vassal king of Xi-Xia. The Tangut ruler had impudently responded that if the Mongols were not strong enough to win wars on their own, they were best advised to refrain from attacking others. In 1226, his wars in the west won, Chinggis Khan turned east with an army of 180,000 warriors to punish the Tanguts and complete a conquest that he regretted having left unfinished over a decade earlier. After routing a much larger Tangut army in a battle fought on the frozen waters of the Yellow River, the Mongol armies overran Xi-Xia, plundering and burning and mercilessly hunting down any Tangut survivors. As his forces closed in on the Tangut capital and last refuge, Chinggis Khan, who had been injured in a skirmish some months earlier, fell grievously ill. After impressing upon his sons the dangers of quarreling among themselves for the spoils of the empire, the khagan died in August 1227.

With one last outburst of Mongol wrath, this time directed against death itself, his body was carried back to Mongolia for burial. The Mongol forces escorting the funeral procession hunted down and killed every human and animal in its path. As Chinggis Khan had instructed, his armies also treacherously slaughtered the unarmed inhabitants of the Tangut capital after a truce and surrender had been arranged.

The vast pasturelands the Mongols now controlled were divided between Chinggis Khan's three remaining sons and *Batu,* a grandson and heir of the khagan's recently deceased son Jochi. Towns and cultivated areas like those in north China and parts of Persia were considered the common property of the Mongol ruling family. A kuriltai was convened at Karakorum, the Mongol capital, to select a successor to the great conqueror. In accordance with Chinggis Khan's preference, *Ogedei,* his third son, was elected grand khan. Though not as capable a military leader as his brothers or nephews, Ogedei was a crafty diplomat and deft manipulator—skills much

This portrait of Ogedei Khan, who was elected to succeed Chinggis Khan as the grand khan of the Mongols, is from a 13th-century album of Chinese emperors.

needed if the ambitious heads of the vast provinces of the empire were to be kept from each others' throats.

For nearly a decade, Ogedei directed Mongol energies into further campaigns and conquests. The areas that were targeted by this new round of Mongol expansion paid the price for peace within the Mongol Empire. The fate of the most important victims—Russia and eastern Europe, the Islamic heartlands, and China—will be the focus of much of the rest of this chapter.

THE MONGOL DRIVE TO THE WEST

Focal Point: While in pursuit of the Khwarazm ruler, Muhammad Shah II, the Mongols had made their first contacts with the rich kingdoms to the west of the steppe heartlands of Chinggis Khan's empire. Raids of reconnaissance into Georgia and across the Russian steppe convinced the Mongol commanders that the Christian lands to the west were theirs for the taking. Russia and Europe were added to their agenda for world conquest. The subjugation of these regions became the project of the armies of the *Golden Horde,* which was named after the golden tent of the early khans of the western sector of the Mongol Empire. The

territories of the Golden Horde made up the four great khanates into which the Mongol Empire had been divided at the time of Chinggis Khan's death. The khanate to the south, called the *Ilkhan Empire,* claimed the task of completing the conquest of the Muslim world that had begun with the invasion of the Khwarazm domains. Though neither Europe nor the Islamic heartlands were ultimately subdued, Mongol successes on the battlefield and the fury of their assaults affected the history of the regions that came under attack, particularly Russia and the Islamic world.

In a very real sense, the Mongol assault on Russia was a side campaign, a chance to fine-tune the war machine and win a little booty while they were en route to the real prize: western Europe. As we saw in Chapter 15, in the first half of the 13th century when the Mongol warriors first descended, a more united Russia had been divided into numerous petty kingdoms, centered on trading cities such as Novgorod and Kiev. By this time Kiev, which had originally dominated much of central Russia, had been in decline for some time. As a result there was no paramount power to rally Russian forces against the invaders. Despite the dire warnings spread by those who had witnessed the crushing defeats suffered by the Georgians in the early 1220s, the princes of Russia refused to cooperate. They preferred to fight alone, and they were routed individually.

In 1236, Chinggis Khan's grandson Batu led a Mongol force of upwards of 120,000 cavalrymen into the Russian heartlands. From 1237 to 1238 and later in 1240, these "Tartars," as the Russian peoples called them, carried out the only successful winter invasions in Russian history. In fact, the Mongols preferred to fight in the winter. The frozen earth provided good footing for their horses, and frozen rivers gave them access rather than blocking the way to their enemies. One after another, the Mongol armies defeated the often much larger forces of local nomadic groups and Russian princes. Cities such as Ryazan, Moscow, and Vladimir, which resisted the Mongol command to surrender, were razed to the ground; their inhabitants were slaughtered or led into slavery. As a contemporary Russian chronicler observed, "no eye remained to weep for the dead." Just as it seemed that all of Russia would be ravaged by the Mongols, whom the Russians compared to locusts, Batu's armies withdrew. The largest cities, Novgorod and Kiev, appeared to have been spared. Russian priests thanked God; the Mongol commanders blamed the spring thaw, which slowed the Mongol horsemen and raised the risk of defeat in the treacherous mud.

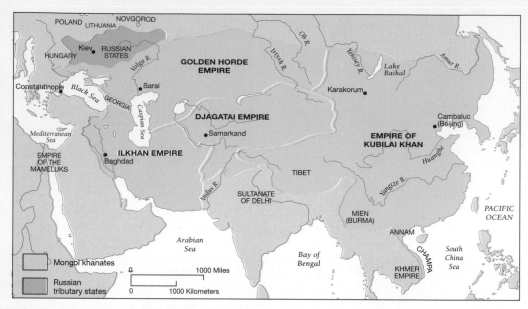

The Four Khanates of the Divided Mongol Empire, c. 1290

Salvation yielded to further disasters when the Mongols returned in force in the winter of 1240. In this second campaign, even the great walled city of Kiev, which had reached a population of over 100,000 by the end of the 12th century, fell. Enraged by Kievan resistance—its ruler had ordered the Mongol envoys thrown from the city walls—the Mongols reduced the greatest city in Russia to a smoldering ruin. The cathedral of Saint Sophia was spared, but the rest of the city was systematically looted and destroyed, and its inhabitants were smoked out and slaughtered. Novgorod again braced itself for the Mongol onslaught. Again, according to the Russian chroniclers, it was "miraculously" spared. In fact, it was saved largely because of the willingness of its prince, Alexander Nevskii, to submit, at least temporarily, to Mongol demands. In addition, the Mongol armies were eager to move on to the main event: the invasion of western Europe.

Russia in Bondage

The crushing victories of Batu's armies initiated nearly two and a half centuries of Mongol dominance in Russia. Russian princes were forced to submit as vassals of the khan of the Golden Horde and to pay tribute or risk the ravages of Mongol raiders. Mongol exactions fell particularly heavily on the Russian peasantry, who had to yield up their crops and labor to both their own princes and the Mongol overlords. Impoverished and ever fearful of the lightning raids of Mongol marauders, the peasants fled to remote areas or became, in effect, the serfs (see

Chapter 15) of the Russian ruling class in return for protection.

The decision on the part of many peasants to become the lifetime laborers of the nobility resulted in a major change in the rural social structure of Russia. Until the mid-19th century, the great majority of the population of Russia would be tied to the lands they worked and bound to the tiny minority of nobles who owned these great estates. Some Russian towns made profits on the increased trade made possible by the Mongol links. Sometimes the gains exceeded the tribute they paid to the Golden Horde. No town benefited from the Mongol presence more than Moscow. Badly plundered and partially burned in the early Mongol assaults, the city was gradually rebuilt, and its ruling princes steadily swallowed up nearby towns and surrounding villages. After 1328, Moscow also profited from its status as the tribute collector for the Mongol khans. Its princes not only used their position to fill their own coffers but annexed further towns as punishment for falling behind on the payment of their tribute.

As Moscow grew in strength, the power of the Golden Horde declined. Mongol religious toleration benefited both the Orthodox church and Moscow. The *Metropolitan,* or head of the Orthodox church, was made the representative of all the clergy in Russia, which did much to enhance the church's standing. The choice of Moscow as the seat of the Orthodox leaders brought new sources of wealth to its princes and buttressed Muscovite claims to be Russia's leading city. In 1380, those claims received an additional boost when the princes of

Moscow shifted from being tribute collectors to being the defenders of Russia. In alliance with other Russian vassals, they raised an army that defeated the forces of the Golden Horde at the battle of Kulikova. Their victory and the devastating blows Timur's attacks dealt the Golden Horde two decades later effectively broke the Mongol hold over Russia. Mongol forces raided as late as the 1450s, and the princes of Muscovy did not formally renounce their vassal status until 1480. But from the end of the 14th century onward, Moscow was the center of political power in Russia, and armies from Poland and Lithuania then posed the main threat to Russian peace and prosperity.

Though much of the Mongols' impact was negative, their conquest proved a decisive turning point in Russian history in several ways. In addition to their importance to Moscow and the Orthodox church, Mongol contacts led to changes in Russian military organization and tactics and in the political style of Russian rulers. Claims that the Tartars were responsible for Russian despotism, either Tsarist or Stalinist, are clearly overstated. Still, the Mongol example may have influenced the desire of Russian princes to centralize their control and minimize the limitations placed on their power by the landed nobility, the clergy, and wealthy merchants. By far the greatest effects of Mongol rule, however, were those resulting from Russia's relative isolation from Christian lands farther west. On one hand, the Mongols protected a divided and weak Russia from the attacks of much more powerful kingdoms such as Poland, Lithuania, and Hungary as well as the "crusades" of militant Christian orders like the Teutonic Knights, who were determined to stamp out the so-called Orthodox heresy. On the other hand, Mongol overlordship cut Russia off from key transformations in western Europe that were inspired by the Renaissance and led ultimately to the Reformation. The Orthodox clergy, of course, would have had little use for these influences, but their absence severely reduced the options available for Russian political, economic, and intellectual development.

Mongol Incursions and the Retreat from Europe

Until news of the Mongol campaigns in Russia reached European peoples such as the Germans and Hungarians farther west, Christian leaders had been quite pleased by the rise of a new military power in central Asia. Rumors and reports from Christians living in the area, chafing under what they perceived as the persecution of their Muslim overlords, convinced many in western Europe that the Mongol Khan was none other than *Prester John*. Prester John was the name given to a mythical rich and powerful Christian monarch whose kingdom had supposedly been cut off from Europe by the Muslim conquests of the 7th and 8th centuries. Sometimes located in Africa, sometimes in central Asia, Prester John loomed large in the European imagination as a potential ally who could strike the Muslim enemy from the rear and join up with European Christians to destroy their common adversary. The Mongol assault on the Muslim Khwarazm Empire appeared to confirm the speculation that Chinggis Khan was indeed Prester John.

The assault on Christian, though Orthodox, Russia made it clear that the Mongol armies were neither the legions of Prester John nor more partial to Christians than to any other people who stood in their way. The rulers of Europe were nevertheless slow to realize the magnitude of the threat the Mongols posed to western Christendom. When Mongol envoys, one of whom was an Englishman, arrived at the court of King Bela of Hungary demanding that he surrender a group of nomads who had fled to his domains after being beaten by the Mongols in Russia, the king contemptuously dismissed them and Batu's demand that he submit to Mongol overlordship. Bela reasoned that he was the ruler of a powerful kingdom, whereas the Mongols were just another ragtag band of nomads in search of easy plunder. As had so often been the case in the past, his foolish refusal to negotiate provided the Mongols with a pretext to invade. Their ambition remained the conquest and pillage of all western Europe. That this goal was clearly attainable was demonstrated by the sound drubbing they gave to the Hungarians in 1240 and then to a mixed force of Christian knights led by the German ruler, King Henry of Silesia.

These victories left the Mongols free to raid and pillage from the Adriatic Sea region in the south to Poland and the German states of the north. It also left the rest of Europe open to Mongol conquest. Just as the kings and clergy of the western portions of Christendom were beginning to fear the worst, the Mongol forces disappeared. The death of the khagan Ogedei, in the distant Mongol capital at Karakorum, forced Batu to withdraw in preparation for the struggle for succession that was under way. The campaign for the conquest of Europe was never resumed. Perhaps Batu was satisfied with the huge empire of the Golden Horde that he ruled from his splendid new capital at Sarai; most certainly the Mongols had found richer lands to plunder in the following decades in the Muslim empires of the Middle East. Whatever the reason, Europe was spared the full fury of the Mongol assault. Of the civilizations that fringed the steppe homelands of the Mongols, only India would be as fortunate.

The Mongol Assault on the Islamic Heartlands

After the Mongol conquest of the Khwarazm Empire, it was only a matter of time before they struck westward against the far wealthier Muslim empires of Mesopotamia and North Africa. The conquest of these areas became the main project of *Hulegu,* another grandson of Chinggis Khan and the ruler of the Ilkhan portions of the Mongol Empire. As we saw in Chapter 12, one of the key results of Hulegu's assaults on the Muslim heartlands was the capture and destruction of Baghdad in 1258. The murder of the Abbasid caliph, one of some 800,000 people who were reported to have been killed in Mongol retribution for the city's resistance, brought an end to the dynasty that had ruled the core regions of the Islamic world since the middle of the 8th century. A major Mongol victory over the Seljuk Turks in 1243 also proved critical to the future history of the region. It opened up Asia Minor to conquest by a different Turkic people, the Ottomans, who would be the next great power in the Islamic heartlands.

Given the fate of Baghdad, it is understandable that Muslim historians treated the coming of the Mongols as one of the great catastrophes in the history of Islam. The murder of the caliph and his family left the faithful without a central authority. The sack of Baghdad and numerous other cities from central Asia to the shores of the Mediterranean devastated the focal points of Islamic civilization. The Mongols had also severely crippled Muslim military strength, much to the delight of the Christians, especially those like the *Nestorians* who lived in the Middle East. Some Christians offered assistance in the form of information; others, especially the Nestorians from inner Asia, served as commanders in Hulegu's armies. One contemporary Muslim chronicler, Ibn al-Athir, found the tribulations the Mongols had visited on his people so horrific that he apologized to his readers for recounting them and wished that he had not been born to witness them. He lamented that:

> . . . in just one year they seized the most populous, the most beautiful, and the best cultivated part of the earth whose inhabitants excelled in character and urbanity. In the countries that have not yet been overrun by them, everyone spends the night afraid that they may yet appear there, too. . . . Thus, Islam and the Muslims were struck, at that time by a disaster such as no people had experienced before.

The Abbasid capital at Baghdad had long been in decline when the Mongols besieged it in 1258. The Mongols' capture and sack of the city put an end to all pretense that Baghdad was still the center of the Muslim world.

Given these reverses, one can imagine the relief the peoples of the Muslim world felt when the Mongols were finally defeated in 1260 by the armies of the *Mamluk,* or slave, dynasty of Egypt at Ain Jalut. Ironically, *Baibars,* the commander of the Egyptian forces, and many of his lieutenants had been enslaved by the Mongols some years earlier and sold in Egypt, where they rose to power through military service. The Muslim victory was won with the rare cooperation of the Christians, who allowed Baibars's forces to cross unopposed through their much diminished Crusader territories in Palestine.

Hulegu was in central Asia, engaged in yet another succession struggle, when the battle occurred. Upon his return, he was forced to reconsider his plans for conquest of the entire Muslim world. The Mameluks were deeply entrenched and growing stronger; Hulegu was threatened by his cousin *Berke,* the new khan of the Golden Horde to the north, who had converted to Islam. After openly clashing with Berke and learning of Baibars's overtures for an alliance with the Golden Horde, Hulegu decided to settle for the sizable kingdom he already ruled, which stretched from the frontiers of Byzantium to the Oxus River in central Asia.

The Mongol Impact on Europe and the Islamic World

Though much of what the Mongols wrought on their westward march was destructive, some benefits were reaped from their forays into Europe and their conquests in Muslim areas. For example, they taught new ways of making war and impressed on their Turkic and European enemies the effectiveness of gunpowder. As we have seen, Mongol conquests facilitated trade between the civilizations at each end of Eurasia, making possible the exchange of foods, tools, and ideas on an unprecedented scale. The revived trade routes brought great wealth to traders, such as those from north Italy, who set up outposts in the eastern Mediterranean, along the Black Sea coast, and as far east as the Caspian Sea. Because the establishment of these trading empires by the Venetians and Genoese provided precedents for the later drives for overseas expansion by peoples such as the Portuguese and English, they are of special significance in global history.

Perhaps the greatest long-term impact of the Mongol drive to the west was indirect and unintended. In recent years, a growing number of historians have become convinced that the Mongol conquests played a key role in transmitting the fleas that carried bubonic plague from south China and central Asia to Europe and the Middle East. The fleas may have hitched a ride on the livestock the Mongols drove into the new pasturelands won by their conquests or on the rats that nibbled the grain transported by merchants along the trading routes the Mongol rulers fostered between east and west. Whatever the exact connection, the Mongol armies unknowingly paved the way for the spread of the dreaded Black Death across the steppes to much of China, to the Islamic heartlands, and from there to most of Europe in the mid-14th century. In so doing, they unleashed possibly the most fatal epidemic in all human history. From mortality rates higher than half the population in some areas of Europe and the Middle East to the economic and social adjustments that the plague forced wherever it spread, this accidental, but devastating, side effect of the Mongol conquests influenced the course of civilized development in Eurasia for centuries to come.

THE MONGOL INTERLUDE IN CHINESE HISTORY

Focal Point: Of all the areas the Mongols conquered, perhaps none was administered as closely as China. Following decades of hard campaigning in the middle of the 13th century, the Mongol interlude in Chinese history lasted only about a century. Though the age-old capacity of the Chinese to assimilate their nomadic conquerors was evident from the outset, the Mongols managed to retain a distinct culture and social separateness until they were driven back beyond the Great Wall in the late 1360s. They also opened China to influences from Arab and Persian lands, and even to contacts with Europe, which would come to full fruition in the following centuries of indigenous Chinese revival under the Ming dynasty.

Soon after Ogedei was elected as the great khan, the Mongol advance into China was resumed. Having conquered the Xi-Xia and Qin empires, the Mongol commanders turned to what remained of the Song empire in south China. In the campaigns against the Song, the Mongol forces were directed by *Kubilai Khan,* one of the grandsons of Chinggis Khan and a man who would play a pivotal role in Chinese history for the next half century (see the Closeup). Even under a decadent dynasty that had long neglected its defenses, south China proved one of the toughest areas for the Mongols to conquer. From 1235 to 1279, the Mongols were continually on the march; they fought battle after battle and besieged seemingly innumerable, well-fortified Chinese cities. In 1260, Kubilai assumed the title of the great khan, much to the chagrin of his cousins who ruled other parts of the empire. A decade later in 1271, on the recommendation of Chinese advisors, he changed the name of the Mongol dynasty to the Sinicized Yuan. Though he was still nearly a decade away from fully defeating the last-ditch efforts of Confucian advisors and Chinese generals to save the Song dynasty, Kubilai ruled most of China, and he now set about the task of establishing Mongol control on a more permanent basis.

As the different regions of China came under Mongol rule, Kubilai promulgated many laws to preserve the distinction between Mongol and Chinese. He forbade Chinese scholars to learn the Mongol script, which was used for records and correspondence at the upper levels of the imperial government. Mongols were forbidden to marry ethnic Chinese, and only women from nomadic families were selected for the imperial harem. Even friendships between the two peoples were discouraged. Mongol religious ceremonies and customs were retained, and a tent encampment in the traditional Mongol style was set up in the imperial city even though Kubilai usually resided in a Chinese-style palace. Kubilai and his successors continued to enjoy key Mongol pastimes such as the hunt, and Mongol military forces remained separate from Chinese.

In the Yuan era, a new social structure was established in China with the Mongols on top and their central Asian nomadic and Muslim allies right below them in the hierarchy. These two groups occupied most of the offices at the highest levels of the bureaucracy. Beneath them came the north Chinese; below them, the ethnic Chinese and the minority peoples of the south. Though ethnic Chinese from both north and south ran the Yuan bureaucracy at the regional and local levels, they could ordinarily exercise power at the top only as advisors to the Mongols or other nomadic officials. At all levels, their activities were scrutinized by Mongol functionaries from an enlarged and much-strengthened censors' bureau.

Mongol women in particular remained aloof from Chinese culture—at least Chinese culture in its Confucian guise. They refused to adopt the practice of footbinding, which so constricted the activities of Chinese women. They retained their rights to property and control within the household as well as the capacity to move freely about town and countryside. No more striking evidence of their independence can be found than contemporary accounts of Mongol women riding to the hunt, both with their husbands and at the head of their own hunting parties. The daughter of one of Kubilai's cousins even went to war, and she refused to marry until one of her many suitors proved able to throw her in a wrestling match. Unfortunately, the Mongol era was too brief to reverse the trends that were lowering the position of Chinese women. As neo-Confucianism gained ground under Kubilai's successors, the arguments for the confinement of women multiplied.

Mongol Tolerance and Foreign Cultural Influences

Like Chinggis Khan and other Mongol overlords, Kubilai and Chabi had unbounded curiosity and very cosmopolitan tastes. Their generous patronage drew scholars, artists, artisans, and office-seekers from many lands to the splendid Yuan court. Some of the most favored came from regional Muslim kingdoms to the east that had also come under Mongol rule. Muslims were included in the second highest social grouping, just beneath the Mongols themselves. Persians and Turks were admitted to the inner circle of Kubilai's administrators and advisors. Muslims designed and supervised the building of his Chinese-style imperial city and proposed new systems for the more efficient collection of taxes. Persian astronomers imported more advanced Middle Eastern instruments for celestial observations, corrected the Chinese calendar, and made some of the most accurate maps the Chinese had ever seen. Muslim doctors ran the imperial hospitals and added translations of 36 volumes on Muslim medicine to the imperial library. Though some of Kubilai's most powerful advisors were infamous for their corrupt ways, most served him well and did much to advance Chinese learning and technology through the transmission of texts, instruments, and weapons from throughout the Muslim world.

In addition to the Muslims, Kubilai welcomed travelers and emissaries from many foreign lands to his court. Like his grandfather, Kubilai displayed a strong interest in all religions and insisted on toleration in his domains. Buddhists, Nestorian Christians, Daoists, and Latin Christians made their way to his court. The most renowned of the latter were members of the Polo family from Venice in northern Italy, who traveled extensively in the Mongol Empire in the middle of the 13th century. Marco Polo's account of Kubilai Khan's court and empire is perhaps the most famous travel account written by a European. Marco accepted fantastic tales of grotesques and strange customs, and he may have cribbed parts of his account from other sources. Still, his descriptions of the palaces, cities, and wealth of Kubilai's empire enhanced European interest in the "Indies" and

Marco Polo and his fellow merchants about to leave from Venice on their lengthy journey to Asia, from a 15th-century English manuscript illumination.

helped to inspire efforts by navigators like Columbus to find a water route to these fabled lands.

Social Policies and Scholar-Gentry Resistance

Kubilai's efforts to promote Mongol adaptation to Chinese culture were overshadowed in the long run by countervailing measures to preserve Mongol separateness. The ethnic Chinese who made up the vast majority of his subjects, particularly in the south, were never really reconciled to Mongol rule. Despite Kubilai's cultivation of Confucian rituals and his extensive employment of Chinese bureaucrats, most of the scholar-gentry regarded the Mongol overlord and his successors as uncouth barbarians whose policies endangered Chinese traditions. As it was intended to do, Kubilai's refusal to reinstate the examination route to administrative office prevented Confucian scholars from dominating politics. The favoritism he showed Mongol and other foreign officials further alienated the scholar-gentry.

To add insult to injury, Kubilai went to great lengths to bolster the position of the artisan classes, who had never enjoyed high standing, and the merchants, whom the Confucian thinkers had long dismissed as parasites. The Mongols had from the outset shown great regard for artisans and because of their useful skills had often spared them the slaughter meted out to their fellow city dwellers. During the Yuan period in China, merchants also prospered and commerce boomed, partly owing to Mongol efforts to improve transportation and expand the supply of paper money. The Mongols developed—with amazing speed for a people who had no prior experience with seafaring—a substantial navy, which played a major role in the conquest of the Song Empire. After the conquest of China was completed, the great Mongol war fleets were used to put down pirates, who threatened river and overseas commerce, and, toward the end of Kubilai's reign, to conduct overseas expeditions of conquest and exploration. Thus, during the Yuan period, artisans and traders enjoyed a level of government backing and social status that was never again equaled in Chinese civilization.

CLOSEUP

Imperial Mediators Between Radically Different Cultures: Kubilai Khan and His Wife, Chabi

Despite his many measures to ensure that the conquering Mongol minority was not completely absorbed by the culture of the defeated, Kubilai Khan had long been fascinated by Chinese civilization. Even before beginning the conquest of the Song Empire, he had surrounded himself with Chinese advisors—some Buddhist, others Daoist or Confucian. His capital at *Tatu* in the north (present-day Beijing) was built on the site occupied by earlier dynasties, and he introduced Chinese rituals and classical music into his own court. Kubilai also put the empire on the Chinese calendar and offered sacrifices to his ancestors at a special temple in the imperial city. He summoned the best Confucian scholars to give his son a proper Chinese education, a move that perhaps more than any other demonstrated his determination to "civilize" his Mongol followers. But he did not then, nor later when he had conquered the south, listen to the pleas of his Confucian advisors to reestablish the civil service exams, which had been discontinued by the Qin rulers.

Thus, from the outset, Kubilai was ambivalent in his attitude toward the ancient civilization that was slipping piecemeal under Mongol control. On one hand, he was determined to preserve Mongol separateness and to keep the scholar-gentry from gaining too much power—hence the refusal to reintroduce the exams. At the same time, he adopted a Chinese lifestyle, was anxious to follow Chinese precedents, and became a major patron of the arts and a promoter of Chinese culture in general.

Kubilai's determination to selectively adopt Chinese culture, without being overwhelmed by it, was bolstered by the advice and example of his wife, *Chabi*. Displaying the independent-mindedness and political savvy of many Mongol women, Chabi gave Kubilai critical advice on how to counter the schemes of his ambitious brother. She also promoted the interests of the Buddhists in the highest circles of government. After the conquest of the Qin, Chabi convinced Kubilai that lenient treatment of the survivors of the defeated royal family was the best way to reconcile the peoples of north China to Mongol rule. On another occasion, she demonstrated that she shared Kubilai's respect for Chinese culture by frustrating a plan to turn cultivated lands near the capital into pasturelands for the Mongols' ponies. Thus, the imperial couple proved a good match of astute political skills and cosmopolitanism, tempered by an abiding respect for their own traditions and a determination to preserve those they found the most valuable.

Ironically, despite the Mongols' ingrained suspicion of cities and sedentary lifestyles, both flourished in the Yuan era. The urban expansion begun under the Tang and Song dynasties continued, and the Mongol elite soon became addicted to the diversions of urban life. Though traditional Chinese artistic endeavors, such as poetry and essay writing, languished under the Mongols in comparison with their flowering in the Tang–Song eras, popular entertainments, particularly musical dramas, flourished. Perhaps the most famous of Chinese dramatic works, *The Romance of the West Chamber*, was written in the Yuan period. Dozens of major playwrights wrote for the court, the rising merchant classes, and the well-heeled Mongol elite. Actors and actresses, who had long been relegated by the Confucian scholars to the despised status of "mean people," achieved celebrity and some measure of social esteem. All of this rankled the scholar-gentry, who bided their time, waiting for the chance to restore Confucian decorum and what they believed to be the proper social hierarchy for a civilized people like the Chinese.

Initially, at least, Kubilai Khan pursued policies toward one social group, the peasants, that the scholarly class would have heartily approved. He issued edicts forbidding Mongol cavalrymen from turning croplands into pasture and restored the granary system for famine relief that had been badly neglected in the late Song. Kubilai also sought to reduce peasant tax and forced-labor burdens, partly by redirecting peasant payments

from local nonofficial tax farmers directly to government officials. He and his advisors also formulated a revolutionary plan to establish elementary education at the village level. Though the level of learning they envisioned was rudimentary, such a project—*if* it had been enacted—would have provided a major challenge to the educational system centered on the elite that hitherto had dominated Chinese civilization.

The Fall of the House of Yuan

Historians often remark on the seeming contradiction between the military prowess of the Mongol conquerors and the short life of the dynasty they established in China. Kubilai Khan's long reign encompassed a good portion of the nine decades that the Mongols ruled all of China. Already by the end of his reign, the dynasty was showing signs of weakening. Song loyalists raised the standard of revolt in the south, and popular hostility toward the foreign overlords was expressed more and more openly. The Mongol aura of military invincibility was badly tarnished by Kubilai's rebuffs at the hands of the military lords of Japan and the failure of the expeditions that he sent to punish them, first in 1274 and again in a much larger effort mounted in 1280. The defeats suffered by Mongol forces engaged in similar expeditions to Vietnam and Java during this same period further undermined the Mongols' standing.

Kubilai's dissolute lifestyle in his later years, partly brought on by the death of his most beloved wife, Chabi, and five years later the death of his favorite son, set the tone for a general softening of the Mongol ruling class as a whole. Kubilai's successors lacked his capacity for leadership and cared little for the tedium of day-to-day administrative tasks. Many of the Muslim and Chinese functionaries to whom they entrusted the finances of the empire enriched themselves through flagrant graft and corruption. This greatly angered the hard-pressed peasantry who had to bear the burden of rising taxes and demands for forced labor. The scholar-gentry played on this discontent by calling on the people to rise up and overthrow the "barbarian" usurpers.

By the 1350s, the signs of dynastic decline were apparent. Banditry and piracy were widespread, and the government's forces were too feeble to curb them. Famine hit many regions and spawned local uprisings, which grew to engulf large portions of the empire. Secret religious sects, such as the *White Lotus Society*, were formed and were dedicated to the overthrow of the dynasty. Their leaders' claims that they had magical powers to heal their followers and to confound their enemies helped encourage further peasant resistance against the Mongols. As had been the case in the past, rebel leaders quarreled and fought with each other. For a time, chaos reigned as the Yuan regime dissolved, and those Mongols who could escape the fury of the mob retreated back into central Asia. The restoration of peace and order came from an unexpected quarter. Rather than a regional military commander or an aristocratic lord, a man from an impoverished peasant family, *Ju Yuanzhang*, emerged to found the *Ming dynasty*, which would rule China for most of the next three centuries.

ANALYSIS

The Eclipse of the Nomadic War Machine

As the shock waves of the Mongol and Timurid explosions amply demonstrated, nomadic incursions into the civilized cores have had an impact on global history that far exceeds what one would expect, given the relatively small numbers of nomadic peoples and the limited resources of the regions they inhabited. From the time of the great Indo-European migrations in the formative epoch of civilized development in the 3rd and 2nd millennia B.C.E. (see Chapters 2, 3, and 4) through the clas-

sical and postclassical eras, nomadic peoples periodically emerged from their steppe, prairie, and desert fringe homelands to invade, often build empires, and settle in the sedentary zones of Eurasia, Africa, and the Americas. Their intrusions have significantly altered political history by destroying existing polities and even—as in the case of Assyria and Harappa—whole civilizations. They have also generated major population movements, sparked social upheavals, and facilitated critical cultural and economic exchanges across civilizations. As the Mongols' stunning successes in the 13th century illustrate, the capacity of nomadic peoples to break through the defenses of the much more populous civilized zones and to establish control over much richer and more sophisticated peoples arose primarily from the advantages the nomads possessed in waging war.

A reservoir of battle-ready warriors and mobility have from ancient times proved to be the key to success for expansion-minded nomads. Harsh environments and ongoing intertribal and interclan conflicts for survival within them produced tough, resourceful fighters who could live off the land on the march and who regarded combat as an integral part of their lives. The horses and camels on which pastoral peoples in Eurasia and Sudanic Africa relied gave them a degree of mobility that confounded the sedentary peoples who sought to ward off their incursions. The mounted warriors of nomadic armies possessed the advantages of speed, surprise, and superior intelligence, which was gathered by mounted reconnaissance patrols. The most successful nomadic invaders, such as the Mongols, also proved willing to experiment with and adapt to technological innovations with military applications. Some of these, such as the stirrup and various sorts of harnesses, were devised by the nomads themselves. Others, such as gunpowder and the siege engines—both Muslim and Chinese—that the Mongols used to smash the defenses of walled towns were borrowed from sedentary peoples and adapted to the nomads' fighting machines.

Aside from the considerable military advantages that accrued from the nomads' lifestyles and social organization, their successes in war owed much to the weaknesses of their adversaries in the sedentary, civilized zones. The great empires that provided the main defense for agricultural peoples against nomadic incursions were, even in the best circumstances, diverse and overextended polities. Imperial control—and protection—diminished steadily as one moved away from the capital and core provinces. Imperial boundaries were usually fluid, and the outer provinces were consistently vulnerable to nomadic raids if not conquest.

Classical and postclassical empires, such as the Egyptian and Han and the Abbasid, Byzantine, and Song enjoyed great advantages over the nomads in terms of the populations and resources they controlled. But their armies, almost without exception, were too slow, too low on firepower, and too poorly trained to resist large and well-organized forces of nomadic intruders. In times of dynastic strength in the sedentary zones, well-defended fortress systems and ingenious weapons—such as the crossbow, which could be fairly easily mastered by the peasant conscripts—proved quite effective against nomadic incursions. Nonetheless, even the strongest dynasties depended heavily on "protection" payments to nomad leaders and the divisions between the nomadic peoples on their borders for their security. And even the strongest sedentary empires were periodically shaken by nomadic raids into the outer provinces. When the empires weakened or when large numbers of nomads were united under able leaders, such as Muhammad and his successors or Chinggis Khan, nomadic assaults made a shambles of sedentary armies and fortifications.

In many ways, the Mongol and Timurid explosions represented the apex of nomadic power and influence on world history. After these remarkable interludes, age-old patterns of interaction between nomads and farming town-dwelling peoples were fundamentally transformed. These transformations resulted in the growing ability of sedentary peoples to first resist and then dominate nomadic peoples, and they mark a major watershed in the history of the human community. Some of the causes of the shift were immediate and specific. The most critical of these was the devastation wrought by the Black Death on the nomads of Central Asia in the 14th century. Though the epidemic proved catastrophic for large portions of the civilized zones as well, it dealt the relatively sparse nomadic populations a blow from which they took centuries to recover. The more rapid demographic (relating to population trends) resurgence of the sedentary peoples greatly increased their already considerable numerical advantage over the nomadic peoples in the following centuries. The combination of this growing numerical advantage, which in earlier epochs the nomads had often been able to overcome, with key political and economic shifts and technological innovations proved critical in bringing about the decline of the nomadic war machine.

In the centuries after the Mongol conquests, the rulers of sedentary states found increasingly effective ways of centralizing their political power and mobilizing the manpower and resources of their domains for war. Some improvements in this regard were made by the rulers of China and the empires of the Islamic belt. But the sovereigns of the nascent states of western Europe surpassed all other potentates in advances in these spheres. Stronger control and better organization allowed a growing share of steadily increasing national wealth to be channeled toward military ends. The competing rulers of Europe also invested heavily in technological innovations with military applications, from improved metalworking techniques to the development of ever more potent gunpowder and firearms. From the 15th and 16th centuries, the discipline and training of European armies also improved markedly. With pikes, muskets, fire drill, and trained commanders, European armies were more than a match for the massed nomad cavalry that had so long terrorized sedentary peoples.

With the introduction early in the 17th century of light, mobile field artillery into European armies, the nomads' retreat began. States such as Russia, which had centralized power on the western European model, as well as the Ottoman Empire in the eastern Mediterranean and the Qing in China, which had shared many of the armament advances of the Europeans, moved steadily into the steppe and desert heartlands of the horse and camel nomads. Each followed a conscious policy of settling part of its rapidly growing peasant population in the areas taken from the nomads. Thus, nomadic populations not only were brought under the direct rule of sedentary empires but saw their pasturelands plowed and planted wherever the soil and water supply permitted.

These trends suggest that the nomadic war machine had been in decline long before the new wave of innovation that ushered in the Industrial Revolution in the 18th century. But that process sealed its fate. Railways and repeating rifles allowed sedentary peoples to penetrate even the most wild and remote of the nomadic refuges and subdue even the most determined and fierce of nomadic warriors, from the Plains Indians of North America to the bedouin of the Sahara and Arabia. The periodic nomadic incursions into the sedentary zones, which had recurred sporadically for millennia, had come to an end.

Questions: What are some of the major ways in which nomadic peoples and their periodic expansions have affected the course of global history? Which of their movements and conquests do you think were the most important? Why were the Mongols able to build a much greater empire than any previous nomadic contender? Why did the Mongol Empire collapse so rapidly, and what does its fall tell us about the underlying weaknesses of the nomadic war machine?

CONCLUSION

The Mongol Legacy and an Aftershock: The Brief Ride of Timur

As we have seen, the Mongols' impact on the many areas where they raided and conquered varied considerably. The sedentary peoples on the farms and in the cities, who experienced the fury of their assaults and the burden of their tribute exactions, understandably emphasized the destructive side of the Mongol legacy. But the Mongol campaigns also decisively influenced the course of human history in the ways they altered warfare and the political repercussions they generated in invaded areas. Mongol armies, for example, provided openings for the rise of Moscow as the central force in the creation of a Russian state, they put an end to Abbasid and Seljuk power, and they opened the way for the Mamluks and the Ottomans. The Mongol empire promoted trade and important exchanges among civilizations, though, as the spread of the Black Death illustrates, the latter were not always beneficial. Mongol rule also brought stable, at times quite effective, government and religious toleration to peoples over much of Asia.

Just as the peoples of Eurasia had begun to recover from the upheavals caused by Mongol expansion, a second nomadic explosion from central Asia plunged them again into fear and despair. This time the nomads in question were Turks, not Mongols, and their leader, *Timur-i Lang,* or Timur the Lame, was from a noble landowning clan, not a tribal, herding background. Timur's was a decidedly divided personality. On one hand, he was a highly cultured individual, who delighted in the fine arts, lush gardens, and splendid architecture and who could spend days conversing with great scholars such as the Muslim historian Ibn Khaldun (see the Document in Chapter 13). On the other, he was a ruthless conqueror, apparently indifferent to human suffering and capable of commanding his troops to commit atrocities on a scale that would not be matched in the human experience until the 20th century. Beginning in the 1360s, his armies moved out from his base at Samarkand to conquests in Persia, the Fertile Crescent, India, and southern Russia.

Though his empire did not begin to compare with that of the Mongols in size, he outdid them in the feroc-

In 1398, Timur-i Lang's central Asian armies left Delhi completely destroyed and India politically fragmented.

ity of his campaigns. In fact, Timur is remembered for little more than truly barbaric destruction—for the pyramids of skulls he built with the heads of the tens of thousands of people slaughtered after the city of Aleppo in Asia Minor was taken, or the thousands of prisoners he had massacred as a warning to the citizens of Delhi in north India not to resist his armies. In the face of this wanton slaughter, the fact that he spared artisans and scientists to embellish his capital city at Samarkand counts for little. Unlike the Mongols, his rule brought neither increased trade and significant cross-cultural exchanges nor internal peace. Mercifully, his reign was as brief as it was violent. After his death in 1405, his empire was pulled apart by his warring commanders and old enemies anxious for revenge. With his passing, the last great challenge of the steppe nomads to the civilizations of Eurasia came to an end.

FURTHER READINGS

A substantial literature has developed on the Mongol interlude in global history. The most readable and reliable biography of Chinggis Khan is René Grousset's *Conqueror of the World* (1966). Grousset has also written a broader history of central Asia, entitled *The Empire of the Steppes* (1970). Peter Brent's more recent *The Mongol Empire* (1976) provides an updated overview and wonderful illustrations. Berthold Spuler's *The Mongols in History* (1971) makes some attempt to gauge their impact on world history, and his *History of the Mongols* (1968) supplies a wide variety of firsthand accounts of the Mongols from the founding of the empire to life in the successor states. T. Allsen's *Mongol Imperialism* provides the best account of the rise and structure of the empires built by Chinggis Khan and his successors.

For specific areas, George Vernadsky's *The Mongols in Russia* (1953) remains the standard, though some of its views are now contested. Morris Rossabi's recent *Kubilai Khan: His Life and Times* (1988) is by far the best work on the Mongols in China. James Chambers's *The Devil's Horsemen* (1979) and Denis Sinor's *History of Hungary* (1957) contain good accounts of the Mongol incursions into eastern and central Europe. The fullest and most accessible summary of the links between Mongol expansion and the spread of the Black Death can be found in William H. McNeill's *Plagues and Peoples* (1976).

21

The West and the Changing World Balance

c. 1266–1337 Giotto

1275–1292 Marco Polo in China

1304–1374 Petrarch; development of Italian Renaissance

1348–1375 Plague spreads in Europe, including Russia

1320s Spread of bubonic plague in Gobi Desert

1258 Mongol conquest of Baghdad; fall of Abbasid caliphate

1291 First Italian expedition seeks route to Indies

1320s First European use of cannon in warfare

1348 Peak of Black Death in Middle East

1330s Black Death reaches China

1290–1317 New famines in Europe

1347 Plague reaches Sicily

1250 C.E.   **1300** C.E.   **1350** C.E.

INTRODUCTION

By the year 1400, partly as a result of the Mongol invasions and their aftermath, it was becoming clear that the balance among civilizations in the world was beginning to change dramatically. This chapter summarizes the leading developments in this new world balance, building on the coverage of specific civilizations in preceding chapters.

This period of transition in the 14th and early 15th centuries was opened by the decline of Arab strength—symbolized by the fall of the last Arab caliphate in 1258—and the disruptions caused elsewhere in Asia and eastern Europe by the Mongol incursions. These developments created new opportunities within the international network that had been established in the post-classical centuries, particularly through the expansive power of Arab religion, trade, and politics. Various candidates emerged to take a new international role, including for a short time China in the early stages of the Ming dynasty, which replaced the Mongol overlords during the 14th century.

The most dynamic new contender for international power was Western Europe, and the conditions that propelled Western civilization toward a new position around 1400 form the second major theme of this chapter. The West was not yet the world's major power; it did not replace the Arabs as international leaders quickly or easily. The first stages of the rise of the West were accompanied by important changes within Western civilization itself, also taking shape by about 1400. At this point, Italy, Spain, and Portugal took a new leadership role in the West, which they would hold for about two centuries.

It is also vital to note the civilizations that were largely or completely outside the international network. Important civilizations in parts of Africa, as well as in the Americas and Polynesia, were independent of larger world connections; yet, the changes they were experiencing by 1400 would feed into the international equation that was taking shape in the 15th century.

THE DECLINE OF THE OLD ORDER

Focal Point: The first steps in the new world order that was beginning to emerge by 1400 involved the major reshuffling in the Middle East and North Africa.

In 1200, this region was still described by two powerful empires, the Byzantine in the northwest and the Islamic caliphate through much of the Middle Eastern heartland. By 1400, this structure was in full disarray. The Byzantine Empire still existed, but it was on its last legs, pressed by invading Ottoman Turks. The imperial capital, Constantinople, would fall to the Turks in 1453, effectively ending the empire. Two centuries earlier, the caliphate, long sapped by increasing reliance on foreign troops and advisors, including the omnipresent Turks, fell to Mongol invasion. Arabs have never since been able to unite all of their region under their own rule.

Social and Cultural Decline in the Middle East

By about 1300, religious leaders in the Islamic Middle East increasingly gained the upper hand over poets, philosophers, and scientists. An earlier tension between diverse cultural elements yielded to the predominance of the faith. The new piety associated with the rising Sufi movement was both the cause and the result of this development. In literature, emphasis on secular themes, such as the joys of feasting and hunting, gave way to more strictly religious ideas. Persian poets, writing now

---

1439 Portugal takes over Azores; increasing expeditions into Atlantic, along northwest African coast

1469 Union of Aragon and Castile; rise of Spanish monarchy

1400 End of Polynesian migrations

1368 Mongols expelled from China; Ming dynasty

1405 Chinese trading expeditions begin

1453 Ottomans capture Constantinople; fall of Byzantine empire

1433 End of Chinese expeditions

1400 C.E.

1450 C.E.

in their own language instead of Arabic, led the way, and religious poetry—not poetry in general—became part of the education of upper-class children. In philosophy, the rationalistic current encountered new attack. In Muslim Spain, the philosopher Ibn-Rushd (Averroës) espoused Greek rationalism, but his efforts were largely ignored in the Middle East. In fact, European scholars were more heavily influenced by his work. In the Middle East proper, a more typical philosopher now claimed to use Aristotle's logic to show that it was impossible to discover religious truth by human reason, in a book revealingly, if not subtly, entitled *The Destruction of Philosophy.*

Thus, Middle Eastern scholarship came to focus on religion and the Islamic legalistic traditions, though a rich artistic production continued. Some interest in science remained, though it too began to fade. In its place, many Sufi scholars wrote excitedly of their mystical contacts with God and the stages of their religious passion, which led to dramatic new statements of Islam.

Changes in society and the economy were as telling as the shifts in politics and intellectual life. As the authority of the caliphate declined, landlords seized power over the peasantry. From about 1100 onward, Middle Eastern peasants increasingly lost their freedom, becoming serfs on large estates. This loss was not the peasants' alone, for agricultural productivity suffered as a result. Landlords turned to sucking what they could from their estates rather than trying to develop a more vital agriculture, and peasants had scant incentive and no means to do better. Tax revenues declined, and Arab and other Middle Eastern traders began to lose ground. Few Arab coins have been found in Europe dating from later than 1100. European merchants began to control their own turf and to challenge the Arabs in other parts of the Mediterranean; initiative in this vital trading area was passing to their hands. Arab and Persian commerce remained active in the Indian Ocean, but the time was not too distant when it would face new competition there as well.

The decline of the Islamic caliphate and its economy was gradual and incomplete. It cannot be compared with the dramatic fall of the Roman Empire in the West many centuries before. Another, more subtle model is needed. The reduction of dynamism in trade, for example, linked to weaker or more limited political and cultural forms, by no means took the Arabs out of major world markets.

Finally, the political fragmentation of the Arab world did not produce prolonged confusion in the Middle East. The emerging Ottoman Turkish state soon mastered most of the lands of the old caliphate as well as the Byzantine corner, expanding into southeastern Europe. (See Chapter 26 in Volume II for the development

This Persian-style painting depicts the Ottoman Turks as they assail the Hungarians with troops and cannons in a battle in 1526.

of the new Ottoman Empire.) It is important to realize, further, that the empire was far more powerful, politically and militarily, than the caliphate had been for many centuries—and proportionately more frightening to observers in neighboring civilizations such as western Europe.

A Power Vacuum in International Leadership

Nevertheless, even the rise of the Ottoman Empire did not restore the full international vigor that the Islamic caliphate had possessed at the height of its powers. Turkish rulers—rather scornful of their Arab subjects though sharing their religion—did not promote trade, particularly maritime trade, as vigorously as in the past. Scientific and philosophical development tended to stagnate in the Middle East. The expansionist power of the Ottoman Empire was very real and would persist into the 17th century, but its bases were somewhat limited. The empire could not serve as the sole hub of an international network, as the Arab caliphate had a few centuries before.

The result, particularly given the Arab decline in international trade, was something of a power vacuum beyond the borders of the Ottoman Empire. A single replacement for the Arabs as hub of the loose international network was not perhaps inevitable, and no other civilization deliberately set out to advance a candidacy as a matter of explicit policy, but in fact a sorting-out process was well under way by 1400, with the West beginning to emerge as the leading beneficiary.

There were several limitations to the list of possible replacements for the Arabs as leading international actors. The Ottoman Empire emphasized trade and cultural dynamism too little. Japan simply did not think in terms of major expansion. India was divided into regional kingdoms, which largely reacted to foreign contacts (particularly from Islamic invaders) rather than initiating them. Russia did not begin an expansionist course until late in the 15th century.

Chinese Thrust and Withdrawal

This left, effectively, only two contenders for the mantle of leading international manipulator: China and the West. China clearly had the edge and for a time took full advantage of the new opportunities in international trade. In a conscious policy decision, however, the new Ming dynasty took itself out of the main international arena, returning to long-standing traditions in the civilization that urged concentration on developing the Middle Kingdom and its evolving internal strengths.

Rebellions in China drove out the deeply resented Mongol overlords in 1368. A rebel leader, born of peasant stock, seized the Mongol capital of Beijing and proclaimed a new Ming—meaning "brilliant"—dynasty that was to last until 1644. This dynasty began with a burst of unusual expansionism. As in earlier dynasties, the initial Ming rulers pressed to secure the borders of the Middle Kingdom. This meant pushing the Mongols far to the north to the plains of what is now Mongolia. It meant reestablishing influence over neighboring governments and winning tribute payments from states in Korea, Vietnam, and Tibet, reviving much of the East Asian

regional structure set up by the Tang dynasty. Far more unusual was a new policy, adopted soon after 1400, of mounting huge, state-sponsored trading expeditions to southern Asia and beyond.

A first fleet sailed in 1405 to India, with 62 ships carrying 28,000 men. Later voyages reached the Middle East and the eastern coast of Africa, bringing chinaware and copper coinage in exchange for local goods. Chinese shipping at its height consisted of 2700 coastal vessels, 400 armed naval ships, and at least as many long-distance ships. Nine great "treasure ships," the most sophisticated in the world at the time in their size and provisions as well as the improved compasses they used for navigation, explored the Indian Ocean, the Persian Gulf, and the Red Sea, establishing regular trade with all.

There is no question that the course of world history might have been immeasurably altered had the Chinese thrust continued, for the tiny European expeditions that began to creep down the western coast of Africa at about the same time would have been no match for this combination of merchant and military organization. But the emperors called the expeditions to a halt in 1433. The bureaucrats had long opposed the new trade policy, out of rivalry with other officials like the admiral Cheng Ho, but there were deeper reasons as well. The costs seemed unacceptable, given the continuing expenses of the campaigns against the Mongols and the desire to build a luxurious new capital city in Beijing. This assessment was not, of course, inevitable. It reflected a preference for traditional expenditures rather than distant foreign involvements. Chinese merchant activity continued to be extensive in Southeast Asia. Chinese trading groups established permanent settlements in the Philippines, Malaysia, and Indonesia, where they added to the cultural diversity of the area and maintained a disproportionate role in local and regional trading activities into the 20th century. China's chance to become a dominant world trading power was lost, however, at least for several centuries, with a decision that in essence confirmed the relatively low status of trade within the official Chinese scheme of things.

To Western eyes, accustomed to judging a society's dynamism by its ability to reach out and gain new territories or trade positions, China's decision may seem hard to understand—the precursor to some inevitable decline. In Chinese terms, of course, it was the brief trading flurry that was unusual, not its cessation. China had long emphasized internal development, amid considerable international isolation, while maintaining suspicion of merchant values and any policy that would unduly elevate commercial activity. Ming emperors consolidated their rule over the empire's vast territory. Internal eco-

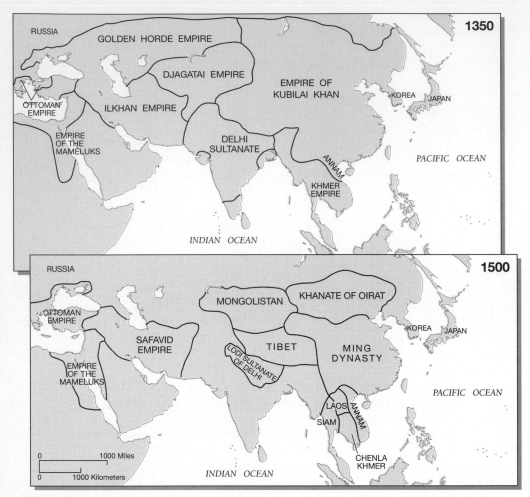

Major Boundary Changes in Asia, 1350–1500

nomic development continued as well, with no need for foreign products. Industry expanded, with growth in the production of textiles and porcelain; ongoing trade with Southeast Asia enriched the port cities; agricultural production and population both increased. Cultural activity showed the only hints that creativity was declining. Intellectuals focused on summing up expanding knowledge in medicine, agriculture, and technology, maintaining interest in drama and poetry, and pursuing philosophical training in Confucianism.

The shift in Chinese policy unintentionally cleared the way for another, in most ways decidedly inferior, civilization to work toward a new international position. With the Arabs in partial eclipse, and with China briefly moving into the resulting trade vacuum but then retreating, hesitant Western expansionism, launched before 1400, began to take on new significance. Within a century, Western explorers and traders had begun directly to seize international trading dominance and had expanded the international network to include parts of the Americas for the first time.

THE RISE OF THE WEST

Focal Point: Western Europe began to undergo important changes in the 14th and 15th centuries. Some involved new problems; others created new opportunities. Examination of the various strengths and weaknesses of this once backward region sets the stage for Europe's new ventures in world trade.

The West's gradual emergence into larger world contacts during the 15th century was surprising in many respects. Westerners remained awed, and rightly so, by the powerful bureaucracies and opulent treasuries of empires

CLOSEUP

Cheng Ho

Cheng Ho was the admiral who commanded China's great expeditions between 1405 and their termination in 1433. A Muslim from western China, Cheng Ho was well suited to deal with Muslims in southeast Asia on his trade route. Cheng Ho was also a eunuch, castrated for service at the royal court. China's Ming emperors retained a large harem of wives to assure succession, and eunuchs were required to guard them without threat of sexual rivalry; many gained bureaucratic powers well beyond this service. Cheng Ho's expeditions usually hugged the coastline, but he had a compass and excellent maps as well as huge vessels that contained ample supplies—even gardens—as well as goods for trade. His fleets must have impressed, even terrified, the local rulers around the Indian ocean, many of whom were enrolled to pay tribute to the Emperor. Several missions visited China from the Middle East and Africa. From Africa also came ostriches, zebras, and giraffes for the imperial zoo—the latter billed as the unicorns of Chinese fable. But Cheng Ho was resented by the Confucian bureaucrats, who refused even to write much about him in their chronicles.

in the traditional civilization centers such as Constantinople. Furthermore, the West was changing in some painful ways. The staples of medieval culture at its height were under new question by 1400. The Church, which had long been one of the organizing institutions of Western civilization, was under new attack. Many popes seemed more interested in advancing their wealth and political position than in religious leadership. Medieval philosophy had passed its creative phase. Warrior aristocrats, long a key leadership group in feudal society, increasingly softened their style of life as military technology began to pass them by, preferring court rituals and jousting tournaments and adopting military armor so cumbersome that real fighting was difficult.

Even more strikingly, the lives and economic activities of ordinary Europeans were in serious disarray. This was a time of crisis, and Europe's expanding world role by no means reversed the fundamental challenges to its internal economic and demographic structure. Europeans began to suffer from recurrent famine after 1300, as population had outstripped the food supply, and no new techniques were discovered to alter the equation. Famine conditions in turn reduced disease resistance, making Europe more vulnerable to the bubonic plagues that spread from Asia.

Bubonic plague, or Black Death, surfaced in various parts of Asia in the 14th century. In China it reduced the population by nearly 30 percent by 1400. Following trade routes, it then spread into India and the Middle East, causing thousands of deaths per day in the larger cities. The plague's worst European impact occurred between 1348 and 1375, by which time 30 million people, one-third of Europe's population, had died. The resulting economic dislocation in turn produced bitter strikes and peasant risings.

Sources of Dynamism: Medieval Vitality

How, then, could the West be poised for a new international role? The answer to that question must embrace several ingredients. First, several key advances of medieval society were not really reversed amid the troubles of the decades around 1400. The strengthening of feudal monarchy, for example, provided more effective national or regional governments for much of the West. The Hundred Years' War between Britain and France stimulated innovations in military organization, including nonaristocratic soldiers recruited and paid directly by the royal government, that enhanced central political power. Strong regional monarchies took hold in parts of Spain and in Portugal as Christian leaders drove back the Muslim rulers of this region. The growth of cities and urban economies continued to spur the commercial side of Western society. Even the Church had made its peace with such key principles of capitalism as profit-seeking.

Technology continued to advance, particularly in ironwork—used for bells and weapons—and timekeeping. Here too, the Hundred Years' War added demands for guns and munitions, spurring this industrial sector. Even in culture, medieval interests in furthering human understanding continued to support advances in scientific research in areas such as optics. The first element of an explanation of new Western vigor involves an understanding that some of the gains the West had achieved during the Middle Ages continued, even as certain characteristic medieval forms wavered.

Demographic Vigor and Technological Imitation

One key durable trend involved population growth, which, beginning about the 9th century, had been a key symptom and cause of other changes in the medieval West. As commerce expanded, agriculture improved, and internal warfare declined, Western population continued to grow. Indeed, between 1000 C.E. and 1700 C.E., Western population expanded at a more rapid rate than that of any other continent. Agricultural shortages and the Black Death temporarily pushed back population growth in the West, but the overall trend was toward expansion. By the end of the postclassical era, European population had already surpassed that of the Middle East. Demographic vigor of this sort helps explain Europe's thirst for expansion and contributed to its growing sense of confidence.

Table 21.1
Population Levels (in millions)

Continents	Years				
	1000	1700	1800	1900	1975
Europe	36	120	180	390	635
Asia (includes Middle East)	185	415	625	970	2300
Africa	33	61	70	110	385
Americas	39	13	24	145	545
Oceania (includes Australia)	1.5	2.25	2.5	6.75	23
Totals	294.5	611.25	901.5	1621.75	3888

Note: Estimates for the earlier dates are only that; they are not precise figures. They indicate comparative magnitudes with reasonable precision.

Source: Adapted from Dennis H. Wrong, ed., *Population and Society* (1977).

Table 21.2
Percentages or Proportions of Total World Population

Continents	Years				
	1000	1700	1800	1900	1975
Europe	12.2	19.6	19.7	24	16.3
Asia	62.9	67.6	69.3	59.8	59.2
Africa	11.2	10.0	7.8	6.8	9.9
Americas	13.4	2.1	2.7	8.9	14.0
Oceania	0.4	0.4	0.3	0.3	0.6

Source: Adapted from Dennis H. Wrong, ed., *Population and Society* (1977).

The Mongol Empire established in Asia and eastern Europe provided, in the late 13th and early 14th centuries, new access to Asian knowledge and technology. Political stability and an openness to foreign visitors by the great khans, along with continued trade through the Mediterranean, helped Westerners learn of Asian technologies, ranging from printing to the compass and explosive powder. Because of a combination of heightened contact and Western eagerness to learn, particularly where technology had military implications, Western technology drew closer to the highest world levels by the early 15th century. Soon it would begin to surpass those levels.

Secular Directions in the Italian Renaissance

The final major ingredient of the West's surge involved changes within the West itself. The decline of medieval society, far from complete in any event, did not signal a narrowing of Western culture or politics but rather an opportunity to innovate. Important dislocations did not prevent some vital new directions. The fact that key innovations occurred in places like Italy, where medieval forms such as Gothic architecture and scholastic philosophy had less intense impact, helps explain how the West was able to begin to change its skin.

Italy, in 1400, was in the midst of a vital cultural and political movement known as the *Renaissance*, or rebirth, and this in turn provides the clearest indication that the West was renewing its society rather than declining. The early phases of the Renaissance, taking shape during the 14th century, involved literature and art friendlier to things of this world, not in opposition to religious goals but with distinctly more secular priorities. Religious art remained dominant but used more realistic portrayals of people and nature, and some nonreligious themes surfaced outright. The doings of human beings deserved attention for their own sake, in the Renaissance view, not as they reflected a divine plan. Artists and writers became more openly ambitious for personal reputation and glory.

Italy was the center of initial Renaissance cultural definitions because it retained more contact with Roman tradition than did the rest of Europe and because it led the West, by the 14th century, in banking and trade. Active commerce and considerable urban manufacturing gave Italian cities the wealth to sponsor new cultural activities; contacts with some foreign scholars, particularly in Byzantium; and a more optimistic view of the power of human endeavor and the validity of earthly goals.

Special political characteristics in Italy contributed to the Renaissance surge. Although northern Italy technically fell into the territory controlled by the German emperors, in fact key city-states had long exercised effective governmental power in the major regions. City-state governments were made up of successful military entrepreneurs, who translated their heroic exploits into political control, or of individual merchants or merchant councils. These governments lacked the support of tradition and had to woo popular backing and undertake an array of new functions, from grain supply to policing, in order to retain power. Furthermore, the city-states were intensely competitive, and while this led to many wars as well as commercial rivalry, it also encouraged sponsorship of cultural achievements as badges of urban greatness. Finally, the attention to government and diplomacy led intellectuals and political leaders to their emphasis on "this-worldly" culture. One of the reasons for the new interest in classical Roman culture was its emphasis on republican virtues, oratorical ability, and other skills useful in successful administration. The Renaissance was very definitely an urban phenomenon, but it also was a result of the special role and organization of Italian cities.

Human Values and Renaissance Culture

For all its political and commercial roots, the Renaissance was first and foremost a cultural movement, launched in Florence and manifesting itself in literature and various arts. The Renaissance focused on a new interest in stylistic grace, an exploration of themes such as romance and nature, and a concern for practical ethics

Giotto's 14th-century Renaissance painting preserves Christian themes in the lamentation over the dead Christ, but with new attention to naturalism and expression in the human figures.

and codes of behavior for urban gentlemen. One leading 14th-century writer, *Francesco Petrarch,* not only took pride in his city and his age but explored the glories of personal achievement with new confidence. The tone of innovation—in style, subject matter, and implicit view of human powers—predominated in the many writings of 14th-century Florentines.

Innovation increasingly prevailed in the visual arts and music as well. The subject matter of art moved toward nature and people, including both cityscapes and the inevitable portraits of the rich and powerful, whether the themes were religious or secular. The Florentine painter Giotto led the way, departing from medieval formalism and stiffness. Other painters, beginning later in the 14th century, started to introduce perspective while also using new colors and other materials. In architecture, favor shifted away from the Gothic to a classicism derived from the styles of Greece and Rome. Vivid, realistic statues complemented the new palaces and public buildings.

As a massive shift in cultural emphases, the impact of the early Renaissance must not be exaggerated. It had little influence, as yet, outside of Italy. Even in Italy, it focused on high culture, not popular outlook. And while it built on distinctive political and economic forms, it did not constitute a full break from medieval tendencies.

Even in Italian intellectual life, important work on science, at places such as the University of Padua, maintained medieval impulses and would gradually lead to later scientific advance outside the most popular cultural themes of the Renaissance.

Nevertheless, the advent of new cultural currents was an important innovation in Western history. The full ramifications of the Renaissance feed into the next period of both world and Western history (see Chapter 22). The movement was only getting started by 1400. The wide range of Italian commerce and shipping proved to be one of the building blocks of European outreach. By the 14th century, ships, particularly from Genoa, which was less well placed than Venice for eastern Mediterranean trade, were ready for new roles. Ambitious city-state governments encouraged new ventures, eager for greater tax money and unembarrassed about promoting commerce as one of their explicit functions. A larger if poorly defined "Renaissance spirit" could also spur innovation. While people like Petrarch defined human ambition mainly in cultural terms, other urban and commercial leaders, including seafaring men like Genoa's Christopher Columbus, might translate some of the same desire for personal glory and confidence in individual ability and in the validity of secular goals to different areas—such as exploration or conquest. It was no accident that Marco Polo, the European who brought new knowledge of China to his civilization, was an Italian inspired by the urban culture of the early Renaissance.

The Iberian Spirit of Religious Mission

Along with Italy, a key center for change by the 14th century was the Iberian Peninsula, where Christian military leaders had for several centuries been pressing back the boundaries of the Muslim state in Spain. Soon after 1400, major regional monarchies had been established in the provinces of *Castile* and *Aragon,* which would be united through royal marriage in 1469, and the Muslims had been pushed out of the entire peninsula save for the region around Granada.

Even before the marriage of Ferdinand and Isabella, Spanish and Portuguese rulers had developed a vigorous military and religious agenda. They supported effective armies, including infantry and feudal cavalry. And they believed that government had a mission to promote Christianity by converting Arabs and Jews or expelling those who held back, and by maintaining doctrinal purity within the Church itself. Close links between church and state provided revenues and officials for the royal government. In return, the government supported church courts in their quest for moral and doctrinal purity. Later in the 15th century, this interaction would lead to the reestablishment of the church-run courts of the Inquisition in Spain, designed to enforce religious orthodoxy and punish deviants. Spain and Portugal, in other words, were developing effective new governments with a special sense of religious mission and religious support. These changes, too, would feed the West's expansion into wider world contacts.

WESTERN EXPANSION: THE EXPERIMENTAL PHASE

Focal Point: Specific European attempts to explore the Atlantic (beyond the earlier Viking voyages in the North Atlantic) began in the later 13th century. While they built on the various changes occurring in European society, they were also designed to solve some practical economic problems. Early discoveries showed rapid interest in setting up a new colonial system.

A Crisis in Economic Position

By 1400, Western Europe was in serious international economic difficulties. From the Crusades onward, Western elites had become accustomed to increasing consumption of Asian luxury products, including spices such as cinnamon and nutmeg, silks, sugar, perfumes, and jewels. In exchange for the luxury items, Europeans mainly had cruder goods to offer: wool, tin, copper, honey, and salt. The value of European exports almost never equaled the value of what was imported from Asia. The resulting unfavorable balance of trade had to be made up in gold, but Western people had only a limited gold supply. By 1400, the constant drain to Asia was creating a gold famine that threatened the whole European economy with collapse.

Furthermore, there were legitimate fears of a new Muslim threat. The *Ottoman Empire* was taking shape, and Europeans began to fear a new Muslim surge. Even before this, the Muslim capture of the last Crusader stronghold (the city of Acre in the Middle East) in 1291 had been a disaster for the Christian faith, but it also gave Muslim traders—particularly Egyptians—new opportunities to serve as middlemen in the oriental trade, for there were no Western-controlled ports left in the eastern Mediterranean. One response to this was a series of conquests by the city-state of Venice along the eastern coast of the Adriatic. A more important and durable response was to begin explorations of alternative routes to

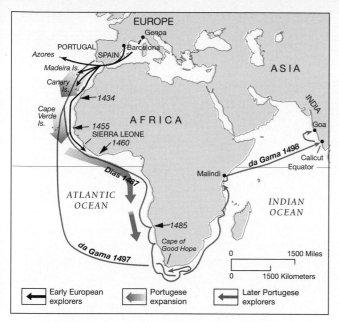

European Exploration of the Atlantic Around Africa

Asia that would bypass the Middle East and the feared and hated Muslim realms altogether.

Early Explorations

As early as 1291, two Italian brothers, the *Vivaldis* from Genoa, sailed with two galleys through the Straits of Gibraltar, seeking a Western route to the "Indies." They were never heard from again, and though they proved to be precursors of a major Western thrust into the southern Atlantic, it is not even entirely clear what they meant by the "Indies."

Early in the 14th century, other explorers from Genoa rediscovered the Canary Islands, populated by a hunting-and-gathering people. These islands had been known vaguely since classical times but had never before been directly opened by Europeans. Genoese sailors also visited the Madeiras and probably reached the more distant Azores by 1351. Soon after this, ships from northeastern Spain, based in the port of Barcelona, sailed along the African coast as far south as present-day Sierra Leone.

Until 1430, technological barriers prevented further exploration for alternative routes. Lacking adequate navigation instruments, Europeans could not risk wider ventures into the Atlantic. They also needed better ships than the shallow-drafted, oar-propelled Mediterranean galleys. Shipbuilding adaptations were under way, however, toward developing an oceangoing sailing vessel. At the same time, the crucial navigational problems were met by new knowledge of the compass and the astrolabe, used to determine latitude at sea by reckoning from the stars. Contacts with Arab merchants (who had learned from the Chinese) provided knowledge of these devices. European mapmaking, improving steadily during the 14th century, was also a key innovation. Because of these advances, Europeans were ready soon after 1400 to undertake voyages impossible just a century before.

Colonial Patterns

Even as these voyages began, in a familiar pattern detailed in Chapter 23, Westerners led by the Spanish and Portuguese began to take advantage of the new lands they had already discovered. Portugal by 1439 had taken control of the Azores and had granted land to colonists. Soon Spaniards and Portuguese had wholly conquered and colonized the Madeiras and Canaries, bringing in, among other things, Western plants, animals, weapons, and diseases. The result was something of a laboratory for the larger European imperialism that would soon take shape, particularly in the Americas. European colonists quickly set up large agricultural estates designed to produce cash crops that could be sold on the European market. First they introduced sugar, an item once imported from Asia but now available in growing quantities from Western-controlled sources. The new supply of sugar launched a progressive Western conversion to a sweet-tooth consumption that remains vigorous to the present day. Ultimately, other crops, such as cotton and tobacco, were also introduced to the Atlantic islands. To produce these market crops, the new colonists brought in slaves from northwestern Africa, mainly in Portuguese ships—the first examples of a new commercial version of slavery that the West would soon expand, and the first sign that Western expansion could have serious impact on other societies as well.

These developments about 1400 remained modest, even in their consequences for Africa. They serve mainly to illustrate how quickly Western conquerors decided what to do with lands and peoples newly in their grasp. The ventures were easily successful enough to motivate more extensive probes into the southern Atlantic as soon as technology permitted. Indeed, voyages of exploration down the coast of Africa and across the Atlantic began to occur as the island colonies were being fully settled. The ventures summed up the swirl of forces that were beginning to reshape the West's role in the world: inferiorities and fears, particularly vis-à-vis the Muslims; new energies

DOCUMENT

Italian Renaissance Culture

Writers in the first phase of the Italian Renaissance were aware that they were defining a culture quite different from that of medieval theologians and philosophers. In the passages that follow, Petrarch (1304–1374) writes about his priorities in literature, including the kind of classical examples he revered, first in a letter to another major writer, Boccaccio, and then in a poem. Petrarch's cultural interests and his definition of personal goals form part of a movement called humanism (see Chapter 22). Judging by the following documents, what defined a Renaissance humanist?

From Petrarch, Letter to Boccaccio (1362)

Neither exhortations to virtue nor the argument of approaching death should divert us from literature; for in a good mind it excites the love of virtue, and dissipates, or at least diminishes, the fear of death. To desert our studies shows want of self-confidence rather than wisdom, for letters do not hinder but aid the properly constituted mind which possesses them; they facilitate our life, they do not retard it. . . . If it were otherwise, surely the zeal of certain persons who persevered to the end could not have roused such admiration. Cato, I never forget, acquainted himself with Latin literature as he was growing old, and Greek when he had really become an old man. Varro, who reached his hundredth year still reading and writing, parted from life sooner than from his love of study. Livius Drusus, although weakened by age and afflicted with blindness, did not give up his interpretation of the civil law, which he carried on to the great advantage of the state. . . .

Besides these and innumerable others like them, have not all those of our own religion whom we should wish most to imitate devoted their whole lives to literature, and grown old and died in the same pursuit? Some, indeed, were overtaken by death while still at work reading or writing. To none of them, so far as I know, did it prove a disadvantage to be noted for secular learning. . . .

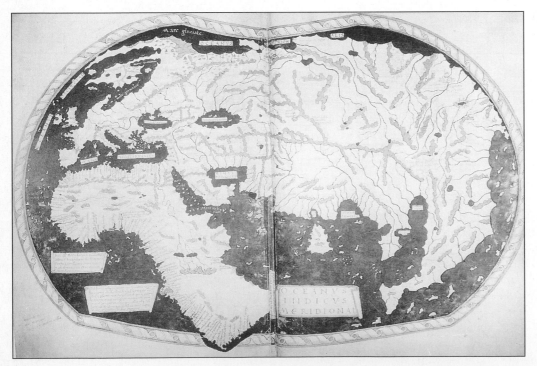

Columbus is supposed to have had a copy of this world map in Spain. The map, dating from about 1489, shows the Old World as Europeans were increasingly coming to know it.

While I know that many have become famous for piety without learning, at the same time I know of no one who has been prevented by literature from following the path of holiness. The apostle Paul was, to be sure, accused of having his head turned by study, but the world has long ago passed its verdict upon this accusation. If I may be allowed to speak for myself, it seems to me that, although the path to virtue by the way of ignorance may be plain, it fosters sloth. The goal of all good people is the same, but the ways of reaching it are many and various. Some advance slowly, others with more spirit; some obscurely, others again conspicuously. One takes a lower path, another takes a higher path. Although all alike are on the road to happiness, certainly the more elevated path is the more glorious. Hence ignorance, however devout, is by no means to be put on a plane with the enlightened devoutness of one familiar with literature. Nor can you pick me out from the whole array of unlettered saints, an example so holy that I cannot match it with a still holier one from the other group.

From Petrarch, the Sonnets (c. 1535)

To a Friend, Encouraging Him to Pursue Poetry

Torn is each virtue from its earthy throne
By sloth, intemperance, and voluptuous ease;
Far hence is every light celestial gone,
That guides mankind through life's
*   perplexing maze . . .*
Who now would laurel, myrtle-wreaths obtain?
Let want, let shame, Philosophy attend!
Cries the base world, intent on sordid gain.
What though thy favourite path be trod by few;
Let it but urge thee more, dear gentle friend,
Thy great design of glory to pursue.

Questions: What are the key purposes of intellectual activity, according to Petrarch? How can these purposes be reconciled with Christianity? How do Petrarch's arguments compare with Cicero's defense of Greek culture (Chapter 8)? To what extent does Petrarch's humanism suggest a more "modern" outlook than that of medieval Western culture?

of Renaissance merchants and Iberian rulers; economic pressures and a long-standing population surge.

ANALYSIS

The Problem of Ethnocentrism

Many cultures encourage an ethnocentric outlook, and the culture of the West is certainly one of them. Ethnocentrism, however, generates problems in interpreting world history. The dictionary definition of ethnocentrism is "a habitual disposition to judge foreign peoples or groups by the standards and practices of one's own culture or ethnic group." Most of us take pride in many of our own institutions and values, and it is tempting to move from this pride to a certain amount of disapproval of other peoples when they clearly do not share our behaviors and beliefs. Many Americans have a difficult time understanding how "other" peo-

ples have failed to establish the stable democratic political structure that we can point to in our own country. Even liberals who pride themselves on a sophisticated appreciation of different habits in some areas may adopt an ethnocentric shock at the seemingly clumsy oppression (by current American standards) of women that is visible in certain societies today or in the past. Indeed, unless a person is almost totally alienated from his or her own society, some tendency to ethnocentric reactions is hard to avoid.

Nevertheless, unexamined ethnocentrism can be a barrier in dealing with world history. Because world history after its early phases often consists of an inquiry into the establishment and evolution of civilizations different from our own, its meaning can be distorted by too much editorializing. We will grasp other times and places better, and perhaps use our own values more intelligently, if we do not too readily dismiss cultures in which "objectionable" practices occur.

Controlling ethnocentrism does not mean abandoning all standards, as if any social behavior were as good as any other. It does involve a certain open-mindedness and sophistication. Reducing distracting levels of ethnocentrism can be aided by some specific procedures. It is important to realize that few cultures behave irrationally over long periods of time. They may differ from our taste, but their patterns respond to valid causes and problems. Our own values are not without complexity. We sometimes believe things about our own society that are not as true as we wish; or, in judging other societies, we forget about drawbacks in our own surroundings. Perspective on our own habits, including awareness of how other cultures might judge us, helps us restrain our ethnocentrism.

Ethnocentrism may become a particularly strong impulse, however, in dealing with some of the changes in world history taking shape about 1400. The West was gaining strength. Since many Americans identify with Western civilization, it will be tempting to downplay some of the subtleties and disadvantages involved in this process or to exaggerate the extent to which the West began to organize world history more generally.

The balance of power among civilizations was beginning to shift about 1400, and it is legitimate—not simply ethnocentric—to note that the West's rise was one of the leading aspects of this change with ultimately international significance. It is unnecessary to neglect the many other patterns continuing or emerging—including new vigor in several other societies—or to gloss over the mixture of motives and results that the West's rise entailed. Ethnocentric impulses can profitably be monitored in grasping the complexity of change in world history, particularly as Western values altered somewhat and at the same time became more important on the world stage.

Questions: Why can ethnocentrism complicate interpretations in world history? How can one balance disapproval and understanding in dealing with practices such as female infanticide? How might a Chinese or Muslim observer have judged some of the cultural innovations of the early Italian Renaissance?

OUTSIDE THE WORLD NETWORK

Focal Point: The international framework that had developed during the postclassical period embraced most of Asia and Europe, North Africa, and portions of Africa south of the Sahara. This network left out important groups and regions which had their own vigorous histories in their centuries.

This 18th-century engraving portrays Vasco da Gama's audience with the Indian ruler of Calicut in 1498.

Developments in the Americas, Polynesia, and several parts of sub-Saharan Africa were simply not affected by the new international exchange. During the next period of world history, these regions would all be pulled into a new level of international contact, but a world balance sheet in 1400 must emphasize their separateness.

At the same time, several of the societies outside the international network were experiencing some new problems during the 15th century that would leave them unusually vulnerable to outside interference thereafter. These problems were entirely coincidental, and they had no larger world significance until Western expeditions redefined the international network. Such problems included new political strains in the leading American civilizations and a fragmentation of the principal island groups in Polynesian culture after several centuries of internal migration and exchange.

Disunity in the Americas and Africa

As discussed in Chapter 17, both the Aztec and the Inca empires ran into increasing difficulties not long after 1400. Aztec exploitation of subject peoples—their exactions of gold, slaves, and religious sacrifices—

roused great resentment. What would have happened to the Aztec Empire if the Spaniards had not intervened after 1500 is not clear, but it is obvious that disunity created opportunities for outside intervention that might not otherwise have existed. The Inca system, though far less brutal than that of the Aztecs, involved an ongoing tension between central leadership and local initiative that was hard to sustain, given the vast expanse of the Inca domains. Here too, probable overextension made change likely by the 1500s—indeed, the empire was already receding somewhat—even aside from European intervention. At the same time, other cultures were developing in parts of the Americas that might well have been candidates for new political leadership, had the dynamics of American history continued to unfold without the complication of contacts with the wider world.

Patterns in sub-Saharan Africa were more complex. The vast continent displayed great diversity. Several regional kingdoms were in decline by 1400, again with little or no involvement with wider world currents. Thus, Zimbabwe began its collapse, while the great Sudanic empire of Mali yielded increasingly to attacks from regional rivals. Another Muslim kingdom, Songhay, soon rose to take Mali's place, however, flourishing between 1464 and 1591, and it increased the effectiveness of the central state by raising royal armies directly instead of depending on alliances with local lords. There was no sense, certainly, that African history was poised in 1400 for major change.

Indeed, in many respects, African history continued a pattern of independent evolution long after the 15th century. Well-organized regional kingdoms maintained substantial control in many areas, even in most of the cases where European traders increasingly intervened. The fact that African society had previously interacted with Mediterranean and Asian cultures precluded the worst potential consequences of isolation. A few European contact points long huddled along the coast, at the sufferance of local rulers and with little interior penetration. Yet, soon after 1500, some important shifts were introduced from the outside. Trade patterns were increasingly redirected in West Africa, from overland contact with the Mediterranean to concentration on opportunities along the Atlantic, and relatedly from Muslim to European hands. The seizure of slaves for European use, already introduced into Spanish and Portuguese island colonies before 1500, touched many regions deeply. Even politics would be affected, as European weapons and troops played an increasing role in regional conflicts including the attacks

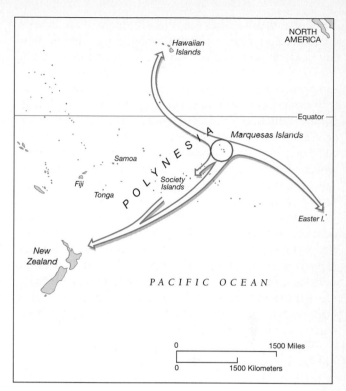

Polynesian Expansion

that at the end of the 16th century brought down Songhay.

Expansion, Migration, and Conquest in Polynesia

A third culture that was later pulled into the expanding world network comprised the islands of Polynesia. Here, as in the Americas, important changes had taken place during the postclassical era but with no relationship to developments in societies elsewhere in the world. The key Polynesian theme from the 7th century to 1400 was expansion, spurts of migration, and conquest that implanted Polynesian culture well beyond the initial base in the Society Islands—as Tahiti, Samoa, and Fiji groups are called collectively (see Chapter 10).

One channel of migration pointed northward to the islands of Hawaii. The first Polynesians reached these previously uninhabited islands before the 7th century, traveling in great war canoes. From the 7th century until about 1300 or 1400, recurrent contacts remained between the Hawaiian islands and the larger Society Islands group, allowing periodic new migration. From about 1400 until the arrival of European explorers in 1778, Hawaiian society was cut off even from Polynesia.

Polynesians in Hawaii spread widely across the islands, in agricultural clusters and fishing villages amid the volcanic mountains. Hawaiians proved inventive in using local vegetation for construction purposes, weaving fabrics as well as making materials and fishing nets from grass. They also imported pigs from the Society Islands—a vital source of meat, though a source of devastation to many plant species unique to Hawaii. Politically, Hawaii was organized into regional kingdoms, which were highly warlike. Society was structured into a caste system with priests and nobles at the top, who reserved many lands for their exclusive use. Commoners were viewed almost as a separate people, barred from certain activities.

Thus, with a Neolithic technology, the Hawaiians created a complex culture on their islands. Lacking a written language, their legends and oral histories, tracing the genealogies of chiefly families back to the original war canoes, were remarkable achievements that formed and preserved their culture.

Isolated Achievements by the Maoris

A second direction of Polynesian migration aimed thousands of miles to the southwest of the Society Islands, perhaps as early as the 8th century, when canoe or raft crews discovered the two large islands that today make up New Zealand. The original numbers of people were small but were supplemented over the following centuries by additional migrations from the Polynesian home islands.

The Polynesians in New Zealand, called Maoris, successfully adapted to an environment considerably colder and harsher than the home islands. They developed the most elaborate of all Polynesian art and produced an expanding population that may have reached 200,000 people by the 18th century, primarily on the northern of the two islands. As in Hawaii, tribal military leaders and priests held great power in Maori society; each tribe also included a group of slaves drawn from prisoners of war and their descendants.

Overall, Polynesian society not only spread but developed increasing complexity in the centuries of the postclassical era. Maoris and others produced a rich oral tradition in which fascinating legends combined with an emphasis on oratorical skill. Woodworking and decoration advanced steadily. The Polynesians did not work metals, but they produced a vigorous economy by combining imported crops and animals with vegetation native to the new settlements. All these achievements, however, were accomplished in isolation—total isolation from the rest of the world and, particularly after 1400, substantial isolation of each major island grouping from the rest of the Polynesian complex. Polynesians were the last of the major isolated cultures to encounter larger world currents brought forcefully by European explorers in the 18th century. When this encounter did come, it produced the same effects that had burdened the Americas: vulnerability to disease, weakness in the face of superior weaponry and technology, and considerable cultural disintegration.

CONCLUSION

Adding Up the Changes

The decades that clustered around the year 1400 clearly constituted a time of transition in world history as well as in the development of many individual civilizations. Shifts in international trade leadership, a rebalancing of power and dynamism, and the impact of spreading technologies all worked to change not just particular societies but the world framework as well.

As a time of transition, the 15th century may be loosely compared with the later 20th century. In each case, a growing series of international contacts, capped by a century of far-flung empires, yielded to a time of rebalancing. The predominant powers of the previous period—the Arabs, and now the West—were challenged by new and more dynamic upstarts. Major changes and dislocations occurred within the rising societies as they prepared, partly unwittingly and partly quite consciously, for unfamiliar world roles. Ordinary people in many parts of the world suffered from new hardships as a result of devastating plagues or wars. At the same time, previous international contacts helped spread technological innovations initially developed by older centers.

The world history framework that began to take shape after 1400 constituted the most important alteration since the fall of the classical empires almost a thousand years before, and it was to last in broad outline until close to our own time.

FURTHER READINGS

On the world network, see Jerry Bentley, *Old World Encounters: Cross Cultural Contacts and Exchanges in Pre-Modern Times* (1993).

Crucial changes in the Middle East are covered in F. Babinger's *Mehmed the Conqueror and His Times*

(1978) on the Ottoman leader who captured Constantinople, and Bernard Lewis's *The Arabs in History* (4th ed., 1958), which offers a brisk interpretation of Arab decline. See also H. Islamoglu-Inan, ed., *The Ottoman Empire and the World Economy* (1987). On China under the early Ming dynasty, see Charles O. Hucker's *The Ming Dynasty: Its Origins and Evolving Institutions* (1978).

An important, highly readable interpretation of the West's rise in a world context is C. Cipolla's *Guns, Sails and Empires: Technological Innovation and the Early Phases of European Expansion, 1400–1700* (1985). See also J. H. Parry's *Age of Reconnaissance* (1963) and *The Discovery of the Sea* (1981). An important interpretation of new Western interests is S. W. Mintz's *Sweetness and Power: The Place of Sugar in Modern History* (1985).

On the Black Death and economic dislocation, see M. W. Dols's *The Black Death in the Middle East* (1977), W. H. McNeill's *Plagues and Peoples* (1976), and the very readable B. Tuchman's *A Distant Mirror: The Calamitous 14th Century* (1979). A provocative study of relevant Western outlook is P. Ariès's *The Hour of Our Death* (1981).

J. Huizinga's *The Waning of the Middle Ages* (1973) deals with the decline of medieval forms in Europe. The early Renaissance is treated in D. Hay's *The Italian Renaissance* (1977); for more cultural emphasis, see C. Trinkhaus's *The Scope of Renaissance Humanism* (1983). On Spain, see F. Braudel's *The Mediterranean and the Mediterranean World* (2 vols. 1978) and R. Altimira's *A History of Spain* (1949).

An excellent overview of the period is Janet L. Abu-Lughod's *Before European Hegemony: The World System A.D. 1250–1350* (1989).

1434–1498 Portuguese expeditions down West African coast

1390 Ming restrictions on overseas trade

1492 Columbus expeditions

1368 Ming dynasty in China

1480 Moscow region free of Mongol control

1281 Founding of Ottoman dynasty

1405–1433 Chinese expedition period

1350s Ottoman invasion of southeastern Europe

1453 Ottoman conquest of Constantinople

1441 Beginning of European slave trade in Africa

1300 C.E.   **1400** C.E.

Many developments highlighted world history between 1450 and 1750, marking a major new period—the early modern period—in the global experience. As in most new world history periods, the balance of power between major civilizations shifted; the West became the most dynamic force worldwide. Largely under Western aegis, contacts among many civilizations intensified; the world became smaller as international trade affected many diverse societies and the speed and range of sailing ships increased. A growth of commerce affected Western Europe and areas under its economic influence, such as Africa; but internal commerce gained in China and Japan as well. Finally, based mainly on new weaponry, particularly gunpowder, new or revamped empires formed important regional political units in many parts of the world—a set of developments especially significant in Asia. The West built a new colonial empire in various parts of the world, using its new maritime muscle combined with naval gunnery. Land-based empires emerged in Russia, now a rapidly rising power; under the Ottoman Turks, in the Middle East, southwestern Europe, and to an extent North Africa; as well as in India, Persia, and China, where this was already a familiar pattern. Gunpowder empires showed new capacities for political integration of substantial territories and cut into traditionally independent areas, notably in central Asia.

The rise of the West, the intensification of international contacts on literally a global scale, the growth of trade, and the formation of new empires marked off the early modern centuries from the previous postclassical period in world history. Many of these developments depended in part on the growing impact of gunpowder. The period was launched during the 15th century, when Western countries, headed by Portugal and Spain, began new explorations and soon new colonization efforts around Africa to Asia and to the Americas. It was launched also by the formation of the powerful new Ottoman Empire in the Middle East and the emergence of Russia from two centuries of Mongol control.

ON THE EVE OF THE EARLY MODERN PERIOD: THE WORLD AROUND 1450

Important new or expanded civilization areas had developed in the postclassical period, in contact with the leading centers. Russia was one, as a Russian monarchy formed. Western Europe, slowly recovering from the 5th-century collapse of the Roman Empire, failed to gain political unity. West Europeans built important regional kingdoms while expanding the role of commerce and city life and establishing an elaborate artistic and philosophical culture around Catholic Christianity. In sub-Saharan Africa, another set of regional kingdoms formed, though vital areas there were organized more

---

1500–1600 Europe's commercial revolution

1519–1521 Magellan circumnavigates globe

1522 Russia begins expansion in central Asia and western Siberia

1509 Spanish colonies on American mainland

1498–1499 Vasco da Gama expedition opens seas to Asia

1570 Portuguese colony of Angola (Africa)

1520–1566 Suleiman the Magnificent (Ottoman)

1510–1511 Portugal conquers Goa (India), Malacca (Malaysia)

1526 Babur conquest in northern India (Mughal)

1501–1510 Safavid conquest of Iran

1517–1541 Protestant Reformation (Europe)

1590 Hideyoshi unifies Japan

1548 Portuguese government in Brazil

1533 Pizarro wins Peru

1519–1524 Cortes conquers Mexico

1591 Fall of Songhay (Africa)

1571 Ottoman naval defeat at Lepanto

1600–1690 Scientific revolution (Europe)

1603 Tokugawa shogunate

1608 First French North American colonies

1637 Russian pioneers to Pacific

1600 Dutch and British merchants begin activity in India

1607 First British colonies in North America

1644 Qing dynasty, China

1642–1727 Isaac Newton

1641 Dutch colonies in Indonesia

1640s Japan isolation

1500 C.E.   **1550** C.E.   **1600** C.E.   CONTINUED

loosely; African trade and artistic expression gained ground steadily. Areas in contact with China, finally, built increasingly elaborate societies. Japan, like Western Europe, emphasized a rather decentralized, militaristic feudal system in politics, but it copied many aspects of Chinese culture and some social principles, including a more patriarchal approach to the status of women.

A third area of the world featured civilizations or elaborate cultures developing in isolation from any international contacts. This was true of parts of sub-Saharan Africa, of the expanding Polynesian zone in the Pacific Islands, and of the brilliant, populous civilizations of the Americas, focused in Central America, under the Aztecs, and in the Andes, which by the 15th century were under the vast Inca realm.

The structure of the postclassical world began to shift between the 13th and 15th centuries, setting the stage for the new world history period. The isolated civilizations were not affected by these changes, precisely because they were isolated; they continued to follow their own dynamic, which culminated in the great Aztec and Inca empires, both of which were showing signs of strain and overextension by the later 15th century. In Asia, Africa, and Europe, the key development was the decline of Arab political power and cultural dynamism. Islam continued to expand, but its political and commercial units fragmented. At the same time, a new round of invasions from central Asia, under the Mongols, attacked China, the Middle East, and eastern Europe, disrupting established political boundaries and allowing new contacts between Asia and Europe.

By 1400 the Mongol threat was receding, though only slowly in Russia. A new empire emerged in China. The Arab caliphate had perished, but a new Islamic political force, under the Ottoman Turks, was taking shape, unifying much of the Middle East and poised to destroy the venerable Byzantine Empire. Utilizing their growing commercial vigor, but also terrified by the emergence of a new Islamic power, west Europeans cast about for ways to gain greater control over their international trade, while possibly winning new areas for the Christian faith and new territories for the competing regional kingdoms. China briefly experimented with a dominant international role early in the 15th century, sending out a series of mighty trading expeditions across the Indian Ocean, but then it pulled back and decided to concentrate on its traditions of internal political, cultural, and commercial development. This, as it turned out, left the way open for the West European probes, as Western leaders benefited from technologies newly learned from China and Islam—such as the compass and explosive powder—while adding important innovations such as guns and faster ocean-going ships.

1689–1725 Peter the Great (Russia)

1652 Dutch colony in South Africa

1682–1699 Turks driven from Hungary

1722 Fall of Safavid dynasty (Iran)

1658–1707 Aurangzeb reign, beginning of Mughal decline

1713 New Bourbon dynasty, Spain

1759–1788 Reforms of Latin American colonial administration

1792 Slave uprising in Haiti

1763 Britain acquires "New France"

1772–1795 Partition of Poland

1775–1783 American Revolution

1764 British East India Company controls Bengal (India)

1781 Indian revolts in New Granada and Peru (Latin America)

1756–1763 Seven Years' War

1770s European-Bantu conflicts in southern A

| 1650 C.E. | 1700 C.E. | 1750 C.E. |

THE RISE OF THE WEST

Between 1450 and 1750 the West, headed initially by Spain and Portugal and then by Britain, France, and Holland, gained control of the key international trade routes. It established colonies in the Americas and, on a much more limited basis, in Africa and parts of Asia.

At the same time, partly because of its new international position and the growing impact of commerce, the West itself changed rapidly, becoming an increasingly unusual kind of agricultural civilization. Commerce began to alter the social structure and also affected basic attitudes toward family life and the natural environment. A host of new ideas, some of them springing from religious reformers, created a novel cultural climate in which scientific principles increasingly held pride of place. The scientific revolution gradually reshaped Western culture as a whole. More effective political structures emerged by the 17th century, as Western monarchs began to introduce bureaucratic principles similar to those pioneered long before in China.

A vital facet of the early modern period, then, consisted of the West's expansion as an international force and its simultaneous internal transformation. Like the previous world-class civilization, Arab Islam, the West developed a diverse and dynamic culture and society, which was both a result and a cause of its ascending international position.

THE WORLD ECONOMY AND GLOBAL CONTACTS

Because of initiatives from the West, the world network set up in the previous period intensified and took on new dimensions. The change involved more than the fact that the Europeans, not the Muslims, dominated international trade. It involved an expansion of the world network to literally global proportions, well beyond the geographical scope of previous linkages. Far more of Africa, and above all the Americas, were brought into contact with other cultures and included in international exchanges for the first time. At the end of the period, in the 18th century, Polynesian and Australian societies began to undergo the same painful integrating experience.

Effectively, by 1750 there were no more fully isolated societies of any great size. The new globalism of human contacts had a host of vital consequences that ran through early modern centuries. The human disease pool became fully international for the first time, and peoples who had previously been isolated from most of the rest of the world suffered immensely from their exposure to diseases for which they had developed no immunities. The global network also permitted a massive exchange of plants and animals. Cows and horses were introduced to the Americas, prompting substantial changes in American Indian habits in economy and warfare alike. American food crops were spread around the world, bringing sweet potatoes, corn, and manioc to China, corn to Africa, potatoes and tobacco to Europe—innovations that in many places prompted great changes in agricultural production. One result through most of the world, beginning in Asia as well as western Europe, was a rapid population expansion that quickly attained unprecedented levels.

Even globalization, though its impact was vast, did not exhaust the changes wrought in the world network during the three centuries after 1450. A set of definite and highly unequal relationships was established among many civilizations. During the postclassical millennium, 450–1450 C.E., a few areas had contributed relatively inexpensive raw materials (including labor power in the form of slaves) to more advanced societies, notably China and the Islamic world; this was true for the West and parts of Africa and Southeast Asia. Though economic relationships in these instances were unequal, they did not constrain the raw-materials-producing societies too severely, because international trade was simply not yet of overriding importance. After 1450 or 1500, as Western commerce expanded internationally, the West began to set up relationships with a number of areas that produced pronounced dependence and subordination in the international economy. Areas such as Latin America depended heavily on sales to export merchants, on imports of processed goods, and on Western ships and merchants to handle international trade. Dependence of this sort might have political ramifications in creating weak governments open to foreign intervention; it certainly affected labor relations by encouraging commercial exploitation of slaves and serfs, and it even tied in with cultural impositions from the West on some of the dependent areas. It is vital to stress that much of the world, particularly in the great Asian civilizations, remained outside this set of relationships, but there was a growing tendency to draw closer toward it, as occurred in India and much of Indonesia by the 18th century, as the level of Western overseas expansion increased steadily. The establishment of a new set of international economic relationships, based on Western preeminence, is discussed explicitly in Chapter 23, but it undergirds analysis of many individual civilizations as well.

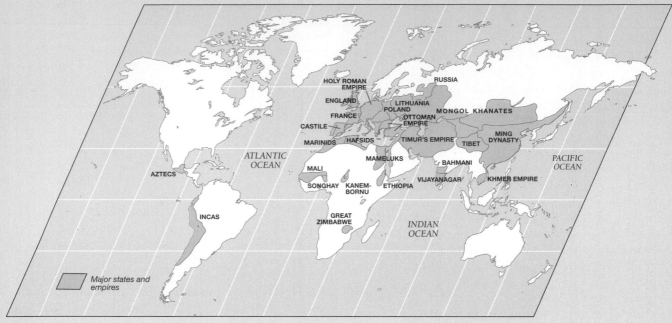

World Boundaries, c. 1453

ANALYSIS

Maps

The period of 1450–1750 saw an unusual number of boundary changes in world history. The spread of Western colonies was the most obvious development, but the establishment or extension of a number of large land-based empires was almost as significant. Compare the two maps by tracing the areas of Western penetration. You will see the different forms this penetration took in different parts of the world. Note also what parts of the world offered particular opportunities for rivalries among the leading Western colonial powers, and what parts were particularly immune to Western expansion of any major sort.

Look also to the land-based empires. What empires were particularly new as they took shape between the 15th and 18th centuries? What parts of the world had the most stable boundaries during these centuries? Why?

Of the boundary changes you can trace during this three-century period, which changes seem particularly important for the world today? What parts of the world look very different today, in terms of the boundaries of major political units, from the form they had achieved by the 18th century?

THE GUNPOWDER EMPIRES

The rise of Western Europe and its growing dominance of world trade did not command all the major themes of early modern world history. The centuries after 1450 could also be designated "the age of the gunpowder empires." The development of cannons and muskets in the 15th and 16th centuries, through the combination of Western technology with previous Chinese invention, obviously spurred the West's expansion. Ship-based artillery was fundamental to the West's mastery of international sea lanes and many ports and islands. But gunnery was picked up by other societies as well. The Ottoman Turks used Hungarian-built cannons in their successful siege of Constantinople in 1453. The subsequent Ottoman Empire relied heavily on land-based guns to supplement trained cavalry. The rise of a new Russian Empire after 1480 also built on the growing use of guns, and the Russian economy was subsequently reshaped to provide the manufacturing basis for the new military hardware. Three other key empires—the Mughal in India, the Safavid in Persia, and the 17th-century Manchu dynasty in China—relied on the new strength of gun-supported land armies. Guns also played a role in Japanese and African history during the period.

Guns supported not only Western colonial empires but also new land agglomerations through much of Asia

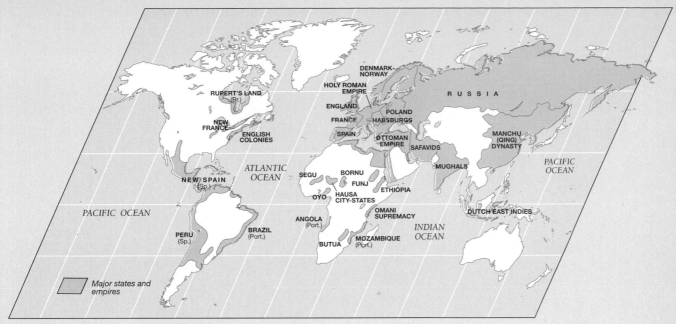

World Boundaries, c. 1700. Compare with the 1453 map. What were the main changes? What areas were most stable? Why did Western colonies spread in some parts of the world and not in others?

and eastern Europe and, to some extent, in Africa. Here were developments largely independent of Western influence, save for some of the initial technologies, and they counterbalanced the growth of Western power to a considerable degree. The rise of the Russian Empire ran through the whole period, and while not as important as the rise of the West it was certainly a vital theme, involving among other things the progressive elimination of an independent central Asia. The rise of the Ottomans, Safavids, and Mughals was a bit shorter-lived but echoed through the first two centuries of the period and, in the case of the Ottomans, created one of the most durable empires known in world history.

COMMERCE AND ITS OUTREACH

One final development deserves note: This was also an age of world commercialization. Market exchange played an increasing role in shaping economic activity. The world remained predominantly agricultural, but agriculture was now modified more than ever by specializations that depended on market transactions as well as by the activities of merchants and the lure of money. Heightened commercial activity was one of the

means by which rising populations could be sustained in advance of major technological change in the means of production. Commerce not only spread knowledge of new foodstuffs but also allowed increased specialization in production that could heighten output, as some regions concentrated on goods they were best suited to grow or manufacture and relied on trade for other materials.

The intensification of international trade, under the sponsorship of Western traders but also involving merchants in other societies, played an important part in the general expansion of commerce. Not only did many Latin Americans produce precious metals and agricultural products for sale to the West; many more Latin Americans produced foods and clothes to sell to workers in the export sectors. Internal trade increased within Latin America, particularly by the 18th century. International trade activities prompted increasing numbers of Westerners, as well, to engage in market activities, at home as well as abroad. Similar patterns emerged in West Africa. Earlier international trade routes, oriented toward North Africa, were diverted to a new Atlantic commerce organized by European merchants. African kings and merchants organized goods to sell in this trade, particularly slaves, and received manufactured

The gun was introduced into Japan in 1542 through the Portuguese. By 1562, 10,000 Japanese soldiers carried muskets. The scenes depicted here are from a military manual written by one of the greatest generals of the period, Nobunaga.

products, including guns, in exchange. Again the West was encouraged in its own commercial expansion, as considerable profits could be realized in the slave trade. The Americas were transformed through the introduction of new African populations and a new kind of slavery, and Africa itself was diversely affected by the new exchange.

The spread of commerce went beyond these Western-dominated transactions, however. Both China and Japan witnessed the rapid growth of market exchanges within their own boundaries, as production and sale of foodstuffs, beverages, and the like expanded. A general trend—the Western-dominated international economy and its growth—was thus supplemented by some parallelisms in some other parts of the world, where internal trade far outweighed international exchange. And this meant not only a surprisingly widespread commercial and urban surge but also some broader effects in terms of culture and society. In most cases without toppling the land-based aristocracy, merchants in several societies, not just the West, gained new influence. Growing trade also played a role in some societies (in the West but also, for instance, in Japan) in en-

couraging some groups to reduce their commitment to religion and otherworldly goals in favor of a focus on secular pursuits. The expansion of commerce, in other words, though not producing a uniform new version of an agricultural economy or society, had wider potential reverberations in many parts of the world.

EVOLUTION OF THE EARLY MODERN PERIOD: CIVILIZATIONS AND LARGER TRENDS

As in earlier world history epochs, many developments during these early modern centuries occurred within individual civilizations, with little or no relationship to more general world trends. Only the Americas came close to being overwhelmed by outside influences. Many of the following chapters, correspondingly, will focus on particular societies.

Nevertheless, the impact of the four international trends—Western expansion, intensification and globalization of the world network, the military and political results of gunpowder, and the spread of commerce—affected patterns in the separate societies in many ways, for the force of international trends was growing. These four trends generate the central questions to be addressed to each major civilization, to see how it fit the larger world picture. Response to the key trends ranged from eager embrace of new international currents, to self-conscious isolation, to forced compliance. A new set of diversities described major societies precisely because of the heightened potency of real or potential international contacts.

By 1700 the West's activities were looming larger, not just in key areas such as the Americas, the Asian island groups, and the coast of West Africa, but in Asia and eastern Europe as well. A new Russian urge to selectively copy aspects of the West, and the establishment of growing British control in parts of India, expressed two facets of this shift. Even Japan, which had responded to the new world economy by effective isolation, began to show modest new openness, rescinding a ban on translating Western books.

With all the advantages historians have of knowing how their stories turn out, it is fair to note that by 1750, civilizations that were not in a position to react effectively to the West's new world role were verging on decline—whereas a mere century before, this would have been a considerable distortion of a more complex international balance. After 1750, in large part because of another major transformation within the West—the emergence of a revolutionary industrial economy—the theme of Western predominance took on new meaning, which is why the periodization of world history breaks at this point once again.

The chapters in this unit focus first on changes within the West and the emergence of Western colonies and Western-dominated world trade. Then, two chapters deal with two societies that had particular links with the West—Russia, whose expansion was such an important theme in its own right, and a new kind of emerging civilization in Latin America. The final group of chapters deals with major societies in Asia and Africa, where contacts with the West and the new world economy were significant, particularly as the early modern period wore on, but where separate patterns of activity remained vital.

22

The Transformation of the West, 1450–1750

1450–1600 Northern Renaissance

1490s France and Spain invade Italian city–states; beginning of Italian decline

1541–1564 Calvin in Geneva

1475–1514 Michelangelo

1515–1547 Francis I of France

1517 Luther's 95 theses; beginning of Protestant Reformation

1300–1450 Italian Renaissance

1469–1527 Machiavelli

1534 Beginning of Church of England

1452–1519 Leonardo da Vinci

1455 First European printing press in Mainz, Germany

1500–1600 "Commercial revolution"

1543 "Copernican revolution"; Copernicus' work on astronomy

1300 C.E.   **1450** C.E.

INTRODUCTION

During the three centuries after 1450, Western civilization—particularly in its core areas such as France, Britain, the Low Countries, and Germany—changed in dramatic ways. Still a largely agricultural society in 1750, the West had become unusually commercially active and had laid out a growing manufacturing sector. Government powers had expanded, and new political ideas and challenges complicated the picture. Beliefs had altered. Science came to form the centerpiece of Western intellectual life for the first time in the history of any society. Popular beliefs, including ideas about personality and family as well as concepts of nature, also had shifted substantially.

In some respects, the West in this period generated capabilities, such as increased bureaucratization in the central state, that other more advanced civilizations had already instituted. But in other areas, such as popular belief and family structure, the West was striking out in new directions. Certainly, Western civilization changed more fundamentally in this period than any of the established societies in Asia, and its innovations prepared further changes—notably, the Industrial Revolution—for the future.

Western Europe in 1450 was politically divided. Regional governments were further decentralized through the powers of the Church and the feudal aristocracy. Its economy, though no longer purely agricultural, lagged well behind those of the other major civilizations in technology and commercial experience. Furthermore, medieval culture had passed its high point. Theology had become less vibrant and more wrapped up in petty debates over trivial definitions. Population and economy had been weakened by major plagues and an inability to produce enough food to sustain previous population growth. Some of these weaknesses, in fact, spurred innovation, including new efforts, through voyages of exploration, to find ways to overcome the West's inferiority in world trade.

Even before 1450, Western culture and the Western economy had been changing. Initially, change focused on Italy and Spain, the former being the leader in cultural innovation, the latter spearheading Europe's overseas expansion along with Portugal. Increasingly, after 1450, change became more general through Western society, and the center of activity shifted northward to France, Britain, and the surrounding areas. Finally, changes within Europe constantly interacted with overseas expansion and the fruits of European dominance of international trade. Europe's steady evolution resulted from its new world power and furthered this power in turn.

Not surprisingly, internal changes in Europe unfolded in somewhat untidy stages. Between 1450 and 1650, a series of cultural shifts hold center stage along with the rise in trade. Thereafter, the scientific revolu-

---

1642–1727 Newton

17th century Scientific Revolution

1730–1850 European population boom

1643–1715 Louis XIV in France; absolute monarchy

18th century Enlightenment

1609 Independence of Netherlands

1776 Adam Smith's *Wealth of Nations*

1688–1690 Glorious Revolution in Britain; parliamentary monarchy; some religious toleration; political writing of John Locke

1555–1603 Elizabeth I, England

1780–1790 Joseph II, Austria and Hungary

1588 Defeat of Spanish Armada by English

1733 James Kay invents flying shuttle loom

1550–1649 Religious wars in France, Germany, and Britain

1670–1692 Decline of witchcraft trials

1736 Beginnings of Methodism

1642–1649 English civil wars

1792 Mary Wollstonecraft's *Vindication of the Rights of Women*

1712–1786 Frederick the Great of Prussia; enlightened despotism

1682–1699 Hapsburgs drive Turks from Hungary

1564–1642 Galileo

1647–1648 Culmination of popular rebellion

1618–1648 Thirty Years' War

1756–1763 Seven Years' War: France, Britain, Prussia, and Austria

1600 C.E.

1750 C.E.

tion and the growth of new political forms introduced additional changes, which were amplified in the 18th-century Enlightenment.

THE FIRST BIG CHANGES: CULTURE AND COMMERCE

Focal Point: During the 15th century Europe began to assume a new role in world trade (see Chapter 23). Internally, the Renaissance emphasized new styles and beliefs. This was followed by even more sweeping cultural and political change in the 16th century, with the Protestant Reformation and the Catholic response to it. A new commercial and social structure grew up as well, creating new opportunities and intense new grievances alike.

The Italian Renaissance

The process of moving away from earlier patterns began with the Renaissance, which first developed in Italy during the 14th and 15th centuries. The significance of this "rebirth" should not be exaggerated; more fundamental changes came later and somewhat separately. But the Renaissance did challenge medieval intellectual values and styles. It suggested a certain amount of political innovation and built on a more commercialized economy. The Renaissance also sketched a new, brasher spirit that may have helped create a new Western interest in exploring strange waters or urging that old truths be reexamined.

Italy was already well launched in the development of Renaissance culture by the 15th century, based on its unusually extensive urban, commercial economy and its competitive city-state politics. Writers such as Petrarch and Boccaccio had trumpeted classical literary canons against medieval logic and theology, writing in Italian as well as the traditional Latin and emphasizing secular subjects such as love and pride. Painting turned to new realism and a host of classical and human-centered themes. Religion declined as a central focus.

The Italian Renaissance blossomed further in the 15th century. This was a great age of Western art, as Leonardo da Vinci advanced the realistic portrayal of the human body and Michelangelo applied classical styles in both painting and sculpture. In political theory, *Niccolo Machiavelli* emphasized realistic discussions of how to seize and maintain power; his work *The Prince* resembled earlier Chinese legalism in urging that rulers do what they must do, without scruple, in order to control undisciplined subjects. Like the artists, Machiavelli bol-

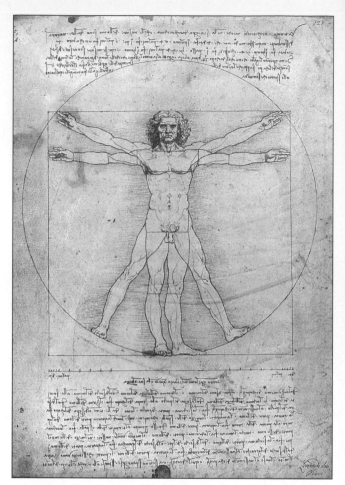

Anatomical sketches by Leonardo da Vinci. Later Renaissance art sometimes turned to science as part of a concern for realism in portraying the human body.

stered his realism with abundant use of Greek and Roman examples. In history, scholars portrayed a past unencumbered by divine intervention and they established new critical standards that could be used to disprove traditional Church claims.

Overall, Italian Renaissance culture stressed themes of *humanism*: A focus on humankind as the center of intellectual and artistic endeavor. Religion was not attacked, but its principles were no longer predominant. Humanists clearly touted the superiority of classical forms over medieval styles. As individuals they could proclaim a pride in their own achievements, which implied an ability of talented people to progress—to advance on the basis of human effort alone.

These Renaissance themes had some bearing on politics and commerce. Renaissance merchants improved their banking techniques and became more unabashedly capitalist in their profit-seeking than their medieval counterparts had been. City-state leaders experimented with new political forms and functions. They justified their rule not on the basis of heredity or divine guidance but more on the basis of what they could do to advance general well-being. Thus, they sponsored cultural activities and tried to improve the administration of the economy. They also developed more professional armies, for wars among the city-states were common, and gave new attention to military tactics and training. They also rethought the practice of diplomacy, introducing the regular exchange of ambassadors for the first time in the West. Clearly, the Renaissance encouraged innovation, though it could also produce some slavish dependence on classical models.

The Renaissance Moves Northward

Italy began to decline as a Renaissance center by about 1500. French and Spanish monarchs invaded the peninsula, cutting down on political independence. At the same time, new Atlantic trade routes reduced the importance of Mediterranean ports—a huge blow to the Italian economy.

As Renaissance creativity faded in its Italian birthplace it passed northward. The *Northern Renaissance*—focused in France, the Low Countries, Germany, and England—opened up after 1450. Renaissance styles also affected Hungary and Poland in east central Europe. Classical styles in art and architecture became the rage. Knowledge of Greek and Latin literature gained ground, though most northern humanists wrote in their vernacular languages. Northern humanists were more religious than their Italian counterparts, trying to blend secular interests with continued Christian devotion. Renaissance writers such as Shakespeare in England, or Rabelais in France, also mixed classical themes with an earthiness—a joy in bodily functions and human passions—that maintained elements of medieval popular culture. Renaissance literature established a new set of classics for literary traditions in the major Western languages: Shakespeare in England, Cervantes in Spain, and so on.

The Northern Renaissance produced some political change. Renaissance kings increased their pomp and ceremony. Kings such as *Francis I* in France became patrons of the arts, even importing Italian sculptors and architects for their classical-style palaces, as these in turn replaced fortified castles. Many Renaissance monarchs tried to impose new controls over the Catholic church, and they also developed some new functions in the areas of economy and welfare. Many monarchs, by the late 16th century, were sponsoring trading companies and colonial enterprises. Interest in military conquest became more blatant than in the Middle Ages. Francis I was even willing to ally in principle with the Ottoman sultan, the key Muslim leader. His goal was to distract his main enemy, the Habsburg ruler of Austria and Spain. In fact, the alliance was an alliance in name only, but it illustrated how power politics was beginning to emerge without some of the feudal or religious justifications that had previously clothed it in the West.

Through most of the West, the Renaissance signaled some vital changes in cultural life. The classical styles favored by Renaissance leaders long prevailed over the medieval Gothic. Upper-class education changed, becoming defined in terms of classical precepts—such as Cicero's advice on moderate morals and devotion to the public good—and literary study, as well as an appropriate dose of Christian morality. Elements of this education would continue to describe the experience of upper-class Westerners into the 20th century. A Renaissance spirit of individual excellence and defiance of tradition influenced other facets of life in the West, including new scientific endeavors.

Yet, the impact of the Renaissance should not be overstated, particularly outside Italy. Renaissance kings had new ceremonies, but they were still confined by the political powers of feudal landlords. A really new political form had yet to emerge. Ordinary people were little touched by Renaissance values; the life of most peasants and artisans went on much as before. Economic life, too, was little altered, particularly outside the Italian commercial centers. Rural people were sometimes pressed for new taxes to support cities and kings. Women, even in the upper classes, sometimes encountered new limits as Renaissance leaders touted men's public bravado over women's domestic roles.

The Commercial Economy and a New Family Pattern

More fundamental changes were brewing in Western society by 1500, beneath the glittering surface of the Renaissance. Spurred by trading contacts with Asia, workers in the West improved the quality of pulleys and pumps in mines and learned how to forge stronger iron products. Printing was introduced in the 15th century when the German *Johannes Gutenberg* introduced movable type, building on Chinese printing technology. Soon books were distributed in new quantities in the West, which helped expand the audience for Renaissance

Western Europe During the Renaissance and Reformation

writers but particularly served to disseminate religious ideas. Literacy began to gain ground and became a fertile source of new kinds of thinking. Technology clearly was poised to spur a variety of changes.

Family structure was also changing. A European-style family pattern came into being by the 15th century. It involved, for ordinary people, a relatively late marriage age and a primary emphasis on nuclear families of parents and children, rather than the extended families characteristic of most agricultural civilizations. These changes emphasized the importance of husband-wife relations. They also linked the family to individual property holdings with new intensity, for most people could not marry until they had appropriate access to property. Late marriage also provided a certain amount of birth control, which prevented vast overcrowding even as economic activity began to speed up again in the West. By the 16th century, most ordinary Europeans did not marry until they were 26 or 27—late by the standards of most societies. Newly formed families were largely independent of older parents, however, which could encourage some sense of division between family and community.

Winds of change were blowing from several directions by the early 16th century. New family habits unseated traditions at one level; new cultural interests challenged them at another. Both elites and ordinary people generated innovation, though in somewhat different manners. It was in the 16th century, however, with religious upheaval and a new commercial surge, that the directions of change began to be more fully defined.

The Protestant and Catholic Reformations

In 1517, a German monk named *Martin Luther* nailed a document containing 95 *theses*, or propositions, to the door of the castle church in Wittenberg. He was specifically protesting claims made by a papal representative in selling *indulgences*, or grants of salvation, for money, but in fact his protest went deeper. Luther's reading of the

Bible convinced him that only faith could gain salvation. Pious actions or Church sacraments were not the path, for God could not be manipulated. Luther's protest, which was rebuffed by the papacy, soon led him to challenge many Catholic beliefs, including the authority of the pope himself. Luther would soon argue that monasticism was wrong, that priests should marry (as he did), and that the Bible should be translated from Latin so ordinary people might have direct access to the teachings of the faith. Luther did not want to break Christian unity, but the church he wanted should be on his terms (or, as he would have argued, the terms of the true faith).

Disputes and heresies were not new in Western Christianity, but always before then, the Catholic church had ultimately managed to contain them. The Renaissance papacy, however, was not interested in compromise and tried to force Luther to back down. At the same time Luther picked up wide support for his views during the middle decades of the 16th century and beyond. Many Germans in something of a nationalist reaction, resented the authority and taxes of the Roman pope. German princes saw an opportunity to gain more power, for their nominal leader, the holy Roman emperor, remained Catholic. Princes who turned Protestant could increase their independence; they also had an excuse to seize Church lands. The Lutheran version of *Protestantism* (as the general wave of religious dissent was called) urged state control of the church as an alternative to papal authority, and this had obvious political appeal.

There were reasons for ordinary people to shift their allegiance as well. Some German peasants saw Luther's attack on authority as a sanction for their own social rebellion against landlords, though Luther specifically renounced this reading. Some townspeople were drawn to Luther's approval of work in the world; since faith gained salvation, Lutheranism could sanction money-making and other earthly pursuits more wholeheartedly than did traditional Catholicism.

Once Christian unity was breached, other Protestant groups sprang forward. In England, Henry VIII set up an *Anglican church*, initially to challenge papal attempts to enforce his first marriage, which had failed to produce a male heir. (Henry would ultimately have six wives in sequence, executing two of them.) Henry was also attracted to some of the new doctrines, and his most durable successor, his daughter Elizabeth I, was Protestant outright. The Anglican church became increasingly, though broadly, Protestant in doctrine as well as in a separate form of church government. Still more important were the churches inspired by *Jean Calvin*, a Frenchman who set his base in the Swiss city of Geneva. Calvinism insisted on God's *predestination*, or prior determination, of those who would be saved. Nothing humans could do, and certainly no sacraments, could win God's favor. At the same time, those elected to God's grace had the obligation to encourage others to behave morally and to gain knowledge of the Bible. Calvinist ministers became moral guardians and preachers of God's Word. Calvinists sought the participation of all believers in local church administration, which had political implications in encouraging the idea of a wider access to government. They also promoted broader popular education so that more people could read the Bible. Calvinism was accepted not only in part of Switzerland but also in portions of Germany, in France (where it produced strong minority groups), in the Netherlands, in Hungary, and in England and Scotland. By the early 17th century, Puritan exiles brought it to North America.

The Catholic church did not sit still under Protestant attack. It did not restore religious unity, but it defended southern Europe, Austria, Poland, much of Hungary, and key parts of Germany for the Catholic faith. Under a *Catholic Reformation*, Church councils revived Catholic doctrine and refuted key Protestant tenets such as the idea that priests had no special sacramental power and could marry. They also attacked popular superstitions and remnants of magical belief, which meant that Catholics and Protestants alike were trying to find new ways to shape the outlook of ordinary folk. A new religious order, the *Jesuits*, became active in politics, education, and missionary work, regaining some parts of Europe for the Church. Jesuit fervor would also sponsor Catholic missionary activity in Asia and the Americas.

The End of Christian Unity in the West

The Protestant and Catholic Reformations had several results within Europe during the later 16th and early 17th centuries. Most obvious was an important series of religious wars. France was a scene of bitter battles between Calvinist and Catholic forces, intertwined with new rebellions by landed nobles against royal authority. These disputes ended only with the granting of tolerance to Protestants through *the edict of Nantes* in 1598—though in the next century, French kings progressively cut back on Protestant rights. Wars raged recurrently in Germany, punctuated by efforts to agree on which states could be Protestant, which Catholic. In 1618, the *Thirty Years' War* broke out, pitting German Protestants and allies such as Lutheran Sweden against the holy Roman emperor, backed by Spain. The war was so devastating that it reduced German power and prosperity for a full century, cutting population by as much as 60 percent in some regions. It was ended only by the 1648 *Treaty of Westphalia*, which agreed to the territorial tolerance concept: some princely states and cities chose one religion, some another. The treaty also reduced Spain's power, after decades during which Spanish armies had been the most powerful in Europe, in favor of France, which had backed the Protestant side. This treaty also finally settled a rebellion of the Protestant Netherlands against Spain, giving the former its full independence.

Religious fighting, finally, punctuated British history, first before the reign of Elizabeth in the 16th century, then in the *English Civil War* in the 1640s. Here too, religious issues conjoined with other problems, particularly in a battle between the claims of parliament to rights of control over royal actions and some rather tactless assertions of authority by a new line of English kings. The fighting of the civil war ended in 1660 (well after King Charles I had been beheaded), but full resolution came only in 1688 to 1689, when limited religious toleration was granted to most Protestant (but not Catholic) faiths.

Religious issues thus dominated European politics for almost a century. The religious wars led generally to a grudging and limited acceptance of the idea of religious pluralism: Christian unity could not be restored, though in most individual countries (the Netherlands came closest to a full exception), any idea of full religious liberty was still in the future. The religious wars persuaded some people that religion itself was suspect; if there was no dominant single truth, why all the cruelty and carnage? The wars, finally, affected the power balance and political structure of Europe. France, after a period of weakness during its internal strife, was on the upswing. The Netherlands and Britain were galvanized toward a growing international role. Spain, briefly ascendant, fell back. Internally, some kings and princes benefited from the decline of papal authority by taking a stronger role in religious affairs. This was true in many Catholic as well as Protestant domains. In some cases, however, Protestant dissent and Protestant-derived political theory that challenged the idea of one-man rule encouraged popular political movements and enhanced parliamentary power.

The impact of religious change went well beyond politics. The way people thought and acted in daily life

Hans Holbein's "The Dance of Death" was encouraged by the continuing plague as well as religious conflict.

began to shift toward new forms. Popular beliefs changed most in Protestant areas, but Catholic reform produced new impulses as well. Several basic shifts were set in motion. Western people gradually became less likely to see an intimate connection between God and nature. Protestants believed fervently in God's power— and in important ways the role of religion in popular belief gained ground for at least a century—but they did not focus on miracles or other disruptive interventions in nature's course. Protestant churches, as physical structures, were more isolated than their Catholic counterparts from market activities in the cities, and this encouraged the idea that religion and daily life were separate. Many Westerners, in sum, gained a new sense of distinction between religious and other activities and tended to see nature in desacralized terms. This could affect, for example, their approach to health problems, encouraging (very gradually) a greater tendency to turn strictly to secular healers rather than priests or religious practitioners when they were ill.

Religious change also promoted greater concentration on family life. Protestant and Catholic leaders began to talk of the family in more positive terms, not simply as an institution necessary because of human lust. Love between husband and wife was encouraged. As one English writer put it, "When love is absent between husband and wife, it is like a bone out of joint: there is no ease, no order." This promotion of the family had ambiguous implications for women. Protestantism, abolishing religious convents, made marriage more necessary for women than before; there were fewer alternatives for women who could not marry. On the other hand, women's emotional role within the family improved with the new emphasis on affection.

Religious change accompanied and promoted growing literacy along with the spread of the printing press. In the town of Durham, England, around 1570, only 20 percent of all people were literate, but by 1630 the figure had climbed to 47 percent. Growing, though still limited, literacy opened people to additional new ideas and ways of thinking. It may have encouraged a new independence, a new belief in the powers of the individual to seek truth. This in turn promoted the idea of the self as a distinct entity separate from church or community.

Without producing sudden or complete revolution in outlook, religious change obviously stimulated a considerable reorientation of the mental map of many ordinary people in the West. This reorientation followed from the important divisions that opened up in formal religious affiliations and the reduced political power of the Christian churches.

The Commercial Revolution

Concurrently with religious upheaval during the 16th century, the economic structure of the West underwent fundamental redefinition. The level of European trade rose sharply, and many Europeans had new goods available to them. Involvement with markets and merchants increased. At the same time, western Europe's growing role in international trade furthered the role of commerce at home.

A basic spur to greater commercialization was a substantial price inflation that occurred throughout western Europe during the 16th century. The massive import of gold and silver from Spain's new colonies in Latin America forced prices up. New wealth heightened demand for products to sell, both in the colonies and in Europe, but Western production could not keep pace—hence the price inflation. Inflation, in turn, while it hurt groups such as landlords who faced fixed rents, encouraged merchants to take new risks, for borrowing was cheap when money was losing value.

Inflation and the new colonial opportunities led to the formation of great trading companies, often with government backing, in Spain, England, the Netherlands, and France. Governments granted regional monopolies to these giant concerns; thus, the Dutch East Indies Company long dominated trade with the islands of Indonesia. European merchants increasingly pushed out Arab and Indian traders in East Asia and the Indian Ocean. They brought new profits back to Europe and developed new managerial skills and banking arrangements.

Colonial markets and generally increasing trade stimulated manufacturing. Most peasants continued to produce mainly for their own needs, but agricultural specialty areas developed in the production of wines, cheeses, wool, and the like. Some of these favored commercial farming and the use of paid laborers on the land. Shoemaking, pottery, metalworking, and other manufacturing specializations arose in both rural villages and the cities. Technical improvements followed in many branches of manufacture, particularly in metals and mining.

The spread of markets and considerable manufacturing had sweeping effects. Population grew by about 20 percent between 1500 and 1650, reversing a long period of decline. Several large urban centers arose. Prosperity increased for ordinary people as well as for the great merchants. English farmers, for example, enjoyed pewter tableware, more feather beds, and other amenities.

One historian has estimated that by about 1600 the average Western peasant or artisan owned five times as many "things" as his or her counterpart in southeastern Europe. Landowning peasants began to commission painters to decorate cabinets and other furnishings, in a popular art style that spread through western and central Europe. People were aware of the change in material standards at the time. A 16th-century Englishman noted that whereas in the past a peasant and his family slept on the floor, having only a pan or two as kitchenware, by the final decades of the century a farmer might have "a fair garnish of pewter in his cupboard, three or four feather beds, so many coverlets and carpets of tapestry, a silver salt, a bowl for wine. . . . and a dozen spoons." It was about this time that French peasants began to enjoy wine on a fairly regular basis rather than simply at special occasions—the result of higher productivity and better trade and transport facilities.

There were victims of change as well, however. Growing commercialization created the beginnings of a new *proletariat* in the West—people without access to producing property. Population growth and rising food prices hit hard at the poor, and many people had to sell their small plots of land. Some proletarians became manufacturing workers, depending on orders from merchant capitalists to keep their tools busy in their cottages. Others became paid labor on agricultural estates, where landlords were eager for a more manipulable work force to take advantage of sales opportunities in the cities. Others pressed into the cities, and a growing problem of beggars and wandering poor began to affect Western society. A new, tough attitude toward poverty crystallized that has lasted to some extent to the present day. New methods of disciplining elements of the proletariat, including institutional prisons, emerged to counter those features of proletarianization that impacted unfavorably on the rest of society. Governments began to organize some aid to the poor, exercising an important new function.

Commercialization, besides moving European society farther away from older traditions of community solidarity, had other results. Growing prosperity for some groups helped support a more elaborate family life. Better furnishings encouraged people to spend more time at home—at family meals for example—and many women were prompted to become regulators of domestic social routine. More market involvement encouraged greater belief in personal achievement and in the demystification of nature. Economic change, in other words, intertwined with some of the alterations in outlook that were also wrapped up in the religious upheaval.

Finally, the shifts in popular economic and cultural traditions provoked important outcries, for these were fundamental challenges to sanctioned behaviors and values. A huge wave of popular protest in Western Europe developed at the end of the 16th century and extended until about 1650. Peasants and townspeople alike rose in defense of noncommercial economic motives and greater protection from poverty and proletarianization. The risings did not deflect the basic currents of change, but they revealed the massive dislocation involved.

A huge outburst against suspected witches arose in the same decades in various parts of western Europe and also in New England. While attacks on witches had developed before, the new scale reflected intense social and cultural upheaval. More than 100,000 suspected witches were accused and killed. The *witchcraft hysteria* reflected new resentments against the poor, who were often accused of witchcraft by communities unwilling to accept responsibility for their poverty. The hysteria also reflected new uncertainties about religious truth, for the trials were particularly common in areas converted to Protestantism. It even showed new tensions about family life and the role of women, who were the most common targets of persecution.

The West, in sum, was moving toward new economic structures and a new belief system, both of which promised further change in the future. Many people greeted the changes with dismay and sought ways of expressing their insecurity and fear, for the changes reached deeply into their personal lives and intimate beliefs.

New Social Divisions

The Renaissance, the Reformation, and economic change had combined to produce new divisions in Western Europe by the 17th century. The Renaissance created some new wedges between the educated elite and the mass of ordinary people. Traditionally, Europe's aristocracy had shared in popular culture, enjoying peasant festivals and an earthiness that embraced ribald jokes and even public urination—as in Wales, where a young man might urinate on his betrothed's dress as a sign of possession. By the 16th century, many aristocrats and religious leaders began to pull away from popular culture, urging more refined manners and/or a purer religious spirit. Both the Protestant and the Catholic Reformations picked up on this latter tone, attacking popular dancing and other customs that had mixed in with religious ceremonies.

In response to elite disapproval and to the growth of a propertyless proletariat, the popular rebellions of the 17th century expressed significant social tension. Peasant songs expressed such sentiments as this: "The whole country must be overturned, for we peasants are now to be the lords, it is we who will sit in the shade." Risings in 1648 produced demands for a popular political voice; an English group called the Levelers gained 100,000 signatures on a petition for political rights. Elsewhere, common people praised the kings while attacking their "bad advisors" and high taxes. One English agitator said that "we should cut off all the gentlemen's heads . . . we shall have a merrier world shortly." In France, Protestant and Catholic peasants rose together against landlords and taxes: "They seek only the ruin of the poor people for our ruin is their wealth."

New social divisions were not, however, completely straightforward, which is one reason the popular risings ultimately failed. Growing wealth spread to property-owning peasants and craftsmen, who also gained increasing literacy. Urged by religious leaders, these people might be attracted to some of the new ideas about tighter family structures. These groups could readily share the suspicions of government leaders about the irresponsibility of the poor. Western social alignments were in flux, which most obviously produced impressive popular protest and new divisions over beliefs, but which also generated audiences for various other new ideas.

SCIENCE AND POLITICS: THE NEXT PHASE OF CHANGE

Focal Point: As the impact of the Reformation and commercialization continued, new scientific discoveries and political forms took shape, from 1600 onward. These two forces shaped a new round of change, that continued into the 18th century.

Religious disruptions had produced major changes in Western intellectual life, and the related shifts in popular culture involved even more fundamental new directions. It was the revolution in science, culminating in the 17th century, that set the seal on the cultural reorientation of the West. While the *scientific revolution* most obviously affected formal intellectual life, it also furthered some of the key changes in popular outlook.

At the same time, after the political upheavals occasioned by the Reformation, a more decisive set of new government forms arose in the West, centering on the emergence of the nation-state. The functions of the state and its contacts with popular loyalties expanded. The Western nation-state was not a single form, as key variants such as absolute monarchies and parliamentary regimes emerged, but there were some common patterns beneath the surface. Continued cultural change, then, and new roles for the state defined the second major phase in the transformation of the early modern West during the late 17th and early 18th centuries.

Science: The New Authority

During the 16th century, important scientific research had continued the traditions of the later Middle Ages, although the results were somewhat obscured by the more striking developments in art and religion. A Polish clergyman, *Copernicus*, used astronomical observation and mathematical calculation to disprove the Hellenistic belief that the earth was the center of the universe. Rather, the earth moved around the sun. Also in the 16th century, anatomical work by the Belgian Vesalius overturned many medical ideas. These key discoveries not only advanced knowledge but also implied a new power for scientific research in its ability to test and often overrule accepted ideas.

These implications won full attention in a dizzying series of empirical advances and wider theoretical generalizations from the 1590s onward. New instruments such as the microscope and improved telescopes allowed gains in biology and astronomy. Scientists throughout the Western world participated in a surge of excited discovery. The Italian *Galileo* publicized Copernicus's discoveries while adding his own basic findings about the laws of gravity and planetary motion. Condemned by the Catholic church for his innovations, Galileo nevertheless definitively proved the inadequacy of traditional ideas about the universe. He also showed the new pride in scientific achievement, writing modestly how he, "by marvelous discoveries and clear demonstrations, had enlarged a thousand times" the knowledge produced by "the wise men of bygone ages." Chemical research advanced understanding of the behavior of gases. The English physician *John Harvey* demonstrated the circular movement of the blood in animals, with the heart as the "central pumping station."

These advances in knowledge were accompanied by important methodological statements about science and its impact. Francis Bacon urged the value of careful empirical research and predicted that scientific knowledge could steadily advance, producing improvements in technology as well. *René Descartes* established the importance of a skeptical review of all received wisdom, arguing that human reason could then develop laws that would explain the fundamental workings of nature. Descartes included a proof of God in his rationalistic generalizations, but his system allowed no real room for divine interventions.

The capstone to the 17th-century scientific revolution came in 1637, when *Isaac Newton* published his *Principia*. This work drew the various astronomical and physical observations and wider theories together in a neat framework of natural laws. Newton set forth the basic, simple principles of all motion: that a body in motion maintains uniform momentum unless affected by outside forces, that changes in rates of motion are proportional to the outside force, and that to every action there is always opposed an equal reaction. Newton defined the forces of gravity in great mathematical detail and showed that the whole universe responded to these

DOCUMENT

Controversies About Women

Changes in family structure and some shifts in the economic roles of women, as well as ambivalent Protestant promptings about women that emphasized the family context but urged affection and respect between wives and husbands, touched off new gender tensions in Western society by the 17th century. Some of these tensions showed in witchcraft trials, so disproportionately directed against women. Other tensions showed in open debate about women's relationship to men; women not content with a docile wifeliness vied with new claims of virtue and prowess by some women. Though the debate was centered in the upper class of Protestant nations such as England, it may have had wider ramifications. Some of these ramifications, though quieter during the 18th century, would burst forth again in arguments about inequality and family confinement in the 19th century, when a more durable feminist movement took shape in the West. In the selections below, the antiwoman position is set forth in a 1615 pamphlet by Joseph Swetham; the favorable view implicitly urging new rights is in a 1640 pamphlet pseudonymously authored by "Mary Tattle-Well and Ioane Hit-him-home, spinsters."

Swetnam's "Arraignment of Women"

Men, I say, may live without women, but women cannot live without men: for Venus, whose beauty was excellent fair, yet when she needed man's help, She took Vulcan, a clubfooted Smith. . . .

For women have a thousand ways to entice thee and ten thousand ways to deceive thee and all such fools as are suitors unto them: some they keep in hand with promises, and some they feed with flattery, and some they delay with dalliances, and some they please with kisses. They lay out the folds of their hair to entangle men into their love; betwixt their breasts in the vale of destruction; and in their beds there is hell, sorrow and repentance. Eagles eat not men till they are dead, but women devour them alive. . . .

It is said of men that they have that one fault, but of women it is said that they have two faults: that is to say, they can neither say well nor do well. There is a saying that goeth thus: that things far fetched and dear bought are of us most dearly beloved. The like may be said of women; although many of them are not far fetched, yet they are dear bought, yea and so dear that many a man curseth his hard pennyworths and bans his own heart. For the pleasure of the fairest woman in the world lasteth but a honeymoon; that is, while a man hath glutted his affections and reaped the first fruit, his pleasure being past, sorrow and repentance remaineth still with him.

Tattle-Well and Hit-Him-Home's "Women's Sharp Revenge"

But it hath been the policy of all parents, even from the beginning, to curb us of that benefit by striving to keep us under and to make us men's mere Vassals even unto all

forces, which among other things explained the planetary orbits. Finally, Newton stated the basic scientific method in terms of a mixture of rational hypothesis and generalization and careful empirical observation and experiment. Here was a vision of a natural universe that could be captured in relatively simple laws (though increasingly complex mathematics accompanied the findings). Here was a vision of a method of knowing that might do away with blind reliance on tradition or an acceptance of the need for religious faith.

The scientific revolution was quickly popularized among educated Westerners, though not yet the wider populace. New scientific institutes were set up, often with government aid, to advance research and disseminate the findings. Lectures and easy-to-read manuals publicized the latest advances and communicated the excitement that researchers themselves shared. The results fed into some of the wider shifts in outlook, at least among literate, urban people. Attacks on beliefs in witchcraft became more common, and magistrates grew increasingly reluc-

posterity. How else comes it to pass that when a Father hath a numerous issue of Sons and Daughters, the sons forsooth they must be first put to the Grammar school, and after perchance sent to the University, and trained up in the Liberal Arts and Sciences, and there (if they prove not Blockheads) they may in time be book-learned? . . .

When we, whom they style by the name of weaker Vessels, though of a more delicate, fine, soft, and more pliant flesh therefore of a temper most capable of the best Impression, have not that generous and liberal Education, lest we should be made able to vindicate our own injuries, we are set only to the Needle, to prick our fingers, or else to the Wheel to spin a fair thread for our own undoing, or perchance to some more dirty and debased drudgery. If we be taught to read, they then confine us within the compass of our Mother Tongue, and that limit we are not suffered to pass; or if (which sometimes happeneth) we be brought up to Music, to singing, and to dancing, it is not for any benefit that thereby we can engross unto ourselves, but for their own particular ends, the better to please and content their licentious appetites when we come to our maturity and ripeness. And thus if we be weak by Nature, they strive to make us more weak by our Nurture; and if in degree of place low, they strive by their policy to keep us more under.

Now to show we are no such despised matter as you would seem to make us, come to our first Creation, when man was made of the mere dust of the earth. The woman had her being from the best part of his body, the Rib next to his heart, which difference even in our com-

plexions may be easily decided. Man is of a dull, earthy, and melancholy aspect, having shallows in his face and a very forest upon his Chin, when our soft and smooth Cheeks are a true representation of a delectable garden of intermixed Roses and Lilies. . . . Man might consider that women were not created to be their slaves or vassals; for as they had not their Original out of his head (thereby to command him), so it was not out of his foot to be trod upon, but in a medium out of his side to be his fellow feeler, his equal, and companion. . . .

Thus have I truly and impartially proved that for Chastity, Charity, Constancy, Magnanimity, Valor, Wisdom, Piety, or any Grace or Virtue whatsoever, women have always been more than equal with men, and that for Luxury, Surquidant obscenity, profanity, Ebriety, Impiety, and all that may be called bad we do come far short of them.

Questions: Why did such different views about women develop in the 17th century? Why did some women defy patriarchal culture, and what were their main arguments? Did the new arguments in favor of women suggest that their conditions were improving?

tant to entertain witchcraft accusations in court; the public hysteria began to die down after about 1670. There were growing signs of a new belief that people could control and calculate their environment. Insurance companies sprang up to help guard against risk. Doctors increased their attacks on popular healers in the name of a more scientific diagnosis of illness. Newsletters, an innovation by the late 17th century, began to advertise "lost and found" items, for there was no point leaving this kind of problem to blind chance.

The scientific revolution had important implications beyond science in terms of how and what people could know. By the 1680s writers affected by the new science, though not themselves scientists, began to attack traditional religious ideas such as miracles, for in the universe of the scientific revolution there was no room for disruption of nature's laws. Some intellectuals held out a new conception of God, called *Deism*, arguing that while there might be a divinity, its role was simply to set natural laws in motion, not to regulate them once the

CLOSEUP

Johannes Kepler

Johannes Kepler (1571–1630) was an early important figure in the scientific revolution, known for his study of planetary motion. More than Copernicus, Kepler provided an accurate basis for replacing the Ptolemaic, earth-centered view of the universe. Kepler came from a poor family. His father abandoned the family outright, while his mother, once tried for witchcraft, was unpleasant. Kepler made his way to university on scholarship. Initially aiming for the Lutheran ministry, he was drawn to astronomy and mathematics. Using the work of Copernicus and his own and others' observations, he resolved basic issues of planetary motion. Kepler also worked on optics and practiced astrology, casting horoscopes for wealthy patrons.

process was launched. Faith came under direct scrutiny. *John Locke*, in England, argued that people, through their senses and reason, could learn everything they needed to know; faith was irrelevant. Christian beliefs in human sinfulness crumbled in the view of the ascendant intellectuals, for they saw human nature as basically good, given the capacity to learn. Finally, scientific advance created wider assumptions about the possibility of human progress. If knowledge could advance through concerted human effort, why not progress in other domains? Even literary authorities joined this parade, and the idea that past styles set timeless standards of perfection came under growing criticism.

The scientific revolution by no means monopolized the West's intellectual life about 1700. There were important movements in art even with continued reliance on classical styles. Religious authorities were hardly silent, and many attacked the brashness of the new sci-

ence. Unquestionably, however, the balance of intellectual interests was shifting, and science, with its presumed implications for other kinds of knowledge, increasingly ruled the roost.

This realignment was a first in human history. Science had never before been central to intellectual life. Science had played important roles in other civilizations, as in China, classical Greece, and Islam. Generally, however, wider religious or philosophical interests predominated. In China most notably, despite some real interest in generalizations about the physical universe derived from Daoism, science continued to be construed mainly in terms of practical, empirical advances. Chinese science piled up concrete information about astronomy and medicinal drugs. The Western passion for combining empiricism with more sweeping rational formulations—the idea of general laws of nature—clearly built on specific traditions that had come from Greek thought as medi-

Europe Under Absolute Monarchy, 1715

ated by Christian theology and Islamic philosophy during the postclassical period. The West, in sum, was not alone in developing crucial scientific data, but it had become the most vibrant center for scientific advance, and its leading thinkers stood alone for some time in seeing science as the key to gaining and defining knowledge.

Absolute and Parliamentary Monarchies

The feudal monarchy—the balance between king and nobles—that had defined Western politics since the later postclassical period finally came undone in the 17th century. In most countries, after the passions of religious wars finally cooled, monarchs gained new powers, curtailing the tradition of noble pressure or revolt. At the same time, more ambitious military organization, in states that defined war as a central purpose, required more careful administration and improved tax collection.

The prototype for this new pattern was France, now the West's most important nation. French kings steadily built up their power in the 17th century. They stopped calling the medieval parliament and passed laws as they saw fit, though some provincial councils remained strong. They blew up the castles of dissident nobles—another sign that gunpowder was undercutting the military basis of feudalism. They appointed a growing bureaucracy drawn from the merchants and lawyers. They sent direct representatives to the outlying provinces. They professionalized the army, giving more formal training to officers, providing uniforms and logistical support, and creating military hospitals and pensions. The French kings had larger and more reliable military forces than ever before in Western history.

So great was the power of the monarch, in fact, that the French system became known as *absolute monarchy*. Its most glorious royal proponent, King *Louis XIV*, summed up its principles succinctly: "I am the state." Louis became a major patron of the arts, giving government a cultural role beyond any previous levels in the West. His academies not only encouraged science but worked to standardize the French language. A sumptuous palace at Versailles was used to keep nobles busy

Louis XIV's grand 17th-century palace at Versailles represents both absolute monarchy and the classical style in architecture.

with social functions so that they could not interfere with affairs of state.

More substantively, using the new bureaucratic structure, Louis and his ministers developed additional functions for the state. They cut down on internal tariffs, which served as barriers to trade, and created new, state-run manufacturing. The reigning economic theory, *mercantilism*, held that governments should promote the internal economy in order to improve tax revenues and to limit imports from other nations, lest money be lost to enemy states. Hence, absolute monarchs like Louis XIV set tariffs on imported goods, tried to encourage their merchant fleets, and sought colonies to provide raw materials and a guaranteed market for manufactured goods produced at home.

The basic structure of absolute monarchy developed in other states besides France. Spain, after its 17th century decline, tried to imitate French principles in the 18th century, which resulted among other things in efforts to tighten control over its Latin American colonies. The most important spread of absolute monarchy, however, occurred in the central European states that were gaining in importance. A series of kings in Prussia, in eastern Germany, built a strong army and bureaucracy. They promoted economic activity and also began to de-

velop a state-sponsored school system. Habsburg kings in Austria-Hungary, though still officially rulers of the Holy Roman Empire, in fact concentrated increasingly on developing a stronger monarchy in the lands under their direct control. The power of these Habsburg rulers increased after they pushed back the last Turkish invasion threat late in the 17th century and then added the kingdom of Hungary to their domains.

Most absolute monarchs saw a strong military as a key political goal, and many hoped for territorial expansion. Louis XIV used his strong state as the basis for a series of wars from the 1680s onward. The wars yielded some new territory for France but finally attracted an opposing alliance system that blocked further advance. Prussian kings, though long cautious in exposing their proud military to the risk of major war, turned in the 18th century to a series of conflicts that won new territory.

Britain and the Netherlands, both growing commercial and colonial powers, stood apart from the trend toward absolute monarchy in the 17th century. They, too, emphasized the role of the central state, but they also firmed up parliamentary regimes in which the kings shared power with representatives selected by the nobility and upper urban classes. The English civil wars pro-

Civil war resulted in the execution of Charles I in London, England, in 1649.

duced a final political settlement in 1688 and 1689 (the so-called *Glorious Revolution*) in which parliament won basic sovereignty over the king. The English parliament no longer depended on the king to convene, for regular sessions were now scheduled, and it held assured rights to approve taxation that allowed it to monitor or initiate most major policies.

Furthermore, a growing body of political theory arose in the 17th century that built on these parliamentary ideas. John Locke and others argued that power came basically from the people, not from a divine right to royal rule. Kings should therefore be restrained by institutions that protected the public interest, including certain general rights to freedom and property. A right of revolution could legitimately oppose unjust rule.

Overall, while the West developed important diversity in political forms, between absolute monarchy and a new kind of *parliamentary monarchy*, a characteristic tension remained between government growth and the idea that there should be some limits to state authority. This tension was expressed in new forms, but it recalled some principles that had originated in the Middle Ages.

Government growth itself should not be exaggerated. While absolute monarchs had torn down some of the characteristic institutions of feudal days, they lacked the means to gain detailed control over their subjects. Nobles, in fact, continued to play a considerable role in affairs of state. Furthermore, many of the innovations that did occur simply brought to the West the kinds of bureaucratic structures that other civilizations, particularly China, had developed long before.

It was significant, nevertheless, that at a time in world history when governments in many civilizations were entering a period of decline, those in the West were on the upswing. It was significant also that Western governments gained new powers to influence wider spheres of activity. They affected economic life and the treatment of the poor. They increasingly defined the way prisoners should be treated. They played some role in cultural trends. They also gave merchants a political role, as bureaucrats or parliamentary representatives, that was unusual in world history to that point.

The Nation-State

Furthermore, both the absolute monarchies and the parliamentary monarchies shared important characteristics as nation-states. Unlike the great empires of many other civilizations, they ruled peoples who shared a common culture and language, some important minorities apart. They thus could appeal for a certain loyalty that linked cultural and political bonds. This was as true of England, where the idea of special rights of Englishmen helped feed the parliamentary movement, as it was of France. Not surprisingly, ordinary people in many nation-states, even though not directly represented in government, showed increasing belief that government should act for their interests. Thus, Louis XIV faced recurrent popular riots predicated on the assumption that, when bad harvests drove up food prices, it was the obligation of government to help people out. Thus, the English parliamentary system, though monopolized by the upper classes, opened the way to frequent popular petitions about various grievances.

Nation-states, in sum, developed a growing list of functions, particularly under the banner of mercantilism, whose principles were shared by monarchists and parliamentary leaders alike. They also promoted new political values and loyalties that were somewhat less common among the political traditions of other civilizations. They certainly kept the West politically divided and frequently at war.

ANALYSIS

Elites and Masses

What caused the end of witchcraft hysteria in the West by the later 17th century? Did wise rulers calm a frenzied populace or did ordinary people themselves change their minds?

One explanation focuses on new efforts by elites, such as local magistrates, to discipline mass impulses. Authorities stopped believing in demonic disruptions of natural processes, and so forced an end to persecutions. But many ordinary people were also thinking in new ways. Without converting fully to a scientific outlook, they became open to new ideas about how to handle health problems, reducing their belief in magical remedies; they needed witches less. Potential "witches" may have become more cautious. Older women, for example, threatened by growing community suspicion, learned to maintain a lower profile and to emphasize benign, grandmotherly qualities rather than seeking a more independent role. Without question, there was a decline both in witchcraft beliefs, once a key element in the Western mentality, and in the hysteria specifically characteristic of the 16th and 17th centuries. This decline reflected new ways of thinking about strangeness and disruption. It involved complex interactions among various segments of Western society—magistrates and villagers, scientists and priests, husbands and widows.

The transformation of Western society after 1450 raises fascinating questions about the role of elites—particularly powerful groups and creative individuals—versus the ordinary run of folk in causing change. The growing importance of social history has called attention to ordinary people, as we have seen, but it has not answered all the questions about their actual role. This role varies, of course, by place and time. But some social historians tend generally to see ordinary people as victims of change, bumped and beleaguered by the power groups. Others, in contrast, tend generally to stress the positive historical role of ordinary people in partly shaping the context of their own lives and in affecting the larger course of history as well.

It is easy to read the early modern transformation of western Europe as an operation shaped by elites, with the masses as passive or futilely protesting clay. Not only the Renaissance and Reformation, but also the commercial revolution, entailed decisive action by key leadership groups. Leading merchants spurred economic change, and they ultimately began to farm out manufacturing jobs. The resultant proletarianization—which tore a growing minority of Western Europeans away from property and so from economic control of their lives—graphically illustrated the disparities of power in Western society, as capitalist merchants and landowners gained a more manipulable labor force. Ordinary people knuckled under or protested, but they were reacting, not initiating.

The rise of science rivets our attention on the activities of extraordinarily creative individuals, such as Newton, and elite institutions, such as the scientific academies. Some historians have suggested that the rise of science opened a new gap between the ways educated upper classes and masses thought.

Yet, the ordinary people of western Europe were not inert, nor did they simply and abortively protest change in the name of the tried and true. Widespread shifts came from repeated decisions by nameless peasants and artisans, not just from those at the top. The steady technological improvements in manufacturing thus flowed upward from practicing artisans, not downward from formal scientists. The European-style family, an innovation by ordinary people the elite long ignored, encouraged new parent–child relations and new tensions between young adults and the old, that might spur other innovations—including a willingness to settle distant colonies in search of property. The fact that young people often had to wait to marry until their property-owning fathers died could induce many to seek new lands or new economic methods. Ordinary people, in other words, changed their habits too. They created a new climate for generating as well as receiving new ideas about medicine, witchcraft, and how to handle emotions in the family. They created new motives and rhythms for work. In mentalities, changes at the popular level were clearly related to elite currents, despite clashes and discontinuities.

Finally, the dichotomy of elites and ordinary people was bridged in important new ways during the early modern centuries, and particularly after about 1650. The spread of literacy facilitated interchange, first in religion and then in science. While the rise of a proletarian minority constituted a new rift, growing prosperity and commercial-mindedness among many middle-level property owners complicated any claim to growing economic inequality overall. Gender divisions increased in some respects, as women became more fully associated with domestic functions, but the emphasis on family values encouraged men and women to participate in some shared experiences. Western society was generating some new middle ground in outlook and power. Commercial contacts even eased, without fully eliminating, one of the oldest divisions in agricultural civilization: that between country and town. Rural people gained access to new and sometimes disturbing urban habits and forms of leisure.

The new Western patterns were obviously complex, as any sweeping transformation must be. Changes emanated from various levels, moved in various directions, and created new groupings as well as new disparities. The active involvement of ordinary people warrants comparison with transformations in other key junctures of world history. It also explains why other civilizations, later seeking to imitate certain features of the new Western society, faced important choices about whether and how to involve the masses—choices in which the masses would have their own contributions to make.

Questions: Did elites gain new power over the masses in early modern Western society? Are ordinary people more conservative by nature, more suspicious of change, than groups at the top? Can you describe at least two other historical cases in which it is important to determine whether change was imposed on ordinary people from above, or whether ordinary people themselves produced important innovations?

THE WEST BY 1750

Focal Point: The three great currents of change—commercialization, cultural reorientation, and the rise of the nation-state—continued to operate in the West after 1700, along with the growing international influence of the West. Each strand, in fact, produced new ramifications that furthered the overall transformation of the West.

Political Patterns

On the whole, during the middle decades of the 18th century, political changes seemed least significant. During much of the century English politics settled into a rather turgid parliamentary routine, in which key political groups competed for influence without major policy differences. Some popular concern for greater representation surfaced in the 1760s, as a movement for democracy surged briefly, but there was as yet no consistent reform current. Absolute monarchy in France changed little institutionally, but it became progressively less effective. It was unable to force changes in the tax structure that would give it more solid financial footing, because aristocrats refused to surrender their traditional exemptions.

Political developments were far livelier in central Europe. In Prussia, *Frederick the Great*, building on the military and bureaucratic organization of his predecessors, introduced greater freedom of religion while expanding the economic functions of the state. His government actively encouraged better agricultural methods; for example, it promoted use of the potato as a staple crop. It also codified its laws toward greater commercial coordination and greater equity; harsh traditional punishments were cut back. Later in the 18th century, an Austrian emperor, *Joseph II*, tried a similar program of state-sponsored improvements, including a major effort to roll back the power of the Catholic church. Rulers of this sort claimed to be enlightened despots, wielding great authority but for the good of society at large.

Enlightened or not, the policies of the major Western nation-states produced recurrent warfare. France and Britain squared off in the 1740s and again in the *Seven Years' War* (1756–1763); their conflicts focused on battles for colonial empire. Austria and Prussia also fought, with Prussia gaining new land. Wars in the 18th century were carefully modulated, without devastating effects, but they demonstrated the continued linkage between statecraft and war that was characteristic of the West.

Enlightenment Thought and Popular Culture

In culture, the aftermath of the scientific revolution spilled over into a new movement known as the *Enlightenment*, centered particularly in France but with adherents throughout the Western world. Enlightenment thinkers continued to support scientific advance. While there were no Newton-like breakthroughs, chemists gained new understanding of major elements, and biologists developed a vital new classification system for the natural species.

The Enlightenment also pioneered in applying scientific methods to the study of human society, sketching the modern social sciences. The basic ideas were that rational laws could describe social as well as physical behavior and that knowledge could be used to improve policy. Thus, criminologists wrote that brutal punishments failed to deter crime, whereas a decent society would be able to rehabilitate criminals through education. Political theorists wrote about the importance of carefully planned constitutions and controls over privilege, though they disagreed about what political form was best. A new school of economists developed. The

Scottish philosopher *Adam Smith* set forth a number of invariable principles of economic behavior, based on the belief that people act according to their self-interest but, through competition, work to promote general economic advance. Government should avoid regulation in favor of the operation of individual initiative and market forces. Here was an important specific statement of economic policy and an illustration of the growing belief that general models of human behavior could be derived from rational thought.

More generally still, the Enlightenment produced a set of basic principles about human affairs: Human beings are naturally good and can be educated to be better; reason is the key to truth, and religions that rely on blind faith or refuse to tolerate diversity are wrong. Enlighten-

CLOSEUP

Denis Diderot

Denis Diderot (1713–1784) was a multifaceted leader of the French Enlightenment, best known for his editorial work on the *Encyclopédie*, a basic compendium of scientific and social scientific knowledge. Trained initially by the Jesuits, Diderot wrote widely on philosophy, mathematics, and the psychology of deaf-mutes and also tried his hand at literature. An active friend of other philosophers, Diderot also traveled to foreign courts as advisor and visiting intellectual. A visit to Catherine the Great of Russia in 1773–1774, to thank her for generous patronage harmed his health, though he maintained his eloquent liaison with his mistress, Sophie Volland.

ment thinkers attacked the Catholic church with particular vigor. Progress was possible, even inevitable, if people could be set free. Society's goals should center on improvements in material and social life.

Enlightenment thinkers showed great interest in technological change, for greater prosperity was a valid and achievable goal. Coercion and cruelty could be corrected, for the Enlightenment encouraged a humanitarian outlook that was applied in condemnations of slavery and war.

Though it was not typical of the Enlightenment's main thrust, a few thinkers applied these general principles to other areas. A handful of socialists argued that economic equality and the abolition of private property must become important goals. A few feminist thinkers, such as *Mary Wollstonecraft* in England, argued—against the general male-centered views of most Enlightenment thinkers—that new political rights and freedoms should extend to women.

The Enlightenment, summing up and extending earlier intellectual changes, became an important force for political and social reform. It did not rule unchallenged. Important popular religious movements, such as Methodism in England, showed the continued power of spiritual faith. Many writers, particularly those experimenting with the novel as a new literary form in the West, rebelled against Enlightenment rationality to urge the importance of sentimentality and emotion. These approaches, too, encouraged people to rethink the traditional styles.

The popularization of new ideas encouraged further changes in the habits and beliefs of many ordinary people. Reading clubs and coffeehouses allowed many urban artisans and businessmen to discuss the latest reform ideas. Leading writers and compilations of scientific and philosophical findings, such as the *Encyclopaedia Britannica*, won a wide audience and, for a few people, a substantial fortune from the sale of books. Groups and individuals that promoted better agricultural or industrial methods on the winning of new political rights referred directly to Enlightenment thinking. Some groups of artisans and peasants also turned against established churches and even withdrew from religious belief as secular values gained ground.

Other changes in popular outlook paralleled the new intellectual currents, though they had deeper sources than philosophy alone. Attitudes toward children began to shift in many social groups. Older methods of physical discipline were criticized, in favor of more restrained behavior that would respect the goodness and innocence of children. Swaddling began to decline as parents became interested in freer movement and greater interaction for young children; no longer were infants tightly wrapped during their first months. Among wealthy families, educational toys and books for children reflected the idea that childhood should be a stage for learning and growth. At the most basic level, parents became increasingly likely to give young children names at birth and to select names different from those of older relatives—a sign of a new affection for children and new belief in their individuality. These changes were gradual, and they involved more adult control of children as well as a more humane outlook. The idea of shaping children and instilling guilt-stimulated consciences gained ground. Unquestionably, the net effect was to alter parent–child relations and also to produce novel personality ideals for adults themselves.

Family life generally was altered by a growing sense that old hierarchies needed to be rethought and revised toward somewhat greater equality in the treatment of women and children within the home. Love between family members gained new respect, and an emotional bond in marriage became more widely sought. Parents, for example, grew more reluctant to force a match on a son or daughter if the emotional vibrations were not right. Here was a link not only with Enlightenment ideas of proper family relations but with the novels that poured out a sentimental view of life.

Ongoing Change in Commerce and Manufacturing

Ongoing economic change, finally, paralleled the ferment in popular culture and intellectual life. Commerce continued its spread. Ordinary Westerners began to buy processed products, such as refined sugar and coffee or tea obtained from Indonesia and the West Indies, for daily use. Here was a sign of the growing importance of Europe's new colonies for ordinary life and of the beginnings of mass consumerism in Western society. Another sign of change was the growing use of paid professional entertainment as part of popular leisure, even in rural festivals. Not accidentally, circuses, first introduced in France in the 1670s, began to redefine leisure to include spectatorship and a taste for the bizarre.

Agriculture began to change. Until the later 17th century, Western Europe had continued to rely largely on the methods and techniques characteristic of the Middle Ages—a severe economic constraint in a still agricultural society. Now, first in the Netherlands and then elsewhere, new procedures for draining swamps added available land. Nitrogen-fixing crops were introduced to reduce the need to leave land fallow. Stock-breeding improved, and new techniques like seed-drills,

CLOSEUP

The New Manufacturer

Around 1700, most manufacturers who made wool cloth in northern England were artisans, doing part of the work themselves. By 1720, a group of loom owners were becoming outright manufacturers with new ideas and behaviors. Here was a sign of the continuing changes in Europe's economy. How was a manufacturer different? He spent his time organizing production and sales rather than doing his own work. He moved work out of his home. He stopped drinking beer with his workers. And he regarded his workers as market commodities, to be treated as the conditions of trade demanded. In 1736, one such manufacturer coolly wrote that because of slumping sales, "I have turned off a great many of my makers, and keep turning more off weekly."

and simply the use of scythes instead of sickles for harvesting, heightened productivity. Some changes spread particularly fast on large estates, which was one reason that in England more and more land was enclosed and ordinary farmers served as tenants or laborers rather than owners. Other changes affected ordinary peasants as well. Particularly vital in this category was the spread of the potato from the late 17th century onward. A New World crop, the potato had long been shunned because it was not mentioned in the Bible and was held to be the cause of plagues. Enlightened government leaders, and peasants' desire to win greater economic security and better nutrition, led to widespread adoption of this efficient crop. The West, in sum, improved its food supply and also its agricultural efficiency, leaving more labor available for other pursuits.

These changes, along with the steady growth of colonial trade and internal commerce, spurred increased manufacturing. The 18th century witnessed a rapid spread of household production of textiles and metal products, mostly by rural workers who alternated manufacturing with some agriculture. Hundreds of thousands of people were drawn into this domestic system, in which capitalist merchants distributed supplies and orders, and workers ran the production process for pay. While manufacturing tools were still operated by hand, the spread of domestic manufacturing spurred important technical innovations designed to improve efficiency. In 1733, James Kay in England introduced the flying shuttle, which permitted automatic crossing of threads on looms; with this, an individual weaver could do the work of two. Improvements in spinning soon followed as the Western economy began to escalate toward a full-fledged Industrial Revolution.

Finally, agricultural changes, commercialism, and manufacturing combined, particularly after about 1730, to produce a rapidly growing population in the West. With better food supplies, more people survived—particularly with the aid of the potato. More commercial motives helped prompt landlords and some ambitious peasants to acquire more land and to push unneeded labor off, heightening proletarianization but also reducing the restraints some parents could impose over the sexual behavior of their children. In essence, as some groups grew unsure of inheritance, they sought more immediate pleasures and also hoped to use the labor of the resultant children. Finally, new manufacturing jobs helped landless people support themselves, promoting in some cases earlier marriage and sexual liaisons. Population growth, in turn, promoted further economic change, heightening competition and producing a more manipulable labor force. The West's great population revolution, which would continue into the 19th century, both caused and reflected the civilization's dynamism, though it also produced great strain and confusion.

Western society was still essentially agricultural by the mid-18th century. Decisive new political forms had yet to be introduced, and in many ways government policies failed to keep pace with cultural and economic change after 1700. Established churches were still forces to be reckoned with. Even new developments, such as the spread of domestic manufacturing, functioned because they allowed so many traditional habits to persist. Thus, while new market relationships described this growing system, the location and many of the methods of work as well as the association of family with production were not altered. Western society hovered between older values and institutions and the full flowering of change. Decades of outright political and economic revolution, which would build on these tensions and cause a fuller transformation, were yet to come.

CONCLUSION

Innovation and Instability

By the 18th century, the various strands of change were increasingly intertwined in Western civilization. Stronger governments promoted agricultural improvements, which helped prod population growth. Changes in popular beliefs were fed by new economic structures; both encouraged a reevaluation of the family and the roles of children. New beliefs also raised new political challenges. Enlightenment ideas about liberty and fundamental human equality could obviously be directed against existing regimes. New family practices might have political implications as well. Children, raised with less adult restraint and encouraged to value their individual worth through parental love and careful education, might see traditional political limitations in new ways. There was no perfect fit, no inevitable match, in the three strands of change that had been transforming the West for two centuries or more: the commercial, the cultural, and the political. Clearly, however, by 1750, all were in place. The combination had already produced an unusual version of an agricultural civilization, and it promised more upheaval in the future.

The Western package of change had also produced a society unusually dynamic in the world at large. Two cautions should be given here. First, other societies had changed rapidly before, and some displayed great vigor after 1450; the West in no sense invented change. Second, Western change depended heavily on the position it won in the wider world. Commercialization, for example, built on the West's ability to extract wealth from other societies. It remained true that internal shifts helped explain the West's course in the wider world, and here the key connection was the West's instability and tension, not its smooth course. Religious disputes, political rivalries, and economic dislocations all helped explain why Westerners reached out, as individuals and in groups, for new roles in international trade, explorations, or colonies. International activity flowed not from serene strength but from recurrent disruption, and this activity in turn served the West as a vital outlet. Only in the 20th century have Westerners faced the obvious resultant question: What will happen to the West and its crosscurrents once the civilization's international role meets new challengers?

FURTHER READINGS

For an overview of developments in Western society during this period, with extensive bibliographies, see Sheldon Watts's *A Social History of Western Europe, 1450–1720* (1984), Michael Anderson's *Approaches to the West European Family* (1980), and Peter N. Stearns's *Life and Society in the West: The Modern Centuries* (1988). Charles Tilly's *Big Structures, Large Processes, Huge Comparisons* (1985) offers an analytical framework based on major change; see also Tilly's edited volume, *The Formation of National States in Western Europe* (1975).

On more specific developments and periods, J. H. Plumb's *The Italian Renaissance* (1986), F. H. New's *The Renaissance and Reformation: A Short History* (1977), O. Chadwick's *The Reformation* (1983), and Steven Ozment's *The Age of Reform, 1520–1550* (1980) are fine introductions to early changes. See also Hubert Jedin and John Dolan, eds., *Reformation and Counter Reformation* (1980). Later political changes are sketched in M. Beloff's *The Age of Absolutism* (1967) and R. Hatton's *Europe in the Age of Louis XIV* (1979). On England in the Civil War period, see Christopher Hill, *A Nation of Change and Novelty* (1990).

Key aspects of social change in this period can be approached through Peter Burke's *Popular Culture in Early Modern Europe* (1978), Robin Biggs's *Communities of Belief: Cultural and Social Tensions in Early Modern France* (1989), Keith Thomas's *Religion and the Decline of Magic* (1971), and Lawrence Stone's *The Family, Sex and Marriage in England 1500–1800* (1977). On popular protest, see Charles Tilly's *The Contentious French* (1986) and H. A. F. Kamen's *The Iron Century: Social Change in Europe 1550–1660* (1971).

On science, A. R. Hall's *From Galileo to Newton, 1630–1720* (1982) is a fine introduction. Relations between science and technology are covered in C. Cipolla's *Before the Industrial Revolution* (1976).

23

The West and the World

1434 Portugal extends expeditions
down West African coast

1519–1521 Magellan circumnavigates globe   **1562** Britain begins
its slave trade

1497–1498 Vasco da Gama to India   **1542** Portuguese reach Japan

1514 Expedition to Indonesia   **1571** Ottoman
fleet defeated in
Battle of Lepanto

1394–1460 Prince Henry the Navigator   **1488** Portuguese round Cape of Good Hope

1433 China ends great expeditions

1492 Columbus's first expedition   **1534** First French explorations in Canada

1509 First Spanish colonies on Latin American mainland

1400 C.E.   1500 C.E.

INTRODUCTION

One of the ways Westerners have long used history to make themselves feel good involves the recounting of the great explorations and conquests accomplished by Western stalwarts from the late 15th century onward. School children are steeped in the voyages of Columbus, the empires hacked out in Central and South America by Spanish conquerors, and the work of Christian missionaries in Asia and the New World.

The rise of the West between the 15th and the 18th centuries also involved other developments of crucial importance in world history: the heightening and redefinition of interchanges between world societies and civilizations.

Previous periods had witnessed important steps toward greater diffusion of goods and ideas. During the classical era, most attention was given to the development of larger regional economies and cultural zones, such as the Chinese Middle Kingdom and the Mediterranean basin. Wider international contacts existed, but they were not of fundamental importance to the societies involved. The level and significance of contacts increased during the postclassical era. Missionary religions spilled across civilization boundaries, as with Buddhism in eastern and southeast Asia and above all with Islam. For the Middle East, parts of Africa, and much of India, international trade became an important feature of the basic economic structure, with some regions garnering particular profits.

Despite these important precedents, the kind of world relationships that developed after 1450, mainly though not exclusively sponsored by Western leaders, spelled a new period in world history. Most obviously, new areas of the world were for the first time brought into the international complex, particularly the Americas but also new parts of Africa and ultimately Polynesia. The rate and impact of international trade also increased in some portions of the Old World, such as the islands of southeast Asia. Furthermore, international trade now became so significant that it forged different relationships between key societies based on the kind of goods and amount of control contributed to the surging world economy. These new economic relationships, in turn, prompted some societies to reconsider older political and cultural traditions in light of patterns—again, particularly those of the West—that seemed compellingly successful. This kind of differential interchange had occurred before in world history—witness the Japanese imitation of China and the impact of Islam in East Africa—but it now spread more widely—more literally, internationally.

This chapter, accordingly, deals with several interrelated developments during the centuries between about 1450 and 1750—the same centuries when the West was changing rapidly within its own borders. Topic one is simply the West's next explorations and acquisitions as it became the world's leading international trader and colonial power. Topic two involves the larger international economic system the West created, which turned out to have a life of its own. New contacts in terms of exchanges of ideas, foods, and diseases followed from the emergence of this new system. Topic three, finally, involves sorting out the different kinds of responses generated outside the West to the new economic framework, and the West's role, ranging from attempts at isolation to outright subjection. The possibilities were considerable, and no society's history was fully described by Western activities or international economics. The new developments did, however, set part of the environment in which individual civilizations continued to evolve.

1588 British defeat Spanish Armada

1641 Dutch begin conquests on Java, in Indonesia

1607 First British colony in Virginia

1597 Japan begins isolation policy

1652 Dutch launch colony in southern Africa

1608 First French colonies in Canada; first trading concession in India to England

1756–1763 Seven Years' War, in Europe, India, and North America

1744 French–British wars in India

1763 British acquire New France

1756 "Black hole" of Calcutta

1775–1783 American Revolution

1764 East India Company control of Bengal

1600 C.E.

1700 C.E.

509

THE WEST'S FIRST OUTREACH: MARITIME POWER

Focal Point: Between 1450 and 1650, various West European nations gained unprecedented mastery of the world's oceans. Trading patterns and colonial expansion focused on Europe's maritime power. Pioneering efforts by Spain and Portugal were followed by the surge of Britain, Holland, and France.

Various Western leaders, particularly merchants but also some princes and churchmen, had become increasingly aware of the larger world around them since the High Middle Ages. The Crusades brought knowledge of Islam's superior economic levels and the goods that could be imported from the Middle East and Asia for the delectation of the West's increasingly sophisticated aristocracy. The Mongol Empire, which sped up exchanges between the civilizations of Asia, also spurred European interest. The fall of the Khans in China disrupted this interchange, as China became once again a land of mystery to Europeans. Europe's upper classes had by this time become accustomed to imported products from Southeast Asia and India, particularly spices. These goods were transported by sea to the Middle East in Arab ships, then brought overland, where they were loaded again onto vessels (mainly from Genoa and Venice, in Italy) for the Mediterranean trade.

Europeans entered into this era of growing contacts with the wider world network with several disadvantages. Their ignorance of the wider world remained vast. To be sure, Viking adventurers from Scandinavia had crossed the Atlantic in the 10th century, reaching Greenland and then North America, which they named Vinland. However, they quickly lost interest beyond establishing settlements on Greenland and Iceland, in part because they encountered Indian warriors whose weaponry was good enough to cause them serious problems. And many Europeans continued to believe that the earth was flat, though scientists in more advanced civilizations knew otherwise; their beliefs made them fearful of distant voyages lest they fall off the world's edge.

Europeans did launch a more consistent effort at expansion from 1291 onward, as was discussed in Chapter 21. They were pressed by new problems: fear of the strength of the emerging Ottoman Empire and the lack of gold to pay for Asian imports. Initial settlements in island groups in the south Atlantic fed their hopes for further gains. The first expeditions were limited, however, by the small, oar-propelled ships used in the Mediter-ranean trade, for they could not press far into the oceans.

New Technology: A Key to Power

During the 15th century, a series of technological improvements began to change the equation. Europeans developed deep-draft, round-hulled sailing ships for the Atlantic, capable of carrying heavier armaments than the ships they and most other peoples had previously used. They also began to use a compass for navigation (an instrument they copied from the Arabs, who in turn had gained it from the Chinese). Mapmaking and other navigational devices improved as well. Finally, European knowledge of explosives, another Chinese invention, was adapted into gunnery. European metalwork, steadily advancing in sophistication, allowed Western craftsmen to devise the first guns and cannon. European technology, initially employed to produce bells, had introduced heavier castings than the finer Asian or African metalwork, and those castings were adaptable to gunnery. Though not initially very accurate, this weaponry was awesome by the standards of the time (and more than a bit terrifying to many Europeans, who had reason to fear the new destructive power of their own armies and navies). The West began to forge a weapons advantage over all other civilizations of the world, at first primarily on the seas—an advantage it would retain into the 20th century. With an unprecedented ability to kill and intimidate from a distance, the West was ready for its big push.

Portugal and Spain Lead the Pack

The specific initiative came from the small kingdom of Portugal. The rulers of this country had driven out the Muslims, who still threatened Europe from north Africa. This threat, the surge of energy that sometimes accompanies expulsion of an occupation force, and Christian missionary zeal prompted the Portuguese to look for conquests in Africa during the 15th century. Portugal's rulers were drawn by the excitement of discovery, the harm they might cause to the Muslim world, and a thirst for wealth—a potent mix. A Portuguese prince, *Henry the Navigator*, directed a series of expeditions along the African coast and also outward to islands such as the Azores. Beginning in 1434 the Portuguese began to press down the African coast, each expedition going a little farther than its predecessor. They brought back some slaves, spices such as pepper, and many stories of gold hoards they had not yet been able to find.

Prince Henry the Navigator, of Portugal, sent annual expeditions down the western coast of Africa.

Later in the 15th century, Portuguese sailors ventured around the *Cape of Good Hope* in a plan to find India, where direct contact would give Europeans easier access to luxury cloths and spices, and also to reach the African east coast, held to be the source of gold. They rounded the Cape in 1488, but weary sailors forced the expedition back before it could reach India. Then, after news of Columbus's discovery of America for Spain in 1492, Portugal redoubled its efforts, hoping to stave off the new Spanish competition. *Vasco da Gama's* fleet of four ships reached India, with the aid of a Hindu pilot picked up in East Africa, in 1497. The Portuguese mistakenly believed that the Indians were Christians, for they were confused by the Hindu temples they saw and thought they were churches. They faced the hostility of Muslim merchants, who had long dominated trade in this part of the world, but they managed to return with a small load of spices.

This success set in motion an annual series of Portuguese voyages to the Indian Ocean. One expedition, blown off course, reached Brazil, where it proclaimed Portuguese sovereignty. Portugal began to set up forts on the African coast and also in India—the forerunners of such Portuguese colonies as Mozambique, in East Africa, and Goa, in India. By 1514 the Portuguese had reached the islands of Indonesia, the center of spice production, and also China. In 1542 one Portuguese expedition arrived in Japan, where a missionary effort was launched that met

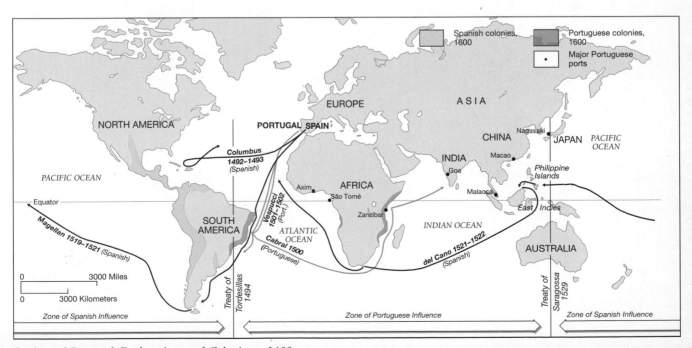

Spain and Portugal: Explorations and Colonies, c. 1600

with some success for several decades. In the space of roughly a century, Portugal had traveled to almost every part of the world; as a Portuguese poet later said, "And if there had been more world they would have found it."

Meanwhile, only a short time after the Portuguese quest began, the Spanish reached out with even greater force. Here was a country only recently freed from Muslim rule, full of missionary zeal and a desire for riches. The Spanish had traveled into the Atlantic during the 14th century. Then in 1492—the same year that the final Muslim fortress was captured in Spain—the Italian navigator *Christopher Columbus*, sailing in the name of the newly united Spanish monarchy and its rulers, Ferdinand and Isabella, set sail for a westward route to India, convinced that the round earth would make his quest possible. As is well known, he failed, reaching the Americas instead and mistakenly naming their inhabitants Indians. Although Columbus believed to his death that he had sailed to In-

dia, later Spanish explorers brought a firm realization that they had voyaged to a region where Europeans and Asians had not traveled previously. One expedition, headed by Amerigo Vespucci, gave the New World its name. Spain, eager to claim this new land, won papal approval for Spanish dominion over most of what is now Latin America, though a later treaty awarded Brazil to Portugal.

Finally, a Spanish expedition under *Ferdinand Magellan* set sail westward in 1519, passing the southern tip of South America and sailing across the Pacific, reaching the Indonesian islands in 1521 after incredible hardships. It was on the basis of this voyage, ultimately the first trip around the world, that Spain claimed the Philippines, which were to be Spanish territory until 1898.

Portugal emerged from this first round of exploration with coastal holdings in parts of Africa and in the Indian port of Goa, a lease on the Chinese port of Macao, short-lived interests in trade with Japan, and, fi-

This is the earliest European sketch of American Indians at the time of a Portuguese expedition to northern South America about 1500. "The people are thus naked, handsome, brown. . . . They also eat each other . . . and hang the flesh of them in the smoke. They become a hundred and fifty years of age, and have no government."

nally, the claim on Brazil. Spain asserted its hold on the Philippines, various Pacific islands, and the bulk of the Americas. During the 16th century, the Spanish moved to back up these claims by military expeditions to Mexico and South America. The Spanish also held Florida and sent expeditions northward from Mexico into California and other parts of what later became the southwestern United States.

Northern European Expeditions

Later in the 16th century, the lead in further exploration passed to northern Europe, as newly strong monarchies, such as France and England, got into the act, and zealous Protestants in Britain and Holland strove to rival Catholic gains. In part this shift in dynamism occurred because Spain and Portugal were busy digesting the gains they had already made; in part it was because northern Europeans, particularly the Dutch and the British, improved the design of oceanic vessels, producing lighter, faster ships than those of their Catholic adversaries. Britain won a historic sea battle with Spain in 1588, in which the British navy and adverse weather routed a massive Spanish Armada. From this point onward, the British, the Dutch, and to some extent the French vied for dominance on the seas, though in the Americas they mainly aimed northward because they could not challenge the Spanish and

Portuguese colonies. Only in the sugar-rich West Indies did northern Europe seize islands initially claimed by Spain.

French explorers crossed the Atlantic first in 1534, reaching Canada, which was claimed in France's name. French voyages increased in the 17th century as various expeditions pressed down from Canada into the Great Lakes region and the Mississippi valley.

The British also turned their attention to North America, starting with a brief expedition as early as 1497. The English hoped, in vain, to discover a northwest passage to India, and in fact accomplished little beyond exploration of the Hudson Bay area of Canada during the 16th century. England's serious work began in the 17th century, with the colonization of the east coast of North America. Holland also had holdings in North America and, for a time, in Brazil.

The Dutch entered the picture after winning independence from Spain, and Holland quickly became a major competitor with Portugal in Southeast Asia. The Dutch sent substantial numbers of sailors and ships to the region, ousting the Portuguese from the Indonesian islands by the early 17th century. Voyagers from the Netherlands explored the coast of Australia, though without much immediate result. Finally, toward the middle of the 17th century, Holland established a settlement on the southern tip of Africa, mainly to provide a relay station for its ships bound for the East Indies.

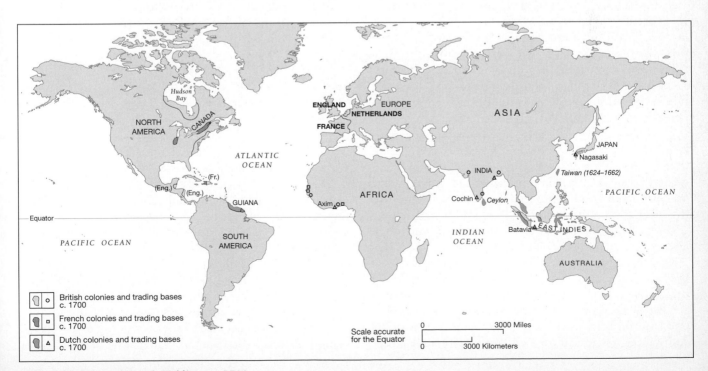

French, British, and Dutch Holdings, c. 1700

Dutch and British exploration and trade were sponsored by the government, but they also owed much to the private initiative of merchant groups. The Netherlands, Britain, and France all chartered great trading companies, such as the *Dutch East India Company* and the British firm of similar name. These companies were given government monopolies of trade in the regions designated, but they were not rigorously supervised by their own states. Thus, semiprivate companies, formed by pooling merchant capital and amassing great fortunes in commerce, long acted almost like independent governments in the regions they claimed. For some time, a Dutch trading company virtually ruled the island of Taiwan off the coast of China; the *British East India Company* played a similar role in parts of India during much of the 18th century. The companies in North America traded actively in furs.

ANALYSIS

Causation and the West's Expansion

Because of their central interest in social change, historians inevitably deal with causation. What prompted the fall of Rome? Why did Islam spread so widely? What factors explain why most agricultural civilizations developed patriarchal family structures?

Historical causation differs from the kinds of causation many scientists test. When experiments or observations can be repeated, scientists can gain a relatively precise understanding of the factors that produce a phenomenon and their exact priority: Remove an ingredient and the product changes. Historical causation is more slippery. Major developments may resemble each other, but they never happen the same way twice, and so definitive proof that factor X explains 40 percent of the spread of Buddhism in East Asia is impossible. Despite the fact that historians cannot prove definitively that they have their causation right—and hence often disagree—the attempt to fathom the process continues, for if precision is impossible, high probability is not. Further, probing causation helps us explore the phenomenon itself. We know more about the nature of Western expansion in the 15th and 16th centuries if we discuss what caused it.

Some historians and other social scientists look to one kind of cause as the key to explain a variety of circumstances. Some anthropologists are cultural determinists. They judge that a basic set of cultural factors, usually assumed to be very durable, causes the ongoing differences between societies: Chinese and Greeks, on average, respond differently to emotional stimuli because of their different cultural conditioning. Some historians, in explaining change, also look to the primacy of cultural causation, assuming that a change in ideas or values leads to other developments such as revolutions or inventions. More common is a technological or economic determinism. Some historians regularly look to technological change as setting other changes in motion. Others, including Marxists, argue that economic arrangements, in terms of the way the economy is structured and what groups control it, produce at least the basic framework for innovations. At another pole, some historians used to look to "great men" as the prime movers in history. The causes of change thus became Chinggis Khan or Ashoka, with no need to look much farther.

Various approaches to causation have been applied to the West's explorations and colonial conquests in the early modern period. There is room, certainly, for a "great man" analysis. Many descriptive accounts that dwell on explorers and conquerors—Vasco da Gama and Cortez, for example—and on leaders who sponsored them—such as Henry the Navigator—implicitly suggest that the key cause of the West's new world role stemmed from the daring and vision of exceptional individuals.

Cultural causation can also be invoked. Somehow, Europe's expansion must relate to the wonders of innovation introduced by the Renaissance. A society that spawned humanistic fascination with the power of individuals to achieve and innovate, and to challenge past constraints, also yielded efforts to challenge the spatial limits of Western civilization. Not accidentally, early explorers came from Renaissance Italian city-states. The link with Christian culture is even easier to prove, for a missionary spirit quickly supplemented the efforts of early explorers, leading to more voyages and settlement in Asia and the Americas.

Political causation enters in, if not in causing the initial surge, at least in confirming it. Through the 16th century and beyond, rivalries between the nation-states helped impel a continuing quest for new trade routes and colonies.

There is also room, however, for a simpler, technologically determinist approach. Europe's gains, in this view, came from a handful of new inventions. Benefiting from knowledge of advances in China and the Middle East, Europeans acquired improved navigational techniques, such as the compass. They also adapted explosives by introducing gunnery with special effect in naval cannon. Along with steady improvements in ship design, new techniques explain why Europe gained as it did. Save in the Americas, where they had larger technical and organizational advantages, Europeans advanced in areas they could reach by sea and dominate by ships' cannon—port cities, islands, and trade routes—and not elsewhere. In the simplest rendering of technological determinism, Europe gained simply because of these few technical edges.

Like all determinisms, however, this technological approach raises as many questions as it answers. Why were Europeans so ready to adopt new inventions? Why did other societies that were quickly aware of Europe's innovations, such as China, show little interest in imitation? Chinese policy successfully aimed at containing Europe's penetration by political arrangements, especially in granting limited access through Macao; it deliberately scorned any adoption of Western naval techniques. Here a different culture, plus China's past decision not to expand its seaborne trade, determined a reaction different from that of the West. Technology and culture went hand in hand. Clearly, some combined causal framework is required in this case, with room for individual factors such as the special position of Spain and Portugal after the expulsion of the Muslims.

Finally, the world history context requires the addition of causes resulting from the West's ambiguous position in the interchanges among key civilizations by the 15th century. Europe expanded from special weakness as well as some new strengths. Explorations were goaded by a fear of Muslim superiority and heightened by the impact of the Turkish conquest of Constantinople. Westerners wanted trade routes that would free them from any dependence on the Islamic powerhouse. They also needed new trading strength, for their economic inferiority required them to pay in gold for costly goods such as spices—hence the greed for precious metals that drove so many early expeditions. The results of expansion changed Europe's economic position in the world dramatically, but these should not be confused with initial causation.

Students of history must sort through the factors involved in a development as complex as the West's expansion to refine the list and try to set priorities. We cannot expect uniform agreement on a precise ordering of causation, but we can expect fruitful debate—the kind of debate that has already moved our understanding beyond surface causation, like the powerful personalities of a few people, to a grasp of more underlying contexts.

Questions: If you had to choose a single determinism (cultural, technological, or economic) as basic to social change, which one would you pick? Why? In what ways might the professed motives of Western explorers and colonists have differed from their real motives? Would they necessarily have been aware of the discrepancy?

TOWARD A WORLD ECONOMY

Focal Point: Europe's maritime dominance and the opening of the Atlantic and Pacific oceans had three major consequences in world history. It created a new international pool for basic exchanges of foods, diseases, and a few manufactured products. It created a new *world economy*, involving of course the fuller inclusion of Africa and the first embrace of the Americas in international trade, but setting a different framework even for Europe and Asia. And it created the conditions for direct Western penetration of some parts of the world through the formation of colonies.

The "Colombian Exchange" of Disease and Food

The impact of wider exchange became visible quite quickly. Just as earlier European contacts with Asia, a few centuries previously, had helped spread new plagues, so the extension of international interaction facilitated disease. Here the tragic victims were millions of native Americans who had not previously been exposed to diseases such as smallpox and measles and who therefore had no natural immunities. During the 16th and into the 17th centuries, they died in huge numbers. Overall, in North and South America, well over half the native population would perish; some estimates run as high as 80 percent. Whole island populations in the West Indies were wiped out. Here was a major blow to earlier forms of civilization in the Americas as well as an opportunity for Europeans to forge a partially new population from their own ranks and the ranks of slaves imported from Africa. The devastation occurred over a 150-year period, though some areas were depleted quickly. When Europeans gained contact with Polynesians and Pacific coast Indians in the 18th century, the

DOCUMENT

Western Conquerors: Tactics and Motives

In the first passage, Columbus writes to the Spanish monarchy on his way home from his 1492 expedition. In the second passage, the brother of Francisco Pizarro, the Spanish conqueror of Peru, describes in 1533 how the Inca ruler, Atahuallpa, was defeated.

Columbus's 1492 Expedition

SIR, Believing that you will take pleasure in hearing of the great success which our Lord has granted me in my voyage, I write you this letter, whereby you will learn how in thirty-three days' time I reached the Indies with the fleet which the most illustrious King and Queen, our Sovereigns, gave to me, where I found very many islands thickly peopled, of all which I took possession without resistance for their Highnesses by proclamation made and with the royal standard unfurled. To the first island that I found I gave the name of *San Salvador*, in remembrance of His High Majesty, who hath marvelously brought all these things to pass; the Indians call it *Guanaham*. . . .

Espanola is a wonder. Its mountains and plains, and meadows, and fields, are so beautiful and rich for planting and sowing, and rearing cattle of all kinds, and for building towns and villages. The harbours on the coast, and the number and size and wholesomeness of the rivers, most of them bearing gold, surpass anything that would be believed by one who had not seen them. There is a great difference between the trees, fruits, and plants of this island and those of *Juana*. In this island there are many spices and extensive mines of gold and other metals. The inhabitants of this and of all the other islands I have found or gained intelligence of, both men and women, go as naked as they were born, with the exception that some of the women cover one part only with a single leaf of grass or with a piece of cotton, made for that purpose. They have neither iron, nor steel, nor arms, nor are they competent to use them, not that they are not well-formed and of handsome stature, but because they are timid to a surprising degree. . . .

Although I have taken possession of all these islands in the name of their Highnesses, and they are all more abundant in wealth than I am able to express . . . yet there was one large town in *Espanola* of which especially I took possession, situated in a locality well adapted for the working of the gold mines, and for all kinds of commerce, either with the main land on this side, or with that beyond which is the land of the great Khan, with which there is great profit. . . .

I have also established the greatest friendship with the king of that country, so much so that he took pride in calling me his brother, and treating me as such. Even should these people change their intentions towards us and become hostile, they do not know what arms are, but, as I have said, go naked, and are the most timid people in the world; so that the men I have left could, alone, destroy the whole country, and this island has no danger for them, if they only know how to conduct themselves. . . . Finally, and speaking only of what has taken place in this voyage, which has been so hasty, their Highnesses may see that I shall give them all the gold they require, if they will give me but a very little assistance; spices also, and cotton, as much as their Highnesses shall command to be shipped; and mastic, hitherto found only in Greece . . . slaves, as many of these idolators as their Highnesses shall command to be shipped. . . .

But our Redeemer hath granted this victory our illustrious King and Queen and their kingdoms, which have acquired great fame by an event of such high importance, in which all Christendom ought to

---

same dreadful pattern played out—again cutting back vibrant cultures.

Other exchanges were less dire. New world crops were spread rapidly via Western merchants. American corn was taken up widely in China (where merchants learned of it from Spaniards in the Philippines), the Mediterranean, and parts of Africa. In some cases this productive new crop, along with local agricultural improvements, triggered substantial population increases. China, for example, began to experience long-term population pressure in the 17th century, and new crops played a key role. Europe itself, ironically, was slower to

rejoice, and which it ought to celebrate with great festivals and the offering of solemn thanks to the Holy Trinity with many solemn prayers, both for the great exaltation which may accrue to them in turning so many nations to our holy faith, and also for the temporal benefits which will bring great refreshment and gain, not only to Spain, but to all Christians.

Why and How Atahuallpa Was Defeated

The messengers came back to ask the Governor to send a Christian to Atahuallpa, that he intended to come at once, and that he would come unarmed. The Governor sent a Christian, and presently Atahuallpa moved, leaving the armed men behind him. He took with him about five or six thousand Indians without arms, except that under their shirts they had small darts and slings with stones.

He came in a litter, and before went three or four hundred Indians in liveries, cleaning straws from the road and singing. Then came Atahuallpa in the midst of his chiefs and principal men, the greatest among them being also borne on men's shoulders. . . . A Dominican Friar, who was with the Governor, came forward to tell him, on the part of the Governor, that he waited for him in his lodgings, and that he was sent to speak with him. The Friar then told Atahuallpa that he was a Priest, and that he was sent there to teach the things of the Faith, if they should desire to be Christians. He showed Atahuallpa a book . . . and told him that book contained the things of God. Atahuallpa asked for the book, and threw it on the ground, saying: "I will not leave this place until you have restored all that you have taken in my land. I know well who you are, and what you have come for. . . . " The Friar went to the Governor and reported what was being done, and that no time was to be lost. The Governor sent to me; and I had arranged with the Captain of the artillery that, when a sign was given, he should dis-

charge his pieces, and that, on hearing the reports, all the troops should come forth at once. This was done, and as the Indians were unarmed, they were defeated without danger to any Christian. Those who carried the litter, and the chiefs who surrounded Atahuallpa, were all killed, falling around him. The Governor came out and seized Atahuallpa, and in protecting him, he received a knife cut from a Christian in the hand. The troops continued the pursuit as far as the place where the armed Indians were stationed, who made no resistance whatever, because it was night. All were brought into town, where the governor was quartered.

Next morning the Governor ordered us to go to the camp of Atahuallpa, where we found forty thousand pesos worth of gold and two or three pounds of silver. . . . The Governor said that he had not come to make war on the Indians, but that our Lord the Emperor, who was Lord of the whole world, had ordered him to come that he might see the land, and let Atahuallpa know the things of our Faith. . . . The Governor also told him that that land, and all other lands, belonged to the Emperor, and that he must acknowledge him as his Lord. He replied that he was content, and, observing that the Christians had collected some gold, Atahuallpa said to the Governor that they need not take such care of it, as if there was so little; for that he could give them ten thousand plates, and that he could fill the room in which he was up to a white line, which was the height of a man and a half from the floor.

Questions: What were the main bases for initial European judgments about the characteristics of American Indians? How might the Indians have judged the Europeans? What motives does Columbus appeal to in trying to interest Spanish rulers in the new land?

take advantage of new crops. The use of tobacco, sugar, and coffee spread, but corn and particularly the potato began to win adoption only in the late 17th century, at which point they spurred major population upheaval in Europe as well.

Animal husbandry became more similar across the world as European and Asian animals, such as horses and cattle, were introduced to the New World. The dissemination of basic products and diseases, then, formed an important backdrop to world history from the 16th century on, with massive effects on population structures in various regions.

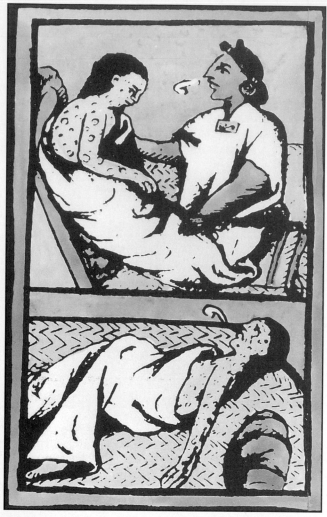

A 16th-century print of Aztec Indians suffering from smallpox during the Cortés invasion (1518–1519).

The West's Commercial Outreach

The development of a new kind of world economy related more directly to European naval advantages. Here, in turn, the key point was the ability of the Europeans to dominate most international trade while steadily increasing its overall levels. Westerners did not displace all Asian shipping from the coastal waters of China and Japan, nor did they completely monopolize the Indian Ocean (see Chapter 28). Along the East African coast, while a few European bases were established, Muslim traders remained active, and the orientation of commerce continued to veer toward the Middle East. Generally, however, the West dominated a great deal of oceanic shipping, even muscling in on trade between other societies, as between India and southeast Asia. This greatly improved Europe's overall profit situation and increased the European ability to determine the framework for international trade, based on disproportionate control of the great merchant companies.

Military muscle backed the surge of trade. In the Mediterranean, for example, a Spanish-directed fleet inflicted a decisive defeat on the navy of the Ottoman Empire in the battle of *Lepanto* in 1571. With this setback, any hope of successful Muslim rivalry against European naval power ended. The Turks rebuilt their fleet and continued their activity in the eastern Mediterranean, just as India and China maintained a stake in Asian shipping, but they could not challenge the Europeans on the larger international routes. Competition for international trade continued among the European powers, not across civilizations. Spaniards vied with English merchant shippers and pirates, and then as Spanish shipping declined, competition among English, Dutch, and French shippers heated up.

Sheer control of the seas and the bulk of international trade involved other incursions of Western power. While the West did not conquer much inland territory in Africa or Asia, it did seek a limited network of secure harbors. Led by Spain and Portugal, then followed by the various northern powers, European ports spread along the west coast of Africa, several parts of the Indian subcontinent, and the islands of Southeast Asia by the 17th century. Even in China, where unusually strong governments limited the Europeans' ability to seize harbors outright, the Portuguese won effective control over the island port of Macao.

European-controlled ports, in turn, brought some fortifications as well as supplies for the omnipresent shipping. They also served as contact areas with overland traders (usually local merchants) and so brought access to inland goods not directly within the reach of the West.

Where scattered ports were not feasible because of effective governments that did not want this kind of foreign interference, European influence and the lure of the trade involved led to the formation of special Western enclaves in existing cities, where Western traders won special rights, often including the ability to regulate themselves rather than be subject to local law. This was the pattern in the Ottoman Empire, where Western merchants set up virtual colonies within Constantinople, and also in Russia, where Western factors (shipping agents) set up first in Moscow and then in St. Petersburg. Elements of this system even emerged in Japan after a firm isolationist policy was launched about 1600, as Dutch traders had some special access to the port of Nagasaki. The point was obvious: Virtually worldwide, international trade gained growing importance in supplementing regional economies. Since the West now ran this trade, the West won special rights of access.

Imbalances in World Trade

What was emerging by the 17th century was a new layering of the world economy, with key Western nations on top. Spain briefly held top position in the 16th century as it brought in silver from the New World. However, its own economy and banking system could not easily accommodate this new wealth—among other things, there was not enough local manufacturing to meet demand—so Spain, like Portugal, declined in economic vitality even while continuing to administer huge colonial empires. The more durable set of economically dominant powers emerged with the second round of exploration and commercial expansion. England, France, and Holland pulled in the lion's share of profits from world trade. Furthermore, these nations and some other parts of western Europe quickly expanded their manufacturing operations so that they were able to export relatively expensive, processed goods—such as guns or manufactured cloth—as well as some high-fashion artisan products in return for cruder unprocessed goods, such as silver or sugar, traded by many other societies. Here, too, was a tidy profit margin.

These dominant core areas in the new world system supplemented their growing economic prowess by self-serving political policies. The doctrines of *mercantilism*, which urged that a nation-state not import goods from outside its own empire but sell exports as widely as possible in its own ships, both reflected and encouraged the new world system. Tariff policies, designed to discourage manufacturing in colonial areas as well as to compete with other Western nation-states, actively furthered the new layering of the world economy.

Beyond Western Europe lay areas that were increasingly enmeshed in the world economy but on a strictly dependent basis. These areas produced low-cost goods in growing quantity: precious metals, and cash crops such as sugar, spice, tobacco, and later cotton. These goods were of course carried in European vessels, with shipping arranged by European agents. In a special though vitally important case, human labor was the item of exchange. Parts of sub-Saharan Africa entered the new world economy mainly on the basis of supplying slaves. In return for relatively unprocessed products—including human beings—Europeans traded their manufactured items while profiting from their control of commercial and shipping services.

The rise of core and dependent economic zones was a vitally important development in world history in the 16th and 17th centuries. Europe's new world economy uprooted many older trade patterns. In West Africa, for example, the earlier orientation toward trading across the Sahara yielded to a dominant focus on the Atlantic and therefore to activities organized by Western shippers. Some parts of West Africa suffered dearly from the decline of the old routes.

A System of International Inequality

Disruptive as they often were at first, the new world economic relationships proved highly durable. Most of the areas established as dependent by the 17th century still, in the late 20th century, suffer some special burdens in world trade. Core and dependent statuses tended to reinforce each other, making it hard to break out of their grasp.

The core-dependent system should not of course be exaggerated, quite apart from the fact that, as we will see, most of the world was not yet fully embraced in it. In dependent areas like Latin America and the slave-supplying parts of Africa, not all people were mired in deepest poverty. African slave traders and princes who taxed the trade might grow rich. In Latin America the silver mines and commercial estates required regional merchants and farmers to supply food. Not all market activity was directly ensnared in Western-dominated world trade, which means that internal social and economic structures could be fairly complex. Further, there were many peasants in Latin America and even more in Africa who were not yet involved in a market economy at all—whether regional or international—but rather produced for local subsistence with traditional motives and methods. It was true, however, that important minorities were wrapped up in production for the world market. It was also true that most African and Latin American merchants and landlords did not fully control their own terms of trade. They might prosper, but their wealth did not stimulate much local manufacturing or general economic advance. Rather, they tended to import European-made goods, including (in the case of American planters) art objects and luxury items.

Moreover, dependence in the world economy had implications beyond the economy itself. It helped determine a coercive labor system. Because dependent economies relied on cheap production of unprocessed goods, there was an inevitable tendency to build a system of forced labor that would cost relatively little even when the overall labor supply was a bit precarious. In the Americas, given the population loss due to disease, this led to the massive importation of African slaves, which brought Africa as well as the Americas into the dependent economic network. Also in the Americas, for many Indians and *mestizos* (people of mixed European and Indian blood), systems of estate management developed that exacted large amounts of labor service and high rents, usually through payments in kind. Systems of this sort not only generated marketable foods such as sugar but also staffed the great silver mines in the Andes. While outright slavery and coercive estate systems developed most fully in the Americas and West Indies, more limited examples of estate agriculture, in which peasants were forced into labor without the legal freedom to leave, arose also for the production of spices in the Dutch East Indies and, by the 18th century, in British-dominated agricultural operations in India.

Forced labor plus the high degree of European influence in economic affairs tended to generate or maintain relatively weak government structures in the dependent areas. Weak governments in Latin America, for example, allowed estates a relatively free hand in regulating their labor force, while substantial poverty among the masses limited the tax revenues available to governments and thus, restricted the effective outreach of governments themselves. In contrast, *core nations*, with growing trade revenues, tended to generate increasing government strength, as in France's absolute monarchy or the nation-state operations of Britain or Holland.

How Much World in the World Economy?

Huge areas of the world were not yet caught up in any intense contact with the world economy. In these areas, the new framework did not significantly influence politics or culture, nor did it prevent vigorous regional economic life. The societies that were external to the world system did not gain ground as rapidly as the core areas of Europe because they did not have the profit opportunities in international trade. Their commercial operations expanded less rapidly, and they did not have the same spurs to additional technological change in transport and manufacturing. Their lag, at least until the 18th century, was relative, not direct; it did not force any particular response, and indeed the societies involved were often blissfully unaware of the gradual shift in relative economic balance.

Dependent economic zones arose mainly in areas where civilizations had developed late and in some isolation, with resultant technological lags behind the Eurasian world. The leading Asian civilizations, in contrast, had ample political strength and economic sophistication to avoid dependent status. They had little need for goods manufactured in Europe. Most trade and production were either aimed at local consumption or destined for regional markets, carried by local shippers overland, by river, or in coastal waters.

East Asia constituted the civilization that remained most fully and consciously external to the burgeoning world economy. The Chinese government, having renounced large-scale international trade of its own early in the 15th century when the great Indian Ocean expeditions were halted just before western Europe began its surge, was resolutely uninterested in elaborate involvement with international trade on someone else's terms. It did copy some firearms manufacturing from the Europeans, though at a fairly low level. Beyond this it depended on extensive government regulation, backed up by a coastal navy, to keep European activities in check. Most of the limited trade that existed was channeled through Macao. European visitors wrote scornfully of China's disdain for military advances. A Jesuit wrote that "the military . . . is considered mean among them." The Chinese were also disparaged for their adherence to tradition. One Western missionary in the 17th century described how, in his opinion, the Chinese could not be persuaded "to make use of new instruments and leave their old ones without an especial order from the Emperor to that effect. They are more fond of the most defective piece of antiquity than of the most perfect of the modern, differing much in that from us who are in love with nothing but what is new."

So China opted out, not keeping up with European developments but also not subservient to European merchants. The world economy thus had little to do with Chinese history through the 18th century. Indeed, at the end of the 18th century, a famous British mission, appealing to the government to open the country to greater trade, was treated to a perfectly accurate rebuff. The imperial court, after insisting on the most abject abasement by the British envoy, haughtily informed him that the Chinese had no need for outside goods. European eagerness for Chinese goods—attested to by the habit adopted in the 17th century of calling fine porcelain "china"—was simply not matched by Chinese enthusiasm, though a trickle of trade continued. Westerners compensated in part by developing their own porcelain industry by the 18th century, which con-

Japanese artists in the 16th century depicted the Europeans and their African slaves as exotic and unfamiliar.

tributed to the early Industrial Revolution, particularly in Britain. Still, there were hopes for commercial entry to China that remained unfulfilled.

Japan, though initially attracted by Western expeditions in the 16th century, also quickly pulled back. The Japanese displayed some openness to Christian missions, and they were also fascinated by Western advances in gunnery and shipping. Guns had particular relevance to Japan's ongoing feudal wars, for there was no disdain here for military life. Yet, Japanese leaders soon worried about undue Western influence and the impact this could have on internal divisions among warring lords, as well as the threat guns posed to samurai military dominance. They encouraged a local gunmaking industry that matched existing European muskets and small cannon fairly readily, but having achieved this they cut off all but the most vestigial contact with any world trade. Japanese were forbidden to travel or trade abroad, the small Christian minority was suppressed, and from the 17th until the 19th centuries, Japan entered a period of almost complete isolation except for some Chinese con-

tact and trading concessions to the small Dutch enclave near Nagasaki.

Several other societies remained substantially untouched by new world trade, participating if at all at levels too low for significant internal impact. The rulers of India's new Mughal Empire in the 16th century were interested in Western traders and even encouraged the establishment of small port colonies, but the bulk of their attention was riveted on internal development; world trade was but a sideline. The same held true for the Ottoman and Safavid empires in the Middle East through the 17th century; their essential dynamics had nothing to do with the West's trading activities, despite the presence of small European enclaves in key cities. Russia also lay outside the world economic orbit. A substantially agricultural society, Russia conducted much of its trade with nomadic peoples in central Asia, which further cushioned it against West European demands. Finally, much of Africa, outside the slave-trading orbit in western regions, was simply untouched by world trade patterns.

The Expansionist Trend

Yet, the world economy was itself not stationary; it tended to gain ground over time. While South America, the West Indies, a part of North America, and some regions in West Africa were first staked out as dependencies beginning in the 16th century, the list subsequently expanded. Portions of Southeast Asia that produced for world markets, under the dominance of the great Western trading companies, were brought into the orbit by the 17th century.

By the late 17th century, Western traders were advancing in India as the Mughal Empire began falling apart. The British and French East India Companies staked out increasing roles in internal trade and administration. Early in the 18th century, Britain began to apply legislation to India that was clearly designed to fit Britain's holdings into a dependent status in the world economy. Notably, tariffs were passed against the import of cotton cloth manufactured in India as a means of protecting Britain's own infant cotton textile industry. The intent was to beat down Indian manufacturing that might have export potential in favor of using India as a market for British-processed goods and a source of outright payments of gold, which the British were exacting in some quantity by the later 18th century. Indian observers were themselves quite aware of the shifting balance. An 18th century account noted:

> But such is the little regard which they [the British] show to the people of this kingdom, and such their apathy and indifference for their welfare, that the people under their dominion groan everywhere, and are reduced to poverty and distress.

India maintained a complex regional economy still, with much internal manufacturing and trade; it was not forced into such complete dependency as, say, Latin America. Nor did coerced labor become as widespread there. Clearly, however, what had initially been a position external to the world economy was being modified, and on the whole to India's disadvantage.

Eastern Europe constituted another area brought into a growing relationship with the world economy and the West European core. The growth of manufacturing in the West, with considerable attendant expansion of cities, created a growing market for imported grains by the 18th century. Much of this market was filled by East European growers, particularly in Prussia and Poland but also to some extent in Russia. Export grains, in turn, were produced mainly on large estates by serfs, who were subjected to increasingly coercive controls, including prolonged periods of labor service. The exports in turn were handled by Western shippers, who also imported Western-made products, including art objects and furnishings for aristocrats. There was no small resemblance between this relationship and that which prevailed in Latin America, with one exception: Outside of Poland, East European governments were considerably stronger than their Latin American counterparts.

The rise and evolution of the world economy thus set a partial, but increasingly important, framework for world history in the centuries after 1500. Along with purely regional developments, as in Japan, it extended the importance of commercial arrangements in many otherwise different societies. It definitely set up a new pecking order among world societies, with the Western core, a number of external societies that lagged in comparison with the West, and finally, several societies in considerable economic dependency. Never before had a single economic system exerted so much effect on such a variety of civilizations, while still, admittedly, falling short of fully determining regional patterns.

COLONIAL EXPANSION

Focal Point: Along with the larger world economic system, a new wave of colonialism took shape following the early Spanish and Portuguese explorations. Key Western nations developed direct overseas empires.

Western colonial outreach began at the same time as the Russian expansion and the spread of the Ottoman and Mughal empires, which also had vital consequences. But the Western colonial pattern, based as it was on naval supremacy, was unusual in bringing considerable Western dominance over a variety of peoples and cultures. It also reinforced the larger world economy, for most colonial areas were quickly placed in a dependent status. Colonial administrations encouraged the production of unprocessed materials and the development of cheap labor systems. The world economic system did not in fact necessitate outright colonies, for certain areas could be brought into partial dependency while retaining their own governments. However, many Western leaders believed that direct control was the only sure way of guaranteeing markets for European products and assuring access to cheap supplies of precious metals, cash crops, timber, and other vital items.

The Americas: Loosely Controlled Colonies

Opportunities for colonies were particularly inviting in the Americas, where European guns, horses, and iron weapons offered special advantages and where in many

Europeans in Florida during the 1590s scorned American Indians for worshipping a column set up by an earlier explorer.

cases political disarray, soon exacerbated by the population losses caused by new disease, provided openings (see Chapter 25). Spain moved first. The Spanish colonized several West Indian islands soon after Columbus's first voyage, starting with Hispaniola and then extending their settlement to Cuba, Jamaica, and Puerto Rico. Only in 1509 did they begin settlement on the mainland, in search of gold; the first colony was established in what is now Panama, under an able if unscrupulous adventurer, *Vasco de Balboa*. Several expeditions fanned out in Central America, and then a separate expedition from Cuba launched the Spanish conquest of the Aztecs in Mexico. Explorations and some settlements in northern Mexico and what is now the American Southwest followed. Another expedition headed toward the Inca realm in the Andes in 1531, where hard fighting was needed before ultimate victory. From this base several colonial expeditions spread to Colombia, other parts of the Andes, and portions of Argentina.

Portugal moved more slowly in Brazil, being initially content with a few small coastal settlements. The need to protect their claim against other European powers like the Dutch, as well as gradual realization of the wealth that could be found in the interior, caused more substantial settlement and a more formal administration.

Early colonies in the Americas were typically developed by small bands of Europeans, often loosely controlled by colonial administrations in the mainland. Thirst for gold drew many adventurers, whose behavior toward each other, as well as toward American Indians, was frequently violent and duplicitous. Where Indian populations were substantial and not totally decimated by disease, the colonial rulers often established only loose controls at first, content to exact tribute without

CLOSEUP

Francisco Pizarro

Francisco Pizarro (1478?–1541) was in many ways a typical Spanish adventurer in Latin America, though an unusually successful one. He first came to the Americas in 1502 and settled on the island of Hispaniola. Later, he joined Balboa's colony in what is now Panama where he received a cattle ranch. Learning of wealth in Peru, he joined with an illiterate soldier and a priest, mounting two expeditions that failed. In 1528 he returned to Spain to gain the king's support and also his agreement that he would be governor of the new province. With these pledges and a force of about 180 men, he attacked the divided Inca empire. Capturing the emperor Atahuallpa, he accepted a large ransom and then strangled him. Several revolts followed during Pizarro's rule from Lima, a coastal city he founded. But the Spanish king ennobled Pizarro for his success. At dinner in 1541, Pizarro was assassinated by a group of Inca rebels.

imposing detailed administration and sometimes leaving existing leaders in place. Gradually, somewhat more formal administration spread, as agricultural settlements were established and official colonial systems took shape under control of bureaucrats sent from Spain and Portugal. Active missionary endeavor, which formed parish churches and a host of missions designed to Christianize the Indians, added another layer of detailed administration throughout the Spanish holdings in North and South America.

France, Britain, and Holland, though latecomers to the Americas, also staked out colonial settlements. French explorations along the St. Lawrence River in Canada led to small colonies around Quebec, from 1608 onward, and explorations in the Mississippi River basin. Dutch and English settlers moved into portions of the Atlantic coastal regions early in the 17th century. Also in the 17th century, all three countries seized and colonized several West Indian islands, which they soon involved in the growing slave trade.

Africa and Asia: Coastal Trading Stations

While Europeans for the most part contented themselves with small coastal fortresses in Africa, negotiating with African kings and merchants but not attempting to claim large territories on their own, there were two important exceptions. From initial coastal settlements, Portugal sent expeditions into Angola in search of slaves. These expeditions had a more direct and more disruptive impact in this part of southwestern Africa than was characteristic elsewhere along the Atlantic coast. More important still was the *Cape Colony* planted by the Dutch on the Cape of Good Hope in 1652. The intent was to form another coastal station in order to supply Dutch ships bound for Asia. But some Dutch farmers were sent, and these *Boers* (the Dutch word for farmers) began to fan out on large farms in a region still lightly populated by Africans. They clashed with local hunting groups, enslaving some of them. Only after 1770 did the expanding Boer settlements directly conflict with Bantu farmers, opening a long battle for control of southern Africa that still raged until recently in the nation of South Africa. South Africa was exceptional, however, because of its mild climate and scant population. Generally, Europeans were deterred by climate, disease, and unnavigable rivers from trying to reach into the interior. The real scramble to colonize Africa came later.

European colonies in Asia were also exceptional. Spain set up an administration for the Philippines, and the Dutch East India company, one of the great government chartered trading units that had sprung up all over western Europe, ousted the Portuguese and administered portions of the main islands of present-day Indonesia and also Taiwan, off the China coast. These holdings, while economically important, did not compel extensive government efforts or substantial settlements from Europe, though the Spanish in the Philippines also mounted a successful missionary effort in the name of the Catholic church.

Colonization in Asia entered a new phase as the British and French began to struggle for control of India, beginning in the late 17th century when the Mughal Empire weakened. Even before the Mughals faltered after the death in 1707 of their last great emperor, Aurangzeb, French and British forts dotted the east and west coasts, along with Portuguese Goa. The Dutch presence in India, briefly a factor, had declined, given the Netherlands' primary focus in the East Indies. As Mughal inefficiency increased, with a resultant surge of regional states ruled by Indians, portions of the subcontinent became an arena for the growing international rivalry between Britain and France.

The British East India Company had two advantages in this competition. Through negotiation with local princes, it had gained a station at *Calcutta*, which gave it some access to the great wealth of the Ganges valley.

Further, the company had enormous influence over the British government and, through Britain's superior navy, excellent communication on the ocean routes. Its French rivals, in contrast, had less political clout at home, where the government was often distracted by European land wars. The French were also more interested in missionary work than the British, who like most Protestants became deeply committed to efforts at conversion in colonial territories only in the 19th century. Before then, the British were content to leave Hindu customs alone and devote themselves to commercial profits.

French–British rivalry raged bitterly through the middle decades of the 18th century. Both sides recruited Indian princes and troops as allies. Outright warfare erupted in 1744 and then again during the Seven Years' War. British officials had become alarmed at growing French influence with local princes and troops. They were also roused by the capture of Calcutta in 1756 by an Indian official, who imprisoned English captives in a "black hole"—a guard room used as a jail by the English themselves; 120 Englishmen suffocated. The East India Company's army recaptured Calcutta and then seized additional Indian and French territory, aided by abundant bribes distributed to many regional princes. French power in India was destroyed, and England was committed—without plan or clear intent as the East India Company dragged the government in its wake—to administration of the region called Bengal, which stretched inland from Calcutta. Soon after this, the British also gained the island of Ceylon (Sri Lanka) from the Dutch. Although the British military force remained small, its superior weaponry, including field artillery, together with tight military organization and alliances with many local leaders, had proved decisive in battles with hostile Indian rulers. At the same time, more sophisticated naval power allowed Britain to outdistance its European rivals. Thus, from 1764 onward, a British empire in India was truly launched. Along with Indonesia and the Americas, India became one of the great territorial acquisitions of the West prior to 1800.

The full history of British India did not begin until late in the 18th century, when the British government took a more active hand in Indian administration, supplementing the quasi government of the East India Company. Indeed, British control of the subcontinent was incomplete. The Mughal Empire remained, though it was increasingly hollow and it controlled scant territory, as did other regional kingdoms, including the Sikh state. Britain gained some new territories by force of arms but was also content to form alliances with local princes without disturbing their internal administration.

This Indian portrait of two ladies in European dress illustrates the English influence in 18th-century India.

British, and to some extent French and Dutch, commercial activities in India had an important effect even before the full implications of India's new colonial status were worked out. Throughout the 18th century, much of India was increasingly drawn into the world trading patterns dominated by the West. Like Indonesia, but unlike the Americas, India offered a well-developed manufacturing economy along with a vast population and a solid agricultural base. European merchants were eager to exploit India's wealth, but were concerned lest India compete with their own manufacturing capabilities. This caused the tariff barriers on Indian exports. By limiting Indian access to a British market, London effectively reduced India's opportunities in world trade. British-made goods, including textiles, were widely sold on the subcontinent. British agents also took growing command over Indian textile production, dictating wages and conditions to the workers, while the British East India Company exported Indian gold as a payment for their costs of administration.

In most cases, European administration of African and Asian colonies remained rather loose. Colonial officials were few in number and were backed by small armed forces supplemented by the omnipresent navies, which could rush in as enforcers in case of emergency. Most administrators depended heavily on deals with local princes; they did not interfere directly in regional affairs or in most aspects of village life. Political and, in many cases, cultural impacts were limited in this situation. In Africa, established kingdoms still held sway. In Asia, significant conversions to Christianity occurred only in the Philippines, and they were even more limited in Africa. European influence was too small, and attachment to established beliefs too great, to effect extensive change. The chief result of colonial acquisitions for the world at large involved the redirection of economic patterns as the new colonies were fit into the world economy.

Few colonies received much European settlement. In Asian holdings, a few merchants and planters joined the sketchy governmental staffs and missionary groups. Dutch South Africa was unusual in that an initially small settler group grew and was joined by some new European immigration (including French Protestants) in the later 17th and 18th centuries. Most West Indian islands drew only small European settlements of plantation owners and the like, though in a few cases, such as Bermuda (previously unpopulated), a relatively large European population lived alongside imported African slaves. Latin America drew somewhat larger groups of Spaniards and Portuguese, and by the 17th century their intermarriage with Indian groups created the largest population segment, the mestizos. People of "pure" European stock continued to hold a special place in Latin American economic and political life, but they were a small minority compared to mestizos, Indians, and (in many areas) imported African slaves. Western impact in terms of sheer numbers of settlers, then, was also limited throughout most of the new colonial holdings.

Impact on Western Europe

Western Europe, of course, was affected by its own colonial success not only economically but also diplomatically. Colonial rivalries and wars added to the endemic hostilities among key nation-states. England and Holland early turned against Spanish success, with great effect. The Dutch and the English competed, engaging in many skirmishes in the 17th century. Then attention turned to the growing competition between the British and the French. This contest had such extensive geographical ramifications—with the Seven Years' War fought in Europe, India, and North America—that it presaged later world wars precipitated in Europe. Economically, colonies supplemented the effects of the overall world economy by bringing new wealth into Europe, encouraging a merchant class, and promoting domestic manufacturing.

There were humbler effects in European society. For example, from the mid-17th century onward, the use of colonially produced sugar spread widely, particularly in countries like Britain with relatively cold climates. Previously, sugar had been a costly, upper-class item. Now for the first time, except for salt, a basic product available to ordinary people was being traded over long distances. The spread of sugar had cultural as well as social and economic significance in giving ordinary Europeans the ability to obtain pleasurable sensations in relatively quick doses—an interesting foreshadowing of later features of Western consumer behavior.

In the world at large, however, the impact of European expansion must be treated in terms of interaction, not simple Western dominance. European penetration affected the history of key civilizations, such as India, but did not bring these civilizations even close to a Western framework. Nor was there any European intent to do so, for the goal was economic differentiation between the West and its colonies, not a merger of equals. Even in Latin America, where the Western impact was far greater than in Africa or Asia, a separate historical record must be written in which the Western share forms only part of a complex story. Western colonialism was an important development in world history by the 18th century, in part because of its role in creating the new world economic system, but it by no means dictated this history even in the regions where it was most pervasive.

British and French North America: Backwater Colonies

One set of colonies stands out from the general pattern in that a fuller development of Western institutions and values took place as part of the early modern colonial experience. In essence, with important modifications suitable to the new location, Western civilization was extended to the Atlantic coast of North America, in the French and particularly in the British colonies, from the 17th century onward.

Colonial holdings in North America—aside from Spain's crucial Mexican colony with its northerly extensions—were generally of least interest to Western colonial powers in the 17th and even the 18th centuries. The Dutch had settlements in what is now New York and New Jersey but were more attached to their Asian colonies. British and French leaders valued their West Indian holdings well above their North American colonies. North America was judged in terms of mercantilism and the world economy and was regarded as a source of crude goods, such as timber and furs, and as a market for costlier imports. But the fact was that the value of North American products was not nearly as great as those available from the Indies or Latin America, and therefore, much less attention was given to careful controls—a crucial ingredient in allowing some merchant and manufacturing activities to emerge among new Americans themselves.

North America remained relatively unimportant in world history through the 18th century. The American colonies that would become the United States had a population of a mere 3 million, far smaller than the powerful colonies in Latin America. The value of imports and exports also remained relatively insignificant. Southern colonies that produced tobacco and sugar, and then cotton, did win importance. Patterns emerged there quite similar to those of Latin America, with large estates based on imported slave labor, a wealthy planter class bent on importing luxury products from western Europe, and relatively weak formal governments. Still, in world historical terms the Atlantic colonies in North America remained something of a backwater amid the larger colonial holdings staked out in the early modern centuries.

Yet, partly because unimportance permitted some freedom of maneuver, the extent to which Western civilization was spread to this new land was important for the future. Driven by religious dissent, ambition, and other motives, Europeans, many from the British Isles, colonized the Atlantic coastal region, where Indian populations were quickly reduced by disease and war. The society that developed in the British colonies was far closer to West European forms than was that of Latin America. The colonies operated their own assemblies, which provided the people with considerable political experience. Local town governments were also active, as, in many cases, were Calvinist church assemblies that gave governing power to groups of elders or wider congregations. Many colonists thus had reason to share with some West Europeans a sense of the importance of representative institutions and self-government. They were also avid consumers of political theories written in Europe, such as the parliamentary ideas of John Locke.

Trade and some manufacturing developed widely. While most international trade was carried in British ships, merchants in the mid-Atlantic colonies and New England made forays of their own. By the late 18th century, some were even trading with China, their ships picking up medicinal herbs along the Pacific coast and exchanging them for Chinese artifacts and tea. Great Britain attempted to impose firmer limits on this modestly thriving local economy, trying to win greater tax revenues and to guarantee markets for British goods and traders, but the effort came too late and helped encourage rebellion in key colonies. Unusual among the West's colonies, North America developed a merchant class and some stake in manufacturing in a pattern similar to that taking shape in western Europe.

North American colonists also retained vigorous cultural ties with western Europe, particularly with Britain and France, where so much cultural action centered in the 17th and 18th centuries. Thanks to Protestant encouragement, an unusual percentage of the colonists were literate, which promoted this kind of cultural exchange. Most Americans focused primarily on religious writings, but even they gave Americans some link to European religious currents, including such later Protestant movements as Methodism. There was also wide reading and discussion of Enlightenment materials, and institutions like the American Philosophical Society formed in the 18th century in deliberate imitation of European scientific institutes. Hundreds of North Americans contributed scientific findings to the British Royal Society. The colonies remained somewhat modest in certain cultural attainments. Art was rather primitive, though many stylistic cues came from Europe. There was no question that in formal culture, North American leaders saw themselves as part of a larger Western world.

The spread of Western values in the Atlantic colonies and in British and French settlements in Canada was also facilitated by the relatively slight ongoing impact of native Americans in these settled areas. The Indian population of this part of North America had always been less dense than in Central America or the Andes region. Because few Indian groups in these regions practiced settled agriculture, instead combining hunting with a slash-and-burn corn-growing complement, European colonists found it relatively easy to displace them from large stretches of territory. The ravages of European-imported disease reduced the Indian population greatly. Furthermore, some Indian groups moved out of the coastal forests spontaneously, from the mid-17th century onward, heading for the plains farther west. Various plains Indians began to adopt the horse after Indians in Mexico first gained its use from the Spanish conquerors. The horse, once present in North America but becoming extinct just as the first Indian settlers arrived from Asia, gave Indian hunters immense advantages in killing bison. Combined with European pressure on the coasts, this induced many forest people to abandon agriculture. Many territorial wars resulted between the North American Indian groups. The net result of all these factors was that while colonists certainly interacted with Indians, learned from them, and feared and misused them, they did not combine with them to forge new cultural amalgams like those in much of Latin America.

By 1700, the importation of African slaves proved to be a more important modification of Western habits, particularly in the southern colonies. The practice of slaveholding and interactions with African culture would mark off North American life from its European counterpart.

North America and Western Civilization

On balance, most white settlers intended to transplant key Western habits into their new setting and managed to do so. Family patterns, for example, were similar. American colonists were able to marry slightly earlier than ordinary West Europeans because of the greater abundance of land, and they had larger families. Still, they reproduced most features of the European-style family, including the primary emphasis on the nuclear unit. The new Americans did display unusual concern for children, if only because they depended so heavily on their work in a labor-scarce environment. European visitors commented on the child-centeredness of American families and the freedom of children to speak up. These variations, while significant, played on trends also becoming visible in Europe, such as the new emphasis on family affection. In other respects, as coastal colonies became more crowded in the 18th century, American families reverted more closely to European patterns, such as marrying later to limit the pressure of large numbers of children on property. In the basic features of life, then, such as family behavior, North American colonists and their European counterparts moved from essentially the same base in very similar directions.

Americans were conscious of some distinctiveness. They lacked Europe's elaborate art and great cities, though they were eager to imitate them. They felt somewhat inferior to the more-powerful mother countries, but they also took pride in what they claimed was greater freedom (slavery was conveniently set apart in a highly racist culture that judged itself by the conditions of whites alone) and a more youthful vigor. The habit of looking to Europe, as well as the spontaneous parallels between key European and American developments in economic, social, and intellectual life, modified the claims to a totally new civilization. Even when key colonies rebelled against European control, as they did in 1776, they moved in the name of Western political ideas and economic goals against the dependency the British belatedly tried to impose, and they proceeded to establish a government that remained within the range of Western political values even though it pioneered some distinctive features.

Crucial diversities arose among the Atlantic colonies. The most important divided the cash-crop, slave-holding colonies, clearly enmeshed as dependents in the European-dominated world economy, from those to the north. There were divisions as well between the colonies that would become the United States and those in Canada.

In Canada, the first substantial European settlements were launched by the French government under Louis XIV. The initial plan involved setting up manorial estates under great lords whose rights were carefully restricted by the state. French peasants were urged to emigrate, though it proved difficult to develop an adequate labor force. However, birth rates were high, and by 1755 *New France* had about 55,000 settlers in a peasant society that proved extremely durable as it fanned out around the fortress of Quebec. Strong organization by the Catholic church completed this partial replica of French provincial society. France lost its colony under the terms of the *Treaty of Paris,* which in 1763 settled the Seven Years' War. France eagerly regained its West Indian sugar islands, along with trading posts in Africa, while Britain took control of Canada and the Mississippi basin. Relations between British officials and the French Canadian community remained strained as British settlements developed in eastern Canada and in Ontario. The flight of many American loyalists after the 1776 revolu-

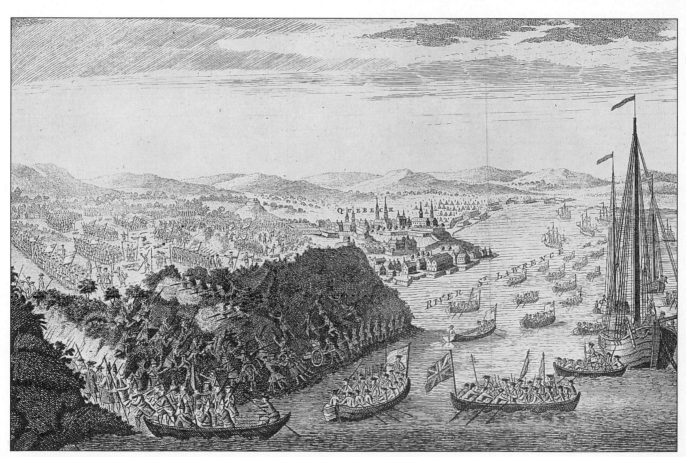

British naval power allowed the light infantry to scale the French fort from the St. Lawrence River and capture Quebec in 1759.

tion added to the English-speaking contingent in Canada.

Many English colonies along the Atlantic seaboard began much as the French in Canada had begun, with grants of land to major proprietors, such as William Penn, who then set about recruiting settlers. New England was an exception, having its early base in Calvinist refugees from religious tensions in Britain. New York began as a Dutch settlement but was taken over easily by an English expedition in 1664. Whatever the initial origins, however, the thirteen colonies that were ultimately set up along the coast all developed local representative assemblies with considerable influence over the governors appointed by the English crown. Economic conditions were considerably more equal than in Europe, and there was no formal aristocracy; only the 23 percent of the population held as slaves stood clearly apart from the mass. This was a new kind of colonial setup, based on significant settlement and on displacement, rather than use or conversion, of the original Indian population. This fact, combined with the loose rule of the British crown, assured a trajectory for this part of North America considerably different from that of the other European holdings. One of the first concrete results of this difference came in the rebellious reaction of many colonists when Britain at last, in 1756, after its expenses in the Seven Years' War, attempted to treat these colonies more similarly to its other vast holdings in order to win clearer economic advantages and also to recoup administrative costs.

CONCLUSION

The Impact of a New World Order

Important as Europe's colonies were in bringing Western influences to new areas of the world, the larger development of the world economy stands as the West's most important, and in some ways most durable, incursion onto the world scene during the centuries after 1500. Like all major shifts in human history, the world economy brought both advantages and disadvantages in its wake. Some societies definitely suffered as economic inequalities between key regions increased. Latin America, major parts of Africa, and even the southern colonies of what became the United States were drawn into the world economy as inferiors, with harsh labor systems and political limitations as a result. Many of these economic inferiorities proved to be self-perpetuating, for few of the initially dependent regions have even today fully achieved economic parity with world economic leaders

or substantial control over their own economic destinies. Correspondingly, the West—ultimately to include much of North America—became a long-term beneficiary in world economic relationships, in a pattern that still substantially prevails today.

The world economy also created new links, mainly through rising commerce, among key societies. Knowledge of new foodstuffs as well as increased trade helped many agricultural societies expand their populations and deal with some problems of scarcity that had previously been irremediable.

Above all, the creation of the world economic framework presented key challenges to virtually every civilization in the world. While not yet a dominant factor in all regions, the world economy, supplemented by the West's military advantages and thirst for colonies, did raise new questions about how to react. Even when the choice involved a new effort at isolation, some innovation was required. The West's new world role, in sum, unleashed an important force for change. Responses varied because of varying conditions and prior traditions, and other changes developed that had little to do with the West one way or the other. Even societies that sought stability above all, however, found their environment shifting, so that some new policies were essential simply to enable them to stand still.

FURTHER READINGS

Excellent discussions of Western exploration and expansion are Carlo Cipolla's *Guns, Sails and Empires: Technological Innovation and the Early Phases of European Expansion 1400–1700* (1965); J. H. Parry's *The Age of Reconnaissance* (1982), and D. Boorstin's, *The Discoverers*. Recent works include Alan K. Smith's, *Creating a World Economy: Merchant Capital, Colonialism and World Trade 1460–1825* (1991) and James Tracy, ed. *The Rise of Merchant Empires* (1986) and the *Political Economy of Merchant Empires* (1991). Somewhat more specific facets are treated in D. K. Fieldhouse's *The Colonial Empires* (1971), J. H. Parry's *The Discovery of South America* (1979), and S. Subrahmanyam's, *The Portuguese Empire in Asia, 1500–1700* (1993). A vital treatment of the international results of new trading patterns of foods and disease is Alfred Crosby's *The Columbian Exchange: Biological and Cultural Consequences of 1492* (1972).

On slavery and its trade, see Eric Williams's *Capitalism and Slavery* (1964), Orlando Patterson's *Slavery and Social Death: A Comparative Study* (1982), and D. B.

Davis's *Slavery and Human Progress* (1984)—the last two being important comparative and analytical statements in a major field of recent historical study. See also Philip D. Curtin's *Atlantic Slave Trade* (1972) and his edited volume, *Africa Remembered: Narratives by West Africans from the Era of the Slave Trade* (1967). A good recent survey of developments in Africa and in the period is Paul Bohannan and Philip Curtin's *Africa and Africans* (3d ed., 1988).

New world trading patterns are discussed in K. N. N. Shanduri's *Trade and Civilization in the Indian Ocean* (1985) and Philip Curtin's *Cross-Cultural Trade in World History* (1984). A controversial theoretical state-

ment about new trade relationships and their impact on politics and social structure is Immanuel Wallerstein's *The Modern World System: Capitalist Agriculture and the Origins of the European World Economy in the Sixteenth Century* (1974) and *The Modern World System: Mercantilism and the Consolidation of the European World Economy 1600–1750* (1980); see also his *Politics of the World Economy: The States, the Movements and the Civilizations* (1984).

For discussions on where colonial North America fits in this period of world history, see Jack Greene and J. R. Pole, eds., *Colonial British America: Essays on the New History of the Early Modern Era* (1984).

Epilogue

The repositioning of western Europe in the world was unquestionably the most important single development in global history during the early modern centuries. The West's new power over international trade and colonial territories was coupled with the unusual dynamism of Western society itself, its ability to innovate in culture, social structure, and political forms. Long-standing relationships began to shift as a result of these changes. The West became the world's center for technological innovation, replacing the various parts of Asia (the Middle East, China, and occasionally central Asia) from which most basic innovations had emanated since the Neolithic revolution. Further change was virtually inevitable, as the West's vigor brought this society closer to more radical shifts in economic forms and to further colonial outreach. The expansion of the West in India during the 18th century—the first significant penetration of a great Asian center—was a portent of more power plays to come.

Yet a whole variety of historical developments took shape in the early modern period, and many of them had little or nothing to do with the West's surge. The complexity and diversity of the world must not be neglected even as due recognition is given to the extraordinary patterns of Western society.

The West thus gained extensive control over only one major area outside its own boundaries, though its conquests were vitally important in the world at large. Technological superiority through guns, iron weaponry, and horses, plus the crushing impact of disease on American populations gave European conquerors a fairly free run through many sections of the Americas. They were able to decapitate the most structured existing civilizations, those of the Aztecs and Incas. Important Indian societies persisted in mountainous regions of Latin America and in much of the North American West, and these would survive for several centuries. Nevertheless, the formal political structures and most elaborate cultures of the Americas now formed under Western influence. They combined with remnants of prior traditions plus the distinctive economic exploitation of American resources, through forced labor and the importation of slavery, to form the first statement of a new American civilization.

This pattern developed nowhere else in the world during the early modern period, for the simple reason that nowhere else did the West have this kind of overwhelming advantage. Western merchants, aided by Western-run coastal settlements along parts of the Atlantic coast of Africa, managed to divert international trading patterns through much of this subcontinent. Routes that once ran up to North Africa across the Sahara, now receded in favor of oceanic trade carried in Western vessels. Further, the most popular cargoes now consisted of slaves, carried to the Americas in huge numbers between the 16th and the 18th centuries—with substantial impact on overall African population size and economic vigor. Nevertheless, Africans continued to run their own societies. Western representatives used care and respect in dealing with local leaders, often genuinely impressed with their canny negotiations and their regal aura. African princes and merchants organized the internal slave trade, often gaining considerable wealth or power in the process. Several kingdoms expanded on the basis of guns imported from the West, and the network of regional monarchies persisted. Major developments occurred independent of Western contacts; thus, late in the 18th century, a wave of popular conversions to Islam occurred south of the Sahara, bringing this religion to ordinary people in the region for the first time.

In Asia, along with limited European penetrations, the big news in the 15th and 16th centuries involved new or revived empires. China underwent territorial expansion and enjoyed great internal commercial prosperity under the Ming dynasty. The Chinese emphasis on "change within tradition" continued to work well, though it was notable that the pace of technological change slackened compared to the postclassical period.

Innovation was the rule in India and the Middle East. The Mughal dynasty in India, produced by Muslim invaders, brought one and one-half centuries of great political stability, economic advance, and cultural creativity. Leading Mughal emperors became great patrons of the arts, and classic Indian monuments such as the Taj Mahal were built during this period. Other empires founded by invaders and bolstered by the use of guns divided the Middle East, with the Safavids holding the

Persian Gulf area and the Ottoman Turks claiming a huge stretch of territory down the eastern Mediterranean to parts of North Africa, including a substantial part of southeastern Europe. Muslim political power reached new heights with these three empires. The Ottomans pushed out the boundaries of their empire for over a century, beginning to stabilize and then modestly recede only in the 17th century; despite the beginning of decline, the Ottoman Empire would last for almost 500 years, a record for regimes in this region.

Innovation described Japanese development, particularly from about 1600 onward when a brief period of contact with Western merchants was replaced by a policy of virtually complete isolation. Internal warfare declined as a central state, the shogunate, gained considerable control over the feudal lords. Government bureaucracy expanded, and Confucian doctrine, imported long before from China but limited in impact at the height of Japanese feudalism, gained ground. Japanese culture became more secular, while artistic creativity persisted at high levels. Internal commerce and agriculture improved as well, in what was proving to be a very dynamic society.

Russia, finally, entered a period of rapid expansion and internal transformation. Russia's achievement of new power was less dramatic than the West's—like all the new empires other than those of western Europe, Russia focused on overland rather than maritime expansion—but it was substantial nevertheless. Russian kings chased out their Mongol rulers in the 15th century, and then began to add to Russian territory in central Asia, eastern Europe, and Northeast Asia. The kings took the title *tsar*, meaning caesar, to celebrate their growing empire and to claim affinity with the great accomplishments of Rome and Byzantium in earlier times. To sustain expansion and improve internal government, Russia by 1700 began to copy selected features of Western structures. Western science and mathematics became standard parts of upper-class education. Western manufacturing was imported to expand Russia's iron production and weapons output. Western dance and art increasingly embellished aristocratic life. Russia did not in the process become Western: it used Western features to establish closer relations with the rest of Europe and to improve its own military prowess and political efficiency. Russian leaders had no desire, however, to promote massive commercial expansion or to experiment with parliamentary political forms. Aristocratic power and tsarist authority were prime goals. Further, Russia's economy depended on an increasingly harsh system of serfdom for peasants and many manufacturing workers, in contrast to the class divisions and wage labor becoming common in Western society. Despite its distinctive features, however, Russia had demonstrated not only the capacity for steady territorial expansion, becoming one of the world's vast land masses, but also the ability to change many long-established aspects of political, cultural, and economic life.

The centuries between 1450 and 1750 were crucial in world history for a host of reasons besides the rise of the West. Western expansion affected several regions significantly; Russia's ability to appropriate certain Western features without becoming Western was an example of complex impact. Developments elsewhere in the world, however, reflected vital innovations quite separate from the Western example. The establishment of new empires, indeed, helps explain why most Asian leaders largely ignored Western initiatives, as they embellished their own new power base. The fact that they were failing to rival Western dynamism did not enter their consciousness and did not, during the bulk of the early modern period, pose a problem for them. Patterns being established in places such as Japan and Africa would, further, have ongoing impact on the societies involved. The importance of popular Islam in sub-Saharan Africa continued to grow, for example, to the end of the 20th century. Japanese secularism and government efficiency played a vital role in developments after the early modern period had ended.

World history, by the 18th century, retained complex patterns. No force organized all developments. Both well-established traditions in key civilizations and capacities to innovate described most major societies, even as the balance of initiatives shifted farther toward the West.

Three developments during the 1790s, after the early modern period was over, neatly suggested the complexity of world relationships and the different definitions that were still being used to measure a society's success. In 1798 a small French expeditionary force easily defeated Egyptian troops, occupying the country for several years despite Ottoman objections and clearly demonstrating a new balance of power between the West and Islam. It was only five years before that the representative of Great Britain, clearly the West's leading commercial power, gained his audience with the Chinese emperor to seek access to the vast Chinese markets. He was treated as if he brought tribute from an inferior state, forced to kowtow as envoys from Korea and Vietnam were required to do. Then, after all his pains, he was treated to the justly famous lecture from the emperor rejecting his argument for more trade, and enjoined to carry the long, patronizing letter to the British King explaining that China had no need for barbarian goods. Finally, in 1796, Toussaint L'Ouverture, a black leader in Haiti, inspired by radical Western political ideas and by fury at the pervasive slave system that ensnared his people, proclaimed national independence and the end of slavery. The result was the second successful rebellion against Western colonialism and the first black-ruled state in the New World. Diversity of power and purpose still ran strong as the early modern period closed.

Glossary

Pronunciation guidance is supplied in square brackets, [ ], after difficult words. The symbols used for pronunciation are found in the table below. Syllables for primary stress are *italicized*.

a	act, bat, marry	i	if, big	u	sum, up
AY	age, rate	I	bite, ice	U	sue, blew, through
âr	air, dare	j	just, tragic	ûr	turn, urge, cur
ä	ah, part, calm	k	keep, coop		
				zh	vision, pleasure
ch	chief, beach	ng	sing		
		o	ox, hot	uh	*a*lone, syst*e*m, eas*i*ly, gall*o*p, circ*u*s
e	edge, set	O	hope, over		
EE	equal, seat, bee	ô	order, ball	A	as in French *a*mi
EER	here, ear	oi	oil, joint	KH	as in German a*ch*, i*ch*
		oo	book, tour	N	as in French bo*n*
g	give, trigger	ou	plow, out	OE	as in French d*eu*x
h	here	sh	she, fashion	R	as in French *r*ouge
hw	which, when	th	thin, ether	Y	as in German f*üh*len

Abbasid [uh bas *id*, ab *uh* sid] Dynasty that succeeded the Umayyads as caliphs within Islam; came to power in 750 C.E. (p. 274)

Abelard, Peter Author of *Yes and No;* university scholar who applied logic to problems of theology; demonstrated logical contradictions within established doctrine. (p. 355)

absolute monarchy Concept of government developed during rise of nation-states in western Europe during the 17th century; featured monarchs who passed laws without parliaments, appointed professionalized armies and bureaucracies, established state churches, imposed state economic policies. (p. 497)

Adena culture First of the mound-building cultures; originating in southern Ohio; lasted until 700 C.E. in some regions. (p. 194)

Aeschylus Greek writer of tragedies. (p. 128)

agrarian revolution Occurred between 8000 and 5000 B.C.E.; transition from hunting and gathering to sedentary agriculture. (p. 13)

Akhenaton [äk *nät* n, ä kuh-] Egyptian pharaoh of the New Kingdom; attempted to establish a one-god religion, replacing the traditional Egyptian pantheon of gods. (p. 34)

al-Ghazali Brilliant Islamic theologian; struggled to fuse Greek and Quranic traditions; not entirely accepted by ulama. (p. 293)

al-Mahdi [al-*mä* dEE] Third of the Abbasid caliphs; attempted but failed to reconcile moderates among Shi'is to Abbasid dynasty; failed to resolve problem of succession. (p. 284)

al-Rashid [al-rä *shEEd*] Most famous of Abbasid caliphs; renowned for sumptuous and costly living; dependent on Persian advisors early in reign; death led to civil wars over succession. (p. 285)

Alexander the Great Successor of Philip II; successfully conquered Persian Empire prior to his death in 323 B.C.E.; attempted to combine Greek and Persian cultures. (p. 122)

Alexandria, Egypt One of many cities of that name founded by Alexander the Great; site of ancient Mediterranean's greatest library; center of literary studies. (p. 122)

Ali Cousin and son-in-law of Muhammad; one of orthodox caliphs; focus for Shi'is. (p. 264)

ali'i [*ä* lEE, *ä* luh EE] High chiefs of Hawaiian society who claimed descent from the gods and rested their claims on their ability to recite in great detail their lineages. (p. 227)

Allah Supreme God in strictly monotheistic Islam. (p. 259)

Almohades [*ä*l mO hädEEz] A reformist movement among the Islamic Berbers of northern Africa; later than the Almoravids; penetrated into sub-Sahara Africa. (p. 310)

Almoravids [al muh *räv* udz] A puritanical reformist movement among the Islamic Berber tribes of northern Africa; controlled gold trade across Sahara; conquered Ghana in 1076; moved southward against African kingdoms of the savanna and westward into Spain. (p. 310)

alpacas Along with llamas, domesticated animals of the Americas; basis for only form of nomadic pastoralism in the New World until European importation of larger animals in 15th century C.E. (p. 197)

Amaterasu [*ä* mä te *Rä* sU] Sun goddess of the Shinto religion. (p. 219)

Anasazi "The ancient ones"; culture located in southwestern United States; flourished from 200 to 1200 C.E.; featured large multistory adobe and stone buildings built in protected canyons or cliffs. (p. 195)

Anglican church   Form of Protestantism set up in England after 1534; established by Henry VIII with himself as head at least in part to obtain a divorce from his first wife; became increasingly Protestant following Henry's death. (p. 489)

animism   A religious outlook that sees gods in many aspects of nature and propitiates them to help control and explain nature; typical of Mesopotamian religions. (p. 27)

Antigonids   One of the regional dynasties that followed the death of Alexander the Great; founded in Macedonia. (p. 123)

Aquinas, Thomas   Creator of one of the great syntheses of medieval learning; taught at University of Paris; author of several *Summas;* believed that through reason it was possible to know much about natural order, moral law, and nature of God. (p. 357)

arabic numerals   Actually an Indian system of numerical notation transported by Arabs to West; central to two scientific revolutions. (p. 280)

Aragon   Along with Castile, a regional kingdom of the Iberian peninsula; pressed reconquest of peninsula from Muslims; developed a vigorous military and religious agenda. (p. 468)

Archaic cultures   Hunting-and-gathering groups dispersed over the American continents by 9000 B.C.E. (p. 184)

Aristophanes   [ar uh *stof* uh nEEz] Greek writer of the comedies; author of *The Frogs.* (p. 125)

Aristotle   Greek philosopher; teacher of Alexander the Great; knowledge based on observation of phenomena in material world. (p. 124)

Arthashastra   [är thä *shäs* trä] Political treatise written during reign of Chandragupta Maurya; advocated use of spies and assassins, bribery, and scientific forms of warfare. (p. 149)

Aryans   Indo-European nomadic pastoralists who replaced Harappan civilization; militarized society. (p. 7)

Ashikaga, Takuaji   [ä shEE kä gä tä kwä ji] Member of the Minamoto family; overthrew the Kamakura regime and established the Ashikaga Shogunate from 1336–1573; drove emperor from Kyoto to Yoshino. (p. 425)

Ashoka   [uh *sO* kuh] Grandson of Chandragupta Maurya; completed conquests of Indian subcontinent; converted to Buddhism and sponsored spread of new religion throughout his empire. (p. 149)

Atlantic colonies   British colonies in North America; originally restricted to coastline of Atlantic Ocean from New England to Georgia. (p. 528)

Augustine (Saint) 354–430 C.E.   Influential church father and theologian; born in Africa and ultimately Bishop of Hippo in Africa; champion of Christian doctrine against various heresies and very important in the long-term development of Christian thought on such issues as predestination. (p. 247)

Augustus Caesar   Name given to Octavian following his defeat of Mark Anthony and Cleopatra; first emperor of Rome. (p. 165)

Austronesian   Family of 30 related languages found in the Philippines, Indonesia, and Southeast Asia; people of this linguistic group migrated throughout Pacific. (p. 225)

Axum   Kingdom located in Ethiopian highlands; replaced Meroe in first century C.E.; received strong influence from Arabian peninsula; eventually converted to Christianity. (pp. 40, 211)

ayan   [ä yän] The wealthy landed elite that emerged in the early decades of Abbasid rule. (p. 277)

ayllus   [äy zhoos] Households in Andean societies that recognized some form of kinship; traced descent from some common, sometimes mythical ancestor. (p. 201)

Aztecs   The Mexica; one of the nomadic tribes that used political anarchy after fall of Toltecs to penetrate into the sedentary agricultural zone of Mesoamerican plateau; established empire after 1325 around shores of Lake Texcoco. (p. 194)

Babylonian empire   Unified all of Mesopotamia c. 1800 B.C.E.; collapsed due to foreign invasion c. 1600 B.C.E. (p. 30)

Baghdad   Capital of Abbasid dynasty located in Iraq near ancient Persian capital of Ctesiphon. (p. 275)

Baibars   [bI *bars*] Commander of Mamluk forces at Ain Jalut; originally enslaved by Mongols and sold to Egyptians. (p. 451)

Bakr, Abu   [*bak* uhr, uh bU] One of Muhammad's earliest converts; succeeded Muhammad as first caliph of Islamic community. (p. 268)

bakufu   Military government established by the Minamoto following the Gempei Wars; centered at Kamakura; retained emperor, but real power resided in military government and samurai. (p. 422)

Balboa Vasco de   First Spanish captain to begin settlement on the mainland of Mesoamerica in 1509; initial settlement eventually led to conquest of Aztec and Inca empires by other captains. (p. 523)

Balkan   Peninsula located in southeastern Europe, including Macedonia and Greece, plus what became Bulgaria; controlled by Byzantine Empire. (p. 330)

ball games   Ritual elements of many American cultures; played on formal courts; religious significance required that losing teams pay penalty of forfeiture of goods or their lives. (p. 190)

band   A level of social organization normally consisting of 20 to 30 people; nomadic hunters and gatherers; labor divided on a gender basis. (p. 10)

Bantu   Originated in eastern Nigeria in West Africa; migrated into central and southern Africa using rivers—particularly the Congo Basin; village dwellers who depended on agriculture and fishing. (p. 206)

Basil   Patriarch at Constantinople in mid-4th century; responsible for development of rule for Christian monasticism in Byzantine Empire. (p. 329)

Battle of River Zab   Victory of Abbasids over Umayyads; resulted in conquest of Syria and capture of Umayyad capital. (p. 274)

Battle of Siffin Fought in 657 between forces of Ali and Umayyads; settled by negotiation that led to fragmentation of Ali's party. (p. 270)

Batu Ruler of Golden Horde; one of Chinggis Khan's grandsons; responsible for invasion of Russia beginning in 1236. (p. 446)

bedouin Nomadic pastoralists of the Arabian peninsula; culture based on camel and goat nomadism; early converts to Islam. (p. 261)

Belisarius One of Justinian's most important military commanders during period of reconquest of western Europe; commanded in North Africa and in Italy. (p. 330)

Benedict of Nursia Founder of monasticism in what had been the western half of the Roman Empire; established Benedictine Rule in the 6th century; paralleled development of Basil's rules in Byzantine Empire. (pp. 247, 348)

Benin City-state formed in 14th century under Ewuare the Great (1400–1473); control extended from Niger River to coast near modern Lagos. (p. 323)

Berke [*ber* kuh] Ruler of the Golden Horde; converted to Islam; his threat to Hulegu combined with the growing power of Mamluks in Egypt forestalled further Mongol conquests in the Middle East. (p. 451)

St. Bernard of Clairvaux [bûr *närd* uhv klär *vO*] Emphasized role of faith in preference to logic; stressed importance of mystical union with God; successfully challenged Abelard and had him driven from the universities. (p. 355)

bhaktic cults [*buk* tEEk] Groups dedicated to gods and goddesses; stressed the importance of strong emotional bonds between devotees and the god or goddess who was the object of their veneration; most widely worshipped gods were Shiva and Vishnu. (p. 299)

bishops Headed Christian churches and regional centers and supervised the activities of other churches within the jurisdictional area. (p. 177)

Black Death Plague that struck Europe in 14th century; significantly reduced Europe's population; affected social structure. (p. 366)

bodhisattvas [bO duh *sut* vuhs] Buddhist holy men; built up spiritual merits during their lifetime; prayers even after death could aid people to achieve reflected holiness. (p. 246)

Body of Civil Law Justinian's codification of Roman law; reconciled Roman edicts and decisions; comprehensive system made Roman law coherent basis for political and economic life. (p. 330)

Boers Dutch settlers in Cape Colony. (p. 525)

boyars Russian aristocrats; possessed less political power than did their counterparts in western Europe. (p. 340)

British East India Company Joint stock company that obtained government monopoly over trade in India; acted as virtually independent government in regions it claimed. (p. 513)

Bronze Age From 4000 to 3000 B.C.E.; increased use of plows, metalworking; development of wheeled vehicles, writing. (p. 14)

Buddha Creator of major Indian and Asian religion; born in 6th century B.C.E. as son of local ruler among Aryan tribes located near Himalayas; became an ascetic; found enlightenment under bo tree; taught that enlightenment could be achieved only by abandoning desires for all earthly things. (p. 146)

Bulgaria Slavic kingdom established in northern portions of Balkan peninsula; constant source of pressure on Byzantine Empire; defeated by Emperor Basil II in 1014. (p. 331)

bushi Regional warrior leaders in Japan; ruled small kingdoms from fortresses; administered the law, supervised public works projects, and collected revenues; built up private armies. (p. 419)

Buyids Regional splinter dynasty of the mid-10th century; invaded and captured Baghdad; ruled Abbasid Em-

pire under name of sultan; retained Abbasids as figureheads. (p. 287)

Byzantine Empire Eastern half of Roman Empire following collapse of western half of old empire; retained Mediterranean culture, particularly Greek; later lost Palestine, Syria, and Egypt to Islam; capital at Constantinople. (pp. 242, 328)

Caesar, Julius Roman general responsible for conquest of Gaul; brought army back to Rome and overthrew republic; assassinated in 44 B.C.E. by conservative senators. (p. 165)

Calcutta Headquarters of British East India Company in Bengal in Indian subcontinent; located on Ganges; captured in 1756 during early part of Seven Years' War; later became administrative center for all of Bengal. (p. 525)

caliph The political and religious successor to Muhammad. (p. 268)

calpulli Seven clans in Aztec society, later expanded to more than sixty; divided into residential groupings that distributed land and provided labor and warriors. (p. 378)

Calvin, Jean French Protestant who stressed doctrine of predestination; established center of his group at Swiss canton of Geneva; encouraged ideas of wider access to government, wider public education; spread from Switzerland to northern Europe and North America. (p. 489)

camel nomads Nomadic pastoralists dependent on domesticated camels; common to Arabian peninsula and Sudanic Africa; associated with development of major trade routes. (p. 78)

cannibal kingdom Modern interpretation of Aztec society created by Marvin Harris; based on observation that Mesoamerica lacked cattle and sheep that replaced human sacrifice in the Old World. (p. 384)

Cape Colony Dutch colony established at Cape of Good Hope in 1652 initially to provide a coastal station for the Dutch seaborne empire; by 1770 settlements had expanded sufficiently to come into conflict with Bantus. (p. 525)

Cape of Good Hope Southern tip of Africa; first circumnavigated in 1488 by Portuguese in search of direct route to India. (p. 511)

Carolingians Royal house of Franks after 8th century until their replacement in 10th century. (p. 348)

Carthage Originally a Phoenician colony in northern Africa; became a major port and commercial power in the western Mediterranean; fought the Punic Wars with Rome for dominance of the western Mediterranean. (p. 163)

caste system Rigid system of social classification first introduced into Indian subcontinent by Aryans. (p. 139)

Castile Along with Aragon, a regional kingdom of the Iberian peninsula; pressed reconquest of peninsula from Muslims; developed a vigorous military and religious agenda. (p. 468)

Çatal Huyuk [*chät* l hU *yook*] Early urban culture based on sedentary agriculture; located in modern southern Turkey; was larger in population than Jericho, had greater degree of social stratification. (p. 18)

Catholic Reformation Restatement of orthodox Catholic beliefs in response to Protestant Reformation; established councils that revived Catholic doctrine and refuted Protestant beliefs. (p. 489)

cattle herders Nomadic pastoralists dependent on domesticated cattle; common to region from upper reaches of Nile to southern Africa; little impact on civilizations until later date. (p. 78)

Celts Inhabited most of Britain and Ireland; organized in small regional kingdoms; featured mixed agricultural and hunting economies; replaced in most places by Germans. (p. 215)

Chabi Influential wife of Kubilai Khan; promoted interests of Buddhists in China; indicative of refusal of Mongol women to adopt restrictive social conventions of Chinese. (p. 454)

Chams Indianized rivals of the Vietnamese; driven into the highlands by the successful Vietnamese drive to the south. (p. 436)

Chan Buddhism Known as Zen in Japan; stressed meditation and appreciation of natural and artistic beauty; popular with members of elite Chinese society. (p. 397)

Chandragupta Maurya [chun druh *gUp* tuh *mour* EE uh] Founder of Maurya dynasty; established first empire in Indian subcontinent; first centralized government since Harappan civilization. (p. 149)

Changan Capital of Tang dynasty; population of two million, larger than any other city in the world at that time. (p. 396)

Charlemagne [*shär* luh mAYn] Charles the Great; Carolingian monarch who established substantial empire in France and Germany c. 800. (p. 348)

Chavín culture Appeared in highlands of Andes between 1800 and 1200 B.C.E.; typified by ceremonial centers with large stone buildings; greatest ceremonial center was Chavín de Huantar; characterized by artistic motifs. (p. 200)

Chichen Itzá Originally a Mayan city; conquered by Toltecs c. 1000 and ruled by Toltec dynasties; architecture featured pyramid of Feathered Serpent (Quetzalcoatl). (p. 194)

chichimecs American hunting-and-gathering groups; largely responsible for the disruption of early civilizations in Mesoamerica. (p. 78)

chiefdom Widely diffused pattern of social organization in the Americas; featured chieftains who ruled from central towns over a large territory including smaller towns or villages that paid tribute; predominant town often featured temples and priest class. (p. 200)

Chimu state Regional Andean chiefdom that flourished from 800 to 1465 C.E.; fell to Incas. (p. 201)

chinampas Beds of aquatic weeds, mud, and earth placed in frames made of cane and rooted in lakes to create "floating islands"; system of irrigated agriculture utilized by Aztecs. (p. 376)

Chinggis Khan [*jeng* guhs *kän*] Born in 1170s in decades following death of Kabul Khan; elected khagan of all Mongol tribes in 1206; responsible for conquest of northern kingdoms of China, territories as far west as the Abbasid regions; died in 1227, prior to conquest of most of Islamic world. (pp. 88, 293, 440)

Choson Earliest Korean kingdom; conquered by Han emperor in 109 B.C.E. (p. 428)

Cicero Conservative Roman senator; Stoic philosopher; one of great orators of his day; killed in reaction to assassination of Julius Caesar. (p. 165)

city-state A form of political organization typical of Mesopotamian civilizations; consisted of agricultural hinterlands ruled by an urban-based king. (p. 26)

civilization Societies distinguished by reliance on sedentary agriculture, ability to produce food surpluses; and existence of nonfarming elites, as well as merchant and manufacturing groups. (p. 6)

Classic Period in Americas from 150 to 900 C.E.; period of greatest cultural achievement. (p. 188)

clientage The social relationship whereby wealthy Roman landholders offered protection and financial aid to lesser citizens in return for political support and labor. (p. 163)

Clisthenes [*klis* thuh nEEz] Athenian reformer of late 6th century B.C.E.; established democratic Council of 500 in Athens. (p. 117)

Clovis Early Frankish king; converted Franks to Christianity c. 496; allowed establishment of Frankish kingdom. (p. 347)

Cluny Monastery in France; site of religious reform movement aimed at restoring purity of monastic movement and removing secularism. (p. 353)

Columbus, Christopher Genoese captain in service of king and queen of Castile and Aragon; successfully sailed to New World and returned in 1492; initiated European discoveries in Americas. (p. 511)

Confucius Also known as Kung Fuzi; major Chinese philosopher; born in 6th century B.C.E.; author of *Analects;* philosophy based on need for restoration of order through advice of superior men to be found among the shi. (p. 92)

Constantine   Roman emperor from 312 to 337 C.E.; established second capital at Constantinople; attempted to use religious force of Christianity to unify empire spiritually. (p. 240)

consuls   Two chief executives or magistrates of the Roman republic; elected by an annual assembly dominated by aristocracy. (p. 163)

Copernicus   Polish monk and astronomer; disproved Hellenistic belief that earth was the center of the universe. (p. 493)

Copts   Christian sect of Egypt; tended to support Islamic invasions of this area in preference to Byzantine rule. (p. 310)

core nations   Nations, usually European, that enjoyed profit from world economy; controlled international banking and commercial services such as shipping; exported manufactured goods for raw materials. (p. 520)

Corinthian   Along with Doric and Ionian, distinct style of Hellenistic architecture; the most ornate of the three styles. (p. 126)

Council of Nicaea   Christian council that met in 325 C.E. to determine orthodoxy with respect to persons of Trinity; insisted on divinity of all persons of the Trinity. (p. 247)

courage cultures   Cultures dominated by warlike males bound to each other by strong ties of personal loyalty; such cultures place emphasis on personal honor and physical courage; typical among pastoral nomads. (p. 80)

Crusades   Series of military adventures initially launched by western Christians to free Holy Land from Muslims; temporarily succeeded in capturing Jerusalem and establishing Christian kingdoms; later used for other purposes such as commercial wars and extermination of heresy. (pp. 288, 352)

culture   Combinations of the ideas, objects, and patterns of behavior that result from human social interaction. (p. 6)

cuneiform   [kyU *nEE* uh fòrm , *kyU* nEE uh-] A form of writing developed by the Sumerians using a wedge-shaped stylus and clay tablets. (p. 26)

curacas   Ayllu chiefs with privileges of dress and access to resources; community leaders among Andean societies. (p. 202)

Cyril   Along with Methodius, missionary sent by Byzantine government to eastern Europe and the Balkans; converted southern Russia and Balkans to Orthodox Christianity; responsible for creation of written script for Slavic known as Cyrillic. (p. 336)

Cyrus the Great   Established massive Persian Empire by 550 B.C.E.; successor state to Mesopotamian empires. (p. 114)

da Gama, Vasco   Portuguese captain who first reached India in 1497; established early Portuguese dominance in Indian Ocean. (p. 511)

daimyos   Warlord rulers of 300 small states following Onin War and disruption of Ashikaga Shogunate; holdings consolidated into unified and bounded ministates. (p. 425)

Damascus   Capital of Umayyad caliphate. (p. 270)

Daoism   Philosophy associated with Laozi; stressed need for alignment with Dao or cosmic force. (p. 94)

Dasas   Aryan name for indigenous people of Indus valley region; regarded as socially inferior to Aryans. (p. 54)

Deism   Concept of God current during the scientific revolution; role of divinity was to set natural laws in motion, not to regulate once process was begun. (p. 495)

Delian league   Alliance formed by Athens after the Persian wars; cities contributed to unified treasury on island of Delos to support alliance fleet; later taken over by Athens and became Athenian Empire. (p. 120)

Demak   Most powerful of the trading states on north coast of Java; converted to Islam and served as point of dissemination to other ports. (p. 301)

Demographic Transition   The change from a high birth rate and high

infant mortality to low rates, as in western Europe and U.S. in late 19th century. (p. 320)

demography   The study of population. (p. 320)

dependent economic zones   Those regions within the world economy that produced raw materials; dependent on European markets and shipping; tendency to build system of forced, inexpensive labor. (p. 520)

Descartes, René   [dAY *kärt*] Established importance of skeptical review of all received wisdom; argued that human reason could then develop laws that would explain the fundamental workings of nature. (p. 493)

Devi   Mother goddess within Hinduism; widely spread following collapse of Guptas; encouraged new emotionalism in religious ritual. (p. 236)

dharma   [*där* muh, *dur*-] The caste position and career determined by a person's birth; Hindu culture required that one accept one's social position and perform occupation to the best of one's ability in order to have a better situation in the next life. (p. 142)

dhimmis   Literally "people of the book"; applied as inclusive term to Jews and Christians in Islamic territories; later extended to Zoroastrians and even Hindus. (p. 271)

dhows   Arab sailing vessels with triangular or lateen sails; strongly influenced European ship design. (p. 276)

Diocletian   Roman emperor from 284 to 305 C.E.; restored later empire by improved administration and tax collection. (p. 240)

direct democracy   Literally rule of the people; as interpreted in Athens, all decisions emanated from popular assembly without intermediation of elected representatives. (p. 117)

Doric   Along with Ionian and Corinthian, distinct style of Hellenistic architecture; the least ornate of the three styles. (p. 126)

Dutch East India Company   Joint stock company that obtained government monopoly over trade in Asia;

acted as virtually independent government in regions it claimed. (p. 512)

East African trading ports   Urbanized commercial centers sharing common Bantu-based and Arabic-influenced Swahili language and other cultural traits; included Mogadishu, Mombasa, Malindi, Kilwa, Pate, and Zanzibar. (p. 319)

edict of Nantes   Grant of tolerance to Protestants in France in 1598; granted only after lengthy civil war between Catholic and Protestant factions. (p. 489)

English Civil War   Conflict from 1640 to 1660; featured religious disputes mixed with constitutional issues concerning the powers of the monarchy; ended with restoration of the monarchy in 1660 following execution of previous king. (p. 490)

Enlightenment   Intellectual movement centered in France during the 18th century; featured scientific advance, application of scientific methods to study of human society; belief that rational laws could describe social behavior. (p. 501)

Epic of Gilgamesh   The first literary epic in Western civilization; written down c. 2000 B.C.E.; included story of Great Flood. (p. 26)

Ethiopian kingdom   A Christian kingdom that developed in the highlands of eastern Africa under the dynasty of King Lalaibela; retained Christianity in the face of Muslim expansion elsewhere in Africa. (p. 310)

Etruscans   Culture that ruled Rome prior to republic; ruled through powerful kings and well-organized armies; expelled by Romans c. 510 B.C.E. (p. 163)

eunuchs   Castrated males used within the households of Chinese emperors, usually to guard the emperors' concubines; became political counterbalance to powerful marital relatives during Later Han. (p. 109)

extended families   Consisted of several generations, including the family patriarch's sons and grandsons with their wives and children; typical of Shang China elites. (p. 57)

fallow   Fields allowed to remain uncultivated; utilized as a means of restoring fertility to the soil during the Middle Ages; until 8th century normally one-half of fields; after 8th century only one-third of fields. (p. 347)

feudalism   The social organization created during the Middle Ages by exchanging grants of land or fiefs in return for formal oaths of allegiance and promises of loyal service; typical of Zhou dynasty; greater lords provided protection and aid to lesser lords in return for military service. (p. 350)

five pillars   The obligatory religious duties of all Muslims; confession of faith, prayer, fasting during Ramadan, zakat, and hajj. (p. 267)

flying money   Chinese credit instrument that provided credit vouchers to merchants to be redeemed at the end of the voyage; reduced danger of robbery; early form of currency. (p. 405)

foot-binding   Practice in Chinese society to mutilate women's feet in order to make them smaller; produced pain and restricted women's movement; made it easier to confine women to the household. (p. 408)

Forbidden City   Imperial precinct with the capital cities of China; only imperial family, advisors, and household were permitted to enter. (p. 106)

Francis I   King of France; regarded as Renaissance monarch; patron of arts, imposed new controls on Catholic church; ally of Ottoman sultan against holy Roman emperor. (p. 487)

Frederick the Great   Prussian king; attempted to introduce Enlightenment reforms into Germany; built on military and bureaucratic foundations of his predecessors; introduced freedom of religion; increased state control of economy. (p. 501)

Fujiwara   Japanese aristocratic family in mid-9th century; exercised exceptional influence over imperial affairs; aided in decline of imperial power. (p. 419)

Galileo   Published Copernicus's findings; added own discoveries concerning laws of gravity and planetary motion;

condemned by the Catholic church for his work. (p. 493)

Gempei Wars   [gem pe] Waged for five years from 1180, on Honshu between Taira and Minamoto families; resulted in destruction of Taira. (p. 422)

Germans   Resided outside the northern boundaries of the Roman Empire; featured mixed agricultural and pastoral economies; moved southward into Roman Empire in course of 4th and 5th centuries C.E. (p. 215)

Ghana   First great sub-Saharan state; created by Soninke people; by 9th century C.E. a major source of gold in the Mediterranean world. (p. 209)

Ghazni Empire   Dynasty and empire founded from Turks who were originally slaves; seized power in 962 in Afghanistan north of Indus valley; later invaded Indian subcontinent. (p. 297)

Glorious Revolution   English overthrow of James II in 1688; resulted in affirmation of parliament as having basic sovereignty over the king. (p. 499)

Golden Horde   One of the four regional subdivisions of the Mongol Empire after Chinggis Khan's death; territory covered much of what is today south central Russia. (p. 447)

Gothic   An architectural style developed during the Middle Ages in western Europe; featured pointed arches and flying buttresses as external supports on main walls. (p. 358)

Gracchus, Gaius   Along with Tiberius, tribune who attempted to introduce land and citizenship reform within the Roman republic; killed on the command of the Senate. (p. 165)

Great Wall   Chinese defensive fortification intended to keep out the nomadic invaders from the north; initiated during Qin dynasty and reign of Shi Huangdi. (p. 97)

Great Zimbabwe   Bantu confederation of Shona-speaking peoples located between Zambezi and Limpopo rivers; developed after 9th century; featured royal courts built of stone; created centralized state by 15th century; king took title of Mwene Mutapa. (p. 323)

Greek fire   Byzantine weapon consisting of mixture of chemicals that ignited when exposed to water; utilized to drive back the Arab fleets that attacked Constantinople. (p. 331)

Gregory VII   Pope during the 11th century who attempted to free Church from interference of feudal lords; quarreled with Holy Roman Emperor Henry IV over practice of lay investiture. (p. 353)

griots   [grEE O, *grEE* O, *grEE* ot] Professional oral historians who served as keepers of traditions and advisors to kings within the Mali Empire. (p. 316)

guilds   Sworn associations of people in the same business or trade in a single city; stressed security and mutual control; limited membership, regulated apprenticeship, guaranteed good workmanship; often established franchise within cities. (p. 360)

Guptas   Dynasty that succeeded the Kushanas in the 3d century C.E.; built empire that extended to all but the southern regions of Indian subcontinent; less centralized than Mauryan Empire. (p. 153)

gurus   Brahmans who served as teachers for the princes of the imperial court of the Guptas. (p. 146)

Gutenberg, Johannes   Introduced movable type to western Europe in 15th century; credited with greatly expanded availability of printed books and pamphlets. (p. 487)

hadiths   Traditions of the prophet Muhammad. (p. 272)

Hagia Sophia   [hä juh sä *fEE* uh] New church constructed in Constantinople during reign of Justinian. (p. 330)

hajj   Pilgrimage to the holy city of Mecca to worship at the Ka'ba. (p. 267)

Hajjaj   [KHaj *jäj*] Umayyad viceroy for eastern provinces; launched punitive campaign against king of Sind in India that resulted in first Islamic conquest in subcontinent. (p. 295)

Hammurabi   The most important ruler of the Babylonian empire; responsible for codification of law. (p. 30)

Han dynasty   Chinese dynasty that succeeded the Qin in 202 B.C.E.; ruled for next 400 years. (p. 101)

Hangzhou   [*häng jO*] Capital of later Song dynasty; located near East China Sea; permitted overseas trading; population exceeded one million. (p. 406)

Hannibal   Great Carthaginian general during Second Punic War; successfully invaded Italy but failed to conquer Rome; finally defeated at Battle of Zama. (p. 164)

Hanseatic League   An organization of cities in northern Germany for the purpose of establishing a commercial alliance. (p. 360)

hapu   Primary social unit of Maori society in New Zealand; divisions of tribes consisting of extended families; land allotted to extended families in common. (p. 228)

Harappa   Along with Mohenjo-daro, major urban complex of the Harappan civilization; laid out on planned grid pattern. (p. 48)

Harappan civilization   First civilization of Indian subcontinent; emerged in Indus River valley c. 2500 B.C.E. (p. 51)

Harsha   Descendent of Guptas in India; briefly constructed a loose empire in northern India between 616 and 657 C.E. (p. 294)

Harvey, John   English physician who demonstrated the circular movement of blood in animals, function of heart as pump. (p. 493)

Hausa states   Combined Muslim and pagan traditions; emerged following the demise of Songhay Empire among the Hausa peoples of northern Nigeria, based on cities such as Kano. (p. 311)

Heian   [*hAΥ* än] Capital city of Japan under the Yamato emperors, later called Kyoto; built in order to escape influence of Buddhist monks; patterned after ancient imperial centers of China; never fully populated. (pp. 221, 417)

Hellenism   Culture derived from the Greek civilization that flourished between 800 and 400 B.C.E. (p. 123)

Hellenistic period   That culture associated with the spread of Greek influence as a result of Macedonian conquests; often seen as the combination of Greek culture with eastern political forms. (p. 123)

helots   Conquered indigenous population of Spartan city-state; provided agricultural labor for Spartan landowners; only semi-free; largest population of Spartan city-state. (p. 120)

Henry the Navigator   Portuguese prince responsible for direction of series of expeditions along the African coast in the 15th century; marked beginning of western European expansion. (p. 510)

hieroglyphs   The form of writing developed in ancient Egypt; more pictorial than Mesopotamian cuneiform. (p. 34)

hijra   [*hij* ruh] Flight of Muhammad and followers in 622 C.E. from Mecca to Yathrib or Medina; marks first year of Islamic calendar. (p. 258)

Himalayas   Mountain region marking the northern border of the Indian subcontinent; site of the Aryan settlements that formed small kingdoms or warrior republics. (pp. 48, 139)

Hittites   An Indo-European people who entered Mesopotamia c. 1750 B.C.E.; destroyed the Babylonian empire; swept away c. 1200 B.C.E. (p. 31)

Hojo   Warrior family closely allied with Minamoto; dominated Kamakura regime and manipulated Minamoto rulers; claimed to rule in name of emperor at Kyoto. (p. 425)

holding ecological adaptation   Human adaptation to an environment in such a way that the original environment is drastically transformed and replaced with a new, human-oriented ecology; typical of sedentary agricultural communities. (p. 75)

holy Roman emperors   Emperors in northern Italy and Germany following split of Charlemagne's empire; claimed title of emperor c. 10th century; failed to develop centralized monarchy in Germany. (p. 348)

Homo sapiens   The human species man that emerged as most successful at the end of the Paleolithic period. (p. 5)

Honshu   Largest of the Japanese islands; most heavily populated. (p. 218)

Hopewell culture   Second of the mound-building cultures; lasted from c. 200 to 500 C.E.; more complex than Adena culture. (p. 194)

Horace   Poet who adapted Greek poetic meters to the Latin language; author of lyrical poetry laudatory of the empire; patronized by Augustus. (p. 167)

horse nomads   A form of pastoralism dependent on domesticated horses; common to Indo-European peoples of central Eurasia. (p. 76)

Hsiung-nu   [shEE *oong* nU] Also known as the Huns; horse nomads responsible for the disruption of Chinese, Gupta, and Roman civilizations. (p. 102)

huacas   Sacred spirits and powers that resided or appeared in caves, mountains, rocks, rivers, and other natural phenomena; typical of Andean societies. (p. 202)

Huanghe River basin   [hwäng] Also known as Yellow River basin; site of the development of sedentary agriculture in China. (p. 55)

Huanghe River valley   River source in Tibetan plateau to mouth in China sea; site of early Chinese sedentary agricultural communities. (p. 56)

Huari   Along with Tihuanaco, large center for regional chiefdoms between 300 and 900 C.E.; located in southern Peru; featured large ceremonial center supported by extensive irrigated agriculture; established widely diffused religious and artistic symbols spread all over Andean zone. (p. 200)

Huitzilopochtli   [wEE tsEE lO *pOch* tlEE] Aztec tribal patron god; central figure of cult of human sacrifice and warfare; identified with old sun god. (p. 375)

Hulegu   Ruler of the Ilkhan khanate; grandson of Chinggis Khan; responsible for capture and destruction of Baghdad. (p. 450)

humanism   Focus on humankind as center of intellectual and artistic endeavor; method of study that emphasized the superiority of classical forms over medieval styles, in particular the study of ancient languages. (p. 486)

Hundred Years' War   Conflict between England and France from 1337 to 1453; fought over lands England possessed in France and feudal rights versus the emerging claims of national states. (p. 352)

hunting and gathering   Means of obtaining subsistence by human species prior to the adaptation of sedentary agriculture; normally typical of band social organization. (p. 7)

Ibn Batuta   Arabic traveler who described African societies and cultures in his travel records. (p. 313)

Ibn Khaldun   [i buhn kal *dUn*, KHUn] A Muslim historian; developed concept that dynasties of nomadic conquerors had a cycle of three generations—strong, weak, dissolute. (pp. 88, 289)

iconoclasm   Religious controversy within the Byzantine Empire in the 8th century; emperor attempted to suppress veneration of icons; literally "breaking of images"; after long struggle, icon veneration was restored. (p. 334)

icons   Images of religious figures that became objects of veneration within Christianity of the Byzantine Empire; particularly prevalent in Eastern monasticism. (p. 334)

ideographic writing   Pictographic characters grouped together to create new concepts; typical of Chinese writing. (p. 59)

Ifriqiya   [if ree *ki* uh] The Arabic term for eastern North Africa. (p. 309)

Iliad* and *Odyssey   Two Greek epic poems attributed to Homer but possibly the work of many authors; defined gods and human nature that shaped Greek mythos. (p. 115)

Ilkhan Empire   One of four regional khanates, or subdivisions of the Mongol Empire after Chinggis Khan's death; located south of the Golden Horde; eventually conquered much of territory of Abbasid Empire. (p. 447)

Inca   Group of clans centered at Cuzco that were able to create empire in Andean civilization c. 1438. (p. 384)

Inca socialism   A view created by Spanish authors to describe Inca society

as a type of utopia; image of the Inca Empire as a carefully organized system in which every community collectively contributed to the whole. (p. 383)

Indian   Misnomer created by Columbus referring to indigenous peoples of New World; implies social and ethnic commonality among Native Americans that did not exist; still used to apply to Native Americans. (p. 371)

Indra   Chief deity of the Aryans; depicted as a colossal, hard-drinking warrior. (p. 53)

Indus River valley   River sources in Himalayas to mouth in Arabian Sea; location of Harappan civilization. (p. 48)

investiture   Practice of state appointment of bishops; Pope Gregory VII attempted to ban the practice of lay investiture, leading to war with Holy Roman Emperor Henry IV. (p. 353)

Ionic   Along with Doric and Corinthian distinct style of Hellenistic architecture; more ornate than Doric, but less than Corinthian. (p. 126)

Islam   Major world religion having its origins in 610 C.E. in the Arabian peninsula; meaning literally submission; based on prophecy of Muhammad. (pp. 233, 259)

Jericho   Early walled urban culture site based on sedentary agriculture; located in modern Israeli-occupied West Bank near Jordan River. (p. 18)

Jesuits   A new religious order founded during the Catholic Reformation; active in politics, education, and missionary work; sponsored missions to North America and Asia. (p. 489)

Jesus of Nazareth   Prophet and teacher among the Jews; believed by Christians to be the Messiah; executed c. 30 C.E. (p. 176)

jihad   Islamic holy war. (p. 269)

jinshi   [chin shEE] Title granted to those students who passed the most difficult Chinese examination on all of Chinese literature; became immediate dignitaries and eligible for high office. (p. 396)

jizya   [*jiz* yuh] Head tax paid by all nonbelievers in Islamic territories. (p. 271)

Jomon culture   Created by early migrants to Japan after 3000 B.C.E.; hunting-and-gathering people, produced distinctive pottery form. (p. 218)

Joseph II   Enlightened monarch of Austria; attempted to introduce reforms into Austria such as limitation of powers of Catholic church, restructuring of peasantry. (p. 501)

Ju Yuanzhang   [jU yU *än jäng, yYän*] Chinese peasant who led successful revolt against Yuan; founded Ming dynasty. (p. 456)

junks   Chinese ships equipped with watertight bulkheads, sternpost rudders, compasses, and bamboo fenders; dominant force in Asian seas east of the Malayan peninsula. (p. 405)

Jurchens   Founders of the Qin kingdom that succeeded the Liao in northern China; annexed most of Yellow River basin and forced Song to flee to south. (p. 404)

Justinian   Eastern Roman emperor between 527 and 565 C.E.; tried to restore unity of old Roman Empire; issued most famous compilation of Roman law. (p. 242)

juula   [jUlä] Malinke merchants; formed small partnerships to carry out trade throughout Mali Empire; eventually spread throughout much of West Africa. (p. 312)

Ka'ba   Most revered religious shrine in pre-Islamic Arabia; located in Mecca; focus of obligatory annual truce among bedouin tribes; later incorporated as important shrine in Islam. (p. 262)

Kabir   Muslim Mystic during 15th century; played down the importance of ritual differences between Hinduism and Islam. (p. 299)

Kamasutra   Written by Vatsayana during Gupta era; offered instructions on all aspects of life for higher caste males including grooming, hygiene, etiquette, selection of wives, and instruction on love-making. (p. 156)

Kamehameha I   Hawaiian monarch who united all of the islands under his rule in 1810. (p. 227)

Kanauj   [ku *nouj*] Capital of Harsha's empire; featured formidable walls, palatial homes, and beautiful gardens. (p. 295)

kapu   Complex set of social regulations in Hawaii which forbade certain activities and regulated social discourse. (p. 227)

Karakorum   Capital of the Mongol Empire under Chinggis Khan. (p. 446)

Karbala   Site of defeat and death of Husayn, son of Ali; marked beginning of Shi'i resistance to Umayyad caliphate. (p. 270)

karma   The sum of merits accumulated by a soul at any given point in time; determined the caste to which the soul would be assigned in the next life. (p. 142)

Kautilya   Political advisor to Chandragupta Maurya; one of authors of *Arthashastra;* believed in scientific application of warfare. (p. 149)

khagan   Title of the supreme ruler of the Mongol tribes. (p. 442)

khanates   Four regional Mongol kingdoms that arose following the death of Chinggis Khan. (p. 439)

Khmers   Indianized rivals of the Vietnamese; moved into Mekong River delta region at time of Vietnamese drive to the south. (p. 431)

Kiev   Trade city in southern Russia established by Scandinavian traders in 9th century; became focal point for kingdom of Russia that flourished to 12th century. (p. 338)

kivas   Circular pits in Anasazi communities used for religious meetings by the men in the society. (p. 195)

Koguryo   Tribal people of northern Korea; established an independent kingdom in the northern half of the peninsula; adopted cultural Sinification. (p. 428)

Kongo   Kingdom, based on agriculture, formed on lower Congo River by late 15th century; capital at Mbanza Kongo; ruled by hereditary monarchy. (p. 323)

Kubilai Khan   Grandson of Chinggis Khan; commander of the Mongol forces responsible for the conquest of China; became khagan in 1260; established Sinicized Mongol Yuan dynasty in China in 1271. (p. 451)

Kumbi Saleh   Capital of empire of Ghana; divided into two adjoining cities—one for the king, court, and indigenous people, one for the merchants, scholars, and religious leaders. (p. 213)

Kung Fuzi   Also known as Confucius; major Chinese philosopher; born in 6th century B.C.E.; author of *Analects;* philosophy based on need for restoration of order through advice of superior men to be found among the shi. (p. 92)

kuriltai   Meeting of all Mongol chieftains at which the supreme ruler of all tribes was selected. (p. 442)

Kush   An African state that developed along the upper reaches of the Nile c. 1000 B.C.E.; conquered Egypt and ruled it for several centuries. (p. 39)

Kushanas   Dynasty that succeeded the Mauryas in northwestern India; sponsors of Buddhism; empire did not extend to Ganges River valley. (p. 152)

Laozi   Major Chinese philosopher; recommended retreat from society into nature; individual should seek to become attuned with Dao. (p. 92)

Legalists   Chinese school of political thought; served Qin dynasty and subsequent dynasties; stressed need for the absolute power of the emperor; power enforced through strict application of laws. (p. 96)

Legions   The basic military unit of the Roman military; developed during the republic. (p. 163)

Lepanto   Naval battle between the Spanish and the Ottoman Empire resulting in a Spanish victory in 1571; demonstrated European naval superiority over the Muslims. (p. 518)

Li Bo   Most famous poet of the Tang era; blended images of the mundane world with philosophical musings. (p. 410)

Li Yuan   Also known as Duke of Tang; minister for Yangdi; took over empire following assassination of

Yangdi; first emperor of Tang dynasty; took imperial title of Gaozu. (p. 395)

Liu Bang   Founder of the Han dynasty in 202 B.C.E. (p. 101)

Livy   Roman historian who linked empire to traditions of republican past; stressed republican virtues popular in early empire. (p. 167)

llamas   Along with alpacas, domesticated animals of the Americas; basis for only form of nomadic pastoralism in the New World until European importation of larger animals in 15th century C.E. (p. 197)

Locke, John   English philosopher during 17th century; argued that people could learn everything through senses; argued that power of government came from the people, not divine right of kings; offered possibility of revolution to overthrow tyrants. (p. 499)

loess   [*IO* es, les, lus] Fine grained soil deposited in Ordos bend by winds from central Asia; created fertile soil for sedentary agricultural communities. (p. 56)

long count   Mayan system of dating from a fixed date in the past—3114 B.C.E.; marked the beginning of a great cycle of 5200 years; allowed precision dating of events in Mayan history. (p. 189)

Longshan culture   One of the formative Chinese cultures located at Ordos bend c. 2000 to 1500 B.C.E.; based primarily on cultivation of millet. (p. 56)

Louis XIV   French monarch who personified absolute monarchy. (p. 497)

Loyang   Along with Xian, capital of the Zhou dynasty. (p. 58)

lunar cycle   One of the principal means of establishing a calendar; based on cycles of moon; differed from solar cycles and failed to provide accurate guide to round of the seasons; required constant revision or intercalation. (p. 196)

Luther, Martin   German monk; initiated Protestant Reformation by nailing 95 theses to door of Wittenberg church; emphasized primacy of faith over works stressed in Catholic church; urged state control of Church. (p. 488)

Macedon   Kingdom located in northern Greece; originally loosely organized under kings, became centralized under Philip II; served as basis for unification of Greece and later Macedonian Empire. (p. 121)

Machiavelli, Niccolo   [mak EE uh *vel* EE] Author of *The Prince;* emphasized realistic discussions of how to seize and maintain power; one of the most influential authors of Italian Renaissance. (p. 486)

Magellan, Ferdinand   Spanish captain who in 1519 initiated first circumnavigation of the globe; died during the voyage; allowed Spain to claim Philippines. (p. 511)

Maghrib   [*mug* ruhb] The Arabic word for western North Africa. (p. 309)

Magna Carta   Great Charter issued by King John of England in 1215; confirmed feudal rights against monarchical claims; represented principle of mutual limits and obligations between rulers and feudal aristocracy. (p. 364)

Mahabharata   [muh *hä bär* uh tuh] Indian epic; written down in the last centuries B.C.E.; previously handed down in oral form. (pp. 99, 144)

Mahayana   Chinese version of Buddhism; placed considerable emphasis on Buddha as god or savior. (p. 245)

Mahmud of Ghazni   Third ruler of dynasty; led invasions of northern India; credited with sacking one of wealthiest of Hindu temples in northern India; gave Muslims reputation for intolerance and aggression. (p. 296)

maize   One of the staple crops of sedentary agriculturists in the Americas; domesticated by 4000 B.C.E. in central Mexico. (p. 184)

Malacca   Powerful trading city on mainland of Malaya; established smaller trading empire after fall of Shrivijaya. (p. 301)

Mali   Empire centered between the Senegal and Niger rivers; creation of Malinke peoples; broke away from control of Ghana in 13th century. (pp. 209, 311)

Mamluks   Muslim slave warriors; established a dynasty in Egypt; defeated the Mongols at Ain Jalut in 1260 and halted Mongol advance. (pp. 293, 450)

mana   Power of ali'i; emanated from their lineages and enabled them to extract labor or tribute from their subjects. (p. 227)

mandalas   Cosmic diagrams of the Hindu natural and spiritual world; Hindu temple complexes during the Gupta Empire were laid out in this fashion. (p. 154)

Mandate of Heaven   The divine source for political legitimacy of Chinese rulers; established by Zhou to justify overthrow of Shang. (p. 60)

manioc   One of staple crops of sedentary agriculturists in the Americas; principal crop of peoples of the lowlands of South America and the islands of the Caribbean. (p. 184)

manorialism   System that described economic and political relations between landlords and their peasant laborers during the Middle Ages; involved a hierarchy of reciprocal obligations that exchanged labor or rents for access to land. (p. 347)

Maoris   Residents of New Zealand; migrated to New Zealand from Society Islands as early as 8th century C.E. (p. 226)

Marius   Successful Roman general during the last century B.C.E.; introduced the concept of using paid volunteers in his army rather than citizen conscripts; created military force with personal loyalties to commander. (p. 165)

Martel, Charles   Carolingian monarch of Franks; responsible for defeating Muslims in battle of Tours in 732; ended Muslim threat to western Europe. (p. 348)

matrilineal   Family descent and inheritance traced through the female line. (p. 12)

matrilocal   A culture in which young men upon marriage go to live with the brides' families. (p. 12)

Mauryas   Dynasty established in Indian subcontinent in 4th century B.C.E. following invasion by Alexander the Great. (p. 148)

mawali   Non-Arab converts to Islam. (p. 271)

Maya   Classic culture emerging in southern Mexico and Central America contemporary with Teotihuacan; extended over broad region; featured monumental architecture, written language, calendrical and mathematical systems, highly developed religion. (p. 188)

mayeques   Class of agricultural laborers or serfs created to work on lands belonging to the Aztec nobility; controlled no land of their own. (p. 379)

Mecca   City located in mountainous region along Red Sea in Arabian peninsula; founded by Umayyad clan of Quraysh; site of Ka'ba; original home of Muhammad; location of chief religious pilgrimage point in Islam. (p. 262)

Medina   Also known as Yathrib; town located northeast of Mecca; grew date palms whose fruit was sold to bedouins; became refuge for Muhammad following flight from Mecca (hijra). (p. 262)

Mencius   Also known as Meng Ko; follower of Confucius; stressed consent of the common people. (p. 94)

Meng Ko   Also known as Mencius; follower of Confucius; stressed consent of the common people. (p. 94)

mercantilism   Economic theory that stressed governments' promotion of limitation of imports from other nations and internal economies in order to improve tax revenues; popular during 17th and 18th centuries. (p. 498)

Mesoamerica   Mexico and Central America; along with Peru, site of development of sedentary agriculture in Western hemisphere. (p. 182)

Mesopotamian   Literally "between the rivers"; the civilizations that arose in the alluvial plain of the Tigris-Euphrates river valleys. (p. 23)

mestizos   People of mixed European and Indian ancestry in Mesoamerica and South America; particularly prevalent in areas colonized by Spain; often part of forced labor system. (p. 520)

Methodius   Along with Cyril, missionary sent by Byzantine government to eastern Europe and the Balkans; converted southern Russia and Balkans to Orthodox Christianity; responsible for creation of written script for Slavic known as Cyrillic. (p. 336)

Metropolitan   Head of the Russian Orthodox church; located at Moscow. (p. 448)

Middle Ages   The period in western European history from the decline and fall of the Roman Empire until the 15th century. (p. 367)

Ming dynasty   Succeeded Mongol Yuan dynasty in China in 1368; lasted until 1644; initially mounted huge trade expeditions to southern Asia and elsewhere, but later concentrated efforts on internal development within China. (p. 456)

Ministry of Rites   Administered examinations to students from Chinese government schools or those recommended by distinguished scholars. (p. 396)

Minoan   A civilization that developed on the island of Crete c. 1600 B.C.E.; capital at the palace complex of Knossos. (p. 42)

Mississippian culture   Last of the mound-building cultures of North America; flourished between 800 and 1300 C.E.; featured large towns and ceremonial centers; lacked stone architecture of Central America. (p. 195)

mita   Labor extracted for lands assigned to the state and the religion; all communities were expected to contribute; an essential aspect of Inca imperial control. (p. 386)

mitmaq   Inca colonists in new regions; could be Quechua-speakers; used to pacify new conquest or conquered population moved to new home. (p. 386)

moa   Large, wingless birds native to New Zealand; hunted to extinction by early settlers; extinction established need to develop new sources of protein. (p. 227)

Mochica state   Flourished in Andes north of Chavín culture in Moche valley between 200 and 700 C.E.; featured great clay-brick temples; created military chiefdom supported by extensive irrigated agriculture. (p. 200)

Mohenjo-daro   Along with Harappa, major urban complex of the Harappan civilization; laid out on planned grid pattern. (p. 48)

moldboard   Heavy plow introduced in northern Europe during the Middle Ages; permitted deeper cultivation of heavier soils; a technological innovation of the medieval agricultural system. (p. 347)

Mongols   Central Asian nomadic peoples; smashed Turko-Persian kingdoms; captured Baghdad in 1258 and killed last Abbasid caliph. (p. 293)

monotheism   The exclusive worship of a single god; introduced by the Jews into Western civilization. (p. 40)

monsoons   Seasonal winds crossing Indian subcontinent and Southeast Asia; during summer bring rains. (p. 48)

montaña   Located on eastern slopes of Andes mountains; location of cultivation and gathering of tropical fruits and coca leaf. (p. 197)

Monte Alban   Chief center of Zapotec culture in southern Mexico during preclassic period; contemporary with Olmec culture; based on irrigated agriculture, calendrical, and writing systems. (p. 187)

Mu'awiya   [mU *ä*'wEE ä] Leader of Umayyad clan; first Umayyad caliph following civil war with Ali. (p. 270)

Muhammad   Prophet of Islam; born c. 570 to Banu Hashim clan of Quraysh tribe in Mecca; raised by father's family; received revelations from Allah in 610 C.E. and thereafter; died in 632. (p. 259)

Muhammad ibn Qasim   Arab general; conquered Sind in India; declared the region and the Indus valley to be part of Umayyad Empire. (p. 295)

Muhammad of Ghur   Military commander of Persian extraction who ruled small mountain kingdom in Afghanistan; began process of conquest to establish Muslim political control of northern India; brought much of Indus valley, Sind, and northwestern India under his control. (p. 297)

Muhammad Shah II   Turkic ruler of Muslim Khwarazm kingdom; attempted to resist Mongol conquest; conquered in 1220. (p. 445)

Muhammad the Great   Extended the boundaries of the Songhay Empire; Islamic ruler of the mid-16th century. (p. 315)

mummification   The act of preserving the bodies of the dead; practiced in Egypt to preserve the body for enjoyment of the afterlife. (p. 34)

Muslims   Followers of Islam. (p. 259)

Mycenae   [mI *sEE* nEE] The first civilization to emerge on the Greek mainland; destroyed c. 1000 B.C.E. (p. 42)

Nahuatl   [*nä* wät l] Language spoken by the Toltecs and Aztecs. (p. 194)

Nara   Along with Heian, capital of the Yamato emperors; patterned after ancient imperial centers of China; never fully populated. (p. 221)

Narmer   First pharaoh of Egyptian Old Kingdom; ruled c. 3100 B.C.E. (p. 32)

Natufian complex   Preagricultural culture; located in present-day Israel, Jordan, and Lebanon; practiced the collection of naturally present barley and wheat to supplement game; typified by large settlement sites. (p. 12)

natural law   General principles of law applicable to all societies; a fundamental concept of the Roman legal system under the empire; related to Stoic ethical theory. (p. 169)

Neanderthals   Species of genus *Homo* that disappeared at the end of the Paleolithic period. (p. 8)

Neolithic Age   The New Stone Age between 8000 and 5000 B.C.E.; period in which adaptation of sedentary agriculture occurred; domestication of plants and animals accomplished. (p. 5)

Nestorians   A Christian sect found in Asia; tended to support Islamic invasions of this area in preference to

Byzantine rule; cut off from Europe by Muslim invasions. (p. 450)

New France   French colonies in North America; extended from St. Lawrence along Great Lakes and down Mississippi River valley system. (p. 529)

Newton, Isaac   English scientist during the 17th century; author of *Principia;* drew the various astronomical and physical observations and wider theories together in a neat framework of natural laws; established principles of motion; defined forces of gravity. (p. 493)

Nezhualcoyotl   [nez wät l coiOt l] Leading Aztec king of the 15th century. (p. 375)

Nguyen   [ngI *en, ngu yen*] Rival Vietnamese dynasty that arose in southern Vietnam to challenge traditional dynasty of Trinh in north at Hanoi; kingdom centered on Red and Mekong rivers; capital at Hue. (p. 436)

niche ecological adaptation   Human adaptation to an environment in such a way that there is minimal impact on the ecology; normally typical of hunting-and-gathering groups. (p. 75)

nirvana   The Buddhist state of enlightenment, a state of tranquility. (p. 147)

Nok   Culture featuring highly developed art style flourishing between 500 B.C.E. and 200 C.E.; located in forests of central Nigeria. (p. 322)

nomads   Cattle- and sheep-herding societies normally found on the fringes of civilized societies; commonly referred to as "barbarian" by civilized societies. (p. 73)

Northern Renaissance   Cultural and intellectual movement of northern Europe; began later than Italian Renaissance c. 1450; centered in France, Low Countries, England, and Germany; featured greater emphasis on religion than Italian Renaissance. (p. 487)

nuclear families   Consisted of husband and wife, their children, and perhaps a grandmother or orphaned cousin; typical of Chinese peasantry. (p. 144)

Octavian   Julius Caesar's grandnephew and adopted son; defeated con-

servative senators following Caesar's assassination; later defeated forces of Mark Anthony and Cleopatra in Egypt; offered title of Augustus by Senate; became first Roman emperor. (p. 165)

Ogedei   Third son of Chinggis Khan; succeeded Chinggis Khan as khagan of the Mongols following his father's death. (p. 446)

Olmec culture   Cultural tradition that arose at San Lorenzo and La Venta in Mexico c. 1200 B.C.E.; featured irrigated agriculture, urbanism, elaborate religion, beginnings of calendrical and writing systems. (p. 186)

Olympic games   One of the pan-Hellenic rituals observed by all Greek city-states; involved athletic competitions and ritual celebrations. (p. 119)

Onin War   War between rival heirs of Ashikaga Shogunate; fought between 1467 and 1477; led to warfare between rival headquarters and Kyoto and destruction of old capital. (p. 425)

oracle at Delphi   Person representing the god Apollo; allegedly received cryptic messages from the god that had predictive value if the seeker could correctly interpret the communication. (p. 119)

oracles   Shamans or priests in Chinese society who foretold the future through interpretations of animal bones cracked by heat; inscriptions on bones led to Chinese writing. (p. 59)

Ordos bulge   Located on Huanghe River; region of fertile soil; site of Yangshao and Longshan cultures. (p. 56)

Ottoman Empire   Turkic empire established in Asia Minor and eventually extending throughout Middle East; responsible for conquest of Constantinople and end of Byzantine Empire in 1453; succeeded Seljuk Turks following retreat of Mongols. (p. 468)

Ovid   Roman poet exiled by Augustus for sensual poetry considered out of touch with the imperial policies stressing family virtues. (p. 167)

Pachacuti   Ruler of Inca society from 1438 to 1471; launched a series of military campaigns that gave Incas control of the region from Cuzco to the shores of Lake Titicaca. (p. 384)

pahi   Double canoes used for long-distance voyaging; carried a platform between canoes for passengers or cargo. (p. 226)

Paleolithic Age   The Old Stone Age ending in 12,000 B.C.E.; typified by use of crude stone tools and hunting and gathering for subsistence. (p. 5)

parliaments   Bodies representing privileged groups; institutionalized feudal principle that rulers should consult with their vassals; found in England, Spain, Germany, and France. (p. 364)

pastoral nomads   An intermediate form of ecological adaptation dependent on domesticated animal herds that feed on natural environment; typically more populous than shifting cultivation groups. (p. 76)

pastoralism   A nomadic agricultural life-style based on herding domesticated animals; tended to produce independent people capable of challenging sedentary agricultural societies. (p. 14)

patriarchal   [*pAY* trEE är k'l] Societies in which women defer to men; societies run by men and based on the assumption that men naturally directed political, economic, and cultural life. (p. 37)

Paul   One of the first Christian missionaries; moved away from insistence that adherents of the new religion follow Jewish law; use of Greek as language of Church. (p. 178)

Peloponnesian War   War from 431 to 404 B.C.E. between Athens and Sparta for dominance in southern Greece; resulted in Spartan victory but failure to achieve political unification of Greece. (p. 120)

Pericles   Athenian political leader during 5th century B.C.E.; guided development of Athenian Empire; died during early stages of Peloponnesian War. (p. 118)

period of the Six Dynasties   Era from 220 to 589 C.E.; featured endless wars fought by the patchwork of regional kingdoms that followed the fall of the Han in China. (p. 393)

Persian Wars   Two wars fought in early 5th century B.C.E. between Persian Empire and Greek city-states; Greek victories allowed Greek civilization to define identity separate from the Asian empire. (p. 119)

Petrarch, Francesco   One of the major literary figures of the Western Renaissance; an Italian author and humanist. (p. 467)

Philip II   Ruled Macedon from 359 to 336 B.C.E.; founder of centralized kingdom; later conquered rest of Greece, which was subjected to Macedonian authority. (p. 122)

Phoenicians   Seafaring civilization located on the shores of the eastern Mediterranean; established colonies throughout the Mediterranean. (p. 42)

pipiltin   [pipiltin] Nobility in Aztec society; formed by intermarriage of the Aztecs with the leading families of the Culhuacan who could trace lineage back to the Toltecs; achieved dominance in society as result of conquest of Azcapotzalco. (p. 377)

Pisastratus   Athenian tyrant of the 6th century B.C.E.; gained popular support against traditional aristocratic councils of Athenian government. (p. 117)

Plato   Greek philosopher; knowledge based on consideration of ideal forms outside the material world; proposed ideal form of government based on abstract principles in which philosophers ruled. (p. 124)

plebeians   Ordinary citizens; originally those Roman families that could not trace their relationship to one of the major Roman clans. (p. 163)

pochteca   [poKH tAY cä] Special merchant class in Aztec society; specialized in long-distance trade in luxury items. (p. 376)

polis   City-state form of government; typical of Greek political organization from 800 to 400 B.C.E. (pl. **poleis**). (p. 116)

polyandry   [*pol* EE an drEE, pol EE *an-*] Marriage practice in which one woman had several husbands; recounted in Aryan epics. (p. 54)

polygamy   Marriage practice in which one husband had several wives; practiced in Aryan society. (p. 54)

Polynesia   Islands contained in a rough triangle whose points lie in Hawaii, New Zealand, and Easter Island. (p. 225)

pope   Bishop of Rome; head of the Christian Church in western Europe. (p. 247)

potter's wheel   A technological advance in pottery-making; invented c. 6000 B.C.E.; encouraged faster and higher-quality ceramic pottery production. (p. 24)

Preclassic   Period in Americas from 2000 to 300 B.C.E.; period of Olmec culture, also Monte Alban culture in Oaxaca. (p. 187)

Prester John   Name given to a mythical Christian monarch whose kingdom had supposedly been cut off from Europe by the Muslim conquests; Chinggis Khan was originally believed to be this mythical ruler. (p. 449)

proletariat   Class of people without access to producing property; typically manufacturing workers, paid laborers in agricultural economy, or urban poor; product of economic changes of 16th and 17th centuries. (p. 492)

Protestantism   General wave of religious dissent against Catholic church; generally held to have begun with Martin Luther's attack on Catholic beliefs in 1517; included many varieties of religious belief. (p. 489)

Ptolemies   One of the regional dynasties that followed the death of Alexander the Great; founded in Egypt. (p. 123)

puna   High valleys and steppes lying between the two major chains of the Andes mountains; site of South American agricultural origins, also only location of pastoralism in Americas. (p. 197)

Punic Wars   Fought between Rome and Carthage to establish dominance in the western Mediterranean; won by Rome after three separate conflicts. (p. 163)

pure land Buddhism   Emphasized salvationist aspects of Chinese Buddhism; popular among masses of Chinese society. (p. 397)

Pygmies   One of few pure hunting societies left in Africa following Bantu migration. (p. 210)

pyramids   Monumental architecture typical of Old Kingdom Egypt; used as burial sites for pharaohs. (p. 33)

Qin dynasty [chin] Established in 221 B.C.E. at the end of the Warring States period following the decline of the Zhou dynasty; fell in 207 B.C.E. (p. 96)

Quetzalcoatl   [ket säl kO *ät* l] Toltec deity; Feathered Serpent; adopted by Aztecs as a major god. (p. 372)

quipu   System of knotted strings utilized by the Incas in place of a writing system; could contain numerical and other types of information for censuses and financial records. (p. 388)

Quran   [koo *rän*, -*ran*] Recitations of revelations received by Muhammad; holy book of Islam. (p. 259)

Quraysh   [koor *Ish*] Tribe of bedouins that controlled Mecca. (p. 262)

Qutb-ud-din Aibak   [kUt bUd *dEEn* I *bäk*] Lieutenant of Muhammad of Ghur; established kingdom in India with capital at Delphi; proclaimed himself Sultan of India. (p. 297)

Rajput   [*räj* pUt] Regional princes in India following collapse of empire; emphasized military control of their regions. (p. 236)

Rama   Major figure in the popular Indian epic *Ramayana*. (p. 141)

reincarnation   The successive attachment of the soul to some animate form according to merits earned in previous lives. (p. 142)

reindeer-herding nomads   Nomadic pastoralists dependent on domesticated reindeer; common to tundra of northern Europe; generally isolated from civilizations. (p. 78)

Renaissance   Cultural and political movement in western Europe; began in Italy c. 1400; rested on urban vitality and expanding commerce; featured a literature and art with distinctly more secular priorities than those of the Middle Ages. (p. 466)

republic   The balanced constitution of Rome from c. 510 to 47 B.C.E.; featured an aristocratic Senate, a panel of magistrates, and several popular assemblies. (p. 163)

Ridda Wars   Wars that followed Muhammad's death in 632; resulted in defeat of rival prophets and some of larger clans; restored unity of Islam. (p. 268)

The Romance of the West Chamber   Chinese dramatic work written during the Yuan period; indicative of the continued literary vitality of China during Mongol rule. (p. 453)

Rurik   Legendary Scandinavian, regarded as founder of the first kingdom of Russia based in Kiev in 855 C.E. (p. 338)

Russian Orthodoxy   Russian form of Christianity imported from Byzantine Empire and combined with local religion; king characteristically controlled major appointments. (p. 339)

Sahara   Desert running across northern Africa; separates the Mediterranean coast from southern Africa. (p. 207)

Sahel   The extensive grassland belt at the southern edge of the Sahara; a point of exchange between the forests to the south and North Africa. (p. 311)

saints   Holy men and women, often martyrs, who were revered in Christianity as models of Christian lifestyles; built up treasury of merit that could be tapped by more ordinary Christians. (p. 246)

Saladin   Muslim leader in the last decades of the 12th century; reconquered most of the crusader outposts for Islam. (p. 288)

samurai   Mounted troops of the bushi; loyal to local lords, not the emperor. (p. 419)

Sanskrit   The sacred and classical Indian language. (p. 154)

Sargon I   Ruler of city-state of Akkad; established the first empire in Mesopotamian civilization c. 2400 B.C.E. (p. 30)

Sassanid Empire   Replaced Parthian Empire in 227 C.E. in northeastern portion of Middle East; shared border with Byzantine Empire. (p. 242)

sati   Ritual in India of immolating surviving widows with the bodies of their deceased husbands. (p. 299)

savages   Societies engaged in either hunting and gathering for subsistence or in migratory cultivation; not as stratified or specialized as civilized and nomadic societies. (p. 6)

scholar-gentry   Chinese class created by the marital linkage of the local landholding aristocracy with the office-holding shi; superseded shi as governors of China. (p. 104)

scholasticism   Dominant medieval philosophical approach; so-called because of its base in the schools or universities; based on use of logic to resolve theological problems. (p. 357)

scientific revolution   Culminated in 17th century; period of empirical advances associated with the development of wider theoretical generalizations; resulted in change in traditional beliefs of Middle Ages. (p. 493)

secret societies   Chinese peasant organizations; provided financial support in hard times and physical protection in case of disputes with local aristocracy. (p. 109)

Seleucids   [si *IU* sids, -cids] One of the regional dynasties that followed the death of Alexander the Great; founded in Persia. (p. 123)

Seljuk Turks   Nomadic invaders from central Asia via Persia; staunch Sunnis; ruled in name of Abbasid caliphs from mid-11th century. (p. 288)

Senate   Assembly of Roman aristocrats; advised on policy within the republic; one of the early elements of the Roman constitution. (p. 163)

sepukku   Ritual suicide or disembowelment in Japan; commonly known in West as hara-kiri; demonstrated courage and a means to restore family honor. (p. 421)

serfs   Peasant agricultural laborers within the manorial system of the Middle Ages. (p. 347)

Seven Years' War   Fought both in continental Europe and also in overseas colonies between 1756 and 1763; resulted in Prussian seizures of land from Austria, English seizures of colonies in India and North America. (p. 493)

Shah-Nama   Written by Firdawsi in late 10th and early 11th centuries; relates history of Persia from creation to the Islamic conquests. (p. 291)

Shang   First Chinese dynasty for which archeological evidence exists; capital located in Ordos bend. (p. 55)

Sharia   [shä *rEE* ä] Islamic law; defined among other things the patrilineal nature of Islamic inheritance. (p. 316)

shaykhs   [shAYks] Leaders of tribes and clans within bedouin society; usually men with large herds, several wives, and many children. (p. 261)

shi   Probably originally priests; transformed into corps of professional bureaucrats because of knowledge of writing during Zhou dynasty in China. (pp. 58, 91)

Shi Huangdi   [*shOE hwäng dEE*] Founder of the brief Qin dynasty in 221 B.C.E. (p. 96)

Shi'is   Political and theological division within Islam; followers of Ali. (p. 270)

shifting cultivators   An intermediate form of ecological adaptation in which temporary forms of cultivation are carried out with little impact on the natural ecology; typical of rain forest cultivators. (p. 73)

Shinto   Religion of early Japanese culture; devotees worshipped numerous gods and spirits associated with the natural world; offers of food and prayers made to gods and nature spirits. (p. 219)

Shiva   The Brahman, later Hindu, god of destruction and reproduction; worshipped as the personification of cosmic forces of change. (pp. 152, 299)

shoguns   Military leaders of the bakufu. (p. 424)

Shrivijaya   [srEE wi *jô* yuh] Trading empire centered on Malacca Straits between Malaya and Sumatra; controlled trade of empire; Buddhist government resistant to Muslim missionaries; fall opened up southeastern Asia to Muslim conversion. (p. 301)

Signet Ring of Rakshasa   One of great dramas produced during the

Gupta Empire; dramatized authority of Brahmans. (p. 153)

Silk routes   The most famous of the trading routes established by pastoral nomads connecting the European, Indian, and Chinese civilizations; transmitted goods and ideas among civilizations. (p. 86)

Silla   Independent Korean kingdom in southeastern part of peninsula; defeated Koguryo along with their Chinese Tang allies; submitted as a vassal of the Tang emperor and agreed to tribute payment; ruled united Korea by 668. (p. 428)

Sinification   Extensive adaptation of Chinese culture in other regions; typical of Korea and Japan, less typical of Vietnam. (p. 428)

Skanda Gupta   Last of the able rulers of the Gupta dynasty; following his reign the empire dissolved under the pressure of nomadic invasions. (p. 158)

slash-and-burn farmers   A system of cultivation typical of shifting cultivators; forest floors cleared by fire are then planted. (p. 76)

Slavs   Indo-European group; ultimately dominated much of eastern Europe from the Balkans northward; formed regional kingdoms by 5th century C.E. (p. 215)

Smith, Adam   Established new school of economy; argued that government should avoid regulation of economy in favor of the operation of the laws of market forces. (p. 502)

Socrates   Athenian philosopher of later 5th century B.C.E.; tutor of Plato; urged rational reflection of moral decisions; condemned to death for corrupting minds of Athenian young. (p. 117)

solar cycle   Calendrical system based on solar year; typical of all civilizations; variations of solar calendars in Western civilization are Julian and Gregorian calendars; Mayas also constructed solar calendar. (p. 196)

Solon   Athenian reformer of the 6th century; established laws that eased burden of debt on farmers, forbade enslavement for debt. (p. 117)

Songhay   Successor state to Mali; dominated middle reaches of Niger val-

ley; formed as independent kingdom under a Berber dynasty; capital at Gao; reached imperial status under Sunni Ali (1464–1492). (p. 311)

Sophocles   Greek writer of tragedies; author of *Oedipus Rex*. (p. 125)

southern Song   Rump state of Song dynasty from 1127 to 1279; carved out of much larger domains ruled by the Tang and northern Song. (p. 404)

split inheritance   Inca practice of descent; all titles and political power went to successor, but wealth and land remained in hands of male descendants for support of cult of dead Inca's mummy. (p. 385)

stateless societies   African societies organized around kinship or other forms of obligation and lacking the concentration of political power and authority associated with states. (p. 308)

stelae   Large memorial pillars erected to commemorate triumphs and events in the lives of Maya rulers. (p. 189)

Stoics   Hellenistic group of philosophers; emphasized inner moral independence cultivated by strict discipline of the body and personal bravery. (p. 124)

stupas   Stone shrines built to house pieces of bone or hair and personal possessions said to be relics of the Buddha; preserved Buddhist architectural forms. (p. 145)

Sudanic states   Kingdoms that developed during the height of Ghana's power in the region; based at Takrur on the Senegal River to the west and Gao on the Niger River to the east; included Mali and Songhay. (p. 312)

Sufis   Mystics within Islam; responsible for expansion of Islam to southeastern Asia. (p. 293)

Sui   Dynasty that succeeded the Han in China; emerged from strong rulers in northern China; united all of northern China and reconquered southern China. (p. 235)

Sulla   Conservative military commander during last century B.C.E.; attempted to reinforce powers of the Senate and to undo influence of Marius. (p. 165)

Sumerians   People who migrated into Mesopotamia c. 4000 B.C.E.; created first civilization within region; organized area into city-states. (p. 25)

Sundiata   The "Lion Prince"; a member of the Keita clan; created a unified state that became the Mali Empire; died about 1260. (p. 312)

Sunnis   Political and theological division within Islam; followers of the Umayyads. (p. 270)

Sunzi   Author of *The Art of War*; argued that war was extension of statecraft; taught war according to scientific principles. (p. 100)

Taika reforms   [*tI* kä] Attempt to remake Japanese monarch into an absolute Chinese-style emperor; included attempts to create professional bureaucracy and peasant conscript army. (p. 416)

Tale of Genji   Written by Lady Murasaki; first novel in any language; relates life history of prominent and amorous son of the Japanese emperor; evidence for mannered style of Japanese society. (p. 420)

tambos   Way stations used by Incas as inns and storehouses; supply centers for Inca armies on move; relay points for system of runners used to carry messages. (p. 386)

Tang   Dynasty that succeeded the Sui in 618 C.E.; more stable than previous dynasty. (p. 235)

Tangut   Rulers of Xi-Xia kingdom of northwest China; one of regional kingdoms during period of southern Song; conquered by Mongols in 1226. (p. 445)

Tatars   Mongols; captured Russian cities and largely destroyed Kievan state in 1236; left Russian Orthodoxy and aristocracy intact. (p. 341)

Tatu   Mongol capital of Yuan dynasty; present-day Beijing. (p. 454)

Temple of the Sun   Inca religious center locates at Cuzco; center of state religion; held mummies of past Incas. (p. 386)

Tenochtitlan   [tAY nôch tEE *tlän*] Founded c. 1325 on marshy island in Lake Texcoco; became center of Aztec power; joined with Tlacopan and Texcoco in 1434 to form a triple alliance that controlled most of central plateau of Mesoamerica. (p. 373)

Teotihuacan   [tAY O tEE wä *kän*] Site of Classic culture in central Mexico; urban center with important religious functions; supported by intensive agriculture in surrounding regions; population of as much as 200,000. (p. 186)

Thirty Years' War   War within the Holy Roman Empire between German Protestants and their allies (Sweden, Denmark, France) and the emperor and his ally, Spain; ended in 1648 after great destruction with Treaty of Westphalia. (p. 14)

three estates   Typical social organization of Middle Ages after 10th century; included military nobility, clergy, and ordinary people. (p. 364)

three-field system   System of agricultural cultivation by 9th century in western Europe; included one-third in spring grains, one-third fallow. (p. 347)

Tian   Heaven; an abstract conception in early Chinese religion; possibly the combined spirits of all male ancestors; first appeared during Zhou dynasty. (p. 62)

Tiberius Gracchus   Along with Gaius Gracchus, tribune who attempted to introduce land and citizenship reform within the Roman republic; killed on the command of the Senate. (p. 165)

Tihuanaco   [*tEE* uh wuh *nä* kO] Along with Huari, large center for regional chiefdoms between 300 and 900 C.E.; located in southern Peru; featured large ceremonial center supported by extensive irrigated agriculture; established widely diffused religious and artistic symbols spread all over Andean zone. (p. 200)

Timbuktu   Port city of Mali; located just off the flood plain on the great bend in the Niger River; population of 50,000; contained a library and university. (p. 313)

Timur-i Lang   Leader of Turkic nomads; beginning in 1360s from base at Samarkand, launched series of attacks in Persia, the Fertile Crescent, India, and southern Russia; empire disintegrated after his death in 1405. (p. 458)

Tlacaelel   [tlä ka elAYl] Advisor to Aztec rulers from 1427 to c. 1480; had histories of Mexico rewritten; expanded cult of human sacrifice as effective means of political terror. (p. 374)

Tlaloc   [tlä *lOk*] Major god of Aztecs; associated with fertility and the agricultural cycle; god of rain. (p. 374)

Tlatelolco   [tlä te lolko] Originally a separate island city in Lake Texcoco; later incorporated into Tenochtitlan; market remained most important in combined city. (p. 373)

Toltec culture   Succeeded Teotihuacan culture in central Mexico; Nahuatl-speaking people; established political control over large territory after 1000 C.E.; declined after 1200 C.E. (p. 342)

Toltecs   Nomadic peoples from beyond the northern frontier of the sedentary agricultural area in Mesoamerica; established capital of Tula following migration into central Mesoamerican plateau; strongly militaristic ethic including cult of human sacrifice. (p. 194)

Topiltzin   Religious leader and reformer of the Toltecs; dedicated to god Quetzalcoatl; after losing struggle for power, went into exile in the Yucatan peninsula. (p. 372)

totem   Most commonly an animal utilized by nomadic tribesmen as a representation of mythic ancestor of the group; venerated as a progenitor and protector. (p. 82)

Trajan   Emperor from 101 to 106 C.E.; instituted more aggressive imperial foreign policy resulting in expansion of empire to its greatest limits. (p. 171)

transhumance   A form of pastoralism common to the Mediterranean basin and the Sahara; involves moving from one region to another according to the season. (p. 208)

transmigration   The belief in the successive reincarnation of the soul in different bodies. (p. 142)

Treaty of Paris   Arranged in 1763 following Seven Years' War; granted New France to England in exchange for return of French sugar islands in Caribbean. (p. 529)

Treaty of Westphalia   Ended Thirty Years' War in 1648; granted right to individual rulers within the Holy Roman Empire to choose their own religion—either Protestant or Catholic. (p. 490)

tribunes   Plebeian representatives in the Roman republic; elected in the Councilium Plebis Tributum on an annual basis. (p. 163)

Trinity   Christian doctrine that held that God had three persons—Father, Son, Holy Ghost—all equally divine. (p. 355)

Trung sisters   Leaders of one of the frequent peasant rebellions in Vietnam against Chinese rule; revolt broke out in 39 C.E.; demonstrates importance of Vietnamese women in indigenous society. (p. 434)

tsetse fly   [*tset* sEE, *tet-*, *tsEE* tsEE] Flourished in wet lowlands; carried sleeping sickness that severely limited pastoralism in western and central Africa. (p. 209)

tumens   Basic fighting units of the Mongol forces; consisted of 10,000 cavalrymen; each unit was further divided into units of 1000, 100, and 10. (p. 442)

Twantinsuyu   [twän tin sUyU] Word for Inca Empire; region from present-day Colombia to Chile and eastward to northern Argentina. (p. 384)

ulama   Orthodox religious scholars within Islam; pressed for a more conservative and restrictive theology; increasingly opposed to non-Islamic ideas and scientific thinking. (p. 293)

Umayyad   [U *mI* yad] Clan of Quraysh that dominated politics and commercial economy of Mecca; clan later able to establish dynasty as rulers of Islam. (p. 262)

umma   Community of the faithful within Islam; transcended old tribal boundaries to create degree of political unity. (p. 266)

untouchables   Lowest caste in Indian society; performed tasks that were con-

sidered polluting—street sweeping, removal of human waste, and tanning. (p. 141)

Upanishads   [U *pan* i shad, U *pä* ni shäd] Later books of the Vedas; contained sophisticated and sublime philosophical ideas; utilized by Brahmans to restore religious authority. (p. 153)

Urban II   Called First Crusade in 1095; appealed to Christians to mount military assault to free the Holy Land from the Muslims. (p. 352)

Uthman   Third caliph and member of Umayyad clan; murdered by mutinous warriors returning from Egypt; death set off civil war in Islam between followers of Ali and the Umayyad clan. (p. 270)

varnas   Clusters of caste groups in Aryan society; four social castes—Brahmans (priests), warriors, merchants, and peasants; beneath four Aryan castes was group of socially untouchable Dasas. (p. 141)

vassal retainers   Members of former ruling families granted control over the peasant and artisan populations of areas throughout Shang kingdom; indirectly exploited wealth of their territories. (p. 57)

vassals   Members of the military elite in the Middle Ages who received land or a benefice from a lord in return for military service and loyalty. (p. 351)

Vedas   Aryan hymns originally transmitted orally but written down in sacred books from the 6th century B.C.E. (pp. 53, 140)

vendettas   Blood-feuds between families or clans of nomadic pastoralists; created a major barrier to interclan and tribal cooperation. (p. 80)

Vergil   One of greatest of Roman poets during "Golden Age" of Latin literature; patronized by Augustus; author of *Aeneid*. (p. 166)

Vikings   Seagoing Scandinavian raiders from Sweden, Denmark and Norway that disrupted coastal areas of western Europe from the 8th to the 11th centuries. (p. 346)

Vishnu   The Brahman, later Hindu, god of sacrifice; widely worshipped. (pp. 152, 299)

Vivaldis   Two Genoese brothers who attempted to find a Western route to the "Indies"; disappeared in 1291; precursors of thrust into southern Atlantic. (p. 470)

Vladimir I   Ruler of Russian kingdom of Kiev from 980 to 1015; converted kingdom to Christianity. (p. 338)

Völkerwanderungen   [*fölk* er van der Ungen] Movement of Germanic peoples southward into the Roman Empire; resulted from population growth, pressure of Asian groups on eastern flanks of Germanic regions. (p. 216)

Wang Anshi   Confucian scholar and chief minister of a Song emperor in 1070s; introduced sweeping reforms based on Legalists; advocated greater state intervention in society. (p. 403)

Wang Mang   Member of one of the powerful families related to the Han emperors through marriage; temporarily overthrew the Han between 9 and 23 C.E. (p. 109)

Warring States period   Period of warfare between regional lords following the decline of the Zhou in the 8th century B.C.E.; ended with rise of Qin. (p. 91)

wazir   Chief administrative official under the Abbasid caliphate; initially recruited from Persian provinces of empire. (p. 275)

Wendi   Member of prominent northern Chinese family during period of Six Dynasties; proclaimed himself emperor; supported by nomadic peoples of northern China; established Sui dynasty. (p. 394)

White Lotus Society   Secret religious society dedicated to overthrow of Yuan dynasty in China; typical of peasant resistance to Mongol rule. (p. 456)

William the Conqueror   Invaded England from Normandy in 1066; extended tight feudal system to England; established administrative system based on sheriffs; established centralized monarchy. (p. 351)

witchcraft hysteria   Reflected resentment against the poor, uncertainties about religious truth; resulted in death of over 100,000 people between 1590 and 1650; particularly common in Protestant areas. (p. 492)

Wollstonecraft, Mary   Enlightenment feminist thinker in England; argued that new political rights should extend to women. (p. 503)

world economy   Established by Europeans by the late 16th century; based on control of seas including the Atlantic and Pacific; created an international exchange of foods, diseases, and manufactured products. (p. 515)

Wu   First of the Zhou to be recognized as king, 1122 B.C.E. (p. 58)

Wuzong   Chinese emperor of Tang dynasty who openly persecuted Buddhism by destroying monasteries in 840s; reduced influence of Chinese Buddhism in favor of Confucian ideology. (p. 398)

Xia   [*shEE ä*] China's first, possibly mythical, kingdom; no archeological sites have been connected to it; ruled by Yu. (p. 56)

Xian   [*shEE än*] Along with Loyang, capital of the Zhou dynasty. (p. 106)

Xuanzong   [*shU än jonh*, shwantsong] Leading Chinese emperor of the Tang dynasty who reigned from 713 to 755 though he encouraged overexpansion. (p. 400)

Xunzi   [hsun tzu, shUn] Follower of Confucius; stressed need for authoritarian government. (p. 94)

Yahweh   The single god of the Hebrews; constructed a covenant with Jews as his chosen people. (p. 40)

Yamato   Japanese clan that gained increasing dominance in the 4th and 5th centuries C.E.; created imperial cult around Amaterasu and Shinto; brought most of the lowland plains of the southern islands under control. (p. 220)

yanas   A class of people within Inca society removed from their ayllus to serve permanently as servants, artisans, or workers for the Inca or the Inca nobility. (p. 387)

Yang Guifei   [*yäng gwä fä*] Young woman belonging to harem of Tang prince; raised to status of royal concubine during reign of Xuanzong; introduction of relatives into royal administration led to revolt. (p. 400)

Yangdi   Second member of Sui dynasty; murdered his father to gain throne; restored Confucian examination system; responsible for construction of Chinese canal system; assassinated in 618. (p. 394)

Yangshao culture   [*yäng shou*] One of formative Chinese cultures located at Ordos bend c. 2500 to 2000 B.C.E.; primarily an intensive hunting-and-gathering society supplemented by shifting cultivation. (p. 56)

Yaroslav   Last of great Kievan monarchs; issued legal codification based on formal codes developed in Byzantium. (p. 339)

Yathrib   [*yath* ruhb] Also known as Medina; town located northeast of Mecca; grew date palms whose fruit was sold to bedouins; became refuge for Muhammad following flight from Mecca [hijra]. (p. 262)

Yayoi epoch   [ya yU] Last centuries B.C.E.; featured introduction of wet-rice cultivation, iron working; produced wheel-turned pottery and sophisticated bronzeware. (p. 218)

Yellow River basin   Also known as Huanghe River basin; site of the development of sedentary agriculture in China. (p. 55)

Yellow Turbans   Chinese Daoists who launched a revolt in 184 C.E. in China promising a golden age to be brought about by divine magic. (p. 234)

Yi   Korean dynasty that succeeded Koryo dynasty following period of Mongol invasions; established in 1392; ruled Korea to 1910; restored aristocratic dominance and Chinese influence. (p. 431)

Yoruba   City-states developed in northern Nigeria c. 1200 C.E.; Ile-Ife featured artistic style possibly related to earlier Nok culture; agricultural societies supported by peasantry and dominated by ruling family and aristocracy. (pp. 209, 322)

Yu   A possible mythical Chinese ruler revered for the construction of an effective system of flood control along the Huanghe River valley; founder of the Xia kingdom. (p. 431)

Yueh-chih   [*yU* zhih] Nomadic invaders of Indian subcontinent; invasions gave rise to Kushana dynasty. (p. 151)

Yupanqui, Topac   [yU *pän* kEE] Ruled as Inca from 1471 to 1493; conquered the northern coastal kingdom of Chimor by seizing its irrigation system. (p. 384)

zakat   Tax for charity; obligatory for all Muslims. (p. 267)

Zanj   Arabic term for the East African coast. (pp. 277, 319)

Zhao Kuangyin   [jaoo *kwän yin*] Founder of Song dynasty; originally a general following fall of Tang; took title of Taizu; failed to overcome northern Liao dynasty that remained independent. (p. 401)

Zhou   Originally a vassal family of Shang China; possibly Turkic in origin; overthrew Shang and established second historical Chinese dynasty. (p. 58)

Zhu Xi   [tsU shEE, ju shEE] Most prominent of neo-Confucian scholars during the Song dynasty in China; stressed importance of applying philosophical principles to everyday life and action. (p. 402)

ziggurats   Massive towers usually associated with Mesopotamian temple complexes. (p. 27)

Zoroastriansim   [zôr O *as* trEE uh niz uhm, zOr-] Animist religion that saw material existence as battle between forces of good and evil; stressed the importance of moral choice; righteous lived on after death in "House of Song"; chief religion of Persian Empire. (p. 269)

Credits

LITERARY CREDITS

PART I

CHAPTER 1

From William H. McNeill, *A History of the Human Community: A Prehistory to the Present,* 4th ed. Copyright © 1993, pp. 9, 16. Adapted by permission of Prentice Hall, Englewood Cliffs, NJ.

CHAPTER 2

Excerpts from *The Babylonian Laws,* edited and translated by G. R. Driver and John C. Miles. Copyright © 1955 Oxford University Press. Reprinted by permission of Oxford University Press.

CHAPTER 3

From A. L. Basham, *The Wonder That Was India.* London Sidgwick and Jackson Ltd., 1954. Poem "Big Rat" from *Sources of Chinese Tradition,* Vol. I, compiled by Wm. T. de Bary, W. Chan and Burton Watson, pp. 13–14. Copyright © 1960 Columbia University Press. Reprinted by permission.

PART II

CHAPTER 4

Poem from *Nomads and the Outside World* by A. M. Khazanov, p. 235. Copyright © 1983 Cambridge University Press. Reprinted by permission of Cambridge University Press.

CHAPTER 5

From *Tao Te Ching* by Gia-Fu Feng and Jane English. Copyright © 1972 by Gia-Fu Feng and Jane English. Reprinted by permission of Alfred A. Knopf, Inc.

Poem No. 33 from *The Way of Life* by Lao Tzu, translated by Raymond B. Blakney. Translation copyright © 1955 by Raymond B. Blakney, renewed © 1983 by Charles Philip Blakney. Used by permission of New American Library, a division of Penguin Books, USA, Inc.

CHAPTER 6

Excerpt from *The Greek Way* by Edith Hamilton. Reprinted with permission of W. W. Norton and Company, Inc. Copyright 1930, 1943, and renewed © 1958 by W. W. Norton and Company, Inc.

CHAPTER 7

From play "Shakuntala" from *Great Sanskrit Plays* by P. Lal. Copyright © 1957, 1959, 1964 by P. Lal. All rights reserved. Reprinted by permission of New Directions Publishing Corporation.

CHAPTER 8

From Cicero, *Pro Archia Poeta,* translated by N. H. Watts, Loeb Classical Library. Cicero, *Pro Archia* (Harvard University Press, 1965), pp. 12–14, 16, 23–24.

CHAPTER 9

From *The Blood of Kings* by L. Schele and M. E. Miller, p. 187. Copyright © 1986 Kimball Art Museum. Reprinted by permission.

CHAPTER 10

Map "Past Climates and Vegetarian Changes" from *Historical Atlas of Africa* edited by Paul Richards, et al. Copyright © 1985. Longman Group Ltd. Reprinted by permission of Cambridge University Press.

Bantu migration myth from Luc de Heusch, *The Drunken King or the Origin of the State* (Bloomington: Indiana University Press, 1982), pp. 11–12.

Germanic myth adapted from A. and E. Keary, *The Heroes of Asgard: Tales from Scandinavian Mythology* (New York: Macmillan Co., 1909), pp. 1–4.

Japanese creation story from Helen and William McAlpine, *Japanese Tales and Legends* (London: Oxford University Press, 1958), pp. 13–14.

Polynesian creation story from Anthony Alpers, *Legends of the South Seas* (New York: Thomas Crowell, 1970), pp. 51–54.

CHAPTER 11

Excerpt from *Chinese Civilization and Society: A Sourcebook* by Patricia Buckley Ebrey. Reprinted with permission of The Free Press, a Division of Simon & Schuster from *Chinese Civilizations and Society: A Sourcebook* by Patricia Buckley Ebrey. Copyright © 1981 by The Free Press.

PART III

CHAPTER 13

Poem by Sa'di from *Introduction to Islamic Civilisation* edited by R. M. Savory, p. 74. Copyright © 1976 Cambridge University Press. Reprinted by permission.

From Khaldûn, Ibn, *The Muqaddimah: An Introduction to History,* Vol. I, Bollingen Series XLIII, translated from the Arabic by Franz Rosenthal. Copyright © 1958, 1967 by Princeton University Press. Reprinted by permission of Princeton University Press.

CHAPTER 16

From *The Goodman of Paris,* translated by Eileen Power. London: George Routledge and Sons, 1928.

CHAPTER 17

Map of Inca Empire from *Atlas of Ancient America* by Coe, Snow and Benson, p. 196. Copyright © 1986. Reprinted by permission of Andromeda Oxford Ltd., Abington, UK.

CHAPTER 18

Cited in *Chinese Civilization* translated by Janet Seligman. Copyright © 1969 by Faber & Faber.

CHAPTER 19

From *The Tale of Genji* translated by Edward G. Seidensticker. Copyright © 1976 by Edward G. Seidensticker. Reprinted by permission of Alfred A. Knopf, Inc.

From *The Tale of Kieu* translated by Huynh Sanh Thong. Copyright © 1973 by Huynh Sanh Thong. Reprinted by permission of Vintage Books, a Division of Random House, Inc.

Poem by Ki no Tomonori from *Japanese Literature from the Earliest Era to the Nineteenth Century* edited by Donald Keene. Copyright © 1955 by Grove Press, Inc. Used by permission of Grove Press, Inc.

Poem by Ki no Tsurayuki from *Japanese Culture* by H. Paul Varley. Copyright © 1977 by H. Paul Varley. Reprinted by permission of Henry Holt and Company, Inc.

Poem by Ho Xuan cited in *Vietnam and the Chinese Model* by A. Woodside. Cambridge, MA.: Harvard University Press, 1971, p. 48.

Poem cited in *From the Vietnamese: Ten Centuries of Poetry* translated by Burton Raffel. Copyright © 1968 by October House.

From *Cultural Atlas of Japan* by Martin Collcutt, et al., 1988. Copyright © 1988. Reprinted by permission of Andromeda, Oxford Ltd., Abington, UK.

CHAPTER 21

Adaptation of map "The Old World." Copyright © 1970 George Philip & Son Ltd. Reprinted by permission.

PHOTO CREDITS

Unless otherwise acknowledged, all photographs are the property of Scott Foresman. Page abbreviations are as follows: (T) top, (C) center, (B) bottom, (L) left, (R) right.

PART I

CHAPTER 1

8 Reprinted from *Life: Introduction to Biology,* 3rd ed., by Beck, Liem & Simpson ©1991/Reprinted by permission Harper-Collins Publishers, Inc.; **9** Musée de l'Homme, Paris; **11** Ralph Morse; **12** From *Past Worlds: Archaeology,* Time Books, London; **16** British Crown Copyright, reproduced by permission of The Department of Environment; **18** *Encyclopaedia Universalis;* **20** Archives Photographiques, Paris; **21** From *The Neolithic of the Near East* by James Mellaart

CHAPTER 2

27 ALL University Museum, University of Pennsylvania; **30** Directorate General of Antiquities, Baghdad, Iraq; **32** Hirmer Fotoarchiv, Munich; **35** Egyptian Museum, Cairo;

Index

Note: Italicized page numbers refer to figures.